British Colonial Rule

1838	John Deere's first plow
1831	McCormick's first reaper
1830	Baltimore & Ohio Railroad opened
1825	Erie Canal opened
1812–15	War of 1812
1804	Louisiana Purchase
1793	Eli Whitney invents the cotton gin
1789	U.S. Constitution adopted
1776	Declaration of Independence
1774	First Continental Congress
1733	Georgia, last English colony, chartered
1690	First Massachusetts paper money
1681	Penn's Colony chartered
1630	Massachusetts Bay Colony founded
1620	Plymouth Colony founded
1619	First black slaves imported
1607	Jamestown settlement established

AMERICAN ECONOMIC HISTORY

THE ADDISON-WESLEY SERIES IN ECONOMICS

Abel/Bernanke
Macroeconomics

Bade/Parkin
Foundations of Microeconomics

Bade/Parkin
Foundations of Macroeconomics

Bierman/Fernandez
Game Theory with Economic Applications

Binger/Hoffman
Microeconomics with Calculus

Boyer
Principles of Transportation Economics

Branson
Macroeconomic Theory and Policy

Bruce
Public Finance and the American Economy

Byrns/Stone
Economics

Carlton/Perloff
Modern Industrial Organization

Caves/Frankel/Jones
World Trade and Payments: An Introduction

Chapman
Environmental Economics: Theory, Application, and Policy

Cooter/Ulen
Law and Economics

Downs
An Economic Theory of Democracy

Eaton/Mishkin
Online Readings to Accompany The Economics of Money, Banking, and Financial Markets

Ehrenberg/Smith
Modern Labor Economics

Ekelund/Tollison
Economics: Private Markets and Public Choice

Fusfeld
The Age of the Economist

Gerber
International Economics

Ghiara
Learning Economics: A Practical Workbook

Gordon
Macroeconomics

Gregory
Essentials of Economics

Gregory/Stuart
Russian and Soviet Economic Performance and Structure

Hartwick/Olewiler
The Economics of Natural Resource Use

Hubbard
Money, the Financial System, and the Economy

Hughes/Cain
American Economic History

Husted/Melvin
International Economics

Jehle/Reny
Advanced Microeconomic Theory

Klein
Mathematical Methods for Economics

Krugman/Obstfeld
International Economics: Theory and Policy

Laidler
The Demand for Money: Theories, Evidence, and Problems

Leeds/von Allmen
The Economics of Sports

Lipsey/Courant/Ragan
Economics

McCarty
Dollars and Sense: An Introduction to Economics

Melvin
International Money and Finance

Miller
Economics Today

Miller/Benjamin/North
The Economics of Public Issues

Mills/Hamilton
Urban Economics

Mishkin
The Economics of Money, Banking, and Financial Markets

Parkin
Economics

Parkin/Bade
Economics in Action Software

Perloff
Microeconomics

Phelps
Health Economics

Riddell/Shackelford/Stamos/Schneider
Economics: A Tool for Critically Understanding Society

Ritter/Silber/Udell
Principles of Money, Banking, and Financial Markets

Rohlf
Introduction to Economic Reasoning

Ruffin/Gregory
Principles of Economics

Sargent
Rational Expectations and Inflation

Scherer
Industry Structure, Strategy, and Public Policy

Schotter
Microeconomics: A Modern Approach

Stock/Watson
Introduction to Econometrics

Studenmund
Using Econometrics: A Practical Guide

Tietenberg
Environmental and Natural Resource Economics

Tietenberg
Environmental Economics and Policy

Todaro/Smith
Economic Development

Waldman/Jensen
Industrial Organization: Theory and Practice

Williamson
Macroeconomics

AMERICAN ECONOMIC HISTORY

Sixth Edition

Jonathan Hughes
Late, Northwestern University

Louis P. Cain
Loyola University of Chicago
and Northwestern University

Boston San Francisco New York
London Toronto Sydney Tokyo Singapore Madrid
Mexico City Munich Paris Cape Town Hong Kong Montreal

Editor in Chief: Denise Clinton
Assistant Editor: Jennifer Jefferson
Production Supervisor: Meredith Gertz
Marketing Manager: Adrienne D'Ambrosio
Supplements Editor: Andrea Basso
Design Manager: Regina Hagen Kolenda
Senior Media Producer: Melissa Honig
Project Coordination and Text Design: Electronic Publishing Services Inc., NYC
Cover Designer: Leslie Haimes
Cover Photo: Corbis Images/PictureQuest
Senior Manufacturing Manager: Hugh Crawford
Electronic Page Makeup: Electronic Publishing Services Inc., NYC

For permission to use copyrighted material, grateful acknowledgment is made to the copyright holders on pp. 642–644 , which are hereby made part of this copyright page.
Library of Congress Cataloging-in-Publication Data

Hughes, Jonathan R. T.
American economic history / Jonathan Hughes, Louis P. Cain.
—6th ed.
p. cm.
Includes bibliographical references and index.
ISBN 0-321-08822-0
1. United States—Economic conditions. I. Cain, Louis P. II. Title.
HC103 .H75 2002
330.973—dc21 2002021447

ISBN 0–321–08822–0

4 5 6 7 8 9 10—HT—06 05 04

CONTENTS

PART THREE
THE RISE OF AN INDUSTRIAL SOCIETY, 1861–1914 253

PART FOUR
THE EXPANSION OF FEDERAL POWER, 1914–1945 425

PREFACE

Since the "Cliometric Revolution" of the 1950s, research in American economic history has been revising our view of the nation's past. A key reason for writing *American Economic History*, Sixth Edition, is to integrate these continuing contributions into a general picture of economic development and change. Neither John Hughes (before his untimely death) nor I have any intention of "throwing the baby out with the bath water;" large parts of our economic biography have not been revised. The ideal, as Douglas C. North writes, is to "explain the structure and performance of economies through time."[1]

A second motivation for writing this book is the modern problems faced by the United States. For the most part, our present is explained by our past. A textbook on American economic history should take us from the earliest beginnings to the present. The story of U.S. economic achievement in per-capita income, technological leadership, and dynamic entrepreneurship—a thriving free-market economy, together with a generous welfare state securely anchored in a growing economy—is the picture one finds in the textbooks circa 1960. It is now early in the twenty-first century, and the situation is not as it was. The roots of the changes over the past four decades lie before 1960, and we must find those roots and explore them in order to understand our present—or to speculate about our future.

It is most unlikely, after all, that an entire society could produce one result and then turn in its track and, using the same institutional technology, produce an entirely different outcome. The country's current attempt to manage the federal government's budget is a product of our past, particularly the seeming fiscal policy triumphs of the early 1960s. The perspective of American economic history today is different from that when an earlier generation chronicled the victorious march through the troubles of the 1930s to the apex of American world prestige at the end of Eisenhower's presidency. As the twenty-first century begins, it is important to understand what has happened in the context of economic history. Thus, this account devotes relatively more space to the twentieth century than has been true of similar texts in the past. In addition, there is a more extensive treatment of the law and of institutional developments.

Since cliometrics has produced massive and fascinating revisions of our economic history, the text reports the major conclusions without emphasizing the background economic analysis. The intent is to make cliometric findings accessible to students and to instructors who are not specialists in economics. Although this approach does slight some powerful and elegant work, many instructors will introduce cliometric fireworks in their classrooms. Meanwhile, everyone else can learn, in summary, what the cliometricians have achieved by way of historical revision.

ORGANIZATION OF THE TEXT

The history of America's economy is presented here in mainly chronological order. That history has been divided into five major parts: The Colonial Period (1607–1783); the National Period (1783–1861); the Civil War and post-Civil War Period (1861–1914); World War I to World War II (1914–1945); and the post-World War II Period (1945–present). Each part begins with a short "Main Currents" essay in which relevant political and social themes are introduced to give the reader some insight into the time period.

Although the text is structured chronologically, by necessity, it occasionally overlaps. For example, the discussion of the participation of women in the tertiary sector (Chapter 28) includes a discussion of events at the turn of the twentieth century. To preserve continuity in a case such as this, the discussion runs behind the straight chronological sequence.

NEW IN THIS EDITION

It is hoped that this revised edition adequately illustrates the vigor and originality of the new research by economic historians. That work has been integrated into the text where it is relevant. There is relatively little change in the first three parts beyond such updating. In particular, Chapter 6 now includes Robert Margo's wage study; Chapter 13 reports the outcome of a retrospective conference on Roger Ransom and Richard Sutch's *One Kind of Freedom*; Chapter 19 incorporates the work that has been done on banking before the Great Depression, while Chapter 20 includes the results of Doug Irwin's continuing examination of free trade's potential impact in those same years.

Perhaps the biggest change to Part 4 is that, beginning in 1929, the Bureau of Economic Analysis' GDP statistics replace the GNP statistics reported in previous editions. By necessity, earlier years still utilize GNP statistics rather than GDP. This introduces minor changes in the narrative, but it does not change the bigger picture.

There are a few minor changes in Chapters 23 and 24 to make the argument more systematic and reduce some duplication. The international argument concerning the origins of the Great Depression has been updated.

The greatest change in this edition is to Part 5. In addition to the use of GDP data, Chapter 27 has been reorganized. It is now divided into three sections: a macroeconomic review of the relatively stable growth that took place in the immediate postwar years plus discussions of the changes in domestic and international policy.

Chapter 28 still emphasizes the tertiary sector, but the chapter is now organized around the population and labor force themes of earlier chapters. There is a new first section on population that discusses births and the baby boom/bust, deaths, and immigration in the twentieth century. The labor section includes more of Claudia Goldin's recent research on education in general, the high school movement in particular. The subsection on blacks and the labor market has been expanded. There is a new subsection on retirees, and the income distribution subsection has been substantially rewritten.

In Chapter 29, the material on the steel and automobile industries has been condensed to make room for a new section on electronics: the semiconductor, computer, and software industries. The intent is to show both the declining and expanding portions of the American economy at the end of the twentieth century. The material on agriculture has been expanded to cover most of the twentieth century.

Chapter 30, like Chapter 27, has been rewritten and restructured. The former chronological orientation has been changed to a more topical orientation. The first section discusses the "new wave of controls" that began in the 1960s and includes a new subsection on the transportation sector. The second section discusses the fiscal policy innovations of the Kennedy-Johnson administrations. The third section investigates the "long peacetime inflation," and includes an expanded subsection on inflation and the financial sector that documents the many changes that have taken place there. The final major section investigates "stagflation" and the movement to supply-side economics. This includes a new subsection on the energy sector that was one source of the supply shock that hit the economy in the 1970s. This section also has an expanded discussion of the "twin deficits"—the federal budget and the balance of trade.

The final chapter has been condensed with the intent of leaving the reader with a bit more optimism about the future than has been true in previous editions.

New research findings can be surveyed only briefly in a textbook such as this. A textbook can never be the same as a thorough reading of the original material itself. The expectation is that instructors who have adopted this book will direct interested students toward the sources listed in the Notes and Suggested Readings that accompany each chapter. As in earlier editions, some fascinating new research on specialized topics has not been included due to space limitations. Fortunately, more and more colleges and universities offer computerized library searches. Most of those more specialized titles can be found by a search beginning with the titles that are cited.

There is a great deal of information that can be obtained through the Internet. Any discussion of that here is likely to be dated before this can be read. Both the *Journal of Economic History* and *Economic History Review* are among the economics journals on JSTOR (www.jstor.org). Many college libraries make this available to students. The general policy is to maintain a five-year moving wall; as each new issue appears, the corresponding issue from five years earlier appears on JSTOR. Past issues of *Explorations in Economic History* are available through "IDEAL," and this also requires a subscription.

There is also a large amount of historical data available on the Internet through the Web sites of many government agencies. Among the sites consulted during this revision are two from bureaus within the Department of Commerce. The first is the Bureau of the Census (www.census.gov), particularly the current issue of the *Statistical Abstract of the United States* (www.census.gov/prod/www/statistical-abstract-us.html). The second is the Bureau of Economic Analysis (www.bea.doc.gov). Data on federal finance can be accessed at the site maintained by the Congressional Budget Office (www.cbo.gov).

A potentially useful site for many students is Economic History Net (www.eh.net). One of their many features is "Ask the Professor," through which students can get information from the profession at large. Another useful feature allows readers to compare the cost of something over time.

The companion Web site to this text may be found at www.aw.com/hughes_cain. It provides additional resources for professors and students that include chapter quizzes, PowerPoint slides, and a forum for questions and discussion.

There are a large number of additional relevant Web sites on the Internet; students should be encouraged to make use of this remarkable resource. Many institutions, and many professors, maintain sites with a wealth of information. To take but one example, the Chicago Historical Society's site (www.chicagohistory.org) has comprehensive features on the Chicago Fire of 1871 and the Haymarket Square Riot of 1886.

BENEFITS FOR STUDENTS

There is an additional reason for the chronological organization of this text—many students have only sketchy memories of their high-school American history classes. The chronological approach gives students a sense of the evolution of events, of how the economic and historical changes have been intertwined throughout nearly four centuries of America's development. A time line has been included on the inside front cover of the book as a visual reference for students, to remind them of the sequence in which these changes occurred.

Important economic terms have been emphasized in the text in boldface type and are defined as they are introduced to help students with a limited economics background more readily grasp their significance. The boldface terms appear in the Glossary at the end of the text. Students may wish to scan this Glossary before beginning the text, and to revisit it as needed when the terms appear in various chapters.

As noted, there are lists of Suggested Readings at the conclusion of each chapter, both articles and books. These readings are closely tied to the topics discussed in the chapter and can be assigned as additional readings for class discussions. They provide the bibliographical foundation for research papers. These readings also offer the student whose curiosity is piqued the opportunity to pursue a particular issue in the original sources. Additional resources can be found on the Web site for this text as discussed above.

American economic history is our "clinical experience" in the effort by theorists and policymakers to continue the work of improving the national economic performance and the welfare of Americans. The experience of the past is a vital part of our knowledge of the economy—how it works and how its functioning can usefully be improved as new problems arise. As someone once said, "You can't know where you're going until you know what road you're on."

L. P. C., Glenview, Illinois

Notes

1. Douglas C. North,. *Structure and Change in Economic History* (New York: Norton, 1981), p. 3. North and Robert W. Fogel were awarded the 1993 Nobel Prize in Economics in honor of their contributions to economic history.

ACKNOWLEDGEMENTS

When John Hughes asked me to collaborate with him on the Fourth Edition of this text, we discussed at length what was to be done. That edition, and part of the fifth, reflected mutually agreed intentions. Sadly, the execution was left to me. John was my teacher, my colleague, and my friend. I wish we could have done more together. This Sixth Edition is the first I have had to do without any input from John, but I hope his presence is still evident to those who knew him—if only through his writing.

This is the second edition published by Addison-Wesley. I thank Denise Clinton and Jennifer Jefferson of Addison-Wesley and the staff of Electronic Publishing Services Inc. for their time and talent.

Tom Geraghty provided exemplary research and editorial assistance in producing this edition, and I am grateful for the many hours he spent on this project.

Gina Germane's revision of the tables and figures for the Fourth Edition remains a singular accomplishment.

John Wallis (University of Maryland, College Park) has been a valued advisor to this project from the First Edition. This time around he provided comments on the new material in Part 5, as did Ray Cohn (Illinois State University), Lea Templer (College of the Canyons), and Robert Whaples (Wake Forest University). Detailed comments on Part 1 were provided by Tawni Hunt Ferrarini (Northern Michigan University), Gary Libecap (University of Arizona), and Lea Templer. Also contributing comments were Lee Alston (University of Illinois, Urbana-Champaign), William Phillips (University of South Carolina), Anthony O'Brien (Lehigh University), and Mark Thomas (University of Virginia). I am indebted to all of them. The Sixth Edition has benefited from the care they took in supplying their comments, and I hope they recognize their contributions in this edition.

Others to be thanked for their contributions to previous editions are:

Hugh Aitken, late of Amherst College
John Altazen, University of New Orleans
Hank Ammerphol, Central Piedmont Community College, North Carolina
Terry Anderson, Montana State University
Jeremy Atack, Vanderbilt University
Fred Bateman, University of Georgia
Jack Blicksilver, late of Georgia State University
Stuart Bruchey, Columbia University
Luvonia Casperson, Louisiana State University, Shreveport
David Chaplin, Colorado State University
Barry Eichengreen, University of California, Berkeley
Robert Fogel, University of Chicago
Robert Gallman, late of University of North Carolina, Chapel Hill
Robert C. Graham, University of North Carolina, Chapel Hill
John R. Hansen, Texas A & M
James Livingston, North Central College, Illinois
Stephen McCloy, Oklahoma City Community College
James McLain, University of New Orleans
Lee Melton, Louisiana State University, Baton Rouge
Douglass C. North, Washington University, St. Louis
Martha Olney, University of California, Berkeley

Anna Orrison, Saddleback College
Stanley B. Parsons, University of Missouri, Kansas City
Roger Ransom, University of California, Riverside
Hugh Rockoff, Rutgers University
Elyce Rotella, University of Indiana, Bloomington
Morton Rothstein, University of California, Davis
Lester Saft, California State University, Northridge
Daniel Shiman, Federal Communications Commission
Richard Steckel, Ohio State University
Dana Stevens, New College, University of South Florida
Thomas Ulen, University of Illinois, Urbana
Samuel Williamson, Miami University, Ohio
Gavin Wright, Stanford University

I would invite any instructor to forward his or her comments and criticisms of this edition to me.

I want to thank my colleagues and students at Loyola, Northwestern, and U.B.C. for their help in shaping my views.

The contribution of those, past and present, in the economic history group at Northwestern is inestimable. Joel Mokyr has made more contributions to this project in more dimensions than any one could ask. Joe Ferrie, Dave Haddock, Hilarie Lieb, and Chiaki Moriguchi are as congenial colleagues and critics as an author could hope to find. Dan Barbezat (Amherst College), Joyce Burnette (Wabash College), Charlie Calomiris (Columbia University), Carmella Chiswick (University of Illinois, Chicago), Ann Hanley (Northern Illinois University), Betsy Hoffman (University of Colorado), Eric Jones (University of Melbourne), Brooks Kaiser (Gettysburg College), Laura Owen (DePaul University), and Alan Taylor (University of California, Davis), and a host of graduate students are all part of a legacy that began with Harold Williamson, passed to John, Joel, and Joe, and continues each Thursday afternoon when Northwestern is in session. Large parts of this book were born of seminar discussions, and I hope each member can find some part that brings forth a memory of the camaraderie that exists among us. I thank them for their friendship and for contributions that go well beyond what you see on the printed page.

My wife and daughter continue to be unwavering in their support—even in the face of whimpering cantankerousness.

Finally, Mary Gray Hughes passed away after the last edition appeared. Her calm, insightful manner is deeply embedded in this book. She was a vital partner in this endeavor from the First Edition onward, and she is missed. This edition is dedicated to her memory.

INTRODUCTION

The subject matter of American economic history is the growth and development of a giant economy from small, inconsequential beginnings. In quantitative measurements, that economic history is largely a "success story." The result is an economy that provides its present population with one of the highest living standards known in history.

It is also an economy with problems. But all economies this side of utopia have problems; ours are mainly the ones we have created for ourselves, very largely as a result of solving earlier problems. For example, our growing population needed an industrialized economy with its huge payoff of manufactured goods. To solve that problem, we built our giant infrastructure of basic metals, chemicals, and energy distribution systems. The resulting standard of life, with its proliferation of employment and consumer options, also produced, as an unwanted side effect, pollution of the air, water, and, in some locations, the earth itself.

The internal-combustion engine—in cars, trucks, and tractors—was a solution to the desire for more flexible and dependable power sources for transportation and other work needs. Better highways, serving the need for stable surfaces on which to move cars and trucks, stimulated suburban living. Convenient neighborhood shopping malls eliminated the need to drive "downtown." All this further stimulated the demand for cars and trucks. More efficient farm machinery was developed to better utilize the mobile power source in the farm tractor, and some self-propelled equipment appeared. Coal-fired boilers were replaced by gas- and oil-fired burners. This further increased the demand for petroleum and substituted one form of air pollution for another. Now we struggle to find solutions to those problems. American economic history provides a continuous record of such problem-solving, problem-producing solutions to the challenges of economic development. It is a study of the down-to-earth processes that lie beneath our larger cultural and political life.

Some who study economic history's gentle art complain of its pedestrian flavor, of its tendency toward dullness compared to other kinds of history. Now, admittedly, there is a certain scarcity of the sublime in economic history. Its great figures, like Eli Whitney, Henry Ford, and Benjamin Strong lack the dramatic flavor. Those who have labored in Mammon's vineyard inspire only small admiration in us compared, say, to the adoration given military heroes like Ike or to political figures like FDR. The subject matter of economic history, individuals apart, includes such topics as historical demography, technological change, institutional development—pale stuff compared to the movements of armies, the fall of empires, the rhetoric of political campaigns, or the romance of great love affairs. Moreover, the connecting logic of economic history is economic analysis, which can seem like dry stuff in itself.

A tree, standing alone upon a windswept ridge, may inspire the poet to supreme flights of creative genius. To a biologist, though, that same tree invokes a more lowly muse. Yet, the biologist's knowledge is perhaps more important than the poet's if what we desire is an understanding of forest ecology. So it is with economic history. Its everyday facts tell us why economies flourish, why they stagnate, why they die. So, if a flourishing economy is the object of public policy, that economy's history is of vital importance. Where it will go depends a great deal upon what road has been taken in the past.

The existing economy, after all, is an artifact. It is the debris of the past. The distribution of incomes, location of industry, dispersion of cities, networks of transport and communications, age structure and ethnic composition of its population, balance of private and collective economic interest—all these things and more, as they stand in our time, are the consequences of decisions made in the past. The vast majority of those decisions were made by people now long dead. If we want to preserve our present, or even to change the course of our future economic affairs intelligently, it is best that we understand why the present relationships came into existence. These relationships are the survivors of history's gristmill; they were not easily achieved and probably should not be altered without a thorough understanding of why they exist in their present forms. Such knowledge is the meat of economic history, and its importance can scarcely be overvalued. We have an economic past, and a long one.

Oddly enough, though, Americans tend to think of their country as somehow young. Partly this conception is due to a fundamental reality, and that reality is incessant economic and social change. During our entire history we have been a nation of dramatic change. Population increase alone has been so powerful a force that every 50 years have produced fundamental alterations in the way we live.

In 2000, we had 281 million people; in 1930, 123 million; in 1880, 50 million. In 2000, we worried about the ecology and whether the energy crisis of recent memory would return. In 1930, such problems were only on the horizon; in 1880, they were unimaginable. From 1776 to our bicentenary in 1976, our population increased by an astounding factor of 85, while Europe's population grew only by a factor of 4. We also have undergone an industrial revolution and become a predominantly urban people. Now, only about 3 percent of our labor force works on farms; that number was as high as 25 percent in 1920. Today, almost three-fourths of our labor force is engaged in services and professions; we no longer need their labor in the making of either food or goods.

As a nation we are lovers of gadgets, so we continually make and buy new things. We move about within the country as much as we ever did during the pioneering epoch, and we have no coherent class structure that can be passed from generation to generation. Instead, we are a society of socially mobile people, both upward and downward. Such constant change motivates us to emphasize how new everything seems to be.

Yet, American economic history actually is the study of a primarily European society, continuous on this continent for almost 400 years in the English-speaking part (Jamestown, Virginia, was settled in 1607), at least as long among French speakers (Quebec City was founded in 1608), and longer still among those who are descended from the Spanish (St. Augustine, Florida, was founded in 1565, and Santa Fe, New Mexico, has been continuously occupied since 1610). Nor should it be forgotten that there is an even older North American history that can be accessed through archaeology. And none of it can be understood without investigating how the continent forced all peoples who arrived here to adjust to its requirements. The federal Constitution of the United States (1789) is the oldest document of its kind in continuous use by any major nation, and much of our law, descending directly from its English ancestors, still bears the recognizable stamp of the Magna Carta (A.D. 1215).

So we are a paradox as a nation, as a living society, old in origin, long-lived in continuous institutions, yet continually renewed in structure and spirit. The study of this complex society's economic evolution will necessarily be a taxing one, and we shall come across remote and archaic origins of vital contemporary realities in our study—strange words and ideas transformed into the rules of daily life in the early twenty-first century. To really understand our modern American economy, we need to study almost four centuries of continuous social evolution.

Every economy has a history, of course, and to some extent, the knowledge gained in studying any single economy's development is helpful in understanding the history of other economies. Therefore, the study of economic history is of general use, like the study of basic economic theory. But even economic theory has its limits. Supply and demand may not explain price determination in a planned economy; the theory of the firm in competition will not explain pricing and output decisions in a regulated industry. Similarly, there are characteristics unique to each society that must be learned, by way of background information, before we can understand why that society's economy grows at rates and in structural forms different from others.

When one considers the radically different economies of the United States and Mexico, side by side in North America, the need for such background information is painfully obvious. The same is true even of cross sections in American history itself. Land settlement in seventeenth-century New England and Virginia and land settlement in nineteenth-century Iowa were so different in character that we will need to seek out knowledge of legal history as well as of changes in population and technology. Similarly, the labor force participation rates of white females are now so different from those that prevailed even 50 years ago that deep-seated economic and social changes must be considered. The role played by government in the modern economy is so much greater than it was before the Great Depression that we must ask penetrating questions about political change. Even "high culture" must fall into focus if we are to comprehend fully the great increase during this century in formal education among the American population.

Other topics (e.g., geology, geography, climatology, agronomy, plant and animal genetics), fundamental changes in science and technology, must also be considered. Over the long history of the American economy, the labor contract has changed radically, the form of business organization has been fundamentally altered, and even the relationship between the individual and the state has changed incredibly, despite the continuous use of the same Constitution as the basic law of the land. So, even if economic history may appear to be a relatively narrow subject, in reality it is not.

Finally, we must keep in mind that we use history to understand ourselves. Since, in the broadest sense, we are the product of our past, we should reasonably expect the study of that past to lead to the present, *as it is*, and not as someone might wish it to be. This point is very important. Many who study and write about history try to pull it this way and that to fit preconceived ideas about how it ought to have come out. For example, leftist writers have hoped again and again in our history—in the late nineteenth century, in the 1930s, during the upheavals of the Vietnam War—that our response to the problems of late twentieth-century American capitalism would lead to socialism. It did not happen. If logic really were on the side of the development of American socialism, why have we been so bull-headed? American economic history should answer such a question.

Similarly, the developing mixed economy, or "welfare state," of the last six decades has dismayed free-market theorists who believe that the expanding role of government is both wasteful and illogical. So why have Americans persisted in their construction of an economy that so runs against the principles of free enterprise? We hope to answer such questions. If the mixed economy was supposed to solve our problems, why do we still have them? Why, after more than seven decades of progressive taxation and redistribution of income, are wealth and income so unevenly distributed? Why, after four decades of electing fearless inflation fighters to the White House, do we still have as much, if not more, inflation than when we first started electing such people? Our study should provide some answers to those questions, too. All such problems are history's consequences, and it is in the study of history that we will understand those problems. There is no other way.

We begin our journey in the distant past, when the first group of people, complete with their laws and institutions, were transplanted from England. In 1682, William Penn, the founder of Pennsylvania, wrote about government something that could be said of all societies:

> Governments, like clocks, go from the motion men give them; and as governments are made and moved by men, so by them are they ruined too. Wherefore governments rather depend upon men, than men upon governments. Let men be good, and the government cannot be bad; if it be ill, they will cure it. But if men be bad let the government be [ever] so good, they will endeavor to warp and spoil it to their turn...[1]

More than three centuries after Penn launched his "Holy Experiment," the government and colony of Pennsylvania, we are still testing the wisdom of those propositions, in economics, in law, in morals and justice. In the processes of American economic history, we will see the dialectical play, to and fro, of people and their institutions in the unending search for justice and equity.

Note

1. Francis Newton Thorpe, ed., *The Federal and State Constitutions, Colonial Charters, and Other Organic Laws* (Washington, D.C.: Government Printing Office, 1909), p. 3054.

11
8
31
10
12
16
9
14
13
29
26
27
25
24

PART ONE

THE COLONIAL PERIOD, 1607–1783

The discovery and colonization of the American continents by the North Atlantic European powers were part of the processes of population growth and nation-building that gripped Europe from the latter part of the fifteenth century onward. The results of those efforts differed widely. The areas colonized by the English developed and grew to a much greater extent than those colonized by other European powers. In particular, the colonies that became the United States of America attained a standard of living similar to that in Europe while they were still colonies. Other former colonies in the New World are categorized even today as "developing" or "transitional."[1] Our study of American economic history must investigate those factors that contributed to successful economic growth and development.

In this section we shall concentrate our discussion on three major topics:

1. The character of the initial institutions and the economic behavior that shaped the future of American development
2. The regional and occupational specializations that enabled the colonial economy to grow internally and to fit itself into the world economy that nurtured it in its infancy
3. The forces of growth that pushed the colonial economy into independence from England, its original founder and sponsor

For the future American economy, it was the period of English history from Elizabeth I to George III that mattered most. The policies of those sovereigns determined the nature of the laws in this country governing land acquisition and ownership, commercial practices, and population growth through immigration. To this day major characteristics of the American economy derive from these remote origins. Both the population and the economy have grown and developed mainly along lines first established in the colonial era. Such things as the common law and secure property rights help explain why the distribution of wealth in the United States. is relatively more equitable than in many other parts of the New World.

Natural endowments necessarily determined patterns of growth. The Eastern Seaboard and its immediate hinterland (the site of the original colonies) provided a variety of soils, minerals, and climates. In adapting to the natural realities the colonies became specialized in economic activity in different ways, which produced long-lasting regional characteristics that sharply distinguished the New England, Middle Atlantic, and Southern economies from each other. In part, these regional economies were internally complementary; they were advantageous to each other. But the initial differences depended greatly for success upon the participation of the regional economies in the larger international economy. In trade, the regions depended more on the outside world than upon their neighbors on the North American continent. The colonies were on the fringe of the Atlantic basin, and their ships, once at sea, were very nearly as close to Europe as to each other.

As historians John McCusker and Russell Menard persuasively argue, "the colonial economy was successful, grew rapidly by eighteenth-century standards, and generated a fairly widespread prosperity." These characteristics, in turn, made "independence thinkable by the 1770s."[2] They also generated social change. Historians Marc Egnal and Joseph Ernst have emphasized two elements of this social change. The first is "the growth of a colonial elite" composed of merchants and wealthy landowners. The second is "the active and self-conscious involvement of the 'lower orders' in the Revolutionary movement."[3] This emphasis is quite different from that of the Progressive historians (e.g., Charles Beard, Louis Hacker) who emphasized the colonies' indebtedness to the mother country.

By the mid-eighteenth century, particularly after the end of the French and Indian War in 1763, the perceived economic needs of the rapidly growing colonial populations increasingly came into conflict with the larger imperial designs of the mother country, England. Conflicts over western lands (that is, west of the Appalachian Mountains), internal economic specialization, plus shipping and international commerce added to and supported the political motivations of those who agitated against the administration of the Empire.

By the mid-1770s, with 2.5 million people, the 13 colonies were a third as populous as England and Wales and had a greater population than did countries such as Sweden, Denmark, Switzerland, and Portugal. The westward movement was already beginning; land companies were formed to settle beyond the Alleghenies, and settlers streamed over the mountains. In fact, the Quebec Act of 1774, which reserved the western lands to the government of Quebec and, hence, British imperial control, was itself considered an act of war, as was the closing of the port of Boston that year. But these were not all. To quote McCusker and Menard again:

> The rapacious behavior of metropolitan [London] merchants in the 1760s and 1770s threatened the abilities of Americans to engage in new or, in some cases, even traditional pursuits. Parliamentary restrictions and predatory British merchants fueled fears of a conspiracy to subvert American liberties and to turn American resources entirely to the benefit of corrupt politicians and metropolitan freebooters.[4]

The Revolution ensued. The British had created, largely by mismanagement, the first of the independent overseas nations forever cast in England's mold by language, law, and custom.

Notes

1. There is a good deal of recent comparative work on why some colonies succeeded and others did not. For example, Stephen Haber, ed., *How Latin America Fell Behind* (Stanford: Stanford University Press, 1997); Kenneth Sokoloff and Stanley Engerman, "Institutions, Factor Endowments, and Paths of Development in the New World," *Journal of Economic Perspectives*, vol. 14, no. 3, Summer 2000; and Engerman, Haber, and Sokoloff, "Inequality, Institutions, and Differential Paths of Growth Among New World Economies," in Claude Menard, ed., *Institutions, Contracts, and Organizations* (Cheltenham, England: Edward Elgar, 2000).
2. John McCusker and Russell Menard, *The Economy of British America, 1607–1789* (Chapel Hill: The University of North Carolina Press, 1985), pp. 351–58.
3. Marc M. Egnal and Joseph A. Ernst, "An Economic Interpretation of the American Revolution," *William and Mary Quarterly*, vol. 29, no. 1, January 1972.
4. McCusker and Menard (1985), p. 352.

CHAPTER ONE

Overseas Empire

American economic history has European roots. Transplanted in American soil, they produced a similar, but not identical, harvest to those in Europe. The same was not true in other parts of the New World. Since that harvest has played (and continues to play) an important role, our story begins with a superficial tour of European history to gain a necessary perspective.

EUROPEAN EXPANSION AND DISCOVERY

In Europe, the epoch known as "antiquity" ended with the overthrow of the Roman emperor Romulus Augustus by the barbarian leader Odoacer in A.D. 476. During the three centuries of bloody history that followed, the peoples of Western Europe survived in the cultural and legal ruin of the old Roman Empire in the West. On the other hand, the Roman Empire in the East, based in Constantinople, flourished in even greater glory.

In the seventh century, most of the old Roman Empire, East and West, was overturned by the relentless force of Islam. Within a century following Mohammed's death in 632, Muslim armies swept the world, wiping out the cultures and dynastic structures of preceding millennia. The old Persian Empire was conquered in 634; Cadiz, in Spain, fell in 711. The next step was France, but there, according to historian Henri Pirenne, the tide of history changed. The victory of Charles Martel at the Battle of Tours in 732 marked the end of the Muslim expansion.

To Pirenne, it was the European response to Islam that created modern Western civilization. Beginning with Charlemagne (742–814), the thousand-year process of uniting European peoples into *nation states*—political and economic groupings of similar language, custom, culture, and dynastic linkages—ensued.

At first, the organization of land and labor in Northern Europe became what is called *feudal*, a complex and pyramidal hierarchy of mutual obligations and rights with respect to both labor and land that extended from the peasant to the king. In simplest terms, peasants farmed the land assigned to them by manorial lords and, in return, received protection and some supplies. Manorial lords received their land from the king.

Surrounding this system was the spiritual force of the Roman Catholic religion and its supranational organization, one of history's greatest and most long-lived bureaucracies. In 1492, when Queen Isabella of Spain granted Christopher Columbus a patent to work his will on "some islands and a continent in the ocean," it was the right of conquest of a Christian sovereign that was invoked—together with a promise to indemnify any Christian prince injured by the forceful actions of Isabella's agent, Columbus. That same year, Christian Spain captured Granada from the Moors, ending more than 700 years of Muslim rule in Spain.

During the centuries, European sovereigns had developed certain rules of the game. Foremost among them was disdain for all non-Christian societies. This was to be continued in the Americas. The right of conquest of any Christian prince looms large in early American history, for it was that power that legitimized the European colonial acquisitions in the Americas. The Europeans might fight among themselves, but their right to subdue and rule the American "savages" was not seriously in question—not in 1521 when Cortez subjected Mexico to Spanish rule, nor in the late nineteenth century in the United States when the surviving American Indians were herded onto reservations. The military response of the West to non-Christian conquest, begun with its response to the Muslims, had an incredibly long historical legacy.

Movement toward the modern European nation state began in the late fourteenth century. The Renaissance bloomed in the fifteenth century as Europe surged ahead in many humanistic, political, and military areas. Historians customarily mark this as the end of feudalism and the beginning of **mercantilism**, the term usually applied to the intellectual and institutional environment that accompanied the emergence of strong, centralized nation states. Mercantilists believed that international trade was a zero-sum game; they believed in the necessity of governmental regulation to maximize the wealth of the nation. These beliefs held center stage until the American Revolution, which occurred at the same time that Adam Smith first argued that less regulation would lead to wealthier nations.

The Nation State

The counterplay of Roman Catholicism and Islam reflects, in the broadest possible brush strokes, the historical transformation of the early modern European world. European culture had evolved as a blend of old and new—the Roman alphabet and Arabic numerals. By the end of the fifteenth century, the nation state was emerging in Europe; national rulers appeared in Sweden, England, Russia, France, and Spain, together with groupings of German-speaking peoples under their own kings and nobles. The movement was accelerated by the Protestant Reformation, beginning in 1519, which underpinned the independent power of the English, Dutch, Swedes, and major German principalities. The power of the city-state was fading, as was that of the great supranational rulers. The nation state extended the reach of the market; in comparison to the city-state, larger areas were subject to uniform laws governing property, contracts, and commerce.

By the end of the fifteenth century, Northern Europe already had become a center of commercial growth. Greater security of persons and property at home and abroad had resulted from the centuries-long legal evolution of the more stable governments into recognized political configurations. Long-distance trade was growing at sea and along the rivers, especially in the North Sea and Baltic, under the laws of the Hanse cities. These laws included rules for insurance, negotiable instruments, and, especially, individual property rights. The latter are the rights of an owner to use, sell, or exchange property. Stable law makes the world less uncertain. The evolution of such law enhanced the economic development of Western Europe. As Adam Smith later argued, a legal system that protects private property and allows property owners to pursue their private self-interest is led, as if by an *invisible hand*, to increase national wealth.

Other necessary institutions developed with the law. As early as the fourteenth century, Italian merchant bankers had branches all over Western Europe, including some in England. They financed manufacturing as well as trade; they lent money to kings and commoners alike. In particular, they utilized the **bill of exchange**, a dated order to pay against the shipment of goods, to cut down on the need for shipping coin and bullion to make payments, greatly simplifying the conduct of foreign trade.

Population Patterns

The growth of commerce implies the growth of cities and population. Despite its agrarian base, the organization of late medieval Europe, before the time of the nation state, contained suitable provision for urban growth. Bologna in the early thirteenth century may have numbered 64,000 persons. Paris at the beginning of the fourteenth century numbered 60,000 people; Cologne, 50,000. In addition, thousands of market towns and villages were the sites of production—food processing, milling, wood and metal fabrication—and the accumulation of tradable goods, such as textiles. From these towns and cities, trade spread back into the hinterland (the area surrounding the town with which it trades) and down the rivers to the oceans and more distant markets.

The development of towns and trade was uneven because of the uneven fate of the population. The story of European population growth is not a story of steady growth. Evidence shows that from the middle of the tenth century to the early fourteenth century, strong growth nourished the civilization of the late Middle Ages. This was a time of massive growth and permanent investment, shown not only in new, enlarged city boundaries, but also in the great Gothic cathedrals. This brilliant episode ended relatively suddenly because of famine, then the plague, in the fourteenth century. The most famous disaster was the Black Death of 1347–1348, which may have killed half of Europe's population. It was said that as many as 200,000 smaller medieval towns and villages were completely depopulated. Recuperation took generations.

Recovery from that catastrophe provided a rising base for further commercial and productive development in the fifteenth century, just at the time the new nation states were engaged in active overseas expansion. By 1545, Britain had 3.2 million people and had not yet recovered entirely from the plague. With minor setbacks, primarily due to the incredible destruction of life caused by the religious wars of the late sixteenth century, European population growth provided the strength for the commercial expansion that would characterize the years of discovery and colonial settlement of the Americas.[1]

The Discoveries

According to mercantilist thought, material resources were to be employed to foster the economic and political strength of the nation state. To that end, nation states undertook exploration, discovery, and, ultimately, colonization. Mercantilists believed in the fundamental lesson of the **quantity theory of money**, that the price level was directly related to the money supply. Rising prices usually meant brisk trade, good business, and increased taxes. Consequently, one factor that motivated European expansion in the Americas was international trade and finance, in particular the acquisition of precious metals. Mercantilism was an alliance of power between the king and the merchant capitalists. The king depended on the merchants to build the national treasury, while the merchants depended on the king to protect their economic interests.

In 1415, the Portuguese crossed over to North Africa and captured Cuenta, marking the beginning of permanent European expansion overseas. After Columbus returned to Spain from his first voyage, an arrangement was concluded in 1494 between the Spanish and the Portuguese (the Treaty of Tordezillas) in which Spain was granted all lands discovered more than 370 leagues west of the Cape Verde Islands, a measurement that in time gave Portugal claim to Brazil. De Soto landed in Florida in 1539, then discovered the Mississippi River before dying in what is now Arkansas. Working north from Mexico by land, the Spanish crossed the Southwest, going as far as modern Kansas. A Spanish officer serving under Francisco Coronado discovered the Grand Canyon in 1540. These discoveries established Spanish claims to large portions of what is now the United States. Thus, in one century, primarily because of the Spanish and Portuguese, the dimensions of the world in European eyes had completely changed.

Other European monarchs followed suit. The English were the first to organize. In 1496, penny-pinching Henry VII issued letters of patent to the Genoese adventurer Giovanni Caboto (John Cabot) "to seeke out, discover and finde whatsoever isles, countries, regions or provinces of the heathen and infidels, which before this time had been unknown to all Christians."[2] On 24 June 1497 Cabot reached Cape Breton, Nova Scotia, which he claimed for Henry VII. His discovery (and later voyages by him and his sons) established the initial English claim in the New World and again altered the course of history—but not for another century. The English continued to hope that a northwest passage, a shortcut to Asia, could be found in the continent's northern waters. After several futile attempts by agents of Henry's son and his granddaughter Elizabeth to find this shortcut, the first permanent English settlement was established in Virginia in 1607 by a company with a charter from James I.

England was not the only European nation with designs on North America. In 1608, the French founded Quebec. The Dutch, long in the Hudson River for trade purposes, established what became New York City in 1624. A Swedish colony, established in 1643 in what became Pennsylvania, was passed to the Dutch in 1655 and, then, to the English.

By 1650 the Spanish, English, Dutch, and French were all established in what would become the United States and Canada. All four powers were nation states in the modern sense (the Dutch had a republic). The Spanish and French represented European military prowess, actually their main interest. The Dutch and English represented the commercial revolution that was sweeping Northern Europe (in part fueled by Spanish gold from the Americas). England would have the most impact on our history.

ENGLAND OVERSEAS

The Investors

By the time the English followed Cabot's discoveries with actual colonization, the riches of the New World had become legendary. Gold and silver shipped to Spain (some of it intercepted by English privateers) had found its way into circulation all over Europe. Following the defeat of the Spanish Armada in 1588, English merchants, whose ships and money had been engaged in the war effort, began a search for potentially profitable investments.[3] The maps and writings of Richard Hakluyt and others had familiarized English leaders with the prospects of North American colonies. They had good information regarding some of the resources they would find in North America, particularly the potential for supplying ship timbers, masts, and naval stores. They had good information on settlement locations north of the Spanish colony in Florida. In addition, they still had some hope of finding a northwest passage to the Orient. The English had picked up furs from trade with the Indians at temporary fishing camps and abandoned settlements along the northeast coast; furs from French trading in Canada also were available in Europe. Many English ship captains had visited the mainland for trading, and, in 1605, the explorer Sir George Weymouth brought back five Indians, who were put on display in London. Despite the earlier failures, there were merchants and other capitalists ready to risk money on colonizing ventures.

Shepherd and Walton offer an economic explanation for the English colonial experiments.[4] The English economy was diversified, but remained predominantly agricultural. It was well endowed with both labor and capital, but had relatively smaller quantities of natural resources. These authors assume that agricultural goods were produced under increasing cost conditions, whereas manufactured goods were produced under constant costs. Income levels and population densities were large enough to provide a dispersed market for manufactured goods at minimum cost.

Agricultural goods, on the other hand, were subject to diminishing returns and incurred cost (and therefore price) increases as the demand for them increased. The North American continent was well endowed with natural resources, but had neither labor nor capital (that is, no labor the English planned to use). Initially, high costs (including subjective risks and uncertainties) discouraged migration and the development of colonial agriculture. As the demand for British agricultural output increased, however, British costs increased, and the relative cost of colonial agriculture decreased. At some point, a colonial venture proved profitable. Learning-by-doing (including the knowledge freely shared by the natives) helped resolve the theretofore subjective risks and uncertainties of producing in an unknown land and shipping across a great ocean and led to further reductions in the cost of colonial agriculture. More colonies were established.

These colonies were enclaves in the customary sense of being detached from the domestic economy. In many ways, the analogy between what development economists term "enclave activities" and the initial North American colonies is apt.[5] In the modern sense, an enclave typically exists for the removal and, possibly, partial processing of extractive products in a nonindustrial environment. The establishment of an enclave is profitable because of the high value of the products on the export market. This value compensates for the increased production costs attributable to the absence of an industrial sector and a market in the host nation and the increased transportation costs to a distant home market. There is little need for the enterprise to adapt to the local environment. Equipment, supplies, and professional-technical labor are imported; the enterprise builds its own transport-port facilities.

There are, however, significant differences between an industrial enclave in a developing country now and North American colonization then. English colonization in the 1600s was biased toward agriculture, although raw materials extraction was one expected source of revenue. The attitude of the colonizers was different from that of a corporation establishing an enclave today and different from that of European colonizers in other parts of the New World then. English colonizers assumed that North America could be considered open land and that, in general, the indigenous labor would not be utilized. Indeed, there were few attempts to develop that labor supply, although the natives played an important role in the fur trade and provided necessary technical information with respect to agriculture. Except for defense, colonizers assumed that their decisions could be made independent of their "host's" wishes, that they could go about their business without courting favor in the native society.

The English organized their overseas ventures in several ways. The first colonies were financed by individuals via an incorporated company. The method used, the **joint-stock company** with a royal charter, was a form of partnership in which shares were issued to each partner up to the amount of his investment. The work of Ann Carlos and others has demonstrated how many English companies of this period (e.g., the Hudson's Bay Company, the Royal African Company) adopted practices that seem quite modern.[6] A joint-stock company like the Virginia Company of London began with a royal charter, but private capital and initiative motivated it. The charter defined and delimited the company's rights, privileges, obligations, and localities of operation. Merchants and other private individuals assumed the risks and uncertainties of building the British Empire.

Later, in Virginia and elsewhere, the government of the colony was taken over and operated directly by the Crown, making each a **royal colony**. In some cases, extensive rights and great tracts of land were granted as personal favors by the king to individual grant proprietors such as Sir Ferdinando Gorges, Lord Baltimore, and William Penn. Although these **proprietary colonies** were in some respects like little kingdoms, their citizens enjoyed all the rights of other Englishmen, including institutions of representative government.

The establishment of a colony involved a substantial capital outlay. If a colony did not survive, such outlays had to be duplicated, since little could be reused. The maintenance of a colony involved additional annual outlays for supplies. Without the discovery of an exploitable mineral resource, colonies were unlikely to be viable commercial propositions until staple production could be established. There also had to be investment in social overhead capital to serve an **entrepôt** function (that is, a trading point or a port). The needs of commerce between England and its colonies dictated the immediate installation of an entrepôt.

The risks and uncertainties of life in an alien land also demanded the reconstruction of European town life in the New World. The unfamiliar environment peopled by natives whose intentions were often incongruent with an Englishman's sense of fair play led colonists to build enclosed, defensible settlements. To ensure a "just and profitable distribution" of the land, to "preserve and promote" their religion, and to resist the lure of "pride and profit" in the new land, they banded together in a few central locations rather than scattering themselves on the abundant land. In short, the town was the mode of settlement; anything less would jeopardize the expected profits from colonizing. As Jackson and Schultz aver, "From the beginning, America was an exercise in community settlement, an experiment in social order."[7]

Public funding, either directly or through subsidy, was a possible alternative, but not a likely one. This is not to say that the public interest was ignored.[8] Quinn argues that, even for the chartered English companies, "the creation of a bulwark against the further extension of Spanish colonial power along the Atlantic coast and a base…for attacks on existing Spanish colonies and the valuable plate-fleets that sailed from them" was an important factor.[9] A second factor was the establishment of a "new Mediterranean type of agriculture." If North America could produce such goods as wine, olive oil, figs, citrus fruits, and sugar, England could simultaneously expand its trade and lessen its dependence on others. Both factors argued for a location to the north of the Spanish colonies.

Whether the merchant adventurers were motivated by a spirit of adventure in the exploration of new land or truly felt they were acting in the best long-run interests of Britain is not clear. The historical record portrays these merchants as prime examples of *homo economicus*; the payoff for successfully assuming risk was profit, but, as it turned out, there was probably more risk and less profit than they had anticipated. The period over which even the most far-sighted investor could be expected to wait for a return in many cases proved to be less than the period investors had to wait for a return.

The location of the initial Virginia colonies of 1584–1587, 36° north latitude, was free from the threat of constant Spanish attacks, close enough for English attacks on the plate-fleets, and temperate enough for a Mediterranean-type agriculture. The enterprises, however, were poorly planned and financed. The chosen site lacked efficient harbor facilities, a serious weakness since the main financing apparently was to be derived by plunder from the Spanish. Further, few Englishmen were familiar with the high degree of organization and specialization associated with Mediterranean-type agriculture, although that problem did not manifest itself until later.[10] The Jamestown settlement (1607) began with several advantages over its predecessors, yet that settlement survived only because of continued pump-priming from England. There was still much to be learned — and much to do.

The People

Especially at the beginning, the English were hard put to find sufficient colonists willing to supply their labor. Early reports home from Virginia and Plymouth cannot have been very optimistic. Those who signed up to sail to America came originally from many walks of life, and they came with very different motives. Some came for religious reasons, seeking freedom to practice faiths that were frowned upon in Europe. The English Puritans, French Protestants, Catholics, Quakers, and Mennonites from Germany were examples of these. Some came as independent settlers with sufficient capital to buy land, then set up as merchants or followed other professions. Possibly half or more of whites came as indentured servants, working off the price of passage by their labor in the New World. Africans came as slaves. Also, some thousands of prisoners of the Crown—debtors, condemned criminals, and prisoners of war—came under bonds of indenture, gaining freedom by their labor. We will discuss them all in due course.

Free Population. Of those who came to America on their own funds, just coming across the Atlantic made them eligible for headright land grants (a grant of land to an individual) in most colonies, and land could be purchased from most colonial governments. Not only farmers came, of course; from the beginning there was (apart from the first Virginia settlement) an immigration of artisans of all sorts—merchants, sailors, carters and draymen, and scholars. The entire array of developed English commercial life appeared on the colonial scene, especially in the seaports. Those who came independently were free, as in England, to contract for their services, although, following English law and custom, there were extensive controls over prices, wages, business licensing, and quality of production (to be discussed in the next chapter).

Indentured Servants. Labor was always in short supply in the colonies. The institutional arrangement developed to increase the migration of white European laborers was **indentured servitude**. Individuals contracted to do certain work for a term of years (usually between four and seven) in return for transportation across the Atlantic and specified payments, mainly food, clothing, housing, or perhaps some education or training in a craft or skill.[11] Indenture contracts often included "freedom dues," a specific amount of money or land to be paid upon successful completion of the contract. David Galenson argues that indentures were an extension and adaptation of the English notion of "service in husbandry," essentially an agricultural apprenticeship.[12] At the end of the contract period, the servant became part of the free population and part of the pool of free labor.

With the rise of the plantation system in the colonies surrounding the Chesapeake Bay, the demand for indentured servants increased dramatically. Indeed, the majority of the over 20,000 servant registrants analyzed by Galenson went to the Chesapeake. They were predominantly males in their late teens and early twenties. The most commonly listed occupations were farmer, artisan, (unskilled) laborer, and domestic servant.

Work by Galenson and Robert Heavener shows in detail the extent of the organized markets available for this form of unfree labor.[13] Thousands of people came over this way; Galenson estimates net white migration to have been 600,000 between 1650 and 1780. Estimates of the proportion of indentured servants among the white immigrants to the Chesapeake area range from one-half to three-quarters. Those who signed indenture contracts of their own free will could do so in England with sea captains or merchants in the servant trade. Galenson found a good deal of bargaining between potential servants and those offering contracts. The cost of passage was paid by the holder of the indenture contract in England, and, upon arrival in American ports, the contracts (and the people) were sold, usually on the ships before the servants disembarked. The purchase price was equal to covered costs plus an approximate 50 percent markup. Generally, the price fetched depended upon the age, sex, and skills of the servant, given the market conditions in the colonies. Indenture contracts had status in courts of law, and servants could appeal to the courts for violations of their rights. Children born of indentured servants during servitude were born free, but it was customary, especially in New England, to place teenagers into apprenticeships to learn trades. Edmund Morgan, in *The Puritan Family*, suggests this was done in part to relieve parents of the problems of coping with their own teenagers!

Farley Grubb and Tony Stitt attribute the rather abrupt shift from reliance on white servants to black slaves at the turn of the eighteenth century to the wars of King William III and, especially, Queen Anne. These wars reduced the supply of prime-aged males, which in turn reduced contract lengths.[14] With the return of peace, the market for indentured servants revived, but not to its previous numbers.

Redemptioners. Immigrants from the European continent, especially Germans, came to the colonies with a status different from that of English immigrants. Known as **redemptioners**, they were brought over by ship captains who then allowed them time to arrange to pay for their passage after arrival. Payment was often made by placing one or more of their children into indenture to raise the money. Whereas English servants usually came over alone, the Germans came in families, bringing their own supplies and movable property with them.[15]

Prisoners. A less common, but perhaps more widely known (thanks to Hollywood), method of getting labor to the colonies was to send convicted felons. The convicts were sold as indentured servants at dockside. These cases, called "His Majesty's seven-year passengers," were men and women convicted of one of the 300-odd crimes punishable by death in England, who were allowed to live on condition that they would transport themselves elsewhere.

This group of immigrants was unpopular in the colonies, but efforts there to legislate against them were thrown out repeatedly by the Board of Trade lawyers who oversaw colonial operations from England. The shipments stopped during the Revolution, but following the signing of the Treaty of Paris (sometimes confusingly called the Treaty of Versailles) in 1783, British courts, oblivious to the meaning of American independence, resumed shipments. Finally, in 1788, Congress, by resolution, forbade further convict transports from England, and the British turned to Australia as a dumping ground.

There were also the special categories of rebels and prisoners of war. A letter written by the Massachusetts Bay Colony Puritan leader, John Cotton, to his friend Cromwell, provides a glimpse of this particular segment of the early colonial labor supply. Unlike convicts, military prisoners, mainly young males, were particularly desirable:

> The Scots, whom God delivered into your hands at Dunbarre, and whereof sundry were sent hither, we have been desirous (as we could) to make their yoke easy. Such as were sick of scurvy or other diseases have not wanted physick and Chyurgery. They have not been sold for slaves to perpetuall servitude, but for 6 or 7 or 8 years, as we do our owne; and he that bought the most of them (I heare) buildeth houses for them, for every 4 an house, layeth some acres of ground thereto, which he giveth them as their owne, requiering 3 dayes in the weeke to worke for him (by turnes) and 4 dayes for themselves, and promiseth, assone as they can repay him the money he layed out for them, he will set them at liberty.[16]

Ship captains wanted servants and prisoners as cargo and no doubt traded them directly for colonial produce to take back on their return voyage. The trade was profitable for all. Later on, by the mid-eighteenth century, improved conditions at home, natural population growth in the colonies, increasing colonial demand for shipments of European goods, and an increasing abundance of black slaves made white indentured servants less desirable than in earlier times. Black slaves cost more than white servants, on the average, because their "contract" to the buyer was superior to that of white servants. Thus slaves tended to be more profitable.

Slaves. African slaves were not protected as British subjects; they were human beings without the right to contract their own labor. Their term of service soon came to be for life, and children, if born to a slave mother, were slaves for life—no matter who was the father. The idea that children follow the condition of the mother was of Biblical origin. Thus, the purchaser of a female slave's "life contract" also received the natural increase if the slave was a woman. This rule lasted until the American Civil War ended slavery.

African slaves had no status at all in court. There were no British laws governing them, and the colonials developed laws of their own that did not allow slaves redress of grievances. The law did allow, however, dismembering, disfiguring, and, occasionally, death to slaves who "disobeyed." In classical Roman slavery, a master might put to death a disobedient slave; in colonial America, this extreme was not usually forbidden, but it was assumed that no man would do such a thing, to "destroy his own estate" without sufficient cause.

Much has been written about American slavery, and we will discuss it at length in later chapters. It is enough to say here that it was considered absolutely necessary to colonial economic development. Slavery began in Virginia in 1619 and, as Edmund Morgan says, developed hand in hand with colonial American ideas of freedom. Farming in the North tended to be based upon smaller, family-sized plots of land; labor was mainly supplied by the families themselves. Slavery existed in all the colonies, but it was on a larger scale in the South. Although no doubt fueled by inherent racism from the beginning, labor was needed, especially on the Southern tobacco, rice, and indigo plantations. African slavery was a response to that need.

In Virginia, both land and labor could be had with a single purchase. An imported slave was also good for a headright grant, as in the case of imported servants. Because the net yield from a slave purchase was far superior to that of an indentured servant, slave prices were accordingly higher. Transportation costs for slaves were minimal, food and clothing outlays by owners were not subject to legal oversight, and the term, expiring at death, cost no freedom payments beyond simple graves.

James Kent, the great American jurist, was embarrassed by the persistence of American slavery when he wrote his *Commentaries* in 1826. There is probably no more illuminating description, even in the most lurid writings, of the legal status of the American slave than in Kent's spare lines:

> Slaves are considered...though not in criminal prosecutions as things or property, rather than persons, and are vendible as personal estate. They cannot take property by descent or purchase, and all they find, and all they hold, belongs to the master. They cannot make law-

> ful contracts, and they are deprived of civil rights. They are assets in the hands of executors, for the payment of debts, and cannot be emancipated by will or otherwise, to the prejudice of creditors. Their condition is more analogous to that of the slaves of the ancients than to that of villeins of feudal times, both in respect to the degradation of the slaves and the full dominion and power of the master.[17]

The laws of the colonies, until 1776, could not be repugnant to the laws of England. In 1772, in the Sommersett case heard in London, Chief Justice Lord William Mansfield held that English law did not support slavery. The ruling led ultimately to compensated emancipation in the British Caribbean Islands in the 1830s and to the peaceful extinction of African slavery in the British Empire. But it came too late for the Americans. Slavery passed through the Revolution, was recognized in the federal Constitution (for congressional apportionment, each slave was worth three-fifths of a person), and, nine decades after the Sommersett case, in a blending of slavery with states' rights, the Americans solved their own problem by a bloody civil war. The international slave trade had been prohibited by the Constitution since 1808, but statesmanship and jurisprudence could not find a peaceful way to root the institution out of American society.

The Land

From the outset, the colonists were considered English subjects and the colonies English land. King James was perfectly clear about this in the charter of 1606. He said that the colonists departing for Virginia "shall have and enjoy all Liberties, Franchises and Immunities, within any of our other Dominions...as if they had been abiding and born, within this our Realm of England."[18]

As we noted, Europeans considered conquest, if it was from non-Christian occupiers of land, a legitimate transfer of ownership to Christians. If no non-Christian owner could be identified, then discovery alone was sufficient. Such was as true of any other Europeans as of the English. For example, the English claimed New York by right of discovery and considered the Dutch settlement there usurpation. They eventually took New York from the Dutch by war and treaty. As for the Indians living in New York at the time, they either received land from the English (as did the Iroquois), or they were simply killed or driven off.

Property Rights. In theory, all English land belonged to the king. He was the sole and absolute owner. Only he, as the Lord Paramount, was beholden to no one save God for his property rights. He was the "donor," and without his authority, there were no land ownership rights for his subjects. According to English feudalism, all land ownership was a grant for services from the king. All Englishmen were the king's tenants on their land; Englishwomen generally did not hold title to land. This is most easily understood in the colonial inheritance laws and customs. When a man died, he conventionally willed his real estate to his sons, but his widow was allowed to use some or all of the property until her death or remarriage. The widow was granted a right to the flow of income generated by the land, but not a right to the land itself.[19] The English developed elaborate techniques for transfers of rights to land, including written deeds of ownership after passage of *The Statute of Frauds* in 1677. Secure property rights in land established a precedent for the establishment of secure property rights in general.

In the United States today, the role of the king has evolved in some sense to that of the state. Thus, if you do not pay your property taxes, your rights are annulled for the amount of the taxes. In other countries, land can be owned *allodially*—by absolute right—but not in the United States. This is an uncelebrated part of our English heritage. To these authors' knowledge, the American people were never asked by what right they wanted to own their land.

Indian Land. European techniques of land transfer were of crucial importance in the dispossession of the Indians, since they had no tradition of private property, no written evidence of ownership. They might obtain land (their own, or someone else's) from the king (or his agents, including colonial governments) by grant or purchase or treaty, but they had no "natural rights" to the land they had long hunted over except the right of "occupancy"—which was feeble indeed, since European law did not recognize the manner in which the Indians "occupied" their lands. In the beginning, indeed into the nineteenth century, as Terry Anderson and Fred McChesney demonstrate, this right of occupancy was respected, and Europeans were inclined to acquire the land through trade.[20] All colonial governments attempted (with uneven success) to restrict purchases from the Indians by private settlers. This policy was necessary because claims of specific tribes could not be shown by any written instruments except those acquired from the whites themselves.

Although the Indians farmed a portion of their land (after all, they shared their techniques with the first European settlers), they logically preferred their traditional diet, which included the meat of wild animals. The European preference for the meat of domesticated animals meant that the Indian diet required significantly more land per capita. Stanley Lebergott reports that, while Europeans needed about 2 acres per person, the Indians required 1,000 to 2,000 times as much.[21] The value of North American land, as Europeans planned to use it, was greater to them than it was to the Indians. This is not an argument that it was acceptable for Europeans to take the land. It simply points out that the acquisition through trade (or purchase) of even a few acres of Indian land at prices an Indian would find reasonable gave rise to the promise of a long-term capital gain. As the European population grew relative to the Indian, the latter's land-intensive lifestyle was increasingly threatened.[22]

Land Acquisition by Individuals. Apart from the acquisition of Indian land, white Europeans acquired original titles to land in America in five major ways, by: (1) ownership shares in the founding colonization companies; (2) headright grants; (3) purchase from governments; (4) preemption ("squatters' rights"); and (5) special purpose grants of governments.

1. *Ownership shares.* In the cases of Virginia and Plymouth, some land rights were assigned on a per-share basis. In Virginia, land was also granted in large blocks in consideration for subscriptions in cash that did not entitle the subscribers to full membership in the company. Thousands of acres originally were assigned in this manner.

2. *Headright grants.* In the case of headright land grants, 50 acres were commonly given to, or for, each man, woman, or child who crossed the ocean. (There was considerable variation, especially in Virginia.) If the grant was 50 acres and one man came, he got 50 acres. If he brought over four other people, he would acquire 250 acres by headright. Such was the policy in Virginia, New York, New Jersey, the Carolinas, and to some extent in Maryland, Pennsylvania, and Georgia. Initially, in Virginia, there were few limits on the amount of headright land granted, but this was modified following charges the privilege was being abused. In a country that needed both land settlement and people, the headright system was a powerful stimulus for colonization.

3. *Purchase from governments.* All colonies finally developed techniques for outright sales of land by the colonial governments. The first of the colonies to attempt to transfer nearly all of its land by sale alone was Pennsylvania. William Penn had a grant of 47 million acres and hoped to sell most of it. By the mid-eighteenth century, all the colonies had developed the practice of land disposal for cash payment only.

4. *Preemption.* Attitudes regarding preemption, or land transfers to individuals for actual settlement, varied. In the Southern and Middle colonies, preemption came to be encouraged, but not in New England. The issue of "squatters' rights" came to the fore by the third quarter of the eighteenth century, when a rapidly growing population faced a largely empty wilderness to the west. This circumstance produced a number of settlers who, for lack of money or knowledge of the law, or because of indifference to the law, began moving into empty lands. By the end of the Revolutionary period, the trickle became a flood.

There had always been **squatters**, those residing on land to which they had no title. In fact, there were squatters in Massachusetts before 1630. The original settlers of Connecticut were technically squatters—they had moved into that territory without leave. Vermont, as early as 1752, had a large population of squatters. The famous armed militia, the Green Mountain Boys, was a band of armed squatters prepared to defend their cleared lands. In New England, squatter settlements were resisted by government, but in the Middle colonies and the South, especially in Virginia, squatters were desired as pioneers, and land-rich governments were generous with preemption land transfers.

5. *Special-purpose grants.* Colonial governments also granted lands for various special purposes, such as to encourage settlement or industry or bridges or ferries or whatever. In Massachusetts, grants were made to form new congregations in frontier townships. Land, called a *glebe*, was granted to help support churches. Soldiers were commonly awarded land in payment for their services. Land was also given to encourage special trades or services: Colonel Williams, founder of Williams College, received 200 acres to build a fort and grist mill; in Massachusetts, an Indian named Hobbamock received land in payment for his services as an interpreter.

By all such means, the colonial land was slowly filled with people. Their rights in that land are of crucial importance as a background to subsequent American economic development. Colonial land ownership contained the seeds of the American capitalism that was to come.

It is customary to think of individual ownership in real property as a "bundle of rights." A buyer has a bundle different from that of a landlord or a sharecropper. In England, during the centuries after the Norman Conquest, a complex net of feudal relationships based upon mutual obligations produced an intricate set of rights in real property. Those rights, the content of ownership, are called the **tenure**. Fortunately, colonial land laws were relatively simple because the Crown permitted only one tenure to be established in America, **free and common socage**. In other parts of the New World many more tenures existed; in such places a far more unequal distribution of land wealth persists to this day. The main distinguishing characteristics of free and common socage were:

1. It was perpetual (not limited to any term of years).
2. It was directly heritable by heirs (it did not need to be regranted by the donor).
3. It could be passed by will.
4. All the obligations on it had to be "fixed and certain."
5. The right of waste existed fully.
6. Socage land was freely *alienable* (it could be sold) by its owner.

These characteristics were shared by military tenures in fee simple (that is, the "simple feud," or direct inheritance) in England. In time, Americans came to call their tenure **fee simple**, and the word *socage* vanished from common use.

By whichever name it is called, the incidents (the costs) of this tenure generally included fixed payments on the land alone, known as *reserved ground rents*, which were annually due to the donor. In colonial America, the bundle of fixed incidents was combined into singular periodic payments called **quit rents**, which meant that the owner who paid them was "quit and free" of all other obligations. These rents eventually became the local property taxes of modern America. If the donor (now the state government and its local units) does not receive tax payments for these obligations, the tenure simply vanishes and ownership reverts to the donor. Some colonists resisted paying these taxes because they considered them "foreign" and unjust. In some colonies, the isolation of settlements made collections difficult.

We need not go further into the complex topic of land law to get the gist of it for our purposes.[23] Americans who bought land could sell it if they wished; buyers had the same rights as sellers. The land could be divided, or its nature changed (trees cut, fields planted, ores mined, wells drilled, ponds constructed). All that was due the seller was the sale price. Sellers could, and still can, reserve certain rights—for example, mineral rights. Since taxes are due in order for the tenure to be maintained, the tenure imposes a cost for holding land idle, and there is an inducement to keep only as much land as will yield more than the taxes on it. This force was commonly thought to have favored the development of family farms as the main vehicle of land settlement unless there were sufficient amounts of other exploitable resources on the land—such as timber, minerals, water—or unless the land could be rented, leased, or sharecropped at rates that exceeded the taxes.

Socage tenure made American land a commodity almost from the beginning, one unencumbered by other rights and obligations to it. Active land markets became characteristic of American economic history, and land **speculation** at times came close to being the main national industry. Individuals purchased land, not because they planned to use it, but because they expected that increased demand would raise its price, thereby creating a capital gain.

The freedom of the tenure also defined the freedom of its owners, causing Americans early on to view land ownership and personal freedom as linked. This relationship became a powerful tradition in American economic history, to be eroded slowly in the twentieth century as land became encumbered by the larger needs of society. For the most part, though, from colonial times until the mid-twentieth century, the land itself was a major commodity in the developing market economy and the base for exploitation of its natural resources by individual enterprises. At the time of colonization, a fifth of all newly discovered precious metals had been reserved for the Crown, but few such reservations remained for the state when coal, oil, iron, and other minerals began to be extracted and refined by private owners in the years of American industrialization.

The Colonies

The sequence of colonization was more or less a matter of chance, depending upon events in Europe as well as in America. However, there is a problem with the founding dates of the individual colonies. The question is whether the year of the charter or that of the first permanent settlement should be considered. We will follow the custom of dating by the settlement (see Figure 1.1). Virginia, in 1607, was supposed to be a profit-making enterprise for a joint-stock company. The Plymouth Colony (1620) and the Massachusetts Bay Colony (1630) were of religious origins, created by the flight from the persecution of the established church in England. Let's take a look at each of these to see at a more detailed level what it took to be successful in the New World.

FIGURE 1.1 Colonial Cities and Their Founding Dates

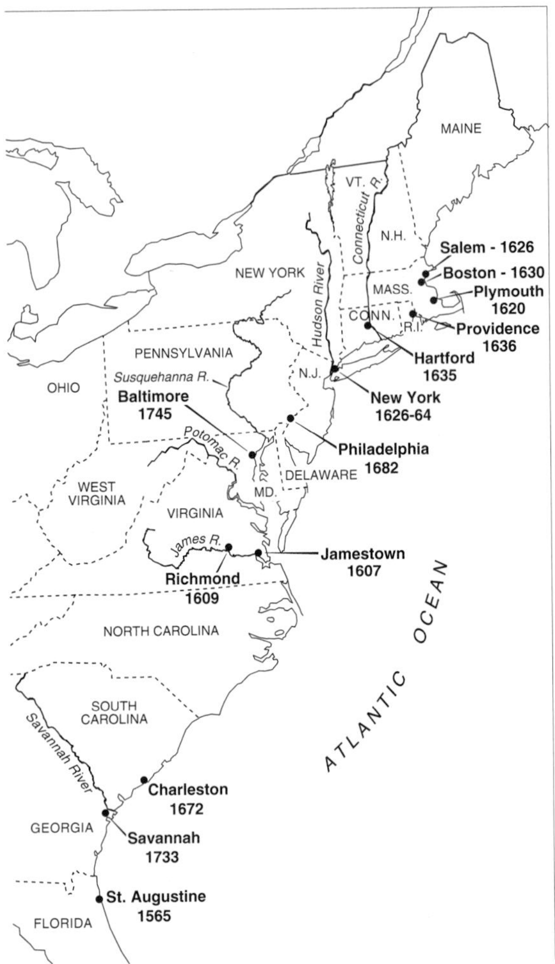

The earliest colonial cities were either seaports or were situated on water routes leading to the sea. St. Augustine was a Spanish settlement. The English settlements began with Jamestown in 1607, followed by Richmond, Plymouth, Salem, and Boston. The final English colony was founded in Savannah in 1733.

Jamestown. A patent was issued to the Virginia Company of London on 6 April 1606 "to reduce a colony of sondry of or [our] people to yt [that] part of America commonly called Virginia."[24] The advisory paper prepared for the company's officers, similar to those prepared for the East India Company and other merchant adventures, contains passages that reveal the investors' commercial intentions. The choice of a site was to be such that an entrepôt could be established:

"...you shall do your best endavor to find out a safe port in the entrance of some navigable river making choice of such a one as runs farthest into the land..."[25]

On 13 May 1607 the settlement at Jamestown was founded, and, within two years, a second settlement was formed 20 miles from the Jamestown fort. Economic and political control over the colony was vested in a governor, the company's man in Virginia. Between 1607 and 1622 there were two periods when the company's methods were revised to incorporate lessons from its learning-by-doing.

The first of these, in 1609, gave the adventurers full political and economic control. The reorganization reduced expectations of sudden wealth and focused attention on the need for a labor supply to produce staples that would find a market in England. The model became more a plantation and less a pirates' den. Indentured servants supplied the labor; they were expected to draw their food supply from the company's common land plus the contiguous forests and water. Naval stores (pitch and tar) from the forests were to supply the initial staple production necessary to provide the company's revenue.

After a slow start, the company's production diminished. Many of the original adventurers dropped out, and few new ones appeared to take their place. As a result, few new colonists were sent, and the numbers (350 in 1616 and 400 in 1618) were deemed insufficient for staple production. In 1614, the initial settlers' seven-year indentures expired, and many elected to remain in Virginia. By the end of that year, there were 81 "free" settlers in the colony. It became the practice to allot these people tenant farms on the assumption that encouraging private enterprise might develop the colony faster than the existing policy of farming the land as a large plantation. As more settlers fulfilled the terms of their indentures, and few new ones arrived to take their place, the number of tenant farms increased dramatically while the company's plantation diminished. A Royal Investigation revealed there was only one plow in the colony in 1618. If there had been more at an earlier date, they had not been replaced. By 1619, the plantation had disappeared for all intents and purposes.

At the same time, the private sector turned to tobacco production. By 1613, Virginians discovered their tobacco was of marketable quality, and a few pounds were taken to England a year later. After 1616, the quantity increased dramatically. Tobacco appeared to be the staple the colony needed, but more and more labor and land devoted to tobacco production meant less food. As early as 1616, Governor Dale was forced to require each man to plant two acres with wheat to minimize the degree of dependency on English food supplies. Such edicts were difficult to enforce, and dependency increased. The colony's economy became one-sided, with too much dependence on supplies from England. This was viewed as bad, both economically and politically. The colony's production was devoted almost exclusively to supplying a vice that the adventurers (and a majority of Englishmen) condemned at that time.

The reforms of 1618, like those of 1609, resulted from the colony's failure to live up to the adventurers' expectations. Reorganization necessitated study of why the colony was failing and what could be done to accomplish its objectives. Land had to be diverted to the production of food and staples other than tobacco. Adequate food supplies were essential for the existing colonists and the potential colonists who had been dissuaded by conditions within the colony. Public lands had to be reoccupied to generate revenue for the company. All these required an increase in the labor supply. This may have been futile, for as Morgan pointed out, "Englishmen simply did not envisage a need to work for the mere purpose of staying alive."[26] Colonists' complaints about economic, political, and social conditions suggested the efficacy of a definite and permanent land tenure policy, clearly established property rights, the abolition of martial law, and the establishment of the Virginia Assembly.

The first assembly passed laws restricting tobacco production. There were expectations the colony could produce iron, silk, wine, naval stores, salt, and several other items that would help make the colony self-sufficient while producing a profitable trade surplus. These expectations were doomed to disappointment. The company advertised for new settlers, especially those in skilled trades. Six hundred new settlers were sent to Virginia in 1619, and more newcomers arrived over the next few years.

In 1622, the company wrote to the leaders at Jamestown inquiring as to when they could expect a return. The company felt that too much effort was going into agriculture and not enough into commerce, that domestic concerns were of greater import to the colonists than was international trade. Although a self-sufficient entrepôt was desired, it was being neglected. The letter "intreats" the Virginians to find a profitable staple; it speaks of necessary urban improvements at the entrepôt.

In March 1622, an Indian massacre disrupted the company's reorganization plans as well as the day-to-day life of the colony. Many private settlements were abandoned. Colonists unable to provide for themselves became wards of the essentially bankrupt company. Even without the massacre, it is doubtful the reorganization scheme would have proved successful. The massacre's significance was that, had the company benefited from learning-by-doing (a dubious assumption), it was no longer able to use the information.

The King and privy council began a Royal Investigation into the Virginia Company in 1623 that became a long political wrestling match between opposing factions. Jamestown's location was deemed unhealthy; its defenses were deemed inadequate. There was no inn or guesthouse for newly arriving colonists, and the houses themselves provided a minimum standard of accommodation. Few staples were produced on the dispersed settlements. The company had transported 6,000–10,000 people (there was disagreement on how many), and, at most, 2,500 remained. Tobacco remained the only profitable staple, and many people still considered that undesirable. Accordingly, the King recalled the Virginia Company's charter, and, in 1624, Virginia became the first royal colony. It was the first government bailout in North America. Thereafter, the colony was permitted to develop as a commonwealth of dispersed tobacco plantations. It is debatable whether Virginia would have survived in the absence of government sponsorship.

Plymouth. The Virginia Company's charter provided for a northern colony. The attempt by the Plymouth (U.K.) Company to establish a settlement at Sagadahoc, Maine, on the Kennebec River, proved unsuccessful and was abandoned. The Pilgrims were the next group to attempt settlement in New England. Pursuing their religious beliefs, they left England for Holland, but, at the beginning of the Thirty Years War, they returned to England, then sailed to the New World. The Pilgrims hoped to settle in the northern part of the Virginia Company's territory, but three problems stood in their way: (1) They needed a patent from the Virginia Company granting them permission to settle on its land. (2) They needed the King's permission, and he was not receptive to the idea. (3) They needed money.

As we have seen, the Virginia Company was anxious to have additional signed-up settlers. The patent granted to the Pilgrims has not survived, but a few sentences in Bradford's history lead to the conclusion that the land must have been near the mouth of the Hudson River; the Virginia Company could not offer a patent for land north of the forty-first parallel. They also could not offer religious toleration without the King's permission. The Pilgrims were forced to "accept" religious principles that were against their beliefs, particularly the supremacy of the King and the Archbishop of Canterbury over their church. Part of the transportation cost was hypocrisy.

The most important question was who would advance money for the voyage and supplies until the new colony became self-sufficient. All previous experience suggested that a large outlay was required, and the Pilgrims' resources were barely sufficient to get them back to England. Even in 1619, the Virginia Company could not divert funds to a northern colony. Enter Thomas Weston, citizen of London, ironmonger, and minor merchant adventurer; a man who had helped the Pilgrims once before. Weston headed a ten-year-old company that was looking for such an investment opportunity. The 70 small subscribers Weston organized were described in Captain John Smith's *Generall Historie* as "...not a corporation but knit together by a voluntary combination without restraint or penalty, aiming to do good and plant religion."

Weston's terms were harsh, but they were similar to those of the Virginia Company.[27] Weston's adventurers would pay for the hiring of a ship, supplies, and transportation. In exchange, the colonists were bound to work for seven years at fur trading, fishing, lumbering, or whatever other profitable employment they could discover. All profit over bare subsistence went to the company. These terms must be viewed as highly speculative. The Pilgrims were predominantly cloth and silk workers; some knew a bit about farming, but they knew nothing about the kinds of employment that might prove profitable in North America.

The Pilgrims reached New England in late 1620, far to the north of their original destination, on land to which they had no title. Too late to gather what had grown naturally, the Pilgrims experienced a terrible first winter in which as many as half of them died. With a preoccupation on survival, little was produced. When the *Mayflower* returned to England in April 1621, and it was learned that the colony had been established north of the Virginia grant, Weston and his group immediately obtained a new patent from the Council for New England, a group to whom the King had granted all land in North America between 40° and 48°.[28] The fact that the Mayflower returned empty caused Weston to write a letter of complaint threatening to cease shipments of supplies if the colony failed to ship furs promptly.

In November 1621, the *Fortune* arrived in Plymouth with the new patent, 36 new settlers, and no provisions. Governor William Bradford warned Weston that the combination of additional people and no provisions would prove a severe hardship. By spring 1622, famine struck the colony. Meanwhile, the *Fortune* sailed back to England with a full cargo of cedar clapboard and beaver and other pelts, but the French captured it, and the cargo was confiscated.[29]

For the first two years, the Pilgrims lived communally. All worked for the company, and all assets were divided equally. In 1623, the settlers requested that they be permitted to work for themselves and be taxed. They felt that some had not contributed their fair share of the labor since they could not see any direct return to their personal welfare. As a result, each family was assigned a plot of land; the size of the plot depended on the size of the family. The assignment was for their present use and could not be passed on to heirs.[30] Assets continued to be held communally until 1627. The shift to private property increased the colony's output, but as a commercial venture, the colony never yielded a dividend on the investment.

Plymouth seemed like a satisfactory site for a plantation, but the bay did not provide good port facilities for ships engaged in the transoceanic trade. The soil near Plymouth was poor. While it was sufficient to grow the colony's food and some surplus corn to trade with the natives, it was too rocky to grow exportable staples that would provide a base for economic growth. Thus, in their search for an exportable staple, the colonists turned primarily to fishing and the fur trade.[31]

In spite of its location near the north Atlantic fishing grounds, Plymouth never profited from fishing. The colony lacked a source of capital to acquire a fishing fleet. More to the point, most Pilgrims were not sailors and preferred to earn their livelihood off the land. The beaver trade proved more promising. Within a year of their arrival, the Pilgrims began to explore the possibility of trade with the natives. Over the next 15 years, they established several permanent trading posts where factors traded tools and cloth for furs. Plymouth came to control the fur trade of New England, but, as more settlers arrived, that trade dwindled. It was successful while it lasted; Bradford estimated that £10,000 in beaver and otter pelts were shipped to England between 1631 and 1636.[32]

Such mercantile operations depended upon English credit, but Plymouth lacked commercial contracts with English trading houses. Plymouth merchants developed some trade with the Caribbean islands, but it was always small. After 1630, Plymouth became involved in a coastal trade with the Massachusetts Bay colony.[33]

Weston's original set of adventurers dissolved their partnership in December 1624, after four years of "losses and crosses at sea." The official reason was the colony's religious practice, but the lack of any return had to be just as compelling. A group of sympathetic adventurers bought out those anxious to separate. Plymouth became self-sufficient at an earlier date than did Jamestown, but neither colony could be termed successful.

Massachusetts Bay. In 1624, Captain John Smith gave the name "Massachusetts" to the coast with the rich fishing grounds he explored. The previous year, the Council for New England awarded a patent to the Dorchester Company, which planned to establish a settlement on Cape Ann, near present-day Gloucester. This company was founded to provide a Puritan refuge from religious difficulties in England, but it folded in 1626. Only a few colonists remained in 1628 when the Council granted a patent to the New England Company, a group of Puritan merchants from Boston in Lincolnshire, who assumed the responsibilities of the Dorchester Company. This group, all good businessmen, recognized the area's potential profitability. They checked to make sure they had a valid patent, and, to make doubly sure, they obtained a Royal Charter confirming the grant of all land between the Merrimac and the Charles Rivers, from sea to sea. In the process, they obtained a new title, "The Governor and Company of the Massachusetts Bay in New England."

The Royal Charter recognized 20 patentees as constituting the company. Seven of the 18 "assistants" plus the governor and deputy governor constituted a quota for business purposes. The company was free to choose how many more "freemen," stockholders with voting rights, there would be. The officers were to be elected by the freemen at meetings called the "General Courts." The charter granted the company full executive and legislative power, subject only to the laws of England. It was the company that was given "full and absolute power and authority, to correct, punish, pardon, and rule" all English subjects who inhabited or visited land within its jurisdiction. The charter also required that the company protect its colonists, to adopt protective measures "for their special defense and safety, to encounter, expulse, repulse, repel, and resist by force of arms, as well by sea as by land, and by all fitting ways and means whatsoever, all such persons as shall at any time hereafter attempt or enterprise the destruction, invasion, detriment, or annoyance of the members of the Massachusetts Bay Company."[34] It was decided that the charter would move with the company to Massachusetts; the General Courts would be held there. Thus, only those stockholders who made the journey would be able to attend the meetings and vote. Consequently, effective power was to be in New England, not in England.[35]

The leaders of Massachusetts Bay were wealthy and prominent people; 17 large ships brought over 1,200 settlers during 1630. In spite of superior planning and resources, this group also experienced a hard first winter. This colony was distinctly different from Virginia, a fact that was recognized by the Puritans. In a 1633 letter to the company's London secretary, a Boston Puritan alleged that Virginia was settled purely for profit, but the Massachusetts Bay settlers went "some to satisfy their own curiosity in point of conscience, others, which was more general, to transport the Gospel to those heathen that never heard thereof."[36] In fact, most of them went to establish a church (and commonwealth) on Calvinist principles and to escape from the policies of Charles I and Archbishop Laud. Over the decade of the 1630s, thousands of Puritans fled to New England. By 1640, with the outbreak of civil war in Scotland and then England, migration ceased.

The economic success of Massachusetts Bay is well known. The ample means of the founders, the desire to colonize rather than to profit, the large numbers of colonists compared with earlier settlements, and the celebrated "Yankee ingenuity" of the colonists all contributed to its success. Plymouth and Jamestown, both established on the profit motive, looked like withered oldsters in comparison to this vigorous youth.

Throughout the first year, seven towns, including Shawmut (Boston), were established.[37] Originally the main encampment was at Charlestown, directly across the Charles River, but Boston became the colony's political center during the first year when Governor John Winthrop moved there. The site of Boston proved ideal for trade. The peninsula was at the center of the network of settlements; it was the crucial link in communication between towns, and between those towns and the rest of the world. While travel by land was cumbersome, travel by water was easy, and ferry service between the peninsula and nearby towns commenced at an early date. Furthermore, Boston Bay afforded an ideal harbor. Near the shore, the bay was shallow; piers and wharves could be easily constructed. Farther out, the bay was deep; the largest ocean-going ships could find safe anchorage.

By 1640 Boston had grown to almost 2,000 and the colony to 12,000. Boston attracted a merchant class, including several from London, the vast majority with good connections in England.[38] Newcomers typically brought little but cash with them; most of what they needed they could obtain once they arrived, quite the opposite of the experiences of Jamestown and Plymouth. Their cash purchased necessities from established settlers who then used the cash to purchase English goods that were often carried on the same ships as newcomers. Boston became the starting point for new settlers, the marketplace for the goods to initiate settlement, and the entrepôt for English goods and the colony's agricultural surplus.

With the arrival of the Massachusetts Bay Puritans, the Plymouth Pilgrims received an economic boost. The Boston market, 40 miles to the north, proved more profitable than the English market 3,000 miles to the east. For example, Boston provided an external market for Plymouth livestock and, therefore, a source of money income. In time, the value of the livestock trade and other agricultural produce surpassed that of Plymouth's beaver trade with the Indians.

During the first decade, the market was focused on newcomers. Demand often exceeded supply, with inflation the inevitable result. As the rate of settlement slackened, the domestic market for the colony's agricultural surplus weakened. Staple agricultural production for the English market was as infeasible for Massachusetts Bay as for Plymouth. This caused difficulties in the short run, but, in the long run, Boston merchants found other outlets. Three major markets developed in the years after 1640. Contacts with English merchants provided information about a market for wood products in Spain and in the Atlantic islands. These same contacts also provided information about a market for the cheap wheat and other grains that made up the bulk of the colony's surplus. A second market developed in outfitting and provisioning ships. This market grew continuously throughout the 1640s as Boston improved its harbor facilities. The third market developed when Caribbean planters began to specialize in sugar production and had to import food. By 1650, Massachusetts Bay's exports to the Caribbean were greater than their exports to Europe.

The overseas trade accelerated change within the colony and, less than 20 years after its founding, Boston was a commercial city with tradesmen and craftsmen who transformed the agricultural surplus into leather, flour, and the like. Shipbuilding developed to complement the outfitting, provisioning, and repairing functions. And, as the Dorchester Company had hoped, the fishing industry developed a firm base. Boston was the political and economic capital not only of the commonwealth, but also of all of New England. In 1691, the Massachusetts Bay Colony was combined with Plymouth to form the "Province of Massachusetts Bay," a province that would find its executive and legislative independence increasingly subjected to the laws of England.[39]

Other Colonies. The establishment of the colony of Maryland in 1634 was partly motivated by Lord Baltimore's desire to find a haven for Roman Catholics, but it was also meant to be profitable, the profits to come from land sales, feudal taxes, and fees of all sorts. The flight of Roger Williams from Puritan Massachusetts (he was banished) to Rhode Island (1644, a charter granted in 1663) was again motivated in part by religious differences, this time exclusively in the New World.

Connecticut was an offshoot of the Massachusetts Bay Colony. In 1639, settlers in New Haven organized themselves into a permanent government. Then, in an amended constitution of 1643, only "members of some or other of the approved churches of New England" were allowed to vote and hold office. In 1662, Connecticut was granted a more liberal charter by Charles II.

Religion again was the major force behind the proprietary colony of Pennsylvania, founded in 1681, the year of William Penn's takeover; the Swedes and the Dutch had already been there some four decades. Pennsylvania began as a huge land grant awarded to Penn by Charles II in payment of an old debt owed to Penn's father, Admiral Sir William Penn. The Quaker leader dreamed of a haven for his persecuted co-religionists and other Protestant groups. Penn also hoped, vainly, that he would make a profit from land sales and rents.

Delaware came into existence in 1702 (charter signed in 1701) after separation from Pennsylvania, due in part to a boundary dispute between Penn and Lord Baltimore's heir. Georgia (1773) began mainly as a charitable enterprise, with both slavery and rum forbidden, but ended up as a royal colony with a more lowly end, such as money, on everyone's mind.

The Stadhuys of New Amsterdam (New York City) in 1679 reflects the cultural and economic endowment of the Dutch.

That was clear when black slavery was introduced in order to make the colony pay. To make life there more bearable, rum imports and consumption also came to be allowed.

New York was settled by charter from the Dutch West India Company. The charter was granted in 1621; settlement at Albany dates from 1624, and permanent settlement on Manhattan is dated from a fort built there in 1626. The British took over the New York Colony in 1664. It continued as a proprietary colony of James, Duke of York, until he became King of England in 1685.

New Jersey began with Dutch and Swedish settlers. Then, for a short time, it had several English proprietary owners. Part of the colony was appended to Penn's grant in 1681. In 1702, the remainder became a royal colony.

South and North Carolina came from the original grants to a group of proprietors for Carolina in a charter of 1663. A permanent settlement was made in 1670. By 1719, South Carolina had a royal charter, and, ten years later, the same was true of the mainly backwoods settlements that would become North Carolina.

The Colonial Empire in Retrospect

As we noted earlier, England had the greatest impact on American economic history. While other European powers established colonies as ports from which the continent's wealth could be extracted, the English inhabited the continent. As the experience of Massachusetts Bay reveals, a successful colony required a critical mass of people and of wealth; both were missing in Virginia and Plymouth. As in Plymouth, the settlers of Massachusetts Bay had an incentive that surpassed mercantilism. Their religious beliefs made it important to succeed in the New World; they did not want to return to England. The Virginia Company was a quintessential mercantilist endeavor, and it failed.

Not one of the original colonies began as a royal colony. All were private ventures, either proprietary or joint stock. But by the time of the Revolution, the problems of colonization led to crown takeovers in all but Rhode Island, Connecticut, Pennsylvania, Delaware, and Maryland. The colonies, for the most part, had existed as so many separate appendages of England, all governed from London. The scheme to unite the northern colonies under Governor Edmund Andros in 1686–1689 died when James II was driven from the throne of England. The earlier Confederation of New England (1643–1684) had come to nothing, and Benjamin Franklin's later plan to unite the colonies in 1754 at the beginning of new troubles with the French and Indians was overturned by the Board of Trade.

The British did not want a separate union on the North American continent, even a union of loyal British subjects. The sugar-producing plantation colonies of the Caribbean isles long seemed more valuable to the Crown than the backwoods settlements on the mainland. Sugar and rum were cash-earning commodities in great demand. But by the mid-eighteenth century, much had changed. What was of fundamental importance at the beginning was the mutual tie of the separate colonies to England. This would give the Americans a common pool of language, laws, customs, and business morality and practice—mutually understood foundations upon which to build their own constitutions and laws when the time came. English institutions, transplanted overseas, would continue to grow, for the most part, changed over time by new challenges met in the American environment.

NOTES

1. Francis Newton Thorpe, ed., *The Federal and State Constitutions, Colonial Charters and Other Organic Laws* (Washington: Government Printing Office, 1909), p. 46.
2. *Ibid.*
3. See Francis Dillon *A Place for Habitation, the Pilgrim Fathers and their Quest* (1973), p. 23, and David Beers Quinn, *England and the Discovery of America, 1481–1620* (1974).
4. James Shepherd and Gary Walton, *Shipping, Maritime Trade and the Economic Development of Colonial North America* (1972).
5. See, for example, Stephen Lewis, Jr., "Primary Exporting Countries," in Hollis Chenery and T. N. Srinivasan, eds., *Handbook of Development Economics*, vol. II (New York: North-Holland, 1989).
6. Ann Carlos and Stephen Nicholas, "Giants of an Earlier Capitalism: The Chartered Trading Companies as Modern Multinationals," *Business History Review*, vol. 62, no. 3, Autumn 1988, and "Theory and History: Seventeenth-Century Joint-Stock Chartered Trading Companies," *Journal of Economic History*, vol. 56, no. 4, December 1996.
7. Kenneth Jackson and Stanley Schultz, eds., *Cities in American History* (New York: Alfred A. Knopf, 1972), p. 41.
8. See Wesley Frank Craven, *Dissolution of the Virginia Company: The Failure of a Colonial Experiment* (1964), pp. 24ff. Nearly all the colonies were subsidized to some extent. The remission of taxes for the initial seven years was common, and England bore a significant portion of the cost of government, particularly defense.
9. Quinn (1974), p. 288.
10. *Ibid.*, pp. 289 and 294.
11. Either party to the contract could take the other to court if the terms of the contract were not fulfilled.
12. David Galenson, *White Servitude in Colonial America: An Economic Analysis* (1981), p. 9.
13. David Galenson, "Immigration and the Colonial Labor System: An Analysis of Length of Indenture," *EEH*, October 1977; Robert Heavener, "Indentured Servitude: The Philadelphia Market, 1771–1773," *JEH*, September 1978.

14. Farley Grubb and Tony Stitt, "The Liverpool Emigrant Servant Trade and the Transition to Slave Labor in the Chesapeake, 1695–1707: Market Adjustments to War," *EEH*, July 1994.
15. See Farley Grubb, "The Auction of Redemptioner Servants, Philadelphia, 1771–1805," *JEH*, September 1988.
16. Thomas Hutchinson, *The Hutchinson Papers* (Albany, NY: The Prince Society, 1865), vol. 1, p. 264.
17. James Kent, *Commentaries of American Law* (Boston: Little, Brown, 1884), vol. II, p. 253.
18. Thorpe (1909), p. 3788.
19. Marylynn Salmon, *Women and the Law of Property in Early America* (1986). A possible exception arose if a man died without a will. His widow was entitled to a dower's share, but the right was only for her life. She was entitled to use her share, but she could not sell or will the land to anyone else. After her death, title reverted to her husband's heirs. See also Carole Shammas, Marylynn Salmon, and Michel Dahlin, *Inheritance in America* (1987), and Alice Hanson Jones, "The Wealth of Women, 1774," in Claudia Goldin and Hugh Rockoff, *Strategic Factors in Nineteenth Century American Economic History* (1992).
20. Terry Anderson and Fred McChesney, "Raid or Trade? An Economic Model of Indian-White Relations," *Journal of Law and Economics*, April 1994.
21. Stanley Lebergott, *The Americans: An Economic Record* (New York: W. W. Norton, 1984), p. 16.
22. A good survey of the economic position of the native tribes in these years is Neal Salisbury, "The History of Native Americans from Before the Arrival of the Europeans and Africans Until the American Civil War," in Stanley Engerman and Robert Gallman, eds., *The Cambridge Economic History of the United States*, vol. 1 (1996).
23. For an analysis of the differences in inheritance practices across all the colonies, see Lee Alston and Morton Owen Shapiro, "Inheritance Laws Across the Colonies: Causes and Consequences," *JEH*, June 1984.
24. Quoted in Edward Neill, *History of the Virginia Company of London* (1968), p. 3.
25. *Ibid.*, pp. 9–10.
26. Edmund Morgan, "The Labor Problem at Jamestown, 1607–1618," *American Historical Review*, vol. 76, 1971, p. 600.
27. The terms exacted from the Pilgrims can be found in Dillon (1973), p. 120.
28. If this had been a Royal Charter, Plymouth would have been a fourteenth state. See Frances Rose-Troup, *The Massachusetts Bay Company and Its Predecessors* (1930).
29. Barbary pirates captured a second ship, the *Little James*, in 1625 in the English Channel. It was another two years before a fully laden ship from Plymouth reached England safely. See Samuel Eliot Morison, *The Story of the "Old Colony" of New Plymouth* (New York: Alfred A. Knopf, 1956), p. 124, and George Langdon, Jr., *Pilgrim Colony: A History of New Plymouth* (1966), p. 27.
30. Direct inheritance by heirs is a characteristic of socage; distribution in socage could not take place until the seven-year indenture period elapsed. See Jonathan Hughes, *Social Control in the Colonial Economy* (1976), pp. 59–65.
31. Clapboard and salt were also included in the colony's list of potential staples.
32. Quoted in Langdon (1966), p. 26.
33. See Bernard Bailyn, *The New England Merchants in the Seventeenth Century* (1955), pp. 34–35.
34. The complete charter is reprinted in Edmund Morgan, *The Founding of Massachusetts: Historians and the Sources* (Indianapolis: Bobbs-Merrill, 1964), pp. 303ff.
35. In fact, less than a dozen of the actual proprietors were present at the first meeting of the General Court held on American soil, 18 May 1631. At that meeting, 116 persons applied to be admitted as freemen. See Emmet Robert Wall, *Massachusetts Bay: The Crucial Decade, 1640–1650* (New Haven: Yale University Press, 1972), p. 6.
36. Rose-Troup (1930), p. 96.
37. See Walter Muir Whitehill, *Boston: A Topographical History* (Cambridge: The Belknap Press of Harvard University Press, 1968), p. 3, and Darrett Rutman, *Winthrop's Boston: Portrait of a Puritan Town 1630–1649* (1965), p. 27.
38. See Bailyn (1955).
39. See Rutman (1965), chap. 7. The Province of Massachusetts Bay also included Nantucket, Martha's Vineyard, and the provinces of Sagadahoc and Maine.

SUGGESTED READINGS

Articles

Alston, Lee J., and Morton Owen Shapiro. "Inheritance Laws Across the Colonies: Causes and Consequences." *Journal of Economic History*, vol. XLIV, no. 2, June 1984.

Anderson, Terry, and Fred McChesney. "Raid or Trade? An Economic Model of Indian-White Relations." *Journal of Law and Economics*, vol. XXXVII, no. 2, April 1994.

Galenson, David. "Immigration and the Colonial Labor System: An Analysis of Length of Indenture." *Explorations*

in Economic History, vol. 14, no. 4, October 1977.
———. "The Rise and Fall of Indentured Servitude in the Americas: An Economic Analysis." *Journal of Economic History*, vol. XLIV, no. 1, March 1984.
Grubb, Farley. "The Auction of Redemptioner Servants, Philadelphia, 1771–1804." *Journal of Economic History*, vol. XLVIII, no. 3, September 1988.
———,. and Tony Stitt. "The Liverpool Emigrant Servant Trade and the Transition to Slave Labor in the Chesapeake, 1695–1707: Market Adjustments to War." *Explorations in Economic History*, vol. 31, no. 3, July 1994.
Heavener, Robert. "Indentured Servitude: The Philadelphia Market, 1771–1773." *Journal of Economic History*, vol. XXXVIII, no. 3, September 1978.
Jones, Alice Hanson. "The Wealth of Women, 1774." In Claudia Goldin and Hugh Rockoff, eds. *Strategic Factors in Nineteenth Century American Economic History: A Volume to Honor Robert W. Fogel*. Chicago: University of Chicago Press, 1992.
Morgan, Edmund. "The First American Boom: Virginia 1618 to 1630." *William and Mary Quarterly*, vol. XXVIII, no. 2, April 1971.
Potter, Jim. "The Growth of Population in America, 1700–1860." In D. V. Glass and B. E. C. Eaversley, eds. *Population in History: Essays in Historical Demography*. Chicago: Aldine, 1960.
Salisbury, Neal. "The History of Native Americans from Before the Arrival of the Europeans and Africans Until the American Civil War." In Stanley Engerman and Robert Gallman, eds., *The Cambridge Economic History of the United States*, volume 1. New York: Cambridge University Press, 1996.

Books

Bailyn, Bernard. *The New England Merchants in the Seventeenth Century*. Cambridge: Harvard University Press, 1955.
Boorstin, Daniel. *The Americans: The Colonial Experience*. New York: Vintage Books, 1958.
Craven, Wesley Frank. *Dissolution of the Virginia Company: The Failure of a Colonial Experiment*. Gloucester, MA: Peter Smith, 1964 (reprinted from 1932).
Curtin, Philip. *The Atlantic Slave Trade: A Census*. Madison: University of Wisconsin Press, 1969.
Dillon, Francis. *A Place for Habitation, the Pilgrim Fathers and their Quest*. London: Hutchinson of London, 1973.
Ford, Amelia Clewly. *Colonial Precedents of Our National Land System as It Existed in 1800*. Philadelphia: Porcupine Press, 1976.
Galenson, David. *White Servitude in Colonial America: An Economic Analysis*. New York: Cambridge University Press, 1981.
Hughes, Jonathan. *Social Control in the Colonial Economy*. Charlottesville: University Press of Virginia, 1976.
Jones, Eric L. *The European Miracle*. Cambridge: Cambridge University Press, 1981.
Langdon, George D., Jr. *Pilgrim Colony: A History of New Plymouth*. New Haven: Yale University Press, 1966.
Morgan, Edmund S. *The Puritan Family: Religion and Domestic Relations in Seventeenth-Century New England*. New York: Harper & Row, 1966.
———. *American Slavery, American Freedom: The Ordeal of Colonial Virginia*. New York: Norton, 1975.
Morris, Richard. *Government and Labor in Early America*. New York: Columbia University Press, 1946.
Neill, Edward D. *History of the Virginia Company of London*. New York: Burt Franklin, 1968 (reprinted from 1869).
Notestein, Wallace. *The English People on the Eve of Colonization*. New York: Harper & Bros., 1954.
Pirenne, Henri. *A History of Europe from the Invasions to the XVI Century*. New York: University Books, 1956.
Powell, Sumner Chilton. *Puritan Village: The Formation of a New England Town*. Middletown, CT: Wesleyan University Press, 1963.
Quinn, David Beers. *England and the Discovery of America, 1481–1620*. London: George Allen & Unwin, 1974.
Rose-Troup, Frances. *The Massachusetts Bay Company and Its Predecessors*. New York: The Grafton Press, 1930.
Rutman, Darrett B. *Winthrop's Boston: Portrait of a Puritan Town 1630–1649*. Chapel Hill: University of North Carolina Press, 1965.
Salmon, Marylynn. *Women and the Law of Property in Early America*. Chapel Hill: University of North Carolina Press, 1986.
Shammas, Carole, Marylynn Salmon, and Michael Dahlin. *Inheritance in America from Colonial Times to the Present*. New Brunswick, NJ: Rutgers University Press, 1987.
Shepherd, James F., and Gary M. Walton. *Shipping, Maritime Trade and the Economic Development of Colonial North America*. New York: Cambridge University Press, 1972.
Smith, Abbot Emerson. *Colonists in Bondage: White Servitude and Convict Labor in America, 1607–1776*. Chapel Hill: University of North Carolina Press, 1947.

CHAPTER TWO

Colonial Development

To understand how the colonial economy developed, we need to explore in detail the pattern of settlement. Where the colonists lived, why they lived there, what they produced, and the legal framework within which they operated are all relevant parts of this pattern. After the first few decades, most colonists did not live in towns. The first census (1790) found only 24 places with populations of 2,500 or more. Yet those towns, many of them seaports, attracted concentrations of economic activity that proved vital for sustained economic life.

TOWNS AND SEAPORTS

In a predominantly agricultural society, if resources are evenly distributed across a flat plain, we might expect that people also would be evenly distributed. Human populations, however, are rarely distributed spatially in equal portions. People build communities, villages, towns, and cities to take advantage of commerce, government, and medical care. Even in an area such as rural Iowa that, to an Easterner, seems completely homogeneous, towns and villages are not distributed evenly. Why are they located where they are?

Location Determinants

Economists have found that a primary determinant for the location of towns is the presence of a **break-in-transport**, essentially a place of unloading and loading, as from an ocean-going ship to a riverboat. Since the original English access to this continent was by water, it is no surprise that the earliest settlements—Jamestown, Plymouth, Boston, New Amsterdam—occurred at the water's edge. But they did not occur at *random* points along the shore, for two reasons: (a) There were several possible ports in any location, depending upon the topography. (b) Some *hinterlands*, the areas surrounding towns, had access to more local produce than others. Those towns at a break-in-transport with hinterlands better able to support two-way commerce, imports *and* exports, were favored.

At first, such commerce was Indian-white—that is, furs for European goods. The colonists soon engaged in primary economic activity—farming, timbering, fishing, and mining—wherever possible. The exchange of goods that took place at the break-in-transport justified the establishment of substantial distribution and collection facilities there, such as docks, warehouses, and stores. Thus, the area surrounding those harbors with exploitable hinterlands was dominated by primary activities. Even an entrepôt location like Newport, Rhode Island, was capable of considerable growth since its port was excellent and so were its seaborn connections to other entrepôts. The eastern shore of the American continent was not a flat plain with evenly distributed resources. Because of irregularities in terrain, such as rivers and mountains, the ocean (bays, inlets) and the rivers had to be the highways. Road-building to the interior was an arduous task, and it developed only as population grew and labor became available.

The concentration of economic activity at a town might also attract governmental activity, such as a military establishment (for example, a fort with supplies) or a place where regular courts of law could meet and the civil activity of government could be transacted. At a seaport, there might be some sort of customs control and facilities for naval stores. This added to the volume of transactions at that site compared to other locations. The fact that the American colonies were offshoots of imperial England would guarantee those kinds of activities.

The number of possible sites for early settlements, a break-in-transport together with a rich hinterland and its developmental capabilities, was limited in a world of differentiated topography. Some locations were favored over others, such as waterside locations: Boston on its bay, Hartford on its river, New York and Philadelphia near the meeting of rivers and ocean, Charleston with its excellent harbor and several rivers stretching into its hinterland.

The exception was Virginia, which had the fewest towns of reasonable size in spite of having the largest colonial population (and, by that measure, the richest hinterland). Urbanization was slow in coming to Virginia because the tobacco plantations along the rivers and bays served entrepôt functions. Such waterways provided the main avenues of commerce, and even small isolated farmhouses were built with a view of the water. Ocean-going ships could easily reach a planter's dock and barter.[1] Our model needs to be altered only slightly to allow for plantations to substitute for towns in an area with an abundance of rivers, bays, coves, and inlets.

Production from the hinterland, whether it came merely to a trading post or to a collection point for more substantial activities, such as facilities to handle agricultural and timber products, in turn created the conditions for a market. Given the established property rights of colonial America (which we reviewed in the previous chapter), landowners had items to sell, and it was profitable for sellers and buyers to concentrate those activities in towns where marketing would naturally arise. If an activity enhanced the value of traded goods or provided services for traders or others, it paid a merchant to locate such activities, in most cases, in a town; the search and transactions costs (e.g., looking for custom or recording a change in ownership) of doing such business were reduced by the concentration of potential customers and suppliers. Such cost-reducing elements in economic life are called **external economies**. Their presence enhanced the possibilities that towns would grow—the greater the external economies, the greater the growth possibilities.[2]

Townships and Counties

Soon after primary economic activities were established, towns began to grow. Their density helped determine the legal and political organization of everyday life. Economics determined many locations, but there also were important noneconomic forces at work that had lasting effects. For many decades, the New England Puritans established new settlements only when there was sufficient demand to create new congregations. Religious conflicts as well as population growth helped this process along. When new congregations applied to the colony government, they were granted enough land for a new town. As a result, for a long time, New England expanded in chunks; new towns were copies of older ones. A town not only was what New Englanders called the "center," but also the supporting land around it. The result was a miniature form of government below that of the colony, yet larger than that of the village or borough.

In other colonies, expansion into the interior tended to be more continuous, but piecemeal, so that population was thinly settled. For administrative purposes, and for protection as well as for trading, a town was established, but it encompassed a larger and more heterogeneous area, the county. Since both township- and county-size units existed in England (the "hundred" and the county), these developments were not new inventions, just institutional applications to differing circumstances. One long-term result, though, was that as the Americans moved into the interior, township government prevailed where New England influence was strongest, and county government prevailed elsewhere. To this day, in states such as Illinois and Indiana, whose northern areas were settled by New Englanders and whose southern areas were settled by transplants from old Virginia, there exists a dizzying mixture of overlapping political and taxing jurisdictions. Further west, county government prevails for the same reason it did originally in Virginia: political life began with population spread thinly over large areas.

The tendency to lay areas out in rectangles of curious dimensions came from colonial practice. The rectangular township covering 36 square miles began in New England in the eighteenth century (Bennington, Vermont, was apparently the first one), and the idea of the 640-acre section (1 square mile) seems to have had its origins in North Carolina. These early beginnings were to have lasting organizational consequences when, in the Land Ordinances of 1785 and 1787, Americans determined the future layout of the continent on the basis of the colonial experiences.[3] The townships were squares, 6 miles by 6 miles, and the 36 sections were 640 acres each. A quarter section—160 acres—became a typical farm.

TABLE 2.1 Town and City Colonial Populations

Town/City	*Year*	*Population*
Philadelphia	1775	40,000
New York City	1775	25,000
Boston	1775	16,000
Charleston	1775	12,000
Newport	1775	11,000
New Haven	1771	8,300
Norwich	1774	7,000
Norfolk	1775	6,200
Baltimore	1775	6,000
New London	1774	5,400
Salem	1776	5,300
Lancaster	1776	5–6,000
Hartford	1774	4,900
Middletown	1775	4,700
Portsmouth	1775	4,600
Marblehead	1776	4,400
Providence	1774	4,400
Albany	1776	4,000
Annapolis	1775	3,700
Savannah	1775	3,200

Source: Carl Bridenbaugh, *Cities in Revolt* (New York: Oxford University Press, 1971), pp. 216–217.

The Major Towns

As noted, when the first national census was taken in 1790, there were only 24 places with population in excess of 2,500 persons. Out of a total population of 3,929,000, only 202,000 (a mere 5 percent) could be classified as "urban" residents. Fifteen years earlier, the proportion was even smaller. If we consider the 20 largest towns at the end of the 150-year colonial period, it is clear how important the role of water transport had been in their establishment and growth (see Table 2.1).

The interior cities were all located on major navigable rivers, but most urban locations were still seaports. Note also the predominance of urban centers in the Middle and New England colonies (see Figure 2.1). Philadelphia, with its rich hinterland and solid base of fabrication and primitive manufacturing, was founded late, in 1681 (survivors of earlier Dutch and Swedish groups were living in caves along the river); yet, by the Revolution, it had overtaken all. In fact, in 1776, Philadelphia was second in population only to London itself. Williamsburg, Virginia's capital and second city, contained only 1,500 inhabitants, whereas Norfolk, the seaport at the mouth of the James River, had more than 6,000. Already, the institutional wherewithal of urban life—fire departments and fire regulations, a night watch for protection against crime, almshouses for poor relief, and attention to the provision of water supplies—were developing. As Carl Bridenbaugh shows in his books *Cities in the Wilderness* and *Cities in Revolt*, the major cities were well developed as places of urban civilization by the end of the colonial period. Later in this chapter, we will examine this developing institutional structure in some detail.

Early Manufacturing

Serving primarily as points of exchange between the mainly agricultural colonies and the external world, the centers of urban life also were developing into centers of fabrication—manufacturing using the technology of the time: handwork, waterpower, and animal power. As the work of Diane Lindstrom and John Sharpless suggests, the colonial heritage, spilling over into the early national period, was one of mixed commercial manufacturing enterprises in these cities.[4] Merchants, because of the break-in-transport feature of their loca-

FIGURE 2.1 Twenty Colonial Cities

The colonial cities were primarily trading centers. Of the 20 largest, note the concentration in New England, where domestic manufacturing, processing of fish and wood products, and shipbuilding predominated. Providence was a center of the slave trade. Production of naval stores and distilling were also prominent New England economic activities.

tions, had been joined by artisans of all sorts. (The existence of external economies would lead us to expect this clustering.) Both sectors served each other and developed together; milling, leather tooling and woodworking, distilling, sugar refining, shipbuilding, spinning, hatmaking—such activities characterized the larger colonial cities. Exceptions were trades like ironworking (to some extent) and timbering, where transportation costs dictated that, because the final product weighed less than the resources used to make it, production took place at the sites of initial extraction.

Smaller villages and farmsteads also were locations for manufacturing, especially in the Middle colonies and New England. For both local needs and for export, American colonists were well along the road to industrial development, even according to European standards of the time. Carl Bridenbaugh estimates that "in the four commercial cities of the North [Boston, New York, Newport, and Philadelphia], between one-third and one-half of the gainfully employed—thousands of citizens—were artisans."[5]

Future urban growth would depend upon both commerce and manufacturing. Centers like Newport, whose hinterland would not support an urban manufacturing center, were destined to lag behind. Ultimately, in the late nineteenth century, when the Industrial Revolution came to America, it would be mainly an urban phenomenon. Even in colonial times, though, the attractiveness of external economies served to concentrate primitive manufacturing in and around the commercial towns. A crucial consequence was that British efforts in the late 1760s and early 1770s to suppress and control manufacturing fell upon these *concentrations* of artisans, craftsmen, and shop and forge workers. The close contact of the aggrieved parties produced a powerful response—thousands of angry workers joined the radicals and contributed to a revolution.

REGIONAL SPECIALIZATION

As we have discussed, the small cities and towns of colonial America served as the market for the main event of the colonial economy. *Primary production*, which employed more than nine-tenths of the population, included the major occupations of agriculture, fishing, mining, and timbering (together with the processing and shipping of the surplus for export).

Comparative Advantage

The boundaries of the original colonies were set in England by men who had never been to America and who did not even have adequate maps of the lands they granted. Their decisions were based on political expediency, not economics. Within those boundaries,

The southeast corner of Third and Market streets in Philadelphia in 1799.

however established, the towns appeared at breaks-in-transport. The question is, "What was being transported?" That was determined by economic realities. The *natural endowment*—the climate, distribution of soil, topography, kinds and quantities of trees and minerals—was a given. Its exploitation, using the knowledge, techniques, and machinery of the time, was guided by Ricardo's principle of **comparative advantage** (that one specializes in producing those goods and services in which one is relatively more efficient) to determine the direction of primary development.

In the mercantilist world, the principle of comparative advantage provided the basis for trade between two individuals or between a mother country and colony; trade between nations was restricted. If each individual or region specializes in producing those goods and services in which it is relatively more efficient, for which it has lower **opportunity costs** (costs measured in terms of the alternative foregone), trade will be profitable for both parties.

Since private profit was the main object of most colonial economic activity—the exploitation of those property rights vested in the charters—maximum profits were most desirable. Development at first proceeded on the basis of trial and error. As we discussed, the first English settlers faced a new environment and a different climate and, therefore, many unknowns. The only way to learn which strain of wheat could be grown; which native crops such as maize, potatoes (native to South America, introduced to North America by the colonists), and squashes, could be used for human food; where the great native weed, tobacco, could best be grown; what could be used as fodder for animals; and which animals could best suit colonial uses, was to try everything, learn from failure, and try again. Because the English were anxious to find ways to eliminate their dependence upon their European rivals, efforts were made by subsidy and protective measures to cultivate such exotics as mulberry trees (for the silkworm) and ginger. In the South, there was great success with two exotic imports, rice and indigo. There also was continuing hope for gold and silver discoveries; small amounts of gold were found intermittently, along with abundant supplies of the ores of baser metals.

Gradually, as the colonists learned what could be produced profitably, the next question became, "Which of those products are the *most* profitable?" If a field in Virginia or Maryland grew both wheat and tobacco successfully, profit maximization still required the determination of which crop paid more. Most Virginia tobacco growers could be wheat growers on the same land, but, given the relative costs of production and the state of the markets for wheat and tobacco, they opted for tobacco, even at the risk of starvation. As we have seen, early governors of Virginia had to order the cultivation of more wheat; in 1616 no man was allowed to plant tobacco until he had planted two acres of wheat. Tobacco farming was tried in all colonies, but, in most places outside the South, its yields were poor compared to those of other field crops. The English, seized hard and early by "Lady Nicotine," tried growing it in England, but the colonies were protected from this unlikely source of competition by appropriate legislation.

Tobacco continued to be grown in the Middle colonies and even in New England, especially in the valley of the Connecticut River, where the long, sweltering summer days rival the Congo. The choice of tobacco over wheat in Virginia, even when wheat was profitable, showed that Virginia's comparative advantage was in tobacco. When prices changed, so did the choice of crops. When tobacco prices fell relative to wheat in the mid-eighteenth century, Virginians shifted crops and surpassed Pennsylvania in wheat exports. The market changed, and with it the comparative advantage. In some places, sheep grazed instead of cattle. In others, farmers abandoned agriculture to follow trades; elsewhere, as on the Yankee hill farms, activities were diversified so that trades could be followed *on the farm*. If nothing could be done competently, and families were still determined to remain on their land, then it paid to specialize in those things that were done *least incompetently*.

Given the other factors discussed and the variance in climate, colonial development based on comparative advantage produced a fairly distinct regional specialization. It must be added that such specialization was also due to the "empire connection." The colonists traded with England, with the rest of the empire, with the Caribbean islands, and even with Europe, more than they did with each other. Thus, the specialization that developed (e.g., tobacco, rice, and indigo in the South, wheat and livestock in the Middle colonies, shipbuilding and fishing in New England) did so from the very beginning largely in response to the international market. The early Virginians needed some way to reimburse the company in London. The Plymouth colonists reorganized their company internally so that furs and other products could be sent to England to pay their debts. It was many decades after independence before purely domestic demand dictated the output patterns of the American economy. In the colonial era, the colonies grew as part of the world market and to some extent, the needs of that market dictated the way the colonies grew. New Englanders exported fish products, small manufactures, ships and shipping services, and imported food. Southerners exported rice, tobacco, indigo, and forest products, and imported manufactures.

New England

At first the colonial settlement had only one concern: simply finding the means of survival. For all the colonists, this meant acquiring food through farming, fishing, and hunting. After the bare requirements of life were found, the forces of the market and comparative advantage began to work. In New England, which had very little good-quality agricultural land, expansion of the economy quickly focused on other gifts of nature. New England's lack of quality farmland was unique. Rocks and mountains made farming a subsistence occupation at best. While the great majority of New Englanders were engaged in agriculture, most Yankee farmers had to find subsidiary occupations, such as lumbering in winter; gathering and refining maple syrup in earliest spring; running a forge, distillery, a woodworking or farm shop, or perhaps a small foundry or grist mill. Many farm families, the women in particular, became involved in manufacturing through the *putting-out system*. Entrepreneurs found it was more efficient to take (put out) the materials into the farm homes than to require the workers to come to the materials. For example, almost every step in the making of a garment, especially spinning the yarn and weaving the cloth, was accomplished with labor that was not needed for agriculture, and that included the men during the winter.

New England farmers had to use their wits to stay on the land. Corn and summer vegetables were the main field crops. The inhospitable climate, with late frosts in spring, early frosts in the fall, and rocky soil, made New England agriculture a difficult, marginal activity. When land across the mountains became available in the early nineteenth century, much of New England was simply abandoned by the backwoods Yankees who gave up the uneven struggle and fled west. Lonely stone walls and foundations, deep in the woods and now overgrown, stand as mute witnesses to their failed efforts to grow crops on stones. Among those who stayed behind, livestock raising (sheep), dairying, and lumbering kept rural New England from being totally abandoned.

Those Yankees living near the sea were quickly drawn into fishing, which had, after all, attracted Europeans to the New England shores long before there were any permanent settlements. As early as 1700, the New England fishing fleet produced 10 million pounds of fish for export, surpassing England itself. By 1775, the New England cod fishery alone employed 4,400 men and had 665 vessels. Shore stations—for salting, drying, smoking, and packing—employed many more. Whaling also became a major New England industry, with 360 ships by the 1770s. Whale oil, used for candles and lighting fuel for lamps, was the product of an industry destined for a long nineteenth-century life.

With an abundance of timber for ships and barrels, the Yankees quickly became skilled at making barrel staves, cooperage (binding barrels), and shipbuilding. The other forest products, tar and pine pitch, used to caulk and line ship hulls, added to the strength of the New England shipping industry. Sawmills were placed along streams and rivers. Shipyards appeared in places such as Newburyport, Salem, Marblehead, and New Haven, as well as in larger centers such as Boston, Portsmouth, and Newport. The native white pine was unrivalled for masts. Bog iron ore in abundant supply, along with woods for charcoal, supported an iron industry. That industry, together with a host of other trades related to shipbuilding, such as wagonmaking, ships' stores, brewing, and distilling, gave New England a base for manufacturing that supported its abundance of small towns and seaports. Farm wives spun wool, mixed it with linen threads, and wove cloth for sale in New England markets. Sheep, cattle, and hogs provided meat; cattle also supported leather tanning and shoemaking. Even before an elementary factory system appeared at the end of the eighteenth century, these town and cottage industries laid the groundwork for the industrial, commercial, and sea-going Yankee nation to come.

Winifred Rothenberg's studies of developing New England farm labor markets led her to argue that the increased productivity that came, finally, from market utilization and better farm management, even without significant technological change, freed New England farm labor for other uses, including factories, when they came. Because the available resources were being used more intelligently, a lack of technological advance did not necessarily impair productivity increases.[6]

New England's misfortune—its poor land endowment—led its colonial settlers to an adaptation that would be New England's fortune by the early nineteenth century.[7] Its merchants developed a market in the Caribbean for the surplus foodstuffs produced in New England and in the Middle colonies; its shipbuilders provided the means to get there.

The Middle Colonies

New York, New Jersey, Pennsylvania, and Delaware did contain good land. The first three had sufficient agricultural land to make a large and expanding agricultural base possible. Pennsylvania's liberal rules for land acquisition encouraged a flood of immigration. As agriculture expanded, augmented by mining, immigration swelled. There were, in addition, essentially the same trades as in New England, including shipbuilding. These, together with an abundance of land for diversified farming, supported the rapidly growing population. The two largest seaports, New York and Philadelphia, did a thriving commercial and entrepôt trade.[8] During the eighteenth century, ironmaking in Pennsylvania and New Jersey began in earnest. Trades such as shoemaking, pottery, glassmaking, woodworking, leather tanning, and the like served the bustling interior. German immigrants came in the tens of thousands to settle the rich valleys of Pennsylvania, contributing their language, architecture (the great stone barns), cuisine, and culture to Penn's colony.

The Middle colonies were especially important for the wheat grains and flour they produced in mills along the splendid rivers and creeks like the Schuylkill and the Brandywine. They were known as the "breadbasket" of the colonies.[9] The Middle colonies also were the major colonial sources of the cattle, hogs, and sheep exported to Europe and, particularly, the Caribbean, and also of dressed and salted meats. By the end of the colonial period, these colonies already had surpassed New England in population, and their growth, rooted in a diversified and expanding agricultural sector and characterized by family farming, provided a powerful internal market for growing commerce and industry in the future.

The South

The comparative advantage of the South was in plantation agriculture—tobacco—and plantation agriculture had come to mean slavery. The colonial South had an abundance of rich, arable land, raw materials, and timber. These the colonies worked not only to provide a self-sufficiency in food staples and animal husbandry, but also to produce a rich export trade in tobacco (primarily Maryland and Virginia) and rice (primarily South Carolina). Indigo was introduced into South Carolina in 1743 by Eliza Lucas, and, after 1748, it was supported by an English bounty. Pitch, turpentine, tar, and resin were produced from Southern pine forests. The cash export crops were most effectively worked by relatively unskilled labor in groups, or "gangs," because of **scale economies**: Within the limits of the land, large groups of workers produce more per worker by cooperative effort than would be true if the land and work were divided and each worker produced only from the worker's own portion. Most agricultural fieldwork using animal power and appropriate tools and machinery is subject to scale economies.

Georgia was a good example of the presence of scale economies in slave labor. The Georgia planters were originally prohibited from using slaves. After some years of failure in nearly every crop, the British finally acceded to their agitation for slavery in 1749. Georgia colonists then reported immediate agricultural success. In 1753, only four years later, there were 1,066 slaves in Georgia and 2,381 whites. Rice production thrived. By 1770, Georgia's population was 23,400, growth by a factor of 10 in less than a generation; 45 percent of that population were slaves.

The South was a region with extensive land resources, and the labor needed to exploit them, using scale economies, was to be found in the Atlantic slave trade. European immigrants wanted land for themselves. There were not sufficient indentured servants available to make up the massive labor force that Southern expansion required.

Colonial Maryland shared many of the characteristics of the Middle colonies, but one statistic, the slave population, marked it as a Southern colony.[10] In 1770, Pennsylvania, with a population of 240,000, had 5,761 slaves; the adjacent colony, Maryland, with 203,000 people, had a slave population of 64,000. To understand the Southern economy, even in the eighteenth century, we must come to grips with the uses of black slavery there. Consider the data shown in Table 2.2.

The great difference between the South and the other colonies in the number of black slaves distinguished not only the Southern labor force from that of the others, but also the economy in which that labor force was employed. Overall, as discussed earlier in this chapter, the South was even more rural than the other colonies, with few urban settlements of note. Yet, Virginia and Maryland were heavily populated. These two colonies had been major destinations for indentured servants in the seventeenth century. However, in the eighteenth century, when servants had more choice and a greater proportion of those coming in were free, the South, apart from the Chesapeake region, was not a favored destination.

TABLE 2.2 Percentage of Black Slaves in Total Population of 1770

Colonies	*Percentage*
New Hampshire	1.0
Massachusetts	2.0
Connecticut	3.1
Rhode Island	6.5
New York	11.7
New Jersey	7.0
Pennsylvania	2.4
Delaware	5.2
Maryland	31.5
Virginia	42.0
North Carolina	35.3
South Carolina	60.5
Georgia	45.5

Source: *Historical Statistics of the United States* (Washington D.C.: United States Government Printing Office, 1975), series Z 1–19.

Southern landowners faced this situation and perhaps encouraged it by adapting the Atlantic slave trade to their needs. The relative efficiency of slavery, once laws to control it sufficiently were in place, made the Southern colonies predominantly slave colonies.

Why European immigrants avoided the Southern colonies is not entirely clear. Pennsylvania, the main destination of white immigrants in the eighteenth century, had developed relatively liberal institutions, and land was readily and easily available. But Virginia was no different in these respects. Jefferson's famous comment in *Notes on the State of Virginia*, "In a warm climate, no man will labour for himself who can make another labour for him," is hardly to be taken seriously.[11] In the first place, it is true of cold climates, too, and, in any case, the fact that the South is warmer than the North from November through May should have been an attraction to Europeans. The summer temperature-humidity indexes of Maryland, Virginia, North Carolina, and Pennsylvania are as abominable as those further south, not to mention New York City and the entire Hudson Valley. Also, wages paid could be used to "make" others labor, if the wages were high enough.

The growing dependency upon slave labor in the Southern colonies seems to have been a more complicated matter than the absence of European immigrant labor. First, the prevalence of large-scale landholding required labor beyond that of the immediate family. Large holdings in Maryland, and especially Virginia, originated in headright land grants (slaves were counted as "servants" for this purpose, making an imported slave bought at dockside worth 50 acres). Second, adherence in the South to the common-law rule of descent, called **primogeniture** (that land goes to the oldest son), meant that estates were not automatically broken up upon the deaths of the landholders. In contrast, in the Middle colonies and New England, equal division with a double portion to the oldest son was generally followed. In Europe, daughters were customarily provided a dowry, but in the cash-starved, land-rich colonies, daughters received a share equal to the younger sons.[12]

Comparatively, primogeniture tended to produce larger landed estates, other things being equal, than the double portion method. We would expect, a priori, a larger concentration of landed wealth (and other wealth, too, since land was its ultimate source) in the South than elsewhere after the lapse of several generations, and, indeed, such is the finding of Alice Hanson Jones, the leading modern scholar of the subject. She found that, by 1774, the private nonhuman wealth per *free* wealth holder in the South was 46 percent greater than in the Middle colonies and 63 percent greater than in New England (the Jones' data are reported in Table 3.3).[13] About a quarter of Southern wealth was the estimated value of slaves, and a quarter was land. However, since nearly half the population of the South were slaves, the importance of these comparative wealth figures should not be exaggerated.

On a strict per-capita basis, the South was still wealthier than the rest of the colonies, even if we exclude slaves as countable wealth. Slave-produced wealth in these figures accrued to the slave owners, and primogeniture ensured that estates would not be automatically broken apart and easily squandered by heirs.

Wealth is the sum of net saving (nonconsumption) from income over time. It is either inherited or earned, and any institutional device to hold it together over the generations helps it accumulate. In 1774, in the Middle and Northern colonies, half of the value of wealth was land. With respect to other evidences of wealth (such as livestock, farm tools and implements, crops, and consumer durables), the Southern colonies were also marginally higher per white capita. These data show what the planters knew: that slavery paid, at least for them.

Slave codes were developed to control this labor input and to direct it specifically to those places where the South had a comparative advantage. The colonial Georgia slave code read:

> No Artificer shall be suffer'd to take any Negro as an Apprentice, nor shall any planter lend or let out a Negro or Negroes to another planter, to be employ'd otherwise than in manuring and cultivating the Plantations of the Country.[14]

It is obvious that slaves could be profitably employed at *all* employments (hence the restriction), but the most powerful interest in Georgia was agricultural. Then, as now, vested interests manipulated governments to gain their own ends at others' expense.

To explain the Southern preference for slaves, we must seek *general* arguments that point out characteristics of the Southern colonies that made them different from the others. The combination of headright land acquisition, inheritance rules, the nature of main-crop cultivation, and, finally, institutional adaptation to these over time, seem to be sufficient. Tobacco cultivation required constant clearing of new lands, and rice cultivation needed much labor. Slaves were the answer. The argument that the Southern climate directly encouraged slavery, favored by Jefferson and by generations of succeeding historians, can be abandoned.

In the Constitutional Convention discussions of 1787, it was held that slavery was not a moral issue but a matter of "interest" only. After all, in 1787, there were slaves in every state. The discussion shows that some delegates believed that slavery was going to die out. Virginia had attempted several times unilaterally to end the Atlantic slave trade to Virginia ports, but it had been overruled by the Board of Trade lawyers in London, who followed the early eighteenth-century dictum of Chief Justice Holt: "Negroes are merchandise and within the Navigation Acts." Virginia could not annul the Navigation Acts except in the way it finally did it, by force of arms. By then, the die was cast. Within a decade of the Constitutional Convention, Eli Whitney, a Yankee visiting Georgia, invented a machine—the cotton gin—that changed everything. Because of the nature of their colonial development, the Southern states already had a labor system whose efficiency in cotton production would astound the world and produce a rupture in the 1787 constitutional agreements that only a bloody Civil War would close.

The Direction of Colonial Trade

In Figure 2.2 we see the overall direction of colonial commodity trade flows in 1768–1772. As we will discuss in Chapter 4, the English Navigation Acts of the 1600s forbade trade with English ports, but, in the

FIGURE 2.2 Percentage Distribution of Total Colonial Trade (1768–1772)

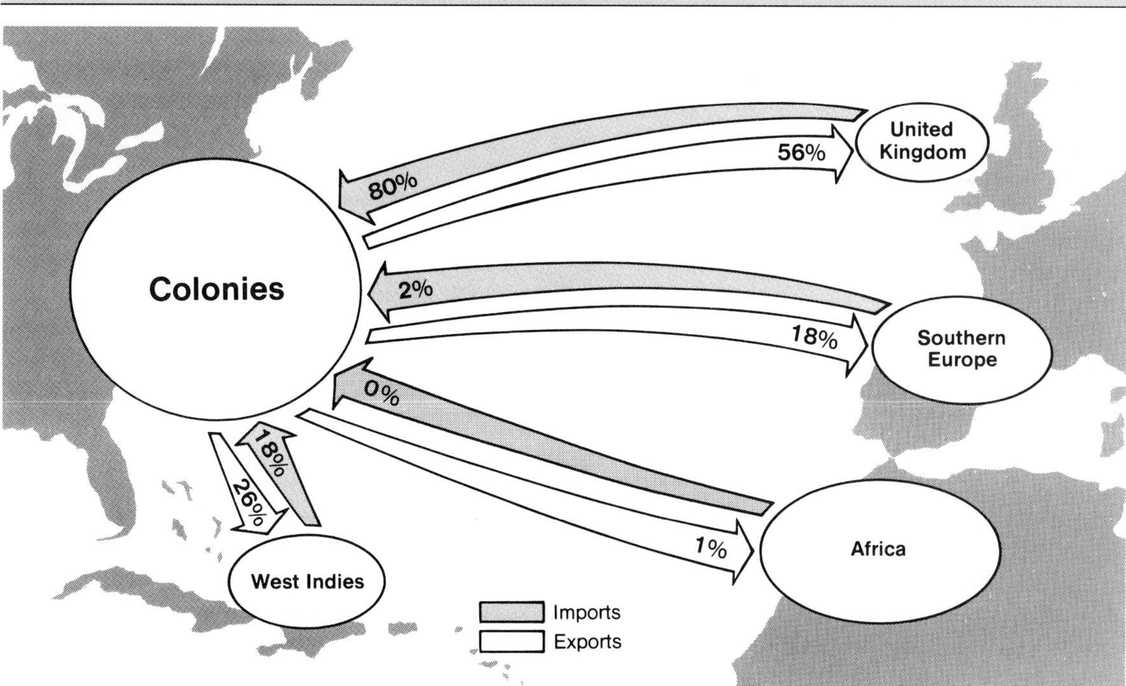

Source: James F. Shepherd and Gary M. Walton, *Shipping, Maritime Trade, and the Economic Development of North America* (Cambridge: Cambridge University Press, 1972), pp. 160–161.

The United Kingdom was colonial America's dominant trading partner in exports and imports, followed by the West Indies and southern Europe.

FIGURE 2.3 Percentage Distribution of Colonial Trade 1768–1772 by Region

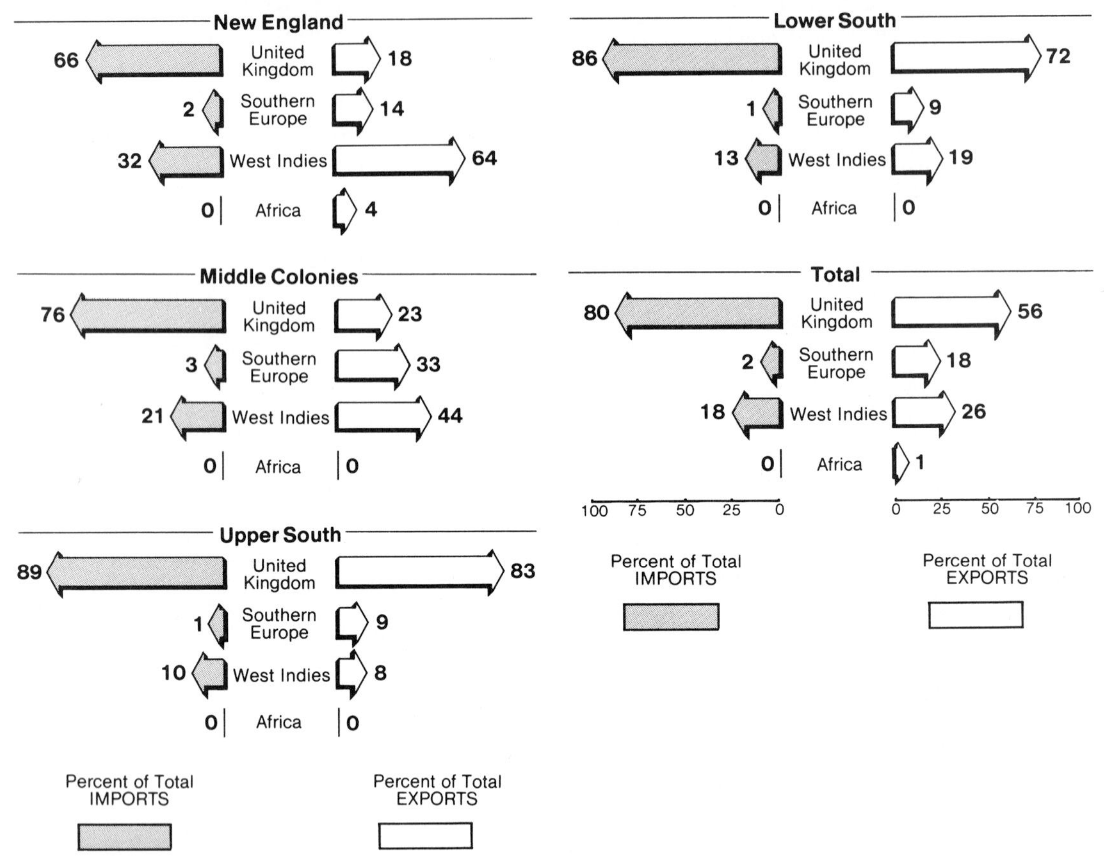

Source: James F. Shepherd and Gary M. Walton, *Shipping, Maritime Trade, and the Economic Development of North America* (Cambridge: Cambridge University Press, 1972), pp. 160–161.

The United Kingdom dominated the colonial trade market as both importer and exporter in all regions except New England, where the West Indies had a sizable share of the market.

1730s, these were amended to allow some direct colonial trade with Europe south of Cape Finisterre (near the northwestern tip of the Spanish Peninsula). Some 56 percent of colonial exports went to the United Kingdom, 18 percent to southern Europe, 26 percent to the West Indies, and less than 1 percent directly to Africa. In return, four-fifths of colonial imports came from the United Kingdom, 18 percent from the West Indies, and much smaller proportions from Africa and southern Europe. The work of economic historians James Shepherd and Gary Walton enables us to get a more refined look at these trade patterns and to grasp their larger implications. Figure 2.3 depicts the regional trading breakdowns.

The regional differences in overseas trading patterns reflect each region's comparative advantage. New England's largest customer for exports was the West Indies. There, the products of New England lumbering, woodworking, fishing, small manufacturing, and naval stores and supplies found their readiest markets. Direct shipments to the United Kingdom and southern Europe were far smaller. Yet fully two-thirds of New

FIGURE 2.4 Average Annual Trade Balances in the Colonies 1768–1772 by Region

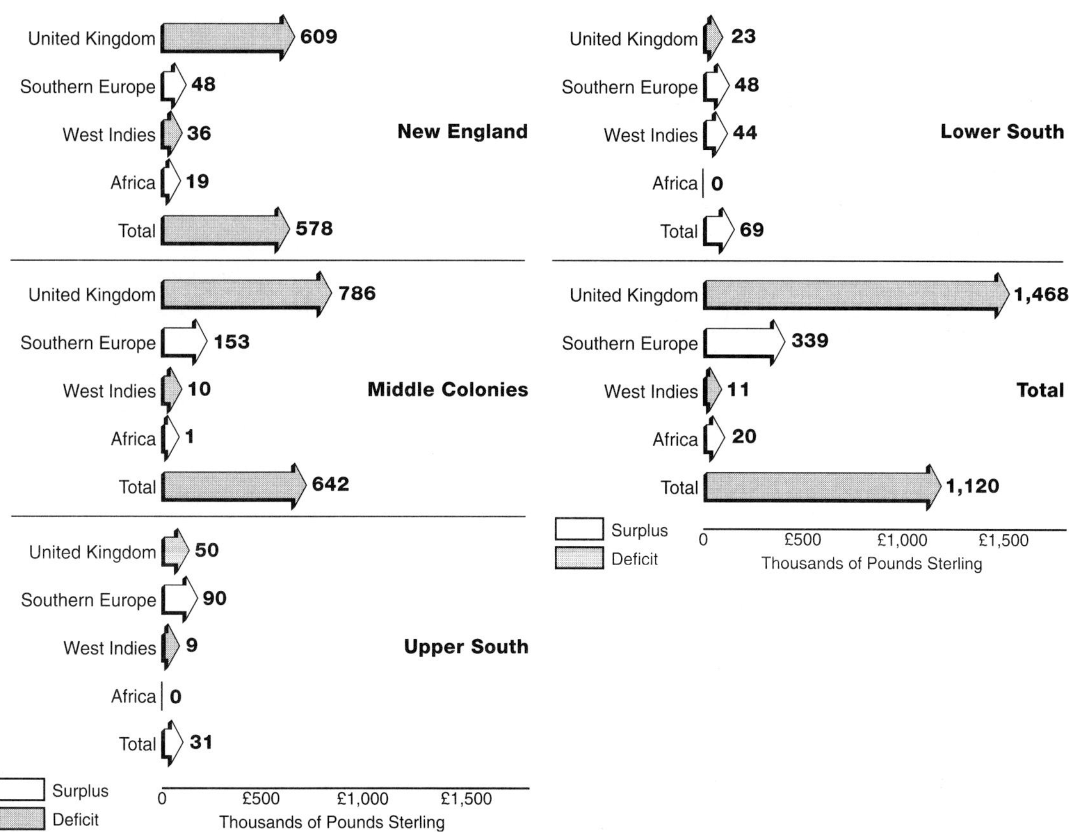

Source: James F. Shepherd and Gary M. Walton, *Shipping, Maritime Trade, and the Economic Development of North America* (Cambridge: Cambridge University Press, 1972), pp. 115.

The deficit in commodity trade was mainly in bilateral trade with the United Kingdom, primarily by New England and the Middle colonies. The Southern colonies had small net surpluses in their trade with southern Europe. Three-fourths of the net overall deficit in commodity trade alone came from trade with the United Kingdom.

England's imports came from the United Kingdom, and nearly a third from the West Indies.

Middle colony exports—grains, hides, flour, livestock, and small manufactures—were more nearly balanced between the United Kingdom, southern Europe, and the West Indies, but fully 76 percent of Middle colony imports came from England. Twenty-one percent of imports were the products of the West Indies.

The more exotic Southern exports (especially tobacco, which was largely reexported to the Continent), went in overwhelming proportions to England, and, in return, the United Kingdom supplied more than 80 percent of Southern imports.

Walton's work indicates that previous ideas about trading "triangles" were too restrictive.[15] There were such triangular routes, as we know (e.g., New England rum taken to Africa and traded for slaves that were shipped to the West Indies and traded for sugar and molasses to be imported into New England to make rum), but the evidence shows that colonial shipmasters mainly were itinerant voyagers. Their trading patterns were similar to those of modern "tramp" steamers; they picked up and discharged cargoes where and when opportunities allowed, given the law and ship captains' calculations about the probability of getting caught with contraband.

The colonies had a large trade deficit in commodity trade alone. They imported more visible commodities from the external world than they exported to it, but by far the greater portion of the commodity-trade deficit grew out of their trade with the United Kingdom. The trade in commodities left the colonies in a deficit position. The annual regional deficits from 1768 to 1772, together with the totals, are shown in Figure 2.4. Of total deficits in those years, three-fourths occurred in bilateral trade with the United Kingdom. The largest area of surplus came from trade with Europe. It is fair to assume that the surplus arose because of the prohibitions within the Navigation Acts against direct imports of northern European goods into the colonies and that part of the deficit with the United Kingdom was due to the extra costs of transshipping those goods through the United Kingdom.

Then, as now, commodity trade was only part of the story, and the deficit was offset by other factors. The actual annual net indebtedness of the colonies was relatively small. What was the sum of all transactions, the overall **balance of payments**? Walton and Shepherd have made this calculation, and it is most instructive.[16] For the years 1768–1772, the average annual commodity-trade deficit of £1,121,000 was almost entirely offset by ship sales of £140,000 together with net shipping earnings and merchant commissions of £880,000. Net payments by colonial importers for slaves (£200,000, mainly from the West Indies) and for indentured servants (£80,000) totaling £280,000 were nearly offset by a single item, British military expenditures of £230,000 in the colonies. In addition, British naval expenditures in the colonies averaged a net £70,000. If we add up the pluses and minuses, the increase in net colonial indebtedness was only about £40,000 annually, a figure representing mainly mercantile credits extended by the British to the Americans.

The figure for annual net increase of foreign indebtedness in 1768–1772 is not nearly as large as historians once believed it was. Obviously, in overall payments, the colonies were prospering from their empire connection.

THE COMMON-LAW HERITAGE

An important part of economic development in the colonial era was the use and consequences of the background of English common law. This is one of the most important factors that differentiated the English colonies from the others. Consequently, it is one of the factors that must be investigated to understand why the English colonies developed faster and grew at a greater rate than other New World colonies.

The common law was the law in all of the colonies for customary relations between persons and government and for disputes between private persons. It was law developed in the age of mercantilism, when economic life was regulated in the interest of the nation state. When mercantilism was superseded by the classical liberalism of Adam Smith and others, the emphasis shifted toward **laissez-faire**, governmental noninvolvement in the private economy. Yet that involvement persisted; the U.S. Constitution adopted the common law. It persisted at the level of local and state governments until it reappeared at the national level in the late nineteenth century. Quite an astonishing amount of modern economic life is still powerfully influenced by this remote source; for example, the "police power" of government to regulate and control everything from the issuance of licenses to barbershops to the Environmental Protection Agency. Yet the same source gave rise to our modern system of markets for both consumption and investment goods. The common law tradition is an integral part of the evolution of the American economy. It is a tradition well worth a few pages in any American history book and some considerable thought by any student of American economics.

Markets and *Caveat Emptor*

We saw in the previous chapter how our land tenure fit into the English land-ownership system. But what about chattel goods—movable property? When was the right to property in commodities or livestock legally transferred from one person to another? There could never be extensive commercial development without secure titles to chattels, providing protection for both buyer and seller.

In England, the problem had been solved by the system of established markets, the **market overt**. Certain towns were designated market towns, and certain days were fixed as market days in those towns. Outside London, market days and market towns were the only places chattels could be legally sold without each transaction being observed by three witnesses, as required for deeds and wills. In London alone, every day was a market day and every shop a market overt. In addition, larger marketing areas were merged occasionally by the appointment of fairs at specific times and places. Market overt and fairs solved two basic problems. Business activities were regulated, and full title passed when goods changed hands. According to English law, all transfers at those times and places were considered to have been witnessed, and the property rights, negotiated by sale or trade, were secure.

In a largely static society, most of whose population was illiterate, the system of market overt was a satisfactory solution. Since professional merchants and occasional sellers such as peasants bringing their own produce to market were largely itinerant, a special set of courts was established to render justice when disputes arose. These courts, called *courts of pie powder* (*pied poudre*, "dusty foot"), were courts of record with rights of appeal. A law of Edward III in 1353 set the system on a formal basis: "[Because] the merchants cannot often tarry in one place in hindrance of their business, we will and grant, that speedy right be to them done from day to day and from hour to hour."[17] These adjustments were the early beginnings of equity proceedings in courts of law.

The entire English system was initially transferred to American shores. When the colonists first began to organize their settlements, it was natural that they would try to reestablish a system whose workings they understood. Accordingly, we find market overt and fair days set up in all the colonies. In Massachusetts in the 1630s and 1640s, the laws read: "There shall henceforth be a market kept at Boston... upon the fifth day of the week... at Salem... upon the fourth day... And at Linn upon the third day...." Boston was to have two fairs a year "on the first third day of the third month, and on the first third day of the eighth month from year to year to continue for two or three days together."[18] Similar fairs were provided for Salem, Watertown, and Dorchester.

The colonial economy became one of vast physical expansion. In a frontier society, transactions took place wherever buyers and sellers met. The ruling that only chattel property rights exchanged in established markets were of guaranteed legality was unrealistic as American trade evolved. Farmers objected, saying that market days glutted the towns with produce, placing sellers at a disadvantage, forcing them to sacrifice their perishable goods in order to sell them all before the end of the market day.

By the close of the seventeenth century, New England farmers were allowed to sell directly to customers on their farms on whatever days the customers appeared. Slowly, intermediary merchants, wholesalers, and then retailers appeared on the scene to profit from such market imperfections and, thus, to eliminate them. Colonial towns became places where regular sales of country produce could take place on a wholesale or retail basis. Artisans in the town also objected to marketing requirements. They developed a "bespoke" trade, doing agreed-upon amounts of work for specific customers. This, too, developed into retailing from shops. In 1789, for example, the master shoemakers of Philadelphia refused membership to any who sold shoes "in the public market of this city."

By then, market overt had become an impediment to regular and expanding trade. Part of the English rule of markets had always been *caveat emptor*, "let the buyer beware." In an open market, if the buyer had a fair chance to examine the goods (and there were rules to ensure that was the case), then the buyer assumed responsibility for the quality of the commodity once the property right in it had been transferred by sale. This principle could be applied anywhere, without the protective regulations of market overt. By late colonial times, market overt had been largely abandoned because the rule of *caveat emptor* protected both buyer and seller. *Caveat emptor* was never meant to be a cover for fraud, and aggrieved buyers could always sue sellers in civil courts for damages.

Towns and cities continued to pass quality-control ordinances and to control the times and days when trade could take place, as they still do. So-called blue laws, preventing many types of trade on Sundays, exist in many towns and states. The "police powers" of government to control business never lapsed—the wide extent of *caveat emptor* until recent decades allowed an expanding economy greater freedom to do business wherever the opportunity arose. Market overt still exists in public and farmers markets all across the country. The states, and now the federal government, have replaced the colonial market officials, imposing safety and quality standards upon manufacturers and sellers of services and commodities. The Occupational Safety and Health Administration, Consumer Product Safety Commission, and Environmental Protection Agency, to name a few, are modern clerks of the market in this respect. *Caveat emptor* still exists, but only where there are no other regulations.

Licensing and Other Controls

In colonial times, as today, licensing restricted access to business opportunities. Today, a butcher shop, barbershop, and bank all require official permission, a license, to do business. Why not just "let 'er rip," and let anyone who can find customers do business of any sort? This is not allowed now and never has been in American history. Since antiquity, there seem to have been four primary motives for the population to seek government protection, to prohibit by force of law, the real or imagined abuses of markets characterized by laissez-faire. These restrictions of free trade are government controls related to: (a) monopoly power, (b) quality controls, (c) morals, and (d) taxes.

Monopoly Power. It was, and is, in the interests of persons in trades and services to gain monopoly power whenever possible in order to charge higher prices and restrict competitors into the market. The most effective form of monopoly is that created by government itself. Typical restrictions of this sort in colonial towns were to prevent outsiders from moving in or local residents from entering protected businesses. Such restrictions were commonly achieved by organized trade groups. These obvious prohibitions could be reinforced by restricting access to trades with rules of apprenticeship imposed by law. Entry was then controlled by those already established. Apprenticeship requirements were easily achieved because of concerns related to quality.

Quality Control. Colonial governments were genuinely concerned that colonial exports achieve a reputation for quality. In addition to apprenticeships, governments routinely passed ordinances to guarantee quality by requiring that inspectors examine merchandise for sale to ensure its quality—to be sure that it gained "the public mark," as Penn put it. The public commonly was enlisted in the enforcement effort by splitting the fines of those convicted between informers and the courts. This tactic sharply reduced enforcement costs.[19]

Morals. Then, as now, certain goods, services, and actions were deemed offensive to public morals, and laws restricted those trades. Today, we restrict the sale of alcohol, tobacco, and adult magazines and films to minors. In colonial times, forbidden practices included unlicensed preaching, sales of spirits to minors, lending money to seamen, wearing luxurious clothing if you were poor (sumptuary laws), keeping "disorderly" houses, riotous behavior, and "lewd dancing." Americans have always believed that morals can be legislated.

Taxes. Whenever a license can be issued, a fee can be collected. Such a fee is a tax on that business. Then, as now, governments found license fees to be a steady source of revenue.[20]

In addition to these sorts of routine controls, the kind of government intervention we now call *public utility regulation* was universally engaged in by colonial governments. Again, the custom was ancient in England and was begun immediately in the colonies. Draymen, porters, carters, coachmen, and innkeepers were licensed, and their rates were controlled by public bodies. Similarly, where competition was limited by nature—at docks and wharves or toll bridges or ferries—charges and services were restricted by the ancient English rule that service must be supplied to all who apply, competently, and at reasonable rates. As Jefferson reported in his *Notes on the State of Virginia*,

"Ferries are admitted only at such places as are appointed by law, and the rates of ferriage are fixed." When, in later years, canals, railroads, telegraphs, telephones, airplanes, central power and water sources, and gas facilities were created by the processes of technological change, no new concepts of control were needed. The Federal Aviation Administration, Federal Communications Commission, and Federal Power Commission are merely modern versions of the seventeenth-century selectmen of colonial Massachusetts who "shall have power to regulate" because there was found to be "a very great abuse in the Townes of Boston and Charleston, by Porters, who many times do require and exact more than is just and righteous."[21] Nowadays, we have public service commissions to exact a "reasonable" rate of profit from the consuming public in such cases. Rightly or wrongly, such rates were not left to the impersonal determination of the market—nor are they now.

Employment, Wages, and Income Supports

Captain John Smith is reported to have laid down the rule in the early days of the Virginia settlement, "He that will not work shall not eat." In colonial America, work was required, at least for the lower classes, even for whites not bound in servitude. The background law was Queen Elizabeth's *Statute of Artificers and Apprentices* (1562) containing "divers orders for artificers, labourers, servants of husbandry and apprentices." This law, by requiring all to have some means of support, was designed to prevent pauperism and civil unrest. In the statute, after a long enumeration of those who were exempt (e.g., persons of noble origin, persons with specified wealth and income, military people, clergy, scholars, mariners, miners, fishermen, persons in trades, masters, journeymen or apprentices in cities, corporate, or market towns), all others could be compelled to labor in agriculture. Men between the ages of 12 and 60, and single women between the ages of 12 and 40, could be so compelled. Hours of daily labor were prescribed, as were conditions of job mobility. Agricultural laborers could not leave employment without prescribed exit papers (as in the former USSR). In the harvest weeks, artisans could be compelled to go into the country and work. Wages were to be set by local authority. Those offering higher than legal wages were to be fined, the fines being split between the courts and the informers. Those refusing such work could be adjudged vagabonds. Under the "charitable alms" law of Henry VIII (1535), as amended by Elizabethan statutes, penalties for vagabonds were whipping, branding, ear lopping, and hanging for the third offense. Merrie olde England.

In colonial America, many of these early English laws were in force. Jefferson pointed out in *Notes on the State of Virginia*, "I never saw a native American begging in the streets or highways." In Virginia, he wrote, "...vagabonds, without visible property or vocation, are placed in work houses, where they are well clothed, fed, lodged and made to labor."[22] In Massachusetts, the laws stated that idle persons were to be committed to prison, with ten lashes, and put to work to earn "necessary bread and water, or other mean food." Apprenticeships were prescribed for those whose parents were lax in their duties. The selectmen of each township could judge which children were not being suitably instructed "in some honest lawful calling, labour, or employment, either in husbandry or some other trade, profitable to themselves or the commonwealth."[23] Such children could be taken from their parents and bound by the courts "with some masters for years," girls to age 18, boys to age 21.

Compulsory labor at wages fixed by courts, selectmen, or local magistrates was, by law, the fate of those who had no other place in society. In a less-developed economy very close to subsistence, such rules seemed to make sense. Subsidized unemployment, whether by charity or by unemployment insurance, is in some sense a luxury, either of the rich or of a rich society. Colonial society provided for its aged and sick poor; others had to work. As late as the 1930s, idle persons were still being jailed in this country for the crime of having "no visible means of support." The idea of the work ethic, an idea resurrected by the Reagan administration, had such origins. Many Americans doubtless believe, as did Henry Ford, that "work is our salvation." But for the doubters, there was always compulsion.

Such rules, when enforced, could surely reduce the amount of charity required of society. That was important because, from Henry VIII onward, English communities (originally parishes) were compelled to tax themselves to provide for the poor and destitute. This practice was also true in the colonies. If the freedom to starve is considered of little value, then the theory behind compulsory labor in colonial America is difficult to condemn on economic grounds.

The colonial years were strewn with efforts to control wages and prices by governmental authority. Labor organizations were considered, by law, criminal conspiracies against society, and so strikes for higher wages were both rare and generally unsuccessful. We already have noted the element of compulsion in the vast unfree labor force of indentured servants and slaves. The element of compulsory labor for those who were neither slaves nor in servitude must be added. The poor did not starve in colonial America when it was unnecessary, nor were they idle when work could be found or created by authorities.

NOTES

1. It has been traditional to blame this trading pattern for the lack of intercolonial and interregional trade in the Southern colonies. It is this trade that is cited as the reason why the South failed to develop an urban economy. Joseph Ernst and H. Roy Merrens, "Camden's Turrets Pierce the Skies." *William and Mary Quarterly*, vol. 30, October 1973, p. 550.
2. Historically, the American diamond business grew in New York City; it was the largest retail market. Once jobbing and cutting started in New York, other dealers and cutters located there to take advantage of labor, communications, buyers and sellers, and finally the trade was there because it was there. Although other locations may offer lower rents and lower crime rates, they lack external economies.
3. For a fascinating essay on the colonial experience and its consequences, see Amelia Clewly Ford, *Colonial Precedents of Our National Land System as It Existed in 1800* (1976).
4. Diane Lindstrom and John Sharpless, "Urban Growth and Economic Structure in Antebellum America," in *REH*, 1978, vol. 3.
5. Carl Bridenbaugh, *Cities in Revolt: Urban Life in America*, 1743–1776 (1955), p. 272.
6. Winifred Rothenberg, *From Market-Places to a Market Economy* (1992), pp. 166–174.
7. New England's shortage of good arable land did not induce a decline in per-capita wealth in the eighteenth century as population increased, as some scholars have believed. Adaptations were made soon enough to avoid impoverishment imposed by poor farmlands. Gloria Main, "The Standard of Living in Colonial Massachusetts," JEH, March 1983. There is also evidence, fragmentary at first, of a developing market in farm labor, a good indicator of developing specialization among the farm population. Rothenberg (1992), chap. 6.
8. Thomas Doerflinger, *A Vigorous Spirit of Enterprise: Merchants and Economic Development in Revolutionary America* (1986). This book, slightly mistitled, is a close examination of merchants, especially in Philadelphia, and the world they made.
9. The evidence indicates a modest growth of agricultural productivity, even in the seventeenth century. Duane Ball and Gary Walton, "Agricultural Productivity Changes in Eighteenth Century Pennsylvania," *JEH*, March 1976.
10. For an interesting view of a family living on the Maryland frontier in the mid-seventeenth century that examines the connections between agriculture and societal development, see Lois Green Carr, Russell Menard, and Lorena Walsh, *Robert Cole's World: Agriculture and Society in Early Maryland* (1991).
11. Thomas Jefferson, *Notes on the State of Virginia* (London: John Stockdale, 1788), pp. 271–272.
12. See Carole Shammas, Marylynn Salmon, and Michel Dahlin, *Inheritance in America* (1987), p. 34, and Salmon's *Women and the Law of Property in Early America* (1986).
13. Alice Hanson Jones, *Wealth of a Nation to Be: The American Colonies on the Eve of the Revolution* (1980), p. 58, Table 3.7. On a strict per-capita basis, total wealth in the 13 colonies averaged £46.5 in 1774. On a regional basis, it was £36.6 in New England, £41.9 in the Middle colonies and, with the slaves, £54.7 in the South. See Jones, p. 54, Table 3.5.
14. Charles Jones, *The History of Georgia* (Boston: Houghton Mifflin, 1883), p. 423.
15. Gary Walton, "New Evidence on Colonial Commerce," *JEH*, September 1968.
16. Walton and Shepherd, *The Economic Rise of Early America* (1979), p. 101.
17. Edward Adler, "Business Jurisprudence," *Harvard Law Review*, vol. 28, 1914–1915, p. 139.
18. William Whitmore, ed., *Colonial Laws of Massachusetts* (Boston: Boston City Printers, 1889), p. 150.

19. In colonial times, both Virginia and Maryland introduced schemes to restrict tobacco output and to control the quality of the marketed product. Mary McKinney Schweitzer, "Economic Regulation and the Colonial Economy: The Maryland Tobacco Inspection Act of 1747," *JEH*, September 1980.
20. For examples of all such colonial regulation, see Jonathan Hughes, *Social Control in the Colonial Economy* (1976), chap. 9.
21. Whitmore (1889), p. 185.
22. Jefferson (1788), p. 220.
23. Hughes (1976), pp. 96–111 and footnotes.

SUGGESTED READINGS

Articles

Anderson, Terry. "Wealth Estimates for the New England Colonies, 1650–1709." *Explorations in Economic History*, vol. 14, no. 4, October 1977.

Ball, Duane, and Gary Walton. "Agricultural Productivity Change in Eighteenth Century Pennsylvania." *Journal of Economic History*, vol. XXXVI, no. 1, March 1976.

Henretta, James. "Economic Development and Social Structure in Colonial Boston." *William and Mary Quarterly*, vol. XXII, no. 1, January 1965.

Jones, Alice Hanson. "Wealth Estimates for the New England Colonies About 1770." *Journal of Economic History*, vol. XXXII, no. 1, March 1972.

Lindstrom, Diane, and John Sharpless. "Urban Growth and Economic Structure in Antebellum America." In Paul Uselding, ed., *Research in Economic History*, Greenwich, CT: JAI Press, 1978, vol. 3.

Main, Gloria L., "The Standard of Living in Colonial Massachusetts," *Journal of Economic History*, vol. XLIII, no. 1, March 1983.

Schweitzer, Mary McKinney. "Economic Regulation and the Colonial Economy: The Maryland Tobacco Inspection Act of 1747." *Journal of Economic History*, vol. XL, no. 3, September 1980.

Shepherd, James, and Samuel Williamson. "The Coastal Trade of the British North American Colonies 1768–1772." *Journal of Economic History*, vol. XXXVII, no. 4, December 1972.

Walton, Gary M. "New Evidence on Colonial Commerce." *Journal of Economic History*, vol. XXVIII, no. 3, September 1968.

Books

Abernathy, Thomas Perkins. *Western Lands and the American Revolution*. New York: Appleton-Century, 1937.

Bridenbaugh, Carl. *Cities in the Wilderness*. New York: The Ronald Press, 1938 (reprinted by New York: Alfred A. Knopf, 1964).

———. *Cities in Revolt*. New York: Alfred A. Knopf, 1955 (reprinted by New York: Oxford University Press, 1971).

Bruchey, Stuart, ed. *The Colonial Merchant: Sources and Readings*. New York: Harcourt, Brace, Jovanovich, 1966.

Carr, Lois Green, Russell R. Menard, and Lorena S. Walsh. *Robert Cole's World: Agriculture and Society in Early Maryland*. Chapel Hill: University of North Carolina Press for the Institute of Early American History and Culture, 1991.

Doerflinger, Thomas M. *A Vigorous Spirit of Enterprise: Merchants and Economic Development in Revolutionary America*. Chapel Hill: University of North Carolina Press, 1986.

Ford, Amelia Clewly. *Colonial Precedents of Our National Land System as It Existed in 1800*. Philadelphia: Porcupine Press, 1976.

Hughes, Jonathan. *Social Control in the Colonial Economy*. Charlottesville: University Press of Virginia, 1976.

Jones, Alice Hanson. *American Colonial Wealth: Documents and Methods*. New York: Arno Press, 1977.

———. *Wealth of a Nation to Be: The American Colonies on the Eve of the Revolution*. New York: Columbia University Press, 1980.

Katz, Michael B. *In the Shadow of the Poorhouse: A Social History of Welfare in America*. New York: Basic Books, 1986.

Kulikoff, Allan. *Tobacco and Slaves: The Development of Southern Cultures in the Chesapeake, 1680–1800*. Chapel Hill: University of North Carolina Press, 1986.

McCusker, John J., and Russell R. Menard. *The Economy of British America, 1606–1789: Needs and Opportunities for Study*. Chapel Hill: University of North Carolina Press, 1986.

Rothenberg, Winifred B. *From Market-Places to a Market Economy: The Transformation of Rural Massachusetts, 1750–1850*. Chicago: University of Chicago Press, 1992.

Salmon, Marylynn. *Women and the Law of Property in Early America*. Chapel Hill: University of North Carolina Press, 1986.

Shammas, Carole, Marylynn Salmon, and Michael Dahlin. *Inheritance in America from Colonial Times to the Present*. New Brunswick, NJ: Rutgers University Press, 1987.

Walton, Gary M., and James F. Shepherd. *The Economic Rise of Early America*. New York: Cambridge University Press, 1979.

CHAPTER THREE

America on the Eve of Revolution

We are accustomed to viewing our Revolutionary ancestors as quaint picture-book figures in homespun knee breeches, rough frontier types who tossed out the rich and effete English. However, the evidence, using a modern frame of reference, suggests that colonial life was far more than just the bare essentials.

POPULATION SOURCES AND GROWTH

Who were these Americans? Where were they from? One way to answer the question of the origins of the colonists is to examine the population at the end of the colonial period. Table 3.1 shows the composition of the population (excluding Indians) in 1790, the year of the first national census.

White Origins

In 1790, just over four-fifths of the population was of European origin, and just under one-fifth was of identifiable African origin. White immigration data are at least as vague as those for black slaves. However, because of the white use of surnames, it is possible for scholars to say something about the remote European origins of the existing population in 1790. If we assume that an O'Hara was of Irish origin; a McDougall, Scottish; a von Schlieben, German; a van Ryswick, Dutch; and a Westwick, English; the estimates are that 60.9 percent of the white population had English surnames. Of the others, 8.3 percent were Scottish, 9.7 percent were Irish, 8.7 percent were German, 3.4 percent were Dutch, 1.7 percent were French, and 0.7 percent were Spanish. The remaining 6.6 percent were not assigned. We might suspect that since common names like Hughes and Smith could be English, Irish, or Scottish, it would be safer to have one category representing all the British Isles. Grouped in this way, the British made up 78.9 percent of the total. We find that in the Northwest Territory (now the Upper Midwest), surnames were 57.1 percent French, and in Louisiana, surnames were 64 percent French. In those areas acquired from the defunct

TABLE 3.1 U.S. Population in 1790

	Nonwhites		*Whites*		*Totals*	
Year	**Count**	**Percentage**	**Count**	**Percentage**	**Count**	**Percentage**
1790	757,000	19.3	3,172,000	80.7	3,929,000	100.0

Source: *Historical Statistics of the United States* (Washington, D.C.: United States Government Printing Office, 1975), series A91–104.

Spanish Empire, about 96 percent of the names were Spanish. Among the original colonies, Pennsylvania surnames were 33 percent German, compared to 35 percent English. New York still had 17 percent Dutch names in 1790. New Jersey, with 16.6 percent, had nearly as many. English names were most prevalent in New England and Virginia—82 percent in Massachusetts, 76 percent in what is now Vermont, 71 percent in Rhode Island, and 68.5 percent in Virginia.

Thus, of the whites documented in the 1790 census, just under three-fourths of the population descended from immigrants from the British Isles. It is little wonder that English institutions were utilized for colonial economic development; the people were already familiar with them. So far as scholars can tell, the other Europeans, naturalized by conquest or voluntarily by immigration, adapted well to English laws and practices. Blacks, mostly slaves, had no say in the matter.

Slave Origins

The blacks mainly were shipped from West Africa, but there was also a slave trade from Madagascar and Zanzibar to the New World. Most slave-trading ports were on the west coast of Africa, but it is known that slaves sold there for transport to the New World also came from distant parts of the interior. Thus, African ancestors of modern Americans may well have come from most parts of that continent below the Sahara Desert. It is estimated that 10 million, perhaps 15 million, African slaves were transported to the Americas from 1501 to 1865. How many came to what became the United States? Robert Fogel and Stanley Engerman report that 6 percent of the Atlantic slave trade was with the original 13 colonies. That would indicate total imports of more than 600,000 individuals, possibly too high a figure.[1] Others estimate that, by 1700, there were about 28,000 blacks in the colonies and that 250,000 were imported in the period 1700–1790. Most blacks were slaves: 59 percent of those in the North and 95 percent of those in the South. Fogel and Engerman think that between 1780 and 1807 many more slaves were imported. If this is correct, we might conservatively estimate that at least a half million, possibly more, were brought in by 1807, which would be less than the number imported (but how much less?) in the colonial years. Efforts to be precise about these figures are doomed to failure.

Population Growth

Since immigration records were irregular or nonexistent, figures for the total colonial white immigration must be taken with a grain of salt, especially in the early years. We know that the Puritan immigration to New England was perhaps 35,000 persons. Estimates of total white immigration between 1700 and 1775 center on the number 300,000. Although white immigration was much larger than black immigration in the seventeenth century, the reverse was true in the eighteenth century. It seems fair to suppose that as many whites as blacks immigrated—altogether, perhaps a half million would be a conservative estimate. David Galenson has estimated total white immigration between 1650 and 1780 to have been about 600,000.[2] If that figure is correct, then Fogel and Engerman's estimate of 600,000 for black immigration is more reasonable. Thus, with natural increases, the proportion of whites in the total population remained overwhelming.[3]

Since death rates among immigrants in the seventeenth century were so stupendous in each colony, it is difficult to say what is meant by *immigrant*. If a person died (or returned to Europe) before he or she could make any meaningful contribution, was that person an immigrant in an economic sense? Suppose that, as Edmund Morgan reports, 15,000 stepped ashore in Virginia between 1625 and 1640, and suppose that there were only about 7,000 alive in 1640. Were those who departed so quickly immigrants in the sense that they added to the population or to colonial economic growth? Earlier immigration was equally luckless. For example, 143 left London for Virginia in December 1606. By the fall of 1607, only 50 were still alive. As we have seen, at Plymouth, many colonists died the first winter. Accepted population estimates for the colonies are shown in Table 3.2.

Birth and Death Rates

Despite the early mortality history, population grew prodigiously. By the end of the colonial period, only one white in ten had been born abroad. Blacks born abroad were two in ten, which shows that the slave trade was still more important to black population growth than immigration was to white population growth. It is generally agreed that once populations were firmly established, relatively low mortality and high birth rates, rather than immigration, accounted for the remarkable increase of colonial population. From 1700 to 1780, the rate of population increase was about 30 persons per 1,000 (3 percent per annum). This population growth rate is not much lower than those typical of modern less-developed countries such as Ghana or Liberia. The colonial growth rates were sufficient to double the population about every 25 years.

Of course, in early decades, the rate of population increase was much higher, high mortality or not, since it started from zero in each colony. The birth rate ranged from 35 births per 1,000 of population per year to as high as 50 births per 1,000 in some areas; 40 per 1,000 per annum seems an accurate average figure. These were very high birth rates, a third or more higher than such rates in Europe at that time. (In contrast, the American birth rate in 1998 was estimated to be 14.6 per 1,000.)

Colonial death rates in the eighteenth century were 20 to 25 per 1000 per annum, below those of Europe.[4] As Billy Smith and others have shown, though, death rates in cities like Philadelphia and Boston could well have been twice as high as the average, which included mostly farmers living in relative isolation.[5]

TABLE 3.2 Estimated Population of the American Colonies 1610–1780

Colonies	*1610*	*1630*	*1650*	*1680*	*1700*
New England Colonies					
Maine	—	400	1,000	(———	——— included
New Hampshire	—	500	1,305	2,407	4,958
Vermont	—	—	—	—	—
Massachusetts	—	506	14,037	39,752	55,941
Plymouth	—	390	1,566	6,400	(———
Rhode Island	—	—	785	3,017	5,894
Connecticut	—	—	4,139	17,246	25,970
Total New England Colonies	0	1,796	22,832	68,822	92,763
Middle Colonies					
New York	—	350	4,116	9,830	19,107
New Jersey	—	—	—	3,400	14,010
Pennsylvania	—	—	—	680	17,950
Delaware	—	—	185	1,005	2,470
Total Middle Colonies	0	350	4,301	14,915	53,537
Southern Colonies					
Maryland	—	—	4,504	17,904	29,604
Virginia	350	2,500	18,731	43,596	58,560
North Carolina	—	—	—	5,430	10,720
South Carolina	—	—	—	1,200	5,704
Georgia	—	—	—	—	—
Kentucky	—	—	—	—	—
Tennessee	—	—	—	—	—
Total Southern Colonies	350	2,500	23,235	68,130	104,588
Total Colonial Population	350	4,646	50,368	151,867	250,888
Total Black	—	60	1,600	6,971	27,817
Percentage Black	—	1.3	3.2	4.6	11.1

Source: *Historical Statistics of the United States* (Washington, D.C.: United States Government Printing Office, 1975), series Z1–19.

Given the primitive medicine of the time, colonial population growth must be attributed to a better climate, better food and water, and less damage from epidemic diseases such as influenza, smallpox, malaria, and diphtheria. Survival rates were about the same for blacks and whites, but if you were destined to be a slave, you were better off in the Southern colonies than in the Caribbean. Fogel and Engerman found that, if mortality rates among mainland black slaves had equaled the terrible rates of the West Indies, the surviving black population of 1 million in 1800 would have been only 186,000. In addition to lower death rates, fertility rates among mainland black slaves exceeded those on the Caribbean islands.

1720	*1750*	*1760*	*1780*
in Massachusetts ———)			49,133
9,375	27,505	39,093	87,802
—	—	—	47,620
91,008	188,000	202,600	268,627
——— included in Massachusetts ———)			
11,680	33,226	45,471	52,946
58,830	111,280	142,470	206,701
170,893	360,011	429,634	712,829
36,919	76,696	117,138	210,541
29,818	71,393	93,813	139,627
30,962	119,666	183,703	327,305
5,385	28,704	33,250	45,385
103,084	296,459	427,904	722,858
66,133	141,073	162,267	245,474
87,757	231,033	339,726	538,004
21,270	72,984	110,442	270,133
17,048	64,000	94,074	180,000
—	5,200	9,578	56,071
—	—	—	45,000
—	—	—	10,000
192,208	514,290	716,087	1,344,682
466,185	1,170,760	1,573,625	2,780,369
68,839	236,420	325,806	575,420
14.8	20.2	20.4	20.7

Marriage and Fertility

It was long assumed by historians that high colonial birth rates were due to couples in America marrying at a younger age than those in Europe. Yet the work of Robert Higgs and Louis Stettler has shown that, at least in New England, women married, on the average, at age 21, and men, at age 24. Although these averages are three or four years younger than present-day numbers, as recently as the 1970s, the age at first marriage was approximately the same as that in colonial New England. Fertility in colonial marriages was very high compared to either contemporary Europe or modern America. Women died more often than now in childbirth, and men remarried. Families were large; as Higgs and Stettler laconically put the matter, "the number of children born to a man in all his marriages being about seven on the average."[6]

The vital data are very rough, but the population aggregates are solid and are justified when compared with the first American census of 1790. Thus, we see colonial population growth as very powerful. This natural vitality continued in the United States into the nineteenth century before it began to slow down.

Regional Distribution

Note in Table 3.2 the relative population sizes of Virginia, Massachusetts, and New York by 1780, a comparison that explains a lot about this country's early political history and the powerful contribution of rural Virginia, even with more than a third of its population still enslaved. Pennsylvania's growth from 1681 was very strong; even though it was founded later than New York, Massachusetts, Maryland, and Virginia, by 1780 it had overtaken all but Virginia. Note also by the end of the period the movement of population into Vermont and across the Appalachians into Kentucky and Tennessee. The westward movement was already underway.

By the end of the colonial period, New England had fallen behind the Middle colonies in population. Southern population growth continued to dominate. Virginia, along with North and South Carolina, comprised some 40 percent of the total colonial population growth in the two decades before American independence was recognized by the Peace of Paris (1783). At the end of the colonial period, nearly half the total population resided in the five Southern colonies.

WEALTH AND INCOME

When we look at structures dating from the colonial period that have survived to modern times, we see evidence of past solidity and wealth in Portsmouth, Newburyport, Boston, Philadelphia, Georgetown, and Charleston. We suppose that only the best buildings survived. Yet these solid structures were places of everyday business and the houses of common persons—who were not princes or feudal lords. A surrounding social and economic infrastructure had voluntarily supported such opulence. Common sense alone suggests that colonial society, by the end of the period, must have been prosperous.

Colonial Growth

American economic history is the story of **economic growth**, of increases in total output per capita. Economic growth does not necessarily measure an improvement in the quality of life; it merely initiates the potential for improvement. The great French Postimpressionist painter Paul Gauguin (1848–1903) traded the comforts and amenities of Western civilization for the simplicity of Tahiti in 1891. Conventional measures of growth consider an employed man or woman living in the pollution and congestion of modern Tokyo to be "better off" than a suntanned artist watching yet another glorious sunset on the beach in Tahiti.

This frame of mind is reflected in American economic history. Until very recently, no one questioned that trees felled, prairies plowed, rivers dammed, and suburbs extended were measures of progress. That kind of thinking was characteristic of colonial times. Well-being was not measured by the number of standing available trees per person, but by the amount of forest cleared per family. American economic history is written in that tradition: Plowing furrows in cleared land is progress.

The sum of all such activity evaluated at market prices is the **Gross Domestic Product (GDP)** for a given year.[7] For most of American history, GDP can only be roughly estimated because our information is incomplete. The value of aggregate output must be equal in value to the aggregate income of all participating **factors of production**—conventionally labor, capital, and natural resources (including land). All output comes from combining factors in given production processes. Consider an example: A man plows a field by hand. The number of furrows is the output of the production process. The man's work is labor, the plow is capital, and the unplowed field is a natural resource. The number of furrows plowed per hour is the output per man hour, what is termed **labor productivity**. If the man acquires an ox (additional capital) to help him propel the plow through the field, the number of furrows plowed per hour should increase, as should his income. Such is the nature of economic growth.

Income received is either consumed or saved. Net saving over time adds up to the stock of **wealth**. Whether it is in solid structures or livestock, it is society's wealth. It is also called **capital**, the stock of "goods that are used to produce other goods" at a given moment of time. Colonial wealth has been roughly estimated in various ways. One method is to use the surviving records of wills from estates that passed through probate court.

The leading modern student of such data is Alice Hanson Jones, and her estimates of colonial wealth are astonishingly large.[8] She found that the average free person in colonial America owned perhaps £76 in real wealth. Now, if we accept that amount as the best number available, some interesting information emerges with a little arithmetic. Following Walton and Shepherd, £76, in 2000 prices, equals $11,100.[9] A tidy sum! If we consider this figure a measure of capital per head, then dividing it by various capital/output ratios produces a result that is a measure of output (income) per head in 1774. Historic capital/output ratios fall somewhere between the boundaries 3 to 1 and 5 to 1.[10] Using the former figure, income per capita in 1774 was £25; using the latter, £15. If we use Walton and Shepherd's conversion to "modern values" and extrapolate to 2000, colonial Americans had incomes per capita in 1774 in the range of $3,875 to $7,250 per capita (again, these have been converted to 2000 prices). These amounts would have given colonial Americans a possible standard of life similar to that today in Botswana, Brazil, or Poland with the lower figure and like that of Argentina or Saudi Arabia with the higher one. Of course, the colonists would have had the consumer and capital goods of 1774, not those of 2000, to absorb their incomes. Admitting, as we must, the large margin of error in such calculations, it is still the case that Americans two centuries ago achieved a level of affluence at least as great as their British cousins. If we adjust our calculation for the lower tax rates paid in the colonies, the disposable incomes of Americans were surely among the highest in the world of the early 1770s. Indeed, our crude estimates suggest their real incomes then were far higher than those of two-thirds of the world's population today.

Most estimates of per-capita growth in the eighteenth century are in the neighborhood of 0.3 to 0.6 percent per annum, slightly above the contemporary English growth rates.[11] Such rates imply a doubling of per-capita output in approximately 140 years, a healthy rate for a largely agricultural economy with little technological change.

By 1774, the Southern colonies had the largest share of total wealth and the highest wealth per capita (see Table 3.3). Land was the largest single component of wealth, even in the South. Terry Anderson found that total wealth in New England in the late seventeenth century was already growing at a robust 1.6 percent per annum, a rate that would double wealth in two generations.[12]

The long colonial years had been an epoch of economic achievement when measured from the "starving time" in Virginia and Plymouth. The handful of survivors from those early settlements, their descendants, and new immigrants, both slave and free, had grown to a population of some 2.5 million.

TABLE 3.3 Private Wealth Per Capita in 1774

	Thirteen Colonies	*New England*	*Middle Colonies*	*South*
Land	£25.6	£26.1	£25.9	£25.1
Livestock	4.3	2.8	4.8	4.8
Equipment	1.6	1.7	1.7	1.5
Inventories	2.3	1.5	3.9	1.8
Consumers' goods	3.7	4.4	4	3.1
Slaves	9.1	0.2	1.6	18.4
Total	£46.5	£36.6	£41.9	£54.7

The numbers may not total perfectly because of rounding.

Source: Alice Hanson Jones, *Wealth of a Nation to Be* (New York: Columbia University Press, 1980), Table 4.2, p. 96.

These numbers indicate that the colonists, deploying European technology, raised per-capita output *very quickly* to English levels in whatever enterprises they formed and developed in new areas of settlement. Growth then *slowed down* to levels justified by the state of existing technology and its gradual improvement. Such a pattern explains both high apparent output levels and relatively slow growth once initial settlements were made. It is not an unreasonable pattern of growth. If a large body of modern Americans were transplanted to a less-developed country, we would expect strong immediate improvements in economic development to occur, since the Americans would employ their own technology and not that of a less-developed country.

Such a pattern of growth explains testimony quoted by Stuart Bruchey in *The Colonial Merchant.* In 1663, just three decades after landing, Reverend John Higginson of Boston said, "We live in a more plentiful and comfortable manner than ever we did expect."[13] While he was clerk of the Pennsylvania legislature, Ben Franklin observed in 1740, only 60 years after Penn's charter for the colony, "The first drudgery of settling new colonies, which confines the attention of people to mere necessaries, is now pretty well over: and there are many in every province in circumstances that set them at ease."[14]

The Standard of Life

In his examination of *The Roots of American Economic Growth,* Stuart Bruchey, having surveyed the historical evidence available in the early 1960s, concludes with what was then a somewhat risky statement, "Probably in few societies in history have the means of subsistence been so widely distributed among the mass of the people as in colonial America."[15] As we shall see, he was not describing an equal distribution of domestic resources, but an abundant and largely sufficient one.

How were these resources deployed? Evidence of the technology available shows that Americans were abreast of Europe. The colonists had come to a new land with the technology and commercial institutions of contemporary England, and what they did with their available resources represented the "best practice" of that time. Colonial agriculture, once European methods were adapted to American climate and soils, was very productive. But the colonists also fabricated products of the farm, forests, mines, and fisheries. They made iron and iron products; they built ships; they made bricks; they wove cloth in abundance—wool and linen—on the farmsteads; and they made weapons. They built mills and slaughterhouses, converted timber into lumber, fished, and maintained a large export industry in seafood, dried and salted meat, and hides. They had tanneries and salteries, made shoes, printed newspapers, and made their own glassware and pewter ware. Wherever they settled, Americans quickly replicated their civilization economically, just as they carried with them their relations, property laws, levels of education, and moral code.[16]

In 1782, Hector Saint-John de Crèvecoeur, who had served as a French officer under Montcalm at Quebec and stayed on to farm in New York until 1780, published 12 essays addressed to Europeans called *Letters from an American Farmer*:

> A Hundred families barely existing in some parts of Scotland, will here in six years, cause an annual exportation of 10,000 bushels of wheat; 100 bushels being but a common quantity for an industrious family to sell, if they cultivate good land...[a hired man would be] well fed at the table of his employer, and paid four or five times more than he can get in Europe.[17]

Modern research supports Crèvecoeur's eyewitness account.

Edwin Perkins convincingly argues that, in addition to its affluence, colonial America enjoyed a high *quality* of life.[18] The abundance of fertile land meant food was bountiful, wood (the primary energy source) was plentiful and cheap, and the population density was low. This healthy environment led, as we have seen, to high birthrates and low mortality rates for both infants and adults. Further, as we shall discuss in Chapter 6, heights have been found to be a good measure of a society's nutritional status. Kenneth Sokoloff and Georgia Villaflor, using the muster rolls for the French and Indian War and the Revolutionary War, estimate that the average colonial recruit was 5 feet, 8 inches tall, quite close to modern heights and a full 2 inches taller than those mustered into the British Royal Marines at the same time.[19]

The distribution of wealth and income in colonial America by the end of the period was uneven. Unequal income distribution is the case in most societies today, even in China. Depending upon tastes and social choices, together with the distribution of resources, skills, talents, and the demand for them, almost any economy will produce differential rewards to participants. When the residues of unequal incomes and different consumption habits—wealth—are inherited, wealth holdings are also, obviously, going to be unequal. James Henretta found that, in 1771, the top 10 percent of wealth holders in Boston owned 57 percent of the wealth.[20] Alice Hanson Jones found that, in 1774, the top 10 percent in New England owned 46.8 percent of the wealth; in the Middle colonies, 35.1 percent; and in the South, 46.9 percent.[21] In a study of American wealth holdings in modern times, Robert Lampman found that, in 1953, the top 10.8 percent of the "top" wealth holders had 46.4 percent of the estates subject to wealth taxes.[22] It is a vexing question among economists whether such inequality helps, hinders, or is generated by the processes of economic growth.[23] We will return to this question in later chapters.

It is perhaps worth a few more lines here to illustrate more completely the colonial experiences regarding inequality. As we already noted, in early Virginia, attempts at equal distribution of the social product were unsatisfactory. When Captain John Smith said that the individual colonists must work to eat, he was expressing a present social need. In Plymouth Colony, early attempts to distribute work assignments and rewards equally resulted in a deficient agricultural output Governor Bradford recorded in his journal the changes they made and the results. The year was 1623.

> So they begane to thinke how they might raise as much corne as they could, and obtaine a beter crope then they had done, that they might not still thus languish in miserie. At length, after much debate of things, the Governor...gave way that they should set corne every man for his owne perticuler, and in that regard trust to them selves; in all other things to goe on in the generall way as before. And so assigned to every family a parcell of land, according to the proportion of their number for that end, only for present use (but

> made no devission for inheritance), and ranged all boys & youth under some familie. This had very good success; for it made all hands very industrious, so as much more corne was planted then other waise would have bene by any means the Governor or any other could use, and saved him a great deall of trouble, and gave farr better contente. The women now wente willingly into the feild, and tooke their litle-ons with them to set corne, which before would aledg weaknes, and inabilitie; whom to have compelled would have bene thought great tiranie and oppression.
>
> The experience that was had in this commone course and condition, tried sundrie years, and that amongst godly and sober men, may well evince the vanitie of that conceite of Platos & other ancients, applauded by some of later times;—that the taking away of propertie, and bringing in communitie into a comone wealth, would make them happy and flourishing; as if they were wiser then God. For this comunitie (so farr as it was) was found to breed much confusion & discontent.... For the yong-men that were most able and fitte for labour & service did repine that they should spend their time & streingth to worke for other mens wives and children, with out any recompence. The strong, or man of parts, had no more in devission of victails & cloaths, then he that was weake and not able to doe a quarter the other could; this was thought injuestice.... Let none objecte this is men's corruption, and nothing to the course it selfe. I answer, seeing all men have this corruption in them, God in his wisdome saw another course fiter for them.[24]

Bradford might have noted God's injunction to Adam when he and Eve were tossed out of Paradise: "In the sweat of thy face shalt thou eat bread." From Plymouth Colony until now, apart from a few utopian experiments like Brook Farm and the later Mormon United Orders, the dream of Plato and other ancients has been confounded by the superior economic achievement of distribution according to individual contribution. An unending question has been, and is, "Where does justice lie in income distribution?"[25] Is justice equality, payment for work done, risks taken, or what? To the colonials, a more pressing question was, "What will we use as money to facilitate transactions between individuals?"

WAS THERE A MONEY SHORTAGE IN COLONIAL AMERICA?

The quantity theory of money argues that a growing economy requires a growing money supply to keep prices stable. The basic equation ($MV = PQ$) argues that if economic growth leads to increases in output (Q), and if the velocity of money (V) is stable, then the money supply (M) must rise by an amount equal to Q in order to keep prices (P) stable. It follows from this that an increase in M, again assuming V is stable, could lead to either an increase in Q (economic growth) or an increase in P (inflation). Colonial areas have always demanded more money as the supply of investment funds traditionally has been relatively limited and, consequently, interest rates have been relatively high. The colonists believed, as have generations of historians, that there was a scarcity of **specie**, gold and silver in coin form. Some, including Ben Franklin, thought that British incompetence on the colonial money issue contributed to the desire for independence. Also, there are two important facts about colonial money:

1. The colonists discovered how to use officially engraved pieces of paper as substitutes for coins.
2. In 1781, the Revolutionary Congress chartered a joint-stock, note-issuing bank that was the origin of American commercial banking.

These two precedents were destined to have enormous consequences in American economic history.

Money

Money, conventionally, is any item that performs four functions:

1. It serves as a medium of exchange.
2. It is a unit of account.
3. It performs as a store of value.
4. It is acceptable as a standard of deferred payment.

It is remarkable how many items in history besides coins have been acceptable as money: animal skins, tobacco, cowry shells, wampum (strings of small shells), rocks with holes bored through them, and engraved bits of paper issued by princes, dictators, republics, and private persons. These and many more have served as a medium of exchange. The only requirement is acceptability, and it need not even be voluntary. Armies of occupation have long extracted real produce from conquered peoples by issuing paper money that is acceptable—or else. In fact, any money called **legal tender** is prescribed in law as what may be offered and must be accepted in payment of both private and public debts. It is coercively circulated; refusal to accept it in payment is a crime—even in modern America.

Specie

Historically, some types of money have tended to be preferred, and specie payments, payment in quantities of precious metal, lead that list.

During the colonial period, the British were on a **bimetallic** (two-metal) **monetary standard**. The mint, the treasury, and (after 1694) the Bank of England bought and sold both gold and silver at fixed prices. The buying price of an ounce of gold was 3 pounds, 17 shillings, 9.5 pence—the price fixed by Sir Isaac Newton as the "right" standard of England. A gold coin known as a *sovereign*, of standard weight and fineness, was worth 1 pound sterling. Each pound was divided into 20 silver shillings. There were coins of multiples of shillings and several coins of less than a shilling: the sixpence, the penny, the farthing, and halfpenny. A "Guinea" gold coin was worth 21 shillings because it was a sovereign made of Guinea gold, of greater fineness than ordinary gold. The original Guinea gold was brought from west Africa during the reign of Charles II in connection with the slave trade.[26]

The English did not allow their coins to be exported legally, even to the colonies, but made no objections to the export or import of foreign coins and bullion (bars) since all could be valued by weight and fineness. Hence, *to pay in specie* meant to pay in some form of gold or silver. The two metals were not always equally preferred, a problem with bimetallism: If the world gold supply expanded at a faster rate than did that of silver, it took more gold to buy a given amount of silver, and the gold price of silver rose. Expanded silver production relative to gold tended to produce the opposite result.

Other Means of Payment

Payments could be made in other ways. The main method, the bill of exchange (a dated order to pay), was well known in colonial times. For example, suppose that A, a Carolina planter, ships rice to B, an English merchant. A draws an order for B to pay, say, £100. (This is exactly what happens today when you write a check or use a debit card; it is an order from you to your bank to pay a given amount out of the funds you have deposited.) In the case of a bill of exchange representing sale of commodities, it was standard practice to place a date, such as three months, four months, or even six months, on the bill as the due date. The length of time stated was the bill's maturity. A "three months bill" matured three months after it was drawn. The next step was to get the bill "accepted," affirmation by B (or more likely B's agent, C, in Charleston), that B will pay. B (or C) signs the bill, and it now becomes money, if B is a person of good credit.

Several things could then happen. A could hold the bill himself until it matured and then present it for payment to B or to B's agent, C. A could sell the bill to someone else, D, for cash as soon as it has been accepted, and D would then wait for the due date and collect. If the bill were for three months, A would normally sell it to D for a discount. The amount of the discount could be any mutually agreeable sum, but the basic price would usually be determined by the current short-term rate of interest. If the current rate of interest were 8 percent, the interest on a three months bill of £100 would be £2: 8 percent times 0.25 (since three months is one-fourth of a year) times 100. Thus, D would give A £98 cash now and collect £100 on the due date.

An importer in Charleston might want to pay someone in England. Instead of shipping gold or silver, he could buy the bill from D (or from A, depending on who was holding it) and send it to his supplier in England in payment for goods shipped to Charleston. The supplier would receive the bill and present it to B or his banker on the due date and receive payment. He also could discount the bill with someone else in England and get cash, and the discounter would then wait for the bill to mature and present it to B.

Any person owning the bill at various points along its path had to endorse it to transfer it to another.

According to English law, *all* signatories to the bill would be liable for payment if B defaulted when the payment came due. In general, the bill of exchange was thus an excellent form of "merchant money" and could be used to finance trade in all directions.

The important point is that international transactions could take place *without any shipments of specie.* That is how most transactions were accomplished—by remission of bills of exchange for payment. Such bills were also used for purely domestic trade. There were many variants of the basic form we have discussed. The point to remember is that bills of exchange fit our definition of money, and, therefore, as long as they were current (not in default), they were money. Their amount at any time depended not upon banks or mints but upon merchant credit.[27]

The Bank of England (founded in 1694) did not issue its own paper as current money in colonial times. Nor, so far as we know, did any other English bank issue such small denomination promissory notes. The "paper pound," the first paper money issued by the Bank of England, appeared in 1791 when the Bank was forced to suspend specie payments. As far as we know, colonial paper money was the first in the British Empire's history. But other things served as "near-moneys." Governments in England and in the colonies issued scraps of engraved paper, evidences of debt, in anticipation of further income (and payment) and promised to pay these off when they matured. They were interest-bearing and, obviously, they also could be considered money if they were transferable and payable to the bearer, except that no one was *forced* to take them in payment (they were not legal tender), and they usually were in denominations too large to be of use as money to the ordinary person. Finally, book credit, like that given by your corner grocer, could be granted by any seller to any buyer. Thus, when we speak of the colonial "money supply" we are not necessarily speaking of specie. But let us speak of the colonial specie problem explicitly.

The Colonial Specie Problem

One difficult task with money in the form of specie is knowing how much of it is around. The amount minted into coins is not necessarily the amount available in coins. Gold and silver can be, and were, used for purposes besides money. Coins can be melted down to make jewelry, sword hilts, and other objects. Also, specie is easily hidden (for example, from tax collectors) or exported, and people have a lamentable tendency to be less than honest about how much they own, in what forms, or where it is. Given that tendency, there is probably no better-known characteristic of colonial money than the much-discussed "shortage" of it. By *money* in this context, colonials meant *specie*, especially English coins.

The nature of the money shortage may be illustrated by the following. Benjamin Franklin returned to his home in Boston briefly in the spring of 1724 after having spent a short period in Philadelphia. He visited his brother's printing shop, and the journeyman printers there questioned Franklin about Pennsylvania:

> ...asking what kind of money we had there, I produc'd a handful of silver, and spread it before them, which was a kind of rareeshow they had not been us'd to, paper being the money of Boston.... I gave them a piece of eight to drink, and took my leave.[28]

Economic historians have scoffed at colonial complaints about a shortage of money primarily for three reasons. First, interest rates in colonial times remained moderate, and with usury laws in all colonies placing ceilings on interest rates (8 percent in seventeenth-century Massachusetts, 5 percent a century later in Pennsylvania), a real money shortage that inhibited trade would have produced significant evidence of violations of the usury laws. There is no such evidence. People would have found ways around the laws, or violated them, as they did when commodities were smuggled into the colonies in violation of the navigation laws. There would have been a record of such activities. Secondly, according to the quantity theory, a money shortage, even with constant real incomes, should have resulted in falling prices. The trend of prices in colonial America, however, was upward. With long-term rising prices and falling nominal interest rates, the *real* rate of interest cannot have been a serious inhibiting factor to borrowers. Finally, the rate of real growth of the colonial economy at rising prices also is not evidence of a money shortage. We have seen that there were many ways to have command over real resources without defining money in terms of specie.

The Balance of Payments and Specie

Were the colonists imagining that they suffered from a money shortage? No, not necessarily. The colonists could only obtain major long-term increases in specie supplies by selling more goods and services to the world than they bought. They seem to have had a small deficit on current account, at least by the end of the colonial period.[29] There is no reason to suppose there was any earlier period of substantial surpluses. Without gold or silver mines, net accumulation of coin could occur only through trade, piracy, or accumulated indebtedness. Your pockets can bulge with coins if your banker lends them to you on credit, and this is what the British did—they gave the colonies credit.

Meanwhile, there were opportunities to get specie from trade with southern Europe and the Caribbean, making Spanish, French, Portuguese, and Dutch coins common in circulation. (The Spanish-milled dollar of 1728 was so acceptable and useful that it became the standard when the American dollar was adopted in 1792.) Year-to-year specie supplies could come from those sources. As we shall see, the overwhelming source of bilateral trade deficit was with England, and that was financed by sales of services and by the long-term accumulation of American debt instruments in English hands. The British extended credit, and they also spent large sums on administration and military operations in the colonies. As Larry Neal has pointed out, a large proportion of that British money landed in American hands.[30] Walton and Shepherd find net American indebtedness growing at a maximum rate of about £40,000 a year in the early 1770s, but the net was no doubt slightly less since some small part of the deficit would have been covered by net specie shipments, the source of the colonial complaint. According to Walton and Shepherd, in 1776, British merchants claimed about £2.5 million in outstanding debts owed by Americans.[31] This amount, which translates into about £1 per person in the colonial population at that time, was no doubt a considerable exaggeration.

Devaluation

The colonials tried several monetary tricks to attract coin. The obvious tactic was **devaluation**: to raise (or attempt to raise) the domestic price of foreign money by law. In the late seventeenth century, New York, Massachusetts, and Pennsylvania all tried to attract Spanish coins by offering a premium (from one-third to as much as one-half of a percent). In 1704, the British issued a proclamation setting official (lower) rates on foreign coins. These exchange rates, known as "Queen Anne's Money," merely made a confusing situation worse. The system was flexible enough for trade to flourish despite governments, and foreign coins came by way of that trade, attracted by something real—colonial commodities at prices dictated by the market. The Massachusetts mint, in existence from 1652 to 1684, made silver coins: shillings and half- and quarter-shillings. Given the same name as the standard English coin, it is said that they were about 23 percent underweight to prevent their being shipped to England. They were shipped anyway, by their actual weight.

Payments-In-Kind

As has been noted, many things besides coins served as money. The coin shortage tested colonial creativity.

Country Money. In the colonial countryside, payment was made in corn, wheat, skins, livestock, and almost anything else that could serve as a substitute for specie. Massachusetts laws, in recognition of the irregularities that could arise from debts accumulated through such media of exchange, contain a wonderful statute from the year 1654:

> All *contracts* and *engagements*, for *money, corn, cattle,* or *fish* shall be satisfied in kinds according to Covenant, or in default of the very kind contracted for, in one of the said kinds, provided that in such cases, where payment in kind is not made according to Covenant; all just damage shall be satisfied...according to bargain.[32]

In modern parlance, such contracts were **indexed**—that is, if the relative values of the kinds of commodities and livestock changed, those who promised to pay at the old ratios were committed to try to honor the value of the original commitment.

In Virginia, tobacco, of course, quickly came to serve as money. But as Studenski and Krooss wrote, there could be no long-term future for tobacco money in the place where it was grown:

> Since anyone with a modicum of ambition could grow money in his own back yard, the cultivation of tobacco increased so rapidly that its price in terms of silver fell 80 percent within a few years.[33]

No controls, no matter how stringent, could hold back tobacco planting, and tobacco long served as money in Virginia and on the frontier. Studenski and Krooss also cite early livestock payments for tuition at Harvard College and for the building fund, "a goat 30s plantations of Watertown rate which died."[34] Commodity moneys were thus imperfect and probably made the "shortage" of specie seem worse because of **Gresham's law** ("Bad money chases out good"): You hoarded your coins if you could pay with a sick goat or a pile of your own tobacco leaves.

Wampum. There is an excellent example of Gresham's law at work in the colonial annals of wampum money. The Dutch at New Amsterdam, trading with the Indians, accepted and paid out wampum—shells strung beadlike into chains—as the medium of exchange.[35] The Indians, wanting more European goods, "devalued" the currency by offering short strings and unstrung wampum in exchange, thus undervaluing the superior wampum and driving it out of circulation. In reply, Wilhelm Kieft, the wily Dutch governor, ordered a 50-percent increase in the quoted prices of European goods against such inferior moneys. Since strung wampum was no longer undervalued at the Dutch trading posts, it returned to circulation.[36]

The Pilgrims in Massachusetts had first been introduced to wampum in 1623 by a Dutch visitor from New Amsterdam named De Rasieres. Finding that the Massachusetts Indians would indeed accept wampum for their goods, the Pilgrims tried to go directly "to the mines" by picking up the right shells and stringing their own wampum. They soon discovered that they had the wrong factor combinations for this endeavor ultimately to pay. Wampum was cheaper when acquired in exchange for their own goods than when it was "manufactured." Consequently, comparative advantage took over, and the Pilgrims traded goods for wampum, wampum for furs, and furs in England for more European goods. Wampum continued to be strung by Indian women and maintained its career as money whenever and wherever it was mutually acceptable.

Paper Money, Bills of Credit, and Banks

The colonists' truly fateful discovery was paper money. As the Chinese had had it centuries earlier, perhaps it was a case of unnecessary originality. Nevertheless, in 1690 the government of Massachusetts issued 7,000 one-year notes, yielding 5 percent, redeemable at par (face value), and acceptable at par for taxes. The government had borrowed from merchants in anticipation of revenues as early as 1676, and these notes had been used among merchants like bills of exchange—as money. In 1690, the government of Massachusetts needed to pay soldiers returning from an unsuccessful campaign against Quebec, but there was no specie to use for this purpose. The soldiers accepted small-denomination bills of credit, the bills passed current as money, and the follies in America of **fiat money** (paper money with no specie backing) had begun. It was a wonderful thing: interest-earning cash. The other colonies noted this phenomenon and quickly followed with issues of their own: South Carolina in 1703; Connecticut, New York, New Hampshire, and New Jersey in 1709; Rhode Island in 1710; North Carolina in 1712; and Pennsylvania in 1723. Apparently, private citizens joined in on an irregular basis with their own issues, since Quaker pacifists in Pennsylvania were moved in 1767 to legislate the death penalty for counterfeiting, per-

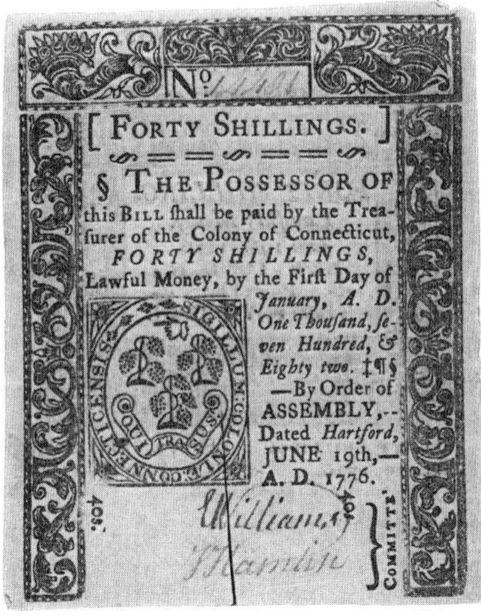

Colonial paper currencies of Connecticut and New Jersey from 1776.

haps the most severe penalty for plagiarism in American history.

Money and Colonial Inflation

Inflation in the colonies meant a general rise in the prices of commodities *and* a reduction in the exchange rates between colonial money and specie. In 1751, the British Parliament prohibited the status of legal tender from being applied to the paper money of New England and, in 1764, extended that prohibition to all the colonies. But the bills themselves were not prohibited. There seems to be little doubt that this addition to the money supply contributed to the rising prices of produce. First, there was a depreciation against specie; how much depended upon circumstances in each colony. It was most severe in New England. In Rhode Island, the extreme of depreciation against specie was 26 to 1; in Massachusetts, the paper fell to 7.5 to 1 against specie. But in the Middle colonies, where the money was better managed and sinking funds were provided, the record was much better. Money issues had even been made in a counter-cyclical way "to steady the rate of business expansion."[37]

In Figure 3.1, we see the exchange rate of Pennsylvania paper against British pounds sterling. Although the pound rose strongly at the beginning of colonialism, after the 1740s, the rate was stable. Fifty-five years after the issues began, there had been no runaway depreciation, and the Pennsylvania currency was only a bit less than one-third depreciated against the pound—against specie. In 1932 in the United States, you could buy an ounce of gold for $20.67; today, it costs almost 13 times as much. In comparison with modern-day American currency, colonial Pennsylvania currency was the acme of fiscal conservatism and integrity. Further, the colonial price trend was indeed upward, but again, by modern standards, it is difficult to take seriously writers who overemphasize such a gentle wafting. Wholesale prices in Philadelphia (Figure 3.2) did not double in more than half a century.[38] Some specific prices, such as that of bread (Figure 3.3), did rise more strongly. Overall, the experience was mixed and seemed to fascinate the English (who would soon enough make abundant use of paper money). Better than any central-bank policy statement in the subsequent two centuries was Ben Franklin's summation of the colonial experience in his *A Modest Inquiry into the Nature and Necessity of a Paper Currency*:

> There is a certain proportionate quantity of money requisite to carry on the trade of a country freely and currently; more than which would be of no advantage to trade, and less, if much less, exceedingly detrimental to it.

The Massachusetts land bank of 1740 did alarm the British and some Americans, and it was put down by Parliament a year later by "An Act for Restraining and Preventing Several Unwarrantable Schemes and Undertakings in His Majesty's Colonies and Plantations in America." The "unwarrantable schemes and undertakings" consisted of the formation of a private, joint-stock company issuing its own paper money secured by mortgages on land, a prototype of frontier banking to come. The English prohibited such ventures in England after 1720 by the "Bubble Act," which was prompted by the sensational financial manipulations, company boom, and subsequent panic called the "South Sea Bubble."

FIGURE 3.1 Annual Rate of Exchange in London for Pennsylvania Currency 1720–1775

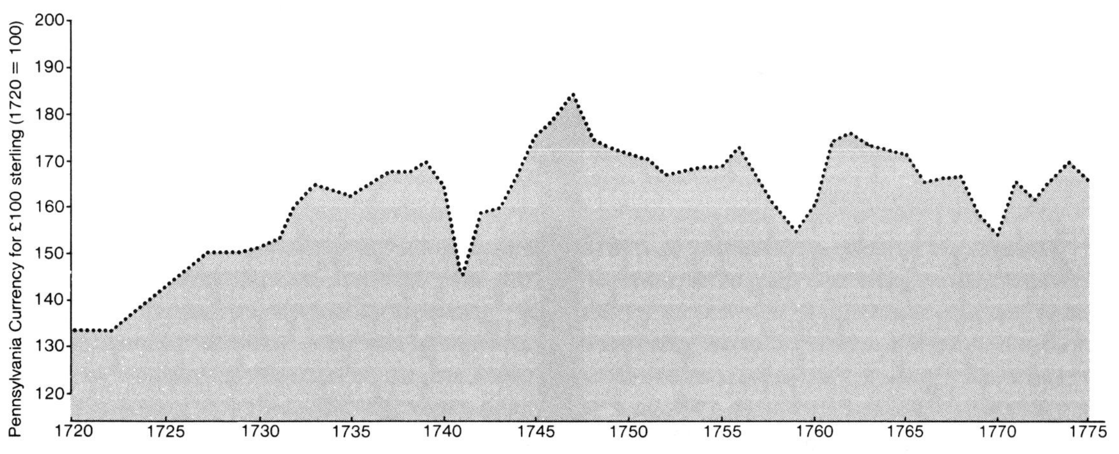

Source: *Historical Statistics,* series Z 585.

The trend of exchange rates between English sterling and Pennsylvania paper currency shows an irregular upward movement. Over time, it took more Pennsylvania money to buy an English pound, but there were periods when the sterling rate fell.

FIGURE 3.2 Wholesale Prices 1720–1775

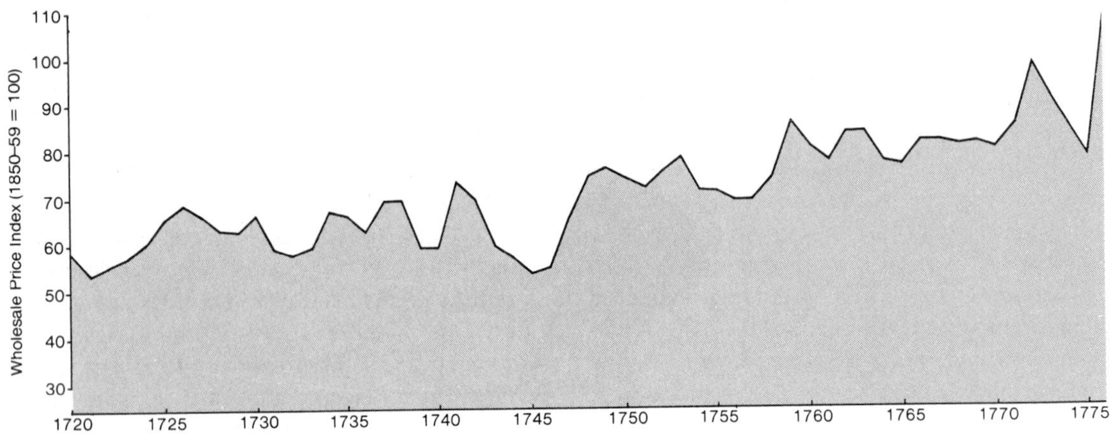

Source: *Historical Statistics,* series Z 557.

The mild long-run inflation of the period shows more clearly in wholesale prices, with a dip just before the Revolution.

It was then decided that the government must protect people from themselves, and, in 1741, the Bubble Act was applied to the colonies. However, private banking did exist in all the colonies, if not in joint-stock form. In 1733, a group of Boston merchants issued notes redeemable in silver (which, naturally enough, were hoarded, like the silver they represented). They opposed the land bank, and they had the ear of Parliament. Joint-stock banking would have to wait for 1781 and the power of the Continental Congress to create a banking corporation, the Bank of North America.

FIGURE 3.3 Price of Bread in Pennsylvania 1720–1775

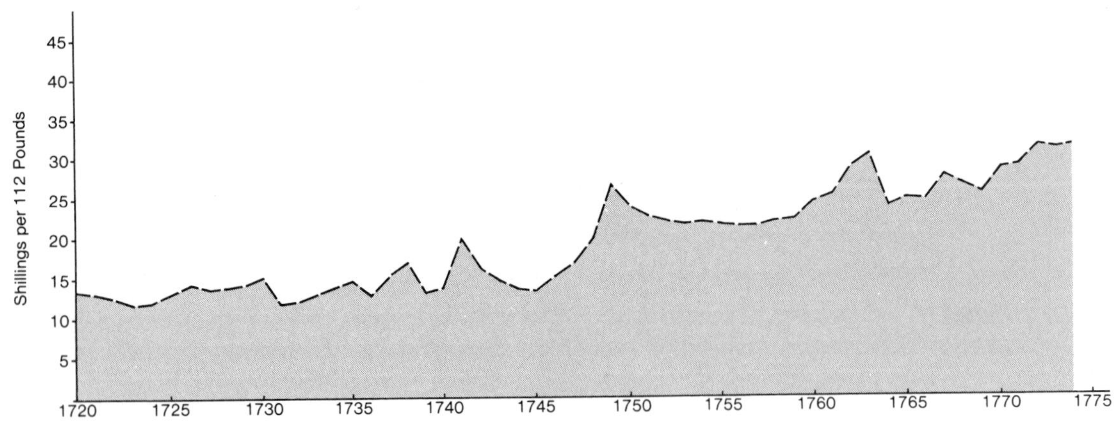

Source: *Historical Statistics,* series Z 562.

The price of bread in Pennsylvania rose over time, but just slightly, indicating only a mild long-run inflation.

In Conclusion

In a later chapter, we will examine another period of American financial history (1789–1863) known as "financial chaos." Yet, there is no evidence, as we shall see, that the long-term effects of such financial disorder were adverse to economic growth and development. The same must be said of the colonial period. Paper money was a substitute for the elusive coins and the clumsy "country" money of tobacco and goats, and it served variously, as it does today, according to how rapidly it was issued relative to the increase in what it bought. What cannot be said is that economic growth was harmed by it, and as Franklin said, in some circumstances, it served well. In fact, he thought a worse problem would be insufficient amounts of money. Modern political leaders all over the world must certainly agree with him.

Inflation in colonial times, as now, eased the problems of debtors against their creditors. Then too, as now, the rich favored fiscal conservation, while those not so wealthy favored liberal money issues. When the Revolution came, Congress issued so much paper money that its value against specie fell drastically, but that Continental currency was redeemed and absorbed by land sales and economic growth. The product of colonial monetary genius, the invention of paper money, must be recognized as one of the greatest legacies the colonists left to their heirs. The concerns of writers in the past who were scandalized by the "inflationary" consequences of colonial moneying need not be taken seriously today. From 1720 to 1775, the annual compound rate of price increase was, on the average, just over 1 percent, less than one-tenth the inflation rates of the late 1970s.

NOTES

1. Robert William Fogel and Stanley Engerman, *Time on the Cross: The Economics of American Negro Slavery* (1974).
2. David Galenson, *White Servitude in Colonial America: An Economic Analysis* (1981), p. 18.
3. Most whites had the option of returning to the countries they had left; many exercised that option.
4. Colonial death rates rose to perhaps as high as 24 per 1,000 in the seventeenth century. Robert Paul Thomas and Terry Anderson, "White Population, Labor Force and Extensive Growth of the New England Economy in the Seventeenth Century," *JEH*, September 1973.
5. Billy Smith, "Death and Life in a Colonial Immigrant City: A Demographic Analysis of Philadelphia," *JEH*, December 1977.
6. Robert Higgs and Louis Stettler, "Colonial New England Demography: A Sampling Approach," *William and Mary Quarterly*, April 1970, p. 291.
7. Before the early 1990s, the U.S. government reported Gross National Product (GNP) rather than GDP. For the years before World War II, estimates of GNP are more common than estimates of GDP. This book will follow the now-current usage and use GDP where possible.
8. Alice Hanson Jones, *American Colonial Wealth: Documents and Methods* (1977).
9. Walton and Shepherd ,*The Economic Rise of Early America* (1979). See their Chapter 7 for an excellent survey and analysis of the data and issues on this subject. This paragraph states only their major conclusions. It also should be noted that not all scholars have made estimates as high as those of Dr. Jones. Yet she has made a most thorough and careful search of the records, and her conclusions must be given primary attention, as the issue now stands.
10. The capital/output ratio purports to show the amount of net savings over time—the stock of capital—a society uses to produce income. If it is 3/1, then $3.00 of "capital" in a given period produces $1.00 of output. It is a very crude and questionable analytical device, but useful for some purposes. Even using modern data, one must be careful with it. The selected boundaries are very conservative.
11. See Peter Mancall and Thomas Weiss, "Was Economic Growth Likely in Colonial British North America?" *JEH*, March 1999, who challenge this finding. They argue that the growth rate for colonists and slaves was much lower, close to zero. Mancall, Weiss, and Joshua Rosenbloom have undertaken a study of the American Indian economy on a regional basis. In the Lower South, where exports were of greater importance than in many other colonies, real output per capita appears to have grown at less than 0.3 percent per annum (See "Conjectural Estimates of Economic Growth in the Lower South, 1720–1800," National Bureau of Economic Research Working Paper No. HO126, June 2000). Population in the eighteenth-century was growing at mean annual rates of more than 3 percent (see Table 3.2).

12. Terry Anderson, "Wealth Estimates for the New England Colonies, 1650–1709," *EEH*, April 1975. The land, relatively poor for agriculture, still produced a capital gain, on average, as population increased. Land, it has been shown, was the main source of increase in heritable wealth in southern New England. Gloria Main and Jackson Turner Main, "Economic Growth and the Standard of Living in Southern New England," *JEH*, March 1988. The increase in inheritable wealth was relatively quick. Lorena Walsh, "Urban Amenities and Rural Self Sufficiency: Living Standards and Consumer Behavior in the Colonial Chesapeake, 1643–1777," *JEH*, March 1983. Evidence of estates shows that by the mid-eighteenth century, rural households in the Chesapeake area enjoyed physical appurtenances like furniture and kitchen equipment at a level indicating a lifestyle about equal to those of urban populations of the same period. A high standard of consumerism was apparent in rural households.
13. Stuart Bruchey, ed., *The Colonial Merchant: Sources and Readings* (1966), p. 1.
14. *Ibid.*
15. Stuart Bruchey, *The Roots of American Economic Growth* (1965), p. 65.
16. Carl Bridenbaugh, *Cities in The Wilderness: The First Century of Urban Life in America, 1625–1742* (1971) and *Cities in Revolt: Urban Life in America 1743–1776* (1971) provide a wide range of evidence on this issue.
17. Henry Steele Commager, ed., *America in Perspective* (New York: Mentor Books, 1964), pp. 34–35.
18. Edwin Perkins, *The Economy of Colonial America* (1988), chap. VIII.
19. Kenneth Sokoloff and Georgia Villaflor, "The Early Achievement of Modern Stature in America," *Social Science History*, Fall 1982. Additional evidence can be found in Farley Grubb, "Lilliputians and Brobdingnagians, Stature in British Colonial America: Evidence from Servants, Convicts, and Apprentices," *REH*, 1999.
20. James Henretta, "Economic Development and Social Structure in Colonial Boston," *William and Mary Quarterly*, January 1965.
21. Alice Hanson Jones, *Wealth of a Nation to Be* (1980), Table 6.2, p. 164.
22. Robert Lampman, *The Share of Top Wealth-Holders in National Wealth 1922–56* (New York: National Bureau of Economic Research, 1962), p. 109. According to the Bureau of the Census, the top quintile held 44.1 percent of median net worth in 1993; the bottom quintile, 7.2 percent.
23. Bruce Daniels found that among the upper strata of the colonial wealth distribution, concentration (inequality) increased from 1700 to 1776. As the economy expanded, inequality grew. "Long Range Trends of Wealth Distribution in 18th Century New England," *EEH*, Winter 1973–1974.
24. William Bradford, *Of Plymouth Plantation* (New York: Capricorn Books, 1962), pp. 90–91.
25. In recent years, American philosophers have taken up this question in earnest once more. John Rawls, *A Theory of Justice* (Cambridge: Harvard University Press, 1971); Robert Nozick, *Anarchy, State and Utopia*, (New York: Basic Books, 1974). Rawls would disapprove of the Pilgrims' solution; Nozick would approve of it.
26. As the modern American tourist in the United Kingdom soon discovers, items priced in guineas (which haven't circulated for a long, long time) cost 5 percent more than those priced in pounds.
27. Colonial understanding of such finance may be illustrated by the following Massachusetts ordinance of 1647: "Any debt, or debts due upon bill or other specialty assigned to another, shall be as good a debt and estate to the Assignee, as it was to the assigner, at the time of its assignation; and that it shall be lawful for the said Assignee, to sue for, to recover the said debt due upon bills, and so assigned, as fully as the original creditor might have done; provided the said assignment be made upon the backside of the bill or specialitie." William Whitmore, ed., *The Colonial Laws of Massachusetts* (Boston: Boston City Printers, 1889), p. 125.
28. Benjamin Franklin, *The Autobiography of Benjamin Franklin*, edited by Charles Eliot, *The Harvard Classics, vol. I* (New York: P. F. Collier and Son, 1937),p. 30.
29. The Southern colonies had a surplus and would be, other things being equal, a net receiver of specie, but they were not. The lack of internal roads meant that Southern trade with the Northern colonies was by ship, and that trade was, in volume, equal to about one-third of overseas trade. Earnings to Northern ship owners from this trade should have siphoned off a good deal of Southern coin. James Shepherd and Samuel Williamson, "The Coastal Trade of the British North American Colonies 1768–1772," *JEH*, December 1972.
30. Larry Neal, "Interpreting Power and Profit in Economic History: A Case Study of the Seven Years' War," *JEH*, March 1970.
31. Walton and Shepherd (1979) p. 109.
32. Whitmore (1889), p. 183.
33. Paul Studenski and Herman Krooss, *Financial History of the United States* (1963), p. 13.
34. The passage might be translated thus: "A goat, valued at 30 colonial shillings, in the accepted rate of exchange then current between colonial and English money at Watertown, Massachusetts, had been contributed to the college. The goat died."
35. The Indians also used wampum to trade with one another.
36. John Romeyn Broadhead, *History of New York* (New York: Harper & Bros., 1859), vol. 1, p. 304, for a more extensive discussion of this episode.

37. Richard Lester, "Currency Issues to Overcome Depressions in Pennsylvania, 1723 and 1729," *JPE*, June 1963.
38. The extent to which colonial money issues inflated commodity prices seems to have depended to some extent on how the money was "backed." Sinking funds made people more willing to hold money than more nebulous promises to pay. Bruce Smith, "Some Colonial Evidence on Two Theories of Money: Maryland and the Carolinas," *JPE*, December 1985. The role of fiscal and monetary policies in determining the value of money is discussed in Charles Calomiris, "Institutional Failure, Monetary Scarcity, and the Depreciation of the Continental," *Journal of Economic History*, vol. XLVIII, no. 1, March 1988.

SUGGESTED READINGS

Articles

Anderson, Terry L. "Wealth Estimates for the New England Colonies 1650–1709." *Explorations in Economic History*, vol. 14, no. 4, October 1977.

Burstein, M. L. "Colonial and Contemporary Monetary Theory." *Explorations in Entrepreneurial History*, 2nd series, vol. III, no. 3, Spring 1966.

Cole, Arthur H. "Trends in Eighteenth-Century New England." *Economic History Review*, 2nd series, vol. X, no. 3, April 1958.

Daniels, Bruce D. "Long-Range Trends in Wealth Distribution in Eighteenth-Century New England." *Explorations in Economic History*, vol. XI, no. 2, Winter 1973–1974.

Gilbert, Geoffrey. "The Role of Breadstuffs in American Trade, 1770–1790." *Explorations in Economic History*, vol. 14, no. 4, October 1977.

Greene, Jack P., and Richard M. Jellison. "The Currency Act of 1764 in Imperial-Colonial Relations, 1764–1776." *William and Mary Quarterly*, 2nd series, vol. XVIII, no. 4, October 1961.

Grubb, Farley, "Lilliputians and Brobdingnagians, Stature in British Colonial America: Evidence from Servants, Convicts, and Apprentices." *Research in Economic History*, vol. 19, 1999.

Henretta, James. "Economic Development and Social Structure in Colonial Boston." *William and Mary Quarterly*, vol. XXVII, no. 1, January 1965.

Higgs, Robert, and Louis Stettler. "Colonial New England Demography: A Sampling Approach." *William and Mary Quarterly*, vol. XXVII, no. 2, April 1970.

Jones, Alice Hanson. "Wealth Estimates for the New England Colonies About 1770." *Journal of Economic History*, vol. XXXII, no. 1, March 1972.

———. "Wealth Estimates for the American Middle Colonies," *Economic Development and Cultural Change*, vol. XVII, no. 4, July 1970.

Land, Aubrey C. "The Tobacco Staple and the Planter's Problems: Technology, Labor and Crops." *Agricultural History*, vol. 43, no. 2, January 1969.

Lester, Richard. "Currency Issues to Overcome Depressions in Pennsylvania, 1723 and 1929." *Journal of Political Economy*, June 1963. Reprinted in Ralph Andreano, ed., *New Views on American Economic Development*. Cambridge: Schenkman, 1965.

Main, Gloria L., "The Standard of Living in Colonial Massachusetts," *Journal of Economic History*, vol. XLIII, no. 1, March 1983.

———, and Jackson T. Main. "Economic Growth and the Standard of Living in Southern New England, 1640–1774," *Journal of Economic History*, vol. XVIII, no. 1, March 1988.

Mancall, Peter C., and Thomas Weiss. "Was Economic Growth Likely in Colonial British North America?" *Journal of Economic History*, vol. 59, no. 1, March, 1999.

Morgan, Edmund. "The First American Boom: Virginia 1618 to 1630." *William and Mary Quarterly*, vol. XXVIII, no. 2, April 1971.

Neal, Larry. "Interpreting Power and Profit in Economic History: A Case Study of the Seven Years' War." *Journal of Economic History*, vol. XXXVII, no. 1, March 1977.

Nettels, Curtis P. "British Policy and Colonial Money Supply." *Economic History Review*, vol. III, no. 2, October 1931.

Shepherd, James F. "Commodity Exports from the British North American Colonies to Overseas Areas, 1768–1772: Magnitudes and Patterns of Trade." *Explorations in Economic History*, vol. 8, no. 1, Fall 1970.

———, and Samuel Williamson. "The Coastal Trade of the British North American Colonies, 1768– 1772." *Journal of Economic History*, vol. XXXVII, no. 4, December 1972.

Smith, Billy G. "Death and Life in a Colonial Immigrant City: A Demographic Analysis of Philadelphia." *Journal of Economic History*, vol. XXXVIII, no. 4, December 1977.

Smith, Bruce D. "Some Colonial Evidence on Two Theories of Money: Maryland and the Carolinas." *Journal of Political Economy*, vol. 93, no. 6, December 1985.

Sokoloff, Kenneth, and Georgia Villaflor. "The Early Achievement of Modern Stature in America." *Social Science History*, vol. 6, no. 4, Fall 1982.

Thomas, Robert Paul, and Terry Anderson. "White Population, Labor Force and Extensive Growth of the New England Economy in the Seventeenth Century." *Journal of Economic History*, vol. XXXIII, no. 3, September 1973.

Walsh, Lorena S., "Urban Amenities and Rural Self Sufficiency: Living Standards and Consumer Behavior in the Colonial Chesapeake, 1643–1777," *Journal of Economic History*, vol. XLIII, no. 1, March 1983.

Walton, Gary M. "New Evidence on Colonial Commerce." *Journal of Economic History*, vol. XXVII, no. 3, September 1968.

———. "Sources of Productivity Change in American Colonial Shipping, 1675–1775." *Economic History Review*, 2nd series, vol. XX, no. 1, April 1967.

Weiss, Roger. "The Issue of Paper Money in the American Colonies, 1720–1774." *Journal of Economic History*, vol. XXX, no. 4, December 1970.

———. "The Colonial Monetary Standards of Massachusetts." *Economic History Review*, 2nd series, vol. 27, no. 4, November 1974.

Books

Bridenbaugh, Carl. *Cities in the Wilderness*. New York: The Ronald Press, 1938 (reprinted by New York: Alfred A. Knopf, 1964).

———. *Cities in Revolt*. New York: Alfred A. Knopf, 1955 (reprinted by New York: Oxford University Press, 1971).

Bruchey, Stuart. *The Roots of American Economic Growth 1607–1861: An Essay in Social Causation*. London: Hutchinson University Library, 1965.

———. *The Colonial Merchant: Sources and Readings*. New York: Harcourt Brace, 1966.

Fogel, Robert William, and Stanley Engerman. *Time on the Cross: The Economics of American Negro Slavery*. Boston: Little, Brown, 1974, 2 vols.

Galenson, David. *White Servitude in Colonial America: An Economic Analysis*. New York: Cambridge University Press, 1981.

Jones, Alice Hanson. *American Colonial Wealth: Documents and Methods*. New York: Arno Press, 1977.

———. *Wealth of a Nation to Be: The American Colonies on the Eve of the Revolution*. New York: Columbia University Press, 1980.

Lester, Richard A. *Monetary Experiments: Early American and Recent Scandinavian*. Princeton: Princeton University Press, 1939.

Nettels, Curtis C. *The Money Supply of the American Colonies Before 1720*. Madison: The University of Wisconsin Press, 1934.

Perkins, Edwin J. *The Economy of Colonial America*. Second edition. New York: Columbia University Press, 1988.

Shepherd, James F., and Gary M. Walton. *Shipping, Maritime Trade, and the Economic Development of Colonial North America*. New York: Cambridge University Press, 1972.

Studenski, Paul, and Herman Krooss. *Financial History of the United States*. Second edition, New York: McGraw-Hill, 1963.

Ver Steeg, Clarence. *The Formative Years, 1606–1763*. New York: Hill & Wang, 1964.

Walton, Gary M., and James F. Shepherd. *The Economic Rise of Early America*. New York: Cambridge University Press, 1979.

CHAPTER FOUR

Gaining Independence

The move toward independence accelerated after 1763. Once we understand what was unleashed in 1763, it is clear that British policy was doomed. Whether that policy should have led Americans to seek independence is another question.

EXPANSION AND THE WESTERN LANDS

If we were to argue that, for economic reasons, the American Revolution was inevitable, the easiest place to begin would be the question of the land beyond the Appalachians.[1]

Across the Appalachians

Interior settlement was a political, a legal, and, of necessity, a military matter. George Washington's experience in western Pennsylvania was a case in point. By the 1740s, Virginians had become interested in their trans-Appalachian lands. Thomas Lee, president of the Virginia Council of State, had organized an Ohio Company in 1747 whose object was trading with the Indians and exerting Virginia's territorial claims there. A year later, this company received a royal grant of 200,000 acres in the Ohio Valley on condition that it be settled.

The French responded by occupying and fortifying various strong points. It was in the interests of the proposed Virginia settlement that, in October 1753, Governor Dinwiddie sent 21-year-old George Washington to discuss with the French their occupation of Virginia's territory. Washington was treated hospitably and sent home. A few months later, he returned with a small force, started building a fort, attacked the French, was beaten, and then surrendered his fort, his men, and himself in July 1754. Again, he was sent home, as were the Virginia soldiers. The fort he built, renamed Fort Duquesne, was completed and staffed by the French. A year later, Washington was back in the area again as an aide to General Braddock, only to meet defeat once more. The survivors escaped back to Virginia. Pennsylvania settlers pulled back to a line of forts in the mountains planned and partly built under the personal direction of an unlikely military engineer, Benjamin Franklin. In 1758, Fort Duquesne was taken by General John Forbes and renamed Pittsburgh.

Montreal fell to the English in 1760; then came the great Indian uprising led by Pontiac. Only after the end of the *French and Indian War* in 1763 (also called the Seven Years' War) was colonizing on any scale reasonably safe in the area. However, Washington reported attempting (unsuccessfully) conversations with German-speaking settlers in 1754 in this back country. Already the movement west was evident.

Further south, the problems impeding westward movement were Indians, the Appalachian Mountains, and the unknown. Virginia's claim was the relevant one, again. In 1750, Thomas Walker found the Cumberland Gap, which provided an accessible passage through the Appalachians. In 1752, John Finley reached the present site of Louisville, journeying down the Ohio River by canoe. His description inspired Daniel Boone's trek in 1769 (he had been a wagoner with Braddock and Washington). In 1774, the town of Harrodsburg was established. By then, Pittsburgh was a going concern. A year later, Richard Harrison and a company of North Carolinians made a treaty with the Cherokee (declared void by the government of Virginia) for a colony they called Transylvania. The way west was opened at the same time the American Revolution got underway. The two events became indissolubly linked because those western lands were a prime reason for the war and were the occasion for acceptance of the Articles of Confederation by the warring colonists.

Even though, by 1776, colonial eyes were fixed on lands west of the Alleghenies, there were few Europeans living beyond the Atlantic fall line. There were permanent populations in Kentucky, Tennessee, and Vermont (a temporary escape hatch for land-hungry settlers fleeing from Massachusetts, New Hampshire, and the Hudson Valley to escape politics, Indians, land scarcity, and overlapping claims). It had taken a century for Americans to begin a serious movement from the early seacoast settlements across the Appalachian barrier and into the interior. The Spanish and French were already established in the Mississippi basin and in the Southwest by the mid-eighteenth century. English fur traders were aware of the interior's riches, too. But until population increase made good settlement lands scarce in the Atlantic coastal areas, there was not sufficient incentive to provoke settlement of the interior.

There was, in addition, the matter of legal jurisdiction. As we have seen, colonial land settlement was not the disorderly affair suggested by Hollywood epics. Secure land titles had to come from established authority, and authority was not always easy to establish beyond the Appalachians. Throughout most of the colonial period, both the English and the French laid claim to most of the Mississippi watershed, and there were periodic skirmishes between the two rivals. To make matters more complicated, the area was already occupied by Indian tribes. When, in 1763, the English emerged victorious in the French and Indian War, the French claim effectively ended.

The original grant to the Virginia Company had been "from sea to sea." This grant of King James, by his Majesty's "merest motion," no doubt reflected his and his advisors' vast ignorance of what the North American continent might be or contain. This ignorance would come back to haunt the descendants of all concerned. The claims of Virginia, and those whose original patents came from the Virginia charter, Massachusetts and Connecticut, were abruptly restricted by the royal *Proclamation Line of 1763*, limiting trans-Appalachian settlement to lands attained by Crown approval. Settlers were not to venture west of the rivers that flow into the Atlantic. The line, drawn in the wake of the French and Indian War, proved much less effective a barrier to westward movement than the armed conflicts that preceded it. Having elected to take over French interests in Canada as a spoil of victory, the English undertook to establish a government in Roman Catholic Quebec. The *Quebec Act of 1774* gave that province all the land west of the Ohio River, a move that incensed the Protestants of New England. The Quebec Act, along with the Port of Boston Act (closing it) issued the same year, were considered acts of war, pure and simple, by the colonists.

British Land Policy

The sudden reality of its possession of the Northwest Territories in 1763 presented the British Crown with new responsibilities and with opportunities undreamed of under the old land grants, which had not been acted upon until the Virginia colonists themselves moved against the French and Indians. The Proclamation of 1763 had been a holding effort, an attempt to restrict entry to property rights granted directly by the Crown, to protect the newly acquired fur trade (in the interest of an old English-chartered company, Hudson's Bay), and to keep peace with the Indian tribes. The colonists, wanting the land, cared nothing for the Hudson's Bay Company or for peace with the Indians, now by far the weaker population contending for the land. The Quebec Act of 1774, an "intolerable" act, was an effort, once and for all, to separate the Americans from their ancient claims.

What did George III and his ministers care about promises made to the colonists by James I more than a century and a half earlier? But the Quebec Act robbed Virginians of millions of acres. George Washington (himself an owner of western lands) said in 1774 that he was prepared to outfit 1,000 men at his own expense and lead them personally to Boston to fight the British. He did more than that. British land policy after 1763 must be counted a disaster. The colonial governments had successfully granted land and settled populations for a century and a half. The old system might have been adapted to post-1763 conditions. It was not. The British tried to change it; the Americans changed it even more, and changed history in the bargain.

BRITISH TRADE POLICY

What was true of the land was also true of trade and commerce. By the 1770s, British policy had become insupportable after a long period of relative success. But, unlike the issue of land policy, it is not so easy to argue that colonial objection to the British trade policies of the 1770s was simply a matter of economics. These policies did not take away American rights so much as they attempted to tax the exercise of them.

We discussed the theory of British colonization in Chapter 1: that the colonists were, and their descendants would remain, the king's subjects under the laws of England, with the rights of English citizens. It must be emphasized again how well the scheme worked for a very long time. But in trade, as in land policy, the French defeat and the end of Pontiac's rebellion meant that, after 1763, the English were free to change their policies drastically, and that the colonials, no longer in danger from the French in Canada and the interior, were free to resist that change if they so desired. Both things happened.

The Navigation Acts

In 1651, Oliver Cromwell, The Lord Protector, was building an empire overseas. The Navigation Act of that year defined that empire, restricting shipping and trade between it and the external world. In 1660, with Cromwell dead, the English decided that they were a monarchy after all, sent a fleet to Holland for Charles II, and brought him home. That year was counted as the twelfth year in the reign of Charles II (his father was executed in 1648). Parliament was busy re-passing the Commonwealth laws it wanted retained since the laws of Cromwell and the Commonwealth were now in limbo and no longer regarded as law. The eighteenth law of 1660 was a repeat of the 1651 Navigation Act, "An Act for the Encouraging and Increasing of Shipping and Navigation."

The Navigation Act's immediate object was to reserve the trade in commodities originating inside the empire to the ship owners, mariners, and merchants who owed allegiance to the King of England. More narrowly, they were to enlarge and protect his income derived from customs, fines, confiscations, and taxes. Under the act, the ships and sailors of the colonies were treated as English. Because until 1707, Scotland was a separate kingdom (with Charles as its king), only one port serving Scotland—Berwick on Tweed—was included in the Act's provisions. Of its several parts, the Act's main injunctions relating to the colonies were the following:

1. No commodities originating from the Empire were to be shipped in any but British (including colonial) ships, under a British captain, with at least three-fourths of the crew to be His Majesty's subjects.
2. The same provisions held for imported commodities from Asia, Africa, or parts of America other than the British colonies.
3. None but British subjects were allowed to be merchants or factors in the colonies.
4. None but British ships with their three-fourths British crews were to carry commodities from one English port to another.

Penalties were provided for violations of these provisions. In addition, several enumerated commodities exported from the "plantations" of America, Asia, and Africa could be landed *only* in England. Those commodities were sugar, tobacco, cotton, indigo, ginger, and fustick or other wood products used for dying cloth. A restriction on the carrying trade stated that no goods could be carried from foreign countries into the Empire in English ships except directly from their place of origin. This provision would be greatly restricted in 1663. The Act included special customs

Fur Trappers and Traders. *These entrepreneurs were the economic link between the Europeans and the Indians. Once each year, trappers brought their furs overland by horseback or downriver in boats (above right) to rendezvous with traders and Indians (above). The furs would pass through frontier outposts like "Bellevue" (below), present-day Omaha, and then to a major city like St. Louis (below right).*

duties for fish and whale products, usually caught by English fishermen, which were imported into England in other than English ships, and customs surcharges were placed against French ships entering English ports. The first provision protected the English fishing industry; the second retaliated for the policies of Louis XIV of France against the English.

In 1662 and 1663, the Act was amended to include further enumerated commodities and more rules for shipping and customs. In the amendment of 1663, imports from Europe into the colonial empire were prohibited except in English vessels "laden and shipped" in England. This stringent amendment was enacted to protect English manufacturers and to encourage

> ...vent for English woolen and other manufacturers and commodities, rendering the navigation to and from the same [colonies] more safe and cheap, and making this kingdom a staple, not only of the commodities of those plantations, but also of the commodities of other countries and places, for the supplying of them, it being the usage of other nations to keep their plantations trade to themselves.

Amendments in subsequent years were true to the spirit of these laws. Essentially, the Empire was treated as if it were the domestic coastal trade, the waters connecting the Empire as if they were British coastal or inland waters. That such laws invited smuggling is obvious enough. How much, we will never know.[2] In 1733, to protect West Indies planters, the Molasses Act imposed high duties on foreign sugar, molasses, and rum imported into the colonies. Colonial sea captains flagrantly ignored that law because (a) they had to trade their goods in the Caribbean; (b) there was insufficient production in the British plantations there; and (c) the Americans traded where they could—thus Spanish, French, and Dutch sugar and molasses were traded for American commodities. The English preferred to ignore this trade until 1764, when a new Sugar Act was enforced, and the Americans resisted. The navigation laws were the "rules of the road" for the growing trade of an expanding empire, and, until 1763, they worked well enough, defining and binding together the English world, the mother country and her overseas colonies.

With New England and the Middle colonies hard-pressed to find markets outside the British Empire through the sieve of the Navigation Acts, they had more commercial conflicts with the Crown than did the Southern colonies. When Britain's laws became more restrictive after 1763, their effects were felt more immediately in the North. But, as we already have noted, there also was a major source of conflict between Virginia and England over the western lands.

Was there any profound logic to these laws? As we have discussed, they were part of the contemporary European commercial policy theory called, collectively, mercantilism. Business enterprises had grown up, some of them trading abroad. Governments licensed, regulated, and taxed all such activity to raise money for governmental activity. Some industries were favored by light taxes, some were even subsidized for reasons of state. Perhaps too much has been made of this issue.

By modern standards, there is nothing extraordinary about the Navigation Acts or about English mercantilism. As the 1663 Navigation Act put it, "It being the usage of other nations to keep their plantations trade to themselves." The use of subsidies, tax rebates, tariffs, and quotas to attempt to protect and encourage American industries at the expense of the rest of the world is standard modern practice. If every member of Congress and every president had the economic backgrounds and viewpoints of Adam Smith and David Ricardo (the great theorists of classical economics), we would not pursue such policies. But they do not, and we do pursue them, *as do all other governments in the world today and as they did throughout the seventeenth and eighteenth centuries*. Europeans, and the English, used governmental power to create industries, fleets of ships, and employment for their own nationals that the world market would not have created if market forces alone had decided what would be produced, where, how, and for whom. The prodigious writing on European mercantilism by historians was an attempt to explain why governments did not act according to the precepts of competitive market theory and free trade. Governments almost never do. As a result, world production was (and is) less than it otherwise might have been (or can be). Trade and commerce in the mercantilist age grew more as they were dictated by government policy, or so government leaders believed at the time and continue to believe today as they vigorously pursue such policies.

One item of special note in so-called mercantilist theory is the emphasis upon export surpluses—the "beggar-thy-neighbor policy." In the days before our own Federal Reserve System learned to circulate its notes backed only by holdings of government securities, Americans thought that a "favorable" balance of trade was a good thing. We used gold for money, and one way to get gold was to sell more to foreigners than they sold to you. That way, they shipped you more gold in payment than you shipped to them. This practice would increase your own supply of gold and, therefore, money. From the quantity theory of money, business people knew that more money meant higher prices and brisk trade, which were good for them. As we discussed in the previous chapter, one reason the colonials complained about the Navigation Acts was that they believed the scarcity of English coin in the colonies occurred because the trade deficit was steadily bleeding the colonies of specie. Governments knew that brisk trade yielded higher taxes than did slack trade; thus governments favored export surpluses, too (and laid on tariffs, embargoes, and quotas to help out). The Navigation Acts made sense in mercantilist theory. Trade surpluses made your kingdom rich and powerful; if they made your enemies (almost everyone else in the seventeenth and eighteenth centuries) poor and weak, so much the better.

HOW DID BRITAIN AFFECT AMERICAN ECONOMIC GROWTH?

To help understand the colonial experience on the eve of the Revolution, let's pull back a bit and look at it in a very general way. Did Britain aid American economic growth in the eighteenth century or did it, as the colonists charged, hamper its growth? This controversial question, which has occupied historians since the Revolution, has no "right" answer. Still, it is an issue having important implications that we should examine. Let's start with a little thought experiment.

Perspectives

Suppose that the United Nations created a giant space station containing the population and the necessary resources to support permanent interplanetary life. The station shadows the Earth's orbit, using solar energy for power and exchanging its specialized products with those of Earth. What sorts of institutions would the vehicle be given for self-government and development? What would our expectations for its future be? What would we expect the space colony's relations with us to be five generations from now? Would we try to control its social and political evolution, placing safeguards against the growth of such political excesses as military dictatorships and ideological totalitarianism? Would we try to control its economic evolution so that the colony would remain congenial and mutually interdependent with us and not develop a rival economy? Would we believe that we had a "right" to do that, and that the colony would benefit throughout time from our guiding hand and steadying influence?

We should be able to see the parallel with colonial America—with one important difference. Because transatlantic travel was by sailing ship, it could take a month to send a message from London to Philadelphia. Irregular internal communications made matters worse. There is a record of a complaint sent from the Privy Council to the Governor of backwoods North Carolina in the eighteenth century, reprimanding him for not communicating for two years. His answer, written a year later, professed surprise and protested that he had been a regular correspondent.

Britain expected the American colonies to produce and grow and yet to remain loyal, as we have seen. The British supplied the necessary provisions, in part, sent over people, provided administration and military protection, and hoped to benefit from the enterprise. The colonies were launched with English institutions but were allowed to modify them to meet local needs, with the proviso that they "be not repugnant" to the laws of England. After only 150 years, there was a violent separation of the two systems—the American Revolution. Scholars have studied that upheaval ever since to identify what parts of it originated from economic life and what parts from flaws in the arrangements between England and the colonies. In this section, we will examine some of the main issues in colonial economic growth that are commonly associated with our revolutionary separation from Britain.

"Full Employment" in the Colonies

The colonists had no choice but to work; a subsistence had to be wrested from the wilderness. The colonies, to be self-sustaining, had to earn an amount at least equivalent to the flow of British investment (plus interest) of manpower, provisions, transportation costs, and the like. Ultimately, they yielded far more, as we have seen, and attracted not only continued British investment and immigration, but also domestic wealth accumulations and rising per-capita income. What were the possible effects of this foreign (British) induced growth upon economic structure, and what difference might the American Revolution have made?

Approximately 95 percent of the population labored in primary occupations (agriculture, timbering, and naval stores), but a proportion, approximately 5 percent, lived in towns, implying that a similar (perhaps slightly larger) proportion of output came from urban occupations (trades, crafts, "manufacturing," and services). We are assuming, perhaps unrealistically, that the proportion of "unproductive" populations—the young, aged, and disabled—is the same in both sectors. The purpose of the severe labor regulations mentioned earlier was to maintain employment as close to **full employment** (a balance between job seekers and job vacancies) as possible, and slavery and servitude with severe punishments for vagrancy (unemployment) helped to achieve that goal. If significant malingering were allowed, production would be less. Unemployment was costly, and, in the early stages of colonization, the laws and agencies of government were stringently employed to prevent it.

If there were no technical improvements, then increased population (men and women injected into the economy at first by forced emigration from Britain and then by voluntary emigration, slave imports, and natural growth) would simply increase production possibilities. With technological improvements of any kind, production possibilities would have increased over time by greater proportions than population increased, and there would have been per-capita economic growth.

Had British policy aimed at *increasing* the proportion of primary output at the expense of all other output, colonial America would have become increasingly rural as it grew. This result, in the view of some scholars, would have been the logical outcome of British mercantilism: Allow the colonies to grow only as congenial economic supplements to the domestic British economy, to the output choices made there. By forbidding all output in the colonies that would compete with British domestic production, say of manufactured goods, the British would have forced the colonies to become increasingly specialized primary producers, not because of comparative advantage but because of the law.

A more reasonable British policy would have been to allow proportionately more urban-style output as time passed. This was apparently the reality since, as we have seen, urbanization was proceeding and urban-style production was expanding accordingly. It was, however, the contention of some colonials (and some later historians) that even that growth path was forced upon them by British laws. Prohibitions such as those against the development of banking, manufacture of wrought iron, and export of colonial woolen goods held down the growth of colonial urban-style industry. Hence, they kept the growth path off its "natural" course, which, as output expanded, would have brought an even faster movement toward nonprimary outputs and employments. If the latter were the case, then the effect of the Revolution would have been to accelerate the rate of urban and manufacturing growth compared to that of primary production. There would no longer have been a foreign constraint upon the pace of the shift from primary production to manufacturing.

The American and Industrial Revolutions

Dramatic acceleration of manufacturing of all kinds did, in fact, occur within a half century after 1776 and has continued ever since. But we cannot say with confidence that the American Revolution initiated that shift because of the technological changes associated with a contemporaneous development, the Industrial Revolution. British inventiveness began to result in machine production run by prime movers (waterpower, then steam), and those changes quickly appeared in America.

James Watt's steam engine was patented in Britain in 1769. By 1783, it was used to work a hammer at John "Iron Master" Wilkinson's works, and he already was using it to "blow" his blast furnaces. When

Richard Arkwright, the great English textile innovator, bought Watt's steam engines to run his machinery in 1790, he already had been preceded by at least two other textile magnates, Robert Peel and Peter Drinkwater. By 1800, hundreds of steam engines were at work in British factories. Those factories, grouped together to gain external economies, were producing the first true industrial cities. The Industrial Revolution was on, and Britain soon achieved a power and influence out of all proportion to her relative size in the world. The lost American empire would be replaced by one of vast dimensions, "a third of the earth," in Asia, Africa, Australia, and New Zealand.

The Americans were quick to follow their British cousins when comparative advantage dictated the profitability of such imitation. Samuel Slater, one of Arkwright's English workers, arrived in America in 1789 with Arkwright's machinery designs memorized. By 1790, with American backers, Slater built the machines and launched the spinning factory of Almy and Brown at Pawtucket, Rhode Island. At that point, the Industrial Revolution in America can be said to have begun. In 1793, Eli Whitney's invention of the cotton gin created the supply side of a major American cotton textile industry and, incidentally, fastened slavery onto the South again. Cotton made black slavery a long-lasting success because it gave the Southern states a very profitable commodity that was best cultivated by slave gangs, given the technology of the time. Cotton quickly became the South's staple product, supplying the textile industries of both Britain and the United States.

The Industrial Revolution accelerated the urbanization process on both sides of the Atlantic, and it came so quickly on the heels of the political and military American Revolution that we will never know whether the natural course in colonial America—forbidden by British mercantilism—could have been achieved without violent separation. The evidence indicates that this was extremely unlikely. In any case, even if the American Revolution had not occurred, the British could not have stopped the Industrial Revolution in America, nor, most likely, would they have wanted to. Considering their persistent heavy investment in this country *after* the Revolution, they probably would have spread the Industrial Revolution here themselves.

THE END OF COLONIAL DEPENDENCE

After 1763, the British began what they hoped would be a new phase in their colonial enterprises on the North American continent. What was needed, they believed, was a revision of the old (in part, individual) settlements between the Crown and the colonies. With an expensive war just ended, they wanted a system of colonial revenues that would make colonial government more self-supporting and less costly to England. There followed a series of laws that fostered the American Revolution. Lance Davis and Robert Huttenback show that the American colonists were among the most lightly taxed people in the European world in the 1770s.[3] Therefore, we must deal with more than merely taxation if we are to understand the breakup of the British North American empire.

Viewed from London, the American Revolution was an outcome of political troubles as well as fiscal problems. Evolution toward parliamentary rule was not quite complete, and the king, now the stubborn, 25-year-old George III (grandson of George II, who died in 1760), was determined to rule, not just reign. Old William Pitt had resigned as Prime Minister in 1761. George tried, by interference in parliamentary affairs, to get his way, and finally succeeded. There followed a period of bungling and incompetence at the top almost without precedent in English history. Worse luck, Europe was entering a period of general upheaval that only ended with the Congress of Vienna in 1815. It was an era of war, revolution, and more war.

The American Revolution marked the beginning of this era. What went wrong in America? It can be viewed, in part, as a case of managerial failure. The technique of British rule in North America had become outdated. By the 1760s, there was no unified English colonial government in America. Each colony had its own separate arrangement, its own charter. Ben Franklin's plan to unify the colonial administration, presented in 1754, had been unwisely rejected. The English Privy Council (a formless and long-lasting jumble of English eminences), with the Board of Trade, ruled the Isle of Man, the Channel Islands off the coast of France, the American colonies, the West Indies, and other holdings spread around the world.

The Board of Trade had been established in a general reorganization in 1696, and its conservative management of colonial affairs produced some notable long-term results: its delineation of the Hudson's Bay Company's southern limits in 1719 became the ultimate U.S.-Canada boundary; its review of colonial laws was the origin of our own judicial review; its practice of forbidding the colonies to discriminate in trade *against each other* was the origin of the commerce clause in the federal Constitution.

The board, however, was merely a bureaucracy and had no control over political evolution. As it was, the board's administration was obsolete in the 1770s. By then, British political life was chaotic, and, in America, the colonial assemblies had evolved a level of competence and power undreamed of in 1696.[4] They raised taxes, appointed officials, granted Western lands, and dealt with the Indians. How could they be ruled by an English bureaucracy? Parliament ruled England, Wales, Scotland, and Ireland by the 1760s. The overseas colonies had lobbyists in Westminster (for example, Ben Franklin), but there could be no question of direct colonial representation, as members of Parliament, under the English constitution. Thus, administratively, the British were unable to cope with the consequences of their own actions—as events soon proved.

Eighteenth-century British government, like most governments now, was one of organized special interests gaining advantages for themselves at the expense of the unorganized. Subsidies here, taxes there, prohibitions, special grants of privilege, year after year, decade after decade, had produced the "British government." Prohibitions in the 1750s against colonial iron-goods manufacturing while colonial pig and bar iron were admitted into England duty-free is a typical example—alienating colonial iron workers and owners, together with British pig and bar iron producers, for the benefit of British manufacturers.

From the British viewpoint, nothing made more sense than colonial tax reform. Before 1767, customs revenues in the colonies annually yielded about £2,000 and cost £9,000 a year to collect. What were needed were a set of taxes that could be collected and a new bureaucracy to collect them. The British, after a long and costly war to protect the colonists from the French, now wanted to garrison 10,000 troops in the colonies for their own protection and wanted the colonists to contribute to their support.

The Proclamation of 1763 was meant to move control of Indian affairs from colonial governments to the Crown. The colonists rightly saw their own governmental powers thus reduced. The Currency Act of 1764 was designed to make colonial paper money issues self-limiting by establishing *sinking fund obligations* (reserves that could redeem the notes in coin or English money), a financially sound move that placed restrictions upon colonial fiscal powers. The Sugar Act of 1764 was meant to protect West Indian interests by placing taxes on foreign sugar and molasses, thus restricting colonial sources of supply and providing officials to enforce the law. The Stamp Tax of 1765 was a minor measure to gain revenues from legal documents and newspapers. Colonial officials were to collect the tax. This was viewed in the colonies as more "taxation without representation." A Stamp Tax Congress met in New York, a nonimportation agreement was reached (it was not honored in the Lower South), and British exports to the colonies fell by two-thirds.

The Stamp Tax could not be collected; its collectors were harassed. The British backed down and repealed the tax, but, in 1766, an outraged Parliament passed the Declaratory Act, which, they believed, established legal authority once and for all for them to tax and legislate for the colonies. This new act added more fuel to the fire. In 1767, Chancellor of the Exchequer Charles Townshend pushed legislation through Parliament placing taxes on tea, glass, and paper and establishing a Customs Board in America with rights of general search and seizure—*writs of assistance*. By 1768, these measures produced serious disorders in colonial ports; by 1770, they resulted in the Boston Massacre.

Lord North, George III's favorite statesman, "a good-natured, indolent man, of limited intelligence, but shrewd and businesslike," became Prime Minister in 1770.[5] Until 1782, guided by George III, he piloted the British government from disaster to disaster. In 1773, the Tea Act reduced the price of tea to the colonists but threatened colonial merchants with extinction by granting the East India Company the right to sell its tea directly to the colonies, bypassing the chain of jobbers and merchants the company had formerly supported. The result was the Boston Tea Party.

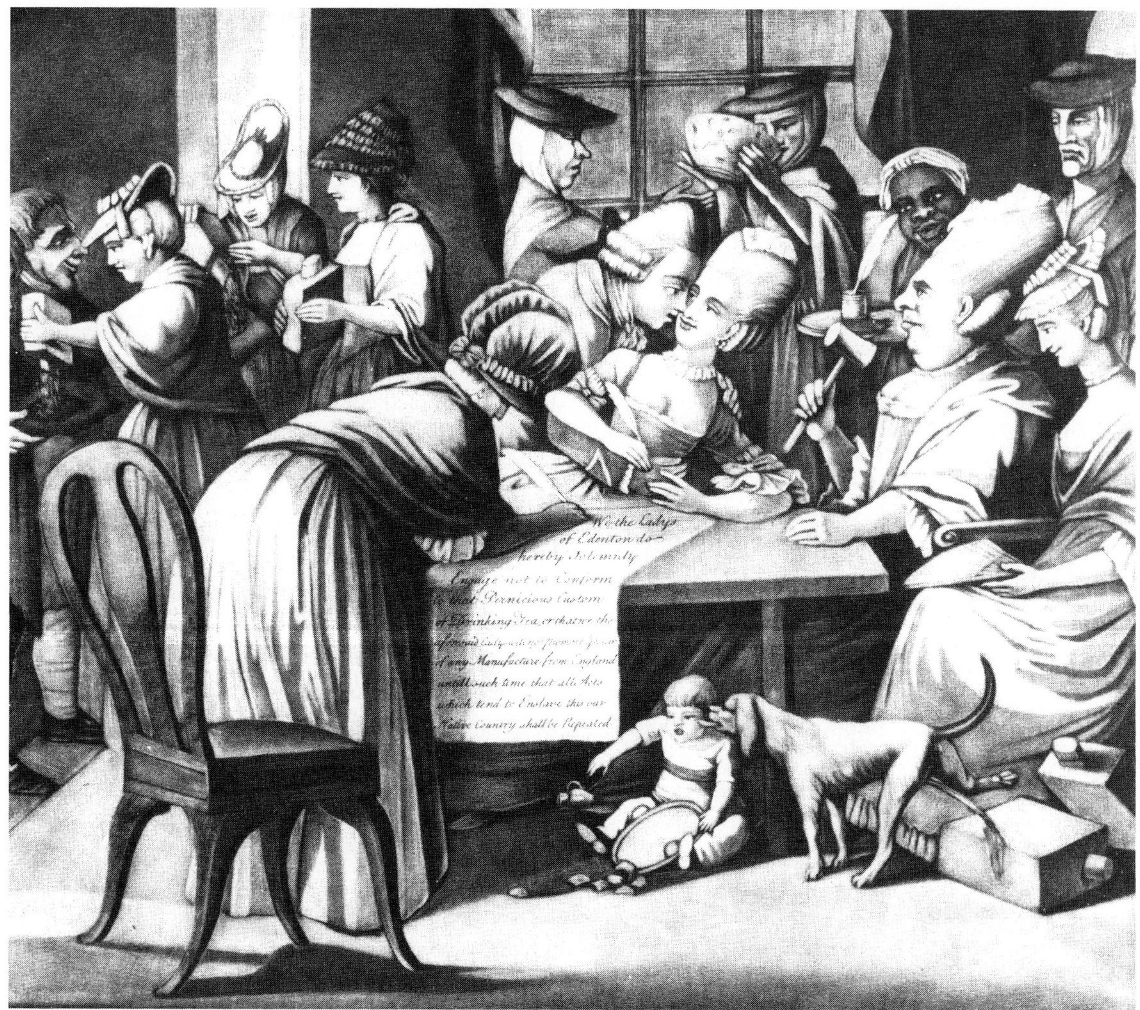

An English artist's view of colonial people and manners portrays colonial women agreeing to give up tea drinking in protest of the Tea Tax.

At this point, in 1774, Lord North and Parliament committed those famous acts of tyranny—the passage of the Port of Boston Act, the Massachusetts Government Act (making Massachusetts a Crown colony), and the Quebec Act—that broke the ties that had bound the colonies and England together for a century and a half. To the British government, the colonists were children who wanted punishment. To the colonists, the British government had become "intolerable." The First Continental Congress met in Philadelphia in September 1774, and on 14 October 1774, listed in plain language its complaints against the British government.

1. Taxes had been imposed upon the colonies by the British Parliament.
2. Parliament had claimed the right to legislate for the colonies.
3. Commissioners were set up in the colonies to collect taxes.
4. Admiralty court jurisdictions had been extended into the interior.
5. Judges' tenures had been put at the pleasure of the Crown.
6. A standing army had been imposed upon the colonies.

7. Persons could be transported out of the colonies for trials.
8. The Port of Boston had been closed.
9. Martial law had been imposed upon Boston.
10. The Quebec Act had confiscated the colonists' western lands.

These complaints were followed by resolutions restating the legal position of the colonies.

> That our ancestors, who first settled these colonies, were at the time of their emigration from the mother country, entitled to all the rights, liberties and immunities of free and natural-born subjects, within the realm of England.
>
> That by such emigration they by no means forfeited, surrendered, or lost any of those rights, but they were, and their descendants now are, entitled to the exercise and enjoyment...of them....

The colonists did not object to the laws of navigation "for the purpose of securing the commercial advantages of the whole empire to England, and the commercial benefits of its respective members," but they rejected "every idea of taxation, internal or external, for raising a revenue on the subjects, in America, without their consent." They further resolved:

> That the respective colonies are entitled to the common law of England, and more especially to the great and inestimable privilege of being tried by their peers of the vicinage, according to the course of that law.

There were more resolutions followed by a listing of eight laws whose repeal the colonists demanded—these laws amounted to virtually all changes in British government in America since 1763.[6] On 6 July 1775, the Congress published the "Declaration of the Causes and Necessity of Taking Up Arms." One year later, on 4 July 1776, independence was declared.

THE WAR FOR INDEPENDENCE

Declaring independence was difficult; achieving it was even more so. The colonial population was divided into three groups: pro-independence, pro-British, and neutral. The pro-independence group was largely composed of middle-class merchants in the North and planters in the South; the pro-British group was largely landed gentry in the North and civil servants and clergymen in both the North and the South. If all three groups were of equal size, and there are many scholars who argue the neutral group was a majority of the population, then the pro-independence faction was a clear minority of the population.

Further, even if the concept of independence enjoyed more popular support, the probability of victory in an armed conflict was low. England had both an army and a navy, command over ample resources, and the wherewithal to finance a war. By contrast, the colonies lacked a central government and had few financial connections outside of England. No effort had been made to prepare for the war that began in April 1775 and was to last for six years. The one advantage they had was, in an era where transportation and communication were difficult, the North American colonies were distant enough from England to create a serious problem for the British. Consequently, when the British forces did not act swiftly to quash incipient rebellion, the colonists had a chance.

How the colonists would finance a war was an important question, an important problem, from the outset. The Second Continental Congress (1775–1781) created the Articles of Confederation, but it took from 1777 to 1781 for each new state to approve them. While they provided for a means of discourse between the former colonies, they created only a very loose tie between them. The power lay within the fundamentally independent states; the central government was powerless. For example, the central government had no independent taxing authority; all taxes had to be requisitioned through the individual states. George Washington's federal troops had to compete for public resources with each state's militia.

Financing the War

In general, there are five ways in which a government can obtain the resources needed to prosecute a war.[7] The first is to reduce nonmilitary expenditures, but the newly formed U.S. government had no such expenditures.

The second is to tax, but, as noted, the U.S. government had no direct access to taxes. The Articles of Confederation contained a system of requisitioning the states for revenue, but states learned to withhold the contributions they were legally bound to pay.[8] Further, since one of the rallying cries of the Revolution was "no taxation without representation," taxation was not a politically feasible alternative.

The third is to borrow the funds, but, at the start, this was not feasible either. The credit-worthiness of a people who just declared independence was an important question, especially since without direct access to tax revenue, it was not clear how the monies would be raised to pay interest and, ultimately, repay principal. But, even if that risk could be resolved, there was the question of whether England would repay the colonists' debt should rebellion fail. Some funds might be raised from wealthy patriots, but the politically conservative side was pro-British, and most colonists did not have funds available to invest in government bonds—that part of the capital market would not develop for many years. Ultimately, some funds were raised from both domestic and foreign sources, but these funds were not forthcoming until the colonists' probability of success increased substantially.

Thus, the fourth and fifth methods were the ones actually used in the first few years of the war. The fourth was the most important method—printing paper money. To pay for goods and services, the United States created "continentals," essentially a bill of credit for specie issued in anticipation of tax revenues that would be used to redeem them. Through 1780, this paper money was almost the only way in which war needs were financed.

Beginning in 1775, $241 million in continentals were issued, but, given some minor redemptions, the amount in circulation was always less. The peak of the issue was reached in 1779 when the new government made 14 different issues totaling $140 million. That same year, Congress voted to limit the total in circulation to $200 million.

Initially, continentals were exchanged 1-for-1 with specie, but, throughout 1776, as more were issued and fewer were redeemed, their value began to decline. The exchange was 3-for-1 by early 1777 and 10-for-1 by late 1778. One year later, at the time of the peak issue, $50 in continentals was equivalent to $1 in specie, but this was not the end of the depreciation. In spite of the "official" exchange of 40-to-1 with respect to the Spanish dollar that Congress established in March 1780, the market exchange continued to fall. In January 1781, it reached bottom, 100-to-1.[9] Thus, the early years of the Revolution were financed largely by printing money!

Because the Continental Congress failed to limit note issue, and because the new states issued an additional $209 million in their own notes, accelerating inflation resulted, as the depreciating value of continentals suggests. Some inflation is probably inevitable during war due to excess demand for many commodities, but this amount was in excess of that. Inflation is an indirect tax that falls on those least able to pay. It can be presumed the government received full value for the currency at first issue, but those who used the same bills later were forced to accept fewer goods and services in exchange for the same pieces of paper. This means that anyone who accepted paper money was contributing, indirectly, to the government. As Charles Calomiris has noted, the hyperinflation of the Revolutionary War era left a legacy of suspicion concerning government monetary management that can still be heard today.[10]

While such contributions were welcome, the inflation also created problems. The indifference of the majority of the population to the cause of revolution meant most farmers and merchants expected to be paid, preferably, in specie. Many refused to accept paper money, which meant that they sold to the British but not to the colonials. Those who would accept paper money often hoarded their goods, for rapidly rising prices created the potential for large profits.

These problems led the government to use the fifth method for obtaining resources, simple confiscation. The poor, hungry soldiers took food; the poor government took land from pro-British sympathizers. Soldiers often went without pay, but, after the war, they were offered land in lieu of back pay.

Economic Effects of the Revolution

In addition to those victimized by inflation, the "widows and orphans" and those on fixed incomes, commerce suffered severely from the war. After two years of closure, U.S. ports were opened in April 1776 to all but British ships. Even so, the British were blockading ports in the North. Privateering was successful, but the fishing, whaling, and trading fleets were very hard hit. Commerce resumed in 1778 when Admiral Howe's fleet relaxed their prosecution of the blockade. In fact, there was a commercial provision included in the 1778 alliance with France, in addition to much-needed funding.[11]

Manufacturing increased during the war as more desirable British goods were generally unavailable. Demand for these goods remained strong, however, and many merchants were willing to accept the risk of supplying them. Given the risk involved, the real price increased dramatically, so domestic manufacturing of an import-substitution variety was encouraged—at least until the end of the war. Thus, supplying British goods and American substitutes proved profitable during the war.

Most colonials were involved in agriculture, and the effect of the war on them depended on how near troops they were. Most farmers benefited from the war, as high wartime demand led to high prices and land values. Given that very little of the fighting took place in New England, times were good through 1780 for those farmers with marketable surpluses. However, most New England farms were too small to benefit. Farmers in the Middle colonies, particularly New Jersey and Pennsylvania, were much nearer the troops. Those who did not sustain property losses, through either troop movements, battles, or confiscation, benefited from the high demand. The same was true in the South, but it was the hardest hit region because its primary crop, tobacco, was subject to the blockade. Both Charleston and Savannah were occupied by the British in 1779–1780, and a great deal of property was lost. In sum, farmers with surpluses gained if they were close enough to the troops to sell those surpluses. When European troops paid in specie, as opposed to paper, there was a double benefit.

War's End

The long war produced few decisive battles, either on land or sea, until the French fleet out-maneuvered the English and cornered Cornwallis at Yorktown in 1781. Even so, the final battle was not fought until August of 1782. The Peace of Paris was signed in September 1783, granting the Americans complete independence together with the western lands they claimed by ancient right. The British ceded Minorca and Florida (obtained from the French in 1763, who had gotten it earlier from the Spanish) to Spain and St. Lucia, Tobago, Senegal (West Africa), and an island off its coast, Goree, to France.

After the war, the new government proved ineffective in dealing with European governments. When the United States refused to restore lands they had taken from British sympathizers (as required in the peace treaty), the English government did not grant the new country a favorable trading status and left its troops on the new country's western frontier. This last irritant would contribute to a second war with Britain three decades later.

HOW MUCH DID IT COST TO BELONG TO BRITAIN?

Was "membership" in the British Empire a good or a bad idea, economically speaking? It is clear that the colonists saw, correctly, that independence *with* access to the western lands would mean a great future for them and their descendants. But could they justify their revolution on the basis of current economic burdens imposed by the British? Actually, they did not need to do so. Revolutions are violent and bloody upheavals, usually between competing evils. If a gang of militant radicals overturns an oppressive dictator and then installs a monstrous regime of firing squads and economic chaos or "planned" economic stagnation or worse, what "good" was served? Measuring the degree of improvement in the quality of life would not be easy. The American Revolution had shades of such a monster in it, but level heads usually prevailed. Assuming that the revolutionaries believed the British were oppressing them economically, were they correct? Based on the information available to would-be revolutionaries in 1774, would income per capita be higher without Empire membership? The answer is not easy to produce.

We discussed earlier how producers in each region discovered, mainly by trial and error, their comparative advantage—those commodities that were best suited to the climate, soil, topography, nature of the available labor force, and institutions that gradually adapted to these activities. In time, fairly distinct economic regionalization developed. Generally speaking, for export purposes, the South specialized in tobacco, rice, indigo, and naval stores; the Middle colonies in grain, animals (and hides), and fabricated products related to domestic primary productions. New England, because of its relatively meager agricultural endowment, became adept at the uses of its rich timber resources, concentrating on shipbuilding and fitting, fishing and whaling, provision of shipping services, and small-shop manufacturing of all sorts.

Such patterns of economic specialization were understandable, especially given trading opportunities between the colonies and overseas. A colony could gain more from specialization and trade than it could from self-sufficient production. Comparative advantage and trade were like technological improvement; each unit of labor could gain more from efficient production and trade than if that labor had been spent on less efficient enterprises. It paid to trade rice for the wines of Portugal, even though wine grapes could have been grown in Virginia and the wine made there.

Enumerated Commodities

English mercantilism did not conform to the principle of comparative advantage. The particular fly in the ointment was the set of (hundreds of) laws that Parliament had produced over the decades to govern economic life in Britain and the colonies. If it is true that the object of those laws was to restrict colonial economic life to patterns complementary to the British home economy, then we would suppose that those laws would apply most stringently to New England and to the Middle colonies, since their products were most similar to domestic British production. Yet from the beginning, the list of commodities contained Southern products—tobacco, rice, indigo, and other dyewoods—items that were most exotic to English agriculture. The cost of the British regulations to the Upper South alone was by no means negligible, as Roger Ransom has shown.[12] However, Parliament had forbidden the growing of tobacco in England to protect the Southern planters! Thus, it is partly misleading to suggest that those laws, "British mercantile policy," were designed to create a strict colony-metropolis relationship—to impoverish, relatively, the overseas dominions for the benefit of domestic British producers and consumers. It was a two-way street.

Nevertheless, free trade (and laissez-faire) was hardly the policy either. The two-way street had twists and turns in it. Over the decades, vested interests in England had managed (as do our own vested interests today) to create distortions in the market by special legislation, creating artificial advantages for themselves and corresponding disadvantages for society at large. When Parliament forbade the working of iron shapes in the colonies (a law flagrantly ignored) or the export of colonial woolen goods, the object was to give favored British industries the advantage. Much has been made of those laws by American writers, but there is little evidence that the colonists found them really burdensome. Besides, some colonial production (pig and bar iron) was favored by such laws. The colonies also were favored by subsidies, bounties, protection from European competition, and *drawbacks*—payments made to colonial producers for goods re-exported from England.

We saw in the Navigation Act of 1660 the beginning of the list of commodities that could be shipped only from the colonies to England. Tobacco and rice were the main ones. Later, rice could be shipped from the colonies directly to southern Europe, but the tobacco merchants of England and Scotland continued to be able to divert all colonial tobacco, aside from that lost to smuggling, to themselves, to be resold at higher prices to European markets.[13] Presumably, the Americans would have been better off absorbing the "middleman" profits by selling directly to the world. But how much better off? That turns out to be very difficult to measure.

All Costs

To understand how much American tobacco producers (and others) lost by having only indirect access to Europe (via England) involves knowledge that we do not now, and never will, have. We do not know what European demand for tobacco would have been at prices that excluded the cost of transshipment through England. We do not know what the American supply prices would have been. One reason we cannot know those prices is that, had America not been an English colonial dependency, the cost of maintaining an independent nation (taxes) would have to be added to the supply prices of Americans. We also would need to know how much, if any, American GDP was reduced, per year, by the payments, out of tobacco (and other commodities) receipts, for transport and administrative costs to the British.

We do not have such GDP figures for the colonies. We would need the equivalent information on colonial imports as well. We also would need an aggregate calculation of the overall costs and benefits of being in the British Empire; all of the taxes (T), costs (C) of the restrictions per year in current prices, and the British expenditures on administration and defense (E) *minus* the sum of all the subsidies (including protection for colonial enterprises estimated in money terms), bounties, and drawbacks (S) and what the colonists would have had to expend to administer and defend themselves (A). In any year, at current prices, the aggregate burden of empire membership (B) would be

$$\mathrm{B} = [(T + C + E) - (S + \mathrm{A})].$$

Then B/GDP would be the net burden in any year. We do not even know whether the sign of B would be plus or minus. Nevertheless, scholars have attempted these heroic calculations, and their efforts form a sizable literature.

The opening shot of the modern debate can probably be dated to 1935 when Louis Hacker baldly asserted that the Americans had been held in "vassalage" by British mercantile policies and that American capitalists would never have gotten control of their own affairs and future if they had stayed in the Empire:

> The interest of colonial enterprises was to be subordinated to every British capitalist group that could gain the ear of Parliament.[14]

To Hacker, the Revolution was fought mainly to remove the British economic yoke from the necks of the colonists. The talk about freedom, inalienable rights, and so forth was just rhetoric to mask the underlying economic realities.

Hacker's thesis was challenged by the historian Lawrence Harper in 1942.[15] He divided "British imperial regulation" into four parts: (1) transatlantic trade, (2) colonial manufactures, (3) taxes on American trade, and (4) the post-1763 changes in policy. Harper concluded that:

1. Americans suffered a "heavy" burden only on their trade with Britain and Europe because of the Navigation Acts; those acts did not reduce trade in the Caribbean or with Africa.
2. British mercantilism on balance probably did more to promote than to hinder colonial industry.
3. Taxes on sugar, molasses, and rum were usually evaded, and in any case, there is no evidence that trade was distorted by the taxes.
4. Post-1763 taxes and restrictions were policy disasters, since they unleashed an "avalanche of agitation."

Harper showed that, overall, British policies probably aided colonial economic growth, although restrictions on trade between the colonies and Europe may have imposed a small net tax burden. Overall, he concluded, "It is difficult to understand how British mercantilism discriminated materially against the colonists." Even though the requirement that enumerated colonial produce be shipped initially to England was a discrimination against the colonists, they had lived with those rules for more than a century without significant complaint against them. Even in the revolutionary rhetoric of 1776, the enumerated commodities were not mentioned.

Could more precise measurements be made? In 1965, Robert Thomas made the pioneering attempts, reopening the subject with a far-ranging effort to quantify the extent of the burden placed on the colonists by the enumerated commodities provisions of the Navigation Acts, together with the net costs of Empire membership.[16] He found them even less burdensome than did Harper. Others entered the debate to expand upon the work of Thomas.[17] Peter McClelland later criticized Thomas sharply for his assumptions and for oversimplifying the scope of the computational problems. In truth, McClelland's analysis of the problem did point out the appalling problems encountered in quantifying the main relationships. McClelland also emphasized the lack of colonial agitation against the British trade laws that were enacted before 1763:

> The Declaration of Independence, for example, makes no mention of the Acts of Trade, and those hardest hit by export restraints—Virginia and Maryland—almost never included those restraints in their list of grievances against the mother country.

In 1971, reprising the issues, Gary Walton estimated that the gross cost to the colonies of British protectionism and regulation might have been 1 percent of annual income in the 1770s. He admitted, however, that the figure would have to be pared down to take into account such factors as British payment for administration, defense, subsidies, and bounties.

Independent America in 1783

The net result of these computations may well be that it paid Americans, in a strictly economic sense, to be in the Empire. Efforts to determine whether this was actually the case were made by Harper and Thomas, based upon American experience of the costs of independent government after 1783. It was clear from those calculations that the net burden may well have been negative, that it paid to be in the Empire and allow the British to foot the big bills. Americans had to tax themselves far more after the Revolution than the British ever did, and land policy north of the Ohio Valley became one of cash sales, which was more restrictive than colonial (British) policies had been before the Quebec Act.

What the Colonists Said

Whether or not it was in our economic interest to remain British is mere speculation. The American Revolution *was* fought, and the colonists did say why, in the Declaration of Independence. Of King George III, they said:

> He has endeavored to prevent the population of these States; for that purpose obstructing the Laws for Naturalization of Foreigners; refusing... to encourage their migrations hither, and raising the conditions of new Appropriations of lands.
>
> He has erected a multitude of New Offices, and sent hither swarms of Officers to harass our people, and eat out their substance.
>
> He has combined with others...
>
> For cutting off our trade with all parts of the world...
>
> For imposing Taxes on us without our Consent.

Complaints about land settlement, population growth, costs and abuses of bureaucracy, restraints of trade, unjust taxation—whether justified or not—reveal why the colonists said they wanted to be independent. And thus they became independent. Fighting started when the Port of Boston was closed under the Act of 1774. By modern standards, closing the port alone would have been more than enough reason to start the shooting. With the return of peace, the new nation would have to devise policies of its own to confront such complaints. Thanks to its English upbringing, it would do so in a growing economy.

NOTES

1. The best survey of the Western lands issue in colonial America is still Thomas Abernathy, *Western Lands and the American Revolution* (1937). It is the main source for the discussion presented here.
2. The evidence of colonial smuggling in the *Reports* of the Admiralty Courts by the 1760s indicates that efforts by Americans to "run" cargoes of contraband into colonial ports had become systematic, frequent, and increasingly bold. British ships and customs officers were hard put to stop it. One judge, after hearing the evidence, acidly accused the Americans of trying to "rid themselves of the Navigation Act." Jonathan Hughes, *Social Control in the Colonial Economy* (1976), pp. 155–156.
3. Lance Davis and Robert Huttenback, "The Cost of Empire," in Richard Sutch, Roger Ransom, and Gary Walton, eds., *Explorations in the New Economic History: Essays*

in Honor of Douglass C. North (1982), p. 44, Table 3.2. Also see their book, *Mammon and the Pursuit of Empire: The Political Economy of British Imperialism, 1860–1912* (New York: Cambridge University Press, 1986).

4. John Brewer, *Sinews of Power: War, Money, and the English State, 1688–1783* (1989) is an interesting discussion of British public policy.
5. Charles Oman, *A History of England* (London: Edward Arnold, 1895), p. 544.
6. *Documents Illustrative of the Formation of the American States* (Washington: Government Printing Office, 1927), pp. 1–4.
7. An excellent review of this topic is Ben Baack, "Forging a Nation State: The Continental Congress and the Financing of the War of American Independence," *EHR*, November 2001.
8. Keith L. Dougherty and Michael J.G. Cain, "Marginal Cost Sharing and the Articles of Confederation," *Public Choice*, vol. 90, March 1997.
9. The outstanding continentals were repudiated in 1783.
10. Charles Calomiris, "Institutional Failure, Monetary Scarcity, and the Depreciation of the Continental," *JEH*, March 1988.
11. Holland and Spain signed treaties with the new country shortly after France.
12. Roger Ransom, "British Policy and Colonial Growth: Some Implications of the Burden of the Navigation Acts," *JEH*, September 1968.
13. David Hancock, *Citizens of the World: London Merchants and the Integration of the British Atlantic Community, 1735–1785* (1995) is a fascinating look at the structure of the British merchant community.
14. Louis Hacker, "The First American Revolution," *Columbia University Quarterly*, September 1935, p. 107.
15. Lawrence Harper, "Mercantilism and the American Revolution," *Canadian Historical Review*, March 1942.
16. Robert Paul Thomas, "A Quantitative Approach to the Study of the Effects of British Imperial Policy on Colonial Welfare: Some Preliminary Findings," *JEH*, December 1965.
17. Peter McClelland, "The Cost to America of British Imperial Policy," including the discussions by Jonathan Hughes and Herman Krooss, *AER*, May 1969. Discussion ranged far and wide: Gary Walton, "The New Economic History and the Burdens of the Navigation Acts," *EHR*, November 1971; Peter McClelland, "The New Economic History and the Burdens of the Navigation Acts: A Comment," *EHR*, November 1973; Gary Walton, "The Burdens of the Navigation Acts: A Reply," *EHR*, November 1973. A broadening of the range from purely economic arguments to politics was achieved by Joseph Reid, Jr., "Economic Burdens: Spark to the American Revolution?" *JEH*, March 1978. Reid shows in a beneficially subtle way how the issues surrounding the Navigation Acts fueled political debate and motivated *some* colonists into action, and that lowered the cost of revolution to the rest.

SUGGESTED READINGS

Articles

Baack, Ben. "Forging a Nation State: The Continental Congress and the Financing of the War of American Independence." *Economic History Review*, vol. LIV, no. 4, November 2001.

Calomiris, Charles. "Institutional Failure, Monetary Scarcity, and the Depreciation of the Continental." *Journal of Economic History*, vol. XLVIII, No. 1, March 1988.

Davis, Lance E., and Robert A. Huttenback. "The Cost of Empire," in Richard Sutch, Roger Ransom, and Gary M. Walton, eds., *Explorations in the New Economic History: Essays in Honor of Douglass C. North*. New York: Academic Press, 1982.

Egnal, Marc M., and Joseph A. Ernst. "An Economic Interpretation of the American Revolution," *William and Mary Quarterly*, January 1972.

Hacker, Louis M. "The First American Revolution." *Columbia University Quarterly*, vol. XXVII, no. 3, part 1, September 1935. Reprinted in Gerald D. Nash. *Issues in American Economic History*. New York: Heath, 1972.

Harper, Lawrence A. "Mercantilism and the American Revolution." *Canadian Historical Review*, vol. XXIII, no. 1, March 1942. Reprinted in Gerald D. Nash. *Issues in American Economic History*. New York: Heath, 1972.

McClelland, Peter D. "The Cost to America of British Imperial Policy," *American Economic Review: Papers and Proceedings*, Vol. LIX, no. 7, May 1969.

———. "The New Economic History and the Burdens of the Navigation Acts: A Comment," *Economic History Review*, vol. XXVI, no. 4, November 1973.

Nettels, Curtis P. "British Mercantilism and the Economic Development of the Thirteen Colonies." *Journal of Economic History*, vol. XII, no. 2 , Spring 1952.

Price, Jacob. "Note on the Value of Colonial Exports of Shipping." *Journal of Economic History*, vol. XXXVI, no. 3, September 1976.

Ransom, Roger. "British Policy and Colonial Growth: Some Implications of the Burdens of the Navigation Acts." *Journal of Economic History*, vol. XXVII, no. 3, September 1968.

Reid, Joseph D., Jr. "Economic Burdens: Spark to the American Revolution?" *Journal of Economic History*, vol. XXXVIII, no. 1, March 1978.

———. "On Navigating the Navigation Acts with Peter D. McClelland." *American Economic Review*, vol. LX, no. 5, December 1970.

Thomas, Robert Paul. "A Quantitative Approach to the Study of the Effects of British Imperial Policy on Colonial Welfare: Some Preliminary Findings." *Journal of Economic History*, vol. XXV, no. 4, December 1965.

Ver Steeg, Clarence. "The American Revolutionary Movement Considered as an Economic Movement." *Huntington Library Journal*, vol. 20, August 1957.

Walton, Gary M. "The New Economic History and the Burdens of the Navigation Acts." *Economic History Review*, 2nd series, vol. XXIV, no. 4, November 1971.

———. "The Burdens of the Navigation Acts, A Reply." *Economic History Review*, vol. XXVI, no. 4, November 1973.

Books

Abernathy, Thomas Perkins. *Western Lands and the American Revolution*. New York: Appleton-Century, 1937.

Bailyn, Bernard. *The New England Merchants in the Seventeenth Century*. Cambridge: Harvard University Press, 1955.

Boorstin, Daniel J. *The Americans: The Colonial Experience*. New York: Vintage Books, 1958.

Brewer, John. *Sinews of Power: War, Money, and the English State, 1688–1783*. New York: Knopf, 1989.

Coleman, D. C., ed. *Revisions in Mercantilism*. London: Methuen, 1969.

Dickerson, Oliver Morton. *American Colonial Government 1695–1765*. Cleveland: Arthur H. Clark, 1912.

Egnal, Marc M. *A Mighty Empire: The Origins of the American Revolution*. Ithaca: Cornell University Press, 1988.

Goodwin, John A. *The Pilgrim Republic*. Boston: Ticknow, 1888.

Greene, Jack P., and J. R. Pole, eds., *Colonial British America: Essays in the New History of the Early Modern Era*. Baltimore, The Johns Hopkins University Press, 1984.

Hancock, David. *Citizens of the World: London Merchants and the Integration of the British Atlantic Community, 1735–1785*. New York: Cambridge University Press, 1995.

Harper, Lawrence A. *The English Navigation Laws*. New York: Columbia University Press, 1939.

Hughes, Jonathan. *Social Control in the Colonial Economy*. Charlottesville: University Press of Virginia, 1976.

McCusker, John J., and Russell R. Menard. *The Economy of British North America, 1607–1789*. Chapel Hill: The University of North Carolina Press, 1985.

Miller, John C. *Origins of the American Revolution*. Stanford: Stanford University Press, 1959.

Morgan, Edmund S. *The American Revolution: A Review of Changing Interpretations*. Washington: Service Center for Teachers of History, 1958.

Schlesinger, A. M. *The Colonial Merchants and the American Revolution*. New York: Frederick Unger, 1964.

Shepherd, James F., and Gary M. Walton. *Shipping, Maritime Trade, and the Economic Development of Colonial North America*. New York: Cambridge University Press, 1972.

Ver Steeg, Clarence. *The Formative Years, 1607–1763*. New York: Hill & Wang, 1964.

NATCHEZ

PART TWO

THE NATIONAL PERIOD AND CONSTITUTIONAL CRISIS: 1783–1861

MAIN CURRENTS 1783–1861

Until the outbreak of the Civil War in 1861, the national experience was largely dominated by three forces:

1. The organization and development of appropriate governmental institutions
2. Westward expansion and continuing sectionalism
3. Early industrialization and urban growth

Like most generalizations, this one covers a multitude of sins. But it will prove to be a useful arena within which to consider, in greater detail, the most important forces motivating economic growth and economic and social development during the first seven decades of the life of an independent nation.

Basic constitutional developments—including the Constitution, the great federal document itself, which launched the nation on new legal grounds in 1789—will be our initial concern. We will discuss especially the establishment of secure property rights for persons and institutions. The Revolution broke our bond with the ancient constitution of England. A new basis was required if there was to be a single national government. The colonies had largely been separate powers even under the Articles of Confederation. Before that, they had been unrelated constitutionally, except via their common English connection. England's constitution was (and is) unwritten—a body of laws and practices with Parliament, after 1688, as the direct amending force.

When we observe what the Americans created, we see a cautious spirit at work. The historian Charles Beard and his followers have labeled this caution **conservatism**, which is a misconception. Professional stunt men and women are very cautious. So, too, are representatives trying to create a constitution. What they are doing is dangerous. The great federal charter of 1789 was developed by representatives of states that already possessed full sovereignty. They, the leaders of the victorious rebel colonies, were now in the king's place. Before surrendering that power to another sovereign, they were likely to examine carefully just what they ought not to give up.

The federal Constitution was an agreement among the states about power: how much should be lodged in a single place and how much might be reserved to those entering into the agreement. We see decades of adjustments of power in subsequent court decisions, in new state constitutions, and in private law—adjustments made by broad strokes as well as by subtle ones. The Americans, by written agreement, legislation, and judicial interpretation, had to discover a way to live in peace among themselves during a period of massive economic and geographic expansion, even as new sovereign states were being created within the federal frame. Conflict between the new federal power and those rights reserved by the states to themselves would be the object of recurring dispute and adjustment. Sectional interests were partly incompatible with each other, and the traditional rights of private persons were not entirely consistent with the expressed needs of economic growth. In the first decades, a framework of government and law had to be devised that would enable further economic prosperity to emerge peaceably from the shell of colonial agrarianism.

Such problems pressed for solution, especially because of massive westward expansion in both the North and South, from the Atlantic coastal strip of colonial settlement all the way to the Pacific. When the agreements among the states that were framed in 1789 failed in 1861, the nation had spanned the continent. Compromises finally failed to resolve sectional differences rooted, as we have seen, in colonial times. The tragedy of war between the states of the union, when it came, threatened to create two continent-wide nations out of colonial America's descendants to join the other artifacts of that era: Canada and Latin America.

The third force, industrialization, we have already observed in its infancy in the colonial period. By 1860, the United States was second only to England itself in industrial output—but a far second. Industry meant urban growth for the most part, even at primitive levels. Flour mills and water-driven factories could be placed away from centers of population, and sometimes were. But there were powerful locational reasons to set mills and factories near markets and breaks-in-transport, as there were, of course, for other activities to locate near such processing and manufacturing.

The founders of 1789 cannot have imagined that in a mere seven decades the number of urban places with populations in excess of 2,500 would grow from 24 to 392 (with two cities in excess of 500,000 inhabitants), and that fully one-fifth of the entire population would reside therein. In 1790, after more than 150 years of settlement, only 5 percent of the population lived in such places. The same factors of location and external economies that produced the little colonial towns and cities—specialization of labor and technique, together with breaks-in-transport and trade—would be augmented now by increments of the Industrial Revolution and would start the United States on the path to becoming an industrial state. Thomas Jefferson's dream of an Arcadia was doomed.

CHAPTER FIVE

Westward Expansion

In this chapter, we will examine the intellectual and geographic dimensions of the new national framework the Americans created for themselves after they gained independence. We begin with the new system of law, the federal Constitution, and the resulting authority of the states and the common law. We will then see how the genius of Thomas Jefferson and his colleagues produced, in the Land Ordinances of 1785 and 1787, the means for orderly westward expansion. This was an achievement probably as great as the Constitution itself.

THE CONSTITUTIONAL SETTLEMENT OF 1789–1791

Articles of Confederation

To fight the War of Independence, the 13 colonies had been tied together loosely by the Articles of Confederation and Perpetual Union. Submitted to the colonial legislatures in 1777, the document was finally ratified by all in 1781. The British colonies to the north in what is now Canada were invited to join the Confederation, but declined. The Confederation was too weak to be entirely effective as a frame of national government. In particular, the taxing power to pay for the operations of the central government, "The United States in Congress Assembled," had been left to the individual states; the central government requisitioned taxes from the states. This delegation of responsibility set up crucial **free-rider** problems (individuals enjoying the benefits without incurring the costs of an activity) and left the new nation buried in debt and inflation when the war ended. In addition to the power to levy taxes, the central government needed the power to regulate interstate and international commerce, to provide for the national defense, and to authorize a national judiciary.

The Constitutional Convention

In January 1786, Virginia and Maryland took the lead and appointed commissioners to consider the development of a more adequate form of government. They met with delegates of other states (Delaware, New York, New Jersey, and Pennsylvania) at Annapolis and issued a call for a Constitutional Convention. The first meeting was held at Philadelphia on 14 May 1787 with 55 delegates from seven states in attendance. The major question was whether the strengthened central government would allow for considerable state sovereignty (a federal system) or limited or no state sovereignty (a national system).

James Madison's account of the discussions presents the modern student with a clear picture of that most remarkable assemblage.[1] In slightly more than four months, on 28 September 1787, George Washington, president of the Convention, sent the complete document with a covering letter to the states for ratification. Delaware ratified 7 December 1787, the first state to do so. Rhode Island, on 29 May 1790, was the last of the original 13 colonies to do so. But on 21 June 1788, the crucial ninth favorable vote had already been cast by New Hampshire, and the new Constitution had become effective. The Congress declared the Constitution to be in effect as of 4 March 1789. The first ten amendments, the Bill of Rights, fashioned after the Declaration of Rights of Virginia, were passed by the first Congress and went into effect 15 December 1791.

Charles Beard argued that the economic self-interest of the delegates to the Constitutional Convention played an important role in shaping that document.[2] Merchants and manufacturers, public and private security holders, capitalists and financiers were all likely to be supportive of a national system. Similarly, slaveholders and debtors were likely to oppose such a system. While the Beard hypothesis provoked controversy among historians for most of the twentieth century, it induced little in the way of empirical investigation. Economic historians focused more on the effect than the cause: the new Constitution, by correcting the deficiencies of the Articles of Confederation, helped to create economic conditions that nurtured economic growth.

Through an empirical analysis of 16 key votes on "pro-national" positions at the Constitution Convention, Robert McGuire and Robert Ohsfeldt believe they have "rehabilitated" Beard.[3] They found, "The voting patterns...generally support an economic interpretation of the Constitution because personal and constituent interests affected voting behavior on particular issues primarily when the interests could be significantly advanced by the outcome."[4] In particular, they identify those from larger and coastal states, bankers and other private debt holders, and those who had been officers in the Revolution as most likely to support the new Constitution. Those from smaller states, more inland areas, and slaveholders were most likely to stand in opposition. Farmers and debtors were either opposed or indifferent.

Reserved Rights

The debates of the Convention, according to Madison's account, were a careful discussion of state interests conducted by delegates determined to succeed. They seemed to know well enough what they wanted. They drew on the past when it served well (judicial review) and invented new forms when necessary. Where compromise was required, as in the case of slavery, they compromised. The representatives of the individual states (each with sovereign powers) jealously guarded their power and gave up to the new central authority only those rights they believed would be necessary to create an effective central government. To strengthen their "reserved rights," they added the Tenth Amendment:

> The powers not delegated to the United States by the Constitution, nor prohibited by it to the States, are reserved to the States respectively, or to the people.

The powers reserved to the states were the police powers—local rules, laws, and ordinances that, as in colonial times, included licensing, inspection, and the regulation of local business activities (see Chapter 7). In relations among themselves, the people had the common law, the ancient set of rules their ancestors had found congenial for nearly two centuries in America. In 1774, the Continental Congress had claimed in the "Declarations and Resolves" the "common law of England" as the right of all Americans. Several state constitutions explicitly laid claim to the same body of law. It became policy to leave the development and interpretation of that law to the states. In cases of ambiguity, the Supreme Court of the United States, as in *Robinson v. Campbell* (1818), ordered the state courts to look to England for guidance:

> The remedies in the courts of the United States are to be, at common law or equity, not according to the practice of the state courts, but according to the principles of common law and

equity, as distinguished and defined in that country from which we derive our knowledge of those principles.[5]

The Constitution could be as brief and sweeping as it is because it did not have to be a complete code of law and statement of rights and privileges. Much could be taken for granted—and was.

The Federal Constitution in Brief

The document itself is remarkably simple. We can usefully note here those parts of special significance to our study of American economic history. The powers given explicitly to Congress are in Article I, Section 8, and they number 18. They say, in summary, that Congress shall have the power to:

1. Tax, with the proviso that federal taxes shall be uniform in and among all the states
2. Borrow, from anyone, on the credit of the new government
3. Regulate commerce with foreign countries, among the states, and with the Indian tribes
4. Make rules regarding naturalization and bankruptcy
5. Create money, regulate its value, and fix a standard of weights and measures
6. Provide punishments for counterfeiting
7. Establish post office and post roads
8. Create patent and copyright laws
9. Create courts inferior to the U. S. Supreme Court
10. Define crimes and felonies committed on the high seas and to provide punishments for the same
11. Declare war and to make "rules" regarding it
12. Raise and support armies, but with no single appropriation of money to remain in force for more than two years
13. Create and maintain a navy
14. Create martial law for the military services
15. Provide for militia to "suppress insurrections and repel invasions"
16. Govern the militia employed by the United States, reserving to the states the appointment of officers
17. Exercise sovereign powers over the site of the federal government's installations
18. Make necessary laws to "carry into execution" the powers stated above

The compromise on black slavery is contained in Article I, Section 9, paragraph 1. The Atlantic slave trade could continue for 20 years, but it would be taxed.

> The migration or importation of such persons as any of the States now existing shall think proper to admit, shall not be prohibited by the Congress prior to the year one thousand eight hundred and eight, but a tax or duty may be imposed on such importation, not exceeding ten dollars for each person.

In Article I, Section 9, paragraph 5, Congress is forbidden the power to lay duties on exports from any state. The next paragraph prohibits Congress from creating regulations under the commerce power (Article I, Section 8, number 3 of the enumerated powers) in a discriminatory way between the states and also forbids interstate duties for vessels clearing a port in one state and entering another.

Such sweeping powers required restrictions upon the sovereignty of the states. These are given in Article I, Section 10. The first paragraph restricts dealings with foreign powers; prohibits creation of state bills of credit (state paper money), legal tender except gold and silver coins, bills of attainder, and ex post facto laws; and includes the famous contract clause: No state shall make a "law impairing the obligation of contracts." The idea of contract permeates English history; the sanctity of contract lay at the very root of the developing idea of government by law and not by men. With the inclusion of this clause, the common law was legislated for the new republic. Paragraph 2 prohibits restrictions on interstate commerce except as "may be absolutely necessary for executing its inspection laws." The latter was consistent with the reservation of police powers by the states.

Article II sets up the executive branch; Article III sets up the judiciary. Article IV contains the "Full

Faith and Credit" provisions, ordering each state to recognize the laws and judicial practices of the others. The citizens of each state have the rights of the citizens of the others. The ancient English doctrine of "hue and cry" (the pursuit of felons across state lines) is enshrined in Section 2, paragraph 2, of this Article. In paragraph 3, the continuation of the colonial practices of servitude and slavery is again recognized.

> No person held to service or labor in one State, under the laws thereof, escaping into another, shall in consequence of any law or regulation therein, be discharged from such service or labor, but shall be delivered up on claim of the party to whom such service or labor may be due.

Application of this rule in the Dred Scott case in 1857 would, in part, launch the American Civil War. Article IV also provides for the entry of new states and the guarantee of a "Republican form of government." Article V provides for amendment. Article VI provides in paragraph 1 for continuation of debt obligations made under the Confederation into the federal era. The second paragraph is the "supremacy clause":

> This constitution, and the laws of the United States...shall be the supreme law of the land.

The Fifth Amendment, famous in political history for the lines:

> ...nor shall any person be subject for the same offense to be twice put in jeopardy of life and limb, nor shall be compelled in any criminal case to be a witness against himself....

is equally famous in economic history for the words that follow:

> ...nor be deprived of life, liberty, or property, without due process of law; nor shall private property be taken for public use without just compensation.

Subsequent Economic Development

The Constitution, this amazingly brief and clear document, has been, as amended and interpreted, the "supreme law of the land" for over two centuries now. Along with the settled and reserved rights of the states and citizens with knowledge of the common law and their rights under it, the federal Constitution secured property rights and the rights of persons. A fundamental element of economic development, the reign of calculable law, was to continue. In Chapter 8, we will see how lawmakers and judges used the Constitution to maintain the orderly growth and development of a massive economy in the decades to come. The practice continues. We will be referring again and again to the clauses dealing with commerce, contracts, reserved rights, and due process as our study proceeds.

THE LAND ORDINANCES OF 1785 AND 1787

Agreement among the states regarding the forms and powers of the federal union had been preceded by agreement about the western lands. What the colonists got from the British in settlement in 1783 was less than the "sea to sea" of the Virginia grant because of the British settlement of 1763 recognizing French and Spanish claims (and those of the Indian tribes) west of the Mississippi and reserving the old Northwest to Quebec (1774). To be settled first, however, was the territory below the Canadian boundary between the Mississippi and the Alleghenies. Who owned it, and how was it to be settled? At stake was the nation's future social and economic structure: From the land and its resources would come income, wealth, cities, and future populations. The nature of the land policy was crucial.

Cessions of Western Lands

The process of agreement was begun before peace actually was achieved, since, after 1781, the British cause was irretrievably lost. Seven of the colonies had claims on the western lands from their original grants or from dealings with the Indians. Virginia's claim included everything north of its southern border, thereby overlapping the claims of other colonies. As we have seen, settlers were moving into

Indians and whites mixed peacefully at Fort Snelling (Minneapolis), as American civilization moved westward.

the western lands even before the Revolution. The Articles of Confederation contained a clause stating that the western lands should not be taken from the states for the benefit of the national government. Not only land speculators favored the opposite policy; some statesmen with purer motives also wanted the new government to be endowed with the public lands so that a national policy might evolve in the west.

Maryland (a state with no western lands) would not ratify the Articles until the land question was settled. New York's claims were based upon treaties with the Iroquois nation, and, when it gave over those claims to the national government in 1781, Maryland responded by ratifying the Articles. In the same year, Virginia offered to contribute its enormous claim, and a national policy was assured. Virginia's gift was accepted in 1784. The Virginians wisely stipulated that their lands were not to be granted by the national government to those who had made private deals for land with the Indians in what are now Illinois and Indiana. To enforce such shoddy claims against the resident Indians, the speculators would have needed the backing of federal troops.

Collective Property Rights and the Public Domain

Before we examine the disposal of the public domain, it is useful to consider briefly the problem in the abstract. The public domain was an enormous expanse of community property, one that *no one had an incentive to conserve* unless the communal rights could somehow be transferred to others by assigning them secure private rights. Why should one person restrain his or her own use of an asset that all others could freely exploit or even destroy? Unless private rights could be assigned, free riders could never be excluded, and it would pay each person to overuse the communal rights of the rest as long as private profit exceeded the cost of use. A free-for-all would end in violence. It was unthinkable that the public domain would remain in government ownership; we had no Tsar to own it all, no hereditary feudal nobility whose assigned property rights would be paramount over those of the common people. In fact, such a development was feared, and the creation of titles of nobility was prohibited in the rules for the public lands.

A way would have to be found to distribute the land. Each piece of land opened to bona fide settlers

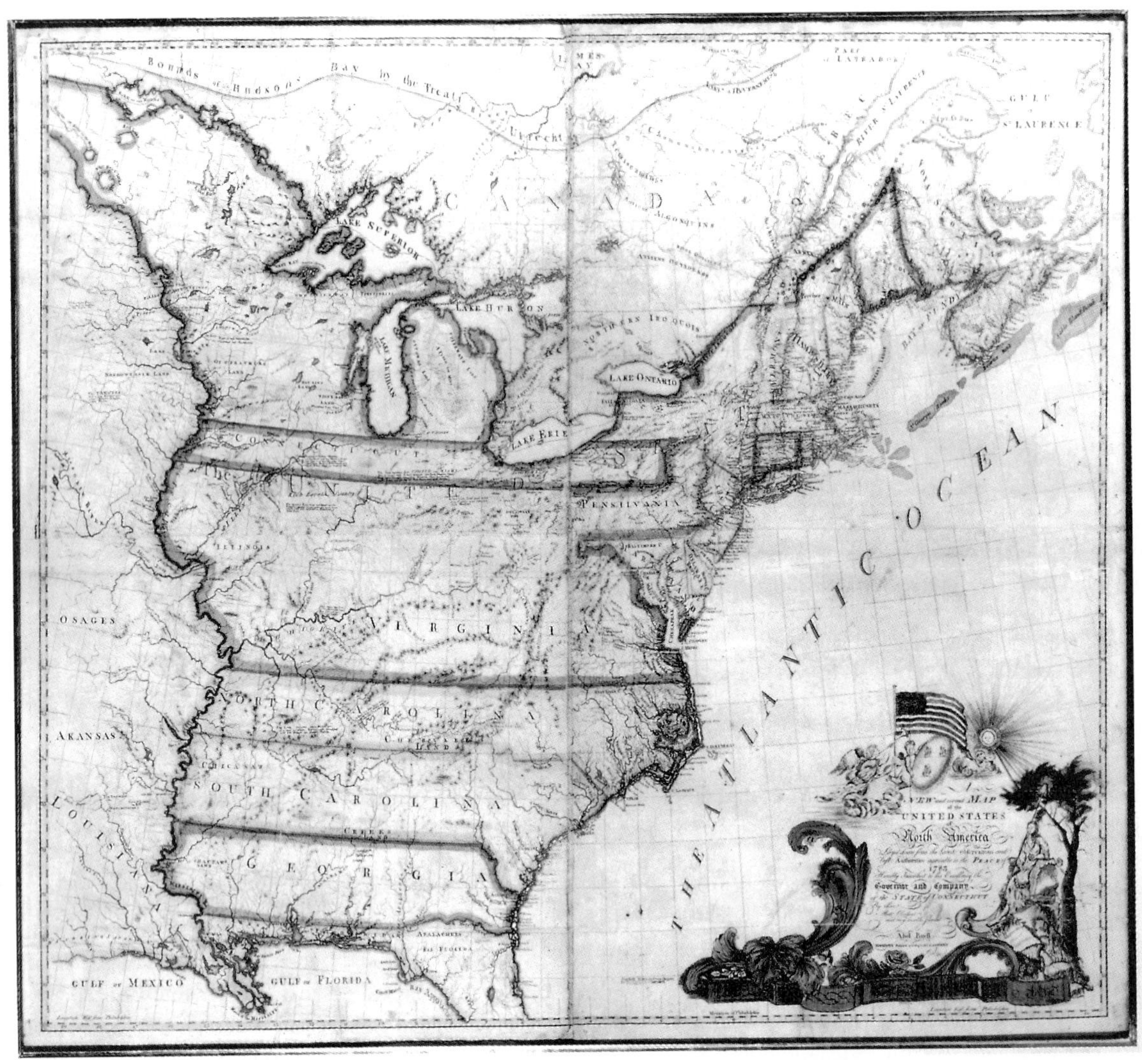

This map is titled: "A new and correct map of the United States of North America. Layed down from the latest observations and best authorities agreeable to the Peace of 1785."

instantly became a ripe plum to be expropriated individually by those with the qualifications or money. Consequently, there was no way in a free society to prohibit speculation—psychological waves of optimism and pessimism (as in modern gyrations in stock-market prices, exchange rates, and commodity prices). That was the first problem. It was part of the process of assignment of rights. Those who bought the public lands resold them at the highest prices they could get. The second problem, apparent since colonial times, was the white settlers' continued attempts to expropriate the public (and Indian) lands individually. The squatter families, steadily knifing their way into the wilderness, were the cutting edge. The British could not keep them out nor, as the white population multiplied, could the Indians. What was needed was a policy that could serve as an overall rule. The public domain was destined to be cut into millions of pieces by private owners. How was it to be done? Only when the best lands were gone and the private costs of expropriation rose sufficiently, would occupation of the empty spaces slow down or cease.

Jefferson and the Ordinances of 1785 and 1787

What would the land policy be? Here again the nation is in debt to Thomas Jefferson of Virginia, the guiding spirit behind the great Land Ordinances of 1785 and 1787. Had he been a student of modern theories of property rights, he could scarcely have done better in theory. No one, and certainly no force, could have made the disposal of the public domain more fair than it was. There were too many pressures at work. Jefferson realized that the "donation" (sovereign sources of clear titles) would begin with the national government. The government, now legatee of this power, had inherited control from the king of England through the colonial charters and the surrender of that power by states like Virginia whose claims came from the British crown.

Jefferson wanted the land (a) to be a one-time source of revenue to the national government, (b) to become the seat of republican government and democratic institutions, and (c) to be a secure property to the private owner. He feared the potential abuse of power by the national government and wanted the land, wherever possible, to be removed from its grasp. His most important ideas about the land may be summed up as follows:

1. Tenure in the lands acquired by private persons from the national government should not be further subject to that government once titles were secured.
2. The distribution should be orderly, with scientific survey before sale and with boundaries marked by that survey rather than by the "metes and bounds" of colonial times.[6]
3. Populations occupying the public lands would make those territories eligible to become new states, formed on an equal basis with the old.

Thus, the lands of the west would produce a lateral expansion of the American democracy and not become the basis for radical departures in government and social or economic policy or practice.

Jefferson's 1784 memorandum on the public lands outlined his policy. He was the leading member of a congressional committee charged with formulating a land policy. Essentially, he viewed the national government's own tenure in the public lands to be fee simple, with the rights transferred to the private buyer by sale. The national government then stepped out, and the donor became the present or future state government. The land was then to be "holden of" the state. Taxes were due to the state, and the land should, in Jefferson's words, "never after, in any case, revert to the United States."[7] By this single act, the new states would be endowed with a future tax base, and property owners would be subject to their state and local governments. The danger that the federal government's power would increase over private citizens was much reduced. Following colonial precedent, an initial attempt was made to reserve one-third of all gold, silver, and other mineral discoveries, together with salt springs, but no settled policy ever developed that reserved mineral rights to the government. Holders in fee simple owned their own minerals, a fact of capital importance when the nation began to develop heavy industry on the basis of privately owned minerals.

Both the 1785 Ordinance and the 1787 Ordinance (the Northwest Ordinance) were revisions, expansions, and readoptions of an ordinance Jefferson's committee proposed in 1784. This ordinance included a provision to ban slavery after 1800 in all lands west of the Alleghenies. It lost in Congress by a single vote. Jefferson later wrote about that defeat:

> There were ten states present. Six voted unanimously for it, and one was divided; and seven votes being requisite to decide the proposition affirmatively, it was lost. The voice of a single individual of the state which was divided, or one of those which were of the negative, would have prevented this abominable crime from spreading itself over the new country. Thus we see the fate of millions unborn hanging on the tongue of one man—and Heaven was silent in that awful moment.[8]

FIGURE 5.1 System of Land Survey 1796

1. SECTIONS OF A TOWNSHIP

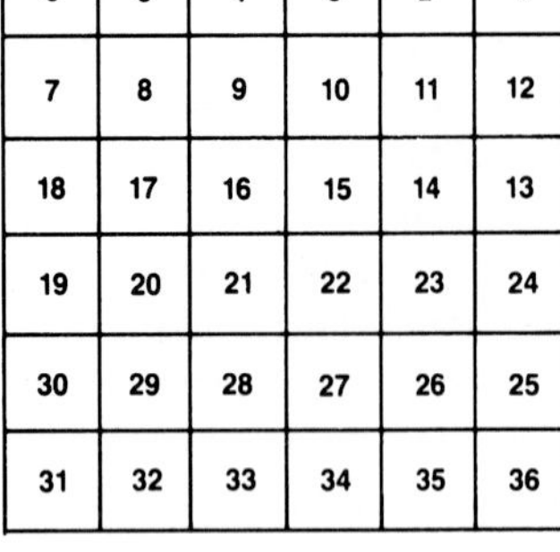

2. SUBDIVISIONS OF A SECTION

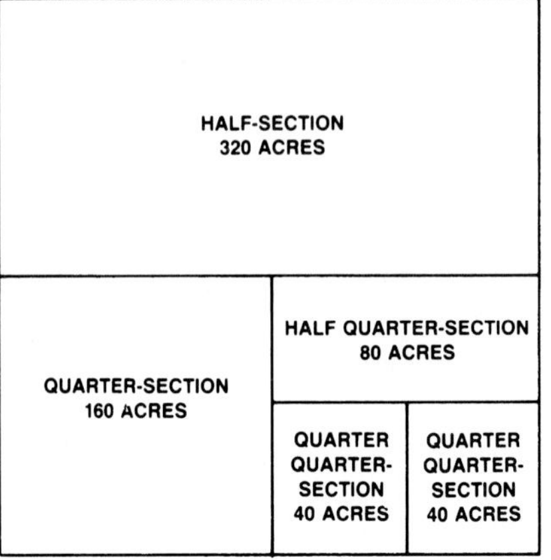

3. DESIGNATING OF TOWNSHIPS

T. 5 N.
T. 4 N.
T. 3 N.
T. 2 N.
T. 1 N.
PRINCIPAL MERIDIAN
BASE LINE
R.III. W. R.II. W. R.I. W. R.I. E. R.II. E. R.III. E.
T. 1 S.
T. 2 S.
T. 3 S.
T. 4 S.
T. 5 S.

Source: Charles O. Paullin, *Atlas of the Historical Geography of the United States* (Washington, D.C. and New York: Carnegie Institution of Washington and the American Geographical Society of New York, 1932), plate 48.

The basic survey scheme for the public lands under the Land Act of 1796 (which followed the outline of the Northwest Ordinance in 1785) is shown here. Each township is 36 square miles. A section, 1 square mile, contains 640 acres. Divided into four farms, it was the "squatter" 160 acres, which still prevailed as the basic homestead in the Homestead Act of 1862. The base and meridian survey lines are division lines used to number the townships.

Thus did Jefferson miss being the man in American history who did more than any other to determine the peaceful demise of chattel slavery. In the 1787 ordinance, slavery was excluded only from the territories north of the Ohio River.[9]

It was planned that the lands would be surveyed and then sold at auction. In the Ordinance of 1785, Jefferson's original plan of 10-square-mile townships was modified to the New England custom of 6-mile-square townships, each with 36 sections of 640 acres (see Figure 5.1). A half-section was 320 acres, and a quarter-section, 160 acres. When the Homestead Act became law in 1862, 160 acres would be a standard family homestead. Later on, in the arid west, the assignment of irrigation water rights from government projects would be for the same-sized "family farm." One section in each township was to be set aside for the support of public schools (following traditions in Virginia and New England) and four sections for government uses. A proposal to include *glebeland* to support churches, common practice in colonial New England, was defeated, in anticipation, perhaps, of the First Amendment.

The Northwest Ordinance of 1787 embraced Jefferson's plan to divide the western lands into several roughly rectangular areas that would become states in due course. In 1784, Jefferson's committee proposed that the Northwest Territory be divided into *ten* parts (see Figure 5.2). Two years later, James Monroe sent a letter to then Ambassador Jefferson

FIGURE 5.2 The Northwest Territory under the 1784 Ordinance

The ten proposed states in the draft ordinance of 1784.

in Paris indicating he feared the creation of *ten* new states was impolitic. Given that the 1784 ordinance met defeat over the slavery issue, he argued that the addition of ten new states would increase the likelihood of sectional division and reduce the new government's probability of success.[10] A year later, Monroe submitted a motion that passed Congress limiting the number of new states in the Northwest Territory to between three and five.

The Northwest Territory was to be organized as a district; Congress would appoint a district governor and judges. When one of the three-to-five districts contained 5,000 male residents of voting age, an elected territorial legislature would be established and a nonvoting delegate would be sent to Congress. The executive and judicial functions were still to be filled by federal government appointees. When the territorial population reached 60,000 free inhabitants, the territory would become a state "on an equal footing with the original states, in all respects whatever." Although a territory had considerable control over its internal affairs, it did not have a vote at the federal level; under the Constitution, a state was guaranteed two senators and one representative. Furthermore, territories were still subject to executive and judicial appointments, which were dependent on federal, not local, concerns; a state was not. Thus, there was a benefit to achieving statehood.

Land grants to war veterans were to be honored—the size to vary according to military rank.[11] Lands, military "reserves," were set aside for this purpose. Because the soldiers could sell their patents to private speculators for cash, most veterans never settled their lands. The land was strictly payment for their services. Although Jefferson had wanted restrictions on the alienation and inheritance of the military portions of the western lands, in the end, the tenure was one of (a) perpetual possession (no time limit in fee simple), (b) direct inheritance, (c) freedom of alienation, (d) right of waste, and (e) inheritance in cases of intestacy (no will) in equal degrees of consanguinity both male and female, without regard to half-blood, together with the right to devise lands by will. Primogeniture and entailment were abandoned.[12] Giving a double portion to the eldest son was also left to the history books; those states that had practiced it dropped the custom by the early nineteenth century. In her study of the relationship of women to property law, Marylynn Salmon notes that the abolition of primogeniture and a double share for the eldest son were among the most significant post-Revolutionary legal changes favoring women.[13]

The western territory south of the Ohio River was organized in steps. In 1792, Virginia consented to statehood for its territory of Kentucky. North Carolina gave over its claims to Tennessee in 1790, and the latter was organized as a territory along the lines of the Northwest Ordinance, except that slavery was not prohibited and the survey system was not applied there. The southern territory, previously disputed with Spain, was organized as the Mississippi Territory in 1798, and Georgia gave over its claim in 1804. The principles again were those of the Northwest Ordinance, save for the clause prohibiting slavery.

Thus, in a single decade after peace in 1783, the entire territory between the Alleghenies and the Mississippi River was organized, in theory, on "American principles," with guaranteed constitutional rights and forms of government and the method devised whereby the land could pass into secure private ownership and development. The foundation of future American capitalism—private ownership and control of productive resources—was created. Since most property rights known to most people were the real property rights imbedded in free and common socage, it was natural that rights to other forms of property were derived from that basic form. An ancient English land tenure became the basis of American capitalism.

At first, lands in the Northwest Territory were to be sold only in sections, then half-sections, and, by the 1830s, in parcels as small as 40 acres; the new states were destined to have their lands filled and owned by a nation of family farmers. Of the present 50 states, 31 came into existence under the organizing principles of the Northwest Ordinance—an incredible achievement from the minds and pens of our eighteenth-century statesmen.[14]

In theory, it was a social mechanism designed to settle a continent on a lawful and orderly basis with secure property rights for individual owners. It was a great gift to the future. The world today is still strewn east to west, from the *taiga* of Russia to the deserts of South Africa, with nations whose political malignancy reflects failure to solve the problems of land ownership with secure titles for individuals. In reality, the disposal of the American public domain was not what Jefferson might have dreamed, but despite a century and more of graft and corruption in the process, his principles prevailed in the final settlement. Those who live west of the Alleghenies do so mostly in the framework of the Northwest Ordinance.[15]

TERRITORIAL GAINS 1790–1853

Acquisition of the continental territory came within six decades of the Constitution (see Figure 5.3, for the acquisitions made between 1790 and 1853). By treaty with England, the territory of the original colonies, together with the land up to the Mississippi River, contained nearly 889,000 square miles. By purchase from Napoleon (for a mere $15 million, with only $11.3 million net of United States claims against France), the Louisiana Purchase of 1803 nearly doubled the national territory, adding 827,000 square miles. In 1819, by treaty with Spain, another 72,000 square miles—Florida—were added.

The Texans revolted against Mexico in 1836, became an independent nation, and nine years later joined the United States, adding another 390,000 square miles. In 1846, settlement of the longstanding dispute with Britain over the Oregon border added an additional 286,000 square miles. War with Mexico began that year. The settlement with Mexico added what became the states of California, Nevada, and Utah, and parts of Wyoming, Colorado, and New Mexico—an enormous 529,000-square-mile domain. The Gadsden Purchase from Mexico in 1853 added some 27,000 square miles.

By 1853, the land area of the United States was 1.9 billion acres. As late as the Civil War, fully two-thirds of it was still empty and in the public domain. The national enterprise until the early twentieth century and, to a large extent, even today, has been filling out this great territory with cultivation and habitation. Russian rights in Alaska were purchased in 1867, adding a massive 586,000 square miles, which are still barely inhabited. Annexation of Hawaii in 1898 and Puerto Rico in 1899 brought the total area now having the status of states of the Union (the Commonwealth of Puerto Rico is an associated state) to some 3,628,000 square miles.

The Philippines were annexed as a territory in 1898 in our spasmodic phase of imperialism. They were given their independence in 1946. Apart from small holdings, like the Virgin Islands, Guam, and American Samoa, the national surge for territory, which began in Virginia in 1607, seems to have spent itself. In all the places the country occupied, the organizational scheme of Jefferson and his colleagues reigned—over land tenure, surveys, support of public schools, sizes of townships, and the rest. The Ordinances of 1785 and 1787 laid out the ground rules.

DISPOSAL OF THE PUBLIC LANDS

During the actual processes of land disposal, almost nothing went exactly according to plan. The government apparatus was too slow off the mark in setting up the system, too cumbersome, and when there were finally sufficient land offices established, too slow in the recording and granting of titles. Events moved too quickly. It is worth noting that overall, the federal government seems to have spent more money disposing of the lands than was received in sales revenues. If you add the annual figures up to 1880, expenses total about $322 million and revenues total about $201 million, for a loss of $121 million. This figure excludes the administrative costs associated with land grants, such as those made to canal and railroad companies. Those who paid the taxes that supported the government subsidized those who bought the lands from the government.[16] Not even the transactions costs were met by sales revenues.

Speculation

Much has been written of speculation in public lands, as though it were a national disgrace. Such an evaluation might bear some weight, *if* the system had ever worked as planned. *If* there had been a survey of all the land before settlement, *if* all the lands had been sold at public auction to actual settlers, the orderly plans might have worked. As it was, they didn't have a chance. The government's various **reservation**

FIGURE 5.3 U.S. Territory by 1853

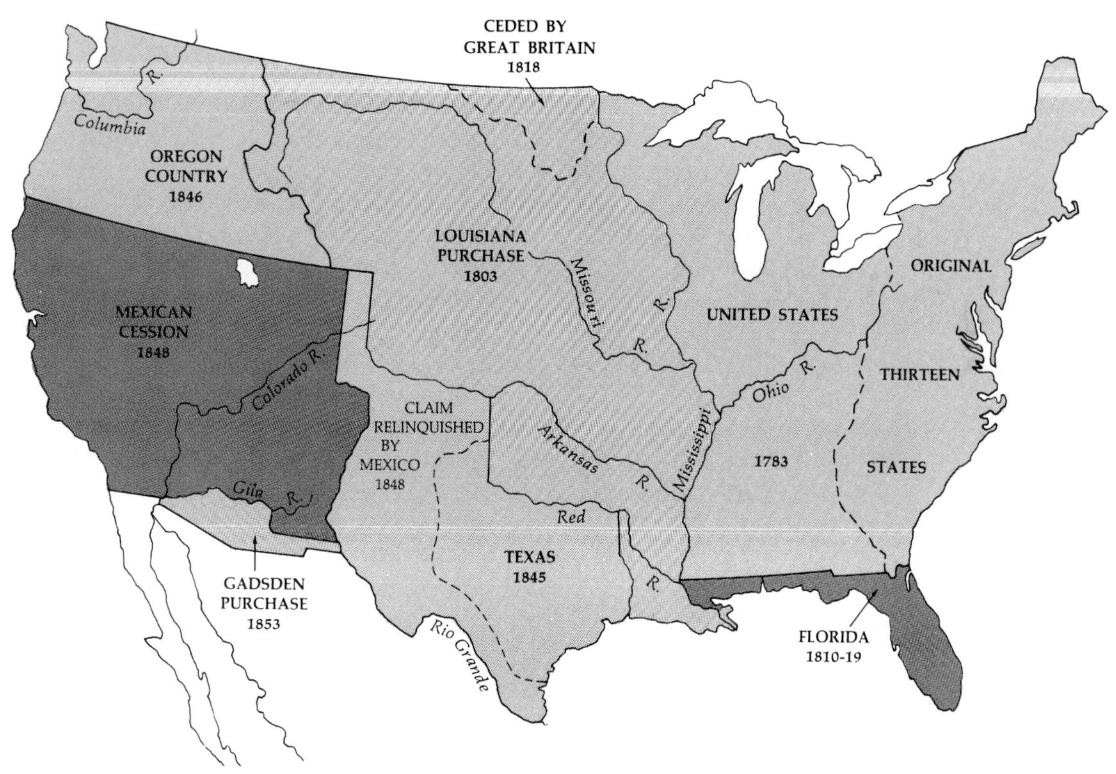

U.S. territories were acquired by various methods. Some—such as Florida, Oregon, the northern section west of the Mississippi, and the Gadsden Purchase—were peaceful transactions; others—New Mexico, Arizona, Utah, Nevada, California, and part of Texas—were the result of various military actions. The Louisiana Purchase was, of course, a cash deal.

prices—minimum prices set by Congress below which no bids were accepted—could not encompass differing qualities of land in different areas. As a result, prices were inevitably too high for some lands (which went unclaimed) or too low for others (which resold, often on the spot, at prices that represented actual market demand and supply). Malcolm Rohrbough, in his book *The Land Office Business,* gives an account of sales in Kalamazoo, Michigan, in 1836, at the height of the land boom of that period. The office had been closed to catch up on record-keeping, but the registrar bowed to the demands of the throng on his doorstep and reopened the bidding. He "accepted numerous applications, marked the tracts as sold on the maps of the office, and watched helplessly while the prospective purchasers speculated with the approved applications."[17] In that case, the reservation price was clearly far too low.

Parcel Size

Disposal of public lands by Congress opened in 1787 with a sale of 1 million acres to the Ohio Company of Associates at about 10 cents an acre. Two more sales of similar size were made that year to the Scioto Company and to John Symmes. It was left to these buyers, as in colonial times, to find settlers and to resell the lands at prices and on terms the new buyers would accept. This arrangement was hardly what Jefferson and his colleagues had anticipated, but it was a portent of things to come. Despite pressures in Congress for sales in parcels affordable by small farmers, the minimum-size purchase was set initially at 640 acres at a government reservation price of $1.00 per acre. Credit terms were available beginning in 1796, at which time the price was raised to $2.00 per acre. In 1800, the minimum parcel size was reduced to 320 acres, in 1804 to 160 acres, and in 1820 to 80 acres, at which time the minimum price was reduced to $1.25 per acre and the credit terms repealed. Speculation—free market sale—was the method of adapting farm size, price, and location to individual demand. In 1832, the minimum size was reduced to 40 acres, cash only, and a 160-acre limit was placed on lands bought by right of **preemption**, the right to buy, at the minimum price, the land one had already settled. There was no upper limit on lands bought for cash.

It seems clear that the public land auction, which in good years attracted huge throngs of prospective buyers for lands being opened, was seen merely as the *initial* transaction necessary to move land out of the public domain into the free market. It was not uncommon, officials charged, for buyers to agree to submit low bids for reservation prices only at the auctions and then to bid among themselves for the newly released lands at much higher prices. But, after the General Preemption Act of 1841, nothing prevented informed buyers from bidding higher at auction (except threats of violence) for choice lands when there were no preemption claims.

Preemption and Graduation

Settlers in colonial times had commonly "squatted" on lands, as we have seen. Except for Massachusetts, state governments tended to deal generously with them, valuing their pioneering labors. The federal government was far less generous—troops were sent out to burn farmsteads and villages. But the squatters returned, for they saw no legitimacy in the federal government's claims to the land. From the beginning, demands for preemption were heavy and, from time to time, were honored by special preemption acts (for example, 1813 legislation covering settlers in Illinois, Missouri, and the Florida Territory). After 1815, the gradual but steady removal of Indian tribes and the nullification of their claims to tribal lands led to a flood of squatters and to demands for a general preemption law.[18] The government, while continuing to pass special preemption acts for specific groups in specific places, resisted the demand for general preemption—the opening of all lands to squatters.

As late as 1830, President Jackson was threatening to use troops to clear the lands of squatters. Instead, that year Congress passed the broadest preemption act yet, to be renewed biennially.[19] It included a proviso that where two squatters' claims overlapped in a single quarter-section, the claim would be divided and each would be allowed to find 80 acres "elsewhere in the said land district." Not surprisingly, a vigorous market in these 80-acre "floaters" quickly developed. In 1841, a general preemption act was passed, limiting preemption to 160 acres but allowing cash sales at $1.25 per acre on parcels as small as 40 acres.[20]

Since much land remained unsold or the titles were never completed, in 1854, Congress passed the Graduation Act, which lowered the reservation price on public land according to the time the land had remained unsold since the district was opened for sale: $1.00 per acre on land ten years unsold, and 12.5 cents per acre on land 30 or more years unsold.

The 1862 Homestead Act opened the remaining public domain to settlers on terms of occupation and improvement only, a century after the Proclamation of 1763 had closed the interior. By then, most of the good lands east of the Mississippi, indeed east of the 100th meridian through the middle of Kansas and Nebraska, were in private hands.

But there is something else to consider here. The return to colonial methods—land grants for settlement and services performed—embodied in the 1862 Homestead Act has always been something of a puzzle, especially so because the Civil War was raging when a congressional act was passed diverting populations away from the cockpit of war, away from the East and Midwest. Why then? Perhaps it is not such a mystery. The homestead lands were in the domain of the plains and mountain Indians. Although those lands had been claimed by the United States since 1781, effective control over them was never established. Homesteaders were, in many respects, an army of occupation, and far cheaper than the one later represented by George Armstrong Custer and Phil Sheridan. Homesteaders paid most of their own way and tended to drive out the Indians. Thus, the homesteaders were loosed upon the West, as the backwoods squatters had been in colonial times. A thousand or so battles later (about three decades), the frontier was closed, the Indians were on reservations, and the federal government ruled all. Homesteading after 1862 was a way for a weak (or preoccupied) government to establish its property rights—by supporting those of the homesteaders—in disputed lands. So says Douglas W. Allen, and the argument makes sense.[21]

Questions of Efficiency and Justice

Studies of the General Land Office and its procedures agree that its administration was deficient throughout. The staff was too small, and settlers constantly pressed into choice areas faster than the land could be surveyed. It took as long as five years after purchase to gain title. At first, each patent to land had to be signed personally by the president of the United States. In 1832, the General Land Office needed to issue 42,000 patents to keep pace. From December to June, President Jackson had signed 10,000 patents, there were 10,590 awaiting his signature, and the number was climbing. Congress then passed a law allowing a secretary to sign on the president's behalf.

Land officers commonly were corrupt, selling information on lands privately and speculating in the lands themselves to augment their salaries. It is charged that, at least until the General Preemption Act of 1841, the system was designed to line the pockets of the rich (speculators who could pay cash for large blocks of land and then resell parcels to small holders) at the public expense.

Was a system that embraced greater justice and equity possible? No doubt. Any system less corrupt might have been an improvement. But in part, the question is strictly academic. Most of the public domain was taken by force from the English, Mexicans, or from the American Indians. For example, what were the American Indians' compensations in the Louisiana Purchase? Treaties were broken, and Indian populations were forcibly evicted from their lands; the Indian Removal Act of 1830 had as its object the transfer of *all* Indians to land west of the Mississippi River. The just distribution of lands thus gained was to become an interesting problem of ethics. In any case, Congress in 1850 with the Illinois Central Railroad, in 1862 with transcontinental railroads, and in later grants to railroads by the states proceeded to give away 10 percent of the continental land mass (about 190 million acres) to subsidize railroad construction. The search for justice and equity there would become even more complex.

If we consider what was going on—the wholesale "privatization" of communal property—we should agree that our system had one overriding virtue; as Lance Davis said, "At least it was fast."[22] There were, however, curious inconsistencies in the policies. The farmers wanted more and more land, since clearing it gave them financial gain. According to Stanley Lebergott, a farmer in the North Central region could clear 10 to 12 acres a year, a gain of between $140 and $200, or more than an adult son could earn in a year as an agricultural laborer. On the other hand, the policy of selling off the public domain undermined this effort, since new lands were constantly being added to supply, reducing land prices overall from the levels they might have otherwise been.[23]

In the end, the land was occupied in *form* as specified by the Ordinances of 1785 and 1787, and that was a great achievement. The *process* as it actually happened was no more a national disgrace than is any modern river and harbor appropriation by Congress. The public lands were in the nineteenth century what the spending power of Congress would become in our own era, the place where private interests were satisfied because no public interest could be agreed upon or even identified. Jefferson would have been appalled then, as he no doubt would be today. Vernon Carstensen quotes with approval a 1915 statement by Dean Eugene Davenport of the College of Agriculture of Illinois: "But we have these farms, these cities, the railroads, and this civilization to show for it, and they are worth what they cost."[24] We could spend much time imagining a system that could have done it better, considering the vastness of the task to be done.

Land Sales Patterns

Westward expansion was a matter of people as well as land. More people were needed as the nation moved westward; thus, time was involved. Until the late 1840s, immigration was not of great significance; natural increase and the migration of native populations moved the nation westward. Consider the data in Table 5.1.

By 1840, the flood of people into the East North Central region (Ohio, Indiana, Illinois, Michigan, Wisconsin) and into the East South Central region (Kentucky, Tennessee, Alabama, Mississippi) had created populations there of nearly 6 million.[25] By 1860, those two regions, together with the West North Central region (Minnesota, Iowa, Missouri, North Dakota, South Dakota, Nebraska, Kansas) and the West South Central region (Arkansas, Louisiana, Oklahoma, Texas), had so grown that nearly half of the U.S. population lived in areas that in 1800 and mainly even in 1820 contained only negligible numbers.

With settled constitutional and legal systems, secure property rights, land settlement laws uniformly applied, no significant internal shocks (wars, revolutions) to the economic system, and population growth mainly based upon natural increase, there would seem to have been conditions for more or less steady westward expansion. *Such was not the case.* The expansion and sales of lands came before 1860 in three waves centered on the dates 1818, 1836, and 1854–1855. Land sales from 1800 to 1860 are plotted in Figure 5.4.

Here we meet, for the first time in this book, the phenomenon in American history known as the **business cycle**, the recurrence of upswings and downswings in economic activity. Before 1860, three strong peaks had occurred—in 1818, 1836, and 1854–1855—with monetary crises followed by depressions in 1819, 1837, and 1857. Minor cycles producing no major monetary crises had also occurred before the Civil

TABLE 5.1 Regional Populations 1800–1860

Colonies	*1800*	*1820*	*1840*	*1860*
Old Areas				
New England	1.2	1.7	2.2	3.1
Middle Atlantic	1.4	2.7	4.5	7.5
South Atlantic	2.3	3.1	3.9	5.4
Total	4.9	7.5	10.6	16.0
New Areas				
East North Central	0.0	0.8	2.9	6.9
West North Central	0.0	0.0	0.4	2.2
East South Central	0.3	1.2	2.6	4.0
West South Central	0.0	0.2	0.4	1.7
Mountain	—	—	—	0.2
Pacific	—	—	—	0.4
Total	0.3	2.2	6.3	15.4

Note: Population figures are in millions of persons.

Source: *Historical Statistics,* series A 195.

TABLE 5.2 Land Sales Around Three Peaks

Year	*Acreage*	*Year*	*Acreage*	*Year*	*Acreage*
1815	1.3	**1833**	3.9	**1851**	2.1
1816	1.7	**1834**	4.7	**1852**	0.9
1817	1.9	**1835**	12.6	**1853**	3.8
1818	3.5	**1836**	20.1	**1854**	12.8
1819	3.0	**1837**	5.6	**1855**	12.0
1820	0.8	**1838**	3.4	**1856**	5.2
1821	0.8	**1839**	5.0	**1857**	4.2

Note: Acreage figures are in millions of acres.

Source: *Historical Statistics,* series J 20.

FIGURE 5.4 Public Land Sales and Farm Products Prices 1800–1860

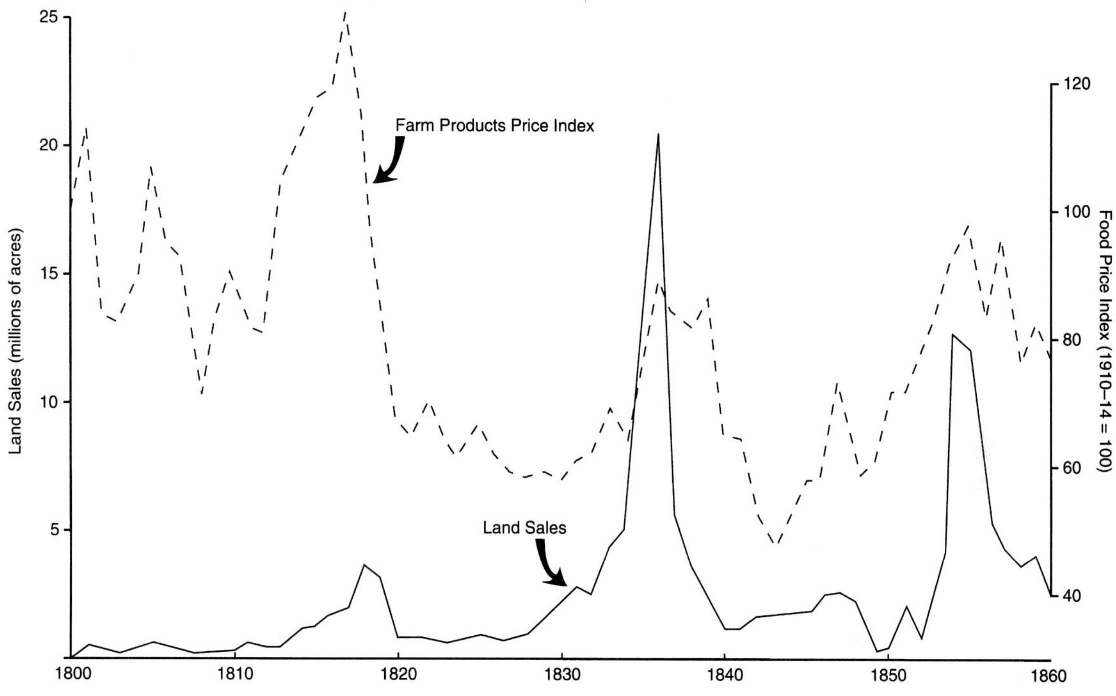

Source: *Historical Statistics,* series E53, J20.

There was a (rough) correspondence before 1860 between westward surges of settlement and rising agricultural prices. The correspondence is especially marked in the mid-1830s and mid-1850s by sales of public lands and the index of food prices. Before 1815, westward movement was blocked by disputed claims to the western lands, lack of government land sale surveys and offices, and hostile Indian tribes.

War. In 1818, 1836, and 1854–1855, the upswings in land sales were dramatic. Note the data in Table 5.2.

Several obvious explanations for this pattern spring to mind. Since the demand for land is to some extent (apart from "land hunger") derived from the prices of its products, we would expect some correlation between movements in food prices and sales of land. Such was the case in 1836 and 1854, as we see in Figure 5.4, but only in an unconvincing way; the magnitude of increases in land sales was out of all proportion to price changes and, of course, in 1818, the relationship did not hold at all.

People need land, but the only source of *variation* in population growth that might be sudden and large (like the increases in land sales) is immigration. Immigration was not important relative to land sales before or after the Irish and Germans came in the late 1840s and early 1850s because these groups stayed mainly in the cities. There is no evidence that their arrival pushed others out onto the public domain. Land availability increased with improved transportation—internal improvements like roads, canals, and railroads—but these improvements were not in the right locations or timed correctly to account for the sudden huge changes in western land sales. Expenditures on canals, roads, and railroads occurred in years when there were no upsurges in land sales; thus, even though they no doubt supported the expansions of activity that underlay the booms in land sales, such expenditures could not have been the cause of the booms.[26]

Arthur Cole, examining all these phenomena in a famous study published in 1927, concluded that speculation was the cause.[27] He noted, using monthly and quarterly data, that increased sales of land *preceded* the boom increases in commodity prices and other evidences of economic activity, and that land sales also started their declines *before* the general downturns in economic activity in 1819, 1837, and 1857. Surviving eyewitness accounts of these episodes certainly support Cole's conclusions. Whole town sites were laid out overnight in the wilderness, some of which never developed; the streets were thronged with buyers one year and were empty the next. Harriet Martineau was in Chicago in 1836 just as it was rising from the muck at the junction of the Chicago River and Lake Michigan.

> I never saw a busier place than Chicago was at the time of our arrival..... The streets were crowded with land speculators, hurrying from one sale to another. A negro dressed up in scarlet, bearing a scarlet flag, and riding a white horse with housings in scarlet, announced the times of sale.... As the gentlemen of our party walked the streets, store-keepers hailed them from their doors with offers of farms, and all manner of landlots, advising them to speculate before the price of land rose higher.[28]

One hopes that someone in her party seized the opportunity, Chicago real estate being what it is now. But what of Allegan, Michigan, a tract of 20,000 acres on the Kalamazoo River, all laid out in town lots and ready to go? A survivor of that fiasco, George C. Bates, later wrote:

> You were not old enough to appreciate the different phases of the inflation, beginning with a gentle breeze in 1834, increasing to a gale in 1835, to a storm in 1836, to a change of wind and an adverse tornado in 1837, leaving wrecks on every hand, succeeded by a dead calm which lasted up to 1844....[29]

The pattern of land sales—borrowing and spending money (debt creation)—was part of the overall cycle in business activity. As we shall see, of the many contributing causes to business cycles, no single force has ever been isolated and agreed upon among economists, except perhaps among the monetarists, economists who see the behavior of the stock of money as an important determinant of macroeconomic activity. Nor has the *periodicity*, the timing of business cycles, ever been satisfactorily explained. The business cycle is a nuisance, but it happens and cannot be rubbed out of economic history just because it inconveniently cannot be explained. Observers all agree that economic growth in unregulated capitalist economies occurs in cycles of expansion and contraction around a rising trend.

Thus, in conclusion, we are left with the fact that although constitutional, legal, and demographic factors laid the groundwork for a steady absorption of the public domain into private hands as the nation grew and spread westward, and, although actual settlement followed this pattern of slow but constant spread, the pattern of land sales actually was markedly cyclical. We will meet the problem of the business cycle again and again, intertwined in nearly all social, political, and economic issues in the growing economy. In the twentieth century, the modern welfare state developed partly as a defense against this force. It is an interesting historical and social fact that the business cycle appeared so early and with such power in our history in something so fundamental as the private occupation of the public domain. Because our land tenure made land into a commodity, for sale like any other commodity, the forces of commercial growth, in cycles, could and did reach it.

NOTES

1. James Madison, *Documents Illustrative of the Formation of the Union of the American States* (Washington, D.C.: Government Printing Office, 1927).
2. Charles A. Beard, *An Economic Interpretation of the Constitution* (1935).
3. Robert McGuire and Robert Ohsfeldt, "An Economic Model of Voting Behavior at the Constitutional Convention of 1787," *JEH*, March 1986. McGuire and Ohsfeldt report similar voting behavior at the state ratifying conventions in "Self-Interest, Agency Theory, and Political Voting Behavior: The Ratification of the United States Constitution," *AER*, March 1989.
4. McGuire and Ohsfeldt (1986), p. 110.
5. *Robinson v. Campbell*, 3 Wheaton 212 (1818).
6. "Metes and bounds" is a system for identifying land that makes use of more or less permanent natural objects such as creeks, trees, and rocks.
7. Quoted in Marshall Harris, *Origin of the Land Tenure System in the United States* (Westport, CT: Greenwood Press, 1970), p. 389.
8. "The Ordinance of 1784 and Jefferson's Services for the Northwest Territory," *Old South Leaflets*, vol. 6, no. 127, Boston: The Directors of the Old South Work, Old South Meeting-house, 1905, p. 23.
9. The ten states Jefferson proposed all had classical names and reasonably complete boundaries. The present city of Chicago, for example, was to be included in the state of Assenisipia, the area "thro' which the Assenisipi or Rock river runs." Directly to the east, and with the same northern and southern boundaries, was the state of Metropotamia, "in which are the fountains of the Muskingum, the Miamis of Ohio, the Wabash, the Illinois, the Miami of the lake and Sandusky rivers." See Louis Cain, "Carving the Northwest Territory into States," in Joel Mokyr, ed., *The Vital One: Essays in Honor of Jonathan R. T. Hughes* (1991), p. 156.
10. Monroe also offered a second reason for reducing the number of new states: "A great part of the territory is miserably poor, especially that near lakes Michigan and Erie and that upon the Mississippi and the Illinois consists of extensive plains which have not had from appearance and will not have a single bush on them, for ages. The districts therefore within which these fall will perhaps never contain a sufficient number of inhabitants to entitle them to membership in the confederacy...". Quoted in *Ibid.*
11. A total of some 9.5 million acres of public land was reserved for veterans of the Revolution and their descendants. The last land warrant for the Revolution was taken out in 1886, over a century after independence. Jerry O'Callaghan, "The War Veteran and the Public Lands," in Vernon Carstensen, *The Public Lands* (1962), p. 112. The vets could, and did, sell their claims to others for cash.
12. "Entailment" limited which line of heirs could inherit property.
13. Marylynn Salmon, *Women and the Law of Property in Early America* (Chapel Hill: University of North Carolina Press, 1986), p. 190. While those changes were important for daughters, she notes that South Carolina adopted an intestacy statute that made wives more nearly the equal of husbands with respect to inheritance.
14. This is not to argue that each new state was a carbon copy of the last. Each state negotiated a separate deal with Congress. Paul Gates, *History of Public Land Law Development* (1968) provides an interesting discussion of the differences.
15. Jonathan Hughes, "The Great Land Ordinances: America's Thumbprint on History," in David C. Klingaman and Richard K. Vedder, eds., *Essays on the Economy of the Old Northwest* (1987).
16. Carstensen (1962), p. xviii.
17. Malcolm Rohrbough, *The Land Office Business* (1968), pp. 245–246.
18. David Wishart, "Evidence of Surplus Production in the Cherokee Nation Prior to Removal," *JEH*, March 1995, argues one reason for the removal was the existence of significant economic rents that could be captured by whites. Wishart is one of a number of authors that contributed to Linda Barrington, ed., *The Other Side of the Frontier: Economic Explorations into Native American History (*Boulder, CO; Westview Press, 1998).
19. Mark Kanazawa, "Possession is Nine Points of the Law: The Political Economy of Early Public Land Disposal," *EEH*, April 1996, discusses the role squatters played in public land policy formation up to the 1830 preemption act. He also presents an analysis of the Congressional vote on the act.
20. For a study of the imperfect results of the 1841 act in the hands of speculators in frontier lands who managed to acquire lands far in excess of 160 acres, see Allan Bogue, "The Iowa Claim Clubs: Symbol and Substance," *Mississippi Valley Historical Review*, 1958, reprinted in Carstensen (1962).
21. Douglas W. Allen, "Homesteading and Property Rights: or, 'How the West was Really Won,'" *Journal of Law and Economics*, April 1991.
22. Lance E. Davis, personal communication. Since "equitable distribution" of stolen goods among the thieves is a

matter of pure fancy, the country was benefited by getting quickly past the act.

23. Stanley Lebergott, "The Demand for Land: The United States, 1820–1860," *JEH*, June 1985. Jeremy Atack and Fred Bateman, *To Their Own Soil* (1987), pp. 7–10, also note this perverse consequence of continuous releases of new land into the market by the government's policy; rents—income from working land—derived from "eastern lands" were reduced accordingly, and transferred west.
24. Carstensen (1962), p. xxvi.
25. An interesting study on this issue is Susan E. Gray, *The Yankee West: Community Life on the Michigan Frontier* (Chapel Hill: University of North Carolina Press, 1997).
26. Carter Goodrich, Julius Rubin, Jerome Cranmer, and Harvey Segal, *Canals and American Economic Development* (New York: Columbia University Press, 1961).
27. Arthur Cole, "Cyclical and Sectional Variations in the Sale of Public Lands, 1816–1860," *REStat*, 1927; and Paul W. Gates, "The Role of the Land Speculator in Western Development," *Pennsylvania Magazine of History and Biography*, 1942, both reprinted in Carstensen (1962). Gates shows the various roles, virtuous and deplorable, of the frontier professional land speculator.
28. Quoted in Rohrbough, *The Land Office Business* (1968), p. 240.
29. Quoted in *Ibid.*, p. 243.

SUGGESTED READINGS

Articles

Allen, Douglas W. "Homesteading and Property Rights; or, 'How the West was Really Won.'" *Journal of Law and Economics*, vol. XXXIV, no. 4, April 1991.

Billington, Ray A. "The Origin of the Land Speculator as a Frontier Type." *Agricultural History*, vol. XIX, no. 4, October 1945.

Bogue, Allan G. "The Iowa Claim Clubs: Symbol and Substance." *Mississippi Valley Historical Review*, vol. 45, no. 2, September 1958, reprinted in Carstensen, *The Public Lands* (1962).

Cain, Louis P. "Carving the Northwest Territory into States." In Joel Mokyr, ed., *The Vital One: Essays in Honor of Jonathan R. T. Hughes*. Greenwich, CT: JAI Press, 1991.

Cole, Arthur H. "Cyclical and Sectional Variations in the Sale of the Public Lands, 1816–1860." *Review of Economics and Statistics*, vol. 9, no. 1, January 1927, reprinted in Carstensen, *The Public Lands* (1962).

Gates, Paul W. "The Role of the Land Speculator in Western Development." *Pennsylvania Magazine of History and Biography*, vol. LXVI, 1942, reprinted in Carstensen, *The Public Lands* (1962).

———. "Charts of Public Land Sales and Entries." *Journal of Economic History*, vol. XXIV, no. 1, March 1964.

Hughes, Jonathan. "The Great Land Ordinances: America's Thumbprint on History." In David C. Klingaman and Richard K. Vedder, eds., *Essays on the Economy of the Old Northwest*. Athens: Ohio University Press, 1987.

Kanazawa, Mark T. "Possession Is Nine Points of the Law: The Political Economy of Early Public Land Disposal." *Explorations in Economic History*, vol. 33, no. 2, April 1996.

Lebergott, Stanley. "The Demand for Land: The United States, 1820–1860." *Journal of Economic History*, vol. XLV, no. 2, June 1985.

McGuire, Robert A., and Robert L. Ohsfeldt.. "An Economic Model of Voting Behavior at the Constitutional Convention of 1787." *Journal of Economic History*, vol. XLVI, no. 1, March 1986.

———. "Self-Interest, Agency Theory, and Political Voting Behavior: The Ratification of the United States Constitution." *American Economic Review*, vol. 79, no. 1, March 1989.

O'Callaghan, Jerry A. "The War Veteran and the Public Lands." *Agricultural History*, vol. 28, no. 4, October 1954, reprinted in Carstensen, *The Public Lands* (1962).

Treat, Payson Jackson. "Origin of the National Land System Under the Confederation." *American Historical Association Report, 1905*, reprinted in Carstensen, *The Public Lands* (1962).

Wishart, David M. "Evidence of Surplus Production in the Cherokee Nation Prior to Removal." *Journal of Economic History*, vol. 55, no. 1, March 1995.

Books

Atack, Jeremy, and Fred Bateman. *To Their Own Soil: Agriculture in the Antebellum North*. Ames: Iowa State University Press, 1987.

Beard, Charles A. *An Economic Interpretation of the Constitution*. New York: Macmillan Company, 1913.

Carstensen, Vernon, ed. *The Public Lands: Studies in the History of the Public Domain*. Madison: University of Wisconsin Press, 1962.

Gates, Paul W. *History of Public Land Law Development*. Washington, D.C.: Public Land Law Review Commission, 1968.

Rohrbough, Malcolm. *The Land Office Business: The Settlement and Administration of American Public Lands, 1789–1837*. New York: Oxford University Press, 1968.

Turner, Frederick Jackson. *The Frontier in American History*. New York: Holt, Rinehart, Winston, 1921.

CHAPTER SIX

Population and Labor Force

Two major trends and characteristics of American population growth that we saw in colonial times continued from independence to the Civil War: (a) growth was very rapid; and (b) populations living in urban places increased, even though this was a period of extensive settlement in the open country. Additionally, a massive change in the sources of immigration occurred. In 1860, there were more than 4 million persons living here who had been born in Europe, a figure nearly equal to the nonwhite population. The proportion of European-born had more than doubled since 1790, and the proportion of nonwhites had fallen by a fourth. This change was the inevitable result of the end of the legal Atlantic slave trade in 1808 and the expansion of free European immigration. Birth rates were beginning their secular decline in all parts of the population, as was the size of the average family. The processes that would produce major twentieth-century population characteristics (such as smaller families) were already apparent.

SIZE AND NATURAL INCREASE

Major population data are given by census years in Table 6.1. This table shows the total population as well as the percentage of white and nonwhite. It also shows the percentage living in urban areas. By 1860, the population of the United States exceeded that of the United Kingdom, and the white population exceeded that of England and Wales. Of the European countries, only France and Russia had populations larger than ours (German-speaking central Europe was still divided into many small states). The rate of population growth after 1790 continued at about 3.3 percent per annum, compounded, doubling roughly every 23 years, about the same rate as that during the latter part of the colonial era. After the Civil War, the rate slowed even though the absolute increases became very large. Prior to 1860, no European nation sustained such an increase. According to Richard Easterlin, one leading scholar of the subject,

TABLE 6.1 Basic Population Data, 1790–1860

	Total[a]	*White*	*Nonwhite*	*Urban*
1790	3.9	82.1%	17.9%	5.2%
1800	5.3	81.1	18.9	6.1
1810	7.2	81.9	18.1	7.3
1820	9.6	82.3	17.7	7.2
1830	12.9	81.4	18.6	8.7
1840	17.1	83.0	17.0	10.8
1850	23.2	84.5	15.5	15.3
1860	31.4	85.7	14.3	19.8

[a]The total is in millions of persons.

Source: *Historical Statistics,* series A2, 57–72, 91–99.

no European country maintained half our overall population growth rate. Since the evidence indicates that American death rates were comparable to those in Europe, the primary causes of the powerful growth of population had to be immigration and a (continuing) high birth rate.[1]

Data on birth rates before the mid-nineteenth century are still fairly conjectural. Available evidence points to a birth rate of perhaps 55 per 1,000 per annum in the early nineteenth century (compared to 30 per 1,000 in 1910 and a mere 15.7 per 1,000 in 1993). The data indicate a slow but steady decline thereafter, down to 41.4 per 1,000 in 1860. There are several reasons for the high fertility of the early population. First, of course, is the fact that more than half of the population were at ages where fertility is high. The median age of the population in 1790 was only 15.9 years, and even in 1860 it was 19.4 years (compared to 35.7 and climbing in 2000, the highest in our history). In 1820, when the nation began its westward movement in earnest, the median American was less than 17 years old. In a sense, we were a nation of teenagers—and younger.

Economic historians have argued that plentiful, relatively inexpensive land (and the opportunity to own it) lay at the root of our high fertility.[2] A nation composed mainly of farmers and people planning to farm, in the presence of a vast quantity of empty land, had every reason to create large families. There was the labor of the young while they remained at home and the hope of their settling nearby after they left home to create families of their own. The availability of land at a time when most of the country was rural (and technological change in agriculture had not yet impressively raised productivity) was undoubtedly a main basis for expectations about the future. Available land was prospective family income. Although it may seem difficult to credit Americans in the early nineteenth century with such extraordinary sensitivity to their environment, this apparently was the case.

Urban dwellers were not farmers. Why should they have been so sensitized to land availability (or the lack of it, in their case)? The differences between urban and rural birth rates and family sizes are very impressive (see Table 6.2); thus there must have been other factors at work. Was it really more difficult to raise a family in a town than in the country? If so, why were towns growing so rapidly in number and population when so much good and cheap land was available? One answer is that children can be considered **durable goods** (like refrigerators or cars in our time) upon which consumers might spend money. There were more options in towns, more ways to spend money than in the countryside; accordingly, urban families were smaller. A second answer is that children can be considered **investment goods** (like plant and equipment) that can be used to produce revenue. Given that they could do chores at a relatively early age on the farm, such as help grow their own food (an option largely denied to urban children), the rate of return on a child born

TABLE 6.2 Number of Children Under 5 Years of Age per 1000 Women 20–44 Years of Age, 1810, 1840, and 1860

	Total				Percent
	1810	*1840*	*1860*	*Ratio 1860/1810*	*Urban of Rural 1840*
Northeast	1052	752	622	0.591	78.7
Middle Atlantic	1289	940	767	0.595	75.6
East North Central	1702	1270	999	0.587	66.2
West North Central	1810	1445	1105	0.610	48.8
South Atlantic	1325	1140	918	0.693	67.5
East South Central	1700	1408	1039	0.611	61.0
West South Central	1383	1297	1084	0.784	65.2
Mountain			1051		
Pacific			1026		
Total United States	*1290*	*1070*	*886*	*0.687*	*65.5*

Source: *Historical Statistics,* series B67–98.

to a farm family should be greater; accordingly, rural families were larger.

Data on the number of young children tend to verify these findings. In each case in Table 6.2, the number of children under the age of 5 per 1,000 women in the childbearing years (a proxy for birth rates and family size) is significantly smaller in settled than in frontier areas, smaller in urban areas than in rural. Note in particular the Mountain and Pacific regions, where new land was acquired after 1848.[3] The age of females at first marriage rose throughout the nineteenth century, and this also tended to reduce fertility rates.[4] From what is known, it appears that trends in fertility rates (but not absolute levels) among blacks, both slave and free, were roughly the same as among whites.[5] After 1860, when better data are available, the same trends continue; both birth and death rates fall and so do family sizes, on average.

Using data from northern family farms in 1860, Lee Craig estimated a dollar value for the household labor of various types of family members; they are reported in Table 6.3. The value of an adult male between the ages of 19 and 54 is reported in the top line; those of other family members are reported as a percentage of that amount. Craig's estimates are consistent with what is known about the division of labor on northern farms.[6] Field work was generally the responsibility of men, while women and children performed tasks closer to the house and garden:

> A field hand during harvest consumed around 4,000 calories a day from three full meals and two "lunches" (one before and one after a midday dinner). The farm wife and any children, particularly teenage daughters, or hired domestic help she may have had available often served the midday meals in the field. Since the preparation, delivery, and cleanup of these meals involved a considerable amount of time, it paid the family to have one group specialize in field work while another focused on domestic production.[7]

This is not to say that women and children could not, or did not, do field work. They were more likely to work in the fields (or to participate in land-clearing activities) in less settled areas where labor was relatively scarce.

Craig's results suggest that, on average, the value of women's labor (excluding the value of domestic production and housework) was about two-thirds that of adult men; those in the Midwest, however, were below two-fifths.[8] Children and teenage girls did not contribute much, but their contribution was greatest in the Midwest (roughly half that of their mothers). Midwestern teenagers of both sexes were more frequently involved in market-production and land-clearing than in the Northeast, where boys were more likely to specialize in market- and girls in household-production. Thus, the lower value for Midwestern women is in part attributable to their having to substitute for their teenage daughters. It is also attributable to the fact that they were more fertile; the average Midwestern farm wife could expect to give birth to almost half again as many babies as one in the Northeast.[9]

Something as important as the long-term fertility decline deserves a believable explanation. Why should the birth rate be in *any* way related to available arable

TABLE 6.3 Dollar Value of Household Labor in Northern Agriculture, 1860

	North	*Northeast*	*Midwest*	*Frontier*
Adult males (age 19–54)	$229.09	$294.77	$186.44	$193.66
Children (0–6)	−8.6%	−7.1%	4.6%	−3.3%
Children (7–12)	7.2	7.7	14.9	14.0
Teenage females	9.6	7.8	21.3	9.1
Teenage males	25.5	37.7	25.5	25.3
Adult females	66.6	52.3	37.7	76.1
Adult males (age 55 and up)	76.7	49.5	65.4	69.9

Northeast: townships in Connecticut, New Hampshire, New Jersey, New York, Pennsylvania, and Vermont.
Midwest: townships in Illinois, Indiana, Ohio, southern Michigan, and Wisconsin.
Frontier: townships in Iowa, Kansas, Minnesota, northern Michigan, and Wisconsin.

Source: Lee A. Craig, *To Sow One Acre More* (Baltimore: The Johns Hopkins University Press, 1993), Table 4.2, p. 80.

land? The answer is that parents had a bequest motive, either a "strategic" or a "targeted" bequest.

Targeted bequests were altruistic; at the time their children left home to start a household, parents chose to give their children an amount at least equal to what they received from their parents. Easterlin noted that this practice would lead to declining fertility rates in settled areas because, in such areas, the high and rising relative price of good farm land increased the price of bequests and reduced the demand for extra children. In newer areas, on the other hand, the relative price of land was lower, making it easier for parents to provide for their children.[10]

Strategic bequests were an incentive for children to behave in a certain way or to supply a particular set of goods and services. As Craig notes:

> Parents view children as a source of income while children remain in the household and as a source of financial security once they grow up and the parents reach old age. Children view their parents as providers of an endowment or bequest, the cost of which is the provision of farm labor while young and possibly old age care for parents later.[11]

Strategic bequests lead to decreasing fertility rates in more settled areas because settlement increases the number of non-farm alternatives, which increases the children's bargaining power.

Paul David and William Sundstrom offer a "life cycle" explanation stressing strategic bequests. Suppose, they argue, that large families were designed to be old-age insurance for the parents. Again, the growing shortage of arable land could be associated with a declining fertility rate. At the time the country gained its independence, the superabundance of arable land meant that land already owned (by the parents) would not rise in price over time sufficient to be a nest egg for old age, and children would, or could, be induced to care for their aged parents. When, late in the nineteenth century, the best lands were growing scarce, then the rent, and therefore the price, of land already owned and settled would increase; it became a nest egg due to its capital gain. Thus, one invested in land as a substitute for more children. The scarcer the land, the higher the economic rent and capital gain, and the fewer children needed to provide for the declining years of the parents.[12]

IMMIGRATION BEFORE 1860

A second source of population increase, of course, was immigration. After independence, immigration continued to be unrestricted and remained so until after the Civil War. Scholars in the past 25 years have raised new and intriguing questions about this massive migration of human beings and what it meant to the economic growth and development of the United States.

The Data

First, we should note that we are speaking only of immigrants about whom some quantifiable evidence remains. We shall never know what the unrecorded flow was across the Canadian and Mexican borders, although literary evidence indicates it was considerable. There is also the question of continued slave cargoes landed after the end of legal imports in 1808. There is no doubt that slave imports continued illegally, but they were apparently very limited in number. The British vigorously suppressed the Atlantic slave trade after 1820, and shipments to the United States, although they continued, were reduced to a trickle. The evidence put together by scholars indicates that imports of slaves after the American Revolution (nearly all of them before 1808), along with their American descendants, may have added from a third to a half of the total nonwhite population.[13] It is estimated that by 1860, 99 percent of America's black population was native and, of course, had *mainly* colonial ancestors. In fact, by 1860, a higher percentage of blacks than of whites were native.[14] The contribution of immigration to population increases up to 1860 is shown by decades in Table 6.4.

Before the decade of the 1830s, immigration was a relatively minor source of population increase. It then expanded rapidly, and the increase built steadily. The annual average number of immigrants in the period 1821–1825 was 8,000; in 1826–1830 it was up to 20,587. In the next five years, 1831–1835, it rose to 50,498, then to 69,330 between 1836 and 1840. By 1841–1845, the expansion had grown to an average of 86,067 per year. At that point in history, a series of poor harvests and the failure of the potato crop in northern Europe disrupted European society and produced the first real deluge of immigrants—1.4 million between 1845 and 1850, a portent of those to come. During the

TABLE 6.4 Net Immigration as a Percentage of Population Increases, 1800–1860

Years	*Percentage of Increase by Decade*
1800–1810	3.3
1810–1820	2.6
1820–1830	3.8
1830–1840	11.7
1840–1850	23.3
1850–1860	31.1

Source: Calculated from Richard Easterlin, "The American Population," Lance E. Davis et al., *American Economic Growth: An Economist's History of the United States* (New York: Harper & Row, 1972). Table 6.1.

next seven years, there was an enormous immigration of 2.2 million from Europe. The major features of this wave of immigration are shown in Table 6.5.

The first upsurge came from the British Isles. The British government proved itself utterly indifferent to the famine in Ireland, and Joel Mokyr estimates that more than 1 million died in the late 1840s as a result.[15] Those who could fled the Emerald Isle, either to other parts of the United Kingdom, to Canada, or the United States. In the ten years 1846–1855 inclusive, nearly 1.3 million Irish are known to have immigrated into the United States. Uncounted additional thousands entered the country from Canada. During the same decade, the German-speaking regions of Europe produced nearly 1 million immigrants to the United States. Political upheavals in 1848 contributed some famous names to this flow (for example, Carl Schurz, later U.S. Senator from Missouri). However, most of this migration was due to harvest failures, as indicated by the fact that the flow from Scandinavia and other countries in northern Europe more than doubled before the wave died down at the end of the 1850s.

Table 6.6 shows the proportions of this flow by countries of origin. Note that the United Kingdom's share (column 5) is more than 50 percent of the total in every year save 1846 and 1854. Note also that Ireland and Germany together (column 6) normally accounted for 65 to75 percent of total immigration. The ordinary share of just three countries in these years (column 7) was from 79.4 to more than 90 per-

TABLE 6.5 Immigration 1845–1860 by Origin[a]

Year	*Total*	*Great Britain*	*Ireland*	*Scandinavia*	*Other Northwestern Europe*	*Germany*
1845	114.4	19.2	44.8	1.0	9.5	34.4
1846	154.4	22.2	51.8	2.0	12.3	57.6
1847	235.0	23.3	105.5	1.3	24.3	74.3
1848	226.5	35.2	112.9	1.1	9.9	58.5
1849	297.0	55.1	159.4	3.5	7.6	60.2
1850	370.0	51.1	164.0	1.6	11.5	78.9
1851	379.5	51.5	221.3	2.4	20.9	72.5
1852	371.6	40.7	159.5	4.1	11.3	145.9
1853	368.6	37.6	162.6	3.4	14.2	141.9
1854	427.8	58.6	101.6	4.2	23.1	215.0
1855	200.9	47.6	49.6	1.3	14.6	71.9
1856	200.4	44.7	54.3	1.3	12.4	71.0
1857	251.3	58.3	54.4	2.7	6.9	91.8
1858	123.1	29.0	26.9	2.7	4.6	45.3
1859	121.3	26.2	35.2	1.6	3.7	41.8
1860	153.6	29.7	48.6	0.8	5.3	54.5

[a] Counts are in thousands of persons.

Source: *Historical Statistics,* series C 89–119.

cent. Other northern European nations accounted for most of the remaining immigration.

Based upon what we know of the colonial white population, which was mostly English- and German-speaking peoples (see Chapter 3), these immigrants should have been received congenially in America. But nativism resulted, as the anti-slave, anti-Catholic, anti-immigrant Know-Nothings—members of a secret society whose main goal was to prevent "foreigners" from gaining political power—demanded a 21-year residency requirement for naturalization in the 1850s. Indeed, in a recent article, Raymond Cohn argues that the downturn in the immigration cycle beginning in the mid–1850s is attributable to the rise of the nativist movement.[16]

The main bone of contention in the 1850s was religion. With the influx of the Irish and the Rhineland Germans, the old nonconformist Protestant sects of the United States were about to be swamped by Roman Catholicism. There was talk that the nation would fall to the legions of Rome. Later, when the countries of origin were Italy, Greece, and those of eastern Europe, the talk became straight racism. By then, the children of the Irish and German immigrants had joined the native white Americans in demanding an end to the flow of people from southern and eastern Europe.

Ferrie's "Yankeys"

Joseph Ferrie's study of these immigrants, *Yankeys Now*, is illuminating.[17] Linking the records of passenger ships arriving in New York City in the 1840s with the manuscript schedules of the 1850 and 1860 federal population censuses, Ferrie compares a sample of 2,594 European immigrants with a sample of native residents linked from the 1850 census to the 1860 census. Although all those in the immigrant sample disembarked in New York City, approximately two-thirds immediately headed elsewhere. More than half went to the states of New York, Ohio, and Pennsylvania alone. In percentage terms, more immigrants than natives were found in urban areas.

The immigrants were more mobile geographically than natives: Almost 70 percent of the immigrant

TABLE 6.6 Proportional Immigration, 1845–1860[a]

	(1)	(2)	(3)	(4)	(5)	(6)	(7)
Year	*Great Britain*	*Ireland*	*Germany*	*All Other*	*Columns 1 + 2*	*Columns 2 + 3*	*Columns 1 + 2 + 3*
1845	16.8	39.2	30.1	13.9	56.0	69.3	86.1
1846	14.4	33.5	37.3	14.8	47.9	70.8	85.2
1847	9.9	44.9	31.6	13.6	54.8	76.5	86.4
1848	15.5	49.8	25.8	8.9	65.3	75.6	91.1
1849	18.6	53.7	20.3	7.4	72.3	74.0	92.6
1850	13.8	44.3	21.3	20.6	58.1	65.6	79.4
1851	13.6	58.3	19.1	9.0	71.9	77.4	91.0
1852	11.0	42.9	39.3	6.8	53.9	82.2	93.2
1853	10.2	44.1	38.5	7.2	54.3	82.6	92.8
1854	13.7	23.7	50.3	12.3	37.4	74.0	87.7
1855	23.7	24.7	35.8	15.8	48.4	60.5	84.2
1856	22.3	27.1	35.4	15.2	49.4	62.5	84.8
1857	23.3	21.6	36.5	18.6	44.9	58.1	81.4
1858	23.6	21.9	36.8	17.7	45.5	58.7	82.3
1859	21.6	29.0	34.5	14.9	50.6	63.5	85.1
1860	19.3	31.6	35.5	13.6	50.9	67.1	86.4

[a] Figures are percentages of total immigration, 1845–1860.

Source: Calculated from *Historical Statistics*, series C 89–119.

sample changed counties at some time between the 1850 and 1860 censuses, compared to 43 percent of the native population. They were also mobile occupationally. For the Germans and Irish in the sample, most of the mobility was observable immediately; their occupations changed little as their time in the United States increased. In the Ferrie sample, relatively more British and Germans were upwardly mobile than Irish; relatively fewer were downwardly mobile than Irish.

As time passed, the immigrants accumulated wealth. Ferrie estimates wealth increased at an annual average of nearly 15 percent among the most recent arrivals, and that wealth grew with time in the United States during an immigrant's first 20 years there. Those who migrated to specific, fast-growing, local economies in the western states fared better than most. In particular, those who settled and remained in rising western cities such as Milwaukee and St. Louis were, by 1860, several times wealthier than those who remained in the east.[18]

Origins of the Atlantic Migration

The data in Table 6.5 record the first great migratory wave from Europe in the nineteenth century. More such waves would come. Between 1815 and 1914, an estimated 50 million persons emigrated out of Europe, and some 35 million were destined to come to the United States. Why? Brinley Thomas, in his book *Migration and Economic Growth*, fashioned an elegant explanation based upon European population growth, occupational and class rigidities in Europe ("noncompeting groups"), the 18- to 20-year "long wave" cycles in such activities as investment and house-building, free trade, free migration, and foreign investment.[19] His thesis will be discussed in some detail in Chapter 16, but it is worth pausing and considering for a moment now because we have just seen the basic anatomy of the first of his cycles. He measured four major pre–1914 waves of Atlantic migration; the last one ended by the outbreak of World War I. The dates of the long waves, trough to trough, are 1844 to 1861, 1862 to 1877, 1879 to 1897, and 1898 to 1914.

Suffice it to say at this point that a combination of "push" from Europe (harvest failures) and "pull" from the United States (an expanding economy—recall the land-sales data for the 1850s) in the presence of a continuously growing European population explains the wave of migration between 1844 and 1861. In Europe, it meant fewer mouths to feed. What did it mean in the United States?

The Walker and Uselding-Neal Theses

Again, we shall anticipate Chapter 16 for a moment to consider briefly the thesis of Francis Walker—economist, statistician, and president of MIT. In the late nineteenth century, Walker put forward the thesis that, given American conditions, there was some maximum rate of population growth. Therefore, each European immigrant filled a place that would otherwise have been occupied by a native American. Other things being equal, each European immigrant meant one less native American into the population.

Paul Uselding countered with two proposals, that: (a) the maximum growth rate never existed, and (b) each European immigrant represented a capital transfer from Europe to America essentially equal to the cost of raising the migrant to the age of migration.[20] Since the immigrants were mainly young males ready to enter directly into the labor force, they were Europe's "gift" to American economic growth. America got the benefit without paying the cost.

Uselding traced the idea to the Italian statistician Augostino De Vita, who argued that the great stock of capital characteristic of the American economy by 1914 was no more than the accumulated cost of rearing, feeding, educating, and transporting the millions of European migrants to the United States. The Atlantic migration had thus "freed" American resources to build the capital equipment these immigrants used in their work here, enabling the United States to pull ahead of the Europeans economically.

Uselding did not accept De Vita's bold conclusions, but pursued the basic idea with several complex econometric models, using the known data concerning immigration from 1839 to 1859. He concluded that, by 1859, the additional capital formation due to immigration was within the range of 5 to 10 percent of the GNP. Larry Neal joined him in the effort, and, in 1972, they published a paper carrying the calculations from 1790 to 1912, concluding that the additional capital stock created by immigration was in the range of 10 to 20 percent of GNP by the end of the period.[21] It thus was true, they argued, that the American economy grew faster than it otherwise would have grown because of the immigration.

Not everyone benefited. Ferrie's work indicates that the arrival of immigrants during the 1850s, Irish immigrants in particular, had a negative impact on native craft workers. This seems to be a result of the fact that the highest rates of immigration in our history occurred at exactly the same time the economy began to industrialize:

> Though their [the Irish] arrival apparently led to some down-grading of native skilled workers, they may have also paved the way for less skilled natives to enter factory work as well, by being available just as employers were preparing to change their production processes.[22]

William Lazonick and Thomas Brush suggested these immigrants were more easily "driven" by foremen to greater effort and individual productivity increases than was true of native Americans.[23]

Robert Gallman, in a critical analysis of the Uselding-Neal work, pointed out various plausibilities, including that, by 1860, probably 35 percent of the adult males in the Northern states were foreign-born (he also noted that half the Union army was foreign-born).[24] Gallman added an additional caveat to the Walker thesis: Since most of the immigrants stayed in the cities, the migration of native Americans to urban areas was less rapid than it would have been otherwise. Thus, *the birth rate for native Americans was higher than it would have been* (urban birth rates being so much lower than rural) if the "places" in urban growth had been filled by native Americans.

Richard Easterlin added a number of objections to the Walker thesis. The decline in native American birth rates was more likely due to the end of the frontier, a reduced availability of land, and the acceleration of urbanization, than to any presumed economic competition with European immigrants.

We will return to these issues in Chapter 16 when we have seen the results of the subsequent three "long waves" in European immigration. Prior to 1860, however, according to Uselding and Neal, the positive impact of immigration on U.S. economic growth was already strong.

Destinations of Immigrants Up to 1860

Census returns show that most of the pre–1860 European immigration went to the Northern states. In 1860, of a total population of 31.5 million, 3.6 million foreign-born whites lived in the northeast and east north central states, a mere 391,000 lived in the South. There were 144,000 people in the West, of which 64,000 were individuals of "other races," largely Chinese. Table 6.7 shows the percentages in each region in 1850 and 1860 by place of birth. Proportionately, the big increases in the white foreign-born population appeared in the North and the West. In the South, the proportional increase in the white foreign-born population was relatively small. At this time, the black population was mainly in the South, in agriculture and in slavery. Was there a connection between the continuation of slavery in the South and the lack of significant European immigration there?

TABLE 6.7 U.S. Population: Nativity, 1850 and 1860[a]

Population Segment	*Northeast* 1850	1860	*North Central* 1850	1860	*South* 1850	1860	*West* 1850	1860
Native-born								
White	82.9	79.5	87.1	82.0	60.0	59.7	84.3	70.4
Nonwhite	1.7	1.4	0.9	0.8	37.3	36.8	0.5	0.7
Foreign-born								
White[b]	15.4	19.1	12.0	17.2	2.7	3.5	15.2	28.9

[a] Figures are percentages of regional totals for each census year rounded to the nearest 0.1%.
[b] Less than 0.1% of the foreign-born population was nonwhite.

Source: Calculated from *Historical Statistics,* series A 190–94.

THE END OF WHITE SERVITUDE AND THE CONTINUATION OF BLACK SLAVERY

The additional contribution of European immigration was to hasten the decline of white indentured servitude inherited from the colonial era. Even by the end of that period (1783), white servitude was declining in competition with free wage labor. David Galenson points out that in the free market white skilled workers became able to negotiate wages that were higher than the comparable real income derived from a contract of indenture.[25] Rising demand for labor drove up the price of *nonfree* white labor compared to that of black slaves. The supply of indentured whites was thus more restricted than that of blacks. Slavery continued to grow as white servitude diminished.

Servitude and Competition

In 1787, when the Constitution was being written, white servitude still had to be taken into account. It lingered on for some decades as a social institution, used primarily to bind vagrants and orphans into productive employment and to enforce apprenticeships in trades. Farley Grubb, in a study of German redemptioners, dates the end as coming about 1820.[26] The supply of servants increased for a few years following 1816, "the year without a summer" that devastated European agriculture; more than 300 arrived in Philadelphia each year between 1816 and 1819, when better conditions returned to Europe. Only 18 indentured servants arrived in 1820, and only 19 in total during the following ten years. Most of these were children. Adults found it easier to finance their passage through family and friends in America.

In addition, judges began to refuse to imprison people for debt. If the contract was not recoverable when breached, the contract lost its value. Negotiated wages were more efficient, especially when they were for long periods (up to a year), and any break by the employee before the time was up released the employer from the obligation to pay wages earned to date.[27] Such a contract was pretty much self-enforcing. Of course, the old ancillary obligations of indenture—such as room, board, clothing, medicine, education in a trade, and payment at the end of the indenture—did not apply with hired labor. The steadily increasing flow of free immigrants entering the labor market made white indentures unnecessary, and they slowly vanished.

Christopher Hanes argued that, as indentures disappeared, turnover costs increased, especially for employers who required more labor than their families could supply for more than a few days. Where the costs associated with searching for workers and the costs of going without labor during a critical period were especially high, employers, such as Southern plantation owners, were attracted to slavery as a way of mitigating these costs.[28]

Apprehension About Slavery

Eli Whitney's invention of the cotton gin in 1793 made the short-staple upland cotton grown in the South a new bonanza, and the South's major agricultural labor form—slavery—evolved with cotton cultivation. We will go more deeply into this topic in Chapters 9 and 10. For now, let us note the consequences in terms of overall population trends. For a country that in 1860 was mainly occupied by Europeans, the United States was unusual, if not unique, in having some 13 percent of its total population owned in chattel slavery. However, the whole world benefited economically from that slavery, wherever European or American cotton cloth was bought.

The enslavement of Africans in the United States began in 1619 at Jamestown when a Dutch man-of-war sold the colonists 20 African prisoners. Slave codes developed. Black slaves were made servants for life; their children were born into slavery. By the end of the colonial period, the country was faced with a social, political, and human problem that vexed the best thinkers. With more than a half million slaves in 1780, most of them concentrated in the South, the way out was unclear. George Washington said in 1794 of his own situation as a slave owner: "Were it not then, that I am principled against selling…[slaves] as you would do cattle in the market, I would not, in twelve months from this date be possessed of one, as a slave."[29]

Before Whitney's gin, there was much sentiment in the South against slavery and a belief that it could not last. The decline of the older tobacco-growing regions threatened to produce a surplus of slave labor in those areas. Diversified farming, which used less labor than had tobacco, was spreading. But there also was a deep fear of any change. Straightforward emancipation (unless compensated by taxpayers, as the British would do in 1834) would mean great capital losses to slave owners. There was also the question, unanswered then because it was untried, whether there could be any peaceful future with former slaves settled among their former masters. Jefferson expressed his fears in *Notes on the State of Virginia*:

> Deep rooted prejudice entertained by the whites; ten thousand recollections by the blacks, of the injuries they have sustained; new provocations; the real distinctions which nature has made; and many other circumstances, will divide us into parties, and produce convulsions which will probably never end but in the extermination of the one or the other races....

Even more dramatically, he wrote elsewhere his most frequently quoted dread of slavery's consequences: "I tremble for my country, when I reflect that God is just; that his justice cannot sleep forever." It slept a bit longer, though, as Whitney's gin loosed the cotton culture upon the Southern states.

Expansion of Slavery

Cotton did not set fears at rest, but it did make the old South's "peculiar institution" extremely profitable. In 1784, eight bales of American cotton had been seized in Liverpool on grounds of false documentation—everyone knew you couldn't grow commercial quantities of cotton in the United States! In 1792, American cotton exports were 138,000 pounds; in 1794, 1.6 million pounds. By 1800, the United States exported 18 million pounds, and a new way of life was about to begin. The rush into new cotton lands carried the slave system with it. Alabama, Mississippi, western Georgia, Louisiana, East Texas—all got cotton, and all got slavery as the labor system designed to grow it.

Even though *most Southern whites owned no slaves*, it is surprising how evenly the slave population came to be distributed among the Southern states (see Table 6.8). The increase was most dramatic in the newer areas. In 1860, slaves were more than 50 percent of the populations of South Carolina and Mississippi and well over 40 percent in Alabama, Georgia, and Louisiana. Widespread as ownership was, proportional ownership within those states actually declined in the 1860s as slave prices rose.[30]

Law and Political Compromise

As a form of labor, American slavery has rarely been acclaimed as a paradigm for others to follow.[31] In Chapter 1, we saw James Kent's view of it as a legal matter. In law, slaves simply were "things or property, rather than persons, and are vendible as personal estate."[32] Black slavery was history's intellectual handicap that scarred the land of Jefferson and Madison.

By 1860, it was mainly a problem in the South, but there had been slavery and slaves in every part of the country earlier. The South simply could not find a way out of it. Modern Americans sometimes find it unreal that less than a century and a half separates them from a slave-owning society. In the

TABLE 6.8 Southern Slave Population, 1790–1860[a]

Year	*Virginia*	*South Carolina*	*North Carolina*	*Georgia*	*Mississippi*	*Alabama*	*Louisiana*
1790	292.6	107.1	100.8	29.3	—[b]	—	—
1800	345.8	146.2	133.3	59.4	3.5	—	—
1810	392.5	196.4	168.8	105.2	17.1	—	34.7
1820	425.1	258.5	204.9	149.7	32.8	41.9	69.1
1830	469.8	315.4	245.6	217.5	65.7	117.5	109.6
1840	449.0	327.0	245.8	280.9	195.2	253.5	168.5
1850	472.5	385.0	288.5	381.7	309.9	342.8	244.8
1860	490.9	402.4	331.1	462.2	436.6	435.1	331.7

[a] Figures are for thousands of persons, 1790–1860.
[b] No data.

Source: Harold D. Woodman, ed., *Slavery and the Southern Economy: Sources and Readings* (New York: Harcourt, Brace & World, 1966). Table 2, p. 13.

North, where slavery had not taken hold so firmly, most slaves were freed by degrees, and the system vanished. In the old Middle colonies, the process of freeing the slaves was slow, but it was finished, for the most part, by 1860. Black exclusion laws, forbidding the settlement of freed slaves, were in force in most states in the North in the hope of avoiding the race problem as more slaves got their freedom in the South.

The courts, following the reservation of powers to the states, continued more or less automatically to enforce slave codes and laws, upholding slavery. In the Dred Scott decision of 1857, the courts denied freedom to Scott, a Missouri slave whose master had taken him to the Wisconsin Territory during the 1830s. The Supreme Court noted that blacks could not sue since they were not citizens, and, more ominously, Congress lacked the power to prohibit slavery in Wisconsin. This absence of power effectively negated the provision in the Northwest Ordinance of 1787 and the Missouri Compromise of 1820. In the process, it pushed the country toward civil war. The political system had attempted compromise again and again, not just in 1820, but in 1850 when California was admitted to the Union and in the Kansas-Nebraska Act of 1854 ("popular sovereignty"). In the end, no compromise prevailed. War did.

Slavery and European Immigration

We see the differing fates of colonial America's two unfree systems of labor. One died out as it became uneconomical, while the other thrived precisely because it became so economical. The system of free wage labor in the North flourished as immigrant labor poured into the Northern cities by the tens of thousands, then millions. As we have seen, European immigrants did not seek out the South before 1860, perhaps because it had few cities of any size before that time. Scholars often write that the immigrants shunned competition with slave labor. It is more than likely that, coming into the country relatively poor, they went where they could find jobs with the greatest ease and least cost. Primarily, that was in the cities where they landed or inland along established transport routes.

For the most part, European immigrants shunned agricultural labor as their ticket to the good life. Few of them had sufficient funds to buy land before 1860. Even in 1910, of the foreign-born stock in the labor force, only 13 percent were in farming; 87 percent had chosen other employment. It may well be true, of course, that immigrants had a distaste for slave labor not shared by native Americans and thus shunned places where it existed, but this question is strictly academic. Given the *numbers* of slaves in 1780, the nature of the constitutional settlement, the evolution of law and institutions, and the growth of the slave population, it is difficult to imagine that European immigrants could have voluntarily gone south into agricultural labor in numbers sufficient to have made slavery unprofitable. It is not even obvious that slavery would be unprofitable now, if it were not illegal.[33]

LABOR IN AMERICAN SOCIETY BEFORE 1860

By 1860, those in the U.S. labor force, counting all persons over 10 years of age, numbered just over 11 million, about 35 percent of the total population. Roughly 79 percent of these (58 percent free and 21 percent slave) were engaged in agriculture. Within 40 years, the proportion in agriculture would be cut in half. The rise of manufacturing, transportation, construction, and services would account for this change, and it would continue. Today, agriculture accounts for less than 3 percent of total employment, and services and transportation for almost 70 percent. As far as employment is concerned, modern economic growth consists of rising efficiency in the production of food and goods (including trading for them) at such a pace that most labor and capital are "freed" for other employments. Even by 1860, we are able to see the beginnings of this process.

The Lebergott-Weiss Labor Force Data

It is to Stanley Lebergott's pioneering work on labor force data and to Thomas Weiss's careful reworking of the data that we owe the information in Table 6.9. Note that employment in agriculture grew at a slower rate than did the total labor force; the agricultural labor force has been a declining share of the total. In the 1850s, employment in manufacturing grew at a

A proslavery cartoon illustrates the advantages of slavery for American blacks compared to working-class life in industrial England.

greater rate (42.5 percent) than that in agriculture (28.8 percent), but at only a slightly greater rate than the total labor force (37.8 percent).

By contrast, in the 1840s, manufacturing employment grew more rapidly than any other sector (123.2 percent), increasing its share of total employment from 8.9 percent to 14.0 percent. The relative slowdown in the growth of manufacturing employment in the decade of the 1850s probably reflects three forces at work: (a) a renewed land boom in the early part of the decade was followed by depression after the panic of 1857; (b) construction, services, and transportation also expanded at comparatively unheard-of rates as millions of new immigrants flooded into the urban labor force; and (c) textile manufacturing growth slowed, while heavy industry had not yet begun its great expansion (which came in the 1870s).

The service sector grew quite rapidly in the 1840s (55.8 percent) and 1850s (62.9 percent). One reason for this growth is that services include transportation and trade. These two industries accounted for just over one-quarter of the service sector in 1840 and just under one-third in 1860. The other sector is the sum of employment in construction, fishing, and mining. Between 1840 and 1860, the labor force in construction grew by 79.3 percent; fishing, by 29.2 percent; and mining, by 450 percent. The enormous growth in mining is attributable to the growth of iron and coal as inputs in American manufacturing.

Lebergott argues that this labor force distribution represents mainly the *domestic demand* for output since, at its peak before 1860, employment in the production of raw cotton (the leading U.S. export) accounted for little more than 5 percent of the labor force while exports as a whole (including cotton) probably did not employ more than 10 percent.[34] Unlike most countries experiencing rapid economic growth and development in the nineteenth century, the demand for labor in the United States would be dictated by the domestic economy. This trend began before the Civil War and would continue for the rest of the century.

Claudia Goldin and Kenneth Sokoloff have advanced the argument that the first areas to industrialize were those where the wages, therefore the marginal products, of women and children were low relative to adult males.[35] As they note, the relative productivity of women and children in the hay, wheat, and dairy areas of the North was low; it was much higher in the plantation agriculture areas of the South. Northeastern women became actively involved in the "putting-out" system; Goldin and Sokoloff describe them as "redundant" agricultural laborers. Around 1810, the percentage of young Northeastern women (ages 10 to 29) engaged in wage work was quite small. Over the next two decades, with the shift away from artisan shops to small factories, the percentage increased 10 to 30 percent, depending on location. By 1832, young women and children comprised 40 percent of the industrial work force in the Northeast, but their incomes typically were pooled with other family members. The "family economy" of the farm and artisan shop became the "family wage economy."[36] A Massachusetts census of 1837 suggests that almost half of the wage-earning women in that state were engaged in the production of palm-leaf hats and straw bonnets, the primary "putting-out" industry. Approximately one-sixth were involved in textile production, which had moved to factory production, and one-seventh were involved in the production of boots and shoes, which remained homebound until the 1850s.[37]

The first American textile mill, that of Almy and Brown, opened in 1790 in Pawtucket, Rhode Island. Although it was relatively small, it established the Providence-Pawtucket area as an important one for textile production. The first of the large-scale New England industrial towns was Lowell, Massachusetts, owned by the Lowells of Boston, a successful commercial firm. The initial Lowell firm in Waltham, Massachusetts, was the first to integrate spinning and weaving (it was also the first to use power looms). This integration produced scale economies, particularly in the use of

TABLE 6.9 Labor Force Distribution, 1800–1860

Year	*Total*	*Agriculture*	*Non-Agriculture (in thousands of employed persons)*	*Manufacturing*	*Service*	*Other*
1800	1,712	1,274	438	—[a]	—	—
1810	2,337	1,690	647	—	—	—
1820	3,150	2,249	901	—	—	—
1830	4,272	2,982	1,290	—	—	—
1840	5,778	3,882	1,896	513	1,037	346
1850	8,192	4,889	3,303	1,145	1,616	543
1860	11,290	6,299	4,991	1,632	2,632	727
			(in percentages)			
1800	100	74.4	25.6	—	—	—
1810	100	72.3	27.7	—	—	—
1820	100	71.4	28.6	—	—	—
1830	100	69.8	30.2	—	—	—
1840	100	67.2	32.8	8.9	17.9	6.0
1850	100	59.7	40.3	14.0	19.7	6.6
1860	100	55.8	44.2	14.5	23.3	6.4

[a] No data.

Source: Derived from Stanley Lebergott, *Manpower in Economic Growth: The American Record Since 1800* (New York: McGraw-Hill, 1964), p. 510, and Thomas Weiss, "U.S. Labor Force Estimates and Economic Growth," in R. Gallman and J. Wallis, editors, *American Economic Growth and Standards of Living Before the Civil War* (Chicago: University of Chicago Press, 1992), pp. 37, 51.

labor. That labor was largely single New England farm girls for whom Lowell constructed clean, well-supervised dormitories. The labor of the "Lowell girls" might have appeared relatively cheap to Lowell, but the wages he paid were higher than they could have earned by staying home on the farm. In contrast, the Rhode Island firms typically hired entire families.

Lee Craig and Elizabeth Field-Hendry subjected the Goldin-Sokoloff hypothesis to several tests and found considerable support. They note that the industries in which women were initially employed, particularly textiles, were the most capital-intensive and mechanized of the day.[38] Consequently, not only were women's wages "bid up" as predicted, they experienced large increases in their productivity. When industrialization reached the Midwest in the years just before the Civil War, unskilled male immigrants were more likely to be employed than native women, both in the Midwest and in the Northeast. By 1850, young women and children comprised only 35 percent of the industrial workforce in the Northeast. Craig and Field-Hendry also note that, by drawing some women out of the Northeastern agriculture labor force, the relative value of those that remained increased. As staple production moved westward, Northeastern farms shifted toward dairy and garden products, production in which women were relatively more valuable.

Early Organized Labor Activities

Before 1860, those who were not owners of land or other real assets primarily were engaged in selling their labor. They were selling in an expanding market, to be sure, but one in which large-scale immigration meant increasing competition. As was true of other sellers, they sought to create collective goods through labor organization.[39] In this effort, they faced great obstacles.

Labor in colonial America was largely self-employment, work for relatives, or servitude. (Remember who worked for others in the colonial economy and who worked for themselves.) The common law and its enforcement were meant primarily for the protection of rights in real property and in chattel goods, although those in skilled trades attained a fairly solid social base. Their skills were many times recognized by special laws protecting entry into their trades, and they enjoyed a fairly widespread system of guilds. But in these guilds, the roles of worker, master (employer), manufacturer, and even merchant were intermixed. One of the most significant developments in the world of laboring people before the Civil War was the emergence of clear differentiation of these roles. This took place in the early textile mills and factories, especially as more goods were made commercially and outside the home. Increasing numbers of urban centers led to widespread retailing by specialists, who bought from producers and even from wholesale merchants.

One of the first recorded labor strikes, that of the New York bakers in 1741, was the refusal of those who owned the equipment and flour to bake and sell bread at a price set by municipal authority. Employer and employee roles were still intermingled. In the 1805 strike of the Philadelphia cordwainers (tried in 1806), it was the journeymen against the masters in the same guild, as was the case with the strike of the Pittsburgh cordwainers in 1815. In both cases, the court held, in accord with the common law, that a formal combination of journeymen against masters was a criminal conspiracy. It was not until the Massachusetts case of *Commonwealth v. Hunt* (1842) that the criminal conspiracy doctrine was dropped from automatic application in American labor law. Chief Justice Lemuel Shaw ruled:

> We think, therefore that associations may be entered into, the object of which is to adopt measures that may have a tendency to impoverish another, that is, to diminish his gains and profits, and yet so far from being criminal or unlawful, the object may be highly meritorious and public-spirited.[40]

An attempt to organize workers on a national scale, the National Trades Union, vanished after the panic of 1837. The early labor organizations were largely a mishmash of secret society hocus-pocus, political agitation, and cooperative economic ventures. By 1860, only about 5,000 workers belonged to what today are called *labor unions*, and these unions' powers to improve the lives of their members by collective action were nil, so far as is known. Nevertheless, organizing activity was at times brisk;

Philadelphia and New York both had citywide trade union councils. The competitive ethos—"competition is the life of trade"—worked against labor organizations while the nonagricultural labor force was so small. When male shoemakers in Lynn, Massachusetts, went on strike in 1860, the single women who worked in the trade formed a union of their own.[41] Also, early American unions were not destined to succeed as political organizations in the relatively classless American democracy. It would be a hard-nosed labor organization, the American Federation of Labor, devoted to bread-and-butter issues, that finally would succeed in establishing itself in 1886.

However, the adoption of *mechanic lien laws* in state after state early in the nineteenth century indicated that property rights in labor that were recognized by law and society at large were possible, despite the colonial background. As James Kent described mechanic lien laws in 1826: "It is now the general rule, that every bailee for hire, who by his labor and skill, has imparted an additional value to the goods, has a lien upon the property for his reasonable charges."[42] Such ideas were fitting in Jacksonian America, and their appearance was an omen of the recognition that labor rights were to receive later.

Finally, a national market for labor developed as the country's geographic expansion continued. Laborers (apart from slaves and indentured servants) were free to migrate from low-wage areas to high-wage areas or to the moving frontier, where new settlements were steadily springing up. Transportation improvements (discussed in Chapter 8) hastened this process, but a single wage level for any given grade of labor (the characteristic of a perfect market) was never achieved, not then or now. Labor markets were not perfectly competitive in the early nineteenth century, nor are they today.

Education

According to Albert Fishlow, America's efforts to educate its pre–1860 labor force consumed perhaps 1 percent of the GNP (compared to perhaps 7 percent today).[43] By the 1850s, publicly supported common schools were relatively widespread in the North, although they still were rare in most of the South. Lebergott estimates that, even by 1870, the average school child in the Northern states was in a classroom only three months each year. On the other hand, even as scarce as it was, education seems to have been more readily available in America than it was in Europe. By 1850, the United States actually led the world with an average of 18 percent of its total population (all ages) enrolled in schools of some sort. (Germany was second with 16 percent. The United Kingdom had 12 percent.) In New England, the proportion was even higher.

Nathan Rosenberg, in his book *Technology and American Economic Growth*, emphasizes the peculiar effectiveness of this primary education, as far as economic development before the Civil War was concerned.[44] It was technology, not science, that was needed, and the common schools seem to have served that purpose; at least they were better than anything else. Lebergott and Rosenberg both hold, in fact, that the easy adaptability of American workers and mechanics to technical change in the early nineteenth century was due in large part to high literacy and numeracy not connected to preconceived notions of how economic processes *ought* to be carried out. Lack of a thorough educational structure beyond the "three Rs" perhaps had its advantages.

POPULATION EXPANSION AND OVERALL ECONOMIC GROWTH

The growth of real output per capita is both helped and hurt by rapid population growth. On the one hand, more labor is available to produce goods and services, but, on the other, there are more mouths to feed. Unfortunately, the data are almost too poor to be accepted with confidence, despite ingenious explorations by a number of gifted scholars.

Sources of Early Growth

The long period (1607–1860) that has been considered lacks scope for the development of sources of growth of the kind we later find, such as great new industrial innovations in areas that form the dynamic core of an integrated commercial economy. For most of the period before 1860, the American economy, apart from the small industrial sector, used techniques known for centuries and spread over a vast area with poor internal transportation. Indeed, as Douglass North argued, there really were three separate economies: Northeast, South, and West.[45] How could economic growth occur in this sort of world? There is no doubt that output per capita grew throughout the period. Since agriculture was still of overwhelming importance until at least the 1850s, the question is a difficult one.

The answer seems to be that growth was the result of a multitude of small local improvements. Better livestock strains, more appropriate field crops adapted to climate and soils, capital accumulation (giving each succeeding generation more productive "tools" to work with), even movement from poor to better land would yield growth, if the process were more or less continuous. Even on the same land, more settlement (if the soil were not exhausted) could, for some period of time, contribute to rising productivity as trees were felled, rocks were cleared, fields were expanded, ditches and drainage were improved, roads were made more passable, access to water transport was improved, bridges and ferries were built.

Improved organization, together with efficient structures (like those enabling improved turnaround times for colonial shipping) could raise output per head. So could external economies, although their effect was slight before the 1820s. Even better storage facilities (barns and granaries, for example) reducing losses of stored crops, would raise output per head. The economic history of these early times is filled with such suggested sources of increased overall productivity. There were substantial advances in manufacturing as well, but that sector was too small to have real overall impact.

Most scholars agree that the first decade or so after independence, up to 1790 at least, was a difficult time, with little net growth. Then improvement occurred, but in patterns that are still in dispute among the experts. Paul David supports a strong overall annual growth rate from 1790 to 1860 of perhaps 1.3 percent.[46] By 1840, says David, real product per capita was already 60 percent above that of 1790. Robert Gallman, however, considers David's rate of increase too high.[47] Support for Gallman's position comes from the work of Thomas Weiss. David's conjectures are based on the Lebergott labor force data. When we use Weiss's revisions, the growth rate falls to just about 1 percent.[48]

Apart from the continuing need for better data, the most important issue is the manner in which expansion took place between 1790 and 1860, whether by slow but accelerating growth or by bursts of economic vigor followed by intervals of lassitude, as David suggests.[49]

INCOME AND WEALTH DISTRIBUTION BY 1860

There are only fragmentary data on the distribution of income and wealth from the end of the colonial period (see Chapter 3) to the Civil War. Foreign visitors during this period remarked on the social and political egalitarianism of antebellum America and assumed that it must have a common basis in a widespread equality of economic condition. And why not? Land was the primary income-earning asset and, in the North, the major form of wealth—and it was readily available. Rapid economic and spatial expansion provided abundant opportunities for new ventures of all kinds. There had been few chances for a class of wealth owners to appear that could sustain itself by inheritance alone, outside the slave-owning South. But even in colonial times, as we already have seen, there was the inevitable bunching of wealth. Equality of economic condition was more apparent in manners and dress than in the realities of probate records. Growth of income was destined to be unequally distributed.

Atack and Bateman have shown that, in 1860, wealth in the rural North was more equally distributed than in the cities, or in the rural South, and more equally distributed than it later would be.[50] They suggest that a large portion of westward migration came from middle-income farm families who, fairly equal in wealth holding even before they migrated westward, tended to perpetuate the Jeffersonian ideal of a sturdy yeomanry without great wealth differentials among themselves. However, even in Northern rural areas, there was unequal distribution. The poorer rural families tended to be headed by women, recent immigrants, young people, or the aged. The picture of the ideal rural America of the antebellum period is summed up thusly: "To be wealthy in this egalitarian society of historical tradition was to be a middle-aged, native, white, literate, male farmer."[51]

With the rapid growth of population, real income growth *per capita* was substantial enough. As we have seen, Thomas Weiss estimated that it grew at 1 percent per annum. After 1850, there seems to have been some acceleration. Robert Margo's recent work on antebellum wages suggests that real wages grew at approximately the same rate between 1820 and 1860, but fell during the decade of the 1850s.[52]

There were significant regional differences in growth rates. Richard Easterlin's estimates of levels of income by region are shown in Table 6.10. These estimates are not adjusted for regional differences in the cost of living. Margo's work shows that one reason why workers migrated west (where personal income per capita was lower than average) is that real wages initially were higher on the frontier than on the East Coast.[53]

These data have been variously grouped and interpreted over the years for different purposes.[54] They clearly show that New England strongly, and the Middle Atlantic and East North Central states barely, grew more rapidly than did other regions between 1840 and 1860. Income per capita was higher than the national average in the West South Central states in 1840 and in 1860, but less so in 1860. Moreover, New England and the Middle Atlantic states had higher per-capita and more rapidly rising income in 1860 than did the West South Central states. The Old South and the newer states of the high plains were the poorer areas in 1840, and they were poorer still, comparatively, in 1860. Some parts of the South, the best cotton-growing areas, were exceptions to this general pattern, and we will deal with them later. The point here is that even regional differences in the pace of economic growth would most likely ensure unequal overall income distribution—the mean-income family in New England would have had a higher money income than the average family in the South Atlantic region. Present evidence indicates that both income and wealth distributions were *more unequal* by 1860 than they had been at the end of the colonial period.

The data for income distribution are very poor in most of the years before the Civil War, but the ingenuity of scholarship has produced valuable inferences from what data there are. In particular, Robert Margo's work on wages goes some distance toward explaining the increased inequality of wealth distribution, for which we have somewhat better data.

Margo notes that in the period from 1820 to the Civil War, there was "a widening of the wage structure in favor of white-collar labor and periods of stagnation in real wages, one of which (the 1850s) was associated with a wave of immigration and a rapid increase in reliance on poor relief, prompted, in part, by adverse movements in the real wages of unskilled labor."[55] Over the entire period, real wages for all the groups he studied rose, as can be seen in Table 6.11. The table makes clear the overall increase, as well as the decline of the 1850s. It reveals some differences across occupations with clerks, the white-collar, educated group experiencing the largest increases. It also reveals differences across regions. In particular, artisans in both the Midwest and South Atlantic experienced little change in real wages over the entire period, a pattern that should not be too surprising given the pattern of immigration and internal migration.

The fact that the real wages of artisans did not grow as fast as those of common laborers is consistent with the movement away from artisanal shops and toward factories. With the growth of internal trade—the growth of production as a result of the factory system and the growth of distribution as a result of the expanding transportation network, both canal and

TABLE 6.10 Regional Personal Income per Capita as Percentages of the National Average

Regions	*1840*	*1860*
New England	132	143
Middle Atlantic	136	137
East North Central	67	69
West North Central	75	66
South Atlantic	70	65
East South Central	73	68
West South Central	144	115
Total United States	*100*	*100*

Source: Richard Easterlin, "Regional Income Trends, 1840–1850," *American Economic History*, edited by Seymour Harris (New York: McGraw-Hill, 1961).

TABLE 6.11 Real Wage Indices

	Northeast	*Midwest*	*South Atlantic*	*South Central*
Common Labor				
1821-30	73.4	85.0	85.8	79.6
1831-40	77.2	90.7	76.1	82.0
1841-50	116.5	114.8	101.8	104.9
1851-60	100.0	100.0	100.0	100.0
Artisans				
1821-30	75.0	104.2	97.8	85.9
1831-40	80.4	99.0	98.9	91.3
1841-50	107.1	104.0	122.1	114.8
1851-60	100.0	100.0	100.0	100.0
Clerks				
1821-30	66.4	85.3	78.5	72.7
1831-40	70.5	76.3	83.5	80.6
1841-50	106.6	124.7	126.8	120.3
1851-60	100.0	100.0	100.0	100.0

Source: Robert Margo, *Wages & Labor Markets in the United States,* 1820-1860 (2000), pp. 71-73.

rail—the demand for clerks (record keepers and managers of supplies) initially outstripped the available supply. This pattern of real wage changes would have contributed to a more unequal wealth distribution, other things being equal.

Williamson and Peter Lindert find that the wealth distribution was marked by increasing inequality up to 1860 (strongest from the 1820s to the late 1840s).[56] For example, according to Alice Jones's figures, the top 10 percent of all wealth holders in 1774 held just under 50 percent of total real wealth.[57] Williamson and Lindert find that in 1860, the top 10 percent's share had increased to more than 70 percent of total real wealth. Williamson and Lindert questioned the plausibility of such a large shift in wealth distribution but found that it is "no mirage." Data errors cannot account for it. Moreover, neither can a single, simple explanation. They considered several outstanding wealth distribution explanations, and we will discuss three of them here. They found none of them convincing.

First is the relative-income movement argument, which is implied by Margo's work. Wealth is the sum of net saving over time. Other things being equal, Margo's data indicate that the unskilled (and, by implication, lower income) families would have had less (proportional) opportunity to accumulate wealth from savings prior to 1860 than did those who were financially better off. Why? As real incomes rise, for example, the proportion spent on food falls. Since the wealthy spent proportionately more of their incomes on machine-made products, whose prices fell relatively, there was in this group a greater possibility for wealth accumulation.[58]

The second explanation is that the increasing age of Americans would have meant simply that a large proportion of the population was old enough by 1860 to have accumulated property (in 1820 the median age of males was 16.6 years; it was 19.8 in 1860). Williamson and Lindert are unimpressed by these possibilities, as they are by the third theory: that urbanization produced a great rise in **rent**—a revenue in excess of the competitive alternative—as populations concentrated on small amounts of land, and that urban land has always been unequally held. Wealth was most unequally distributed in the cities in 1860, followed by the rural South, and then rural areas elsewhere.[59] Farmers, on average, were the wealthiest Americans in 1860. In the South, wealth concentration increased from 1790 to 1860 as a smaller proportion of families acquired more and more of the main form of wealth—slaves.

But it must be admitted that none of these explanations appears to be sufficient, especially since increasing concentration ceased after the Civil War.[60] Nor can immigration trends explain it, as Lee Soltow points out.[61]

There is no doubt that unequal wealth and income distributions, as long as there is sufficient wealth at all, are correlated with high economic growth in the early stages of development.[62] Thus, the trends of income and wealth distribution up to 1860 underpinned the nation's main interest, growth and development. Mrs. Frances Trollope, a visiting Frenchwoman who didn't much like the United States, made the following observations of the citizens of Cincinnati in 1829:

> Some of the native political economists assert that this rapid conversion of a bear-brake into a prosperous city, is the result of free political institutions...a more obvious cause suggested itself to me, in the unceasing goad which necessity applies to industry in this country, and in the

absence of all resource for the idle. During nearly two years that I resided in Cincinnati, or its neighborhood, I neither saw a beggar, nor a man of sufficient fortune to permit his ceasing his efforts to increase it; thus every bee in the hive is actively employed in search of that honey...vulgarly called money; neither art, science, learning nor pleasure can seduce them from its pursuit.[63]

Americans wanted growth. With ability being unequally distributed and luck dealt at random, unequal rewards are not surprising in a country with few mechanisms for taxing and redistribution. There appears to be evidence, indirectly, that the growing antebellum inequality had a different source: physiological data.

The Evidence of Stature

It should be apparent that data for our conventional measures of aggregate income are linked to census years. Because those measures were not developed until the twentieth century, economic historians can only make estimates of, say, personal income per capita and its distribution when adequate data are available (as from a census). In the past few decades, an additional data source has provided a more complete picture. A variety of studies suggest that measures of stature—a person's height—are highly (positively) correlated with measures of income and wealth.

Differences in stature attributable to nutritional deprivation, for example, provide a measure of income inequality. If all classes of the population had equal access to all kinds of nutrition, and equal information about its effects, then, *ceteris paribus*, we would expect those who were malnourished were so because of income constraints upon outlays for nutrition. That is, populations would not voluntarily impose malnutrition in any degree upon themselves if they had an option—we can assume that there were no calorie-deficient diet fads at work among the poor in the antebellum period. Of course, income is not the only factor that affects stature. Richard Steckel points to several others:

Personal hygiene, public health measures, and the disease environment affect illness, and work intensity is a function of technology, culture and methods of labor organization. In addition, the relative price of food, cultural values such as the pattern of food distribution within the family, methods of preparation, and tastes and preferences for foods may also be relevant for net nutrition.[64]

As we saw in Part 1, the colonial economy experienced slow, steady growth. The stature evidence is consistent. The average adult height of those born between 1720 and 1740 was relatively constant at about 171.5 centimeters, but those born in the mid–1750s were about a centimeter taller. The average for those born between 1780 and 1830 was relatively constant at about 173 centimeters.[65] These are very similar to contemporary heights. Further, the death rate per 1,000 had fallen to 23 by 1850 (compared to 40 in 1700).[66] The improvement is customarily attributed to the general rise in well-being in the nation's predominantly rural population (a sound diet, reduced risk of epidemic disease, and easy access to land).

What John Komlos has termed the "antebellum puzzle" is that stature then decreased, reaching a minimum of, say, 169.5 centimeters in the 1880s. This is a puzzle because "the nutritional status of a population was hardly expected to decrease when per-capita output was increasing by some 50 percent between 1830 and 1860."[67] In addition, life expectancy fell on the average for those born between 1820 and 1860.[68] Robert Fogel notes, while average food consumption (gross nutrition) remained high during these years, the average amount of nutrients (net nutrition) most likely fell. Fogel attributes this to increased claims on food intake due to the spread of malaria and the rise of diarrheal diseases.[69]

It initially appeared that a setback in nutritional standards could account for this phenomenon. In a comparison of West Point cadets and Harvard students, Komlos found West Point cadets lost about 3.5 centimeters in height between those born in the 1820s and those born in the 1850s. Moreover, West Point cadets of the mid-century, only about 5′ 5″ tall, were also underweight, many in the range of 100 to 120 pounds. Contemporary Harvard students did not display either characteristic, loss of height or weight.[70] Robert Gallman raised serious questions concerning Komlos's explanation for the decline.[71] He notes that there were few Southern-born West Point cadets during the Civil War and that Southerners were taller, on average, than other Americans. Komlos pointed to the

20 to 40 percent increase in food prices during the antebellum period as the likely source of the decline. In particular, ordinary families substituted cheaper foods for more expensive ones, especially animal protein; parents of Harvard students apparently did not make such a substitution.

Both Komlos and Gallman agree, however, that a diminution in stature occurred in the antebellum period, that a puzzle exists. Gallman and John Wallis note that it is also a puzzle that the stature evidence is the only evidence to suggest that there was a decline in personal income and wealth.[72] Komlos, however, remains convinced there is a link to growing inequality: "The 'antebellum puzzle' implies...that during the early stages of modern economic growth, progress was not uniform in all dimensions of human existence."[73]

NOTES

1. Robert Fogel, "Nutrition and the Decline in Mortality since 1700: Some Preliminary Findings," in Stanley Engerman and Robert Gallman, eds., *Long Term Factors in American Economic Growth* (1986), p. 440. Fogel shows that American death rates per 1,000 were 40 in 1700 compared to 28 in the United Kingdom that year. By 1850, the U.S. death rate was down to 23 compared to 24 in the United Kingdom.
2. Richard Easterlin, "Population Change and Farm Settlement in the Northern United States," *JEH*, March 1976; Lee Craig, *To Sow One Acre More* (1993).
3. For an extended argument along these lines, see Easterlin (1976); Richard Steckel, "Antebellum Southern White Fertility: A Demographic and Economic Analysis," *JEH*, June 1980; or Don Leet, "The Determinants of Fertility Transition in Antebellum Ohio," *JEH*, June 1976.
4. This had an approximately equal effect in rural and urban areas. Michael Haines and Barbara Anderson, "New Demographic History of the Late 19th-Century United States," *EEH*, October 1988, p. 342.
5. Richard Steckel, in work discussed in Chapter 10, argues that the *absolute* levels of fertility rates among slave women must have been *much* higher (on his evidence, perhaps twice as high) than among contemporary white women, and much higher than had been previously thought.
6. The products resulting from "women's work" were a larger share of the value of output on farms in the Northeast, and these farms were more profitable than those in the other two regions. Craig (1993), p. 80.
7. Craig (1993), p. 36.
8. Dairy products, poultry and eggs in particular, occupied a large amount of the time women and children spent in market-production.
9. Jeremy Atack and Fred Bateman, *To Their Own Soil* (1987), pp. 49–55, underscores these findings. Among all populations, fertility was lowest in New England.
10. Easterlin's thesis was supported by Morton Owen Shapiro, "A Land Availability Model of Fertility Changes in the Rural Northern United States, 1760–1870," *JEH*, September 1982, and Craig (1993), p. 96. Given the dependent role accorded women in the common law, particularly in New England, parents who chose to make a bequest of land to a daughter would distribute it, with restrictions, to the control of their son-in-law.
11. Craig (1993), p. 23.
12. Paul David and William Sundstrom, "Bargains, Bequests, and Births: An Essay on Intergenerational Conflict, Reciprocity, and the Demand for Children in Agrarian Societies," Stanford Project on the History of Fertility Control, Working Paper No. 12. We are indebted to the authors for permission to cite this work.
13. Robert Gallman, "Human Capital in the First 80 Years of the Republic: How Much Did America Owe the Rest of the World?" *AER*, February 1977.
14. Robert Fogel and Stanley Engerman, *Time on the Cross*, vol. 1, (1974), pp. 23–24.
15. Joel Mokyr, "The Deadly Fungus," in Julian L. Simon, ed., *Research in Population Economics* (Greenwich, CT: JAI Press, 1980), p. 248.
16. Raymond Cohn, "Nativism and the End of the Mass Migration of the 1840s and 1850s," *JEH*, June 2000. Robert Fogel addresses the goals of the Know-Nothings and the general agenda of the "second" great awakening in *The Fourth Great Awakening and the Future of Egalitarianism* (2000).
17. Joseph Ferrie, *Yankeys Now: Immigrants in the Antebellum U.S., 1840–60* (1997).
18. A considerable amount of work has been done recently on mobility and wealth. In addition to Ferrie, see Timothy Conley and David Galenson, "Nativity and Wealth in Mid-Nineteenth-Century Cities," *Journal of Economic History*, vol. 58, no. 2, June 1998; Steven Herscovici, "Migration and Economic Mobility," *Journal of Economic History*, vol. 58, no. 4, December 1998; and Thomas R. Walker, "Economic Opportunity on the Urban Frontier: Wealth and Nativity in Early San Francisco," *Explorations in Economic History*, vol. 37, no. 3, July 2000.
19. Brinley Thomas, *Migration and Economic Growth* (1954).

20. Paul Uselding, "Conjectural Estimates of Gross Human Capital Inflow to the American Economy," *EEH*, Fall 1971.
21. Larry Neal and Paul Uselding, "Immigration, A Neglected Source of American Economic Growth: 1790–1912," *Oxford Economic Papers*, March 1972.
22. Ferrie (1997), p. 208. See also Chapter 8.
23. William Lazonick and Thomas Brush, "The 'Horndal Effect' and Early U.S. Manufacturing," *EEH*, January 1985.
24. Gallman (1977), p. 31. The estimate is based on the work of Lee Soltow, *Men and Wealth in the United States, 1850–1870* (1975).
25. David Galenson, "White Servitude and the Growth of Black Slavery in Colonial America," *JEH*, March 1981.
26. Farley Grubb, "The End of European Immigrant Servitude in the United States: An Economic Analysis of Market Collapse, 1772–1835," *JEH*, December 1994.
27. Morton Horwitz, *The Transformation of American Law, 1780–1860* (Cambridge: Harvard University Press, 1977), p. 186.
28. Christopher Hanes, "Turnover Costs and the Distribution of Slave Labor in Anglo-America," *JEH*, June 1996.
29. Quoted in Harold Woodman, ed., *Slavery and the Southern Economy: Sources and Readings* (New York: Harcourt Brace & World, 1966), p. 3.
30. Gavin Wright, *The Political Economy of the Cotton South: Household, Markets, and Wealth in the Nineteenth Century* (New York: Norton, 1978), pp. 34, 42.
31. See Stanley Elkins, *Slavery: A Problem in American Intellectual and Institutional Life* (Chicago: University of Chicago Press, 1959), chap. 3, for a psychological comparison with Nazi detention camps.
32. James Kent, *Commentaries on American Law* (Boston: Little, Brown & Co., 1873), chap. 1, fn. 12.
33. In January 1982, three men who worked as bosses of farm laborers and who had hired from the ranks of illegal immigrants were sentenced to long prison terms for charges that included slavery.
34. Stanley Lebergott, "Labor Force," in Davis et al., *American Economic Growth* (1972), p. 191; see also Lebergott, *Manpower in Economic Growth* (1964). Thomas Weiss, "U.S. Labor Force Estimates and Economic Growth, 1800–1860" in Robert Gallman and John Wallis, eds., *American Economic Growth and Standards of Living before the Civil War* (1992).
35. Claudia Goldin and Kenneth Sokoloff, "Women, Children, and Industrialization in the Early Republic: Evidence from the Manufacturing Censuses," *JEH*, December 1982; and by the same authors, "The Relative Productivity Hypothesis of Industrialization: The American Case, 1820 to 1850," *QJE*, August 1984.
36. The terms are those of Louise Tilly and Joan Scott, *Women, Work, and Family* (New York: Holt, Rinehart, and Winston, 1978).
37. See Thomas Dublin, *Transforming Women's Work: New England Lives in the Industrial Revolution* (1994), p. 20. Dublin's study of the "Lowell girls" remains the definitive study of the period, *Women at Work: The Transformation of Work and Community in Lowell, Massachusetts, 1826–1860* (1979).
38. Lee Craig and Elizabeth Field-Hendry, "Industrialization and the Earnings Gap: Regional and Sectoral Tests of the Goldin-Sokoloff Hypothesis," *EEH*, January 1993.
39. See Mancur Olson, *The Logic of Collective Action: Public Goods and the Theory of Groups* (New York: Schocken Books, 1971), chap. III, on this characteristic activity of labor organizations.
40. Stephen Mueller, *Labor Law and Legislation* (Cincinnati: Southwestern Publishing Co., 1949). p. 42.
41. Dublin (1994), p. 13.
42. Kent, *op. cit.*, vol. 2, p. 914.
43. Albert Fishlow, "Levels of Nineteenth Century American Investment in Education," *JEH*, December 1966.
44. The data are Richard Easterlin's, presented in Nathan Rosenberg's *Technology and American Economic Growth* (1971), Table 1. For his discussion on the effectiveness of the common school education, see chap. II, "The Economic Matrix," in that volume.
45. Douglass North, *The Economic Growth of the United States 1790–1860* (New York: Norton, 1966), chap. IX–XII; Richard Sutch, "Douglass North and the New Economic History," in Roger Ransom, Richard Sutch and Gary Walton, eds., *Explorations in the New Economic History: Essays in Honor of Douglass C. North* (New York: Academic Press, 1982), chap. 2; Lloyd Mercer, "The Antebellum Regional Trade Hypothesis: A Reexamination of Theory and Evidence," in the same volume, chap. 4.
46. Paul David, "The Growth of Real Product in the United States Before 1840: New Evidence, Controlled Conjectures," *JEH*, June 1967, p. 155, Table 1.
47. Robert Gallman, "The Statistical Approach," in George Rogers Taylor and Lucius Ellsworth, eds., *Approaches to American Economic History* (1971).
48. Weiss (1992).
49. As we noted earlier, Gloria Main does not find evidence of a growth slow-down in the early 18th century in the data on estates. Gloria Main, "The Standard of Living in Colonial Massachusetts," *JEH*, March 1983.
50. Atack and Bateman (1987), p. 269; and by the same authors, "The 'Egalitarian Ideal' and the Distribution of Wealth in the Northern Agricultural Community: A Backward Look," *REStat*, February 1981.
51. Atack and Bateman (1987), p. 129. Donghyu Yang finds that, in the South, the "land owning yeoman farmer class," was "substantially poorer than was its northern counterpart." "Notes on the Wealth Distribution of Farm Households in the United States, 1860: A New

Look at Two Manuscript Census Samples," *EEH*, January 1984, p. 99.

52. Robert Margo, *Wages & Labor Markets in the United States, 1820–1860* (2000), pp. 142–143.
53. Margo (2000), pp. 100–102.
54. See Robert Fogel and Stanley Engerman, "The Economics of Slavery," in Fogel and Engerman, eds., *The Reinterpretation of American Economic History* (New York: Harper & Row, 1971), pp. 333–338.
55. Margo (2000), p. 158.
56. Jeffrey Williamson and Peter Lindert, "Three Centuries of American Inequality," in Paul Uselding, ed.. *REH* (1976), vol. 1, pp. 101–102.
57. Alice Hanson Jones, *Wealth of a Nation to Be: The American Colonies on the Eve of the Revolution* (New York: Columbia University Press, 1980), p. 259, Table 8.1.
58. Robert Margo and Georgia Villaflor, "The Growth of Wages in Antebellum America: New Evidence," *JEH*, December 1987, pp. 883–884, 895, argue that their wage data do not support this argument. They show an increase of about 33 percent in skilled wages and about 48 percent in unskilled in the antebellum period.
59. A recent symposium examines one consequence of this inequality, the development of various forms of public relief. See Kyle Kauffman, ed., "Before the Welfare State: Learning from Early Experiments with Public Relief in the Nineteenth Century," *Quarterly Review of Economics and Finance*, vol. 37, no. 2, Summer 1997, particularly the contribution coauthored by Lynne Kiesling and Robert Margo and the case study by Joan Hannon on the rise of the poorhouse.
60. Williamson and Lindert (1976), pp. 77, 83.
61. Lee Soltow (1975), pp. 107, 145. After 1860, wealth was slightly more evenly distributed among the foreign-born than it was before 1860. Large-scale immigration by itself did not increase inequality. Also see Soltow, "Inequalities in the Standard of Living in the United States, 1798–1875," in Gallman and Wallis (1992); and Margo (2000), pp. 19–22.
62. Simon Kuznets, *Six Lectures on Economic Growth* (New York: The Free Press, 1961), p. 55. As industrialization proceeds, the tendency is that *income* distribution becomes more equal. Such also happened in the United States, as we shall see later.
63. Frances Trollope, *Domestic Manners of Americans*, edited by Donald Smalley (New York: Alfred Knopf, 1949), p. 43.
64. Richard Steckel, "Stature and the Standard of Living," *JEL*, December 1995 is an excellent summary of this research; the citation can be found on p. 1911.
65. Dora Costa and Richard Steckel, "Long-term Trends in Health, Welfare, and Economic Growth in the United States," in Richard Steckel and Roderick Floud, eds., *Health and Welfare during Industrialization* (1995).
66. Fogel (1986), p. 440.
67. John Komlos, "Anomalies in Economic History: Toward a Resolution of the 'Antebellum Puzzle'," *JEH*, March 1996, p. 202.
68. Fogel (1986), p. 466.
69. Fogel, (2000), p. 164–165.
70. John Komlos, "The Height and Weight of West Point Cadets: Dietary Change in Antebellum America," *JEH*, December 1987.
71. Robert Gallman, "Dietary Change in Antebellum America," *JEH*, March 1996.
72. Robert Gallman and John Wallis, "Introduction," in Gallman and Wallis (1992), pp. 12–16. Margo (2000), p. 152, notes that adverse short-term movements in real wages during the 1850s could have contributed to the puzzle.
73. Komlos (1996), p. 212.

SUGGESTED READINGS

Articles

Adams, Donald R. "Earnings and Savings in the Early 19th Century." *Explorations in Economic History*, vol. 17, no. 2, April 1980.

Anderson, Terry L. "Economic Growth in Colonial New England: Statistical Renaissance." *Journal of Economic History*, vol. XXXIX, no. 1, March 1979.

Atack, Jeremy, and Fred Bateman. "The 'Egalitarian Ideal' and the Distribution of Wealth in the Northern Agricultural Community: A Backward Look." *Review of Economics and Statistics*, vol. LXIII, no. 1, February 1981.

Ball, Duane, and Gary Walton. "Agricultural Productivity Change in Eighteenth Century Pennsylvania." *Journal of Economic History*, vol. XXXVI, no. 1, March 1976.

Craig, Lee, and Elizabeth Field-Hendry. "Industrialization and the Earnings Gap: Regional and Sectoral Tests of the Goldin-Sokoloff Hypothesis." *Explorations in Economic History*, vol. 30, no. 1, January 1993.

Cohn, Raymond. "Nativism and the End of the Mass Migration of the 1840s and 1850s." *Journal of Economic History*, vol. 60, no. 2, June 2000.

Costa, Dora, and Richard Steckel. "Long-term Trends in Health, Welfare, and Economic Growth in the United

States." In Richard Steckel and Roderick Floud, eds., *Health and Welfare During Industrialization*. Chicago: University of Chicago Press, 1995.

Crowther, Simeon J. "Urban Growth in the Mid-Atlantic States, 1785–1850." *Journal of Economic History*, vol. XXXVI, no. 3, September 1976.

David, Paul. "The Growth of Real Product in the United States Before 1840: New Evidence, Controlled Conjectures." *Journal of Economic History*, vol. XXVI, no. 2, June 1967.

Easterlin, Richard A. "Influences in European Overseas Emigration Before World War I." *Economic Development and Cultural Change*, vol. 9, no. 3, April 1961.

———. "The American Population." In Lance E. Davis et al., *American Economic Growth: An Economist's History of the United States*. New York: Harper & Row, 1972.

———. "Population Change and Farm Settlement in the Northern United States." *Journal of Economic History*, vol. XXXVI, no. 1, March 1976.

Egnal, Marc. "The Economic Development of the Thirteen Continental Colonies, 1720–1775." *William and Mary Quarterly*, vol. 32, 3rd series, April 1975.

Fishlow, Albert. "The Common School Revival: Fact or Fancy?" In Henry Rosovsky, ed., *Industrialization in Two Systems*. New York: Wiley, 1966.

———. "Levels of Nineteenth-Century American Investment in Education." *Journal of Economic History*, vol. 26, no. 4, December 1966.

Fogel, Robert William, "Nutrition and the Decline in Mortality Since 1700: Some Preliminary Findings." In Stanley L. Engerman and Robert E. Gallman, eds., *Long-Term Factors in American Economic Growth*, NBER *Studies in Income and Wealth*, vol. 51, Chicago: University of Chicago Press, 1986.

Galenson, David W. "White Servitude and the Growth of Black Slavery in Colonial America." *Journal of Economic History*, vol. XLI, no. 1, March 1981.

Gallman, Robert. "The Statistical Approach." In George Rogers Taylor and Lucius Ellsworth, eds., *Approaches to American Economic History*. Charlottesville: University Press of Virginia, 1971.

———. "The Pace and Pattern of American Economic Growth." In Lance E. Davis et al., *American Economic Growth: The Economist's History of the United States*. New York: Harper & Row, 1972.

———. "Human Capital in the First 80 Years of the Republic: How Much Did America Owe the Rest of the World?" *American Economic Review*, vol. 67, no. 1, February 1977.

———. "Dietary Change in Antebellum America." *Journal of Economic History*, vol. 56, no. 1, March 1996.

Goldin, Claudia, and Kenneth Sokoloff. "Women, Children, and Industrialization in the Early Republic: Evidence from the Manufacturing Censuses." *Journal of Economic History*, vol. 42, no. 4, December 1982.

———. "The Relative Productivity Hypothesis of Industrialization: The American Case, 1820 to 1850." *Quarterly Journal of Economics*, vol. 99, no. 3, August 1984.

Grubb, Farley. "The End of European Immigrant Servitude in the United States: An Economic Analysis of Market Collapse, 1772–1835." *Journal of Economic History*, vol. 54, no. 4, December 1994.

Haines, Michael R., and Barbara A. Anderson. "New Demographic History of the Late 19th-Century United States." *Explorations in Economic History*, vol. 25, no. 4, October 1988.

Hanes, Christopher. "Turnover Costs and the Distribution of Slave Labor in Anglo-America." *Journal of Economic History*, vol. 56, no. 2, June 1996.

Komlos, John. "The Height and Weight of West Point Cadets: Dietary Change in Antebellum America." *Journal of Economic History*, vol. XLVII, no. 4, December 1987.

———. "Anomalies in Economic History: Toward a Resolution of the 'Antebellum Puzzle.'" Journal of Economic History, vol. 56, no. 1, March 1996.

Kulikoff, Alan. "The Economic Growth of the Eighteenth Century Chesapeake Colonies." *Journal of Economic History*, vol. XXXIX, no. 1, March 1979.

Lazonick, William, and Thomas Brush. "The 'Horndal Effect' and Early U.S. Manufacturing." *Explorations in Economic History*, vol. 22, no. 1, January 1985.

Lebergott, Stanley. "Labor Force." In Lance E. Davis et al., *American Economic Growth: An Economist's History of the United States*. New York: Harper & Row, 1972.

Leet, Don R. "The Determinants of the Fertility Transition in Antebellum Ohio." *Journal of Economic History*, vol. XXXVI, no. 2, June 1976.

Lindstrom, Diane. "American Economic Growth Before 1840: New Evidence and New Directions." *Journal of Economic History*, vol. XXXIX, no. 1, March 1979.

Main, Gloria L. "The Standard of Living in Colonial Massachusetts." *Journal of Economic History*, vol. XLIII, no. 1, March 1983.

Margo, Robert A. "Wages and Prices during the Antebellum Period: A Survey and New Evidence." In Robert Gallman and John Wallis, eds., *American Economic Growth and Standards of Living before the Civil War*. Chicago: University of Chicago Press, 1992.

———, and Georgia C. Villaflor. "The Growth of Wages in Antebellum America: New Evidence." *Journal of Economic History*, vol. XLVII, no. 4, December 1987.

Neal, Larry, and Paul Uselding. "Immigration, A Neglected Source of American Economic Growth: 1790 to 1912." *Oxford Economic Papers*, 2nd series, vol. 24, March 1972.

Potter, J. "The Growth of Population in America, 1700–1860." In D. V. Glass and D. E. C. Eversley, eds., *Population in History*. New York: Aldine, 1965.

Shapiro, Morton Owen. "A Land Availability Model of Fertility Changes in the Rural Northern United States, 1760–1870." *Journal of Economic History*, vol. XLII, no. 3, September 1982.

Soltow, Lee. "Economic Inequality in the United States in the Period from 1790 to 1860." *Journal of Economic History*, vol. XXXI, no. 4, December 1971.

———. "Inequalities in the Standard of Living in the United States, 1798–1875." In Robert Gallman and John Wallis, eds., *American Economic Growth and Standards of Living before the Civil War*. Chicago: University of Chicago Press, 1992.

Steckel, Richard H. "Antebellum Southern White Fertility: A Demographic and Economic Analysis." *Journal of Economic History*, vol. XL, no. 2, June 1980.

———. "Stature and the Standard of Living." *Journal of Economic Literature*, vol. XXXIII, no. 4, December 1995.

Taylor, George Rogers. "American Economic Growth Before 1840: An Exploratory Essay." *Journal of Economic History*, vol. XXIV, no. 4, December 1964.

Uselding, Paul. "Conjectural Estimates of Gross Human Capital Inflow to the American Economy." *Explorations in Economic History*, vol. 9, Fall 1971.

Weiss, Thomas. "U.S. Labor Force Estimates and Economic Growth, 1800–1860." In Robert Gallman and John Wallis, eds., *American Economic Growth and Standards of Living before the Civil War*. Chicago: University of Chicago Press, 1992.

Williamson, Jeffrey. "American Prices and Urban Inequality Since 1820." *Journal of Economic History*, vol. XXXVI, no. 2, June 1976.

———, and Peter Lindert. "Three Centuries of American Inequality." In Paul Uselding, ed., *Research in Economic History*, vol. 1. Greenwich, CT: JAI Press, 1976.

Yang, Donghyu. "Notes on the Wealth Distribution of Farm Households in the United States, 1860: A New Look at Two Manuscript Census Samples." *Explorations in Economic History*, vol. 21, no. 1, January 1984.

Books

Atack, Jeremy, and Fred Bateman. *To Their Own Soil: Agriculture in the Antebellum North*. Ames: Iowa State University Press, 1987.

Coale, Ansley J., and Melvin Zelnik. *New Estimates of Fertility and Population in the United States*. Princeton: Princeton University Press, 1963.

Craig, Lee A. *To Sow One Acre More: Childbearing and Farm Productivity in the Antebellum North*. Baltimore: The Johns Hopkins University Press, 1993.

Dublin, Thomas. *Women at Work: The Transformation of Work and Community in Lowell, Massachusetts, 1826–1860*. New York: Columbia University Press, 1979.

———. *Transforming Women's Work: New England Lives in the Industrial Revolution*. Ithaca: Cornell University Press, 1994.

Ferrie, Joseph P. *Yankeys Now: Immigrants in the Antebellum U.S., 1840–60*. New York: Oxford University Press, 1997.

Fogel, Robert. *The Fourth Great Awakening and the Future of Egalitarianism*. Chicago: University of Chicago Press, 2000.

———, and Stanley Engerman. *Time on the Cross*, vol. 1. Boston: Little, Brown, 1974.

Gallman, Robert E., and John Joseph Wallis, eds. *American Economic Growth and Standards of Living before the Civil War*. Chicago: University of Chicago Press, 1992.

Handlin, Oscar. *Boston's Immigrants, 1790–1880*. Cambridge: Harvard University Press, 1959.

Lebergott, Stanley. *Manpower in Economic Growth: The American Record Since 1800*. New York: McGraw-Hill, 1964.

Margo, Robert A. *Wages & Labor Markets in the United States, 1820–1860*. Chicago: The University of Chicago Press, 2000.

Rosenberg, Nathan. *Technology and American Economic Growth*. New York: Harper, 1972.

Soltow, Lee. *Men and Wealth in the United States, 1850–1870*. New Haven: Yale University Press, 1975.

Thomas, Brinley. *Migration and Economic Growth*. New York: Cambridge University Press, 1953.

Yasuba, Yasukichi. *Birth Rates of the White Population of the United States, 1800–1860: An Economic Study*. Baltimore: Johns Hopkins University Press, 1962.

CHAPTER SEVEN

Law and the Rise of Classical American Capitalism

The United States has a written constitution, difficult to amend, against which the laws reflecting political, social, and economic change over time are measured. This measurement results in tailoring, the processes of lawmaking and judicial review, to make the law "fit." The student of American economic history must come to grips with the major advances, twists, and turns in the relevant parts of our legal history, since every piece of legislation that enters the stream of American life ultimately passes through court review. Changes in American society that require a change in the law receive definition through the courts. This is a vast subject that, after a long hiatus, has recently gained recognition as a tool of historic and economic understanding. In the past, economic history scarcely addressed the contents of this chapter. However, in recent years, the processes of law and public choice have come to the fore. Here, we cannot do more than review a basic outline of this subject from our colonial roots up to 1860.[1]

One of the economic wonders of the nineteenth century was the appearance of classical American capitalism in all its forms: the giant entrepreneurial business firm, the industrial labor force concentrated in the great manufacturing centers, the complete commercialization of agriculture and extractive industries, and the rise of big-time finance and giant transportation systems.[2] The little agrarian world of Jefferson and Madison at the turn of the nineteenth century became, by the end of that century, the world of J. Pierpont Morgan, John D. Rockefeller, Andrew Carnegie—and also of Samuel Gompers, Eugene V. Debs, the Interstate Commerce Commission, and the Sherman Antitrust Act. Incredible growth was accompanied by incredible change. It is the province of economic history to explain that change, and the law is a necessary part of that explanation.

Even though the full flowering of classical American capitalism came only in the latter decades of the nineteenth century, the roots were well developed by 1860. Whether or not we approve of nineteenth-century American capitalism, we must understand it if we are to make any coherence of what comes later. We live today, institutionally, in its shadow. Most of the language and ideologies—pro and con—of public economics and policymaking to this day have their origins before 1914. In the first few decades after independence, changes occurred that turned colonial America into the seedbed of classical American capitalism.

THE COLONIAL PROPERTY RIGHTS HERITAGE

Although important changes came about within the definitions of the property rights that Americans claimed, the basic ideas established in the colonial era remained untouched by the Revolution (apart from the abolition of primogeniture and perpetual entailment). It was from those property rights that the modern American economy developed. As Chief Justice John Marshall stated in *Dartmouth College v. Woodward*: "It is too clear to require the support of argument that all contracts, respecting property, remained unchanged by the revolution."[3]

The American Revolution was not against the law but against a particular alien authority. The Americans were not going to throw away the common law.

REAL PROPERTY RIGHTS

Even though the tenure in real property originally had been developed in a small rural society of feudal structure, it proved capable of extraordinary flexibility in meeting the changing needs of modern capitalism. Recall from Chapter 1 the basic nature of the real property tenure that was transferred here from England. For the purchaser, or heir in socage (from now on called *fee simple*), there were five vital characteristics of ownership:

1. The maturity of ownership by purchase was perpetual, in theory, as long as incidents (taxes) due the "donor" were met.
2. The rights of both buyer and seller were "fixed and certain.
3. Land could descend to heirs from earlier generations either by will or inheritance. The latter was direct: The property right did not go back (escheat) to the donor to be regranted.
4. Ownership included both surface and subsurface resources, and the right to exploit them (waste) was complete. The reserved rights of the king to a fifth of the precious metals vanished in American practice.
5. Rights were completely alienable—by sale or trade—and reserved rights (minerals) had to be explicit and were limited.

Apart from ungranted public lands, there were no residual rights of government, only the "police powers" and the power to tax, and those were held by the state and local (not federal) government. The power of government to condemn property by the right of eminent domain was mainly a post-Revolutionary American innovation; it was not a reassertion of the donor's rights but of the sovereign power of government to take property (commonly land) by forced purchase (and sometimes outright expropriation).

This form of ownership was almost ideal as the base for a free-market economy. The rewards from all economic activity related to property and its production were "commodities" in the sense that they were easily bought and sold, with few restrictions that mattered. The tenure allowed property to be leased, rented, let out on a sharecropping contract, subdivided, or amalgamated with other properties. Water and mineral rights could be owned separately. All this freedom was the property right of anyone with the purchase price. It is difficult to imagine a superior tenure for an individual. The only weakness (for the owner) was the donor's right of "reentry" (confiscation of rights) upon nonpayment of taxes. This condition, on the other hand, ensured that American local governments had a solid tax base as development and population increase augmented the demands for public services. In any case, as long as the taxes imposed by popularly elected governments were reasonable in amount, they posed no barriers to economic development.

As the nation expanded laterally by land settlement and farming, the American land tenure proved the perfect vehicle for economic growth. With the arrival of heavy industry based upon the extraction of minerals, the tenure gave rewards (which could be great) to those fortunate people who owned or acquired gold, silver, copper, coal, oil, iron ore, and other resources—just as it long had done for land owners, farmers, and timbering interests. Not surprisingly, the wealth and income derived from such exploitation of real property rights were unevenly distributed because those minerals, by nature, were not homogeneously present in the soils. Private persons owned the land, controlled it, and exploited it, and that property right was the basis of American capitalism in its classic form: the unquestioned right of individuals to do with their property whatever they wished and to enjoy the fruits of their enterprise by themselves. It was a system in which self-interest was exalted, and the tenure of real property was ideally designed for that system.

BASIC LEGAL DEVELOPMENTS

Constitutions are the basic framework of law. The day-to-day interpretation and application of those fundamental rules, the substantive contents of them, were (and are) matters for legislatures and the courts. We inherited from the English practice of common law a system of judge-made law. To this day, theoretically, legislation is not "law" until it has been interpreted in court tests. For this reason, we are known as a common-law country, even though we operate by positive statute law and written constitutions. The division of American government into three parts, with separate and independent powers bestowed upon the judiciary, is recognition and reinforcement of common-law principles. Another and related source of authority in economic life is the tradition of police power.

The Police Power

The right of government to maintain settled and peaceable conditions for all the polity, by force if necessary, is called the **police power**. Application of this power over time has covered everything from weights and measures to sexual behavior. It has been used to order and control business activity since "time out of mind." We have already considered many of its uses in colonial America. Even though the police power has been primarily the regulatory power of state and local governments, eventually it was elevated to the federal level (for example, pollution-control regulation). This power is not a trivial one, even at the local level, since by means of licensing, zoning, and controls over conditions of trade and manufacturing, the police powers could be, were, and are used by government to control entry into business and thus, to control economic structure.

At the beginning of the federal era, the colonial police powers remained in effect in the settled areas. There has been some confusion about this concept among historians, some of whom incorrectly associated such regulations with "mercantilism" and supposed that they had been overthrown by the Revolution. After all, the Revolution was not waged against colonial governments, but against the British. The police power regulations were part and parcel of colonial government and the common-law tradition. There was no question of some mythical "break for freedom" into a world of true laissez-faire once the Revolution was won. The ideas of laissez-faire were not widely known or espoused in colonial times. Regulation was the right of government and its duty. State and local governments did not change when the British were driven out.[4]

In their classic study of Massachusetts from the end of the colonial era to the Civil War, Oscar and Mary Handlin found such continuity for most colonial controls over inns, taverns, public transportation, harbors, and wharves—special franchise monopolies.[5] Massachusetts town governments even "retained the Medieval right to control and organize markets, regulating in great detail the conditions of sale."[6] Manufacturing was controlled, as of old, by inspection. By 1816, "the governor appointed inspectors of pot and pearl ash, or pork and beef, nails, butter and lard, pickled fish, each with a retinue of deputies."[7]

There were, indeed, significant extensions of police powers over economic life. Informers were still used and rewarded by the courts for their support of the controls. Lawyers were in danger of losing their monopoly of knowledge when Joseph Story's treatise on common pleading was published. In the fashion of a medieval guild, lawyers demanded the creation of a collective good for themselves and were rewarded when the Massachusetts Supreme Court set up formal examinations and required completion of a three-year apprenticeship for entry before the Massachusetts bar.

Louis Hartz, in a similar study of Pennsylvania, found the same continuity for the police powers exercised over economic life in that state. Hartz wrote:

> "It is the duty and interest of all governments," asserted a Pennsylvania statute of 1781, "to prevent frauds, and promote the interests of just and useful commerce." The colonial tradition of licensing, inspection, and similar regulations was maintained steadily from the Revolution to the Civil War and was in certain instances appreciably expanded.[8]

Hartz argued that in Pennsylvania, these sentiments had been "taken for granted." Licensing, inspection, occasional government price-fixing—all such police-power exercises continued unabated. An act of 1835 set up a very extensive and detailed inspection for all items manufactured for export from the Commonwealth. There was no questioning of such power. Indeed, we will see the Supreme Court of the United States (in *Hammer v. Dagenhart*, 1918) uphold this power of the states to regulate manufacturing, and it continued to do so until 1942.

However, there was also sentiment for greater freedom from control. We saw the beginning of this counterforce developing in the colonial economy: in the markets for labor, in the abolition of markets overt, and the growing strength of the idea that *caveat emptor*—buyer beware—protected the bargain and warranted the legitimate transfer of title where there was no overt fraud. New York State, in its constitutional revision of 1846, abolished outright many of its police-power controls: "All offices for the weighing, gauging, measuring, culling or inspecting any merchandise, produce, manufacture or commodity, whatever, are hereby abolished, and no such office shall hereafter be created by law."[9]

Commerce and manufacturing became more complex before the Civil War. As the number and kinds of manufacture proliferated in a society without modern record-keeping and communications technology, the old police-power controls by detailed inspection became increasingly difficult to maintain. The outstanding exceptions were controls over common carriers (public utility control). These carriers were special franchise monopolies, most of them with eminent domain powers over private-property owners, and there never was any question of their being free of regulation. In fact, this form of regulation received very extensive development, especially in connection with canals and railroads in the decades before 1860. However, in other areas, free-markets increasingly were seen as a cheaper method of social control than was regulation. Hartz suggested that free-market sentiment simply developed "naturally" as business enterprise grew and became less exceptional. Proprietors began to believe that their own property in business establishments ought to be as free as was property in real estate. The Handlins noted the confusion in Massachusetts that had arisen by 1860 after extensive economic development:

> It was as if, imperceptibly, all the familiar metes and bounds that marked off one man's estate from another vanished to leave a vast and open space, familiar but with the old landmarks gone. Somewhere, everyone knew, the state could act directly, somewhere it could legislate as arbiter, and somewhere it had no place at all. But where one field ended and another began, no one knew; the master map was not yet drawn....[10]

The main point to remember about the police powers is that they are and were unquestioned prerogatives of government. American capitalism *never* knew a time when it was free of these controls. But it did know a time when such controls were not applied by the federal government. The police powers were applied then, as they often are today, by local government to force notions of propriety on business as well as on morals. Like most of our ancient legal background, the police powers were capable of *development*. The precedent was all-important, as we shall see when we examine the great watershed case of state control powers, *Munn v. Illinois*, in Chapter 17. The federal government today in its regulation of product safety is entirely within the police-power tradition. During the rise of the free-market economy, the police powers continued to be imposed, although sporadically; they were part of the rules of the game. They also had wasteful side effects.

Privilege and Rent-Seeking

The police powers could be, and were, used to create privileges that could then be exploited by those to whom the privileges were granted.[11] Suppose only one barber is allowed to cut hair in a town. He or she has a monopoly created by government. At the lowest level of privilege, it is specific individuals who are thus favored. With the lawyers in Massachusetts in 1816, as we have just seen, an organized group received a collective privilege or good from government. They could charge higher fees because entrance to the bar was restricted.

Consider an example from colonial America. The records of Massachusetts contain the following ruling by the colony government in 1641: A certain William Davis "was denied libertie to sell drinke, or ale, or to keep a cookes shopp, because there are others sufficient in the towne of Boston, and his carriage hath been formerly offensive."[12] From this ruling, we see that:

1. To sell drink, ale, or food, permission (a license) was required.
2. Because those already in the business were considered "sufficient," their profits were protected from Davis's competition—his application was denied.
3. The moral tone of Boston was upheld when Davis was turned away because of his "offensive" behavior on previous occasions.

Those already in business gain a **rent** that would not be there without the regulation. In the case of William Davis, this rent would have been lost if Davis's entry into competition with the others had been allowed to increase supply, given Boston's demand for such services. Any kind of business licensing or regulation produces such rents. Thus, it would be difficult indeed for the police power to be economically neutral. Its exercise creates, by definition, circumstances different from those that the free market produces. Otherwise, the regulation would be pointless.

Clearly, in 1641, not many of Boston's socially productive resources were diverted to create or to gather such rents. Even outright bribery for such privileges would cost little in 1641, and the extra price of "drinke," ale, and goodies from the already existing "cookes shopps" did not amount to much. Most of Boston's resources were devoted to creating positive new production in other sectors of the economy.

Rent-seeking is an inefficient way for a society to use its resources. For such rents to be gained, some resources are necessarily wasted, simply transferred from productive uses. Also, note that the returns to the rent-gainers, which are above the competitive levels, are "transferred" to them from the rest of society *only because of the regulation*. Society supposedly is compensated for this social cost by the provision of such things as better health, safety, good order, and higher morals.

In a mainly agricultural and extractive society, a society of small cities and governments with (geographically) limited powers, not many resources were expended on rent-seeking. It is more appropriate to call the receipt of such rents "privilege." However, as American society grew, there were important changes. No longer were government-created privileges available to a few select persons, as in colonial Boston. Bigger stakes were involved as economic life expanded and organizations became larger. It paid for whole classes of people, organized groups, to agitate for privileges from government, for what Mancur Olson calls **collective goods**.[13] It originally occurred in land sales and happened again in the pursuit of special-franchise monopolies to build canals, railroads, and bridges. And as it happened, the United States was developing a large rent-seeking sector.

According to Terry Anderson and Peter J. Hill, this characteristic becomes important mainly after 1870 with the exercise of *federal* police power.[14] Agitation for collective goods is an economically wasteful by-product of political authority exercised to control the market. For now, we will be seeing the origins of this rent-seeking sector in the privileges created by the police power. Competitive rent-seeking will produce both waste and corruption. According to E. A. J. Johnson, the first congressional meeting under the new federal Constitution was alive with competitive rent-seekers.[15] Their first triumphs on a large scale were public land sales to groups of speculators, and the protective tariff.

LAW, INCOME, AND WEALTH TRANSFERS

When the existing states elected their first president and launched a new form of government in 1789, they did not seem to recognize that a dynamic interpretation of their new Constitution could make the law an instrument for the redistribution of wealth and income. As Charles Beard pointed out in his *Economic Interpretation of the Constitution*, a reasonable person might see it as a very conservative document intended to preserve the status quo. Of course, such was not to be the case. It was the genius of American jurists that they could stay within the general boundaries of the constitutional settlement and yet modify the substantive content of the law enough to release the powerful forces of change and development that underpinned the expansion of American capitalism within the framework of a growing economy. This freedom to interpret the law, called "judicial instrumentalism," found its greatest impact in the century between 1780 and 1880.[16] Without it, the American economy could never have developed as it did. Judicial instrumentalism gave advantage to some at the expense of others, and, thus, changed the distribution of wealth and income from that which would otherwise have prevailed.

Property Rights: From Prescriptive Rights to Priority Rights

Judicial instrumentalism amounted to, in the words of Harry Scheiber, "pragmatic concern to advance productivity and material growth." Since the Constitution was concerned with preventing the redistribution of wealth and income in the interests of order and stability, and since economic growth *meant* dynamic instability, it was left to the courts to encourage entrepreneurial activity by judicial interpretation. So thoroughly was judicial discretion used in this regard that by 1820, as Horwitz puts it in *The Transformation of American Law*, "the legal landscape of America bore only the faintest resemblance to what existed forty years earlier."[17] This change was accomplished in large part by judges placing social weights upon property rights that favored some more than others.

Suppose there were two landowners, existing side by side, with equal amounts of land. In the common law of England, within the tenure rights, each had "absolute dominion" over his or her property. Under the common-law doctrine of "ancient lights," one neighbor could not build a structure that would obscure the sunlight already enjoyed by the other. That ancient usage, that enjoyment of the sunlight, was a **prescriptive right**, and it must prevail over the ambition of the neighbor to change it. Scenery, clear air, quiet enjoyment—these were the amenities of real property and the seated property owner. They had real, monetary value and could not be disturbed without compensation. People could not use their property in ways that damaged the amenity rights of others without being liable for damages. The same argument would prevail if one neighbor wanted to build a mill dam that flooded the other's meadow. The use of the meadow is a prescriptive right. As William Blackstone, the great English jurist, wrote in 1765 in his *Commentaries on the Laws of England*, any injurious act by one owner against another might be prohibited "for it is incumbent on a neighboring owner to find some other place to do that act, where it will be less offensive."[18]

Now, in such a world you won't build a Gary, Indiana, or a Pittsburgh or a Houston or a Los Angeles. If the country is to grow economically, some property must be commercially developed, even to the detriment of the amenity rights of others. Adverse spillovers, or what economists call **negative externalities**, such as smoke, noise, congestion, and all the other unlovely consequences of economic growth, are inevitable. The prospect is expressed by the old English saying "Where there's muck there's brass." Vested property rights would have to be dislodged. Rights long enjoyed, prescriptive rights, would have to be weakened to make way for other rights, **priority rights**, to grow where there was conflict. Trees had to be cut, streams and rivers dammed up, mines dug, and factories built.

In our own time, with 275 million people, there is great concern about finding ways to adjust and reduce priority rights in the interests of environment and ecology. Between 1780 and 1860, when Americans faced an undeveloped continent, the sentiments were the opposite. The doctrine of ancient lights had to go. Horwitz cites a case in New York State in 1838, *Parker v. Foote*, in which the judge wrote that the doctrine of ancient lights "cannot be applied in the growing cities and villages of this country without working the most mischievous consequences."[19]

What judicial instrumentalism meant, in fact, was that the entrepreneurial costs of economic development were destined to be subsidized by the public at large. Rivers and lakes might be polluted with industrial wastes, pastoral views obscured, the air made foul so that there could be cities and jobs. Fortunes would be made by entrepreneurs who were not required to compensate other property owners for damage, *unless negligence could be proved in courts*, which was hard to do. People had the right to develop their own property commercially if they did so with reasonable care. A stable next door was noisy because horses are noisy; that noise was not negligence. A nuisance might still be abated by lawsuit, but judges became increasingly tolerant about such matters in the interests of economic growth. "You can't stop progress."

These changes in property rights were accomplished by judges in private law cases.[20] The content of the law was altered, and not subtly, but no changes were made in the constitutional guarantees of the sanctity of property. Some sanctities became greater than others, in the eyes of the law. The meaning of rights changed in accord with the felt needs of nineteenth-century economic development, even though, in theory, eighteenth-century conceptions of property as "absolute dominion" remained. In the twenty-first century, we continue to change these ideas. In an age of environmental concerns, "progress" is commonly stopped by the courts—despite the old adage—proof that we live in a different era.

An example of the change in attitudes about the social value of material improvements was already noted in the appearance of mechanic lien laws. Another concrete example is the case of *Van Ness v. Pacard* (1829) in which Justice Joseph Story rejected the common-law doctrine that improvements to rental property made by a tenant belonged to the landlord and that the tenant need not be compensated. Nineteenth-century Americans wanted improvements made, just as they valued the frontier squatter's labor when he or she trespassed upon the property of another. The squatter was rewarded for trespass with preemption rights; the tenant must be rewarded as well.[21]

A point to bear in mind is that American ideas of private property rights had been developed in England, then a small, stable, rural society of rigid social-class structure. Americans, with a roughly democratic society, experiencing unheard-of growth on an undeveloped continent, changed the content of the law, strengthening the rights they wanted developed, weakening those they thought were less *economically* efficient. That we might want to change the social weights of these rights again today may be considered entirely reasonable in our circumstances, since our needs in present-day America do not reflect our ancestors' needs. They wanted factories, not forests.

The Changing Nature of Contracts

Another instrumental change of great consequence concerns contracts. Blackstone wrote of English contract law:

> ...a contract for any *valuable* consideration, as for marriage, for money, for work done, or for reciprocal contracts, can never be impeached at law; and, if it be of sufficient adequate value, is never set aside in equity.[22]

Who could make a valid contract? Children, the mentally impaired, and, in many cases, women were not considered competent to make valid contracts. This ruling was based on the assumption that the contracting parties would be too unequal. Such a contract was void for lack of equity. The notion that a valid contract should be equitable, that the contracting parties should be in some sense equal in contracting ability, was a medieval idea, and it stood in the way of economic development. Could a factory worker make an equitable labor contract with a corporation? One argument used to this day favoring unions and collective bargaining is that it is necessary to equalize the strength on both sides of the bargaining table by combining labor, just as capital is combined. In 1898, in the case of *Holden v. Hardy* (upholding Utah's right to regulate employment conditions in mines to protect health and safety), the U.S. Supreme Court ruled that

> ...the fact that both parties are of full age and competent does not necessarily deprive the state of the power to interfere where the parties do not stand upon an equality, or where the public health demands that one party to the contract shall be protected against himself.[23]

The Court argued that in such cases, "self-interest is often an unsafe guide, and the legislature may promptly interpose its authority."[24] Health and safety were involved, but note that the equity argument is added for extra weight. We hear echoes of the equity idea even today, for example, in cases of consumer fraud.

In the eighteenth century, the tradition of equity had prevailed, according to Horwitz, on grounds of "natural justice," and also because so many prices were customary ones. Three changes came quickly:

1. The "meeting of wills" generally ruled against ideas of equity. If two free persons of legal age made a contract without compulsion, it was considered in most cases to be valid. Factory owners could thus contract with masses of employees for wages, hours, and working conditions if the terms were made known and the laborers agreed to them.
2. The meeting of wills was also important in advancing the rule of *caveat emptor* in the markets.

If a vendor *unknowingly* sold defective goods, the buyer's opportunity to inspect the goods before purchase would ensure the vendor's innocence of overt deception.

3. Contracts for sale and purchase made on the basis of current *market* prices ruled. If prices later changed, the original contracted price still held. This change opened the way for the trading of futures contracts of all sorts.

These and other changes facilitated free-market determinations of wages and prices, determinations now freed from older "natural rights" ideas of justice. To some people, of course, this utter commercialization seemed, and still does seem, immoral. In theory, the new ideas of contracts meant that subsequent changes altering the advantages and disadvantages of the contracting parties became irrelevant to the obligations of the contracting parties. For people in business, the passing of bankruptcy laws brought relief from the rigors of contract. Builders who could not complete their work were allowed by the courts to recover "off the contract" for work they had done. Workers simply lost wages if they violated their employment contracts.[25]

Contracts: Employer Liability

Two doctrines developed that relieved employers of liability from the dangers of the workplace and job. First, the courts began to assume that danger was encapsulated in the wage; the greater the danger, other things being equal, the higher the wage. "Normal risk" also was subsumed in the wage, and employees' agreement to the wage contract implied their acceptance of the risks involved. Secondly, the employer's danger of liability for employee injury was reduced by contributory negligence, the negligence of another worker on the job, also known as the "fellow servant doctrine." Injuries in factories (or most other employments) were rarely free of this element. Since injured workers not compensated by their employers were thrown upon society at large for their maintenance, these legal doctrines produced yet another public subsidy for business. To this day, workers are not entirely free of the assumption of normal risk or contributory negligence, either by themselves or by another worker on the job.

These changes, like the triumph of priority rights over those of prescription, were what Scheiber calls the "intangible contributions" to economic growth made by the courts in private law cases. They reduced the risks and the costs of business and made business enterprise more daring (and profitable) than it would otherwise have been.

EMINENT DOMAIN

Other aids to business came from direct government redistribution through eminent domain proceedings. The Fifth and Fourteenth Amendments to the Constitution ensure that private property will not be taken by the federal or state governments without just compensation and due process of law. The technique used to obtain that property, already present in colonial times, is condemnation by right of **eminent domain**. The power of eminent domain is the unusual case where the costs are concentrated and the benefits, diverse. The history of the exercise of this power shows that it was ill-defined and irregular but that, gradually, the process of jury awards became standard in cases where the owner of the condemned property refused the government's offer price. What never became clear is the *limit of the use* to which such property may be put by government after it has been sequestered. The power of eminent domain never was, nor is it now, limited to public purposes. Land may be taken for a canal, railroad, grain elevator, toll road, public housing, or slum clearance. Eminent domain has always been a significant rent-seeking sector; some gain while others lose. The federal government, perhaps honoring Jefferson's desire that it "never after, in any case" regain property sold out of the public domain, did not exercise eminent domain power directly until the 1870s. But states and municipalities did from the beginning.[26]

INCORPORATION

The privilege of incorporation is the gift of the state to collective business ventures. By special dispensation, an enterprise organized in the corporate form is granted *perpetual life* and diversified ownership, each part of which has *limited liability* for the debts and other liabilities of the firm. A corporation is treated in the law as a legal person; it can sue and be sued in its own name. It is, in Chief Justice Marshall's words, "an artificial being, invisible, intangible and existing only in contemplation of the law." He wrote those words in *Dartmouth College v. Woodward* (1819) while upholding that corporation's (the college's) charter, granted by King George III, against an attempt by the state of New Hampshire to overthrow it. From that point on, the corporation emerges in American history as a vivid reality. It develops, legally and in adaptability, until it, and not the traditional proprietorship, becomes the most important form of business enterprise. It is a being with the rights of a citizen, but with its limited liability and perpetual life, it has superhuman economic powers. It is a center of economic power inside the state, created by the state. As Arthur Selwyn Miller describes corporations, they are "feudal entities within the body politic."[27]

There had long been corporations in Europe and in England. Colonial governments granted the rights to private companies seven times. By 1790, there were 40 American corporations. Between 1790 and 1800, nearly 300 new charters were issued. After that, the volume increased. Each charter was a special act of a state legislature (except in New York and Connecticut). Usually, the charter stated the nature of the business venture: its purpose, its location, and the amount of capital it could employ. The charter was a license to do the business in a specified manner. These limitations seemed reasonable at the time, given that the act of incorporation was an extension of the state's sovereign power to a group of private persons.

At first, special franchises were deemed to be grants of monopoly and, therefore, in the province of the sovereign power. The federal government also had the power to incorporate enterprises, as it did in the case of the First (1791–1811) and Second (1816–1836) Banks of the United States. But in the nineteenth century, and generally until World War I, the federal government was reluctant to use its chartering power. In modern times, of course, federally chartered corporations are commonplace; for example, the Commodity Credit Corporation was given a federal charter in 1948.

Beginning in 1811, the state of New York allowed general rules of incorporation, without the need of special legislative charters. Connecticut passed a similar law in 1837, but generalized incorporation did not become common in these states until the 1870s (why this is so will be discussed in Chapter 18). For now, it is sufficient to note that American businesses in the antebellum period had access to incorporation if they wanted it, but the process usually required a special act of legislation, a sometimes expensive, sometimes corrupt, procedure.

Thousands of special-franchise corporations were produced by the state legislatures between 1790 and 1860, probably half of them in the 1850s. The law regarding them was almost uniquely an American product, even though incorporation under English law was known in colonial times. The British Parliament was extremely cautious about allowing limited liability, and from 1720 to 1825, joint-stock enterprises were not allowed in financial business, except for the Bank of England. Since each American state was free to create corporations, it was natural that a good deal of originality would be involved. According to the great legal historian James Willard Hurst, American corporation law owed almost nothing to the English.[28]

Development of new laws for incorporation was a necessity because the U.S. Constitution viewed the individual person as the agent of economic life, as an autonomous, self-motivating creature, and, apart from the state government, it made no provisions for groups. Since the corporation is a group of people who have intermingled their capital under a single legal charter, making them a collective person, new thinking was required. From *Dartmouth College v. Woodward* onward, the law on corporations began to build. We will meet it again shortly.

THE SUPREME COURT AND ECONOMIC GROWTH BEFORE 1860

As previously noted, the federal Constitution was a general, limited document agreed to by sovereign states that already had legal systems of their own. The Constitution was the "supreme law of the land," to be sure, but much was left unsaid. Soon enough, constitutional problems arose that required solutions of *national* scope if the new nation was to remain a coherent political entity as it grew and changed. Given an independent judiciary, and the provision of judicial review, the natural forum for settling disputes of a national character was the Supreme Court of the United States.

Beginning with the reign of Virginian John Marshall as Chief Justice, the Court was not diffident about its powers. In *Marbury v. Madison* (1803)—the "midnight judges" case—Marshall ruled that the U.S. Supreme Court's review powers extended to actions by the other two branches of the federal government and not merely to the laws of the states. Marshall wrote in ringing words in *McCulloch v. Maryland* (1819) the classic statement of "implied powers," while upholding the charter of the Second Bank of the United States:

> We must never forget that it is a constitution we are expounding—(and it is)…intended to endure for ages to come and, consequently, to be adapted to the various crises of human affairs.

Marshall followed a "large policy": that the constitutional power would always be sufficient to meet the need. Since provision was made to amend the Constitution, he could hardly be wrong.

Commerce

By our own era, it became apparent that the broadest power in the federal Constitution is the commerce clause:

> The Congress shall have power…to regulate commerce with nations, and among the several States, and with the Indian tribes…[Article I, Sec. 8, No. 2 of the enumerated powers].

The test case was *Gibbons v. Ogden* (1824), which overturned New York's grant of a steamboat monopoly on the Hudson River, which touches both New York and New Jersey. Only Congress could regulate commerce between the states. In *Cooly v. Board of Wardens* (1851), Chief Justice Roger Taney upheld the powers of the port of Philadelphia to impose controls reflecting its own special needs. But any regulation with national implications, such as of a seaport, was within the regulatory power of Congress. In the case of *Brown v. Maryland* (1827), the Court had held, in connection with the commerce power, that no state could license and tax importers. Once the commerce power was set, it lay mainly in the background until 1887, when it resurfaced with a vengeance upon the establishment of the Interstate Commerce Commission. For long decades after *Gibbons v. Ogden*, business enterprises with national or interstate scope were freed of many of the vexations of state police powers. As Harry Scheiber said of *Gibbons v. Ogden*, it ensured the United States of an internal common market.[29] This situation would prove of immense importance as transportation and production technologies made it possible for local firms to grow and serve a national market.

The Contract Clause

The contract clause contained in Article I, Section 10, of the Constitution reads (by careful excision):

> No state shall pass any…law impairing the obligation of contracts….

The first two cases concerning contract that came before the Marshall Court were *Fletcher v. Peck* (1810) and *Dartmouth College v. Woodward* (1819). The first case was a complex one involving two states and American Indian lands. The definitive case was *Dartmouth College*. Great issues were at stake because Dartmouth's claim to legitimacy, a grant from King George III, also involved by implication every land grant held under this authority. If the patent for Dartmouth College could be overturned by a state legislature, what of the rest? The Court held, as already noted, that the charter of Dartmouth College was a valid contract and was subject to the constitutional prohibition.

Marshall wrote that it was "too clear to require the support of argument" that a mere revolution did not upset vested property rights. Associate Justice Story added that it was a "settled principle of the common law that the division of an empire works no forfeiture on previously vested rights of property."[30] He further added that he considered the idea "monstrous" that a successful revolution would upset arrangements already set in place by the government that had been overthrown. Modern revolutionaries must find the American Revolution a fairly odd thing as revolutions go, restricted as it was by the law.

Commercial Law

The rules by which merchants dealt with each other had evolved separately, for the most part, from other branches of the law. As we saw in Chapter 1, certain

In *Gibbons v. Ogden* (1824), the U.S. Supreme Court secured a single national economy, applying the commerce clause to overturn the steamboat monopoly on the Hudson River that had been granted by New York State to Robert Fulton and his financial backer, Robert Livingston. Shown here is Fulton's first steamboat, the *Clermont*, named after Livingston's estate on the Hudson.

international rules had prevailed by the time of the American colonization, especially the rules of negotiable instruments and shipping derived from the practices of the Hanseatic League. As the U.S. economy grew under the separate commercial experiences of the states, a clumsy variability began to appear. In *Swift v. Tyson* (1842), Justice Story argued that there must be a general "Law Merchant" in the United States. When the state laws conflicted with each other, the Supreme Court had the obligation to rule for all so that the right rules could be found by the Court in the "general principles of commercial law." Again, the national economy felt the unifying force of the Constitution. The Court, until the 1930s, tended to honor states' rights wherever possible, but in matters economic the idea that a single national market must prevail is evident from the beginning.

Business Enterprise

Within a few decades of its founding, the Court began to favor a competitive national market. In *Charles River Bridge v. Warren Bridge* (1837) the Court overturned the ancient conception that a state special-franchise charter *implied* a grant of monopoly. The Court held that a state might incorporate competing enterprises if it so wished. This was a vitally important development, especially in transportation. Soon there were *competing forms of transportation*, with corporate charters, whose efforts "damaged" each other's property rights (profits). Ferries competed with bridges, railroads with canals; later on, airplanes and trucks competed with railroads and each other; wire-transmitted communication systems vied first with wireless and underground cable systems and now with satellite transmissions. It could no longer be, as the common law held, that a franchise was automatically a grant of exclusive right.

The *Charles River Bridge* case also involved two other important issues: (a) A prescriptive right, a previously vested property right, was lost, and (b) it was argued in the case that the "public good" had to be considered, that it was best served by competition, and that it must be an issue in considering the validity of vested property rights. This issue loomed large in years to come when the states, and then the federal government, expanded their powers to regulate the private exploitation of private property—the rates, prices, and profits of business enterprises.

Finally, in the case of *Bank of Augusta v. Earle* (1839), the states were allowed to legislate against out-of-state corporations doing intrastate business, but could not restrict the movements of agents of corporations between the states. Each corporate being became a "person," was "domiciled" in the state of its charter, and was free to do business in other states, unless doing so was specifically prohibited by state legislation. The case has always been celebrated for its ambiguity, and the states continue to this day to pass discriminatory legislation whenever possible, thereby suppressing competition by creating in-state rents for their own corporate creatures at the expense of the public. The Court had to bow toward the Full Faith and Credit clause of the Constitution (Article IV, Sec. 1), but it also had to respect the states' powers to regulate under their police powers. Chief Justice Taney backed away from defining a corporate person as a *citizen*, however, and the issue of the full rights of the corporate person was thus deferred until 1886. By then the "person" whose property was protected by the Fifth Amendment was a citizen (if born in the United States or naturalized) under the Fourteenth Amendment. The rights of the citizen were protected against state laws. The corporate persons were then called" "citizens" and given that protection in *Santa Clara County v. Southern Pacific Railroad.* Thus we must consider this issue again later, in connection with railroad regulation.

These cases represent the main trends of judicial review affecting economic development before 1860. Their general tendency took the same direction as the instrumentalism of the state courts—easing the way for business, economic growth, and the creation of an integrated national market. The Marshall Court was especially robust in the nationalism of its decisions. However, there is a certain caution, too, as Harry Scheiber emphasized.[31]

Before the 1870s or thereabouts, the powers of the federal government were still seen as circumscribed by the powers reserved to the states—except on the issues of slavery and withdrawal from the federal agreement by the Southern states. Private rights under the common law were still reserved to the states. The big change in this regard begins in 1877, which we will discuss in due course.

What can be said most generally of the antebellum period is that the law aided the evolution of the main ideas and institutions of developing American capitalism: economic growth based mainly upon private decision making regarding the exploitation of privately owned productive resources. Behind these developments was the assumption that most economic life was a private matter—government aided and supported private economic power and also relied upon that power to produce growth. Only later will we see the older ideas of governmental restraints reemerging, as in colonial times, but this time at the federal level.

NOTES

1. For further study, see, in particular, the articles of Harry Scheiber, a leading scholar in this line of analysis and pioneer of its use in economic history, and the book (1991) of Herbert Hovenkamp, a legal scholar with insight into economic history.
2. Stuart Bruchey emphasizes that such results were aided and abetted by certain *social* consequences of the Revolution: an established "elite" of landed and commercial wealth that had become ensconced in the colonial era, and whose allegiances were to the Crown, was upended, and thousands were driven into exile when the war ended. "Economy and Society in an Earlier America," *JEH*, June 1987.
3. 4 Wheaton, 518 (1819) 651.
4. The argument that regulation was a widely accepted social phenomena is central to William J. Novack, *The People's Welfare: Law and Regulation in Nineteenth-Century America* (Chapel Hill: The University of North Carolina Press, 1995).
5. Oscar and Mary Handlin, *Commonwealth, A Study of the Role of Government in the American Economy: Massachusetts 1774–1861* (1947).
6. *Ibid.*, pp. 93–94.
7. *Ibid.*, p. 70.
8. Louis Hartz, *Economic Policy and Democratic Thought: Pennsylvania, 1776–1860* (Cambridge: Harvard University Press, 1948), p. 204.

9. Francis Newton Thorpe, ed., *The Federal and State Constitutions* (Washington: Government Printing Office, 1909), p. 2662.
10. Handlin and Handlin (1947), p. 260.
11. Lance Davis and Douglass North, *Institutional Change and American Economic Growth* (1971), pp. 74–77.
12. Jonathan Hughes, *Social Control in the Colonial Economy* (Charlottesville: University Press of Virginia, 1976), p. 139.
13. Mancur Olson, *The Logic of Collective Action: Public Goods and the Theory of Groups* (New York: Schocken Books, 1971), chap. 1.
14. Terry Anderson and Peter J. Hill, "Institutional Change Through the Supreme Court and the Rise of Transfer Activity," in Roger Ransom, Richard Sutch, and Gary Walton, eds., *Explorations in the New Economic History* (1982).
15. E. A. J. Johnson, *The Foundations of American Economic Freedom* (Minneapolis: University of Minnesota Press, 1973).
16. For two authoritative treatments of this instrumentalism, see Harry Scheiber, "Federalism and the American Economic Order, 1789–1910," *Law and Society*, Fall 1975, and Morton Horwitz, *The Transformation of American Law, 1780–1860* (1977). Both authors give extensive bibliographies of this literature.
17. Horwitz (1977), p. 30.
18. Quoted in *Ibid.*, p. 31.
19. *Ibid.*, p. 46.
20. See Scheiber's various articles and Horwitz (1977) for examples.
21. Karen B. Clay, "Property Rights and Institutions: Congress and the California Land Act of 1851," *Journal of Economic History*, vol. 59, no. 1, March 1999, provides an interesting case study of the implementation of property rights following California's entry into the union. Mark T. Kanazawa, "Efficiency in Western Water Law: The Development of the California Doctrine, 1850–1911," *Journal of Legal Studies*, Vol. XXVII, no.1, January 1998, examines California's approach to water law at exactly the same time.
22. William Blackstone, *Commentaries on the Laws of England* (Oxford: The Clarendon Press, 1765), book II, p. 443.
23. 169 U.S. 398 (1898).
24. *Ibid.*
25. For a full discussion of contract changes, see Horwitz (1977), chap. 5.
26. Harry Scheiber, "The Road to Munn: Eminent Domain and the Concept of Public Purpose in the State Courts," *Perspectives in American History*, 1971. For a full history, see Errol Meidinger's fine survey, "The 'Public Uses' of Eminent Domain: History and Policy," *Environmental Law*, Spring 1980.
27. Arthur Selwyn Miller, *The Supreme Court and American Capitalism* (1972), p. 14.
28. James Willard Hurst, *The Legitimacy of the Business Corporation in the United States* (1970), p. 1.
29. But, as Scheiber (1975) illustrates, there continued to be cases under the commerce power, and the rule of *Gibbons* was not entirely unambiguous when applied to these cases, especially where police powers were involved.
30. 4 Wheaton 518, 706–707 (1819).
31. For example, see Scheiber (1975).

SUGGESTED READINGS

Articles

Anderson, Terry, and P. J. Hill. "Institutional Change Through the Supreme Court and the Rise of Transfer Activity." In Roger L. Ransom, Richard Sutch, and Gary M. Walton, eds., *Explorations in the New Economic History: Essays in Honor of Douglass C. North*. New York: Academic Press, 1982.

Bruchey, Stuart. "Economy and Society in an Earlier America." *Journal of Economic History*, vol. XLVII, no. 2, June 1987.

Horwitz, Morton. "The Transformation in the Concept of Property in American Law, 1780–1860." *University of Chicago Law Review*, vol. 40, no. 2, Winter 1973.

Lively, Robert A. "The American System: A Review Article." *Business History Review*, vol. 29, no. 1, March 1955.

McGuire, Robert A., and Robert L. Ohsfeldt. "Economic Interests and the American Constitution: A Quantitative Rehabilitation of Charles A. Beard." *Journal of Economic History*, vol. XLIV, no. 2, June 1984.

Mann, W. Howard. "The Marshall Court: Nationalization of Private Rights and Personal Liberty from the Authority of the Commerce Clause." *Indiana Law Journal*, vol. 38, no. 2, Winter 1963.

Meidinger, Errol E. "The 'Public Uses' of Eminent Domain: History and Policy." *Environmental Law*, vol. 11, no. 1, Spring 1980.

Scheiber, Harry. "At the Borderlands of Law and Economic History: The Contributions of Willard Hurst." *American Historical Review*, vol. 75, no. 3, February 1970.

———. "The Road to Munn: Eminent Domain and the Concept of Public Purpose in the State Courts." *Perspectives in American History*, vol. 5, 1971.

———. "Property Law, Expropriation and Resource Allocation by Government, 1789–1910." *Journal of Economic History*, vol. XXXIII, no. 1, March 1973.

———. "Instrumentalism and Property Rights." *Wisconsin Law Review*, vol. 1975, no. 1, 1975.

———. "Federalism and the American Economic Order, 1789–1910." *Law and Society*, vol. 10, no. 1, Fall 1975.

———. "Regulation, Property Rights, and Definition of the Market: Law and the American Economy." *Journal of Economic History*, vol. XLI, no. 1, March 1981.

Umbeck, John. "The California Gold: A Study of Emerging Property Rights." *Explorations in Economic History*, vol. 14, no. 3, July 1977.

Books

Coleman, Peter J. *Debtors and Creditors in America: Insolvency, Imprisonment for Debt and Bankruptcy, 1607–1900.* Madison: State Historical Society of Wisconsin, 1974.

Davis, Lance E., and Douglass C. North. *Institutional Change and American Economic Growth.* New York: Cambridge University Press, 1971.

Friedman, Lawrence. *A History of American Law.* New York: Simon & Schuster, 1973.

Handlin, Oscar and Mary. *Commonwealth, A Study of Government in the American Economy: Massachusetts 1774–1861.* New York: New York University Press, 1947.

Horwitz, Morton. *The Transformation of American Law 1780–1860.* Cambridge: Harvard University Press, 1977.

Hovenkamp, Herbert. *Enterprise and American Law, 1836–1937.* Cambridge: Harvard University Press, 1991.

Hughes, Jonathan. *The Governmental Habit Redux.* Princeton: Princeton University Press, 1991.

Hurst, James Willard. *Law and the Conditions of Freedom in the Nineteenth Century United States.* Madison: University of Wisconsin Press, 1956.

———. *Law and Social Process in United States History.* Ann Arbor: University of Michigan Law School, 1960.

———. *The Legitimacy of the Business Corporation in the Law of the United States 1780–1970.* Charlottesville: University Press of Virginia, 1970.

Johnson, E. A. J. *The Foundations of American Freedom.* Minneapolis: University of Minnesota Press, 1973.

Miller, Arthur Selwyn. *The Supreme Court and American Capitalism.* New York: The Free Press, 1972.

CHAPTER EIGHT

Transportation, Internal Improvements, and Urbanization

Successful economic development depended not only upon the establishment of farms and extractive activities, but also upon the creation of towns at breaks-in-transport. The process discussed in Chapter 2 continued, for the same reasons, as economic activity spread westward. The revenue that firms earn from selling their outputs must cover both production and distribution costs. Transportation is a large component of the latter. **Productivity**, output per unit of input, rises in part as transport costs decrease. Think of how many teamsters and wagons it would take to carry as much freight as one train can hold. The train "frees" labor to pursue a different specialization, say farming. Thus, output increases, and living standards improve, just as the principle of comparative advantage suggests. Americans were aware of this, and no single collective activity was really more striking in the antebellum period than the nation's energetic pursuit of transportation improvements.

The way such activities were organized is of special interest. In England, canals and railroads were built by private capitalism, almost without government participation. But in the United States, overwhelmingly, there was a mixture of enterprise—part private and part governmental. Economic historians have long debated whether these mixtures were examples of successful rent-seeking by private operators who successfully extracted special privileges from governments, or whether wily political leaders, who wanted such improvements for reasons of local or national ambition, coaxed private enterprise out into the open by the offer of special advantages. We cannot resolve the debate; we can only consider a short synopsis of the major arguments of both sides.

Traditionally, it was believed that the sheer size of the investment required for improvements like canals and railroads was beyond the capability of private entrepreneurs acting alone.[1] Because of transaction costs or risk, or both, the theory held that the private sector could not raise the necessary funds in competition with the other available investment opportunities. Governmental units—state, local, or even national—could ease this constraint by giving direct financial contributions or by lending their credit through the issuance of long-term bonds whose proceeds went to pay, in part, for construction.

The legal historian James Willard Hurst advanced a different argument, shifting the initiative from the private sector to government:

> We felt the need to promote a volunteer muster of capital for sizable ventures at a time when fluid capital was scarce and there were severe practical limits on the government's ability to tax in order to support direct intervention in the economy.[2]

By incorporating transportation companies, political leaders could grant privileges and the rights to contract loans, levy tolls, and even (in some cases) print money to support transportation enterprises. Consequently, state and local governments became vitally involved almost from the beginning. In effect, they delegated the taxing power to private companies along with the other forms of government assistance that were provided. Thus, Hurst argues, it is government involving private capital, not vice versa, that explains the vigor of mixed enterprises. Let us now consider the results in detail.

THE INTERNAL IMPROVEMENT ERA

Once settlers began pouring into western lands, the advantages of improved transportation became obvious. At first, it was hoped that the new federal government would play a major role, and, indeed, in 1806, work was underway to build a national road from Cumberland, Maryland, westward to Illinois (ultimately, supporters hoped, all the way to Missouri). That same year, proposals for federal aid in canal building had already been before Congress. The basis for these proposals was that funds from sales of public lands would support such projects.

It often is said that economic planning is somehow foreign to the American scheme of things. Yet, early in the country's independent existence, the United States had a full-scale plan for a comprehensive system of internal land and water transport in the eastern part of the country: the Gallatin Plan. The idea came from the Senate itself. Secretary of the Treasury Albert Gallatin received instruction in 1807 to prepare "a plan for the application of such means as are within the power of Congress, to the purposes of opening roads and making canals...."[3]

Gallatin delivered his plan to the Senate in April 1808. In it he emphasized "the extent of territory compared to the population," and the lack of sufficient private capital to exploit potential opportunities. To sustain private investment, he believed, communications links had to be set up between areas that could readily generate revenues. A time would come when such enterprises would pay, but initially, only the federal government, he believed, could command sufficient resources. To give the country a "tidewater inland navigation" from Massachusetts to Georgia, he proposed that canals be cut through Cape Cod, between the Raritan and Delaware rivers, between Delaware Bay and Chesapeake Bay, and between the Chesapeake and Albemarle Sound. In addition, he suggested major east-west links: a northern link from the Hudson River to Lake Champlain, and from the Mohawk River to Lake Ontario and Lake Erie; and connecting road links between the Allegheny and the Susquehanna (or Juniata) rivers, the Monongahela and the Potomac, the Kanawha and the James, and the Tennessee and the Santee (or the Savannah).[4]

With all the canals and road links, the plan would cost, according to Gallatin, $20 million—an outlay of $2 million per year for ten years. He believed that the federal government could bear the expense and that the advantages would be incalculable. Moreover, once the projects generated sufficient revenues, they could be sold to private companies, and the proceeds could be used to promote further internal improvements.

The plan, ingenious as it was, was not undertaken by the federal government for a variety of reasons, including doubts about its legality. Presidents Madison and Monroe both favored federal participation in internal improvements projects but considered such federal action within the states unconstitutional. The Constitution had been an agreement between existing sovereignties, and expansion of federal power was viewed with deep suspicion. Monroe had wanted the federal Constitution amended to allow for such federal action. However, federal intervention in those days of "strict constructionism" faded in 1830, when President Jackson vetoed the Maysville Road bill, calling it "unconstitutional." Between 1824 and 1828, about $2 million of federal funds had been spent on canals.[5] The national road from Maryland to Missouri was never to be completed as originally planned, but, altogether, some $7 million of federal money had been spent on it.

The federal government's failure to implement the Gallatin Plan was offset by private entrepreneurs. Together with state and local governments, they (as Carter Goodrich showed) completed most of it.[6] Railroads ultimately filled in the gaps. Goodrich argued that politics and sectional rivalries, and not ideology, largely nullified the hope of full-scale federal participation, even at these early dates. Tariff votes for the Northeast were traded for internal improvement votes for the Midwest; the South was left with little to gain from federal expenditures on internal improvements. Gallatin's plan was indirectly influential in charting the future course of events. It just ended up being done in a different way.

ROADS, CANALS, STEAMBOATS, AND RAILROADS

Turnpikes (intercity toll roads) seemed at first to offer a solution to many surface transport problems. They offered a more dependable road surface (stone, gravel, and later, plank) than did the common roads as well as direct links between well-populated and, therefore, profitable areas. Local roads were adequate for local needs. It hardly paid taxpayers in any location to construct better roads for the advantage of others. However, turnpike promoters hoped that the offer of superior quality with greater possible speed and dependability would attract sufficient long- and middle-distance traffic to pay a profit to investors. More than $25 million of private capital was invested by several hundred turnpike companies; turnpike mileage was approximately 4,600 miles in 1810 and about 27,800 miles by 1830.[7] Because most turnpike companies were small and built fairly short roads, a given long-distance route would be served by several such companies, each charging tolls on its own sections. Since tolls were regulated by public officials and activities of the companies were restricted by their charters to road operations, turnpike profits proved disappointing.

The record of turnpike profitability is, in fact, dismal. Most potential traffic at that time consisted of fairly short journeys, and, for these, common (free) roads were an alternative. Costs per ton mile on the turnpikes were lowest for large loads making long journeys. Unfortunately, most turnpike traffic was not of that nature. Albert Fishlow estimated that profit rates were only 3 and 4 percent for turnpikes.[8] By the 1830s, the turnpikes had been overtaken by canals, then by the railroads, and were subsequently abandoned. Most of the funds invested in turnpikes had been private in origin, even in Pennsylvania, where direct state government investment was greatest. Still, it amounted to only 30 percent of the estimated total. In antebellum canal and railroad construction, the proportion of government money to the total was much larger.

Canals

The great canal-building era, roughly 1815 to 1843, had many interesting characteristics that have tantalized modern scholars. (Figure 8.1 shows the canal system of 1800–1860.) It was through turnpikes and canals that mixed enterprises—combinations of private and (state and local) government money and power—entered American history. American canal building in the antebellum period was truly on a large scale. According to Professor Harvey Segal, canal investment from 1815 to 1844 was $31 million, of which 73 percent came from governments. From 1844 to 1860, another $66 million was invested, of which about 66 percent was government money.[9]

Although a few entirely private canals existed, they were fairly inconsequential. The Santee Canal, built in 1800 in South Carolina, and the Middlesex, constructed from Boston to Lowell in 1803, were private. But it was the completion of the Erie Canal in 1825 that pointed to a great future. The cost of shipping a ton of wheat from Buffalo to New York City fell from $100 a ton to $10. Shipping times fell to one-third of what they had been. Settlement in the Northwest Territory, which had been along the Ohio and Mississippi rivers, would shift north to the Great Lakes area.

Hopes for federal aid to build the Erie Canal were dashed in March 1817 when President Madison vetoed a bill that would have provided $1.5 million. A month later, the New York legislature passed the necessary laws to build a canal between the Hudson River and Lake Erie by state action alone. Funds were to come from earmarked taxes, from borrowing on state credit, and from tolls collected as sections of the canal opened. When completed, the canal was 363 miles long and cost $7 million. Initial issues of Erie bonds were in small denominations and were purchased mainly by citizens of New York State. When the success of the canal became evident, large investors and foreign buyers entered. By 1829, foreigners had purchased half of the canal's debt. Then, as now, foreign investment was welcomed as long as it didn't involve control. With success came expansion. Several feeder

FIGURE 8.1 Principal Canals 1800–1860

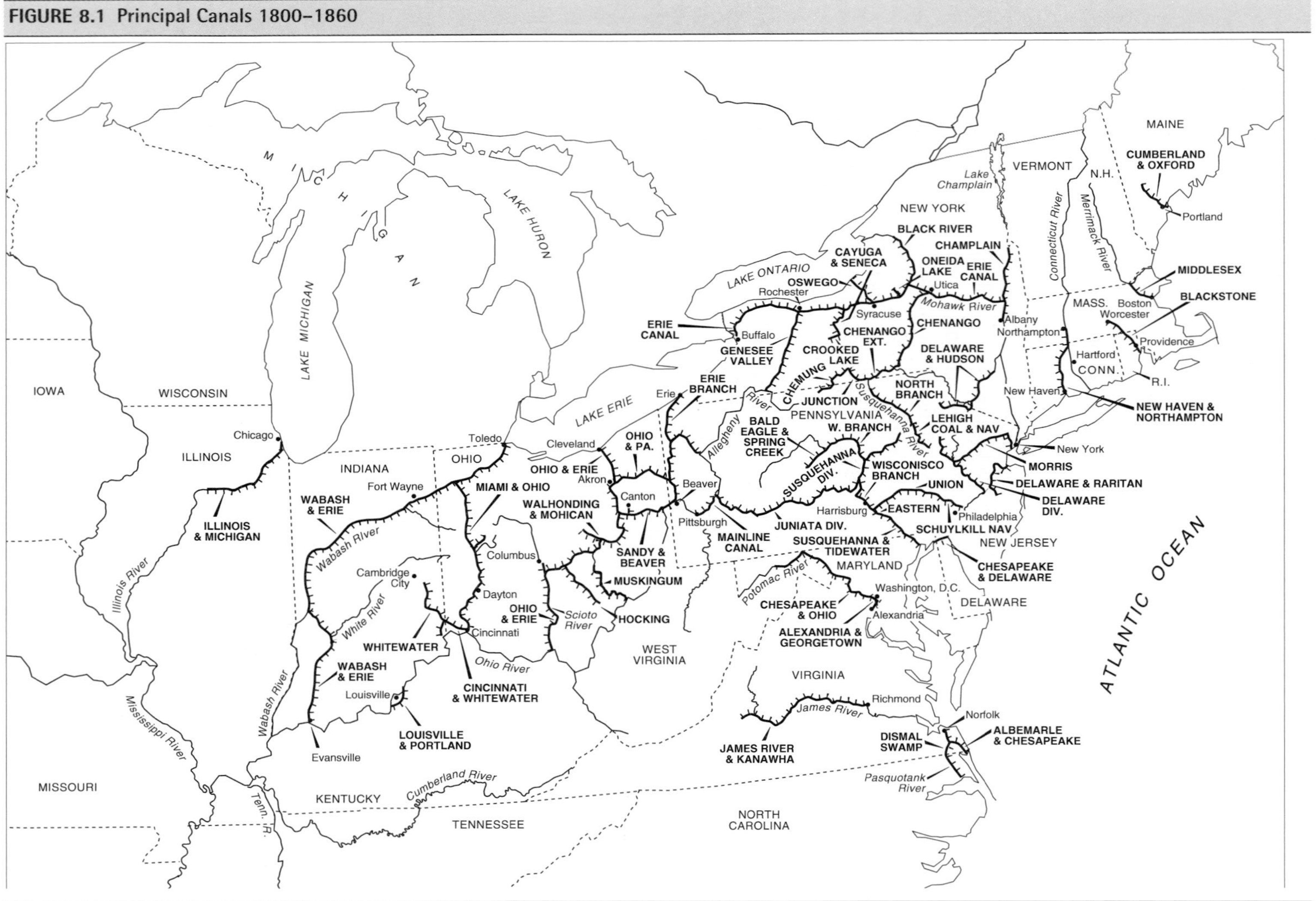

In the antebellum period, an elaborate canal system was built to exploit the country's internal water-transport possibilities, mainly east of the Mississippi River. The longest canal was the Wabash and Erie, from Evansville, Indiana, to Toledo, Ohio.

Canals and Railroads. Mixed transport technologies moved westward in the age of internal improvements in the 1830s (above). Canals formed an internal transportation network in the competitive race with railroads in Pennsylvania (left).

lines were constructed, including a connection to Lake Champlain.[10]

Following the Erie's success, a flurry of canal building began elsewhere. The enterprising citizens of Pennsylvania were early enthusiasts for internal improvements. By 1789, they were benefiting from what later was called a "Gallatin Plan for Pennsylvania," produced by the Society for Promoting Improvement of Road and Inland Navigation. The road west, the Pittsburgh Pike, was completed in 1817. The state had invested tax funds, which by 1825 amounted to \$1.8 million, in 56 turnpike and bridge companies, in cooperation with private capitalists. But the Erie presented a new challenge. Philadelphia's preeminence was now threatened, and in 1826, the legislature voted to build the Main Line Canal with state funds.

Because of the Appalachian barrier's height and width between Pittsburgh and the coastal plain, the

Main Line was a complicated project involving transfers of cargo to surface transport (later to rail links) at several points. These necessary breaks-in-transport would, from the start, put the Main Line at a competitive disadvantage with the Erie. The Main Line, traversing 359 miles, was completed in 1835 at a construction cost of some $12 million. By then, an additional $6.5 million had been spent on smaller canals.

In the aftermath of the Panic of 1837, Pennsylvania, like several other states, failed (in 1842) to meet the interest on the $33 million of state obligations that had accumulated from internal improvements projects. It later redeemed the securities. Overall, the Main Line earned only 3 percent on the original investment of $12 million. It was sold to the Pennsylvania Railroad in 1857 for $7.5 million.[11]

Canal building was also a major state undertaking in parts of the Midwest where natural waterways seemed to offer excellent opportunities for canal improvements. Indiana built the longest waterway, from Evansville on the Ohio River all the way north to Toledo, Ohio. Called the Wabash and Erie Canal, it was 450 miles long. The Wabash and Erie was finished in the 1850s at a cost of $6.5 million and was abandoned a short while later because of railroad competition. In Ohio, canal building was extensive: 761 miles of canals at a cost of $16 million to connect the state's waterways. While the first wave of canal building in Ohio was successful, the second wave of the 1830s was not; railroad competition proved too strong.[12]

Illinois had a federal land grant to support the Illinois and Michigan Canal, linking Lake Michigan to the Mississippi River via the Chicago and Illinois rivers. Like the Wabash and Erie, it cost about $6.5 million and was superseded quickly by the railroad; what remains is now a "national heritage corridor." Experience with this canal finally inspired engineers to dredge the Chicago River, reversing its flow and thus making possible the modern Chicago megalopolis.[13] The original canal, however, was a financial failure.

Other canals experienced the same fate. Both Virginia and Maryland had supported the Potomac Canal Company with state funds, and George Washington himself had been its first president. The company, which built locks around five falls of the Potomac, ended in bankruptcy. In 1825, a new venture, the Chesapeake and Ohio Canal, was underway with an initial grant of $1 million of federal money and an additional $2 million of state and local funds. Private participation was a minority interest, a mere $600,000. The canal was to extend to Cumberland, Maryland. That goal was finally reached 25 years later in 1850 after an expenditure of $10 million, 60 percent of which had been supplied by the State of Maryland alone.

Virginia's internal improvements were, relatively speaking, immense. Goodrich estimates that at the end of the 1850s, the state had contributed, in total, close to $55 million to internal improvements in canals, roads, and railroads. State aid in Virginia was always meant to be bait to draw private funds into action. Virginia was an explicit example of the Hurst thesis (discussed earlier). As an 1815 report stated: "The Commonwealth should subscribe so much...and on such terms as will suffice to elicit individual wealth for public improvement."[14] Virginians made every effort to open up their interior to commerce by public effort. Apparently they were not discouraged by the lack of profitability (by private standards), since at the outbreak of the Civil War, Virginia authorized extensive new outlays from the public funds.

The entire canal system would have made sense if there had been no railroads. As Albert Niemi suggests, these canals fostered a manufacturing sector to serve a regional agriculture made more prosperous by cheaper transport costs. But, as Roger Ransom shows, a major portion of the manufacturing that grew up along the canal routes was the processing of agricultural output for export out of the regions served by the new canals.[15] In both cases, the canals brought greater economic activity by reducing transport costs. But the long-run fate of most canals in the United States was sealed by the railroads, which came along, in many cases, on competitive routes before the canals were even completed. The railroads provided faster, more dependable, year-round service to offset the higher freight charges, and the canals were mainly left in the dust of history.[16]

Steamboats

No account of the country's antebellum growth is complete without an examination of the development of steamboats and their use on the great internal river system—the Ohio, Missouri, and Mississippi rivers—that drains half a continent. Flatboats, keelboats, and the legendary steam-driven paddle wheelers gave farmers in the vast interior cheap transportation for their crops downriver to New Orleans and the sea. They also brought manufactures back from New Orleans into the interior of the country. James Mak and Gary Walton said of this era: "The transformation of these areas, 1815–1860, from unsettled backwoods regions into agricultural heartland was due primarily to improvements in river transportation."[17]

The process began as early as 1811. The supply-side impact of the steamboats is obvious in two separate measures: (a) the carrying capacity of the river steamboat fleet as tonnage (tons of water displaced by the vessels) and (b) the productivity of that tonnage. How efficiently was it used? Both factors could increase the available transport supply at every price. Because the entire supply curve of transportation shifted to the right, increases in tonnage, and/or in its efficiency in use, lowered the costs of food transportation and thus the price of food to the consumer.

Erik Haites and James Mak considerably refined our understanding of the actual river steamboat fleet and its tonnage on the western rivers in the antebellum period. They were able to calculate the *net* additions annually to tonnage and number of steamboats by estimating the number and tonnages of boats removed from service each year. Table 8.1 shows the Haites and Mak data for selected years.

Before 1860, the average working life of a river steamboat was only about 5.5 years.[18] And the boats were not cheap. The capital embedded in the least expensive vessel in a sample reported by Jeremy Atack was greater than that invested in 85 percent of extant manufacturing firms and equal to the price of six average farms. More than half the boats in Atack's sample met their end in an accident. Most were lost as a result of snags in the river, but explosions and fires were also common occurrences.[19]

By the end of the 1850s, a vast fleet of some 800 steamboats serviced the interior rivers of the United States. Freight rates had fallen in real terms by some 90 percent upstream from 1815 to 1860 and by nearly 40 percent downstream (where they already were relatively low because of the highly competitive flatboat market for downstream traffic).[20] The heavy loads, crops and raw materials, tended to go downstream, but the lighter and more valuable (per unit) upstream cargoes gained enormously from steamboat technology. Transit and turnaround times were drastically cut by the steamboats and the technology associated with them.

TABLE 8.1 Steamboats in Operation on Western Rivers, 1811–1860

Years	*Number*	*Tonnage*
1811	1	371
1815	7	1,516
1820	69	14,208
1825	80	12,527
1830	151	24,574
1835	324	50,123
1840	494	82,626
1845	538	96,155
1850	638	134,566
1855	696	172,695
1860	817	195,022

Source: Erik F. Haites and James Mak, "The Decline of Steamboating on the Ante-Bellum Western Rivers: Some New Evidence and an Alternative-Hypothesis," *Explorations in Economic History,* vol. 11, no. 1, Fall 1973. Derived from their Table A-1.

Growth of the river steamboat fleet was not constant, either in construction or in tonnages in service. Haites and Mak found cyclical activity that was roughly in accord with overall economic fluctuations, as did Harvey Segal in his study of canal building.[21] The business cycles were pervasive in their effects upon advances in transport, as we will see shortly in the case of the new railroad system. Steamboat construction boomed during general expansions, and the construction growth lagged a year or so behind general downturns. Boats under construction tended to be carried through to completion, despite worsening prospects in downturns. On the other hand, since crews could be laid off instantly and the boats docked when trade slumped, tonnage in use did not lag behind cyclical downturns.

As was the case with steamship building generally, each new expansion of construction embodied the newest improvements; therefore, productivity per ship tended to rise even more than the increases in tonnage indicate.[22] The operating tonnage of the 1850s was far more efficient than that of earlier periods.

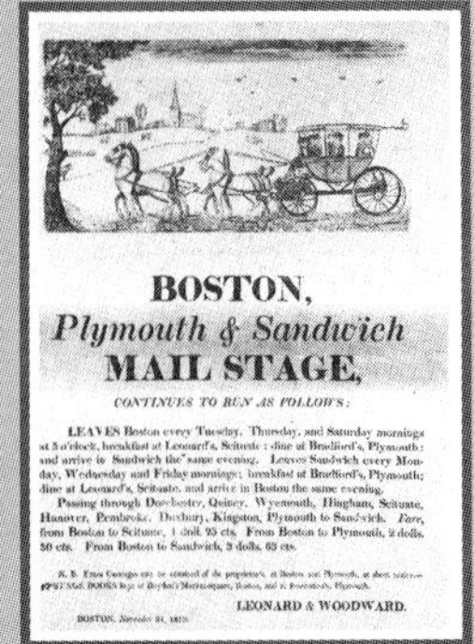

BOSTON,
Plymouth & Sandwich
MAIL STAGE,

CONTINUES TO RUN AS FOLLOWS:

LEAVES Boston every Tuesday, Thursday, and Saturday mornings at 5 o'clock, breakfast at Leonard's, Scituate: dine at Bradford's, Plymouth: and arrive in Sandwich the same evening. Leaves Sandwich every Monday, Wednesday and Friday mornings; breakfast at Bradford's, Plymouth; dine at Leonard's, Scituate, and arrive in Boston the same evening.

Passing through Dorchester, Quincy, Weymouth, Hingham, Scituate, Hanover, Pembroke, Duxbury, Kingston, Plymouth to Sandwich. *Fare*, from Boston to Scituate, 1 doll. 25 cts. From Boston to Plymouth, 2 dolls. 50 cts. From Boston to Sandwich, 3 dolls. 63 cts.

N. B. [illegible]

LEONARD & WOODWARD.

BOSTON, [illegible]

Early Roadways and Waterways. ***Moving people and goods over rutted dirt roads that became dangerously muddy and frequently impassable during bad weather discouraged most early travel. Attempts to bridge mud with corduroy roads of logs laid side by side (opposite, upper left) resulted only in lame horses and rickety wagons. It was not until roads paved with stone and gravel were built by private companies that travel increased. Fees for use of the roads varied for freight, horsemen, and stages, and were collected at tollgates (top left). By 1811, there were 137 such road companies in New York State alone. Numerous inns and taverns opened along the turnpikes to accommodate travelers (below). When***

roadways were impeded by broad, deep rivers that could not be bridged, ferries took travelers across (above right). Coal, grain, and agricultural products were taken to market on flatboats and rafts, which frequently were sold for their lumber, as well. After steamboats were invented, they became the primary mover of goods and people on America's waters (below).

Mak and Walton measure an increase in per-unit productivity of the steamboat fleet by nearly a factor of nine from 1815 to 1860.[23]

Improvements in design (which raised the ratio of net carrying capacity to gross tonnage), together with better engines and improved docking facilities (cutting turnaround times), accounted for most of the productivity increase, and most of that was achieved as early as the 1840s, according to Mak and Walton.[24] The evidence shows that railroad competition did not cause total steamboat freight to fall before the Civil War.[25] But the disruptions of the river system during the war, together with increased railroad building during and after the war, put an end to the glorious era of antebellum steamboating celebrated by Mark Twain and others.

Mak and Walton emphasize that many factors, each working in its own way, produced the golden age of the river steamboat: Externalities like the "growth of market trade and improvements in commercial organization" contributed to improved turnaround times, while design changes, river improvements, better captains and crews, lowered insurance rates, and a host of other small changes made their contributions. Mak and Walton quote from Louis Hunter's classic work, *Steamboats on the Western Rivers*, which says that "plodding progress" was how it was done.[26] Nevertheless, railroads displaced river steamboats after the Civil War in the legendary "transportation revolution" of the American economy.

Railroads

The railroad has long played a pivotal role in American economic history books. No single innovation before, or since, quite gripped the minds of historians, and none seemed to characterize so aptly the adventuresome spirit of the nineteenth century in the United States. Apart from the color (in song and story), there were two bases for the railroad's high place in American historiography: (a) To a much greater extent than the other forms of transportation we have discussed, the railroad was perceived as having "opened the country," building (at great risk) "ahead of demand," gambling on the future. (b) The railroads sharply reduced transportation costs, linking the country together in all directions and spurring the nation's growth far in advance of anything that might otherwise have been achieved. Railroad construction even determined, in its variations, the timing of the nineteenth-century business cycle.[27] However, modern scholarship has sharply deflated all of these appraisals.

The work of Albert Fishlow on antebellum railroads lays to rest the idea that the early railroads were typically built by farseeing geniuses who knew where future development would take place.[28] Fishlow found that the early railroads went mainly into areas that were already populated and developed, even in Illinois, and that the required amount of government money tended to vary inversely with the profitability of the routes: The lower the profit prospects for private investors, the more government money was needed to attract railroad construction.

Where the proportion of government participation was greatest, Fishlow argues, the motives of local governments to invest tax money were mainly "defensive"—to ensure that certain communities would not be bypassed. Railroad planners sometimes assembled routes based solely on the promise of local public participation: In that case, the evidence supports the traditional view that promoters deceived governments into investing in questionable enterprises. But governments also were willing to make financial offers to attract promoters (as they still do with devices like tax increment financing), which is evidence that the deception worked both ways. Obviously, in all cases, the opportunities were mutually, although not necessarily equally, attractive.

For a time, Robert Fogel's work on the social savings created by the railroads threw nearly all historians into a tizzy.[29] The tradition, built up for decades, had placed railroad construction at the very center of explanations of the fantastic economic growth achieved by Americans in the nineteenth century. Instead of recounting once again the truly impressive evidence on American railroad construction, Fogel asked an interesting question: How might the country have developed had there never been any railroads? What was the **social saving** of railroads—the difference between real GNP with the railroad and what it would have been by the next best alternative mode of transportation (in this case, rivers and canals)?

To the surprise of most, Fogel found that the river and canal systems could very nearly have produced the same results. All but 4 percent of existing agricultural land in 1890 would have been cultivated. The social savings would have been roughly 5 percent of estimated GNP by 1890. Moreover, the weight of common nails consumed in the country in 1849, during a period when railroads supposedly were determining the growth of the iron industry, exceeded that of railroad consumption by more than 100 percent. The "backward linkage" of railroads on the iron industry's growth was not that important, says Fogel, nor was it crucial even before 1860 in the lumbering industry, in coal, or even in transportation equipment.[30]

Fogel was not attempting to eliminate the railroad from American economic history, but rather to broaden ideas about causality in economic development. Fogel's message is that no single innovation created American economic growth, especially in "take-offs," or great leaps forward. The country's economic growth was indeed magnificent, and the railroad played its proper role, but so did house-building, and so did the potbellied iron stove. Actually, until 1860, only 40 percent of American rail iron came from domestic sources; the rest was imported from England.

All in all, the railroad is an important example of technology transfer. The first operating railroad, the Stockton and Darlington, was in operation in England in 1825. Five years later, in 1830, the railroad era began in this country when the Baltimore and Ohio began operation. Americans adapted British technology to local conditions. Table 8.2 gives an indication just how rapidly the modified technology diffused throughout the country.[31]

Mileage in 1869 was still only a faint beginning of the 260,400 miles of main track (429,883 miles including all yards, switching track, and so forth) that would be operated in the industry's peak year, 1930. By the Civil War, however, our mileage exceeded that of railroads in the United Kingdom, France, and the German states combined.[32] The distribution of railroad mileage built in the various regions by 1860 is shown in Table 8.3.

Fishlow estimates that total investment in railroads up to 1860 ran to more than $1 billion, more than five times the amount invested in the canals.[33] Government participation was highest in the South: about 50 percent of total investment. There, sparse population and competition with river transport reduced initial profit possibilities. In New England and the major Midwestern routes, government participation was as little as 10 percent of the total. By 1860, Chicago, the new Midwest rail center, had some 4,000 miles of railroads converging on it, but the city never invested a cent of public money in railroads.

The inroads made by the railroads on canal and river traffic were based upon savings in *total* transport costs for shippers. The railroads offered year-round service, whereas the main canals faced ice-bound conditions during the weeks of hard winter. Also, the railroads offered more contact points for producers, thus cutting down the costs of wagon haulage, unloading, and reloading. Therefore, even though the railroads could not match the price, per ton mile, of water transport along the whole route from producer to consumer, railroads reduced shipping costs. From their inception, the railroads began cutting into potential canal revenues as well as sharing in the growth of all trade. Because railroads tended to be built along river routes where the terrain was flat (see Figure 8.2), to a large extent, they actually ran parallel to available water routes.

TABLE 8.2 Miles of Railroad in Operation, 1830–1860

Year	*Mileage*
1830	23
1835	1,098
1840	2,818
1845	4,633
1850	9,021
1855	18,374
1860	30,626

Source: *Historical Statistics,* series Q 321–328.

TABLE 8.3 Distribution of Railroad Mileage, 1830–1860

Region	*Mileage*	*Percentage*
New England	3,660	12.1
Middle Atlantic	6,353	21.0
North Central	9,592	31.7
South	8,838	29.2
West of the Mississippi River	1,840	6.0

Source: *Encyclopaedia Britannica,* 1958 ed., vol. 18, p. 918.

FIGURE 8.2 U.S. Railroads as of 1860

Railroads quickly overtook, and largely displaced, the canal system. By 1860, the major Eastern cities were connected, and the country's developed economic regions were no longer so isolated from each other. The railroad network by 1860 was far more dense in the North than it was in the South.

Even so, it would be misleading to imply that railroad competition alone was responsible for the financial failures of those canals that were abandoned in the antebellum period. Many, such as the Wabash and Erie in Indiana (whose southern part was being abandoned even before the northern parts were completed), were fatally compromised by the very element of government support that made them initially possible. Following the commercial crises of 1837 and 1839, a deep depression lasting into the early 1840s so disrupted state finances that nine states suspended payments on their debts.[34] Included were Illinois, Indiana, Maryland, and Pennsylvania, and their major canals never recovered.

Railroads, too, suffered from that episode, but they were only at the beginning of their great growth experience and, during the next big expansion in the 1850s, were able to attract fresh government funds and foreign investment. Also, in 1850, a huge 3.75 million-acre land grant was made by the federal government to Illinois, Alabama, and Mississippi to finance the building of the Illinois Central Railroad.[35] This was not the first land grant for internal improvements, but it was by far the largest and a harbinger of things to come. The new surge of railroad building that began in the 1850s ultimately would result in tracks that spanned the continent. The details of that growth are considered in a later chapter. By the time of the Civil War, the waterways (including coastal shipping), still carried far more freight than did the new railroads, but the handwriting was on the wall.

Cycles

The construction of internal improvements roughly followed the course of the business cycle, with big expansions in construction outlays during the 1830s and the 1850s. Although there is conflict between cycle movements and investment in canals, the data on railroads show a fairly close relationship.[36] It is not believable, however, that railroad construction was the sole cause of business cycle swings and turning points: The amounts involved relative to GNP were too small, and the question of remote cause remains, with conflicts in other areas, including banking and changes in foreign trade and the supply of money.

As Paul Cootner argues, American demand for transport, including railroads, reflected world demand for American commodities.[37] Railroad construction, like the rest of the economy, reacted to changing market conditions in the aggregate. The appearance of a causal force running from railroads to the economy at large is thus merely a result of the fact that both move with the business cycle. Nevertheless, internal improvements and railroads in the 1830s and 1850s no doubt did underpin the expansions of those years and, thus, sped the processes of economic growth in the antebellum period.

URBANIZATION

As the transportation network spread, the number of possible sites for the establishment of commercial and industrial centers multiplied, and then multiplied again. Every break-in-transport was a possible site, although, as we have seen, other economic factors had to come into play. We would not expect to find a town or city wherever a railroad crossed a river. Nevertheless, if we consider only the U.S. Bureau of Census count of "urban places"—those settlements of 2,500 persons or more—it almost seems that the maximum number of towns and cities *was* being established during the antebellum period. From 1790 to 1860, when the population grew by just slightly more than a factor of 8, the number of urban places multiplied by more than a factor of 16.

Towns and Cities

In 1790, there were 24 American cities with populations in excess of 2,500. By 1830, even before the first real boom in internal improvements, that number had grown to 90. By 1860, the map contained 392 places with populations more than 2,500. The proportion of urban population, a mere 5 percent of the total in 1790, was only 8.7 percent four decades later, but was 19.7 percent, nearly one-fifth, in 1860. Urbanization was already upon us. The raw data for urban places are shown in Table 8.4.

Although this growth was a mere token of the urbanization yet to come, there already were interesting characteristics. Consider Table 8.5, which shows the top ten urban places in 1790 and 1860. The four great urban centers of colonial America still were the largest cities in 1860. New York and Philadelphia had changed positions in the ratings, largely as a result of the Erie Canal. The next six colonial urban centers had vanished from the list, to be replaced by new urban places. Newark was growing as a manufacturing and port city. Buffalo was at the head of navigation on the Great Lakes, connected to the East Coast by canal and railroad. It also was a milling and manufacturing center. The rest of the new top cities were on waterways in the West, and Chicago was already beginning its career as the hub of the country's railroad system. The shift of top urban sites westward reflected the general westward movement of population—by 1860, the country's population-geographical center had shifted from Baltimore to Chillicothe, Ohio.

TABLE 8.4 Size Distribution of Urban Population in 1790, 1830, and 1860[a]

	1790		*1830*		*1860*	
Urban Size by Population	*Number of Places*	*Total Population*	*Number of Places*	*Total Population*	*Number of Places*	*Total Population*
2.5–5	12	44	34	126	163	595
5–10	7	48	33	231	136	976
10–25	3	48	16	240	58	884
25–50	2	62	3	105	19	670
50–100			3	222	7	452
100–250			1	203	6	993
250–500					1	267
500–1,000					2	1,379
Totals	*24*	*202*	*90*	*1,127*	*392*	*6,216*
Percentage of Total U.S. Population		5.1		8.8		19.8

[a] Population figures are given in thousands of persons.

Source: Derived from *Historical Statistics,* series A 43–54, 58, 69.

The Economics of Urbanization

As noted earlier, external economies are the primary, though not the only, reasons for urbanization. Beyond certain *indivisibilities*—such as minimal sizes for efficient water supply, sewerage, and fire protection—there had not yet been sufficient economies internal to city organization to sustain growth to the mammoth sizes now experienced by the largest urban areas in the United States.

It was the force of *external* economies that produced most urban agglomerations. Each firm or economic agent could capture some advantages by locating in urban areas: The net returns for each exceeded the costs of production in part because of location alone. There were clear advantages to co-location; a butcher who located next door to a baker enabled his customers to combine trips and reduce their transportation costs. It also enabled customers to travel longer distances, enlarging the customer base of both the butcher and the baker. This power is evident even before the Civil War. Consider, in Table 8.6, the large proportion of the total urban population concentrated in a few large cities.

In 1790, more than 30 percent of the total urban population resided in Philadelphia and New York

TABLE 8.5 Top Ten Urban Places in 1800 and 1860

Rank Order	*1800*	*1860*	*1800 Top Ten in 1860 List*	*1860 Top Ten Not in 1800 List*
1	Philadelphia	New York City	New York City	
2	New York City	Philadelphia	Philadelphia	
3	Baltimore	Baltimore	Baltimore	
4	Boston	Boston	Boston	
5	Charleston	New Orleans		New Orleans
6	Salem	Cincinnati		Cincinnati
7	Providence	St. Louis		St. Louis
8	New Haven	Chicago		Chicago
9	Richmond	Buffalo		Buffalo
10	Portsmouth	Newark		Newark

Source: Lance E. Davis et al., *American Economic History: The Development of a National Economy* (Homewood, IL: Irwin, 1969), p. 265.

City. In 1830, 37.7 percent of the urban population was in just four places: New York, Philadelphia, Baltimore, and Boston. In 1860, when there were 392 urban places, 46 percent of the urban population resided in only 10 percent of them, and the largest two cities alone contained 22 percent of the total.

We observed in our discussion of colonial America that successful growth settlements needed a hinterland to sustain them. That hinterland was a nearby source of commodities and goods to process and transship as well as a market for services and imported goods. As such, each settlement would begin to acquire distinctive regional characteristics because of specialization and division of labor along the most profitable lines. For example, New Orleans would develop services and ancillary trades associated with cotton; Pittsburgh, with iron; and Chicago, with livestock, wheat, corn, and railroads. Diane Lindstrom's study of Philadelphia from 1815 to 1840 shows that the city's growth was dominated by the exchange of its locally produced manufactures and services with its expanding agricultural hinterland. Philadelphia's foreign and interregional trade declined, and it did not become a specialized exporter of any dominant product.[38]

The process developed among smaller regional urban places as well—settlements within a given market area would begin to specialize. As Eugene Smolensky wrote, after a while no town's existence could be understood by its own characteristics considered in isolation, since each one, as part of a system, would be specialized within a market area and would depend upon the others for some functions:

> All the towns, villages, and cities taken together form a complete system, each with its place in the hierarchy of urban places serving a region. Furthermore, the towns in a region can be understood only when that region is viewed as a subsystem of an interdependent system of regions.[39]

As the economy developed, with this infrastructure of specialized economic subsystems growing within it, urbanization grew as a natural part of economic expansion. There is, as yet, no end to the process; by 1860, of course, the main growth of American cities was still to come. Figure 8.3 shows the principal U.S. cities by 1860. They all were located at breaks-in-transport produced by the ocean, Great Lakes, and main rivers wherever local economic activity was sufficiently intense.

In our own time, advances in transportation and communications have allowed significant decentralization to occur (a topic to be discussed in a later chapter). But until the *diseconomies of size*—typically the disadvantages of excessive taxes, pollution, congestion, and crime—overcome the positive externalities, certain urban places will tend to grow. The most economically advantageous combinations have been those involving transport and communications in addition to manufacturing. Although it has been shown that industrialization alone does not

TABLE 8.6 Size Distribution of Urban Populations

Urban Size by Population	*Urban Population*					
	1790		*1830*		*1860*	
	Number	*Percentage*	*Number*	*Percentage*	*Number*	*Percentage*
2.5–5	12	21.7	34	11.2	163	9.6
5.0–10	7	23.8	33	20.5	136	15.7
10–25	3	23.8	16	21.3	58	14.2
25–50	2	30.7	3	9.3	19	10.8
50–100			3	19.7	7	7.3
100–250			1	18.0	6	16.0
250–500					1	4.3
500–1,000					2	22.1
Total	*24*	*100.0*	*90*	*100.0*	*392*	*100.0*

Source: Table 8.4.

Boomtown. *Chicago was both the most dramatically growing city of the nineteenth century and representative of the way so many American cities grew. Its population increased from 50 people in 1830, to 4,200 at its incorporation as a city in 1837, to 30,000 in 1850, to 300,000 in 1870, to 600,000 in 1880, to 1.2 million in 1890, to 2 million just after the turn of the century. Since Chicago was built next to a waterway and was subject to periodic flooding (like so many cities), in the 1860s, the city was raised by several feet. All buildings near the Chicago River were mechanically raised several inches (above left),*

which left the city on two levels (below left). Chicago is shown (below) a year before the great fire of 1871, which burned a path four miles long and a mile wide, leaving 100,000 people homeless. A similar view taken just after the fire (above) shows the devastation. The Chicago Water Tower is the second tower from the right in the top picture and just to the left of the flagpole in the bottom one.

FIGURE 8.3 Principal Cities in 1860

In 1860, most of the country's cities were in the North; the New West was represented by a ring of cities around the Great Lakes that would prove to be the focal points of the new industrialism that came after the Civil War.

account for urban growth, even in the antebellum period, industrialization was dominant in some cases.[40] As Lance Davis wrote: "As textile production proved possible in New England, cities literally grew out of the fields (Lowell and Lawrence, for example)."[41] In Southern antebellum cities, commerce was predominant.[42]

Industrialization made factories profitable, especially where a central prime mover, such as waterpower or steam power (before 1860), was used. Factories grew because of internal economies of scale. The location of workers near factories—with attendant services, both to human and mechanical needs, brought nearby for reasons of profit—reduced the real costs to others who contemplated joining them. Towns and cities resulted. We saw this process in Chapter 2 in Douglass North's model for regional growth around an export base. As Woytinsky and Woytinsky have concluded, "the pattern of urbanization has been determined by a combination of historical, geographical, and economic conditions."[43]

The list of top cities in 1860 includes no purely commercial, purely transport, or purely industrial centers. Even New Orleans, perhaps the prime candidate as a mainly commercial and transport center in its area, had local industrial activity as well as shipbuilding. In the United States, it was as the great French historian Paul Mantoux said of Great Britain: The seed of industry, cast upon the ground, "gave a harvest of cities."[44] What was already evident in 1860 in this country would become overwhelming in another half century.

Thomas Jefferson's hope for a peaceful Arcadia, a huge nation and millions of farmers, would never be. Its resources, both human and material, would group around the transportation system and produce an urban society. In 1860, the United States was still four-fifths rural, and the South more rural than the North. Internal improvements and the natural system of waterways, even before the appearance of important heavy industry, exerted an urbanizing force.

Railroad construction hit its stride in the 1850s as a national system was developed. The first railroad to leave Chicago did not do so until 1848, the same year the Illinois and Michigan Canal was completed. Within a few short years, it was possible to take a single train from Chicago to New York City. This link, in turn, tied the two cities together even more securely than had the Erie Canal. During the 1850s, the railroad asserted its superiority over the canal. Before that, the problems canals faced were as much a product of their own success (they were expanding by building feeder lines into smaller markets) as they were a product of competition from the railroads.

NOTES

1. Carter Goodrich, *Government Promotion of American Canals and Railroads 1800–1890* (1960), chap. 1. The original scholarship on this point was done by Guy Stevens Callender, "The Early Transportation and Banking Enterprises of the States," *QJE*, 1902.
2. James Willard Hurst, *The Legitimacy of the Business Corporation* (1969), p. 23.
3. Goodrich (1960), p. 27.
4. *Ibid.*, pp. 27–48.
5. Jonathan Hughes, *The Governmental Habit Redux* (Princeton: Princeton University Press, 1991), pp. 68–76 for this episode.
6. Goodrich (1960), pp. 34–35.
7. Albert Fishlow, "Internal Transportation," in Davis et al., *American Economic Growth: An Economist's History of the United States* (1972), pp. 472–475.
8. *Ibid.*, p. 474.
9. Carter Goodrich, Jerome Cranmer, Julius Rubin, and Harvey Segal, *Canals and American Economic Development* (1961), p. 215.
10. Goodrich (1960), pp. 53–56; Julius Rubin, "The Erie Canal," in Goodrich, et al. (1961).
11. Rubin (1961).
12. Goodrich, (1961), pp. 135–137. Roger Ransom, "Interregional Canals and Economic Specialization in the Antebellum United States," *EEH*, Fall 1967.
13. Louis Cain, *Sanitation Strategy for a Lakefront Metropolis: The Case of Chicago* (DeKalb: Northern Illinois University Press, 1978).
14. Goodrich (1960), p. 4; also pp. 87–101 for data in preceding paragraph.
15. Roger Ransom, "Canals and Development: A Discussion of the Issues," *AER*, May 1964; Albert Niemi, "A Further Look at Interregional Lands and Economic

Specialization: 1820–1840," *EEH*, Summer 1970; Roger Ransom, "A Closer Look at Canals and Western Manufacturing," *EEH*, Summer 1971; Albert Niemi, "Reply" to Ransom, *EEH*, September 1972.

16. The Canadians also entered the "transportation revolution" of the antebellum period with canals. Theirs were government financed and financially unsuccessful. Thomas F. McIlwraith, "Freight Capacity and Utilization of the Erie and Great Lakes Canals Before 1850," *Journal of Economic History*, vol. XXXVI, no. 4, December 1976.
17. James Mak and Gary Walton, "Steamboats and the Great Productivity Surge in River Transportation," *JEH*, September 1972, p. 620.
18. Erik Haites and James Mak, "The Decline of Steamboating on the Ante-Bellum Western Rivers: Some New Evidence and an Alternative Hypothesis," *EEH*, Fall 1973, p. 28.
19. Jeremy Atack, "Quantitative and Qualitative Evidence in the Weaving of Business and Economic History: Western River Steamboats and the Transportation Revolution Revisited," *BEH*, Fall 1999, p. 5.
20. Mak and Walton (1972), p. 625.
21. Haites and Mak (1973), p. 30; Goodrich (1961), chap. III, especially Figure 1, p. 173.
22. Jonathan Hughes and Stanley Reiter, "The First 1945 British Steamships," *American Statistical Journal*, June 1958, vol. III, no. 282, pp. 362–375. As the British steam fleet grew over time, iron screw-driven steamers displaced wooden and paddle-wheel ships.
23. Mak and Walton (1972), p. 637.
24. *Ibid.*, Figure 1, p. 624.
25. Haites and Mak (1973), pp. 31–33.
26. Mak and Walton (1972), p. 636. Louis Hunter's great work is *Steamboats on the Western Rivers* (1949). For more recent general analyses of the steamboat industry in the Midwest, see Erik Haites and James Mak, "Ohio and Mississippi River Transportation, 1810–1860," *EEH*, Winter 1970; and by the same authors, "Steamboating on the Mississippi Before the Civil War: A Comparative Study," *BHR*, Spring 1971.
27. Robert Fogel, *Railroads and American Economic Growth: Essays in Econometric History* (1964), pp. 1–10, for a brief survey of the conventional view. On the business cycle, Joseph Schumpeter, *Business Cycles* (New York: McGraw-Hill, 1939), two vols.; Leland Jenks, "Railroads as an Economic Force in American Development," in Frederic Lane and Jelle Riemersma, *Enterprise and Secular Change* (1953).
28. Albert Fishlow, *American Railroads and the Transformation of the Ante-Bellum Economy* (1965). Also, see Fishlow (1972). Lloyd Mercer has shown that the developmental role, "building ahead of demand," cannot be abandoned entirely in the case of railroads financed in large part by government land grants, mainly after the Civil War. Lloyd Mercer, "Building Ahead of Demand: Some Evidence for the Land Grant Railroads," *JEH*, June 1974.
29. Fogel (1964). The critical reaction to this book was, at the time, awe-inspiring. See Peter McClelland, "Railroads, American Growth, and the New Economic History: A Critique," *JEH*, March 1968.
30. See Fogel (1964), chap. VI, for a summary.
31. An interesting view of the early period can be found in Von Gerstner, *Early American Railroads* (1997). This is an English translation of a book first published in German in 1842–43 that looks at both canals and railroads on a geographical basis.
32. In 1860, the U.K. operated 10,410 miles; France, about 5,000 miles; and the German states, approximately 7,000–8,000, depending upon which ones are counted.
33. Fishlow's estimates are as follows: 1828–1843: $137.1 million; 1844–1850: $172.3 million; 1851–1860: $737.7 million. The 1850s alone saw nearly double the amount of total capital investment. Fishlow (1972), p. 496.
34. R. C. McGrane, *Foreign Bondholders and American State Debts* (New York: Macmillan Company, 1935).
35. Paul Gates, *The Illinois Central Railroad and its Colonization Work* (1934). This superb book contains, in rich detail, samples of all the problems associated with mixed enterprises—federal government, state and local government, foreign investment, financial crises, and political consequence.
36. Jonathan Hughes and Nathan Rosenberg, "The United States Business Cycle Before 1860: Some Problems of Interpretation," *Economic History Review*, 2nd series, vol. XV, no. 3, August 1963.
37. Paul Cootner, "The Role of the Railroads in United States Economic Growth," *JEH*, December 1963.
38. Diane Lindstrom, "Demand, Markets, and Eastern Economic Development: Philadelphia, 1815–1840," *JEH*, March 1975, pp. 271–273.
39. Eugene Smolensky, "Industrial Location and Urban Growth," in Davis, et al. (1972), p. 536.
40. Diane Lindstrom and John Sharpless, "Urban Growth and Economic Structure in Antebellum America," in Paul Uselding, ed., *REH* (1978), vol. 3.
41. Lance Davis, Jonathan Hughes, and Duncan McDougall, *American Economic History*, 3rd ed. (Homewood, IL: Irwin, 1969), p. 266.
42. Lindstrom and Sharpless (1978), p. 169.
43. W. S. Woytinsky and E. S. Woytinsky, *World Population and Production, Trend and Outlook* (New York: The Twentieth Century Fund, 1953), p. 125.
44. Paul Mantoux, *The Industrial Revolution in the Eighteenth Century: An Outline of the Beginnings of the Modern Factory System* (London: Jonathan Cape, 1928), p. 368.

SUGGESTED READINGS

Articles

Atack, Jeremy. "Quantitative and Qualitative Evidence in the Weaving of Business and Economic History: Western River Steamboats and the Transportation Revolution Revisited." *Business and Economic History*, vol. 28, no. 1, Fall 1999.

Callender, Guy Stevens. "The Early Transportation and Banking Enterprises of the States." *Quarterly Journal of Economics*, vol. XVII, no. 1, November 1902.

Cootner, Paul. "The Role of the Railroads in the United States Economic Growth." *Journal of Economic History*, vol. XXIII, no. 4, December 1963.

David, Paul. "Transport Innovation and the Economic Growth; Professor Fogel on and off the Rails." *Economic History Review*, 2nd series, vol. 22, no. 3, December 1969.

Fishlow, Albert. "Internal Transportation." In Lance E. Davis et al., *American Economic Growth: An Economist's History of the United States*. New York: Harper & Row, 1972, chap. 13.

Fleisig, Heywood. "The Central Pacific Railroad and the Railroad Land Grant Controversy." *Journal of Economic History*, vol. XXXV, no. 3, September 1975.

Haites, Erik F., and James Mak. "Ohio and Mississippi River Transportation 1810–1860." *Explorations in Economic History*, vol. XIII, No. 2, Winter 1970.

———. "Steamboating on the Mississippi Before the Civil War: A Comparative Study." *Business History Review*, vol. XLV, No. 1, Spring 1971.

———. "The Decline of Steamboating on the Ante-Bellum Western Rivers: Some New Evidence and an Alternative Hypothesis." *Explorations in Economic History*, vol. 11, no. 1, Fall 1973.

Heath, Milton."Public Railroad Construction and the Development of Private Enterprise in the South Before 1861." *Journal of Economic History, The Tasks of Economic History*, vol. X, 1950.

Hidy, Ralph, and Muriel Hidy. "Anglo–American Merchant Bankers and the Railroads of the Old Northwest, 1848–1860." *Business History Review*, vol. XXXIV, no. 2, Summer 1960.

Jenks, Leland H. "Railroads as a Force in American Development." In Frederic C. Lane and Jelle Riemersma, eds. *Enterprise and Secular Change*. Homewood, IL: Irwin, 1953.

Lindstrom, Diane L. "Demand, Markets and Eastern Economic Development, Philadelphia, 1815–1840." *Journal of Economic History*, vol. XXXV, no. 1, March 1975.

———, and John Sharpless. "Urban Growth and Economic Structure in Antebellum America." In Paul Uselding, ed., *Research in Economic History*. Greenwich, CT: JAI Press, 1978, vol. 3.

Mak, James, and Gary Walton. "Steamboat and the Great Productivity Surge in River Transportation." *Journal of Economic History*, vol. XXXII, no. 3, September 1972.

Mercer, Lloyd J. "Building Ahead of Demand: Some Evidence for the Land Grant Railroads." *Journal of Economic History*, vol. XXXIV, no. 2, June 1974.

McClelland, Peter D. "Railroads, American Growth, and the New Economic History, a Critique." *Journal of Economic History*, vol. XXVIII, no. 1, March 1968.

Niemi, Albert W., Jr. "A Further Look at Regional Canals and Economic Specialization: 1820–1840." *Explorations in Economic History*, vol. 7, no. 4, Summer 1970.

———. "A Closer Look at Canals and Western Manufacturing in the Canal Era: A Reply." *Explorations in Economic History*, vol. 9, no. 4, September 1972.

Ransom, Roger L. "Canals and Development, A Discussion of the Issues." *American Economic Review*, vol. LIV, no. 2, May 1964.

———. "A Closer Look at Canals and Western Manufacturing in the Canal Era." *Explorations in Economic History*, vol. 8, no. 4, Summer 1971.

———. "Interregional Canals and Economic Specialization in the Antebellum United States." *Explorations in Economic History*, 2nd series, vol. V, no. 1, Fall 1967.

Smolensky, Eugene. "Industrial Location and Urban Growth." In Lance E. Davis et al., *American Economic Growth: An Economist's History of the United States*. New York: Harper & Row, 1972, chap. 15.

Weiss, Thomas. "Demographic Aspects of the Urban Population, 1800–1840." In Peter Kilby, ed., *Quantity and Quiddity: Essays in American Economic History*. Middletown, CT: Wesleyan University Press, 1987.

Williamson, Jeffrey. "Urbanization in the American Northeast." *Journal of Economic History*, vol. XXV, no. 4, December 1965.

———, and Joseph Swanson. "The Growth of Cities in the American Northeast, 1820–1870." *Explorations in Entrepreneurial History*, 2nd series, 4 (Supplement), 1966.

Books

Fishlow, Albert. *American Railroads and Transformation of the American Economy*. Cambridge: Harvard University Press, 1965.

Fogel, Robert W. *Railroads and American Economic Growth: Essays in Econometric History*. Baltimore: Johns Hopkins University Press, 1964.

Gates, Paul W. *The Illinois Central Railroad and Its Colonization Work*. Cambridge: Harvard University Press, 1934.

Goodrich, Carter H. *Government Promotion of American Canals and Railroads, 1800–1890*. New York: Columbia University Press, 1960.

——. *The Government and the Economy, 1783–1861*. Indianapolis: Bobbs-Merrill, 1967.

——, Jerome Cranmer, Julius Rubin, and Harvey Segal. *Canals and American Economic Development*. New York: Columbia University Press, 1961.

Haites, Erik F., James Mak, and Gary Walton. *Western River Transportation: The Era of Early Internal Development, 1810–1860*. Baltimore: The Johns Hopkins University Press, 1975.

Hunter, Louis. *Steamboats on the Western Rivers*. Cambridge: Harvard University Press, 1949.

Hurst, James Willard. *The Legitimacy of the Business Corporation*. Charlottesville: The University Press of Virginia, 1969.

North, Douglass C. *The Economic Growth of the United States, 1790–1860*. Englewood Cliffs, NJ: Prentice–Hall, 1961.

Taylor, George Rogers. *The Transportation Revolution*. New York: Holt, Rinehart and Winston, 1951.

Von Gerstner, Franz Anton Ritter. *Early American Railroads*. Stanford: Stanford University Press, 1997.

CHAPTER NINE

Agricultural Expansion: The Conflict of Two Systems on the Land

Antebellum America is today a far distant place. No one alive can remember it. It is a land that now belongs entirely to historians, who themselves cannot agree, in some very important respects, about what it was like. We have considered much of this period already, but the heart of the antebellum economy was farms and farmers.

It was the farmers who occupied the continent and brought it into production; whose needs created the demand for industry, towns, cities, finance, and transportation networks; and whose output fed the rising urban masses.[1] In 1850, farmers still numbered almost 60 percent of the labor force. They had acquired an empire but (through their elected representatives) could not agree about one fundamental piece of its organization: whether the labor contract would, or would not, include black slavery. In the end, this issue produced the American Civil War. Was it the sole cause? No. Would there have been a Civil War without the slavery issue? No.[2]

As we have discussed, although slavery existed in the North during colonial times, the nature of comparative advantage in regional agriculture had concentrated the slave population in the Southern colonies. In a sense, history had conspired to encourage slavery's continued expansion where it first had become important in agriculture. The drying-up of the indentured servant supply in the late eighteenth century had made slave purchases all the more necessary in the South. After 1725, natural increase provided most of the slave supply in that region; imports from Africa and the Caribbean, the rest. From Pennsylvania north, the heavy, early immigration of whites laid the foundation for a large and growing white population and consequently, family farming. The passage of time brought an accentuation of the differences in the regional agricultural labor input.

By 1850, nearly 37 percent of the South's population were slaves; in the North, the number of slaves had become negligible. After Eli Whitney invented the cotton gin in 1793 and Southern planters penetrated into Alabama, Louisiana, Arkansas, Mississippi, and east Texas, cotton culture gave the slave South a greatly expandable money crop in addition to sugar production. The expansion of cotton textiles in England, then in New England and continental Europe, kept cotton demand rising, decade after decade, inducing enormous increases in raw cotton output. Slaves were deemed the necessary labor ingredient.

The cotton gin, in common with the harvester and the thresher, began as a simple, hand-operated, wooden machine. These agricultural implements all were aimed at what was, and remains, the bottleneck of agricultural production—the capacity to harvest. The labor a farmer was able to apply at harvest time determined his output for the season, and implements such as the cotton gin increased the productivity of that labor. Much of the difference between North and South is attributable to the fact that, up to 1860, no implement impacted northern agriculture as the cotton gin did southern agriculture. The North, especially on the frontier, remained an area of largely self-sufficient farmers who did not specialize.[3]

The two agricultural systems moved westward in parallel fashion, clashing where they met (geographically in the borderlands and intellectually in the courts and in Congress). This movement created the major political themes of the nation's first seven decades after the new Constitution was ratified in 1789. Ultimately, the conflict over slavery was to rupture that agreement. Already in the Northwest Ordinance of 1787, the conflict was on the horizon; slavery was prohibited in the new territories north of the Ohio. The Missouri Compromise (1820), the Compromise of 1850, and the Kansas-Nebraska Act of 1854 were all legislative efforts to find solutions to a problem planted on the land in the colonial era. The issue was one in which financial interests, political philosophies, morals, religion, and politics were all hopelessly embroiled. Whether a solution short of the Civil War was possible is a moot question since, in the end, war, and only war, resolved it—leaving the nation scarred and wounded for more than a century afterward.

The seemingly inexorable conflict between the two systems is projected in a paper by Peter Temin. He poses antebellum American development as two separate solutions to Evsey Domar's well-known "impossibility theorem": It is not possible to have simultaneously (a) free land, (b) free labor, and (c) a land-owning aristocracy.[4] In the South, the options taken were slave labor and a land-owning aristocracy. In the North the options were free land, free labor, and no aristocracy. Since the incompatible developments occurred within a single constitutional system, the "solution" was the Civil War. Although Domar's theorem was originally designed for Europe, it does shed considerable light on the dilemma facing Americans before 1861.[5]

SETTLEMENT AND POPULATION

In part, the westward movement of farmers was simply the result of organic phenomena: population growth and the attraction of new land. Young people, growing up on farms in the older settled areas, wanted farms of their own. Once the way west was open, the agricultural populations of the East Coast became the major source of colonizing farmers in the Midwest, and then the plains. New Englanders and settlers from Pennsylvania and New York moved into Ohio and Indiana along the rivers. Virginians moved into Kentucky, Tennessee, and Alabama. Eventually, some of these families or their descendants settled Illinois, Iowa, Mississippi, Arkansas, and Missouri. In 1850, there were 1.45 million farms by census count, consisting of 293.5 million acres. A decade later there were 2.04 million farms, totaling 407.2 million acres. Older areas might still be more intensively cleared and farmed, but the better lands were taken long ago. Westward migration was the most attractive course. Townships in the backwoods of New England began to empty out as farmers headed west. The same was true in Pennsylvania, New York, New Jersey, and the Old South.

We can see in Table 9.1 the flavor of the Midwest in 1850, which is to some extent evident to this day. For the moment, we will ignore the proportions of native-born in each state in 1850.[6] However, we should note the relatively heavy concentrations of persons from the South in Indiana and Illinois. The "Southern" politics of Indiana and Illinois in the 1850s have obvious origins. In Wisconsin, Michigan, and Illinois, large portions of the populations were born in Europe, and the old Middle colonies contributed heavy concentrations in the same states. New England people contributed their largest proportions in Michigan and Wisconsin. The effects of western migration were clearly more telling in the dwindling townships of New England than in the lusty new settlements of the Midwest.[7]

In the 1830s, Harriet Martineau wrote of a conversation with a Southern legislator who complained of the steady drain of young people to the West:

> He told me of one and another of his intelligent and pleasant young neighbors, who were quitting their homes and civilized life, and carrying their brides "as bondswomen" into the wilderness because fine land was cheap there.[8]

In addition, there was the ever-present element of land speculation (discussed in Chapter 5). Acquiring land, clearing some of it, building a house and barn,

TABLE 9.1 Midwest Populations by Place of Birth and Domicile in 1850[a]

Domicile in 1850	Area of Birth						
	New England	*Middle States*	*South*	*Northwest*	*Native-Born*	*Europe*	*Total*
Ohio	3.3	15.0	7.5	—	64.2	10.0	100
Indiana	1.2	8.0	18.5	13.7	52.8	5.8	100
Illinois	4.4	13.2	16.2	12.9	40.4	12.9	100
Michigan	7.8	37.7	1.0	4.5	35.2	13.8	100
Wisconsin	8.9	26.2	1.6	7.5	20.7	35.1	100

[a]Figures given are percentages.

Source: Ray Billington and Martin Ridge, *Westward Expansion* (New York: Macmillan, 1982), p. 308.

then selling it to others and moving on to new land—this was a laborious but profitable frontier enterprise for many farm families.

Comparative population data for 16 trans-Appalachian states are shown in Table 9.2. An area that contained less than 15 percent of the nation's population in 1810 had more than 46 percent by 1850. In the last decade before the Civil War, it was still growing in population more rapidly than the rest of the country. In the North, lands that would grow corn and wheat and support livestock attracted family farmers. Among the population in the South, family farmers, too, were attracted into the rich cotton-growing lands of the Mississippi drainage basin. Alabama, Mississippi, and the whole southern part of the great gulf plains received them. Where there was good land in the South, there was opportunity for plantation agriculture, and slave owners were quickly attracted. Claudia Goldin estimated that between 1790 and 1860, an army of some 835,000 slaves moved from the Old South (85 percent from Maryland, Virginia, and the Carolinas). Alabama, Mississippi, Louisiana, and east Texas alone received some 75 percent of this huge black migration.[9]

Looking backward, the trans-Appalachian movement seems logical and obvious. However, certainty was not what prompted people to change their addresses. People moved for opportunity, and that was enhanced periodically by rising prices for agricultural produce. Data for cotton, wool, and wheat prices (see Figure 9.1), together with land sales, show that in both the South and the North the price booms of the antebellum period were closely correlated with big increases in public land sales in 1817–19, 1835–37, and 1852–54. These were big bulges in sales on top of a rising trend. Population was moving westward in any case, but extraordinary opportunities stemming from rising agricultural prices accelerated the movement in both the North and South.

TABLE 9.2 Populations of Trans-Appalachian States[a]

State	*1810*	*1850*	*1860*
Ohio	231	1980	2340
Michigan	5	398	749
Indiana	25	988	1350
Illinois	12	851	1712
Minnesota	—[b]	6	172
Wisconsin	—	305	776
Iowa	—	192	675
Kansas	—	—	107
Kentucky	407	982	1156
Tennessee	262	1003	1110
Alabama	9	772	964
Mississippi	31	607	791
Louisiana	77	518	708
Arkansas	1	210	435
Missouri	20	682	1182
Texas	—	213	604
Total	*1,080*	*9,707*	*14,831*
Total U.S.	*7,224*	*23,261*	*31,513*
Percentage Trans-Appalachia of Total U.S.	15.0	41.7	71.1

[a]Figures given in thousands of persons, excludes Far West and West Coast.
[b]No data.

Source: *Historical Statistics*, derived from series A7, 196.

FIGURE 9.1 Prices for Cotton, Wool, and Wheat, 1815–1860

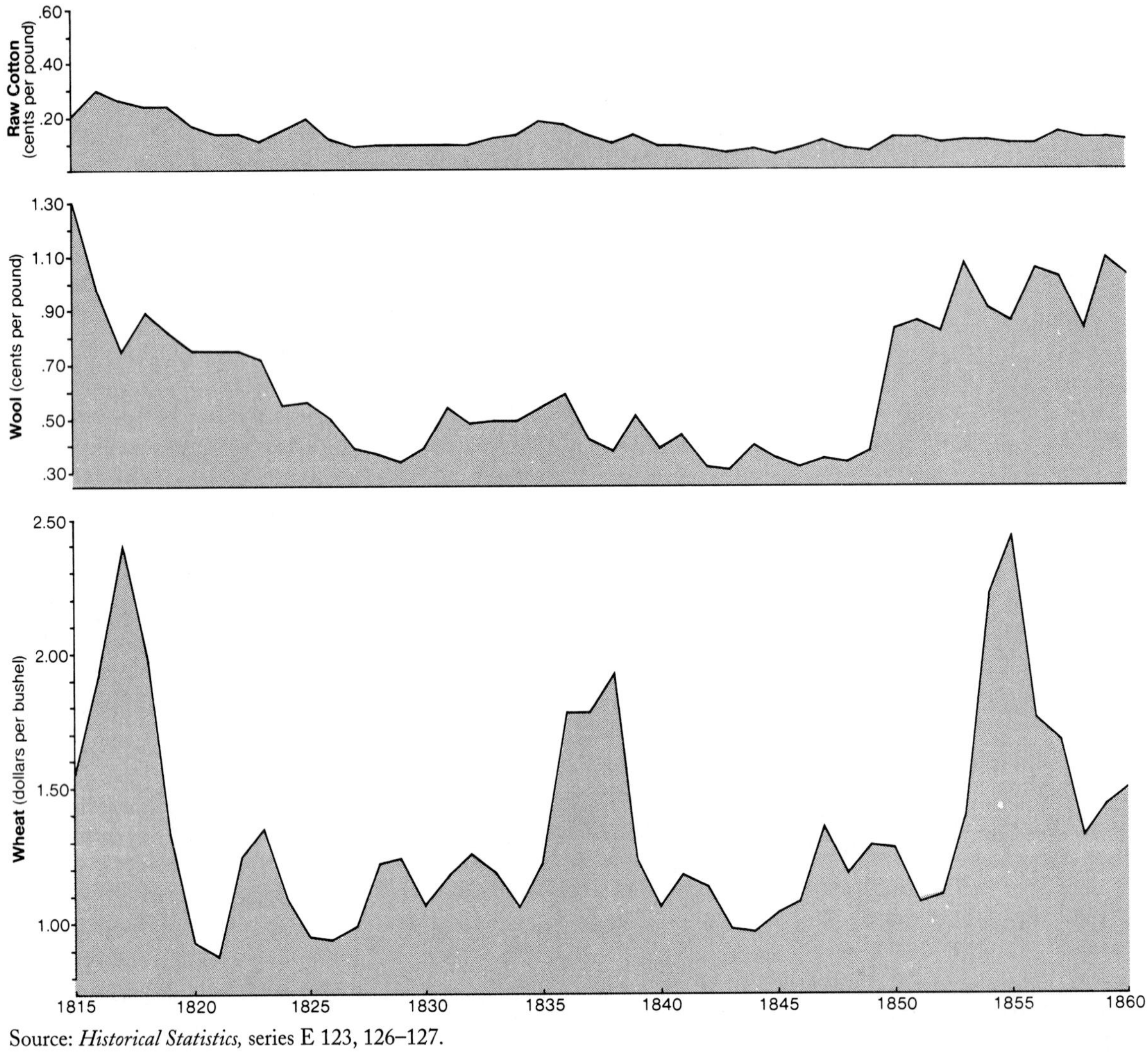

Source: *Historical Statistics*, series E 123, 126–127.

Commodity prices fell between 1816 and 1820. Except for a brief surge in the 1830s, they remained on a plateau until the 1850s, when they showed a renewed upward movement.

Average Farm Size

By 1860, less than one-third of all Southern farms owned slaves; the proportion was higher than in earlier decades. Conversely, in the North, there was an estimated one hired male worker for every two farms. Northern farms were not labor intensive. They grew grains and fed animals. Considerable improvements had been made in farm machinery and tools, and there was sufficient land—Northern family farms could thrive without a huge supply of hired labor. On the other hand, according to Fogel and Engerman, slave labor in cotton, sugar, rice, and tobacco yielded scale economies. They argue that the principal source of these economies was the use of the gang system.

Slave plantations that employed the gang system were estimated to be 39 percent more productive than free farms. Why? Because the plantation owners used the gang system to speed up the rate of production.[10] This finding generated a great deal of controversy, as we shall see in the next chapter. Nonetheless, we should not be surprised that, on average, Southern farms tended to be significantly larger than those in the North. Moreover, one-fourth of cotton plantations and farms in the South were *far* larger than any seen in the North (except in the rarest cases).

The data in Table 9.3 are only a sample of the important work of Gavin Wright, to which the reader is referred for more detail. Wright analyzed the Cotton South according to soil types.[11] *Piedmont area* refers to the Appalachian foothills of southern Virginia, the Carolinas, Georgia, and Alabama. The *sand hills* are just east of the Appalachian divide in the Carolinas and Georgia. *Western upland* refers to land in Arkansas, Louisiana, and east Texas. *Alluvial lands*, the best for growing cotton, are along the Mississippi and Red rivers in Missouri, Arkansas, and Louisiana. The largest plantations and the greatest concentrations of slaves were located there in 1860.

The more complete data in Wright's work tell substantially the same story as our sample. In Midwestern states, very few farms were larger than 500 acres, although in the Cotton South these accounted for nearly 40 percent of the total. In the Piedmont alone, 36 percent of the acreage was in farms of 1,000 acres or more. Minnesota and Wisconsin apart (where farming was still in the early stages in 1860), most Midwest-farming was on tracts of land in the range of 100 to 499 acres.

Apart from the newer areas (western upland), Southern farms in the cotton-growing areas showed a distinct bulge at the top of the distribution. Within some relevant ranges there were, apparently, either constant or increasing returns to scale in the use of slaves. The same sorts of limited internal economies exist today on modern farms employing expensive machinery. Enough acres must be farmed to cover high fixed costs, and, beyond that, it pays a farmer to expand only until the marginal costs are *just covered* by additional revenues derived from that expansion.

The evidence indicates that slave labor produced efficiencies—scale economies—in Southern agriculture, but not infinitely so. There were limits to efficient size even in Southern plantations. Costs ultimately rose with plantation size, even if there were scale economies within limits. Significantly, for example, there were no incorporated slave plantations drawing upon widespread sources of capital by the sale

TABLE 9.3 Distribution of Improved Acreage by Size Class, Cotton South and Other Farm States, 1860

	Percentage of Total Improved Acreage by Improved Acreage Size Class				
Region	*0–49*	*50–99*	*100–499*	*500–999*	*≥1000*
South (Town Areas)					
Piedmont	4.1	8.7	36.6	14.5	36.1
Sand Hills	12.0	17.5	40.5	3.6	26.4
Western Upland	15.5	21.7	49.3	10.2	3.2
Alluvine	4.3	4.7	33.0	24.5	33.5
Cotton South (total)	7.3	11.5	43.5	16.9	20.9
Illinois	8.1	20.7	65.8	4.2	1.3
Iowa	17.8	29.0	52.0	1.0	0.2
Indiana	17.0	28.6	51.5	2.0	0.8
Minnesota	52.0	24.4	23.4	0.2	0.0
Ohio	11.2	28.1	57.8	2.1	0.8
Wisconsin	24.6	27.2	46.7	1.2	0.2

Source: Gavin Wright, "Economic Democracy and the Concentration of Agricultural Wealth in the Cotton South, 1850–1860," in *The Structure of the Cotton Economy of the Antebellum South,* edited by William Parker (Washington, DC: The Agricultural History Society, 1970), derived from Table 4, p. 73.

of stock—what we would expect if scale economies from slavery were not restricted. At some point, the additional costs of size compared to added revenues put a limit on the profitable scale of single plantations.[12] Ideally, with abundant land and a perfectly competitive market in slaves, significant economies of scale would have produced giant plantations.

As far as we can tell, problems of management, slave discipline, and communications all played a role in placing limits on scale economies on the cotton plantation. Scale economies were present, but constrained. Such is suggested, for example, by the work of Jacob Metzer.[13] In fact, 4.7 percent of all farms in the Deep South were 500 acres or more, compared with a mere 0.1 percent of farms in the Northeastern states—a remarkable difference.[14] Since cotton was a labor-intensive crop, the large growing units in the South were cultivated by a large number of workers, compared to northern family farms, and the relative efficiency of gang labor in cotton production made the larger Southern farms profitable.

It is clear from Wright's data that, in the antebellum period, the optimal-sized Southern plantation was far larger than the Midwestern farm. Nevertheless, more than half of Southern acreage fell within the boundaries of the family-sized farm, below 500 acres, and half of the farms in the South had no slaves!

The median farm size in the Cotton South in 1860 was 70.6 acres. In the Midwestern states, median-sized farms were about 70 percent as large, 49.3 acres. But the mean-sized farm in the Cotton South was 135.9 acres, more than twice as large as the mean-sized Midwestern farm of 64.5 acres.[15] The difference between the median and mean ratios reflects the bulge at the top in the Cotton South, the extraordinary number of relatively large-sized Southern farms and plantations worked by slave gang labor.

Farm Wealth Comparisons

Heywood Fleisig estimates that the value of farm implements per worker in 1860 was $66 in the free states, but only $38 in the slave states. But Fleisig does not include women and children in his calculations of capital per worker in the North as he does in his figures for the slave-worked farms in the South. Since slaves were expensive, it should follow that Southern planters used capital to substitute for slaves wherever it was profitable. Slaves, together with land, implements, and buildings, made the market value of a typical slave-state farm $7,101 compared to only $3,311 in the free states. In the Cotton South, the figure was $8,786.[16] What slaves did to differences in wealth holding is described by Wright:

> Slaveholders constituted the wealthiest class in the country by far. The average slaveowner was more than five times as wealthy as the average northerner, more than ten times as wealthy as the average non-slaveholding southern farmer.[17]

The data illustrate the success of slavery as a social mechanism for settlement, hard as that interpretation might be for modern Americans to accept. Slavery was immoral, but it ensured a labor supply. The hard work of settlement, clearing, plowing, building structures—in an age before the internal combustion engine when most farm work was handwork—gave the slave system advantages. As the historian Abbot E. Smith wrote of servitude and slavery in colonial America:

> It is a familiar story that mankind, when confronted in America with a vast and trackless wilderness awaiting exploitation, threw off its ancient shackles of cast and privilege and set forth upon the road to freedom. Among the social institutions found most useful in the course of this march were those of African slavery and white servitude.[18]

By the mid-nineteenth century, servitude was gone, but slavery was not.

The economics of slavery are considered in detail in Chapter 10. The point in comparing the two agricultural systems overall is that slavery and cotton made Southern farming more successful by conventional measures (size of farm and wealth) than northern farmsteads in the era before extensive mechanization.

COTTON AS A FOREIGN-EXCHANGE EARNER

Chapter 12 will discuss in some detail the balance of international payments between 1790 and 1860: what we sold to the world, what we bought from it, and the pattern of those relationships over time. Here, we want to tie agricultural development into the story of domestic growth. Part of its effect is straightforward:

the employment of workers and resources in farming and the demand produced by those activities for services and manufacturers. But part of the impact of American agriculture upon the country's growth was indirect, through the balance of payments, and it was of crucial importance. That impact came from what we now call **foreign-exchange earnings**.

Paying the Bills

When the United States was growing rapidly, as in the 1830s and 1850s, the economy used more economic resources than it produced, so the country was forced to borrow. However, borrowed funds bear interest, which is a net drain on the borrower. Thus, although the loans were timely and enhanced the American economy's growth, the lower the subsequent interest drain (together with repayment of capital), the higher still was the supply of resources available for domestic use in consumption and investment. Hence, exports were of crucial importance. What was imported had to be paid for with something, and exports paid most of the bill. Consider the structure of commodity trade per annum in the 1850s as presented in Table 9.4.

Because the manufacturing sector was not yet able to supply as large a part of the demand as it later would, finished and semifinished goods accounted for 63 percent of imports. Exports were the products of agriculture and extractive industries; crude materials and food alone accounted for about 84 percent of exports.

Cotton's Export Earnings

In the 1850s, exports averaged $211 million, imports averaged $275 million. The difference, $64 million, was made up in part by "invisible" earnings, such as shipping, and the rest by foreign loans, both short-term mercantile credits and longer-term borrowing (such as railroad bonds). *More than half* of those export earnings from crude materials came from cotton exports alone. In the earlier years, the cotton proportion was even higher.

Thus, cotton was by far the most important single export. This would be true throughout the nineteenth century, although in some later years, wheat would run a very close second. Before the Civil War, however, raw cotton directly earned more than half the nation's ability to buy needed goods from abroad. Gold exports, after the California discoveries, became important, too. In 1855, $54 million of gold exports amounted to 61 percent of earnings from cotton. According to Douglass North, earnings from shipping, although rising in absolute amount, were equal to about 10 percent of total export earnings and were actually declining as a proportion of the total.[19]

The annual value of cotton exports increased by a factor of 5 from the period 1815–1820; the volume increased in the same period by a factor of 11. The growth of both cotton output and cotton exports was a major event of the antebellum period (see Table 9.5).

In 1860, the earnings from cotton exports totaled $192 billion, nearly four times the revenues of the federal government. It was quite an incredible situation that a single commodity could so dominate the American economy's position in the world. British industry, expanding again and again through the decades, depended upon the American South for 75 to 80 percent of its raw materials. By 1860, of an employed labor force in England of 10.5 million, nearly one-half million were directly employed in cotton textile manufacturing, and the total in cotton textiles in all stages may have come to 1.5 million.[20] If the South felt confident of cotton's economic power in any conflict between the states, it is not surprising.

TABLE 9.4 Structure of Commodity Trade, 1851–1860[a]

Commodity	*Exports*	*Imports*
Crude materials	61.6	9.6
Crude foodstuffs	6.6	11.7
Manufactured foodstuffs	15.5	15.4
Semimanufactures	4.0	12.5
Finished manufactures	12.3	50.7

[a] Figures are annual averages as a percentage of the total.

Source: *Historical Statistics,* derived from series U214–218, 220–224.

TABLE 9.5 Average Annual Cotton Exports

Period	*Million Pounds*	*Million Dollars*
1815–1820	94	$ 23
1821–1830	204	26
1831–1840	432	53
1841–1850	700	55
1851–1860	1,180	124

Source: *Historical Statistics,* series U275–76.

As David Surdam has demonstrated, cotton was still king in 1860; demand was strong and expected to remain so.[21]

AGRICULTURAL LABOR: DEPENDENCE ON SLAVERY

Farming depends upon energy. Nearly all farm jobs require lifting, digging, pulling, pushing, cutting, chopping, and carrying. Even with modern equipment, farm work is astonishingly hard compared with nearly any other nonpenal employment. The human body has limited strength for this kind of work, and the entire history of agricultural invention is the record of innovations designed to lighten and shorten this labor. Any implement, tool, animal, or natural or synthetic force that relieved human beings of this relentless labor has been welcomed. Sharpened sticks, better cutting and hoeing tools, draft animals, pulleys, wheels, levers, wind, water—over the centuries, every method has been tried. With slavery, *someone* else (the slave) suffered the exertions of agricultural labor.

One slave can substitute for the labor of one slave owner; many slaves are substitutes for many free workers. Concentration on grain and animal production kept Northern farms to a size that could be managed by single families, as we already have noted. In the Cotton South, a competitive market in slaves meant that a labor force was readily available to those who wanted to cultivate beyond the family-farm size and had the money to buy slaves. The problem was to make acquisition of slave labor profitable. Cotton, sugar, and tobacco cultivation would tempt a Southern farmer to purchase the slave capital required. The market for cotton was guaranteed before the Civil War, and there was abundant land for sale. In addition, slave owners could count on a handsome capital gain in the value of their slave property. Plantations, therefore, could be readily established by those who understood the cotton trade. In addition, the widespread use of hired management, white overseers, meant that entry into cotton growing was easily achieved by the wealthy.

Labor-Intensive Slavery

Slaves were substitutes for free labor. Were slaves substitutes for capital equipment, too? Certainly not, if that equipment could increase the profitability of Southern agriculture. No sensible plantation owner would deny workers the use of shovels, hoes, and axes. There were no working mechanical cotton pickers before 1860. Until then, there was only slave gang labor. The example of Whitney's cotton gin shows that Southern farmers would quickly innovate productivity—using machinery when it appeared.

The slave field gang became extraordinarily efficient by reduction of the work to specialized tasks and control of its rhythm. As Robert Fogel says: "Once it is recognized that the fundamental form of the exploitation of slave labor was through speed-up rather than through an increase in the number of clock-time hours per year, certain paradoxes resolve themselves."[22] Those paradoxes include regular rest periods, Sundays off, and probably a shorter work year than that enjoyed by the typical Northern farmer, or Southern free farmer, who still had animals and poultry to tend after the field work was finished. The goal of the slave field gang system was regular *intensive* labor. Cotton production made Southern plantations labor-intensive.

Cotton and the Slave Population

Between 1810 and 1830, cotton production rose from 178,000 bales a year to 732,000 bales, an increase of 311 percent. By 1860, output was 3.8 million bales, an increase of another 435 percent.[23] From 1790, of course, the increase was astronomical (see Table 9.6). Moving south and west, the slave labor force under the direction of its white masters created one of the great successes of American economic history.

TABLE 9.6 Cotton Output

Year	*Thousand Bales*
1790	3
1800	73
1810	178
1820	335
1830	732
1840	1,348
1850	2,136
1860	3,841

Source: *Historical Statistics,* series K554.

After Whitney's cotton gin (1793) enabled short-staple cotton varieties to be separated on a competitive commercial basis by mechanical means, American cotton quickly dominated world cotton textile production. For example, after the 1820s, three-quarters of Britain's massive consumption of raw cotton came from the United States. For decades, world cotton textile development and the expansion of American slave agriculture went hand-in-hand. Indeed, in a forceful essay, Ronald Bailey demonstrates that profits from the international slave trade bolstered a significant part of colonial commercial wealth and provided major capital for early New England industry. Names from the New England pantheon of business history such as Cabot, Lowell, Brown, Perkins, and even Sam Slater were stained by their connections with slavery. From its inception, the new U.S. industrial system indirectly exploited slave labor.[24]

The soils and climate of the cotton-growing areas gave the South an economic rent from cotton—financial returns in excess of alternative competitive uses of resources. From 1820 to 1860, cotton output rose by about a factor of 11.5, and slave population, by only a factor of 2.5. The increase in output of cotton per slave was by a factor of 4.6.

Of course, some cotton was grown by free white farmers, but it probably is accurate to say that most of the cotton was grown by slaves. Half the Southern farms had no slaves, and 28 percent grew no cotton. The evidence suggests that 86 percent of the cotton was grown on farms of more than 100 acres and that 90 percent of the slaves were owned on these farms.[25] The Cotton South was an astounding agricultural success: cheap land, slave labor, hired management, and a strongly rising demand for cotton all combined to make the slave system profitable for slave owners.

Southern population between 1790 and 1860 is shown in Table 9.7. Over the period 1790 to 1860, the slave population increased slightly more rapidly than did that of free whites; thus, the proportion of slaves to free whites rose slightly. An interesting feature of the data is that the population of southern free blacks was growing more than 40 percent more rapidly than either the slave or the free white populations. However, by 1860, the free black population was still negligible in absolute numbers or proportion.

By the 1850s, slave ownership was becoming more concentrated. According to Wright, the number of all Southern families owning slaves declined from 36 percent in 1830 to 25 percent by 1860. By that year, about 48 percent of Southern farmers owned no slaves at all. The slave owners were the wealthiest, by far. Lee Soltow found that, in both 1850 and 1860, between 90 and 95 percent of all the agricultural wealth in the South was owned by slaveholders.[26] It is clear that as cotton output expanded and slave prices rose, fewer Southern farmers could afford to own this species of property. The game was getting more profitable, but the table stakes were rising sharply. As Wright put it: "The very forces that were strengthening the economic incentives for slave owners to retain slavery were slowly weakening the political supports for the institution."[27]

TABLE 9.7 Southern Population[a]

Year	*Free White*	*Slave*	*Free Black*	*Percentage Slave of Free White*
1790	1,271	690	33	54
1800	1,704	918	61	54
1810	2,191	1,268	107	58
1820	2,776	1,644	135	60
1830	3,546	2,162	182	61
1840	4,309	2,642	214	61
1850	5,630	3,352	235	60
1860	7,034	4,097	258	58

[a] Figures given are in thousands of persons.

Source: Derived from *Historical Statistics,* 1960, series A114; 1975, series A175–176.

Southern Self-Sufficiency Before 1860

The cash crops in Northern agriculture were also subsistence crops: Wheat, corn, oats, hogs, and cattle could either be sold for cash or kept on the farm and consumed there by the grower's own family. The market economy for Northern farmers was such that they had only to extend themselves in activities they would be pursuing in any case.

In the Cotton South, the problem was more complex. Hutchinson and Williamson have shown that the South, New Orleans apart, was not necessarily dependent for food upon any other section, despite the importance of the cotton crop.[28] Cotton was not consumed as part of domestic subsistence life. The cotton farmer distributed his resources between growing cotton for cash and, like their counterparts in the North, growing corn and other food items and raising hogs and cattle for subsistence consumption.

In those early times, every farm was in part self-sufficient in foodstuffs, and certain raw materials were processed there. Saw mills, tanneries, blacksmith shops, flour mills, dairies—all were located at sites of primary production. Farmers and plantation owners might include one or several of these specialties in conjunction with other farming operations. The problem was, what mix of cash and subsistence crops was most desirable? Then, as now, the mix chosen depended upon relative prices and costs, but cotton was the main cash crop. Food crops, fodder, and animals could be tended by the slaves, too—by women and children at peak times and by all during slack seasons in the annual cycles of cotton planting, cultivating, and harvesting.

The capacity of any cotton farm or plantation to produce revenues depended upon market prices as well as upon physical crop yields. Then, as now, agricultural prices varied considerably from year to year. Given the transportation system of the time and the restricted storage and credit facilities available to Southern farmers, domestic production of basic foodstuffs used spare labor and saved cash for uses other than purchases of food provisions. Grain besides corn *could* be grown in the cotton belt, too.[29] With larger acreage, cotton as an additional cash crop added another dimension. At the most fundamental level, subsistence food growing enabled the farmer or plantation owner to conserve cash in the years of low cotton prices. Thus, substantial self-sufficiency in food was characteristic of cotton farming. The basic need was labor for picking cotton. Land, the more plentiful factor, could be applied to both food and cotton. Corn was the perfect complement to cotton cultivation.

As it happened, the peak periods of demand for labor during the annual cycles of planting and harvest varied enough so that the same labor force could be kept in steady employment growing *both* cotton and provision crops. Cotton planting began in April, but corn could be planted as early as late February or March. Also, mature corn could be left in the fields while the cotton crop was brought in between August and December. In the other months, there were no peak labor demand periods, and the labor force could be assigned the full range of farm tasks without disrupting essential planting and harvest needs.[30]

Because more labor was available on large plantations in the form of slaves purchased at will, the proportion of land devoted to cotton could be increased according to the marginal product of labor and estimated cotton prices while the basic food and other subsistence needs of the plantations could be covered as well. Hence, the yeoman farmer on a small farm grew relatively little cotton in proportion to other crops, while the slave plantations produced mostly cotton—and *most* of the cotton.

The mutually reinforcing link between slave owning and expansion of the cotton economy was strengthened by the practice of achieving substantial self-sufficiency. The more efficient farms, using greater amounts of land, could devote an increasing proportion of their total effort to the cash crop, thus raising the cash-revenue productivity of the slave labor force.

Until 1860, the demand for cotton reinforced the motives for the expansion of slavery, especially among the wealthy who financed the establishment of large-scale plantations. Cotton was cash, and the larger the slave-owning establishment, the greater the proportion of land used to grow it. Farmers wanted farms, but slave owners wanted *cotton lands.*

WESTERN EXPANSION OF NORTHERN AGRICULTURE

As we saw in Table 9.2, by 1860, population in the new Northern states beyond the Appalachians actually exceeded that of the new Southern states. From Ohio to Kansas, farm families took up the new land. The first settlers shunned the open prairies and settled in forested areas and bottomland along rivers where significant woodlands could be found to provide building materials and fuel.

The Eastern Link

The Erie Canal had first provided a direct east-west link for transportation on a scale beyond oxcarts and poor roads. The result was a significant reduction in transportation costs. As a result, there was a rise in the prices farmers received for wheat and other foods grown on the farm and a decline in those prices to consumers in the Eastern markets. Manufactured goods became cheaper for Midwestern farmers to buy as the transportation links to the East improved. As a result, Thomas Berry found, farmers by 1860 could buy more than twice as many manufactured goods with a given quantity of their products as they could in 1820.[31] These results were augmented by the new canals in Ohio and Indiana and then, very quickly, by direct rail links. By 1853 (as we saw in Chapter 8), Chicago was the Northern center of a rail network stretching from the Mississippi to the East Coast. Farm products could be shipped quickly and regularly to Eastern and world markets, cutting handling and storage costs, instead of just seasonally downriver to New Orleans. More competition for freight, of course, meant alternative buyers for farmers. Connecting railroads such as the Illinois Central were in place or under construction by the 1850s, and the Midwestern agricultural cornucopia was near the beginning of its fantastically productive career.

Pioneering

At first, Midwestern land looked like no wonder of nature or humanity. The early pioneers stayed away from the vast open prairies, where the glaciers had pulverized native limestone into soils of incredible richness and depth. Topsoils were 40 feet deep and awaited the plow. Early settlers preferred lands in or near stands of timber, so that clearing and planting had building materials and fuel production as natural by-products.

The prairies were a puzzle. The deep sod under the natural prairie grasses was a powerful challenge to the traditional wooden plow with its iron-plated moldboard. It took two to three years to get the first full crop of wheat. Initially, the farmer could produce only a "sod crop," cutting the overturned prairie grass roots with an axe to make a slash in which seed was deposited. A year later, with more plowing and working, the soil would begin to yield to regular cultivation as the sod stubble and dry roots decomposed. Danger of prairie fires was constantly present in the summer months, and farms had to be surrounded by plowed strips that served as firebreaks. Also, with 30 to 40 inches of rainfall per year from the Ohio Valley westward to eastern Kansas, the flat prairie lands, when wet, drained poorly and were prolific breeders of mosquitoes and malaria.

In forested areas, such as those of Michigan and Wisconsin, it could take a month of backbreaking labor to clear an acre, from five to ten years to make a modest farm. The prairies were also thought at first to be poor soils, since they did not seem to be able to support a good growth of hardwoods.[32] Time and experience would change that.

The Cost

Long, hard labor faced Midwestern farmers who had to rely primarily on family labor. Progress was slow. Martin Primack estimated that fully a sixth of the Midwestern labor force in the 1850s was constantly engaged in the sole task of clearing land.[33] Such activity required capital and was itself capital formation. Indeed, the family opening a new farm must have spent the majority of its work time and effort on activities we would classify as *investment*: clearing land, constructing fences and buildings, feeding and breeding herds and flocks. If all such output could be measured in terms of an abstract *labor unit*, it is clear that the model of frontier economic growth is one in which the ratio of investment must *fall* initially—the opposite of standard ideas about economic growth.[34]

The farm family that devoted 85 percent of its labor effort to activities meant to sustain current consumption and 15 percent to investment in the pioneering stage probably would have failed. In the five to ten years it took to build a modest frontier farm, the ratio of investment to total activity had to be extraordinarily high. Consuming income instead of reinvesting it in the farm was a luxury to be enjoyed only *after* the more rigorous processes of farm formation were carried through.

It was for that reason that so many hardy farmers profited from a sequence of farm "developments," selling out a finished or partly finished farm at a profit and moving on to a new location. The land-sale history discussed earlier reflects this widespread habit in nineteenth-century America. Primack's estimates show that the time spent on land clearing in the Midwest in the 1850s was 18 percent, compared with about 10 percent in the South and only roughly 7 percent in the Northeast.

This labor had to be accompanied by other investment. The state of Minnesota estimated in 1860 that a hypothetical representative small farm of 160 acres (with one-fourth the acreage fenced) would cost $795 to establish and stock.[35] Since the average annual earnings of a farm laborer in the West North Central region in 1860 was only $165 (with board included), successful farming clearly was an expensive proposition. According to Donald Adams, a factory worker would have needed from five to ten years of average savings to set himself up in "independent agriculture."[36] Atack and Bateman have supplied an abundant set of estimates for farm making in the 1850s.[37] Moving west paid in general; in 1860, a typical 80-acre farm would cost $2,784 in Ohio but only $805 in Minnesota.

> A northeastern farmer who sold and moved west to Ohio could purchase a farm perhaps one-eighth larger than that which he vacated, but if he moved instead west or north of Indiana, he could purchase a farm at least twice as large.[38]

Experienced Pioneers

"Old stock" Americans comprised the majority of pioneer farmers moving westward from the old colonies with their farm animals, tools, and equipment. Given promising places to establish farms, they became a remarkable and, indeed, relentless cutting edge of settlement. Penniless immigrants, even those from European farms, went mainly to the cities to do wage labor by necessity. Successful agricultural pioneering required extensive capital, including working family members.

Let's look at two remarkable examples of evidence that remain. In both cases, the data came from the wreckage of wagon trains that had left the Midwest for California. The first is George R. Stewart's gripping account of the Donner party, which came to grief in the snows of the Sierra Nevada in the winter of 1846.[39] There were 20 covered wagons carrying 87 people. Three families had three wagons each, two with seven yoke of oxen (the number for the third, the "aristocratic" Reed family, is not recorded), milk cows, saddle horses, and beef cattle.

The leading members of the party all had been successful farmers in Illinois. George Donner had grown to adulthood and lived successively in Kentucky, Indiana, and Springfield, Illinois, creating farms and raising in succession three families with three wives. The equipage of this wagon train seems opulent. Yet there is no evidence that it was more than an average pioneering adventure.

In his masterpiece about the Utah Mormons, Leonard Arrington quotes from an account of Howard Stansbury describing roadside scenes west of Fort Laramie during the Gold Rush in 1849:

> Before halting at noon, we passed eleven wagons that had been broken up, the spokes of the wheels taken to pack-saddles, and the rest burned or otherwise destroyed. The road has been literally strewn with articles that have been thrown away. Bar-iron and steel, large blacksmith's anvils and bellows, crowbars, drills, augers, gold-washers, chisels, axes, lead trunks, spades, ploughs, large grind-stones, baking-ovens, cooking-stoves without number, kegs, barrels, harness, clothing, bacon, and beans, were found along the road in pretty much the order in which they have been here enumerated.... In the course of this one day the relics of seventeen wagons and the carcasses of twenty-seven dead oxen have been seen.[40]

Again, there is no reason to suppose that the inventory described came from a wagon train of extraordinary wealth. Pioneering was for generations a way of life. The new farms were made by people who knew how and were equipped to do it. The companies that faced the disasters of the California trail were average American families leaving farms in the Midwest for the Golden State. It remained for successive generations to find ways to turn pioneer farms into what would become the great American breadbasket.

The Importance of Technology

We saw that the cotton economy could expand output by intensive use of slave labor. The Northern family farm had less need for hired labor since the main crops were grain (not labor-intensive) and livestock (a 365-day-a-year job). When improved farm machinery came along, the Midwestern family farm became the great "factory on the farm" we know today. Change came slowly but relentlessly—bigger plows, better cultivating and harvesting machinery, steam engines, then the internal combustion engine, and with it, tractors and trucks. Therein lay the future of Midwestern agriculture.

In modern times, a Midwestern family farm rotating soy beans, wheat, and corn commonly contains 500 acres or more and is mostly worked by a single full-time operator employing farm machinery worth a small fortune: tractors, seeders, massive discs, spraying equipment, air-conditioned combines, even butane dryers for crops in the storage silos. The origin of this economic wonder of mechanization was the chronic Midwest farm labor shortage in the nineteenth century.

Early Inventions

When the pioneer farmers first approached the Midwest, their technology was remarkably medieval: Ground was broken with a small wooden plow sheathed in iron; seeds were sown by hand; grain was cut by scythe and cradle, bound, shocked by hand, and dried, then separated from the shocks and husks by handheld flail, and winnowed and screened in the wind. Farm implements were mainly improved by small changes impossible to locate in remote origin, but there were several "heroic" improvements we do know something about.

In the Midwest, the steel plow was one such improvement. It was lighter and stronger than the old iron-sheathed wooden plows, and the moldboard scoured (cleared itself of mud) more efficiently as it was pulled along. The steel plows, drawn by teams of mules, horses, or oxen, could cut the prairie sod faster and thus extend the practical size of the family farm. By 1857, 20 years after its introduction, the John Deere Company of Moline, Illinois, annually produced 10,000 steel plows.

The horse-drawn reaper was a similar invention. In 1833, Obed Hussey patented one, and in 1834, Cyrus Hall McCormick patented another. The reaper—consisting of reciprocating cutting blades powered by the wheels as the machine was drawn through the grain by a horse—could eliminate the whole harvest force wielding scythes. Yet, by 1850, less than 1 percent of American grain was cut by reaper, and only 3,400 of the machines had been sold. By 1860, some 80,000 had been sold, and in 1859, about 56,000 of those 80,000 were still in working order. Why the long delay and then the sudden splurge?

Economic historians have had fun trying to find the answer; however, it is important to know, since the reaper's history is doubtless representative of most large and relatively expensive pieces of agricultural capital equipment. The traditional view held simply that the upsurge in wheat prices in the 1850s made the purchase of machinery profitable. Yet, as Paul David noted, if the reaper cut production costs, the purchase of a reaper might have been profitable if prices were fixed or falling. In an attempt to answer the question, David's analysis took into account (a) farm terrain, (b) wage costs, (c) interest rates, and (d) useful life of the equipment as well as the rising prices of grain in the 1850s. Terrain was important. Obviously, a farmer facing table-flat, stone-free fields in central Illinois saw more hope from such a device than did the long-jawed Vermonter contemplating rock-encrusted hillside fields. As David puts it:

> ...the efficient use of mechanical reapers required a level, stone-free farm terrain, arranged in large and regularly shaped enclosures—a specific natural resource input that at the mid point of the nineteenth century was obtained much more cheaply (relative to the prices of grain) in the United States than in the British Isles.[41]

Thus, mechanical reaping would spread as Midwestern agriculture came "on line" in the westward movement. With given labor costs (high), given interest rates, and machine life, a single farm would need to reach a certain threshold size before it paid the farmer to invest in a reaper. Only then would expected production be large enough to cover the lifetime cost of the machine and still yield a profit. To David, that size fell from about 46 acres between 1849 and 1853 to 35 acres in the mid–1850s, and because that threshold matched the average size of a large portion of Midwest farms, reaper investment surged.

David's calculations proved controversial. Alan Olmstead argued that reaper life was shorter than David assumed, thus raising the threshold acreage. Further, because reapers were commonly rented and also jointly owned, threshold size was, in fact, largely irrelevant. It held only for single buyers. Moreover, the reapers were constantly being improved and made more efficient, effectively cheaper, and, hence, more profitable.[42] Lewis Jones argued that it was not *average* farm sizes that mattered, in any case, but the sizes of those where reapers were used.[43] There were more than enough Midwestern farms in the 1850s large enough to meet the threshold calculated by either David or Olmstead to account for reaper sales. Therefore, increased prices of grain must also have been an important determinant of reaper sales. Small-scale farmers were left with their scythes, or they could rent or invest jointly with others in reapers.

Steam-powered threshing machines became common in the 1850s, eliminating the flail. These machines were shared out, rented, jointly owned, or otherwise acquired. Also, drill seeders became common, as did cultivators, mowing machines, horse-drawn hay rakes, and improved harrows for working the soil just before planting. Even if Midwestern farmers could not significantly raise yields per acre (and they could not, except with fertilizers) or expand their output by greater labor inputs per farm, machinery allowed them to farm *more acres* and thus to expand their output per farm. They had two expensive factors, labor and capital, and one plentiful factor, land. Adoption of machinery conserved labor, and the addition of plentiful land inputs raised the productivity of both capital and labor. Machinery would become the "slave" of the Northern farmer.

Output

Table 9.8 reports some rough output numbers for the entire country. If we suppose that the numbers for these three crops are representative of the Midwest, we see bigger decade rates of increase for two field grains, wheat and barley, in the 1850s than in the 1840s. Reapers were used for these crops but not for corn. However, because reapers were used to cut oats, perhaps those data show (slightly) the increase in wheat and barley prices compared with oats as well as the consequences of the reaper. Of course, other machinery made a difference, too.

How much of the increased output was produced in the Midwest alone? That we cannot say either, although some stray numbers add to the picture. Data for flour and corn exported from the Midwest and Upper South show the expected big increases: Flour rose from 800,000 barrels in 1839, to 3 million in 1850, to 5 million in 1860. However, corn exports rose from 1 million bushels in 1839 to 24 million in 1860, and reapers were not used in corn.[44]

TABLE 9.8 Output of Major Grains[a]

Year	*Wheat*	*Corn*	*Oats*	*Barley*
Decade				
1839	85	378	123	4
1849	100	592	147	5
1859	173	839	173	16
Rate of Growth per decade				
1839–1849	17.7	56.6	19.5	25.0
1849–1859	73.0	41.7	17.7	220.0

[a]Output figures are for grain only and are given in millions of bushes.

Source: *Historical Statistics,* series K503, 507, 512, 515.

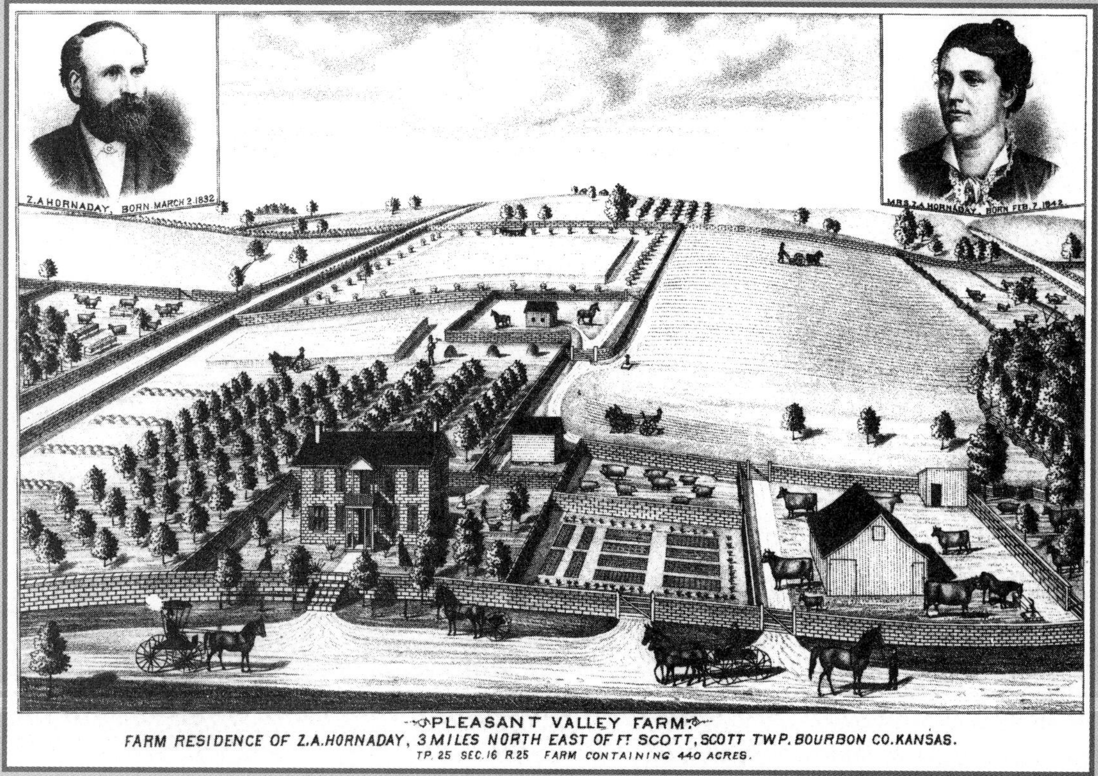

Z.A.HORNADAY, BORN MARCH 2 1832

MRS Z.A.HORNADAY, BORN FEB.7.1842

PLEASANT VALLEY FARM

FARM RESIDENCE OF Z.A.HORNADAY, 3 MILES NORTH EAST OF FT SCOTT, SCOTT TWP. BOURBON CO. KANSAS.

TP. 25 SEC.16 R.25 FARM CONTAINING 440 ACRES.

Two Agricultural Cultures. *An artist's conception of an idyllic Northern farm (above) shows how the concentration on grain crops and animals and the use of farm machinery to increase output reduced the need for hired labor. Labor-intensive agriculture of Southern cotton plantations (below) was the primary economic motive for slavery in the antebellum South.*

The precise impact of mechanization attributed to each individual invention cannot be shown from such data. We can rely only upon common sense. The farmers were buying farm machinery and, in the 1850s, plunged into reapers. They bought farm machinery to use and make a profit. Thus, the machinery must have been financially desirable. Otherwise, they would have stayed with scythes and "saved money."

THE COMPROMISE FAILS

There is an imaginary line between the wheat-growing northern areas of the trans-Appalachian West and the South in the 1850s that extended east and west from Shelbyville, Illinois. This line of demarcation is at the southern edge of the Wisconsin drift of the last glacier. Above that line are flattened prairies, below are hills and mountains, descending into the alluvial and upland regions of the Cotton South. In the 1850s, in the area between wheat and cotton, lay a mixed farming region in which the main grain crop was corn, consumed by both humans and animals. Frederick Merk made an insightful observation about those who lived in that middle ground:

> All the great compromises on the slavery issue came from corn-belt politicians. An Illinois Senator, Jesse B. Thomas, introduced the Missouri Compromise of 1820. A Kentucky senator, Henry Clay, worked out the Compromise of 1850. Another Illinois Senator, Stephen A. Douglas, was the champion of the compromise doctrine of popular sovereignty. A Kentuckian, John J. Crittenden, worked out the Crittenden peace plan of 1860, which failed.[45]

As the line extended roughly westward, the compromises gave out. The Kansas-Nebraska Act of 1854 allowed popular sovereignty in Kansas over the issue of slavery, and gunfire was the result when the two systems of agriculture finally came into direct confrontation. Cotton was not going to be grown in Kansas. But in Texas, Arizona, and California—lands acquired from Mexico in the 1840s—cotton would eventually be an important crop. Slavery already had entered Texas; it was kept out of Arizona and California. Land—who was to own it, how it was to be used, who was to work it—had always been a driving force in American history. As the two systems extended westward in the 1850s, the will to compromise on these issues failed.

As Jennifer Roback emphasizes, to the South, the lands beyond the Missouri were a common property resource, to which the Southern states had an equal claim by virtue of the contract of 1789—the federal Constitution.[46] When Lincoln was elected in 1860, backed by Northern groups determined to keep slavery out of the West, the contract was breached, and the South seceded from the Union. Slavery was abolished by fire and sword.

NOTES

1. These farmers displaced Native American tribes, in both the North and the South east of the Mississippi in the 1820s and 1830s, in episodes like the Black Hawk War and the Cherokee removal that will darken American history forever. Ray Allen Billington, *Westward Expansion: A History of the American Frontier* (New York: Macmillan, 1949), chaps. XIV, XV, XXXII.
2. For those who would like to see such an opinion "costed out," see Gerald Gunderson, "The Origin of the American Civil War," *JEH*, December 1974.
3. Peter McClelland, *Sowing Modernity: America's First Agricultural Revolution* (Ithaca: Cornell University Press, 1997) is a careful study of agricultural innovation, emphasizing agricultural implements.
4. *Free land* in this sense means not land at zero price, but land freely exchanged at market prices and unencumbered by such restraints as feudal obligations.
5. Peter Temin, "Free Land and Federalism: A Synoptic View of American Economic History," *JIH*, Winter 1991.
6. *Native-born* in this table means a resident in 1850 of a given state who also was born in that state. Richard Steckel advances arguments based upon "human capital," mainly in agriculture, to explain the tendency, strong before the Civil War, for the internal migrations to be predominantly east-west, with relatively little north-south migration. "The Economic Foundations of East-West Migration During the 19th Century," *EEH*, January 1983.

7. Jeremy Atack and Fred Bateman, *To Their Own Soil: Agriculture in the Antebellum North* (1987), chap. 5, "Migration and Immigration," for a detailed examination of the general east-west migration. Although families moved around within regions, they note, that within their sample, "...no families...made a long-distance move from a state west of Indiana to one east of that state" (p. 75).
8. Harriet Martineau, *Society in America* (Garden City, NY: Doubleday, 1962), p. 181.
9. See Robert Fogel and Stanley Engerman, *Time on the Cross: The Economics of American Negro Slavery* (1974), vol. I, p. 47, and vol. II, p. 43.
10. Robert Fogel, *Without Consent or Contract* (1989), pp. 78–79, and Fogel and Engerman (1974), vol. 1, pp. 191–196 and 234–237.
11. Gavin Wright, *The Political Economy of the Cotton South: Households, Markets, and Wealth in the Nineteenth Century* (1978), chap. 2, pp. 15–24 for all soil types.
12. *Ibid.*, pp. 74–87.
13. Jacob Metzer, "Rational Management, Modern Business Practices, and Economies of Scale in the Ante-Bellum Southern Plantations," *EEH*, April 1975.
14. Heywood Fleisig, "Slavery, the Supply of Agricultural Labor, and the Industrialization of the South," *JEH*, September 1976, p. 586.
15. Wright (1978), p. 23. The mean-sized farm in 1997 was 487 acres. *Statistical Abstract of the U.S.* (Washington, D.C.: Government Printing Office, 1999) Table 1105.
16. Fleisig (1976), p. 596. Terry Anderson, in a private communication, has emphasized the element of incomparability in these data. Slaves were "capital equipment" and had a known market value, which is included. But what of the "human capital" embodied in the brains and brawn of Northern farmers? That is not counted. If it were, if its market value (the opportunity cost, measured as income potential from alternate employment) were added into the free state data, the force of this argument would be considerably reduced.
17. Wright (1978), p. 35.
18. Abbot Smith, *Colonists in Bondage: White Servitude and Convict Labor in America, 1607–1776* (Chapel Hill: University of North Carolina Press, 1947), p. 226.
19. Douglass North, *The Economic Growth of the United States, 1790 to 1860* (Englewood Cliffs, NJ: Prentice-Hall, 1961), p. 77.
20. Jonathan Hughes, *Fluctuations in Trade, Industry, and Finance: A Study of British Economic Growth 1850–1860* (Oxford: The Clarendon Press, 1960), p. 72.
21. David Surdam, "King Cotton: Monarch or Pretender? The State of the Market for Raw Cotton on the Eve of the American Civil War," *EHR*, February 1998.
22. Fogel (1989), p. 79.
23. The 1859 and 1860 crops were extraordinary and, it has been estimated, exceeded 4 million bales. The data in Table 9.6 are census numbers.
24. Ronald Bailey, "The Slave(ry) Trade and the Development of Capitalism in the United States: The Textile Industry in New England," *Social Science History*, Fall 1990.
25. Wright (1978), Table 2.5, p. 28.
26. *Ibid.*, p. 35.
27. *Ibid.*, p. 42.
28. William Hutchinson and Samuel Williamson, "The Self-Sufficiency of the Antebellum South: Estimates of the Food Supply," *JEH*, September 1971.
29. Southern farms were apparently nowhere as efficient in grain production, on the average, as were farms in the Northeast or North Central states. William Parker and Judith Klein, "Productivity Growth in Grain Production in the United States," in Dorothy Brady, ed., *Output, Employment, and Productivity in the United States After 1800, NBER, Studies in Income and Wealth* (New York: Columbia University Press, 1966), vol. 30.
30. Wright (1978), pp. 164–176.
31. Thomas Berry, *Western Prices Before 1861* (Cambridge: Harvard University Press, 1943), Appendix B, Table 19. Reprinted in North, p. 255.
32. Frederick Merk, *History of the Westward Movement* (1978), chap. 21.
33. Martin Primack, "Land Clearing Under 19th Century Techniques," *JEH*, December 1962, p. 492.
34. For example, W. W. Rostow, *The Stages of Economic Growth* (Cambridge: Cambridge University Press, 1961), pp. 7–9, in which the "take-off" into sustained growth occurs as the rate of investment *rises* into the range of 10 percent plus. If American farmers had had such an investment ratio on the frontier, they might have been overtaken by natural reforestation.
35. See Jeremy Atack and Peter Passell, *A New Economic View of American History* (New York: Norton, 1994), p. 277.
36. Donald Adams, Jr., "Earnings and Savings in the Early 19th Century," *EEH*, April 1980.
37. Atack and Bateman (1987), chap. 8, "Relative Costs of Farm Making."
38. *Ibid.*, pp. 136–137.
39. *Ibid.*, pp. 136–137.
40. Leonard Arrington, *Great Basin Kingdom: An Economic History of the Latter-Day Saints 1830–1900* (Cambridge: Harvard University Press, 1958), p. 70.
41. Paul David, *Technical Choice: Innovation and Economic Growth: Essays on American and British Experience in the Nineteenth Century* (New York: Cambridge University Press, 1975), p. 89.

42. Alan Olmstead, "The Mechanization of Reaping and Mowing in American Agriculture 1833–70," *JEH*, June 1975.
43. Lewis Jones, "The Mechanization of Reaping and Mowing in American Agriculture: A Comment." *Journal of Economic History*, vol. XXXVII, no. 2, June 1977.
44. Diane Lindstrom, "Southern Dependence Upon Interregional Grain Supplies: A Review of the Trade Flows, 1840–1860," Table 7, printed in William Parker, ed., *The Structure of the Cotton Economy in the Antebellum South* (1970).
45. Merk (1978), p. 179.
46. Jennifer Roback, "A Public Choice Perspective on the Coming of the Civil War," manuscript, by permission.

SUGGESTED READINGS

Articles

Adams, Donald R., Jr. "Earnings and Savings in the Early 19th Century." *Explorations in Economic History*, vol. 17, no. 2, April 1980.

Atack, Jeremy, and Fred Bateman. "Egalitarianism, Inequality, and Age: The Rural North in 1860." *Journal of Economic History*, vol. XLI, no. 1, March 1981.

Bailey, Ronald. "The Slave(ry) Trade and the Development of Capitalism in the United States: The Textile Industry in New England." *Social Science History*, vol. 14, no. 3, Fall 1990.

Bogue, Allan G. "Farming in the Prairie Peninsula 1830–1890." *Journal of Economic History*, vol. I, no. 1, March 1947.

Danhof, Clarence. "Farm Making Costs and the Safety Valve; 1855–60." In Vernon Carstensen, ed., *The Public Lands*. Madison: University of Wisconsin Press, 1963.

Fleisig, Heywood. "Slavery, the Supply of Agricultural Labor, and the Industrialization of the South." *Journal of Economic History*, vol. XXXVI, no. 3, September 1976.

Gunderson, Gerald. "Southern Ante-Bellum Income Reconsidered." *Explorations in Economic History*, vol. 10, no. 2, Winter 1973.

———. "The Origin of the American Civil War." *Journal of Economic History*, vol. XXXIV, no. 4, December 1974.

Hutchinson, W. K., and Samuel H. Williamson. "The Self-Sufficiency of the Ante-Bellum South: Estimates of the Food Supply." *Journal of Economic History*, vol. XXXI, no. 3, September 1971.

Metzer, Jacob. "Rational Management, Modern Business Practice, and Economies of Scale in the Antebellum Plantations." *Explorations in Economic History*, vol. 12, no. 2, April 1975.

Olmstead, Alan. "The Mechanization of Reaping and Mowing in American Agriculture 1833–70." *Journal of Economic History*, vol. XXXV, no. 2, June 1975.

Parker, William. "Agriculture." In Lance E. Davis et al., *American Economic Growth: An Economist's History of the United States*. New York: Harper & Row, 1972, chap. 11.

———, and Judith Klein. "Productivity Growth in Grain Production in the United States." In Dorothy Brady, ed., *Output, Employment and Productivity in the United States After 1800*, National Bureau of Economic Research, *Studies in Income and Wealth*. New York: Columbia University Press, 1966, vol. 30.

Passell, Peter. "The Impact of Cotton Land Distribution on the Ante-Bellum Economy." *Journal of Economic History*, vol. XXXI, no. 4, December 1971.

Primack, Martin. "Land Clearing Under 19th Century Techniques." *Journal of Economic History*, vol. XXII, no. 4, December 1962.

Ransom, Roger L., and Richard Sutch. "Growth and Welfare in the American South in the Nineteenth Century." *Explorations in Economic History*, vol. 16, no. 2, April 1979.

Schmitz, Mark D. "Economies of Scale and Farm Size in the Ante-Bellum Sugar Sector." *Journal of Economic History*, vol. XXXVII, no. 4, December 1977.

——— and Donald Schaefer. "Paradox Lost: Westward Expansion and Slave Prices Before the Civil War." *Journal of Economic History*, vol. XLI, no. 2, June 1981.

Steckel, Richard. "The Economic Foundations of East-West Migration During the 19th Century." *Explorations in Economic History*, vol. 20, no. 1, January 1983.

Surdam, David. "King Cotton: Monarch or Pretender? The State of the Market for Raw Cotton on the Eve of the American Civil War." *Economic History Review* vol. 51, no. 1, February 1998.

Temin, Peter. "Free Land and Federalism: A Synoptic View of American Economic History." *Journal of Interdisciplinary History*, vol. 21, no. 3, Winter 1991.

Books

Atack, Jeremy, and Fred Bateman. *To Their Own Soil: Agriculture in the Antebellum North*. Ames: Iowa State University Press, 1987.

Bidwell, Percy, and John Falconer. *History of Agriculture in the Northern United States 1620–1860*. Washington, D.C.: The Carnegie Institution, 1925.

Bogue, Allan G. *From Prairie to Cornbelt: Farming on the Illinois and Iowa Prairies in the Nineteenth Century*. Chicago: University of Chicago Press, 1963.

Danhof, Clarence. *Change in Agriculture: The Northern United States, 1820–70.* Cambridge: Harvard University Press, 1969.

Fogel, Robert W. *Without Consent or Contract: The Rise and Fall of American Slavery.* New York: W. W. Norton, 1989.

—— and Stanley Engerman. *Time on the Cross: The Economics of American Negro Slavery.* Boston: Little, Brown, 1974.

Merk, Frederick. *History of the Westward Movement.* New York: Alfred Knopf, 1978.

Parker, William, ed. *The Structure of the Cotton Economy of the Antebellum South.* Washington, D.C.: The Agricultural History Society, 1970.

Wright, Gavin. *The Political Economy of the Cotton South: Households, Markets, and Wealth in the Nineteenth Century.* New York: Norton, 1978.

CHAPTER TEN

The Debate Over Slavery

Previous chapters have discussed antebellum Southern agriculture. This chapter examines a single topic that has engaged the attention of many—slavery, the main labor input in the cotton crop.

WHY THE CONTROVERSY?

Probably no other topic in American history can produce deep conflict more readily than slavery. So much of the country's past was molded by that institution, and so many modern Americans are descendants of slave ancestors, that the subject is bound to be of continuing interest. While white indentured servitude died out peacefully, black slavery was ended only by civil war and constitutional amendment.

Especially in the last decade before the Civil War, the slave economy flourished as never before. Why was this? Was slavery "efficient" as a system of production? Did it really have a viable, long-term future that was cut off by the Civil War?

Slavery Was ...

What was slavery like? Oddly enough, a question that simple is impossible to answer, partly because "what it was like" was determined by the perceptions of all those who lived in it—each with a different experience—and partly because of the innate problems of historical writing. We will first consider the latter reason, in order to understand with any sympathy the contradictions, distortions, misunderstandings, and disagreements among historians regarding slavery.

Slavery and History

The serious study of historical records involves several extremely difficult intellectual problems. The record of the past lies waiting to answer our questions. However, because historians must choose which questions will be asked, their own preconceptions must influence the written history that results. This is why we have all sorts of mutually incompatible interpretations of the same historical subjects. A liberal, a conservative, and a Marxist historian, all studying the same phenomenon, will probably produce three narratives that contradict each other, yet each account is based on "the facts." A neoclassical economist will write a history unrecognizable to these three because the analysis will make sparing use of institutions, individual experience, time, and legal change.

The careful historian, striving for objectivity, will give special attention to three matters. First, an understanding of the *background conditions* of the period is essential. For example, a new dimension can be added to our understanding of American slavery if we remember white servitude. We then see slavery's colonial origins as part of a more general unfree-labor-supply problem *in addition* to slavery's moral repugnance. Secondly, we must consider those recurring processes over time, the *initial conditions*, that continually motivated the institution. A good example is the secular expansion of demand for raw cotton based upon British, European, and American industrialization. Decade after decade, industrialization helped to make rural American slavery profitable because of the international market for raw cotton.

Finally, we must rely upon a *theory* for our understanding, the generalized set of cause-and-effect relationships we think "explain" the subject, given the background and initial conditions. For example, if a slave plantation were a "business," intent upon maximizing profits, it might then occur to the economist that what is rational behavior to a modern business person would have been equally rational to a plantation owner. The danger of this view is that it ignores the possibility that racism, ignorance, ingrained irrational custom, or laws designed to maintain the discipline of slavery at the expense of more "rational" behavior would prevail. Theory alone can be a dangerous guide and must be treated with great care.

Clearly, there is ample room for disagreement about these elements. And plenty of disagreement exists. A great deal of historical writing in recent years has been done on the economics of slavery, and we now know much more about the subject than we did even 30 years ago. But this increase does not mean that everything is known or that everyone accepts the same explanations. Many questions still exist, and these include some basic ones.

THE SLAVE FAMILY

Between 1790 and 1860, both the free white and slave populations of the South increased by just more than a factor of 5.5; the slave population, in fact, grew slightly more rapidly than did the white population.[1] The similarity of the rates of growth largely disposes of two ideas, that: (a) in general, slaves were "bred" at maximum rates because of their value, and (b) living conditions were generally at "inhuman" physical levels among slaves. Slave families, whatever their condition, reproduced the population at a rate only slightly greater than that of whites.

We know that: slaves had to have slave mothers; they had little or no status in courts of law; their marriages (when there was a ceremony) were not legal (were not binding contracts); their property was not their own; and even their own children were not theirs to control. Slaves were property: They could be sold, willed, or distributed in payment of debts in cases of bankruptcy of the owners.

Because there was no legal international slave trade in this country after 1808, the natural increase of slaves was necessary to maintain the system.[2] Slave owners had to depend upon slave mothers to increase the supply. The bases of the system, then, were slave women and their children. Part of the background information is that Americans were governed by a moral code, derived in part from Christianity, that presumably found slave breeding repugnant (despite lurid modern novels and even eyewitness accounts to the contrary). This meant that some sort of pairing off of men and women into families, even though there was no legal marriage, had to occur. What were these slave families like?

Again, a simple question with no ready answer. Whom do you ask? Each slave narrative is only one example out of the millions possible. Besides, it's like trying to describe today's "average" American family. Which family is typical? We could construct an average from census returns. But, in the case of slave families, there is no official census enumeration listing the names of father, mother, and the date of marriage or, lacking that, the amount of time a couple lived together. The birth dates of the children often were not known. Let us consider some alternatives.

In their 1974 study of slavery, *Time on the Cross*, Robert Fogel and Stanley Engerman concluded that despite the presence of forces that we might suppose would have made stable family formation difficult or impossible, slaves generally did hold families together for periods of years.[3] The sale of young children by owners, they say, was not a common practice.

A basic family system is implied for three fundamental reasons: (a) the natural habits of slaves themselves, which made the family unit a stable relationship; (b) the inclinations of slave owners to maintain some approximation of ordinary American sexual conduct among their property; and (c) the fact that families were more efficient economic units than were other arrangements.[4] According to these authors, alternative family lifestyles—such as communal living with complete sexual freedom for men and women alike, the pairing of unattached women with a sequence of men, or the grouping of several females with one male as a shared mate, were rejected.[5] Fogel and Engerman concluded:

> The belief that slave-breeding, sexual exploitation, and promiscuity destroyed the black family is a myth. The family was the basic unit of social organization under slavery. It was to the economic interest of planters to encourage the stability of slave families, and most of them did so.[6]

Three Eyewitnesses

Fogel and Engerman's description sounds reasonable enough. Why should anyone have thought otherwise? The reason is that observers at that time often presented pictures that differed considerably and that abolitionists used effectively in their literature as evidence of sexual exploitation and irregular family life. Thus, we are left wondering about the matter. Consider the reminiscences of two famous persons born into slavery, Frederick Douglass and Booker T. Washington. Douglass described his parentage in an 1845 book that was a widely used piece of abolitionist literature:

> My mother was named Harriet Bailey. She was the daughter of Isaac and Betsey Bailey, both colored and quite dark. My mother was of a darker complexion than either my grandmother or grandfather. My father was a white man. He was admitted to be such by all I ever heard speak of my parentage. The opinion was also whispered that my master was my father....[7]

Of his family life, Douglass wrote:

> My mother and I were separated when I was but an infant.... It is common custom, in the part of Maryland from which I ran away, to part children from their mothers at an early age. Frequently, before the child had reached its twelfth month, its mother was taken from it, and hired out on some farm ... the child is placed under the care of an old woman, too old for field work.
>
> I never saw my mother, to know her as such, more than four or five times in my life, and each of these times was very short in duration, and at night.... She made these journeys (12 miles) to see me in the night, travelling the whole distance on foot, after the performance of her day's work.[8]

In his autobiography *Up From Slavery*, Booker T. Washington wrote in 1901, more than half a century after the Douglass book:

> I was born near a cross-roads post-office called Hale's Ford, and the year was 1858 or 1859.... Of my ancestry I know almost nothing.... I have been unsuccessful in securing any information that would throw any accurate light upon the history of my family beyond my mother. She, I remember, had a half-brother and a half-sister.... Of my father I know even less than of my mother. I do not even know his name. I have heard reports to the effect that he was a white man who lived on one of the nearby plantations.[9]

How was Family Life?

> The early years of my life, which were spent in the little cabin, were not very different from those of thousands of other slaves. My mother, of course, had little time in which to give attention to the training of her children during the day. She snatched a few moments for our care in the early morning.... One of my earliest recollections is that of my mother cooking a chicken late at night, and awakening her children for the purpose of feeding them. How or where she got it I do not know.... I cannot remember having slept in a bed until after our family was declared free by the Emancipation Proclamation. Three children—John, my older brother, Amanda, my sister, and myself—had a pallet on the dirt floor ... we slept in and on a bundle of filthy rags....[10]

It does not seem, on the face of it, to have been much of a family life. However, perhaps it was no worse than family life among the free working poor in the cities.

A third eyewitness, Frederick Law Olmsted, wrote in 1860 of a large cotton plantation he visited in Mississippi:

> It was a first-rate plantation. On the highest ground stood a large and handsome mansion, but it had not been occupied for several years, and it was more than two years since the overseer had seen the owner. He lived several hundred miles away.... The whole plantation, including the swamp land around it, and owned with it, covered several square miles. There were between thirteen and fourteen hundred acres under cultivation with cotton, corn and other hoed crops, and two hundred hogs running at large in the swamp.... There were 135 slaves big and little, of which 67 went to the field regularly.... There was a nursery for sucklings at the quarters, and twenty women at this time who left their work four times a day for half an hour, to nurse their young....[11]

Of course, labor demand for field work in agriculture is not so intensive the entire year, and during the slack winter months there was more time for "family life" than has been indicated by the descriptions of Douglass and Washington.

Other Evidence

The problem for historians trying to generalize from such evidence is that only isolated examples are available, and they cannot know if the samples are good random choices or merely outlying cases that happened to be in print. While there are many other accounts of plantation life that are in basic agreement with Douglass and Washington, a substantial body of evidence reaches the same conclusion as did Fogel and Engerman.

Herbert Gutman's study of black families on six large plantations showed that after emancipation, most slave families were found to be "double-headed"—that is, a husband and wife lived together monogamously.[12] He found that, among slaves who lived into their forties, most were involved in a long-lasting relationship that ended with the death of one member. Corroborating evidence on this point comes from findings of Richard Steckel and Stephen Crawford. Steckel, investigating Civil War pension files, shows that slave women did not tend to have children as soon as was biologically possible, that slave marriage strongly influenced the birth of the first child, and, after that, births were strongly influenced by work patterns of the slave mothers. There is no case of a former slave woman applying for veterans benefits from more than one man.[13] Moreover, the black veterans' wives, although widowed quite early in life, tended not to remarry. Crawford, investigating the narratives of ex-slaves conducted in the 1920s and 1930s, found that, of 742 slaves under the age of 13, roughly two-thirds lived in two-parent households, and one-quarter lived in one-parent (almost always the mother) households. Of the latter group, roughly three-fifths of the families were broken by the slave trade or the like. Crawford found that the size of the plantation mattered. On plantations with 15 or fewer slaves, only one child in three lived in a two-parent household. On plantations with 25 or more slaves, two children in three did.[14]

There is another problem. When we try to move from numbers to an understanding of the living situations that produced those numbers—to an evaluation of the quality of life—we are moving from quantitative to qualitative evidence. There is no natural intellectual transition for such a move. The truth is that most descriptions of life in the slave quarters are bleak. However, populations can and do increase during incredibly difficult and unhappy circumstances—most of humanity throughout history has done so. Given the problems of moving from quantitative to qualitative evidence, it is difficult indeed to argue that a reasonable physical standard of life for slaves (or anyone else, for that matter) implied any degree of contentment among slave families.[15] What we can ask is, "Where are the slave narratives of 'happy days on the old plantation?'"

The eyewitness accounts that we examined suggest three assumptions: (a) There was no male family head of any importance; indeed, Douglass and Washington did not even know who their fathers were. (b) Institutional provision was made for infants so that even nursing mothers could work nearly full time. (c) One mother had little chance to play that role; the other did so only with difficulty. These are standard criticisms of the slave system in agriculture that have their parallels in some analyses of the modern-day black family: no steady male head, and no adequate home atmosphere provided by the mother because she must be the breadwinner. On the other hand, close examination of the aggregate evidence by scholars such as Gutman, Steckel, and Crawford agree with the judgment of Fogel and Engerman—the typical slave family was headed by an adult couple.

WAS SLAVERY DOOMED WITHOUT CIVIL WAR?

In recent years scholarly interest in slavery has been continuous and intense, and the major questions have been thrown into sharp relief. Some historians long had held that slavery was a terminally ill institution by 1860 and that it would have died from natural causes without the 1861–1865 military intervention. Slavery, these scholars say, was not really profitable enough to continue in the face of better investment opportunities coming down the line with later nineteenth-century industrialization. Historians Charles Sydnor and Ulrich B. Phillips especially were of that conviction.[16] Various "radical" writers found this view congenial because it presented slavery as an anachronism, a pre-capitalist holdover that could have had no place in an industrializing workers' economy. At least, this is how Marx saw slavery. The American South, viewed economically, with no industrial proletariat, was merely a colonial appendage of capitalist Europe.[17]

It is always convenient to believe that whatever has happened in history has been inevitable. This is the road taken by those historians who believe that the Civil War was merely a tragic waste of lives and resources to erase an institution that was already dying. Lewis Gray, in his *History of Agriculture in the Southern United States to 1860*, ruled differently, finding evidence that slavery had been perfectly viable before 1861.[18] Until 1958, the issue was thus largely a matter of disagreements among scholars. Since evidence and argument seem to support every view, people have tended to choose their position on the basis of personal preference and instinct.

Conrad and Meyer

In 1958, the heavy guns of econometrics (applied mathematical statistical analysis guided by economic theory) were zeroed in on antebellum slavery by Alfred Conrad and John Meyer in their famous paper "The Economics of Slavery in the Antebellum South."[19] They found that the annual returns to slave agriculture were competitive with the alternatives available to southern investors and, moreover, that the "whole South" profited from slavery. In the older states, it was the sale of slaves from the existing stock to the new cotton-producing areas south and west that created the profits. Cotton production itself was the main underpinning of the system. In important subsequent critical works by Yasukichi Yasuba and Richard Sutch, capital gains from the stock of slaves were factored into the profit equations, and the viability of slavery was reinforced.[20]

The findings of the econometric work seemed to establish the profitability and viability arguments once and for all. They were based upon numbers, and they meant (or seemed to mean) that institutional and cultural analyses of slavery were largely irrelevant. The simple fact was that slavery had been maintained because it paid slave owners as much as or more than they could earn from any other employment of their capital. Historians continued to reassess their own findings, and some, like Kenneth Stampp in *The Peculiar Institution*, were in substantial agreement with the revisionist view. Slavery was still immoral, repugnant, and sometimes inhuman, but it paid while it lasted.

Time on the Cross: Theses and Rebuttals

Then, in 1974, came *Time on the Cross*. Fogel and Engerman advanced ten major theses about antebellum slavery in a way that produced a virtual avalanche of scholarly criticism. Some of their ideas were not really novel, but they were advanced in so bold a manner, in connection with other more radical findings, that historians were forced to rethink their implications. The "peculiar institution," the critics charged, had never before looked so peculiar. *Time on the Cross* was subjected to a level of criticism that, in fineness as well as vigor and volume, has rarely been known in the scholarship of economic history.

In brief, the ten major theses of Fogel and Engerman are as follows:

1. Slavery was a rational, profitable way for Southerners who knew their own interests to maximize profits and wealth.
2. Before 1861, slavery was thriving and growing economically stronger than ever.
3. Slave owners were not "pessimistic" about slavery's future on the eve of the Civil War.
4. Slave agriculture was more efficient than free agriculture, not only in the South, but also when compared to the family farm in the North. Scale economies explain much of the difference.
5. The average slave field hand was more hardworking and efficient than his "white counterpart."
6. Demand for slaves was increasing more rapidly in urban areas than in rural, and slaves were competitive with free workers in urban employments.
7. Slave breeding and sexual exploitation were myths. Stable slave families were the norm and, being in the best interests of the slave owners, were encouraged. Most sales of slaves were whole families or else "at an age when it would have been normal for them to have left the family."
8. The material conditions of life for slaves compared favorably with those of free whites employed in Northern factories.
9. The rate of exploitation of slave earnings was only 10 percent: The average male field hand received in real income 90 percent of what he produced over a lifetime.
10. The Southern economy was not stagnant; between 1840 and 1860, Southern per-capita income increased more rapidly than did Northern and was relatively high in absolute terms compared to that in the North and in other countries.[21]

Stated bluntly, the main theses of *Time on the Cross* were a clear and irresistible target. Moreover, there were supplementary findings that were really inflammatory to many scholars. For example, Fogel and Engerman suggest that force was seldom used and that generally encouragement to productive effort was in the form of positive economic rewards.[22] Further, they conclude that slaves responded to such good treatment by redoubled efforts to be efficient workers.

A heavy bombardment came as soon as the first reviewers of the book recovered from the initial shock. Fogel and Engerman were accused of implying that slavery was a benign, even progressive, capitalist institution, consisting of diligent well-rewarded workers toiling under the rational and largely benevolent gaze of carefully profit-maximizing Southern entrepreneurs. Their book produced an incredible response. Let us briefly survey, point by point, the major findings on the ten theses before dwelling at greater length on some special points of the debate.

Slavery was a rational way for Southerners to maximize profits and wealth. There had been little disagreement before 1974 on this issue. Cotton production produced a rent due to the climate and soils of the South. As Kenneth Stampp emphasizes, only a small minority of scholars still clung to the idea that Southern slave owners were operating at losses because they were somehow locked into the system.[23]

Slavery was growing stronger economically before the Civil War. Gavin Wright and others argue that there was an element of illusion here.[24] The market for American cotton was extraordinarily strong during the 1850s because of the significant growth of cotton textile manufactures. That situation could not last much beyond the decade and indeed, did not. Supplies of raw cotton caught up with demand after the Civil War, and profits in raw cotton production were greatly reduced for years. If the slave system was getting stronger economically in the 1850s, that was no portent of things to come, since profitability was rooted in cotton cultivation.

Slave owners were optimistic about slavery's future just before the Civil War. Over the usual slave life cycle, the net return to slave purchases was positive, counting potential capital gains from any sales that might take place. Since slave prices were rising in the 1850s even though, by some estimates, slaves yielded less than the return from alternative investments, it must be assumed that continued slave purchases were evidence of optimism on the part of slave owners about the future of the slave system.[25]

Slave agriculture in the South was more productive than was family farming in the North. We know from the previous chapter that plantations employing the gang system were reportedly 39 percent more productive than free farms. As the critics noted, there is no way to make such a comparison, except to define productive as "revenue-earning."[26] Even that, as we have noted, was based upon extraordinary demand in the 1850s and a spectacular crop in 1860 (the main year of comparison) that sold at high prices. Scale economies, according to Gavin Wright and others, were not overwhelmingly important.[27] On the other hand, it seems clear enough that the use of slaves made slave-worked farms in the South more efficient than free farms there, and, within limits, the dominance of large farms and plantations showed significant scale economies.

Slave field hands were harder working and more efficient than were white agricultural workers. The critics argued that slaves, with no choice in the matter, worked longer hours and more days each year than did free whites. Thus, they may have produced more revenues from their labors, but this figure tells nothing about output per hour.[28] Fogel, as we have seen, argues that the gang system led to a "speed-up," a greater work intensity, so that slaves working in gangs produced as much output in 35 minutes as farmers (either free or slave) produced in an hour.

Demand for slaves was increasing more rapidly in urban than in rural areas. Actually, the 1976 work of Claudia Goldin showed the complexity of the situation but supported Fogel and Engerman's conclusion.[29] Demand for slaves was *price elastic* in urban employment; an increase in price caused a large decrease in demand given the number of good substitutes that were available. Conversely, demand for slaves was *inelastic* in agriculture.[30] Higher cotton prices drove up slave prices; as a result, urban slave populations declined between 1840 and 1860.

Slave breeding and sexual exploitation were myths. The works of Richard Sutch, Herbert Gutman, and others argue that the abolitionists' views on this matter have some merit. The evidence does suggest that slaves were encouraged to raise their birth rates by various means with a view to the sale of the children. The ratio of children to adults on slave plantations rose when the ratio of women to men decreased.[31] However, the long-run decline in birth rates among slaves, paralleling the fall in birth rates of free whites, shows that slave breeding did not successfully defeat other forces determining demographic trends. But the evidence does not support the thesis that slave sales rarely broke up slave families.

The material condition of slaves compared favorably with that of free workers. It should be clear that since slaves were an expensive factor of production, it would be economically foolish to deprive them of a nutritious diet, adequate clothing, and housing. To do so would be to jeopardize their ability to perform, now or in the future. Fogel and Engerman, however, went further. They argued the diet was more than simply nutritious; it was balanced and had substantial variety. There is considerable uncertainty on this point, because, in order to reach this conclusion, they had to calculate what slaves ate as a residual. Sutch points out that the data on this issue in *Time on the Cross* compared the largest plantations with the poorest classes of Northern slum dwellers. He also contends that evidence on food, clothing, and medical care is less than supportive of the Fogel and Engerman findings.[32]

Over the course of an entire slave lifetime, the rate of exploitation was only 10 percent for prime field hands. Fogel and Engerman's calculation is based on the present value at birth of the difference between what a slave was expected to produce and the cost of maintaining that slave, totaled over a slave's life. Up to age 9, years that are discounted relatively little, the annual difference is negative. After age 9, it becomes positive, but, given the discounting, the rate of exploitation doesn't reach zero until age 27. Paul David and Peter Temin argue that a 10 percent rate is too low, probably much too low.[33]

The economy in the South was growing more rapidly than that in the North. The accuracy of this statement depends upon which areas are compared. It was true of the Delta region of Louisiana and east Texas but not true of the Old South—the slave states circa 1800. Moreover, the per-capita income of *most of the Southern population* was below that of the United States as a whole. It is clear that the West South Central region, where the big cotton-growing expansion took place from 1840 to 1860, did grow remarkably, and faster than any other section in those years.[34]

These findings amount, in some cases, to a confirmation of and, in others, to a vigorous dissent from the findings of *Time on the Cross*, and here the debate stands. Now let us consider a few of the more interesting parts of the debate in some detail.

From Quantity to Quality

It is understandable that economic historians would try to isolate the purely economic side of slavery. The logic of economic theory allows the economist to make powerful and even definitive deductions from quantitative evidence. However, this can be done only *if* the evidence can be found and *if* it can be analyzed in a world in which the related social facts that produced the evidence *do not matter*. Conrad and Meyer presented evidence on a very general level, and their conclusions produced no great dispute. Subsequent alterations of Conrad and Meyer were also fairly restricted and tied to generally accepted evidence.

Fogel and Engerman were much more ambitious, attempting to illuminate many questions for which the evidence had always been blurred and contested: How often was physical force used to maintain work levels? How well were the slaves fed, clothed, and housed? Was the instability of the slave family responsible for a multitude of social ills that have afflicted the black community ever since? Were those families commonly broken up by slave sales? Were slaves purposely bred like livestock to maximize the capitalized rents? Was infant mortality significantly higher among slaves than among whites? Did approaching urbanization and industrialization inevitably doom slavery in America? Why were there so few slave uprisings?[35] These questions and many more of a very qualitative nature need to be answered if we are really to understand the "peculiar institution" and the hold it had on this country for so long.

In *Time on the Cross*, Fogel and Engerman made a bold attempt to face these questions head-on with deductions drawn from primarily quantitative evidence. As we have seen, they met with very heavy criticism. Referring to the earlier discussion of writing history and its intellectual problems, we can now better appreciate the origins of such massive disagreements. To say "what was" and to have no dissent are almost impossible. Such is the nature of historical research, and we learn from the resulting critical fallout.

A fundamental criticism of *Time on the Cross* came from Paul David and Peter Temin.[36] They argued that, on the basis of economics alone, we simply cannot deduce the comparative welfare of the slaves—how "well off" they were compared to any other groups. For example, David and Temin compare two pieces of information, Engel's Law and the slave diet. Engel's Law is an empirical observation that normally, as real income rises, a decreasing proportion of it is spent on food. In Fogel and Engerman's data, one result of their suggested high real incomes for slaves is the absence of Engel's Law. The slaves ate more: a calorie-charged diet of carbohydrates.

David and Temin ask, "How poor would a free white family need to be to convert such a high proportion of their income into such a diet?" The point David and Temin are making is that slavery was compulsion, and it is not possible to make comparative judgments about welfare implications from any level of real income if it is produced under compulsion and *consumed the same way*. We might go further and argue that since slaves had no property rights—in themselves, their earnings, homes, clothing, children, wives, husbands, animals, or anything else—it is simply folly to impute *any* amount of satisfaction to them regarding their lives. An old antebellum joke still told in Indiana succinctly illustrates the point. A slave escaped from Kentucky and was brought before a Hoosier justice of the peace.

Judge: Were you unhappy there?
Slave: Oh no. I had a good life there.
Judge: Were you mistreated?
Slave: No. Old Massa and me was the greatest friends. Fished and hunted together.
Judge: Did you have good food and housing?
Slave: Sure enough. Ham and 'taters. Molasses. My little cabin had roses over the door.
Judge: I don't understand. Why did you run away?
Slave: Well, your Honor, the situation is still open down there if you'd like to apply for it.

Concerning slave health and diets, even if we were to accept the most optimistic conclusions of *Time on the Cross*, the well-being of the slaves could no more be imputed from such evidence than could that of present-day prison populations, whose standards of "adequate" clothing, food, and medical and dental care often exceed that of the general run of American citizens. However, there is additional evidence to consider.

Steckel's Findings

The work of Richard Steckel has upended our information about the quality of life of American slaves. Previous evidence (mainly from surviving plantation records) indicated that mortality rates in the antebellum black population were not much different from those of contemporary whites.[37] This appeared to explain the very similar population growth rates of antebellum whites and blacks noted earlier. But now Steckel has been able to show that the prenatal and postnatal pictures were drastically different.

Steckel finds that average birth weights of slave babies were only about 5.5 pounds and that 30 to 35 percent of these babies died. He believes that more than half of all slave conceptions must have been lost either by miscarriages or in very early infancy. These losses can be attributed in part to the poor medical knowledge of the era that claimed many children, white and black. However, losses among black children under the age of 5 were roughly twice those of white children, and only about a quarter of the difference is explainable by the harsher disease environment of the South. Another part is attributable to the (presumably profit-maximizing) masters, who pushed slave mothers to work as long before births as they could, and to return to work as soon as possible afterward.[38] These practices produced malnourished fetuses and newborns: "The adverse consequences of the 'wearied mother' for infant health began at conception."[39]

Considering the rate of natural increase of the overall slave population, Steckel concludes that slave women were far more fertile than had previously been thought. Their losses, from stillbirths and neonatal mortality, were in fact 2.5 times as high as similar losses among white women. The difference was made up by new pregnancies. Slave mothers were on average about two years younger than their white counterparts at first conception.[40] The new data on slave children at early ages produce the following conclusion by Steckel:

> At age 3, for example, slave children attained about centile 0.2 of modern height standards, which places them among the poorest populations ever studied by auxologists. Comparative heights suggest that children from the slums of Lagos, Nigeria, and from urban areas of Bangladesh had an environment for growth superior to that of American slave children.[41]

Perhaps more remarkable have been Steckel's discoveries about life-cycle slave nutrition and physical growth. These discoveries are based, as are those just noted regarding birth weights, on 50,606 slave manifests (declarations by shippers), from 1820 to 1860 for individuals transported on coastal and inland waterways, one of the principal ways slaves moved from east to west. A federal law of 1807 provided for the manifests, and thus the data are now available to us. The shipping manifests were created and handed over to the ship's captain at port of origin. The object of the law was to be certain that slaves from the Caribbean or Africa were not being landed as traffic from another U.S. port. The evidence is of disastrous malnutrition among slave children. The survivors, however, caught up in growth and weight once they were old enough to work and were then given proper diets, including meat. A perfectly cold-blooded calculation, had it been consciously made, might have warranted such a feeding policy. The discounted future value of the slave until about age 6 would have justified it. We should note, however, that Steckel does not argue that such a conscious calculation was why slave owners starved the children. Slave children younger than age 6 seemed like dwarfs to observers for good reason: "The stature of slave children would trigger alarm in a modern pediatrician's office."[42] As young children, American slaves were smaller than any of the other populations Steckel examines (European, American, African, Caribbean). Yet by age 16.5 years, American male slaves were taller than factory workers and laborers in England, the poor of Italy, students in Habsburg military schools, the middle class of Stuttgart, German peasants, and factory workers in Russia. As adults, American male slaves also exceeded in height the aristocrats of Stuttgart.[43] Adequate diet after it paid to feed them—after they could work—allowed the slaves to recover their physical stature.[44]

Steckel then speculates about other problems these data might help explain; the reported docility and lassitude of slaves, for example (see the later section "The Elkins Explanation"). Steckel speculates that, following the earlier period of malnutrition, although stature recovered, the possible impairment of the brain's functioning remained, and the adverse consequences of that lasted into adulthood. The poor achievements of blacks immediately after emancipation could be explained, in part, by this factor.[45] It is an appalling possibility. But American slavery was an appalling institution.

WHY DID SLAVERY PERSIST?

Time on the Cross may be thought of as a scenario designed to explain a historical phenomenon: By 1860, black slavery had existed in this country for nearly two-and-a-half centuries and apparently was never more prosperous than in its final decade. In their pioneering quantitative effort, Fogel and Engerman attempted to explain such a remarkable set of facts, given the evidence. Moreover, despite such famous rebels as Nat Turner and Denmark Vesey, million of slaves lived out their lives in bondage, exhibiting very little resistance besides commonly asserted acts of pretended illness and theft.[46]

In thousands of relatively isolated locations, a handful of whites lived in the midst of black slaves many times their number with little fear. How was this possible? A moment's reflection will show that there is no obvious answer. A well-known antebellum Southern view was that slaves were happy, goodhearted, childlike creatures who responded positively to good treatment and a teaspoonful of chastisement.[47] If this was not the reason why slavery endured, what was?

In *Time on the Cross,* we have a model of a world in which slave-operated enterprises paid their labor forces sufficiently with material rewards and occupational mobility to reconcile the slaves to their condition of unfreedom. As Fogel and Engerman put it, the creation of such an overwhelming economic success as the antebellum cotton economy using mainly slave labor was nothing less than "the record of black achievement under adversity."[48] Profit-maximizing slave owners and slaves striving to make the best of their circumstances can explain the high productivity and comparative stability of a gigantic slave economy spread over a third of this country. For this interpretation, Fogel and Engerman were scathingly condemned. Kenneth Stampp writes of *Time on the Cross*:

> ... the book is not a defense of slavery, and its argument is not racist ... but its highly favorable assessment of life in bondage originates in the traditional proslavery interpretation nonetheless[49]

and

> *Time on the Cross* replaces the untidy world of reality, in which masters and slaves, with their rational and irrational perceptions and their human passions, survived as best they could, with a model of a tidy, rational world that never was.[50]

The Elkins Explanation

Are there better overall explanations of slavery's persistence in this country? Perhaps, but they also are disputed. Stanley Elkins argues that slavery crushed out individualism, producing the stereotypical "Sambo" personality—the happy, carefree, clowning slave who loved his or her master, "Ol' Massa."[51] The slave identified with the master's interests and family, devoting his or her life selflessly to the owner's welfare at the expense of all else, including the slave's own family. The reason, simply put, was that dependence was too great for significant self-interested individualism to develop among the slaves. The result was a docile plantation in circumstances where docility paid more than did any of the alternatives. "Toadying" to figures of power and authority pays where anything else is prohibitively expensive. Low-ranking military personnel, people confined to hospitals, and women in nearly all cultures through the ages have experienced similar phenomena.

Elkins compares American slaves to the inmates of Nazi concentration camps. Arbitrary brutality—together with total dependence, total loss of prior identity, and constant humiliation—produced a similarly docile mass of persons, in that case Europeans, who were almost *unable* to resist excessive work demands and even deprivation of life. The prisoner lost name, language (if he or she were not German), and culture—the former life ceased to have any use or meaning. He or she no longer could plan. The future was a blank; the past, meaningless. Survival depended upon instant obedience. All benefits came from the SS guards, whose authority was total. Slowly, the prisoners began to adopt the values of the guards. They began to identify with the interests of the guards and even copy them, to some extent. The prisoners tried to please. In the end, they did not seem to hate the SS. Suicide, an individual decision, was rare in those circumstances because it required a degree of independence that had vanished.[52]

The parallels are indeed striking. The slave child's father and mother could not offer protection; from infancy onward, the child had to depend upon the kindness of the master for whatever good or small favors might come his or her way. The adult slave was conditioned by an entire life's experiences to survive within the system. To disobey was to risk corporal chastisement (beating and whipping, mainly), short rations, perhaps even sale to a slave dealer. Eugene Genovese, in *Roll, Jordan, Roll*, presents a striking account of the slow, almost reluctant way the slaves faced freedom after emancipation, just as the concentration camp prisoners did when liberation came.[53]

The Genovese Thesis

In *From Rebellion to Revolution*, Eugene Genovese tries to explain the apparent lack of slave resistance in a more objective way than the Elkins thesis provides.[54] Slave resistance here, compared with that in the Caribbean and South America, was a minor affair in the century before 1860. Why? Genovese, looking at the slave revolts that occurred, narrows the vital elements to eight factors:

1. The ratio of blacks to whites
2. The size of slave-holding units
3. The nature of the surrounding physical terrain
4. The ratio of African-born slaves to those born in America
5. The presence of slave owners at the work site
6. Conflicts within the "ruling class"
7. Poor economic conditions
8. The structure of social relationships that allowed black leaders to emerge

In the South, compared with the Caribbean and South America, all these factors weighed against slave resistance, against the prospects of even limited success.

In American circumstances, only minor outbreaks were likely to occur. With the prospect so bleak for successful resistance, it paid the individual slave to go along and make the best of it. Except in parts of South Carolina and Mississippi, whites were in the majority. Nearly half of the American slaves were owned in groups of 20 or fewer, making rare a "critical mass" for an uprising. There were few really inaccessible mountains or jungles available to harbor escaped slaves. By the antebellum period, the vast majority of American slaves were natives (no longer trained warriors like the Africans) and a large proportion were of partially white ancestry. In fact, since the late seventeenth century, the majority of American slaves alive at any time were native.[55]

Slave owners usually lived among or near their slaves on Southern plantations. There was little important conflict over slavery among Southern slave owners, or between them and those Southerners who did not own slaves. Economic conditions were good; starvation among adults (apart from punishment) was unknown. Black leaders were limited, for the most part, to slave preachers of pacifist Christian doctrines. In view of these data, there was little reason to expect significant slave resistance or revolt in the South. A Nat Turner might come along, but no one like the great Haitian revolutionary Jean Jacques Dessalines.

Thus, in terms of "slave mentality" or of rational rebellion, resistance made no sense. In the world of *Time on the Cross*, it made even less sense. Why would slavery *not* persist? In addition to all else, it was an institution of private property, protected by law and long usage, and profitable to those who owned the slaves.

PROBLEMS OF THE SLAVE "BUSINESS FIRM"

To some critics, one of the most galling aspects of *Time on the Cross* was its analysis of the Southern slave plantation as a small-scale enterprise run on strict maximizing principles, perhaps along the same lines as a modern rural sawmill. The peculiarities of the institution become cost and revenue functions; slave owners are presented as people who know their opportunity costs and act accordingly. Many critics prefer to think of slavery either as a precapitalist artifact, lost in time, or as a monstrous perversion. However, given acceptance of the neoclassical analysis of *Time on the Cross*, then certain parts of the Fogel and Engerman findings do seem odd, and they do seem to lean toward a more humanitarian interpretation. As noted, the authors insist upon three points, with their reasoning based on a mixture of sound economics and Victorian morality: (a) Force was used only "optimally."[56] (b) Slave sales were not common and rarely broke up families. (c) Slave breeding for profit was a myth. In a purely neoclassical context, where force is a freely available substitute for money or material rewards, it would be employed whenever its marginal product was relatively high. Fogel and Engerman agree and say, thus, it would have been used optimally. Others agree, too, but they point out that, according to the evidence, *optimally* did not mean *rarely*.[57] In any case, the threat of the whips could, and probably did, make every hour of slave labor more intensive than free labor would have been, especially for unskilled physical farm work.

Slave Sales

The manager of a modern business firm who discharges workers will typically be unconcerned about their family relationships. Critics of *Time on the Cross* believe that slave families were commonly broken up by sales of children, wives, and husbands. Such critics are more neoclassical than are Fogel and Engerman, who maintain that efforts were made to hold families together. The issue can be illustrated by a quotation from Olmsted, in which an informant believed a young girl being taken away for sale must have offended her master. "What had she done wrong?" he asked.

> "Done? Nothing."
> "What are you going to do with her?"
> "I'm taking her down to Richmond, to be sold."
> "Does she belong to you?"
> "No; she belongs to ______; he raised her."
> "Why does he sell her—has she done anything wrong?"
> "Done anything? No. She's no fault, I reckon."
> "Then what does he want to sell her for?"
> "Sell her for! Why shouldn't he sell her? He sells one or two every year; wants the money for 'em, I reckon."[58]

How commonly were slaves sold and with what effect on families? The evidence seems to suggest that slave sales were relatively common and that families often were broken up by such sales. Since slave marriages (by whatever authority) had no legal standing, and since the children belonged to the master and not to the slave parents, nothing *except* the humanity of slave owners kept slave families together, at least once the children reached working age. Critics of Fogel and Engerman see common humanity as a much rarer commodity in the Old South than is argued in *Time on the Cross*.

Breeding

What about slave breeding? It was commonly asserted by abolitionists that breeding was the general practice. Consider another quotation from Olmsted:

> A slaveholder writing to me with regard to my cautious statements on this subject, made in the *Daily Times*, says: "In the States of Maryland, Virginia, North Carolina, Kentucky, Tennessee and Missouri, as much attention is paid to the breeding and growth of negroes as to that of horses and mules. Further south, we raise them both for use and for market. Planters command their girls and women (married or unmarried) to have children; and I have known a great many girls to be sold off, because they did not have children. A breeding woman is worth from one-sixth to one-fourth more than one that does not breed."[59]

Richard Sutch, one of the major critics of *Time on the Cross*, describes breeding as any means taken by the owners to increase the fertility of slave women. The profit came from the expected future return from sales over the costs of rearing to the age of sale. By the 1850s, a babe in arms was worth from $150 upward.[60] The slave stock on any plantation was reproducible, just like livestock. Presumably any

An invoice from an 1835 slave sale (right) and a drawing of a small farm with slave housing, c. 1850 (below).

An invoice of ten negroes sent this day to John B Williamson by Geo Kremer named & cost as follows

To wit	Betsey Kackley	$410.00
	Nancy Aulick	515.00
	Harry & Helen Miller	1200.00
	Mary Kootz	600.00
	Betsey Ott	560.00
	Isaac & Fanny Brent	992.00
	Lucinda Luckett	467.50
	George Smith	510.00
		5254.50
Amount of my traveling expences & boarding of lot No 9 not included in the other bills		39.50
Kremers expences transporting lot No 9 to Richd		51.00
Carryall hire		6.00
		$5351.00

I have this day delivered the above named negroes costing including my expences and other expences five thousand three hundred & fifty dollars this May 26th 1835

John W. Pittman

I did intend to leave Nancy child but she made such a damned fuss I had to let her take it I could of got fifty Dollars for so you must add forty Dollars to the above

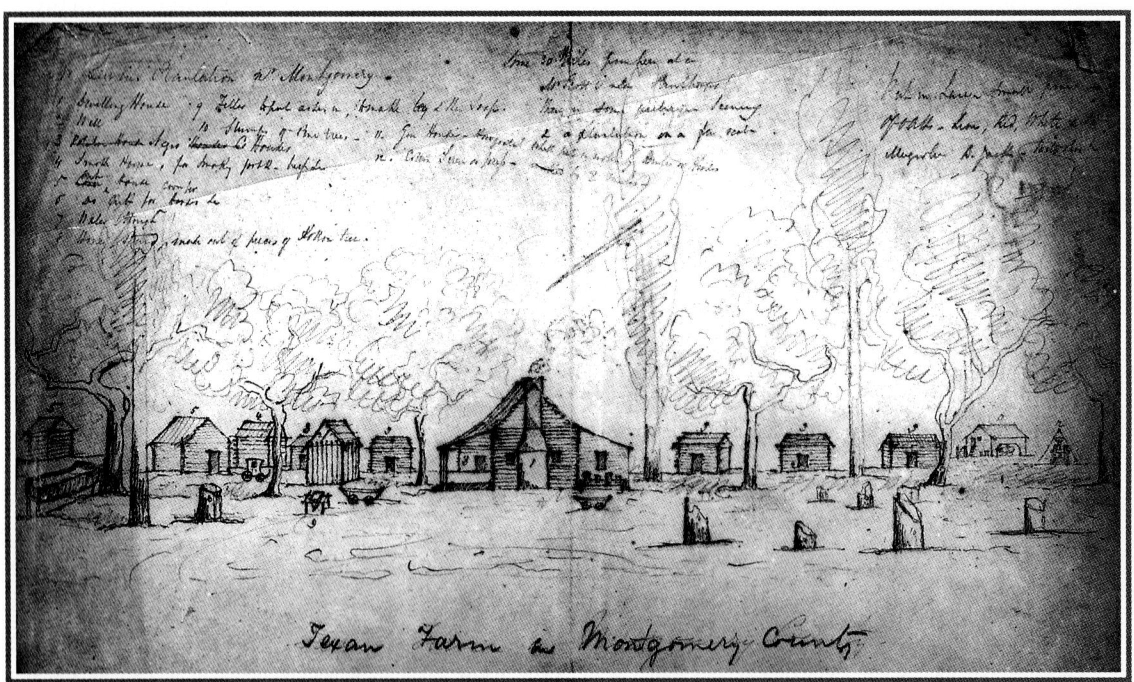

profit-maximizing slave owner would consider breeding that stock as an option.

Not so, say Fogel and Engerman, or at least not commonly so, and they unleash a barrage of contrary arguments and evidence.[61] Conrad and Meyer argue that sales and breeding were integral to the system. The Old South, where cotton was not a major crop, supplied slaves to the cotton-growing regions, and the whole South benefited. Remember also Douglass North's point that the *whole nation* benefited economically. This had been one of the most powerful abolitionist arguments. Victorian Americans were apparently shocked by such immoral rationality. On this issue, Richard Sutch stayed away from the sort of evidence just quoted (which could never be proved typical, or even common) and instead went after the numbers: census figures of slave ages, sex, and residence. He found that:

1. Net slave sales from the Old South to the New South were large.
2. The ratio of children to adults was significantly higher in the selling than in the buying states.
3. In the selling states, the ratio of children to adults was actually higher on plantations where the ratio of men to women was lower.

The conclusions seem inescapable. Sutch concluded with no mincing of words:

> Many slaveowners in the American South systematically bred slaves for sale. These slave breeders were concentrated in the border states and in the states along the Atlantic coast. They held disproportionately large numbers of women in the child-bearing age group. They fostered polygamy and promiscuity among their slaves. The products of this breeding operation were sold or transported to the south-western slave states, predominantly as young adults. There is little possibility that this practice was innocent....[62]

We must keep in mind, however, that this conclusion does not show slave breeding as either common or typical in the American South. What it argues is that slave breeding did exist; it was no myth. Slavery was bad enough without slave breeding, but we cannot ignore the evidence of its presence on at least some Southern farms.

RETROSPECT

This chapter has touched only upon certain vital points of the modern slavery debate. Strictly speaking, many of the most burning issues, like the nature of the slave family, can be only partly a matter of economics. They must be either ignored or analyzed by economic logic in a way that is artificial to many scholars. Those who are interested in gaining more information are urged to read the main literature cited in this chapter. We are far from having settled conclusions on many crucial points, and there may never be general agreement.

For example, how much did the "whole South" really gain from slave sales from the East to the West? To what extent did the loss of top-quality slave labor lower the returns to agriculture in the East while raising it in the West? What were the net results? Passell and Wright, followed by Kotlikoff and Pinera, present evidence and arguments showing that the gain in the Old South from sales of slaves to the New South during the westward expansion of cotton cultivation may well have been offset by declining land values in the Old South as the result of so much of the best slave labor moving out.[63] Steckel's work shows that slave owners, systematically malnourishing the slave population at its source, were more ignorant than murderous. If it can be argued, as he demonstrates, that a strict cost-benefit analysis might have justified the huge death rates of the children from a profit-making viewpoint, it is not proof that slave owners commonly made such analyses of their commissary policies.

In 1994, Robert Whaples surveyed 178 economic historians concerning their opinions on several major debates.[64] The survey made four statements with respect to slavery, and the reactions provide a snapshot of where things stand. Almost all the respondents *disagreed* with the first two:

1. Slavery was a system irrationally kept in existence by plantation owners who failed to perceive or were indifferent to their best economic interests.

2. The slave system was economically moribund on the eve of the Civil War.

Much smaller majorities agree with the other two statements that reflect two of Fogel and Engerman's more controversial findings. Slightly more than two-thirds of those responding agreed, with some provisos, that:

3. Slave agriculture was efficient compared with free agriculture. Economies of scale, effective management, and intensive utilization of labor and capital made Southern slave agriculture considerably more efficient than nonslave Southern farming.

Finally, only a bare majority agreed with the proposition that:

4. The material (rather than psychological) conditions of the lives of slaves compared favorably with those of free industrial workers in the decades before the Civil War.

Slavery is gone, and so are those who can remember it. Historians, economists, sociologists, and others, picking over the charred remains, will continue their efforts to tell us "how it really was." No doubt the shock waves produced by *Time on the Cross* will be equaled by some future investigation.

The ending of slavery more than a century ago did not solve all the problems; it merely wove the future of black America into the mainstream on a new basis. American slavery, however much deplored, was one of the prodigies of history. It was in many respects resolutely illogical and, in terms of general (newly found) European standards of morality by the mid-nineteenth century, repugnant. Slavery was prodigiously productive in its main economic applications in Southern agriculture. Discussions of slavery cannot be avoided if American history is to be understood. As a consequence, all the acrimony and dispute, as well as the shame and anger, must be rekindled again and again. Some would prefer American history to be all heroes and purity. However, it was not, and the ownership of human beings was an important part of the story—along with frontier massacres, injustice to minorities of all sorts, corruption in high places, and crime. History is about human beings, and even economic history cannot escape addressing the blemishes and imperfections.

NOTES

1. The slave population actually grew slightly faster than did the Southern white, rising by a factor of 5.8 between 1790 and 1860, compared to 5.5 for whites. The raw numbers were slaves: 1790, 657,327; 1860, 3,838,765; whites: 1790, 1,271,390; 1860, 7,033,973. *Historical Statistics*, 1960, series A 95–122. Note that this information was not included in the revised version. Overall slave mortality seems to have been similar to general mortality in the antebellum South. Richard Steckel, "Slave Mortality: Analysis of Evidence from Plantation Records," *SSH*, October 1979b, p. 110. But Steckel has radically revised his views of infant mortality among the slaves, as we will see below.
2. Peter C. Mancall, Joshua L. Rosenbloom, and Thomas Weiss, "Slave Prices and the South Carolina Economy, 1722–1809," *Journal of Economic History* (forthcoming), find that the value of slave labor divided by the prices of the goods that slaves produced remained relatively constant over the eighteenth century. In the 1790s, Chesapeake slave prices were below international levels. The banning of international trade in slaves, by restricting supply, was expected to increase the value of domestic slaves and, therefore, was supported by Chesapeake slave owners. The availability of low-priced slaves in the Chesapeake meant that, even though slave prices in South Carolina were high enough to justify continued imports, planters did not oppose the ban, as one might have expected them to do.
3. Robert Fogel and Stanley Engerman, *Time on the Cross: The Economics of American Negro Slavery* (1974), 2 vols. Although Fogel responded to critics of *Time on the Cross* in *Without Consent or Contract* (1989), his more recent opinions do not appear to have changed very much. Consequently, the discussion in this chapter refers to the earlier book.
4. Fogel and Engerman (1974), vol. I, p. 126.
5. For a much-praised, slightly more recent study, see Herbert Gutman, *The Black Family in Slavery and Freedom 1750–1925* (1976). Richard Steckel, "Slave Marriage and the Family," *Journal of Family History*, Winter 1980.

6. Fogel and Engerman (1974), vol. I, p. 5. See Gutman (1976), pp. 418–425, concerning evidence of polygamy and polyandry after the Civil War as black families attempted to sort things out and reestablish themselves. His evidence clearly shows that monogamous families seemed to be the most desired objective, even when sales of slaves had broken up earlier families and multiple husbands and wives had resulted.
7. Frederick Douglass, *Narrative of the Life of Frederick Douglass* (1968), pp. 21–22.
8. *Ibid.*, p. 22.
9. Booker T. Washington, *Up From Slavery* (1963), p. 2.
10. *Ibid.*, pp. 2–3.
11. Frederick Law Olmsted, *The Slave States* (1959), pp. 200–201.
12. Gutman (1976), chap. 1. For evidence of the existence of the "Plantation Stud," etc., see the footnote on p. 59.
13. See Steckel (1980).
14. Stephen Crawford. "The Slave Family: A View from the Slave Narratives," in Claudia Goldin and Hugh Rockoff, eds., *Strategic Factors in Nineteenth Century American Economic History* (Chicago: University of Chicago Press, 1992); and "Quantified Memory: A Study of the WPA and Fisk University Slave Narrative Collections" (unpublished Ph.D. dissertation, University of Chicago, 1980).
15. For a modern study of plantation life written from slave narratives, see John Blassingame, *The Slave Community: Plantation Life in the Antebellum South* (New York: Oxford University Press, 1972).
16. Charles Sydnor, *Slavery in Mississippi* (New York: Appleton Century, 1933), and Ulrich Phillips, "The Economic Cost of Slaveholding in the Cotton Belt," *Political Science Quarterly*, vol. XX, no. 2, June 1905.
17. Karl Marx, *Capital* (London: William Glaisher, 1918), vol. I, p. 790, n. 1.
18. Lewis Gray, *History of Agriculture in the Southern United States to 1860* (1933).
19. Alfred Conrad and John Meyer, "The Economics of Slavery in the Antebellum South," *JPE*, April 1958.
20. Yasukichi Yasuba, "The Profitability and Viability of Plantation Slavery in the United States," *Economic Studies Quarterly*, September 1961; and Richard Sutch, "The Profitability of Antebellum Slavery Revisited," *SEJ*, April 1963.
21. Fogel and Engerman (1974), vol. I, pp. 4–6.
22. *Ibid.*, pp. 144–157.
23. Paul David, Herbert Gutman, Richard Sutch, Peter Temin, Gavin Wright, "Introduction," by Kenneth Stampp, *Reckoning with Slavery: A Critical Study in the Quantitative History of American Slavery* (1975), pp. 12–13.
24. Gavin Wright, *The Political Economy of the Cotton South* (1978), chap. 6, 118–123; David (1978), pp. 308–312.
25. Fogel and Engerman (1974), vol. II, pp. 74–83.
26. Paul David and Peter Temin, "Slavery: The Progressive Institution?" in David (1978), pp. 218–223.
27. Wright (1978), pp. 44–55. One problem concerning scale economies in slave agriculture lay in the lack of substitutability between slave labor and other inputs. Evidently, slave owners were severely constrained and, to expand output, they added slaves instead of adding capital equipment to augment output from the existing slave labor force—hence, labor-intensive agriculture in slavery. Mark Schmitz and Donald Schaefer, "Slavery, Freedom, and The Elasticity of Substitution," *EEH*, July 1978.
28. David and Temin, in David (1978), pp. 202–214.
29. Claudia Goldin, *Urban Slavery in the American South* (Chicago: University of Chicago Press, 1978).
30. In the simplest formulation: If the percentage change in quantity demanded divided by the percentage change in price is greater than 1, then demand is price elastic. If the percentage change in quantity demanded percentage change in price is less than 1, then demand is price inelastic.
31. Herbert Gutman and Richard Sutch, "Victorians All? The Sexual Mores and Conduct of Slaves and Their Masters," in David (1978). See pp. 99–133 in that chapter for a discussion of slave sales and pp. 134–162 for one on slave breeding. Also, in a more extended analysis, Sutch, "The Breeding of Slaves for Sale and the Westward Expansion of Slavery, 1850–1860," in Stanley Engerman and Eugene Genovese, editors, *Race and Slavery in the Western Hemisphere: Quantitative Studies* (1975), chap. VIII.
32. Richard Sutch, "The Care and Feeding of Slaves," in David (1978).
33. David and Temin, in David (1978), pp. 187–202. The average rate of exploitation was the proportion of the competitive wage *not* paid to slaves for their labor at any point in time. Fogel and Engerman allow that figure to rise to perhaps 54 percent overall; Richard Vedder sees it as perhaps 65 percent overall, "The Slave Exploitation Rate," *EEH*, October 1975.
34. Richard Easterlin, "Regional Income Trends, 1840–1950," in Robert Fogel and Stanley Engerman, editors, *The Reinterpretation of American Economic History* (New York: Harper & Row, 1971), pp. 38–45.
35. Discussions of each of these questions appear in Fogel and Engerman (1974), vol. I, pp. 144–157.
36. David and Temin, in David (1978), pp. 183–184 and pp. 223–235.
37. Steckel (1979b).
38. Richard Steckel, "Birth Weights and Infant Mortality Among American Slaves," *EEH*, April 1986. See also his "Stature and the Standard of Living," *JEL*, December 1995.
39. Richard Steckel, "A Dreadful Childhood: The Excess Mortality of American Slaves," *Social Science History*, Winter 1986c, p. 450.

40. *Ibid.*, pp. 451–452.
41. *Ibid.*, p. 430.
42. Richard Steckel, "A Peculiar Population: The Nutrition Health, and Mortality of American Slaves from Childhood to Maturity," *JEH*, September 1986b, p. 726.
43. *Ibid.*, p. 728.
44. Philip Coelho and Robert McGuire, "Diets Versus Diseases: The Anthropometrics of Slave Children," *Journal of Economic History*, vol. 60, no. 1, March 2000, argues that the disease environment of the American South adversely affected slaves. This article is followed by a reply from Steckel.
45. Steckel (1986c). This is Steckel's final conclusion in this remarkable paper, but he emphasizes that it must be speculative.
46. Kenneth Stampp argues that such forms of resistance were more important than is commonly assumed and sharply criticizes Fogel and Engerman for downplaying it. In David (1978), "Introduction," pp. 27–28.
47. Stanley Elkins, *Slavery: A Problem of American Institutional and Intellectual Life* (1959), pp. 2–23.
48. Fogel and Engerman (1974), vol. I, p. 264.
49. Stampp, in David (1978), p. 18.
50. *Ibid.*, p. 30.
51. Elkins (1959), chap. III; a discussion of "Sambo" and slave infantilism appears on pp. 82–89.
52. *Ibid.*, pp. 103–133.
53. Eugene Genovese, *Roll, Jordan, Roll: The World the Slaves Made* (1976), "The Moment of Truth," pp. 97–112. The comparison to concentration camps can be found in Elkins (1959), p. 114.
54. Eugene Genovese, *From Rebellion to Revolution: Afro-American Slave Revolts in the Making of the Modern World* (Baton Rouge: Louisiana State University Press, 1979).
55. We are indebted to Professor Thomas Ulen for emphasis on this point.
56. Fogel and Engerman (1974), vol. I, p. 232. Also force was used *judiciously*, see p. 237.
57. Herbert Gutman and Richard Sutch, "Sambo Makes Good, or Were Slaves Imbued with the Protestant Work Ethic?" in David (1978), pp. 60–67, 90–93. Also Giorgio Canarella and John Tomaske, "The Optimal Utilization of Slaves," *Journal of Economic History*, vol. XXXV, no. 3, September 1975.
58. Olmsted (1959), pp. 49–50.
59. *Ibid.*, see the footnote on p. 49.
60. Gutman and Sutch, in David (1978), pp. 159–160.
61. Fogel and Engerman (1974), vol. I, pp. 78–86.
62. Sutch, "The Breeding of Slaves," in Engerman and Genovese (1975), pp. 195, 198.
63. Peter Passell and Gavin Wright, "The Effects of Pre-Civil War Territorial Expansion on the Price of Slaves," *Journal of Political Economy*, vol. 80, no. 6, December 1972; and Laurence Kotlikoff and Sebastian Pinera, "The Old South's Stake in the Inter-Regional Movement of Slaves, 1850–1860," *Journal of Economic History*, vol. XXXVII, no. 2, June 1977.
64. See Robert Whaples, "Where Is There Consensus Among American Economic Historians? The Results of a Survey on Forty Propositions," *Journal of Economic History*, vol. 55, no. 1, March 1995.

SUGGESTED READINGS

Articles

Aufhauser, R. Keith. "Slavery and Technological Change." *Journal of Economic History*, vol. XXXIV, no. 1, March 1974.

Conrad, Alfred, and John Meyer. "The Economics of Slavery in the Antebellum South." *Journal of Political Economy*, vol. 66, no. 2, April 1958.

Fenoaltea, Stefano. "The Slavery Debate: A Note from the Sidelines." *Explorations in Economic History*, vol. 18, no. 3, July 1981.

Fleisig, Heywood. "Slavery, the Supply of Agricultural Labor, and the Industrialization of the South." *Journal of Economic History*, vol. XXXVI, no. 3, September 1976.

Fogel, Robert William. "Three Phases of Cliometric Research on Slavery and Its Aftermath." *American Economic Review*, vol. LXV, no. 2, May 1975.

———, and Stanley L. Engerman. "The Relative Efficiency of Slavery: A Comparison of Northern and Southern Agriculture in 1860." *Explorations in Economic History*, vol. 8, no. 3, Spring 1971.

———. "Explaining the Relative Efficiency of Slave Agriculture in the Antebellum South." *American Economic Review*, vol. 67, no. 3, June 1977.

———. "Explaining the Relative Efficiency of Slave Agriculture in the Antebellum South: A Reply." *American Economic Review*, vol. 70, no. 4, September 1980.

Schmitz, Mark D., and Donald F. Schaefer. "Slavery, Freedom, and the Elasticity of Substitution." *Explorations in Economic History*, vol. 15, no. 3, July 1978.

Steckel, Richard H. "Slave Height Profiles from Coastwise Manifests." *Explorations in Economic History*, vol. 16, no. 4, October 1979a.

———. "Slave Mortality." *Social Science History*, vol. 3, nos. 3 and 4, October 1979b.

———. "Slave Marriage and the Family." *Journal of Family History*, vol. V, no. 4, Winter 1980.

———. "Birth Weights and Infant Mortality among American Slaves." *Explorations in Economic History*, vol. 23, no. 2, April 1986a.

——— "A Peculiar Population: The Nutrition, Health, and Mortality of American Slaves from Childhood to Maturity." *Journal of Economic History*, vol. XLVI, no. 3, September 1986b.

———. "A Dreadful Childhood: the Excess Mortality of American Slaves." *Social Science History*, vol. 10, no. 4, Winter 1986c.

———. "Stature and the Standard of Living." *Journal of Economic Literature*, vol. XXXIII, no. 4, December 1995.

Sutch, Richard. "The Profitability of Antebellum Slavery Revisited." *Southern Economic Journal*, vol. 31, no. 2. April 1963.

———. "The Treatment Received by American Slaves: A Critical Review of the Evidence Presented in *Time on the Cross*." *Explorations in Economic History*, vol. 12, no. 4, October 1975.

Thomas, Robert Paul, and Richard Nelson Bean. "The Fishers of Men: The Profits of the Slave Trade." *Journal of Economic History*, vol. XXXIV, no. 4, December 1974.

Vedder, Richard K. "The Slave Exploitation (Expropriation) Rate." *Explorations in Economic History*, vol. 12, no. 4, October 1975.

Wright, Gavin. "Slavery and the Cotton Boom." *Explorations in Economic History*, vol. 12, no. 4, October 1975.

Yasuba, Yasukichi. "The Profitability and Viability of Plantation Slavery in the United States." *Economic Studies Quarterly*, vol. 12, no. 3, September 1961.

Zepp, Thomas M. "On Returns to Scale and Input Substitutability in Slave Agriculture." *Explorations in Economic History*, vol. 13, no. 2, April 1976.

Books

David, Paul, Herbert Gutman, Richard Sutch, Peter Temin, and Gavin Wright. *Reckoning with Slavery: A Critical Study in the Quantitative History of American Slavery*. New York: Oxford University Press, 1978.

Douglass, Frederick. *Narrative of the Life of Frederick Douglass*. New York: New American Library, 1968.

Elkins, Stanley M. *Slavery: A Problem of American Institutional and Intellectual Life*. New York: Grosset & Dunlap, 1959.

Engerman, Stanley, and Eugene Genovese. *Race and Slavery in the Western Hemisphere: Quantitative Studies*. Princeton: Princeton University Press, 1978.

Fogel, Robert William. *Without Consent or Contract: The Rise and Fall of American Slavery*. New York: W. W. Norton, 1989.

———, and Stanley Engerman. *Time on the Cross: The Economics of American Negro Slavery*. Boston: Little Brown, 1974, 2 vols.

Genovese, Eugene. *Roll, Jordan, Roll: The World the Slaves Made*. New York: Vintage Books, 1976.

Gray, Lewis. *History of Agriculture in the Southern United States to 1860*. Washington, D.C.: The Carnegie Institution, 1933, 2 vols.

Gutman, Herbert. *The Black Family in Slavery and Freedom*. New York: Pantheon Books, 1976.

Olmsted, Frederick Law. *The Slave States*. New York: Capricorn Books, 1959.

Stampp, Kenneth. *The Peculiar Institution*. New York: Vintage Books, 1964.

Washington, Booker T. *Up from Slavery*. New York: Bantam Books, 1963.

Wright, Gavin. *The Political Economy of the Cotton South*. New York: Norton, 1978.

CHAPTER ELEVEN

The Early Industrial Sector

In order fully to appreciate the level that American industrial output had reached by 1913—nearly as great as that of all the European nations combined—we must step back in time a moment to consider its small beginnings. In 1790, manufacturing activity was primitive for the most part. Alexander Hamilton, in his *Report on Manufactures* (1791), estimated that from two-thirds to four-fifths of the population's clothing was homemade at that time. Apparently, not a spindle in the country was driven by waterpower. As previously discussed, there were water-powered grain milling and the basic fabricating activities associated with agriculture, sacking, and cooperage. Towns contained artisans who made tools, shoes, hats, pots, and pans by hand. Lumber mills on the edges of rivers like the Merrimac resembled small factories, as did (according to old prints) the DuPont powder works on the Brandywine.

In the first years of the new nation, American producers found it difficult to compete with the British. Significant domestic production began in the years just prior to the War of 1812, when Britain was drawn into the European war and the United States decided to assert its rights as a neutral country by legislating an embargo on foreign trade. The vast majority of American establishments were quite small, and they could be replicated quickly when trade was suspended. A brief increase in domestic production had taken place during the Revolution. As late as 1820, the vast majority of manufacturing firms were concentrated in the Northeast and were small-scale enterprises using time-honored processes; textiles were the notable exception.

THE DIRECTION OF CHANGE IN MANUFACTURING

If America's industrial progress in the nineteenth century had been equal to that of Europe, America would have been producing no more than 28 percent of Europe's industrial output, perhaps less, by the early twentieth century. In fact, in 1913, the United States produced 31.9 million metric tons of crude steel, compared with 35.5 million for all of Western Europe; it mined 517 million metric tons of coal, compared with their 493 million. We are looking at the beginnings of an industrial prodigy. It has been estimated that, by 1914, American industrial productivity was double that of Western Europe. In the nineteenth century, the United States astonished the world with its industrial ability. We first look at the factors that shaped nineteenth-century American industrial growth.

The Human Element

We can suppose that Americans in 1790 exhibited an amount of mechanical ability equal to that possessed by Western Europeans. They were, by all accounts, as literate and numerate as the Europeans; schooling at the elementary level (at least in the Northern and Middle Atlantic states) was available in the settled areas. In the arts of commerce and in the application of technology, such as in shipbuilding and war-making, they were equal to the European level. The United States was not a "less developed" country in the modern sense of that term but simply a nation with less industry.

The Spread of the Industrial Revolution

In 1790, the Industrial Revolution was beginning in Europe and was centered in Great Britain, which had created (and was trying to maintain) the technical lead. Not unlike modern governments attempting to hoard newly developed scientific knowledge, the British tried to achieve a technological monopoly. In 1774 and 1781, Parliament passed laws prohibiting the export of the new industrial machinery, imposing a fine of £200 and 12 years' imprisonment for exporting textile machinery. A law of 1782 provided penalties for *labor pirating*, attempts to lure skilled British mechanics abroad. But there was no way for the government to succeed completely in this attempt to control the transfer of technology. Industrialists traveled where the money was and took the British industrial revolution with them, laws or not.

In 1775, William Wilkinson, brother of the famed English industrialist John "Iron Master" Wilkinson, was already in France setting up iron works using British machinery and workers—and teaching the French how to use that machinery to bore cannon. On 3 August 1789, Arthur Young, traveling in revolutionary France, had viewed several of Wilkinson's works and wrote of the facility at Montcenis:

> ... a disagreeable country.... It is the seat of one Mons. *Weelkainsong's* establishments for casting and boring cannon....The French say that this active Englishman is brother-in-law to Dr. Priestly, and therefore a friend of mankind: and that he taught them to bore cannon, in order to give liberty to America. The establishment is very considerable; there are from 500 to 600 men employed, besides colliers; five steam engines are erected for giving the blasts, and for boring.... I conversed with an Englishman ... there were once many, but only two are left at present....[1]

In Belgium, the beginnings of a manufacturing industry are associated with the name and firm of William Cockerill, another emigré from Britain. In the Ruhr Valley, German industry was growing under the direction of W. T. Mulvany, an Irishman. In Russia in the late 1860s, it was John Hughes and a host of Welshmen involved in coal and iron.[2]

The United States also benefited mightily from such out-migration. The brothers Schofield, who arrived in the early 1790s from Yorkshire, built wool-carding machinery driven by waterpower. Notable among others who followed their path was the Scots engineer Henry Burden, who was responsible for crucial innovations in that "cradle of American technology," the Springfield (Massachusetts) armory.[3] He followed a policy of bringing over immigrant mechanics to work there. It was David Thomas, a Welsh immigrant, who first introduced anthracite iron smelting into the Pennsylvania iron industry in 1840. Just over three decades later, the immigrant Scot Andrew Carnegie would launch the Industrial Revolution in steel in this country using English inventor Henry Bessemer's converter, "Bessemer's volcano," where others had tried and failed.

Skilled Yankee observers also imported industrialization. Almy and Brown, the first American textile mill, made use of technology smuggled out of England by Samuel Slater. Francis Cabot Lowell, traveling in England in 1811, was entranced by English weaving machinery and studied it closely. Returning home, he worked with a skilled mechanic named Paul Moody, and, by 1814, they had succeeded in making a loom driven by waterpower. As we saw in Chapter 6, the Lowell firm pioneered large-scale weaving factories in this country as well as significant labor-force innovations.

American Innovations

Although the United States borrowed all it could from Europe, very early peculiar inventions and innovations began to be made here. The word *peculiar* is used to set apart two characteristics of American industry that became predominant: economy of labor by the use of machines and extravagant use of raw material. The United States was "short" on labor and "long" on raw material; therefore, it conserved what was scarce and freely used what was plentiful In brief, good economics were practiced.

One measure of the outcome could already be seen in cotton textiles by 1860. The average English integrated spinning and weaving factory contained 17,000 spindles and 276 looms compared with a mere 7,000 spindles and 163 looms in the average New England factory. The American cotton textile industry (the nation's largest), with 20 percent of the spindles the British employed and perhaps 25 percent of the workers, consumed 40 percent as much raw cotton.[4] Productivity was higher in the United States than in Britain; by 1860, this advantage had already been the subject of great curiosity and remark. In other segments of industry the higher productivity was also noted, as well as the fact that none of these industrial technologies began in the United States.[5] What was going on?

In 1784–1785, inventor Oliver Evans built a flour mill outside Philadelphia run by gravity, friction, and waterpower. Grain was moved from the loading bin throughout the mill's several levels by buckets and leather belts without the intervention of any human effort apart from guiding and regulating. The mill could handle 300 bushels an hour. It was an assembly line more than a century before Henry Ford's Highland Park factory housed the first real automotive assembly line.

Eli Whitney and Simeon North both had contracts from the federal government to make arms. Whitney's was for 10,000 muskets in 1798, and North's for pistols a year later. Both men pursued the idea of interchangeable parts—the use of stamping and cutting machines to make identical parts from a pattern. Unskilled workers with a minimum of hand fitting (filing) could assemble these parts into the final product.

In the case of the mill, the object was in part the substitution of **capital equipment**—machinery—for unskilled workers. In the case of arms manufacturing, the substitution of technology was for *skilled* workers, armorers, who simply were not available in this country. Whitney said of his years of devising machinery to replace human skills, "I have not only the *Arms* but a large portion of the *Armourers* to make."[6] Oliver Wolcott, Secretary of the Treasury, awarded the contracts to Whitney and North. He, at least, had an appreciation for what Whitney was doing. Wolcott wrote to Whitney: "I should consider a real improvement in machinery for manufacturing arms as a great acquisition to the United States."[7] The idea had been tried in France with no known result by Honoré Blanc, and Thomas Jefferson (in France at the time) had talked with him, hoping to get him to emigrate to the United States. French and English officers to whom Whitney explained his ideas scoffed at them. Whitney completed his contract for the 10,000 muskets in 1809; in 1812, the British, using the old methods, had 200,000 muskets in disrepair and were waiting for armorers to fix each part, one at a time.[8] Because the muskets had been made individually, their parts were not interchangeable.

By the 1830s, the ideas of standardization, interchangeability, and division of labor in lengthy production processes were being widely applied in American industry. Their incorporation in the manufacturing sector produced an interesting result that came to characterize much of American economic life: Although as in Europe, skilled labor in the United States tended to fetch a higher wage than did unskilled labor, the *ratio* of skilled to unskilled wages was lower than in Europe.[9] The difference in the two ratios, American and British, reflected the relatively higher productivity of unskilled workers in the United States, who were aided in their labor by machinery that substituted for skill.[10] By the 1840s, the system was being used for locks, clocks, and watches. In 1846, the sewing machine was patented, and it soon worked its way into the making of boots, shoes, harnesses, and belts, as well as into the clothing industry.

At the Great Exhibition in London (1851) American products, not noted for their elegance, were outstanding for their practicality, cheapness, and utility.[11] By then what had become known as the "American System of Manufacturing"—simplicity of design, standardization, interchangeable manufacture, and large-scale output—had taken over in light consumer goods.[12] Later, it would work its way into heavy industry, into machine-making (machines to make machines), and, indeed, into nearly the entire economy. By the end of the nineteenth century, American industry contrasted sharply with European and British in terms of output per unit of labor. Eventually, the United States would become a nation where an unskilled teenager working at a service station might earn as much as a skilled woodworker, and where unskilled assembly line factory "hands" might earn more than bookkeepers, and even schoolteachers.

The American System of Manufacturing

Economic historians, particularly Nathan Rosenberg, have demonstrated a direct line between the introduction of the "American system" of interchangeable parts in the Springfield armory at the start of the nineteenth century, the development of the machine tool industry in the middle of the century, and the emergence of the bicycle, aviation, and automobile industries at the end.[13] Technological historians, such as Merritt Roe Smith and David Hounshell, documented exactly how various steps in this process took place. Smith demonstrated the role the Army Ordnance Department played in promoting interchangeability, while Hounshell established direct connections between the public-sector armories and the private-sector metalworking industries in the Connecticut River valley.[14]

Donald Hoke, another technological historian, has challenged this tradition. Although he is looking at exactly the same facts as the others, Hoke argues that private-sector, profit-maximizing entrepreneurs in the woodworking industries of the Connecticut River valley played the important role. He believes that the American system began with wooden clock making in Bristol in the 1810s and the Collins axe factory near Hartford in the 1830s; "armory practice was not the significant factor previous interpretations have suggested."[15]

The basic difference between Hoke and the others is what each is seeking. Smith and Hounshell try to understand how the "technological convergence" Rosenberg described took place, to explain the long-term movement from small arms production in the early national period to the assembly line at the Ford Motor Company a century later. Hoke does not attempt to develop any linkages between the industries he explores and their neighbors who are part of the "technological convergence" tradition. He wants to know who was the first to tinker with the technology. By asking slightly different questions, by assigning different weights to what is "important," both sides can be "right."

The Importance of Factor Proportions

In recent years scholars have made careful studies of the singular pattern of nineteenth-century American industrial innovation to find its remote sources. Did the difference in availability of labor and land account for the path of development taken by the American manufacturing industry? Sir John Habakkuk, in his trailbreaking book *American and British Technology in the Nineteenth Century: The Search for Labour-Saving Inventions*, argued that the origin of the *need* for labor-cost-reducing (labor-saving) machinery in America was initially the worker's "opportunity cost"—the availability of a viable alternative on the frontier.[16] Cheap land, said Habakkuk, means that wages in manufacturing had to be high enough to keep workers from "going west." The labor market, by implication, was not perfectly competitive. Employers could not hire all the workers they needed at going wages. They had to pay more. Use of machinery by relatively unskilled workers raised their productivity and thus justified the payment of higher wages by profit-maximizing employers. There was, however, a paradoxical result: Labor became even more "scarce"—high priced—and the inducement "to save labor" by raising wages was even greater. Thus, a rapidly increasing industrial labor force was also a "high-wage" labor force because of rising productivity.[17]

As the system became a more general one, it proved profitable for American industrialists to hire workers at wages higher than were typically paid in Europe and to buy machinery at higher interest rates. In a static world, higher interest rates restrict investment. But, as technological change made capital more productive, the investment demand curve *shifted to the right*—increasing both the interest rate and the level of investment. The American economy, because of efficient technology, became one of high wages, high interest rates, high profits, and rapid growth.

The pressures in Great Britain to be efficient with machinery were not so great, argued Sir John, in part because the British worker, lacking easy access to a frontier such as America offered, accepted lower wages for greater skill, thus tempting the British employer to use skilled labor, an abundant resource. As time passed, British industry became a labor-using industry with low wages, while that in America increasingly became a *labor-saving* industry with higher wages.[18]

The question of choice of technique (actually, the whole range of technical change that is adopted) must, of course, involve adoption of the technical apparatus *and* development of knowledge, organization of production, labor force, marketing, finance, and much else. Paul David added to the pioneering work of Habakkuk by offering an explanation of why major departures in technological development prove to be self-sustaining.[19] His work was based on both American and British nineteenth-century technology. A shift in technique could begin with changes in the ratio of labor to capital prices that would induce a switch, such as that from a labor-intensive to a labor-saving manufacturing process. However, there is a difference between possible technologies and *available* technologies. The latter are fewer than the former, and, if the change is to be a fundamental one (for example, from animal to mechanical power), other related activities have to adjust to fully exploit the change. Jobs will change; institutions will adapt. Major locational consequences involving significant population movements, development of appropriate supporting social infrastructure, and a learning-by-doing process to integrate the technological switch into society at large may occur.

Little by little, improvements are made all along the line that commit the economy more steadfastly to the new technology. The older methods and organizations disappear as new processes diffuse themselves in a market economy. As time passes, a whole new system evolves; associated economic activities develop in ways congenial to the new technology, making it increasingly productive socially and more efficient economically. In a way, the first technical switch sets the tone for subsequent development, *if* the learning-by-doing process is set in motion. If factor prices change back toward the old ratios, indicating marginal advantages from a return to older techniques, re-switching most likely will not occur: The economy will not convert back to its old track. Setup costs, involving abandonment of all recent changes, are too high. It is more profitable to continue making cost-saving improvements in what has become a new, and then a general, way of economic organization.[20]

William Lazonick published a fascinating case study of these institutional and technical forces.[21] He adds the reaction of labor and ownership to the background and initial conditions. In the nineteenth-century cotton-spinning industry, we might expect to see a uniform technology on both sides of the Atlantic. However, although the British industry became labor intensive by using inferior raw material, the American industry adopted a technology that utilized better machinery and higher grades of raw material while conserving labor. British labor organized to protect its jobs and cooperated with management by substituting skill and inferior raw material for new technology. Unlike the British, American workers did not unionize; they tended to change jobs and leave the industry for better opportunities elsewhere. American industry could compensate for this mobility through newer machinery, better grade raw cotton, and less reliance on a stable labor force.

An additional labor-force consideration is the Goldin-Sokoloff hypothesis—the first areas to industrialize were those where the wages of women and children were low relative to adult males—introduced in Chapter 6.[22] Almost all manufacturing firms realized significant advances between 1820 and 1860, with textiles doing somewhat better than the others. Consistent with the hypothesis, changes in labor organization appeared to explain this. It was the larger firms, in or near urban areas, that typically used a larger proportion of women and children. Even though they had about the same capital-labor ratio as smaller, artisan enterprises, their larger size allowed them to adopt a more complex division of labor. By moving the production site from people's homes to their own manufactories, they intensified the work pace. Outside of urban areas, women and children were largely part-time, off-peak manufacturing workers who were desirous of flexibility with respect to the time and place of work. Consequently, cottage industry, while less productive, remained a competitive form of organization. The evidence, notes Sokoloff, "would seem to make it increasingly difficult to sustain the view that the onset of industrial expansion in the Northeast was primarily due to the release of labor and other resources from a stagnant and declining agricultural sector."[23]

Productivity and Patents

The productivity studies of Sokoloff agree with the standard view that technological change in industry before the Civil War advanced in two phases. The first phase, which occupied most of the period before the Civil War, reflected the spread of manufactories from textiles to other industries. His estimates suggest that, before the Civil War, increases in total factor productivity were responsible for most of the advance in labor productivity. Efficiency increased without a significant addition to the capital-labor ratio. Further, the rate of technological advance was almost as high before as after the war. The second phase, which began around 1850, reflected the adoption of inanimate power sources and, consequently, more mechanized production techniques with correspondingly higher capital-labor ratios.

Using the surviving quantitative evidence, Sokoloff finds there were some scale economies in the expansion of shop size from the artisan enterprise to a prefactory specialized workshop employing 10 to 15 workers. New England, with its relatively limited supply of good farmland, its "urbanization," and relatively large supply of competent artisans, was subject to these scale economies and so developed a "preindustrial" industry based upon reorganization into specialized workshops. Sokoloff is not certain whether the scale economies came from the greater division of labor and specialization made possible from this reorganization (similar to Adam Smith's famous pin factory described in *The Wealth of Nations*), or the more intensive labor effort per unit of work that shop work with greater supervision and management implies. Similar developments were identified in European industrial history.[24]

Sokoloff has made use of information on U.S. patents to explain the trend toward greater specialization and the diffusion of "modern" industrial techniques.[25] The spread of competitive firms and the improvements in the transportation network are major parts of the explanation for the initial acceleration in the rate of technological change. But, as Sokoloff notes, that rate continued to accelerate. Why?

Patent data have been widely criticized as a measure of technological change since Jacob Schmookler's path-breaking 1966 book *Invention and Economic Growth*.[26] The gist of the argument is that most patents add very little to technological change, and many changes that add a great deal are not patented or are not patentable. Sokoloff argues that we should consider the patent record to be a qualitative reflection "of the resources consumed in inventive activity."

In total, the patent record shows that a sustained acceleration began during the first years of the nineteenth century; the per-capita rate increased by a factor of 15 between 1790 and 1860. This acceleration was not limited to a particular industry, nor was it constant. Sokoloff attributes the expansion of markets associated with early industrialization as playing an important role. With the exception of a marked increase in the years before the War of 1812, patenting activity in general moved together with the business cycle over the period. It was also geographically dispersed. The rate of patenting per capita increased in both urban areas and in areas where access to markets was poor. Nonetheless, southern New England and New York had the highest rates throughout the entire period.

Sokoloff, in collaboration with Zorina Khan, elaborated on the increased importance of what they refer to as investment in "invention-generating capital."[27] The initial expansion of markets broadened the number and type of people who participated in the process; for example, housewives and clergymen held patents. Over time, however, specialization developed in inventing, as in other economic activities. By midcentury, the data indicate an increase in the number of lifetime patents by patentees. The move toward the modern pattern, where specialists undertake the bulk of inventive activity, is evident in the data. So, too, is the move toward cities where more resources are available. All of these factors, however, are more reflective of the post-Civil War years, and we will revisit these data later.

Consumption

In addition to the dramatic changes occurring on the supply side of the market, demand was rising. Demand in America, historians argue, became peculiar; it became demand for mass-produced, standardized products. Edward Ames and Nathan Rosenberg added the element of mass-product demand to the argument.[28] Americans wanted factory-made products instantly to free their own labor for more immediate work in agriculture and extractive industry. If the machine-made tools wore out—and had been profitably used—new ones would be purchased to replace them. Simple designs would suffice. The need was for an immediate availability of the tools. As Ames and Rosenberg asked, "Who used a shotgun in England, and who used one in America?" In England, the shotgun, a weapon used by a limited number of people—landowners— to shoot birds, was also an item of prestige. In America, it was a tool, like the shovel or axe, used by settlers everywhere. The American consumer of durables was not interested in frills. On the other hand, quality clothing cost money, and clothing could easily be replaced, perhaps in a new style:

> The material, being expected to last for a single season, is purchased in a quality to do that, and no more. The next season the customer supplies himself again.... This habit of almost constant change in said to run through almost every class of society, and has ... a great influence upon the character of goods generally in demand which ... are made more for appearance, and less for actual wear and use, than similar goods are in England.[29]

American consumers would buy tools that worked, no matter what the appearance of those tools, and good-looking, factory-made clothes, no matter whether they wore well or not. In both cases the question was simply price and use. Regarding tools, Rosenberg quotes an early twentieth-century British author who noted that Americans allowed machine capability to set their standards:

> ...where mechanical devices cannot be adjusted to the production of the traditional product, the product must be modified to the demands of the machine. Hence the standard American table-knife is a rigid, metal shape, handle and blade forged in one piece, the whole being finished by electroplating—an implement eminently suited to factory production.[30]

These are examples of consumers getting what they want, *if they intend to use it up and buy something else.* Both sorts of demand are ideal for factory production and doubtless are the origin of the famous American "throw-away economy" of the present day that has embraced even automobiles and houses.

Resources

An additional element stressed by Rosenberg in his book *Technology and American Economic Growth* is the use of raw materials, especially *wood.*[31] Wood was in abundant supply compared with other materials for houses, tools, furniture, and transport equipment, and Americans used it freely in the nineteenth century, substituting it for metals wherever possible before 1860. In fact, in 1860, the lumber industry was second only to cotton textiles in creation of market value. Rosenberg estimates that in 1860 American per-capita wood consumption was five times that of England and Wales.[32] Elaborate woodworking equipment had been invented by Americans in pursuit of a cheap resource (just as, in England, an elaborate social structure had been developed to exploit labor, *their* cheap resource). Europeans were appalled by American wastefulness in wood manufacturing. Rosenberg quotes an English observer (writing in 1872): "Lumber manufacture, from the log to the finished state, is, in America, characterized by a waste that can truly be called criminal...."[33] This is true only if you think that lumber is a scarce resource.

Thus, American manufacturing developed on a labor-saving, resource-using basis, buoyed by consumers who accepted the products of machine manufacturing, later to become the products of machine-moving, assembly line manufacture. In the twentieth century, Europeans developed the same tastes, especially for automobiles. As Peter Temin points out, the innovation of characteristic American manufacturing techniques proceeded no more rapidly than was profitable.[34] In his study of the iron and steel industry, Temin found that the iron industry stuck to charcoal as long as it was the most profitable fuel, turning to coking coal only when resources and techniques justified the change.[35] By 1860, therefore, the American iron industry might have *appeared* to be technically backward compared to the British since it still depended upon small furnaces and forges run by anthracite coal or charcoal, again, a wood product.

Once the industry and a large part of its market moved across the Alleghenies, once transportation to the East Coast by rail was developed, and once the right quality of coking coal was discovered, the American iron and steel industry would quickly catch up with and surpass European technical practice. But only when it *paid* to do so. American economic growth was a matter of private profit calculations, not national prestige or planning. The same forces were at work in changing motive power. Even though the steam engine was introduced early in American history and its use was widely diffused, as late as 1869 nearly half the motive power used in industry was water—so good were the country's millrace streams and rivers.[36]

The Course of Expansion to 1860

Figure 11.1 shows the size distribution of ten manufacturing industries in 1860 by *value added* (revenue less the cost of materials). Of a total manufacturing labor force of 1,530,000 (compared to 5,880,000 in agriculture in 1860), some 1,474,000 were employed in these ten industries alone. Cotton goods production, the largest by value added, was second in order of employment (115,000). Cotton textile manufacturing led in the growth of American industry, as it had in England, and would in the future in nearly every industrializing country the world over. The machinery was relatively simple, and little or no skill was required of the labor force.

The largest employer of labor in 1860, boots and shoes manufacturing (123,000), was third in order of

FIGURE 11.1 The Course of Growth by Value Added

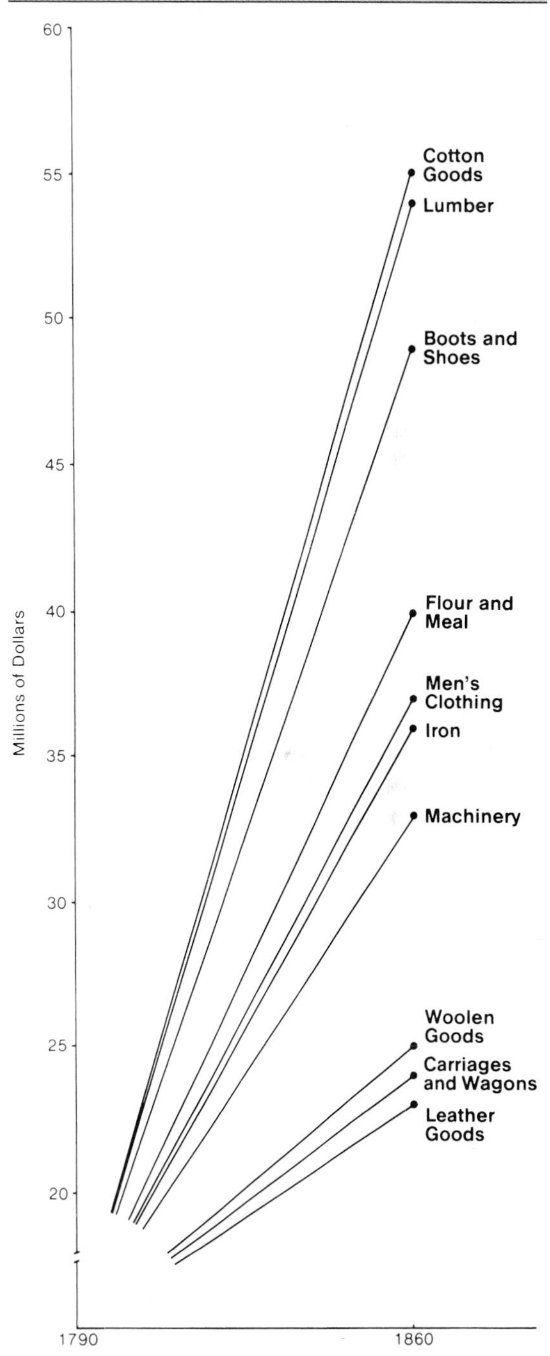

Source: *Eighth Census of the United States,* 1960, vol. 3, Manufactures.

magnitude by value added. By then the sewing machine had been widely adopted in the industry, and factory production was becoming common. The men's clothing industry, by 1860, had also discovered the sewing machine; 115,000 were employed there. Lumbering, second in value added, employed 76,000 men in the exploitation of one of the United States' richest resources and would long remain among the most productive industries. Per worker employed in 1860, though, flour milling and leather goods manufacturing produced the most value added.

Machinery production, seventh in value added (with 41,000 employed), in 1860 was already third in value added per worker. As Rosenberg emphasizes, this industry would become the "focusing" industry of future technological change.[37] It would become increasingly more specialized, developing eventually into the machine-tool industry, where machines were designed to make machines. There would also be specialized branches, such as locomotive building and the canning industry.

In another half century, machine building would become the largest industry by value added. Technical progress would spread through American industry via the machine builders. Americans, already willing to buy standardized products of machine fabrication, increasingly would be paying for the standardization of the machines themselves, and then of the tools that built them. Standardization was effective when it was most widespread. In World War I, the force of defense spending enhanced the process of standardization because the government, which became the largest buyer, *required* uniform sizes for everything from men's underwear to nuts and bolts. Here again we encounter the idea of interchangeability.

The 1860 industrial distribution still shows its close association with agriculture and the forest. We will see more of industries using the products of other manufacturing industries as **inputs**, a half century later.

ENERGY SOURCES

Manufacturing requires energy, and in early factories the central power source, the prime mover, powerfully influenced industrial location. In the United States in the antebellum period, the variety of energy sources employed was striking.

Animal Energy

We can never know precisely the amount of animal energy that was used in the United States. Horses, mules, and oxen could be used for stationary work as well as for traction. Dependable data show that in 1867, there were 6.8 million horses and probably 1 million mules at work in the country. Population then was about 37.5 million; thus, there were about 5.4 persons per horse. Assuming constant technology for those few years, there must have been 5.5 million horses at work by 1860, perhaps a million mules, and many, many oxen. How much of the economy's total work was powered by these animals is unknown. They must have powered most of the traction, and it is estimated that in 1860 they provided an astonishing 63 percent of the total horsepower of prime movers.[38]

Water and Steam

In addition to horses, mules, and oxen, Americans used windmills, waterwheels, and steam engines as prime movers. Scholars have found the official 1838 count of stationary steam engines to be only a partial count. Peter Temin corrected the official report as far as he feels is possible and concluded that at least 1,616 engines could be identified on that basis.[39] Rosenberg is willing to let that figure drift up to 1,800.[40] According to Atack, Bateman, and Weiss, the correct figure is 1,420.[41] The precise count is not important here. If we can picture 1,420 colored pins on a map of the settled regions of the United States in 1838, we can see how abundantly available the steam engine was. In mechanical (nonanimal) energy sources, though, it is clear that waterpower was still predominant over steam.[42] Surviving evidence shows that some 250 firms built the 1838 steam engines. Fully 90 percent of the value added by the machinery industry (seventh largest in the country, see Figure 11.1) in 1860 came from the construction of steam engines alone.[43] The builders were primarily small firms engaged in other work. Foreign supply was also present. Despite widespread familiarity with steam-engine design and construction, the evidence shows that Southern users of steam engines had a distinct propensity to import them from England.[44]

Henry Burden's great waterwheel in Troy, New York (1850) was 60 feet in diameter and 22 feet wide. Its speed could be regulated manually with gears to within a second.

Economic Considerations

Waterpower's tenacious hold as a prime mover has several explanations. First, of course, a waterwheel simply was sufficient mechanical power in small grist mills and similar employments. There are also the geographical considerations; industrial sites in New England and generally down the fall line of the Appalachians were generously endowed with fast-moving streams and rivers and good sites for millrace dams. In the South and Midwest, beyond the Appalachians, the use of stationary steam power was predominant early because of the lack of suitable mill sites. Had those areas been endowed with waterpower like that of the Appalachian fall line, no doubt waterpower would have been more important than steam, but not necessarily in the same ways because of differences in the *work to be done*. We will return to this point later in the chapter.

There were other economic reasons for the persistence of waterpower when the steam option was available. As Temin points out, the total life of these early steam engines may have been only five years or so; thus, even though the initial capital cost of waterpower was higher than steam, the life of the installation was much longer, fuel costs were zero, and the longer depreciation period for waterpower made the annual capital cost where there were good water sites somewhat lower than it was for the steam engine.[45] Especially if the raw material, like cotton, could be easily transported to the factory site (the site of the prime mover), steam engines lost one of their advantages over waterpower–flexibility of location. Thus, cotton textiles were destined for a long life in New England's water-driven mills.[46]

Location

Because of its locational flexibility, the steam engine had many of the advantages of the modern fractional-horsepower electric motor and internal combustion engine. It could be transported *to the site* of the work to be done. Where raw materials were light and easily transported, this was not a great advantage. Where the raw materials were perishable, as in sugar refining, or where weight reduction was important, as in lumbering, cement, and brick manufacturing, the locational flexibility of the steam engine was of great advantage. Of course, its early adaptation to shipping on the country's vast system of inland waterways as well as on the ocean was the logical extreme of carrying the source of the power *to the job*. Accordingly, the permeation of the steam engine into American manufacturing was most rapid in the Midwest, where appropriate waterpower was scarce and, when available, slower than in New England.[47]

By 1869, steam power predominated over waterpower, just as in the twentieth century internal combustion and electrical power would make the steam engine a rarity. The efficiency of any prime mover is the amount and cost of power delivered relative to the work to be done. Waterpower ultimately would be doomed (until it could be generated into electrical energy) by the limitations of the waterwheel itself, no matter how much it was improved. Big factories were difficult to run with waterwheels. Waterpower's last grasp as a direct transmitter of motive force was no doubt the massive waterwheel constructed by the machinery innovator, Henry Burden, to power his machine works in Troy, New York, in 1851.[48] It was an excellent example of the adage that, in technology, old techniques tend to gigantism in their final stages of use.

Finally, steam power, because of its flexibility in location, allowed industry to grow at sites determined by other economic forces, such as markets or transportation advantages, in addition to the considerations we already have discussed.

Low- Versus High-Pressure Steam Engines

Rosenberg's thesis about the American exploitation of abundant resources by the technology adopted plays a part in the history of American steam engines, too. It was somewhat puzzling that Americans, equally adept at designing and making either low- or high-pressure steam engines (some firms made both, according to demand), for the most part opted for high-pressure engines, while in England, low-pressure engines generally prevailed.[49] The advantages of the high-pressure engine were its cheapness and relatively light weight. The main disadvantage was its extravagant fuel consumption. But fuel was no problem in the United States. As Rosenberg writes:

> These characteristics made such engines attractive in the resource-abundant environment of the U.S., where it was worthwhile, in effect, to "trade off" relative large amounts of natural resource inputs for a reduction in fixed capital costs.[50]

The high-pressure steam engine, appearing almost simultaneously in England and in the United States in 1803–1804, was developed in England by Richard Trevithick and in the United States by Oliver Evans. The great advantages of steam over waterpower and animal power were well-appreciated by Evans, who pointed out the lack of sufficient water sites for the long run, the problems of freezing in winter, the inconstancy of wind, and the fact that animals were "tedious" and "subject to innumerable accidents." Steam, Evans wrote, "at once presents us with a faithful servant, at command in all places, in all seasons."[51] Ultimately, his view prevailed since electrical power is now generated by burning coal, oil, and nuclear fuels to produce steam. His kind of steam engine was largely replaced by electrical motors and internal combustion engines. Charcoal, wood, coke, coal—all could "raise steam" by combustion, and did so by 1860. The discovery of commercial quantities of oil in Titusville, Pennsylvania, in 1859 had no effect in the history we have considered. Later on, petroleum produced dramatic changes.

Many Power Sources

That Americans so generally preferred high-pressure over low-pressure engines would have pleased both Trevithick and Evans. That waterpower and animal power would be so long-lasting in the United States might have surprised both. It was a matter of costs and revenues, again, and not technological fashion. Antebellum American industry depended upon many sources of motive and traction power, determined by locational needs and advantages. Since industry grew prodigiously anyhow, there is no evidence that the multiplicity of power sources was any disadvantage to the economy's needs. It is conceivable that modern changes in petroleum prices and availabilities could produce a similar heterogeneous growth of energy sources again. If so, history shows that heterogeneity of power sources is not by itself an economic disadvantage.

INDUSTRIAL LOCATION

Chapter 2 discussed the location of initial settlements and towns on a largely unknown and unpopulated territory, breaks-in-transport, and differentiation of productive capabilities in the natural endowment. On that basis, if we were asked in 1790, "Where will the country's future cities be?" we would probably answer that they would be near rivers, lakes, or the oceans, where roads came to such waters, causing the breaks-in-transport. Road locations, we would say, would be determined by the needs of future economic activity. Looking at a modern map of the United States, we might be largely satisfied with that answer, except for Denver, Salt Lake City, Spokane, Butte, and some cities in the Southwest, such as Amarillo and Lubbock.[52] Can we better explain the location of cities and economic activity in general? In 1955 and 1959, Douglass North published two papers that provide us with a finer focus on the location of economic activity in America throughout its history.[53]

The Regional Export Base

First, consider the idea of a region and its export activity. North looked at the development of specializing regions over the course of American history, noting the distinctly *unbalanced* pattern at the beginning, once the problem of subsistence food growing had been solved. Over and over, a new territory would be developed because of the possibility of exploiting some resource (e.g., fish, timber, cotton, gold, wheat, coal) that could be exported to the more settled areas of the country. Population and investment capital would flow in initially to exploit and develop this single resource (or perhaps linked resources like grains and livestock in the Midwest).

In North's analysis, the future of any region after an export activity develops will turn on three factors: (a) the region's natural endowments (at given levels of technology), (b) the "character" of the export industry, and (c) subsequent changes in technology and transport costs.

If the region has a significant comparative advantage in a single commodity, production will concentrate upon it, and other possibilities will be ignored. The Western mining settlements of Telluride, Colorado; Jarbidge, Nevada; and Silver City, Idaho; are examples. When the richest ore veins gave out, people moved on, leaving ghost towns in their wake. Much later, another change in technology (automobiles and recreational vehicles) brought in tourists. However, at the time of exploitation of the big export commodity, these regions appeared to be limited in their developmental possibilities.

The "character" of an export industry will influence other important features of a region's subsequent economic development. If the export industry has **increasing returns to scale**—that is, a large-scale organization has significant competitive advantages over small-scale activities—income distribution in the region will tend to be relatively unequal and development will produce only a few urban centers where activities are concentrated on processing and shipping the export commodity. If we look at American history specifically, the North contrasts with both the South and the Midwest in this regard. The cotton economy in the South was labor-intensive with scale economies (slavery and large plantations were the most efficient technology), and only a few urban centers devoted mainly to processing and shipping raw cotton were the result. In the Midwest, family-farm agriculture produced a more equal income distribution and, as a consequence, a greater number of possibilities for urban growth. (We will return to this point in detail.)

The comparative advantage originally established can be altered by some changes in technology and transport costs. In some cases, other (secondary) export industries may develop alongside those that first attracted settlers and investment. These secondary industries may ultimately take over the lead in growth or totally supplant the old export sector. The mixture of export and secondary industries can ultimately give the region the appearance of industrial "balance," *masking the*

Towns and Cities. *In the nineteenth century, America's cities grew rapidly into areas of concentrated economic and cultural activities. Retail stores and numerous street vendors supplied the growing population with their household goods and foodstuffs. City workers took their meals at "eating houses," quenched their thirst at root beer stands, or snacked on oysters on the half shell after a night at the theater.*

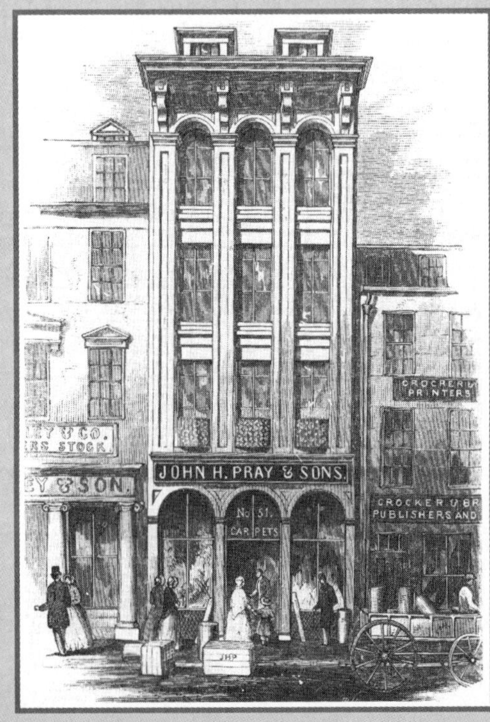

KNICKERBOCKER
ROOT BEER

CHATAM square

CHARLES BROWN.

crucial role played initially by exclusively export activities. Since we've mentioned mining towns in the old West, ski resorts in the modern West make a good example of this point. Transport to ski areas (auto, trains, busses, jets) and the installation of chair and T-bar lifts have brought life back to nearly abandoned mining sites like Ketchum, Alberta and Aspen, Colorado.

Land Ownership, Social Infrastructure, and Location

North argues that the absence of significant scale economies in nineteenth-century agriculture outside the South produced (a) more equal income distribution, (b) millions of family farms, (c) the need for schools and social services, and (d) more widespread marketing possibilities for manufacturers and sellers. As Rosenberg says, "Nineteenth-century American society was dominated by the tastes of rural households...."[54] These households, outside the rural South, were rich by European standards, and they were a huge and growing market. This fact tended to multiply the number of possible sites for cities—sites to be determined less by the needs of a single export commodity than by the needs of millions of families and the opportunities to supply them. The multiplication of possible urban sites also meant that urban-type activities could be supported in many places. Together these factors would multiply the demand for investment in *human capital*, for schools and universities. The more equally distributed incomes among a property-owning citizenry with full political rights and responsibilities equally imposed explain the rich social infrastructure of schools, churches, colleges, and like resources north of the slave-owning area. To the North, the blessing of the American landownership system was the sturdy communal life in places like Indiana, Ohio, and Iowa. One real cost of slavery was the South's lack of such infrastructure west of the tidewater areas—paradoxically *because slavery was so profitable* to those with the capital to engage in it on a large scale. The failure to invest locally in human capital marred Southern society's economic potential well into the twentieth century.

We add now the role of the break-in-transport in determining the location of an urban center. If the earth's surface were homogeneous, then the actual location of such cities would be a curious problem almost entirely solved by transport-cost considerations.[55] But because the continental United States is not a homogeneous surface, nature helps. The continent is carved by rivers and mountain ranges that generally run north and south and are dotted with exploitable natural resources, apart from farmland, in patches—specific locations. Roads, canals, and railroads tend to run east to west, connecting regions to each other where the north-south water transport system has been deemed insufficient to meet the needs of development. Breaks-in-transport between the water and surface routes became the urban sites, locating near export-base regional development. A simplified example is shown in Figure 11.2, where we have only one export-base industry, a single break-in-transport, and several supporting secondary activities. Other things being equal, urban location will be where the railroad crosses the river. Inside the region, transport will radiate out from the urban site. External economies at the site will cause secondary activities to gravitate toward the urban area, where transport costs also are minimized.

The list of American cities resulting from this process as the nation moved west (with Western and Southwestern exceptions already mentioned) is lengthy: Troy, Syracuse, Rochester, Buffalo, Pittsburgh, Wheeling, Youngstown, Cleveland, Akron, Detroit, Chicago, Milwaukee, Minneapolis, Dubuque, Omaha....[56] The list continued to grow in the nineteenth century as the nation continued its westward movement, and railroads, water, and other natural resources were exploited. North's theses, added to the break-in-transport analysis, provide a rich background description of regional growth and urbanization, not only up to 1860, but in subsequent decades.

CONTRASTS BETWEEN THE NORTH AND SOUTH

North's analysis casts a powerful light on differences between antebellum industrialization in the

FIGURE 11.2 Hypothetical Determination of Regional Growth and Urban Location

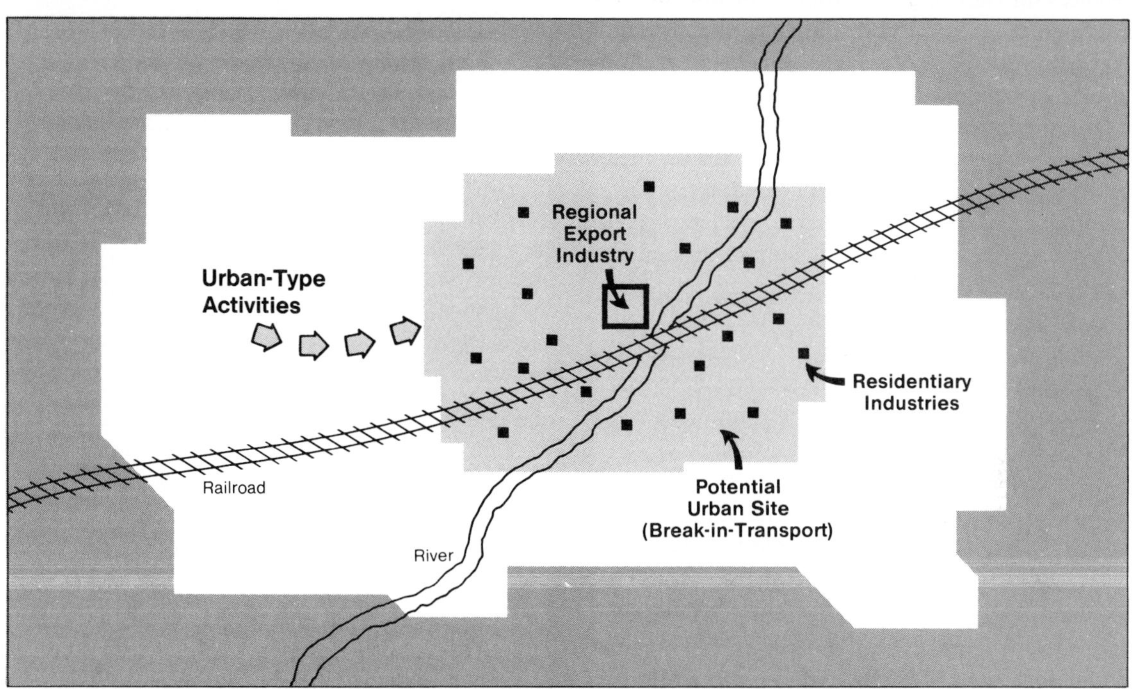

The region's development begins with the exploitation of an export industry. Income from it supports a social infrastructure as well as secondary industries. The break-in-transport, together with local transport costs and topography, will produce the potential urban site. The external economies of the break-in-transport will pull activities toward the urban site wherever profitable.

North and South. It is generally held that, by 1860, industrialization in the South was far below its apparent potential compared to such achievements in the North. The work of Fred Bateman and Thomas Weiss underscores this point, but these authors have demonstrated that the differences are more of a puzzle than initially assumed because of the accepted tradition of "Southern backwardness" in U.S. historiography.[57] In 1860, manufacturing in the South's major industries such as cotton textile production, boots and shoes, clothing, and flour and milling came to only about 20 percent of the national total, and Southern cotton mills were only a third the size of those typically found in New England. Although there were some larger Southern industrial firms, the Southern manufacturing firm typically was smaller than one in New England, or even in the new states of the Northwest, and was often found in an isolated rural location. There is no obvious reason why this size differential should have been so. Bateman and Weiss demonstrate that profitability in Southern manufacturing was comparable to that in the North and West and should have justified a more extensive development than did occur, other things being equal. They offer several possible reasons why it did not:

> Southern investors were exceptionally risk averse, were not knowledgeable about the benefits of diversification, failed to alter their expectations in the light of accumulating evidence on the greater profitability of manufacturing, or attached unagreeably high social costs to industrial diversification.[58]

Jeremy Atack attempted to explain regional differences through an examination of mainly theoretical possibilities and to contend with those who maintain that the very structure of the antebellum South (low population density, lack of consuming power among slaves and poor whites, preference of the rich for imports and handcrafted luxuries, etc.) inhibited Southern industrial development.[59] He found that differences in returns to scale and external economies were not sufficient to explain the Southern deficiency in developing industrial potentials. So far as Atack's evidence goes, the scale and the extent of industry in the South by 1860 were fully justified by existing technical and other conditions. Southern entrepreneurs were neither lax nor sluggish.

The expectation of rents in cotton production and of capital gains in slave-ownership helps to resolve these puzzles. The South did not industrialize as rapidly as the North did before the Civil War for many reasons—some logical, some nonsensical. Virtually all the arguments developed in this chapter about the character of American industrialization could apply equally well in the North and the South, especially once steam power neutralized New England's relative advantage as the owner of more waterpower sites. The South, when it did develop its industrial potential, was typically "American" in its choice of techniques. Sokoloff and Tchakerian find, comparing counties specializing in the same agricultural products, that there is little difference in manufacturing output per capita. In those Southern counties specializing in cotton, manufacturing output per capita was exceptionally low.[60] Before 1860, while there were good, purely business reasons to invest in manufacturing, those who had capital to invest elected in large measure to stay with slavery and cotton production. The export base in the South supported a sufficient number of secondary industries, as Bateman, Weiss, and Atack show. However, it was only after the expectation of greater returns on dollars invested in slave-based Southern agriculture vanished that capital flowed more readily into Southern manufacturing, flowing in sufficient volume to transform local industrial establishments into part of the new export base that was to come from Southern industrialization.

MANUFACTURING AND THE TARIFF QUESTION

To complete our preliminary survey of American manufacturing's origins, we should consider the tariff, not so much because of its purely economic importance in the nineteenth century, but because of its never-ending political interest. To consumers, a **tariff** is a tax they pay on goods imported from other countries. It is a transfer from domestic consumers to protected domestic producers. Those who produce goods that are competitive with the imports can raise their own offer prices because the prices of imported goods are now higher. The tariff is thus a financial umbrella for high-cost domestic producers, or else it adds an element of pure profit to sales and may induce a higher rate of investment in protected industries than otherwise would be warranted.

Consumers who buy the import-competing goods suffer losses in real income because of the tariff-inspired price increases. Foreigners lose income if Americans do not buy as many of their products because of the tariff, and, as a result, American exporters (such as Southern cotton growers) lose customers abroad. Who gains from the tariff? The government gets tax revenue. Producers of import-competing goods get more customers or higher prices or both, those who work in such industries may receive higher wages than they might otherwise, and higher prospective returns resulting from the tariff may induce investors to put their money into protected industries.

To producers, the tariff is a subsidy, and, like most subsidies, it distorts economic processes away from market solutions. As John James has shown, the antebellum tariff shifted resources from the South to industry in the North, a fact Southerners appreciated early in American history.[61]

Why do tariffs exist? Obviously governments want them for revenue (provided they are not *too* protective, stopping imports and revenue altogether). Rent-seeking producers want them for their extra revenues. Who else?

Tariffs have always been popular with politicians as surefire vote-getters. Modern arguments for them usually stress protection of American jobs. If Americans buy foreign cars, American auto workers may be

Exterior and interior views of the Paterson (New Jersey) Iron Works in 1856.

laid off. The argument is absolutely true. The obvious response to it is that American manufacturers should make better, cheaper cars. In earlier times tariffs were needed, it was said, to protect American workers from the products of "cheap foreign labor," which was mainly a bogus argument. Foreign labor was so cheap then because it was so unproductive. The argument was always good for votes, however, because Americans knew that foreign workers had low standards of living; they feared that competition might drive down the American standard. In recent years, this argument is heard less since it is affluent German, Swedish, and Japanese workers who produce the goods Americans want in such volumes, and those workers are both highly competent and highly paid.

The early "unanswerable" argument for tariffs was the "infant-industry" argument—that, as economic development proceeds, a country's new industries may require short-term protection in order to compete effectively against the established industries of other countries. If such industries have to meet international competition in their start-up phase, they will not mature to where they have a comparative advantage. It was stated in the first U.S. tariff act, passed 4 July 1789:

> Whereas it is necessary for the support of the government, for the discharge of the debts of the United States, and the encouragement of manufactures, that duties be laid on goods, wares and merchandise imported....

No question here of consumer welfare, free trade, or economic efficiency. The tariff was to raise money for the government and to protect infant American industry from foreign competition. The revenue-raising and the infant-industry arguments are seldom heard today. Customs duties (tariffs) no longer amount even to 1 percent of federal revenues; in 1790, they were 99.9 percent of total revenues, and in 1860, still 94 percent. In some years, high land sales changed the proportions, but generally, up to 1860, the tariff was the mainstay of federal revenues.

The argument for protection is separate since the "perfectly" protective tariff would kill off imports altogether and would reduce government customs revenues to zero. As for protection, Frank Taussig, studying the lusty infant (still protected) industries nearly a century after the first tariff, doubted that any of them owed their successes to the tariff, apart from the ever-anemic American silk (worm) industry and cotton manufacturing up to 1824.[62] From the 1790s to 1815, American cotton manufacturers had been protected from foreign competition by incessant European wars. When peace came in 1815 and British manufactured textiles hit American shores in full force, the American manufacturers went to Congress with the infant-industry argument, asked for protection, and got it. Peter Temin shows that Francis Lowell, in the tariff of 1816, went after a flat rate, minimum 25 cents per yard on imported cotton cloth. This was a *high* specific tariff for low-count cloth, the kind Lowell's mills produced. It was designed to cut out low-count cloth from places like India, but it did not interfere significantly with the finer cloth imports from places like England. Southerners were satisfied with this tariff, and it produced a transfer to Lowell, while the Rhode Island mills, which produced higher-count cloth, got little protection.[63] Alexander Hamilton, in his *Report on Manufactures*, thought there might be something to the infant-industry argument. In 1816, Lowell seemed to be more "infant" than the fine cloth makers of Rhode Island.

Since the tariff was an income transfer to manufacturing, it was clear at the beginning what part of the country was *not* going to benefit from it. The South sold its products in the international market at international prices and either purchased its manufactured goods from rent-seeking American manufacturers protected by tariffs or else imported the manufactured goods and paid the duties. Because of this situation, the protective element in the tariff rankled Southern political leaders from the very beginning and was a source of increasing sectional division.

Agitation for greater protection of manufacturers in the North tended to be concentrated in or near cyclical depressions; thus, the main protective tariffs were passed in 1816, 1824, 1828, and 1842. The reasons for this singular correlation are obvious: In depressions prices tend to fall (or did, until recently) and tariffs reduce the extent to which they need to fall to meet foreign competition. The 1828 tariff act, known as the "Tariff of Abominations," raised the average rate on dutiable goods to 61 percent of value and inspired Southern statesmen, led by John C. Calhoun, to seriously reconsider the nature of the constitutional bargain that had been struck in 1789, and whether because of this issue the individual states might themselves "nullify" an act of Congress.

Underlining, perhaps, the wisdom of John C. Calhoun, Knick Harley recently revisited the antebellum tariff. Although most historians have argued the tariff had a modest effect on American industrialization, Harley concludes that the protective tariff was responsible for increasing the size of the American manufacturing sector in general, and cotton textiles in particular.

> The tariff reduced American imports and in turn reduced the export of foodstuffs. The main costs of the tariff thus fell on land, as the factor used intensively in food production. The West as well as the South were the principal losers from the protection of manufacturing.[64]

Utilizing a computable general equilibrium model, Harley calculates that, had the tariff been eliminated, the cotton textile industry would have shrunk to at least half its size. In an earlier study (without the aid of econometric analysis), Mark Bils concluded that the protective tariff was about the only reason the United States had a cotton textile industry as late as 1833![65] Compromise in 1833, federal surpluses at embarrassingly high levels, and lower tariffs in 1846 and 1857 blunted the force of the anti-tariff feelings in the South in the 1850s.

By 1860, tariff rates had fallen so low that tariff revenue as a percentage of the value of dutiable imports was a mere 19.7 percent, whereas in 1830, when the nullification controversy raged, that figure was 61.7 percent (see Figure 11.3). Thus, the growth of manufacturing took place in the presence of a declining tariff from 1833 to 1860. Although the tariff declined, it was a political issue of note, and it *did*, after all, gratuitously transfer income from the South and other nonindustrial areas to manufacturers. It is not accidental that when the Confederacy was defeated, rent-seeking manufacturers returned to drink from the tariff trough. The tariff percentage of dutiable import value rose to nearly 50 percent in

FIGURE 11.3 Tariff Revenue to Value of Dutiable Imports, 1820–1860

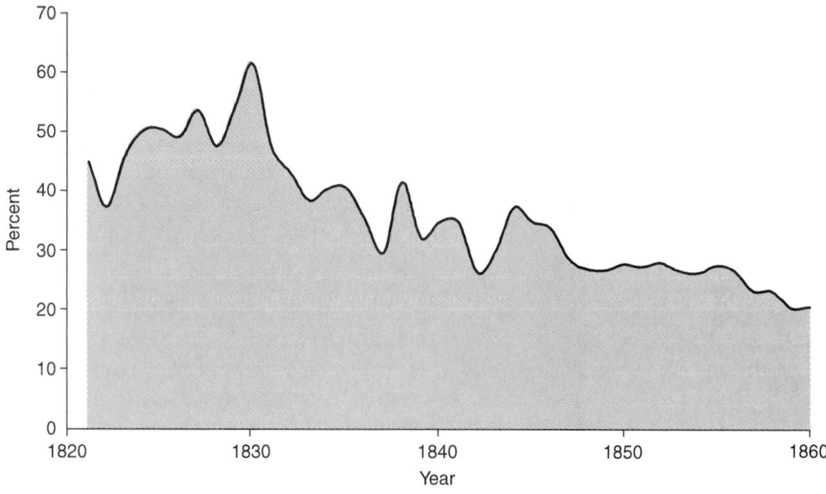

Source: *Historical Statistics,* series U 212

By 1860, tariff revenues as a percentage of dutiable imports were 40 percent of what they had been in the 1820s.

1865 and, with the exception of 1873 and 1874, was never below 40 percent again until the 1920s. The tariff may not have determined the growth of American industry, as Taussig pointed out, but it did generate extra income for manufacturers at the expense of everyone else—a fact that John C. Calhoun had well understood about tariffs designed to encourage "infant industries."

NOTES

1. Quoted in Jonathan Hughes, *Industrialization and Economic History: Theses and Conjectures* (1970), p. 74.
2. For a fuller discussion of entrepreneurial migration and suggested readings on the topic, see Hughes (1970), pp. 71–77.
3. Paul Uselding, "Henry Burden and the Question of Anglo-American Technological Transfer in the Nineteenth Century," *JEH*, June 1970.
4. Hughes (1970), p. 132.
5. For a detailed analysis of this industry, see Robert Brooke Zevin, "The Growth of Cotton Textile Production After 1815," in Robert Fogel and Stanley Engerman, eds., *The Reinterpretation of American Economic History* (1971), chap. 10.
6. Jonathan Hughes, *The Vital Few: American Economic Progress and Its Protagonists* (1986), p. 123.
7. Quoted in Hughes (1986), p. 141.
8. *Ibid.*, pp. 141–142.
9. Nathan Rosenberg, "Anglo-American Wage Differences in the 1820s," *JEH*, June 1967.
10. Moreover, the evidence for 1821–1859 shows that unskilled wages rose at an average annual rate of 1.4 percent compared to 1.0 percent for skilled workers in the antebellum period, reinforcing the pattern. Robert Margo and Georgia Villaflor, "The Growth of Wages in Antebellum America: New Evidence," *Journal of Economic History*, vol. XLVII, no. 4, December 1987. Gerald Friedman's findings show that after the Civil War this pattern was finally reversed, that skilled wages, 85 percent above unskilled in 1903, exceeded unskilled by 80 percent in 1890 and only 61 percent in 1880. The huge influx of unskilled labor in the great Atlantic migration of the late nineteenth century seemed to overwhelm the historic pattern established in the early industrial period. Gerald Friedman, "Strike Success and Union Ideology: The United States and France,

1880–1914," *Journal of Economic History*, vol. XLVIII, no. 1, March 1988.
11. Nathan Rosenberg, *Technology and American Economic Growth* (1972), p. 50.
12. By 1871, Henry Burden's machines, could produce 3,600 horseshoes an hour. Uselding (1970), p. 331.
13. See, for example, Nathan Rosenberg, ed., *The American System of Manufacturers: The Report of the Committee on the Machinery of the United States 1855 and the Special Reports of George Wallis and Joseph Whitworth 1854* (Edinburgh: Edinburgh University Press, 1969).
14. Merritt Roe Smith, *Harper's Ferry Armory and the New Technology* (1977) and "Army Ordnance and the 'American System' of Manufacturing, 1815–1861," in Smith, ed., *Military Enterprise and Technological Change: Perspectives on the American Experience* (Cambridge: MIT Press, 1985); David A. Hounshell, *From the American System to Mass Production, 1800–1932* (1984).
15. Donald Hoke, *Ingenious Yankees: The Rise of the American System of Manufacturers in the Private Sector* (New York: Columbia University Press, 1990), p. 258.
16. H. J. Habakkuk, *American and British Technology in the Nineteenth Century: The Search for Labour-Saving Inventions* (1962). For a qualification of the Habakkuk thesis in bold form, Paul Uselding, "Factor Substitution and Labor Productivity Growth in American Manufacturing 1839–1899," *JEH*, September 1972.
17. Habakkuk (1962), chap. III.
18. Stated thus boldly, the essence of the "Habakkuk thesis" is simplicity itself. Underpinning it with relevant wage data has proved to be a challenging enterprise. Nathan Rosenberg, "Anglo-American Wage Differentials in the 1820s," *JEH*, June 1967; Donald Adams, Jr., "Wage Rates in the Early National Period: Philadelphia 1785–1830," *JEH*, September 1968; Jeffrey Zabler, "Further Evidence on American Wage Differentials, 1800–1830," *EEH*, Fall 1972; Donald Adams, Jr., "Wage Rates in the Iron Industry: A Comment," *EEH*, Fall 1973; Jeffrey Zabler, "More on Wage Rates in the Iron Industry: A Reply," *EEH*, Fall 1973.
19. Paul David, *Technical Choice, Innovation and Economic Growth* (1975).
20. Technologies abandoned in one economy need not be in another, and a technology can be improved over time in one area even if abandoned elsewhere. An interesting example of this, and a rare case of re-switching, came with the reawakened interest in wood stoves for heating in the late 1970s. These stoves had long been abandoned in favor of cheap (and more convenient) oil in New England. When OPEC fuel oil prices became prohibitive in the late 1970s, New Englanders were driven back to their inexhaustible (and labor-using) wood supplies. They were surprised and delighted with wood stoves imported from Scandinavia, where they had not been abandoned and had been enormously improved. A technique viewed as outmoded in the 1930s had been improved to an astonishing degree in 40 years.
21. William Lazonick, "Production Relations, Labor Productivity, and the Choice of Technique: British and U.S. Cotton Spinning," *JEH*, September 1981.
22. Claudia Goldin and Kenneth Sokoloff, "The Relative Productivity Hypothesis of Industrialization: The American Case, 1820 to 1850," *QJE*, August 1984.
23. Kenneth Sokoloff, "Productivity Growth in Manufacturing during Early Industrialization: Evidence from the American Northeast, 1820–1860," in Stanley Engerman and Robert Gallman, eds., *Long-Term Factors in American Economic Growth* (1986), p. 724. See also Sokoloff and David Dollar, "Agriculture Seasonality and the Organization of Manufacturing in Early Industrial Economies: the Contrast Between England and the United States," *Journal of Economic History*, vol. 57, no. 2, June 1997.
24. Kenneth Sokoloff, "Was the Transition from the Artisanal Shop to the Nonmechanized Factory Associated with Gains in Efficiency? Evidence from the U.S. Manufacturing Censuses of 1820 and 1850," *EEH*, October 1984. Herbert Kisch, *From Domestic Manufacture to Industrial Revolution* (New York: Oxford University Press, 1989). Kisch says that the original idea of the "proto-factory" appeared in Fritz Redlich and Hermann Freudenberger, "The Industrial Development of Europe: Reality, Symbols, Images," *Kyklos*, vol. 25, 1964, p. 381. The generalization of an evolutionary route to industrialization in Europe is set out thusly by Joel Mokyr: "… the Industrial Revolution consisted of the emergence of a germinal modern sector, which gradually increased its weight in the economy until it ended up dominating the economy entirely." "Growing-Up and the Industrial Revolution in Europe," *Explorations in Economic History*, vol. 13, no. 4, October 1976, p. 372. For a survey of the idea of "proto-industrialization" in its complete effulgence, D. C. Coleman, "Proto-Industrialization: A Concept Too Many," *Economic History Review*, vol. XXXVI, no. 3, August 1983.
25. Kenneth Sokoloff, "Invention, Innovation, and Manufacturing Productivity Growth in the Antebellum Northeast," in Robert Gallman and John Wallis, eds., *American Economic Growth and Standards of Living before the Civil War* (1992). This essay includes a valuable summary of much of Sokoloff's work on this topic.
26. Jacob Schmookler, *Invention and Economic Growth* (Cambridge: Harvard University Press, 1966).
27. Kenneth Sokoloff and Zorina Khan, "The Democratization of Invention during Early Industrialization: Evidence from the United States, 1790–1846," *JEH*, June 1990.

28. Edward Ames and Nathan Rosenberg, "Changing Technological Leadership and Industrial Growth," *EJ*, March 1963.
29. Habakkuk (1962), p. 123.
30. Rosenberg, *Technology and American Economic Growth* (1972), p. 44.
31. *Ibid.*, pp. 18–24.
32. *Ibid.*, p. 27.
33. *Ibid.*, p. 28.
34. Peter Temin, "Manufacturing," in Davis, et al., *American Economic Growth* (1972).
35. Peter Temin, *Iron and Steel in Nineteenth Century America* (1964).
36. Rosenberg, *Technology and American Economic Growth* (1972), pp. 63–64.
37. Nathan Rosenberg, "Technological Change in the Machine Tool Industry, 1840–1910," *JEH*, December 1963.
38. The number of horses in this country peaked at an incredible 21.4 million in 1915, and there still were 4.7 persons per horse that far into the age of the railroad and the internal combustion engine! The data for animals in this passage are from *Historical Statistics*, series K 564–582; the estimate of total horsepower of all prime movers, from series S 1–14.
39. Peter Temin, "Steam and Water Power in the Early 19th Century," in Robert Fogel and Stanley Engerman, eds., *The Reinterpretation of American Economic History* (1971), p. 231.
40. Rosenberg, *Technology and American Economic Growth* (1972), p. 64.
41. Jeremy Atack, Fred Bateman, and Thomas Weiss, "The Regional Diffusion and Adoption of The Steam Engine in American Manufacturing," *JEH*, June 1980, p. 285.
42. As noted previously, by 1869, steam had only barely surpassed waterpower as prime movers. Atack, Bateman, and Weiss (1980), p. 282, fn. 10.
43. Temin (1971), pp. 230–235.
44. *Ibid.*, p. 231, Table 1.
45. *Ibid.*, p. 197, Table 4.
46. In the New England textile industry, the preferences of industrial lenders also played a part: Lance Davis, "Sources of Industrial Finance: The American Textile Industry, A Case Study," *EEH*, April 1957 and "The New England Textile Mills and the Capital Markets: A Study of Industrial Borrowing, 1840–1860," *JEH*, March 1960.
47. Temin (1971), p. 191, Table 1.
48. Uselding (1970), pp. 332–333.
49. Temin (1971), pp. 232–233.
50. Rosenberg, *Technology and American Economic Growth* (1972), p. 65, fn. 6. Also see Harlan Halsey, "The Choice Between High-Pressure and Low-Pressure Steam Power in America in the Early Nineteenth Century," *Journal of Economic History*, vol. LXI, no. 4, December 1981.
51. Quoted in Temin (1971), p. 228. Rapid innovation in the machine technology did not necessarily mean that American technology was "capital intensive," measured in money terms. For example, in most uses a Honda is more "efficient" than a Rolls Royce, and several Hondas may be purchased with the technical improvements "embodied" in each new model, while one Rolls Royce is being fully depreciated. Perhaps such considerations help explain the recent findings of Alexander Field that nineteenth-century British manufacturing seems to have been more "capital intensive" than American manufacturing, measured either as the money value of installed machinery to output or to labor. Alexander Field, "On the Unimportance of Machinery," *EEH*, October 1985.
52. William Dean was the main innovator of the location paradigm just described. It can be used to explain the location of Chicago. Louis Cain, "William Dean's Theory of Urban Growth: Chicago's Commerce and Industry, 1854–1871," *JEH*, June 1985.
53. Douglass North, "Location Theory and Regional Economic Growth," *JPE*, June 1955; "Agriculture and Regional Economic Growth," *Proceedings of the American Farm Economics Association*, December 1959. The two analyses are combined in *The Economic Growth of the United States 1790–1860* (Englewood Cliffs, NJ: Prentice-Hall, 1961), chap. 1.
54. Rosenberg, *Technology and American Economic Growth* (1972), p. 48.
55. The problem was worked out long ago by the German economist August Lösch. Stefan Valavanis, "Lösch on Location," *American Economic Review*, vol. XLV, no. 4, September 1955.
56. For applications of location theory to Chicago's site and growth, see Louis Cain, *Sanitation Strategy for a Lakefront Metropolis: The Case of Chicago* (DeKalb: Northern Illinois University Press, 1979) and "From Mud to Metropolis: Chicago before the Fire," in Paul Uselding, ed., *REH*, (1986), vol. 10.
57. Fred Bateman and Thomas Weiss, "Manufacturing in the Antebellum South," in Paul Uselding, ed., *REH* (1976) vol. 1.
58. Bateman and Weiss (1976), p. 161.
59. Jeremy Atack, "Returns to Scale in Antebellum United States Manufacturing," *EEH*, October 1977.
60. Kenneth Sokoloff and Viken Tchakerian, "Manufacturing Where Agriculture Predominates: Evidence from the South and Midwest in 1860," *Explorations in Economic History*, vol. 34, no. 3, July 1997.
61. John James, "The Welfare Effects of the Antebellum Tariff: A General Equilibrium Analysis," *EEH*, July 1978. But there were possible effects that aided Southern cotton producers at various points in time, depending

upon the effects on demand for raw cotton produced by the growth of Northern textile manufacturing. Clayne Pope, "The Impact of the Ante-Bellum Tariff on Income Distribution," *EEH*, Summer 1972; Bennett Baack and Edward Ray, "Tariff Policy and Income Distribution: The Case of the United States 1830–1860," *EEH*, Winter 1973–74.

62. Frank Taussig, *The Tariff History of the United States* (1888). Zevin, "The Growth of Cotton Textile Production After 1815," shows a complex shifting of demand, supply, and technical change accounting for the cotton textile industry's growth, with the major technical innovations coming before 1825. Although it would be difficult to prove that these innovations were the *results* of tariff protection, they certainly would not have harmed investors. Would they have taken place in any case? No doubt, but perhaps with different timing. Zevin thinks the initial impetus of growth in this industry was mainly due to factory production itself, which shifted the industry out of people's homes.
63. Peter Temin, "Product Quality and Vertical Integration in the Early Cotton Textile Industry," *JEH*, December 1988.
64. C. Knick. Harley, "The Antebellum American Tariff: Food Exports and Manufacturing," *EEH*, October 1992, p. 398.
65. Mark Bils, "Tariff Protection and Production in the Early U.S. Cotton Textile Industry," *JEH*, December 1984.

SUGGESTED READINGS

Articles

Adams, Donald R., Jr. "Wage Rates in the Iron Industry: A Comment." *Explorations in Economic History*, vol. 11, no. 1, Fall 1973.

———. "Wage Rates in the Early National Period: Philadelphia, 1785–1830." *Journal of Economic History*, vol. XXVIII, no. 3, September 1968.

Ames, Edward, and Nathan Rosenberg. "Changing Technological Leadership and Industrial Growth." *Economic Journal*, vol. 73, no. 289, March 1963.

Atack, Jeremy. "Fact or Fiction? The Relative Costs of Steam and Water Power: A Simulative Approach." *Explorations in Economic History*, vol. 16, no. 4, October 1979.

———. "Returns to Scale in Antebellum United States Manufacturing." *Explorations in Economic History*, vol. 14, no. 4, October 1977.

———, Fred Bateman, and Thomas Weiss. "The Regional Diffusion and Adoption of the Steam Engine in American Manufacturing." *Journal of Economic History*, vol. XL, no. 2, June 1980.

Baack, Bennett P., and Edward J. Ray. "Tariff Policy and Income Distribution: The Case of the U.S., 1830–1860." *Explorations in Economic History*, vol. 11, no. 2, Winter 1973–1974.

Bateman, Fred, James Faust, and Thomas Weiss. "Profitability in Southern Manufacturing: Estimates for 1860." *Explorations in Economic History*, vol. 12, no. 3, July 1975.

Bateman, Fred, and Thomas Weiss. "Comparative Regional Development in Antebellum Manufacturing." *Journal of Economic History*, vol. XXXV, no. 1, March 1975.

———. "Manufacturing in the Antebellum South." In Paul Uselding, ed., *Research in Economic History*, vol. 1, 1976.

Bils, Mark. "Tariff Protection and Production in the Early U.S. Cotton Textile Industry." *Journal of Economic History*, vol. XLIV, no. 4, December 1984.

Brito, D. L., and Jeffrey G. Williamson. "Skilled Labor and Nineteenth Century Anglo-American Managerial Behavior." *Explorations in Economic History*, vol. 10, no. 3, Spring 1973.

Cain, Louis. "William Dean's Theory of Urban Growth: Chicago's Commerce and Industry, 1854–1871." *Journal of Economic History*, vol. XLV, no. 2, June 1985.

———. "From Mud to Metropolis: Chicago before the Fire." In Paul Uselding, ed., *Research in Economic History*. Greenwich, CT: JAI Press, 1986, vol. 10.

David, Paul. "The Horndal Effect in Lowell, 1834–1856: A Short-Run Learning Curve for Integrated Cotton Textile Mills." *Explorations in Economic History*, vol. 10, no. 2, Winter 1973.

———. "Learning by Doing and Tariff Protection: A Reconsideration of the Case of the Antebellum United States Textile Industry." *Journal of Economic History*, vol. XXX, no. 3, September 1970.

Davis, Lance E. "Sources of Industrial Finance: The American Textile Industry, A Case Study." *Explorations in Economic History*, 1st series, vol. LX, no. 4, April 1957.

———. "The New England Textile Mills and the Capital Markets: A Study of Industrial Borrowing, 1840–1860." *Journal of Economic History*, vol. XX, no. 1, March 1960.

Field, Alexander J. "Sectoral Shift in Antebellum Massachusetts: A Reconsideration." *Explorations in Economic History*, vol. 15, no. 2, April, 1978.

———. "On the Unimportance of Machinery." *Explorations in Economic History*, vol. 22, no. 4, October 1985.

Goldin, Claudia D., and Frank D. Lewis. "The Role of Exports in American Economic Growth During the Napoleonic Wars, 1793 to 1807." *Explorations in Economic History*, vol. 17, no. 1, January 1980.

Goldin, Claudia, and Kenneth Sokoloff. "The Relative Productivity Hypothesis of Industrialization; The American

Case, 1820 to 1850." *Quarterly Journal of Economics*, vol. LXIX, no. 3, August 1984.

Harley, C. Knick. "The Antebellum American Tariff: Food Exports and Manufacturing." *Explorations in Economic History*, vol. 29, no. 4, October 1992.

James, John. "The Welfare Effects of the Antebellum Tariff: A General Equilibrium Analysis." *Explorations in Economic History*, vol. 15, no. 3, July 1978.

Lazonick, William H. "Production Relations, Labor Productivity, and Choice of Technique: British and U.S. Cotton Spinning." *Journal of Economic History*, vol. XLI, no. 3, September 1981.

Livesay, Harold, and Glenn Porter. "The Financial Role of Merchants in the Development of U.S. Manufacturing, 1815–1860." *Explorations in Economic History*, vol. 9, no. 1, Fall 1971.

North, Douglass C. "Location Theory and Regional Economic Growth." *Journal of Political Economy*, vol. LXII, no. 3, June 1955.

———. "Agriculture and Regional Economic Growth." *Proceedings of the American Farm Economic Association*, vol. XLI, no. 5, December 1959.

Passell, Peter, and Maria Schmundt. "Pre-Civil War Land Policy and The Growth of Manufacturing." *Explorations in Economic History*, vol. 9, no. 1, Fall 1971.

Pope, Clayne. "The Impact of the Antebellum Tariff on Income Distribution." *Explorations in Economic History*, vol. 9, no. 4, Summer 1972.

Rosenberg, Nathan. "Technological Change in the Machine-Tool Industry, 1840–1910." *Journal of Economic History*, vol. XXIII, no. 4, December 1963.

———. "Anglo-American Wage Differences in the 1820s." *Journal of Economic History*, vol. XXVII, no. 2, June, 1967.

———. "Factors Affecting the Diffusion of Technology." *Explorations in Economic History*, vol. 10, no. 1, Fall 1972.

Sokoloff, Kenneth L. "Was the Transition from the Artisanal Shop to the Nonmechanized Factory Associated with Gains in Efficiency? Evidence from the U.S. Manufacturing Censuses of 1820 and 1850." *Explorations in Economic History*, vol. 21, no. 4, October 1984.

———. "Productivity Growth in Manufacturing during Early Industrialization: Evidence from the American Northeast, 1820–60." In Stanley Engerman and Robert Gallman, eds., *Long-Term Factors in American Economic Growth*. Chicago: University of Chicago Press, 1986.

———. "Invention, Innovation, and Manufacturing Productivity Growth in the Antebellum Northeast." In Robert Gallman and John Wallis, eds., *American Economic Growth and Standards of Living before the Civil War*. Chicago: University of Chicago Press, 1992.

———, and Zorina Khan. "The Democratization of Invention during Early Industrialization: Evidence from the United States, 1790–1846." *Journal of Economic History*, vol. 50, no. 2, June 1990.

Temin, Peter. "Steam and Water Power in the Early 19th Century." *Journal of Economic History*, vol. XXVI, no. 2, June 1966. Reprinted in Robert Fogel and Stanley Engerman, eds., *The Reinterpretation of American Economic History*. New York: Harper & Row, 1971.

———. "Manufacturing." In Lance E. Davis et al., *American Economic Growth: An Economist's History of the United States*. New York: Harper & Row, 1972.

———. "Product Quality and Vertical Integration in the Early Cotton Industry." *Journal of Economic History*, vol. XLVIII, no. 4, December 1988.

Terrill, Tom E. "Eager Hands: Labor for Southern Textiles, 1850–1860." *Journal of Economic History*, vol. XXXVI, no. 1, March 1976.

Uselding, Paul. "Henry Burden and the Question of Anglo-American Technological Transfer in the Nineteenth Century." *Journal of Economic History*, vol. XXX, no. 2, June 1970.

———. "Technical Progress at the Springfield Armory." *Explorations in Economic History*, vol. 9, no. 3, Spring 1972.

———. "Factor Substitution and Labor Productivity Growth in American Manufacturing 1839–1899." *Journal of Economic History*, vol. XXXII, no. 3, September 1972.

———. "A Note on the Inter-Regional Trade in Manufactures in 1840." *Journal of Economic History*, vol. XXXV, no. 2, June 1976.

Zabler, Jeffrey F. "Further Evidence on American Wage Differentials, 1800–1830." *Explorations in Economic History*, vol. 10, no. 1, Fall 1972.

———. "More on Wage Rates in the Iron Industry: A Reply." *Explorations in Economic History*, vol. 11, no. 1, Fall 1973.

Zevin, Robert Brooke. "The Growth of Cotton Textile Production After 1815." In Robert Fogel and Stanley Engerman, eds., *The Reinterpretation of American Economic History*. New York: Harper & Row, 1971.

Books

Clark, Victor S. *History of Manufactures in the United States 1607–1860*. Washington, D.C.: The Carnegie Institution, 1929.

Cole, A.H. *The American Wool Manufacture*. Cambridge: Harvard University Press, 1926.

David, Paul A. *Technical Choice, Innovation and Economic Growth*. New York: Cambridge University Press, 1975.

Habakkuk, H. J. *American and British Technology in the Nineteenth Century: The Search for Labor Saving Inventions*. New York: Cambridge University Press, 1962.

Hounshell, David A. *From the American System to Mass Production, 1800–1932: The Development of Manufacturing Technology in the United States*. Baltimore: Johns Hopkins University Press, 1984.

Hughes, Jonathan. *Industrialization and Economic History: Theses and Conjectures*. New York: McGraw-Hill, 1970.

———. *The Vital Few: American Economic Progress and Its Protagonists.* New York: Oxford University Press, 1986.

Rosenberg, Nathan. *Technology and American Economic Growth.* New York: Harper & Row, 1972.

Smith, Merritt Roe. *Harper's Ferry Armory and the New Technology.* Ithaca, NY: Cornell University Press, 1977.

Taussig, Frank W. *The Tariff History of the United States.* New York: Putnam's Sons, 1888.

Temin, Peter. *Iron and Steel in Nineteenth-Century America: An Economic Study.* Cambridge: MIT Press, 1964.

Ware, C. F. *The Early New England Cotton Manufacture: A Study of Industrial Beginnings.* Boston: Houghton Mifflin Company, 1931.

CHAPTER TWELVE

The Financial System and the International Economy

Let's retrace our steps to follow the financial system's development during the antebellum period. In finance, the Americans relied on their colonial habits and inclinations about paper money, but that money was *privately* issued after 1790. The needs and consequences of Revolutionary War finance had to be accommodated by new institutions, and stresses developed between the sovereign state powers and the pressures to devise a workable set of national practices and institutions related to banking and money.

CURRENCY AND BANKING DEVELOPMENTS

Financing the Revolution was a "near thing," as Wellington said of Waterloo. The Americans barely brought it off. The Continental Congress did not have the authority to levy taxes during the Revolution, nor was there any systematic way to raise financial support from the states. From 1776 to 1780, Congress paid bills by printing paper money. Too much was printed relative to either specie reserves or hope of redemption in specie, and it depreciated badly. A total of $241.6 million was issued by 1780, driving all specie out of circulation (Gresham's Law again).

In 1780, the states were asked to levy taxes to redeem the Continental currency at a ratio of $40 Continental to $1 silver. Congress then issued a new currency to redeem the old from the states at a ratio of $20 to $1. The old bills that were not turned in depreciated finally to about $1,000 to $1—hence the phrase "not worth a Continental." From 1776 to 1782, Congress also borrowed domestically about $63.6 million (worth only $7.7 million in specie). From 1780 to 1783, foreign borrowing ($7.8 million, of which $6.4 million came from France alone) and requisitions (honored only in part) on the individual states were the main sources of national finance. After their surrender at Yorktown, the British lost their taste for any more war with their North American colonies—at least for the next quarter century, and there was no need to raise more funds to extend the fighting.

In addition, the states had borrowed and issued paper money of their own, bills of credit and paper money with a nominal value of $209 million. In its efforts to provide financial organization, Congress chartered the Bank of North America in 1781. The bank was a *limited-liability corporation* that handled the government's finances as best it could and, in most respects, did the chores of a central bank. Studenski and Krooss consider this the first real U.S.

central bank, an appellation usually reserved for the Bank of the United States chartered in 1791.[1] The Bank of North America received a charter from Pennsylvania in 1787 and became a state bank.

Hamilton's Policies

Between 1783 and 1787, the central government's fiscal affairs deteriorated badly; it could not tax, it made little revenue from sales of public lands, and it was forced to borrow from foreign (Dutch) bankers to stay afloat. The new Constitution in 1789 established the federal government on a completely different and potentially powerful financial basis, giving it the authority to levy taxes, to borrow, and to issue money and "regulate" its value. In the process, the states gave up their right to issue money. They did so, according to Rolnick, Smith, and Weber, because, first as colonies and then as states, they had experienced exchange rate variability and had come to prefer a monetary union.[2]

The constitutional powers were followed by vigorous policies devised by Secretary of the Treasury Alexander Hamilton. Only partly achieved (and bitterly opposed by many at the time), Hamilton's policies now have come to be viewed as brilliant in conception, although imperfect in execution. They were: (a) establishment of tariffs and other taxes for federal revenue, (b) complete refunding (with arrangements for redemption) of the wartime debts of the Continental Congress, (c) assumption by the federal government of the states' wartime debts, (d) establishment of a new central bank, and (e) creation of a national currency standard based upon newly minted coins.

Beginning with the tariff law of 1789, Hamilton's immediate designs were realized in part. As discussed in Chapter 11, the tariff yielded nearly all federal government revenues. The internal taxes Hamilton wanted yielded much less, and one—the tax on whiskey—provoked the "Whiskey Rebellion" in 1794 among the farmers of western Pennsylvania. On-the-farm whiskey distilleries were a favored technology at the time for "storing" surplus grains. The rebellion was put down by militia without bloodshed.

Hamilton estimated that the national debt in 1790 was about $54 million, and that the outstanding state war debts totaled about $25 million. In 1790 and 1795, provisions were made to refund all this debt with various new issues and, then, ultimately to retire it by setting money aside in a *sinking fund*. The debt was never completely retired, although it very nearly vanished in 1835–1836 during Andrew Jackson's presidency. Instead, it rose and was replaced with new obligations that sold at high prices. Those who held the old debt profited handsomely since arrangements were made to refund and prices soared. Hamilton was castigated by his opponents, some of whom wanted the original owners of the obligations to be compensated. Jefferson, among others, also greatly doubted the extent to which the Revolutionary expenditures of the states had, in fact, been in the common cause.[3] Nevertheless, Hamilton's system was adopted almost in its entirety.

With their wartime debts taken over by the federal government, the states were placed on a sound financial basis. But, under the new Constitution, they had lost the power to issue their own paper money. The banks they created by acts of incorporation *could* do so, and did.

In 1791, a new central bank, the First Bank of the United States, was chartered for 20 years, with one-fifth of its stock held by the U.S. Treasury. The rest was held by private persons. Jefferson opposed this bank, as did many others, on the ground that the Constitution provided no such power and that the bank threatened to introduce all sorts of alien practices into the country.[4]

In 1792, the Mint Act provided for a mint in Philadelphia and placed the United States on a bimetallic basis: 15 ounces of silver were equal to 1 ounce of gold. The coins were minted on a metric basis. There was to be a ten-dollar gold coin (the Eagle), a silver dollar, and fractional coins. There would be no national paper money.

What can be said of the whole system? As noted, the tariff was long the mainstay of federal finance, but the internal taxes were less successful. The assumption of Revolutionary debt by the federal government did establish the federal credit, as Hamilton had wished. The First Bank of the United States did an excellent job by all accounts but lost its recharter in 1811 (by one vote). In 1812, the United

States again went to war with Great Britain without a central bank and suffered accordingly. The government had difficulty financing the war, and, when specie payment was suspended in 1814, rapid inflation developed. Jenkins and Weidenmier estimate that the absence of a bank cost the government $46 million in that they were unable to sell bonds at par. In 1816, a new bank was chartered, the Second Bank of the United States, but its recharter was vetoed by Andrew Jackson in 1832. The next central bank, the Federal Reserve System, did not come about until 1914.[5]

Richard Sylla argues that Hamilton's policies, by the standard of their time, gave the U.S. a "world class" financial system at a very early date in its history. He emphasizes the close and synergistic ties this system created between the banking system and other financial markets. Whether U.S. economic growth was ultimately "finance-led," as Sylla argues, remains an open question; it is clearly the case that these policies facilitated growth at an early date.[6]

Little need be said here of the Mint Act. Bimetallism is a poor metallic system because the two metals fluctuate in price constantly against each other with strange results (thanks to Gresham's Law: "Bad money chases out good."). In Europe, gold prices rose in terms of silver, and the new gold coins were shipped almost as soon as they appeared in 1796. The silver coins were boxed up and shipped to the Caribbean, where they were exchanged for irregular, tarnished, and heavier Spanish dollars that were brought back to exchange for gold and/or new silver dollars. Thus, for a long time (until the mid–1830s) Americans had no metallic coin of their own in circulation and went back to the colonial practice of using foreign coins, even declaring some of them legal tender.[7] It made little difference, however, because the new state banks provided the currency the people used as a medium of exchange–paper.

Paper Money—State Bank Notes

As we have seen, the states retained the sovereign power to create corporations by special franchise. This power was quickly used to establish state-chartered private banks that issued their own paper money. The paper money was paid out when loans were made, in contrast to the modern practice of establishing a demand deposit against which checks may be written by the borrower. Although the new Constitution forbade the states to issue paper money, their creations, the state banks, supplied the needed amounts of it.[8]

The notes, unless presented for redemption, circulated at whatever value the market gave them. Guides ("currency detectors") for users of paper money were published commercially to indicate the possible market value of a note, based upon known assets, the characters of proprietors, and so forth. Checks and deposits were not much used before the 1830s. Bank loans thus gave rise to immediate circulation until they were presented for redemption in specie, sometimes long after the issuers had vanished into history. By 1860, there were 1,562 state banks in existence, and it is estimated that perhaps 10,000 different kinds of paper money were in circulation.

Much was once written about the colorful state banks and their wild "over-moneying," their notes called names like "blue monkey," or "sick Indian." The demise of the Second Bank has been blamed for all the economic calamities that followed in its wake—the Panic of 1837, the inflation that preceded it, and the depression years of 1839 to 1843. The argument was simply that without the Second Bank's restraining influence, banks, particularly "wildcat banks," took advantage of the situation and increased their note issues beyond what was warranted.[9]

Critics were puzzled by the tendency of the U.S. economy to grow despite its banking system.[10] The paper currency issues of the "wildcat banks" (however much undersecured by reserves they were) produced no sustained inflation at all. Prices moved generally downward throughout the period 1816 to 1860, with only slight cyclical upswings in the 1830s and the 1850s. Moreover, there is not the slightest evidence that "excess money" was the consequence of such liberal banking laws and the absence of a central bank. The money supply did not even grow as fast as did the population after the demise of the Second Bank of the United States (see Table 12.1). By modern standards, this was a most enviable performance, one that the post-World War II Federal Reserve System could not hope to emulate. Scholars such as Hugh Rockoff and Peter Temin show that this characterization of

TABLE 12.1 Population, Banking, and Price Data, 1836–1860

Year	*Population (in millions)*	*Total Bank Deposits (in millions)*	*Bank Note Circulation (in millions)*	*Total Bank Assets (in millions)*	*Wholesale Prices*[a]
1836	15.4	$166	$140	$ 622	$114
1860	31.5	310	207	1000	93
Percentage of Change	+104.7	+86.7	+47.9	+60.8	-18.4

[a] Indexed on the basis of 1910–1914 = 100.

Source: *Historical Statistics*, series A7, E52, X581, 585–586.

events is unfair to the Second Bank.[11] As Richard Sylla pointed out, the critical view of American banking in the antebellum period primarily resulted from public disapproval of bank fraud and failure.[12]

Learning New Techniques

This time of experimentation in the American economy was paralleled by European developments. Throughout the Western world in the first half of the nineteenth century, new financial techniques suitable for industrial economies (given local law and custom) were being tried out. The financial history of that period is strewn with the wreckage of failures, with ideas being abandoned, as well as successes being celebrated.[13] The American state banks were part of that learning process. The best financial technologies had to be found by trial and error.

The state-chartered banks were also part of the development of a system of financial intermediation in the early American economy peculiar to our needs and laws. State chartering created **unit banking**, many small banks, but, in the 1830s, there were several hundred separate banking companies in England, too. For the future, the difference lay in national amalgamation in England, which never occurred in the United States because of the separate powers of the states. Even now, there is little nationwide branch banking in the United States, as there is in England and Canada.

State banks were special-franchise corporations before 1838 and represented obvious rent-seeking behavior on the part of their owners as well as the social need for such financial services. But from 1838 to 1863 (the year of the National Banking Act), the spread of competitive "free banking" among the states represented more the need for financial intermediation than mere rent-seeking on the part of would-be local monopolists.

Both ideas later gave way to state banking control by commission and the national banking system. Both special franchises for banks and free banking were experiments, as were the so-called industrial banks—corporations set up for industrial purposes that contained banking powers in their charters. The idea did not work in the United States, but in Europe, banks that did all sorts of commercial banking (and were deeply engaged in transportation and industrial activities as well) became commonplace. Americans, like their British cousins, came to prefer that their commercial banks stick to banking and that they lend their funds out primarily for short periods only. As Robert Craig West has emphasized, this prejudice underlay, finally, the Federal Reserve legislation in 1913.[14]

The Need for Intermediation

The need for financial intermediation was obvious in colonial times, (a) in the efforts to create banks by charter (which the British stopped when the Bubble Act was applied to the Massachusetts Land Bank) and (b) in the nonincorporated banking business engaged in by groups of colonial merchants. **Intermediation**—all middleman activity between savers and borrowers—is part of the system of general communication in any society. In its purest form, intermediation is mere brokering. Some persons, businesses, or even regions generate a surplus from current business and household management, while others have need for funds beyond their own current *saving* (free resources not needed for current consumption).

Consider, for example, a person who wishes to build a house. This individual will probably need to borrow funds to do it. The property will be mortgaged to a lender on agreed terms, and the amount of the loan plus interest (the cost of the rent of the money) will be paid back over a fixed term of years. The interest here is a price mutually satisfactory to the lender and the borrower for the use of the money—claims over real resources. A lender whoin turn has borrowed the funds from others (as do bankers when they accept deposits) is then the intermediary.

The state banks accepted deposits and paid interest for them. Those who made the deposits earned interest for the use of their deposits. The banks then loaned the money out again at a higher interest charge, completing the circle of intermediation. By this means, the surpluses earned by some were kept "at work" by the industry of others. This function was socially useful, and it speeded up the pace of economic growth, or at least the possibilities for such growth.

Social Considerations

We can consider the intermediary function just described as the *mobilization of capital*. One role of intermediation—by banks, life insurance companies, savings and loan associations, the stock markets—is this mobilization. It is necessary, but the selection of borrowers is not a socially neutral practice. We will encounter much criticism in U. S. financial history (which continues today) of the social consequences of bank lending. The distribution of wealth and income is affected. Those who can pay get the funds and the potential benefit, and those who cannot, do not.

Many early New England banks were credit banks, not deposit banks; that is, their main business was to discount commercial paper rather than to solicit deposits. Naomi Lamoreaux has argued that these banks were extensions of a system of family capitalism, a mixing of banking and entrepreneurial ventures.[15] The bank marketed its shares to outsiders as a way of generating funds to lend to insiders. In the early nineteenth century, this was an accepted practice, but, as we will see in Chapter 19, public opinion had changed by the end of the century. Why, in the early years, did outsiders buy the shares of such banks? Lamoreaux argues that these banks were "investment clubs." Shares in a bank practicing insider lending were similar to shares in a mutual fund whose portfolio consisted of the enterprises of the family running the fund.

> It is important to recognize that early-nineteenth-century banks were not really commercial banks in the modern sense of the term but instead were essentially investment clubs. The sale of bank stock enabled small savers to buy shares in a diversified portfolio of investments, a portfolio whose character differed in important and known ways from one institution to the next. It thereby enabled small investors to participate in the activities of the local entrepreneurs they most admired.[16]

The sums thus raised were not trivial. Lamoreaux estimates the total resources of the banking sector in 1860 were of the same order of magnitude as the capital stock in the region's manufacturing sector.

In his study of New York and Pennsylvania banks, Robert Wright finds that these banks were more widely owned than Lamoreaux's New England banks. They had a large capitalization that forced their lending practices to be less concentrated; they lent to a wide variety of borrowers including small business and farmers. Howard Bodenhorn's study of antebellum banks reaches a similar conclusion, that urban banks largely lent to merchants and rural banks lent to farmers. Both Wright and Bodenhorn believe, like Lamoreaux, that the lending practices of their banks, outsider lending in this case, contributed to the economic development of the region in which they were located.[17]

The state banks, as profit-making institutions, naturally wanted to lend where interest was highest, and that often was where the risks were highest. Because depositors wanted their money back, the safety of the loans made by deposit banks became an issue. Since there was no obvious way to combine total safety with highest earnings, even the process of intermediation gave rise to difficulties. If safety (certainty of repayment on schedule) was the first consideration, then farmers likely would have trouble borrowing against the collateral of farm land. If safety were not a requirement, then banks would fail in hard times as their borrowers went broke, depositors would lose their money, and the entire community would suffer.

We will see how these largely incompatible demands upon banking practice created recurrent problems in American banks, repeated efforts at bank reform and demands by some elements, notably farmers, for government banks to meet their special requirements—once again, rent-seeking.

Fractional Reserve Banking

Banks, as a group, do not simply intermediate: They can also *create money* in multiples of the amounts of deposits through **fractional reserve banking.**[18] Early on, bankers realized that they did not need to keep funds on hand sufficient to repay all deposits at a given moment. Only a fraction of the funds deposited were required to meet any normal day's demand for withdrawals. The rest could be loaned or invested, and banking income from resulting interest payments would be increased. Although no single bank could lend more than was deposited, as a group they could.

Let's think of the entire banking system as a single bank. If there were only one bank in the whole country, and it kept reserves of 20 percent cash against deposits, then for every $100 deposited in cash, it could create loans (or issue its own notes) in the amount of $500. Of course, this bank could not repay its depositors (or redeem notes held by others) if they all came at once to demand the money due them. *No* system of fractional reserve banking could, then or now. Thus, fractional reserve banking was both profitable and potentially dangerous.

The Reserve Ratio

The reserve question, then, centered upon what **reserve ratio** was both safe and profitable for bankers. No one has ever provided an answer. Some reserves were required for daily business, and some extra reserves might be needed in case of emergency. However, cash reserves earned no interest, and bankers had to seek higher-yielding loans to compensate for them.

In large-scale emergencies, no reserve ratio less than 100 percent could suffice, and that was clearly not possible in fractional reserve banking, especially since the promise of redemption was usually given in specie, the legal tender of the country. As a result, when crises came, the banks would tend to stop paying out specie against their notes and deposits. In the panics of 1819, 1837, and 1857, and in 1860, nearly every bank in the country suspended specie payments. This defensive maneuver continued in later crises, all the way to 1933, when every bank in the nation closed its doors.

Leverage

Creation of bank money by fractional reserve methods can be economic leverage since claims on real resources are being created in excess of those set aside by savers. If the country responds by greater production (the bank money is accepted at current prices for goods and services), the leverage produces real growth. If bidding for resources stemming from the creation of money produces no such response, the exchange rate between money and goods and services falls, and **inflation** is the result—more money chases the same volume of goods. Since bank money usually expanded with business demands, and the big economic expansions were associated with rising prices, the state banks were blamed for excessive money creation when the crash came. But in bad times, banks that could not recover all their loans were like other businesses in similar situations, and they had to give up. Widespread bank failures punctuated all nineteenth-century business downturns.

State Bank Growth

Bank formation boomed between independence and the Civil War. Intermediation was needed, and in most circumstances the leverage worked—people accepted the notes of the state banks as money. As a result, apart from periods of crisis and depression, banking was a desirable business. By 1810, there were 88 state-chartered banks, by 1820 more than 300, and by 1860, despite the multitude of failures, at least 1,500 state banks. The notes and deposits of the state

TABLE 12.2 State Bank Notes and Deposits

Year	*Notes Outstanding*	*Deposits*
1834	95	102
1835	104	122
1840	107	120
1845	90	114
1850	131	146
1855	187	236
1860	207	310

Source: *Historical Statistics,* series X437, 585.

banks from 1834 to 1860 are shown at intervals in Table 12.2.

What the data in Table 12.2 do not show, nor do the trends mentioned earlier indicate, is the *volatility* (ups and downs) of state bank behavior. It is in this area that the antebellum state banks were subjected to criticism for recklessness. In Table 12.3, we see rough estimates of volatility based upon the available data for bank liabilities compared to wholesale prices.

In the three big price expansions between 1834 and 1860 (1834–1837, 1843–1847, and 1851–1857) for which we have any corresponding bank data, the increase in demand liabilities of bankers—bank money—was far in excess of increases in the wholesale price level in general. Even though there was some inflation, the slower growth of prices relative to bank liabilities suggests successful leverage in real terms.

TABLE 12.3 Volatility of Bank Liabilities[a]

Volatility	*Wholesale Prices*	*Bank Notes Outstanding*	*Total Deposits*
Price Expansions			
1834–1837	+ 25	+ 54	+ 83
1843–1847	+ 15	+ 47	+ 42
1851–1857	+ 28	+ 60	+ 113
Price Contractions			
1837–1843	− 40	− 90	− 112
1847–1851	− 7	+ 49	+ 55
1857–1860	− 18	− 8	+ 22

[a] Figures represent the percentage of change.

Source: *Historical Statistics,* series E52, X585–586.

In all three economic crises that followed these expansions, it was charged that the state banks had contributed to the excessive optimism by their "over issues."[19] But we might just as well argue that business optimism gave rise to demand for credit and that bankers merely responded. As Peter Temin has shown, the expansion of bank money was solidly based upon increased specie reserves in the banking system, and the economy's response was a heightened demand for resources, using a more plentiful money supply.[20] The small size of the price increases compared to those of bank liabilities suggests that either there were significant real production increases to absorb all the bank money, or else bank money was not that important.

During periods when prices fell, the record is mixed. The severe depression following the panic of 1837 witnessed sharp declines in notes and deposits (and many bank failures) in excess of the fall in prices. The prostrate condition of the economy was doubtless partly the result of the banking crisis indicated by the data. No other explanation seems plausible. Unfortunately, we cannot be more precise, given the data from this period. In the two other periods of falling prices after economic crises, bank note issues continued to increase (although in 1858 they declined in a single year about 15 percent and then made a recovery to 1860). Only between 1857 and 1860 was there a drop in deposits corresponding to declining prices.

Efforts to Regulate

Bank failures created such widespread suffering (for millions of depositors) that efforts were made to force a greater conservatism upon the bankers, by both private actions and the political system. Since the banks were, by their charters, branches of the state sovereignty, the states were considered partly responsible for the consequences if the public was harmed. One major private regulatory effort was the famous **Suffolk System** of the Boston banks.

As early as 1819, country bank notes, issued against small reserves, circulated in Boston, driving notes from the Suffolk Bank of Boston out of circulation (Gresham's Law again). In retaliation, the Suffolk Bank forced higher reserves on the country banks by regularly presenting their notes to their issuers and demanding redemption in specie. In 1824, six other Boston banks joined the fray. The country banks then agreed to keep reserves in the Boston banks against their note issues if they were not presented by the Boston banks for payment in specie. The result was higher country bank reserves (hence, lower loan volumes against given deposits) and fewer country bank notes circulating freely again as the exchange rate fell against country notes.

This system was a forerunner of the modern practice of required nonearning deposits for member banks in the Federal Reserve System. The Suffolk System lasted until the 1850s, when a Boston bank clearinghouse was organized about the same time that clearinghouses were organized in New York, Philadelphia, and other major banking centers. Clearinghouse rules imposed stricter behavior on individual banks and were a force for banker conservatism.[21]

State power, too, was used to regulate banking practices—not surprising when we recall that the state was the origin of the bank charter. In 1827, **double liability** (twice the face value of bank stocks) was imposed on bank stock owners in New York in an effort to encourage prudence among bankers. The idea spread rapidly.[22]

A notable state regulatory experiment was conducted in New York between 1829 and 1839. This innovation was mandatory deposit insurance paid for by the bankers: the New York **Safety Fund**, a forerunner of the modern Federal Deposit Insurance Corporation (FDIC). Each New York bank receiving a charter (or a recharter) was required to deposit into a fund an amount equal to 3 percent of its capital stock as a reserve against note and deposit repudiation by state banks. The idea was a sound one as long as banks failed at a reasonable rate or in reasonable numbers. But in the panic of 1837, so many banks failed that the fund went broke.

State deposit insurance schemes continued to fail in crises, right up to the 1930s when the FDIC was formed by the federal government with authority to borrow from the U.S. Treasury to pay off depositors. State efforts were doomed because their resources were limited to funds deposited. With the U.S. Treasury behind the FDIC, its funds are potentially limited only by the discretion of government—a very liberal backing.

Efforts to require higher legal reserve ratios produced some successes, most notably, the **Forstall System** in Louisiana.[23] It was first organized in 1842 after all banks in Louisiana had closed their doors. The Forstall System required one-third specie reserves against notes and deposits, and also restricted state bank loans of deposited funds to commercial paper with maturities of 90 days. Such conservatism paid off. During the panic of 1857, Louisiana banks continued specie payments when most other banks in the country (all but one in New York, for example) closed their doors. Safety, it seemed, paid for note holders and depositors, and bankers, too. High cash reserves became a feature of the national banks after 1863, and the success of the Forstall System probably was the main reason for it.

In 1838, New York led the movement toward competitive **free banking**, a system by which any group of persons could acquire a banking charter by following some general rules to register their group, to agree to conduct banking business according to state regulations, and, in some states, to agree to maintain specified reserves. Other states followed New York, and the number of banks multiplied again. Legislators believed, rightly, that free banking contained less favoritism and temptation to corruption than the old system of special franchise chartering. By 1838, the Safety Fund was dead, and so was the Second Bank of the United States.[24]

The First and Second Banks

A great deal has been written about the two "central" banks chartered by Congress in 1791 and in 1816.[25] The obvious question to ask is, "Would U.S. economic history have been significantly different without them?" The answer may well be no, since from 1836 to 1914—a period of dramatic change and enormous economic growth—there was no trace of central banking in this country. However, the two banks continue to be of interest in a historical perspective as part of the nation's learning process about finance, and, of course, there were great personalities involved:

Hamilton and Jefferson in the First Bank, and Biddle and Jackson in the Second.

There is no doubt that the Bank of England was the paradigm for both banks; Jefferson charged that Hamilton was simply infatuated by English example in his advocacy of the First Bank of the United States.[26] Like the Bank of England, it was a direct competitor with the commercial banks and was expected to turn a profit. Because both the First and the Second banks were direct competitors with private business, the rest of the banking community generally was opposed to their recharter.

Some lessons were learned from this. The idea of joint public-private ownership, embodied in both the First and the Second Bank charters, was entirely suitable to democratic ideas about the partnership between government and business. But the sale of bank stock to foreigners in both cases raised hostility to these banks. Therefore, when the Federal Reserve System was organized in 1914, stock ownership was limited to member banks, transfer restricted, and government ownership was limited to the headquarters in Washington, D.C. Also, when the Federal Reserve was organized, it was a bank for bankers only and did not compete for business with private bankers.

Why did both the First and Second banks vanish from the scene after a single, 20-year charter? Even though their respective histories are very different, the one thing they did have in common, the 20-year federal charter, was fatal. In both cases, politics made survival impossible. Hamilton's ideas were vigorously opposed by Jefferson, who believed that the First Bank was simply an unconstitutional assumption of powers that were reserved to the states. When the bank was chartered in 1791, Federalists controlled the government. When it came time to recharter the bank, Jeffersonians were in control, and they (urged on by banker competitors) were not disposed to do so. The First Bank was huge compared with the private banks, and its business was a juicy morsel the private banks longed to gobble up, and would if the charter was not renewed. There were 88 private state banks when the recharter was lost in 1811, and 250 of them five years later.

Historians have generally agreed that, in all of the First Bank's career, the central banking operations it performed were done well. It conducted most of the federal government's fiscal business with efficiency and provided a brake on the expansionary pace of the state banks by shrewdly sending back state bank notes for redemption in specie when the rate of growth was deemed excessive. But that, in fact, was the rub. The bank had not been chartered as a *regulatory* agency, and those activities of central bank control so approved of by modern historians were considered usurpations of power by contemporaries.

The Second Bank, chartered in 1816, also performed its central banking operations well, especially during the bank presidencies of Langdon Cheves and Nicholas Biddle. The attempt to recharter the Second Bank was killed in 1832 by a single lethal dose of politics, Andrew Jackson's veto of the recharter legislation, and subsequent withdrawal of federal moneys from the Bank's management.[27] Jackson's vigorous veto message was a concentrated attack on the Second Bank's power over the country, but he emphasized also that it was a *privileged* monopoly, its stock largely owned by foreigners and the "rich."

When Jackson was elected President of the United States in 1828, the Bank, under the cosmopolitan Biddle, was prosperous and was generally considered to be doing the job for which it was chartered. After a year in office, in a message to Congress, Jackson resurrected the constitutional objections from Jefferson's time and noted he would prefer a government-owned bank, if such a monopoly were needed in the future. Biddle tried unsuccessfully to win Jackson's support, but the president remained steadfast. (He was no friend of banking. Early in his life, he had accepted what turned out to be worthless notes in exchange for a sizable amount of land.) Biddle then turned to Henry Clay, who was to be Jackson's foe in the 1832 election. Clay obtained Biddle's permission to use rechartering as a campaign issue. Although they were able to win sufficient congressional support to pass a rechartering bill in the summer, Jackson won a decisive victory in what history has termed the "Bank War" at the polls that November.

Taking his victory as a mandate on the bank, Jackson almost immediately began to remove federal moneys from the Second Bank, depositing them in favored state banks. The Second Bank of the United

States received a Pennsylvania charter after 1836 and expired in 1841, after an unsuccessful attempt to use its funds to corner the market in raw cotton.

The Second Bank, like the First, was huge compared to the state banks. By using its drafts on its branches as money, it was, in fact, creating a uniform currency, a practice much feared by the private bankers.[28] The Bank's branches were resented as privileged intrusions into local economic life. Monopoly on money is what a central bank *ought* to have, by modern standards. But such was not the prevailing view in the 1830s. As a result, from then until 1914, the United States had no central bank. Instead, the Treasury Department tried to conduct its affairs independently of the banking system. The independent Treasury became another experiment left in the dust of history when in 1914 the country returned to central banking with the Federal Reserve System. It had also learned from the Second Bank that regulatory powers should be in the charter, so far as possible, and that was done in 1914 (although they were changed greatly afterward).[29]

The two banks chartered by Congress, modeled after the Bank of England, left one more legacy. The Federal Reserve System has a virtually perpetual charter. The charter can be amended, but the Fed does not come up for recharter every 20 years as did the First and Second Banks of the United States, or it no doubt also would have passed into history along with its ancestors. Of course, Congress could abolish the present system if that were the "will of the people."

OTHER INTERMEDIARIES

Other kinds of intermediation were needed to serve other parts of the social system. The state banks were commercial banks, operating, as the name suggests, as intermediaries primarily in the world of business and as instruments of commerce. To borrow long-term moneys and sell equities (shares of ownership), businesses and governments needed organized capital markets. The new transportation companies and, increasingly, the rising manufacturing firms required a forum. The evolution of capital markets went hand-in-hand with markets for short-term money. Short-term finance was the lubricant for long-term borrowing and equity sales. New York, Boston, Philadelphia, Baltimore, and New Orleans were early centers.

The New York Stock Exchange Board was formally organized in 1817 after 20 years of less formal existence.[30] It slowly forged ahead of the others as the center of the nation's capital markets—just as New York City itself took the lead in commerce and growth. Stock exchanges grew up in other cities as well to serve local needs. In time, the major centers were linked by telegraph, with the focus on the New York exchange. *Common stocks* were sold from the beginning, as were bonds. During the 1830s, *preferred shares* (with a preferred claim to dividends) appeared, and, later, industrialists followed the lead of governments and began issuing long-term bonds for subscription in the public capital markets.

Such specialized activities appeared wherever there were need and imagination. *Mutual savings banks*, carefully governed depositories for the savings of the poor, appeared early in the American scene. The first one was organized in Philadelphia in 1816. Emphasis was on the safety of the loans, even if earnings were deliberately low, and these institutions produced an enviable record of trustworthiness compared to the oft-failing commercial banks. By 1860, there were 278 mutual savings banks in the country, with combined assets approximately 15 percent of those of the state banks. According to Lance Davis, the leading expert on the subject, nine of the ten largest businesses in the country by 1860 were savings banks.[31] The idea, imported from England, was to provide the small saver with a secure way to practice thrift and frugality. The huge funds generated by such virtue went into the most secure forms of investment. In England they had been limited to investment in government bonds. Here, the conservative investments of the savings banks freed other funds for more speculative uses.

Life and fire insurance companies were formed in the early nineteenth century, along with burial societies, building societies, and private fire engine companies. All were techniques for mobilizing the funds of a group against disasters that struck individual families. Since fire was not necessarily an individual hazard in towns, municipalities took over the chores of operating fire-fighting equipment in self-defense. The "free rider," the owner of a house not covered by a private engine company, became a real danger. An uninsured house on fire, if not attended to, would ignite insured houses. Private engine companies in towns had to douse the fires of those who did not purchase their service in order to protect the houses of those who did. Nevertheless, insurance against fire losses continued on a private basis.

The list of intermediation attempts is a long one. The point is that experimentation was necessary as new needs developed, and the American economy before 1860 was alive with such experimentation.[32]

How Integrated Was the Antebellum Capital Market?

In a recent paper, Howard Bodenhorn and Hugh Rockoff have asserted that the financial markets of New England, the Middle Atlantic, and the South were reasonably integrated with that of New York City as early as 1850.[33] Integration in this context is measured by a narrow interest rate differential. This is a surprise. Most scholars have argued that capital markets were not integrated until about 1900, but Bodenhorn and Rockoff's data suggest smaller differentials in 1850 than 1900. Further, the 1850s were years of great expansion of the railroad and telegraph networks which are thought to have facilitated this integration. The telegraph, invented by Samuel F. B. Morse in the 1840s, significantly reduced the time it took for a message to travel between two points, and the vast majority of messages using the new technology were commercial messages. News of New York City interest rates moved across telegraph lines, usually constructed adjacent to rail lines, as fast as operators could push the keys. Evidence from the Midwest, where a good deal of the rail construction of the 1850s was concentrated, suggested rates were a bit higher there than along the Atlantic Coast. Evidence from the Pacific region, which would not be connected to the East by rail or telegraph until after the Civil War, suggested rates there may have been substantially higher. As might be expected, the Civil War significantly altered this pattern, particularly in the South. Bodenhorn and Rockoff's research raises the question of why reintegration took so long in the post-bellum years. That is a question we will address in Chapter 19.

THE FINANCIAL LINK: U.S. AND WORLD ECONOMICS

The modern student may well be perplexed that private banks in the nineteenth century issued their own promissory notes as "money." To comprehend the history of banking in this period, we must understand that practice. In addition, we must go further into the matter of specie redemption because that promise made by state banks when their notes were issued firmly tied the heterogeneous American monetary system to the international economy. When a state banker in, say, Georgia paid out gold coin on demand for the return of his own notes, he was paying out international money.[34] If he observed a given reserve ratio, that gold flowing from his vault decreased his ability to lend—that is, it *contracted his note issues.*

Bimetallism and the Gold Standard

When the Bank of England suspended gold payments in 1797, England was a bimetallic country, with fixed prices for both gold and silver at the Bank. England was, therefore, on the same monetary standard as the United States. When payments were resumed finally in 1821, only the gold price was fixed at the Bank, and England was on a straight gold standard.[35] By then, other countries—France and the German states, for example—were still bimetallic.

As long as the price of one metal was fixed, stable exchange rates between currencies could exist. The Bank of England's gold price was £3-17-10$^1/_2$ (three pounds, seventeen shillings, ten and one-half pence) per troy ounce. The U.S. mint price was $20.67 for an avoirdupois ounce. If we adjust for differences in ounces and gold quality, the British pound was worth $4.87, each English shilling was worth 24.35 cents, and each English penny worth slightly more than two American cents. Other currency exchange rates could be similarly calculated, once gold prices were fixed.

If an American merchant wanted to remit specie to England in payment for goods, and the English free-market silver price was too low, the merchant could always trade silver for gold, ship it, and receive credit at £3-17-10$^1/_2$ an ounce. Thus, the nineteenth-century international financial system was based on a fixed gold price and stable exchange rates.

Apart from temporary dislocations (like the American suspension of gold payments between 1861 and 1879), stable and fixed exchange rates were the norm during most of the nineteenth century. Even though some countries were bimetallic (or even on a straight silver standard after the California and Australian gold discoveries of 1849–1851 lowered the price of gold in terms of silver), the system has come to be known simply as the **gold standard**.

The Gold Points

As in colonial times, most international payments among merchants in the nineteenth century were not made by shipping specie but by purchasing and remitting bills of exchange. American supplies of sterling (claims on London) came primarily from the export of a single commodity—raw cotton—and from shipping services. The bills of exchange were not themselves fixed in price. What it cost to buy one was determined by its *face value* (the amount payable on the date of maturity), discounted by an interest charge (since it was payable in the future), and then by the haggling between seller and buyer.[36] Therefore, what a merchant, say, in Philadelphia paid for sterling was to some extent determined by free-market forces. The qualifier, "to some extent," is present because shipping specie was always an alternative to purchasing exchange.

The trouble involved in buying specie and packaging, insuring, and shipping it set a limit on the possible price of exchange. If, for example, the price of sterling bills rose to the point where it was as cheap or cheaper to ship specie in payment, then such shipments occurred, and either the bills were offered cheaper or the owners had the trouble themselves of collecting when they became due. The upper limit on foreign exchange prices was the *gold export point*. Similarly, if American bills were too expensive in London, gold flowed to the United States. That threshold was the *gold import point*. The two gold points ensured the stability of foreign exchange rates under the gold standard. The gold points were the exchange rate extrema, beyond which exchange rates, by definition, did not go.

Because of fixed gold prices and the possibility of gold shipments, nineteenth-century merchants enjoyed an element of stability in their calculations that was most valuable in a time of slow communications. The known limits of the various exchange rates were called the *solidarity* of the gold points. However, since the possibility of gold shipments created that solidarity, there were numerous occasions before the Atlantic cables were laid in the 1860s (allowing fast transfers of bank credit) when exchange rates became unstable because gold was temporarily unavailable for shipment.

During monetary crises like the panics of 1837 and 1857, the banks refused specie payments, and gold could be acquired only at a premium. Accordingly, the gold points drifted away from their normally narrow range.[37] This was the free market's way of holding the international financial system together in times of stress, and it meant that the state banks' freedom to pursue their own lending policies was restricted by international conditions—as long as reserve ratios were maintained. The only way to escape the international influence was to abandon specie payments.

When American currency was at the gold export point, usually during times of rapid economic growth when the balance of payments ran into strong deficits (the country was consuming more goods and services than it produced), gold losses from domestic supplies produced tight money, higher interest rates, restricted lending, and a curb upon further immediate expansion. The process was reversed in times of stagnation; gold inflows would encourage greater growth by easing the monetary situation. It is for such reasons that the gold standard was called *self-adjusting*.

Thus it was that the American monetary system and economy were integrated into the world market with a specie standard. It was both an advantage and a disadvantage. The United States benefited from foreign economic expansions, but it was set back by foreign economic troubles (except for harvest failures abroad, which always raised demand for American food). The gold standard automatically transmitted monetary shocks, and they reverberated back again via the financial markets. It became common in London to blame the Americans for monetary troubles and in America, at the same time, to blame the British. The truth is that the gold standard was an *integrated* financial system that transmitted the good and bad with equal efficiency.

Southern Cotton Finance

Before 1860, a special element in the U.S. financial system, interesting in itself, played an important role in antebellum Southern economic expansion. Great Britain was the greatest producer of cotton textiles, and in normal years more than three-quarters of its raw cotton was shipped from American ports in the South. *Big money* was involved; it was perhaps the antebellum equivalent of financing modern international oil shipments from OPEC nations to the industrial countries.

An intricate system of finance grew up, with agents (factors) of British banks, discount houses, and cotton importers located throughout the cotton-growing and -shipping portions of the South. Thus, finance was always available, from international sources as well as Southern cotton growers and shippers. The cotton factor arranged immediate payment in cash to Southern growers. Agents usually "accepted" (endorsed) the bills on behalf of their British principals, and the cotton market was thus instantly infused with British credit.

The cotton was shipped, and the bills of exchange arising from it either were sold to American importers in both the North and South or were purchased by specialized British houses who undertook to wait for payment in England. The cotton bills were discountable in

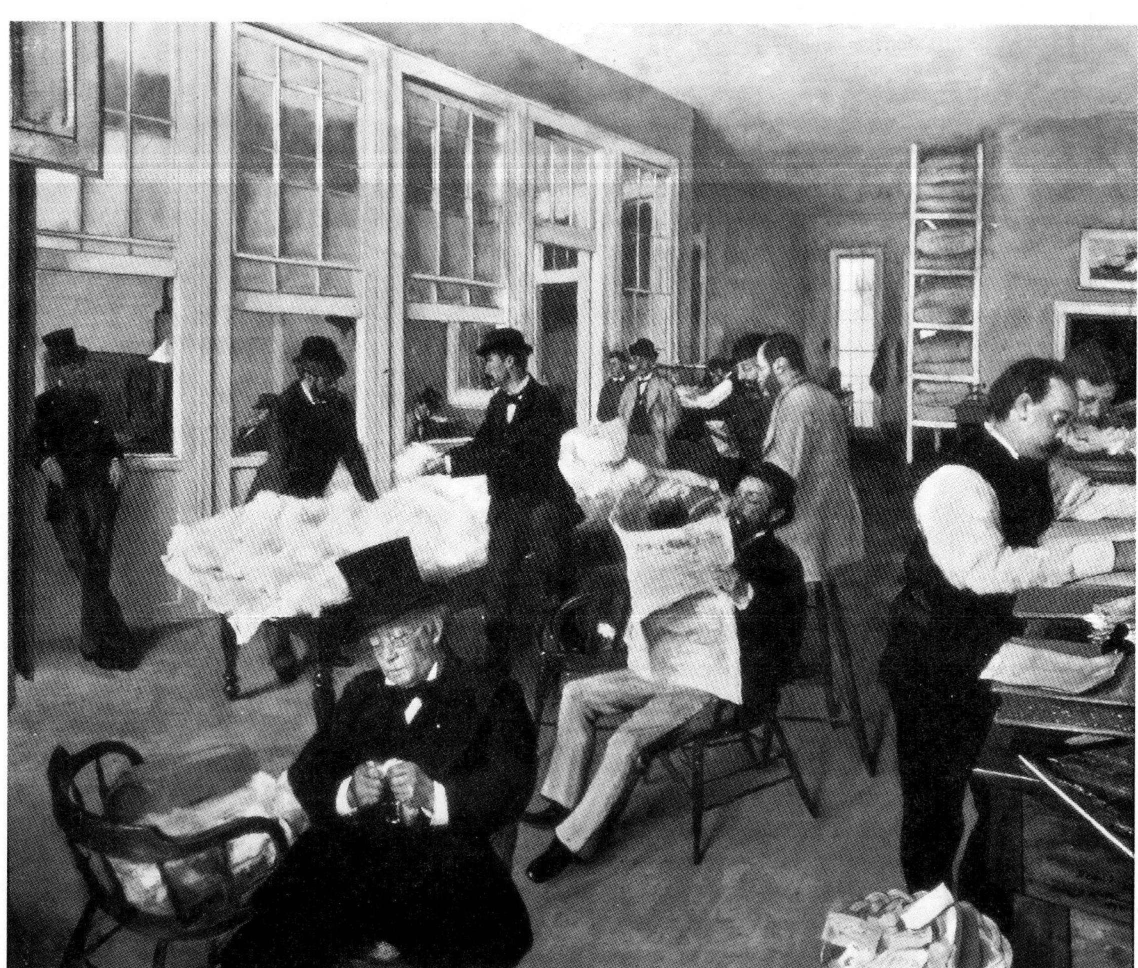

The Cotton Bureau at New Orleans by Edgar Degas (1873)

The California Gold Rush. *The discovery of gold brought people from around the world and permanently changed the West. Entire rivers were diverted to wash the gravel for gold (above right). San Francisco's harbor (above) was filled with hundreds of deserted and rotting ships that had brought nearly 40,000 people in just six months. Colorado and Nevada (below right) were the next boom areas. Nevada's Comstock Lode alone yielded over $300 million worth of gold and silver over 20 years. A cutaway view of this mine is shown below.*

England since they bore British signatures and were the stock in trade of the discount house there. Credit flowed both ways, of course, and the Cotton South was provided with a more efficient financial system before 1860 than it would experience for many decades after 1865.[38]

The Northern economy also benefited. It was generally in deficit with its trade with England—the largest trading partner by far before 1860—while the South was in surplus. English credit was available to the North, too, and, of course, the North generally had a surplus in its trade with the South. Southern prosperity thus fueled Northern economic growth. As Douglass North has shown in his book *The Economic Growth of the United States 1790–1860*, the Southern trade surplus with Europe was largely responsible for Northern industrial and agricultural progress before 1860.[39] The South earned the foreign exchange that the North used for imports of machinery and manufactures. Since the Southern surplus was based upon slavery and the entire system was serviced by British finance, it has not been much celebrated in American history.

American bankers slowly worked their way into the system, although it remained primarily a British show before the Civil War. The historical tendrils from the cotton finance were long, and, eventually, were a primary origin of American investment banking. One example will have to suffice. Here we need the detail of personal histories, and our discussion must move from *macro*economic to *micro*economic history.

George Peabody, a Yankee financier from Salem, Massachusetts, had a long and successful career in London. His firm, Peabody & Company, was an "American house" that, for the most part, dealt in cotton finance. In 1854, he invited a new American partner to London, Junius Spencer Morgan, grandson of the founder (in 1819) of the Aetna Fire Insurance Company of Hartford, Connecticut.

In 1857, J. S. Morgan's son, Pierpont, was at loose ends after studying mathematics at Göttingen University. Young Morgan joined his father in London in time to observe the Bank of England's dramatic actions during the panic of 1857 (which included a large loan to Peabody & Company to keep it afloat). After two years' apprenticeship in London, in the fall of 1859, Pierpont Morgan went to New Orleans with the cotton shipping firm of Duncan Sherman to learn cotton finance from the American side. He immediately got involved in other things, and he arrived in New York City during the Civil War.

Peabody & Company became J. S. Morgan & Company in 1865. With offices in London and Paris, it became a leading European merchant banking house, financing, among other things, a $50-million loan to the French in 1870 at the time of the Franco-Prussian War. When Junius Morgan died in 1890, his firm was coequal with the Rothschilds and Barings in European finance. Pierpont became the primary founder of modern American investment banking and was the greatest financier in American history.

Early in his career, Pierpont, together with his father, had helped the young Andrew Carnegie sell Pennsylvania Railroad stocks in London. In 1900, that kindness was repaid when Carnegie turned over his affairs in Carnegie Steel to Morgan for $500 million. The formation of the United States Steel Corporation was underway with that transaction, quarterbacked by Morgan. When he died in 1913, the name J. P. Morgan was already a legend in American financial history and has so remained to this day.[40]

As previously noted, nineteenth-century American finance was a learning experience. We will meet Mr. Morgan and Mr. Carnegie again in later chapters.

THE FINANCIAL SYSTEM AND THE BUSINESS CYCLE

The solidarity of the gold points was very much like a good electrical connection, except that, in the case of the foreign exchanges, the current passing through was made up of economic impulses. Because of the South's cotton connection with England, the rhythm of economic fluctuations between the American and British economies was bound to be easily communicated. How deeply into the real economic life of a mainly agricultural nation these variations in the pace of economic growth were felt in the earlier years is difficult to assess. Even though money incomes were affected, farming activities continued in the North as well as in the South when prices fell. In fact, it has been a historical pattern, prevailing until quite recently, that farm output was fairly insensitive to price changes.[41] Southern agriculture was perhaps more commercially sensitive than were the mainly self-sufficient farmsteads of the North in the antebellum period, but fixed costs were so relatively high in the slave economy that variations in prices would affect the scale of output only in the most extreme circumstances. Planters would not typically sell off their slaves because of a temporary dip in cotton prices.

Wholesale Price Fluctuations

Figure 12.1 is a chart of annual wholesale prices from 1790 to 1860. These data mask a host of exceptions, and we will use them here only as a general guide. In an economy as free to respond to the signals of the market as was the antebellum economy, general price movements roughly indicate changes in the pace of economic life. The record of prices at the beginning is overshadowed by the sharp variations after 1793, when European wars were in progress and Jefferson's embargo—which disrupted the markets on a month-by-month basis—was in force.

The small seaboard economy, mainly agricultural and tied closely to international markets, was extremely sensitive to such influences. Next came the inflation of 1812–1815, when the wartime American market was largely cut off from European goods, the domestic manufacturing establishment was very small (but thriving in the circumstances), and state banks were free to expand their issues after the demise of the First Bank of the United States. Appearing in 1816 were two general forces that would drive prices down until the 1830s: (a) the return of European manufactured goods to the American market and (b) the gradual recovery of European agriculture. This recovery increased supplies of foodstuffs in Europe and caused farm products to glut the American markets for more than a decade after 1818.[42]

Three major expansions in activity are indicated by these data: (a) the strong expansion ending in 1837 and the panic of that year (followed by a small peak in 1839), (b) a relatively weak expansion between 1843 and 1847, and (c) the double-headed affair of the 1850s, with price peaks in 1855 and 1857. During this period, the British had major monetary crises

FIGURE 12.1 Wholesale Prices 1790–1860

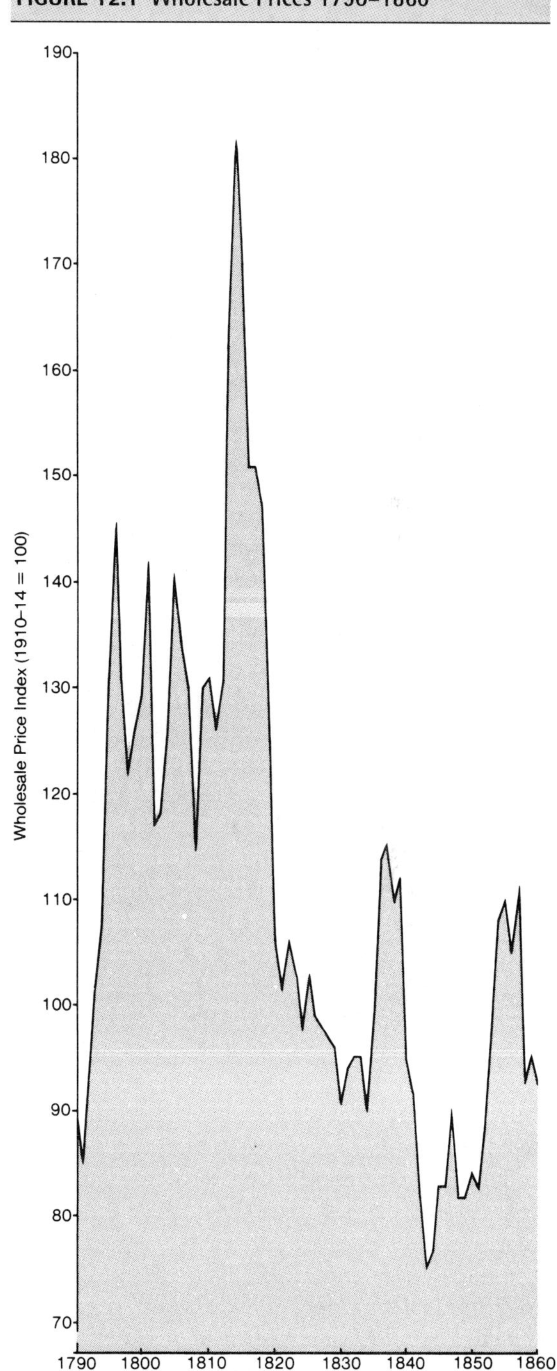

Source: *Historical Statistics,* series E 52.

(in 1825, 1837, 1847, and 1857). The first big American financial crisis was in 1819; followed by a major crisis in 1837 and then, in 1847, a minor one. The panic of 1857 was international, severe in both the United States and Europe.

The crises of 1837 and 1857 in this country and in England were closely linked by the financial connection, but *real* activities in the two countries were, at best, only vaguely related, economically speaking. In the 1830s, the British were pursuing a major industrial expansion, and the Americans, a boom in internal improvements and sales of Western lands. That these real activities somehow were coordinated cannot be proved, but all observers agree that the monetary connection detonated the panics in both countries.

In Britain in 1847, the monetary blowup came as the boom in railroad stocks passed its peak and turned into a sell-off. The Bank of England, operating under its new charter (1844), which totally restricted its ability to expand its own note issues except against deposits of specie, very nearly suspended payments.[43] There were other troubles in Britain, too, including bad harvests, the flood of starving Irish immigrants, and a sharp decline in railway investment.

In the United States, the 1840s had begun with a severe depression (some historians think it rivaled that of the 1930s).[44] But war with Mexico in 1846 produced higher expenditures and higher prices. Then, in 1849, there came a new surge in activity related to the California gold discoveries and, once again, a major westward movement. The U.S. gold production of 43,000 ounces in 1847 rose by a factor of more than ten to 484,000 ounces in 1848. That was only the beginning. In 1849, an incredible 1.9 million troy ounces were produced, and the figure kept rising until 1853, when production reached 3.1 million troy ounces—12 ounces to the pound. It declined after that peak, but it was still at 2.2 million ounces in 1860.[45]

Gold was also discovered in Australia in 1851. By 1857, the world's supply of monetary gold had been increased by a third, an unheard-of increase for a single decade.[46] The United States became a gold-producing gold exporter, and the new gold, together with rising government expenditures in Europe during the Crimean War (1854–1855), gave the early 1850s an aura of renewed prosperity all over the commercial world. As backing for currency, the new gold reserves allowed for a rise in U.S. currency circulation from $226 million in 1847 to $475 million in 1857. That prices rose only about 50 percent under such a monetary onslaught indicates a great rise in real output in the 1850s.[47]

In the United States, the cotton economy was never more prosperous than in the 1850s. American cotton output doubled in a single decade, yet the expansion of world cotton consumption was so great that raw cotton prices continued to rise. In the 1850s, it was nearly double those that had ruled a decade earlier. There was a new minor outburst of sales of public lands, but it did not approach the scale of the 1830s. The best lands were gone, and, in 1862, the Homestead Act was passed to encourage people to settle in the West on *free* land. An era was ending.

Then, in 1857, came what many scholars have considered the first worldwide economic convulsion.[48] The British blamed the Americans, because the banking panic started in late summer in the United States, and the first big failures in England were American houses. By November, the panic was raging all over Western Europe. However, research has shown that an economic downturn was clearly underway in Britain, from the spring of 1857 onward, for complex reasons (partly related to the abrupt ending of government expenditures when the Crimean War ended in 1855) that had little connection with the Anglo-American financial network. Britain began a quick recovery in 1858, based on renewed textile exports, and American cotton prices did not fall to pre-1856 levels. Apparently the American economy was still suffering from this financial convulsion when it was overtaken by war in 1861.

Interdependence

Although we could hardly call the international cycles of the antebellum period synchronized, the strongest impulses in the 1830s and 1850s were effectively transmitted by the gold standard mechanism.[49] Such is probably true of the American depression of the early 1840s, too.

It is important to realize that these fluctuations in economic activity, the "business cycle," have never

The China Trade. *After independence, American merchants were free to trade with China. The first American ships to reach Canton's factories carried a cargo of ginseng, woolen garments, cotton, furs, and lead. (The Canton waterfront is shown above.) The return cargo was black and green tea, handwoven cotton cloth, silk, cinnamon, and porcelain. Chinese porcelain became so popular that it was soon produced specifically for the export market, as shown in the plate depicting the Salem merchant ship* Friendship *and the vase with an image of the signing of the Declaration of Independence.*

been really understood as a sequence. They have perplexed economists for more than a century. Whereas the cycles tend to look alike superficially, each time they have had different origins in economic behavior and structural change.[50] The increases in the money supply and prices that occurred in each upswing are like a fever, but fevers occur with many illnesses. There is no doubt, though, that a world of growing interdependence, brought about by greater specialization and growing trade on the basis of comparative advantage, emerged. That world effectively used a single currency, specie within the gold standard mechanism, which made it a world that would necessarily become more vulnerable to the transmission of cyclical disturbances.

THE BALANCE OF PAYMENTS AND THE CYCLE

The growing U.S. economy looked very much like a modern "developing" country in its international relations. During expansions, it used more goods and services than it produced; and trade deficits appeared prominently in the 1830s and 1850s (see Figure 12.2). When growth was sluggish, as in the early 1840s, trade surpluses appeared. The reason for this pattern was the secular growth of the world's demand for U.S. exports, particularly raw cotton, together with the tendency of the U.S. economy to grow in spurts—"booming" periodically and running ahead of the world's growth pace. Foreigners were willing to finance this growth by lend-

FIGURE 12.2 U.S. Balance of Merchandise Trade

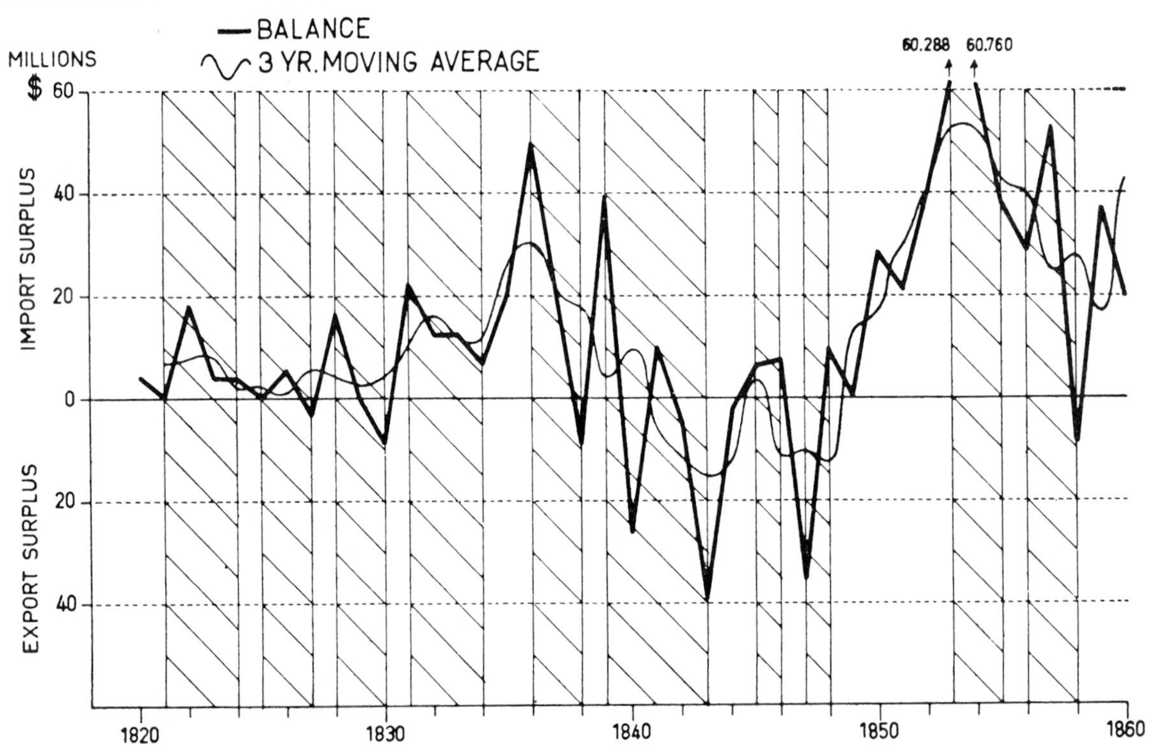

Source: *Historical Statistics*, series U 196.

During the antebellum period, the U.S. economy performed in its international transactions much like a modern "less-developed" country, using relatively more of the world's goods than it produced itself in expansion. The shaded areas are cyclical contractions. The three-year moving average smooths out the cycles and makes the development features more visible.

ing the United States money and by investing in the country. What would have been a serious specie loss in the 1830s, imposing a correction upon the United States before 1837, was offset, as Peter Temin has shown, by its bimetallism. Mexican silver "filled up" the bimetallic U.S. currency as gold flowed out, enabling the dynamic increase in state-bank note issues noted earlier.[51]

In the 1850s, gold production did slacken a bit, in time to be partly blamed for the U.S. financial debacle of 1857 and for a tightening of monetary conditions in the face of a mounting trade deficit. As always, the banks were blamed for "over issue." Such explanations are not entirely convincing, and that episode, the American side of the 1857 crisis, requires a closer examination.

From the viewpoint of modern Keynesian theory, an oddity of the antebellum period is the entirely virtuous performance of the federal government's financial system (see Figure 12.3). The ideal countercyclical policy by modern standards would be to create federal

FIGURE 12.3 Total Federal Receipts and Expenditures

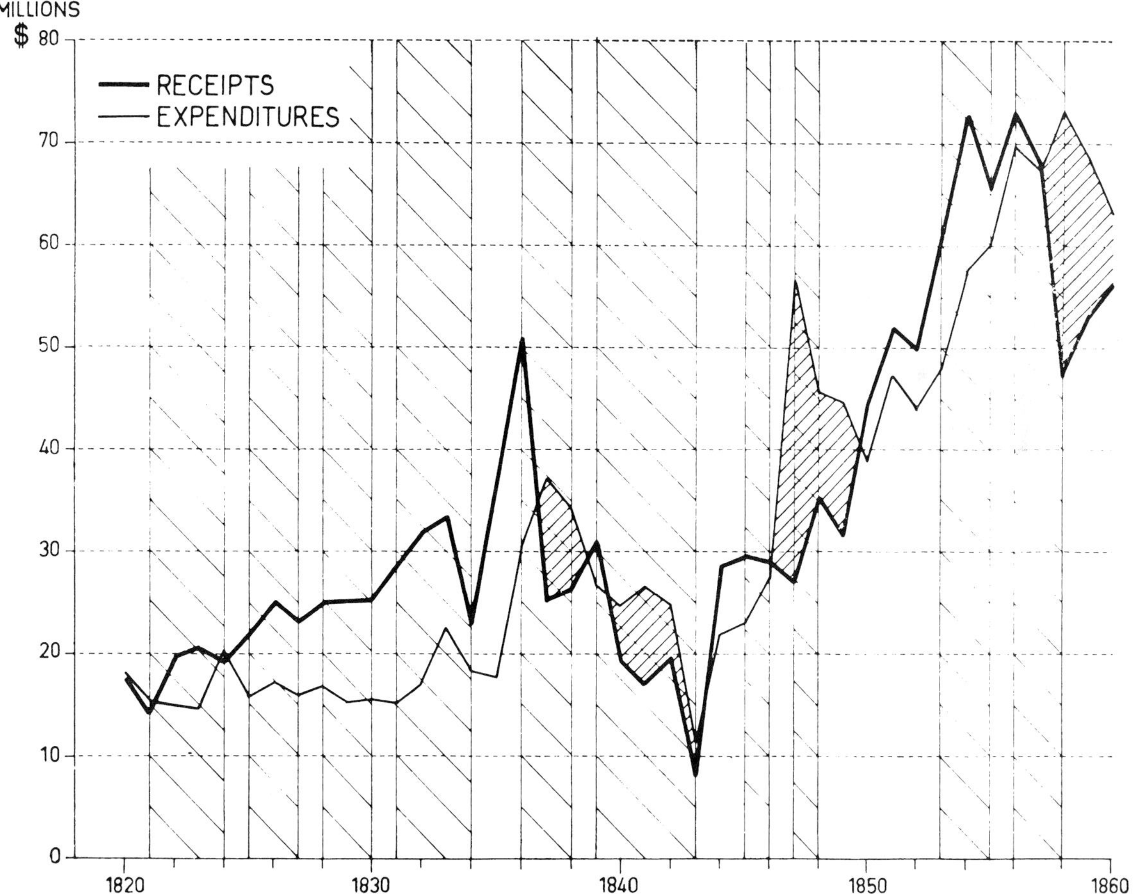

Source: *Historical Statistics,* series Y 335–336.

The federal government was accidentally operating a "cyclically balanced budget" from the 1830s until the Civil War. There were deficits (shaded areas) in largely depressed periods and surpluses in the mainly expansionary periods. The "exemplary behavior" occurred in large part because receipts were more income elastic than were expenditures.

government surpluses in periods of cyclical expansion by withdrawing funds from circulation and moderating the boom. In recessions, federal deficits should be encouraged to moderate the depth and length of the downswing by adding deficit-financed federal expenditures to the spending system. In the big expansions of 1825–1846, 1844–1846, and 1850–1857, the economy was (theoretically) braked by federal surpluses. In the major downswings of 1820–1821, 1837–1843, 1847–1849, and 1858–1860, deficits were run that should have stimulated the underemployed economy.

This enviable macroeconomic record, never equaled by modern governments, was apparently an accident. The federal government was then very small relative to total economic activity. Expenditures were, for the most part, insensitive to changes in domestic income. They went mainly to pay interest on the national debt and the salaries of the bureaucracy and military. After Jackson's veto of the expenditures on the Maysville Road (1830), federal spending on internal improvements remained small. As a result, expenditures more or less kept pace with the country as it grew, and the government responded to provide minimal necessary services.

Revenues, on the other hand, came mainly from customs receipts. Imports, sensitive to income changes, rose as domestic income increased: These great internal expansions caused government revenues to soar. Figure 12.4 tracks the ratio of customs rev-

FIGURE 12.4 Ratio of Customs Revenue to Merchandise Imports Before the Civil War

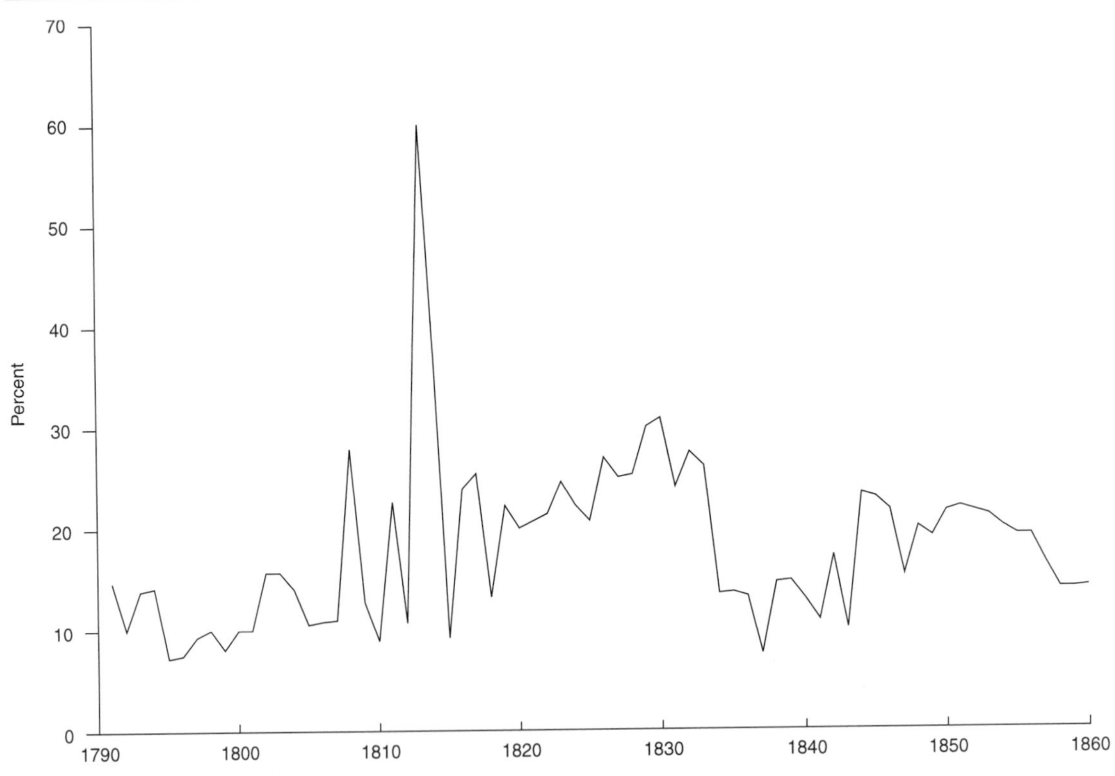

Source: *Historical Statistics,* series U 9 and Y 353.

This has been calculated by dividing the customs revenue collected by the merchandise imports in each year. The quotient is less than the average tariff rate because not all imports were subject to tariffs.

enue to merchandise imports before the Civil War. The large spike occurs during the War of 1812 when the denominator falls. There is a smaller spike in 1807 when Congress passed the Embargo Act in an attempt to get England and France to recognize that the United States should be granted the rights of a neutral country. Once again, the spike is attributable to a decrease in imports. The other relatively high point occurs in 1828 when Congress passed the "Tariff of Abominations," which raised average tariff rates above 50 percent on dutiable goods. Although we can also observe the tariff bills of 1816, 1824, and 1842 in the figure, it is clear that the 1828 rates were the highest in the years before the Civil War.

Since there was no felt need to increase expenditures just because revenues were increasing, the federal budget ran into surplus during good times, just as macroeconomics teaches.[52] We should notice, though, that this government behavior tends to offset the "self-correcting" gold standard mechanism by making expansions and depressions weaker than they otherwise would be. Keynesianism and the classical gold standard were ill-suited to one another.

RETROSPECT

The antebellum financial system was a laboratory of change; by 1860, it scarcely resembled that of 1790. In large part, it had been a chaotic episode. We should consider one final point that remains a puzzle: *There is no evidence that the financial chaos slowed down the economy's long-term growth or development.* Britain had a far more sophisticated and institutionally "correct" system—with a central bank, amalgamated branch banking, a strict gold standard, and conservative ideas at the Exchequer—yet U.S. growth in the period simply outstripped that of Great Britain, the world's first industrial nation. If "money matters," as modern monetarists like to say, U.S. history up to 1860 suggests the question: "Does it matter what kind of money it is?"

NOTES

1. Paul Studenski and Herman Krooss, *Financial History of the United States* (1952), p. 31.
2. Arthur Rolnick, Bruce Smith, and Warren Weber, "In Order to Form a More Perfect Monetary Union," Federal Reserve Bank of Minneapolis, *Quarterly Review*, Fall 1993. The authors note such a union would also avoid the seigniorage problem inherent in a fixed exchange rate system. For more on the exchange rates between the colonies, see John McCusker, *Money and Exchange in Europe and America, 1600–1775: A Handbook* (Chapel Hill: University of North Carolina Press, 1978).
3. Richard Hofstadter, editor, *Great Issues in American History from the Revolution to the Civil War 1765–1865* (New York: Vintage Books, 1958), part III, document 3, p. 155.
4. For a look into the first years of the bank, see David J. Cowen, "The First Bank of the United States and the Securities Market Crash of 1792," *Journal of Economic History*, vol. 60, no. 4, December 2000.
5. In Jeffery Jenkins and Marc Weidenmier, "Ideology, Economic Interests, and Congressional Roll-Call Voting: Partisan Instability and Bank of the United States Legislation, 1811–1816," *Public Choice*, September 1999, vol. 100, no. 3–4, the authors examine the votes to recharter the First Bank and to charter the Second Bank. They find the former vote followed ideological lines, but not the latter. In between, the Federalist party collapsed.
6. See, for example, Richard Sylla, "U.S. Securities Markets and the Banking System, 1790–1840," *Review*, May/June 1998.
7. Studenski and Krooss (1952), pp. 62–63; David Martin, "The Changing Role of Foreign Money in the United States, 1782–1857," *JEH*, December 1977.
8. The view that the states used bank charters to get around the prohibition against printing their own notes has now been buttressed by research showing that the states not only taxed the capital of the banks, but sometimes invested in the banks themselves. It is now estimated that the states, in the antebellum period may have raised as much as 20 percent of their finances from bank-chartering. Richard Sylla, John Legler, and John Wallis,

"Banks and State Public Finance in the New Republic: The United States, 1790–1860," *JEH*, June 1987.

9. The use of the adjective "wildcat" is uncertain, but it appears to be related to the frontier.
10. The actual reserve ratios maintained by the antebellum banks seem to have varied widely. Roger Hinderliter and Hugh Rockoff, "The Management of Reserves by Antebellum Banks in Eastern Financial Centers," *EEH*, Fall 1973.
11. Hugh Rockoff, *The Free Banking Era: A Reexamination* (1975); and Peter Temin, *The Jacksonian Economy* (1969).
12. Richard Sylla, "American Banking and Growth in the Nineteenth Century: A Partial View of the Terrain," *EEH*, Winter 1971–1972. Also, Paul Trescott, *Financing American Enterprise: The Story of Commercial Banking* (New York: Harper & Row, 1963), chap. 2.
13. Examples of unsuccessful systems: in England after the 1837 crisis, the abandonment of the "Palmer Rule" for governing the Bank of England; in France, the failure of bimetallism to stabilize the French currency in the 1850s; also in France, the national development bank, the Credit Mobilier, was founded in 1852—it failed 15 years later. Jonathan Hughes, *Fluctuations in Trade, Industry and Finance* (1960), chaps. 2 and 10.
14. Robert Craig West, *Banking Reform and the Federal Reserve, 1863–1923* (Ithaca, NY: Cornell University Press, 1977), chap. 7. Also, Sylla (1971–1972) contains a discussion of origins, rationale, and relevant literature on the short-term credit, or "real bills" doctrine in American banking.
15. Naomi Lamoreaux, *Insider Lending: Banks, Personal Connections, and Economic Development in Industrial New England* (1994).
16. *Ibid.*, p. 82.
17. Robert Wright, "Bank Ownership and Lending Patterns in New York and Pennsylvania, 1781–1831," *BHR*, Spring 1999, and Howard Bodenhorn, *A History of Banking in Antebellum America* (2000), particularly chaps. 2 and 3.
18. Richard Timberlake, Jr., *Money, Banking, and Central Banking* (New York: Harper & Row, 1965), chaps. 5–7.
19. Jonathan Hughes and Nathan Rosenberg, "The United States Business Cycle Before 1860: Some Problems of Interpretation," *EHR*, April 1963.
20. Temin (1969). See also, Hugh Rockoff, "Money, Prices, and Banks in the Jacksonian Era," in Robert Fogel and Stanley Engerman, eds., *The Reinterpretation of American Economic History*, (1971), chap. 33.
21. Studenski and Krooss (1952), pp. 88–99; Wilfred Lake, "The End of The Suffolk System," *Journal of Economic History*, vol. VII, no. 2, November 1947. Arthur Rolnick, Bruce Smith, and Warren Weber, "The Suffolk Bank and the Panic of 1837," *Quarterly Review*, Federal Reserve Bank of Minneapolis, Vol. 24, No. 2, Spring 2000, argues that by acting as a clearing house for the banknotes of the area, the Suffolk Bank made reserves available to other New England banks during the Panic of 1837 and kept the payments system operating. In this respect, it supplied a service now associated with central banks. Two other recent studies make use of the Suffolk System to examine contemporary issues. Charles Calomiris and Charles Khan, "The Efficiency of Self-Regulated Payments Systems: Learning from the Suffolk System," *Journal of Money Credit and Banking*, vol. 28, no. 4, Nov 1996, Part 2, examine it as a self-regulatory clearing system, while Bruce Smith and Warren Weber, "Private Money Creation and the Suffolk Banking System," *Journal of Money, Credit and Banking*, vol. 31, no. 3, August 1999, Part 2, examine the private money issue (which has an electronic counterpart today).
22. Double liability for stockholders lasted generally until 1933. The Emergency Banking Act of that year removed double liability for new stocks issued by national banks. The national banking law of 1935 enabled national banks to drop this requirement for all their stocks by 1937. State banks followed suit later.
23. George Green, "The Louisiana Bank Act of 1842: Policy-Making During Financial Crisis," *EEH*, Summer 1970; Irene Neu, "Edmund Jean Forstall and Louisiana Banking," *EEH*, Summer 1970.
24. Studenski and Krooss (1952), p. 89; A. Barton Hepburn, *History of Currency in the United States* (1924).
25. John Holdsworth and Davis Dewey, *The First and Second Banks of the United States* (Washington, D.C.: Government Printing Office, 1910); Ralph Catterall, *The Second Bank of the United States* (1903); A. M. Schlesinger, Jr., *The Age of Jackson* (1945); Bray Hammond, *Banks and Politics in America from the Revolution to the Civil War* (1957); Bray Hammond, "Jackson, Biddle, and the Bank of the United States," *JEH*, May 1947; Marie Elizabeth Sushka, "The Ante-Bellum Money Market and the Economic Impact of the Bank War," *JEH*, December 1976.
26. "Jefferson," in Hofstadter, *op. cit.*, p. 158.
27. George Rogers Taylor, ed., *Jackson and Biddle: The Struggle over the Second Bank of the United States* (Boston: D. C. Heath, 1949); see also Schlesinger (1945).
28. Also, according to David Martin, Jacksonians viewed the Second Bank as a transgressor for not ridding the country of small-note paper currency. "Metallism, Small

Notes, and Jackson's War with the B.U.S.," *EEH*, Spring 1974.

29. The Federal Reserve Act became law 23 December 1913 when Woodrow Wilson signed the Act. It has become common practice to say that the Federal Reserve System began in 1914 with the commencement of its operations.
30. Stuart Banner, "The Origin of the New York Stock Exchange, 1791–1860," *Journal of Legal Studies*, vol. xxvii, January 1998.
31. Lance Davis, Jonathan Hughes, and Duncan McDougall, *American Economic History*, 3rd ed. (Homewood, IL: Irwin, 1969), chap. 13.
32. A particularly interesting case is Karen Clay's study of merchant activity in early California, "Trade, Institutions, and Credit," *Explorations in Economic History*, vol. 34, no. 4, October 1997.
33. Howard Bodenhorn and Hugh Rockoff, "Regional Interest Rates in Antebellum America," in Claudia Goldin and Hugh Rockoff, eds., *Strategic Factors in Nineteenth Century American Economic History* (1992). They find that, using the simplest definition of integration, Philadelphia and South Carolina were integrated with New York City as early as 1820. See also Bodenhorn (2000), particularly chap. 4.
34. Thomas Willett, "International Specie Flows and American Monetary Stability," *JEH*, March 1968.
35. Sir Albert Feavearyear, *The Pound Sterling: A History of English Money* (Oxford: The Clarendon Press, 1963), chap. IX.
36. The interest discount a bill's buyer would desire would be the one equal to his or her "opportunity cost," the return the money would bring from an alternative investment of equal quality. This calculation would depend upon the buyer's options. If a seller wanted to be charged a lower price for cash, he or she would need some alternatives. In Lance Davis and Jonathan Hughes, "A Dollar-Sterling Exchange 1803–1895," *EHR*, August 1960, domestic rates were thus used to determine exchange rates implicit in prices of bills purchased in the United States. For the view and supporting arguments that English rates would better serve the purpose, see Edwin Perkins, "Foreign Interest Rates in American Financial Markets: A Revised Series of Dollar-Sterling Exchange Rates, 1835–1900," *Journal of Economic History*, vol. XXXVIII, no. 2, June 1978; Lawrence Officer, "Dollar-Sterling Mint Parity and Exchange Rates, 1791–1834," *Journal of Economic History*, vol. XLIII, no. 3, September 1983; and Michael Collins, "Sterling Exchange Rates, 1847–80," *The Journal of European Economic History*, vol. 16, no. 3, Winter 1986.
37. Davis and Hughes (1960), Table A-2.
38. Normal Buck, *The Development of the Organization of Anglo-American Trade, 1800–1850* (New Haven: Yale University Press, 1925); R. C. O. Matthews, *A Study in Trade-Cycle History* (Cambridge: Cambridge University Press, 1953), chap. V.
39. Douglass North, *The Economic Growth of The United States 1790–1860* (1961); also, a shorter version, Douglass North, "The United States Balance of Payments, 1790–1860," in *Trends in the American Economy in the Nineteenth Century*, NBER, *Studies in Income and Wealth*, (Princeton: Princeton University Press, 1960), vol. 24.
40. Jonathan Hughes, *The Vital Few* (New York: Oxford University Press, 1986), chap. 9.
41. This relationship was discussed by Gardiner Means in 1935 in Senate Document No. 13, 74th Congress, 1st session, "Industrial Prices and Their Relative Inflexibility," reprinted and elaborated in Means's book, *The Corporate Revolution in America* (New York: Collier Books, 1964), chaps. 4 and 5.
42. W. B. Smith and A. H. Cole, *Fluctuations in American Business 1790–1860* (Cambridge: Harvard University Press, 1935), section I.
43. On the pattern of British cycles in this period, A. D. Gayer, W. W. Rostow, and A. J. Schwartz, *Growth and Fluctuation of the British Economy 1790–1850* (Oxford: The Clarendon Press, 1952); W. W. Rostow, *British Economy of the Nineteenth Century* (Oxford: The Clarendon Press, 1952); R. C. O. Matthews, *op. cit.*; Jonathan Hughes, "The Commercial Crisis of 1857," *Oxford Economic Papers*, vol. 2, June 1956; Peter Temin, "The Anglo-American Business Cycle, 1820–1860," *EHR*, May 1974.
44. Ira Ryner, "On the Crises of 1837, 1847 and 1857," *University of Nebraska Studies*, vol. 5, April 1905; Temin (1969).
45. Robert A. Margo, *Wages & Labor Markets in the United States, 1820–1860* (Chicago: The University of Chicago Press, 2000), chap. 6, provides an interesting view of the California gold rush.
46. Hughes (1960), chap. 1.
47. Gold and currency figures taken from *Historical Statistics*, 1960, series M 268; X 420.
48. Hughes (1956).
49. Temin (1974).
50. Wesley Clair Mitchell and Arthur Burns, the leading American students of business cycles, attempted to reduce the evidence to those elements common to all cycles. They concluded that business cycles "can be seen through a cloud of witnesses only by the eye of the mind." *Measuring Business Cycles* (New York: National Bureau of Economic Research, 1947), p. 12.
51. Temin (1969), pp. 80–81.
52. Hughes and Rosenberg (1963).

SUGGESTED READINGS

Articles

Bodenhorn, Howard, and Hugh Rockoff. "Regional Interest Rates in Antebellum America." In Claudia Goldin and Hugh Rockoff, eds., *Strategic Factors in Nineteenth Century American Economic History*. Chicago: University of Chicago Press, 1992.

Bordo, Michael, and Anna J. Schwartz. "Money and Prices in the Nineteenth Century: An Old Debate Rejoined." *Journal of Economic History*, vol. XL, no. 1, March 1980.

Davis, Lance E., and Jonathan Hughes. "A Dollar-Sterling Exchange 1803–1895." *Economic History Review*, vol. XIII, no. 1, August 1960.

Green, George D. "The Louisiana Bank Act of 1842: Policy Making During Financial Crisis." *Explorations in Economic History*, vol. 7, no. 4, Summer 1970.

Hammond, Bray. "Jackson, Biddle, and the Bank of the United States." *Journal of Economic History*, vol. VI, no. 2, May 1947.

Hinderliter, Roger H., and Hugh Rockoff. "The Management of Reserves by Banks in Ante-Bellum Eastern Financial Centers." *Explorations in Economic History*, vol. 11, no. 1, Fall 1973.

Hughes, Jonathan. "The Commercial Crisis of 1847." *Oxford Economic Papers*, vol. 8, no. 2, June 1956.

———, and Nathan Rosenberg. "The United States Business Cycle Before 1860: Some Problems of Interpretation." *Economic History Review*, vol. XV, no. 3, August 1963.

Lamoreaux, Naomi R. "Banks, Kinship, and Economic Development." *Journal of Economic History*, vol. XLVI, no. 3, September 1986.

Martin, David A. "1853: The End of Bimetallism in the United States." *Journal of Economic History*, vol. XXXIII, no. 4, December 1973.

———. "Metallism, Small Notes, and Jackson's War with the B.U.S." *Explorations in Economic History*, vol. 11, no. 3, Spring 1974.

———. "The Changing Role of Foreign Money in the United States, 1782–1857." *Journal of Economic History*, vol. XXXVII, no. 4, December 1977.

Neu, Irene D. "Edmond Jean Forstall and Louisiana Banking." *Explorations in Economic History*, vol. 7, no. 4, Summer 1970.

North, Douglass C. "The United States Balance of Payments, 1790–1860." *Trends in the American Economy in the Nineteenth Century*, NBER, *Studies in Income & Wealth*. Princeton: Princeton University Press, 1960, vol. 24.

Redlich, Fritz. "American Banking and Growth in the Nineteenth Century: Epistemological Reflections." *Explorations in Economic History*, vol. 10, no. 3, Spring 1973.

Rockoff, Hugh. "Money, Prices and Banks in the Jacksonian Era." In Robert Fogel and Stanley Engerman, eds., *The Reinterpretation of American Economic History*. New York: Harper & Row, 1971, chap. 33.

———. "Varieties of Banking and Regional Economic Development in the United States, 1840–1860." *Journal of Economic History*, vol. XXXV, no. 1, March 1975.

Roll, Richard. "Interest Rates and Price Expectations during the Civil War." *Journal of Economic History*, vol. XXXII, no. 2, June 1972.

Rolnick, Arthur, Bruce Smith, and Warren Weber. "In Order to Form a More Perfect Monetary Union." Federal Reserve Bank of Minneapolis, *Quarterly Review*, Fall 1993.

Sushka, Marie Elizabeth. "The Ante-Bellum Money Market and the Economic Impact of the Bank War." *Journal of Economic History*, vol. XXXVI, no. 4, December 1976.

Sylla, Richard. "American Banking and Growth in the Nineteenth Century: A Partial View of the Terrain." *Explorations in Economic History*, vol. 9, no. 2, Winter 1971–1972.

———. "U.S. Securities Markets and the Banking System, 1790–1840." *Review*, Federal Reserve Bank of St. Louis, vol. 80, no. 3, May/June 1998.

———, John B. Legler, and John J. Wallis. "Banks and State Public Finance in the New Republic: The United States, 1790–1860," *Journal of Economic History*, vol. XLLVII, no. 2, June 1987.

Temin, Peter. "The Anglo-American Business Cycle, 1820–1860." *Economic History Review*, 2nd series, vol. XXVII, no. 2, May 1974.

Willett, Thomas D. "International Specie Flows and American Monetary Stability." *Journal of Economic History*, vol. XXVIII, no. 1, March 1968.

Wright, Robert E. "Bank Ownership and Lending Patterns in New York and Pennsylvania, 1781–1831." *Business History Review*, vol 73, no. 1, Spring 1999.

Books

Bodenhorn, Howard. *A History of Banking in Antebellum America: Financial Markets and Economic Development in an Era of Nation-Building*. New York: Cambridge University Press, 2000.

Catterall, Ralph. *The Second Bank of the United States*. Chicago: University of Chicago Press, 1903.

Hammond, Bray. *Banks and Politics in America from the Revolution to the Civil War*. Princeton: Princeton University Press, 1957.

Hepburn, A. Barton. *History of Currency in the United States.* New York: Macmillan, 1915.

Hughes, Jonathan. *Fluctuations in Trade, Industry and Finance.* Oxford: The Clarendon Press, 1960.

Lamoreaux, Naomi. *Insider Lending: Banks, Personal Connections, and Economic Development in Industrial New England.* New York: Cambridge University Press, 1994.

North, Douglass C. *The Economic Growth of the United States 1790–1860.* Englewood Cliffs, NJ: Prentice-Hall, 1961.

Redlich, Fritz. *The Molding of American Banking: Men and Ideas.* New York: Hafner, 1947 and 1951, 2 vols.

Rockoff, Hugh. *The Free Banking Era: A Reexamination.* New York: Arno Press, 1975.

Schlesinger, A. M., Jr. *The Age of Jackson.* New York: Mentor Books, 1945.

Studenski, Paul, and Herman Krooss. *Financial History of the United States.* New York: McGraw-Hill, 1952.

Sumner, William Graham. *A History of American Currency.* New York: Putnam's Sons, 1878.

Temin, Peter. *The Jacksonian Economy.* New York: Norton, 1969.

PART THREE

THE RISE OF AN INDUSTRIAL SOCIETY, 1861–1914

MAIN CURRENTS

Even though the Civil War's impact on the country's economic growth was negative, the war's end, in a very imprecise way, was a turning point. The Old South was "gone with the wind," and that region's economic well-being would compare poorly with the rest of the nation for decades to come. Northern agriculture came into its own in terms of production; by the 1880s wheat exports alone ran a close second to raw cotton, the country's leading staple export. In fact, farming's economic and social dominance was reaching its apex. The next generation of Americans would be the first to live in an industrial nation in which the growth of cities and an urban life and culture really dominated the nation's life and politics. A few figures will illustrate the nature of the change.

In 1870, there were 14 cities with 100,000 or more in population, and only 26 percent of the population lived in urban places of 2,500 or more. A person born that year turned 40 years of age in 1910, when there were 50 cities of more than 100,000 in the country and nearly half the population, 46 percent, lived in urban places. Three cities (New York, Chicago, and Philadelphia) had more than 1 million inhabitants, and five more had populations between 500,000 and 1 million.

In 1870, the United States made a mere 77,000 short tons of steel. In 1910, U.S. output of steel ingots and castings exceeded 28 million tons, more than Germany and Great Britain combined. Indeed, by 1913, the United States produced some 36 percent of the entire world's manufactured goods. In 1860, Great Britain alone surpassed American output of iron and coal by more than four times. However, by 1913, the United States produced more coal than did all of Europe, and it also produced more than half the world's petroleum output. These changes did not come overnight, but they did come easily within a single lifetime. The pace was fast enough to produce considerable social disruption as the nation's agrarian-based laws and institutions strained to adapt.

Although farmers would make one last heroic stand to achieve their collective aims, in the years after the Civil War, the focus was, appropriately enough, on the burgeoning powers of the federal government. The control powers of state governments would no longer be sufficient. An industrial and urban society would be one in which the federal power waxed at the expense of all other. It was the power to redistribute wealth and income, to create rents and disburse them on a political basis.

In his insightful book *The Search for Order, 1877–1920*, Robert Wiebe documents the breakdown of the old, unwritten "constitutional settlement" of antebellum America, a settlement based upon demography and land ownership.[1] The farmers and small-town political coalitions were fated to lose their influence. Railroads, cities, mines, factories, heavy industry, great financial combines, and the giant corporations would be the major origins of the nation's economic growth in the half-century following Appomattox. Immigrants would pour in by the millions, mainly into the cities and industrial regions.

Twenty years after Appomattox the old conflict of free soil versus slavery and westward expansion seemed as long gone as the Puritan forefathers. "Cousin Jonathan's Great Farm," as the English had called antebellum America, had been replaced by the world's major industrial nation, a dynamic volcano of technical and social change. American farmers were not victimized by railroads, bankers, or big business. In spite of roughly equal increases in labor productivity, the agricultural sector did not grow as rapidly as manufacturing, and farmers were aware of the declining importance of their sector. In many respects, the period from 1870 to 1914 was, as Robert Higgs celebrated it, truly the transformation of America.[2] Across the entire time span of American history, the transformation was briefly executed. Jefferson's ideas and hopes for a land of property-owning yeomen were largely forgotten.

Notes

1. Robert Wiebe, *The Search for Order* (New York: Hill & Wang, 1967).
2. Robert Higgs, *The Transformation of the American Economy 1865–1914: An Essay in Interpretation* (New York: Wiley, 1971).

CHAPTER THIRTEEN

Economic Effects of the Civil War

The most direct economic consequence of the Civil War was the ending of chattel slavery in the South, a labor system that had prevailed for nearly 250 years. Southern agriculture, the region's primary enterprise, was organized around forced labor. The supply of slaves in combination with the profitability of cotton determined the "choice of technique." The availability of slave labor conditioned the market values of real estate, personal wealth, and specialized tools and equipment. A whole society, class structure, system of manners, law, education, and expectations for the future, were rooted in the existence of property rights in human beings.

The Old South as a "going concern"—in an accounting sense—was an economy of compulsion at the fundamental level of real output. When the slaves were no longer compelled to work, when the capitalized value of their labor ceased to be an article of commerce in which a slave did not share, two-and-a-half centuries of historical development, measured in every conceivable way, dissipated. The slaves were free, but all Southerners, black and white alike, had to make a whole new start.

MEASURES OF THE WAR'S COSTS

What did the war cost? It is not foolish to try to calculate the cost of a war. War has been among the largest economic enterprises of the modern state. The cost of things matters. The Civil War wasted men and resources on a vast scale. The attempts that have been made to calculate the cost will seem both cold-blooded and artificial, but we need some figures to answer important questions about the war and subsequent economic development.

The Cost of Carnage

Approximately 600,000 died on both sides, 9 percent of the male population aged 15 through 39 as reported in the 1860 Census. The official numbers for the Union forces are that 140,000 troops died in battle, and another 224,000 died of other causes—16.5 percent of the total men in uniform. Another 282,000 were wounded.[1]

What were these lives worth? If they were valued at the price of a prime field hand in the 1860 market for slaves, about $2,000 each, the outright loss of that "human capital" would have been about $1.2 billion. Another 500,000 were wounded. How should the cost of those wounds be measured? Such intellectual calculations are, on the face of it, absurd. What family would have been willing to sell the life of a son or father for $2,000 in 1860? (This is equal to 20 years' consumption expenditures for each person at 1860 rates—perhaps it is just as well that the question remains rhetorical.) However, any attempt to say what the war cost must begin with such calculations.

Fortunately, Claudia Goldin and Frank Lewis have made the attempt.[2] Calling the excess of soldiers' pay over normal (peacetime) earnings to be a "risk premium" for the 600,000 dead, they estimate a loss of human capital of $1.06 billion for killed and wounded in the North and $767 million for the South, or about $1.8 billion in human loss for both sides combined. They estimate direct government expenditures were $2.3 billion in the North and $1 billion in the South. Physical destruction of property was mostly limited to the South and was estimated at $1.5 billion.

The Total Cost

Summing up all their figures, Goldin and Lewis estimate the direct Northern cost at $3.4 billion and the direct Southern cost at $3.3 billion, or perhaps $6.7 billion in all at war's end. What was that cost, in some real measure, in prices of 1860? The sum of $6.7 billion was more than *double* the total of U.S. exports in the 11 years between 1850 and 1860, and it was probably *double* the national income of 1860. It was more than *four times* the sum of all federal government expenditures from 1789 to 1860. It was more than *eight times* the value added by all U.S. manufacturing enterprises in 1860. It was nearly *seventeen times* the total value of U.S. exports in 1860.

We are considering, in strictly economic terms, what we might consider a sheer waste of resources. The sum of accumulated costs after 1865—that is, the opportunities and talents forever lost, the accumulated interest charges, and payments to veterans—have been omitted. Atack and Passell note that the war's cost could have purchased all the slaves from their owners at 1860 prices, given each slave family 40 acres and a mule, and still had $3.5 billion left over for "reparations"—back wages.[3]

Such was the cost of revising American history to exclude slavery. Americans have never known whether it was the price of virtue or the wages of sin. Either way the American Civil War was one of history's long bills that finally came due.

FINANCING THE CIVIL WAR

In the Civil War, as in all wars, *all* of the money actually paid out in the purchase of material and labor was *received* by someone. Thus, when we say that the war was a great cost to the participants, we also are saying that it was a great source of income for someone, too. An army contractor buying beef from farmers and selling it at a handsome profit to Uncle Sam clearly gained from the war if his income rose more than his taxes. An individual working in the private sector selling to people who received no war-related income paid out taxes that went toward the war, but received no war-related income in return. Destruction of life and property was a dead loss to those who paid. When a town's flour mill was destroyed, the owner lost the mill, and his neighbors had to incur the search, transactions, and transportation costs of finding an alternate mill to grind their wheat. For society as a whole, these losses must be subtracted from any gains that might have been achieved—as must the external diseconomies of the losses to third parties.

Taxes and Inflation

Financing a war means expropriating resources. Beyond death or wealth taxes, very little can be done to collect money from the past population. The present population can be taxed either directly or indirectly. Direct taxes include such devices as sales or income taxes, while indirect taxes include those raised by the inflation that inevitably results when defense expenditures surge ahead of tax collections. This is especially true if governments "pay" for the excess expenditures with freshly printed money. Alternatively, a government can raise the necessary resources from future populations by increasing net government borrowing, by increasing the *national debt*. In either case, the government buys what it wants, and the population must make do with less. The purchasing power of money decreases. As a result, it takes more and more newly printed money to buy a given bundle of goods. This is inflation. Both the federal and confederate governments tried this method of taxing—as have nearly all governments financing a war.

Federal Finance

As the Civil War began, both sides grossly underestimated the magnitude of coming events. On a current basis, neither the federal nor the confederate government contrived tax programs that came anywhere

The Real Financial Costs of War. Cleaning up the battlefield (above). The hundreds of thousands of young men slaughtered in the Civil War were an "expenditure" of human capital. How does one measure the dollar cost? The loss of physical capital could be measured by replacement cost (see below, Richmond in 1865).

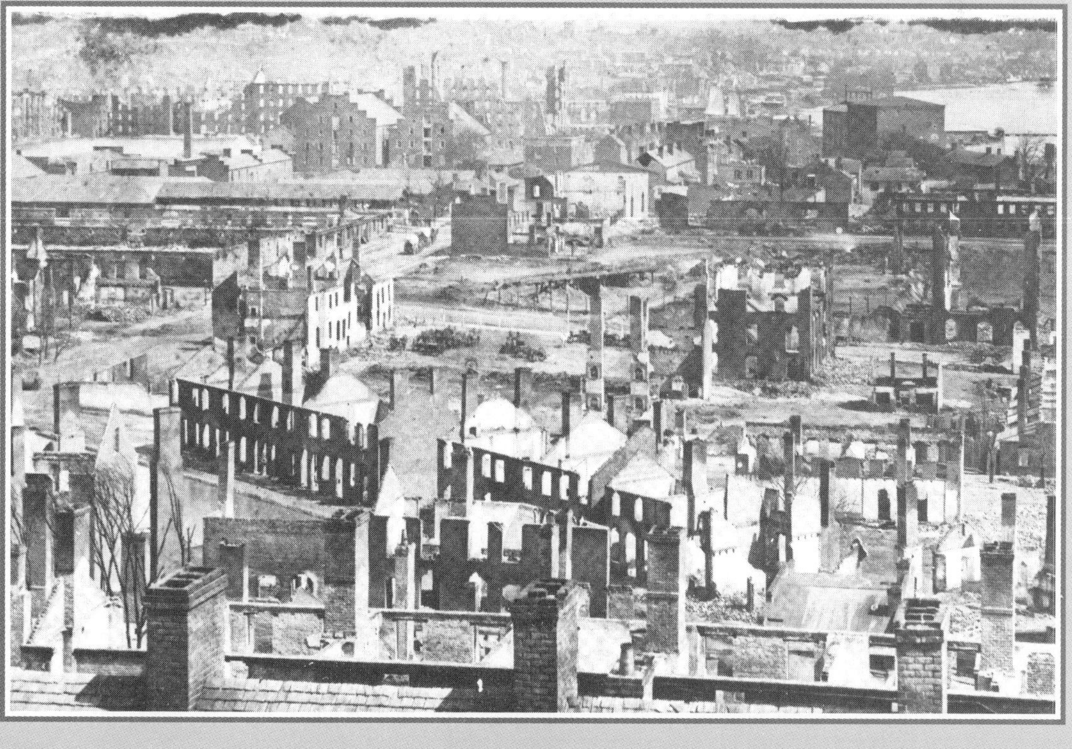

near to paying the bills. The result was debt and money creation in order to pay for more soldiers and more equipment. Inflation and borrowing on the future were necessary. Compare the federal budget results in the two years 1860 and 1865, as presented in Table 13.1.

Expenditures in 1865 were more than 20 times the level of 1860. Even though taxes were imposed on everything imaginable—including a slightly progressive income tax, increased customs, excises, extended federal licensing requirements for merchants, and taxes on whiskey and beer—the federal government by 1865 had been able to raise tax revenues over 1860 levels by only a factor of 5.9. Thus, the deficit increased by unimaginable proportions, and the gross debt grew by a factor of 41 in a mere five years. It is a wonder that the federal government could cope at all with increased financial necessities of such magnitude. Salmon P. Chase, Lincoln's Secretary of the Treasury, has suffered considerable criticism from historians for his programs. These included the "farming out" of bond sales to the financier Jay Cooke; the suspension of specie payments; the printing of federal legal-tender money (U.S. notes, popularly called *greenbacks*). In addition, the private banking system was officially harnessed to the war effort in 1864 by the establishment of the National Banking System and the force-feeding of more of the enormous bond issues into the nation's financial system. Yet, if we look back over more than a century (and several wars), Chase and his colleagues did a relatively good job.

The federal government squeezed the required resources from the economy by methods that were necessarily inflationary. With the suspension of specie payments in December 1861, the issue of $415 million in greenbacks in 1864, and an additional issue of $146 million of national bank notes by 1865 (with government bonds as their main security), the money supply had been increased from $442 million in 1860 to $1,180 million in 1865. Prices rose by a less than equal amount (see Table 13.2).

In 1860, with the country still suffering some unemployment in the aftermath of the 1857 panic, it was possible for an increase in the money supply to be absorbed by a considerable expansion of real goods and services. However, prices rose when the money stock rose and fell when the money stock fell, even if the proportions were not exactly the same. Also, as Stanley Engerman has shown (to be discussed in a later section), a reduction in the growth rate of the government's demand for other goods and services offset the increased demand for specifically military goods and services. Thus, on the federal side the inflation was surprisingly restrained, especially if we consider the scale of possible increase in the money supply derived from the debt increase (see Table 13.1). Greenbacks fell against gold on the free market to a maximum discount of 65 percent, but then recovered by war's end. **Hyperinflation**—price increases of truly extraordinary amounts (as in Germany in 1923, when prices were billions of times higher than they had been in 1914)—did not occur.

The Confederacy

For the South, the financial circumstances were far more difficult, but they finally did end in a disastrous hyperinflation.[4] Whereas the federal government had been able to raise taxes enough to cover more than 20 percent of the war expenditures, the government in Richmond, Virginia, its ports cut off by the federal

TABLE 13.1 Federal Government Budgets and Debt[a]

Year	*Revenues*	*Expenditures*	*Surplus (+) Deficit (–)*	*Gross Debt*
1860	$ 56.1	$ 63.1	$– 7.0	$ 64.8
1865	333.7	1,297.6	–963.9	2,677.9
1865 data / 1860 data	5.9	20.6	137.7	41.3

[a] Amounts given are in millions of dollars.

Source: *Historical Statistics,* derived from series Y 335–38.

TABLE 13.2 Money and Prices[a]

	Index Numbers—Federal Side		
Year	*Money Stock*	*Wholesale Prices*	*Cost of Living*
1860	100	100	100
1865	267	199	167
1869	198	162	156

[a] Amounts given are in millions of dollars.

Source: *Historical Statistics*, derived from series X 420, 585–586; E 52, 183.

blockade and a war raging through its territories, could raise only about 12 percent of its expenditures by taxation. Confederate debt totaled more than $2 billion when the war ended.[5] Prices had risen by a factor of 92.[6] The Confederate monetary officials had neglected to make their notes legal tender—a major management error—and as the South's military fortunes sank, the currency became worthless. According to Eugene Lerner's calculations, before the war's end the Confederate notes fell to a level of nearly 1/1000 against gold.[7] In the South the financial rout was probably worse than the military debacle. Lee negotiated for an army in the field at Appomattox. The same cannot be said for Confederate finances.[8] Holders of Confederate financial assets were wiped out. The victorious federal Congress did nothing to redeem the "rebel" currency and bonds.[9]

The Real Burden

Economic historians have puzzled over who paid for the Civil War. The dead, those who owned Confederate financial assets, those whose crops and farm animals were sequestered, and those whose homes and farm buildings were destroyed, of course, paid terrible prices. Slave owners parted with their property without compensation. What of the North? The billions spent became income for some, but not for all, nor in equal portions.

The decline of greenbacks against gold just noted was a measure of the *rise* in foreign exchange prices. Americans, for the most part, paid premium prices for imported goods. Some scholars have considered the resulting decline in purchasing power an important part of the real burden of the war. Table 13.3 shows the relevant available balance of payments data.

The data in Table 13.3 are five-year averages of Douglass North's estimates for foreign transactions in goods and services. It is clear that the war produced a sharp reduction in exports. Imports also fell, but to a lesser degree. These imports were more expensive because of the decline in greenback prices against gold. Alchian and Kessel have estimated that as much as 40 percent of the real income lag during the Civil War inflation came from this source.[10] If they are correct, then we must also consider the foreign transactions of the immediate postwar years to be part of the war burden. Note the huge decrease in the trade balance during the first five peacetime years. U.S. prices fell *immediately* from 1865 into 1866, and foreign prices did not generally decline until 1873. As the gold value of the U.S. dollar rose in the postbellum years, in part because of foreign investment in the renewed expansion in the North and West, the market for U.S. cotton, even at lower domestic prices, must have been adversely affected.[11] In short, the South was disproportionately harmed.

In terms of relative prices and exchange-rate problems, Americans may have been as badly off from 1866 to 1870 as they were from 1861 to 1865. The deficit was bigger, exports earned fewer imports, and the real burden of interest rates was higher because of falling domestic prices. The years 1866–1870 were distinctly years of recovery and economic expansion. That the internal economy expanded in the face of a trade deficit is not impossible, of course, but it does make the balance-of-payments argument concerning the real burden of the war far more complex than first seems to be the case.

Another older argument, stemming from Wesley Clair Mitchell's early work and given further support by Stephen DeCanio and Joel Mokyr, is that wage earners, suffering declining real earnings as wages

TABLE 13.3 U.S. Trade 1856–1870, Five-Year Averages[a]

	Goods and Services		
Period	*Exports*	*Imports*	*Balance*
1856–1860	383.2	396.4	−13.2
1861–1865	294.2	353.4	−59.2
1866–1870	442.4	560.4	−118.0

[a] Amounts given are in millions of dollars.

Source: *Historical Statistics*, series U 1, 8.

lagged behind the inflation, bore a major direct real cost of the war.[12] Fully two-thirds of the decline in real wages resulted from price increases fueled by monetary expansion.

In addition, the U.S. Treasury's conservative postwar policy of reducing the debt (see Table 13.1) by applying the proceeds of regressive taxation (taxing the poor to pay the rich) added to the real burden placed upon those who worked and paid taxes. Bonds purchased with inflated greenbacks were paid off in postwar dollars that had considerably higher real value (that is, purchasing power) in exchange for domestically produced goods. In the South, the war had been called "a rich man's war and a poor man's fight."[13] In the North, those conscripted could actually pay substitutes, poor men, to go in their places, and many did. As in most wars, those who could not escape the fighting and those who paid taxes picked up the tab. Others did well for themselves on the home front. Those whose income and wealth kept ahead of inflation did especially well.

DID THE WAR AID INDUSTRIALIZATION?

An older generation of historians saw in the Civil War itself the origin of the great wave of industrialization that came to the United States in the nineteenth century's final quarter. Many leading industrialists and financiers of that era, such as Andrew Carnegie and Pierpont Morgan, had made considerable financial gains during the war (but nothing like the amounts they would make later). War, these historians believed, must have raised enormous demands for the productions of manufacturing industry: all the army shoes, guns, uniforms, wagons, and food.

Historically speaking, agrarian America seemed to have been launched upon the road to industrialization almost in a flash. It happened in a single generation. Muckrakers like Matthew Josephson, who saw little of virtue or honor in the lives of the late-nineteenth century *nouveau riches* (those made wealthy in finance and industry), found special motivation in the idea that the American industrial state should have been launched by something so foul and tragic as the Civil War.[14] Even in poetry, such as Stephen Vincent Benét's *John Brown's Body*, it was the world of factories and workers that had beaten back the flashing sabers of the Southern cavaliers.

The Tradition and Engerman

Among American historians, the link between the Civil War and industrial expansion is most commonly attributed to Charles A. Beard and Louis Hacker.[15] The so-called Beard-Hacker thesis makes a splendid and vulnerable target. Writing in the 1920s and 1930s, with the economic growth of World War I in the immediate background, and arguing along the "industrial North" lines turned to verse by Benét, Beard and Hacker saw the Civil War as a major stimulus to industry, even though they lacked reliable data. The problem was that the war was fought *in the United States* and drew millions of people away from productive labor. For example, the million-odd men under arms in the Union army in 1865 were perhaps 20 percent of the total male population of military age. The war was, in fact, a great drain. As Stanley Engerman has shown, it stalled U.S. economic development.

Engerman could find few signs of the Civil War gains postulated in the Beard-Hacker thesis. Robert Gallman's total commodity output figures show an increase of 4.6 percent per annum between 1840 and 1860, a decrease to a mere 2 percent between 1860 and 1870, and then recovery to an annual average of 4.4 percent in the decades 1870–1900.[16] Engerman says of these, "The 1860s were uniquely low for the nineteenth century."[17] It would seem, by these measures, that the war cost the country about five years' growth. Real growth per capita was perhaps 1.5 percent per annum between 1850 and 1860. The war cut that rate sharply. On a per-capita basis, the "non-South" grew less than 1 percent per annum in the 1860s.

Output in the South, of course, fell absolutely. Indeed, it is Engerman's opinion that the revived growth rates after the war were, in part, merely "catching up." As for the Confederacy, Engerman writes:

> It is in the South that the destructive effects of the war were most severely felt. Per capita commodity output declined by 39 per cent in the Civil War decade, and in 1880 was still 21 percent below the 1860 level.[18]

He estimates that had the South maintained its prewar per-capita income growth, the 1870 level would have been *double* what it actually was. Edwin Frickey's index of industrial production rises a mere 6 percent from 1860 to 1865, but from 1865 to 1870 the increase is a robust 47 percent.[19] Data for fixed capital show an annual increase of 8.5 percent in the 1850s and less than half that rate (4.1 percent) in the 1860s.[20]

War Industries Alone

Attempts to narrow the search for benefits down to "war industries" alone show that, apart from woolens (millions of uniforms), the 1860s were slump years. Between 1855 and 1865, the Massachusetts boot and shoe industry showed a decline of some 30 percent in output and about the same in employment. Farm output increased little. The country was well fed when the war broke out. The North, despite rising prices for food, produced little additional output. For example, wheat flour output, at 41.6 million barrels in 1861, was 42.5 million in 1865.[21] After the 1864 harvest, Cyrus McCormick was carrying an unsold reaper inventory equal to 40 percent of his sales. Iron for guns was in fact a trivial portion of annual iron sales (1 percent) and railroad building, already down from the 1857 commercial crisis, sagged lower (below 1,000 miles) in the war years (see Figure 13.1).

The South suffered badly. Its exit from the national market was, of course, an additional blow. What it did to regional trade can be shown by the change in import quantities of a standard consumer item, coffee. Coffee imports were 180 million pounds in 1860, about 11 pounds per capita per annum. In 1862, the figure was, appropriately, cut nearly in half, to 94 million pounds. Coffee was part of a famous front-line swap in which the men in blue traded coffee for the tobacco of the men in gray. By 1870, imports had returned to 272 million pounds, roughly 6.8 pounds per capita per annum, about three-fourths what it is today.[22] All nonlocal trade must have been severely constrained by the absence of the South—the absence of its foreign-exchange earning ability and the absence of its market.

Real Wages and Profits

Engerman disputes the idea that falling real wages must have meant rising real income in other sectors of economic life—the **residual claimant hypothesis**.[23] He points out the obvious possibility that no one gained, that income shares remained unchanged, while the real growth of income declined overall.

FIGURE 13.1 Miles of Railroad Built 1850–1870

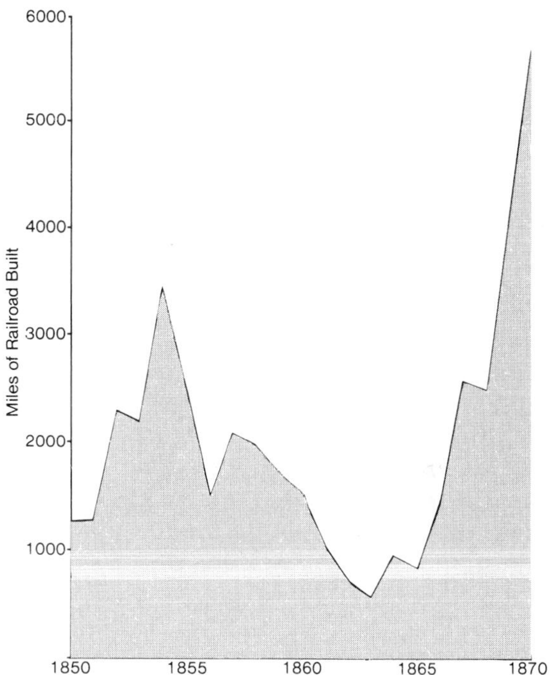

Source: *Historical Statistics*, series Q329.

Railroad construction declined after 1854 (although there was a temporary rally in 1857) and then fell even more drastically in the first years of the Civil War. The erea of the transcontinentals began after the war, and the statistic "miles of new railroads built" boomed until the Panic of 1873 played havoc with the economy.

Here the Kessel and Alchian argument is most effective. The turning of the terms of trade (export prices/import prices) against the United States during the war could have reduced the real level of wages, profits, interest, rents—everything. If the United States traded one bushel of wheat for eight English shirts, and then its export prices (the price of its currency) fell 25 percent against the pound, it would get only six shirts for a bushel of wheat. *Everyone* would share the loss of two shirts per bushel of wheat, regardless of income distribution. Actually, estimates of income distribution by Edward Budd show a slight rise in labor's income share during the war years.[24] Therefore, the admittedly small, available evidence does not support the residual claimant thesis.

Wartime Economic Legislation

Engerman also examined the major wartime economic legislation that was not strictly temporary—legislation written in the absence of Southern congressmen and senators. Some historians have seen in that legislation a device to further the interest of industrialists against the agrarians (the Beard-Hacker thesis again). The explanation sounds good, but it really does not work. The main legislation passed was the National Bank Act, Homestead Act, Morrill Act, Morrill Tariff, and the Pacific Railroad Act. The Morrill Tariff aside, this legislation produced no strictly pro-industry results, and, indeed, much of it satisfied old agrarian demands. The Morrill Tariff was as much (perhaps more) a measure to generate federal revenue than to aggrandize Northern capitalists.

Jeffrey Williamson argues, however, that improvements in federal debt financing augmented the country's ability to build its real capital structure after the war.[25] Interest payments and debt retirement, paid out of postwar revenues, made available about 1 percent of GNP annually to private capital formation between 1866 and 1872, and 0.8 percent between 1872 and 1878. The government, through its fiscal policy, acted as a capital mobilization machine.

From our modern perspective, the fact that the Civil War freed the slaves sanctifies its sacrifices. We do not question their freedom. However, because in 1860 Americans did question it, it is worthwhile to consider the economic costs. They are a part of our history, the great past, and they had consequences.[26]

COMPARATIVE RECOVERY: THE NORTH AND THE SOUTH AFTER THE WAR

Between 1860 and 1870, the nation's population grew by 8.4 million, or nearly one-fourth. The East North Central and West North Central states alone accounted for 3.8 million, or 45 percent, of the increase. The Southern states grew only by 1.1 million persons, 10 percent of its 1860 population, which contributed a mere 13 percent to the national increase. Yet before the war, as we have seen, the Southern population had grown about as rapidly as had the Midwest region. The data reflect a host of influences that blighted the South, but they also measure a sad problem that would vex the country for decades after the Civil War.

The South's agrarian vigor seemed to vanish with the slave-based plantation system. For a century thereafter, the South lagged behind the rest of the country by almost every measure of social and economic well-being.[27] One caveat is worth considering; Jay Mandle emphasizes that within the South, those states that experienced the least impact of the slave system, those with the fewest cotton plantations, showed the best record of growth and development in the postbellum period.[28]

Measures of Physical Growth

Per-capita commodity output showed an incredible reduction in the South. In 1860, the South actually had led the non-South by \$78 to \$75. In 1870, the South trailed, \$48 to \$82. Even in 1880, when the numbers were \$62 and \$106, the South had yet to recover to its prewar level, while the rest of the nation had raised its per-capita commodity output by 41 percent over the prewar figure. Growth of per-capita GNP in the country as a whole ranged between 4.4 and 5.2 percent per annum between 1871 and 1879, but gross Southern crop output increased by less than 2 percent per annum in the same period.[29] Table 13.4

TABLE 13.4 Commodity Output by Region and Industrial Sector[a]

Year	*Total*	*Mining and Agriculture*	*Manufacturing*
Non-South			
1860	100	100	100
1870	140	146	133
1880	232	218	245
South			
1860	100	100	100
1870	75	75	80
1880	118	115	141

[a] Amounts given are in millions of dollars.

Source: Calculated from Robert W. Fogel and Stanley Engerman, "The Economic Impact of the Civil War," reprinted in *The Reinterpretation of American Economic History*, edited by Robert Fogel and Stanley Engerman (New York: Harper & Row, 1971), p. 371.

shows gross commodity output converted to indexes of 1860.

The South's failure to recover is apparent by these measures. Even in 1880, when the non-South had more than doubled its output over 1860 in the agricultural and the industrial sectors, the South had gained only 15 percentage points in agricultural and 41 points in industrial output. Looking at these numbers, we are studying a failure of giant magnitude.

Wartime Destruction

The problem of war-related destruction has been considerably illuminated by recent research, some of it producing very surprising conclusions. The commonsense place to look for the origins of the South's postwar backwardness is in the actual wartime destruction of life, wealth, animals, buildings, and the functioning organizational networks for finance, commerce, and the like. These were grievous losses. James Sellers estimated that the money value of total wealth in the South declined by 30 percent as a result of the war. The South lost 20 percent of its sheep, 30 percent of its mules, 32 percent of its horses, 35 percent of its cattle, and 42 percent of its swine. Farm real estate fell in value by 50 percent.[30] These losses were of catastrophic proportions. Except in the most extraordinary circumstances, it would take some years to rebuild the animal herds alone. There was no postwar Marshall Plan to rebuild the South as there was for Europe after World War II.

In addition, the financial structure of the region was wrecked by the fiscal disaster of the Confederacy. Nine-tenths of the state banks of the South, which were larger on average than those of the North before the war, vanished.[31] The old labor-force organization was, of course, disestablished. How was the land to be farmed? No one knew. With peace came the mighty job of rebuilding, a situation similar to that in Germany and Japan in 1945.[32] The difference is that by 1950, the West Germans had reestablished real output at 1938 levels. As we have seen, the South had not really recovered 1860 levels of per-capita output by 1880. What went wrong?

Cotton

One problem was the long-term decline in raw cotton prices as the South recovered production. Cotton prices were very high in 1860. Output was the problem. Cotton crops of the size achieved in the late 1850s were only produced again in the late 1870s. By then, the prices were below the 1850s levels and far below those of the war and the immediate postwar years. In 1869, cotton still averaged 16.5 cents per pound (in 1865 it had been 43.2 cents). By the late 1870s, the price was half that and generally stayed between 8 cents and 9 cents per pound for the rest of the century.[33] Roger Ransom and Richard Sutch showed that cotton prices fell generally, even more than other prices, in a period of declining farm prices.[34] To actually gain in such a market, producers would have needed extraordinary increases in efficiency. Such were not forthcoming in the postwar years. As a result, King Cotton was no longer the sure source of prosperity it once had been.

Despite these figures, cotton was still the premier cash crop in the South, and producers redoubled their efforts to raise total output. As Gavin Wright emphasized, the old self-sufficiency of the prewar cotton culture was sacrificed to make more cotton per farm.[35] With prices falling for their cash crop, cotton growers increasingly had to buy food and provisions, and, as we shall see, under onerous conditions. Southern *poverty* associated with cotton now became a fixed feature of the South. Before the war, cotton had meant riches. In 1866, 7.7 million acres were planted in cotton, in 1870, more than 9 million. By 1875, the figure was more than 11 million acres, but the 1875 crop, 4.6 million bales, was probably smaller than that of 1859.[36] Output per acre had fallen sharply. Why?

Emancipation without Compensation

The Southern slave system, rooted in the oppression of black workers, had evolved over two-and-a-half centuries into a powerful engine of economic expansion that was nourished by the market for raw cotton. When that engine was shattered by military defeat and emancipation, there were many possibilities open for the reordering of economic life. Although the South grew during the postwar years, and blacks experienced substantial gains, the chosen system restricted growth.

Like iron filings under the force of a magnet, a new pattern formed, and unfortunately that pattern was one of relatively low productivity, poverty, and social backwardness. In *One Kind of Freedom,* a study of the remarkable institutional transformation of the postbellum South, Roger Ransom and Richard Sutch argue that the magnetic force was racism. "Keeping the Negro in his place" gave the American economy a huge island of rural backwardness within the larger mold of dynamic American capitalism in the later decades of the nineteenth century. While the Northern and Western states produced the world of U.S. Steel, General Electric, and Standard Oil, a unique phenomenon in world history of financially integrated economic growth and change, the agrarian South evolved into a pattern of relative poverty.

Before the war, ideas for "buying out" slavery had focused upon compensating slave owners for the loss of their human property. The war ended that approach. The slaves were freed unconditionally, their rights established by constitutional amendment. Southern slave owners were forced to absorb personally the financial loss, estimated at perhaps $1.6 billion (at 1860 slave prices), or perhaps 40 percent of the total property loss in the South.[37]

Like their owners, slaves also were not compensated—in their case, for the centuries-long oppression of themselves and their ancestors. Ransom and Sutch estimated the rate of exploitation (slave "wages" below the market value of their labor) at about 54 percent.[38] While the entire nation had benefited from the slaves' labor, no debt was paid. Blacks were left to fend for themselves in the market economy. Without property, without money, without skills (in 1870 more than 90 percent could only be laborers), without experience in the most ordinary decision-making processes of economic life (bargains for their labor, for example), they were uniquely unprepared for the lives they now had to find for themselves.[39] In 1870, more than 90 percent of black males over 20 were illiterate (compared to 20 percent for poor Southern whites in the same age group).[40]

At the end of the war, not one Southern state contained a statewide system of public education. The victorious federal Congress, sunk in corruption and incompetence, did next to nothing to remedy the situation. For Southern whites, peacetime life began with destruction, poverty, and defeat. For blacks, peacetime life began in a void. They were free but without property, skills, or education.

Peacetime Progress for Southern Blacks

The stark picture this conjures is overstated. For Southern blacks, freedom began the process of reaching equality with white Americans that would last for generations to come and that is still incomplete. The important point is that there was some progress. In the years before World War I, the economic position of Southern blacks advanced more rapidly than that of whites, as might be expected given the small base from which they began. Culling data from reports of the Comptroller-General of Georgia, Robert Higgs reported that, by 1880, Southern blacks accumulated a total of $5.8 million worth of property, roughly $8 per capita. Over the next 30 years, assessed value of property increased by a factor of 3.3 for blacks but only by 1.4 for whites.[41] Higgs calculated that the level of black income per capita more than doubled between the end of the Civil War and 1900.[42]

One explanation for this was the rapid rise of literacy among blacks. With literacy came the ability to process information. At emancipation, most blacks lacked the ability and experience to be successful farmers. The increase in literacy reflects a major investment in human capital. In his study of education in the South, Robert Margo notes that over three-fourths of blacks were illiterate in 1880, in contrast to one-fifth of whites. Twenty years later, over one-half of Southern blacks are reported as literate in contrast to seven-eighths of whites. Beginning in 1880, each successive generation of black children had higher rates of school attendance and, therefore, literacy. Up to the turn of the century, Southern schools were "separate, but equal." This status changed in the twentieth century as whites came to demand more education and blacks were disenfranchised. Nevertheless, Margo estimates that, by 1950, black literacy had reached 90 percent.[43] As Higgs comments:

> Perhaps the widespread failure to recognize the genuine economic gains of the first half century of freedom springs from an exclusive concentration on certain obstacles to even greater black progress.... To catalog the major barriers blocking more rapid progress is to identify important elements of what might conceivably have been but was not accomplished.[44]

A second factor was migration, as blacks responded to interstate differentials in agricultural productivity. Blacks migrated westward into Arkansas, Oklahoma, and Texas. Many were searching for a farm of their own, either to own or to rent. Others sought opportunities in the newly emerging urban centers of the Southwest.

Labor and Sharecropping

Initially the problem was determining how to work the land. Defeated or not, the South was still part of the American economy. Because it was mainly rural, farming had to be the basis of the immediate future. The right to use land had to come, as before, from ownership or from some tenure that was a derivative of ownership: lease, rental, or working on shares.

The land still belonged to those whose titles were derived from antebellum ownership. Blacks needed to work for others, initially at least. Various schemes were tried—wages by the month, wages with food and lodging thrown in. A government agency, The Freedman's Bureau, tried to set a minimum wage of $8 to $10 per month. (Freedmen had bargained for as low as $2 per month in Georgia in 1865). No uniform system of wage payment was found, of course. In a competitive market, the wage was determined, in part, by the productivity of the land in question. Wages would necessarily differ in different locations and circumstances. No general rule was possible.

At this point, the South (and some later historians) should have recognized the role *force* had played under slavery. Force meant more hours, and more days, for more people, in common labor than would have been the case in a "free market." Once set free, the former slaves made labor-leisure choices similar to those of whites. Women and children quit the fields, and men opted for more time off, exchanging leisure for money earnings. Here was born the opposite, racist myth that the freedmen were lazy! Like anyone else, they no longer would work like slaves once they had the freedom to choose between work and leisure. The extra days, long hours, and extra hard work had been the special contribution of force to slavery's remarkable overall productivity *per head*.

Thus, one immediate result of emancipation was a labor "shortage," although it was an intentional shortage. Since workers withdrew the extra work time that was compulsory under slavery, per-capita output fell from antebellum levels in the five states of the Cotton South and *never recovered* during the rest of the nineteenth century. In 1900, it stood at 69 percent of the 1859 level; in earlier years it had been lower.[45] As Ransom and Sutch pointed out, the withdrawal of about one-third of the potential black labor input rendered irrelevant much of the wartime losses of animals, implements, and buildings.[46] With less available labor, these items could hardly have been employed, in any case. Yet, even by working less, the freedmen raised their real standards of life considerably above anything enjoyed during slave times.[47] One publication quoted by Ransom and Sutch noted with muted outrage in April 1866: "Most of the field labor is now performed by men, the women regarding it as the duty of their husbands to support them in idleness."[48]

After mixed, and largely unhappy, experiences with attempts to institute work for hire, even efforts to restore gang labor, the South fell back upon alternate methods of putting its lands and people to work: ownership and various forms of tenancy, including sharecropping.[49] As Higgs points out, "wage payments proved unsatisfactory to both employers and employees."[50] Given the pace they had demanded of their slaves, planters complained that freedmen shirked. For their part, the freedmen complained that the planters cheated on the wage contract.

Ownership of land was still highly concentrated, but the old plantation lands were now largely subdivided into thousands of family-size farms.[51] In general, freedmen lacked the resources to buy equipment or livestock, and they had little to employ at first. After many experiments, the more or less standard agreement for sharecropping was a fifty-fifty split of the crop, and the landowner furnished the farm and buildings, seed and equipment, and provisions for the year. The freedman furnished his own and his family's labor. The contracts were almost universally renewable every year.[52] In 1860, more than 80 percent of all improved lands had been in farms of 100 or more acres. By 1870, nearly 40 percent of the farms were less than 100 acres; 73 percent of the land was owned by the wealthiest 20 percent of the population. In 1860, it had been 75.1 percent.[53] Thus, the war, whatever it did to individual landowners, did little to "democratize" land ownership. By 1880 in the Cotton South, 69.5 percent of the

FIGURE 13.2 Cotton South in 1880: All Land in Crops and the Tenure

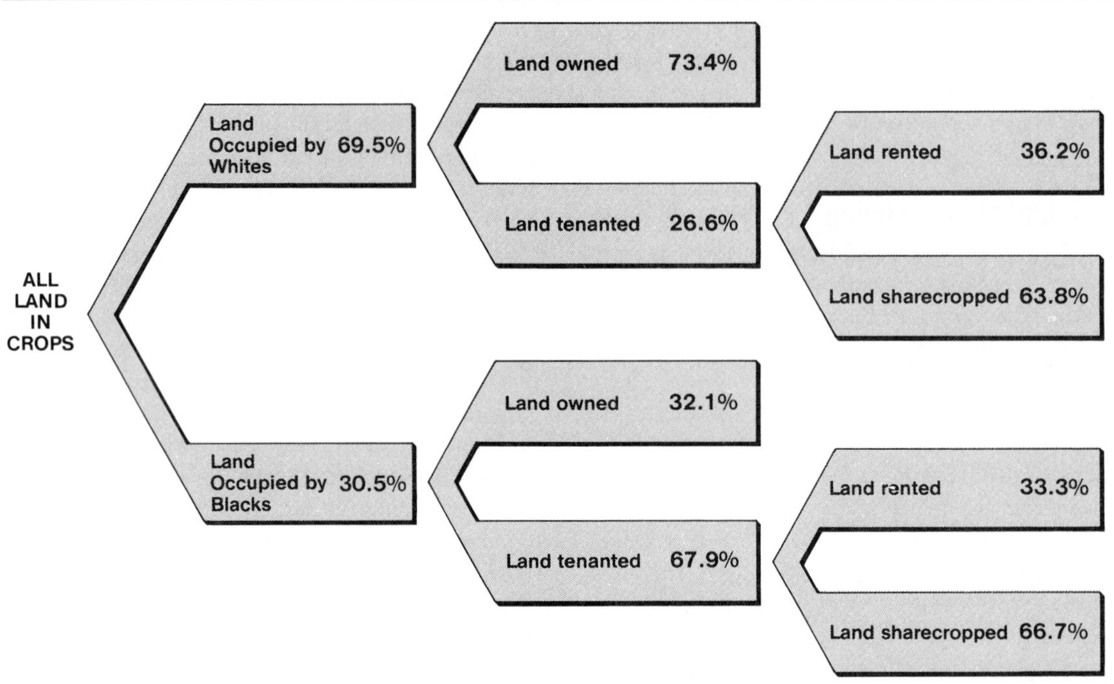

Source: Roger L. Ransom and Richard Sutch, *One Kind of Freedom: The Economic Consequences of Emancipation* (New York: Cambridge University Press, 1977), derived from Table 5.1, p. 84.

Of Southern land tenanted, more than 60 percent of that held by both whites and blacks was sharecropped. Most of the farmland (69.5 percent) was occupied by whites. Of that portion held by whites, 73.4 percent was owner operated. For blacks, the ownership figure was only 32.1 percent (which was less than 10 percent of total Southern farmland.

farms were operated by whites and 30.5 percent by blacks (see Figure 13.2). The average landowner in 1880 who employed tenants employed 4.7 of them. Some of the old plantations had been held together by the use of tenant and hired labor, and, in 1880, they still managed to produce about 14 percent of the cotton grown.[54]

Blacks made up half of the Southern population and were probably more than 70 percent of the agricultural labor force. By 1880, they owned 32.1 percent of the 30.5 percent of land occupied by blacks. They owned, therefore, 9.8 percent of the Cotton South's land sown in crops by 1880. If we consider conditions in 1865, it seems remarkable that *so much* of the land had come into black possession in ownership by 1880. Not only was land expensive, but resistance, sometimes violent, to any black ownership at all was widespread.[55] Note in Figure 13.2 that of the land tenanted, the proportions of the tenanted land rented out and sharecropped were about the same among poor whites and blacks.[56] As Ransom and Sutch commented, sharecropping may well have given poor white farmers their chance too![57]

The sharecropping agreement was a form of labor-force organization and control. Management basically remained with the landowner, who could, by provisioning of the farms, determine what and how much could be planted. There has been considerable debate about the origin in the United States of the sharecropping agreement. Joseph Reid and others have argued that the final form was an optimal outcome of free-agent bargaining.[58] Others have seen different origins. Without presuming to settle the matter, the following, regarding the *first* sharecropping agreement in American history (in the Virginia colony), is of interest:

> After 1618 and until the crown took over in 1625, indentured servants who were farmers and worked the company's land ... were furnished with a year's provision, tools, and indentured for seven years on condition that they turn half of their product over to the company. At the end of their indentures they received a grant of land. Until then they were sharecroppers.[59]

In the Virginia example, the sharecropper was granted land after seven years. Therefore, we actually might view the postbellum agreement, coming 250 years later, as a step backward! Ransom and Sutch demonstrated that, once set in motion, the institution of sharecropping spread rapidly throughout the Cotton South. It gave the freed slave and poor white a chance to earn a living and independence from day-to-day supervision, on the job and otherwise in life. Risk of failure was shared by both parties: sharecropper and landlord. The landowners got their property worked and a chance to change tenants in cases of unsatisfactory performance.

It was to no one's benefit under sharecropping to make extensive improvements. Since tenants might be evicted at any time, they were not motivated to make improvements (with only the uncertain prospect of a lawsuit to realize the value of their improvements). The landlords were also unlikely to make improvements because they would have been trusting their own invested capital into the hands of tenants perhaps indifferent to its long-run value. In any case, the effect of grinding poverty on the South's sharecroppers renders such speculation largely superfluous. Stephen DeCanio, in his study of the South after the Civil War, estimated that mere ownership of land would have doubled sharecropper incomes and that ownership of both capital and land would have tripled it. The failure to compensate former slaves with property for the generations of forced labor launched the blacks into poverty as well as into freedom.[60] Forty acres and a mule would have made a difference.

Country Finance and Debt Peonage

The antebellum cotton economy with its large plantation "management units" had been well served financially by an international network of banking houses and agents representing the cotton-spinning industry in this country and abroad. English banks commonly held, under discount in import centers such as Liverpool, masses of American paper, paper that had originated in the South to move raw cotton. State-chartered banks in the South also granted credit (discounted their paper) to those who had cotton to ship.

At the end of the Civil War, hardly a trace of the old financial system remained. The old state banks, filled with Confederate debt, failed utterly. The representatives of cotton-spinning firms had long since left the scene of devastation. It is not entirely clear why the old system did not revive in some form.[61] In fact, Southern banking made a very poor recovery. With the atomization of cotton-growing plantations into family-sized farms (the disappearance of the plantation system), an equally atomized financial system appeared that lasted through the rest of the century.

A large part of *One Kind of Freedom*, indeed a most controversial part, is a study of postbellum Southern finance.[62] Ransom and Sutch argued that the basic financial unit became the local provisioning merchant—essentially a country store—which could provide supplies to tenants and sharecroppers. The security taken was a lien against the forthcoming crop.

The postwar Southern banking system, when it did finally appear, was concentrated in urban areas. The national banks needed initial capital of $50,000 to start, and that limited their appearance to those areas. The South had far fewer urban centers than the North, as we have already seen. Without a system of nationally organized branch banking (as existed in England at the time), it was left to local initiative to produce financial intermediation from the materials at hand. Smaller private and state banks appeared in the smaller towns. However, mortgages on land were no longer primary debt instruments in the South. Loans were made on personal notes and other collateral for those who had sufficient standing. These excluded the mass of sharecroppers and tenant farmers located in isolated country locations.

The South was bereft of normal banking services and remained largely in that condition. In 1880, when there were 2,061 national banks in the country, only 126 were in the 12 states of the old Confederacy, and only 42 were in the five cotton-growing states. Unlike the situation in the antebellum period, Southern banks were now smaller, on the average, than banks elsewhere in the country. But small or large, obviously too few existed for the job at hand.

The vacuum was filled by a more elementary form of financial intermediation, *commodity credit* at excessive markups. Nearly 8,000 country stores appeared that gave credit to poor sharecroppers and tenants, at "normal" markups of from 40 to 70 percent per annum.[63] (Both eyewitnesses and the calculations of Ransom and Sutch produced such estimates.) Poor Southern farmers were paying these interest rates while, in cities 50 or 100 miles away, interest rates were one-tenth of those levels.[64] An atomized economic system needed an atomized financial underpinning. Decentralized financial management would be created to match the atomization of decision-making units. That is what happened, except that the financial institution was not a deposit bank at all, but a distributor of real commodities. Competitive intermediation between the consumer and commodity source vanished. The result was usury.

What is probably most remarkable about this system of country finance is that it simply "sprang up" in response to changing local needs. The states passed laws establishing crop liens as primary charges on the assets of sharecroppers. Deposits and checks had not been widely used in the South in antebellum times. With state bank notes taxed out of existence and few national banks in the territories of the South circulating their own promissory notes, this primitive and usury-laden system of barter prospered. The merchants themselves spontaneously became shippers of cotton.

The old system, with its large-scale units, had been serviced by traveling "cotton factors," who had issued paper against the movement of cotton. That paper "money" had been discounted at banks in the South, on the East Coast, or even abroad, and the South had been provisioned. But, because tenancy and sharecropping produced such a vast multiplication of the number of "management units," the system of factors could not be efficiently reestablished. Someone who knew the actual tenants and sharecroppers by sight, name, and reputation had to provide finance. The country storekeeper was that person. As a result, this suboptimal form of noncompetitive intermediation appeared and dominated the rural South through the rest of the century. Other changes, especially new ginning and bailing equipment and the burgeoning Southern railway system (12,842 miles in 1860 and 56,786 miles by 1890), cut the cost of bailing cotton and shipping, and multiplied the number of shipping points—any stop on a railroad line—and thus helped to localize the postbellum cotton industry.

Ransom and Sutch argued that this system gave the country storekeeper monopoly power. The basis of that power was apparently a combination of high transactions costs and rural isolation with poor transportation. As in the location theory of August Lösch discussed in Chapter 8, country stores sprung up approximately a half day's journey apart, depending on the topography. Any closer and competition might have become possible—the farmer could have "shopped around" for better prices—but only if the farmer were *equally* creditworthy in more than one locality. The roads were poor, and there was no significant mail-order service (or even enough post offices) until late in the century.

The result of sharecropping and monopoly country finance was what Ransom and Sutch called "debt peonage," which arose, "Because the farmer ended each year with insufficient food reserves and insufficient cash to purchase the necessary food at cash prices, he was forced into borrowing to feed his family during the subsequent year."[65] Since cotton was the cash crop, credit was given for *cotton growing*. The result was a reduction in the amount of land and resources applied to self-sufficiency in food.[66] Unlike in the antebellum period, the small growing units were now maximizing their cotton acreage. The sharecropper and tenant sank into continuous indebtedness. Effective economic power slipped into the hands of those who had nothing to gain from "progress." What was needed at the country store was a continually impoverished clientele, as long as they could still grow cotton.[67] With this new system, the economics of the South had been stood on its head. Cotton was now a poverty crop; the production of it was at the expense of food growing.[68] Finance became small-scale and local.

How strong is the Ransom and Sutch case against the country storekeeper? Are annual interest rates of 60 percent and more, as implied by the difference between cash and credit prices, sufficient to determine culpability? Claudia Goldin noted most scholars attribute these rates to difficulties in determining risk rather than monopoly power. Further, whether they had a serious economic impact depended on the percentage of total supplies acquired on credit. She presented evidence indicating that only 20 percent was purchased on credit, far lower than the amount calculated by Ransom and Sutch.[69] Robert Higgs argued that direct evidence contradicts the idea that these rates discriminated against blacks, while Peter Temin commented that there is no evidence rural merchants grew rich at the expense of their black customers. Further, Higgs took issue with the idea that merchant pressure led to an "overproduction" of cotton. He believes a more plausible hypothesis is that blacks were overrepresented on the land best suited to cotton production.[70]

Clearly, the Southern labor market remained a separate entity, shunned by Northern and immigrant labor. In his book *Old South, New South,* Gavin Wright argued that the South became a low-wage labor market, with Southern entrepreneurship geared to exploit it.[71] Thus, for seven decades after the Civil War, until the 1930s, there remained a distinctive Southern economy. Southern workers migrated out of it, but high birth rates in the predominantly rural South filled up the labor force with replacements for the emigrants. Wages fell so low in the sugarcane plantations and refineries that the hired Chinese laborers abandoned the industry and migrated to the West Coast. Farms in the South actually decreased in average size while Northern farms were growing steadily larger with the application of successive generations of farm machinery to the land. Under the pressure of abundant rural population, Southern farms actually became smaller on average than Northern farms, the reverse of the antebellum situation. Cotton production was labor-intensive and nonmechanized, and Southern farming became a fountain of poverty.

Starting from very small beginnings, Southern manufacturing, also labor-intensive, grew at respectable rates, sometimes faster than growth in comparable Northern industries. But there was far to go. The Southern manufacturing sector in the postbellum years remained too small to be the salvation of the Southern economy. Southern industry developed and perpetuated patterns of racial segregation (whites only in textiles, large numbers of blacks in steel) that can only be understood through social history. Economics alone cannot explain such curiosities.[72] Also, the relative lack of cities and small trading towns (another legacy of slavery), and of a financial infrastructure, meant there were few commercial foci for a transformation to a modern economy.

Also, the South was not making the kinds of investment in human capital that characterized the Northern states. The South's lack of an extensive system of public schools was another legacy of slavery. Such schools were irrelevant in slave times, and the South resisted establishing them. According to Wright, for decades after the Civil War in the Old South, such schooling was considered a luxury and a waste. Education for the poor merely encouraged the beneficiaries to migrate to the North and higher wages. One result was that wage disparity between the North and the South grew, even though within each region the disparities of wages between states tended to narrow, as we would expect from economic theory.

Northern investors, according to Wright's account, tended to avoid the South and its poverty. Ransom and Sutch argued that wealthy Southerners, on the other hand, invested generously in Northern industry in the postbellum period. When these patterns finally were reversed after the 1930s, the distinctive Southern economy itself vanished from the American scene. Until the 1930s, the postbellum South, mainly a world of small farms and labor-intensive industry, was a paradigm of economic and social backwardness.[73]

In the later nineteenth century, given the technology, the culture, and the traditions, perhaps the old Cotton South really had no better alternatives. Stephen DeCanio argued along these lines. He emphasized that cotton farming was still the most "productive" activity available for Southern farmers; cotton farmers (both white and black) were more prosperous than were those of either race who did not grow cotton.[74]

CONCLUSION

A great opportunity was lost by the nation as a whole in the postbellum American South. Until well into the twentieth century, it was a region noted for wasting human and natural resources, a region scarred by backwardness and brutal racism. What the white racist said of the black: "He's lazy, shiftless, and ignorant," the Northerner and Westerner said of the white Southerner.

In the twentieth century, with the automobile, paved roads, and jobs in the industrial cities, the spell was broken. Mechanization came to Southern agriculture, and industry arrived at the region's great ports and commercial centers. Moving to the cities, particularly to Northern cities, the descendants of the freedmen became primarily urban dwellers. In the South, *Jim Crow laws,* which determined where blacks could eat and drink, live, work, and even sit on public transportation, were passed.[75] As Ransom and Sutch wrote, "Nearly 15 percent of the black population must have left the cotton south between 1910 and 1930. The black exodus was one of the larger migrations in human history." Thousands of poor Southern whites cleared out, too.

The Civil War is a never-ending tragedy in American history whose seeds were planted in colonial times. It was the only (to date) breakdown in the constitutional settlement of 1789. The appalling human and economic costs of the war were augmented by the costs of the system that grew up in the ruins of the Old South. To this day, the scars are not erased, and the human and financial costs of the disaster continue.

NOTES

1. Official numbers are not available for Confederate troops, and the estimates are quite broad (for example, total men in uniform are estimated as being between 600,000 and 1.5 million. For enlistees in the Union army, Chulhee Lee has found that the probability of dying (the disease environment was often more deadly than battle) was a function of age, place of birth, occupation, and household wealth; "Selective Assignment of Military Positions in the Union Army," *SSH,* Spring 1999.
2. Claudia Goldin and Frank Lewis, "The Economic Cost of the American Civil War," *JEH,* June 1975. Goldin and Lewis also estimated the "indirect," long-term costs: How much did the Civil War extract from future income? Peter Temin has argued that these figures are overestimated by a factor of four; see "The Post-Bellum Recovery of the South and the Cost of the Civil War," *JEH,* December 1976. Goldin and Lewis and Temin had a further exchange on the war's cost: See *JEH,* June 1978, pp. 487–493.
3. Jeremy Atack and Peter Passell, *A New Economic View of American History,* 2nd ed. (New York: Norton, 1994), pp. 360–363.
4. A footnote to Confederate financial history: In 1979, it was reported that surviving Confederate dollars were selling at $1 Confederate to $8 Federal Reserve, someone quipped, because of the conservative money supply policies followed by the Confederate Treasury after 1865.
5. Marc Weidenmier, "The Market for Confederate War Bonds," *EEH,* January 2000, notes that one issue of Confederate bonds underwritten by the French firm of Emile Erlanger and Company were redeemable in cotton.
6. Richard Burdekin and Farrokh Langdana, "War Finance in the Southern Confederacy, 1861–1865," *Explorations in Economic History,* vol. 30, no. 3, September 1993, argue that Confederate debt and note-issue decisions were driven by the state of the budget, but the inflation rate driven by "news."
7. Eugene Lerner, "Money, Wages and Prices in the Confederacy," *Journal of Political Economy,* vol. LXIII, no. 1, February 1955.
8. For a concise survey of Civil War finance, see Paul Studenski and Herman Krooss, *Financial History of the United States* (New York: McGraw-Hill, 1952), pp. 137–160. The exceptions to the Confederate currency debacle came in private wartime note issues in Texas, Louisiana, and Arkansas, which depreciated less than did the Confederate currency. Gary Pecquet, "Money in the Trans-Mississippi Confederacy and the Confederate Currency Reform Act of 1864," *EEH,* April 1987.
9. Let it be noted that, after 1945, Germans got a better deal from the United States, exchanging the financial assets of the 12-year "Thousand-year Reich" for post-war currency at ratios of 100/1 for bonds and 10/1 for currency.
10. Reuben Kessel and Armen Alchian, "Real Wages in the North During the Civil War: Mitchell's Data Reinterpreted," *Journal of Law and Economics,* vol. 2, October 1959.
11. Mark Aldrich, "Flexible Exchange Rates, Northern Expansion, and the Market for Southern Cotton: 1866–1879," *Journal of Economic History,* vol. XXXIII, no. 2, June 1973.
12. Stephen DeCanio and Joel Mokyr, "Inflation and Wage Lag During the American Civil War," *EEH,* October 1977.
13. Stanley Lebergott shows that Southern cotton planters kept the manpower equivalent of "the entire Confederate army" at home growing cotton and stayed home themselves. "Through the Blockade: The Profitability and Extent of Cotton Smuggling, 1861–1865," *JEH,* December 1981. John James concludes that retiring the debt after the war increased the rate of capital growth in the private sector significantly. Debt retirement policy, in effect, mobilized capital by taking broadly by

taxation and transferring narrowly to bondholders. James calls this the "crowding in" effect. The consequences, by increasing productive investment in the private sector (former bondholders now had to invest in the private sector) were to increase the postbellum rate of economic growth. "Public Debt Policy and Nineteenth Century Economic Growth," *EEH,* April 1984, p. 210.

14. Matthew Josephson, *The Robber Barons* (New York: Harcourt Brace, 1934).
15. Charles Beard and Mary Beard, *The Rise of American Civilization* (1930); and Hacker, Louis. *The Triumph of American Capitalism* (1940). A quarter century later, Hacker put more emphasis on the way Republican judges interpreted the law. See Hacker, *The World of Andrew Carnegie, 1865–1901* (Philadelphia: Lippincott, 1968).
16. Stanley Engerman, "The Economic Impact of the Civil War," reprinted in Robert Fogel and Stanley Engerman, eds., *The Reinterpretation of American Economic History,* (1971). Gallman's figures are cited p. 371.
17. *Ibid.,* p. 371, note 1.
18. *Ibid.,* p. 373.
19. *Historical Statistics,* series P 17.
20. Engerman (1971), p. 374.
21. *Historical Statistics,* series P 231.
22. *Historical Statistics,* series P 227.
23. Engerman (1971), p. 376.
24. Cited in Engerman (1971), p. 376.
25. Jeffrey Williamson, "Watersheds and Turning Points: Conjectures on the Long-Term Impact of Civil War Financing," *JEH,* September 1974.
26. A survey of the quantitative research on the economic impact of the Civil War can be found in Patrick O'Brien, *The Economic Effects of the American Civil War* (Atlantic Highlands, NJ: Humanities Press International, 1988).
27. James Irwin, "Explaining the Decline in Southern per Capita Output after Emancipation," *EEH,* July 1994, argues that the decrease in Southern production has more to do with loss of the plantation system than with freeing the slaves.
28. Jay Mandle, "The Plantation States as a Sub-Region of the Post-Bellum South," *JEH,* September 1974. The plantation states are Alabama, Arkansas, Georgia, Louisiana, Mississippi, and South Carolina. Mandle suggests "the possibility that the institutions associated with plantation agriculture might be growth retarding" as a general possibility, anywhere in space or time (pp. 737–738).
29. Engerman (1971), pp. 371–372.
30. James Sellers, "The Economic Incidence of the Civil War in the South," *Mississippi Valley Historical Review,* September 1927.
31. Roger Ransom and Richard Sutch, *One Kind of Freedom: The Economic Consequences of Emancipation* (1977), pp. 108–109.
32. Jonathan Hughes, *Industrialization and Economic History: Theses and Conjectures* (New York: McGraw-Hill, 1971), p. 269.
33. Ransom and Sutch (1977), pp. 326–327, n. 30; *Historical Statistics,* series K 555.
34. Ransom and Sutch (1977), p. 192.
35. Gavin Wright, *Political Economy of the Cotton South* (1978). Wright thinks the concentration upon cotton at the expense of other crops resulted from falling prices—an effort to maintain cash income. Ransom and Sutch have a more institutional explanation.
36. *Historical Statistics,* series K 553–554; a difference in sources between the two years makes it impossible to say for sure.
37. Sellers (1927).
38. Ransom and Sutch (1977), p. 212. By way of contrast, Fogel and Engerman, *Time on the Cross,* vol. 1 (Boston: Little, Brown, 1974) estimate that "12 percent of the value of the income produced by slaves was expropriated by their masters" (p. 153).
39. Ransom and Sutch (1977), p. 31.
40. *Ibid.,* p. 30.
41. Robert Higgs, "Accumulation of Property by Southern Blacks before World War I," *AER,* September 1982. Robert Margo, "Accumulation of Property by Southern Blacks before World War I: Comment and Further Evidence," *AER,* September 1984, confirms Higgs's findings with data from five additional states. This essay is followed by a reply from Higgs.
42. This is the intermediate estimate reported in Robert Higgs, *Competition and Coercion* (1977), p. 102.
43. Robert Margo, *Race and Schooling in the South, 1880–1950: An Economic History* (1990), pp. 8, 130.
44. Higgs (1977), p. 123.
45. Ransom and Sutch (1977), Table F. 2, pp. 258–259.
46. Their estimates range from 28.3 to 37.2 percent as the amount of black labor "withdrawn" from free market. Ransom and Sutch (1977), p. 45; argument about the irrelevance of Southern losses of capital stock, p. 47.
47. Ransom and Sutch (1977), pp. 6–7.
48. Cited in Ransom and Sutch (1977), p. 45.
49. Gerald David Jaynes provides an interesting interpretation of the emergence of black sharecropping. The slave capital had been transferred to the ex-slave by the emancipation. It was no longer available to the former slave owner as collateral for credit. The black sharecropper, acquiring credit on the promise of his own labor output, was now utilizing that capital as his own collateral. *Branches Without Roots: Genesis of the Black Working Class in the American South* (1986).
50. Higgs (1977), p. 45.

51. Ransom and Sutch (1977), pp. 78–87.
52. *Ibid.*, pp. 89–105, on sharecropping, with examples of agreements.
53. *Ibid.*, pp. 71, 79.
54. Nancy Virts, "Estimating the Importance of the Plantation System to Southern Agriculture in 1880," *JEH*, December 1987.
55. Ransom and Sutch (1977), p. 81–87.
56. In a study based on evidence on black occupations in the Virginia Piedmont, James Irwin argues that Ransom and Sutch may have overstated the situation by classifying as "farmers" many of those enumerated as "farm laborers." Irwin, "Farmers and Laborers: A Note on Black Occupations in the Postbellum South," *AgHist*, Winter 1990, note 14.
57. Ransom and Sutch (1977), p. 104.
58. Joseph Reid, "Sharecropping as an Understandable Market Response: The Postbellum South," *JEH*, March 1973. Robert Higgs, "Race, Tenure and Resource Allocation in Southern Agriculture," *JEH*, March 1973; and "Patterns of Farm Rental in the Georgia Cotton Belt, 1880–1900," *JEH*, June 1974. See Ransom and Sutch (1977), p. 339, note 67, for further discussion.
59. Jonathan Hughes, *Social Control in the Colonial Economy* (Charlottesville: University Press of Virginia, 1976), p. 57.
60. Stephen DeCanio, "Productivity and Income Distribution in the Post-Bellum South," *JEH*, June 1974.
61. Ransom and Sutch (1977), p. 113, Table 6.4.
62. At a 1999 conference revisiting their research, Ransom and Sutch presented "One Kind of Freedom: Reconsidered (and Turbo Charged)," *EEH* January 2001, in which they redid several of the calculations from the original study, but they employed a much larger database. Inasmuch as Ransom and Sutch did not change their basic conclusions, the discussion in this chapter refers to the original work. It should be noted that their published paper is followed by discussion from Gavin Wright, Harold Woodman, Peter Coclanis, and Stanley Engerman.
63. Ransom and Sutch (1977), p. 129–130.
64. *Ibid.*, p. 130.
65. Ransom and Sutch (2001), p. 22; see also Ransom and Sutch (1977), chap. 8. Utilizing the larger dataset, they estimate an "astonishing" 46.2 percent of the small-scale, family operated farms in the Cotton South, both Black and White, were operating inefficiently as a result of the credit system.
66. Ransom and Sutch (1977), p. 151–159. Both William Brown and Morgan Reynolds, "Debt Peonage Reexamined," *Journal of Economic History*, vol. XXXIII, no. 4, December 1973, and Gavin Wright, *Old South, New South: Revolutions in the Southern Economy* (1986) would argue that the force of country finance was not needed. According to them, the South, by growing cotton for cash, was still pursuing comparative advantage. But, if that were so, why the complete turnaround? Before the war, small farmers devoted a relatively small part of their lands to cotton; after the war, a relatively large part. If self-sufficiency paid before 1860, why not afterward, too? It makes little economic sense to say that Southern farmers became uniquely unable to understand their own self-interest. It was the boll weevil that finally put an end to the system.
67. Why was there no amalgamation? Why not more entry? Why did the local merchants not expand operations? High transactions costs must be the answer. Until communications improved, it paid no one to undertake a business of financial intermediation that required such detailed, strictly local information. Finally, of course, these changes came about. Sufficient banking facilities grew up in rural towns. Farmers could travel to towns, and where there was banking competition, take advantage of it. In part, the phenomenon described so graphically by Ransom and Sutch was a product of three factors: (a) geography, (b) the land tenures adopted to put the postbellum Cotton South under the plough, and (c) the war itself, which destroyed any chance for the antebellum Southern banking system to evolve as the needs of intermediation changed.
68. Suppose we assume that emphasis shifted to cotton at the expense of food because Southern farmers became more willing to gamble for a good cash-crop year in the competitive economy of postbellum farming. Gavin Wright and Howard Kunreuther, "Cotton, Corn and Risk in the Nineteenth Century," *JEH*, September 1975; Robert McGuire and Robert Higgs, "Cotton, Corn and Risk...Another View," *EEH*, April 1977; Wright and Kunreuther, "... A Reply," *EEH*, April 1977; Robert McGuire, "A Portfolio Analysis of Crop Diversification and Risk in the Cotton South," *EEH*, October 1980.
69. Claudia Goldin, "'N' Kinds of Freedom, An Introduction to the Issues," *EEH*, January 1979. The entire issue is devoted to the proceedings of a conference on *One Kind of Freedom*. This collection was reprinted as Gary Walton and James Shepherd, editors, *Market Institutions and Economic Progress in the New South, 1865–1900* (New York: Academic Press, 1981).
70. Higgs (1977), p. 71; Peter Temin, "Freedom and Coercion: Notes on the Analysis of Debt Peonage in One Kind of Freedom," *EEH*, January 1979.
71. Gavin Wright (1986).

72. Gavin Wright, "Postbellum Southern Labor Markets," in Peter Kilby, ed., *Quantity and Quiddity: Essays in U.S. Economic History* (1987).
73. For further discussion on institutional barriers to progress in the postbellum south and to the 1930s, see Lee Alston and Joseph Ferrie, *Southern Paternalism and the American Welfare State* (1999); William Phillips, "The Labor Market of Southern Textile Mill Villages: Some Micro Evidence," *EEH,* April 1986, and Warren Whatley, "Southern Agrarian Labor Contracts as Impediments to Cotton Mechanization," *JEH,* March 1987.
74. Stephen DeCanio, *Agriculture in the Postbellum South: The Economics of Production and Supply* (1974), pp. 12–14.
75. Robert Higgs (1977) for an analysis and survey.

SUGGESTED READINGS

Articles

Cochran, Thomas. "Did the Civil War Retard Industrialization?" *Mississippi Valley Historical Review,* no. XLVIII, no. 2, September 1961.

DeCanio, Stephen. "Cotton 'Overproduction' and Late Nineteenth-Century Southern Agriculture." *Journal of Economic History,* vol. XXXIII, no. 3, September 1973.

——. "Productivity and Income Distribution in the Post-Bellum South." *Journal of Economic History,* vol. XXXIV, no. 2, June 1974.

——, and Joel Mokyr. "Inflation and Wage Lag during the American Civil War." *Explorations in Economic History,* vol. 14, no. 4, October 1977.

Engerman, Stanley. "The Economic Impact of the Civil War." Reprinted in Robert Fogel and Stanley Engerman, eds., *The Reinterpretation of American History.* New York: Harper & Row, 1971.

Goldin, Claudia. "'N' Kinds of Freedom, An Introduction to the Issues." *Explorations in Economic History,* vol. 16, no. 1, January 1979.

——, and Frank Lewis. "The Economic Cost of the American Civil War." *Journal of Economic History,* vol. XXXV, no. 2, June 1975.

Higgs, Robert. "Race, Tenure, and Resource Allocation in Southern Agriculture." *Journal of Economic History,* vol. XXXIII, no. 1, March 1973.

——. "Patterns of Farm Rental in the Georgia Cotton Belt, 1880–1900." *Journal of Economic History,* vol. XXXIV, no. 2, June 1974.

——. "Accumulation of Property by Southern Blacks before World War I." *American Economic Review,* vol. 72, no. 4, September 1982.

Irwin, James R. "Farmers and Laborers: A Note on Black Occupations in the Postbellum South." *Agricultural History,* vol. 64, no. 1, Winter 1990.

——. "Explaining the Decline in Southern per Capita Output after Emancipation." *Explorations in Economic History,* vol. 31, no. 3, July 1994.

James, John A. "Public Debt Policy and Nineteenth Century Economic Growth." *Explorations in Economic History,* vol. 21, no. 2, April 1984.

Lebergott, Stanley. "Through the Blockade: The Profitability and Extent of Cotton Smuggling, 1861–1865." *Journal of Economic History,* vol. XLI, no. 4, December 1981.

Lee, Chulhee. "Selective Assignment of Military Positions in the Union Army: Implications for the Impact of the Civil War." *Social Science History,* vol. 23, no. 1, Spring 1999.

Mandle, Jay R. "The Plantation States as a Sub-Region of the Post-Bellum South." *Journal of Economic History,* vol. XXXIV, no. 3, September 1974.

Margo, Robert. "Accumulation of Property by Southern Blacks before World War I: Comment and Further Evidence." *American Economic Review,* vol. 74, no. 4, September 1984.

McGuire, Robert A., and Robert Higgs. "Cotton, Corn, and Risk in the Nineteenth Century: Another View." *Explorations in Economic History,* vol. 14, no. 2, April 1979.

——. "A Portfolio Analysis of Crop Diversification and Risk in the Cotton South." *Explorations in Economic History,* vol. 17, no. 4, October 1980.

Pecquet, Gary M. "Money in the Trans-Mississippi Confederacy and the Confederate Currency Reform Act of 1864." *Explorations in Economic History,* vol. 24, no. 2, April 1987.

Phillips, William H. "The Labor Market of Southern Textile Mill Villages: Some Micro Evidence." *Explorations in Economic History,* vol. 23, no. 2, April 1986.

Ransom, Roger, and Richard Sutch. "The Impact of the Civil War and of Emancipation on Southern Agriculture." *Explorations in Economic History,* vol. 12, no. 1, January 1975.

——. "One Kind of Freedom: Reconsidered (and Turbo Charged)." *Explorations in Economic History,* vol. 38, no. 1, January 2001.

Reid, Joseph. "Sharecropping as an Understandable Market Response: The Postbellum South." *Journal of Economic History,* vol. XXXIII, no. 1, March 1973.

Sellers, James L. "The Economic Incidence of the Civil War in the South." *Mississippi Valley Historical Review,* vol. 14, no. 2, September 1927.

Temin, Peter. "The Post-Bellum Recovery of the South and the Cost of the Civil War." *Journal of Economic History,* vol. XXXVI, no. 4, December 1976.

———. "Freedom and Coercion: Notes on the Analysis of Debt Peonage in One Kind of Freedom." *Explorations in Economic History,* vol. 16, no. 1, January 1979.

Virts, Nancy. "Estimating the Importance of the Plantation System to Southern Agriculture in 1880." *Journal of Economic History,* vol. XLVII, no. 4, December 1987.

Weidenmier, Marc D. "The Market for Confederate War Bonds." *Explorations in Economic History,* vol. 37, no. 1, January 2000.

Whatley, Warren C. "Southern Agrarian Labor Contracts as Impediments to Cotton Mechanization." *Journal of Economic History,* vol. XLVII, no. 1, March 1987.

Williamson, Jeffrey. "Watersheds and Turning Points: Conjectures on the Long-Term Impact of Civil War Financing." *Journal of Economic History,* vol. XXXIV, no. 3, September 1974.

Wright, Gavin. "Postbellum Southern Labor Markets." In Peter Kilby, ed. *Quantity and Quiddity: Essays in U.S. Economic History.* Middletown, CT: Wesleyan University Press, 1987.

———, and Howard Kunreuther. "Cotton, Corn, and Risk in the Nineteenth Century." *Journal of Economic History,* vol. XXXV, no. 3, September 1975.

Books

Alston, Lee J., and Joseph P. Ferrie. *Southern Paternalism and the American Welfare State: Economics, Politics, and Institutions in the South, 1865–1965.* New York: Cambridge University Press, 1999.

Andreano, Ralph, ed. *The Economic Impact of the Civil War.* Cambridge, MA: Schenkman, 1964.

Beard, Charles A., and Mary R. Beard. *The Rise of American Civilization.* New York: Macmillan, 1930.

DeCanio, Stephen. *Agriculture in the Postbellum South: The Economics of Production and Supply.* Cambridge: MIT Press, 1974.

Hacker, Louis. *The Triumph of American Capitalism.* New York: Simon & Schuster, 1940.

Higgs, Robert. *Competition and Coercion: Blacks in the American Economy, 1865–1914.* New York: Cambridge University Press, 1977.

Jaynes, Gerald David. *Branches Without Roots: Genesis of the Black Working Class in the American South.* New York: Oxford University Press, 1986.

Margo, Robert. *Race and Schooling in the South, 1880–1950: An Economic History.* Chicago: University of Chicago Press, 1990.

Ransom, Roger L. *Conflict and Compromise: The Political Economy of Slavery, Emancipation, and the American Civil War.* New York: Cambridge University Press, 1989.

———, and Richard Sutch. *One Kind of Freedom: The Economic Consequences of Emancipation.* New York: Cambridge University Press, 1977.

Stampp, Kenneth. *The Era of Reconstruction, 1865–1877.* New York: Knopf, 1966.

Walton, Gary, and James Shepherd, eds. *Market Institutions and Economic Progress in the New South, 1865–1900.* New York: Academic Press, 1981.

Woodward, C. Vann. *The Strange Career of Jim Crow.* New York: Oxford University Press, 1966.

Wright, Gavin. Old South, *New South: Revolutions in the Southern Economy.* New York: Basic Books, 1986.

———. *The Political Economy of the Cotton South.* New York: Norton, 1978.

CHAPTER FOURTEEN

Railroads and Economic Development

By 1860, the American railroad network stretched into the Midwest and South, as we saw in Chapter 8. There were about 30,000 miles of track in operation, already the most extensive railroad system in any single country. By 1910, the United States had a tremendous 351,767 miles of track, of which 266,000 miles were main track. The nation had far more miles of railroad track than it had of surfaced roads: 204,000 miles.

Constructing the American railroads was such a giant effort that the story of it has become simply overpowering in its influence upon American history. And, indeed, why not? There had never before been anything like it. A whole continent was bound together by steam engines and bands of steel. The products of farm and factory, thousands of miles apart in their origins, were now easily mixed in the country's new establishments of manufacturing and distribution. Via the railroads, which connected the interior to the ports and docks, the produce of the whole economy could regularly and conveniently reach the world. Isolation in the United States was almost a thing of the past. The river steamers and canal barges seemed (to many writers) almost as remote as the era of the pyramids. The railroad had written a new chapter in world history.

In recent years, economic historians who reexamined the railroads and American economic growth, using quantitative methods, concluded that far too much interpretive weight had been placed on the railroad by historians and economists, to the detriment of an understanding of economic development processes. The purpose of dismantling the legend of the railroad was not debunking for its own sake. It was a necessary next step, once economists and historians had concentrated their attention on the mysteriously different histories of world economic development after World War II.

With the United Nations attempting to spread knowledge of economic development to the world at large, scholars in those countries that had created high per-capita incomes, who had largely taken such progress for granted, began to investigate their own records of economic growth. Some countries were (and still are) desperately poor; some are relatively rich. Why? Modern technology is available to all. Was there some magical element in the past histories of the industrial nations that explained their success? The rich countries of the West all shared a history of extensive "railroadization" in the nineteenth century that ran parallel to their own industrialization. Was this the answer?

The income effects of the railroad investment—for example, industries supplying railroad equipment were stimulated, users of railroad transport were supplied with regular and dependable communications—

suggested an obvious key. In the histories of the main industrial countries of the West—the United Kingdom, France, the United States—and in Eastern Europe, Russia, and Japan, the processes of railroad building seemed to be central explanatory themes, the indispensable factor that led the way to all other forms of modernization. Would a new railway system in East Africa produce the same progressive side effects? And if not, why not?

The importance of such considerations caused the work of Robert Fogel and Albert Fishlow on American railroads to hit the history and economics professions like a bombshell.[1] When the scholarly fallout finally settled, many of their colleagues realized that successful economic development had not been achieved cheaply in the United States by the concentrated development of a single sector or a few "leading" sectors, even one as basic as transportation. In the end, these economists and historians began to worry about "human capital," honest and efficient government, and agriculture—to the great delight of those who had never accepted the railroad story.

COMPLETION OF THE RAIL NETWORK

Looking back at the era of American railroad construction, we are struck by the tumultuous pace. It is a prime example of the way "waves" of innovation have come to the American economy. Under *unfettered capitalism*—in which the returns accrue to the entrepreneurs, with no limit placed by government or other planning agencies on profit levels—high profit prospects in an innovative sector (such as the railroad) attract capital and enterprise. The sector expands until the prospective returns fall back to the competitive level. If a government subsidy is involved (as in the case of the railroads), the rush to invest is that much greater.

During periods of entrepreneurial exhilaration, when high profits beckon, the innovative sector grows in a spectacular way. The tobacco culture of the colonial South, the slave-worked cotton culture, the steam engine applied to industry, the westward movement of Northern farmers, the application of electricity to industry and households, the automobile culture in the 1920s, television after World War II, fast-food chains, personal computers and the Internet—are other examples of the explosive surges of innovation that have influenced American economic growth.

Somehow, the historian must give credit where it is due without being swept away by the glamour of the great innovative sectors in their time. Some sectors grow and some decline and vanish, even while spectacular innovations or waves of innovations dominate. The phenomenon of simultaneous growth and decline is well known to scholars. Pioneering studies of it were published half a century ago by Simon Kuznets and Arthur F. Burns.[2] Growth is the algebraic sum of expansions and contractions over time. Joseph Schumpeter's work on secular growth and the pattern of cycles was powerfully influenced by these great innovative waves.[3] Schumpeter argued that the innovative waves were necessary to offset stagnant tendencies among the older and more conservative sectors of the economy. The railroad in the late nineteenth century seemed to be an indisputably dominating innovative sector.

The Pace and Pattern of Construction

In Table 14.1, we see the growth of the railroads from 1860. The main-track mileage rose until World War I, when the railroads, in precarious financial condition, were taken over by the federal government on national defense grounds. After the war, financial troubles mounted, and the huge system went into a financial decline that continues to the present. Abandoned lines

TABLE 14.1 Main Track Railroad Mileage Operated, 1860–1915

Year	*Mileage*[a]	*Year*	*Mileage*[a]
1860	30.6	**1890**[b]	166.7
1865	35.1	**1895**	180.7
1870	52.9	**1900**	193.3
1875	74.1	**1905**	218.1
1880	93.3	**1910**	240.3
1885	128.3	**1915**	253.8

[a] Amounts given are in thousands of miles of track.
[b] After 1890, yard tracks and sidings omitted from amount.

Source: *Historical Statistics,* series Q 287, 321.

became a serious problem in the early 1920s; *total* mileage—including main track, yards, and sidings—reached a peak of 429,883 miles in 1929 (17 times the earth's circumference) and then began to decline as abandonments exceeded new construction. By then, the automobile and truck had cut into railroad growth prospects, and air travel was on the horizon.

In 1915, half the existing main-track mileage had been built between 1885 and that year. Professor Fishlow's study of construction patterns within the sector revealed three major waves in the late nineteenth century: 1868–1873, 1879–1883, and 1886–1892. Since the railroads were built primarily with borrowed money, it is not surprising that these construction booms were terminated by the major financial crises of 1873, 1882, and 1893. However, each time the economy began a recovery, railroad construction boomed again. The twentieth-century crises of 1903 and 1907, dramatic as they were, failed to stop the railroad expansion. The downturn of 1929–1932 did, but by then the railroads faced new competing forms of transportation.

The regional construction patterns in the Fishlow postbellum waves are illustrated in Figure 14.1. The railroad is largely a piece of continuous, linear physical capital. Since population and economic activity (the sources of freight earnings) are not homogeneously distributed, the financial prospects and problems of the different lines varied in a bewildering way. Also, the geography of the United States placed practical limits on the routes the railroads could take across the continent.

All these considerations had their effects on the financial histories of the different railroad systems, and it is most hazardous to attempt to generalize

FIGURE 14.1 Three Postbellum Railroad Construction Booms by Region

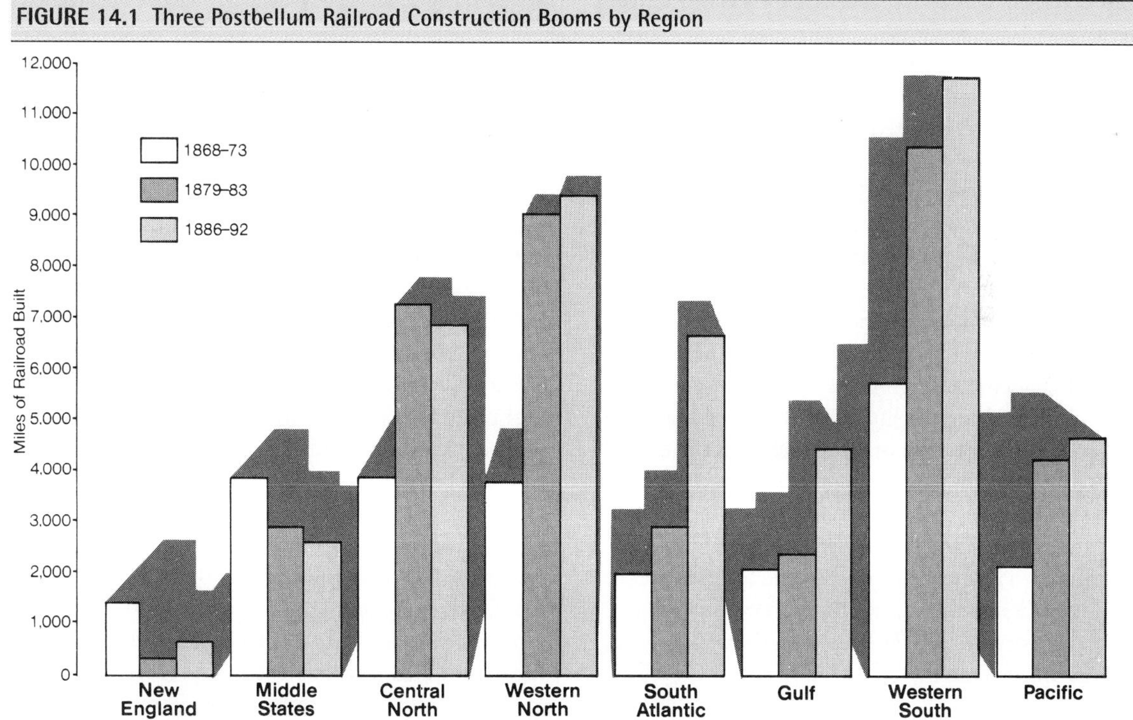

Source: Albert Fishlow, "Internal Transportation," Lance E. Davis, et al., *American Economic Growth* (New York: Harper & Row, 1972), Table 13.12.

Regional figures for miles of railroad built between 1868 and 1892 show that the country's vast midsection—both North and South—the Far West, the Southwest, and the Pacific states dominated. By 1868, the Eastern tracks (apart from the South Atlantic region) had been built, for the most part.

about them. For example, Figure 14.1 shows that the postbellum railroad construction booms occurred mainly in the Southwestern and Northwestern regions. In these areas distances were vast, and railroads had to be long to exist at all. However, miles of track do not indicate financial success. Fishlow points out that in 1873, measured by earnings, the Northeastern region had 60 percent of the nation's effective railroad service.[4] With its concentrated populations and relatively heavy industrialization, the Northeastern region generated massive revenues. Because the area was small and compact, and because little new construction was needed to earn a dollar as compared to an area such as western Nebraska, success or failure depended upon management.

James J. Hill's Great Northern railroad never went bankrupt. The Union Pacific, reorganized by Edward Harriman in 1897, went from years of bankruptcy to unprecedented financial success. By 1906, its dividend was 10 percent, and Harriman had made a killing. Besides financial reorganization, Harriman had carried out a huge program of physical reconstruction of the old "rusted streak of iron."[5] The Erie, on the other hand, was in continuous bankruptcy for generations, despite its advantageous location. Its early financial management, led by James Fisk and Jay Gould, reigns as one of the most scandalous in U.S. financial history.

Success or failure depended upon a combination of building costs, the character of the financial structure, management, freight returns, and economic development along the lines as well as terminal linkups with other systems of transport. After the 1893 panic, 153 U.S. railroads were in bankruptcy, each for its own reasons. As we will see, Robert Fogel found that the Union Pacific's freight earnings could easily have justified its great cost of construction, despite the amount of its track that ran through empty deserts.[6] Its bankruptcy in 1895, as Harriman showed, was due to poor management.

Land Grants and Construction

Chapter 8 discussed the question of private-sector finance versus government construction aid in railroad building and whether governments cleverly seduced railroad builders with subsidies, or railroad builders demanded and got government aid where their own money was at greater risk. The practice (whichever it was!) continued at the national level, with the giant federal land grants after the Civil War. Following the Illinois Central railroad grants in 1851, Congress gave to the four transcontinental railroads alone 100 million acres—10 percent of the public domain—in order to encourage railroad construction. Land grants by the federal government to all railroads totaled 131 million acres, and the states added an additional 49 million acres. Figure 14.2 shows where that land was located. Clearly the object was to tie the country together internally by rail.[7]

The land grants tended to be in areas where the greatest mileage was added (see Figure 14.1). The federal subsidy produced railroad *construction*, at least. According to Lloyd Mercer, the railroad grants had the intended effect but may not have been the most efficient kind of subsidy.[8] However, land is what governments had in abundance, and if construction was the object of the land grants, the huge railroad mileage measured the success of policy. In 1869, the first transcontinental link was forged at Promontory Point, Utah, when two heavily subsidized railroads, the Central Pacific (building eastward) and the Union Pacific (building westward), met. Other transcontinental roads, north and south, followed in succeeding years. The policy of railroad land grants was praised as a crucial government subsidy or criticized as a giveaway (depending on your position), without which the transcontinental roads might not have been built.[9]

Despite the appalling financial history of the railroads, most historians regard it favorably.[10] Though great stretches of the transcontinental roads were built "ahead of demand" by public resources, in subsequent years the whole country benefited as settlers populated the land, bankrupt railroads reorganized, and freights were increased. That favorable view has occupied American historians ever since.[11] As Stanley Engerman emphasizes, the problems in estimating the social gains and costs, compared to the sum of the gain and opportunity costs to both builders and users of railroads, leave wide open the issues of social profitability and equity in the land-grant policies.[12]

FIGURE 14.2 Federal Land Grants for Railroads

Source: Charles O. Paullin, *Atlas of the Historical Geography of the United States* (Washington, D.C. and New York: Carnegie Institution and the American Geographical Society of New York, 1932), plate 56D.

RAILROADS AND ECONOMIC GROWTH

Probably no single investigation in economic history since World War II has had a greater impact on the *techniques* of research and analysis than that of Robert Fogel. Published in 1964, his book outlined his estimate of the quantitative importance of nineteenth-century railroads to overall economic growth. The following year, Albert Fishlow's book on antebellum railroads appeared. Both studies downgraded the railroad as *the* overwhelming influence on nineteenth-century U.S. economic growth. The drama was no doubt heightened because one of Fogel's main targets was Walter Rostow, a distinguished economic historian whose work had largely dominated the writing of economic history in the 1940s and 1950s. Rostow's work was a pioneering effort to employ economic theory to interpret history.

Rostow and Leading Sectors

Fogel's and Fishlow's contributions to our understanding of American economic history are best appreciated if we consider, first, the work of Professor Rostow and some of his predecessors and, second, the reasons for their views. The story really begins with the generally unsuccessful efforts of earlier generations of economists to explain the causes of the cyclical growth that characterized the nineteenth-century capitalist nations. There is a huge, and now largely unread, literature from these earlier efforts. Expansions and contractions of the business cycle had been explained by an extraordinary range of causes, from sunspots and "manias" to cyclical changes in such "real" factors as harvests and, of course, the condition of the money supply and the practices of bankers.[13] Then, in 1936, John Maynard Keynes's *General Theory of Employment, Interest, and Money* riveted attention upon investment and its determinants.

In 1939, the young Paul Samuelson showed that the cycle could be generated by a simple combination of two economic phenomena, the *multiplier* and the *accelerator*, both of which represented known real phenomena.[14] The *multiplier*, the relationship between the initial change in an expenditure and ultimate change in income, determined by society's consumption and saving habits, had figured centrally in Keynes's *General Theory*. The main expenditure whose variations over time combined the right amount of volatility, cyclical timing, and relations with price and monetary phenomena was private investment. The *accelerator* was a secondary investment effect, induced investment brought about by the using up of excess capacity in expansions. New capacity had to be created, and that was brought about by added investment and more income effects.

To understand the historic role of **investment** (the creation of new plant and equipment), we must identify the kinds of investments being made—cotton textile machinery and factories in one epoch, railroads or steel mills in another—and why. Over time, different types of real investment came to the fore during different cycles as technology changed and so did consumer tastes.

In a capitalist economy, investment is made by private persons. Here Joseph Schumpeter's ideas were crucial. Since the publication of his *Theory of Economic Development* in 1914, Schumpeter had emphasized the central role of the entrepreneur, the individual capitalist who introduced change into the flow of economic life in the form of new commodities, techniques, and ideas in pursuit of his or her own private gain.[15] The result of all such entrepreneurial activity was the economic change that in fact occurred. The history of industrial development is filled with great entrepreneurial figures, from James Watt to Henry Ford.

In 1939, Schumpeter had pieced together a lifetime's research in his great two-volume *Business Cycles*, in which the innovative entrepreneur played the central role in determining the direction of investment. The cyclical quantitative results had already been shown by Samuelson. All that was left was the later emphasis upon the net results over time: economic growth.

Subsequent detailed studies of cycles by economists seemed to justify identification of each cyclical upsurge with innovative industries that pulled in resources and produced net growth over time. An influential article by Leland Jenks showed a very close identity between the timing of waves of railroad building and the general business cycle.[16] The general inference was that causation ran from the railroads to the cycle, and not that railroad construction merely passively reflected general movement in the economy. Again, investment was the centerpiece.

Rostow's own *British Economy of the Nineteenth Century* (1948) and his collaborative work with A. D. Gayer and Anna J. Schwartz, *The Growth and Fluctuation of the British Economy 1790–1850* (1953), emphasized the determinants of investment and the time pattern of industrial change produced by those activities.[17] Then, in his *Process of Economic Growth* (1953), Rostow developed his "leading sector" thesis, which suggests that the major growth episodes in cyclical history are motivated by the income effects emanating from the booming innovative sectors.[18] So far, so good.

In 1960, Rostow went a step further and developed a generalized "explanation sketch" of economic development, *The Stages of Economic Growth*.[19] Central to Rostow's general scheme was the idea of *take-off*, the point at which each economy could sustain a sufficient ratio of investment to income to propel it (via multiplier-accelerator interactions) into the career of secular economic progress that characterized all industrial countries. Innovation and resulting leading sectors continued the process.

Rostow's work integrated decades of progress on the understanding of cycles and growth. He then charted out the main historical outlines of the process in several countries. In the case of the United States the take-off occurred in the final decades before the Civil War, and investment in railroads was "indispensable" to the process. The railroads consumed iron, labor, and fuel; spun off other innovations, reduced transportation costs; and quickly developed into giant companies with vast resources. Railroads dominated the era. What was begun before 1860 continued through the rest of the century. For Schumpeter, painting on a huge historical canvas, the long cycle beginning in 1875 was due to the "railroadization of the world." Rostow's "stages" scheme and leading sector idea identified a similar process earlier in the American economy.

Fogel and Fishlow

How big would an indispensable leading sector be? What proportion of the national income was indeed produced by all railroad activity in the nineteenth century? Providing precise answers to these questions was the ambition of both Fogel and Fishlow in their separate research efforts.

The initial results were a shock, forcing a total reappraisal of ideas about the country's growth in the nineteenth century. Fogel began his work to demonstrate by econometric methods how right the traditional view of the "railroadization of the world" really was. He wanted to nail down the numbers once and for all. At first, no one was more dismayed than Fogel with his results. No statement was more repeated and less questioned by historians than the one that railroad construction had played a central role in the growth of the iron and steel industries. The reverse was just axiomatic: Where would the iron industry have been without the iron road? Douglass North, in 1961, had shown that in 1860 railroad iron brought the iron industry no more revenues than did sales of iron to make iron stoves.[20] On that basis, could you make any generalizations?

Fogel focused on railroad iron used, taking into account the scrapping and rerolling of old rails. Of the total pig iron produced between 1840 and 1860, railroad production used less than 5 percent.[21] It seemed that 95 percent of iron output went elsewhere. Economic historians had to think about that one. The weight of iron nails used in building construction, Fogel discovered, was greater than the weight of iron used in the railroads.[22] If the railroads had played as dominant a role in the demand for iron as had been believed by even the most eminent historians, the iron industry would have gotten nowhere.

What about coal? The coal used to make iron for rails was less than 6 percent of total coal output. The wood requirement (all those ties) for the railroads was an almost inconsequential part of total lumber production. As Fogel put it: "The modest position of railroads in the market for lumber products emphasizes the scale of lumber consumption by other sectors of the economy."[23]

In 1859, the value of output of railroad equipment was only a quarter of the market value of all transportation equipment produced. Railroads accounted for a mere 6 percent of the output of machinery. Fogel concluded that, in 1859, output generated by the railroads accounted for less than 4 percent of the GNP.

What was the opportunity cost of the railroads? Perhaps they were like imported coffee beans: expensive but much less so than if they had been grown in greenhouses in Kansas. Perhaps the service provided by the railroad was much cheaper than an equivalent amount of wagon and canal service would have been. Perhaps, then, the *real and indispensable* contribution of the railroad can be determined by how much it would have cost to haul an equivalent amount of freight on the least expensive, alternative transportation route. The difference between that figure and the actual cost of using the railroads is what Fishlow and Fogel termed the **social savings** of the railroads to the economy. For the movement of freight, rates by water were lower than freight rates by rail. This advantage, however, was lost when the additional costs were included. These costs were attributable to items such as additional wagon hauling, transshipment, cargo lost in transit, a reduced season of navigation, and the need to carry additional inventory because deliveries were slower. For passengers, the calculation emphasized the time they saved by taking the railroad.

Fishlow, in his careful study of the antebellum railroads, estimated the social savings of the railroads at 4 percent of GNP in 1859. The great railroad construction booms followed. With the huge system of 1890 in place, how much had the picture changed? (Remember, *all* of the economy had grown.) Fogel found that the social savings from railroads in 1890 was less than 5 (actually 4.7) percent of GNP.[24]

Fogel's investigation produced a methodological revolution in the study of economic history. He made elaborate **counterfactual** (a plausible, but not factual, alternative) expansions of canal, river, and wagon transport to replace the railroads that had actually been built and then studied the differences in costs and benefits. Three-quarters of the farm output of 1890 took place within 40 miles of navigable (or potentially navigable) water, a manageable distance by wagon. Thus, the epic stories about opening the land with the iron horse on prairie, farm, and mountain valley had to be diluted. It *could* have happened otherwise. Fogel concluded that without the railways, the GNP of 1890 would not have been reached until 1892.[25]

The "greatest" innovation of the nineteenth century, steam traction applied to land transport, was only one piece of the total mosaic of economic growth. The unrivaled economic expansion of the nineteenth-century United States was not due to railroads in the way we had believed; they were "indispensable" only if the 1892 GNP was desired as early as 1890. Other scholars, studying comparative productivity, showed that the railroads were unremarkable in that regard. This is not surprising, since they were, in the main, a huge application of contemporary technology.[26]

Salvaging the Myth

Any student of nineteenth-century railroads in this country or in other countries would conclude that they were in some sense a "leading sector." Neither Fishlow nor Fogel would be willing to relegate them to the dustbin of history, even though they have been lowered drastically in our estimation as growth producers. After all, 5 percent of GNP is a *very large* percent for a single industry. No single industry in this country today accounts for anything like that proportion of total output.

As Alfred Chandler emphasized, the railroads were our first giant enterprises.[27] Their management problems and methods sent all U.S. industrial entrepreneurs to school. Their securities were for some time the dominant commodity traded in the growing U.S. capital markets. Their relentless expansion in good times, for such a long time, helped establish the nineteenth-century American ethos of boundless growth and opportunity. But they were perhaps *too* visible. The growth of an entire economy is a complex phenomenon, involving all the inputs.

However, pursuing angles others ignored, Jeffrey Williamson argues that in various intervals up to 1890 the railroads could have enhanced the nation's growth by more than is implied by Fogel's calculation of the social savings. Williamson emphasizes that the growth of agricultural products would not have occurred without the construction of the railroads in the West. Thus, according to Williamson, the railroads were more "indispensable" than Fogel would allow.[28]

RAILROADS AND THE ATTACK ON BIG BUSINESS

The railroads in the late nineteenth century placed all sorts of dramatic problems on the public table. When those problems were solved, there was really no way that the railroads could go on as ordinary capitalistic business ventures. Oddly enough, the railroads were not even "indispensable" in the evolution of public policy toward big business. It is easily shown that law and practice growing out of the government regulation of the railroads was already extant from past legal history.[29] However, what happened in the area of public policy happened *as it did* largely because of the nation's experience with the railroads. Here, without question, the railroads left an indelible mark on U.S. history.

The railroads entered a gray area of combined private ownership and government regulation. In reality, it is hard to imagine any other fate for them, for several reasons:

1. The railroads were *all* government creatures—they were publicly licensed corporations with the accompanying privileges and liabilities. They were extensions of the sovereign power, having even the right of eminent domain over the property of others. Their government sponsorship, while necessary and profitable, left them singularly vulnerable to changes in, or additions to, public policy—that is, politics.
2. They had been built, in large part, with government subsidies and land grants and came to be seen as unfairly privileged.
3. Competing, parallel lines and rate wars were loathed by railroad management, yet consolidations and amalgamations tended to establish regional monopolies that were easy targets of public complaint.

4. Their natural oligopolistic tendencies—rate-fixing pools to "stabilize" revenues, rate discriminations, and kickbacks (the normal activities of the discriminating monopolist)—left their managements very far from common notions of fair play.
5. Like the modern automobile, they went from a novelty to a necessity, and their activities came to be seen as the public's business.

There is one other reason why the railroads met the fate—government regulation—they did. Those who built them included a fair share of notorious scoundrels and rough characters whose careers, attitudes, and *nouveau riche* lifestyles got them little public sympathy. In some cases the leading railroad figures had reputations little better than those of common criminals. The railroads were easy targets of public hatred, and when the time came, they became simply puppets of public policy. The problem was that policy had no particular object to it. The great railroad system became a pitiful giant whose future was to be determined by the vagaries of politics and public opinion.

The Monopoly Issue

Strictly speaking, a *monopolist* is a single seller. It is true that along the isolated trunk lines, there was only one railroad. If you bought the railroad's services, you were buying a monopoly service. What would the monopoly price be? For the railroad, with many kinds of services for many kinds of customers, there was the tantalizing prospect of attempting to be a perfectly discriminating monopolist, to provide services at varying prices to all who applied. The old rule-of-thumb in railroad pricing was to "charge what the traffic will bear." How much is that?

Figure 14.3 shows a profit-maximizing monopolist who charges a single price for service. Such a monopolist operates at point *a*, at the quantity (q_1) where MC = MR. At that quantity, the price p_1 is what the traffic will bear. Total revenue, price times quantity, is the area op_1aq_1. Total cost, average cost times quantity, is the area $oceq_1$. Therefore, profit is the area cp_1ae.

The demand curve shows *all* prices and quantities wanted by the railroad's customers, and it is clear that some customers are willing to pay a price higher than

FIGURE 14.3 Two Cases of Monopoly Pricing

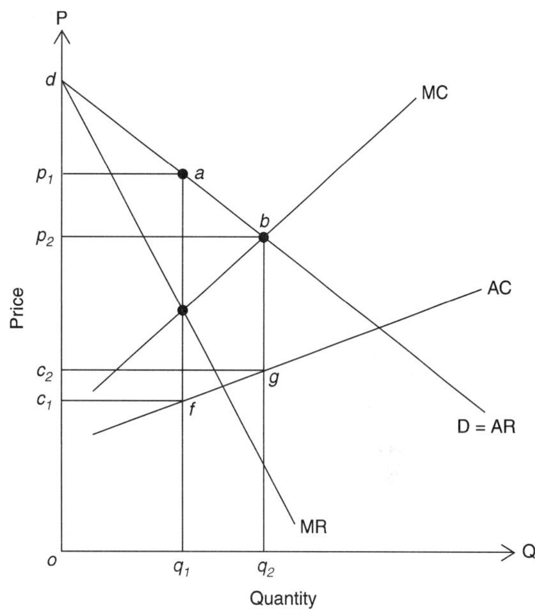

A profit-maximizing monopolist who charges a single price will operate at point a at the output where MC = MR. A perfectly discriminating monopolist who charges each customer his or her demand price will operate at point b where MC = AR. The profit of the former is c_1p_1 af; that of the latter is $c_2$dbg.

p_1. Now, the thinking monopolist must regret that loss of potential revenue. If the monopolist's marginal cost for additional service is small (typical of railroads, an extraordinarily large part of their total costs are fixed), the monopolist may begin to think about providing services to all potential customers at prices they are willing to pay, instead of just charging one price, p_1. Country doctors who, knowing their patients' wealth and incomes, fit their fees to their patients' abilities to pay are a close approximation.

Think of modern "deregulated" airline fares. We see surcharges for top service, "supersavers" for cheap seats, and cheaper round-trip fares from New York to Los Angeles than from Chicago to Bozeman, Montana. Ideally, the perfectly discriminating monopolist would force every customer to pay his or her demand price. The perfectly discriminating monopolist operates at point *b*, at the quantity (q_2) where MC = AR.

At that quantity, the price to the last customer is p_2. Total revenue is now the area $odbq_2$. Total cost, average cost times quantity, is the area $ocfq_2$. Therefore, the profit is the area *cdbf*; the perfectly discriminating monopolist is much more profitable than the single-price monopolist. Area *cdbf* includes area cp_1ae.

Old-time railroads engaged in price discrimination. They charged lower rates in areas where there was competition, higher rates where there was none. Rebates were given to the larger customers, who could go elsewhere for service; higher rates were charged for short hauls than for long ones—the whole bag of tricks.[30] Airlines do it now, and railroads did it then. The resulting outcry from disgruntled shippers and travelers produced government regulation.

To be fair, the railroads tried to solve the problems of pricing their services through mutual consultation and cooperation. Where Mammon got the upper hand, they resorted to conspiracy. Professor Thomas Ulen has shown that some price cartels were long lasting and relatively stable, despite a great temptation for cartel members to cheat, to shave prices below cartel levels.[31] There were many such price-fixing rings among the old railroads.

The economist's rule-of-thumb, that the competitive (and therefore "fair") price is always equal to marginal cost, was of no help to the railroads. Imagine two passengers waiting for a train in Wolf City, Wyoming. They buy two tickets to Omaha, Nebraska, and stand on a Union Pacific station platform. The train stops. How much should the first passenger pay? What is the marginal cost of the second ticket? Is it different from that of the first one? Now multiply this problem across all stations, all passengers, and all types of freight, and you can understand why no one—railroad owners, judges, state or Interstate Commerce Commission officials—*ever* figured out what were fair or "reasonable" rates for railroad service.

Edward Harriman, our greatest railroad financier by a country mile, once tried to defend his own rate-setting policies by a unique standard, the maximum (presumably) rates that his customers could afford to pay him and still be competitive in their own markets:

> It would be suicidal for a railroad to throttle or paralyze the industries along its lines by charging exorbitant rates. Even if there be no direct competition by parallel roads, every industrial plant located along a line of railroad is competing with plants located on other lines, and every railroad is forced to make such low and reasonable rates as will permit the industries in the territory tributary to it to make sales in competitive markets, and thus furnish the traffic from which the railroad company derives its earnings. It is impossible for a railroad company to sever its interests from those of its patrons.[32]

The trouble with this standard, apart from its vagueness and irrelevance for the discriminating monopolist (customers' demand prices already reflect their own competitive positions), is that the customers still knew they were vulnerable to rate-setting agreements among the railroads. These agreements allowed *all* rates or particular classes of rates to be raised in unison, thus transferring income *en masse* from railroad users to railroad owners. Cartels could still work perfectly. Because railroads are vulnerable to political pressure, the result was public regulation.

The Coming of Regulation

By 1890, there were about 1,000 separate railroad companies. Together, they were the railroad system, moving goods and people across the land. Were they really supposed to operate like 1,000 corner grocery stores, without mutual evaluation and collaboration? These companies were the survivors of a colorful and chaotic past that had included incredible episodes like the Susquehanna War (in which rival railroad investors hired small armies of roughhewn men to fight it out for physical control of railroad property). They had allegedly bribed judges and individual politicians and "salted" whole legislatures. They had purposely built lines parallel to each other to engage in rate wars and takeovers. Despite their collective vigor, many, including huge systems like the Union Pacific, had finally become financial basket cases, ruining thousands of investors in the process. Their discriminatory rate-setting practices had made many enemies.

The Granger Cases

Public antagonism to these new corporate giants was not long in coming; the public turned to government for remediation.[33] In the 1870s, the state legislatures passed laws to allow state agencies to control various aspects of railroad operation, including rate setting. The railroads fought this kind of regulation in the courts, and, in the fall of 1876, five of these cases reached the U.S. Supreme Court together and became known as the "Granger Cases." They were so named because they were largely the result of farmer discontent, focused by the National Grange leaders of the period. (Granges were local organizations of farmers that were originally established for social and educational purposes. They became political forums and channels for farmer protest—and the railroad was a frequent adversary.) The cases were: (a) *Munn v. Illinois*, (b) *Chicago, Burlington, and Quincy Railroad v. Iowa*, (c) *Peik v. Chicago and Northwestern Railroad*, (d) *Chicago, Milwaukee, and St. Paul Railroad v. Ackley*, and (e) *Winona and St. Peter Railroad v. Blake*.[34]

In March 1877, the five cases were reported out. We can see, in retrospect, that they sealed the fate of the U.S. railroad system. The court covered all five cases in its ruling in *Munn v. Illinois*, which was actually a case involving a grain elevator. But the rule of *Munn* was then applied by the court across the board to the four railroad cases. Even though *Munn* became inoperative for railroads a decade later (because of *Wabash v. Illinois*, discussed in the next section), the principle remained that railroads were unquestionably subject to permanent regulation.

Chapter 6 noted the legal foundations of public control over private property employed in business ventures. The railroads in the Granger decision were seen as private property that had mutated into public property. Chief Justice Waite ruled that any business firm whose property and activities were crucial to the public at large, any firm "clothed in the public interest," was, by ancient tradition, subject to government regulation. The relevant government in the *Munn* ruling was state government, and, by 1886, there were 25 state railroad commissions.

Wabash, Legal Persons, and the ICC

In 1886, a Supreme Court decision involving discriminatory pricing (our discriminating monopolist at work), *Wabash, St. Louis, and Pacific Railroad v. Illinois*, set the stage for federal regulation. The Supreme Court held that the railroads, being mainly in interstate commerce, were only properly subject to congressional regulation on their interstate business, under the federal Constitution's commerce clause. In the same year, in *Santa Clara County v. Southern Pacific Railroad*, special local taxes on railroad property were held to be in violation of the Fourteenth Amendment, the protection of the property of "persons" from state power without due process of law.[35] The amendment was meant to protect the property of former slaves, and the Court simply defined the Southern Pacific Corporation as a legal person. The marvelous subtlety of the legal mind in this decision did nothing for the image of the railroads in that Populist era.

The timing was accidental, but historically fateful. A year later, in 1887, Congress established the Interstate Commerce Commission (ICC), the first permanent independent federal regulatory agency. Given the interstate nature of railroads, the regulation the public demanded from the states simply passed to the federal government. Although at first the ICC lacked the power to set railroad rates, its founding marked the beginning of a kind of federal government power capable of almost infinite expansion.

In recent years, the origins of the ICC have been the subject of debate. Thomas Gilligan, William Marshall, and Barry Weingast argue that the Interstate Commerce Act resulted from a compromise between the railroads and the short-haul shippers, the two economic interests with a direct interest in the issue. Keith Poole and Howard Rosenthal argue that the act resulted from a coalition of much broader political and economic interests, that the other side places too much emphasis on narrowly defined interest groups.[36] To Poole and Rosenthal, there was widespread interest in bringing the federal power to bear on important issues.

Noted historian Gabriel Kolko and others have argued that the railroad operators saw the Commission as an opportunity to coerce the federal power into solving the problems of cartel management.[37] The ICC could provide a national and federally funded forum for the railroad interest. The ICC was, in this view, the first case of the "capture" of a regulatory commission by the regulatees.

In 1898, the case of *Smythe v. Ames* was initially considered as a solution to the dilemmas of rate setting

Railroad Expansion. *The railroads engaged the country's resources to expand commerce. From Chinese laborers building the roads (above left) and the business talents of railroad agents (below left), the railroads soon carried Western products to Eastern markets for consumption and export. The Grangers believed that the cost of transportation was too high relative to the value of the products, as shown in this 1873 cartoon "The Grange Awakening the Sleepers" (below right). In the case of* Munn v. Illinois, *the Supreme Court confirmed the right of states to regulate commerce because, at the connection between rail and lake transport in Chicago (above right), the grain elevators stood astride the very "gateway of commerce."*

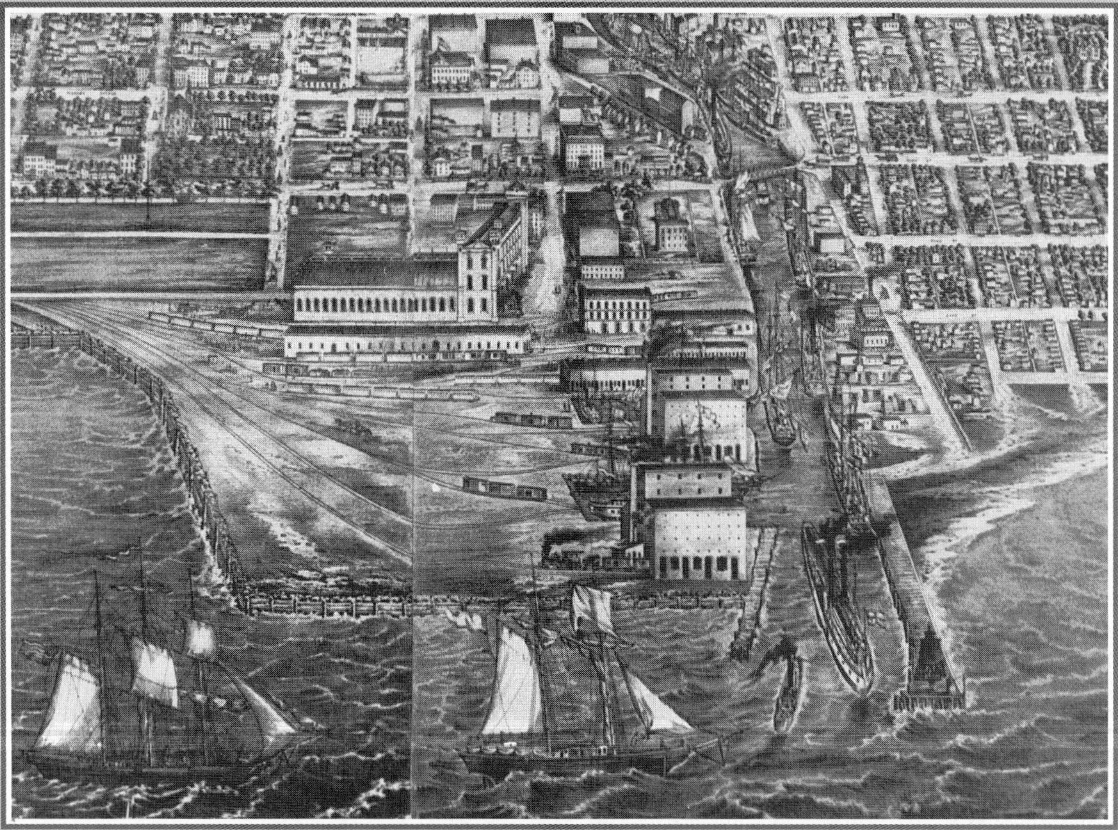

OPPRESSION
USURPATION
BRIBERY.
EXTORTION
CONSOLIDATION TRAIN
GRANGE
THE PARTISAN

that had been attempted by the courts. The standard set was that rates were to be sufficient to provide a "fair" rate of return upon investment.[38] In fact, this attempt at a solution merely shifted the ground for debate. The question now became valuation of railroad assets, whether original or replacement cost was to form the rate base. In 1906, the power to set maximum rates was given to the ICC by the Hepburn Act.

Albro Martin and the Capture Thesis

How did the "captured" federal control agency act? Were rates raised sufficiently to guarantee profitable operation? Here the work of Albro Martin is crucial evidence. Martin, in *Enterprise Denied*, shows that the ICC, if it was captured by anyone, was captured by the users of the railroads—passengers and shippers.[39] As prices rose after 1896, railroad rates fell behind, first because of rate setting by the courts, then by the ICC. After the Hepburn Act, the ICC refused to grant the rate increases the railroads said they needed. According to Martin, repair and replacement of capital equipment could not be sustained, and, by 1914, the railroads were financially strapped and physically disabled. This predicament set the stage for the federal takeover in 1917 in the interest of national defense.

The Sherman Act and the Long Future

In the *Northern Securities* case of 1904, the Sherman Antitrust Act was employed to block the formation of a giant holding company uniting the interests of the Union Pacific, Northern Pacific, Great Northern, and Burlington roads.[40] The Court argued that such a combine would tend to reduce competition. In 1913, the 1901 purchase and reorganization of the Southern Pacific railroad by Harriman's Union Pacific were dissolved on similar lines—that Harriman's last masterpiece of organization reduced competition.[41] Railroad amalgamation seemed a natural course for railroads all over the world, since economic forces were propelling them toward fewer operating units in all the major countries and, finally, toward state monopoly ownership. Application of the Sherman Act and, after World War I, the lodging of veto power over railroad mergers in the hands of the ICC, meant that railroad amalgamation in the United States would not proceed at the pace it had in Europe.

Use of the Sherman Act in its early years to constrain railroad amalgamation reflected an understandable fear of monopoly, even government-regulated monopoly. But this left the railroads dependent upon government initiative where the scale economies and externalities to be gained by car pooling, terminal sharing, and continuous service were concerned. That initiative proved to be sluggish. Only in our own time, through government subsidies, planning, and management, were amalgamation and rationalization finally carried out on the scale that the old-time tycoons had tried in the Northern Securities Trust. Amtrak and other government-sponsored and subsidized systems designed to save the remnants of the great railroad network seem to summon up the ghosts of Harriman, Hill, and Pierpont Morgan for one last cheer. By the 1960s, when Amtrak was organized, the American railroad system was in a state of financial desperation.[42] Things are somewhat brighter today, but the relevant question remains, "What might have been?"

Some, like Martin, argue that the railroads were never given the chance. Government regulation was imposed early and continuously. On the other hand, Henry Ford—who bought a railroad, ran it on *his* principles, made it profitable, and was forced by the ICC to sell it—argued that *both* the traditional railroad management and the government control agency were utterly incompetent. He may well have been correct. His brief experience as a railroad magnate is the one example we have of a modern railroad run on straight, twentieth-century business principles, without regulation, without collusive arrangements with other roads, and with no unions or work rules. Ford was satisfied with his little railroad, but the ICC was outraged.[43]

The United States never adopted all the Populist demands; it never nationalized the railroad system. To this day, American railroads are privately owned, although management remains largely a creature of regulatory agencies. The main problem with the method, private ownership and development on the one hand and government control on the other, is that no one got what they wanted—not the investors in the railroad companies, nor their management, their users, nor the government—since it never really had a policy.

NOTES

1. Robert Fogel, *Railroads and American Economic Growth: Essays in Econometric History* (1964); Albert Fishlow, *American Railroads and the Transformation of the Ante-Bellum Economy* (1965).
2. Simon Kuznets, "The Retardation of Industrial Growth," *Journal of Economic and Business History*, August 1929; Arthur F. Burns, *Production Trends in the United States Since 1870* (New York: National Bureau of Economic Research, 1934), chap. IV, "Retardation in the Growth of Industries."
3. Joseph Schumpeter, *Business Cycles* (New York: McGraw-Hill, 1939), 2 vols. Others followed his lead. For example, Thomas Wilson, *Fluctuations in Income and Employment* (New York: Pitman, 1949).
4. Fishlow, "Internal Transportation," in Lance Davis et al., *American Economic Growth: An Economist's History of the United States* (1972), p. 500.
5. Jonathan Hughes, *The Vital Few* (1986), pp. 374–379.
6. Robert Fogel, *The Union Pacific Railroad* (1960).
7. Stanley Engerman, "Some Economic Issues Related to Railroad Subsidies and the Evaluation of Land Grants," *JEH*, June 1972, p. 444, n. 2.
8. Lloyd Mercer, "Land Grants to American Railroads: Social Cost or Social Benefit?" *BHR*, Summer 1969.
9. State and local governments also invested in railroads. Jac Heckelman and John Wallis, "Railroads and Property Taxes," *Explorations in Economic History*, vol. 34, no. 1, January 1997, estimate that the increase in property values attributable to railroad construction could have generated sufficient property taxes to cover the majority, if not all, of the construction costs.
10. When live cattle were shipped east by rail, they were taken off the train at regular intervals for food and fluids. Since cattle were sold by the pound, unscrupulous sellers would fill them full of water just before they were sold, hence the phrase "watering the stock." The first corporate stock to be "watered"—where capitalization was increased without a concomitant increase in plant and equipment—was that of the railroads. Tycoons such as Daniel Drew and Jay Gould reputedly manipulated railroad stock in an attempt to maximize their own profits. In the recession of 1873, many American railroads went into receivership.
11. J. Hayden Boyd and Gary Walton, "The Social Savings from 19th Century Rail Passenger Services," *EEH*, Spring 1972; Gerald Gunderson, "The Nature of Social Saving," *EHR*, August 1970; E. H. Hunt, "Social Savings in 19th Century America," *AER*, September 1967; Stanley Lebergott, "United States Transport Advance and Externalities," *JEH*, December 1966; Peter McClelland, "Railroads, American Growth, and the New Economic History: A Critique," *JEH*, March 1968.
12. Engerman (1972), p. 463.
13. Gottfried von Haberler, *Prosperity and Depression* (Cambridge: Harvard University Press, 1958).
14. Paul Samuelson, "Interaction of the Multiplier and Accelerator," *Review of Economics and Statistics*, vol. XXI, no. 2, May 1939.
15. Joseph Schumpeter, *Theory of Economic Development*, English edition (Cambridge: Harvard University Press, 1934).
16. Leland Hamilton Jenks, "Railroads as an Economic Force in American Development," in *Views of American Economic Growth* (1966), vol. 2.
17. W. W. Rostow, *British Economy of the Nineteenth Century* (Oxford: Clarendon Press, 1948); and A. D. Gayer, W. W. Rostow, and Anna J. Schwartz, with the assistance of Isaiah Frank, *The Growth and Fluctuation of the British Economy 1790–1850: An Historical, Statistical, and Theoretical Study of Britain's Economic Development* (Oxford: Clarendon Press, 1948).
18. W. W. Rostow, *The Process of Economic Growth* (Oxford: Oxford University Press, 1953).
19. W. W. Rostow, *The Stages of Economic Growth: A Non-Communist Manifesto* (1960). Rostow returned to these themes in his massive work, *The World Economy* (1978).
20. Douglass C. North, *The Economic Growth of the United States: 1790–1860* (New York: W.W. Norton, 1966), p. 164.
21. Fogel's main findings were reported in Fogel (1964). The iron measurement is on pp. 230–233.
22. Fogel (1964), p. 233.
23. *Ibid.*, p. 234.
24. For Fogel's social savings estimate and commentary on Fishlow, see *Ibid.*, pp. 219–224.
25. *Ibid.*, p. 92 for a map of his hypothetical canal system.
26. Trevor Dick, "United States Railroad Inventions' Investment Since 1870," *EEH*, Spring 1974. As Dick points out, the dependence of railroads on capital from the money markets for investment funds made them unlikely candidates to lead the rise in productivity. They followed the cycle.
27. Alfred Chandler, *The Railroads: The Nation's First Big Business* (1965).
28. Jeffrey Williamson, *Late Nineteenth-Century American Development: A General Equilibrium Approach* (New York: Cambridge University Press, 1974), p. 193. Rostow (1978) replied to Fogel's criticism in a long footnote, pp. 748–749, and in Chapters 13 and 14 of his text. Rostow sticks to his leading sector analysis and places the railroads preeminently as a leading sector.
29. Jonathan Hughes, *The Governmental Habit Redux* (1991), pp. 102–109.

30. The most famous of these, the "midnight rebates," were paid to Standard Oil by the railroads, who had to deal with John D. Rockefeller, Sr.
31. Thomas Ulen, "Railroad Cartels Before 1887: The Effectiveness of Private Enforcement of Collusion," *REH* (1983).
32. Quoted in Hughes (1986), p. 391.
33. Anne Mayhew, "A Reappraisal of the Causes of Farm Protest in the United States, 1870–1900," *JEH*, June 1972; Robert McGuire, "Economic Causes of Late Nineteenth Century Agrarian Unrest," *JEH*, December 1981.
34. Hughes (1991), pp. 12–15.
35. 118 U.S. 394 (1886).
36. Thomas Gilligan, William Marshall, and Barry Weingast, "Regulation and the Theory of Legislative Choice: The Interstate Commerce Act of 1887," *JLE*, January 1989. Keith Poole and Howard Rosenthal, "The Enduring Nineteenth-Century Battle for Economic Regulation: The Interstate Commerce Commission Act Revisited," *JLE*, April 1993; and "Congress and Railroad Regulation: 1874 to 1887," in Claudia Goldin and Gary Libecap, eds., *The Regulated Economy: A Historical Approach to Political Economy* (1994).
37. Gabriel Kolko, *Railroads and Regulation 1877–1916* (1965).
38. 169 U.S. 466 (1898). The famous phrase is "a fair return upon the value of that which it (the company) employs for the public convenience."
39. Albro Martin, *Enterprise Denied* (1971). For an earlier critique of the Kolko thesis, Robert Harbeson, "Railroads and Regulation 1877–1916; Conspiracy or Public Interest?" *JEH*, June 1967.
40. 193 U.S. 197 (1904).
41. 226 U.S. 86 (1913).
42. Paul MacAvoy, *The Economic Effects of Regulation* (1965); Thomas McCraw, "Regulation in America," *BHR*, Summer 1975, for surveys of regulation and its long-run consequences.
43. Henry Ford, *My Life and Work* (New York: Doubleday, 1922).

SUGGESTED READINGS

Articles

Boyd, J. Hayden, and Gary Walton. "The Social Savings from 19th Century Rail Passenger Services." *Explorations in Economic History*, vol. 9, no. 3, Spring 1972.

David, Paul. "Transport Innovation and Economic Growth: Professor Fogel On and Off the Rails." *Economic History Review*, second series, vol. 32, no. 3, December 1969.

Dick, Trevor J. O. "United States Railroad Inventions' Investment Since 1870." *Explorations in Economic History*, vol. 11, no. 3, Spring 1974.

Engerman, Stanley L. "Some Economic Issues Relating to Railroad Subsidies and the Evaluation of Land Grants." *Journal of Economic History*, vol. XXXII, no. 2, June 1972.

Fishlow, Albert. "Internal Transportation." In Lance E. Davis et al., *American Economic Growth*. New York: Harper & Row, 1972.

Fogel, Robert W. "Notes on the Social Savings Controversy." *Journal of Economic History*, vol. XXXIV, no. 1, March 1979.

Gilligan, Thomas W., William J. Marshall, and Barry R. Weingast. "Regulation and the Theory of Legislative Choice: The Interstate Commerce Act of 1887." *Journal of Law and Economics*, vol. 32, no. 1, April 1989.

Gunderson, Gerald. "The Nature of Social Saving." *Economic History Review*, second series, vol. 23, no. 2, August 1970.

Harbeson, Robert. "Railroads and Regulation 1877–1916; Conspiracy or Public Interest?" *Journal of Economic History*, vol. XXVII, no. 2, June 1967.

Hunt, E. H. "Social Savings in 19th Century America." *American Economic Review*, vol. 57, no. 4, September 1967.

Jenks, Leland Hamilton. "Railroads as an Economic Force in American Development." Reprinted in Thomas Cochran and Thomas Brewer, eds., *Views of American Economic Growth*. New York: McGraw-Hill, 1966, vol. 2.

Lebergott, Stanley. "United States Transport Advance and Externalities." *Journal of Economic History*, vol. XXVI, no. 4, December 1966.

Mayhew, Anne. "A Reappraisal of the Causes of Farm Protest in the United States, 1870–1900." *Journal of Economic History*, vol. XXXII, no. 2, June 1972.

McClelland, Peter D. "Railroads, American Growth, and the New Economic History: A Critique." *Journal of Economic History*, vol. XXVIII, no. 1, March 1968.

McCraw, Thomas. "Regulation in America, a Review Article." *Business History Review*, vol. 49, no. 2, Summer 1975.

McGuire, Robert A. "Economic Causes of Late Nineteenth Century Agrarian Unrest." *Journal of Economic History*, vol. XLI, no. 4, December 1981.

Mercer, Lloyd. "Land Grants to American Railroads: Social Cost or Social Benefit?" *Business History Review*, vol. 43, no. 2, Summer 1969.

———. "Building Ahead of Demand: Some Evidence for the Land Grant Railroads." *Journal of Economic History*, vol. XXXIV, no. 2 June 1974.

Poole, Keith T., and Howard Rosenthal. "The Enduring Nineteenth-Century Battle for Economic Regulation:

The Interstate Commerce Commission Act Revisited." *Journal of Law and Economics*, vol. 36, no. 2, October 1993.

———. "Congress and Railroad Regulation: 1874 to 1887." In Claudia Goldin and Gary Libecap, eds., *The Regulated Economy: A Historical Approach to Political Economy*. Chicago: University of Chicago Press, 1994.

Ulen, Thomas. "Railroad Cartels Before 1887: The Effectiveness of Private Enforcement of Collusion." *Research in Economic History*, vol. 8. Greenwich, CT: JAI Press, 1983.

Weiss, Thomas. "United States Transport Advance and Externalities: A Comment." *Journal of Economic History*, vol. XXVIII, no. 4, December 1968.

Books

Chandler, Alfred D. *The Railroads: The Nation's First Big Business*. New York: Harcourt, Brace & World, 1965.

Cochran, Thomas C. *Railroad Leaders, 1845–1890, The Business Mind in Action*. Cambridge: Harvard University Press, 1953.

Fishlow, Albert. *American Railroads and the Transformation of the Ante-Bellum Economy*. Cambridge: Harvard University Press, 1965.

Fogel, Robert W. *The Union Pacific Railroad: A Case of Premature Enterprise*. Baltimore: Johns Hopkins University Press, 1960.

———. *Railroads and American Economic Growth*. Baltimore: Johns Hopkins University Press, 1964.

Grodinsky, Julius. *Transcontinental Railway Strategy*. Philadelphia: University of Pennsylvania Press, 1962.

Hughes, Jonathan. *The Vital Few: American Economic Progress and Its Protagonists*. New York: Oxford University Press, 1986.

———. *The Governmental Habit Redux: Economic Controls from Colonial Times to the Present*. Princeton: Princeton University Press, 1991.

Kolko, Gabriel. *Railroads and Regulation, 1877–1916*. Princeton: Princeton University Press, 1965.

Martin, Albro. *Enterprise Denied: Origins of the Decline of American Railroads, 1897–1917*. New York: Columbia University Press, 1971.

———. *James J. Hill and the Opening of the Northwest*. New York: Oxford University Press, 1976.

MacAvoy, Paul. *The Economic Effects of Regulation*. Cambridge: MIT Press, 1965.

Ripley, W. Z. *Railroads: Rates and Regulations*. New York: Longmans, Green, 1912.

Rostow, Walter W. *The Stages of Economic Growth: A Non-Communist Manifesto*. New York: Cambridge University Press, 1960.

———. *The World Economy: History and Prospect*. Austin: University of Texas Press, 1978.

Stover, John. *American Railroads*. Chicago: University of Chicago Press, 1961.

CHAPTER FIFTEEN

Post-Civil War Agriculture

The discussion of American agriculture in Chapter 10 centered on the parallel westward movements of two agrarian social systems: the family farm of the North and the largely slave-based plantation of the South. The extreme scarcity of hired labor in the North—one laborer for every two farms—already had produced a trend toward relatively capital-intensive agriculture there. Slavery seemed to be creating a remarkably labor-intensive agriculture in the South. In the antebellum period, both systems "made sense."

The Civil War eliminated the South's slave-based plantation agriculture. The conversion from plantation slavery to sharecropping and a system of hired agricultural labor was relatively unsuccessful, and Southern agriculture became a relatively depressed area in the American economy that was not reformed until well into the twentieth century. In the North, two more great stages of agricultural expansion awaited: The first was dry-land farming of basic grains and livestock feeding, followed in the mid-twentieth century by large-scale, government-aided water control and irrigation systems, true engineering marvels of our era.

THE HOMESTEAD AND THE END OF THE FRONTIER ERA

At first, American agriculture grew in the form of continued extensive cultivation, which resulted in a huge expansion of farm output. In the period up to World War I, a remarkable phenomenon occurred: The ratio of increases in the acreage of basic crops under cultivation to increases in output was nearly 2 to 1. Let's consider the data in Table 15.1.

As we can see, the output of wheat per acre increased only by roughly 12 percent in the four decades from the end of the Civil War to 1910, and corn output per acre seems to have declined for at least part of this period. These changes occurred when farmers substituted the level, glacially ground acres of the Midwest for the stones and mountainsides of the East Coast.

The farmers continued the westward push into new lands recently vacated by the Indians and the great buffalo herds, both of which suffered near-extinction. The Homestead Act of 1862 changed the process of land acquisition, but it was not the utopian dream of previous generations. Most new settlement *did not* come from homesteads. Making a farm was an expensive, risky, and time-consuming proposition. Besides, the lands open to homesteading were mainly beyond the 100th meridian in the middle of Kansas and Nebraska, where rainfall is sharply lower than in the central and eastern parts of the country. Farmers had to learn new techniques to farm these relatively dry regions without irrigation.

The Western railroads had been granted vast amounts of land. They were anxious to sell those

TABLE 15.1 Corn and Wheat Acreage and Output, 1866–1990

	Corn			*Wheat*		
Year	*Acreage Harvested (in millions)*	*Output (millions of bushels)*	*Bushels per Acre*	*Acreage Harvested (in millions)*	*Output (millions of bushels)*	*Bushels per Acre*
1866	30	731	24.4	15	170	11.0
1890	75	1650	22.1	37	449	12.2
1910	102	2853	27.9	46	626	13.7
1950	82	3075	37.5	62	1019	16.4
1970	66	4099	61.9	44	1370	31.1
1990	67	7934	118.5	69	2736	39.5

Source: *Historical Statistics,* series K 502, 503, 506–507: *Statistical Abstract,* 1992, Table 1115.

lands, and they produced a market in competition with homesteading. The railroads provided financing and helped with problems of settlement. They wanted not only to profit from their land sales but also to promote economic development along their lines in the interest of generating freight. Even though the homestead land was granted without a money payment, for a long time it was the railroad lands that provided most new farms in the West.

Extensive Growth

The absence of basic chemical and biological improvements to raise output per acre before World War I meant that the ratio of output growth to additional land inputs in American agriculture grew almost in a straight line—a remarkable phenomenon. Roughly measured between 1866 and 1910 (see Table 15.1), the secular increase in land under cultivation produced an increase in the physical output of almost equal proportion, so there was little change in the number of bushels per acre.

Figure 15.1, a generalized view of this situation, conceptually transforms the physical output and land input numbers for the other years in Table 15.1 into the percentages of 1866, assuming, for the moment, that wheat and corn are representative of all grains. Had the growth rates been exactly equal, the final numbers would have fallen at the tip of a ray drawn from the origin with a slope of 45 degrees (line *B*). It was very nearly so. Had the quality of the new land brought down the average, other things equal, the rate of increase in output should have dropped, say, to curve *C*. Had the land quality improved significantly on average, output may have risen disproportionately, say, to curve *A*. It is conceivable that steady substitutions of curve *A* land offset the extensions of grain farming on curve *C* land, resulting in the growth of outputs and inputs by equal proportions.[1] Later on, the biochemical revolution in agriculture would produce a phenomenon like curve *A*.

From the end of the Civil War until 1910, the great expansion in output of wheat and corn was accompanied by only a small increase in yields per acre. The major source of the increase in total output was simply the increased land input. More land was being planted in corn and wheat. By the mid-twentieth century (again, see Table 15.1), the biochemical revolution had occurred in American agriculture. Yields rose phenomenally, and acreage devoted to these basic food crops was actually reduced as output soared. But, until 1910, it was increased land input with a fairly constant yield per acre that enabled the great growth of Northern agriculture to occur. In the final westward thrust of the Northern family farm, the *overall* result was almost as represented by line *B* in Figure 15.1.

The physical nature of the land suggests that in the antebellum period the expansion westward from the old colonies into the Midwest at first shifted total output above the 45-degree line, to something like curve *A*. That change reflects an initial improvement in land quality. Why else abandon Vermont to embrace Iowa? From the Civil War onward, as the

FIGURE 15.1 Increase of Agricultural Land Inputs and Physical Outputs 1866–1910 As a Percentage of 1866

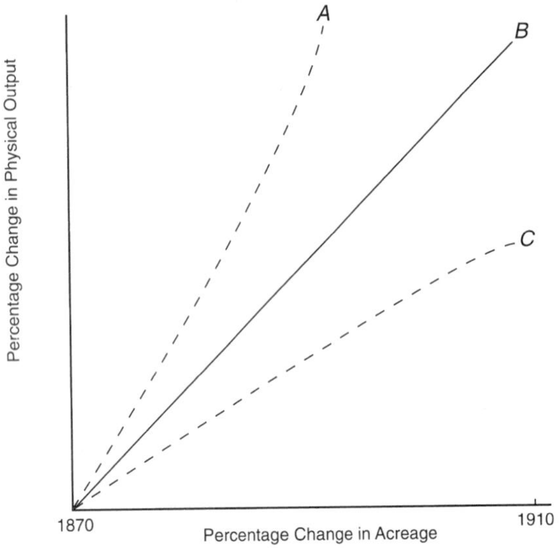

If the percentage increase in acreage were just matched by the percentage increase in output, line *B* would describe the advance in output as the area of cultivation grew. Line *A* shows a set of cases where the percentage increases in output exceed those of the acreage increases. Line *C* is the reverse: Along it, the percentage increase in output is less than the percentage increase in acreage.

system of agriculture spread across prairie and plain, the product of the land constantly increased—but in proportion to the increased land input.

Agricultural Efficiency

The westward movement was accompanied by a small increase in the efficiency of Northern farming; as we have seen, output per acre was relatively constant over these years. Output per worker-hour rose as the number of acres per farmer increased as a result of innovations in horse- and mule-drawn implements and machinery. Even if the output of the land variable was constant, average costs of output could be reduced by adding other inputs of increasing efficiency. Better plows, steam threshing, more effective reapers, then combined reaper-binders, better cultivating equipment, improved transport—all these things raised total farm productivity and released the Northern farmer from the labor constraint.[2] Therefore, even though output per acre was almost constant, output per worker-hour rose and so did the potential for profits in farming. As a result, farming attracted more people and more investment. Table 15.2 shows the advances made in output per worker-hour.

Even in cotton, where fundamental mechanization was slow in coming at the level of actual field work, worker-hour productivity rose. In corn and wheat, it rose markedly. Farmers could hope to become increasingly effective by acquiring more land over which to spread the cost of their draft animals and equipment. Land in farms was truly a variable input in this period of economic history. The land's own fertility was relatively fixed, but changing the proportions of the rest of the input mix could produce rising profits in farming.

Using a regionally weighted index of the average labor input per bushel, William Parker and Judith Klein estimated that, between 1840 and 1860 and 1900 and 1910, labor productivity grew a little over 2 percent in wheat and about 1.8 percent in both corn and oats.[3] These are high rates by agricultural standards, as high as those observed in other sectors of the economy. In their history of Northern agriculture, Jeremy Atack and Fred Bateman reworked these estimates using exactly the same estimating formula with two changes. They used their estimates of regional yields and excluded the South. As a result, the rate for wheat was unchanged, but, as they expected, those for corn and oats both decreased.[4]

Increasing productivity and profitability resulted in an increase of acres in farms and homesteads, as shown in Table 15.3. Note that the increase in farmland was not mainly due to homesteads. The

TABLE 15.2 Agriculture: Output per Worker-Hour

	Bushels per Worker-Hour		
	Wheat	*Corn*	*Cotton*
1840	0.43	0.36	0.23
1880	0.66	0.56	0.33
1900	0.93	0.68	0.35

Source: *Historical Statistics,* series K 449, 454, 459.

TABLE 15.3 Land in Farm and Homesteads[a]

Year	*Land in Farms*	*Increase per Decade*	*Final Homestead Entries per Decade*
1860	407.2	—	—
1870	407.7	0.5	1.4
1880	536.1	128.4	17.9
1890	623.2	87.1	29.0
1900	841.2	218.0	31.9
1910	881.4	40.2	38.8
1920	958.7	77.3	74.3

[a] Figures for land are in millions of acres.

Source: *Historical Statistics,* series K 5, J 15.

additional farmland came primarily from cash sales by the government, from railroad grants, and from lands ceded to the states and then sold to individuals. Moreover, three-fourths of the homesteads were taken up after 1890, when the unbroken line of the physical frontier had vanished. The greatest decade of homesteading was, in fact, 1910–1920, at a time when high prices for farm products finally returned. Taking up land and making farms, even when the land was free, were *market decisions* because they involved costs. The other inputs were not free, and the opportunity costs of farm-making were not zero. Homesteading was never a utopian solution to land hunger.

Of all the public lands, homesteads totaled 285 million acres, while cash sales totaled 300 million acres. Between 1860 and 1920, land in farms increased by 548.2 million acres, of which homesteads were only 192.3 million acres. From 1860 to the end of the nineteenth century, cash sales, and not homesteads, accounted for the preponderance of new farms.

Patterns of Regional Agricultural Production

One consequence of extensive farming was the creation of the "farm belt," a phenomenon that dominated postbellum American agricultural history. In Figures 15.2 and 15.3, the farm belt is the mass of black dots, each representing 25,000 acres, that runs right across the center of the country from Ohio through the Midwest, thinning out as an east-west finger on the Nebraska-Kansas border to the west, with a separate extension running northward into the Red River wheat country of Minnesota and the Dakotas. The basic grains, corn and wheat (and sorghum in the western part) were the root of this great development.

Wheat and corn are used directly for human consumption and are joined by sorghum as livestock feed. They form the base upon which the great Midwestern food industry grew. As we see in Figure 15.4, by 1920, cattle production, ubiquitous in American agriculture (even on the dry ranges of the Western highlands), became concentrated in a Midwestern band running north-eastward from Texas to Illinois. Chicago, Omaha, and Kansas City became the centers of the great meatpacking industry.

The advance of refrigeration into railroad cars and steamships, beginning in the 1880s, contributed to the Midwest grain and livestock industries' dominance of their markets in the United States and in international trade. Railroads, grain elevators, and river and lake steamers connected the Midwest to the world, and supporting financial services grew up with their center in the Chicago commodities market. In the late nineteenth and early twentieth centuries, these commodities markets, which the Chicago Board of Trade organized, did for food what the New York Stock Exchange had done for securities. We can see the expansion of basic grain output in Table 15.4.

The Wheat Cycle

Midwest American grain farmers developed remarkable regional specialization in the late nineteenth century

TABLE 15.4 Output of Basic Grains[a]

Year	*Wheat*	*Corn*	*Oats*	*Barley*
1859	173	839	173	16
1870	254	1125	268	29
1880	502	1707	418	45
1890	449	1650	609	70
1900	599	2662	945	97
1910	625	2853	1106	142
1914	897	2524	1066	178

[a] Figures are in millions of bushels.

Source: *Historical Statistics,* series K 503, 507, 512, 515.

FIGURE 15.2 Improved Land 1870

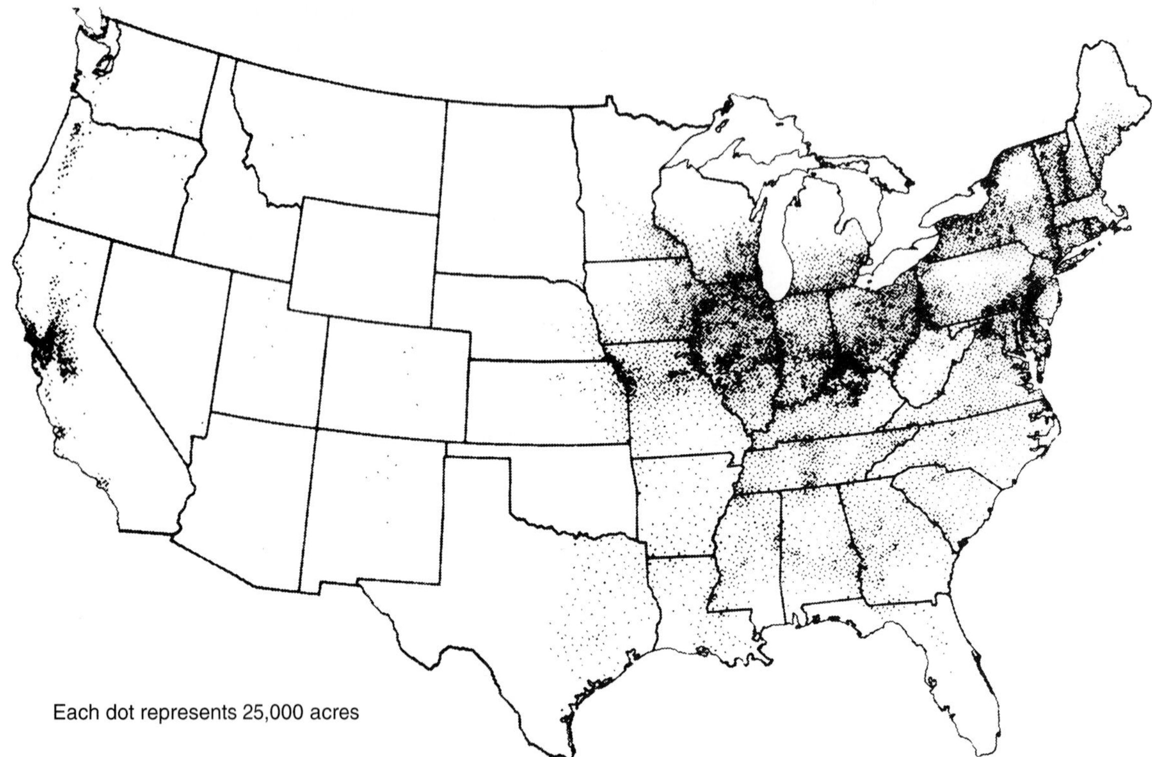

Source: Charles O. Paullin, *Atlas of the Historical Geography of the United States* (Washington, D.C. and New York: Carnegie Institution and the American Geographical Society of New York, 1932), plate 144E.

In 1870, improved acreage west of the Mississippi was fairly well restricted to Minnesota, Iowa, Missouri, Arkansas, Louisiana, and east Texas—together with Oregon's Willamette Valley and the Central Valley in California.

that is still followed: corn in the prairies, sorghum on the high plains, winter wheat in the warmer parts of the midsection, spring wheat in the North. These formed the base of the livestock and poultry industries that were created to exploit the grain output. Other rotations were mixed in later (especially soybeans in the corn belt), but the wheat schedule became basic.[5] Winter wheat was planted in the late fall in Texas, Oklahoma, and Kansas and ripened in late spring, while wheat planted in the spring in the Northern regions was ready for harvest by August. The great harvesting began in June in the South for the winter wheat and moved north as the hot Midwestern summer advanced. By fall, the harvest was in, and the cycle was ready to begin again.

Grain elevators along the rail routes and in the milling centers made massive storage and shipping possible.[6] Futures trading in grain allowed farmers access to an extended schedule of net receipts. Futures also allowed buyers of grains to contract ahead of need and, to some extent, control the net cost of their purchases. The element of gambling in the futures market, although incidental to the commodities trade, seemed to disrupt it, to the anger of alert political leaders. As a result, abuses and controls of this element appeared early in the history of futures trading.[7] Nevertheless, futures trading attracted nonagricultural money to the financing of grain and livestock as the market increasingly commercialized Midwest agriculture.

FIGURE 15.3 Improved Land 1900

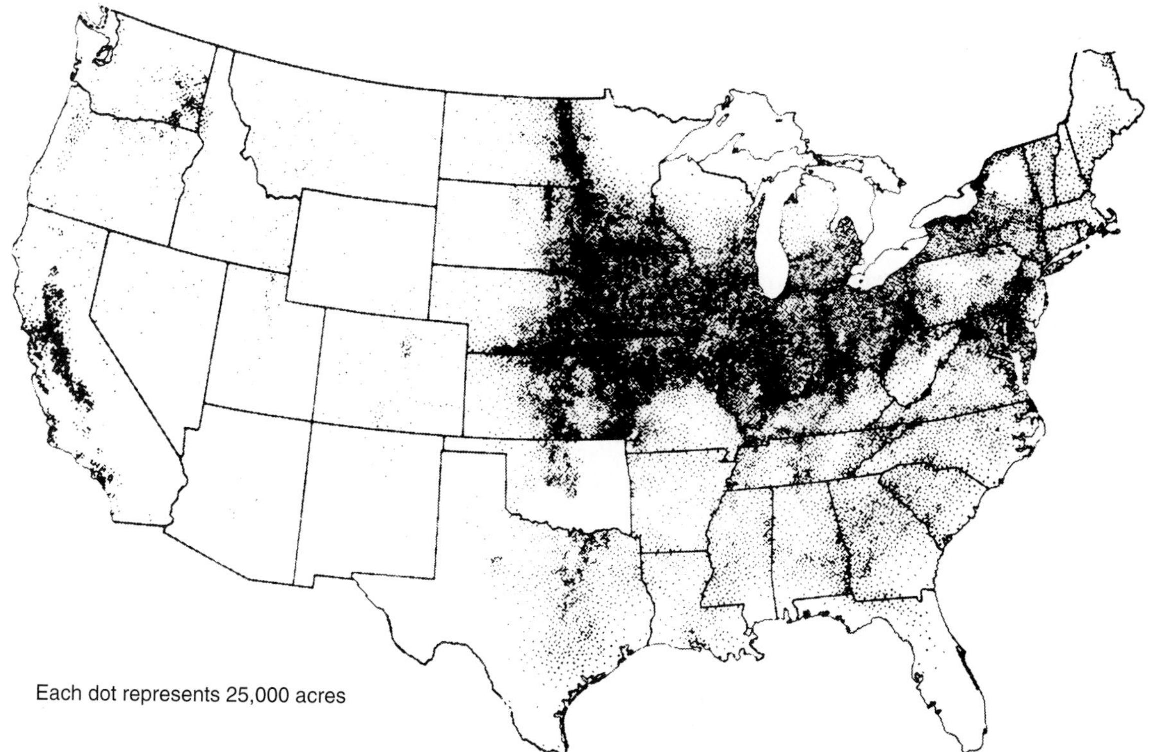

Source: Charles O. Paullin, *Atlas of the Historical Geography of the United States* (Washington, D.C. and New York: Carnegie Institution and the American Geographical Society of New York, 1932), plate 144H.

By 1900, although there was more extensive cultivation on the high plains and in the West than was true in 1870, the lack of rainfall from the Cascades and Sierra Nevada ranges eastward to the Midwest farm belt clearly defined those continuing features of dry land and irrigation farming that came to characterize agriculture in the Great Basin, Southwest, and high plains states.

Learning-by-doing in agriculture meant experimentation and change. The story of hybrid corn has been much discussed in the literature.[8] As for wheat, in the nineteenth century, the Northern grain belt benefited from the introduction of hard red wheats, which were rich in gluten, for bread. The red wheats came from southern Russia, imported at first by Mennonite farmers who had emigrated from that region. In addition, other drought- and rust-resistant strains that thrived on the Great Plains were imported. Important new strains were developed there by plant geneticists with the Department of Agriculture and Kansas State University. A whole new world of wheat growing was born, and the most ancient approach to agriculture was transformed.

Sorghum corn brought from Africa in the 1870s was found to thrive in relatively dry, hot areas. With its introduction, in the winter, high plains ranchers could feed cattle off the range with a locally grown row crop. Improved breeding raised cattle and hog slaughter weights in the Midwest. The extraordinary efficiency of the new Midwest grain belt forced farmers in the East and near urban centers to shift into dairying, poultry, vegetables, and fruit.[9] Growing urban populations supported this shift, and since this increased specialization paid (that is, raised the opportunity costs of grain production outside the

FIGURE 15.4 Cattle (Excluding Dairy Cows) 1920

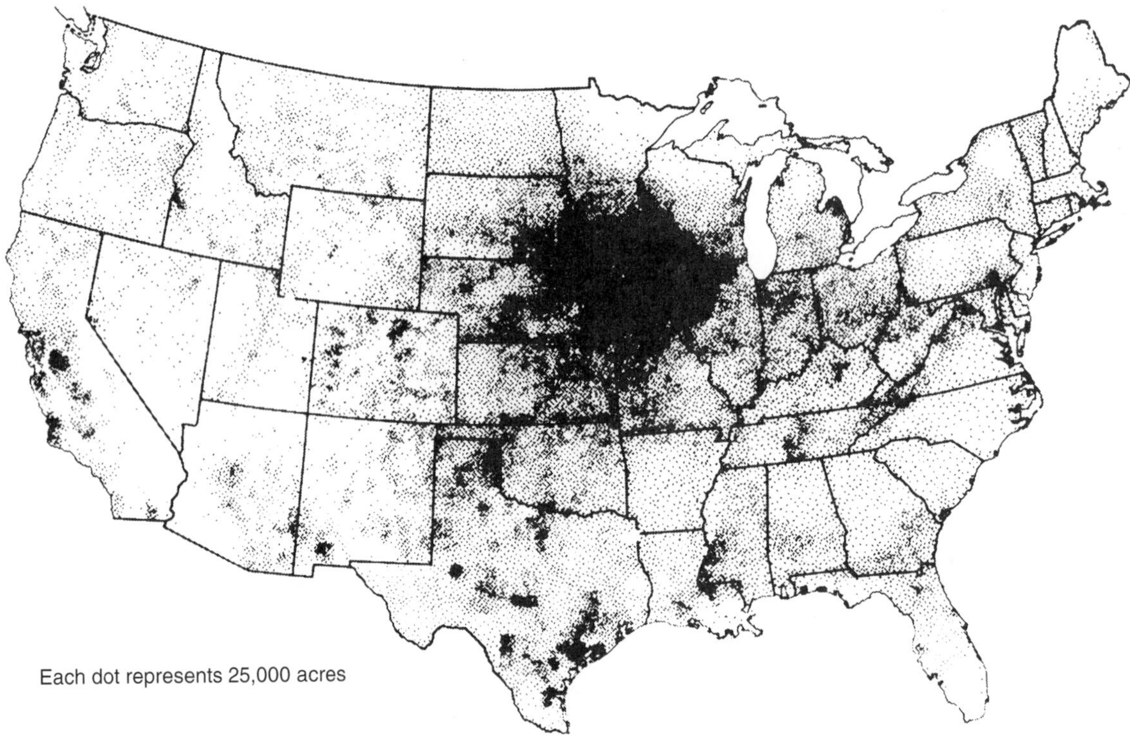

Source: Charles O. Paullin, *Atlas of the Historical Geography of the United States* (Washington, D.C. and New York: Carnegie Institution and the American Geographical Society of New York, 1932), plate 143C.

Cattle production for beef, although very widespread, was dominated in 1920 by feed grains. As a result, cattle production for beef shows a band of concentration from the Texas panhandle north-northeast through the farm belt states. The slaughtering and beef-packing industries were also concentrated in this area—especially in Chicago, Omaha, and Kansas City.

Midwest), American agriculture in its entirety became more commercialized and less subsistence oriented. Other regions benefited secondarily from Midwest agriculture: New England dairy farmers fed their milk cows with Midwestern grains to supplement hay.[10]

Table 15.5 shows how the North Central states came to absolutely dominate the production of basic grains and livestock. Even in livestock sales, the potential product of nearly every American farm, the specialization of the Midwest won out. Then, when the internal combustion engine appeared, oats—a primary fuel for horses and mules—were replaced by gasoline. The adoption of the internal combustion engine liberated millions of acres, formerly in oats, for other uses.

EXPANDING AGRICULTURE AND THE PRICE DILEMMA

If we consider agriculture in physical dimensions alone, the numbers, from the 1870s onward, begin to sound like the basic ingredients of a resounding success story. But the actual history of the United States—dotted with the Greenback, Granger, and Populist Movements—shows that the farmers, or a large part of them, thought otherwise.[11] In 1860,

TABLE 15.5 Regional Grain and Livestock Production[a]

	Northeast		*North Central*		*South*		*West*	
Product	*1880*	*1900*	*1880*	*1900*	*1880*	*1900*	*1880*	*1900*
Corn	91.0	90.7	1,285.3	1,941.2	374.8	629.7	3.5	4.7
Wheat	34.2	33.1	329.6	441.3	52.8	93.8	42.9	90.3
Oats	84.0	87.3	270.2	764.3	43.6	62.3	10.1	29.6
Livestock	286.0	320.5	772.5	1,557.0	392.7	810.8	125.7	367.2

[a] Figures of corn, wheat, and oats are in millions of bushels; those for livestock are in millions of dollars. Total across the U.S. for corn, wheat and oats do not agree with totals given in Table 15.5 because of the use of different government sources. Niemi's numbers are from the U.S. Bureau of the Census, selected years.

Source: Albert Niemi, *U.S. Economic History*, 2nd ed. (Chicago: Rand McNally, 1979), Table 13.3.

there had been 2.04 million farms. By 1890, the number had reached 4.58 million, and the Populist movement was in full cry, demanding basic changes in income and wealth distribution by the federal power. What had gone wrong?

The problem was that supply was shifting to the right faster than demand; the domestic market for food had not grown as rapidly as had output. Consequently, prices of farm products generally declined (with only a few years of upward movement here and there) from the end of the Civil War all the way to the late 1890s. Although other prices also fell, farmers believed that they were the hardest hit. As a result, farmers' fixed costs—interest and amortization of equipment and livestock—had to be paid in the face of declining prices. The problem was not, of course, insurmountable. If average cost falls more rapidly than average revenue (prices), increased output can still occur, with increasing profitability. But a lag of (relatively) high fixed costs made that increased output more difficult for the average farmer to achieve. It would have been easier if there had been rising prices, automatic capital gains, and no pressure on the cost side.

What the great American historian Richard Hofstadter called the "paranoid strain" in American politics took over. The farmers, if we are to take seriously the platforms of Populist Party contentions, believed themselves to be the victims of various conspiracies, not just of the state of the market. What do the price patterns in Figure 15.5 and the output data in Table 15.4 suggest if, for the moment, we ignore the various supposed conspiracies?

We know from the data that, over time, supplies increased and prices fell. Demand was increasing, too. More and more products were sold at the lower prices. As we noted, through 1895, supply simply increased faster than demand. Each outward shift of demand *could* have produced *higher* prices had there been less supply in any year. Because there was not, the trend of prices was downward for more than two decades. To reverse this trend, as indeed happened in the late 1890s, demand somehow had to rise more rapidly than did supply.

Even though the American population had grown by a factor of 4.8 between 1850 and 1910, agricultural production outran it. The increased incomes of the larger population were not spent proportionally upon food (remember Engel's law). In addition, increases in productivity may have reduced costs and thus lowered farmers' offer prices across the board. When prices did turn upward in the late 1890s, foreign demand had increased significantly, and, in general, as Jeffrey Williamson argues, the years of price recovery could not have come in any other way.[12]

The rush of farmers into the Midwest and plains after the Civil War created temporary excess supplies of farm products, even with constant output *per acre*. The export markets became increasingly important, and, in the end, expanding foreign markets pushed up prices. As Williamson put it, "In the long run, grain prices were primarily determined by conditions exogenous to both the Midwest and America."[13] The Populists sought a primarily domestic solution (which will be discussed in Chapter 19). They wanted their problems solved by the direct action of the federal

FIGURE 15.5 Farm Prices 1870–1914

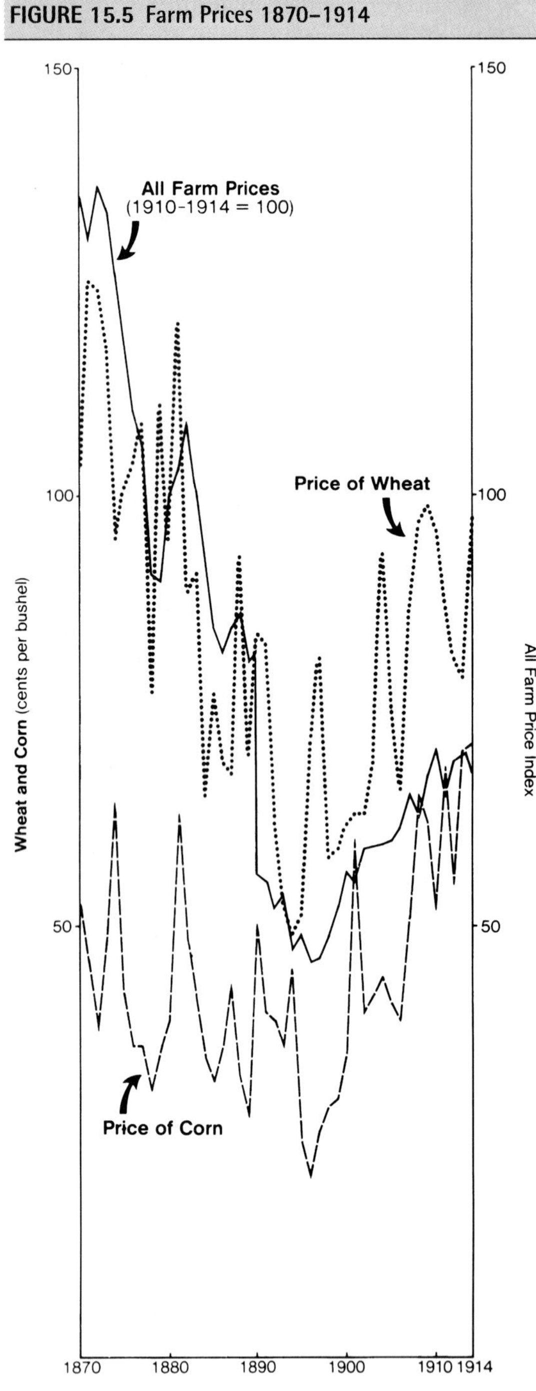

Source: *Historical Statistics*, series E 53, K 504, 508.

The trend of farm prices fell off rather sharply from the end of the Civil War to the mid-1890s, followed by a recovery. It was in the era of falling farm prices that the great agrarian political movement of the nineteenth century came into existence.

government, by measures that were meant mainly to redistribute domestically produced income to the farm sector. Later, in the 1920s—and to this day—American farmers realized that foreign markets were the best way to sell their excess product. We became the *only one* of the world's giant nations (consider China, India, and Russia) that could not consume all the food product it created.

Had the expansion of output been more profitable for farmers (for example, if there had been rising prices or more rapidly falling average costs), it is conceivable that the great farmer protest movements of the late nineteenth century would not have occurred. But, as we have seen, farm income was rising more slowly than incomes in other sectors, the farmer's share of the GNP was falling, and farm life was hard. Also, it seems clear from the Populist platforms that the farmers simply believed they were losing, did not relish the prospect, and sought rent creation by government action to relieve them of a market outcome they had created but resented.

THE FARMERS' COMPLAINT

Scholars have paid a great deal of attention to the Populist complaints. In the long run, those complaints produced such a change in American public policy that it is important to understand their nature. The results of our inquiry will be, not surprisingly, somewhat of a mixed bag.[14]

Railroad Rates

Robert Higgs found some justification, prior to 1896, for the Populists' arguments that railroad costs were too high. Analyzing changes in farm prices relative to changes in railroad rates in the postbellum period, Higgs confirmed that the farmers' position did not improve. This finding ran against the grain of conventional modern thought:

> Farmers did not benefit from lower transportation charges over the three decades before 1897. The amounts of cotton, corn, or wheat exchanges for a ton-mile of railroad transportation remained substantially unchanged throughout the Gilded Age. This finding makes the farmers' complaint about "high" railroad freight rates somewhat more comprehensible.[15]

After 1906, the farmers gained from lower *real* freight rates as the politically motivated Interstate Commerce Commission (ICC) acquired rate-setting power and the commissioners refused to raise railroad rates as prices soared. The railroads' rates fell behind the rise in their operating costs, and investment in roadbeds and equipment languished. By 1917, when the federal government took over the railroads, their rolling stock (the railroad cars) was a shambles.[16] But the farmers had enjoyed approximately ten years of favorable freight rates at their expense.

The Terms of Trade for Farmers

Jeffrey Williamson's calculations show that Midwestern farmers' **terms of trade**—changes in the prices of farm products relative to changes in the costs (to them) of manufactured articles—were not adverse and even improved up to 1890.[17] However, as Higgs emphasizes, farm real income, while growing, was rising more slowly than were incomes in other sectors; the farmers' relative position was declining.[18] They knew it, and they resented it.

Interest Rates and Land Monopoly

Higgs does not view sympathetically complaints by farmers that they were paying usurious rates of interest—after 1870 those rates actually declined faster than did farm prices. Despite this decrease, the longstanding belief that all interest on money is immoral existed in fundamentalist, as well as strict Roman Catholic, thought. Short mortgages, which prevailed after the Civil War, meant higher pay-off schedules but also the chance to renegotiate mortgages over time as mortgage rates fell.[19] Scholars cannot substantiate the farmers' charges of "land monopoly" against railroads and corporations. Although it is true that nonhomestead land had a positive price (and homestead land a positive opportunity cost), there is no evidence of any general monopoly element in land prices.[20] There was plenty of land, and, as we have seen, it was rapidly being converted into farms throughout the period from the Civil War to World War I.

On the other hand, the findings of Margaret and Allan Bogue and Robert Swierenga on the profits of land speculation in the Midwest cut both ways.[21] Although "Eastern investors" did profit from capital gains in land speculation, so, by the same token, did the farmers who later resold their lands. After all, most of the resale land was sold after initial settlement by the settlers themselves. Robert Fogel and Jack Rutner found that *annual capital gain* on Western land—the difference between the buying price plus carrying charges over the years owned and the sale price divided by the number of years owned—was in excess of 2.3 percent per annum between 1869 and 1889.[22] This is a respectable figure during a time of low interest rates. In local situations, of course, individual farmers could be, and no doubt were, deceived by moneylenders and monopolists, among others.

The Farm Revolt: Why?

When is dissatisfaction about economic matters justified? There is really no way to answer such a question. *Any* losses may be considered just cause for complaint if they come in a supposedly riskless enterprise (e.g., money left in a federally insured demand deposit). But farming has never been a low-risk venture. Moreover, anyone can complain that *any* positive profits are too small, any interest payment excessive. Farmers, like all of us, did not enjoy paying interest. (Besides, they moralized that hardworking sodbusters were paying idle fat cats for the privilege of working hard.) The Populist position on this subject is consistent with that of the IRS, which views interest as "unearned income." Moreover, the farmers believed that they were being denied their just rights in the matter because the national banks, institutions created by the federal power, were not allowed to accept farm mortgages as loan collateral. That policy was discriminatory, and the farmers knew it.

The farmers' other financial complaints can easily be justified.[23] As Robert Wiebe argued, this was a time when the old consensus was breaking up, and among those being brushed aside were the nation's farmers.[24] They objected, even though their predicament was created by their own abundant productivity. Anne Mayhew argues for an umbrella interpretation—that farmers objected to the "commercialization" of their lives as farming became more sensitive to developing market structures.[25] As we already have noted, McGuire argues that repeated bouts of income instability fueled farmer discontent, a finding not inconsistent with that of Mayhew.[26]

It is one of the great paradoxes of American economic history that the tremendous agricultural development of postbellum America ended with political fratricide and social upheaval. The Grangers, the Populists, and their allies declared war on the economics of the Gilded Age, and by the end of the New Deal, when their major demands had been met, the country had undergone fundamental change. Americans have the Populists to thank for secret ballots, direct election of senators, federal land banks, the Commodity Credit Corporation, the Federal Reserve note, the Export-Import Bank, and a host of other institutions and basic changes created since 1892 by the federal government in the name of reform. Important, in the end, is not whether their complaints were justified, but the practical consequences of their extensive effort to capture and manipulate federal power. In 1896, it looked like the Populists were going nowhere: By 1936, however, they were everywhere.

CLOSING THE FRONTIER: A GLIMPSE OF THE FAR FUTURE

In older textbooks, American history is a beautiful and inspiring pageant that began in 1607. The binding element is the frontier, ever there, ever moving westward: good, brave people crossing the wilderness in wagons, claiming and clearing the land, then pushing the railroads through it. Finally, at the turn of the century, it ends with the closing of the continuous line of forts and army camps and the Populist revolt.[27] The rest is only an epilogue. Of course, this is a romanticized version of the American past. As we have already seen, most of the homesteading occurred after 1890, when the buffalo and the Indians were long gone from the plains and prairies. The greatest expansion of agricultural output came long after the farm population began to decline, and, in fact, wheat and corn output have gone up more in the past 30 years than they did from 1800 to 1910. The drama of American farming was only beginning when the frontier closed.

Mining the Land

At this point let us consider some possible scenarios for the land and its uses. Basic grain yields per acre were relatively constant from the Civil War to World War I. Because of the modern revolution in agroscience, this potential long-run barrier never became operative. The nature of the land input itself was changed. The process actually began with irrigation quite early in the nineteenth century, and, with the development of irrigation schemes linked with conservation policies, the future was radically altered.

What the "closing of the frontier" measured, in part, was simply severely diminishing returns to the purely lateral expansion of traditional American agriculture. Extensive farming methods meant that the land was being *mined* of its creative power. That process started in colonial Virginia with the migration of tobacco crops from exhausted soils to ever newer fields, and it moved westward for nearly three centuries.

On the prairies and high plains, the problem of obtaining fertilizer constrained specialization in grain rotations by the need to keep animals for manure. Where rain was irregular or insufficient, crop yields varied widely from year to year. Artificial fertilizer (and machinery to spread it) was needed, and the water supply had to be stabilized. In Illinois, farmers had to cut the prairie sod, plant a sod crop, and then harrow, disk, and plow year after year, depending upon nature's normally abundant rains and sunshine, in addition (they hoped) to some natural fertilizer to make nutrients for the crops.

To farm in the Snake River Valley of Idaho or the Imperial Valley of California, someone had to create a water supply. Nature had provided almost no water, but it did provide plenty of sun. By the 1930s, erosion from wind and water was wasting the potential of millions of acres in the semiarid parts of the farm belt. The problem was attacked by a massive government intervention: Reclamation policies would produce the water, and soil conservation practices would check the erosion.

The Beginnings of Irrigation and Water Conservation

The processes of putting surface water where nature did not provide it have now changed the character of farming from the high plains to the Pacific Ocean. Although the acreage involved is a relatively small part, 4 percent of total farmland (approximately 40 million acres), a whole new set of possibilities for American settlement and development have been created.

From its beginnings, American economic history has involved the partly coordinated development of urban life in connection with farming. The American land tenure, together with the commercial character of agriculture, has assured that. In the West, a new irrigated agricultural empire produced watered fields and suitable habitat for vast populations of urban dwellers where nature had put only harsh desert. These sun-bathed lands now support huge populations, and, by present judgment, much more of this country's future growth lies in these former deserts than was imagined even 30 years ago.

The conservation of water by gravity irrigation has been known since antiquity in arid lands such as Sumeria. The Spaniards, entering the desert of Southern California, produced small-scale irrigation in the Los Angeles area. When the Mormons entered the dry basin of the Great Salt Lake in 1847, they planted potatoes immediately and irrigated them with the dammed-up waters of City Creek. They then systematically reorganized their society to allocate property rights (and obligations) in the irrigation systems.[28] From that point, the dry deserts of the country's western third became a challenge, and no longer an insurmountable barrier to development. Here was a problem that could be solved by a combination of government action and the granting of property rights to private persons.

Early Acts

In 1877, Congress passed the Desert Land Act in response to these prospects. Under this law, 640 acres of semiarid and arid public land were sold for $1.25 an acre to anyone who would reclaim a third of it by irrigation within three years. Title passed in this case partly by cash payment and partly by "service" (the reclamation). By 1880, Americans had irrigated 1 million acres of Western farmland, and, by 1890, 3.36 million acres. The Cary Act of 1894 sped the process by granting a million acres to any Western state that agreed to reclaim it by grants for irrigation.

In 1902, the Newlands Reclamation Act set up a reclamation fund in the U.S. Treasury to receive and allocate funds to assist new irrigation schemes. Procedures were created for the building of storage dams by the federal government. Affected lands were temporarily withdrawn from homestead entry (to prevent speculation), but participants could file for 160-acre homesteads after the basic irrigation works were in place. The settlers organized irrigation districts. They repaid the costs of the works (apart from the storage dams, which the government maintained) and took title to the lands once the majority had repaid their pro-rata shares of the costs.

From such beginnings, by 1919, some 19 million acres of land were actually under irrigation, and the way was open for joint government-private allocations of property rights to irrigate the land.[29] Dams had to be built, the lands settled, the processes of payment completed, and secure property rights assigned. The whole system then fit into our standard ways of owning and exploiting the land.

The Future in Brief

The results of these beginnings would lie in the mid-twentieth century and the more distant future. The greatest engineering works in history were developed from those beginnings—giant multipurpose dams for land reclamation, power generation, conservation, and recreation. By the 1980s, the deserts and mountains were decorated with huge artificial lakes, and millions of acres of rich, irrigated farmland had been produced. Boulder Dam (now Hoover Dam), finished in 1936, created a lake 150 miles long.[30] As a result, major parts of Arizona and southern California became garden spots, and Phoenix, Las Vegas, Los Angeles, and lesser urban areas grew. By 1941, the Imperial Dam on the Gila River, together will the All American Canal, assured California's Imperial

Farm Technology Moves West. *The hand-held cradle, a scythe with fingers to guide the cut wheat, was apparently introduced in America in the 1770s (above left). The later horse-drawn reaper soon was adapted to mechanized binding (lower left). In the massive farms of the upper Great Plains and Pacific Northwest, capital intensity was profitable in combined reaping and threshing machines drawn by teams of 20 to 30 horses (above right). Family farming still required intensive labor when farms were first settled, as shown by a family of former slaves seated before a typical Nebraska sod house (below right).*

Valley of a controlled water supply. In 1937, Congress appropriated funds to build the fantastic Big Thompson Project in Colorado. Water was pumped up 186 feet from the Colorado River, dropped through a 13-mile-long tunnel under the Rocky Mountains, and routed into storage dams and farms irrigated on the Big Thompson and South Platte rivers across the Continental Divide. In 1956, Congress passed the Colorado River Storage Project Act, which created the Glen Canyon and Navajo dams on the San Juan River, Flaming Gorge Dam on the Green River, and Blue Mesa Dam on the Gunnison. The Southwest was flush with water.

The Pacific Northwest, east of the Cascades, contained great tracts of arable lands that were dry-farmed. Grand Coulee Dam on the Columbia River, authorized in 1935, was built to provide irrigation water to those farms on the surrounding table lands. Although the distribution of property rights was complex, by 1948, it was under way. Grand Coulee generated power, as did Bonneville Dam downriver. For power generation, smaller dams were also built on the Columbia and its tributaries. The result, as in the Southwest, has been the creation of an "artificial" world of irrigated agriculture in the formerly desolate (but beautiful) wastes of the Northwest. Also in 1935, the Central Valley Project, a giant storage dam below Mount Shasta intended to generate power and regulate the flow of water from Shasta Lake down the center of the Golden State, was authorized by Congress. The San Joaquin Valley was placed under more extensive irrigation.

In the East, the giant reclamation projects were along the watersheds of the Missouri, Arkansas, and Tennessee rivers. The Tennessee Valley Authority (TVA) was established in 1933 to take over the World War I Dam at Muscle Shoals, Alabama, and its power-generating facilities. Because the TVA's great system of dams (with their power-generating capacity) was created by the federal sovereignty in an already settled part of the country, where established property rights were of relatively ancient lineage (by American standards), great controversy surrounded it, and still does. The TVA created rents, destroyed rents, and made massive changes in the demography, industrial structure, and economic future of the entire area.

Another major reclamation project was the Missouri Valley Project, which set up a system of dams and reservoirs along the course of the Missouri River. Flood control was its basic aim. The Public Works Administration dam at Fort Peck, Montana, was completed in 1937. In subsequent decades, more dams were created by the federal government under the control of a complex, intergovernmental agency called the Missouri Basic Inter-Agency Committee. By 1973, the system was largely complete, and flooding was nearly ended.

The last major project to be nearly completed to date is the Arkansas River Project, 13 dams and a system of locks making that river navigable from the Mississippi River to central Oklahoma, controlling floods, and providing water supplies to a huge region. The 1965 Water Resources Planning Act opened the way for more river basin commissions to be created by executive order and the process to be repeated wherever future needs arise.

Even with these advances, the applications of this technology are still in the infant stage. The possibilities of water resource planning, conservation, and irrigation are enormous.

The Question of Environment

All these monumental engineering achievements had to be compromises between nature lovers, already vested holders of property rights in the regions affected, and the urge to use federal power to continue the process of creating American civilization from nature's raw materials. Much of this process involved the creation of public goods; some involved the destruction of them (the drowned glories of Glen Canyon). There were free-rider problems, and problems with the distribution of economic rents through the political system at taxpayer expense. Such conflicts produced abundant fodder for endless political disputes and fortunes in lawyers' fees as injured persons test the courts. In *Oklahoma v. Atkinson* (1941), the U.S. Supreme Court opened the way for the federal power to extend into almost any water system via the commerce clause: "Congress may exercise its control over the nonnavigable stretches of river to preserve and promote commerce on the navigable portions."[31]

What will society want to do with its natural endowment now? The energy crisis of the 1970s and 1980s changed ideas about the arid and semiarid parts of the continental domain. The huge dams and irrigation systems greatly extend the possibilities for continued population growth there.[32] Ubiquitous capture of solar energy is an obvious long-run prospect in these regions. Joint government-private enterprise is an old American tradition that is congenial and easily achieved within the constitutional system.

Recall the era of internal improvements in the 1830s. Economic, social, political, and cultural problems are normal outcomes of *any* process of change. After all, the entire westward movement involved three centuries of such conflict. Democratic processes enabled the United States to resolve the conflicts in peace, Indian wars and the American Civil War apart. Thus, the tale of the closing of the frontier to American agriculture and settlement in the late nineteenth century was really the opening chapter of a new era—the *intensive* use of the land and its resources with the aid of science and engineering. More than a century later, Americans are still seeing only glimmerings of the constructive future that is possible.

Remaining Public Land

Finally, there is the question of the remaining public lands that were never sold. Of the total land area of 2,271 million acres, about 775 million remain in the public domain, roughly 34 percent of the total land area. Alaska contains an enormous 359 million acres of public land. About 71 million acres are now vested in national park lands, and about 53 million acres are in Indian tribal and trust lands. The Forest Service has custody of roughly 191 million acres, and about 30 million acres are assigned to the Pentagon. Other holdings, including huge areas of grazing lands, are mainly under the control of the Department of the Interior. These public lands contain vast natural resources, timber, minerals, wildlife, and priceless scenic assets that can be exploited for settlement, agriculture, and grazing. Policies developed on the uses of this vast *common property* can never be free of controversy, threats of corrupt use, or the danger of destruction from overuse—the *inevitable* fate of common property resources if they are left unregulated.

Our knowledge of the economic problems associated with the use of such common property has been greatly enlarged by the work of Gary Libecap.[33] In two papers with Ronald Johnson, Libecap notes that conservationists were critical of the rate at which forests in the Great Lakes and Pacific Northwest were harvested. According to Johnson and Libecap, perhaps one-half of the land claims in the Pacific Northwest fraudulently used the Homestead, Preemption, and Timber and Stone acts in an attempt to circumvent the limitations placed on claiming and patenting forest lands. They estimate that this fraud cost $17 million between 1881 and 1907 and delayed the establishment of clear rights for up to six years. As a result, this valuable resource was susceptible to a rapid rate of exploitation.[34]

Further, there are the seashores and underwater lands (and their resources—for example, oil and gas). An increasingly urban nation has changed its attitudes several times in recent decades about the acceptable uses of these common resources. These issues are fuel for endless controversy. A wilderness area is by definition inaccessible to the automobile-bound general public. Such exclusivity is by its own nature discriminatory and undemocratic—the wilderness cannot be experienced by those who cannot, or will not, enter it on foot, horseback, rubber raft, kayak, horseback, or skis. Turned over to private interests, the common property is a "giveaway." Developed by government, it is "socialism." Jefferson wanted the federal government's ownership of the land extinguished. That is now an impossibility. Many chapters on the public lands remain to be written.[35]

NOTES

1. For a further discussion of such hypothetical possibilities, see William Parker, "Agriculture," in Lance Davis et al., *American Economic Growth* (1972), pp. 376–379.
2. Wayne Rasmussen, "The Impact of Technological Change on American Agriculture, 1862–1962," *JEH*, December 1962.
3. William Parker and Judith Klein, "Productivity Growth in Grain Production in the United States, 1840–1860 and 1900–1910," in National Bureau of Economic Research, *Output, Employment and Productivity in the United States after 1800*, Studies in Income and Wealth no. 30 (New York: Columbia University Press, 1966).

4. Jeremy Atack and Fred Bateman, *To Their Own Soil* (1987), pp. 188–191.
5. The introduction of nitrogen-fixing soybeans in the twentieth century expanded the rotation to wheat, corn (as sorghum), and soybeans.
6. An excellent discussion of the Midwestern grain trade can be found in William Cronon, *Nature's Metropolis: Chicago and the Great West* (New York: W. W. Norton, 1991), chap. 3.
7. Jonathan Lurie, *The Chicago Board of Trade, 1859–1905* (1979); Richard Zerbe, "The Chicago Board of Trade Case, 1918," *Research in Law and Economics*, vol. 5 (1983).
8. Zvi Griliches, "Hybrid Corn and the Economics of Innovations," *Science*, vol. 132, 29 July 1960. The analysis developed by Griliches emphasized the role of market forces in spreading scientific advance. Allan Bogue widened our knowledge of this accomplishment by showing the importance of mechanization in the corn belt which prepared the way for hybrid corn, "Changes in Mechanical and Plant Technology: The Corn Belt, 1910–1940," *JEH*, March 1983.
9. Fred Bateman, "Improvements in American Dairy Farming, 1850–1910: A Quantitative Analysis," *JEH*, June 1968. As Bateman demonstrates, technical improvements were slow in coming to dairying, making the painful adjustment to changing comparative advantages within agriculture.
10. Philip Coelho and James Shepherd, "Differences in Regional Prices: The United States, 1851–1880," *JEH*, September 1974; John Bowman and Richard Keehn, "Agricultural Terms of Trade in Four Midwestern States, 1870–1900," *JEH*, September 1974. Coelho and Shepherd find consistent price differentials, but they are not systematically against the farm states. Bowman and Keehn find no secular turning of the terms of trade against the Midwest farmers but do find episodes within the period that corresponded to short-term increases of farm belt unrest associated with the Grangers and Populists.
11. The Patrons of Husbandry (the Grange) arose shortly after the Civil War as a movement whose objective was to improve the condition of farmers. The People's Party of the 1890s (the Populists) became the political expression of the farmers' desires, many of which were first articulated within the Grange.
12. Jeffrey Williamson, "Greasing the Wheels of Sputtering Export Engines: Midwestern Grains and American Export Growth," *EEH*, July 1980, p. 200.
13. *Ibid.*, p. 197.
14. Robert McGuire, "Economic Causes of Late Nineteenth Century Agrarian Unrest," *JEH*, December 1981, argues that instability of farm income over time correlates most highly with the various episodes of agrarian unrest on the form of political movements.
15. Robert Higgs, *The Transformation of the American Economy, 1865–1914: An Essay in Interpretation* (1971), p. 89.
16. Albro Martin, *Enterprise Denied: Origins of the Decline of American Railroads, 1897–1917* (New York: Columbia University Press, 1971).
17. Williamson (1980), p. 200.
18. Higgs (1971), p. 100.
19. Douglass North, *Growth and Welfare in the American Past: A New Economic History*, 2nd ed. (Englewood Cliffs, NJ: Prentice-Hall, 1974), p. 133.
20. Higgs (1971), pp. 90–102.
21. Allan Bogue and Margaret Bogue, "Profits and the Frontier Speculator," *JEH*, March 1957; and Robert Swierenga, *Pioneers and Profits* (1968).
22. The estimates are adjusted for losses on mortgages. Robert Fogel and Jack Rutner, "The Efficiency Effects of Federal Land Policy, 1850–1900," in W. O. Aydelotte, A. G. Bogue, and R. W. Fogel, eds., *The Dimensions of Quantitative Research in History* (1972).
23. For a brief summary of Populist complaints and the consequences, see Jonathan Hughes, *The Governmental Habit Redux* (Princeton: Princeton University Press, 1991), pp. 98–117. The classic is John Hicks, *The Populist Revolt* (1961). More recently, Anne Mayhew, "A Reappraisal of the Causes of Farm Protest in the United States, 1870–1900," *JEH*, June 1972.
24. Robert Wiebe, *The Search for Order* (1967).
25. Mayhew (1972), pp. 469–475.
26. Dennis Halcoussis, "Economic Losses Due to Forecasting Error and the U.S. Populist Movement," *EI*, April 1996, shows that, at the peak of the Populist movement, the economic loss attributable to forecasting error increased. Like Mayhew, Halcoussis focuses on new market opportunities. As transportation costs decreased, agricultural technology improved, and farmers became integrated into a national market, their expected mean incomes increased. So did the cost of price uncertainty; greater participation in cash markets meant they were more dependent on prices. After the peak, diversification into livestock helped reduce the loss.
27. Frederick Jackson Turner, *The Frontier in American History* (1921).
28. Leonard Arrington, *Great Basin Kingdom* (1958).
29. Frederick Merk, *History of the Westward Movement* (1978), p. 508.
30. For greater detail and coverage of the entire development of irrigation, reclamation, and conservation, see Merk (1978), chaps. 5–7.
31. 313 U.S. 508 (1941) 525.
32. Not without difficulties, of course. The newly husbanded water supplies of the Sun Belt are expensive.

They are economic goods with positive prices assembled largely by government expenditures, and their distribution must necessarily be partly political. Since the overall process is mainly unplanned, populations will not necessarily grow where the water is most abundant. We might suppose that, in the long run, a specific area could outgrow its water supply. Should that happen, population *must* decline.

33. Gary Libecap, "Property Rights in Economic History: Implications for Research," *EEH*, July 1986, is an excellent review of this literature.
34. Ronald Johnson and Gary Libecap, "Efficient Markets and Great Lakes Timber: A Conservation Issue Reexamined," *EEH*, October 1980; and Libecap and Johnson, "Property Rights, Nineteenth-Century Federal Timber Policy, and the Conservation Movement," *JEH*, March 1979.
35. There is much excellent material about problems of common property resources. Among the best are Garrett Hardin, "The Tragedy of the Commons," *Science*, 13 December 1968, and Libecap (July 1986). In addition, Libecap has several other specific papers these issues: "Government Policies on Property Rights to Land: U.S. Implications for Agricultural Development in Mexico," *Ag. Hist.*, Winter 1986; with George Alter, "Agricultural Productivity, Partible Inheritance, and the Demographic Response to Rural Poverty: An Examination of the Spanish Southwest," *EEH*, April 1982; and with Ronald Johnson, "Legislating Commons: The Navajo Tribal Council and the Navajo Range," *EI*, January 1980. Also, on the exhaustion of the California fisheries, see Arthur McAvoy, "Law, Public Policy, and Industrialization in the California Fisheries, 1900–1925," *Business History Review*, vol. 57, no. 4, Winter 1983.

SUGGESTED READINGS

Articles

Bateman, Fred. "Improvements in American Dairy Farming, 1850–1910: A Quantitative Analysis." *Journal of Economic History*, vol. XXIII, no. 2, June 1968.

Bogue, Allan G. "Changes in Mechanical and Plant Technology: The Corn Belt, 1910–1940." *Journal of Economic History*, vol. XLIII, no. 1, March 1983.

———, and Margaret Bogue. "Profits and the Frontier Speculator." *Journal of Economic History*, vol. XVII, no. 1, March 1957.

Bowman, John. "An Economic Analysis of Midwestern Farm Land Values and Farmland Income, 1890–1900." *Yale Economic Essays*, vol. 5, no. 2, Fall 1965.

———, and Richard H. Keehn. "Agricultural Terms of Trade in Four Midwestern States, 1870–1900." *Journal of Economic History*, vol. XXXIV, no. 3, September 1974.

Coelho, Philip, and James Shepherd. "Differences in Regional Prices: The United States, 1851–1880." *Journal of Economic History*, vol. XXXIV, no. 3, September 1974.

DeCanio, Stephen. "Productivity and Income Distribution in the Post-Bellum South." *Journal of Economic History*, vol. XXXIV, no. 2, June 1974.

Fogel, Robert W., and Jack Rutner. "The Efficiency Effects of Federal Land Policy, 1850–1900." In W. O. Aydelotte, A. L. Bogue, and R. W. Fogel, eds., *The Dimensions of Quantitative Research in History*. Princeton: Princeton University Press, 1972.

Halcoussis, Dennis. "Economic Losses Due to Forecasting Error and the U.S. Populist Movement." *Economic Inquiry*, vol. XXXIII, no. 2, April 1996.

Hardin, Garrett. "The Tragedy of the Commons." *Science*, 13 December 1968.

Harley, C. Knick. "Western Settlement and the Price of Wheat, 1872–1913." *Journal of Economic History*, vol XXXVIII, no. 4, December 1978.

Johnson, Ronald N., and Gary D. Libecap. "Efficient Markets and Great Lakes Timber: A Conservation Issue Reexamined." *Explorations in Economic History*, vol. 17, no. 4, October 1980.

Libecap, Gary D. "Economic Variables and the Development of the Law: The Case of Western Mineral Rights." *Journal of Economic History*, vol. XXXVIII, no. 2, June 1978.

———. "Bureaucratic Opposition to the Assignment of Property Rights: Overgrazing on the Western Range." *Journal of Economic History*, vol. XLI, no. 1, March 1981.

———. "Government Policies on Property Rights to Land: U.S. Implications for Agricultural Development in Mexico." *Agricultural History*, vol. 60, no. 1, Winter 1986.

———. "Property Rights in Economic History: Implications for Research." *Explorations in Economic History*, vol. 23, no. 3, July 1986.

———, and George Alter. "Agricultural Productivity, Partible Inheritance, and the Demographic Response to Rural Poverty: An Examination of the Spanish Southwest." *Explorations in Economic History*, vol. 19, no. 2, April 1982.

———, and Ronald N. Johnson. "Property Rights, Nineteenth-Century Federal Timber Policy, and the Conservation Movement." *Journal of Economic History*, vol. XXXIX, no. 1, March 1979.

——. "Legislating Commons: The Navajo Tribal Council and the Navajo Range." *Economic Inquiry*, vol. XVII, no. l, January 1980.

McGuire, Robert A. "Economic Causes of Late Nineteenth Century Agrarian Unrest." *Journal of Economic History*, vol. XLI, no. 4, December 1981.

Mayhew, Anne. "A Reappraisal of the Causes of Farm Protest in the United States, 1870–1900." *Journal of Economic History*, vol. XXXII, no. 2, June 1972.

Parker, William. "Agriculture." In Lance E. Davis et al., *American Economic Growth: An Economist's History of the United States*. New York: Harper & Row, 1972.

Rasmussen, Wayne D. "The Impact of Technological Change on American Agriculture, 1862–1962." *Journal of Economic History*, vol. XXII, no. 2, December 1962.

Williamson, Jeffrey G. "Greasing the Wheels of Sputtering Export Engines: Midwestern Grains and American Export Growth." *Explorations in Economic History*, vol. 17, no. 3, July 1980.

Winters, Donald L. "Tenancy as an Economic Institution: The Growth and Distribution of Agricultural Tenancy in Iowa, 1850–1900." *Journal of Economic History*, vol. XXXVII, no. 2, June 1974.

Zerbe, Richard. "The Chicago Board of Trade Case, 1918." *Research in Law and Economics*, vol. 5. Greenwich, CT: JAI Press, 1983.

Books

Arrington, Leonard. *Great Basin Kingdom*. Cambridge: Harvard University Press, 1958.

Atack, Jeremy, and Fred Bateman. *To Their Own Soil: Agriculture in the Antebellum North*. Ames: Iowa State University Press, 1987.

Bogue, Allan. *From Prairie to Cornbelt: Farming on the Illinois and Iowa Prairies in the Nineteenth Century*. Chicago: University of Chicago Press, 1963.

Hicks, John D. *The Populist Revolt*. Lincoln: University of Nebraska Press, 1961.

Higgs, Robert. *The Transformation of the American Economy, 1865–1914: An Essay in Interpretation*. New York: John Wiley & Sons, 1971.

Lurie, Jonathan. *The Chicago Board of Trade, 1859–1905*. Urbana: University of Illinois Press, 1979.

Merk, Frederick. *History of the Westward Movement*. New York: Alfred Knopf, 1978.

Shannon, Fred A. *The Farmer's Last Frontier, 1860–1897*. New York: Harper & Row, 1968.

Swierenga, Robert P. *Pioneers and Profits: Land Speculation on the Iowa Frontier*. Ames: Iowa State University Press, 1968.

Turner, Frederick Jackson. *The Frontier in American History*. New York: Henry Holt, 1921.

Wiebe, Robert. *The Search for Order*. New York: Hill & Wang, 1967.

CHAPTER SIXTEEN

Population Growth and the Atlantic Migration

Demographic trends established before the Civil War continued without abatement through World War I. The differing rates of change of the component variables produced, over the long run, important changes in the total profile and structure of the American population.

TRENDS

The established demographic trends had four major effects:

1. The trends produced a continuing rise in the population living in urban areas.
2. The country continued spreading out geographically, and the East Coast proportion continued to decline. The Midwest, West, and Southwest were producing an internal empire, the promise of which was already extant when the Civil War intervened.
3. The percentage of foreign-born rose, as Europe continued to supply most of the immigrants.
4. The nonwhite portion of the population continued to fall.

We can see these results in aggregate in Table 16.1.

Probably the most surprising conclusion from the numbers in Table 16.1 is that the proportion of those born abroad and still living in 1910 was only a small percentage increase over the 1860 proportion. Actually, the 1860 number was extraordinarily high because of the influx of Irish and Germans in the late 1840s and the 1850s—nearly 4 million between 1845 and 1860. These immigrants, who came to the United States following the potato blight in northern Europe in the mid–1840s (as noted in Chapter 6), really were the beginning of mass European immigration. In 1850, the proportion of foreign-born had been only 9 percent. In 1910, approximately 40 percent of white Americans were either foreign-born or had at least one foreign-born parent. According to Easterlin, by 1910, half of the American population were the product of the European immigrants who came into the country after 1790.[1]

Birth Rates and Immigrant Vitality

Immigrants continued to make a major contribution to the total population stock, in part because the vital force of the original colonial stock, both white and black, continued to decline. Their birth rates per 1,000 population in the late eighteenth century had been 50 or above. These high birth rates declined

TABLE 16.1 Overall Population Changes

		Percentages of Total					
Year	*Total Population*[a]	*Urban*	*Rural*	*White*	*Nonwhite*	*Foreign-Born*	*Residence: East Coast*
1860	31,444	19.8	80.2	85.6	14.4	13.2	33.7
1910	91,972	45.7	54.3	88.9	11.1	14.7	28.1

[a] Figures for total population are in thousands of persons.

Source: *Historical Statistics,* series A 57, 69, 92, 99, 105, 112, 195.

steadily all through the nineteenth century (see Table 16.2). Death rates also declined. As basic health conditions improved, death rates fell from about 22 per 1,000 per year to about 16 per 1,000 per year between 1870 and 1910.[2] Population rose, but its high rate of increase required steady infusions from foreign stock.

Also, the rate of increase of the colonial black stock was so similar to that of the colonial white stock that the ratio between the two (their descendants) was about the same in 1920 as it had been in 1790.[3] Both the colonial black and white populations were destined to be enveloped by the nineteenth-century European immigrants and their descendants.

In 1980, the birth rate (14.6 per 1,000) was half of what it had been in 1910, and we should recall that the rate in 1910 was approximately half of what it had been in 1800. The children of those women, as well as the children of immigrants, tended to cut *their* family sizes. The pattern became established in the years between 1860 and 1910.

Population Increase and Economic Growth

During the decades 1860 to 1900, when population nearly tripled, real output grew even more rapidly under the push of rapid industrialization. National product per capita grew at rates varying between 1.4 and 1.6 percent per annum. The growth was not steady—there were serious cyclical problems—but expansion resumed after each downturn. Over time, real output stayed ahead of the rise in population. This result is contrary to economist Thomas Malthus's theory that population will increase at high rates to absorb any surplus output until all population exists nearly at the starvation level. The United States, in fact, enjoyed the opposite of the Malthusian nightmare: As population rose, its means to provide increased even faster.[4] It shared this experience with the other major industrial nations. That is what distinguished these countries from the nations of Asia and Latin America, which were nearly swamped by population increase in the twentieth century.

The data in Table 16.3 illustrate these changes in a very simple way. From 1860 to 1910, the work force grew faster than did total population; the national income grew faster still, and the workday shortened. The use of power sources, such as steam and then

TABLE 16.2 Live Births per 1000 Population per Annum

Year	*Number of Births*
1800	55.0
1860	41.4
1880	35.2
1900	30.1
1910	29.2

Source: *Historical Statistics,* series B 6, white only.

TABLE 16.3 Evidences of Growth: 1910 Data as Multiples of 1860

Area of Growth	*1910 data / 1860 data*
Population	2.93
Employed workers	3.43
Annual hours of work	2.76
National income in 1950 prices	6.00
Horsepower of installed prime movers	8.27

Source: L. E. Davis et al., *American Economic History: The Development of a National Economy* (Homewood, IL; Irwin, 1969), p. 388, Table 20.3.

electric power, increased more rapidly than did any other area shown in the table. This increase provides a clue to understanding the rest of the information. Because mechanical power was a substitute for human energy, it was applied so that more people were employed, worked shorter hours, and were better paid for their efforts.

During most of the period, the growth of aggregate real product was extraordinarily high. In fact, of the industrial nations, only Japan maintained as high a growth of GDP in the late nineteenth and early twentieth centuries as the United States did. From the late 1860s until 1900, American GDP grew at about 4 percent per annum, compounded; between 1893 and 1907, it grew at more than 5 percent. At the latter rate, GDP was doubling every 14 years. Although huge increases in population cut these rates down on a per-capita basis, the economy maintained sufficient momentum to produce net economic growth decade after decade.[5]

IMMIGRATION AND GROWTH

In Figure 16.1, the raw immigration data are plotted for each year from 1865 to 1914 on an arithmetic scale. These numbers have been so analyzed by economic historians that the nature of the actual achievement tends to be lost within specialized books and papers. Twenty-four million immigrants came here between 1840 and 1914. In the last decade and a half before World War I, the U.S. admitted 12.9 million immigrants, equivalent to the populations of a medium-sized European nation or that of all Scandinavia at the

FIGURE 16.1 U.S. Immigration, 1865–1914

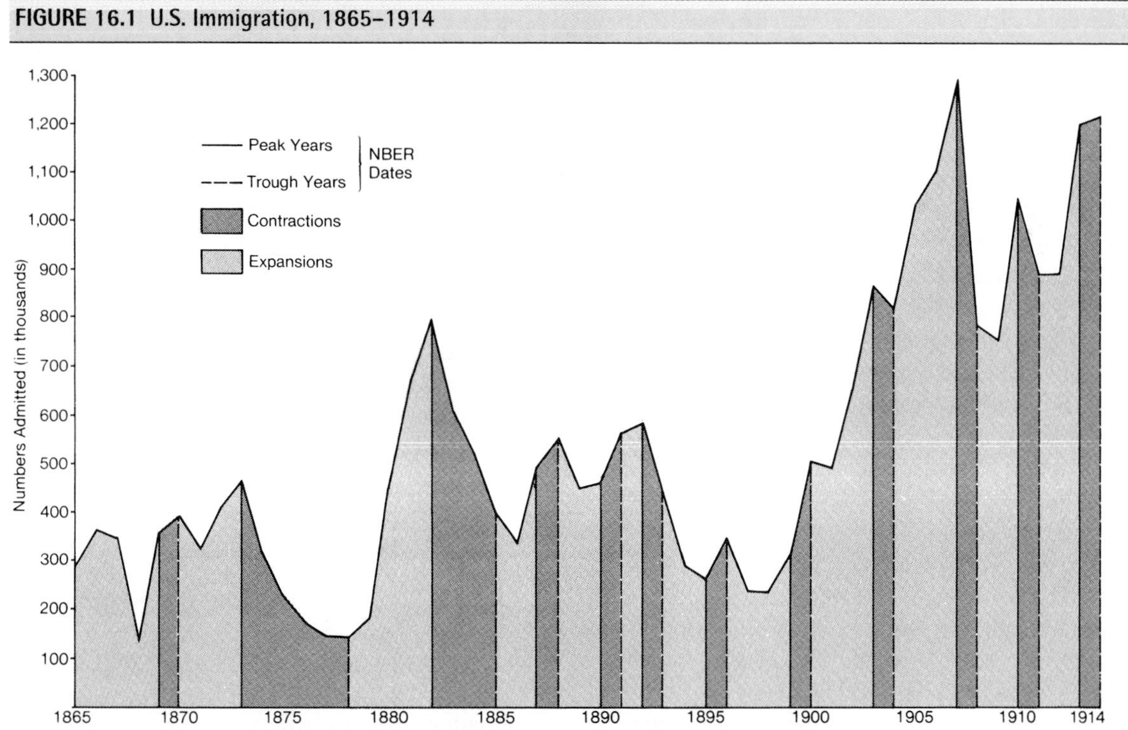

Source: *Historical Statistics*, series C 89; business cycle dates: A.F. Burns and W. C. Mitchell, *Measuring Business Cycles* (New York: NBER, 1947), p. 78.

The great waves of immigration show plainly, even in the raw data. The theories of Brinley Thomas comprise the leading set of explanations of these immigration waves.

time. In 1905, 1906, 1907, 1910, 1913, and 1914, immigration added more than 1 percent a year to the U.S. population. It was a magnificent wave unequaled in all of human history. These millions came voluntarily and were admitted voluntarily.

Raw Data and the Cycle

The expanding economy utilized the millions of immigrants. It could have grown without them, of course, but its growth would have been different, and probably not as great as it was.[6] The pattern of the migration has long fascinated economists. We considered earlier the great surge in the late 1840s and in the 1850s, as the first millions poured out of Europe following the potato blight. The pace fell to less than 100,000 per year in the initial years of the Civil War, then picked up again. Since the migration was a purely economic phenomenon (backed by no significant governmental policy actions on either side of the Atlantic), we would expect the attraction of the United States to wax and wane somewhat with general business conditions—that is, to fit the changes in the ordinary business cycle.[7] We might think that if immigrants had the choice, they would prefer to migrate to a country experiencing prosperity rather than one in the throes of a depression. Was this generally so?

For the most part, yes. Note in Figure 16.1 the strong peaks in immigration in 1873, 1882, 1892, 1903, 1907, and 1910. These were indeed peaks in business cycle activity, and after each one there was a large downturn in immigration. In bad times, letters sent home by earlier immigrants warned off younger brothers and sisters, or parents. In good times, enthusiastic letters home urged relatives to emigrate. Using data from the *Annual Report of the Commissioner-General of Immigration* and focusing on the year 1898, James Dunlevy and Henry Gemery find that this "family-friends effect" is an important determinant of immigrant destinations.[8] There were other peaks and downturns without any corresponding turn of the immigration tide. Information lags, extra-strong "push" effects (for example, bad harvests and pogroms or massacres between 1898 and 1910 in eastern Europe) clearly overwhelmed many other influences. What we can say, then, is that there were *some* major correspondences between short-term American business activity and the immigration inflow.

Long Swings

Looking at Figure 16.1, we should be impressed by the longer-term bulges and slumps, next to which the shorter peaks and troughs appear relatively insignificant, like individual waves moving against changes in the ocean tides. As discussed in Chapter 6, these "long swings" came in roughly four cycles, measured trough to trough: 1844–1861, 1862–1877, 1879–1897, and 1898–1914. The duration runs from 16 to 18 years.

What accounts for these swings? The economist Simon Kuznets (after whom these cycles have been named) found corresponding long swings in overall U.S. economic growth and related movements in such fundamental forces as population increase and immigration. He wrote of the underlying processes:

> The long swings in addition to per capita flow of goods to consumers resulted, with some lag, in long swings first in the net immigration balance and then in the natural increase, yielding swings in total population growth. The latter then induced, again with some lag, similar swings in population-sensitive capital formation, which caused inverted long swings in "other" capital goods to consumers. The swing in the net migration balance, and in natural increase, and so on.[9]

Kuznets's study shows that, generally, immigrant waves swelled when the worldwide growth of real incomes was upward and fell back in the secular downswing. Such fundamental forces ruled, even though individual peaks and troughs in domestic economic activity and immigration might not be in strict correspondence. The main attraction, or disattraction, of the United States to potential foreign migrants was the secular trend of U.S. real wages and incomes.

The Thomas Model

In 1954, the noted Welsh economist Brinley Thomas published the book *Migration and Economic Growth*, which may, in the long run, stand as one of the works of genius in empirical economics.[10] In it, Thomas saw the Atlantic economy (which consisted of all nations near enough to the ocean for their people to reach and cross it) as a single economic unit, with flows of people and capital moving in a self-nourishing rhythm of Kuznets cycles. This migration takes center stage for Thomas, whereas Kuznets was fairly reserved about its importance.

Thomas noted that the immigrant labor force and its supporting flow of European investment capital pushed the American economy in its upswings. Cheap labor and demand for food and housing gave the American expansion extra impetus.[11] There was a corresponding lull in the European rate of growth. When the American economy's secular growth rate was subsiding (the Kuznets cycle downswing), there was a corresponding expansion of the European secular growth rate as demand for food and housing rose in Europe—demand from those who now stayed home rather than emigrating. With the free flow of commodities, capital, and *people*, the nineteenth-century Atlantic economy grew in inversely related Kuznets long cycles, even though the ordinary business cycles were largely synchronized, at least on an annual basis.

International Capital Flows

Thomas emphasizes that individual investors responded as the migrants did. They were all reacting to market conditions, and they all sought the highest return. Thus, when the American economy was expanding relative to trend, European investment capital flowed copiously into the American economy and helped to employ, feed, clothe, and house the arriving immigrants. There was no plan to this, just thousands of persons, rich and poor, reacting to market opportunities. Immigrants poured into the expanding cities of the booming American industrial economy. During these periods, Thomas argues, investment tended to be *labor-using*—more labor per unit of investment was used. Thomas calls this phenomenon the "widening" of capital.

In the reverse circumstances, fewer immigrants came. They worked in Europe, thus food, clothing, and housing were needed there. Wages were lower than they otherwise would have been, and European investment stayed home. In those periods, American investment tended to be *labor-saving*—machines were substituted for workers. Thomas calls this the "deepening" of capital. Thus, the rhythm of the Atlantic economy's growth was established by the utterly free flow of people and capital, in addition to the normal growth attributes usually credited by economists to the relatively free trade in commodities in the nineteenth century.

In fact, according to Thomas, it was the disruptive force for freer trade itself that initially launched this pattern of Atlantic migration. Food, raw materials, and some manufactured goods entered the European economy and disrupted the lives of the growing European peasant population by lowering farm incomes just when that population was entering a phase of rapid growth. European agriculture could not expand in those circumstances, and the new population faced the need to find different employment. Since mobility between social classes and occupations was so limited in European countries, Europeans found it more efficient to migrate to the relatively open and unrestricted U.S. economy than to try to change occupations and locations within the small national and linguistic cells of the European countries. Thus, populations dislodged by economic change found the highest net marginal returns to their labor *across the Atlantic Ocean*. The same was true of investors. Improvements in communications and transportation facilitated both forms of "employment search."

Thomas's grand thesis (only briefly outlined here) has withstood well the test of critical examination by scholars for nearly half a century and remains intact.[12] The inverse rhythms of the Kuznets cycle, says Thomas, explain the nineteenth-century Atlantic economy's pattern of growth (and hence the immigration shown in Figure 16.1). The completely open (to Europeans) U.S. immigration policies, the gold standard (complete currency convertibility, assumed in perpetuity), the complete freedom for the international movement of investment capital, and the fact that the United States was a "melting pot" society, enabled Europe to adjust to its own population and industrial growth patterns. Europe's unemployed were free to migrate.

Before it was disrupted by World War I, subsequent immigration restrictions, the rise of protectionism in the 1920s, as well as the shattering of the international gold standard and its institutions, the Atlantic was truly a European-American lake. Movement across its surface enabled the economies along its edges to grow and develop at rapid long-term rates. The marginal adjustments made growth easier on both sides of the ocean.

Now, if we add the arguments of Larry Neal and Paul Uselding, discussed in Chapter 6, that the immigrants themselves were also a major form of capital transfer from Europe to America—human capital provided cheaply to the Americans—we begin to see why the United States thrived from its nineteenth-century European immigration. Even if it could be argued that the same is true of the millions of Latin Americans (and others) who recently came to the United States, the difference is that this latest wave of human capital typically does not have the force of investment *from* the Latin American countries—they are largely unskilled laborers—to help support it. Moreover, American companies have been investing in labor-using factories abroad. Accordingly, recent migrants have received perhaps a less cordial welcome than might otherwise have been the case.

The Migration's Changing Composition

The cycles of immigration appear in aggregated data as a homogeneous stream from Europe. Actually, that was not so. Internally, the stream's composition changed over time. At first it looked very much like the colonial immigration, being mainly from the British Isles with marginal contributions from northern Europe and little or no immigration from the countries of southern and eastern Europe. Since the northern countries were mainly Protestant (apart from Ireland) and the culture of the people was congenial to colonial-stock Americans, the immigration aroused little resistance. Indeed, in the first decades after independence, immigrants were generally welcomed, as in colonial times, as necessary and sought-after additions to help conquer and fill up an empty continent.

Beginning with the Irish and Rhineland Germans of the 1840s and 1850s, however, a change occurred. Religion was still a major concern to Americans and so, accordingly, was religious prejudice. Because the Germans were Protestant, their large numbers attracted little resistance; however, between 1845 and 1860, 1.5 million Irish Catholics appeared. The result, as discussed in Chapter 6, was the "Know Nothing" nativist movement.

Anti-immigrant sentiment welled up again later in the century.[13] This time Italians, Greeks, and southern Slavs—peoples from the Balkans and Russia—raised nativist ire. These were peoples depicted by Senator Lodge of Massachusetts as "races with which the English-speaking people have never hitherto assimilated and who are most alien to the great body of the People of the United States."[14] Demands increased for restrictions (the Chinese had already been restricted by the Chinese Exclusion Act of 1882).[15] Laborers feared the competition of fresh millions; business owners wanted their cheap labor.

By the late 1890s, most of the immigrants were coming from southern and eastern Europe. The 1913 figure, 1,198,000, contained a mere 15 percent from the old immigration area of northwestern Europe; about 70 percent, more than 800,000 persons, came from central Europe, Russia, and Italy.

The end of the Atlantic migration was near, in part because Americans (already safely ashore) wanted no more of such peoples. Seventy-seven percent of American whites could trace their national origins to the British Isles in 1790; by 1920, that figure was down to 41 percent; more than 30 percent had their origins in central and southern Europe.[16] In 1921, the first law to generally restrict immigration (the Emergency Quota Act) passed Congress with "National Origins" quotas designed to halt further innovations in the American ethnic mix.[17]

Accounting for the change in immigration flow from northwest to southeast Europe was a complicated mixture of rapid population growth—throughout the nineteenth century, from west to east—and spreading industrialization, trade, and other factors that cut death rates. Toward the end of the century, political upheavals added to the forces of "push" from the east. However, France, which had plenty of political upheaval, contributed few American immigrants. France had a very slow population growth and stable agricultural conditions. Presumably the "pull" was of the same force for the French, but there was no significant "push," and push mattered.

John Tomaske's study refines this analysis.[18] He argues that emigration from various European countries to the United States was *positively* related to the stock of immigrants already here from a given country (who sent information home) and *inversely* related to the ratio of per-capita income in any given country at any point in time and U.S. per-capita income at the same point in time. Hence, information plus

TABLE 16.4 Annual Combined Immigration from European Areas: 1895–1907[a]

Year	*"Old Area" Country (Great Britain, Ireland, Scandinavia, Germany)*	*"New Area" Country (Central Europe,[b] Russia, Italy)*
1895	134.2	105.5
1896	129.9	185.3
1897	84.8	122.4
1898	74.4	133.0
1899	84.8	200.9
1900	97.9	305.8
1901	106.4	334.6
1902	128.4	457.7
1903	186.7	572.7
1904	194.1	515.6
1905	238.3	682.1
1906	192.5	753.9
1907	201.3	883.1

[a] Figure for immigrants per year are in thousands of persons.
[b] Includes Czechoslovakia, Yugoslavia, Austria, and Poland.

Source: *Historical Statistics,* series C 91–93, 95, 96, 98, 100.

opportunity cost affected the patterns of emigration to the United States.

In Table 16.4, we examine the effect of the Kuznets cycle upswing of 1898–1907 by comparing "old" and "new" areas as sources of immigration. We begin with the lull in 1895 at the end of the previous long swing. The pull effects might be expected to have been generally felt in Europe. At first, the "new area" numbers are similar in magnitude to the "old area" data. Then, a great surge from southern and eastern Europe is evident as early as 1899. The numbers quickly become immense. There was clearly more push at work there than in northern Europe. In Table 16.5, we see the long-run changes in immigrant origins.

Thomas would not be surprised by these changes. Nor would Tomaske, since the growth of "new area" population relative to "new area" GDP would have reduced the opportunity cost of emigration.[19] Kuznets, relying on American expansion to pull the Europeans, might not have expected such a difference between old and new areas. Perhaps push begins the migration from the new area; then pull dominates everything as the new American upswing is under way. The Thomas model embraces the total phenomenon. Political upheaval is something separate from pure economics; thus, the increase of immigrants from Russia, numbering 25,800 in 1897 and 258,900 in 1907 following Russia's defeat in the Russo-Japanese War, was no accident.

There is another point to make here. Thomas argues that U.S. immigration restrictions after 1921 enhanced the rise of totalitarianism in central and eastern Europe. This last part of his book has never been a great favorite among American economists. According to Thomas, the Malthusian wave continued after 1918 in central, southern, and eastern Europe, but now, because there was no open escape route to America, local European governments were forced to make places at home for these rising populations. The results were protectionism, large-scale government intervention in economic life, and, ultimately, totalitarianism. Even if the facts *are* correct, since the United States had no obligation to continue its immigrant inflow, it can hardly be held responsible for European political aberrations. This really is too heavy a load for the American Congress of 1921 to bear.

The important question is why the United States ended the immigration when it did. If the Atlantic migration was good for American economic growth up to 1914, why was it stopped in the 1920s? The

TABLE 16.5 Immigrant Origins by Percentage of Total

	Europe				
Year	*North & West*	*East & Central*	*South*	*Other American Countries*	*Asia*
1821–1890	82	5	3	8	2
1891–1920	25	39	25	8	3

Source: *Historical Statistics,* series C 89–114.

usual answer was that a combination of nationalism and chauvinism had developed during World War I. Fear of European "radicalism" and the resurgence of protectionist sentiment, together with organized labor's resistance to the influx of any new waves of immigrants on the prewar scale, produced sufficient political support for restriction.[20]

Attempts to close the door had been ongoing for at least a quarter century prior to World War I. A literacy test, generally the ability to read a part of the U.S. Constitution in a language of the immigrant's choice, became law in 1917. As Claudia Goldin notes:

> The ultimate switch in policy is not hard to explain. The perplexing part of the legislative history of immigration restriction is its timing.[21]

A similar act first passed both houses of Congress in 1892. Although the House voted to override President Grover Cleveland's veto, the Senate took no action, and the bill died. For most of the remainder of the 1890s, similar bills had the support of both organized labor and capital. The latter were reacting to events such as the 1886 Haymarket Square Riot in Chicago, which occurred during a rally at which a number of German anarchists spoke. Robert Wiebe observes that the capitalists reverted relatively quickly to their earlier view as the economy recovered from the downswing of the 1890s.[22] In 1912, both houses once again passed legislation mandating a literacy test. Once again, the president (now William Howard Taft) vetoed the legislation. This time, it was the Senate that overwhelmingly voted to override the veto, whereas the measure failed by six votes in the House. When the bill finally became law in 1917, it did so over President Woodrow Wilson's veto.

Goldin's analysis of the several recorded votes on this measure indicates that the Northeast, a good portion of the Middle Atlantic, and roughly half the Midwest initially favored the test, while the South opposed it. Fifteen years and a good deal of immigration later, the Northeast and Midwest were split—with the rural areas in favor of the test and urban areas, particularly the large cities to which the immigrants flocked, opposed. The South remained steadfast and was joined by the Mountain and Pacific states, which had been too few to categorize in the initial period. The battle lingered longer in the larger cities, but as war approached, the rest of the country came to favor restrictions.

Immigration resumed again after World War II, but on a much-reduced scale. Table 16.6 dramatizes the astonishing phenomenon of the old Atlantic migration. (Recent immigration, legal and illegal, is considered in Chapter 28.) It was a fundamental determinant of this country's historical experience. From 1841 to 1920, the rate of immigration per 1,000 of total population was never less than three times the 1951—1960 rate.

It is possible to take one final look at the echo of the great migration. It is 1930, the census year in which the maximum number of children of immigrants—25.9 million—were alive. These children reported their parentage as shown in Table 16.7.

By 1930, the number of Americans with German parents equaled those whose parents had come from the British Isles. Italy, central Europe, and the USSR together accounted for a larger portion than did either the British Isles or Germany. By then, most Americans, particularly those with white or nearly white skins, had little idea of the proportions of their ethnic history.[23] Table 16.7 shows the final traces in the American genetic pool of the great nineteenth-century Atlantic migration, which brought the ancestors of so many millions to these shores.

TABLE 16.6 Immigrants per 1000 Population: 1820–1960

1820–1830	1.2
1831–1840	3.9
1841–1850	8.4
1851–1860	9.3
1861–1870	6.4
1871–1880	6.2
1881–1890	9.2
1891–1900	5.3
1901–1910	10.4
1911–1920	5.7
1921–1930	3.5
1931–1940	0.4
1941–1950	0.7
1951–1960	1.5

Source: *Historical Statistics,* series A 7, C 89.

TABLE 16.7 Native White Population of Foreign or Mixed Parentage by Country of Parents' Origin, 1930

Countries	*Number*	*Percentage of Total*
British Isles	5,295,000	20.4
Germany	5,264,000	20.3
Italy	2,756,000	10.6
Central Europe	2,555,000	9.9
Scandinavia	2,247,000	8.7
USSR—Post-1918 Territory	1,516,000	5.9
Other Northwestern Europe	701,000	2.7
All Other Europe	252,000	1.0
Asia	152,000	0.6
French Canada	735,000	2.8
Other Canada	1,324,000	5.1
Mexico	583,000	2.3
All Other	2,525,000	9.7
Total	*25,905,000*	*100.0*

Source: *Historical Statistics,* series C 195–227.

THE URBAN MAGNET

Even though the European immigrants came primarily from rural areas and small villages, they settled in U.S. cities. By 1890, according to Easterlin, the majority of the nation's urban populations, 53 percent, were foreign-born.[24] On the other hand, three-fourths of the native white stock still lived in rural areas, and a mere 8 percent lived in cities of more than 100,000.[25]

Political Implications

The foreign-born dominating the cities, and the native whites living mainly in rural areas and small towns, would determine the political flavor of the country for decades. After the Civil War, the Republicans were the majority party, and their strength lay in the areas dominated by native white stock. The Democrats, searching for a clientele, catered to the rising urban populations with their foreign-born majorities. Later in the 1930s, the immigrants and their descendants would give the Democrats huge majorities in national politics. The GOP, rooted in small-town and (dwindling) rural America, would have to struggle for majorities. This pattern lasted far into the twentieth century.

Regional Distribution of the Foreign-Born

The absolute numbers of foreign-born began to dwindle after the census of 1930 because of death rates and the restrictive immigration legislation of the 1920s. Half of all immigrants remained in the Northeastern states after their arrival, near the ports of entry for Europeans. From 1870 to 1920, the foreign-born made up about one-fifth of the total population of those states. Table 16.8 shows the patterns of regional settlement.

Although the largest concentrations of immigrants remained in the Northeast, the North Central states, with their huge new industrial cities and fertile agricultural lands, attracted many. In 1880 and 1890, more foreign-born actually were located there than in the Northeast. The sparser populations of the West also had a relatively high proportion of foreign-born in the total population from the beginning. On the coast—California, Oregon, and Washington—the foreign-born traditionally played leading roles; in fact, whole sections of some cities had a foreign flavor (for example, San Francisco's Chinatown, Seattle's Ballard). Logging towns and fishing villages attracted large proportions of Swedes, Norwegians, Finns, Portuguese, and Italians.

The South attracted relatively few immigrants before the Civil War, and Appomattox appears to have had no effect on this locational preference. For most of the decades covered in Table 16.8, the proportion of foreign-born residents in the South was less than 6 percent of the total foreign-born population. Of course, as a whole, the percentage of foreign-born in the Southern population was minuscule. The South's lack of attraction to European immigrants before 1860 may have had more to do with job opportunities and climate than with slavery, the explanation usually given.

After 1865, farming was expanding in the Midwest and Great Plains, but it required considerable capital. Many immigrants managed to establish themselves there, as the growth of Minnesota, Wisconsin, and Iowa can well attest. But most immigrants were without capital when they arrived, and their skills (if they had them) could more easily be used in cities. Employment in urban services and in industry were the places where opportunity was greatest, for both the skilled and unskilled, and there the immigrants concentrated.[26] For them the "golden shore" was a

Immigration and the Urban Market. *As immigrants began pouring into the expanding economy, New York City was the first stop for most, beginning with "the pens" at Ellis Island for "processing" (above left). Many went on to tenement life (below left) which, while noisome, was alive with economic activity, as shown by this view of Hester Street (above right). A civilization dependent on horses for transport faced the daily problems of removing manure and sometimes the beasts themselves (below right).*

TABLE 16.8 Regional Settlement of the Foreign-Born: 1860–1950

		Foreign-Born Percentage of Regional Populations				*Regional Percentage of Total Foreign-Born Population*			
Census Year	*Total Foreign-born*[a]	*Northeast*	*North Central*	*South*	*West*	*Northeast*	*North Central*	*South*	*West*
1860	4.0	19.1	17.0	3.5	28.9	50.7	38.7	6.1	4.5
1870	5.6	20.5	18.0	3.3	31.6	45.3	41.9	7.2	5.6
1880	6.7	19.4	16.8	2.7	27.8	42.1	43.7	6.7	7.5
1890	7.8	22.3	18.1	2.6	24.6	50.1	37.6	5.8	6.5
1900	10.3	22.6	15.8	2.3	19.6	46.1	40.2	5.6	8.2
1910	13.5	25.8	15.7	2.5	19.9	49.4	34.7	5.5	10.4
1920	13.7	23.1	13.5	2.6	17.3	50.1	31.9	6.3	11.7
1930	14.2	20.9	11.3	2.2	14.8	50.7	30.7	5.7	12.8
1940	11.6	17.0	8.4	1.5	10.4	52.6	29.0	5.5	12.9
1950	10.3	13.4	6.1	1.6	7.9	51.1	26.2	7.4	15.3

[a] Figures for total foreign-born population are in millions of persons.

Source: *Historical Statistics*, series A 172, 191, 194.

town or city, and for about half the entire immigration from Europe, that town or city was located east of the Appalachians.

Whether there was discrimination against immigrants remains an open question. McGouldrick and Tannen find a "moderately" successful amount of discrimination against newly arrived immigrants from southern and eastern Europe.[27] Others have found little support for the thesis that employers successfully discriminated against immigrants. Robert Higgs, in particular, vigorously argues there was no discrimination.[28]

Joan Hannon's investigation of Michigan's agricultural implements and ironworking industries at the end of nineteenth century—industries that contained a large number of immigrants—led her to argue that the forms of discrimination associated with emerging labor management systems were responsible for the lower occupational mobility she found in small cities. In those cities, immigrants were prevented from even getting a foot on the occupational ladder, whereas in large cities, they were only prevented from climbing very high.[29] In a recent study, David Buffum and Robert Whaples find that employers in Michigan's furniture industry paid a wage premium of 0.1 percent if the share of employees from one's own ethnic group fell by 1.0 percent.[30] The effect was even more pronounced in smaller firms and smaller towns. Not surprisingly, Protestants received such a premium when they had to work with Catholics. It proved cheaper to pay the premium than to segregate the laborers by ethnic group. It is nearly impossible for employers to racially discriminate with respect to wages in a perfectly competitive market; few would be willing to work at the lower wage. However, this is not the only way discrimination arises, as the Buffum-Whaples study demonstrates.[31] Labor markets are not, of course, perfect markets.

The once widely circulated idea that the immigrants went to the urban areas because they were incapable of any except unskilled factory labor has long since been abandoned.[32] The nation was industrializing, cities were growing, and immigrants proved to be flexible and responsive; they settled where wages were highest.[33] The urban concentrations may also have represented the attraction of ethnic-group cultures in the cities, but real economic opportunities mattered, too. For example, Basque shepherds went to the wide-open spaces out West. Opportunity for their specialty attracted them there, and they did not settle for factory jobs in the Eastern cities. Each immigrant contributed to the country's economic growth.

NOTES

1. Richard Easterlin, "The American Population," in Lance Davis et al., *American Economic Growth* (1972), pp. 124–127. A useful survey of recent research in historical demography is Michael Haines and Barbara Anderson, "New Demographic History of the Late 19th-Century United States," *EEH*, October 1988.
2. Robert Higgs, in an important paper, attributes the decline in rural death rates to a general increasing healthiness of the population due to improvements in nutrition and housing resulting from the growth of real income. "Mortality in Rural America, 1870–1920: Estimates and Conjectures," *EEH*, Winter 1973. The phenomenon of falling death rates in urban areas is more generally attributed to these factors together with improvements in water supplies and urban sanitation. Edward Meeker, "The Improving Health of the United States, 1850–1915," *EEH*, Summer 1972. In 1998, the death rate per 1,000 population was 8.7.
3. Easterlin (1972), p. 127. The same author provides a useful survey of much of the material treated in this chapter in "Population Issues in American Economic History," in *REH*, Supplement 1 (1977).
4. Allen Kelley argued that strong population growth in the nineteenth century stimulated economic growth (rising incomes per capita) via inventive activity. Allen Kelley, "Scale Economies, Inventive Activity, and the Economics of American Population Growth," *EEH*, Fall 1972.
5. Simon Kuznets, "Notes on the Pattern of U.S. Economic Growth," reprinted in Robert Fogel and Stanley Engerman, eds., *The Reinterpretation of American Economic History* (1971), Table 1, pp. 18–19.
6. Jeffrey Williamson, "Migration to the New World: Long-Term Influences and Impact," *EEH*, Summer 1974; similarly, "Immigration and American Growth," Chapter 11 in his book, *Late Nineteenth-Century American Development: A General Equilibrium History* (1974).
7. Harry Jerome, *Migration and Business Cycles* (1926).
8. James Dunlevy and Henry Gemery, "The Role of Migrant Stock and Lagged Migration in the Settlement Patterns of Nineteenth Century Immigrants," *REStat*, May 1977. Dunlevy and Richard Saba, "The Role of Nationality-Specific Characteristics on the Settlement Patterns of Late Nineteenth Century Immigrants," *EEH*, April 1992, argues that the "family-friends effect" was particularly important for migrants who planned only a temporary stay. More recently, Simone Wegge, "Chain Migration and Information Networks: Evidence from Nineteenth-Century Hesse-Cassel," *Journal of Economic History*, vol. 58, no. 4, December 1998, provides a detailed look at the decision to leave Europe by what she terms "networked" and "non-networked" migrants.
9. Simon Kuznets, "Long Swings in the Growth of Population and in Related Economic Variables." *Proceedings of the American Philosophical Society*, February 1958, p. 34.
10. Brinley Thomas, *Migration and Economic Growth* (1954).
11. "Cheap labor" means merely that added supplies made wages lower than they otherwise might have been.
12. Richard Easterlin, "Economic-Demographic Interactions and Long Swings in Economic Growth," *AER*, December 1966.
13. See, in particular, John Higham, *Strangers in the Land* (1955).
14. Quoted in Jonathan Hughes, *The Governmental Habit Redux* (Princeton: Princeton University Press, 1991), p. 65.
15. The conflicts between Chinese laborers in the western states and Caucasian Americans were extremely complex. In addition to the usual racial problems, Chinese language and customs were incomprehensible to the Caucasians. When they wanted Chinese labor, they could not utilize it within their own system of wage labor contracting. Nor could they return to the old system of indentures. Cloud and Galenson argue that indentures could not be reintroduced into the United States economically by the 1860s because of the cost of enforcing performance. In the case of West Coast Chinese, a system developed in which the cost of performance was shifted to a middle-man, the "tong." They show a fascinating insight into a labor contracting system of extraordinary eccentricity. In the end, racial bias won, and the Chinese Exclusion Act was the result. Their paper is a model of common sense in the face of facts that would make any narrowly theoretical applications extremely artificial. Patricia Cloud and David Galenson, "Chinese Immigration and Contract Labor in the Late Nineteenth Century," *EEH*, January 1987.
16. Easterlin (1972), Table 5.2, p. 125.
17. The National Origins Act was passed in 1929.
18. John Tomaske, "The Determinants of Intercountry Differences in European Emigration, 1881–1900," *JEH*, December 1971.
19. Irving Howe's *World of Our Fathers* (New York: Harcourt, Brace, Jovanovich, 1978) implies such a situation existed for late-nineteenth- and early-twentieth-century Jews emigrating from eastern Europe. See also Barry Poulson and James Holyfield, "A Note on European Migration to the United States: A Cross Spectral Analysis," *EEH*, Spring 1974.

20. Jeremiah Jenks and Jeff Lauck, *The Immigration Problem* (1926); Edward Hutchinson, "Immigration Policy Since World War I," *Annals of the American Academy of Political and Social Science*, vol. 262, March 1949.
21. Claudia Goldin, "The Political Economy of Immigration Restriction in the United States, 1890 to 1921," in Goldin and Gary Libecap, eds., *The Regulated Economy* (1994), p. 225.
22. Robert Wiebe, *Businessmen and Reform* (1962).
23. A fifth-generation American would have had 16 American ancestors; a seventh-generation, 64 ancestors.
24. Easterlin (1972), p. 136.
25. Native whites, however, were increasingly migrating to cities, and the immigrant decision to locate there reflected the same attractions that were pulling in the native-born: economic opportunities. Lowell Gallaway, Richard Vedder, and Vishwa Shukla, "The Distribution of the Immigrant Population in the United States: An Economic Analysis," *EEH*, Spring 1974.
26. David Brody, *Steelworkers in America* (1960), "The Immigrants." For a more recent survey of all the tangled issues surrounding the employment of immigrants in the American manufacturing industry, together with a survey of their indicated skill levels, see Albert Niemi, *U.S. Economic History: A Survey of the Major Issues*, 2nd ed. (Chicago: Rand McNally, 1980), chap. 15. In 1920, immigrants provided roughly 25 percent of the labor force in manufacturing, over 30 percent of the miners, and more than 30 percent of railroad laborers.
27. See Paul McGouldrick and Michael Tannen, "Did American Manufacturers Discriminate Against Immigrants Before 1914?" *JEH*, September 1977.
28. Robert Higgs, "Landless by Law: Japanese Immigrants in California Agriculture to 1941," *JEH*, March 1978. A similar result is reported in the case of immigrant women by Martha Norby Frauendorf, "Relative Earnings of Native and Foreign-Born Women," *EEH*, April 1978. Taking age and skill levels into account, Peter Hill also finds no strong evidence of successful labor-market discrimination against immigrants, "Relative Skill and Income Levels of Native and Foreign-Born Workers in the United States," *EEH*, January 1975.
29. Joan Hannon, "City Size and Ethnic Discrimination: Michigan Agricultural Implements and Iron Working Industries," *JEH*, December 1982. In a series of related papers Hannon examined poor relief in New York State over the nineteenth-century. Relief measured by the benefits-earnings ratio was, in the early years of the century, similar to what was available a century and a half later at the beginning of the "War on Poverty." Joan Hannon, "The Generosity of Antebellum Poor Relief," *JEH*, September 1984. The ratio fell through mid-century. Coincidentally, the poorhouse increased in importance; Hannon, "Poor Relief Policy in Antebellum New York State: The Rise and Decline of the Poorhouse," *EEH*, July 1985. Hannon attributes the increase in the number of short-term, able-bodied paupers to the rise of market production and the spread of wage labor in both urban and rural areas; urbanization and industrialization were less important factors. Hannon, "Poverty in the Antebellum Northeast: The View from New York State's Poor Relief Rolls," *JEH*, December 1984.
30. David Buffum and Robert Whaples, "Fear and Lathing in the Michigan Furniture Industry: Employee-Based Discrimination a Century Ago," *EI*, April 1995.
31. For a brilliant demonstration of the fact that the force of necessity has a way of wiping out the hope of wage discrimination by employers on the basis of race, see Yuzo Mutayama, "Contractors, Collusion, and Competition: Japanese Immigrant Railroad Laborers in the Pacific Northwest, 1898–1911," *EEH*, July 1984.
32. Lowell Gallaway and Richard Vedder, "The Increasing Urbanization Thesis: Did 'New Immigrants' Have a Particular Fondness for Urban Life?" *EEH*, Spring 1971; James Dunlevy and Henry Gemery, "Economic Opportunity and the Responses of 'Old' and 'New' Migrants to the United States." *JEH*, December 1978.
33. Arcadius Kahan, "Economic Opportunities and Some Pilgrims' Progress: Jewish Immigrants from Eastern Europe in the U.S., 1890–1914," *JEH*, March 1978; Gordon Kirk and Carolyn Kirk, "The Immigrant Economic Opportunity, and Type of Settlement in Nineteenth Century America," *JEH*, March 1978.

SUGGESTED READINGS

Articles

Buffum, David, and Robert Whaples. "Fear and Lathing in the Michigan Furniture Industry: Employee-Based Discrimination a Century Ago." *Economic Inquiry*, vol. XXXIII, no. 2, April 1955.

Cloud, Patricia, and David Galenson. "Chinese Immigration and Contract Labor in the Late Nineteenth Century." *Explorations in Economic History*, vol. 24, no. 1, January 1987.

Dunlevy, James A., and Henry A. Gemery. "The Role of Migrant Stock and Lagged Migration in the Settlement Patterns of Nineteenth Century Immigrants." *Review of Economics and Statistics*, vol. LIX, no. 2, May 1977.

———. "Economic Opportunity and the Responses of the 'Old' and 'New' Migrants to the United States." *Journal of Economic History*, vol. XXXVIII, no. 4, December 1978.

Dunlevy, James A., and Richard P. Saba. "The Role of Nationality-Specific Characteristics on the Settlement Patterns of Late Nineteenth Century Immigrants." *Explorations in Economic History*, vol. 29, no. 2, April 1992.

Easterlin, Richard. "Economic-Demographic Interactions and Long Swings in Economic Growth." *American Economic Review*, vol. 56, no. 5, December 1966.

———. "The American Population." In Lance E. Davis et al., *American Economic Growth: An Economist's History of the United States*. New York: Harper & Row, 1972.

———. "Population Issues in American Economic History: A Survey and Critique." In Robert Gallman, ed., *Recent Developments in the Study of Economic and Business History: Essays in Honor of Herman E. Krooss. Research in Economic History*, Supplement 1. Greenwich, CT: JAI Press, 1977.

Frauendorf, Martha Norby. "Relative Earnings of Native and Foreign-Born Women." *Explorations in Economic History*, vol. 15, no. 2, April 1978.

Gallaway, Lowell, and Richard Vedder. "The Increasing Urbanization Thesis: Did 'New Immigrants' to the United States Have a Particular Fondness for Urban Life?" *Explorations in Economic History*, vol. 8, no. 3, Spring 1971.

———. "Emigration from the United Kingdom to the United States, 1860–1913." *Journal of Economic History*, vol. XXXI, no. 4, December 1971.

———, and Vishwa Shukla. "The Distribution of the Immigrant Population in the United States: An Economic Analysis." *Explorations in Economic History*, vol. 11, no. 3, Spring 1974.

Gallaway, Lowell, and Richard Vedder. "Population Transfers and the Post-Bellum Adjustments to Economic Dislocation, 1870–1920." *Journal of Economic History*, vol. XL, no. 1, March 1980.

Goldin, Claudia. "The Political Economy of Immigration Restriction in the United States, 1890 to 1921," in Goldin and Gary Libecap, eds., *The Regulated Economy*. Chicago: University of Chicago Press, 1994.

Haines, Michael R., and Barbara A. Anderson. "New Demographic History of the Late 19th-Century United States." *Explorations in Economic History*, vol. 25, no. 4, October 1988.

Hannon, Joan U. "City Size and Ethnic Discrimination: Michigan Agricultural Implements and Iron Working Industries." *Journal of Economic History*, vol. XLII, no. 4, December 1982.

———. "The Generosity of Antebellum Poor Relief." *Journal of Economic History*, vol. XLIV, no. 3, September 1984.

———. "Poverty in the Antebellum Northeast: The View from New York State's Poor Relief Rolls." *Journal of Economic History*, vol. XLII, no. 4, December 1984.

———. "Poor Relief Policy in Antebellum New York State: The Rise and Decline of the Poorhouse." *Explorations in Economic History*, vol. 22, no. 3, July 1985.

Higgs, Robert. "Mortality and Rural America, 1870–1920: Estimates and Conjectures." *Explorations in Economic History*, vol. 10, no. 2, Winter 1973.

———. "Landless by Law: Japanese Immigrants in California Agriculture to 1941." *Journal of Economic History*, vol. XXXVIII, no. 1, March 1978.

———. "Cycles and Trends of Mortality in 18 Large American Cities, 1871–1900." *Explorations in Economic History*, vol. 16, no. 4, October 1979.

Hill, Peter J. "Relative Skill and Income Levels of Native and Foreign-Born Workers in the United States." *Explorations in Economic History*, vol. 12, no. 1, January 1975.

Kahan, Arcadius. "Economic Opportunities and Some Pilgrims' Progress: Jewish Immigrants from Eastern Europe in the U.S., 1890–1914." *Journal of Economic History*, vol. XXXVIII, no. 1, March 1978.

Kelley, Allen C. "Scale Economies, Inventive Activity, and the Economics of American Population Growth." *Explorations in Economic History*, vol. 10, no. 1, Fall 1972.

Kirk, Gordon W., and Carolyn J. Kirk. "The Immigrant, Economic Opportunity, and Type of Settlement in Nineteenth-Century America," *Journal of Economic History*, vol. XXXVIII, no. 1, March 1978.

Kuznets, Simon. "Long Swings in the Growth of Population and Related Economic Variables." *Proceedings of the American Philosophical Society*, vol. 102, no. 1, February 1958.

———. "Notes on the Pattern of U.S. Economic Growth." In Robert Fogel and Stanley Engerman, eds. *The Reinterpretation of American Economic History*. New York: Harper & Row, 1971.

McGouldrick, Paul F., and Michael B. Tannen. "Did American Manufacturers Discriminate Against Immigrants Before 1914?" *Journal of Economic History*, vol. XXXVII, no. 3, September 1977.

Meeker, Edward. "The Improving Health of the United States, 1850–1914." *Explorations in Economic History*, vol. 9, no. 4, Summer 1972.

Mutayama, Yuzo. "Contractors, Collusion, and Competition: Japanese Immigrant Railroad Laborers in the Pacific Northwest, 1898–1911." *Explorations in Economic History*, vol. 21, no. 3, July 1984.

Neal, Larry, and Paul Uselding. "Immigration, A Neglected Source of U.S. Economic Growth, 1790–1913." *Oxford Economic Papers*, 2nd series, vol. 24, no. 1, March 1972.

Niemi, Albert W. "The Role of Immigration in United States Commodity Production, 1869–1929." *Social Science Quarterly*, vol. 52, no. 1, June 1971.

Poulson, Barry W., and James Holyfield, Jr. "A Note on European Migration to the United States: A Cross Spectral Analysis." *Explorations in Economic History*, vol. 11, no. 3, Spring 1974.

Tomaske, John A. "The Determinants of Intercountry Differences in European Emigration, 1881–1900." *Journal of Economic History*, vol. XXXI, no. 4, December 1971.

Williamson, Jeffrey D. "Migration to the New World: Long-Term Influences and Impact." *Explorations in Economic History*, vol. 11, no. 4, Summer 1974.

Books

Brody, David. *Steelworkers in America*. Cambridge: Harvard University Press, 1960.

Easterlin, Richard. *Population, Labor Force, and Long Swings in Economic Growth: The American Experience*. New York: Columbia University Press, 1968.

Erickson, Charlotte. *American Industry and the European Immigrant, 1860–1885*. New York: Russell and Russell, 1967.

Higham, John. *Strangers in the Land: Patterns of American's Nationalism, 1860–1925*. New Brunswick, NJ: Rutgers University Press, 1955.

Jenks, Jeremiah, and Jeff Lauck. *The Immigration Problem*. New York: Funk & Wagnalls, 1926.

Jerome, Harry. *Migration and Business Cycles*. New York: National Bureau of Economic Research, 1926.

Kuznets, Simon, and Ernest Rubin. *Immigration and the Foreign Born*. New York: National Bureau of Economic Research, 1954.

Taylor, Phillip. *The Distant Magnet: European Emigration to the United States*. London: Eyre and Spottiswood, 1971.

Thomas, Brinley. *Migration and Economic Growth*. Cambridge: Cambridge University Press, 1954.

Wiebe, Robert H. *Businessmen and Reform*. Cambridge: Harvard University Press, 1962.

Williamson, Jeffrey G. *Late Nineteenth Century American Development: A General Equilibrium History*. New York: Cambridge University Press, 1974.

CHAPTER SEVENTEEN

Industrialization and Urban Growth

From the Civil War to World War I, American economic history of necessity concentrates on, and is colored by, industrialization. After the preliminary murmurings, big industry, big business, and the related social and political problems and benefits came to this country. Within a half century, the America of Abraham Lincoln, a largely agrarian country, was transformed into that of Theodore Roosevelt, an urban industrial society.

PRELIMINARY OBSERVATIONS

A few rough generalizations offer useful insights. We need a "big picture" to work with, so we will examine the trees that together make up the hypothetical forest.[1] What makes the forest—an industrializing urban society—grow in that form? Forests are not linear, nor are cities of infinite size. There are shapes, structures, limits. It long has been argued that two elementary economic forces governed the processes of industrialization in this period of American history: (a) internal economies, which made production in factories more profitable than production in scattered small-scale facilities; and (b) external economies, which made production in *groupings* of factories more profitable than the same production would have been if conducted in isolated installations.[2]

Recently, Paul Krugman has developed models of urban systems in which economies of scale at the firm level, transportation costs, and factor mobility interact to produce a system of cities in the absence of external economies.[3] In related research, Sukkoo Kim demonstrates that the long-term trend in regional specialization and localization developed in the United States was the result of internal economies and interregional trade. Kim finds little evidence that external economies mattered.[4]

What created the internal economies? A firm chooses a location for production on the basis of minimizing both production and transportation costs. The first factories in England resulted from Richard Arkwright's invention of the water frame (1769) and Samuel Crompton's spinning mule (1779), both of which revolutionized spinning. With the new machinery, supervision and quality control were essential, and the cost per unit of managing production was reduced by grouping the workers in a single place. Hence the factory, but where to place it?

Power sources are not homogeneously distributed in nature. Since Arkwright's water frame used a natural power source (the power in a moving body of water), a factory adopting this technology was forced to locate its physical capital (buildings and equipment) adjacent to the power source. Those whose employment involved those buildings and equipment installations had to travel to where they were located.

Beginning with James Watts's steam engine, also patented in 1769 (Joel Mokyr terms it the *annus mirabilis*—wondrous year), and continuing to today's electrical engines, a firm's location has depended less and less on where Mother Nature placed the ultimate power sources. Since coal and, later, electricity were both portable, location came to depend more and more on transportation costs. When firms were no longer tied to sites of particular power sources, they were liberated to move closer to either the input markets or the market for its product, whichever was less costly.

The steam engine can be viewed as a transport-cost-reducing technology. Its application to water transport (steamboats) and land transport (railroads) caused transportation costs to fall throughout the nineteenth century. In modern times, good highways, dependable long-distance communications networks, jet airplanes, computers, and satellite communications have relaxed the power of these forces even more. However, in the late nineteenth and early twentieth centuries, we are looking at an economy whose industrial locations were strongly influenced by water and rail transport and by what quickly became the major energy source, the burning of bituminous coal to raise steam.

By the Civil War, firms in cities like Chicago found that they could market their output in even more distant markets at the same (or lower) costs. As the nineteenth century unfolded, such firms adopted new production processes that made it possible to manufacture larger outputs at lower cost. Throughout the century, production and transportation costs fell, to each other's benefit.

What produced external economies? As noted earlier, industrial locations tend to be grouped, not scattered at random over the continent. Factories tend, other things being equal, to locate near each other. Each one gains from the others' presence; the joint use of transportation facilities, labor force concentrations, and social overheads reduces cost. Historically, the first step was the primary locational activity, and that productive activity usually was pinpointed upon a regional export industry. Once that step was taken, a successful industrial network tended to develop as export industries and their supporting residentiary industries grew and multiplied. While the work of Krugman and Kim leads to the conclusion that these effects were relatively unimportant, it does not argue that they were absent.

For the most part, the economy at that time was one in which factories *meant* cities. Industrializing America accelerated the processes of urban growth already started, even in colonial times, by commerce, transportation, and small-scale fabrication. Navigable waterways and railroads, raw materials including fuel, and product markets were prime determinants of location for most nineteenth-century cities.

Concentrations in the old Northeast, at ports, along rivers in the mid-Atlantic states, bordering the Great Lakes, in the Gulf ports, at major river junctions in the Mississippi basin, in addition to a few inland locations (Dallas, Denver, and Birmingham, Alabama), accounted for most of the population growth in the industrial cities. In proportion to the total land area, very little actual space was changed by industrialization. If we omit the 20 or 30 largest industrial locations, by 1914, the country might have seemed to a visitor to be as rural and unspoiled as it had at the end of the 1820s. Indeed, in places like the backwoods of New England and in Appalachia, the country reverted to forest as the populations left, heading for urban employment or better farms further west.

THE RISE OF HEAVY INDUSTRY

Henry Ford was born in 1863, the year of the Battle of Gettysburg. In the model year 1913–1914, Ford Motor Company, an 11-year-old endeavor, shipped 248,307 completed automobiles from its plants. Each working day, Ford shipped nearly 800 cars, one car every 36 seconds. Ten years later, the Ford assembly line reached its peak production: a Model T every 15 seconds. The moving assembly line at the Highland Park, Michigan, factory began operating in 1913. With it, long-time American experimentation with interchangeable manufacture, labor-saving specialization, and capital-intensive and resource-using choices of technology triumphed: Mass production had changed industry completely as the "American system" reached its zenith on Ford's assembly line. A man born when the country still had slaves had lived through an industrial revolution and would live to fly in airplanes of his own manufacture. But, let us note, the great change had occurred *before* the moving assembly line was introduced. The "American system" drew considerable comment at London's Crystal Palace Exhibition in 1851 where products such as McCormick's reaper, Colt's revolver, and Singer's sewing machine were displayed, all of which included interchangeable parts.

Growth of Industry

If we index the basic numbers related to economic growth between the Civil War and World War I on an 1860 base, we roughly observe the outcomes shown in Figure 17.1. For example, population almost tripled between 1860 and 1914. If we set the 1860 population (31.5 million) equal to 100, the 1914 population (92.4 million) is equal to 293. We can interpret the other numbers in the same way.

Between 1860 and 1910, food production grew slightly faster than population. Textile production, however, grew faster than population by a factor of 3.7; total manufacturing, by a factor of 9; industrial and commercial activities, by a factor of 12.9; iron and steel output, by a factor of 19.9. What Americans had accomplished with cotton textile production before 1860, they now did with the known range of industrial and manufacturing commodity production. In the process, the mainly agrarian nation transformed itself into an industrial giant.

Factor Inputs

To raise production output by these amounts, the country had to increase the quantity of inputs it used. What can we say about the proportions by which those inputs were increased? Robert Gallman reduced

FIGURE 17.1 Course of Growth by Value Added 1860–1910

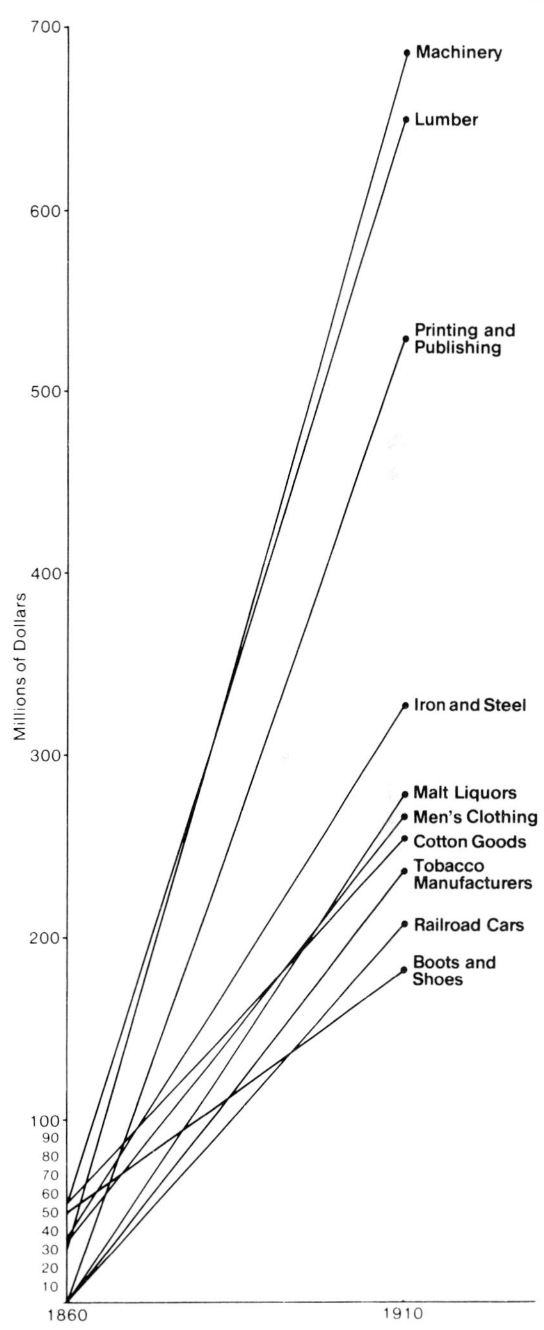

Source: *Census of Manufactures*, 1910.

By 1910, machinery, lumber, printing, and publishing—together with iron and steel production—had taken the lead in value added among American manufacturing industries. The industrial revolution had moved beyond the predominantly light manufacturing of the antebellum era.

the number of inputs in net national product (NNP) to three. When we divide the 1910 value in his data series by the 1860 value, the results are labor, 3.4; land, 3.7; capital, 10.3; NNP, 6.2.[5] In these numbers, we see the relatively high increase in the use of capital, compared to either land or labor. If we substitute capital for scarcer resources, particularly skilled labor, an increase of capital inputs by a factor of 10.3 produced an increase in NNP of slightly more than a factor of 6 in conjunction with the other two inputs.

The sine qua non of industrialization is the increased use of capital, particularly factories, to produce final output. Where did the capital come from? It takes the production of output above current consumption to produce capital investment. Families, businesses, and government must save to release the necessary resources for investment. In economics, an older idea of the measurement of growth requirements of this sort was called the *capital-output ratio.* How much invested capital does it take to produce a dollar of final output? If it is 2 : 1, two dollars of capital to create one dollar of output, it takes a 2 percent increase in investment to create a 1 percent increase in final output. To measure this ratio, we need a defensible notion of capital. We must assume that incentives to save exist and that the actual processes of investment will not reduce the average output over time. It is also clear that increasing technical efficiency in investment can *lower* the capital-output ratio.

Sumner Slichter measured the amount of *industrial capital* as the replacement values of physical plant equipment, machinery, and unsold inventories. He found an increase in industrial capital per dollar of national income from 41 percent to 75 percent between 1850 and 1912, depending upon the estimates he used.[6] Had income been fixed, such increases in capital equipment would have called for big increases in the proportion of every dollar of income produced and *not* consumed—that is, invested.

With *growing income*, however, consumption and investment can increase simultaneously. Since each family has more income, an increase in the proportion saved (not consumed) does not have to reduce total consumption. For example, assume that income in year T_1 is \$100; \$80 is consumed, and \$20 is saved. In year T_2 income grows to \$150. Consumption that year is \$112.50, and \$37.50 is saved. The ratio of savings to income is 20 percent in year T_1 and 25 percent in year T_2, while consumption actually increases from \$80 to \$112.50. The growth of NNP—by a factor of 6.2 between 1860 and 1910—enabled producers to create a massive amount of capital and consumers to acquire substantially more goods and services.[7]

Jeffrey Williamson argues that the increase in the ability to invest came more from reductions in the relative prices of capital goods than from any other single source.[8] Rising productivity of physical capital, itself the result of industrial development, opened the way for the great increase in income, aggregate investment, and savings rates.

Even now, attempts to attribute increases in income to specific factors with pinpoint accuracy are

TABLE 17.1 Selected Measures of Industrial Expansion: 1910 Data as Multiples of 1860[a]

Part I: Labor Force		*Part II: Basic Physical Output*	
Total	3.3	Iron ore	19.8
Agriculture	1.9	Crude petroleum	405.0
Mining	6.7	Bituminous coal	46.1
Construction	3.7	Pennsylvania anthracite	7.7
Total manufacturing	5.8	Cement	70.7
Trade	6.3	Copper ore	67.5
Railroad	24.3		

[a] All multiples were calculated from the original data.

Sources: Part I: Calculated from Stanley Lebergott, "The American Labor Force," in Davis et al., *American Economic Growth* (New York: Harper & Row, 1972), Table 6.1, p. 187; and Thomas Weiss, "U.S. Labor Force Estimates and Economic Growth," in R. Gallman and J. Wallis, editors, *American Economic Growth and Standards of Living before the Civil War* (Chicago: University of Chicago Press, 1992), pp. 37, 51. Part II: Calculated from *Historical Statistics,* series M 77–79, 188, 205, 235. Part III: Calculated from Edwin Frickey, *Production in the United States, 1860–1914* (Cambridge: Harvard University Press, 1947), pp. 38–43, 54.

not convincing. Although the available data are scant for this early period, we have Robert Gallman's own heroic efforts to explain the growth of NNP.[9] He calculates that from 1870 to 1930 roughly 43 percent of the increase in output came from increased labor inputs, 4 percent from land, 27 percent from the surge in capital usage, and an additional 27 percent from such unmeasurable sources as better education of the labor force, more efficient forms of economic organization, and improvements in design.

Other Measures of Change

Although significant technological changes had occurred (which we will discuss later), the great increase in industrial output was based mainly upon the availability of labor and the exploitation of cheap raw materials. Let us repeat the same operations that produced Figure 17.1, but this time using labor-force inputs (Stanley Lebergott's data) as our basis for comparison. The result is Table 17.1, in which we can get an overall sense of the changes with a bit more precision than shown in Figure 17.1.

In Table 17.1, we can observe the statistical evidence of the shift of resources as America industrialized. Note first under the Labor Force section, that the increase in the agricultural labor force is smaller than that of the total labor force.The agricultural labor force of 11.9 million in 1910 was still roughly double the 1860 figure of 5.9 million, but it had not grown proportionately with the total labor force, which had

Part III: Physical Output Manufactured	
Total manufacturing output	10.8
Food and kindred products	3.7
Textiles and their products	6.2
Iron, steel, and their products	25.2
Other metals and metal products	26.0

risen from 11.1 million to 37.5 million.[10] Abstracting from changes in technology and productivity, we could say simply: Although the agricultural labor force doubled between 1860 and 1910, its increase was only about 59 percent as great as that of the total labor force. We can interpret other data in the same way.

Workers generally made their way into the industries experiencing the most rapid growth and demand for labor, producing relatively rapid labor force expansion. As Victor Clark put it, "the industrial progress of the United States was the result of carrying labor to raw materials."[11] Thus, even if agriculture's 11.9 million workers in 1910 dominated absolutely mining's 1 million in total numbers, the expansion of labor forces in mining, by a factor of 6.7, indicates that there was an equally extraordinary growth in mining output (and/or in profitability). Was there? Observe in Table 17.1 the expansion numbers for mining activity shown in the Basic Physical Output section and compare them to total labor force expansion. They are huge. During this period, the country turned to its great store of natural resources to extract the basic materials for industrial expansion.

Apart from food production (see Table 17.1, Physical Output Manufactured section), the physical output of manufactured products far outstripped the increase in labor force (and population). Even textile output, the oldest manufacturing industry, grew at more than half again the rate of growth of the total labor force (and of the increase in cotton textile workers). The growth of metals production generally was more than seven times the growth of the labor force.

Labor Saving Again

As noted earlier, Nathan Rosenberg's improvement of the "choice of technique" argument emphasized that Americans were conserving a relatively scarce factor—labor—by extensively utilizing the most plentiful ones—capital and raw materials. Although most of his discussion was based upon antebellum materials, it is in the late-nineteenth-century industrialization that we see the wisdom of his approach. Americans were still using wood nearly as extravagantly as before (lumber output from 1870 to 1910 rose by a factor of 3), but they now turned to their (at that time) superabundant resources of coal and metal ores to produce the great industrialization. Cain and Paterson reaffirmed the pervasive biases in American industry toward labor-saving and material-using technology.[12] Elizabeth Field-Hendry has shown that, over exactly the same period (1850–1919), the aggregate labor-saving bias is the result of a labor-saving male bias through 1890, a male-using bias from 1900–1919, and a labor-using female bias over the entire period.[13]

Motivations to create giant-sized corporate enterprises were justified, according to Alfred Chandler, by both reductions in transportation costs and scale economies emerging from "continuous process production technology." In those few industries where such forces prevailed—such as tobacco products, steel, and meatpacking—giant corporations appeared between 1870 and 1900. In a separate study, Jeremy Atack shows that among those industries, the *average* firm in 1900 was nearly as large as were the very largest plants in 1870. In industries not subject to decisive improvements in transport costs and the opportunity for such scale economies, the size of individual plants and their management organizations changed little.[14]

The literature discussed above generally argues that, in the late nineteenth century, physical capital and human skill were substitutes. On the other hand, as Claudia Goldin and Lawrence Katz note, it is more common today to find these two considered to be complements. In an attempt to explain the transition between these two, they view the process of technological change as having occurred in two stages. The first consists of installing the machines. This requires the use of skilled machinists as complements to the machines. The second stage is the use of the machines by unskilled labor. The machines substitute for the skilled labor (for example, a weaver) that formerly produced the good. Their research reveals that the more capital-intensive industries, the ones using batch and continuous-process technologies, the ones emphasized by Chandler as requiring more managerial and professional workers, were also the "high-education" industries.[15]

Energy

Such an expansion of output required a similar growth of energy consumption. Between 1860 and 1910, the production of energy from mineral resources rose by a factor of 26.4.[16] The use of soft bituminous coal for energy production rose by a factor of 43.8, and, by 1910, fully 64 percent of all nonanimal energy production in the United States came from bituminous coal. Surprisingly, the United States still produced about 11 percent of its nonanimal energy by burning wood to raise steam. Hard anthracite coal produced 12.4 percent; oil, 6.1 percent; natural gas, 3.3 percent; and hydroelectric power, 3.3 percent. The coal-burning railroad system had grown from 30,626 miles of track in 1860 to a gigantic 351,767 miles (including railroad yards) in 1910, an expansion by a factor of 11.5 with a labor force expansion by a factor of 23.2 (see Table 17.1).

Before the diesel engine was applied to railroads in the 1920s, virtually all this mileage was worked by burning coal. An abundant resource, coal was cheap to acquire in money terms (workers killed and injured were another matter altogether, of course), and before environmental restrictions were imposed, energy for American industrialization was mainly derived from that source. The mere consumption of bituminous coal does not measure a remarkable transformation that was underway in energy use: the generation of electric power using mainly coal (and later) oil-fired central generating plants throughout the country. Ever-cheaper electric power combined with fractional-horsepower motors enabled energy sources to be localized throughout manufacturing plants virtually at will. Plant design and layouts were now freed from the need to conform to the central power source (instead of the production processes). By 1909, electric power already accounted for 21 percent of primary horsepower in manufacturing, a figure that would reach 50 percent in 1919, and 75 percent by 1929. As Arthur Woolf shows, electrification would be almost an additional industrial revolution, and its impact was felt even before World War I.[17]

Change in Industrial Income

Table 17.2 compares Peter Temin's compilations, from the census returns, of *value added*—revenues received minus the cost of materials—by industry in 1860 and 1910. Here we can see the changes in another measure: how much net income was added to raw materials by manufacturing processes that made the finished products of the economy.

Note that by 1910 four entirely new industries had moved into the top ten: printing, malt liquors, tobacco products, and railroad cars. Flour and meal, woolen goods, carriages and wagons, and leather goods, in the top ten in 1860, had dropped to lesser positions. These changes mirrored the transformation of society.

The new big industries represented a society with mass communications and transportation and "higher" consumption standards (for luxuries like alcoholic beverages from identifiable sources, cigars, and cigarettes) than that of 1860. Flour and meal output, exports apart, could not be expected to grow much more rapidly than population, and certainly not as rapidly as income when income per capita was rising (Engel's law again). Straight woolen goods were less needed with higher incomes because of the use of different clothing for summer and winter (cottons and linens for summer), improved household and office heating, and the mixing of cotton and woolen yarns to make lighter and more flexible clothing. Also, the Goodyear welt seam, better sewing machines, and superior distribution raised boots and shoes into the top ten. Mechanization of boot- and shoe-making resulted in factory production.[18] The revolutionary adoption of paper made from wood pulp encouraged the expansion of printing and publishing beyond what was possible with the superior quality paper made from cloth rags.

The machinery industry alone by 1910 created value added equal to 85 percent of the top ten industries *together* in 1860. As Rosenberg pointed out, the machine tool industry, which came into its own with automatic and semiautomatic technology by the end of the nineteenth century, served as a focusing and diffusion force in the revolutionary growth of standardized machines.[19] Lumber held its place as the second major income-producing industry. Renewable wood resources were abundant, and Americans continued to use lumber lavishly. It became adaptable to many new uses as cutting and shaping machinery improved. By 1910, steel had become the basic metal of American manufacturing industry.

Finally, these industries were merely the ten largest in 1910. Others were coming down the track with compelling force by the late nineteenth century—petroleum, chemicals, electricity for lighting and power, the automotive industry (with all its supporting infrastructure, including public agencies building highways)—that soon would disrupt and change the industrial world of 1910 beyond all recognition. They were part of the total onslaught of industrialization, if not yet leaders in sheer size. There was no rest. American industrialization had become a world of constant innovation, with far-reaching social and political consequences.

Technological Change

To achieve manufacturing technology with true interchangeability of parts, great technical progress

TABLE 17.2 Ten Largest Industries by Value Added[a]

1860		*1910*	
Industry	***Value Added***	***Industry***	***Value Added***
Cotton goods	55	Machinery	690
Lumber	54	Lumber	650
Boots and shoes	49	Printing and publishing	540
Flour and meal	40	Iron and steel	330
Men's clothing	37	Malt liquors	280
Iron	36	Men's clothing	270
Machinery	33	Cotton goods	260
Woolen goods	25	Tobacco products	240
Carriages and wagons	24	Railroad cars	210
Leather	23	Boots and shoes	180
All manufacturing	*815*	***All manufacturing***	*8529*

[a] Figures for value added are in millions of dollars.

Source: Peter Temin, "Manufacturing," in Davis et al., *American Economic Growth* (New York: Harper & Row, 1972), pp. 433, 447.

Factories and Mass Production. *Early industrialists attempted to improve living conditions for their workers with model, planned urban living. Lowell's mills in Massachusetts (above) and later workers' houses at Pittsburgh's Homestead Works (below) contained examples of this attempt to stabilize industrial living conditions. Mass production in a simple form may be seen on the floor of a rail mill (above right). In its more complex form, mass production came to the steel industry at U.S. Steel's Gary, Indiana, plant, where these Bessemer converters were located (below right).*

beyond antebellum industry was necessary.[20] As Paul Uselding describes it, the intent of the term "American system" is to capture the unique elements in our mechanical technology:

> The main elements of machines or products falling under this rubric were: 1) standardization or rendering uniform the product to be manufactured, 2) division of labor and specialization of function, 3) uniformity of work method and 4) mechanization of the routinized and standardized work tasks.[21]

What truly distinguished the American system from the late stages of handicraft production or from the English system was the use of special-purpose machinery that produced interchangeable parts.

In particular, Americans had developed a process through which unwanted metal was removed by milling. Developed around the time of the War of 1812, milling machinery was common in the United States by the 1830s. One of the most important contributions of Nathan Rosenberg was his explanation of how advances in metalworking technology were diffused throughout American industry.[22] Rosenberg focused on the role of the machine-tool industry in meeting its customers' specialized needs with specific machine tools. These tools, capital goods, originally were custom-made. As the specialized, technical needs of one customer were met, it became clear the technology could be transferred to meet a similar need in another industry. The technology began to diffuse. Ultimately, the configuration of particular machines became standardized, and those machines could be produced in volume. Standardized machinery lowered production costs and market price, creating a further diffusion of the technology, a process Rosenberg called *technological convergence*.

Uselding differentiates between accuracy in "making" machines (one at a time to order) and "manufacturing" them in production batches for all buyers. The economics are familiar. Americans become adept at innovating European measurement devices for use in an extensive market. Europeans, Uselding notes, made impressive measuring devices to improve the accuracy of fittings in machine making. Over and over again, Americans imported these devices, then found ways to incorporate them in machines that could produce interchangeable replicas of various parts. The market dictated the nature of these developments. Americans wanted machines everywhere possible to save labor. Adopting ever finer standards of measurement in machine manufacturing was part of the process.

Uselding doubts that there was true interchangeability anywhere in American manufacturing "at the shop level," even by 1860. Parts still had to be filed and fitted, even in such standardized productions as muskets. Devices for measurements to fine tolerances had to be invented and manufactured. Lathes, milling machines, plug and ring gauges, screw calipers, even accurate flat rules of steel were only commonly available to machinists and manufacturers in the later nineteenth century.

American society embraced change and improvement in the nineteenth century. As noted in an earlier chapter, the notion "you can't fight progress" had even infiltrated courts of law where property rights were concerned—it was priority over prescription. New products and techniques multiplied as the economy grew. A complete catalog of even the major late-nineteenth-century technological improvements is beyond the scope of this chapter. For more detail, see Paul Uselding's masterful survey essay on research in the history of technology.[23]

In iron and steel, the basic changes are both well known and terribly dramatic. First, the expansion of output had been accompanied by the development of astounding scale economies. According to Temin, a "good" American blast furnace of 1860 produced 7 to 10 tons of pig iron per day. By 1910, that figure was 500 tons, and it was being produced more efficiently by the associated technology of conserving and using the hot gases that were released (which formerly had been wasted).[24] In steelmaking, two great innovations—the Bessemer converter and the Siemens open-hearth furnace—occurred in succession. The Bessemer converter, invented in 1856, was successfully introduced in the United States after the Civil War, and it made the American steel industry the world's largest. However, no sooner had the Bessemer triumphed than it was outstripped by open-hearth technology, as shown in Table 17.3.

Andrew Carnegie, the greatest steel manufacturer of the era, dominated the industry on the basis of the Bessemer converter. Sir Henry Bessemer himself had

TABLE 17.3 Steel Production, 1870–1913[a]

Year	Total	Bessemer Converter	Open-Hearth Furnace	Percentage: Bessemer Converter	Percentage: Open-Hearth Furnace
1870	77	42	2	54.5	2.6
1880	1,397	1,203	113	86.1	8.1
1890	4,779	4,131	566	86.4	11.8
1900	11,227	7,481	3,638	66.6	32.4
1910	28,330	10,478	17,672	37.0	62.4
1913	34,087	10,604	23,340	31.1	68.5

[a] Figures are in thousand short tons unless otherwise indicated.

Source: *Historical Statistics,* series P 265–267.

convinced the young Carnegie that "Bessemer's volcano" could work with American iron, and Carnegie had come back to Pittsburgh to install his first great Bessemer works in the early 1870s.

In a competitive market, output expands and prices fall, as the gains go mainly to the most efficient. Steel rails sold at $120 a ton in 1873 and had fallen as low as $17 a ton in 1898. During that period, Andrew Carnegie had entered the steel industry as a novice and surpassed every steel producer in the world. He had done it by ruthless use of the market, telling his sales force to accept the market price and his managers to meet it profitably. Every time his furnaces were rebuilt, Carnegie demanded improvements in their design.

In the 1890s, there was a tariff of $28 a ton on steel rails, and the industry hankered after a price-fixing pool, such as the Organization of Petroleum Exporting Countries (OPEC) was in the 1970s and still attempts to be so today. Such pools had existed in Pittsburgh traditionally, although after the Sherman Antitrust Act of 1890 joining them was risky. Carnegie knew that his cost-cutting innovations and expansion into open-hearth technology could give him all the sales he wanted. He told a competitor he wanted no more pooling agreements: "The market is mine whenever I want to take it. I see no reason why I should present you with my profits."[25]

Carnegie freely scrapped his massive Bessemer plants to install the Siemens open-hearth furnaces and, in the process, was reported to have opened a board meeting with, "Well, what shall we throw away this year?"[26] Technological change produced rapid obsolescence, and a competitive economy forced new innovations to be adopted.[27] Those who fell behind the pace had to give up.

Andrew Carnegie was the classic nineteenth-century American tycoon, the Horatio Alger rags-to-riches success story, the entrepreneur whose competitive methods were characterized by the great economist Joseph Schumpeter as "creative destruction." If new inventions are to be introduced into the stream of economic life, less efficient processes must be retired. The innovative economy necessarily leaves a trail of obsolescent junk. Kenneth Sokoloff and Zorina Khan's research, using the evidence in U.S. patent records, suggests that the first half of the nineteenth century was a period of considerable invention.[28] Patent activity generally was procyclical, entrepreneurial, and positively correlated with the growth of markets. These criteria are true whether the frame of reference is the complete record or limited to those of 160 "great" inventors.

In a competitive market, the measure of need is profit. It can be increased by cutting costs, and that is what the new technologies did in the nineteenth century. Steel was perhaps the most dramatic example. Vast quantities of money were involved—thousands of workers, coal, coke, railroads, lake steamers, barge lines—whole communities and cities appeared as the industry grew. Great fortunes were made (and lost) from it, and dramatic confrontations in social relations occurred—for example, the famous and violent Homestead strike of 1892, in which Carnegie Steel used the Pinkerton agency and the National Guard to protect "scab" workers and break the strike.

In the 1890s, production of special alloy steels increased, and then electric furnaces were introduced.

The constant pressure was to reduce the time (and need for reheating) between ingot production, rolling, shaping, and drawing. Progress was steady, competition was intense, and the industry continued its cost-reducing expansion.

Reductions in production costs, passed on to buyers, are the private economy's version of *subsidies*, except that no forced transfers of income are involved. Instead, the buyer's real income is increased. Competition forced producers to pass the gains on to their customers. Judge Elbert H. Gary, then head of Illinois Steel, said it all, commenting upon the results of Carnegie's competitive onslaught. It no longer would be possible "to do business on the basis of high profits for comparatively small tonnage."[29] Even when J. P. Morgan bought out Carnegie and put together two-thirds of the industry's ingot capacity as United States Steel, the industry kept expanding.

Improvements in agricultural machinery, steam threshing, and better reapers and harvesters kept agricultural machinery a growing industry as the Midwest wheat and corn economy expanded. The introduction of refrigeration in meatpacking, beginning in the 1870s, opened up a national market to packers, and the race for amalgamation produced such names as Swift and Armour. The petroleum industry's John D. Rockefeller was slowed by a successful antitrust prosecution in 1911, and that industry was not monopolized.[30] Discoveries of oil in the Southwest gave it further impetus. In textiles, the latter decades of the century saw the further development of automatic power looms, better sewing machines, and cutting tools reduce the cost of manufacture in clothing. Standard sizes in men's wear had resulted from the experience of making uniforms for the Union army, thus increasing the possibilities of mass production, including boots and shoes.

By the last part of the century, standardization and interchangeable parts, an older American tradition, had finally become characteristic of American manufacturing. Production for a national market had been the object of the growth and merger of industrial firms, increasing the drive for standardization of sizes in producer goods, consumer durables, clothing, and tools. These made mass production possible as the huge American market grew and eased the problems of industrial expansion by simplifying product designs.[31]

EXPANSION OF THE MARKET

Where did all the growth of output go? Since the cost of output is income to the factors used to produce it, the answer is simply that it was sold in the American market. The incentive to invest and expand output was there because the incomes that were produced were distributed in such a way that the product found profitable sales. Probably Adam Smith's most-quoted maxim has been: "The division of labor is limited by the extent of the market." In this case, the market was massively extended.

Between the Civil War and World War I, the population grew by a factor of 2.93. Net national product in constant prices grew by a factor of 6. Average persons could thus buy two times as much in 1914 as could their counterparts in 1860, and there were nearly three times as many people. Even if there had been no *substitution effects* (one product bought at the expense of another), the expansion of the domestic market would have given splendid scope for new industries, products, and techniques. In fact, some products and industries declined as others came to the fore, so there were *product displacement effects* as well. Other things being equal, the resulting increase of per-capita incomes was mostly available for the purchase of manufactured goods or services. The income elasticity of demand for food was less than one, Engel's law yet again. Americans were already reasonably well fed in 1869.

Professor Gallman's estimates of real GNP (at prices of 1860) are shown in Table 17.4 in overlapping

TABLE 17.4 GNP, 1834–1908 (Prices of 1860)

Overlapping Decades	*$ Billions*
1834–1843	1.56
1849–1858	3.30
1869–1878	6.40
1874–1883	8.40
1879–1888	10.6
1884–1893	12.7
1889–1898	14.4
1894–1903	17.3
1899–1908	21.8

Source: Robert E. Gallman, "Gross National Production in the United States 1834–1909," Dorothy S. Brady, ed., *Studies in Income and Wealth* (New York: N. B. E. R., Columbia University Press, 1966), vol. 30, Table A 1.

Scale Economies in the Retailing Revolution. *Mass production presupposed mass consumption and a national market. In 1876, Wanamakers in Philadelphia was the epitome of the big-city department store (above). But even in the more humble circumstances of a National Tea Company store in Chicago (below), the customer had the advantages of food preparation and standardized packaging.*

decades. The estimates reveal an expansion of roughly the order of 5 to 6 between 1858 and 1903. Pushed back to the 1830s, Gallman's estimates show that by 1840 U.S. GNP was probably just below the GNP of Britain and of France. GNP *per capita* was from 25 to 40 per cent higher than France and somewhere near the British. Gallman concludes: "Very early in her history the United States was one of the great economic powers."[32]

The rate of growth of GNP was about 48 percent per decade in 1834–1843 to 1894–1903, and slowed to 34 percent per decade in 1894–1903 to 1944–1953. However, with the *rate of growth* of population also decelerating, per-capita growth was about constant, at 16 percent per decade from 1834 to 1953.

In the entire period there was one really striking change: a powerful increase in the share of capital formation. Gallman is not certain just exactly when this occurred, but it centered around the era of the Civil War. In the pre-Civil War decades, gross capital formation was about 14 to 15 percent; after the Civil War it rose to 24 to 28 percent, and that high rate continued into the twentieth century until 1914. Gallman notes of this phenomenon that it was "... from a high level to an exceptionally high level."[33] This originated almost entirely from an increase in domestic savings rates.

As economic growth proceeded, it was striking that the supply of manufactured producer durables was produced domestically, in the main. Americans produced their own machines, for the most part, as they industrialized.

In addition to the domestic market growth, there was a massive expansion of the markets for manufactured and semimanufactured goods abroad.[34] Between 1860 and 1914, exports of manufactured food grew by a factor of 7.5, from $39 million to $293 million; exports of semimanufactured goods expanded from a mere $13 million to $374 million, or by a factor of 28.8. Exports of finished goods grew by an extraordinary factor of 20.1, from $36 million to $725 million. Crude materials, the antebellum winner in international trade, only increased from $217 million to $800 million in the same period, by a factor of 3.7. The farmers did well enough—crude food exports increased from $12 million to $137 million. Thus, by 1914, manufactured food, semimanufactures, and finished manufactures together actually earned 49 percent *more* than did crude food and raw materials combined. In 1860, exports of manufactured materials and food had equaled only 12 percent of the combined exports of crude materials and crude food. In that era of fairly free trade, American manufacturers had done well indeed in the foreign economy, while constantly pressing for unnecessary protective tariffs at home!

Simon Kuznets estimated NNP at market prices at an annual average of $6.20 billion in the years 1869–1873 (his earlier published figures) and $34.6 billion in 1912–1916.[35] This rise by a factor of 5.6 is on the same order of magnitude, given the differences in dates (and uncorrected prices), as our other estimates. Every dollar of potential market in 1860 had become five to six dollars by 1914. American industrialists faced the prospect of secular rising demand for their product.

Other things being equal, innovations in technology, together with steady labor force increases in a competitive market, can be considered bright market conditions for Adam Smith's extended divisions of labor—investment in new technologies to make new products. There were the great cyclical swings, but as Schumpeter argued, they actually *helped* the processes of growth in a capitalist economy. The massive expansion of American manufacturing seems to have been in the cards toward the end of the nineteenth century, once the country's first "great game," the public domain and its private expropriation, had been attended to. Extensive acquisition of the best publicly held resources was nearly over, and it was time for intensive processes of growth to take over, those characterized by the rise of the manufacturing industry.

URBAN GROWTH

That urban places are also industrial places is nearly a truism, since (in Douglass North's terminology) even a Florida city consisting of the retired elderly and winter tourists would grow to support secondary employment.[36] Given any scale economies at all, some of these employments would produce agglomerations of workers—factory-style grouped employment. Some secondary industries would then achieve regional and national status as their products penetrated the market. What has been really rare has been industrialization *without* accompanying urban growth. With modern communications, it would seemingly be possible, but it has seldom occurred.

For example, England, during the Industrial Revolution, experienced a general population growth of 130 percent (1751–1831). London, an already huge and ancient city in the mid-eighteenth century when the process of industrialization accelerated, by 1831, had grown 170 percent over the 1750 figure. However, in that same period, populations of the industrial county of Lancashire expanded by a factor of 5. Manchester, its largest city, expanded by more than a factor of 6.7. All over Europe, once industrialization spread, new cities grouped around factories appeared where formerly only sleepy medieval villages had existed.[37]

In this country the westward movement of populations and industry produced the same effects: Troy and Buffalo, then Erie, Youngstown, Cleveland, Toledo, Detroit, Gary, Chicago, Milwaukee, and Duluth grew up around the Great Lakes and in the North. Scranton, Allentown, Pittsburgh, Akron, Wheeling, Columbus, Fort Wayne, Indianapolis, Minneapolis, and Cincinnati developed inland along the rivers. Birmingham, Mobile, New Orleans, Shreveport, and Houston appeared in the South and along the Gulf. Thus, the list of cities of late-nineteenth- and early-twentieth-century America grew as populations flocked to the centers of industrial activity. By 1960, 160 metropolitan areas contained some 90 percent of the American population.[38]

The process is never finished. As technologies change, some older cities decline, while new ones expand. The "energy crisis" of the late 1970s is credited with locating many new manufacturing enterprises in the Sun Belt of the American South and West, abandoning the grimy old steel and coal towns of the upper Midwest and East. Some older industries have proved to be migratory, like machine tools, whose centers have moved many times to follow their customers: leaving Troy, Cincinnati, and then Chicago behind as the population moved to Houston and Los Angeles. Textiles and clothing manufacturing have also proved to be remarkably mobile.[39] Cotton textiles brought urbanization to the South, dominating Southern industrial life, just as earlier in history, raw cotton dominated Southern rural life.[40] Table 17.5 outlines urban growth from 1790 to 1910.

By 1910, three cities—New York, Philadelphia, and Chicago—had over a million in population and together contained very nearly 10 percent of the nation's entire population. There were already 50 urban places with populations in excess of 100,000, containing 22 percent of the total population. By 1910, one of five Americans lived in a large urban place. It might have seemed at the time that the whole country would evolve into a few great cities. But that did not happen, and even in the nineteenth

TABLE 17.5 Urban Growth

	Incorporated Places, 2,500 and Over		*Incorporated Places, 100,000 and Over*		*Incorporated Places, 1,000,000 and Over*	
Year	*Number*	*Percentage of Total Population*	*Number*	*Percentage of Total Population*	*Number*	*Percentage of Total Population*
1790	24	5.4	—[a]	—	—[a]	—
1840	131	10.8	3	3.0	—[a]	—
1860	392	19.8	9	8.4	—[a]	—
1880	939	28.2	20	12.3	1	2.4
1890	1,348	35.0	28	15.4	3	5.8
1900	1,737	39.7	38	18.7	3	8.5
1910	2,262	45.7	50	22.1	3	9.2

[a] No urban areas of this size yet existed.

Source: *Historical Statistics,* derived from Series A 57–69.

Early Urban Mass Transit. *Urban public transportation soon enough produced suburbs. The early horse-drawn omnibus (introduced in the 1820s) was succeeded by the horse-drawn trolley on tracks that operated from the 1850s until about 1900. In 1887, the first electrified trolley system was introduced in Richmond, Virginia. By 1890, it had spread like wildfire to nearly every American city.*

Shown above is an electrified trolley in Oak Park, Illinois, in 1890. Within 20 years, this open country had become suburbanized. Real estate speculators immediately got the point, as shown in the advertisement (below) for lots along Chicago's Lincoln Avenue.

century, the vigor of smaller urban places was apparent in the data. Urban places of more than 2,500 but smaller than 25,000 managed to hold more than 30 percent of total urban population, even while the big cities were growing most rapidly.[41]

The maximum city size had not yet been tested in the United States. That would come later in the twentieth century when the giants would stop growing and lose population, and smaller cities would take over the processes of urban growth. Nevertheless, the chronicles of the nineteenth century already revealed the familiar urban problems of crime, congestion, and pollution, the *dis*economies of urban life. The advantages of urban life prevailed, although already draining the *increase* of population out of the countryside (in another half century, the countryside would experience absolute decreases in numbers and appear to be largely abandoned).

The significant scale economies of cities included transport, education, medicine, central water and sewerage systems, "culture," communications—all the amenities that attracted people.[42] But most of all, the cities meant jobs and varieties of opportunity for the growing population of the country. The large tertiary sector—services, trades, and professional employments that service the industrial base—was clearly evident. Lebergott's labor force data show that by 1914, fully 54 percent of the nonfarm labor force was in tertiary employment, and these jobs tended to be concentrated in urban areas. Thomas Weiss's research on the origin of the increase in tertiary sector employment shows that, in the main, it is the result of the rise in per-capita income attendant to the growth of cities and the urban workforce.[43]

By the mid-twentieth century, about two-thirds of *all* employment would be in the tertiary fields.[44] Such employments are based upon the productiveness of extractive industries, manufacturing, and primary industry. Essentially, the tertiary sector consists of services traded for food, clothing, shelter, and other services. Notice in Table 17.6 that tertiary employment (either including or excluding transport and utilities) expanded, while the proportion in manufacturing *actually declined.* This trend would continue and is, in fact, typical of successful industrialization.[45] Rising productivity frees labor for employments besides making food and goods.

Tertiary employments tend to require specialized education and/or training and, therefore, to cluster in cities. Industrial activity attracts them and pays them. They are the creatures of external economies and tend to locate near each other—for example, advertising in New York City and television production in Hollywood. Thus, urban growth created more urban growth. The industrialization of American life sealed American society as an urban one. People whose ancestors had cut down the woods and plowed up the prairies would typically be uncertain whether cheese

TABLE 17.6 Employees in Nonfarm Establishments[a]

Area of Employment	*1900*				*1914*
	Number	*Percentage*			*Number*
Mining	637	4.2			1,027
Contract construction	1,147	7.6			1,267
Manufacturing	5,468	36.0			8,210
Transport and utilities	2,282	15.0			3,445
Trade	2,502	16.5			4,128
Finance	308	2.0	37.2	52.2	657
Service	1,740	11.5			2,647
Total civilian government	1,094	7.2			1,809
Total	*15,178*	*100.0*			*23,190*

[a] Figures that are not percentages are in millions of persons.

Source: Stanley Lebergott, "The American Labor Force," in Davis et al., *American Economic Growth* (New York: Harper & Row, 197 derived from Table 6.2, p. 192.

and butter had a common origin. It was, however, information they no longer needed for survival.

INDUSTRIAL GROWTH UNDER CAPITALISM

For the most part, the country's growth and development patterns and structure simply resulted from the sum, over time, of individual's reactions to their own desires and opportunities. A notable phenomenon in American economic development was the absence, during most of its history, of any effective centralized economic planning. Governments taxed and spent (on a small scale), passed tariff laws, gave some subsidies, and sold part of the public domain to private owners. Under police powers, certain businesses were regulated or required to have licenses by state and local governments. Apart from the spate of internal improvements in the 1830s and 1840s, there was little more that one might call central direction. Growth resulted from individual initiative.

Why did they do it? Economic discussions focus on purely economic stimuli to human action. Of course, reality is far more complex. For example, something as supposedly unrelated to economics as religion directed the enterprise of thousands of people from Plymouth Colony onward. Individual motivations are complex beyond imagination, and people entered into economic enterprises for the full range of possible reasons. However, in American society, there was always one powerful centralizing force: private rights in property of all sorts, well understood and protected. Thus, such universal motivations as survival, greed, avarice, and envy, as well as more elevated impulses, could always be counted on to focus and produce economic increase in all but the most difficult circumstances.

Wealth and Entrepreneurial Supply

As we have seen from very earliest colonial times, wealth was unequally divided among the population by inheritance, hard work, or blind luck. After all, in every population, some are very risk averse, most are cautious, and a small portion always are gamblers and plungers. Throughout American history, when knowledge and opportunity were present, and distributive rights to the profits settled and assured, entrepreneurial activity would occur. This force has long been the dominant power shaping the country's development, but there was far more to it than unequal wealth distribution.[46] It is impressive that until recent times, when American innovative and entrepreneurial powers seemed to weaken (see Chapter 29), virtually no comment was made about the effectiveness of its entrepreneurial prowess.[47] It was just there, always, whenever it was needed.

Images of the great entrepreneurs are contradictory. On the one hand, they were held in high esteem as the helmsmen of a corporate culture. Continued economic growth fostered a faith in free enterprise. The Horatio Alger legend of a common man rising to the top of the corporate culture was much more myth than reality; most business leaders came from well-to-do backgrounds.[48] On the other hand, the great entrepreneurs tended to be the focus of popular envy and abuse. As Theodore Roosevelt said of the railroad financier Edward Harriman, "[He is] a malefactor of great wealth." The explanation for this paradox lies in Americans' fear of size, a fear debated publicly from the time of the First Bank of the U.S. What proved acceptable as long as it was small and local grew more sinister as it became large and national. As Robert Wiebe observed in *The Search for Order*, there was a "belief that great corporations were stifling opportunity, and no one cried his resentment

Percentage			*Percentage Increase (1916 over 1900)*
4.4			61.2
5.5			10.5
35.4			50.1
14.9			51.0
17.8			65.0
2.8	39.8	54.7	113.3
11.4			52.1
7.8			65.4
100.0			

more persistently than the local entrepreneur." As a national network of transportation and communication brought the economy closer together, "almost every small enterprise bound its sponsor into a bewildering complex of business relationships which seemed to restrict rather than extend his freedom."[49]

Since successful entrepreneurs tended to be famous and wealthy, they were the butt of acid commentary and ridicule. Today, their descendants are venerated. No one is laughing at the Harrimans, Goulds, and Vanderbilts in the *New York Times* social pages, but those who earned that money have been treated in American history much like common criminals. Society is more apt to think of them as "robber barons" than "captains of industry." Only during the 1970s when the American steel industry needed a new Carnegie and the automobile industry needed a new Henry Ford—*and no one stepped forward*—did we begin to worry about entrepreneurship, call conferences, award government grants to study the problem, and otherwise sound the alarm.

Invention and Innovation

The leading student of capitalist entrepreneurship was the economist Joseph Schumpeter (recall Chapter 14). In three of his books, *The Theory of Economic Development*, *Business Cycles*, and *Capitalism, Socialism, and Democracy*, as well as in many shorter works, Schumpeter expounded his analysis of the entrepreneurial role in the development of modern capitalism.[50] The end of a chapter on late nineteenth-century industrialization is a good place to pause a moment and consider Schumpeter's thesis in brief outline.

The period from 1842 to 1897 was the one that most fascinated Schumpeter, a time of the building of an international "bourgeois culture" (his nonpejorative term). By *bourgeois* he meant the middle class—its values, culture, ideals—the whole package of liberal democracy, representative government, open societies that encouraged social mobility, easy access to education, personal freedom, toleration of diversity, and secure property rights. To Schumpeter, a student of history, these were unique creations of nineteenth-century capitalism. No other kind of economic system had created, or could create, this type of society.

What motivated the growth of bourgeois society? To Schumpeter, the driving force was the innovating capitalist entrepreneurs. They were the risk-takers. If they succeeded, their visions of the future—for themselves, their families, and their associates—created the future. The weapon they used to force change into the competitive marketplace was innovation—new products, new ideas, new services, new technologies.

Invention and *innovation* were two separate things. Invention was a passive employment of human talent. A "better mousetrap" made no difference to society at large or to economic growth if it remained in the workshop. To produce and sell it in the competitive marketplace took a different kind of talent, entrepreneurial ability. An invention successfully placed into the stream of economic life diverted that stream, changed the allocation of resources, and became an innovation. Those innovating entrepreneurs (some of whom, like Bell and Edison, were also inventors) who were able to succeed on a gigantic scale became the "natural" leaders of bourgeois civilization because of their success.

Nineteenth-century industrialization was created by individual business firms, which had been created by individual persons: the entrepreneurs.[51] People started businesses—"conditions" started nothing. Therefore, those who were the "robber barons" to critics of bourgeois civilization were to Schumpeter its heroes. Cyrus McCormick and John Deere in farm machinery; Cornelius Vanderbilt in steamships and railroads; Collis Huntington, Leland Stanford, Edward Harriman, James J. Hill, even Jay Gould and Jim Fisk in railroads; Carnegie and Henry Frick in steel; John Pierpont Morgan, August Belmont, Andrew Mellon in finance; John D. Rockefeller in oil—all Schumpeterian entrepreneurs. That energy was motivated by the opportunity for pure *entrepreneurial profit*, returns to entrepreneurial activity in excess of those possible from any other use of resources.[52]

It was a competitive world, not zero-sum, but one in which the inefficient were "driven to the wall," a necessary result of the capitalist growth process. The disruption caused by competitive battles was the price of progress. Entrepreneurs reacted to the signals of the marketplace. That was the only "planning" there was. The economy grew in response to consumer demand expressed in dollar votes, either because successful entrepreneurs discovered what consumers wanted or because they *convinced* consumers, by sales techniques, that the new innovations were essential. Moreover, innovation led to even more innovation by the mechanism of derived demand.[53]

The Entrepreneurial Role

Americans have always relied upon entrepreneurship and respected it—so long as it was not *too* successful.[54] The great wealth in the United States is nearly all derived from successful entrepreneurship, but the amount of special social position enjoyed by its wealthy entrepreneurs is trivial, except very locally. People such as William Bradford, John Winthrop, William Penn, even Thomas Jefferson and George Washington, played entrepreneurial roles in addition to their other contributions to the country's history. *So did millions of others whose names are not remembered.* The crucial point about entrepreneurship in American history is not who the entrepreneurs were, but that they existed and were able to achieve what they did.[55] *There was no plan for the economic development of the United States.* There was only an original frame of laws and constitutions, which included the developmental rights of property owners. We have seen how that system evolved.

Property owners were left to achieve their own destinies. Sometimes they did it alone, sometimes with the help of family labor. Sometimes government subsidies (expropriation and distribution of the taxpayers' money by government officials) played critical roles, but the decision making was always left to those who hoped to profit. In the main, the nation's economic history is what its people achieved, guided by their own entrepreneurial spirits. That some entrepreneurial spirits were greater than others was always true, as it is today.

Not all people are constitutionally set up to be entrepreneurs.[56] A trip to Atlantic City or Las Vegas would make us quickly aware that attitudes toward risk-taking vary widely. Many people, probably most, prefer life without a great amount of *conscious* risk. Yet all entrepreneurship involves risk-taking, just as gambling does.[57] Risk-averse entrepreneurs will try to reduce the element of pure luck by advertising, by price competition, by higher quality at given prices, but also by collusion, oligopolistic practices, price rigging, and mergers to attain monopoly. American society, through such policies as antitrust and regulation, has tried to limit the extent of risk-reducing activity among entrepreneurs on the grounds that it is antisocial.

Creative Destruction and Schumpeterian Growth

Schumpeter referred to the entrepreneurial role as "creative destruction" because, in the capitalist process of growth, competitive users of resources were driven out of business by more successful entrepreneurs. Henry Ford not only put many worthy carriage makers into bankruptcy, he also drove hundreds of other automakers out of business. Television decimated the weekly and monthly magazine business like the Black Death. Small, fuel-efficient Japanese and European auto imports very nearly left Detroit a basket case by the early 1980s. And who knows how many of yesterday's dot-com millionaires are looking for a job today?

People do not keep everything. New ideas, new products, and new techniques are adopted, and the old ones are abandoned. Schumpeterian entrepreneurs were the ones who correctly foresaw opportunity and made their moves. The country grew in *a different way* because of their actions. Over time, apart from government-induced constraints, the country's economic growth was the consequence of entrepreneurial decision making. The market always provided choices, but some were taken, and some were not. The net result is what is now called "Schumpeterian growth"—a business cycle upswing during which there are waves of innovations, sometimes functionally linked with each other (for example, steel, chemicals, electricity, autos), followed by a downswing in which only the most efficient survive. However, since some survive, each new wave begins at a higher output per capita than the previous one.

Recession itself was thus a critical part of the Schumpeterian growth process because it precipitated creative destruction.[58] Those who had been swept along in the boom, whose ventures were unsound, or whose older businesses had become obsolete, were generally forced to liquidate. The workers and resources they had employed were free to be bought up (perhaps at cut rates) by more efficient firms or by new ones coming on line in the ensuing business upswing. Alert operators bought out the losers—as Andrew Carnegie bought the Homestead works and

Invention and Innovation. *To Schumpeter, the marriage of invention and innovation, of human talent and entrepreneurial ability, sparked the growth of bourgeois society. The financial risks taken by Edison, Ford, and the Wright brothers, for example, paid off handsomely in profits for them and external benefits for society. A photo taken on a 1918 camping trip (above right) shows, left to right: Thomas Edison, Harvey Firestone, Jr., Prof. R. DeLoach, John Burroughs, Henry Ford, and Harvey Firestone, Sr. Not all entrepreneurial ventures got their ideas "off the ground." The 16-flapping-disc helicopter (below right) of Mr. Scott of Chicago failed. Technological progress embraces failure as part of its cost.*

Duquesne Steel—during recessions. One of Carnegie's managers said of his methods:

> The real time to extend your operations was when no one else was doing it. Whenever there would be a boom in the steel trade most manufacturers would start in and build new steel works. They would have to pay the very highest prices for the materials that entered into these constructions on account of boom times, and about the time they were ready to operate the bloom was off the peach and the works would have to lie idle.[59]

That's when Carnegie made his bid. Other successful entrepreneurs understood this.[60] Those who did not, failed. It was hard, ruthless, and, Schumpeter argues, effective in the creation of economic growth of unimaginable dimensions. The great growth period from 1842 to 1896 (trough to trough) saw vast industrialization all over the commercial world, as well as in the United States.

The Classical Entrepreneurs

When Pierpont Morgan died in March 1913, the London *Economist* wrote:

> Mr. Morgan was undoubtedly a man of genius, with strong will power and a commanding personality. He will stand, as a contemporary remarks, with Carnegie the manufacturer, Rockefeller the commercial organizer, Harriman the railway man, as one of the four most original and typical products of modern America.[61]

By 1913, the world had come to recognize in the great American entrepreneurs a social force that had changed the world. The greatest entrepreneurs, or at least those who made the most money, had organized the huge new American industrial economy, root and branch, into vast companies under unified managements that were capable of expansion and diversification. A company like Carnegie Steel was in a dozen different industries: building bridges and skyscrapers, mining and shipping ores by lake steamers, operating railroads. Men such as Pierpont Morgan were the financial organizers and controllers of economic activities that ranged from coal mining to banking.

Where there are economies of scale, the first firm to expand along its long-run, downward-sloping average cost curve will be able to undersell all rivals and drive them from the market—as long as the scale economies persist. That situation will lead to domination by a single firm, and under late nineteenth-century conditions, most likely a dominant entrepreneur.[62]

Unequal entrepreneurial ability poses a serious problem for the economic analysis of industry growth. Entrepreneurship is not one of the variables commonly found in the toolbox of microeconomic theory. Yet, in the history of nearly every industry, unequal entrepreneurship has played a dominating role, although it shifts with time. Henry Ford was the terror of the automobile industry until the mid–1920s. By then, in his sixties, he began to lose his lead and was overtaken by people like Alfred Sloan and William Knudsen at General Motors (the latter had been fired by Ford), Walter Chrysler, and the Dodge brothers. In the ensuing struggle, other automobile firms and entrepreneurs vanished without a trace.

Thus, while it is not necessarily true that any one entrepreneur in a particular industry will produce permanent domination, it is very likely that every new firm in an industry will not be entrepreneured equally well. As the industry expands, some firms will grow disproportionately as a result of their superior management. In some cases, the perpetual life of the (usually) resulting corporation enables firms brought to dominance by great entrepreneurship to survive for decades as leaders, far beyond the lifetimes of their founders. General Electric (Thomas Edison), Westinghouse (George Westinghouse), Firestone Rubber (Henry Firestone), U.S. Steel (Andrew Carnegie and Pierpont Morgan), Standard Oil (John D. Rockefeller) are examples. The great entrepreneurs were clearly survivors in a Darwinian sense. We can see the logic without accepting the justice of the legendary homily given by John D. Rockefeller to his Sunday school class: The American beauty rose can only be produced by nipping off the smaller blossoms as the rose develops. He nipped many a smaller bud to make his great rose, Standard Oil.

For more than two centuries, American society and its laws have encouraged the entrepreneur, and the nation has grown and prospered from the consequences.

NOTES

1. For the best short, but elegant, survey of the period and issues covered in this chapter, see Robert Higgs, *The Transformation of the American Economy 1865–1914* (1971).
2. For a world in which no cities would develop, see *ibid.*, pp. 59–61. Heterogenous physical features and internal and external economies are sufficient to produce cities in a commercial world.
3. Krugman has published a series of influential papers. Two recent examples are "On the Number and Location of Cities," *European Economic Review*, April 1993; and "First Nature, Second Nature, and Metropolitan Location," *Journal of Regional Science*, May 1993.
4. Sukkoo Kim, "Expansion of Markets and the Geographic Distribution of Economic Activities: The Trends in U.S. Regional Manufacturing Structure, 1860–1987," *QJE*, November 1995.
5. Robert Gallman, "The Pace and Pattern of American Economic Growth," in Lance Davis et al., *American Economic Growth: An Economist's History of the United States* (1972), calculated from Table 2.9, p. 34.
6. Sumner Slichter, *Economic Growth in the United States and Its History Problems and Prospects* (Baton Rouge: Louisiana State University Press, 1961), p. 62. His capital-output ratio for industrial capital was 1.63 in 1850 and ranged from 2.3 to 2.9 for 1900.
7. Robert Gallman estimates that savings rates in fact did increase powerfully as industrialization proceeded, as in the example in the text. He estimated savings rose from about 14 percent of NNP in the 1860s to more than 25 percent in the 1880s. "Gross National Product in the United States, 1834–1909," National Bureau of Economic Research, *Studies in Income and Wealth*, vol. 30 (1966).
8. Jeffrey Williamson, "Inequality, Accumulation, and Technological Imbalance: A Growth Equity Conflict in American History?" *Economic Development and Cultural Change*, vol. 27, no. 2, January, 1979, p. 249.
9. Robert Gallman, "The Pace and Pattern of American Economic Growth," in Davis (1972), pp. 33–39. The calculation for the years 1870–1910 is that of Jeremy Atack and Peter Passell, *A New Economic View of American History*, 2nd ed. (New York: W.W. Norton, 1994), Table 1.5.
10. Agriculture generated 61 percent of value added, to industry's 39 percent, measured in constant dollars. By 1909, these numbers were 26 and 74—more than a reversal of roles. Robert Gallman and Edward Howle, "Trends in the Structure of the American Economy Since 1840," reprinted in Robert Fogel and Stanley Engerman, eds., *The Reinterpretation of American Economic History* (1971), p. 26.
11. Victor Clark, *History of Manufactures in the United States* (1929), p. 2.
12. Louis Cain and Donald Paterson, "Biased Technical Change, Scale, and Factor Substitution in American Industry, 1850–1919," *JEH*, March 1986. Gavin Wright has emphasized the critical role American natural resources played in late nineteenth century growth: "The Origins of American Industrial Success, 1879–1940," *AER*, September 1990; and, with Richard Nelson, "The Rise and Fall of American Technological Leadership: The Postwar Era in Historical Perspective," *JEL*, December 1992.
13. Elizabeth Field-Hendry, "The Role of Gender in Biased Technical Change: U.S. Manufacturing, 1850–1919," *Journal of Economic History*, vol. 58, no. 4, December 1998.
14. Alfred Chandler, Jr., *The Visible Hand* (1977); and Jeremy Atack, "Industrial Structure and the Emergence of the Modern Industrial Corporation," *EEH*, January 1985.
15. Claudia Goldin and Lawrence Katz, "Technology, Skill, and the Wage Structure: Insights from the Past," *AER*, May 1996. See also their "The Origins of Technology-Skill Complementarity," *Quarterly Journal of Economics*, vol. 113, no. 3, August 1998.
16. Data from *Historical Statistics*, Series M 83–92.
17. Arthur Woolf, "Electricity, Productivity, and Labor Saving: American Manufacturing, 1900–1929," *EEH*, April 1984.
18. William Mulligan, Jr., "Mechanization and Work in the American Shoe Industry: Lynn, Massachusetts, 1852–1883," *Journal of Economic History*, vol. XLI, no. 1, March 1981.
19. Nathan Rosenberg, *Technology and American Economic Growth* (1972).
20. Paul Uselding, "Measuring Techniques and Manufacturing Practice," in Otto Mayr, ed., *The American System of Manufacturing* (1981). The improved quality of American manufactured metal products in the late nineteenth century *and* their competitive prices in the British market is documented by Roderick Floud, "The Adolescence of American Engineering Competition, 1860–1900," *EHR*, February 1974.
21. Paul Uselding, "Studies of Technology in Economic History," in *REH*, supplement 1 (1977), p. 168.
22. Nathan Rosenberg, "Technological Change in the Machine Tool Industry," *JEH*, December 1963.
23. Uselding (1977).
24. For perhaps the best modern study, Peter Temin, *Iron and Steel in Nineteenth-Century America: An Economic Inquiry* (1963). For an excellent study of blast-furnace

technology: Robert Allen, "The Peculiar Productivity History of American Blast Furnaces 1840–1913," *JEH*, September 1977.

25. Jonathan Hughes, *The Vital Few* (1986), p. 239.
26. *Ibid.*, p. 259.
27. Americans also took a different view of the purpose of blast-furnace linings. By raising air pressure in the blast, the amount of pig iron per charge could be increased, but the blast furnace linings were worn out more rapidly. The American iron masters raised the pressure, called "hard driving," and their profits, too. British observers were critical of the technique, but the Americans could sell iron cheaper, even at the expense of new blast-furnace linings. Peter Berck, "Hard Driving and Efficiency: Iron Production in 1890," *Journal of Economic History*, vol. XXXVIII, no. 4, December 1978.
28. Kenneth Sokoloff, "Inventive Activity in Early Industrial America: Evidence from Patent Records, 1790–1846," *JEH*, December 1988; Sokoloff and Zorina Khan, "'Schemes of Practical Utility': Entrepreneurship and Innovation among 'Great Inventors' in the United States, 1790–1865," *JEH*, June 1993.
29. Hughes (1986), p. 238.
30. Joseph Pratt, "The Petroleum Industry in Transition: Antitrust and the Decline of Monopoly Control in Oil," *JEH*, December 1980.
31. The new American technological advances were not universally adopted by her trading partners. For example, in clock and watch manufacturing, the Swiss copied American techniques, but the British did not. Donald Hoke, *Ingenious Yankees* (1990). The selective international spread of "best practice" technology in these cases remains a mystery. Hoke argues that the savings from this technology were so great as to overwhelm any imaginable differences due to differing factor endowments. There are other similar puzzles in areas like textiles: Gregory Clark, "Why Isn't the Whole World Developed? Lessons from the Cotton Mills," *JEH*, March 1987; Mira Wilkins, "Efficiency and Management: A Comment on Gregory Clark's 'Why Isn't the World Developed?'" *JEH*, December 1987; and John Hanson II, "Why Isn't The Whole World Developed? A Traditional View," *JEH*, September 1988.
32. Gallman (1966), p. 7.
33. *Ibid.,* p. 14.
34. *Historical Statistics*, series U 214–18.
35. *Historical Statistics*, series F 99.
36. And perhaps even relevant inventions! Irwin Feller found that inventing activity tended to be urban-concentrated, but *not* that inventions in any particular city influenced its growth. "The Urban Location of United States Invention, 1860–1910," *EEH*, Spring 1971.
37. Jonathan Hughes, *Industrialization and Economic History: Theses and Conjectures* (New York: McGraw-Hill, 1970), pp. 60–62.
38. Eugene Smolensky, "Industrial Location and Urban Growth," in Davis (1972), p. 582. See also David Meyer, "Midwestern Industrialization and the American Manufacturing Belt in the Nineteenth Century," *JEH*, December 1989.
39. Leonard Carlson, "Labor Supply, The Acquisition of Skills, and the Location of Southern Textile Mills, 1880–1900," *JEH*, March 1981.
40. Kenneth Weiher, "The Cotton Industry and Southern Urbanization, 1880–1930," *EEH*, April 1977.
41. From 1860 to 1910, fully 90 percent of the number of urban places continued to be small towns, between 2,500 and 25,000 in population. Proportionately, of course, their influence declined: These small towns contained 40 percent of the urban population in 1860 and still contained 32 percent by 1910. *Historical Statistics*, series A 43–67. The growth of cities drew little from the normal economic activity of rural America and its small towns. John Ermisch and Thomas Weiss, "The Impact of the Rural Market on the Growth of the Urban Workforce, U.S., 1870–1900," *EEH*, Winter 1973–1974.
42. Celeste Gaspari and Arthur Woolf, "Income, Public Works, and Mortality in Early Twentieth-Century American Cities," *JEH*, June 1985.
43. Thomas Weiss, "The Nineteenth Century Origins of the American Service Industry Workforce," *Essays in Economic and Business History* (1984); see also "Urbanization and the Growth of the Service Workforce," *EEH*, Spring 1971; and "The Industrial Distribution of the Urban and Rural Workforces: Estimates for the United States, 1870–1910," *JEH*, December 1972.
44. Jonathan Hughes, "Industrialization. Part I: Economic Aspects," *International Encyclopedia of the Social Sciences*, 1968 edition, vol. 7, pp. 252–263.
45. *Ibid.*
46. For more on the distribution of wealth in this era, see Richard Steckel and Carolyn Moehling, "Rising Inequality: Trends in the Distribution of Wealth in Industrializing New England," *Journal of Economic History*, vol. 61, no. 1, March 2001. Steckel and Moehling test several labor market based hypotheses for the growth of inequality in this period, but conclude in favor of a new mechanism based on "luck, rents, and entrepreneurship."
47. Times change. Consider the following from a Japanese industrial leader: "Our processing industries are simply better than [those] in the United States.... If the United States wants to sell us finished consumer products, they don't have a chance.... The Americans are good at inventing new machines, but in the ability to apply those

inventions, well, maybe the Japanese have more ability." *The Washington Post*, 31 July 1978. So much for the legacy of Carnegie and Ford.

48. The main statistical studies are Frances Gregory and Irene Neu, "The American Industrial Elite in the 1870s," and William Miller, "The Business Elite in Business Bureaucracies." Both are included in William Miller, ed., *Men in Business* (1962). See also Ralph Andreano, "A Note on the Horatio Alger Legend," in Louis Cain and Paul Uselding, eds., *Business Enterprise and Economic Change* (1973).
49. Robert Wiebe, *The Search for Order* (New York: Hill & Wang, 1967).
50. Joseph Schumpeter, *The Theory of Economic Development* (1949); *Business Cycles* (1939), 2 vols.; and *Capitalism, Socialism, and Democracy* (1943), chap. 7, "The Process of Creative Destruction." A more recent contribution is Israel Kirzner, *Competition and Entrepreneurship* (1973).
51. James Willard Hurst argued that the greatest change in the nineteenth century wrought by legal reform was the release of entrepreneurial energy that followed the instrumental decisions of the courts favoring economic development at the expense of all other property rights, *Law and the Conditions of Freedom in the Nineteenth Century United States* (Madison: University of Wisconsin Press, 1964).
52. Kirzner (1973), chaps. 1–2.
53. Ross Thomson, "Learning by Selling and Invention: The Case of the Sewing Machine," *JEH*, June 1987. The phenomenon continued into modern times: Daniel Nelson, "Mass Production and the U.S. Tire Industry," *JEH*, June 1987.
54. The mainstream of American writing on the nation's great entrepreneurs had been mainly in the spirit of the muckraking historians of the early twentieth century—deeply hostile. The best are T. W. Lawson, *Frenzied Finance* (New York: Ridgeway Thayer, 1905); Henry Clews, *Fifty Years in Wall Street* (New York: Irving, 1908); Gustavus Myers, *History of the Great American Fortunes* (Chicago: Charles Kerr, 1910); W. Z. Ripley, *Trusts, Pools and Corporations* (New York: Ginn & Co., 1916); John Moody, *The Masters of Capital* (New Haven, CT: Yale University Press, 1919); Ida M. Tarbell, *History of the Standard Oil Company* (New York: Macmillan, 1925); C. W. Baron, *They Told Baron* (New York: Harper & Bros., 1930); and Matthew Josephson, *The Robber Barons* (New York: Harcourt Brace, 1934).
55. Arthur Cole, *Business Enterprise in its Social Setting* (1959). For a sympathetic view of American entrepreneurs, see Jonathan Hughes, *The Vital Few* (1986).
56. Much has been written about these differences in people's attitudes toward risk-taking. The student might be interested in the work of Reuven Brenner in this regard: *History—The Human Gamble* (Chicago: University of Chicago Press, 1983); *Betting on Ideas: Wars, Inventions, Inflation* (Chicago: University of Chicago Press, 1985).
57. See John Nye, "Lucky Fools and Cautious Businessmen: On Entrepreneurship and the Measurement of Failure," *Research in Economic History*, Supplement 6 (Greenwich, CT: JAI Press, 1991).
58. The classic critique of Schumpeter's huge system is Simon Kuznets, "Schumpeter's 'Business Cycles,'" reprinted in Simon Kuznets, *Economic Change: Selected Essays in Business Cycles, National Income, and Economic Growth* (London: William Heinemann, 1954). Kuznets noted that Schumpeter's analysis implied that the supply of entrepreneurial talent would not always be forthcoming (p. 112), although Kuznets thought the implication was a cyclical one.
59. Hughes (1986), p. 237.
60. See *ibid.*, pp. 315–317 on Henry Ford in the 1921 recession and pp. 370–374 on Harriman's acquisition of the Union Pacific after the Panic of 1893.
61. Hughes (1986), p. 454.
62. For evidence of industrial concentration in the late nineteenth century, see F. M. Scherer and David Ross, *Industrial Market Structure and Economic Performance*, 3rd ed. (Boston: Houghton Mifflin, 1990), pp. 153–156.

SUGGESTED READINGS

Articles

Allen, Robert C. "The Peculiar Productivity History of American Blast Furnaces, 1840–1913." *Journal of Economic History*, vol. XXXVII, no. 3, September 1977.

Andreano, Ralph C. "A Note on the Horatio Alger Legend: Statistical Studies of the Nineteenth Century American Business Elite." In Louis Cain and Paul Uselding, eds., *Business Enterprise and Economic Change*. Kent, OH: Kent State University Press, 1973.

Asher, Ephraim. "Industrial Efficiency and Biased Technical Change in American and British Manufacturing: The Case of Textiles in the Nineteenth Century." *Journal of Economic History*, vol. XXXII, no. 2, June, 1972.

Atack, Jeremy. "Industrial Structure and the Emergence of the Modern Industrial Corporation." *Explorations in Economic History*, vol. 22, no. 1, January 1985.

Cain, Louis P., and Donald G. Paterson. "Biased Technical Change, Scale, and Factor Substitution in American Industry, 1850–1919." *Journal of Economic History*, vol. XLVI, no. 1, March 1986.

Carlson, Leonard A. "Labor Supply, the Acquisition of Skills, and the Location of Southern Textile Mills, 1880–1900." *Journal of Economic History*, vol. XLI, no. 1, March 1981.

Clark, Gregory. "Why Isn't the Whole World Developed? Lessons from the Cotton Mills." *Journal of Economic History*, vol. XLVII, no. 1, March 1987.

Ermisch, John, and Thomas Weiss. "The Impact of the Rural Market on the Growth of the Urban Workforce, U.S., 1870–1900." *Explorations in Economic History*, vol. 11, no. 2, Winter 1973–1974.

Feller, Irwin. "The Urban Location of United States Invention, 1860–1910." *Explorations in Economic History*, vol. 8, no. 3, Spring 1971.

Floud, Roderick C. "The Adolescence of American Engineering Competition, 1860–1900." *Economic History Review*, vol. XXXVII, no. 1, February 1974.

Gallman, Robert E., "Gross National Product in the United States, 1834–1909." In Dorothy Brady, ed., *Studies in Income and Wealth*, vol. 30, National Bureau of Economic Research. New York: Columbia University Press, 1966.

———. "The Pace and Pattern of American Economic Growth." In Lance Davis et al., *American Economic Growth: An Economist's History of the United States*. New York: Harper & Row, 1972.

———, and Edward S. Howle. "Trends in the Structure of the American Economy Since 1840." In Robert Fogel and Stanley Engerman, eds. *The Reinterpretation of American Economic History*. New York: Harper & Row, 1971.

Gaspari, K. Celeste, and Arthur G. Woolf. "Income, Public Works, and Mortality in Early Twentieth-Century American Cities." *Journal of Economic History*, vol. XLV, no. 2, June 1985.

Goldin, Claudia, and Lawrence F. Katz. "Technology, Skill, and the Wage Structure: Insights from the Past." *American Economic Review*, vol. 86, no. 2, May 1996.

Gregory, Frances W, and Irene D. Neu. "The American Industrial Elite in the 1870s: Their Social Origins." In William Miller, ed., *Men in Business*. New York: Harper, 1962.

Hanson, John R., II. "Why Isn't the Whole World Developed? A Traditional View." *Journal of Economic History*, vol. XLVIII, no. 3, September 1988.

Hughes, Jonathan. "Industrialization: Economic Aspects." *International Encyclopedia of the Social Sciences*, 1968 ed., vol. 7.

Kim, Sukkoo. "Expansion of Markets and the Geographic Distribution of Economic Activities: The Trends in U.S. Regional Manufacturing Structure, 1860–1987." *Quarterly Journal of Economics*, vol. 110, no. 4, November 1995.

Krugman, Paul. "On the Number and Location of Cities." *European Economic Review*, vol. 37, no. 2, April 1993.

———. "First Nature, Second Nature, and Metropolitan Location." *Journal of Regional Science*, vol. 33, no. 2, May 1993.

Meyer, David. "Midwestern Industrialization and the American Manufacturing Belt in the Nineteenth Century." *Journal of Economic History*, vol. XLIX, no. 4, December 1989.

Nelson, Daniel. "Mass Production and the U.S. Tire Industry." *Journal of Economic History*, vol. XLVII, no. 2, June 1987.

Pratt, Joseph A. "The Petroleum Industry in Transition: Antitrust and the Decline of Monopoly Control in Oil." *Journal of Economic History*, vol. XL, no. 14, December 1980.

Rosenberg, Nathan. "Technological Change in the Machine Tool Industry." *Journal of Economic History*, vol. XXIII, no. 4, December 1963.

———. "American Technology: Imported or Indigenous?" *American Economic Review*, vol. 67, no. 1, February 1977.

Smolensky, Eugene. "Industrialization and Urban Growth." In Lance Davis et al., *American Economic Growth*. New York: Harper & Row, 1972.

Sokoloff, Kenneth. "Inventive Activity in Early Industrial America: Evidence from Patent Records, 1790–1846." *Journal of Economic History*, vol. XLVIII, no. 4, December 1988.

———, and Zorina Khan. "'Schemes of Practical Utility': Entrepreneurship and Innovation among 'Great Inventors' in the United States, 1790–1865." *Journal of Economic History*, vol. 53, no. 2, June 1993.

Temin, Peter. "Manufacturing." In Lance Davis et al., *American Economic Growth*. New York: Harper & Row, 1972.

Thomson, Ross. "Learning by Selling and Invention: The Case of the Sewing Machine." *Journal of Economic History*, vol. XLVII, no. 2, June 1987.

Uselding, Paul. "Studies of Technology in Economic History." In Robert Gallman, ed., *Recent Developments in the Study of Economic and Business History: Essays in Honor of Herman E. Krooss. Research in Economic History*, supplement 1. Greenwich, CT: JAI Press, 1977.

———. "Measuring Techniques and Manufacturing Practice." In Otto Mayr, ed., *The American System of Manufacturing*. Washington: The Smithsonian Institution, 1981.

———, and Bruce Juba. "Biased Technical Progress in American Manufacturing." *Explorations in Economic History*, vol. 11, no. 1, Fall 1973.

Weiher, Kenneth. "The Cotton Industry and Southern Urbanization, 1880–1930." *Explorations in Economic History*, vol. 14, no. 2, April 1977.

Weiss, Thomas. "Urbanization and the Growth of the Service Workforce." *Explorations in Economic History*, vol. 8, no. 3, Spring 1971.

———. "The Industrial Distribution of the Urban and Rural Workforces: Estimates for the United States, 1870–1910." *Journal of Economic History*, vol. XXXII, no. 4, December 1972.

———. "The Nineteenth Century Origins of the American Service Industry Workforce." *Essays in Economic and Business History*, vol. III (1984).

Wilkins, Mira. "Efficiency and Management: A Comment on Gregory Clark's 'Why Isn't the World Developed?'" *Journal of Economic History*, vol. XLVII, no. 4, December 1987.

Woolf, Arthur G. "Electricity, Productivity, and Labor Savings: American Manufacturing, 1900–1929." *Explorations in Economic History*, vol. 21, no. 2, April 1984.

Wright, Gavin. "The Origins of American Industrial Success, 1879–1940." *American Economic Review*, vol. 80, no. 4, September 1990.

———, and Richard R. Nelson. "The Rise and Fall of American Technological Leadership: The Postwar Era in Historical Perspective." *Journal of Economic Literature*, vol. 30, no. 4, December 1992.

Books

Chandler, Alfred D., Jr. *The Visible Hand: The Managerial Revolution in American Business.* Cambridge: Harvard University Press, 1977.

———. *Scale and Scope: The Dynamics of Industrial Capitalism.* Cambridge: Harvard University Press, 1990.

Clark, Victor S. *History of Manufactures in the United States, 1607–1914*, 2 vols. Washington, D.C.: Carnegie Institution, 1928.

Cole, Arthur. *Business Enterprise in Its Social Setting.* Cambridge: Harvard University Press, 1959.

Frickey, Edwin. *Production in the United States, 1860–1914.* Cambridge: Harvard University Press, 1947.

Higgs, Robert. *The Transformation of the American Economy 1865–1914.* New York: Wiley, 1971.

Hoke, Donald R. *Ingenious Yankees: The Rise of the American System of Manufactures in the Private Sector.* New York: Columbia University Press, 1990.

Hounshell, David A. *From the American System to Mass Production, 1800–1932: The Development of Manufacturing Technology in the United States.* Baltimore: Johns Hopkins University Press, 1984.

Hughes, Jonathan. *The Vital Few: American Economic Progress and Its Protagonists.* New York: Oxford University Press, 1986.

Kirzner, Israel. *Competition and Entrepreneurship.* Chicago: University of Chicago Press, 1973.

Pred, A. R. *The Spatial Dynamics of U.S. Urban-Industrial Growth, 1800–1914.* Cambridge: MIT Press, 1966.

Rosenberg, Nathan. *Technology and American Economic Growth.* New York: Harper & Row, 1972.

Schumpeter, Joseph. *Business Cycles*, 2 vols. New York: McGraw-Hill, 1939.

———. *Capitalism, Socialism, and Democracy.* New York: Harper, 1943.

———. *The Theory of Economic Development.* Cambridge: Harvard University Press, 1949.

Temin, Peter. *Iron and Steel in Nineteenth-Century America: An Economic Inquiry.* Cambridge: MIT Press, 1964.

CHAPTER EIGHTEEN

Big Business and Government Intervention

Looking back more than a century to the 1880s and the relative positions of private business and the federal government in Washington, D.C., we are struck by a singular realization: There was little federal government control over the daily operations of private economic activity. *None* of the massive modern array of control agencies existed. A scholar would be hard-pressed to locate half a dozen permanent federal agencies that had any control over business in this country a century ago. There were no antitrust laws. There was no federal income tax. The federal government did not license businesses. There were no federally chartered corporations extant. By current standards, we can almost say that there was *no* federal government intervention in the economy. We cannot go quite that far, however. Even by the early 1880s, the federal power was evident. By then, for example:

1. The federal government was in control of the public domain—its resources and its disposition.
2. Through subsidies, the federal government had already produced business configurations that the free market might never have produced.
3. By tariff legislation, federal government rules determined the flow of commodities into the country and, consequently, created extra profitability—rents in domestic productions—which would not otherwise have existed.
4. The federal government reorganized the nation's banking system, thereby producing a pattern of banking different from the one the states and free market had produced. The entire financial structure of the country was profoundly affected.
5. The federal government's determination of the monetary standard influenced wages, prices, interest rates, and all else that depended upon them.
6. After the Civil War, the federal government's policies (and lack of them) had undermined the South's recovery. A whole section of the nation was depressed for decades.
7. Federal immigration policies actively encouraged a mass migration of Europeans into the country.

Thus, it was not really true that there was *no* federal influence in the economy. In fact, *if the federal government had done none of these things, that decision would have been a policy as well.* And, indeed, not a neutral one, because the classes favored by the existing policies would not have been favored—to the benefit of someone else.

We already know that since the earliest colonial times, governments at some level controlled businesses—regulated them, licensed them, and abolished them. The federal government, though, had been founded in 1789 by other governments, many of them already more than a century old. And, as we have already seen, at first the sovereign states were jealous of the powers they surrendered to the new federal establishment. Among the powers withheld were those regulating businesses in small detail. The federal government set the general background—the list of interventions just mentioned—but had neither the precedent, resources, nor inclination to be involved in the regulation of everyday business affairs.

Beginning in the 1880s, the status quo changed, and the intrusive regulatory powers of the states and local governments slowly but surely ascended to the federal level. The Occupational Safety and Health Administration (OSHA) is perhaps an excellent example of this transformation. The goal of "deregulation" proclaimed by federal administrations since the late 1970s thus amounts to nothing less than a desire to reverse the direction of a century of American history. Not surprisingly, there is considerable resistance to deregulation since generations of American business and labor leaders have known little else.

LEGAL CHANGES: CORPORATIONS AND THE LAW

Between the Civil War and World War I, two streams of American legal development, priority right and the privileges of incorporation, fused into a mighty current that would mold the future in ways no founder could have imagined. The courts, according to modern scholars, attempted to impose conservatism where earlier there had been pragmatic innovation, but they met with limited success.[1] By 1914, the giant enterprises celebrated by Alfred Chandler dominated the American economy.[2] Such an enterprise was usually a corporation with generalized powers or even a group of corporations locked into pools, cartels, trusts, and other arrangements (by then, in theory illegal) making resource allocations that affected the lives of millions. They were a capital-saving innovation, in the view of Alexander Field, with corporate management as the efficiency-promoting device: more income from less capital expenditure.[3]

Others believed, however, that monopoly was the game afoot, and that the great merger wave of the 1890s, which came *after* passage of the Sherman Antitrust Act, proved it.[4] The giant corporations, called by Arthur Selwyn Miller "feudal entities within the body politic" seemed likely to take over that body.[5] The corporate enterprise became the "agenda setter" of the American economy for many decades to come. In major part, the American economy became what the nation's corporations decided it would be in response, of course, to consumer choice. In the struggle to control the resulting power of "big business," the nation slowly changed again, into the modern regulated economy. Indeed, it is Miller's opinion, baldly stated, that modern "big government" is simply the consequence of government's interaction with big business.[6]

The Rise of Big Business

Alfred Chandler, as noted in the previous chapter, believed that big business—giant corporate organizations—could be justified, at least in part, by scale economies emerging from "continuous process production technology." In *Scale and Scope*, he argues that successful corporations made investments in production, distribution, *and* management:

> The first was an investment in production facilities large enough to exploit a technology's potential economies of scale or scope. The second was an investment in a national and international marketing and distribution network, so that the volume of sales might keep pace with the new volume of production. Finally, to benefit fully from these two kinds of investment the entrepreneurs also had to invest in management: they had to recruit and train managers not only to administer the enlarged facilities and increased personnel in both production and distribution, but also to monitor and coordinate those two basic function activities and to plan and allocate resources for future production and distribution.[7]

Like Schumpeter, Chandler believes big business plays an important role in economic growth, but Chandler's successful firm is responding to innovation, not leading it. In *The Visible Hand*, Chandler argues:

> The visible hand of management replaced the invisible hand of market forces where and when

The Gilded Age. *The dominant entrepreneurs of this period were often portrayed in an unflattering light. The political cartoon above shows Pierpontifex Maximus—J. P. Morgan—attempting to do for ocean shipping what he had already done for a large part of American railroads: Morganization. The caption of the cartoon below reads "Let them have it all, and be done with it!"*

> new technology and expanded markets permitted a historically unprecedented high volume and speed of materials through the process of production and distribution. Modern business enterprise was thus the institutional response to the rapid pace of technological innovation and increasing consumer demand in the United States during the second half of the nineteenth century.[8]

According to William Lazonick's attempt to bridge Schumpeter and Chandler, big business emerges from a world of decentralized markets in an act of innovation that creates economic capabilities within the firm. These capabilities set the stage for the ultimate realization of scale economies "through the process of production and distribution."[9]

As Richard Langlois has noted, this approach varies from neoclassical theories of industrial organization. It is concerned with the ways an institution, such as big business, generates growth (or fails to generate growth). The economic capabilities Lazonick's firms create lie at the center of this analysis. Chandler's analysis is comparative and tightly focused on which forms of organization best create growth on the basis of their *internal* capabilities. Yet, as Langlois argues, an alternative tradition traces its roots to the economist Alfred Marshall. While never denying the existence of internal scale economies, Marshall also looked at the interactions between competing and cooperating firms to check for the existence of *external* economies.[10]

Naomi Lamoreaux's research on the "great merger movement" is an attempt to explain why so many big businesses appeared in a relatively short period of time as a result of horizontal mergers.[11] During the nine years she studied (1895–1904), over 1,800 manufacturing firms relinquished their separate identities and combined with former rivals. One-third of these combinations resulted in a market share in excess of 70 percent.

Three historical "events" explain this phenomenon. The first event, the one on which Chandler focuses, is the emergence of capital-intensive, mass-production technologies that raised the proportion of fixed to total cost. If the economy is in a recession, one expects to find a direct relation between how prone an industry is to "serious pricing discipline breakdowns" and the proportion of fixed to total cost.[12] High fixed-cost firms are viewed as generally aware of their position and exercise considerable restraint. When, however, such restraint falters, they are most likely to "scurry into formal collusive agreements."

The second event is the extremely rapid growth of a large number of capital-intensive industries in the years following 1887 and the consequent uncertainty as to the probability of retaliation in these nascent oligopolies. In particular, where there were new firms in new industries with high fixed costs, sales revenue was a necessity; thus, the probability of price wars was extremely high. Margaret Levenstein compares the bromine, bleach, and salt markets through the records of the Dow Chemical Company. She suggests that national distributors with established reputations facilitated the entry of small producers into integrated markets. They also facilitated collusion. Large producers like Dow joined the collusion in the short run, but not the long. As Dow introduced new production processes, it integrated the production and distribution functions to avoid the restrictions imposed by the collusive agreements.[13] Levenstein notes that, beginning in 1885, price wars in the bromine industry resulted from bargaining or coordination problems. When firms in the industry agreed to cooperate, price wars became less likely.[14]

The third event of Lamoreaux's schema, the depression of the 1890s, was the trigger for the consolidation movement. The reduction in demand made high fixed cost ratios a much greater problem. With the return of better times, American politicians, beginning with Theodore Roosevelt, looked to bigger government as a way to cope with the economic power of these concentrated industries.

The Governmental Response

It is possible to generalize the development of bigger government from the materials we already have studied regarding the American tradition of nonmarket control—the use of government rather than market decisions to allocate resources. As the economy grew, businesses followed the line of settlement westward, or even led it, in cases of regional export industries. The "business society" became familiar in most sections of the country. The policy power we studied in Chapter 6 was the common law, and that power to control, forbid, and discriminate existed wherever there were courts and legislatures. However, economies of scale—either in production, in organization, or even in collusive action between rivals—made possible business organizations whose affairs simply overlapped many jurisdictions, creating a power potentially above any law, called the *size effect*.[15]

The only way to control this power was with an equally broad political force—federal control. The alternative was giant enterprise uncontrolled. Federal power could cross state lines and move internationally, in response to the organizational genius of American business owners, whose masterpiece, the huge American corporation, was an economic wonder of the late nineteenth century. The consequences of the size effect were first seen in railroads, and here we can gain perspective from Harry Scheiber:

> Organized across nearly half a continent, aggregating millions in capital, and controlling bureaucracies much larger than those of any state government, the giant railroad firms outdistanced the objective capacity of the states ... to exercise controls over them.[16]

If there were not to be businesses with power beyond that of the political system's control, then the federal government would have to expand. *And it could.*

Recall Chief Justice Marshall's view in *McCulloch v. Maryland* (1819) that the Constitution was "intended to endure for ages to come and, consequently, to be adapted to the various crises of human affairs." The federal government's powers, in his view, would always be sufficient to the need at hand.

Privilege, Power, and Suspicion

The states chartered corporations indiscriminately by special franchise, creating a new piece of legislation for each case. It was cumbersome and corrupt. But, as early as 1811, New York had made provision for incorporation by simple registration, adhering to generalized rules. There was no need for an act of legislature for each incorporation. In 1837, Connecticut also provided for general incorporation.

In its 1846 constitution, New York State further liberalized the rules. It lifted restrictions on the different kinds of business that corporations could do under a single charter, on locations, and on capital requirements. In 1875, New Jersey eliminated capital restrictions and in 1888 allowed its corporations to do all their business outside the state. Delaware followed with similar rules. Gradually, the special privileges of incorporation, once strictly limited and jealously guarded, were becoming available for any business group who sought them.[17]

Another line of legal evolution now came abreast of these developments. The federal Constitution had provided only for relations between *individuals* and the sovereign power. There was no conception of private *collective* economic entities in 1789. In 1819, Marshall, in *Dartmouth College v. Woodward*, had said that a corporation was in law an intangible "being." It was thus an individual, but not a Constitutional *citizen*. This interpretation squared reality with the abstraction. A series of Supreme Court cases (as we saw in Chapter 5) clarified the position of corporate enterprises with the law.

In 1851, Chief Justice Roger B. Taney had written in *Cooly v. Board of Wardens of the Port of Philadelphia* that, logically, controls by states and cities could not be extended beyond their own jurisdictions and that the need for greater power would have to be met by Congress. Then, in 1886, in *Santa Clara County v. Southern Pacific Railroad*, the Supreme Court held that the corporate person was protected by the due process clause of the Fourteenth Amendment: State and local governments thus were further limited in their abilities to regulate corporations.

The stage was very nearly set for a reversion to ubiquitous government regulation as in the colonial era, but this time with federal agencies playing the roles of boards of selectmen determining by their own deliberations the "public interest." We might object to the *ways* in which controls were imposed, but, in truth, it is inconceivable that no controls would have been imposed.

The big new companies were adept at market manipulations of all sorts—price fixing by pooling agreements, monopoly price, and output controls by cartel agreement. The pooling of the voting stock of competitive firms in trust allowed a more rigorous control, essentially the creation of a single management where formerly there had been competing firms. These devices, in a time of trouble in the agrarian sector, gave rise to a stiff hatred and envy of the corporation itself, as was manifested in the demands of the Populist platforms. The American corporation came to be viewed as alien to the rest of American life.[18]

The general public believed that American industry was being monopolized, that output was restricted, that prices were excessive, and that farmers, laborers, and consumers were being cheated by bloated plutocrats. There *was* a high degree of "concentration" of industrial power. Whether it was exploitive is unknowable. But even by early dates, scale economies were at work, and large firms succeeded. For example, in 1880, although some 1,900 firms made farm implements, the top four made 65 percent of the industry's entire output. In 1890, the copper industry was dominated by a few giant firms; three-fourths of all copper was produced by the top four. Standard Oil in 1879 refined 90 percent of all domestically pumped crude oil and owned 80 percent of the country's pipelines.[19] The sinister caricature of John D. Rockefeller, Sr., did nothing to help his firm's public image.

Such signs of private economic power were terrifying to some. It seemed that a new oligarchy would rise up and feudalize Jefferson's Arcadia. President Cleveland said of corporations in his message to Congress in 1888:

> As we view the achievements of aggregate capital, we discover the existence of trusts, combinations, and monopolies, while the citizen is struggling far in the rear, or is trampled to death beneath an iron heel. Corporations, which should be the carefully restrained creatures of the law and the servants of the people, are fast becoming the people's masters.[20]

As William Vanderbilt had said, "The Public be damned." It is naive to suppose that the federal government's powers would not be used to intervene. But, by 1888, intervention was already coming down the line, and from several different directions.

THE PIVOTAL POINT: *MUNN v. ILLINOIS*

The case of *Munn v. Illinois* (1877) was ultimately left in the dustbin of history, but to an economic historian, it is of particular interest. On it is focused 270 years of the Anglo-American tradition. It is a pivotal point in regulatory history. In the end, the effort to make the doctrine of *Munn* work as government regulation was a failure, and American history in these matters depended upon subsequent innovations.

Agrarian interests after the Civil War suffered from falling prices and from discriminatory rate-fixing by the railroads, or so the farmers and their supporters believed. Where the agrarians had the power in state legislatures, they took action. The laws they passed came to be identified with the Patrons of Husbandry, a.k.a. the Grange.[21] Laws were passed regulating railroad rates. Illinois, in its 1871 constitutional revision, provided for the licensing of grain elevators and control of their prices. Two Chicago elevator operators, Munn and Scott, refused to comply, and the results were the "Granger Cases" discussed in Chapter 14.

Munn v. Illinois and After

Many facets are touched upon but not developed in the majority opinion of the *Munn* decision, including the issue of monopoly power. Chief Justice Morrison Waite fell back upon the Anglo-American tradition of the police power. He saw nothing novel in the Granger laws, except that they dealt with giant businesses. From "time out of mind," local governments in this country, and the government in England before that, had regulated businesses in the interests of health and safety. The power was unquestioned. It was not so much a matter of "natural monopoly," as some textbooks still argue, as it was the historic basis of public utility regulation.[22] Inns, taverns, carters, draymen, bake shops, brewers, barbers—all had been subject to public regulation. Railroads and grain elevators were no different.

Waite quoted extensively from an essay by Lord Hale, a seventeenth-century English jurist who advanced the doctrine that any private property was subject to government regulation if the public had come to depend on its use. If that property became "affected with a public interest," it lost its private character. There could be no question of this power. As Waite wrote:

> [Such powers had been used] in England from time immemorial, and in this country from its colonization to regulate ferries, common carriers, hackmen, bakers, millers, wharfingers, innkeepers ... and in so doing to fix a maximum charge to be made for services rendered, accommodations furnished, and articles to be sold. To this day, statutes are to be found in

> many of the States upon some or all of these subjects; and we think it has never been successfully contended that such legislation came within the constitutional prohibitions against interference with private property.[23]

Harry Scheiber has shown that Chief Justice Waite was not as original as was thought at the time and that American courts had, in fact, utilized Lord Hale's arguments to justify regulation for decades before *Munn*.[24] Contemporaries feared that the doctrine of *Munn* would usher in extreme innovation in government. Associate Justice Field said of it, in a dissenting opinion: "If this be sound law … all property and all business in the state are held at the mercy of a majority of its legislature."[25] Quite.

If you recall from Chapter 1 the character of the original land tenure, free and common socage, you will remember that its incidents *had to be met* for ownership rights to continue. From earliest times, as Waite said, businesses were subject to political controls. Eminent domain proceedings had been regularized over time, but the power of eminent domain went unquestioned. The Constitution's Fifth Amendment prohibited the federal government from taking property without compensation and due process, and the Fourteenth Amendment had likewise constrained the states. But there was no absolute prohibition against government's ultimate power over the rights of private property.

In the decades that followed 1877, a fascinating blind alley of *Munn* doctrine laws and cases developed.[26] One was *Tyson v. Banton* (1927), in which the New York State legislature passed a law holding that ticket scalping on Broadway was clothed in the public interest and therefore was subject to regulation. Associate Justice Oliver Wendell Holmes, Jr., wrote:

> The notion that a business is clothed with a public interest … is little more than a fiction intended to beautify what is disagreeable to the sufferers. The truth seems to me that, subject to compensation when compensation is due, the legislature may forbid or restrict any business when it has a sufficient force of public opinion behind it.[27]

To Holmes, the *Munn* case was a needless complication.

Seven years later, *Nebbia v. New York* reached the Supreme Court.[28] The case involved an attempt to hold milk prices artificially high to the apparent benefit of large milk processors. New York State farmers were told that this was also to their benefit. The Court ruled this scheme to be well within the police powers and, agreeing with Holmes, said of *Munn*: "It is clear that there is no closed class or category of business affected with a public interest."[29] Justice MacReynolds saw clearly that *Munn* had in fact restricted the spread of government regulation for half a century, and that *Nebbia* would open the flood gates. He wrote in dissent:

> *Munn v. Illinois* has been much discussed.... And always the conclusion was that nothing there sustains the notion that the ordinary business of dealing in commodities is charged with a public interest and subject to legislative control. The contrary has [now] been distinctly announced. To undertake now to attribute a repudiated implication to [*Munn*] is to affirm that it means what this Court had declared again was not intended.[30]

After *Nebbia*, any and all business and control of private property was potentially subject to control wherever governments wanted it. In *Munn*, Chief Justice Waite reaffirmed the right of government to legitimately apply one of its traditional powers to modern business, with Lord Hale dragged in by his hair to set some kind of limit. Half a century of spreading nonmarket control had been somewhat restricted by that limit. *Munn* was the last gasp of the traditional police powers to counter the size effect of business development. *Nebbia* removed the limit, and the way was open for such phenomena as OSHA.

The Interstate Commerce Commission

By the 1930s, the railroads had already long since escaped the tendrils of *Munn* and had fallen into a different trap, the permanent federal regulatory agency. The first agency of that type was the Interstate Commerce Commission (ICC), founded in 1887.[31] Although at first the ICC had no rate-setting powers, the Hepburn Act changed that in 1906.[32]

In recent years, the creators of the ICC have been given credit for an unlikely amount of rationality. An earlier chapter discussed the opinion shared by historian Gabriel Kolko and his followers that Congress knew what it was doing in 1887: that it was giving the railroads a federal agency to act as their cartel manager.[33] Since the ICC has few friends in any political spectrum, Kolko's thesis is usually unquestioned. There is, however, plenty of contrary evidence.

First, since the Civil War, Congress had been attempting to find a way to regulate the railroads and had even imposed financial organization on the Union and Central Pacific railroads.[34] Second, Kolko's conspiracy theory implies that rustic legislators of the 1880s went along with a scheme to defraud the farmers. What of the cry by Senator Hoar of Massachusetts?

> You give these men power over the business of great towns and great cities and great classes of investments—a power which no Persian satrap or Roman proconsul was ever entrusted with....

Or that of Congressman Oates of Alabama:

> I freely confer, sir, that I am jealous of this eternal tendency to the enlargement and centralization of federal power.[35]

Was this criticism just rhetoric? Perhaps Hoar and Oates had been left out of the conspiracy? But what of this? Richard Olney, Cleveland's Attorney General, had to explain "capture" to a friend—a railroad president, no less—who also had apparently been left out and wanted the ICC abolished. Olney certainly knew what *he* was talking about:

> The Commission, as its functions have been limited by the courts, is, or can be made, of great use to the railroads. It satisfied the popular clamor for a government supervision of railroads, at the same time that supervision is almost entirely nominal. Further, the older such a commission gets to be, the more inclined it will be found to take the business and railroad view of things. It thus becomes a sort of barrier between the railroad corporations and the people and a sort of protection against hasty and crude legislation hostile to railroad interests.... The part of wisdom is not to destroy the Commission, but to utilize it.[36]

But Olney's argument depended upon restrictions imposed by the courts *after* 1887. Moreover, since the ICC was the first case, it was Olney's *wisdom* that led him to believe that the ICC would ultimately be "captured." The fact is that the ICC has only been the worst of many bad examples that followed. Congress no more "knew" what it was doing in 1887 than it does today when it creates a new commission, agency, power, office, or control to conserve energy, stop inflation, boost prices, or defend the homeland.

The regulatory commission is a way to *manage* problems, not solve them. That the commissions get "captured" is not surprising. Although there is no way to know the public interest, those who get regulated at least know their own, and they make their interests known to the agencies in many ways. The latter are left with the responsibility for the welfare of those they control. No regulatory agency wants to destroy the industry whose affairs it is to rule.

The ICC never even managed that much. As a "cartel," it was a terrible failure. Albro Martin, in his book *Enterprise Denied* demonstrates that by 1914, ICC regulation had reduced the railroads to a shambles.[37] Especially devastating had been the denial of rate increases as prices and wages rose in the early twentieth century. The railroads, Martin argues, could not be maintained, but that was early in the game. Thomas Ulen has pointed out that the original legislation, trying to include something for everyone, was hopelessly inconsistent, and its subsequent adjustments and amendments seem not to have served *any* interest![38]

The ICC was the granddaddy of all the permanent federal regulatory agencies. Shortly after its centennial year, it ceased to exist; its functions were absorbed by the Department of Transportation. Its objectives were never known, or knowable. The ICC's fate, however ignominious, should not divert us from its origins. Initially, its commissioners were of high intellectual quality. The ICC was part of a parcel of efforts to offset the size effect and to raise to the federal level direct political control over business. After the Supreme Court made one final effort to spread the umbrella of traditional police power over big business in *Munn v Illinois*, a fresh attack was needed.

One prong of that attack was the developing army of federal regulatory agencies under the commerce clause. The ICC was the first of these. The second prong was the establishment of organizational and behavioral rules for the new corporations.

THE ANTITRUST ACTS

In 1890, Congress passed the Sherman Antitrust Act, whose famous beginning reads:

> Every contract, combination in the form of trust or otherwise, or conspiracy, in restraint of trade or commerce among the several states or with foreign nations is hereby declared to be illegal....[39]

With that, the federal courts were launched upon a continuous career of industrial and economic management from which they have never been able to extract themselves. At the very heights of the corporate economy, it became lawyers and judges who decided if the creations of the nation's industrial leaders would live or die. The fact that most lawyers and judges know little or nothing about the management of huge economic enterprises was not considered relevant then, nor it is now. After more than a century, the resulting body of antitrust law, is nonsensical.[40]

The Sherman Act and its subsequent amendments comprise a vast and complex behavioral sumptuary law for business. Just as the Massachusetts Puritans forbade certain classes of people from wearing certain clothing, so the antitrust laws forbade certain organizational behavior. And, just as the Puritan divines never told the lower orders what they *could* wear, the antitrust laws do not say what actions *are* legal. For example, over and over, businesses have been constrained by the courts under the antitrust acts for reducing competition, but there is no act of Congress that says what competition *is*.

Businesses may not engage in activities that reduce something that is not mentioned in the Sherman Act, something that is unknown outside the ethereal atmosphere of the economics classroom What is legal under the antitrust laws is simply what has not yet been found to be *illegal*. Since an infinity of collusive action is possible, the antitrust laws produced (in theory) an infinity of court actions. The long shelves of thick books called antitrust law comprise the monument to the Sherman Act and its amendments.

The Purpose of Antitrust Laws

Surprisingly, there is no general agreement among scholars about the Sherman Act's precise origins or objectives. We have already noted the agitation of the 1870s and 1880s against trusts, corporations, pools, and cartels. Agitation is a political statement that need not represent anything important to be effective—antivivisectionists, prohibitionists, antifluoridation enthusiasts, free silver proponents, anti-Darwinists—all and more have had their moments. What is important in politics is votes, and, in this country, almost any cause can be pushed for that purpose.

The big "trust buster" politicians, Theodore Roosevelt and William Howard Taft, arrived in the White House long after the Sherman Act was passed. But Populists and labor leaders had agitated against the new corporations and various business alignments before 1890. Eighteen states had passed their own antitrust laws by 1891. Both major political parties included antitrust planks in their platforms in 1888, and Senator John Sherman (R-Ohio) introduced antitrust bills in 1888 and 1889 before succeeding in 1890.[41]

Thus, the historian must presume that there was *something* causing all this agitation, even if it did end up as politics. What was it? The answer seems to be fear of economic size and excessive power in private business. F. M. Scherer, a leading modern scholar of American industrial development, presents an aggregate of causes for the appearance of our antitrust laws:

1. Growth of large-scale firms was based upon "technical innovations in metallurgy, industrial chemistry, energy generation and utilization, and the use of interchangeable parts." Innovations existed that produced scale economies in industry.
2. Declining transportation costs encouraged growth of optimal plant sizes.
3. Developing financial services in the capital markets made it easier for individual firms to achieve economies of scale.
4. Liberalization of state laws of incorporation encouraged professional management (and plowed-back profits) by separating actual control from the stockholder owners of the firms.
5. Expansion of both domestic and international markets made enlarged plant size profitable.

(Recall Adam Smith's dictum about the division of labor and the size of the market.)

6. Depressions from 1873 to 1879 and from 1883 to 1886 had produced price wars among manufacturers—unhappy conditions that led to efforts to control markets by collusion or merger when prospects improved.
7. American law, which made cartel agreement unenforceable in the courts (the opposite was widely true in Europe), led to a tendency for firms to merge to achieve control.
8. Merger, the creation of "big business," was more in line with the "expansive frontier spirit" of American entrepreneurs than was quasi-legal participation in pools and cartels.
9. The extravagant lifestyles of the new corporate elite were an affront to the rest of the electorate. Envy made the anti-big-business stance good politics for aspiring candidates.
10. Farmers, who were the majority in many states, were especially harmed by the depressions of the 1870s and 1880s. Many believed that the growth of big business was against their interests. In the Granger and Populist movements, this political force was an organized one.[42]

Scherer, perhaps wisely, did not attempt to place weights on any one factor. The literature of the time shows little effort by big business leaders to defend their activities on what we now would consider perfectly conventional grounds: job creation, and economic growth, for example. Indeed, they may well have believed much of the charge against them, since it came not only from the daily press and the turmoil of politics and economic life, but even from the White House itself.

The Sherman Act

William Letwin and others have shown the connections between the Sherman Act and the common law.[43] It was perfectly legal for the king, and later Parliament, to grant monopoly privileges to an individual person or company. Privately, a single person could gain in trade what we would loosely call "monopoly power" (for instance, the ability to set his or her own prices locally), so long as it was not deemed "unreasonable." What was not admissible was a single person's gaining the position of a *single seller* on a wide scale (or even locally, if it were done by agreement with potential competitors) by his or her own action without the sanction of Parliament.[44]

When the possibility of monopoly power occurred because of nature—for instance, a toll bridge over a stream or a ferry site on a river—those situations were regulated, and had been since time out of mind, as "natural" monopolies. As we have seen, the English, and the Americans afterward, regulated many private businesses under the police powers for all sorts of reasons, and they also regulated natural monopolies where they occurred. Thomas Jefferson wrote of colonial Virginia: "Ferries are admitted only at such places as are appointed by law, and the rates of ferriage are fixed."[45]

Thus, a federal law passed in 1890 stating that private monopolies, combinations, and other conspiracies in restraint of trade would be henceforth illegal seemed simple enough. This already was the case in common law and had been so since the country was first settled. However, there followed an astounding development called *antitrust law*, which has continued to grow and develop unabated to our own time. Such had not been the intention. In 1911, William Hornblower wrote, somewhat apologetically, in the *Columbia Law Review* that the Sherman Act had been drafted by the ablest lawyers in the Senate.

> One would have supposed that if ever a statute would prove to be unambiguous, intelligible and enforceable, this would be that statute; yet it is safe to say that no statute ever passed since the foundation of the government has been the subject of more difference of opinion or the cause of more perplexity, both to judges and lawyers than the same statute.[46]

Section 1 of the Act prohibits conspiracies, contracts, or combinations in restraint of trade and provides for penalties (which have since been increased). Section 2 prohibits monopoly or actions tending to monopoly. In Section 4, the attorney general of the United States is authorized to institute lawsuits (in equity) against offenders, and Section 7 allows injured private parties to bring suit for recovery of triple damages against offenders under Sections 1 and 2.[47]

The "Billion Dollar Congress" (1889). It was widely believed by Populists and others that big business owned the U.S. Congress and controlled its legislative activities.

Fine-Tuning the Regulation

Experience with the Sherman Act soon made it clear that finer specifications of illegal actions and exemptions, together with more diligent enforcement activity, would be necessary to make a federal antitrust policy effective.[48] In the Clayton Antitrust Act of 1914 (amending the Sherman Act), Section 2 forbids price discrimination that reduces competition. Section 3 outlaws exclusive dealing and tying contracts that reduce competition. Because the Sherman Act had been used against organized labor unions (which either are useless or are successful restraints of trade), Section 6 of the Clayton Act declares grandly (and illogically) that labor "is not a commodity or article of commerce" and that labor unions are not to be considered in law as "illegal combinations or conspiracies in restraint of trade."[49] Section 7 prohibits mergers that would reduce competition, and Section 8 forbids interlocking directorates between firms held to be otherwise competitive (in the same industry).[50]

To police these laws and to intercede by steady surveillance, the Federal Trade Commission (FTC) was also set up in 1914. Its job is to pursue wrongdoers full time. This is a most curious institution, called by one legal writer a case of "multiple impersonation." It is "complainant, jury, judge and counsel."[51] The FTC commissioners can issue "cease and desist" orders to those whose actions are found repugnant and can seek enforcement of their orders in the courts. From 1914 onward, the FTC shared the obligation of enforcing the antitrust laws with the attorney general.

The antitrust laws have been much amended since 1914, but not in any ways that have made them more coherent. Over the years, the FTC has been given more and more authority to enforce virtue, even to the point of prohibiting misleading advertising. By 1980, the FTC had acquired so many enemies that Congress attempted to clip its wings and give itself the power of legislative veto and the power to override FTC rulings, thus adding to the confusion. In 1983, the Supreme Court had to override Congress on this issue.

Exceptions to the Rule

It is not readily apparent what these antitrust laws are, other than lists of problems with which Congress and the courts have tried to cope. Simplistically, they oppose monopoly power. Until 1942, the U.S. Supreme Court held that manufacturing was not commerce.[52] Therefore, apparent violations of antitrust law—beginning with the E. C. Knight case (the Sugar Trust) in 1895 in which the business involved could qualify as manufacturing—could not be forbidden.[53]

From the U.S. Steel case in 1920 to the ALCOA aluminum case in 1945, size alone was not considered evidence of monopoly; there had to be "intent" to monopolize.[54] Organized labor was exempted from antitrust laws in 1914. Combines of Americans fixing prices for foreign markets were exempted by the Webb-Pomerene Act of 1918. Farm cooperatives were allowed to fix prices by agreement among themselves by the Capper-Volstead Act of 1922.[55] Gradually, the government came to accept that industries subject to federal regulatory agencies ought to be exempted from antitrust proceedings. It made little sense for a business to be directed by one regulatory agency into the grip of another, although it has sometimes happened.[56]

At first, lawyers objected that the Sherman Act was inconsistent with common law because there was no "rule of reason" in it. In common law, only "unreasonable" restraint was illegal. The Sherman Act said "every" restraint was forbidden, whether reasonable or not. Thus, in *U.S. v. Trans-Missouri Freight Association* (1897), the Supreme Court rejected a rule of reason.[57] But in *Standard Oil of New Jersey v. U.S.* (1911), a rule of reason, whatever the Court should decide was reasonable, was enunciated.[58] *Both* lines of reasoning have been followed by the courts.

All this confusion would be laughable except that companies have been broken up, fines levied, and people imprisoned as a result. Whatever the antitrust acts mean, the courts take them very seriously.

REMARKS ON GOVERNMENT INTERVENTION

As we know, American business never operated outside a settled form of established legality—except possibly on the remotest edges of frontier settlement, and then only briefly. The social climate for business was the province of the state power from earliest colonial times. The property laws; the common law remedies for injury, fraud, and negligence; and the penchant of American governments to regulate directly meant that entrepreneurs in settled parts of the country lived in a more or less settled legal environment. They knew the law, and their customers and competitors knew it, too.

Just at the time that American business leaders discovered the joys of large-scale organization and proceeded to create the giant manufacturing, transport, and financial combines for which the late nineteenth and early twentieth centuries were famous, popular opinion soured. The very apparatus of the state power seemed to turn against business enterprise. It became profitable for politicians to oppose "big business," at least during election campaigns. Legislation came to reflect this bias, also. As we already noted, by 1914, the main props for federal control over the nation's business activities were already in place. These laws and institutions, and those like them that were soon to follow, were meant to restrain the power of the country's business leadership, to impose political control over it.

Robert Wiebe argues that during the entire period after the Civil War, the basic social structure of the country was undergoing upheaval. Small-town and rural America were trying to maintain their political power, despite the obvious shift of economic power to the burgeoning new urban areas.[59] The federal imposition of nonmarket control, following Wiebe's line of thought, reflected this basically atavistic force.

Douglass North presents a compatible line of thought.[60] North argues that in a popular democracy the *losers* try to recoup their losses from free-market economic processes through the political system, where their vote counts. Clearly, the reach of the giant new industries and the industrial cities they spawned, together with the relative decline in the fortunes of farmers, could have been the source of antibusiness legislation. Although the labor interest could not yet have mobilized decisive political power (as we will see in Chapter 21), labor votes meant something in factory districts. Their representatives could have joined in coalitions to push their interests, minority or not.

In a popular democracy, coalitions of losers can be put together in legislative activities in which voting minority interests are advanced, despite the majoritarian politics that generally prevail.[61] More than one thing can be happening at the same time. Business can get protection from the McKinley Tariff (1890), while at the same time, other interests push through the antitrust law.[62] Such inconsistencies were as true from 1865 to 1914 for special-interest politics as they are in our own time. They help explain why it was in an era of supposedly corrupt Congresses that the first modern moves to impose federal regulation on business were made. George Bittlingmayer's examination of the first 25 years of antitrust enforcement shows that cases filed against large firms coincided with business cycle downturns whereas case filed against small firms did not, a finding that supports the hypothesis that antitrust hurt business activity.[63]

The rise of an antibusiness attitude in government, beginning perhaps with Grover Cleveland and reaching pronounced crescendos with Woodrow Wilson's election in 1912, was clearly good—that is, winning—politics. Both Theodore Roosevelt and William Howard Taft pursued trust-busting rhetoric as the road to election. Farmers' and small-town residents' votes still constituted a majority, if a shrinking one, in this country.

Those in colonial times who gained from the trend toward weakening of strict government control were independent spirits, losers in the grip of the big land grantors, the governments of New England who distributed new lands only in townships. They were mainly land-hungry farmers who wanted, and finally gained, access to the land through the free market by revolution (and via the land auctions, beginning under the land ordinances of 1785 and 1787). They were joined by business people who wanted freedom from the tight nonmarket controls of the colonial towns and cities—freedom from the army of watchers, searchers, viewers, and gaugers of the colonial settlements.

The farmers once again were the losers in the postbellum period, but they now were joined by labor and the urban poor, who fell behind urban commercial interests and industrialists in the battle for distributive income shares. They demanded a return to nonmarket controls over business and a systematic transfer of wealth and income. Such demands underlay the initial demands for state regulation of railroads and continued when that power moved to the federal level. They were present in the demand for a variety of bills affecting agriculture and industry, including the Federal Reserve Act. After winning periodic battles, in the 1930s, they won the war.

For nearly half a century, what reigned next was the American version of the welfare state, but it was a **transfer society** in which only a very small portion of the wealth was transferred from the rich to the poor.[64] The losers in the post-New Deal period of the 1930s were those who worked and earned and were taxed excessively by both direct income taxes and inflation to create rents that were transferred elsewhere: to government contractors; to those with specially protected incomes; to the poor; and, to some extent, even to those abroad, as military and nonmilitary government grants to foreign powers. They were joined by business interests who wanted freedom from expanding regulation, and, as we shall see, by 1980, they were able to swing the system around through political action.

The chaos of the federal regulation and antitrust law is not unique. It is characteristic of federal government intervention by nonmarket control methods, and has been since their inception in 1887. The object of this control is to *manage* problems in perpetuity, not to *solve* them. The entire magnificent array established by 1914—the ICC, Sherman Act, Pure Food Act (1906), Clayton Act, FTC, Federal Reserve System (1914)—was meant to be, and was, ongoing mediation between the agents of the marketplace, the buyers and sellers.

We must keep one point in mind, since there would be much less nonsense in American life and history and economics books if it were faced directly: Nonmarket *control means rejection of the market decision* due to someone's successful appeal for a political, or politicized, solution.[65] Usually the object is straightforward enough: One party in the market wishes to gain an advantage from government intervention that the market alone will not produce. Otherwise, there is no reason for the control, except the employment of lawyers and bureaucrats.

In the late nineteenth century, American capitalism produced giant business firms, usually by way of general laws of incorporation. Americans feared the collective power of these firms, but, at the same time, they wanted:

1. The advantages of large-scale production that only huge firms could provide
2. The virtues of the competitive open market where the consumer interest is protected by the rivalry among sellers.

The two objects conflict with each other.[66] But many desirable things in life are filled with inconsistencies (for example, families and careers). Americans decided to have it all and have managed it until now. The distrust of the free market is obviously deeply rooted in American society and reaches back to the earliest settlements. On the other hand, the complaints against government regulation are nearly universal and are regularly mouthed by presidential candidates of all parties, and independents, too.

This dichotomy is a way of life that is characteristic of the American economic system. When the business firms became gigantic, so did the effort made to control them by the political arm of society. The argument was put bluntly by the U.S. Supreme Court in 1937 when it held that the Wagner Act—which imposed federally established labor unions on businesses—was constitutional:

> When industries organize themselves on a national scale, making their relation to interstate commerce the dominant factor in their activities, how can it be maintained that their industrial labor relations constitute a forbidden field into which Congress cannot enter....[67]

There was to be no area of economic life into which government control could not enter. As we know, this was hardly a new idea, harking all the way back as it did to 1607. Between 1887 and 1914, that power was raised to the *federal* level, and there it has remained, grown, flourished, and multiplied. *Munn v. Illinois* was the end of the ancient system, and the Interstate Commerce Act of 1887, the beginning of the new.

NOTES

1. Harry Scheiber, "Federalism and the American Economic Order, 1789–1910," *Law and Society*, Fall 1975; Herbert Hovenkamp, "The Classical Corporation in American Legal Thought," *The Georgetown Law Review*, June 1988; and Morton Horwitz, *The Transformation of American Law 1780–1860* (1977), chap. VIII.
2. Alfred Chandler, *The Visible Hand* (1977) and *Scale and Scope* (1990).
3. Alexander Field, "Modern Business Enterprise as a Capital-Saving Innovation," *JEH*, June 1987.
4. The evidence is disputed, but there can be no doubt that monopoly power is a *desideratum* for most business people, and the data show that, in the merger wave of the 1890s, there was much added concentration of power. Anthony Patrick O'Brien, "Factory Size, Economies of Scale, and the Great Merger Wave of 1898–1902," *JEH*, September 1988. However, others have found with Alfred Chandler, that the pursuit of scale economies, and not desire for monopoly power, motivated the great mergers. For example, Jeremy Atack, "Industrial Structure and the Emergence of the Modern Industrial Corporation," *EEH*, January 1985.
5. Arthur Selwyn Miller, *The Supreme Court and American Capitalism* (1972), p. 15.
6. *Ibid.*, p. 175.
7. Chandler (1990), p. 8.
8. Chandler (1977), p. 12.
9. William Lazonick, *Business Organization and the Myth of the Market Economy* (1991). Sukkoo Kim argues that the rise of the multiunit firm has more to due with marketing than with scale and scope. See his "The Rise of Multiunit Firms in U.S. Manufacturing," *Explorations in Economic History*, vol. 36, no. 4, October 1999.
10. Richard Langlois, "External Economies and Economic Progress: The Case of the Microcomputer Industry," *BHR*, Spring 1992. See also Langlois and Paul Robertson, "Explaining Vertical Integration: Lessons from the American Automobile Industry," *JEH*, June 1989; and their *Firms, Markets and Economic Change: A Dynamic Theory of Business Institutions* (1995). Langlois and Robertson have found important examples of external economies in the automobile and microcomputer industries. As noted in the previous chapter, Krugman and Kim do not find external effects to be statistically significant in the aggregate.

11. Naomi Lamoreaux, *The Great Merger Movement in American Business, 1895–1904* (1985).
12. The theory in Lamoreaux is derived from the section on the dynamic implications of cost structures in F. M. Scherer and David Ross, *Industrial Market Structure and Economic Performance*, 3rd. ed. (1990).
13. Margaret Levenstein, *Accounting for Growth: Information Systems and the Creation of the Large Corporation* (Palo Alto: Stanford University Press, 1998), chap. 1.
14. Bromine producers elected to form a cartel rather than merge with competitors. Margaret Levenstein, "Do Price Wars Facilitate Collusion? A Study of the Bromine Cartel before World War I," *EEH*, January 1996, and "Price Wars and the Stability of Collusion: A Study of the Pre-World War I Bromine Industry," *Journal of Industrial Economics*, vol. XLV, no. 2, June 1997.
15. Jonathan Hughes, "Transference and Development of Institutional Constraints Upon Economic Activity," in *REH*, vol. 1, 1976, p. 50. The argument is made by Charles McCurdy that even the size effect itself depended upon the courts opening up the national economy to larger scale business operations; "American Law and the Marketing Structure of the Large Corporation," *JEH*, September 1978.
16. Scheiber (1975), p. 99.
17. For a general survey, James Willard Hurst, *The Legitimacy of the Business Corporation in the United States, 1780–1970* (1970). Also, Lawrence Friedman, *A History of American Law* (1973), chap. VIII. An interesting recent perspective is Christopher Grandy, "New Jersey Corporate Chartermongering, 1875–1929," *JEH*, September 1989.
18. See note 54 in chap. 17 for a list of books in the muckraking tradition. For a more modern view, see Louis Galambos, *The Public Image of Big Business in America, 1880—1940* (1975).
19. Willard Thorp and Grace Knott, "The History of Concentration in Seven Industries," in *The Structure of Industry* (1941), part IV.
20. Quoted in Jonathan Hughes, *The Governmental Habit Redux* (1991), p. 112.
21. John Hicks, *The Populist Revolt: A History of the Farmers' Alliance and the People's Party* (1931); also, Irwin Unger, *The Greenback Era* (1964).
22. An interesting, modern exploration into public utility regulation is Werner Troesken, *Why Regulate Utilities?* (1996).
23. *Munn v. Illinois*, 94 U.S. 125 (1877).
24. Harry Scheiber, "The Road to *Munn*: Eminent Domain and the Concept of Public Purpose in the State Courts," *Perspectives in American History*, 1971.
25. *Munn*, p. 136.
26. Maurice Finklestein, "From *Munn v. Illinois* to *Tyson v. Banton*, A Study in the Judicial Process," *Columbia Law Review*, vol. 27, no. 7, November 1927.
27. *Tyson v. Banton*, 273 U.S. 261 (1927), Holmes in dissent, p. 446.
28. *Nebbia v. New York*, 291 U.S. 502 (1934).
29. *Nebbia*, p. 536.
30. *Nebbia*, p. 555.
31. Thomas Gilligan, William Marshall, and Barry Weingast, "Regulation and the Theory of Legislative Choice: The Interstate Commerce Act of 1887," *JLE*, April 1989.
32. An excellent discussion of the Hepburn Act can be found in Martin Sklar, *The Corporate Reconstruction of American Capitalism, 1890–1916: The Market, the Law, and Politics*, (1988).
33. Gabriel Kolko, *Railroads and Regulation 1877–1916* (1965).
34. Hughes (1991), pp. 107–109.
35. Both speeches quoted in Karl Brent Swisher, *American Constitutional Development* (Boston: Houghton Mifflin, 1954), p. 415.
36. L. L. Jaffe, *Judicial Control of Administrative Action* (Boston: Little, Brown, 1965), p. 12.
37. Albro Martin, *Enterprise Denied: Origins of the Decline of American Railroads* (1971).
38. Thomas Ulen, "The Market for Regulation: The I.C.C. from 1887 to 1920," *AER*, May 1980.
39. Milton Handler, *Trade Regulation* (1970), p. 1109.
40. For a sympathetic summary: A. D. Neale, *The Antitrust Laws of the United States* (1970). Also, see Lawrence Friedman, *A History of American Law*, pp. 405–408.
41. F. M. Scherer, *Industrial Market Structure and Economic Performance*, 1st ed. (Chicago: Rand McNally: 1970), p. 424.
42. *Ibid.*, pp. 422–427.
43. William Letwin, *Law and Economic Policy in America: The Evolution of the Sherman Antitrust Act* (1965). See also Handler (1970), chaps. 1–2; and Hans Thorelli, *The Federal Antitrust Policy: Origination of an American Tradition* (1954).
44. Handler (1970), pp. 105–108.
45. Thomas Jefferson, *Notes on the State of Virginia* (London: John Stockdale, 1788), p. 253.
46. William Hornblower, "Anti-Trust: Legislation and Litigation," *Columbia Law Review*, vol. 11, no. 8, December 1911, p. 702.
47. Handler (1970), p. 114. Sec. 4 of the Clayton Act superseded Sec. 7 of the Sherman Act.
48. In a recent article, Carlos Ramirez and Christian Eigen-Zucchi challenge the conventional wisdom. In "Understanding the Clayton Act of 1914: An Analysis of the Interest Group Hypothesis," *Public Choice*, vol. 106, no.1, January 2001, the authors argue that the vote in the Senate was influenced by both small and large manufacturing interests.
49. The Pullman strike of 1894 ended with labor leader Eugene V. Debs being jailed for contempt.

50. Gilbert Montague, "Anti-Trust Laws and the Federal Trade Commission, 1914–1927," *Columbia Law Review*, 1927, p. 661.
51. *Ibid.*, p. 661. For an illuminating study of the FTC's "shakedown cruise," when it first learned the scope and limitations of its power, see Robert Aduddell and Louis Cain, "Public Policy Toward the 'Greatest Trust in the World,'" *BHR*, Summer 1981.
52. *U.S. v. Darby*, 312 U.S. 100 (1941).
53. *U.S. v. E.C. Knight Co.*, 156 U.S. 1 (1895).
54. *U.S. v. U.S. Steel Corp.*, 251 U.S. 417 (1920) and *Aluminum Co. of American v. U.S.*, 148 F.2d. 416 (1945).
55. In addition, in 1936 Congress amended the Clayton Act with the Robinson-Patman Act, aimed directly at the consumer in an attempt to prohibit discounts for large volume purchases by chain stores. Something for everyone. Small business had to be protected from competition by big business. Scherer comments on Robinson-Patman: "There is virtual unanimity among students of the Act that ... its motivation was desire to limit competition, not to enhance it." In 1937, Congress passed the Miller-Tydings Act exempting resale price maintenance agreements (price-fixing) between manufacturers and retailers. F. M. Scherer and David Ross, *Industrial Market Structure and Economic Performance* (1990), p. 509.
56. At one point in the AT&T antitrust case, it was argued that the firm needed to be broken into smaller units as it had become too big to regulate.
57. *U.S. v. Trans-Missouri Freight Association*, 166 U.S. 290 (1897).
58. *Standard Oil of New Jersey v. U.S.*, 221 U.S. 1 (1911).
59. Robert Wiebe, *The Search for Order, 1877–1920* (New York: Hill & Wang, 1967).
60. Douglass North, "Structure and Performance: The Task of Economic History," *Journal of Economic Literature*, vol. XVI, no. 3, September 1978.
61. James Buchanan, *The Limits of Liberty: Between Anarchy and Leviathan* (Chicago: University of Chicago Press, 1975), pp. 100–103.
62. For a structuring of American economic history from this viewpoint, see Stanley Reiter and Jonathan Hughes, "A Preface on Modeling the Regulated United States Economy," *Hofstra Law Review*, vol. 9, no. 5, Summer 1981, especially pp. 1403–1421.
63. George Bittlingmayer, "Antitrust and Business Activity: The First Quarter Century," *Business History Review*, vol. 70, no. 3, Autumn 1996.
64. Alan Blinder, "The Level and Distribution of Economic Well-Being," in Martin Feldstein, ed., *The American Economy in Transition* (Chicago: University of Chicago Press, 1980), pp. 443–447. The term is taken from Terry Anderson and P. J. Hill, *The Birth of a Transfer Society* (1989).
65. Anderson and Hill (1989).
66. Those conflicts are ably summarized by Alfred Chandler and Louis Galambos in "The Development of Large-Scale Economic Organizations in Modern America," *JEH*, March 1970.
67. *NLRB v. Jones and Laughlin Steel Corp.*, 301 U.S. a (1937), pp. 41–42.

SUGGESTED READINGS

Articles

Aduddell, Robert M., and Louis P. Cain. "Public Policy Toward the 'Greatest Trust in the World.'" *Business History Review*, vol. LV, no. 2, Summer 1981.

Atack, Jeremy. "Industrial Structure and the Emergence of the Modern Industrial Corporation." *Explorations in Economic History*, vol. 22, no. 1, January 1985.

Chandler, Alfred D., and Louis Galambos. "The Development of Large-Scale Economic Organizations in Modern America." *Journal of Economic History*, vol. XXX, no. 1, March 1970.

Field, Alexander J. "Modern Business Enterprise as a Capital-Saving Innovation." *Journal of Economic History*, vol. XLVII, no. 2, June 1987.

Gilligan, Thomas W., William J. Marshall, and Barry R. Weingast. "Regulation and the Theory of Legislative Choice: The Interstate Commerce Act of 1887." *Journal of Law and Economics*, vol. 32, no. 1, April 1989.

Grandy, Christopher. "New Jersey Corporate Chartermongering, 1875–1929." *Journal of Economic History*, vol. XLIX, no. 3, September 1989.

Hovenkamp, Herbert. "The Classical Corporation in American Legal Thought." *The Georgetown Law Review*, vol. 76, no. 5, June 1988.

Hughes, Jonathan. "Transference and Development of Institutional Constraints Upon Economic Activity." In Paul Uselding, ed., *Research in Economic History*, vol. 1. Greenwich, CT: JAI Press, 1976.

Langlois, Richard N. "External Economies and Economic Progress: The Case of the Microcomputer Industry." *Business History Review*, vol. 66, no. 1, Spring 1992.

———, and Paul Robertson. "Explaining Vertical Integration: Lessons from the American Automobile

Industry." *Journal of Economic History*, vol. XLIX, no. 2, June 1989.

Levenstein, Margaret C. "Mass Production Conquers the Pool: Firm Organization and the Nature of Competition in the Nineteenth Century." *Journal of Economic History*, vol. 55, no. 3, September 1995.

———. "Do Price Wars Facilitate Collusion? A Study of the Bromine Cartel before World War I." *Explorations in Economic History*, vol. 33, no. 1, January 1996.

McCurdy, Charles W. "American Law and the Marketing Structure of the Large Corporation, 1875–1890." *Journal of Economic History*, vol. XXXVIII, no. 3, September 1978.

Montague, Gilbert H. "Anti-Trust Laws and the Federal Trade Commission, 1914–1927." *Columbia Law Review*, vol. 27, no. 6, June 1927.

O'Brien, Anthony Patrick. "Factory Size, Economies of Scale, and the Great Merger Wave of 1898–1902." *Journal of Economic History*, vol. XLVIII, no. 3, September 1988.

Scheiber, Harry. "Federalism and the American Economic Order, 1789–1910." *Law and Society*, vol. 10, no. 1, Fall 1975.

———. "The Road to Munn: Eminent Domain and the Concept of Public Purpose in the State Court." *Perspectives in American History*, vol. 5, 1971.

Thorp, Willard L., and Grace W. Knott. "The History of Concentration in Seven Industries." *The Structure of Industry*. Temporary National Economic Committee, Monograph No. 23, Washington, D.C.: United States Government Printing Office, 1941.

Ulen, Thomas. "The Market for Regulation: The I.C.C. from 1887 to 1920." *American Economic Review*, vol. 70, no. 2, May 1980.

Books

Anderson, Terry L., and Peter J. Hill. *The Birth of a Transfer Society*. Lanham, MD: University Press of America, 1989.

Chandler, Alfred. *The Visible Hand*. Cambridge: Harvard University Press, 1977.

———. *Scale and Scope: The Dynamics of Industrial Capitalism*. Cambridge: Harvard University Press, 1990.

Friedman, Lawrence M. *A History of American Law*. New York: Simon and Schuster, 1973.

Galambos, Louis. *The Public Image of Big Business in America, 1880–1940*. Baltimore: Johns Hopkins University Press, 1975.

Handler, Milton. *Trade Regulation*. Brooklyn: The Foundation Press, 1960.

Hicks, John D. *The Populist Revolt: A History of the Farmers' Alliance and the People's Party*. Minneapolis: University of Minnesota Press, 1931.

Horwitz, Morton. *The Transformation of American Law, 1780–1860*. Cambridge: Harvard University Press, 1977.

Hughes, Jonathan. *The Governmental Habit Redux: Economic Controls from Colonial Times to the Present*. Princeton: Princeton University Press, 1991.

Hurst, James Willard. *The Legitimacy of the Business Corporation in the United States, 1780–1970*. Charlottesville: University Press of Virginia, 1970.

Josephson, Matthew. *The Robber Barons: The Great American Capitalists, 1861–1901*. New York: Harcourt Brace, 1934.

Kolko, Gabriel. *Railroads and Regulations, 1887–1916*. Princeton: Princeton University Press, 1965.

Lamoreaux, Naomi R. *The Great Merger Movement in American Business, 1895–1904*. Cambridge: Cambridge University Press, 1985.

Langlois, Richard N., and Paul Robertson. *Firms, Markets and Economic Change: A Dynamic Theory of Business Institutions*. New York: Routledge, 1995.

Lazonick, William. *Business Organization and the Myth of the Market Economy*. Cambridge: Cambridge University Press, 1991.

Letwin, William. *Law and Economic Policy in America: The Evolution of the Sherman Antitrust Act*. New York: Random House, 1965.

Martin, Albro. *Enterprise Denied: Origins of the Decline of American Railroads*. New York: Columbia University Press, 1971.

Miller, Arthur Selwyn. *The Supreme Court and American Capitalism*. New York: The Free Press, 1972.

Moody, John. *The Truth About the Trusts*. New York: Moody, 1904.

Myers, Gustavus. *History of the Great American Fortunes*. Chicago: Kerr, 1960.

Neale, A. D. *The Antitrust Laws of the U.S.A.: A Study of Competition Enforced by Law*. Cambridge: Cambridge University Press, 1970.

Scherer, F. M., and David Ross. *Industrial Market Structure and Economic Performance*, 3rd ed. Boston: Houghton Mifflin, 1990.

Sklar, Martin J. *The Corporate Reconstruction of American Capitalism, 1890–1916: The Market, the Law, and Politics*. Cambridge: Cambridge University Press, 1988.

Sobel, Robert. *The Age of Giant Corporations: A Microeconomic History of American Business 1914–1970*. Westport, CT: Greenwood Press, 1972.

Tarbell, Ida M. *History of the Standard Oil Company*. New York: Macmillan, 1925.

Thorelli, Hans B. *The Federal Antitrust Policy: Origination of an American Tradition*. Stockholm: Akademsk Avhandling, 1954.

Troesken, Werner. *Why Regulate Utilities? The New Institutional Economics and the Chicago Gas Industry, 1849–1924*. Ann Arbor: The University of Michigan Press, 1996.

Unger, Irwin. *The Greenback Era*. Princeton: Princeton University Press, 1964.

CHAPTER NINETEEN

Financial Developments 1863–1914

Until the 1863 National Banking Act, banking in the United States was a mixture of (a) licensing by special state charters, (b) banking done by nonchartered private bankers, or under general state rules, and (c) free banking, following New York State's system.[1] Under Civil War legislation, the federal government reentered American banking for the first time since the charter of the Second Bank of the United States had lapsed in 1836, a victim of Jackson's veto.

The national banks created after 1863 were still limited to operations within their state boundaries, and, even there, they were forbidden to have branches. They were "national" simply because of their federal charters. The rival state banking systems continued, thus maintaining the American tradition of confusion in banking. Even in the nationwide **Federal Reserve System** (the central bank of the United States that began operations in 1914 and in which the national banks were forced to participate) the state boundaries prevailed. The National Bank Act banned branch banking across state lines; it was prohibited in most states to protect the local monopoly rents derived from the unit-bank charters.

Since the expanding economy required financial intermediation, the financial history of the United States in the period 1863–1914 is essentially the story of creating that intermediation within the constraints of the continuing regime of unit banking. It is an odd but, nevertheless, fascinating tale.

CREATING FINANCIAL INTERMEDIATION

In 1912, the National Monetary Commission report ripped into the existing American commercial banking system, denouncing it root and branch, and liberally crediting it with a multitude of crimes and errors. After a recital of 17 specific points of gross deficiency in the existing system, the report then generalized:

> The methods by which our domestic and international credit operations are now conducted are crude, expensive and unworthy of an intelligent people.... The unimportant part which our banks and bankers take in the financing of our foreign trade is disgraceful to a progressive nation.... The disabilities from which our producers suffer in our foreign trade also apply largely to domestic transactions.[2]

If all these charges were correct, we might fairly ask, how did the American legislatures, federal and state, manage to create such a marvel? In part, the answer is they thought it up, but they also blundered into it. It was (and is) characteristic of American government to try to give everyone what he or she wants by legislation. Economic institutions created by our legislative processes usually are not designed to achieve economic goals exclusively; they also are meant to satisfy the more effectively organized vested interests and, at the same time, garner votes (and sometimes financial support) for those who draft the laws. Not surprisingly, the results of such activity tend to vary remarkably.

The National Bank Acts

As we already know from Chapter 12, by 1860, there existed more than 1,500 separate state banks that had survived the various financial crises of the past. They were note-issuing institutions that circulated their own promissory notes, of many denominations, as money. By 1860, there may have been 10,000 different kinds of bank notes in circulation.

The federal government's fiscal position was nevertheless strained. Efforts to raise money by sales of long-term bonds were only partly successful, and borrowing on short-term simply multiplied the problems of federal finance.[3] In 1861, some $189 million of long-term bonds bearing 6 percent interest were sold. In 1862, the financier Jay Cooke contracted to sell a huge issue and succeeded, by a door-to-door campaign, in placing $362 million. In that year, the Treasury also sold an additional $150 million worth of bonds. However, that same year, the Treasury, desperate for funds, borrowed an additional $682 million on short-term notes and issued $915 million in legal tender notes (a maximum of $447 million outstanding at any time.)[4] There were objections to "farming out" any new long-term issues to operators like Cooke.

Because all this preceded the pivotal Battle of Gettysburg in 1863, several war years had yet to be financed, and a new method had to be found to harness the banking system to the federal Treasury's needs. The obvious answer would be somehow to force-feed federal securities into the state banks. The method chosen was the National Bank Act of 1863 (and subsequent amendments), which, it was envisaged, would blend the federal Treasury's fiscal requirements with the country's need to rationalize the currency. The notes of the Bank of England under the Bank of England Act of 1844 (which provided for ultimate elimination of private bank notes) might have been an inspiration. The thousands of state bank notes could be eliminated at a stroke by the issue of a national uniform bank currency. The way to do this was to have the state banks rechartered by the federal government.[5]

The outbreak of war had removed the Southern legislators temporarily from Congress and, thus, the representatives of those states most opposed to a reappearance of a "monopolistic" Bank of the United States. Their absence facilitated the passage of the new banking legislation. The National Bank Act was passed in 1863 but produced only a small response; thus, in October 1864, the Act was revised. A new office was established, that of the comptroller of the currency. Under the revised Act, the national banks would have capital requirements according to the size of the cities in which they were located (initially the range was from $200,000 for a city of 50,000 or more down to $50,000 for a city with a population of 6,000). By purchasing U.S. bonds equal to at least one-third the required bank capital and then *hypothecating* (depositing) the bonds with the comptroller, each bank would receive back national bank notes (with each bank's name embossed thereupon) equal to 90 percent of the face value of the bonds thus immobilized. This feature was copied from the free banking system of New York; the Safety Fund feature of New York's banking system, the deposit insurance feature, was not copied.

The national bank notes were to be legal tender for all except customs payments. To make the system seem more sound than the state banking system, legal reserve requirements were imposed upon the national banks, and double liability was imposed on the stock of the national banks. These features were supposed to attract deposits to the national system. A small semiannual tax of one-half percent was placed upon the national bank note circulation—one-quarter percent on capital in excess of the government bonds deposited with the comptroller and one-quarter percent against deposits. In addition, a tax of 2 percent was levied against state bank notes in June 1864.

Because bankers received the scheme with little enthusiasm, in March 1865, the tax on state bank notes was increased from 2 percent to 10 percent. The high cost of continuing to operate with a state charter now overcame the previous lack of enthusiasm. Membership in the national system was soaring as the Civil War came to an end. At first it must have seemed that the national bank system would finally eliminate the bank-chartering business of the state legislatures. Instead, there now were two systems, adding to the complexity (see Table 19.1).

At first the state system dwindled rapidly, but as early as 1870, once state bankers learned how to earn

TABLE 19.1 National and State Banks

Year	Total		National Banks		State Banks		Percentage National Bank Assets of Total
	Number	Assets[a]	Number	Assets[a]	Number	Assets[a]	
1860	1,562	$ 1,000	—	—	—	—	—
1861	1,601	1,016	—	—	—	—	—
1862	1,492	1,012	—	—	—	—	—
1863	1,532	1,209	66	$ 17	1,466	$ 1,192	0.1
1864	1,556	973	467	252	1,089	721	25.9
1865	1,643	1,358	1,294	1,127	349	231	83.0
1866	1,931	1,673	1,634	1,476	297	197	88.2
1867	1,908	1,674	1,626	1,494	272	180	89.2
1868	1,887	1,736	1,640	1,572	247	164	90.6
1869	1,878	1,736	1,619	1,564	259	171	90.1
1870	1,937	1,781	1,612	1,566	325	215	87.9
1880	3,355	3,399	2,076	2,036	1,279	1,364	59.9
1890	8,201	6,358	3,484	3,062	4,717	3,296	48.2
1900	13,053	11,388	3,731	4,944	9,322	6,444	43.4
1910	25,151	22,922	7,138	9,892	18,013	13,030	43.2
1914	27,864	27,349	7,518	11,477	20,346	15,872	42.0

[a] Assets are given in millions of dollars.

Source: *Historical Statistics*, derived from series X 580, 581, 634, 635, 656, 657. The data for state banks are for "nonnational" banks and include banks other than commercial banks.

a profit without issuing notes, it was making a comeback, and its recovery was dramatic. By 1900, the state banking system held considerably more in total assets than did the national. There were far more state than national banks, although the average state bank was only about half the size of the average national bank. There were an astounding 13,000+ banks in the country then, and the number was still growing by leaps and bounds. What had happened?

Deposits and Checks

In the postwar period, the system of checks and deposits became an increasingly common way to make payments. State banks, which could only circulate their own notes (with a 10 percent federal tax on them), could loan money in the form of **demand deposits**, accounts against which checks could be written. A check on a demand deposit actually is a *financial bill of exchange*, an order from a principal (one who creates the check) to his or her agent (the bank) to disperse funds to a third party. As we saw in Chapter 1, the financial instrument called the bill of exchange had been used by merchants and bankers in Western Europe to make payments long before the discovery of America and was apparently known in antiquity. It could become the main financial instrument used by common citizens once other citizens accepted it in payment instead of demanding coins or the promissory notes of bankers. The law relating to checks was already in place in colonial times.

The common use of checks by ordinary citizens was a major innovation, since it meant that the need for banknotes and coins could be reduced in daily circulation. Two things were necessary. First, bankers had to honor the checks; the principal had to have sufficient bank credit. Second, the seller *trusted* the ability of the principal to make good the amount, either by transfer of bank credit from the principal to the third party (called the *holder-in-due-course*) or by payment in notes or coins by the bank upon whom the check was drawn. Ancillary to the process, of course, was the belief by the seller that the bank itself could pay.

Common use of checks and deposits meant that the state banks no longer needed to print their own promissory notes to create bank credit—money. The demand deposits, since they served all the functions of notes and coins, were themselves "money." The 10 percent tax levied upon state bank notes in 1865 could thus be avoided without diminution of state bank credit *once the checks and demand deposits became acceptable practice.* Within a decade after 1865, the state banks were able to recover the business that formerly had depended upon the issue of their own notes. In Table 19.1 we can see the resulting growth of the state banks, along with the growth of the banking system as a whole up to 1914.

Since the number of banks of all kinds, and their assets, more than doubled even in the final decade-and-a-half before 1914, banking clearly continued to be a growth industry as the economy expanded and became increasingly commercialized in all its aspects. At various points before 1914, efforts were made to reform and control this burgeoning phenomenon. Let's take a look at those attempts.

Currencies and Coins

By the late 1870s, all the state bank notes had vanished from circulation. The national bank notes were based upon deposits of U.S. government bonds with the comptroller. As interest rates fell—from the Civil War into the 1890s—bond prices rose, and the national bankers were loathe to invest in such low-yielding assets, even to circulate national bank notes with their own names embossed thereupon.[6] Instead, the national banks created demand deposits, too. National bank notes in circulation thus declined (see Table 19.2).

The various Secretaries of the Treasury were conservative about any further increases in U.S. notes, better known as *greenbacks*. As will be discussed, these notes, issued during the Civil War, were not convertible into gold or silver until 1879, when the Treasury resumed specie payments.

The currency expanded, mainly by accretions of gold and silver and the warehouse receipts for them: gold and silver certificates. Until the turn of the century, greenbacks and national banknotes remained a stagnant portion of the total means of payment. *After* 1900 there was a large expansion of the national bank note circulation as the numbers of national banks increased (see Table 19.1). With rising interest rates, U.S. bonds were now a better buy for bankers than they had been for a generation, and the cachet "national" over a bank door had come to mean prestige.[7] The national banks had done marginally better than the state banks in surviving the various monetary panics.

Until after 1900, the Civil War national bank "solution" to U.S. currency problems was less than a joke, giving rise to inevitable political movements in favor of other one-shot money solutions to all problems—solid gold, free silver, and commodity money, each of which will be discussed. At present, we need to consider the reappearance of central banking in 1914. According to the arguments of the time, part of the reason was the "inelasticity" of the money supply, the national bank note supply in particular.[8] Over the course of the business cycle, the money supply did not expand (or contract) as fast as the demand for it.

TABLE 19.2 Currencies and Coins in Circulation, 1870–1914[a]

Year	*U.S. Notes*	*National Bank Notes*	*Gold Coin*	*Gold Certificates*	*Silver Dollars*	*Silver Certificates*	*Treasury Notes of 1890*	*Subsidiary Silver*
1870	$325.0	$288.7	$ 81.2	$ 32.1	$ —	$ —	$ —	$ 9.0
1880	327.9	337.4	225.7	8.0	20.1	5.8	—	48.5
1890	334.7	181.6	374.3	130.8	56.3	297.6	—	54.0
1900	317.7	300.1	610.8	200.7	65.9	408.5	75.3	76.2
1910	334.8	683.7	590.9	802.8	72.4	478.6	3.7	135.6
1914	337.8	715.2	611.5	1,026.1	70.3	478.6	2.4	160.0

[a] Amounts given are in millions of dollars.

Source: *Historical Statistics,* series X 424–434.

For those who think expansion of currency and coin is sound economics, it was the mining and coining of precious metals, together with those acquired through the balance of payments, that "solved" the country's economic problems until after 1900 (see Table 19.2). By that year, the ratio of pure paper money to coins and moneys representing precious metals deposited had been cut by more than 90 percent. Whereas in 1870, there were $5 of pure paper afloat for every $1 of some metallic kind, by 1900, there were about 40 cents in paper for every $1 metallic. The largest increases in the circulation came from increased monetary gold supplies together with a (lesser) increase in the uses of monetary silver. When the United States finally adopted the gold standard officially in 1900, the country was well supplied with that metal.

Banking Reforms and the Federal Reserve System

At first the various comptrollers believed that *upper* limits on the number of national bank notes in circulation might be necessary. That idea was dropped in 1875, since note circulation was already declining. There was no evident way to get national banks (and their notes) spread evenly over the country. Studenski and Krooss report that, in 1876, there was a greater national bank note circulation in the town of New Bedford, Massachusetts, than in any Southern *state*. Per-capita national bank note circulation was $77 in Rhode Island and 13 cents in Arkansas.[9] To encourage the growth of national banks, the bond deposit requirement on the smaller banks (those with capital below $150,000) was reduced from one-third to one-fourth of all capital in 1882. Reserve requirements were scaled again according to city size. In 1900, national banks were allowed to issue notes equal to the full par value of deposited bonds.

		Sum of	
Minor Coin	*Paper Money*	*Metallic & Metallic Representative*	*Ratio of Paper to Metallic*
$ —	$ 613.7	$ 122.3	5.0
—	702.1	308.1	2.3
—	516.3	912.9	0.6
26.1	617.9	1,463.5	0.4
46.3	1,018.5	2,130.2	0.5
57.4	1,053.0	2,406.2	0.4

Nevertheless, there was no system to the National Banking System. Its check-clearing activities were slow and expensive, and there was no central institution of coordination. The financial crises of 1873 and 1882 endangered the national banks. They were in deep difficulty again in the Panic of 1893, and, in the Panic of 1907, they came close to universal *suspension of payments*—refusal to return specie in return for bank notes. *Call money rates* (interest charged for loans that could be called in without warning) reached 70 percent in the Panic of 1893; in 1907 they hit 125 percent. Richard Grossman's simulation of the macroeconomy during this period suggests that a minor economic downturn, one characterized by only a few bank failures, would lead to an immediate 2 percent decrease in real GNP. A major downturn with widespread bank failures could have led to a 20 percent decrease.[10]

When the dust of 1907 settled, reforms were demanded. The 1907 panic once again demonstrated the problems of uncoordinated fractional-reserve banking. As the demand for money increased in times of crisis, its supply was reduced. Small-town bankers counted as reserves their deposits in correspondent banks in the cities. Because of its active call-loan market, New York City especially attracted such deposits. In a crisis, country and small-town bankers withdrew their correspondent deposits, city bankers called in their loans to meet demand, and the credit structure collapsed like a house of cards. Despite efforts of the U.S. Treasury to help by allotting emergency deposits here and there and of the banks themselves by issuing clearinghouse certificates to be used as temporary money, there was no way to stop the panics from spreading.[11] They periodically appeared at the peak of the business cycle; many believed (and still believe) such panics were caused by the expansion of bank money (deposits).[12]

In 1907, much of the potential damage was averted by adroit and forceful actions in New York City under the direction of the aging Pierpont

Early in the Civil War, the chaos of the financial system was made worse by private money issues (above). Below is a view of the Populist platform of 1892 as seen by a "regular" Democratic cartoonist.

Morgan.[13] Although it was an extraordinary performance by "Pierpontifex Maximus," the greatest of the old-time financiers, he was not thanked for it. His actions—the pooling of bank funds, rationing of credit, and disciplining of the short interest in the stock market—were, in part, similar to techniques developed by the Bank of England in the decades after 1857, which Morgan knew well. By 1907, he had been spending (for half a century) part of each year in London managing his bank there. He had grasped what there was to learn about crisis management from the Bank of England. He had, in fact, prepared for similar actions in 1903 when conditions were becoming ominous. His method was central banking without a central bank.

A return to some sort of central banking had been discussed for years. The supposed transgressions of Nicholas Biddle and the Second Bank of the United States were forgotten in the terror of 1907 and the memories of 1873 to 1893. In 1908, Congress passed the Aldrich-Vreeland Act, which provided for a temporary emergency currency for the "next time," recommended formation of a National Currency Association of national banks for that purpose, and ordered that a National Monetary Commission be set up to suggest changes in the banking system. What they suggested was the Federal Reserve System.[14]

The Commission's chairman, Senator Nelson Aldrich of Rhode Island, produced a plan in 1911 for a National Reserve Association organized in 15 districts nationwide, to be owned and operated by the private banking interests and to be sponsored by federal action. In fact, the senator's plan was similar to other large-scale financial reorganizations prepared in the past by his old friend Pierpont Morgan.

In 1912, the Commission reported the same proposal. In 1912, however, Woodrow Wilson and the Democrats won the election. They were reform-minded and willing. They took over the congressional work on the legislation and changed it to meet their own standards. The Federal Reserve Act, signed into law by Wilson in December 1913, was the result.

The creation of the Fed was the apparently permanent American contribution to central banking. Much of the Aldrich Plan remained in the final bill, but much was changed, too. Also, an effort was made to politicize the new system by the creation of the

Federal Reserve Board, all political appointees with certain executive powers.

The Federal Reserve Act is a curious hybrid, reflecting well its heterogeneous origins. It is a mixture of private interest and political creativity. The Fed's structure and functions were reformed in 1935, and it has now evolved into something that *looks* like "government." But looks can be deceiving.

At first the Federal Reserve System was no more than an empty framework, apart from its purely technical functions of clearing checks and servicing the federal government's financial operations. Central banking with 12 banks was a slight simplification of the Aldrich scheme; the Fed was not meant to be a monolithic central bank like other contemporary institutions: the Bank of England, Bank of France, Reichsbank, or the Swedish Riksbank. Each of the 12 banks was to be located in the financial center of its district, but, as Odell and Weiman show, this was not necessarily an easy task.[15]

Lessons from the past were embedded in the Federal Reserve Act. Since its charter does not expire, we are spared any more great bank charter crises. The Fed does its business with other banks; it is a bank for bankers. It does not deal with the public directly—that is, it does not *compete* with private bankers as did the earlier central banks. Thus, there is no pressure from the banking sector to abolish it.

Member banks are required to keep non-interest-bearing *cash* reserves in their district banks, a valuable lesson in credit control learned earlier from the Suffolk System discussed in Chapter 12. The required reserves (changed many times and now very complex, indeed) were initially copied from those developed under the National Banking System—that is, scaled by city size. Originally there was to have been a deposit insurance scheme in the Federal Reserve Act, but it had to be dropped from the legislation because of opposition from bankers.[16] After more disaster between 1929 and 1933, this idea reappears in our history as the Federal Deposit Insurance Corporation (FDIC). The original inspiration was New York's Safety Fund, established in 1829.

To please all parties, the ownership and the governance of the Federal Reserve System were, from the beginning, a hodgepodge. The national banks, with their federal charters, were forced to belong to the system. They bought the original stock in the district banks. Each national bank was to purchase Federal Reserve stock equal to 6 percent of its capital and surplus (3 percent paid in, the other 3 percent callable in the future). Each district bank was to have nine directors, three in each of three classes: Class A, representing bankers; Class B, representing business, commerce, and agriculture; and Class C, representing the "public." Class B directors could not be employees, directors, or officers of any bank. Class C directors bore the same constraints and, in addition, could not own stock in any bank. State banks were invited to join the system, keeping their state charters, or to utilize the Fed's check-clearing facilities without even joining the system.

Gluing these together was the Federal Reserve Board: seven members, originally including the secretary of the Treasury and the comptroller of the currency. The president appointed the other five members, with the advice and consent of the Senate. The terms of office were staggered to minimize the possibility that occupants of the White House could gain control over the system through appointments. Top officers of the district banks were appointed subject to approval by the Federal Reserve Board. In addition, there was to be a Federal Reserve Board "agent" in each district bank for liaison purposes. The district banks could give advice and counsel to the Board through the regularly scheduled meetings of the Federal Advisory Council.

The bankers wanted federal sponsorship without federal control, and they wanted private ownership. The Populists in Congress wanted democracy and limited private banking interest at the top. Wilson and the reformers wanted some sort of central bank. Everyone got something.

The district banks were to issue their own promissory notes against the commercial paper they purchased, which was supposed to make the currency "elastic," able to expand when commercial demand increased. But originally there was a requirement—to placate the sound money interests—that the note issues were to be "backed" by gold (originally the gold holdings were included in the "capital" accounts). The "note cover" actually lasted until 1968, having been scaled down by then to 25 percent. District bank profits in excess of 6 percent were to be split evenly with the U.S. Treasury, to be used either to pay off the national debt or to serve as a base for further greenback issues.

Those interested in "easy money" at first expressed dissatisfaction with the prospects of the new Federal Reserve notes. They wanted something as easy to create as the greenbacks had been. Just print them up and pay them out! The Federal Reserve Act was entitled:

> An act to provide for the establishment of Federal Reserve banks, to furnish an elastic currency, to afford means of rediscounting commercial paper, to establish a more effective supervision of banking, and for other purposes....

Many changes in the Fed's structure and functions were to follow. At the outset, a peculiar sort of genius obviously was needed to "find the handle," to discover how to conduct central banking operations from this strange institution. That man, Benjamin Strong, head of the New York Federal Reserve Bank, arrived on history's stage almost instantly. It was he, in the 1920s, who essentially invented the Open Market Committee and its operations.[17] By the 1970s, Federal Reserve notes, based almost exclusively upon purchases of government securities, would achieve an "elastic currency" beyond the wildest fantasies of the greenbackers. If printing more money could have solved economic problems, the Fed would have produced utopia. The year 1914 was only the faint beginning, the return of central banking after eight decades without it.[18]

INVESTMENT BANKING AND THE CAPITAL MARKET

Financial intermediation can take as many forms as there are needs for it to meet, and the varieties of institutions that can be created are almost as numerous. The system the United States finally developed is one of the most complex. In the later decades of the nineteenth century, the growing economy was facile in its ability to create the necessary structures. When the economy was growing on land speculation and agricultural commodity trade, the country developed land mortgage companies and merchant banks. When the transportation system and industrialization grew in tandem, the investment bank appeared.

The Davis Thesis

Lance Davis noticed an interesting difference between American and British experience with respect to the linkage between industrial and financial development.[19] As we have seen, in the late nineteenth and early twentieth centuries, U.S. industrialists participated in a great merger movement during which "giant enterprises" emerged. The same was not true in banking, which proliferated by replication—more and more, hundreds, thousands, of small banks. By 1900 or so, the United States had huge industrial corporations and a plethora of small commercial banks. The opposite was true in Great Britain. The British characteristically did not merge industrial firms into large organizations, but they did amalgamate their commercial banks into a small number of giant banks with numerous branches nationwide and worldwide.

Davis, a student of finance in both countries, noted the crucial link—investment banking. The American investment banker specialized in placing stocks and bonds in the hands of investors, including the thousands of small commercial banks. In Britain, small industrialists in a secondary city such as Wolverhampton or Sheffield, could go to their local branch of Lloyds, Barclays, or the Westminster Bank for all their financial needs. The bank's local branch offices could draw upon the mobilized capital of a giant system. In this way, British industrialists could raise the capital for expansion without surrendering their individual firms to amalgamation. Consequently, Britain's industrial structure consisted largely of small, family firms.

The American industrial firm in similar circumstances had no such local capital source. To raise the capital, the American firm had to create an intangible asset that could be traded elsewhere, in a major center, for capital funds. It created such intangible assets, stocks and bonds, to finance activities such as mergers. American industrialists had access to big money, but not to small. The specialized agencies for such capital-raising industrial reorganizations were the investment banking firms located in the financial centers who did business under names like J. P.

Morgan, Brown Brothers, Harriman, Kuhn-Loeb, and Kidder-Peabody.

People like Pierpont Morgan and Jakob Schiff made their careers in investment banking by merging and reorganizing railroads, mining companies, and manufacturers into firms whose prospects were bright enough for their financial paper to be marketable. Transactions costs were reduced by this intermediation. It was widely believed that the result was reduced competition in industries so organized. Thus, the American investment banking industry, logically following the Davis thesis, grew up with the American manufacturing industry and the transportation network. Big firms were made by investment bankers, and investment banking grew on the proceeds of organizing big firms. In fact, Pierpont Morgan typically insisted upon placing a "Morgan man" on the board of directors of each of his great financial reorganizations to maintain the ties.

The process can be illustrated with a single man: Andrew Carnegie. In the late 1860s, Carnegie, then a Pennsylvania Railroad official, had gone to London to raise money. It could not be done in the United States. In 1900, when Carnegie decided to sell out, he wrote his price, more than $400 million, on a piece of paper, and handed it to his boy-wonder executive, Charles Schwab, who delivered it to Pierpont Morgan. Schwab reported that Morgan merely glanced at the paper and said, "I'll take it." The result was the biggest industrial merger in history to date, United States Steel, which had two-thirds of the industry's ingot capacity, $550 million of common stock, $550 million of preferred stock, and $304 million in bonds. The American capital market, by then centered in Wall Street, had come into its own with investment bankers like Morgan filling the pilot role. It all happened in a single lifetime, in the business career of a single person, such as Carnegie or Morgan. Institutional adaptation, in this case to the remorseless fragmentation of American commercial banking, produced both high finance and big business. So Davis argues, and history seems to support him.[20]

Money and Capital Markets

Two fundamental processes were involved in the process of intermediation: collection and investment. Savers had to find advantages for concentrating their funds in a few collecting institutions, such as banks and insurance companies, before such institutions could become lenders. Borrowers, on the other hand, needed instruments and access to institutional lenders.

All intermediaries are specialized in brokering, borrowing, and lending for various lengths of time. On the short end were the banks, savings institutions, and private bankers like Morgan that took deposits. Then there were houses specializing in commercial paper that borrowed from banks and loaned to merchants. There were nonbank intermediaries, including insurance companies lending at longer term, and houses specializing in the placement of long-term securities, the investment bankers.[21]

Commercial banks, as we already know, had begun shortly after independence. Their clientele primarily was the well-to-do, and their growth in numbers and assets was prodigious.

Savings banks began in this country in 1816. They were designed to receive deposits from the poor. The early ones were organized as mutual companies, with the depositors in the role of owners, and investments were restricted to the lowest risk categories. Because their conservative investment policies provided a maximum of safety, the mutual savings banks had a reputation for soundness not shared by commercial banks. Though relatively few in number, they were in fact among the largest companies in the nation. The mutual savings banks, as a result, played a more important role in the nineteenth century as capital mobilizers than they do today. By 1910, the 628 mutual savings banks had combined assets of $3.6 billion, about a third of those held by the 7,000 national banks.[22]

Although savings and loan associations were in existence, by 1914, they had not yet begun to play the role they played later in the twentieth century. Life insurance companies also were not yet as critical a part of the capital markets as they are now, but they were large institutions by the standards of the time. Life insurance had been sold as early as the 1750s by the Presbyterian Minister's Fund of Philadelphia. A century later, sales of insurance policies had expanded to other forms. Sales of a variety of policies added to the appeal of insurance. By 1910, the insurance companies had assets of $3.9 billion, or slightly more than those of the mutual savings banks.[23] Commercial banks, mutual savings banks, and life-insurance companies were the main intermediaries of collection between 1865 and 1914. The funds of all three were available for lending.

Accumulated funds could be loaned to individuals against personal and (except for national banks) real security (mortgages). Although a large portion of any bank's business might be (and is) done in this manner, it is cumbersome compared to the use of standard financial-market instruments—commercial paper, bonds, stocks—all of which are purchased and sold by qualified specialists. Such specialized evaluation on a steady flow of securities greatly reduced transactions costs for everyone involved.

National banks could not lend against mortgages until 1914, and banks generally were wary of industrial securities until late in the nineteenth century. Organized markets for intermediation were much more efficient. Specialized businesses developed to sort out borrowers for the lenders. **Financial instruments** such as common stocks, preferred stocks, convertibles, debenture bonds, and ordinary bonds were needed that could be readily classified and placed with buyers and lenders. Investment bankers advised their clients on the best ways to borrow.

Markets for "money" (short-term loans) and "capital" (long-term loans) developed in all the major cities. But New York City, with its port, banks, and proliferation of intermediaries, became the real center of all the nation's money and capital markets by the 1870s. Wall Street centralized and dominated the country's finance.[24]

Professor Davis argues that New York's huge money market was the key. In normal times, funds poured in from country and small-town correspondents to the New York banks. Money brokers in New York were sufficiently specialized even in the eighteenth century to have agreed upon a standard scale of commissions for their services. By the mid–1820s, the New York Stock Exchange Board was in business and would dominate the other domestic money centers.[25] Dealers in long-term debts and stocks were constantly in need of short-term funds, and they formed the basis of the New York call-loan market. Funds could be employed by them on the shortest notice.

At first, few industrial shares were listed in New York. Government bonds, issued by public utility companies and railroads, predominated. Davis credits the huge revenue demands of the federal government during the Civil War with the development of investors' sophistication. Once a taste for portfolio purchases by savers developed, it could be exploited by brokers and investment bankers. By the end of the nineteenth century, industrialists, guided by Wall Street specialists, had easy access to the pooled resources of the country's savers, directly and via the intermediaries of collection. The country had a machine for the mobilization of capital. Expansion of it came through the use of the linked money and capital markets. Davis summarizes it as follows:

> The impressive gains chalked up by the markets in the thirty-five years after Appomattox were the result, in large measure, of increasing investor sophistication, the innovation of the new marketing techniques proved during the Civil War, the continued development of the call-loan markets, and the rise of the investment banking house.[26]

THE CURRENCY QUESTION

Success in the building of financial institutions was achieved in the teeth of dysfunctions in the physical supply of the medium of exchange. As we already know, the United States was launched on its career of crankiness in the matter of money when bimetallism was adopted at the beginning of the Republic's independent existence. The experiences of the antebellum period, with thousands of different kinds of (state) bank notes added to the stew, did nothing to simplify matters. Then, during the Civil War, came both greenbacks and national bank notes. From that time until 1933, the position was not stabilized. "Money" invaded politics as never before, and more than one presidential campaign was dominated by the question of what kinds of money the country *ought* to have.

What Kinds of Money?

The United States is not alone in its persistent money madness, by the way. The English version of this derangement was the centuries-long campaigns by various reformers to decimalize that wonderfully exotic old money system. Finally, in the 1960s, success came in England, and the decimal currency was fated to become the vehicle for the worst inflation in that country's history. The nineteenth-century debates caused Prime Minister Sir Robert Peel to observe in the 1840s, "The question of the currency has made more lunatics than love."

In the United States, the advantages of decimalization had been enjoyed from the beginning. Once Americans were able to get their money (coins, paper) denominated in dollars, they cut themselves free from English money: guineas, pounds, crowns, half-crowns, florins, shillings, pence, and farthings. Apart from quarters, which made possible continuation of the old two bits, four bits, and six bits, they had 100 pennies in a dollar and divisions thereof. In America, the problem was deciding what kind of *metal* should be used for the coins. What metal should be the standard?

The Constitution had said that both gold and silver were to be legal tender. That left out copper, lead, and iron. But what about representative moneys like gold and silver certificates? Should they be 100 percent "backed" by deposited precious metal? What about promissory notes of banks? Should they be "backed" by something? By what? Who should issue them? What about the pure fiat issues of the federal government? Who should control those? What parts of all this should be legal tender? What parts not?[27]

To simplify, let us return for a moment to the money question in colonial times (leaving out wampum and deerskins, for example). Debtor classes favored lots of money per capita so that wages would rise. Those who bought and sold commodities (farmers) also favored abundant money supplies, since prices might be raised and automatic capital gains accrued. However, those who had money wealth did not want profligate increases in money supplies because interest rates might fall and their incomes from moneylending might be reduced accordingly. Thus, roughly generalizing, the poor and the farmers wanted increased money supplies per capita, while those who derived income from interest wanted stable or decreased money supplies per capita.[28]

Since gold was the scarcest metal, a gold standard was favored by the wealthy. Since the most plentiful precious metal was silver, it found favor among those who gained from rising wages and prices. It follows that the latter groups also favored paper money from whatever source. Bimetallism was a compromise on the metals; reserve requirements were restrictions on paper-money issues by banks. Other limitations were favored on straight fiat issues: in the nineteenth century, greenbacks; today, Federal Reserve notes.

We might consider at this point that these conflicts have never been resolved altogether. Today, the "neo-Keynesians" represent the old inflationist interest, while the modern Monetarists represent the "sound money" interest. Now let us examine the fun and games the leaders had with the currency between 1862 and 1914.

Greenbacks and Specie Payments

The issuance of United States bank notes, "greenbacks," began in 1862, when gold was flowing out of the country and the banks and the Treasury suspended specie payments. Greenbacks were purely fiat money. There was virtually no silver in circulation in 1862, silver having been undervalued by the Currency Act of 1834. As the issues of greenbacks and national bank notes proceeded, prices zoomed upward (see Figure 19.1). The Civil War inflation set the stage for a half century of further tinkering with the currency. Those who enjoyed increased incomes from the inflation might not have wanted even more inflation, but they surely did not relish what actually happened when peace came. The postwar collapse in prices continued until about 1896, with only partial recoveries in a few cyclical episodes. There was, therefore, steady pressure for 30 years from the inflationists to *do something* to stop the deflation.

The fact that the falling prices reflected rising productivity and produced rising *real* wages and incomes was irrelevant to the inflationists. Those who wanted inflation became enthusiasts for silver and paper money. The "sound-money" interests were for gold, and they had every reason to oppose the silver and greenback interests. The recovery of prices from the late 1890s to 1914, while partially placating the forces of cheap money, came more from the increase in the supplies of gold and silver than from paper. As in the late 1840s and early 1850s, increased supplies of metals proved capable at last of raising prices.

FIGURE 19.1 Prices, 1860–1914

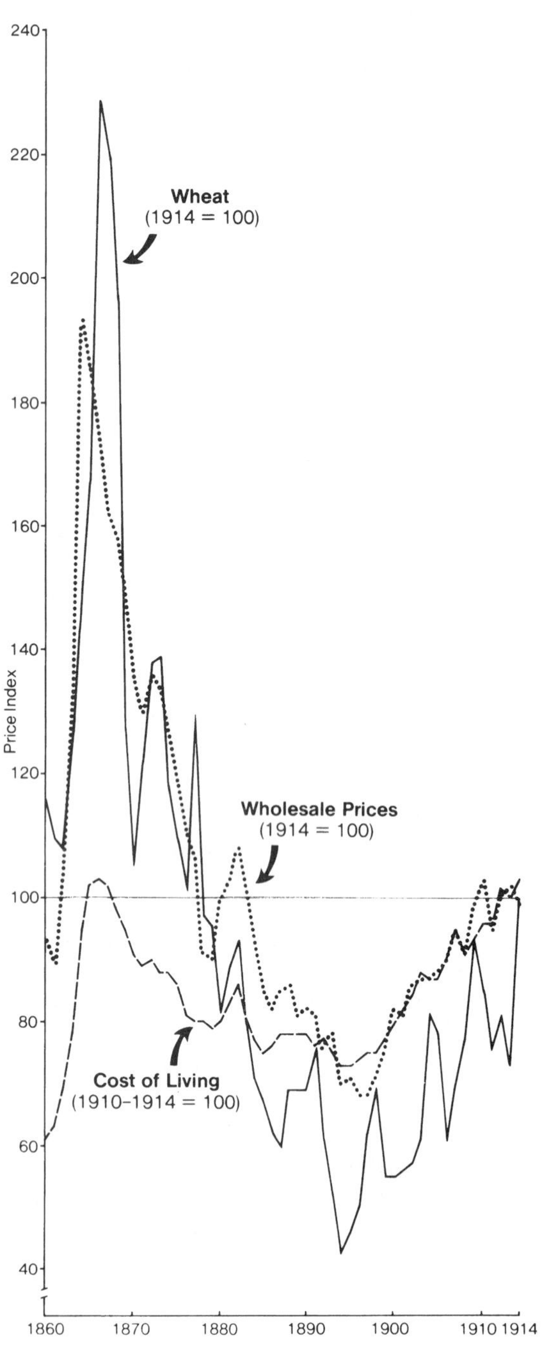

Source: *Historical Statistics*, series E 40, 52, 123, 183.

The object of successive secretaries of the Treasury, once the war ended, was a return to gold payments. Falling prices were necessary to restore the competitiveness of American exports. Therefore, paper money issues had to be constrained. Greenback issues were frozen, then reduced, and, as we have seen, national bank circulation did not expand enough to raise prices. The result was the first "money revolt," the Greenback movement, which advocated expansion of the U.S. note issues to reflate prices.[29] The Panic of 1873 produced another sharp fall in prices and more pressure to expand paper money. In 1874, however, Congress placed an upper limit on greenbacks of $382 million and the next year directed the Treasury to resume gold payments in January 1879. This action was taken after 15 years of suspension. Provision had also been made in the Funding Act of 1870 to retire greenbacks after 1870 until they reached a level of $360 million.[30] They were to be replaced by a presumed increase in the national bank notes (which did not occur until the twentieth century, in fact, as shown in Table 19.2).

The Crime of '73

Silver had been driven from circulation by the rise in gold supplies in the 1840s and 1850s.[31] The Currency Act of 1834 had set the mint ratio at 16 to 1. By 1861, 15.29 ounces of silver bought an ounce of gold (silver was $1.352 an ounce). Silver did not circulate because it was worth more as bullion than as coins. By the early 1870s, as the impact of the California and Australia gold rushes began to wane, the bullion content of each dollar was $1.0312; thus silver still did not circulate. The Coinage Act in 1873 omitted any provision for the resumption of the minting of silver dollars. As a result, the U.S. Treasury had been forced to print paper money in fractions of one dollar to provide a circulating medium.

When the western silver discoveries occurred, output soared, and, by 1874, it took 16.7 ounces of silver to buy an ounce of gold. On the market, silver was down to $1.292 an ounce. The silver producers wanted the subsidy restored. The 1873 Coinage Act, which withdrew the fixed mint silver price, became known as the "Crime of '73," and a new politico-economic force was born, curiously called **free silver**, which sought a restoration of silver's former position. It was "curious" because taking silver off the market was defined as "freedom." It was argued that silver purchases by the mint would raise the quantity of money and, hence, prices. The inflationists had a new target for legislation, the return of the Treasury silver purchases to the mint par of 1834. President Hayes vetoed legislation in 1877 to restore the subsidy, but Congress passed the legislation over his veto a year later.

The Bland-Allison Act of 1878

The Bland-Allison Act also offered something for everyone. It produced what Studenski and Krooss called the "limping standard," not fully bimetallic, but not anything else either.[32] Under the 1878 Act, the Treasury was to purchase $2 million to $4 million of silver a month but *at the current market price*. On the other hand, the silver was to be coined into dollars weighing 412.5 grains (troy ounce = 480 grains), 371.25 grains of which were 0.9 fine (pure) silver. This was the silver dollar weight of the old coin under the Act of 1834: $20.67 worth of silver dollars would buy an ounce of gold at the U.S. mint. Moreover, the silver dollars were full legal tender; however, if they were exchanged for silver certificates ($10 and up), the certificates were not legal tender for private transactions. Banks, for example, would obviously refuse to accept them.

The cry had gone up before 1878 that silver had been "demonetized" because the Treasury could refuse to buy it beyond the needs for coinage. After the Bland-Allison Act, the Treasury was committed to buying silver for coins. The silver flowed in, and the gold flowed out. Prices still fell, and the Treasury was blamed for not buying enough silver at a high enough price. Under Bland-Allison, the price was the market price. By the 1880s, other groups, known collectively as the Populists, came out for restoration of the old price, 16 to 1. They hoped that raising the price of silver might raise the price of other things too, like corn and hogs and cotton.[33]

The Sherman Silver Purchase Act of 1890

Despite the purchase of 291.3 million ounces under the Bland-Allison Act, the price of silver had fallen by 1890 to 93 cents an ounce on the market, and the Treasury had more than $380 million of the white metal in storage. Other prices had not recovered, and the silverites, greenbackers, Populists, and other inflationists were demanding firmer action.

In return for Western votes to support the McKinley tariff (high restrictive duties), the Senate came through with the Sherman Silver Purchase Act of 1890. It doubled the monthly purchase rates—the silver was to be purchased with Treasury notes of 1890, which then could be turned in to the Treasury for gold bullion or coins. As long as silver prices kept falling, it paid to sell silver for Treasury notes, buy gold, use it to buy silver, and then trade it for Treasury notes.

By 1893, when the Sherman Act was repealed because of President Cleveland's urgent appeals to Congress ("Financial distrust and fear have sprung up on every side"), the Treasury's gold reserves were well below the $100-million minimum, a dangerously low level.[34] Reserves continued to decline under balance-of-payments pressures. The government resorted to bond sales. Finally in 1895, President Cleveland went to Wall Street and the investment bankers for aid.[35]

A syndicate was formed by Pierpont Morgan, August Belmont, and others to market U.S. bonds in Europe for gold. The syndicate succeeded temporarily, but a great scandal resulted. Popular opinion considered it disgraceful that the U.S. government should have to turn to private investment bankers for aid. After six months, gold began flowing out again, and Morgan offered to repeat the exercise. President Cleveland instead went back to direct bond sales to the public for gold. The bonds were favorably priced. The public traded in notes for gold and bought the bonds. Had the Treasury refused to give gold for the notes, the silverites would have succeeded in forcing the government away from gold and on to silver.

The balance of payments turned around in late 1896, and gold began flowing back in, relieving the crisis. The Treasury had been through eight years of chaos, several times far below their own minimum gold reserve.

Silver advocates had demanded a restoration of the silver price to 16 to 1 (16 ounces of silver at $1.292 an ounce equals 1 ounce of gold at $20.67 an ounce). By 1896, silver was down to 69 cents an ounce, or nearly 30 to 1. That summer, William Jennings Bryan won the Democratic nomination, uniting all the inflationists behind his "Cross of Gold" speech. It was a wonderfully effective speech, but McKinley won the election, and the forces of gold, "sound money," were on the march.[36] Under the Bland-Allison and Sherman acts, the Treasury had purchased more than $500 million of silver. Now, with the balance of payments in surplus, gold flowing in again, and prices on the rise with the advance of business prosperity, it was the sound money people who had their turn at bat.

The Gold Standard Act of 1900

In 1900, after several abortive attempts, Congress passed the Currency Act, or Gold Standard Act, putting the country legally on the pure gold standard. The dollar was defined as 25.8 grains of 0.9 fine gold. A reserve of $150 million in gold coin was to be set aside for ultimate redemption of the greenbacks and the 1890 Treasury notes. The minimum capital requirements for national banks was reduced to $25,000 in cities of less than 3,000 population, and national banks were authorized to issue notes equal to the par value of deposited bonds. The result was a surge in national bank formation.

Gold continued to flow in, and the currency remained mainly metallic. Then came the panic of 1907, the National Monetary Commission, and the formation of the Federal Reserve System with its new Federal Reserve notes, yet another kind of money.

Epilogue: 1933 and Silver Again

Despite all the jiggering and tinkering, the system crashed again between 1929 and 1933, worse than ever before. Among the new "solutions" came one last blast from the Populist silver "crazies." The market price of silver by 1933 was down to 43 cents an ounce, and the government was raising the price of gold by 69 percent to $35 an ounce. To pacify the Populists, President Roosevelt ordered the Treasury to buy silver again. In June, the Silver Purchase Act of 1933 was passed, which directed the Treasury to buy silver until its holdings equaled 25 percent of the gold stock, or until the market price reached $1.29 an ounce.

Gold poured into the United States as war clouds threatened in Europe and Asia. By 1939, another billion ounces of silver had been purchased by the U.S. Treasury (draining the world's monetary system of the metal), and the price was still 43 cents an ounce in the market. World War II, photography, electronics (providing a huge industrial use), together with inflation, finally "did something for silver." Monetary stocks disappeared from central banks and were melted off the coins. By early 1980, silver was at an all-time peak: $50 an ounce, when the Hunt brothers cornered the market.[37] The U.S. Treasury had purchased more than 460,000 *tons* of it between 1792 and 1939, largely in vain.

WHAT DID THE POPULISTS WANT?

Throughout these dramatic monetary struggles, life went on, and the business cycle continued its course. During the great financial crises, banks closed, railroads went bankrupt, factories shut down, and millions lost their jobs. These events gave rise to labor radicalism and to grave dissatisfaction with the free market's way of producing long-run growth. John James has determined that the increased severity of business cycles in the postbellum period cannot be attributed to increasingly severe shocks; the cause is increased monetary disturbances, whether through the money multiplier, the stock of high-powered money, or money demand.[38] The depression of the 1890s was very severe—the bread lines were long—and a great change occurred. People began to say that the *federal government* had responsibility for the country's economic welfare, and they began to organize on that basis. The largest organization was the People's Party, the Populists, those who had been campaigning for increased government involvement on a number of fronts.

The involvement of the Populists in new regulatory innovations (e.g., the Interstate Commerce Act of 1887 and the Sherman Antitrust Act of 1890) has been discussed in previous chapters. All the currency and banking changes discussed in this chapter were overt attempts by the federal government to intervene in the economy, consistent with the Populists' platform. Despite stout disclaimers from the president on down, many people had noticed that pensions for soldiers, subsidies to shipbuilders and operators, subsidies and special favors to railroads, and tariffs to protect manufacturers from foreign competition, all federal government money and/or power, could produce economic activity and jobs where the market, if left alone, would not. The arrival of "Coxey's Army" of the unemployed in Washington in April 1894, with its demands for massive federal expenditures, produced legislative attempts to print money for direct relief. President Cleveland was appalled, but the point was clear. If the federal power could be used to aid railroad magnates and manufacturers, it could be used for the poor as well. In the depression of the 1890s, a *very different* future was beginning to appear.

After the Panic of 1907, Congress made one last effort to solve economic problems exclusively by fooling with the money and reforming the banks—it created the Federal Reserve System. The 1921 recession was too short to test the new system, but, in 1933, it became clear that "monetary reform" alone would no longer satisfy those who were left destitute by the cyclical downturns. The New Deal would finally legislate much of the Populist platform into being.

The discussion of financial developments in this chapter completes the final piece needed to address a much broader question: What did the Populists want? The Populists were not revolutionaries in the sense that they wanted to overturn the settlement of 1789. They stayed within the bounds of the federal Constitution, for it was a source of *power*.[39] However, they wanted its substantive content very considerably altered.

For example, the Populists wanted a more direct democracy at the federal level. They demanded that the state legislatures be stripped of their powers to appoint the members of the U.S. Senate. By that reasoning, all government (except the federal courts) would be subject to the forces of direct popular democracy. There was to be no area reserved for an establishment based upon economic power and (local) influence. All must be subject to the ballot at regular elections.

Their demand for a secret ballot reinforced the idea of the greater influence of popular democracy. The corrupt practices of the rising urban political machines would be curbed by their inability to monitor the actual votes cast. It was, no doubt, naive to suppose that a secret ballot cast among competing office-seekers would by itself produce good government, but at least bad governments would be more freely chosen.

Women's suffrage was part of the same package—political advantage—which, in addition, would eliminate the obvious disenfranchisement of half the population as things stood. The same could be said of the sympathetic statements in the Populist platforms favoring the cause of labor. The demand for improved public education can probably also be considered basically political. Education was the obvious ladder to success in public service, and, at the turn of the century, the proportion of people who graduated from high school was very small (only 7 percent in 1900). Without a broader educational system, the way was barred to all but a small portion of the children of the poor.

These political demands ultimately were met, and, if it cannot be shown that the quality of American political life was improved thereby, at least it can be argued that bad politics does not now come from lack of opportunity to vote. Likewise, functionally illiterate, modern high-school graduates are not the product of a public education system that *cannot* matriculate and educate the children of the poor. If it *does not*, that is a different matter.

Economic Demands

The Populists' economic demands were a straightforward attempt to use the federal power for income and wealth redistribution. The Populists clearly saw that this already had been accomplished—for industry, by the tariff; for railroads, by subsidies; for corporations, by the courts and legislatures. Inequitable outcomes in the free market were only partially responsible for generating the Populist rage.

Although most extreme Populist demands were never met, they are interesting in their own right:

1. *Abolition of the national banking system.* These federally chartered banks were objects of scorn and hatred because they had not expanded their operations (loans) as the country grew, and, in any case, they systematically discriminated against agriculture by refusing to make mortgage loans on farm real estate. State bank note issues had been taxed out of existence to assure the success of the national bank issues. The national banks were of little help, and possibly much disadvantage, to the Populists.

2. *Nationalization of the railroads and telegraph system.* Railroad and telegraph companies had been the

beneficiaries of government power: rights of way, eminent domain, special franchise monopolies on routes, subsidies of every kind. They were prime cases, from the Populist viewpoint, of abuse of privilege. These businesses were placed under federal regulation, not nationalized. From the Populist viewpoint, the "private" character of these enterprises was a joke.

3. *Prohibition of subsidies to corporations.* No legislature then or since has been found that could meet this demand. Corporations are groups of people whose capital has been intermingled. It makes no sense for government to grant subsidies to single individuals and not to groups. The U.S. Supreme Court's 1886 decision that corporations were individual persons was one of several reasons why this demand, by the end of the 1880s, was unrealistic. Had it been met at the federal level, the subsequent history of the United States could not have occurred. The Commodity Credit Corporation, COMSAT, and the Chrysler Corporation, not to mention the entire aircraft and defense industries, all are monuments to federal subsidization of corporations.

4. *No alien or corporate ownership of land or natural resources.* This was nativism, atavism, *and* early-day environmentalism. The point was that the land should be reserved for farming and conservation. "The land, including all the natural resources of wealth, is the heritage of the people." There are still rumblings on these two issues, including lawsuits in California to restrict the water rights of each farm to the original 160-acre homestead. Foreign owners of American land are widely held to be odious, as in the past.

What ultimately would become the concern of ecologists and environmentalists was not invented for the Populist Party platforms. The Desert Land Act of 1877 and the Timber and Stone Act of 1878 were the beginnings of an effort to "put something back" into the environment as part of the settlement process. By 1868, the people of California already had withdrawn Yosemite from private ownership, and Yellowstone Park was set aside by the federal government in 1872. It is easy now, as we shall see shortly, for us to view the Populist movement as a massive forerunner of modern special-interest politics. However, the Populists also professed deep concerns of a general nature that would in time find broad support in the nation's policies. For example, they recognized that public health measures based on the emerging germ theory of disease would protect workers, poor and rich alike.[40] The picture drawn of the Populist as a "dumb hayseed" is an elitist caricature.

Closer to Home

Where the Populists' demands were narrowly concerned with their own economic interests, we find a model of politics to come. The Populist program was camouflaged by a series of charges against the existing order—big monopolistic (but not small entrepreneurial) business, corruption in the courts and in the legislatures, and the accumulation of "colossal fortunes" therefrom. According to the Populists, "from the same prolific womb of governmental injustice we breed two great classes—paupers and millionaires." Such rhetoric was necessary because the Populist demands were couched in the language of reform. For a reform to take place, something has to be improved, and what the Populists proposed to improve was their share of the national income.

One such "improvement" was currency reform. There were essentially two kinds of currency demands, both for a "commodity money." The various silver proposals were part of that issue. The Populist campaigns of the late 1880s and early 1890s came near the end of the long period of declining prices. The Populists knew that the money stock had to grow as fast as real output, other things being equal, or else prices would fall. The greenback issues were frozen; the national banks had not increased their note issues. The 1878 Silver Purchase Act had been insufficient, and the Populists wanted the Treasury to purchase more silver with new money. Otherwise, the only hope for an increased money supply was gold, which was favored by the Eastern hard-money people but viewed as a dim prospect by the Populists. Hence, they came up with the "sub-Treasury scheme," which would utilize agricultural output to increase the supply of money.

The "sub-Treasury scheme" called for the establishment of regional Treasury offices in farm areas. At harvest time farmers could either sell their crops to the government or use them as collateral for government loans. The Treasury would print new money to be used for these transactions. Crops would thus produce new money. Agricultural prices would no longer be depressed at harvest time, and farmers' incomes would benefit accordingly. The scheme was not adopted until 1933, when the Commodity Credit Corporation was innovated to do this job for the farmers, using the more conveniently "elastic" Federal Reserve notes. It didn't solve the farm problem.

The absence of a secure lending source for agricultural mortgages was to be met in the same way, by direct government loans on farm mortgages. This method would bypass the existing banks and mortgage companies and increase the money supply in the bargain. This scheme was adopted in 1916 when the Farm Loan Act established the Federal Land Banks to make loans on farm mortgages, the first of many federal efforts to come in this service. By 1981, farm organizations were petitioning the government to stop the land banks from foreclosing defaulted mortgages. Even though the land bank system had helped some farmers enormously, it also failed to solve the farm problem.

An interesting forerunner of modern Monetarism was the Populist demand that the currency supply be maintained by the Treasury at $50 per head of population (it is now about $200 per head). The idea was to insure against falling prices, and the Populists were firm "quantity theory" advocates, if nothing else. They, like the Greenbackers before them and hosts of others later on, knew that rising farm incomes—prices times quantities—could not be guaranteed unless the general level of money demand could be kept abreast of farm output. They supposed that an arbitrary sum of currency per head would be some assurance against a continued decline in farm prices as output soared.

As we saw in Chapter 15, it was not just the decline in farm prices that rankled the Populists but also their (often erroneous) belief that they were worse off than others; that farm prices had fallen more than other prices; that their terms of trade against industrial goods, transportation costs, and interest rates had worsened. Since this situation was due in part to the farmers' own prodigious energies in production, which they did not intend to cut back, the way out was to use government power to raise demand.

For the next century, there would be countless efforts by aggrieved groups of "losers" in American society to do the same thing. By the 1970s, it would be widely complained that special-interest politics in the nation's capital was sandbagging Congress, keeping it from governing wisely. The Populists were truly people of our time—a century early.

NOTES

1. Hugh Rockoff, "Varieties of Banking and Regional Economic Development in the United States, 1840–1860," *JEH*, March 1975.
2. *Report of the National Monetary Commission* (Washington, D.C.: United States Government Printing Office, 1912), pp. 28–29.
3. A million dollars borrowed in year T_1 for one year had to be repaid in year T_2, when additional borrowing also was required. Ideally, the Treasury would borrow as far forward as possible, at least shifting the problem of repayment to a period when money would be the only problem.
4. Paul Studenski and Herman Krooss, *Financial History of the United States* (1952), Table 20, p. 156.
5. In *Veazie Bank v. Fenno* (1869) the scheme was declared constitutional by the Supreme Court.
6. Studenski and Krooss (1952), pp. 178–179.
7. From 1863 to 1907, 449 national banks failed; 2,000 state banks passed into oblivion in the same period. Of the national bank failures, 80 percent of their debts were satisfied (*Ibid.*, p. 248).
8. A recent discussion can be found in George Selgin and Lawrence White, "Monetary Reform and the Redemption of National Bank Notes, 1863–1913," *BHR*, Summer 1994.
9. *Ibid.*, pp. 178–181.
10. Richard Grossman, "The Macroeconomic Consequences of Bank Failures under the National Banking System," *EEH*, July 1993.
11. Jon Moen and Ellis Tallman, "Clearinghouse Membership and Deposit Contraction during the Panic of 1907," *Journal of Economic History*, vol. 60, no. 1, March 2000, argues that New York and Chicago banks that were

members of a clearinghouse had smaller contractions than nonmember banks, a fact that generated support for the Federal Reserve Act.

12. Some economists also believe that financial crises are the mere epiphenomena of more deep-seated imbalances. The evidence shows no clear tendency toward either monetary or nonmonetary causation alone. It has been a mixed bag. Michael Bordo, "The Impact and International Transmission of Financial Crises: Some Historical Evidence, 1870–1933," *Rivista di Storia Economica*, 1985.
13. Jonathan Hughes, *The Vital Few* (1986), pp. 439–453.
14. For details on the background and genesis of the resulting Federal Reserve System, see Robert Craig West, *Banking Reform and the Federal Reserve 1863–1923* (1977).
15. Kerry Odell and David Weiman, "Metropolitan Development, Regional Financial Centers, and the Founding of the Fed in the Lower South," *Journal of Economic History*, vol. 58, no. 1, March 1998.
16. For an analysis of the Act, Studenski and Krooss (1952), pp. 258–262. The standard history is H. Parker Willis, *The Federal Reserve System: Legislation, Organization, and Functions* (New York: Ronald Press, 1923).
17. Elmus Wicker, *Federal Reserve Policy 1912–1933* (1966); S. V. O. Clarke, *Central Bank Cooperation, 1924–31* (New York: Federal Reserve Bank of New York, 1968).
18. The idea that the Fed was the inexorable outcome of developing corporate capitalism is set out in James Livingston, *Origins of the Federal Reserve System: Money, Class, and Corporate Capitalism* (Ithaca: Cornell University Press, 1986).
19. Lance Davis, "Capital Immobilities and Finance Capitalism: A Study of Economic Evolution in the United States," *EEH*, Fall 1963.
20. Since power over banking in the United States remained with the states, local interests prevailed. See Charles Calomiris, *U.S. Bank Deregulation in Historical Perspective* (2000).
21. Margaret Myers, *The New York Money Market* (1931), vol. I; John James, "The Development of a National Money Market, 1893–1911," *JEH*, December 1976.
22. Lance Davis, Duncan McDougall, and Jonathan Hughes, *American Economic History: The Development of a National Economy*, 3rd ed., (Homewood, IL: Irwin, 1969), p. 203; Alan Olmstead, "Investment Constraints and New York City Mutual Savings Bank Financing of Antebellum Development," *JEH*, December 1972, on the consequences of restrictions on investments by savings banks.
23. Davis (1969), p. 203.
24. Robert Sobel, *The Big Board: A History of the New York Stock Market* (1965).
25. Kenneth Snowden, "American Stock Market Development and Performance, 1871–1929," *EEH*, October 1987; and "Historical Returns and Security Market Development, 1872–1925," *EEH*, October 1990.
26. Davis (1969), pp. 215–216. Also, Richard Sylla, "Federal Policy, Banking Market Structure, and Capital Mobilization in the United States, 1863–1913," *JEH*, December 1969. The need for investment banking intermediation was no doubt increased by the lack of interstate branch banking, which helped to maintain regional interest rate differentials. Lance Davis, "The Investment Market, 1870–1914: The Evolution of a National Market," *JEH*, September 1965.
27. For two excellent older works covering this material in detail, see A.B. Hepburn, *History of Currency in the United States* (1924), and Davis Dewey, *Financial History of the United States* (1934). Hepburn is particularly good on the madcap consequences of the Sherman Silver Purchase Act.
28. As we will discuss below, one of the Populist demands was for a fixed amount of money ($50) per capita. This idea is still around in current Monetarist thought, although it has been changed to a matching of monetary and population *growth rates*.
29. Irwin Unger, *The Greenback Era* (1964).
30. Numbers in this section from Studenski and Krooss (1952), chap. 16.
31. In fact, we might argue that from the 1850s on, the United States really was no longer on a bimetallic standard. David Martin, "1853: The End of Bi-metallism in the United States," *JEH*, December 1973. See also Milton Friedman, "The Crime of 1873," *JPE*, December 1990. Friedman argues that most of the decline in prices that characterized the remainder of the nineteenth century could have been avoided had a strict bimetallism been retained.
32. Studenski and Krooss (1952), p. 190; see also Milton Friedman and Anna Schwartz, *A Monetary History of the United States* (1963), pp. 113–119 on silver and the currency.
33. In an article in which he analyzes Congressional votes, Jeffry Frieden argues that higher constituent debt levels were not necessarily associated with opposition to gold, while mining and agricultural production levels were. Frieden concludes that the debate was as much about the effect of the exchange rate on relative prices as it was about the inflation of the absolute price level. See Frieden, "Monetary Populism in Nineteenth-Century America: An Open Economy Interpretation," *Journal of Economic History*, vol. 57, no. 2, June 1997.
34. Studenski and Krooss (1952), p. 219.
35. Matthew Simon, "The Morgan-Belmont Syndicate of 1895 and Intervention in the Foreign-Exchange Market," *BHR*, Winter 1968.
36. An interesting discussion of this episode can be found in Hugh Rockoff, "The 'Wizard of Oz' as a Monetary Allegory," *JPE*, August 1990.

37. By January 1980, silver approached $50 an ounce after a spectacular run-up from $5 an ounce in the previous 12 months. Bunker and Nelson Hunt, the Texas oil millionaires, played a vital role in this boom before it collapsed.
38. John James, "Changes in Economic Instability in 19th-Century America," *AER*, September 1993.
39. The following discussion comes largely from the appendices of John Hicks, *The Populist Revolt* (1931).
40. See Robert Higgs, *Transformation of the American Economy, 1865–1914* (1971), pp. 36–39. Barbara Rosenkrantz, *Public Health and the State* (1972) discusses how both science and Massachusetts politics changed between 1842 and 1936.

SUGGESTED READINGS

Articles

Bordo, Michael D. "The Impact and International Transmission of Financial Crises: Some Historical Evidence, 1870–1933." *Rivista Di Storia Economica*, International issue, 2nd series, vol. 2, 1985.

Davis, Lance E. "Capital Immobilities and Finance Capitalism: A Study of Economic Evolution in the United States." *Explorations in Entrepreneurial History*, vol. 1, no. 1, Fall 1963.

———. "The Investment Market, 1870–1914: The Evolution of a National Market." *Journal of Economic History*, vol. 25, no. 3, September 1965.

Friedman, Milton. "The Crime of 1873." *Journal of Political Economy*, vol. 98, no. 6, December 1990.

Grossman, Richard S. "The Macroeconomic Consequences of Bank Failures under the National Banking System." *Explorations in Economic History*, vol. 30, no. 3, July 1993.

James, John A. "The Development of a National Money Market, 1893–1911." *Journal of Economic History*, vol. 33, no. 4, December 1976.

———. "Cost Functions of Post-bellum National Banks." *Explorations in Economic History*, vol. 15, no. 2, April 1978.

———. "Public Debt Management Policy and Nineteenth-Century American Economic Growth." *Explorations in Economic History*, vol. 21, no. 2, April 1984.

———. "Changes in Economic Instability in 19th-Century America." *American Economic Review*, vol. 83, no. 4, September 1993.

Martin, David. "1853: The End of Bimetallism in the United States." *Journal of Economic History*, vol. 33, no. 4, December 1973.

Olmstead, Alan L. "Investment Constraints and New York City Mutual Savings Bank Financing of Antebellum Development." *Journal of Economic History*, vol. 32, no. 4, December 1972.

Rockoff, Hugh. "Varieties of Banking and Regional Economic Development in the United States, 1840–1860." *Journal of Economic History*, vol. XXXV, no. 1, March 1975.

———. "The 'Wizard of Oz' as a Monetary Allegory." *Journal of Political Economy*, vol. 98, no. 4, August 1990.

Selgin, George, and Lawrence White. "Monetary Reform and the Redemption of National Bank Notes, 1863–1913." *Business History Review*, vol. 68, no. 2, Summer 1994.

Simon, Matthew. "The Morgan-Belmont Syndicate of 1895 and Intervention in the Foreign Exchange Market." *Business History Review*, vol. 42, no. 4, Winter 1968.

Smiley, Gene. "Interest Rate Movements in the United States, 1888–1913." *Journal of Economic History*, vol. XXXV, no. 3, September 1975.

Snowden, Kenneth A. "American Stock Market Development and Performance, 1871–1929." *Explorations in Economic History*, vol. 24, no. 4, October 1987.

———. "Historical Returns and Security Market Development, 1872–1925." *Explorations in Economic History*, vol. 27, no. 4, October 1990.

Spencer, Austin H. "Relative Downward Industrial Price Flexibility, 1870–1921." *Explorations in Economic History*, vol. 14, no. 1, January 1977.

Sushka, Marie Elizabeth, and W. Brian Barrett. "Banking Structure and the National Capital Market, 1869–1914." *Journal of Economic History*, vol. XLIV, no. 2, June 1984.

Sylla, Richard. "Federal Policy, Banking Market Structure, and Capital Mobilization in the United States, 1863–1913." *Journal of Economic History*, vol. 29, no. 2, December 1969.

———. "American Banking and Growth in the Nineteenth Century: A Partial View of the Terrain." *Explorations in Economic History*, vol. 9, no. 2, Winter 1971–1972.

Williamson, Jeffrey G. "Watersheds and Turning Points: Conjectures on the Long-Term Impact of Civil War Financing," *Journal of Economic History*, vol. XXXIV, no. 3, September 1974.

Wimmer, Larry T. "The Gold Crisis of 1869: Stabilizing or Destabilizing Speculation Under Floating Exchange Rates?" *Explorations in Economic History*, vol. 12, no. 2, April 1975.

Books

Calomiris, Charles. *U.S. Bank Deregulation in Historical Perspective.* New York: Cambridge University Press, 2000.

Davis, Lance, and Robert Gallman. *Evolving Financial Markets and International Capital Flows: Britain, The Americas, and Australia: 1865–1914.* New York: Cambridge University Press, 2000.

Dewey, Davis R. *Financial History of the United States.* New York: Longmans, Green, 1934.

Friedman, Milton, and Anna J. Schwartz. *A Monetary History of the United States 1867–1960.* Princeton: Princeton University Press, 1963.

Hepburn, A. Barton. *History of Currency in the United States.* New York: Macmillan, 1924.

Hicks, John D. *The Populist Revolt.* Minneapolis: The University of Minnesota Press, 1931.

Higgs, Robert. *Transformation of the American Economy, 1865–1914.* New York: Wiley, 1971.

Hughes, Jonathan. *The Vital Few: American Economic Progress and Its Protagonists.* New York: Oxford University Press, 1986.

James, John. *Money and Capital Markets in Postbellum America.* Princeton: Princeton University Press, 1978.

Myers, Margaret. *The New York Money Market.* New York: Columbia University Press, 1931.

Rosenkrantz, Barbara G. *Public Health and the State: Changing Views in Massachusetts, 1842–1936.* Cambridge: Harvard University Press, 1972.

Sobel, Robert. *The Big Board: A History of the New York Stock Market.* New York: Free Press, 1965.

Studenski, Paul, and Herman Krooss. *Financial History of the United States.* New York: McGraw-Hill, 1952.

Unger, Irwin. *The Greenback Era.* Princeton: Princeton University Press, 1964.

West, Robert Craig. *Banking Reform and the Federal Reserve 1863–1923.* Ithaca: Cornell University Press, 1977.

Wicker, Elmus. *Federal Reserve Policy 1917–1933.* New York: Random House, 1966.

CHAPTER TWENTY

The Giant Economy and Its International Relations

Unlike the other industrializing nations of the late nineteenth century, America was not as heavily dependent upon overseas markets for its economic growth. Most European countries commonly relied upon exports for 20 to 30 percent of the sales of their domestic output, and they imported similar proportions of the goods and commodities used in domestic production and consumption. Comparative advantage thus counted heavily for the Europeans in their efforts to raise living standards by specialization in production. The British had to import textile raw materials, the French, fuel, in order to operate their factories. Proportionately, the United States depended far less on trade.

Throughout the period from the 1820s to the 1920s, U.S. exports were only 6 to 7 percent of GNP. The proportion slowly declined over time; in colonial times the ratios were far higher, 20 to 30 percent in the late 1720s and 10 to 15 percent between 1790 and 1800.[1] Because the raw-material wealth of the interior continental United States was being exploited during the westward movement, Americans needed little beyond exotic (mainly tropical) products and very specialized manufactured imports. However, in certain industries, imports and exports figured more prominently. For example, about 20 percent of agricultural output went to the foreign market, and imports of items like diamonds, coffee, tea, spices, and high-grade china and cut glass dominated some parts of domestic trade.

We should not infer, however, that U.S. foreign trade was unimportant to Americans. Its true value to Americans, since they *did* want to buy foreign wares, was the same as with other marketable goods and services—the *opportunity cost.* If Americans insisted upon drinking tea and coffee and could not import those commodities, the cost to Americans to produce them with American land, labor, and capital would have been very high indeed. Similarly, had American farmers been unable to export 20 percent of their output, their troubles in the postbellum era would have been far worse than they were. Americans had an enhanced standard of life, as did all their trading partners, because of foreign trade. The great difference between the United States and the other industrializing countries was the extent of self-sufficiency.

TRENDS IN TRADE AND PAYMENTS

Over time, each nation—as a result of technological advance and changes in factor proportions—experiences a slow but certain change in comparative advantage. Technological change itself, by redefining the factors of production, changes the factor proportions. Even a Caribbean island that grows nothing but bananas for export may find itself able, because of modern transportation, to export its climate and scenery (especially in wintertime) in the form of a tourist industry. As a result, it will put a smaller proportion of its resources into bananas and a larger proportion into hotels. The island may end up even *importing bananas*, if it is more profitable for all the local labor force to work in hotels and buy bananas from a less fortunate isle.

Changes in U.S. Trade Composition

In Table 20.1, we can see the way comparative advantage shifted from the early nineteenth century through the 1920s—away from agriculture in favor of manufacturing. On the export side the proportion of finished manufactures rose as the country's industrialization proceeded. On the import side the proportion of crude materials rose dramatically as that of finished manufactured goods declined. Exports of food as a proportion of the total peaked toward the end of the nineteenth century. The increase in agricultural protectionism on the European continent played a role in the relative decline of food exports after that.

Although food imports also slowly declined as a proportion of the total, that decline was not a function of U.S. agricultural protectionism. Americans mainly imported tropical and exotic foods that could not be grown in their own country.[2] Demand for imports of tropical and exotic foods, subject to Engel's Law, soon grew less rapidly than did the demand for other imports.

TABLE 20.1 Structure of U.S. Trade[a]

	Crude Materials		*Crude Foodstuffs*		*Manufactured Foodstuffs*	
Years	*Exports*	*Imports*	*Exports*	*Imports*	*Exports*	*Imports*
1821	60.5	4.5	4.8	11.1	19.5	19.7
1851–1860	61.7	9.6	6.6	11.7	15.4	15.4
1881–1890	35.9	21.3	18.0	15.4	25.3	17.8
1901–1910	31.0	34.0	10.6	11.9	20.1	12.1
1921–1930	26.0	37.1	8.5	11.8	11.8	11.4

[a] Figures given are percentages of total U.S. trade.

Source: Lance E. Davis et al., *American Economic History: The Development of a National Economy* (Homewood, IL: Irwin, 1969), Tables 16–3A, B.

TABLE 20.2 Expansion of U.S. Trade[a]

	Total		*Crude Materials*		*Crude Foodstuffs*		*Manufactured Foodstuffs*	
Years	*Exports*	*Imports*	*Exports*	*Imports*	*Exports*	*Imports*	*Exports*	*Imports*
1820	$ 52	$ 55	$ 31	$ 3	$ 2	$ 6	$ 10	$ 11
1851–1860	232	274	143	27	15	33	36	44
1891–1900	1,006	763	296	202	183	129	256	130
1921–1930	4,499	3,742	1,165	1,387	360	445	528	423

[a] Figures given are mean annual rates in millions of dollars.

Source: Lance E. Davis et al., *American Economic History: The Development of a National Economy* (Homewood, IL: Irwin, 1969), Tables 16–3A, B.

Expansion

The figures in Table 20.1 reflect the proportions of a rapidly expanding total trade. In value terms, we see the numbers in Table 20.2. The growth was extraordinary—in one century, exports increased by a factor of 86 and imports by a factor of 68. But, as we have already noted, these increases actually were slightly *slower* than the economy's rate of growth overall. It was in some ways a peculiarity of the American economy in this epoch that its long-run elasticity of imports relative to GNP declined; therefore, its *average propensity to import*, the percentage change in imports relative to GNP, declined. The reason was the long period of relative self-sufficiency of the United States in most raw materials, together with the extraordinary expansion of the economy as industrialization proceeded. The pattern continued until the post-World War II period, when imports of petroleum skyrocketed, and imports of finished manufactures rose again to nineteenth-century proportions. (This dramatic turn of events is covered in Chapter 30). For the late nineteenth century and the first half of the twentieth century, the demand for foreign goods declined relatively as domestic income expanded, as population soared, and as the competitive economy produced the American industrial revolution.

Semimanufactures		*Finished Manufactures*	
Exports	*Imports*	*Exports*	*Imports*
9.4	7.4	5.7	56.8
4.0	12.5	12.3	40.5
5.2	14.8	15.6	30.8
12.8	17.2	25.6	24.8
13.3	18.2	40.8	21.4

Semimanufactures		*Finished Manufactures*	
Exports	*Imports*	*Exports*	*Imports*
$ 5	$ 4	$ 3	$ 31
9	36	29	156
82	106	190	197
600	686	1,916	801

U.S. Share of World Trade

Even though its average propensity to import fell, from the mid-nineteenth century onward, the United States occupied a share of world trade disproportionately large compared to American population. This pattern would be expected in the case of a rich and growing economy with its doors generally open to trade. Some relevant data are shown in Table 20.3.

Only in the case of imports of manufactures did the U.S. share of world trade rise substantially more than did its share of world population. At first this result might seem paradoxical. After all, it was *exports* of manufactures that rose the most rapidly in the country's trade accounts. But per-capita incomes also rose powerfully as the U.S. economy developed.

Manufactured goods are not subject to Engel's law, and, *because of their variety*, they are not really subject to the tendency toward **diminishing marginal utility** (the reduction of satisfaction derived from an additional unit of a good). In the classic example, diminishing marginal utility results from the acquisition of additional units of goods the consumer already owns. In the case of an economy with an endless variety of manufactured goods, boredom hardly applies—as today's economy so well demonstrates. Rising imports of manufactures, logically enough, characterize economies with rising per-capita incomes. The richest industrially developed countries are the most dynamic markets for manufactured goods. Even though manufactured imports declined as a *proportion* of total U.S. imports, they increased over time and absorbed a growing part of the total world trade in manufacture.

The Direction of U.S. Trade

Throughout the years from the Civil War to the post-World War I era, trade with Europe, both exports and imports, dominated, but there was a steady rise in trade with other parts of the world. By the 1920s, inter-American trade, in aggregate (see Table 20.4), accounted for nearly 40 percent of total U.S. imports and nearly a third of exports. Trade with Asia expanded powerfully—especially with Japan, but also with other Asian countries (which were, at that time, mainly European dependencies). Economic development there, as in Canada, Mexico, and Latin America, created both sources for our imports and customers for exports.

As the great Swedish foreign-trade statistician Folke Hilgerdt emphasized, it was economic development, not mere geographical and climatic differences, that created the possibilities of trade.[3] By the 1920s, nearly 90 percent of world trade emanated from the developed countries. Trade *among* the less developed nations was a trivial part of the world total.[4] Producers in various parts of the world that were engaged in foreign trade learned to specialize their outputs to fit the demand of their foreign customers. As incomes rose worldwide, markets expanded, and greater economic development—division of labor—became possible. The U.S. economy benefited from these changes through its foreign trade.

TABLE 20.3 U.S. Share of World Trade[a]

	Manufactured Articles		*Primary Products*		*U.S. Population as a Percentage of Population*
Years	*Exports*	*Imports*	*Exports*	*Imports*	
1876–1880	7.4	3.7	15.4	7.1	**(1850)** 2.0
1881–1885	9.6	3.8	16.0	8.5	
1886–1890	9.1	3.8	14.4	9.5	
1891–1895	8.6	4.4	16.1	10.0	
1886–1900	7.0	6.7	16.7	8.0	**(1900)** 4.7
1901–1905	7.0	7.7	16.0	8.9	
1906–1910	7.2	7.8	14.7	9.6	**(1910)** 5.1
1913	6.4	9.3	14.2	10.0	
1921–1925	7.9	13.2	**(1926–1929)** 18.9	15.1	**(1920)** 5.7

[a] Figures given are percentages of the totals.

Source: Trade Data: Folke Hilgerdt, *Industrialization and Foreign Trade* (Geneva: League of Nations, 1945), derived from Tables VII, VIII, IX, XIII. Population: John V. Grauman, "Population Growth," *International Encyclopedia of the Social Sciences* (New York: Macmillan, 1968), vol. 12, p. 379, and *Historical Statistics,* series A2.

TABLE 20.4 Direction of U.S. Trade, 1860–1925[a]

	Northern North America		*Southern North America*		*South America*	
Years	*Exports*	*Imports*	*Exports*	*Imports*	*Exports*	*Imports*
1860	6.9	6.7	8.8	12.5	4.7	9.9
1901–1905	8.6	5.4	6.7	13.3	3.2	12.5
1921–1925	14.3	11.5	10.1	14.9	6.8	12.2

[a] Figures given are percentages of total U.S. trade.

Source: Lance E. Davis et al., *American Economic History: The Development of a National Economy* (Homewood, IL: Irwin, 1969), Tables 16–4A, B.

The Balance of Payments

As noted earlier, in the antebellum period, the U.S. balance of international payments resembled that of any developing economy. In periods of economic expansion Americans used more of the world's output than they produced, creating current-account deficits and increased foreign debt. In periods of economic stagnation the pattern reversed.

In the postbellum period, as our industrialization expanded, a great change occurred. The powerful rise in exports of food and materials was spurred on by the growth of wheat, dairy products, and meat as big foreign-exchange earners. Cotton exports, although no longer a source of prosperity for Southern farmers, continued to be produced in large amounts and remained the top foreign-exchange earner. In addition, exports of manufactures and semimanufactures grew remarkably as the country's industrialization became more general. As a result, by the late 1870s (see Table 20.2), these forces combined to create a turnaround in the trend of the trade balance. After 1875, the U.S. balance of merchandise trade went into a long-term surplus position (see Table 20.5). By the late 1890s, the overall current-account balance of payments followed.[5]

The big current-account deficits in the late 1880s and early 1890s reflected a temporary weakening in the trade surplus, but they also showed the importance of U.S. foreign indebtedness. Americans had borrowed heavily from foreign nations (mainly England), and the payments of interest and dividends—together with net payments for foreign shipping, insurance, and banking—were sufficient to provide one last string of annual deficits. These very nearly drained the U.S. Treasury of gold, as we saw in Chapter 19. After 1895, the current-account balance of payments moved into a long-term surplus position. In World War I, the country "repatriated" most of its outstanding long-term debt (the Allies exchanged the stocks and bonds for war supplies) and became, for the first time in its history, a creditor nation in long term.[6]

From the 1890s until the 1950s, the U.S. economy, with its unusual self-sufficiency in food and raw materials, absorbed foreign-exchange credits and gold year after year. Recall from Chapter 19 the initial consequences of the financial system: the "filling up" of the currency and banking system with gold and the formal adoption of the gold standard in 1900. For the

TABLE 20.5 U.S. Balance of Merchandise Trade and Current Account Balance of Payments Annual Averages, 1866–1914[a]

Years	*Balance of Trade*	*Balance of Payments on Current Account*
1866–1870	$ −34.8	$ −118.0
1871–1875	−12.8	−137.4
1876–1880	+182.0	+131.2
1881–1885	+114.6	+4.4
1886–1890	+37.8	−115.2
1891–1895	+165.2	−51.4
1896–1900	+419.2	+394.6
1901–1905	+505.6	+322.6
1906–1910	+433.0	+218.2
1911–1914	+575.0	+240.3

[a] Amounts given are in millions of dollars.

Source: *Historical Statistics,* series U 1, 8, 189.

Europe		*Asia*		*Oceana*		*Africa*	
Exports	*Imports*	*Exports*	*Imports*	*Exports*	*Imports*	*Exports*	*Imports*
74.8	61.3	2.4	8.3	1.5	0.3	1.0	1.0
72.3	51.3	5.3	15.4	2.0	0.9	1.9	1.1
52.7	30.4	11.3	27.3	3.2	1.6	1.6	2.1

country's trading partners, the American current-account surplus became a fact of life for half a century. The U.S. economy's tendency to import so little that there was almost no movement toward a balance-of-payments "equilibrium" (exports − imports = zero) placed the continued agitation for import restrictions—protective tariffs—in an odd light.

THE TARIFF QUESTION AGAIN

Recall from Chapter 13 the Morrill Tariff Act of 1861. With Southern legislators temporarily absent from Washington because of the Civil War, resistance to protectionist agitation was weakened. In addition, the Union government hoped both to reduce nonessential imports and to gain revenues from the tariff (a most unlikely outcome). The Morrill Tariff raised tariff levels back to those that had prevailed in the 1830s. In 1860, the average tariff rate on dutiable imports was down to 20 percent; it had been 62 percent in 1830. The 1861 tariff act raised the level to 47 percent, and it stayed above 40 percent from then until World War I. Baack and Ray, in a survey of American tariff history after the Civil War, conclude that protectionism alone accounts for it:

> The fact that tariff cuts were systematically associated with fast growth industries ... lends support to our contention that tariff rates across industries and tariff changes over time were structured to serve the narrow economic protectionist needs of special interest groups.[7]

A temporary war measure, as so often has happened, became a permanent feature, with the result that the United States became a leader in the world of restrictionist trade policies.

Tariff Revenues

The tariff rates remained high for two reasons: revenues and protectionist sentiments. About the first there were no doubts. The scale of federal government expenditures (revenue needs) rose dramatically during the Civil War. As in the case of all the wars, postwar expenditures never fell back to prewar levels. The need for additional revenues remained. The average expenditures in the five years 1856–1860 had been $69 million. After the war ended, the armies were disbanded. Wartime expenditures fell, but they got stuck going down. Between 1866 and 1870, average yearly expenditures came to $378 million; the prewar figures were never seen again.[8]

Revenues from sales of public lands were proportionately trivial after the 1862 Homestead Act (although they rose in some years), and federal expenditures had permanently expanded. The Civil War income tax was dropped in 1872, and all efforts to install a new income tax failed until the Sixteenth Amendment of the U.S. Constitution was ratified in 1913. From 1872 until 1913, the federal government was dependent almost entirely upon taxes from the consumption of goods and services. The tariff, a tax on the consumption of foreign goods, was a mainstay of these regressive taxes. Between 1866 and 1913, the federal government collected just under $21 billion in revenues; $10 billion (nearly half) came from customs duties on imports alone. Until the income tax amendment, given the fiscal technology of the time, tariffs were necessary for revenue purposes. It was either tariffs or close down the federal government.

Protectionism

The second reason for high tariffs was the protectionist sentiment in the United States. In Europe, Great Britain's free-trade policies had considerable impact, and the United States had sharply cut the protectionist element in the tariff act in 1857. Then, in 1860, Britain and France signed the Cobden-Chevalier Treaty, which committed those two nations and their trading partners to extensive, bilateral, tariff-reducing negotiations. In 1862, the German Customs Union made a bilateral tariff-reducing agreement with France. The United States, engulfed in the Civil War in 1861, did not respond to European trade liberalization moves. After the war ended, protectionist pressures were intensified.[9] Those who agitated for freer trade were generally unsuccessful. (A slight tariff reduction in 1870 was negated by an increase in the rates in 1875.)

In 1882, President Chester Arthur appointed a commission to look into the tariff—the government's budget being then in surplus. Although the commission recommended cuts, the McKinley Tariff arrived in 1890, followed by the Dingley Tariff in 1897.[10] The Germans passed protective duties in 1879, while the French passed such measures in 1881 and 1892. By 1914, the British and the Dutch were the only remaining free trade countries in Europe.[11] In 1913, President Wilson pushed for a more liberal policy, but World War I intervened. Rates fell in the 1920s to below 20 percent, but the Smoot-Hawley Tariff, a bold protectionist measure, passed in 1930, raised the rates to nearly 45 percent, putting them back to late-nineteenth-century levels.

The protectionist sentiment, still pushed in Congress, is based upon a simple fact. A tariff creates a rent, thus providing higher profits for those protected and their suppliers, and higher wages for their employees than would be supported by the competitive market. *All other consumers pay for this.* In the distant past, arguments for the tariff included the **infant industry** thesis: New industries could achieve success and produce domestic economic growth only if they were shielded initially from foreign competition.[12] This had been Alexander Hamilton's hopeful argument at the Republic's beginning.

Frank Taussig's study of this position indicated that, except for silk and cotton-spinning before 1842, little or no American industry grew from infancy to adolescence because of protection.[13] No doubt it can be done. A hothouse banana industry in Maine or Minnesota would work if tariffs on bananas were high enough. But U.S. politicians apparently kept rates below those that would have strangled trade completely because the government needed the revenues. Legislators did not want to forego their paychecks.

The main argument used in favor of protection, from the Civil War to the present, has been the "full lunch pail" approach: Tariffs create jobs and prosperity at high American wages. Since this is the solution being pushed these days in defense of American steel, chemicals, textiles, boots and shoes, it is worth consideration. The argument goes thusly: If products made with cheap foreign labor are admitted into the U.S. economy, then American jobs and prosperity are destroyed. Americans are sacrificing their own welfare for the benefit of foreign producers who employ poor wretches in sweatshops. Every imported Volvo is a Buick not bought, causing highly paid union members to face unemployment. This argument, carried to its extreme, would eliminate international trade altogether. But it has always been a powerful vote-getter.

Comparative advantage is not so easily converted into politics. Besides, comparative advantages change over time. Industries like the American steel and auto industries, which at one time were the world's most efficient and the terror of all foreign competitors, fell behind in technology and became uncompetitive. If they then fail, men and women are unemployed, factories close, towns decay, and investments are lost. It is little compensation to these people for some professor to point out that resources would be better employed elsewhere—not locked up in factories that cannot produce efficiently by modern standards. *Total protection*, abolition of all auto imports, solves the problem completely, or so the argument goes. As a result, protectionism remains. Its benefits are concentrated, and its costs are widely spread out.

Comparative Advantage Again

Comparative advantage says that you employ your resources where they are most efficiently used. If your resources are not so employed, the alternative output forgone is just wasted. At the two extremes, comparative advantage says:

1. If you are the most efficient producer of everything in the world, it still pays you to deploy your resources in your own most efficient production and trade your output to others for your other needs.
2. If you are incompetent at all production, it still raises your own income to concentrate your production in areas where you are the least incompetent and trade for the rest of your needs.

The great English economist John Stuart Mill (1806–1873) put it elegantly in 1848:

> We may often, by trading with foreigners, obtain their commodities at a smaller expense of labour and capital than they cost to the foreigners themselves. The bargain is still advantageous to the foreigner, because the commodity which he receives in exchange, though it costs us less, would have cost him more.[14]

It is important for us to consider carefully what Mill wrote while we contemplate the American tariff. Tariffs redistribute income in favor of those protected *and* make total income smaller than it otherwise would be, unless, as a result of a tariff, production springs into existence that is more efficient than those resources could produce in any other application.

The issues become more complex when, as today, all nations have tariffs and bargain with each other over their respective heights. Each country exports. Thus, if a nation whose exports to the United States are constrained by American tariffs counters by placing restrictive duties on American exports, then the two governments must bargain with each other to reduce the *damage to both economies*.[15] If they do not, the harm to both economies is maximized, even though those protected in each economy still gain relative to everyone else in each economy. Since the United States carried out its industrialization after 1866 as one of the world's two most protectionist commercial nations (Tsarist Russia was the other), we might be somewhat taken aback by the thought that it would have done better without tariff restrictions.

Incidence of the Tariff

In reality, those who were protected at the expense of everyone else would not have done as well as they did. Whereas it is difficult to find any American industry between 1866 and 1914 whose existence depended upon protection, it is obvious that the rents created by the tariffs drew resources into the protected industries that would otherwise have been profitably employed elsewhere.

A calculation by Lance Davis roughly measures the extent of the income transfers over time (see Table 20.6). Agriculture received little in the way of tariff protection; manufactures and semimanufactures received the most. In 1890, for example, manufactures were 29.2 percent of total imports, yet duties on manufactures were 41.8 percent of total import duties. Semimanufactures were 14.8 percent of total imports, but they gathered 18.6 percent of total import duties. Agricultural imports, 16.3 percent of the total, yielded only 4.2 percent of the duties. Davis concluded: "Thus it appears that while almost all business received some subsidy (paid for by consumers), manufacturing industry received much more than its proportionate share."[16]

Alternatively, consumers paid far more subsidy—in the form of tariffs—to manufacturing industry than it did to farmers. Farmers were aware of this discrimination and wanted other forms of government subsidies to redress the balance. They failed, for the most part, before 1914. Not surprisingly, the National Association of Manufacturers has been traditionally protectionist.

THE GOLD STANDARD IN 1900

It is useful at this point for us to relate our previous discussions of monetary changes to the balance of payments. International transactions benefit from any simplification. We already have noted that payment in

TABLE 20.6 The Relative Incidence of Tariff Protection, 1860–1920

Year	(1) Manufactured Imports as Percentage of Total Imports	(2) Duties on Manufactured Imports as Percentage of Total Import Duties	(3) Semimanufactured Imports as Percentage of Total Imports	(4) Duties on Semimanufactured Imports as Percentage of Total Import Duties	(5) Total: Column 1 + Column 3
1860	48.7	60.3	9.9	10.2	58.6
1870	39.8	40.8	12.8	12.8	52.6
1880	29.4	40.5	16.6	20.8	46.0
1890	29.2	41.8	14.8	18.6	44.0
1900	23.9	38.6	15.8	18.4	39.7
1910	23.6	37.8	18.3	20.2	41.9
1920	16.6	23.0	15.2	11.8	31.8

Source: Lance E. Davis et al., *American Economic History: The Development of a National Economy* (Homewood, IL: Irwin, 1969), Table 16–2.

commercial bills of exchange facilitated trade in commodities by making credit easily available to growers, shippers, and manufacturers. The bills, when due, were settled either in money or in other bills of exchange. For example, a Liverpool merchant holding maturing American bills payable in England might find it more profitable to take in payment bills payable in the United States and to ship goods to America, rather than to accept payment in cash. Thus did international banking grow in conjunction with the expansion of trade.

Ultimately, such a credit system had to rest upon the expectation of payment in a universally acceptable medium of exchange, and specie played that role up to 1914. A country's basic monetary unit was defined in terms of the weight of either one (monometallic) or both (bimetallic) forms of specie. As such, nearly the entire commercial world was on **fixed exchange rates**. The declining value of silver in the market after the 1870s (as discussed in Chapter 19) made gold the preferable metal. Although the United States was de facto a gold standard country after resumption of Treasury gold payments in 1879, silver continued to play a disruptive role, as we have seen. Most European countries gave up silver and bimetallism and adopted a purely gold standard in the nineteenth century (Russia, as late as 1893).[17]

The United States kept the silver option open at least until 1900, when it finally adopted the pure

(6)	*(7)*	*(8)*
Total: Column 2 + Column 4	*Agricultural Goods Imports as Percentage of Total Imports*	*Duties on Agricultural Imports as Percentage of Total Import Duties*
70.5	12.9	1.3
53.6	12.4	13.0
61.3	15.0	3.2
60.4	16.3	4.2
57.0	11.5	6.1
58.0	9.3	3.9
34.8	10.9	3.0

gold standard. Freedom for anyone to buy gold in any form or quantities anywhere in the commercial world and ship it anywhere, at any time, finally produced gold points within a narrow range and assured the stability, and the solidarity, of the international monetary system.[18] By nineteenth-century standards, this was the ultimate financial achievement, virtually removing purely monetary uncertainty from international transactions. You knew you could get your money at a fixed rate. The gold standard operated with widely dispersed reserves of gold coin and bullion.[19] The Bank of England at the hub of it guaranteed payment in gold, and gunboats at the fringes of the system collected customs from defaulting third-world nations to ensure their adherence to the major virtues.

The gold standard had many advantages and some major disadvantages. The advantages centered upon the fixed exchange rates and the discipline it imposed on banking systems in all countries, requiring them to control their bank money in such a way as to maintain gold convertibility. Governments, for example, could not (as they do now) print money as they pleased to extract real resources at will from the world economy by inflation. Their two alternatives were to borrow from the public at market rates (as the French did from 1871 to 1873 to pay the German indemnity owed as a result of the Franco-Prussian War), or to tax their people to meet financial obligations.[20]

The disadvantages were that losses of gold via the balance of payments required the losing nations to encourage *deflation*, usually by curtailing credit, raising central-bank discount rates, and increasing the amount of unemployment and general business distress. This was the harsh "medicine" the gold standard prescribed for nations whose economies expanded too rapidly relative to others. Modern fiscal techniques, based upon unending deficit spending, were not really possible in such a system. Governments had to remain "honest."

A powerful mystique developed around this system with its "rules of the game" that central banks used to enforce sympathetic movements of international trade and payments. Central banks were supposed to *magnify* gold movements in and out by their own lending policies to make the gold standard

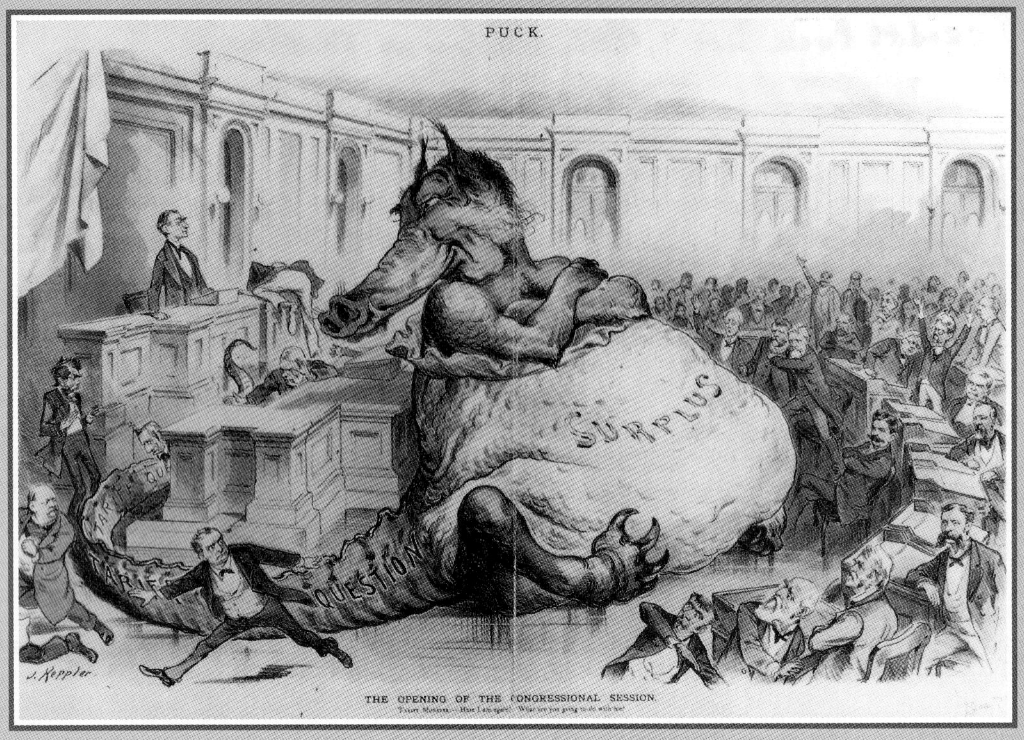

***The Tariff.** As this 1887 cartoon (above) attests, by the late 1880s, the tariff was regularly debated in Congress. McKinley was elected in 1896 as the economy was beginning an expansion phase. Guarded by McKinley (below), the tariff was seen as enabling the greedy monopolist to extract his toll from the honest farmer.*

work.[21] If gold reserves rose, central banks, under the "rules," were supposed to lower their discount rates and increase their loans and investments. If gold reserves fell, central banks were, accordingly, supposed to cut their loans, sell securities, and raise their rates of discount.

It was feverishly believed by financial orthodoxy at the turn of the century that the gold standard and its attendant responsible policies (including liberal trade) would create conditions in which balances of payments would automatically tend toward equilibrium and that very little actual movement of specie between nations would be required. The disequilibrium in the U.S. balance of trade and payments was not supposed to occur. Add to that a system of competitive internal markets and international free trade. Incomes to the factors of production in traded goods tended to become equal internationally because of commodity trade alone, with no need for the factors of production themselves, labor and capital, to be traded. In theory, it was practically utopian.

Utopias, of course, don't exist. There were several reasons why this one did not. Millions of people did migrate internationally, and huge capital flows occurred. And these events took place precisely because balances of payments did not tend toward equilibrium and factor prices did not tend to equality, despite the reign of the most liberal system of international trade the world had known. Moreover, the gold standard's monetary adjustment mechanism, far from being the well-oiled machine of theory, regularly clanked to a grinding halt in the great financial crises of the nineteenth and early twentieth centuries. Finally, the central banks, it turned out, honored the "rules of the game" only when it was convenient. They were loathe to create internal disturbances for some hypothetical international adjustment.

It was the free-rider problem again. Why should a single central bank disrupt the ongoing processes of its own economy for the benefit of its trading partners? It did not, as Arthur Bloomfield showed for the late nineteenth century and Ragnar Nurkse found in the reconstituted gold-exchange standard of the interwar years.[22] In about two-thirds of the relevant cases, central bank reserves moved against the rules of the game in response to balance-of-payments changes. Until 1914, the United States had no central bank, but its balance of payments turned into current-account surpluses every year after 1895, and it steadily accumulated reserves.

The argument is not that the gold-standard mechanism *could not* work according to theory in the way one hopeful writer described it:

> Comparatively small adjustments in credit policy and small transfers in the ownership of gold to offset temporary changes in international balances of payments were usually sufficient to keep international exchange rates and price levels in close conformity with each other.[23]

The point is that the standard *did not*. In the real-life circumstances of the nineteenth century, with trading nations' economies growing at different rates, massive international transfers of people and capital were required to make economic progress happen. Net progress occurred, accompanied by the cycle of boom, financial crisis, depression, and unemployment that characterized the old financial system.[24] That cycle was finally ruptured by World War I.

The Bank of England "suspended" the Act of 1844 (the Bank's way of coping with gold-standard breakdowns) for the last time in 1914, and the pure gold standard was gone with the wind.[25] Attempts have been made ever since 1918 to bring back some facsimile of the old system, since it imposed fiscal integrity upon governments and produced something besides permanent inflation. But, as of now, all such efforts have failed. Central banks have continued to respond more to domestic economic (and political) pressures than to the requirements of international stability. These matters are dealt with again in later chapters.

After the financial disasters of the 1870s, 1880s, and 1890s, the United States participated as a full gold-standard partner in the old system, but its experience was punctuated by the crises of 1903 and 1907. Even with its new central bank in operation, further major disasters came in 1921 and 1929, and the country finally gave up the gold-standard game for good in 1933. Partial gold reserves were continued until 1968, but they were abandoned just as soon as they were in danger of becoming operative.[26]

The myth of the gold standard is powerful. The reality was nineteenth-century economic history as it occurred: Trade expanded as economies grew, and currencies were pure paper, pure gold, pure silver, or bimetallic as events unfolded. The U.S. economy entered this world with a bimetallic standard, slowly left silver, was on an inconvertible standard from 1861 to 1879, and then went to a straight gold standard in 1900 with silver dragged along for auld lang syne. By 1914, the country had been accumulating gold for two decades through its balance of payments.[27]

INTERNATIONAL CAPITAL FLOWS

The current-account surplus after 1895 meant that, to balance, the United States should have been a net lender in international transactions in every year. Net lending is like positive net investment in the national accounts equation. For example:

$$GNP = C_p + I_p + G + (X - Z)$$

Gross national product equals the sum of expenditures on private consumption (C_p) plus private investment (I_p) plus government expenditures (G) plus the remainder of exports minus imports ($X - Z$). Other things being equal, the larger imports, whether goods and services or capital, the smaller is the final GNP—what the United States has produced out of total expenditures. When exports exceed imports, the GNP is greater than domestic consumption, and the country extends credit to its foreign customers to absorb its excess. Thus, in the 1890s, net exports—exports minus imports—became positive and stayed there.

All trading countries give and receive credits. In periods when the United States had current-account deficits, it simply used more of the world's goods and services than it produced. When it had surpluses on current account, it used less than it produced, and the excess was exported. The resulting credits then were balanced over time, either by net specie shipments to the country—which happened extensively after 1895—or by the debts becoming "funded," as long-term debt instruments of all sorts, together with equities.[28] Thus, even before World War I, when evidences of past foreign borrowings were repatriated en masse, the current account surpluses slowly were turning the United States around from its traditional international debtor position. It was becoming a creditor nation because of the long-term change in its balance of payments. Before 1895, foreign savings had aided the growth of the American economy by financing its deficits.[29] After that date, its net savings began to finance the growth of foreign economies.

We need to consider one caveat to explain data for net capital movements that run counter to expectations for current-account, balance-of-payments data. We have discussed the capital flows as if they were merely passive balancing items. Yet, we know from history that such is not the case. Foreign investors in the United States were interested in investment projects independently of current U.S. balance-of-payments movements. Thus, when we were in current-account surplus and were automatically lending as a result, we also were recipients of foreign loans and investments. Jeffrey Williamson's recasting of the available data for the nineteenth century reflects these problems. He produces estimates that are in some instances similar (and in some not) to the data used in Table 20.7; his analysis of the late nineteenth century is similar to the one presented here.[30]

It is difficult to measure these intangibles. Even today—with computers and platoons of trained specialists in places like the Federal Reserve System, Treasury Department, and Commerce Department—trying to count the value of such capital transactions is largely a guessing game. Commodity trade and many capital and financial transactions are now

TABLE 20.7 U.S. Capital Movements Net by Decade[a]

Decade	*Net Outflow*	*Net Inflow*
1820–1830	$ 14	$
1831–1840		186
1841–1850	20	
1851–1860		160
1861–1870		875
1871–1880		332
1881–1890		1,310
1891–1900	393	
1901–1914	41	

[a] Amounts given are in millions of dollars.

Source: *Historical Statistics,* series U 18–23.

countable because of detailed regulation, but from the billions of individual transactions it is impossible to keep track of everything. Before 1914, the official counting procedures were minimal, and attempting believable statistical reconstructions of the international capital flows associated with balance-of-payments outcomes is a challenge to scholarship.[31]

Table 20.7 shows well-known estimates, summed by decade, of U.S. capital transactions indicated by trade data, fragmentary investment estimates, and so forth. No one claims strict accuracy for these figures.[32] But they do underline the point. Notice that before the 1890s, on a decadal basis, the only times the United States consumed less than it produced were during the ragged 1820s and the (mainly) depressed 1840s. In all other nineteenth-century decades until the 1890s, the economy used more of the world's goods and services than it produced, and there were, in consequence, net capital inflows. Then, beginning in the 1890s, the United States assumed its role as a capital exporter on a larger scale.

Foreign Capital Flows

The numbers in Table 20.7 estimate net *flows of credit*. The *stock of foreign investment* at any time was the outstanding sum of the flows, less defaults and repayments. Lance Davis and Robert Cull estimated that approximately $3.1 billion in foreign capital was imported into the United States between 1790 and 1914. As they noted:

> Clearly, in the aggregate, foreign capital cannot have played a major role; and, in fact, the flows of financial capital were almost certainly less significant than the flows of human capital that moved across the Atlantic.... Overall, between 1790 and 1900 the ratio of foreign capital imports to new national capital formation was almost five percent, and, over the last three decades of the century, it was about four-fifths of that amount.
>
> Despite the small relative overall magnitude, ... in some times and in some places those transfers were very important.[33]

The authors emphasized three times and places. First, between 1816 and 1840, capital imports made up 22 percent of new capital, which was skewed largely toward the transportation sector—turnpikes, canals, and railroads. They estimate that in 1838, 40 percent of foreign long-term capital, roughly $45 million, was directed toward the transportation sector. Second, during the 1860s, foreign capital was just under 16 percent of the total; the funds were applied to the Civil War debt, reconstruction, and the first transcontinental railroad. Third, during the 1880s, when the American West was integrated into the union, foreign capital accounted for nearly 9 percent. Most of it continued to go into the railroad sector, but land and industries related to land (particularly in the West) began to see increasing investment. As of 1914, 60 percent of foreign investment was in transportation, but land-related activities attracted over 14 percent.

While Britain was the source of most of these funds, the French and Dutch held a great deal of debt as a result of the American Revolution, the Louisiana Purchase, and the War of 1812. British investors owned 48 percent of the U.S. government debt held abroad in 1818; the Dutch owned 43 percent. Ten years later, the respective percentages were 74 percent and 11 percent. The British share continued to increase until the Civil War, even though the amount of money coming from the Continent increased in the 1840s and 1850s. Britain's share of foreign investment in the United States is estimated to have reached 90 percent in 1861; it remained as high as 74.5 percent in 1900.[34]

Many American issues were floated on the London Stock Exchange, largely because the New York Stock Exchange specialized in railroad stocks until the early years of the twentieth century. In 1880, there were 103 U.S. stock issues trading in New York, 73 of them railroad stocks. Ten years later, there were 15 more stocks listed on that exchange, but the number of railroad stocks increased by 17. In the same year, the London Stock Exchange permitted trading in 47 U.S. stocks, 19 of them railroad issues. Over the next decade, the number of U.S. stocks traded increased by 61, but the number of railroad stocks only increased by 18.[35] One reason for the continued high level of foreign investment is that, at the end of the nineteenth century, even though U.S. saving was exceptionally high, U.S. institutions had not grown as quickly as the demand for capital.

Davis and Cull also discussed foreign investment by Americans beginning at the end of the nineteenth century.[36] From 1790 through 1896, the United States was a net international debtor. From 1897 through 1914, the last 18 years of their study period, the United States became a net capital exporter, a leading international creditor. Over those years, U.S. foreign investments more than quintupled; direct investment quadrupled, and portfolio investment increased by a factor of 17. With all this growth, the geographic pattern remained stable. Approximately 75 percent of long-term foreign investment was located in the Americas, with Canada and Mexico accounting for just under 80 percent of that amount. Mexican investments were primarily in railroads and mines; Canadian investments were much more varied. The majority of the small share invested in Europe was the result of a specific demand for the products of U.S. firms.

The most common American response to foreign investment was simply to request that foreign investors be treated the same as everyone else, but this was not a uniform response. Populists, Western farmers, and workers, particularly in the years of agricultural depression (1885–1895), gave voice to their xenophobia. "Faced with land they could not farm and mortgages they could not pay, the agricultural community, ignoring the geographic and climatic cause of their problems, turned on ... the foreign investor."[37] Both political parties included restrictions on alien land ownership in their platforms, and 30 of the 45 states passed such restrictions into law, regardless of the fact the West was capital-starved.

Convergence

By World War I, U.S. economic development, so long dependent upon foreign lenders, had undergone a transition from a capital-poor to a capital-rich country, at least from the perspective of its capital flows. These capital flows were symptomatic of the globalization of the economy. The research of Jeffrey Williamson and his colleagues suggests this globalization contributed to a convergence in living standards in which the difference between rich and poor nations narrowed.[38] The countries Williamson examines are the Western industrialized nations that contributed to the large flows of labor and capital at the end of the nineteenth century. The path of convergence was neither smooth nor continuous. It reached a peak between 1870 and 1890, but the years during which the two world wars were fought were years of divergence.

The North American experience, that of both the United States and Canada, is somewhat aberrant. As we have seen, after the depression years of the early 1890s, the United States emerged as a capital-rich, net exporter of industrial products.[39] Williamson reports that real wages in the United States were 72 percent greater than those in Britain in 1870, only 63 percent in 1890, and then back to 72 percent in 1913.

Convergence is expected as a result of the Heckscher-Ohlin factor price equalization theorem. Countries will export products making intensive use of their abundant factors and import those using factors with which they are poorly endowed. As transportation costs fall, goods prices are equalized and trade increases. The demand for abundant factors increases (shifts to the right), while that for the less abundant factors decreases. Consequently, as goods prices converge, factor prices converge.

Williamson and Kevin O'Rourke demonstrated that the convergence of commodity prices explained approximately 30 percent of the decline in the real wage gap that existed between the United States and Britain between 1870 and 1895.[40] Williamson, O'Rourke, and Timothy Hatton calculated that the U.S. labor force would have been 13 percent smaller in 1890 (and 27 percent smaller in 1910) without the net immigration that took place after 1870.[41] In turn, the real wage would have been 4 percent higher in 1890 (and more than 9 percent higher in 1910). In brief, migration also tended to create convergence, but how much? Williamson and Alan Taylor went about answering this question contrafactually by asking a different question: How much convergence would there have been in the absence of migration? Assuming the global capital market would have responded, they estimated that migration could explain 40 percent of the decline in the real wage gap. The rest was explained by such "residual" forces as investments in human capital and total factor productivity.[42]

Alone on Top

The disastrous results of World War I left the United States as the world's major creditor nation. Before 1914, the American effort for foreign investment was smaller than the American economy's potential. Its stock of foreign investment in 1913 equaled about 2 percent of its total stock of wealth. The British figure was equal to one-quarter of its national wealth; the German figure was about 7 percent of German wealth; the French figure, about 17 percent of French wealth.[43] Americans had found sufficient investment opportunities at home. Their time as a dominant supplier of international capital lay in the future.

NOTES

1. Robert Lipsey, "Foreign Trade," in Davis et al., *American Economic Growth* (1972), p. 554.
2. Stanley Lebergott, "The Returns to U.S. Imperialism, 1890–1929," *JEH*, June 1980.
3. Folke Hilgerdt, *Industrialization and Foreign Trade* (1945), pp. 23–25. Also, "the growth of manufacturing, far from rendering the countries concerned independent of foreign-produced manufactured articles, stimulated the importation of such articles" (p. 118).
4. Folke Hilgerdt, *The Network of World Trade* (1942), p. 7.
5. Jeffrey Williamson, *American Growth and the Balance of Payments 1820–1913* (1964), Appendix B for yearly data.
6. As a survey in detail of the entire nineteenth century, the classic work is Charles Bullock, John Williams, and Rufus Tucker, "The Balance of Trade of the United States," *REStat*, 1919. For a more recent analysis, see Williamson (1964). Also, Matthew Simon, "The United States Balance of Payments, 1861–1900," *Studies in Income and Wealth*, vol. 24 (1960).
7. Bennett Baack and John Edward Ray, "The Political Economy of Tariff Policy: A Case Study of the United States," *EEH*, January 1983, p. 86.
8. Jonathan Hughes, *The Governmental Habit Redux* (Princeton: Princeton University Press, 1991), p. 189.
9. Gary Hawke, "The United States Tariff and Industrial Protection in the Late Nineteenth Century," *EHR*, February 1975.
10. Douglas Irwin, "Higher Tariffs, Lower Revenues? Analyzing the Fiscal Aspects of 'The Great Tariff Debate of 1888'," *JEH*, March 1998, argues that, in 1888, the actual tariff level was below the maximum revenue tariff level. Thus, any tariff reduction would have reduced customs revenues.
11. S. B. Saul, *Studies in British Overseas Trade 1870–1914* (Liverpool: Liverpool University Press, 1960), chap. VI. For American tariffs, see Frank Taussig, *The Tariff History of the United States* (1932).
12. The American iron industry's turn-of-the-century development was deeply influenced by tariff policy changes. Bennett Baack and Edward John Ray, "Tariff Policy and Comparative Advantage in the Iron and Steel Industry," *EEH*, Fall 1973. More recently, Douglas Irwin, "Could the United States Iron Industry Have Survived Free Trade after the Civil War?" *EEH*, July 2000, argues that, had the tariff been completely removed in 1869, a substantial part of the industry would have remained.
13. William Hutchinson, "Import Substitution, Structural Change, and Regional Economic Growth in the United States: The Northeast, 1870–1910," *JEH*, June 1985. He generally agrees with Taussig, although thinks that the wool industry must also be considered a creature of the tariff only.
14. John Stuart Mill, *Principles of Political Economy* (London: Longmans, Green & Co., 1911), 6th ed., p. 348.
15. Gottfried von Haberler, *The Theory of International Trade with Its Applications to Commercial Policy* (1959), pp. 374–390.
16. Lance Davis, Jonathan Hughes, and Duncan McDougall, *American Economic History: The Development of a National Economy*, 3rd ed., (Homewood, IL: Irwin, 1969), p. 304.
17. Michael Bordo and Hugh Rockoff, "The Gold Standard as a 'Good Housekeeping Seal of Approval,' " *JEH*, June 1996, discusses how peripheral countries with poor records of adhering to the "rules of the game" paid a premium in the capital markets of the core countries.
18. Oskar Morgenstern, *International Financial Transactions and Business Cycles* (1959), chap. V.
19. Arthur Bloomfield, *Short-Term Capital Movements Under the Pre-1914 Gold Standard* (1963), pp. 14–19.
20. Haberler (1959), pp. 92–96.
21. Ragnar Nurkse, *International Currency Experience: Lessons of the Interwar Period* (1944), chap. IV.
22. Bloomfield (1963), p. 19; and Nurkse (1944), pp. 68–88.
23. William Ashworth, *A Short History of the International Economy: 1850–1950* (1952), p. 168.
24. Morgenstern (1959), chap. II.

25. Victor Morgan, *Studies in British Financial Policy, 1914–25* (London: Macmillan, 1952), chap. I.
26. That is, in 1968 the legal "gold cover" in the ratio of gold certificates on the Federal Reserve's balance sheets to its demand liabilities (Federal Reserve notes and demand deposits) was 25 percent. The money supply was rising as the Fed bought government securities to help the Treasury finance the Vietnam War. Since the gold account had no prospect of rising without a "devaluation" (raising the gold price), the gold cover was abandoned.
27. R. G. Hawtrey, *The Gold Standard in Theory and Practice* (1939), chap. III.
28. Jeffrey Williamson, "Real Growth, Monetary Disturbances, and the Transfer Process, 1879–1914," *SEJ*, January 1963, pp. 256–257, shows net specie imports in 1897, 1898, 1899, 1901, 1902, 1904, 1905, 1906, and 1907, after a successive run of net exports from 1889 through 1896.
29. Williamson (1963), pp. 256–257, from 1850 to 1895, 45 years, only the years 1857, 1859, 1861, 1877–1879, 1881, and 1893, eight in all, saw net capital outflows.
30. Williamson (1963), chap. 4, pp. 124–188, and Appendix B. Williamson argues (pp. 175–183) that U.S. gold flows did *not* determine long-term movements in the domestic money stock in strict sympathy to balance-of-payments changes. The conflict between Williamson, and others is analyzed in Bijan Aghevli, "The Balance of Payments and the Money Supply Under the Gold Standard Regime: U.S. 1879–1914," *American Economic Review*, vol. LXV, no. 1, March 1975.
31. For yearly estimates, see Williamson (1963), Appendix B.
32. For other estimates see Williamson (1963), Appendix B; also, *Historical Statistics*, Series U 15–25.
33. Lance Davis and Robert Cull, *International Capital Markets and American Economic Growth, 1820–1914* (1994), p. 111.
34. *Ibid.*, p. 17.
35. Only one stock was traded on both exchanges, the New York Central Railroad.
36. Davis and Cull (1994), chap. 5.
37. *Ibid.*, p. 51.
38. Williamson measures this as a reduction in the percentage difference in real wages. See his presidential address to the members of the Economic History Association: Jeffrey Williamson, "Globalization, Convergence, and History," *JEH*, June 1996. His real wage series can be found in "The Evolution of Global Labor Markets since 1830: Background Evidence and Hypotheses," *EEH*, April 1995.
39. See Moses Abramovitz and Paul David, "Convergence and Deferred Catch-Up: Productivity Leadership and the Waning of American Exceptionalism," in R. Landau, T. Taylor, and G. Wright, *Growth and Development: The Economics of the 21st Century* (1995).
40. Kevin O'Rourke and Jeffrey Williamson, "Late Nineteenth-Century Anglo-American Factor Price Convergence: Were Heckscher and Ohlin Right?" *JEH*, December 1994. O'Rourke, Williamson, and Alan Taylor found that the convergence of commodity prices can explain a quarter of the convergence in the wage-rental rate between the New and Old worlds, "Factor Price Convergence in the Late Nineteenth Century," *International Economic Review*, August 1996.
41. Kevin O'Rourke, Jeffrey Williamson, and Timothy Hatton, "Mass Migration, Commodity Market Integration and Real Wage Convergence," in Hatton and Williamson, eds., *Migration and the International Labor Market, 1850–1939* (1994).
42. Alan M. Taylor and Jeffrey G. Williamson, "Convergence in the Age of Mass Migration," *European Review of Economic History*, April 1997.
43. Data converted at pre-1914 exchange rates from Herbert Feis, *Europe, The World's Banker 1870–1914* (1965). For a summary discussion, see Jonathan Hughes, *Industrialization and Economic History* (New York: McGraw-Hill, 1970), pp. 150–152.

SUGGESTED READINGS

Articles

Abramovitz, Moses, and Paul David. "Convergence and Deferred Catch-Up: Productivity Leadership and the Waning of American Exceptionalism." In R. Landau, T. Taylor, and G. Wright, *Growth and Development: The Economics of the 21st Century*. Stanford: Stanford University Press, 1995.

Baack, Bennett D., and Edward John Ray. "Tariff Policy and Comparative Advantage in the Iron and Steel Industry, 1870–1929." *Explorations in Economic History*, vol. 11, no. 1, Fall 1973.

——. "The Political Economy of Tariff Policy: A Case Study of the United States," *Explorations in Economic History*, vol. 20, no. 1, January 1983.

Bordo, Michael D., and Hugh Rockoff. "The Gold Standard as a 'Good Housekeeping Seal of Approval.' " *Journal of Economic History*, vol. 56, no. 2, June 1996.

Bullock, Charles J., John H. Williams, and Rufus S. Tucker. "The Balance of Trade of the United States." *Review of Economic Statistics*, vol. 1, 1919.

Hawke, Gary R. "The United States Tariff and Industrial Protection in the Late Nineteenth Century." *Economic History Review*, vol. XXVIII, no. 1, February 1975.

Hutchinson, William K. "Import Substitution, Structural Change, and Regional Economic Growth in the United States: The Northeast, 1870–1910." *Journal of Economic History*, vol. XLV, no. 2, June 1985.

Irwin, Douglas A. "Higher Tariffs, Lower Revenues? Analyzing the Fiscal Aspects of 'The Great Tariff Debate of 1888'." *Journal of Economic History*, vol. 58, no. 1, March 1998.

———. "Could the United States Iron Industry Have Survived Free Trade after the Civil War?" *Explorations in Economic History*, vol. 37, no. 3, July 2000.

Lebergott, Stanley. "The Returns to U.S. Imperialism, 1890–1929." *Journal of Economic History*, vol. XL, no. 2, June 1980.

Lipsey, Robert. "Foreign Trade." In Lance E. Davis et al., *American Economic Growth: An Economist's History of the United States*. New York: Harper & Row, 1972.

O'Rourke, Kevin, and Jeffrey G. Williamson. "Late Nineteenth-Century Anglo-American Factor Price Convergence: Were Heckscher and Ohlin Right?" *Journal of Economic History*, vol. 54, no. 4, December 1994.

———, and Timothy J. Hatton. "Mass Migration, Commodity Market Integration and Real Wage Convergence." In Hatton and Williamson, eds., *Migration and the International Labor Market, 1850–1939*. London: Routledge, 1994.

O'Rourke, Kevin, Jeffrey G. Williamson, and Alan Taylor. "Factor Price Convergence in the Late Nineteenth Century," *International Economic Review*, vol. 37, no. 3, August 1996.

Simon, Matthew. "The United States Balance of Payments, 1861–1900." *Studies in Income and Wealth*, vol. 24. National Bureau of Economic Research, Princeton: Princeton University Press, 1960.

Tanner, J. E., and V. Bonomo. "Gold, Capital Flows, and Long Swings in American Business Activity." *Journal of Political Economy*, vol. 76, no. 1, January/February 1968.

Taylor, Alan M., and Jeffrey G. Williamson, "Convergence in the Age of Mass Migration." *European Review of Economic History*, vol. 1, part 1, April 1997.

Williamson, Jeffrey G. "Real Growth, Monetary Disturbances, and the Transfer Process, 1879–1914." *Southern Economic Journal*, vol. 29, no. 3, January 1963.

———. "The Evolution of Global Labor Markets since 1830: Background Evidence and Hypotheses." *Explorations in Economic History*, vol. 32, no. 2, April 1995.

———. "Globalization, Convergence, and History." *Journal of Economic History*, vol. 56, no. 2, June 1996.

Books

Ashworth, William. *A Short History of the International Economy 1850–1950*. London: Longmans, Green & Co., 1952.

Bloomfield, Arthur I. *Short-Term Capital Movements Under the Pre-1914 Gold Standard*. Princeton: International Finance Section, Department of Economics, Princeton University, 1963.

Davis, Lance E., and Robert J. Cull. *International Capital Markets and American Economic Growth, 1820–1914*. New York: Cambridge University Press, 1994.

Feis, Herbert. *Europe, the World's Banker 1870–1914*. New York: Norton, 1965 ed.

Haberler, Gottfried von. *The Theory of International Trade with Its Applications to Commercial Policy*. London: William Hodge, 1959 ed.

Hawtrey, R. G. *The Gold Standard in Theory and Practice*. London: Longmans, Green & Co., 1939.

Hilgerdt, Folke. *The Network of World Trade*. Geneva: League of Nations, 1942.

———. *Industrialization and Foreign Trade*. Geneva: League of Nations, 1945.

Morgenstern, Oskar. *International Financial Transactions and Business Cycles*. National Bureau of Economic Research, Princeton: Princeton University Press, 1959.

Nurkse, Ragnar. *International Currency Experience: Lessons of the Interwar Period*. Geneva: League of Nations, 1944.

Taussig, Frank W. *The Tariff History of the United States*. New York: Putnam's Sons, 1932.

Williamson, Jeffrey G. *American Growth and the Balance of Payments*. Chapel Hill: University of North Carolina Press, 1964.

CHAPTER TWENTY-ONE

Labor and the Law

The United States celebrates its working people every year with a major national holiday, Labor Day. It has been a national holiday since 1894. The Secretary of Labor has existed as a cabinet-level officer since 1913.

The basic facts presented in Table 21.1 are clear enough. The total noninstitutional population increased just under three times between 1870 and 1920, while the total labor force increased by a factor of 3.3. The agricultural labor force increased, but only by a factor of 1.8. Over the same years, the nonagricultural labor force increased by a factor of 4.7. Consequently, the proportion of agricultural workers in the total labor force decreased from just under 50 percent to just over 25 percent. Roughly 90 percent of agricultural workers were male, as were 75 percent of nonagricultural workers. We considered the role of immigration in helping to provide labor (and its relation to the business cycle) in Chapter 16.[1]

There was some movement toward an integrated national labor market, but the presence of large persistent regional differences in average annual earnings was such that we still cannot speak of a national market at the outbreak of World War I. Using a comparison of the average earnings from the *Census of Manufactures,* Joshua Rosenbloom concludes that, at the end of the nineteenth century, there were two large, integrated labor markets in the United States. The first, comprising the Northeast and North Central regions, emerged as early as 1879. The second consisted of the South Atlantic and South Central regions. In a separate study, Rosenbloom and William Sundstrom argue that the West constituted a third regional market.[2]

LABOR'S SOCIAL POSITION

Considering the history of laboring people—the vast majority of whom, in 1790, were self-employed agricultural workers, indentured servants, chattel slaves, or their descendants—the succeeding two centuries witnessed a remarkable improvement in social status. Work, as such, is held in high esteem by Americans. It is a personal accomplishment. "He works hard" or "she works hard" are phrases of respect in this country. The United States has never—yet—had a true leisure class, and it has had no hereditary nobility or aristocracy. As Thorstein Veblen emphasized, it just liked to pretend that it did.[3]

The greatest nineteenth-century family fortunes were accumulated by people who earned the money from scratch, one way or another. Even notorious scoundrels have always gained respect if their money was somehow earned, if they were "self-made." From a log cabin to the White House was supposedly the dream of all red-blooded American boys in the nineteenth century. Americans have never applauded idleness, even for those who had no real need to work for their living. To this day, it is considered scandalous to have no productive occupation, even if one is independently wealthy.[4]

Unionization and the Labor Movement

Attitudes such as admiration for self-made people and disdain for the idle rich are easily understandable in the United States, with its pioneer and frontier traditions. Also understandable, though, is the widespread parallel hostility toward organized labor, since labor unions represent a threat to the rights of real property employed in business enterprise, another part of the "American tradition." When unions achieve "public good"—changes in job conditions such as increased safety or improved health conditions—there are always employers who resist. They do so because these gains will come out of profits, unless they can be passed on to consumers. As a result, labor has been both respected and feared. The two attitudes seem to be paradoxically related. Even though modern union leaders are much more conservative than their predecessors, they have not yet lived down the reputation of being radical: people whose ideas were somehow subversive to right-thinking Americanism. Modern American labor unions are top-heavy with bureaucracy, they rarely change leadership by elections, and they are widely held to be insensitive to their rank-and-file membership.[5] The unions must fight for social respectability, while the occupations of their members suffer no such disabilities. Although a plumber is a valued member of society, his or her union is looked at with deep suspicion. These attitudes may seem confusing, but are easily understood once we consider the history of unions and the labor movement.

The present status of organized labor and the rights of laborers are both consequences of political change. Since 1935, the unions have been protected by a federal law, the National Labor Relations Act (NLRA), which contains provisions for elections by workers to choose their bargaining agents. These agents must be recognized by employers in interstate commerce for union representation and collective bargaining purposes. Furthermore, the NLRA contains provisions and mechanisms for arbitration. The Fair Labor Standards Act of 1938 contains further protections of labor's wages and working conditions. More such protection of employees at their jobs is contained in the Social Security Act of 1936, Civil Rights Act of 1964, Age Discrimination Act of 1967, and Occupational Safety and Health Act of 1970. In fact, employees are now surrounded by a veritable cocoon of governmental protection of health, income, and working conditions. (Discussion of the development of this legislation appears in Chapter 25.)

This concern for labor represents a remarkable reversal of interest in American history. A century ago, one would hardly have argued that American society showed any extraordinary concern for working employees, or for their efforts to combine into

TABLE 21.1 Labor Force Characteristics, 1870–1920

Year	*Total Noninstitutional Population*	*Total Labor Force*	*Agricultural Labor Force*	*Percent of Total Labor Force*	*Percent Male*	*Nonagricultural Labor Force*	*Percent of Total Labor Force*	*Percent Male*
1870	28,229	12,506	5,949	47.6	93.3	6,557	52.4	78.1
1880	36,762	17,392	7,714	44.4	92.3	9,678	55.6	78.8
1890	47,414	23,318	9,148	39.2	91.6	14,170	60.8	77.2
1900	57,950	29,073	10,382	35.7	90.6	18,691	64.3	76.8
1910	71,580	38,167	12,388	32.5	85.4	25,779	67.5	75.7
1920	82,739	41,614	10,666	25.6	89.8	30,948	74.4	75.9

Source: *Historical Statistics,* series D 11, 12, 16, 17.

unions to negotiate. In fact, as seen in legislation and in the courts, one could indeed argue that society seemed hostile to such interests. The change in attitudes toward the social position of labor commonly has been associated with the success of labor unions as bargaining agents for workers. The entire history of the struggle for legislation of unions is called the labor movement. (This history blends the wider struggle to improve the conditions of labor and the narrower development of organized labor.)

The Political Dimension

To understand the labor movement, we must bear in mind that it has been largely a political phenomenon. Presidential candidates and other aspirants to public office now vie with each other for the support of labor unions. A century ago, such support would almost certainly have been a ticket to political oblivion, at least at the national level. In 1880, of a labor force of some 17.4 million, fewer than 1 percent belonged to labor unions. In 1880, there were more independent entrepreneurs than there were workers in industry. Employees in manufacturing numbered 3.3 million. Fully 72 percent of the total population was still rural. In a total population of 50.3 million, there were nearly 3 million independently owned farms and 750,000 small businesses.

In the presidential election of 1880, 9.2 million votes were cast. Thus, perhaps 40 percent of them might have been the votes of independent owners of businesses, who were certainly persons of voting age. The labor vote was smaller—much smaller in an era where women and those under 21 could not vote—and organized labor's political strength was minuscule. If business people and farmers had believed that their interests were in conflict with those of organized labor, politicians would have been wary of labor's cause.

Today the United States is mainly a nation of employees. The vast majority of businesses are small (87.2 percent have fewer than 20 employees), but they account for only 26.9 percent of total employees. Factory employment alone is in excess of 17 million, and what the census calls "managerial and professional specialty" employment is almost 34 million. Of some 123 million persons in the labor force, 13.65 percent are members of labor unions. Smart politicians tailor their appeal to include employees. Therefore, it is not surprising that esteem for the rights of employees includes legislation, promises, and politicians supporting those rights. In a political democracy, those in the minority may be protected and, if well organized, may lobby successfully, but they cannot elect. Owners of independent businesses are now a small minority, and they are unlikely to be served if their ambitions, as a group, conflict with those of labor.

It is interesting to ask whether the interests we historically call "the labor movement" and those of organized labor in the narrower sense are, or ever were, the same thing. The object of unionization is job monopoly, a necessary first step if unions are to achieve their goals by coercion.[6] The historical objectives of the broadly defined labor movement were unorthodox and included demands for more job opportunity, a less unequal distribution of income and wealth, and broadly focused political and social reforms of all sorts. These objectives made strange bedfellows. But with a great historical shift from a structure dominated by self-employment to a nation of employees, the political alliance proved to be effective, however mismatched.

Equal Rights for Workers

Labor's emergence into an improved status in American society was the outcome of a complex legal evolution. The main benchmarks along the way were:

1. A stable and developable political presence
2. A separate identity within economic life
3. Recognition of a valuable property right in the organization of work
4. Elimination of ancient legal encumbrances

Let us consider these briefly.

Political Presence. In Anglo-American tradition, political rights came with property rights. The English in the seventeenth century allowed no rights to vote except by property qualification. Property ownership qualifications were not entirely removed in the United States for free, white, male adults until 1860. And it was another six decades (the Nineteenth Amendment, 1920) before adult women had the vote. The ancient definition of an adult, 21 years of age, was not lowered to age 18 until the 1960s. As Claudia Goldin's important book, *Understanding the Gender Gap*, suggests, the lag in political rights had its parallel in a lag in wages and skill acquisition by working women, together with the increasing participation rates of white women in the labor force. The process of linking political and property rights had a parallel development in the achievement by women of marketable property rights as well as their right to vote.[7]

Since those without property qualifications tended to be laborers, their disenfranchisement was a barrier to full participation in American life. Progress was achieved slowly, state by state, beginning in the 1820s in Massachusetts and New York. Some states required tax payments, some allowed nonowners of property who paid rents above a certain amount to vote, and some required either militia service or payment of a fine. All these requirements were designed to restrict the franchise to those with a permanent, local interest and to exclude laborers. The newer Western states tended to be more liberal with the franchise than were the older Eastern ones.

At first it was real property that counted. Since the valuable property of labor was in skill and effort, it required a considerable liberalization of "the public philosophy" for laborers to be counted as equals with other owners of real property. The idea that labor is a property right remained difficult to fit into the law for a long time. In the Clayton Antitrust Act (1914), Congress (illogically) declared that labor, by then recognized as property, was not an article of commerce (which, of course, it is or can be).

Economic Identity. Who owned such property? The recognition of labor's rights required a clear identification of who the laborers were. In early manufacturing processes, the various species of property rights were commingled. As long as shops were organized in the ancient guild structures (apprentice, journeyman, and master), there was no way to focus separately on labor property. Masters sold the joint product of the entire enterprise.

Early strikes and the withholding of products from the market (usually in opposition to municipal price-fixing) contained no separate definition of employee interest. Indeed, some early trade unions included the masters as well as the workers. The reason labor historians have so emphasized the journeymen cordwainers' strike in 1805 in Philadelphia (discussed in Chapter 6) is precisely because there the separation of interests became clear. The journeymen were striking against the masters for higher wages. From that time onward, disputes between masters and journeymen tended to reflect the standard polarization of employer-employee interests: capital and labor.

By the early 1800s, there were already many masters associations (forerunners of modern employers' trade associations), which were usually concerned with price-fixing in the markets. The journeymen organized their own associations to claim a piece of the pie by attempting to control wages, hours, and working conditions. By the 1820s, strikes by laborers against their employers seem, from the evidence, to have taken the form of standoffs between those who owned the means of production and those whose property was in labor only. Once this increasingly became the case, the separate interest of labor could be pursued.

Property Rights in Labor. The reality and calculable value of labor's own property right were fixed in law by the appearance of mechanic lien laws. If a master went into bankruptcy, the hired workers were allowed to claim their wages against the property of the master's customers.

Mechanic lien laws were an interesting parallel in time and concept to the similar rights of preemption that were being given to squatters on public lands. The federal government passed a general preemption act in 1841; acts specific to various territories were passed earlier. The lien laws were also parallel to laws allowing tenants evicted by their landlords to recover the monetary value of any improvements they had made.

Mechanic liens were, after all, an explicit recognition of property rights in labor alone. They essentially created, involuntarily, a third-party liability in a two-way business transaction. The acceptance of tenants' rights to recover the value of improvements also historically paralleled the switch we noted in Chapter 7 from prescriptive to priority rights in the state courts when two private property rights were in conflict. All these changes were made in the service of economic development. Laborers—like squatters, improving tenants, and entrepreneurial owners—were being encouraged by the courts. They created GNP out of inert property by their own endeavors.

Women and Children in the Labor Force. *Women and children found employment as factory operatives early in American industrial history; later on, the appearance of office machinery placed women near management, but not in it.*

A more difficult and intractable problem was recognition of labor's "corporate" or collective property right in its own organization. It was in some ways similar to the legal recognition of "goodwill" as a valuable property right for ongoing businesses. Insofar as an established labor union can raise its members' wages above those of the unorganized (and the evidence suggests it can), a rent has been created.[8] The rent is an externality of organization that can be internalized only by the union members. The rent is a "collective good" produced by unionization.[9] It is a return to organizational activities above the opportunity cost of those activities applied elsewhere. In this sense it "pays" laborers to unionize. If employers cannot pass this added cost along to their customers, then it must come out of their own returns. There lies the source of what may be a fundamental conflict between employers and their organized workers.

The conflict is over the distribution of the proceeds of selling a product or service made jointly by owned resources and hired labor. The more competitive the industry, the more intense the conflict is likely to be, since absence of monopoly power will force the employer to absorb the added cost of union wage increases. This conflict has never been resolved, and it never can be since organization changes a firm's internal revenue distribution in ways adverse to the claims of ownership. The 1935 National Labor Relations Act compelled employers in interstate commerce to accept the extra cost. Much of the bitterness of employer opposition to organized labor has come simply from this elemental conflict of interests.

The Law of Conspiracy. Among the ancient encumbrances on labor were those associated in common law with the idea of conspiracy: A and B combine to inflict financial damage upon C. Conspiracies by merchants to raise prices had always been unacceptable to common law, and a labor union is nothing if not a conspiracy to achieve collective ends. However, associations of masters in this country had become common by the 1820s. What had to change if unions were to gain legal rights was the law of conspiracy. Some conspiracies had to become legal.

Chapter 6 discussed the 1806 cordwainers' case, in which workers were charged with and convicted of two conspiracies: (a) that they had combined to raise wages and (b) that their combination was designed to injure others. Conspiracy cases continued against unions striking for wage increases and union shops. In 1829, the New York State legislature passed a law making a "conspiracy to commit any act injurious to public morals or to trade or commerce" an offense.[10] That seemed a powerful new barrier to labor unions. But, in 1842, Chief Justice Lemuel Shaw of the Massachusetts Supreme Court cut up the criminal conspiracy doctrine in words that permanently changed the position of organized labor in the law. The case was *Commonwealth v. Hunt*, and the issue was a labor union's attempt to exclude nonunion workers by a strike. Shaw wrote:

> Supposing the object of the association [the union] to be laudable and lawful, or at least not unlawful, are these means criminal? The case supposes that these persons are not bound by contract, but free to work for whom they please, or not to work, if they so prefer. In this state of things, we can not perceive that it is criminal for men to agree together to exercise their own acknowledged rights, in such a manner as best to subserve their own interest.[11]

Shaw then addressed the issue of damage to others property resulting from such a strike:

> We think, therefore, that associations may be entered into, the object of which is to adopt measures that may have a tendency to impoverish another, that is, to diminish his gains and profits, and yet so far from being criminal or unlawful, the object may be highly meritorious and public spirited. The legality of such an association will therefore depend upon the means to be used.... If it is to be carried into effect by fair or honorable and lawful means, it is, to say the least, innocent; if by falsehood or force, it may be stamped with the character of conspiracy....[12]

The remaining issue was, then, what means engaged in by labor unions were illegal? Secondary boycotts might be: A and B block access to D's business in order to enforce a work agreement on C, D's supplier. These boycotts have been favorites of the building trades, for obvious reasons. Tertiary boycotts always have been considered illegal.

Court fights continued until 1947, when, in Section 8b of the Taft-Hartley Amendment to the NLRA, secondary boycotts were outlawed. Court tests of that act made exceptions with the doctrines of freedom of speech and unity of interest. Strikes themselves, restricted in various ways over the years, generally came under the doctrine that peaceful picketing was free speech.[13]

Even though the struggle between labor and its employers is a continuing one, at least by the 1840s, labor had achieved political power in the franchise, and unions per se were not considered in law to be conspiracies and, therefore, illegal.

THE EMERGENCE OF NATIONAL UNIONS

Because the changing status of labor in the early years involved its political legitimacy (the franchise) and acceptance of organized action to achieve its narrower objects, it is not surprising that labor organizations for decades were indecisive about their goals. They had to choose between achieving broad social ambitions or concentrating upon the pursuit of narrow economic interests—"pure and simple" unionism. In the end, it was pure and simple unionism, embodied in the conservative American Federation of Labor, that won out, and that remains the case today. Until the late 1880s, though, nearly every kind of labor philosophy found an outlet in some sort of labor organization.

Early Unions

The earliest written record of organized labor is found in the evidence of strike actions. Few documents remain from the early 1800s. As Selig Perlman suggested, the record of a strike may not really be evidence of any effort at permanent organization.[14] It is easier to organize for a strike than it is to establish and maintain a permanent organization. As far as is known, the Philadelphia Journeymen Cordwainers Union, organized in 1794, was the first U.S. union to achieve any long-term tenure, although it was preceded by several strikes—some against price-fixing and some to increase pay and shorten the workday.

The Matter of Goals

Early local unions tended to concentrate on bread-and-butter issues, but ideological and utopian elements did influence their activities for awhile, as we saw in Chapter 6. Soon enough, unions turned from utopian communities such as Brook Farm and the Oneida Colony, from social issues such as abolishing debtor's prisons and providing public education, to the dream of nationwide organization, One Big Union—with political clout. By the time of the Civil War, ideological factors in the labor movement had achieved successes, and it was not surprising that labor leaders would make a significant move toward national politics.

The National Labor Union

In 1866, the National Labor Union held its first convention. It was an attempt to unite organized labor on a national level to cope politically with the problems of the postwar recession. One of the National's main objectives became the adoption of an eight-hour day in government offices, without wage reductions. Senator Gratz Brown of Missouri introduced a bill into Congress in 1866 to achieve that end. Two years later, after a successful lobbying effort by the National Labor Union, President Andrew Johnson signed a federal eight-hour measure into law for government employees. With such successes, the political method must have seemed effective.[15] Eight-hour laws had been passed in several states, and labor leaders realistically might have hoped for a sympathetic response from the private sector.

The National Labor Union then went off the tracks, politically, by advocating "Greenbackism" at its 1867 convention.[16] The idea, much like that actually followed in this country between 1945 and 1951, was to monetize part of the national debt, refunding it on a 3 percent basis and then converting the resulting bonds into legal-tender notes at face value. Holders of the debt, realizing an immediate capital gain, could be expected to cash in their bonds for U.S. notes and to lend those notes to worthy borrowers.

The resulting sharp reduction in interest rates would bypass the existing banking system (or, if the funds were deposited there, drive down bank interest rates) and, supporters hoped, make investment capital cheaply available to labor cooperatives for expansion of their enterprises. The Greenback movement went nowhere in national politics. But, in 1872, the National Labor Union entered politics wholeheartedly—organizing a National Labor and Reform Party, nominating candidates for president and vice president—and was washed away in the resulting Republican landslide.

The Knights of Labor

In 1873, President Grant's second administration was greeted by a colossal financial panic and an ensuing long and deep depression. By then, a new and even more amorphous labor organization, the Noble Order of the Knights of Labor, was on the scene. Organized in 1869 by Uriah Stephens, it was at first a secret order. The post-Civil War years saw a rich development of these groups. In 1878, the Knights went public with a strong, centralized, national organization and a platform as ambitious as anything ever known in the annals of American social organization. The Knights demanded nothing less than a restructuring of society and the abolition of capitalism.[17]

Nearly anyone (including women and blacks, but not bankers, lawyers, and sellers of alcohol) could join the Knights.[18] They emphasized the uplifting of the unskilled, but with the help of their more fortunate members. As Gerald Grob phrased it:

> The Order was not an industrial union. It was rather a heterogeneous mass that subordinated the economic functions of labor organizations to the primary goal of reforming society.[19]

During the 1870s and early 1880s, the Knights grew and prospered. Their new leader, Terence V. Powderly, the Grand Master Workman, organized diligently and spread the Knights' gospel of uplift, the elimination of the "wage system" altogether, and the reordering of society around cooperative principles.[20] By 1886, the Knights had won some important strikes and face-offs with the most important leaders of the new industrial structure, including a sensational triumph over the "Mephistopheles of Wall Street," Jay Gould.

In 1885, Gould gave in to pressure from the Knights in a strike of workers against his railroads. The result was enormous publicity for the Knights, but then the "Peter Principle" took over.[21] In 1886, Powderly's feckless incompetence as a leader came to the surface in the violent labor upheavals of that incredible year in American labor history. The country was racked by strikes and violence. It was the year of the Haymarket Riot, the great strike of the Chicago meat packers, and strikes across the country by railroad coal handlers. Economist Henry George was running for mayor of New York on a single-tax platform, and the eight-hour day (from which Powderly tried to disassociate the Knights) was a central issue in the wave of strikes. Utopian novelist Edward Bellamy chose 1886 as the year from which the hero of his book *Looking Backward* escaped into the year 2000. Powderly called off the strike against the Chicago meat packers after weeks of bitter struggle when a priest told him that wives and children of the strikers were suffering from their actions. Labor quickly fled from his leadership.

The American Federation of Labor

After 1886, the Knights diminished rapidly, then vanished. Their main antagonists in the business of organizing labor were the skilled craft workers and their trade union. On the one hand, the Knights were inclusive, organized across many occupations, and had a strong central organization aiming at the loftiest goals of moral and social elevation, together with political reform. On the other hand, the craft unions were locally rooted and concerned mainly with the improvement of their own conditions—at the expense of all others, if necessary. They were satisfied with creation of a local by organization and negotiation.

Samuel Gompers of the New York union of cigar makers, a founder of the American Federation of Labor (AFL), argued that unions should control the place of employment; stick to wages, hours, and working conditions in their negotiations; build up "in the imitation of capital;" and win strikes.[22] His tactics were to keep the membership restricted to craft workers, to accumulate large strike funds with high dues requirements, and, in politics, to "reward our friends and punish our enemies." That was the essence of pure and simple unionism, and it was a far cry from the ethereal objectives of the Knights.

By the fateful year 1886, the two traditions were on a collision course and in open conflict. The

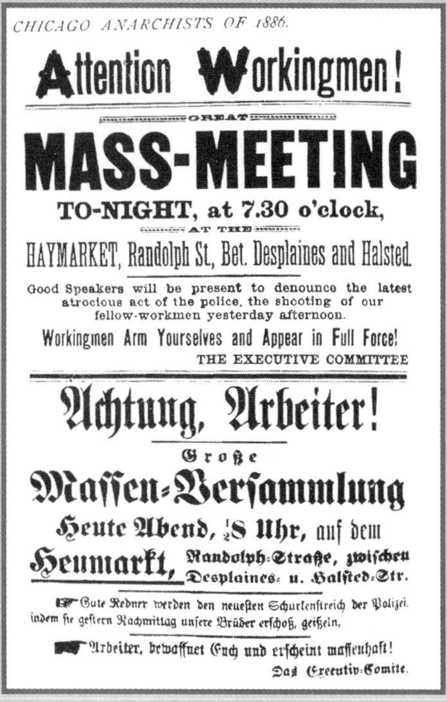
CHICAGO ANARCHISTS OF 1886.
Attention Workingmen!
GREAT
MASS-MEETING
TO-NIGHT, at 7.30 o'clock,
AT THE
HAYMARKET, Randolph St, Bet. Desplaines and Halsted.
Good Speakers will be present to denounce the latest atrocious act of the police, the shooting of our fellow-workmen yesterday afternoon.
Workingmen Arm Yourselves and Appear in Full Force!
THE EXECUTIVE COMMITTEE
Achtung, Arbeiter!
Große
Massen-Versammlung
Heute Abend, ½8 Uhr, auf dem
Heumarkt, Randolph-Straße, zwischen Desplaines- u. Halsted-Str.
Gute Redner werden den neuesten Schurkenstreich der Polizei, indem sie gestern Nachmittag unsere Brüder erschoß, geißeln.
Arbeiter, bewaffnet Euch und erscheint massenhaft!
Das Executiv-Comite.

JEFFERSON ST

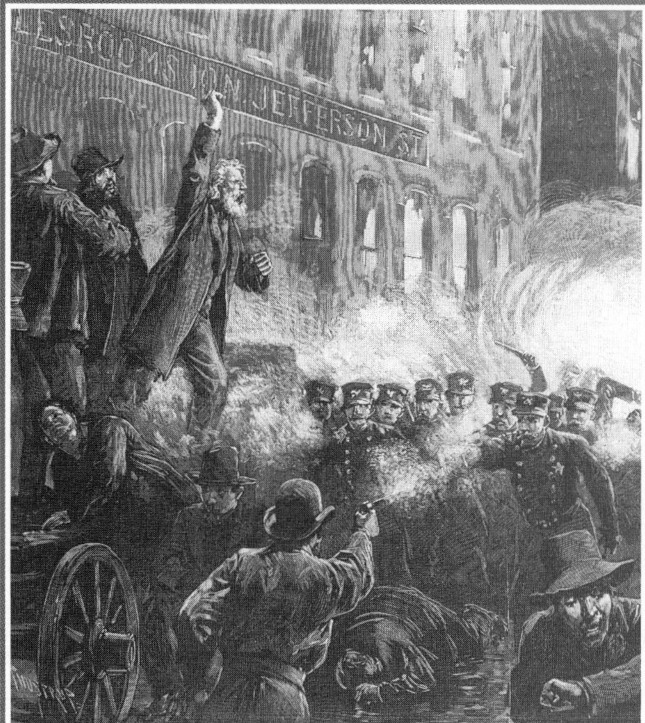

Labor Unrest. ***The explosive mixture of immigrants and American laborers plus foreign and political radicalism produced events such as the Haymarket Square riot (above). Together with native American ideas of industrial rebellion (see IWW slogans below), this kept alive the traditions of violence in American labor relations.***

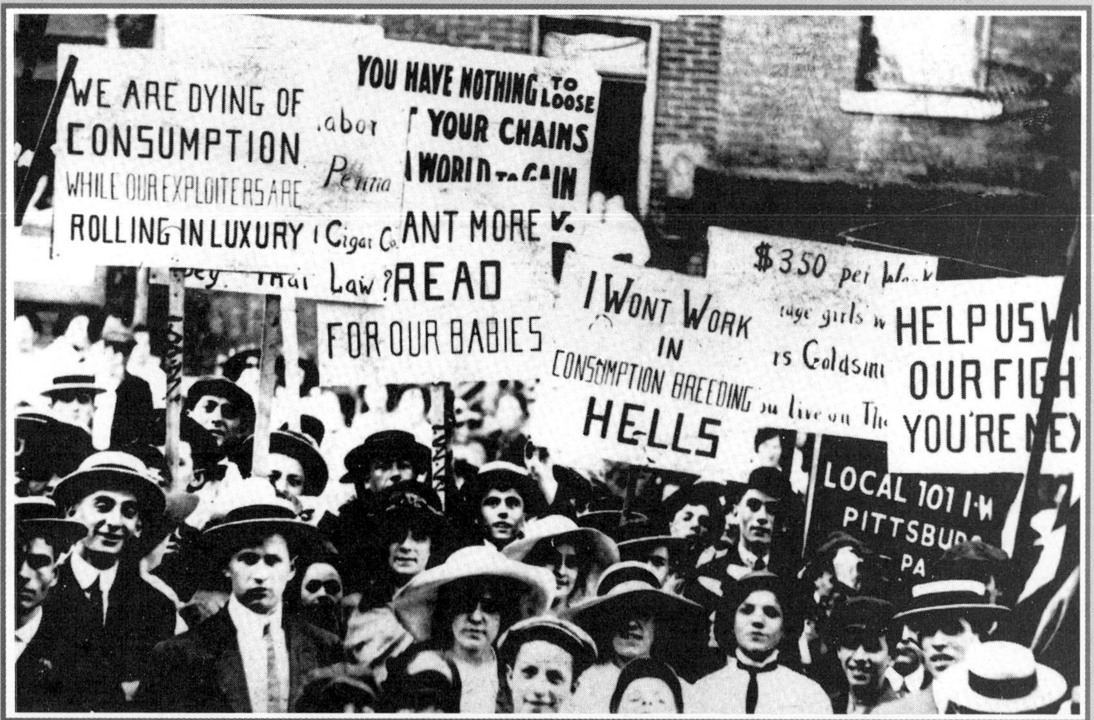
WE ARE DYING OF CONSUMPTION WHILE OUR EXPLOITERS ARE ROLLING IN LUXURY
YOU HAVE NOTHING TO LOOSE
YOUR CHAINS
ANT MORE
READ FOR OUR BABIES
I WONT WORK IN CONSUMPTION BREEDING HELLS
$3.50
HELP US
OUR FIGH
YOU'RE
LOCAL 101 I.W
PITTSBU
PA

Knights were driving to enlist the craft union members into the fold of the One Big Union. A treaty was negotiated between the Knights and the craft unions, but failed, and in December 1886, the AFL was organized. Its object was to maintain craft exclusivity. The Knights faded away, and with them went the long tradition of utopian reformism in the American labor movement. In its conventions in 1930 and 1931, the AFL even rejected compulsory workers' compensation insurance.[23] Apart from heretical groups like the Industrial Workers of the World, some reformist unions like the International Ladies Garment Workers' Union, or some Western unions that continued the tradition, such as the Western Federation of Miners and the International Longshoremen and Warehousemen's Union, craft unionism prevailed for the next half century.[24]

The AFL, rooted in local unions of skilled craft workers and local issues, dominated the labor arena until the movement for industrial unionism began under the leadership of John L. Lewis and the coal miners. In 1935, this movement culminated in the Committee for Industrial Organization, renamed the Congress of Industrial Organization (CIO), under the protection of the National Labor Relations Act. At first the CIO seemed very politically and socially oriented. But, by 1955, it had merged with the AFL and followed that body's tradition of nonaligned political activity. The demise of what Leo Troy calls "the old unionism" is discussed in Part 5.

ANTITRUST LAW AND THE UNIONS

While organized labor struggled to get its own house in order, the country's employers had found new antistrike weapons, first the court injunction and then the Sherman Antitrust Act of 1890. With the appearance of the latter, labor faced not only state courts (and state militias used as strike breakers) but the federal government as well.[25]

The Injunction

We saw that after *Commonwealth v. Hunt* (1842), employers no longer could count upon a favorable response from the courts in labor disputes. Unions were not illegal conspiracies per se, but their actions might be considered illegal. If union actions were illegal, the courts might be brought into labor disputes by the application for injunctive relief.

Injunctions are writs or orders issued in equity proceedings. They are meant to protect property against nuisance or continued trespass. They can be prohibitory or mandatory, either forbidding the performance of a given act or requiring the performance of some act. Failure of an individual so enjoined to adhere places him or her in contempt of court, which is a criminal offense. *Commonwealth v. Hunt* took labor cases out of criminal courts, to the great disadvantage of employers. The use of the injunction brought the element of criminality back into labor disputes to the advantage once again of the employers.

Injunctions began to appear prominently in the late 1880s to halt strikes against railroads. One was issued in Iowa in 1886 to halt a railroad strike. Then, in 1888, the federal courts, appealing to the 1887 Interstate Commerce Act for authority, issued an injunction to suspend a strike against the Chicago, Burlington, and Quincy Railroad.[26] Two years later, the Sherman Antitrust Act opened more possibilities.

The Sherman Act and Labor

It is astonishing that the framers of the Antitrust Act seem not to have foreseen the antilabor possibilities of its Section 1: "Every contract, combination in the form of trust or otherwise, or conspiracy in restraint of trade or commerce ... is hereby declared to be illegal." When a union calls a strike, its object is restraint of trade, in a literal sense. But was it that in a legal sense?

The first major application of the Sherman Act was in the Pullman strike of 1894, but it was not a real test. Federal troops were sent to Chicago to move the mails. In the original action, Attorney General Olney appealed to the Sherman Act for authority. However, once in court, the government shifted its ground and based its case on restraint of commerce, and the Court followed that line. Eugene V. Debs, one of the labor leaders, refused to comply with the prohibitory injunction and was sentenced to prison for contempt. He appealed, but the U.S. Supreme Court upheld the contempt conviction.[27]

Fourteen years later, the Sherman Act was used explicitly against labor. An injunction was secured by the Loewe Company of Danbury, Connecticut, to stop a boycott of its product: hats. The resulting case, *Loewe v. Lawler* (1908), produced an ominously worded Supreme Court ruling:

> The combination [the union] described in the declaration is a combination "in restraint of trade or commerce among the several states" in the sense in which those words are used in the [Sherman] Act.[28]

Labor leaders and sympathizers lobbied Congress for exemption of labor unions from the Sherman Act, and, as we have already noted, this was achieved in 1914 by the Clayton Amendment to the Sherman Act. The Clayton Antitrust Act was hailed as "labor's Magna Carta."

Herbert Hovenkamp argues that labor suffered under the Sherman Act and still suffers under the Clayton Act because of the Supreme Court's belief that combinations of labor and capital should be treated equally as restraints of trade. Labor unions, unincorporated, suffered especially from injunctions, which applied to every individual member, whereas an injunction against a legal-person corporation treated its officers and employees merely as agents of the principal. The officers could arrange a price-fixing scheme internally, among themselves, with perfect safety and not be considered a conspiracy, since the corporation itself would act as a single "person" in the market. Unions refused to incorporate, and thus give state governments legal power to intervene in their internal affairs.

After *Commonwealth v. Hunt* (1842), labor combinations at common law were not per se illegal, and monopoly agreements between businesses were not enforceable at common law. The Sherman Act upset all that. Under the Sherman Act every combination in restraint of trade was illegal. Businesses could evade the impact of the Sherman Act in all sorts of ways: price leadership, merger, incorporation. Moreover, they were often protected from competition by high entry costs. But labor, with no scale economies, and perfect entry and exit from its market, was relatively defenseless against market competition without organization. With organization, combination was obvious, and restraint of trade was obvious. Since unions aimed precisely to weaken the price-taking aspect of their market, they were anticompetitive by their very nature. The unions' problems with the law seemed to be unsolvable in the courts. Hence, only the change in governmental philosophy and law embodied in the 1935 Wagner Act could legitimize labor unions and their ways in the American economy. The applications of old-time restraints by the courts against the unions even in the 1920s neatly illustrate Hovenkamp's thesis.[29] Thus, despite some gains in the nineteenth century, the Clayton Act, and the advances made during World War I, by the end of the 1920s, organized labor's place in law was still nebulous.

PRELUDE TO THE 1930s

The Supreme Court decisions discussed in this chapter are a mere sample of the Court's attitudes toward the ambitions and actions of labor. Even though they were early twentieth-century decisions, their flavor was of the previous century. They form a prelude to the sharp reversal inflicted by Congress in the 1930s, mainly the Norris-LaGuardia Anti-Injunction Law (1932), the National Labor Relations Act (1935), and the Fair Labor Standards Act (1938).

We might fairly ask the question: Why were leaders of the labor movement not beaten down by the Court's adverse positions over such a long stretch of history? The answer is, in part, the experience of World War I, which fell in the middle of this history and was a time when organized labor actually realized a moment of full federal support. It became clear that labor's major ambitions could be achieved by friendly politics. That time came in the 1930s. The experience of World War I showed the wisdom of the conservative Gompers approach to politics—whereas independent labor parties tended to terrify Republicans and Democrats alike, organized labor's support for friendly candidates of the established parties could yield congenial legislation and executive actions. Supreme Court justices did not depend upon votes; elected politicians did.

NOTES

1. Estimates of unemployment for this period reflect macroeconomic fluctuations. See Stanley Lebergott, *Manpower in Economic Growth: The American Record since 1800* (1954); also see J. R. Vernon, "Unemployment Rates in Postbellum America: 1869–1899," *Journal of Macroeconomics*, col. 16, no. 4, Fall 1994. Christopher Hanes, "The Development of Nominal Wage Rigidity in the Late 19th Century," *American Economic Review*, vol. 83, no. 4, September 1993, argues that firms in industries that experienced a great deal of strike activity in the 1880s were less likely to cut wages during the downturn in 1893.
2. Joshua Rosenbloom, "Was There a National Labor Market at the End of the Nineteenth Century? New Evidence on Earnings in Manufacturing," *JEH*, September 1996; and, with William Sundstrom, "Occupational Differences in the Dispersion of Wages and Working Hours: Labor Market Integration in the United States, 1890–1903," *EEH*, October 1993.
3. Veblen, *The Theory of the Leisure Class* (New York: New American Library, 1949), chap. 3, "Conspicuous Leisure."
4. Thus our Rockefellers, Kennedys, and Harrimans are noted for public service in the generations succeeding the founding fathers of those family fortunes.
5. Seymour Lipset, "Trade Unionism and the American Social Order," in David Brody, ed., *The American Labor Movement* (1971).
6. Mancur Olson, *The Logic of Collective Action* (1971), pp. 36–43.
7. Claudia Goldin, *Understanding the Gender Gap* (1990).
8. See, for example, Roy J. Ruffin and Paul R. Gregory, *Principles of Economics*, 6th ed. (Reading, MA: Addison-Wesley, 1997), p. 297. The belief that there is a wage-employment tradeoff suggests that the ability to increase the nominal wage means that fewer people are employed.
9. Olson (1971), especially chaps. I and III.
10. Selig Perlman, *A History of Trade Unionism in the United States* (1922), pp. 146–150.
11. Stephen Mueller, *Labor Law and Legislation* (1949), pp. 43–44.
12. *Ibid.*, p. 44.
13. *Ibid.*, chap. 6.
14. Perlman (1922), chap. 1.
15. Lloyd Ulman, *The Rise of the National Trade Union* (Cambridge: Harvard University Press, 1955).
16. Perlman (1922), pp. 51–52. Irwin Unger, *The Greenback Era* (Princeton: Princeton University Press, 1964).
17. H. A. Millis and Royal Montgomery, *Organized Labor* (New York: McGraw-Hill, 1945), pp. 59–75.
18. The Knights were ambivalent about the inclusion of women, but they did try to organize them. They argued race was not an economic issue, but black workers were largely segregated in separate unions.
19. Gerald Grob, "Knights of Labor Versus American Federation of Labor," in David Brody, ed., *The American Labor Movement* (1971), p. 41.
20. A sympathetic view of the Knights can be found in Robert E. Weir, *Beyond Labor's Veil: The Culture of the Knights of Labor* (University Park: The Pennsylvania State University Press, 1996) which makes extensive use of Powderly's papers.
21. Each person tends to rise in large organizations to the level of his or her own incompetence.
22. For a careful and classic analysis of the AFL, see Selig Perlman, *A Theory of the Labor Movement* (New York: Augustus Kelley, 1949), chap. V. See also Perlman (1922), chap. 5.
23. Harold Laski, *The American Democracy* (New York: Viking, 1949), p. 215.
24. Melvyn Dubofsky, "The Origins of Western Working Class Radicalism," in David Brody, ed., *The American Labor Movement* (1971), pp. 83–100.
25. On strikebreaking, see Joshua Rosenbloom, "Strikebreaking and the Labor Market in the United States, 1881–1894," *JEH*, March 1998; on innovations in state laws, see Janet Currie and Joseph Ferrie, "The Law and Labor Strife in the United States, 1881–1894,"*JEH*, March 2000.
26. Perlman (1922), pp. 155–156.
27. Quoted in Mueller (1949), pp. 172–178.
28. Quoted in Millis and Montgomery (1945), p. 569.
29. Herbert Hovenkamp, "Labor Conspiracies in American Law, 1880–1930," *Texas Law Review*, April 1988.

SUGGESTED READINGS

Articles

Currie, Janet, and Joseph Ferrie. "The Law and Labor Strife in the United States, 1881–1894." *Journal of Economic History*, vol. 60, no. 1, March 2000.

Dubofsky, Melvyn. "The Origins of Western Working Class Radicalism." In David Brody, ed., *The American Labor Movement.* New York: Harper & Row, 1971.

Grob, Gerald N. "Knights of Labor Versus American Federation of Labor." In David Brody, ed., *The American Labor Movement.* New York: Harper & Row, 1971.

Gutman, Herbert G. "Work, Culture and Society in Industrializing America, 1815–1919." *American Historical Review*, vol. 78, no. 3, June 1973.

Hovenkamp, Herbert. "Labor Conspiracies in American Law, 1880–1930." *Texas Law Review*, vol. 66, no. 5, April 1988.

Lebergott, Stanley. "The American Labor Force." In Lance E. Davis et al., *American Economic Growth.* New York, Harper & Row, 1972.

Lipset, Seymour Martin. "Trade Unionism and the American Social Order." In David Brody, ed., *The American Labor Movement.* New York: Harper & Row, 1971.

Pessen, Edward. "The Workingmen's Movement in the Jacksonian Era." *Mississippi Valley Historical Review*, vol. XLIII, no. 3, December 1956.

Rosenbloom, Joshua L. "Was There a National Labor Market at the End of the Nineteenth Century? New Evidence on Earnings in Manufacturing." *Journal of Economic History*, vol. 56, no. 3, September 1996.

———. "Strikebreaking and the Labor Market in the United States, 1881–1894." *Journal of Economic History*, vol. 58, no. 1, March 1998.

———, and William A. Sundstrom. "Occupational Differences in the Dispersion of Wages and Working Hours: Labor Market Integration in the United States, 1890–1903." *Explorations in Economic History*, vol. 30, no. 4, October 1993.

Books

Brody, David. *The American Labor Movement.* New York: Harper & Row, 1971.

Commons, John R., et al. *History of Labor in the United States.* New York: Augustus Kelley, 1921–1935, 4 vols.

Goldin, Claudia. *Understanding the Gender Gap: An Economic History of American Women.* New York: Oxford University Press, 1990.

Lebergott, Stanley. *Manpower in Economic Growth: The American Record since 1800.* New York: McGraw-Hill, 1954.

Mueller, Stephen J. *Labor Law and Legislation.* New York: Southwestern Publishing Co., 1949.

Olson, Mancur. *The Logic of Collective Action.* New York: Schocken Books, 1971.

Perlman, Selig. *A History of Trade Unionism in the United States.* New York: Macmillan, 1922.

Taft, Phillip. *Organized Labor in American History.* New York: Harper & Row, 1964.

When You

BUY an AUTOMOBILE

You GIVE

3 Months' Work

to Someone

Which
Allows
Him to
BUY

OTHER PRODUCTS

PART FOUR

THE EXPANSION OF FEDERAL POWER 1914–1945

MAIN CURRENTS

In the first half of the twentieth century, two great changes occurred that had profound effects on America's economic future:

1. The independent power and influence of business leadership continued to grow and dominate the economy until it was drastically weakened by the Great Depression of the 1930s.
2. The centralizing and social-control powers of the federal government expanded, particularly in the wake of the Great Depression.

It was not until the 1960s and 1970s that the enormous implications, and further development, of these changes became *obvious features* of the nation's economic landscape. However, when we study the economic history of the period 1914–1945, the growth pattern of these changes becomes apparent.

Although these two changes ran somewhat counter to each other, the extent to which they were complementary was most important. Business people resisted the growth of government to a degree, but they also assisted it in crucial ways by contributing their advice and expertise. They wanted the benefit of federal power to organize and stabilize, but they hated the necessary cost—the loss of initiative in the private sector. Modern war, from 1914 to 1918 and again from 1939 to 1945, pushed these changes to the fore, but the Great Depression was probably as decisive as either war—its impact brought permanent political, social, and economic change. As in the two wars, government in the 1930s was called upon to intercede in private economic life, and the advice of business leaders was critical in the planning and shaping of that intervention.

In Part 3 we saw the rise of great business leaders as entrepreneurs and creators of the industrial and financial transformation that occurred in the United States in the years between the Civil War and World War I. These people stepped onto history's stage as natural (but nonpolitical) leaders who seemed destined, by their great economic achievements, to shape the nation's future from their positions in the factories and the countinghouses. Most of the great business leaders, however, those of enormous power and even popular influence, from J. P. Morgan to John D. Rockefeller, avoided the political spotlight. Yet it was to be in politics, in war, and in economic crisis that a wholly new force—great economic power in the hands of the federal government—would come into existence.

Looking back, we can see the early symptoms of this coming change. Between 1875 and 1914, even as the largest industrial corporations were being born (companies like General Electric, Standard Oil, United States Steel, and the Ford Motor Company) and as the names of their entrepreneurs were spread across the front pages of the country's newspapers, the transfer of social-control powers from local governments to Washington was producing the initial critical mass of federal regulatory power: the early regulatory agencies, the Sherman and Clayton antitrust acts, and the federal income tax amendment.

Then, between 1917 and 1919, the demands of modern war generated a full-blown, government-directed "command economy." Business leaders poured into the top levels of the wartime government to "make it work," to produce the armies and weapons that went to France in 1917 and 1918. Economic power in the hands of Woodrow Wilson's second administration seemed to vanish in the peaceful interlude of the 1920s with Harding and Coolidge in the White House. But in 1929, the onset of a great and long-lasting economic crisis brought the command economy back to Washington to create new structures for economic control and (it was hoped) greater stability. World War II brought renewed total mobilization, supported this time by the pay-as-you-earn income tax and highly graduated tax rates. By 1945, the balance of economic power had been altered for good; it shifted from the primacy of private decision making toward the arena of government and politics. The American "welfare state" had come into being, in large part the child of modern war and economic crisis.

CHAPTER TWENTY-TWO

The Command Economy Emerges: World War I

World War I was the first in a sequence of crises that engaged the American economy in the twentieth century. The actions that the war evoked and the lessons it taught provided a rough blueprint of things to come. It is a curiosity of American economic history that much of the war's institutional apparatus has been used to cope with crises since 1918.[1]

By the 1920s, most of the wartime command economy had vanished, and normalcy (President Harding's word) reigned. But in the New Deal emergency of the 1930s, the techniques of war mobilization reappeared in various guises, and these have remained the main options for meeting emergencies by federal action ever since. The importance of World War I for institutional evolution has been neglected in most U.S. economic history textbooks, although it is well known among specialists. Murray Rothbard, one of the more unsympathetic critics of the second Wilson administration (1916–1920), wrote of the "war collectivism" that it was:

> a totally planned economy run largely by big-business interests through the instrumentality of the central government, which served as the model, the precedent, and the inspiration for state corporate capitalism for the remainder of the twentieth century.[2]

Is Rothbard's doleful assessment correct?

THE INCOME TAX AMENDMENT OF 1913

Federal power, beyond "police power" regulation like that of the ICC or the Federal Trade Commission, required a greater control over resources than could be achieved by revenues from land sales and customs and excise taxes, the financing that had been provided by the country's founders. Those taxes fell mainly, and regressively, upon consumers. A tax on general economic activity was needed to give the federal government decisive economic power. A permanent, federal income tax was the choice.[3]

Background

Taxation in its crudest form is simply forcible seizure of property by a monarch for personal use. What the monarch does with the property is the monarch's business, not that of its former owners. This simple explanation is a most useful one for comprehending taxation. Unless the monarch's subjects have equal incomes and identical desires, unless they lose equal amounts of property, there is no way for taxation to be "equal" or "fair."

Any tax in the real world is subjectively unequal. Because taxes inevitably affect relative prices, and we all respond to relative prices, any tax policy affects the way resources are allocated.[4] Self-interested citizens will naturally attempt to direct their activities where taxes are lowest or nonexistent. Similarly, there is no neutral way for the monarch to spend revenue. Thus, taxation is always a burden, and expenditures a boon, to some more than to others. If the monarch invites you to his or her birthday feast, you gain more from the royal largess than those not on the invitation list. The men who drafted the U.S. Constitution in the hot summer of 1787 in Philadelphia had a lively interest in taxation, and they severely restricted the new government's taxing power. Article I, Section 8, Clause I, of the federal Constitution states that all "Duties, Imposts and Excises shall be uniform throughout the United States."

In response to the Civil War emergency, a desperate federal government imposed a progressive income tax. It needed immediate revenues and could worry about lawsuits later. In 1872, Congress abolished the tax. A subsequent Supreme Court ruling in 1881, *Springer v. U.S.*, actually held that the income tax was not a direct tax; therefore, it had been constitutional.[5] Congress passed an income tax in 1894 in conjunction with a reduction in tariff rates, but the U. S. Supreme Court rejected it on constitutional grounds. In *Pollock v. Farmers' Loan and Trust Company* (1895), the Court reversed the *Springer* decision and held that an income tax was a direct tax upon land and its products and must be apportioned equally.[6] The only way out for those who wanted incomes to be taxed would be a constitutional amendment that allowed unequal taxation.

Ben Baack and Edward Ray analyzed how that was achieved. The continued growth of government, in its military building programs, foreign interventionism, military pension systems, and expanding regulatory functions, required a new and renewable revenue source. The need for a Constitutional amendment meant that resistance to an income tax had to be bought off in advance by an adroit targeting of expenditures and proposed expenditures to the high-income, industrial Eastern states. In the main, they opposed another income tax, having paid two-thirds of the Civil War income tax. The newer Western states could be expected to harbor Populist sentiments in favor of taxing and redistributing income. The data show that about two-thirds of the pension outlays and of the new military spending were channeled to those states with a record of opposition to the income tax. The scheme worked.[7]

The Sixteenth Amendment

In 1913, the income tax was ratified. Once again, the occasion was a significant reduction in tariff rates.[8] The income tax amendment to the federal Constitution was a total abridgment of the limitations in Article I of the original document:

> The Congress shall have power to lay and collect taxes on incomes, from whatever source derived, without apportionment among the several states, and without regard to any census or enumeration.

The immediate result: Of total revenues collected between 1915 and 1919—the fiscal years of the war effort—$6 billion of $11.4 billion, or 53 percent, came from income taxes on individuals and corporations.[9] The top marginal rate was only 7 percent, but it was increased to 77 percent to help finance World War I. Rates were reduced after the war, but the top marginal rate only fell to 25 percent. The Sixteenth Amendment was the small beginning of a fiscal revolution that would change the American economy beyond the wildest dreams of those who supported its passage as a needed social reform.

WORLD WAR I: THE NUMBERS

In the early years of the twentieth century, continued European industrialization, conjoined with nationalism, degenerated into an arms race. Germany, in particular, sought a political role consistent with its industrial strength. The assassination of Archduke Ferdinand in Sarajevo on June 28, 1914, was the event that provided the pretext for war. Germany invaded Belgium to outflank France, and that brought Britain into the conflict. Within a month, the two sides dug in for several years of trench warfare. On August 4, 1914, President Wilson officially declared American neutrality. The effectiveness of the British blockade led the Germans to announce unrestricted submarine warfare on January 31, 1917. U-boat attacks on American ships caused the U.S. to break diplomatic ties with Germany a few days later and to declare war on April 6, 1917. The addition of one million American forces to the Allied side tipped the balance in their favor, and, a year later, on November 11, 1918,

Modern War. In the World War I command economy, organizational leadership came from American industry, where the Industrial Revolution went into the armaments business (above). To free resources for the war effort, patriotic bond purchasing was used to raise the savings rate (below).

Germany formally surrendered. All told, the war effort involved 4.7 million Americans and cost the United States $32.7 billion. Nearly 116,700 Americans were among the 10 million military personnel who died during the war.

War—in addition to its human devastation—both influences the amount of real production and diverts resources. In order to build and equip massive military forces, the government requires production quite different from what is produced in peacetime. Countries at war need production in great amounts, and they need it immediately. Therefore, a government cannot wage a major war with normal taxation. Resources and labor must be diverted from their normal occupations; people are conscripted into military service.

For the first time since the Civil War, labor in World War I was diverted by force; the Selective Service Act of May 1917 required the registration of all males aged 21 to 30 (later 18 to 45). The armed forces of the United States averaged 173,000 from 1914 to 1916. In 1917, there were 644,000 men and women under arms; in 1918, there were 2.9 million. By 1922, enlistments had fallen back to 270,000 persons.[10] Military finances to pay, feed, equip, and transport this army rose, as shown in Table 22.1.

TABLE 22.1 Military Expenditures, 1914–1922[a]

Year[b]	*Army*	*Navy*	*Total*
1914	$ 208	$ 140	$ 348
1915	202	142	344
1916	183	154	337
1917	378	240	618
1918	4,870	1,279	6,149
1919	9,009	2,002	11,011
1920	1,622	736	2,358
1921	1,118	650	1,768
1922	458	477	935

[a] Amounts are in millions of dollars.

[b] These are fiscal years ending 30 June (i. e., 1914 includes half of 1913 and half of 1914).

Source: *Historical Statistics,* series Y 458,459.

General Finances

Total war expenditures were about 25 percent of GNP in fiscal 1919.[11] Most of the increase was directly for the war effort, but it included a general expansion of government-associated outlays. To help finance the war, the federal government raised the new income tax and also increased certain excise taxes, laid imposts on the profits of munitions manufacturers, and placed a surtax on income (a rate above the normal income-tax rates that had been provided by Congress).[12] These revenues, however, could not keep up with the rapid increase in expenditures. As a result, the national debt rose by a factor of 21, an increase of $24 billion. Since the financial system absorbed part of the debt by net money creation, the money supply soared. In addition, gold was pouring into the United States from Europe. By 1916, the gold-standard banking system had absorbed some $2 billion, the largest amount of gold ever held by a single nation.[13] Foreign governments, buying armaments from the United States, liquidated the American debts owned by their citizens. The United States became, almost overnight, a "mature creditor nation," having been a long-term net debtor only three years previously. Consider the data in Table 22.2.

The $24 billion debt increase from 1916 to 1919 was achieved by well-organized borrowing. Secretary of the Treasury William McAdoo had learned the lessons of Civil War financing. With a more sophisticated banking system than that of 1861, he was able to produce a well-orchestrated diversion of resources without simply printing money. More greenbacks would not be required. There were now Federal Reserve notes.[14]

If the public would buy the debt directly, then a transfer (temporary diversion) of claims over resources would go from the public to the government. If the Federal Reserve were to absorb the debt, the money supply would increase directly. This increase would result from net Federal Reserve purchases, together with massive purchases of government securities by the commercial banks. Changes were made that enabled the gold reserve to support more than twice as much bank money than the 1914 Federal Reserve Act allowed; the gold reserve backing was changed to 40 percent in support of Federal Reserve notes, and, in 1917, the reserve requirements of the member banks were cut.[15] The result was, of course, a straightforward money-supply increase of massive proportions; currency in circulation and demand deposits in 1920 were 100 percent higher than they had been in 1914.

The government could tax (and did), could borrow (and did), and could tax invisibly by inflating the cur-

TABLE 22.2 Federal Finance and Money Supply, 1914–1922[a]

Year	Expenditures	Revenues	Deficit (–) Surplus (+)	Gross Federal Debt	M_2
1914	$ 726	$ 725	$ –1	$ 1,188	$16.39
1915	746	683	–63	1,191	17.59
1916	713	761	+48	1,225	20.85
1917	1,954	1,101	–853	2,976	24.37
1918	12,677	3,645	–9,032	12,455	26.73
1919	18,493	5,130	–13,363	25,485	31.01
1920	6,357	6,649	+292	24,299	34.80
1921	5,062	5,571	+509	23,977	32.85
1922	3,189	4,026	+737	22,963	33.72

[a] In billions of dollars.

Source: *Historical Statistics,* series Y 335, 336, 493, X 415.

rency. In the latter case the government merely purchased its goods and services at whatever prices were necessary to divert them from other uses to the government. Consumers went without, finding by surprise that they had (forced) savings. If that diversion were insufficient, the government could also resort to various physical allocation devices and did. In World War I, the government never actually needed to resort to ticket rationing—inflation, taxes and borrowing, reenforced by an elaborate system of allocating devices (which will be discussed in the next section), did the job.

Although the economy in 1914 was close to full employment most of the time, it initially dipped into a recession as the European war spread. By late 1916, output and employment had recovered. With subsidies, government contracts in hand, and favorable tax treatment, a great rise in investment did occur. Capital outlays on fixed plant and equipment in manufacturing industries, $600 million in 1915, rose by a factor of four to $2.4 billion in 1920, an astounding increase in just five years. Then disaster struck, and in a single year investment fell 50 percent (to $1.4 billion).[16]

Investment in productive capacity for war goods meant that the increase to 1918 levels could be achieved with a smaller sacrifice of peacetime goods. The great economist John Maurice Clark estimated that about 60 percent of the war goods came from consumer retrenchment in World War I and only 40 percent from increased output.[17] Clark's results are surprising, if we consider the data for physical investment above.

The Inflation

With such a shift in the production possibilities due to new investment, we can appreciate all the more the sheer force of the monetary stimulus produced by war financing. *Real* GNP rose some 22 percent in the period 1914–1918, yet commodity prices in general more than doubled, and the consumer price index just doubled.[18] The data are shown in Table 22.3. As can be seen, wholesale prices increased at a faster rate than consumer prices, then fell faster.

Once the expenditure program was under way and the diversions away from civilian consumption were beginning to take hold, only increases in physical

TABLE 22.3 Wholesale and Consumer Prices, 1914–1922 (1926 = 100)

Year	Wholesale Prices	Consumer Prices
1914	68.1	56.8
1915	69.5	57.4
1916	85.5	61.7
1917	117.5	72.5
1918	131.3	85.1
1919	138.6	97.7
1920	154.4	113.2
1921	97.6	101.1
1922	96.7	94.7

Source: *Historical Statistics,* series E 52, 135.

output proportionate to increased spending could keep prices from rising. Such production increases could, of course, come from existing excess capacity, but that had vanished by 1916 as the United States was busy producing goods for the Allies. Increased productivity from existing labor and capital, or new capacity, could still reduce the inflationary pressures, and must have done so, given the investment data.

In some industries there were significant production increases, but in others, there were not. The inflation in those latter areas was pure, only offset by physical allocation devices imposed during the war. Where such allocations occurred, the lapse of controls in 1919 brought forth a surge of prices as pent-up demand hit the markets. Thus, between 1918 and 1920, there was a huge *postwar* inflation in many commodities. The fast reduction of federal expenditures after the war and the appearance of big budget surpluses produced the price collapse of 1921.

Consider the corn and steel outputs and prices shown in Table 22.4. In the case of corn, output did not increase sufficiently, and prices soared. Food was needed not only for American forces but also for the substantial food assistance the United States gave to its allies then and, in the immediate postwar period, as aid to the hungry millions of war-ravaged Europe, a program administered impressively by Herbert Hoover. The price collapse in 1921 triggered new demands by the farm interest for a federal solution to the suddenly reappearing problem of farm incomes.

Also, as Table 22.4 indicates, shipments of steel ingots and rolled steel increased impressively during the war and immediate postwar years, but so did the demand for these products. Consequently, prices rose despite the output increases.

Hours and Wages

The average number of hours worked each week in manufacturing industries declined, continuing a trend that began long before World War I. The government enforced an eight-hour day in all government employment.[19] As in previous wars when industrial labor was allocated primarily by the market (and was also massively withdrawn from that market at confiscatorily low rates for military levies), wartime inflation created a time of temporary prosperity for wage earners. Hourly wages, however, increased dramatically in both nominal and real terms. In general, World War I brought prosperity to workers; it was arguably the first war to do so.[20] Farm workers did less well than factory workers, but there seems to be little doubt that, on average, even their real wages rose substantially during the war. Other evidence suggests that the income distribution actually shifted toward labor in World War I and its immediate aftermath. Representative wage and hours data are shown in Table 22.5. The deflator used to calculate real average hourly earnings is the CPI from Table 22.3.

TABLE 22.4 Selected Outputs and Prices, 1914–1922

	Corn		*Steel*		
			Output		
Year	*Output (billion bushels)*	*Price ($ per bushel)*	*Ingots* (*million short tons*)	*Rolled* (*million short tons*)	*Rail Prices ($ per gross ton)*
1914	2.5	$ .71	25.6	20.6	$30.00
1915	2.8	.68	35.2	27.3	30.00
1916	2.4	1.14	46.8	36.3	33.33
1917	2.9	1.46	49.8	37.0	40.00
1918	2.4	1.52	49.0	34.9	56.00
1919	2.7	1.51	38.1	28.1	49.26
1920	3.1	0.64	46.2	36.2	53.83
1921	2.9	0.52	21.6	16.5	45.65
1922	2.7	0.73	38.9	29.6	40.69

Source: *Historical Statistics,* series E 130, K 503, 504, P 265, 270.

TABLE 22.5 Selected Hours and Earnings, 1914–1922

	Manufacturing Industry		
	Average Weekly	*Average Hourly Earnings*	
Year	*Hours*	*Nominal*	*Real*
1914	55.2	$0.287	$0.505
1915	55.0	0.287	0.500
1916	54.9	0.320	0.519
1917	54.6	0.364	0.502
1918	53.6	0.448	0.526
1919	52.3	0.529	0.541
1920	51.0	0.663	0.586
1921	50.7	0.607	0.600
1922	51.2	0.574	0.606

Source: *Historical Statistics,* series D 765, 766.

The postwar surge in prices was accompanied by a similar rise in wages. Even with demobilization and the cutbacks in current federal spending (see Table 22.2), pent-up demand resulting from induced physical shortages, together with a greatly expanded money supply, provided a base for continued optimism that the coming of peace would extend the prosperity. Then came the sharp setback of 1921. Wages fell relatively little compared to prices and left labor with net significant gains in real income over the entire course of the war and postwar experience. Indeed, the "normalcy" of the later 1920s, with its aura of great prosperity, was enhanced, many economists believe, by the quick, sharp adjustment of relative prices in 1921, which left employed labor with increased real purchasing power.

War Finance and Income Distribution

War finance, conducted as it was with massive money creation, inflation, and high wartime income and profit taxes, produced some other unexpected results. The new federal income tax reduced effective civilian demand among those groups to whom the taxes applied. The workers whose wages rose faster than prices gained income shares at the expense of the "rentier classes," those who depended on earnings from investments.

Between 1914 and 1920, prices were rising at compound rates of more than 14 percent a year. Stocks and bonds yielded less than half that rate, in part because of corporate profit taxes actually paid to the Treasury. The "capitalist" who paid taxes and made profits from investments in the capital market instruments came out of the war worse off, compared to others. Interest rates in general were far below inflation rates. It would have been an excellent time to borrow and speculate—and not pay taxes—but a poor time to plod along with AT&T and U.S. Steel stocks. Tales of war profiteering and giant fortunes made by the "merchants of death" may well contain their elements of truth, but there was little spillover, apparently, into those financial markets for which we have statistical records.

Consider the data shown in Table 22.6. The inflation rate is simply the rate of change in the CPI given in Table 22.3. In terms of earnings alone, nothing kept up with inflation. Industrial stock prices rose 36 percent from 1914 to 1917 and 28 percent in the single year 1918–1919 as the postwar inflation took hold. Otherwise, the war, financed as it was, proved no friend to the passive capitalist who depended upon the markets for a living. In real terms, the "widows and orphans," and idle millionaires, who lived off the earnings of the markets could have been better served with industrial jobs.

Common stocks in railroads and utilities faded slowly in price because their yields could not keep pace with the inflation. Stanley Lebergott found the same result in his study of wealth and income distributions.[21] In fact, it has been the common experience that the wars of the twentieth century tended to reduce income inequality.[22] If, as Marxists and others claim, capitalists start wars to maintain their class interests, they seem to have chosen a poor vehicle.

In the case of World War I, the strategy of pursuing mobilization with money creation, inflation, and progressive income taxation was a blueprint for income redistribution favoring the wage-earning population. Since it enabled the Treasury's new debt to be sold at relatively high prices (low interest charges), the policy was well chosen from the viewpoint of debt management. It was, in fact, very clever fiscal policy, and it was successfully followed in World War II by another massive debt creation at low charges. That the policy succeeded so well was due in large part to the construction of an elaborate system of nonmarket controls, the command economy of World War I.

TABLE 22.6 The Financial Markets, 1914–1922[a]

Year	Prime Rate	Corporate Bond Yields	Common Stock Yields	Common Stock Prices (1941–1943 = 100 Base)	Inflation Rate
1914	5.47	4.44	5.01	80.8	1.4
1915	4.01	4.62	4.98	83.1	1.1
1916	3.84	4.49	5.62	94.7	7.5
1917	5.07	4.79	7.82	85.0	17.5
1918	6.02	5.23	7.24	75.4	17.4
1919	5.37	5.29	5.75	87.8	14.8
1920	7.50	5.81	6.13	79.8	15.9
1921	6.62	5.57	6.49	68.6	−10.7
1922	4.52	4.85	5.80	84.1	−6.3

[a] Prime rates, corporate bond yields, and common stock yields are given as annual percentage rates.

Source: *Historical Statistics*, series X 445, 476, 479, 495.

THE COMMAND ECONOMY

The federal government did not rely simply upon the market's response. It proved to be a prolific innovator of nonmarket control devices during World War I; nearly 5,000 new federal agencies were created. The government wanted rapid mobilization of resources, whether or not the new allocations were desirable to those whose lives were being changed by them. Coercion was necessary and, thus, so was centralized decision making. To achieve this, a bureaucracy of control had to be created to *direct* the economic mobilization. The extreme example, of course, was the draft of labor into the armed forces.

Eligible men were forced to muster to the colors at wages below opportunity costs. Patriotic fervor was encouraged, and prison sentences awaited those eligible for military service who preferred nonmartial lives. In fact, the government got them cheaply by force, and that was in part the rationale for the creation of the wartime bureaucracy of the command economy.

Boards, Offices, and Administrations

After the failures of the immediate German invasion of Belgium and France in 1914 and the Russian invasion of Germany, the Europeans found themselves locked into a devastating war of attrition that was to last four long years. Vast armies faced each other across thousands of miles of trenches and fortifications.

The United States at first proclaimed neutrality and played the role of banker to the combatants. Slowly, national support swung behind the Allies, and, by 1916, the country began preparations to intervene. To do so, it needed ships, armies, weapons, and supplies. Someone had to plan the amounts and the locations of training and production as well as the transport. Since the federal government was in no way able to supply such expertise, leaders from private business were called to Washington to plan and mount the mobilization.[23]

In 1916, the Naval Consulting Board was formed to evaluate the nation's defense needs.[24] It was composed of senior scientific and industrial luminaries, including even Thomas A. Edison, then in his seventies. A spin-off organization, the Committee on Industrial Preparedness, financed by private industry, was formed to actively plan for war. Late that year, it was transformed into the Council for National Defense, a fully government-funded war organization that included cabinet secretaries.

The Council for National Defense was guided by the Advisory Commission, again composed of senior leaders from the private sector. According to Grosvenor Clarkson, the Advisory Commission had decisive influence.[25] It laid plans for food control, industrial allocation, even press censorship. In the prewar phase the defense effort had to rely largely upon private-sector expertise in a semiofficial way. Later, the industrial sector sent its brightest executives to Washington to serve their country in an official capacity for the duration.

Even in 1916 (after the presidential election that Woodrow Wilson won on the slogan "he kept us out of war"), the writing was on the wall. The National Defense Act of 1916 provided the means for the expansion of the armed forces. The Shipping Act of 1916 organized a formal merchant marine to be controlled by the United States Shipping Board.[26] More appropriations bills followed as the financial scope of the coming war became evident.

The industrialists knew what could be done. Paul Koistinen quotes a letter from Howard Coffin, president of Hudson Motors, to the DuPonts, written in December 1916:

> It is our hope that we may lay the foundation for that closely knit structure, industrial, civil and military, which every thinking American has come to realize is vital to the future life of this country, in peace and in commerce, no less than in possible war.[27]

It truly was a vision of the "military-industrial complex" that so vexed General Eisenhower when he left the White House in 1961.[28]

Carrot and Stick: The Lever Food Control Act

One piece of legislation, the Lever Food Control Act of August 1917, proved to be the primary control legislation. It provided the power to federally license businesses, requisition commodities, even take over factories directly (it also funded the FBI in its earliest stage). Power was given to establish minimum prices for wheat and other crops. Herbert Hoover was appointed head of the United States Food Administration with primary power under the Lever Act. To gain a patina of legitimacy for such legislation, *Munn v. Illinois* was even conscripted: It was written in the Lever bill that food production was "clothed in the public interest."[29] Even in a war emergency, one government eye was focused on the Constitution and the courts.

Fuel supplies could be controlled, outputs determined, and prices set under the Lever Act, and the United States Fuel Administration was established to control output and fix prices of coal. In the summer of 1917, the War Industries Board (WIB) was organized to set production priorities in manufacturing industries, to fix prices, and to coordinate government purchases. This board was headed by the famous financier Bernard Baruch.

The WIB governed contracts for war production according to its own criteria; there was no competitive bidding. It also launched, through its Conservation Division, a campaign to standardize American industrial sizes of everything from drill bits to clothing.[30] The new army provided an excellent opportunity to reappraise (from the Civil War) the standard physical dimensions of American males! In the 1920s, the Commerce Department under Herbert Hoover continued the program for standardization.

In major cases, the problem of ownership of war supplies was solved by creation of quasi-public corporations. The United States Grain Corporation, organized under the laws of Delaware, bought food and other commodities to fix prices and store surpluses. The United States Housing Corporation, incorporated under the laws of New York, used government money to supply housing for defense workers. The Emergency Fleet Corporation, chartered in the District of Columbia, faced the immense problem of organizing shipyards, materials, and labor to build a huge ocean transport fleet. Finally, the War Finance Corporation used federal funds to underwrite bank loans to private industry.

Since the federal government had no tradition of production, or ownership of productive resources beyond the federal armories, these quasi-public corporations turned to another traditional solution for a pattern: They followed the institutional leads of the First and Second Banks of the United States, which had mixed public and private ownership. Although the railroad in the Panama Canal Zone was a wholly government-owned corporation, the main technique was to create corporations that were state-chartered and, superficially at least, seemed private. The command economy was approached gingerly, or so it appeared on paper.

Through licensing, purchase without competitive bid, emergency regulation, and outright seizure where necessary, the government could, in the short run, extract a desired output that the market, in all probability, would not freely provide. Military labor was conscripted; private labor was largely bribed. Labor was placated by being granted its reasonable demands or by the War Labor Board's forcing settlements by arbitration upon both management and labor.[31] The federal government took over the telegraph and railroad systems and imposed its own management rules for the duration.

The War Labor Board upheld union representation throughout the government's domain. The War Labor Policies Board was established to coordinate federal government activities in the field of labor. By 1918, the federal government had become the single largest employer of labor in the country.[32] When states passed laws against union solicitation of workers, the Attorney General ordered U.S. attorneys to defend those union organizers so charged. As noted, workers in government employment were given the eight-hour day, and their unions were recognized as a matter of course. The government wanted production; it did not want labor disputes.

Usually, because the price-setting by government authority was aimed at assuring delivery, prices tended to be minimum prices. Since the output of basic grains scarcely increased at all during the war years, it is entirely probable that food prices would have been inflated without the aid of any policies aimed at that outcome. In other areas, such as steel output, where production did soar, federal price-fixing and price floors may well have been decisive in maintaining and raising prices.[33]

An interesting exception was sugar. There were two markets—foreign (mainly Cuban) and domestic. Among the Allies, an International Sugar Committee was organized as a monopoly buyer in the foreign market to force offshore sellers to deliver at low prices. When the Cubans balked, their food imports from the United States were cut off. They gave in and continued sales at low prices.

American beet-sugar growers, on the other hand, wanted high prices. To meet their demand, the Sugar Equalization Board was established, which sold the cheap Cuban sugar to American refiners at prices high enough to keep a price floor under domestic American growers.[34] Between 1916 and 1918, retail sugar prices rose only about 21 percent under this system (compared with 60 percent for wheat). But, in the two years 1918–1920, after the controls lapsed, sugar prices rose strongly. Then the sugar market fell (see Table 22.7).

The Cubans were obviously cut out of the war boom from 1916 until 1918. They gained between 1918 and 1920 when controls were off; but sugar prices fell 80 percent for them in the next two years. The object of policy was to ensure supplies at prices to foreigners below domestic price; thus, the Sugar Equalization Board was a brilliant success. Fortunately, the United States did not need Cuban goodwill at the time.

THE LEGACY OF WARTIME CONTROL

Woodrow Wilson was an enthusiast for the competitive market throughout his political career. He favored policies that limited, he thought, the potential power of big business. During the war, the goodwill and cooperation of giant American firms had been necessary. The Germans would not have been beaten by ma-and-pa grocery stores, nor would guns, ships, tanks, airplanes, and munitions be made by small firms gambling on competitive bids. It had been a modern war, and the command economy had pulled together a military-industrial complex for the good of the war effort. But when the war ended, Wilson wanted to go back quickly to the previous status quo. He ordered the new command economy dissolved, and it began to vanish quickly. The government's wartime support for organized labor was equally short-lived. In the labor unrest of 1919–1920, the government pulled back into the role of conciliator, and the labor unions were generally subdued. Their membership plunged.[35]

Dismantling the Bureaucracy

Many people, inside and outside the government, considered the system of enforced wartime cooperation between firms and industries, together with government direction (and financing), superior to the old dog-eat-dog tendencies of the prewar competitive economy. But Wilson moved quickly to abolish the command structure. As noted, the armistice took place on November 11, 1918, and on November 23, less than two weeks later, Wilson ordered the WIB to wind up its affairs.[36]

Early in 1919, trying to maintain the "order" of wartime, the Commerce Department bureaucracy set up an Industrial Board of mixed government and private direction. When it became clear that the main object of the Industrial Board was price-fixing, Wilson ordered it dissolved. Baruch and others hoped for some continuation of the wartime system, but the industrialists temporarily in Washington quickly packed up and headed home, especially when it became clear that the system's basis, the wartime presidential power, was no longer there.[37] In any case, the boom of 1918–1920 indicated that no government direction of economic life was required to make the economy prosper.

The U.S. Supreme Court helped push the wartime regime into temporary oblivion by wiping out the 1916 Child Labor Act in *Hammer v. Dagenhart* (1918) and wage and hour legislation in *Adkins v. Children's Hospital* (1923). It also finished off state-level wartime controls over prices in *Wolff Packing Company v. Court of Industrial Relations* (1921). It seemed that World War I was strictly for the history books.

The Legacy

Despite the lessons learned, what happened during World War I would not be forgotten. The WIB would reappear in 1933 as the National Recovery Administration (NRA).[38] The United States Grain Corporation would resurface in the 1930s as the Commodity Credit Corporation. The planning activities of the Food Administration would reappear in the two Agricultural Adjustment Acts. The Emergency Fleet Corporation came back as the National Maritime Administration. The Federal Housing Administration of the 1930s had been born first as the wartime United States Housing Corporation. The Fuel Administration under the Lever Act reemerged in the 1930s as the Bituminous Coal Division in the Interior Department. Senator Joseph Guffey (D, PA), who was instrumental in creating the New Deal laws governing coal and oil output and pricing, had been head of the petroleum division of the WIB.

The list of World War I institutions that reappeared in the 1930s and/or later in World War II is a long one. The people of the wartime regime also served again, and again. Herbert Hoover himself is the most famous case. But there were many others of note. Gerard Swope, the General Electric executive whose ideas later played crucial background roles in the NRA and the Social Security legislation, had worked under Baruch in the WIB. Baruch himself was a tireless planner and enthusiast for the reconstitution of the wartime regime in the crisis of the 1930s. Two Moline Plow executives, George Peek and General Hugh S. Johnson, served under Baruch in the WIB and then in New Deal positions. Peek was the first head of the Agricultural

TABLE 22.7 U.S. Sugar Prices Paid at Retail and Wholesale and on Average for Imported Sugar[a]

Year	*Retail*	*Wholesale*	*Imports*
1914	.059	.047	.020
1915	.066	.056	.033
1916	.080	.069	.041
$\frac{\textbf{1916 price}}{\textbf{1914 price}} \times 100$	135.6	146.8	205.0
1917	.093	.077	.045
1918	.097	.078	.047
$\frac{\textbf{1918 price}}{\textbf{1916 price}} \times 100$	121.3	113.0	114.6
1919	.113	.089	.056
1920	.194	.127	.138
$\frac{\textbf{1920 price}}{\textbf{1918 price}} \times 100$	200.0	162.8	293.6
1921	.080	.062	.039
1922	.073	.059	.026
$\frac{\textbf{1922 price}}{\textbf{1920 price}} \times 100$	37.6	46.5	18.8

[a] All prices are in dollars per pound.

Source: *Historical Statistics,* series E 125, 202, U 300–301.

Adjustment Administration, and Johnson was the head of the NRA. New Dealer Leon Henderson, who headed the Office of Price Administration in World War II, had served in 1918 in the WIB Ordnance Division. There were many more.[39]

The lessons of economic mobilization were not lost, and when a new crisis came—the Great Depression of the 1930s—the emergency institutions and the people who understood them were called to history's stage for a rerun.

But for more than a decade after 1918, it seemed that a new, high level of permanent prosperity had been created and that the wartime experience would never be relevant again.

NOTES

1. Hugh Rockoff, *Drastic Measures: A History of Wage and Price Controls in the United States* (1984), chap. 3; Robert Higgs, "Crisis, Bigger Government, and Ideological Change: Two Hypotheses on the Ratchet Phenomenon," *EEH*, January 1985, and *Crisis and Leviathan: Critical Episodes in the Growth of American Government* (1987), chap. 7.
2. Ronald Radosh and Murray Rothbard, *A New History of the Leviathan* (1972), p. 66. For specific reference to war mobilization and the New Deal, see William Leuchtenberg, "The New Deal and the Analogue of War," in John Braeman et al., *Change and Continuity in Twentieth-Century America* (1967).
3. See Elliot Brownlee, *Federal Taxation in America: A Short History* (1996).
4. For example, Elliot Brownlee, "Income Taxation and Capital Formation in Wisconsin, 1911–1929," *EEH*, Fall 1970. He argues that Wisconsin's state income tax inadvertently shifted expenditures away from capital formation in manufacturing. Industrialists "voted with their feet," and Wisconsin's development fell behind that of its neighboring states.
5. *Springer v. U.S.*, 102 U.S. 586 (1881).
6. *Pollack v. Farmers' Loan and Trust Company*, 157 U.S. 429 and 158 U.S. 601 (1895).
7. Bennett Baack and Edward John Ray, "Special Interests and the Adoption of the Income Tax in the U.S.," *JEH*, September 1985.
8. A concern that high tariffs could return was one of the reasons the Wilson administration created a Tariff Commission. See Karen Schnietz, "Democrats' 1916 Tariff Commission: Responding to Dumping Fears and Illustrating the Consumer Costs of Protectionism," *Business History Review*, vol. 72, no. 1, Spring 1998.
9. See Paul Studenski and Herman Krooss, *Financial History of the United States* (1952), Table 42, chap. 23, for an excellent short study of World War I finance.
10. *Historical Statistics*, series Y 904.
11. Studenski and Krooss (1952), p. 301.
12. Rockoff (1984).
13. *Ibid.*, p. 284.
14. Clemens Kool, "War Finance and Interest Rate Targeting: Regime Changes in 1914–1918," *EEH*, July 1995, dates the beginning of interest rate targeting in the United States to late 1917 after the country entered World War I.
15. Studenski and Krooss (1952), p. 294.
16. *Historical Statistics*, series P 107.
17. Studenski and Krooss (1952), p. 301, n. 16.
18. *Ibid.*, p. 301.
19. A forerunner of federal control of hours and wages made its appearance in the Adamson Act of 1916, which included a federally mandated eight-hour day (with time-and-a-half for overtime) for the railroads under the commerce clause. Jonathan Hughes, *The Governmental Habit Redux* (1991), pp. 115, 130–35. The long quest for an eight-hour day for all workers was realized in the years after the war. See Robert Whaples, "Winning the Eight-Hour Day, 1909–1919," *Journal of Economic History*, vol. L, no. 2, June 1990. The emergence of a national labor market in the prewar period is discussed in Joshua Rosenbloom, "One Market or Many: Labor Market Integration in the Late 19th Century United States," *Journal of Economic History*, vol. XLIX, no. 1, March 1990.
20. Sanford Jacoby points out that during the war, those manufacturers unable to recruit sufficiently from the "outside" labor market developed their own labor forces, an "inside" market to provide sufficient labor input. This accounts for much of the improvement of wages and working conditions for the manufacturing labor force. "The Development of Internal Labor Markets in American Manufacturing Firms," in Paul Osterman, ed., *Employment Practices in Large Firms* (Cambridge: MIT Press, 1984). See also Laura Owen, "Gender Differences in Labor Turnover and the Development of Internal Labor Markets in the United States during the 1920s,"*Enterprise and Society*, vol. 2, no. 1, March 2001.
21. Stanley Lebergott, *The American Economy: Income, Wealth and Want* (Princeton: Princeton University Press, 1976), pp. 205–208.

22. Arthur Stein, *The Nation at War* (Baltimore: The Johns Hopkins University Press, 1980), pp. 82–86.
23. See Rockoff (1984) and Higgs (1987).
24. See Hughes (1991), pp. 126–135; Radosh and Rothbard (1972), pp. 66–110, for most of the information in the subsequent discussion.
25. Grosvenor Clarkson, *Industrial America in the World War* (Boston: Houghton Mifflin, 1923).
26. See Richard Sicotte, "Economic Crisis and Political Response: The Political Economy of the Shipping Act of 1916," *Journal of Economic History*, vol. 59, no. 4, December 1999.
27. Paul Koistinen, "The Industrial-Military Complex in Historical Perspective: World War I," *BHR*, Winter 1967, p. 385.
28. Hughes (1991), p. 211.
29. *Ibid.*, p. 131.
30. Radosh and Rothbard (1972), pp. 75–76.
31. Edwin Witte, "Strikes in Wartime: Experience with Controls," *Annals of the American Academy of Political and Social Science*, vol. 224, November 1942.
32. Karl Brent Swisher, *American Constitutional Development* (Boston: Houghton Mifflin, 1954), pp. 596–598.
33. Robert Cuff and Melvin Urofsky, "The Steel Industry and Price-Fixing During World War I" *BHR*, Autumn 1970.
34. Radosh and Rothbard (1972), pp. 85–88.
35. Edward Berkowitz and Kim McQuaid, *Creating the Welfare State* (1988), p. 59.
36. Robert Himmelberg, "The War Industries Board and the Antitrust Question in 1918," *JAH*, June 1965.
37. Berkowitz and McQuaid (1988), p. 58.
38. For these and other examples, see Leuchtenberg (1967).
39. Radosh and Rothbard (1972), pp. 95–97.

SUGGESTED READINGS

Articles

Baack, Bennett D., and Edward John Ray. "Special Interests and the Adoption of the Income Tax in the U.S." *Journal of Economic History*, vol. 45, no. 3, September 1985.

Brownlee, W. Elliot. "Income Taxation and Capital Formation in Wisconsin, 1911–1929." *Explorations in Economic History*, vol. 8, no. 11, Fall 1970.

Cuff, Robert D., and Melvin I. Urofsky. "The Steel Industry and Price-Fixing During World War I." *Business History Review*, vol. 44, no. 3, Autumn 1970.

Higgs, Robert. "Crisis, Bigger Government, and Ideological Change: Two Hypotheses on the Ratchet Phenomenon." *Explorations in Economic History*, vol. 22, no. 1, January 1985.

Himmelberg, Robert F. "The War Industries Board and the Antitrust Question in 1918." *Journal of American History*, vol. 52, no. 1, June 1965.

Koistinen, Paul A. C. "The Industrial-Military Complex in Historical Perspective: World War I." *Business History Review*, vol. 41, no. 4, Winter 1967.

Kool, Clemens J. M. "War Finance and Interest Rate Targeting: Regime Changes in 1914–1918." *Explorations in Economic History*, vol. 32, no. 3, July 1995.

Leuchtenberg, William E. "The New Deal and the Analogue of War." In John Braeman et al., *Change and Continuity in Twentieth-Century America*. New York: Harper & Row, 1967.

Rockoff, Hugh. "Price and Wage Controls in Four Wartime Periods." *Journal of Economic History*, vol. XLI, no. 2, June 1981.

Books

Berkowitz, Edward, and Kim McQuaid. *Creating the Welfare State: The Political Economy of Twentieth-Century Reform*, 2nd ed. New York: Praeger, 1988.

Brownlee, W. Elliot. *Federal Taxation in America: A Short History*. New York: Cambridge University Press, 1996.

Hardach, Gerd. *The First World War, 1914–1918*. Berkeley: University of California Press, 1977.

Higgs, Robert. *Crisis and Leviathan: Critical Episodes in the Growth of American Government*. New York: Oxford University Press, 1987.

Hughes, Jonathan. *The Governmental Habit Redux: Economic Controls from Colonial Times to the Present*. Princeton: Princeton University Press, 1991.

Nelson, L. Keith. *The Impact of War on American Life: The Twentieth Century Experience*. New York: Holt, Rinehart & Winston, 1971.

Radosh, Ronald, and Murray N. Rothbard, eds. *A New History of the Leviathan: Essays on the Rise of the American Corporate State*. New York: Dutton, 1972.

Rockoff, Hugh. *Drastic Measures: A History of Wage and Price Controls in the United States*. New York: Cambridge University Press, 1984.

Studenski, Paul, and Herman Krooss. *Financial History of the United States*. New York: McGraw-Hill, 1952.

CHAPTER TWENTY-THREE

"Normalcy": 1919–1929

Between the two world wars, the American economic experience was schizophrenic: a decade of apparently limitless economic advance, followed by a decade of baffling and frustrating depression. Then war once again created the conditions for total economic mobilization.

The interwar period contains many ambiguous elements, and you should be forewarned that economists have been more successful in describing the period than explaining it. That inadequacy is surprising. Oceans of ink have been spilled over these events, and, yet, even such a primary question as what caused the 1929 stock market crash cannot be answered with confidence. Many—probably too many—explanations have been proffered, but there is little consensus.

The period 1919–1930 is one of general postwar prosperity. Even the year 1929 was, in most respects, a year of great prosperity, and through most of 1930 there seemed little reason to expect what followed. In 1931, the economy dipped powerfully into depression and was still not fully recovered at the end of 1941, when the Japanese attacked Pearl Harbor. Contemporary politicians could find no way to resolve the mysterious combination that characterized the depression: high unemployment and low levels of investment. The key to the 1930s disaster may well lie in the boom years of the 1920s. If so, it has never been clearly identified.

The next chapter will discuss several weaknesses in the economy of the late 1920s, but none of these, taken by itself, can explain a downtown of the magnitude that was experienced. The event most often thought to be the key, the stock market crash of 1929, is only one such weakness. While a complete explanation of the Great Depression has yet to be written, it is likely that many keys will be required to unlock its mysteries. This chapter will examine the events leading up to the crash and the crash itself.

INCOME DISTRIBUTION

The introduction of the income tax and other techniques of wartime finance leveled, to some degree, the country's income and wealth distributions. In the 1920s, the process was reversed. Once the war's excess demand for labor passed, the claims of others resumed priority.

According to Robert Lampman, the top 1 percent of adults held 32 percent of the nation's wealth in 1922, and they increased that share to 38 percent by 1929.[1] After that date, a secular decline began. Since wealth is the sum of net savings over time, it is not surprising to find that the wealth inequality was in part a reflection of income and savings inequalities. It is easier to save money from a large income than a small one, other things being equal.

In 1922, says Lampman, the top 1 percent of income recipients received 12 percent of all personal income and accomplished 49 percent of the country's saving. By 1928, these numbers were 13.7 percent and an astounding 80 percent, respectively. In 1929, the income share of the top 1 percent was still 13.6 percent, but savings of that group, after the financial disasters of that year, had fallen to 42 percent.[2]

Inequality of income and wealth was present in colonial times, as you learned in Chapter 3, and, although not fixed in constant shares over time, was a persistent feature of the country's long-term economic growth. According to Williamson and Lindert, the path of rising inequality of income and wealth was essentially unbroken until World War I.[3]

Wartime mobilization raised the shares of income going to labor. But when peace came again, the normal American preference for access to saved resources resumed its course, and so did the enhanced income shares accruing thereto. As Williamson and Lindert point out, this was the normal consequence of rapid growth in a gold-standard setting where there is no easy way to increase the money supply, to increase the command over real resources. According to Lampman, the income and wealth structure was a significant feedback mechanism until the onset of the 1930s depression. High incomes led to savings and hence wealth, which produced more income, which produced more wealth.[4] The 1920s saw a resumption of this old pattern.

The evidence for income received shows that inequality increased in the 1920s; the extent of that increase is currently in dispute.[5] Increased income inequality in the 1920s means that consumption expenditures would tend to weaken even though aggregate personal incomes continued to rise. With the 1929 crash and the recession of 1929–1932, there was no question about the future of consumption expenditures—they fell. The Great Depression brought fundamental changes, including high tax rates on interest incomes, which will be discussed in the next chapter. The trend of both the income and wealth distributions reversed and moved in the direction of greater equality until the 1980s.

THE EXPANSION OF THE 1920s

The "Roaring Twenties" is the popular phrase that describes the decade: jazz, bootleg booze, gangsters, F. Scott Fitzgerald, H. L. Mencken, Babe Ruth, and the Great Crash of 1929. It remains a legend in our economic and social history.[6] What shaped it?

Consumer Credit and Consumer Durables

Martha Olney's work adds a new dimension to our understanding of the 1920s economy. It was a time when consumers shifted their household demands dramatically into purchases of durable goods on credit.[7] In the early decades of the twentieth century, products based upon the new network of dependable supplies of electric power, together with internal combustion engines (and fractional horsepower engines), began to flood the market. Automobiles, radios, washing machines, electric refrigerators, and a host of other new electrical household gadgets were creating a bright new world for the ordinary household. Americans waded into installment-plan buying to purchase these durable consumer goods. Instead of the use of interest-earning assets to finance ultimate purchases, a down payment and an installment contract transferred ownership of the assets (with a lien). Consumers *used the assets* while their monthly payments reduced consumption expenditures on other commodities. It was, in effect, a new kind of saving: purchase for future consumption in which investment in the asset substituted for other forms of saving.

As a result, consumer durables purchases increased at 8.3 percent per annum, nearly double the increase in GNP and in consumption from 1922 to 1929. By 1925, 75 percent of automobiles, 70 percent of furniture, 75 percent of radios, 90 percent of pianos, 80 percent of phonographs, and 80 percent of household appliances were purchased on installment credit. A permanent new "American way of life" was born, financed by innovation in the country's financial institutions and a desire by consumers to enjoy now and pay later. The consumer durables revolution added a new flavor to the country's economic life in the 1920s.

The New Leisure. *Radio was one of the industries that flourished after World War I (above). The provision of paved roads by public authorities led eventually to intercity highways and mob scenes on the beaches (below).*

Even Henry Ford arranged for his cars to be bought on the installment plan.[8]

These new durables contributed to the development of a new market in used durables, fed in part by units repossessed from those who missed installment payments. When the economy turned down, people simply stopped making payments. As more used units became available, fewer new ones had to be produced. This, however, is more an effect of depression than a cause. As will be discussed in the next chapter, the timing is wrong for this to have been a key to the Great Depression.

Output and Prices

Automobile production, like that of most other goods, increased dramatically in the 1920s. Manufacturing output very nearly doubled between the 1921 recession and the 1929 crash. Prices were extraordinarily stable, while, by modern standards, the extent of monetary expansion in the 1920s was modest.

Consider the data in Table 23.1. The expansion falls between two sharp downturns in prices and activity. The 1920–1921 recession was short and sharp. In fact, note that prices fell far more between 1920 and 1921 than they did between 1929 and 1930. So also did the money supply. In the 1921 recession, little was overtly done by government to compensate, although Elmus Wicker argues that the Federal Reserve System *accidentally* buffered the decline by maintaining high bank liquidity at high rates of interest.[9] Most of the World War I inflation was blown away in the 1921 recession, and, when recovery came, there had been a drastic realignment of prices.

From 1921 to 1929, manufacturing output rose with only a small check (the mild recession of 1924) and a leveling from 1926 to 1927. Wholesale and consumer prices were remarkably stable in the face of such a powerful expansion of real output and the slower (but still significant) increase in the money supply from its 1921 level. A strong boom in real investment and leftover capacity from the war years made real growth without inflation possible. Even though the money supply increased some 25 percent from the 1920 low, prices actually declined. Real wages rose; with prices stable, average industrial wages increased about 17 percent between 1922 and 1929.[10] Even in 1930, after the crash, the actual money supply and price movements of that year scarcely forecast the depths of the depression.

TABLE 23.1 Money, Prices, and Manufacturing Production, 1919–1930

Year	M_2[a]	*Wholesale Prices*	*Consumer Prices*	*Index of Manufacturing Production*
			(1967 = 100)	
1919	$31.01	71.4	51.8	15
1920	34.80	79.6	60.0	15
1921	32.85	50.3	53.6	12
1922	33.72	49.9	50.2	15
1923	36.60	51.9	51.1	18
1924	38.58	50.5	51.2	17
1925	42.05	53.3	52.5	19
1926	43.68	51.6	53.0	20
1927	44.73	49.3	52.0	20
1928	46.42	50.0	51.3	21
1929	46.60	49.1	51.3	23
1930	45.73	44.6	50.0	19

[a] In billions of dollars.

Source: *Historical Statistics,* series E 23, 135, P 13, X 415.

GNP and Unemployment

Table 23.2 shows GNP and unemployment figures for the period 1919–30. Without the two recession years (1921 and 1924), the average rate of unemployment was about 4 percent. As in the nineteenth century, the boom years reduced unemployment levels to the rates sustained by frictional and technological job disruptions, together with seasonal unemployment. In 1919, 1923, 1926, and 1929, employment must have been *full* by most definitions of the word.

The high unemployment rates of 1921, 1922, 1924, and 1930 reflect the natural adjustments believed to be typical of an economy when the federal government makes no attempts at buffering actions. Resources and workers were quickly thrown into unemployment, prices were reduced, wages were reduced—all to be absorbed in more efficient employment in the ensuing expansions. This explanation was believed by orthodox economists and was the basis of Schumpeter's great system of cyclical analysis, discussed in Chapter 17. The 1920s fit perfectly into his analysis.

Between the 1921 recession and 1929, real GNP (1929 prices) rose 59.3 percent, an average annual rate of 6 percent. In real terms it was a vigorous expansion with the added attractions of stable prices, rising real wages, and, for the most part, "full" employment. Even so, the actual distribution of the gains between the rich and the poor was markedly uneven.

The sharp downturn in 1920–1921—with a jump of 6.5 percent in the unemployment rate and a fall of 37 percent in wholesale prices in a single year—was accompanied by a reduction of only 8.7 percent of real GNP.[11] The 1929–1930 fall in real GNP was 9.9 percent, nearly 14 percent larger, even though prices declined very little (see Table 23.1). The initial rise in the unemployment rate in 1930, nearly tripling the 1929 figure, was still far below that experienced between 1920 and 1921. The supply of money had declined by 3 percent from 1929 to 1930 compared to a whopping 9.3 percent from 1920 to 1921.[12]

At the period's end, by such measures, it might have been thought that a recession was at hand, milder than the one of 1920 and 1921. It would have been reasonable to have every confidence of an ensuing recovery.[13] If you didn't know that the increases in real disposable income were more unequally distributed in the 1920s, the figures for increased per-capita GNP might suggest a particular robustness. If rising GNP per capita alone were really indicative of

TABLE 23.2 Unemployment, GNP, and Federal Finance, 1919–1930

		Gross National Product					
Year	*Unemployed Percentage of Labor Force*	*Current Prices ($ billions)*	*1958 Prices*	*1958 Prices per Capita*	*Federal Receipts ($ billions)*	*Federal Expenditures ($ billions)*	*Federal Surplus(+) Deficit (–) ($ billions)*
1919	1.4	$ 84.0	$146.4	$1,401	$5.1	$18.5	$–13.4
1920	5.2	91.5	140.0	1,315	6.6	6.4	+0.2
1921	11.7	69.6	127.8	1,177	5.6	5.1	+0.5
1922	6.7	74.1	148.0	1,345	4.0	3.3	+0.7
1923	2.4	85.1	165.9	1,482	3.9	3.1	+0.8
1924	5.0	84.7	165.5	1,450	3.9	2.9	+1.0
1925	3.2	93.1	179.4	1,549	3.6	2.9	+0.7
1926	1.8	97.0	190.0	1,619	3.8	2.9	+0.9
1927	3.3	94.9	189.8	1,594	4.0	2.9	+1.1
1928	4.2	97.0	190.9	1,584	3.9	3.0	+0.9
1929	3.2	103.1	203.6	1,671	3.9	3.1	+0.8
1930	8.9	90.4	183.5	1,490	4.1	3.3	+0.8

Source: *Historical Statistics*, series F 1, 3, 4, D 9, Y 335, 336.

economic health (and it is conventionally measured as such), the increase of 42 percent from 1921 to 1929 might suggest an economy of particular strength. Actually, of course, catastrophe was on the way.

The income distribution figures discussed at the beginning of this chapter suggest that such considerations are an illusion. Harry Oshima points out that the mechanization of the 1920s associated with fractional horsepower and internal combustion engines sharply reduced demand for nonskilled and even skilled labor. The idea of "technological unemployment" appeared first in the later 1920s. Such factors must have contributed to the change in income distribution in the 1920s.[14]

Fiscal Results

After 1919, the consequences of the federal government's fiscal policy were deflationary. The federal budget outcomes are shown in the last column of Table 23.2, rounded to the nearest tenth of a billion dollars. There remained a war-related deficit, $13.4 billion, in 1919, but in subsequent years the federal budget was in surplus every year. The net result was mildly deflationary. In 1919, the deficit equaled just under 16 percent of GNP. When the Federal Reserve purchased government-issued debt, there was a powerful inflationary stimulus. Most of the consequences were blown away by the 1921 recession. Only in 1924 and 1927 were the ensuing surpluses as much as 1 percent of GNP.

From the Civil War to 1919, federal expenditures never reached $1 billion a year. However, with the new income tax in 1913, the federal government was funded at a new high level. Thus, according to *Parkinson's third law*, "expenditures rise to meet income," federal expenditures were never again below $1 billion. World War I, like all American wars of this century, caused a fairly large jump in federal expenditures.

The Farm Sector

Conventional wisdom about the 1920s is that the farm sector was a major contributor to the unprecedented collapse in the 1930s. We know that the farmers themselves believed they were falling behind even in the late nineteenth century, and phenomena like the Populist revolt and subsequent reforms were monuments to that agrarian discontent. In the 1920s, the agricultural sector again agitated for special treatment by the federal government. In 1922, with the Capper-Volstead Act, farm-bloc lobbyists succeeded in lifting the threat of antitrust prosecution from farm cooperatives. This bill paved the way for output restrictions and price-fixing by those organizations.[15]

Efforts were virtually continuous to get federal subsidies for exports of food. Both Presidents Coolidge and Hoover vetoed Haugen-McNary bills that sought such support; President Roosevelt signed the bill creating the Export-Import Bank in 1933.

The farmers wanted outright federal purchases of food to create artificial shortages in the markets. The latter scheme was a favorite of the Populists and had been partly achieved during World War I under the Lever Act. In 1929, President Hoover submitted to the pressure, and in the Agricultural Market Act and the Federal Farm Board of that year, provisions were made to lend some $500 million to farm co-ops and stabilization groups. By 1930, the Farm Board owned a third of the nation's wheat supply, all in the interest of supporting farm incomes.[16] The farmers clearly felt aggrieved. Why?

Table 23.3 supplies a shorthand economic history of the 1920s farm problem. All original data are transformed into index numbers based upon 1920, the peak postwar business-cycle year. In Column 1, notice that the volume of farm output rose only moderately in the period; 1928 volume was only 7 percent higher than that of 1920. However, owing to the sharp decline in farm prices, net farm income fell far below that of 1920 and never did recover.[17] Farm prices relative to nonfarm prices fell sharply from 1919 to 1921 (Column 8, farm net barter terms of trade) but recovered fairly steadily until 1930. The lack of output expansion meant that even though farm income rose from the low of 1921, it never regained the level of 1919, or even that of 1920. As a result, the farm share of national income steadily eroded (see Column 9 in Table 23.3) throughout the 1920s.

Fixed charges measured against farm income rose disastrously between 1920 and 1925 (Columns 10, 11, 12). Real estate debt, interest charges, and taxes on real estate pressed against reduced farm income and produced hard times in American agriculture, even though the strict terms of trade of farmers

TABLE 23.3 The Farm Economy, 1919–1930: Selected Indicators (1920 = 100 Base)

	(1)	(2)	(3)	(4)	(5)	(6)	(7)
						Prices	
Year	*Farm Output*	*Net Farm Income*	*Farm Debt Outstanding*	*Interest Payable on Farm Loans*	*Real Estate Taxes per Acre*	*Nonfarm*	*Farm*
1919	94.3	134.9	84.5	82.9	80.4	80.0	104.6
1920	100.0	100.0	100.0	100.0	100.0	100.0	100.0
1921	88.6	55.4	121.0	113.6	105.9	65.0	58.7
1922	97.1	62.5	126.7	118.3	105.9	63.5	62.3
1923	98.6	71.9	127.7	118.3	107.8	64.9	65.5
1924	97.1	75.1	126.1	112.5	107.8	62.0	66.3
1925	100.0	89.6	117.3	106.4	109.8	63.7	72.8
1926	104.3	83.4	115.0	104.2	109.8	62.1	66.5
1927	102.9	82.7	114.3	103.3	111.8	58.3	65.9
1928	107.1	82.2	115.5	102.6	113.7	57.5	70.3
1929	105.7	88.3	115.5	101.2	113.7	56.7	69.5
1930	102.9	63.7	114.0	99.1	111.8	52.7	58.8

Source: *Historical Statistics,* series K 284, 361, 372, 374, 415; E 24, 25; F 125, 127.

actually improved considerably after the collapse of 1920–1921. These hard times contributed to the failure of a series of southern banks, but, as we shall see in the following chapter, these are not the bank failures that play a crucial role in the Monetarist's explanation of the Great Depression.

Thus, the farm disaster of the 1930s did have strong roots in the 1920s.[18] The high prices occurring between 1899 and 1919 had lent a temporary respite to the problems of the previous generation. But the troubles of the 1920s, tied peculiarly to long-term debt and taxes, prepared the way for the tidal wave of farm foreclosures of the 1930s.

Building Construction, Population, and Immigration

The one indicator nearly every writer has fixed upon as an ominous sign of disaster is the great building boom of the 1920s and its peak from 1925 to 1927, *preceding* the Great Crash. This phenomenon is shown in Table 23.4.

Building construction is so ubiquitous that a change in its fortunes affects all communities almost instantly. Building has been subject to long cycles (18 to 22 years) of duration in the American economy, a famous phenomenon among economists. Indeed, Arthur F. Burns and Wesley C. Mitchell concluded in *Measuring Business Cycles* that the building cycle is the most regular and clearly defined of all cyclical activity in the American economy.[19] The great building boom of the 1920s raised total income generated from construction by 80 percent. The value of new construction permits rose by a phenomenal 192 percent between 1919 and 1926.

Then the boom faded. It was not killed by rising building costs, as the composite cost index shows. Costs were stable. Demand simply died off, slowly but remorselessly.[20] As was discussed in Chapter 16, there was a legislated decrease in immigration following World War I. Table 16.6 noted that the rate of immigration was 10.4 per thousand population in the first decade of the 20th century. The rate was only one-third of that in the 1920s, and one-twenty-fifth of that in the 1930s. This contributed to a deceleration in the rate of population growth. Between 1890 and 1915, the total resident population grew at an average annual rate of just less than 2 percent, but the average annual rate for the decade 1919–1929 was only in the neighborhood of 1.5 percent. The deaths of young Americans in the war (the population growth rate for 1918

(8) Farm Net Barter Terms of Trade (Column 7 / Column 6) x 100	(9) Farm Output as Percentage of GNP	(10) Farm Debt as Percentage of Farm Income (Column 3 / Column 2)	(11) Interest Payable as Percentage of Farm Income (Column 4 / Column 2)	(12) Real Estate Taxes as Percentage of Farm Income (Column 5 / Column 2)
130.8	13.2	74.4	5.0	4.1
100.0	13.0	117.4	8.0	6.7
90.3	12.6	259.7	16.6	13.0
98.1	12.8	240.8	15.3	11.5
100.9	12.0	210.9	13.3	10.1
106.9	11.1	199.9	12.1	9.6
114.3	11.6	155.6	9.6	8.1
107.1	10.8	163.8	10.1	8.9
113.0	11.0	164.4	10.1	9.3
122.3	10.6	167.0	10.1	9.5
122.6	10.3	155.5	9.3	9.1
111.6	10.6	212.7	12.6	12.5

was negative) and the decrease of immigration caused a decline in the rate of household formation beginning in the early 1920s.[21] The construction industry did not perceive this decrease. By the middle of the 1920s, an excess supply of housing had developed, one that grew worse as incomes fell in the Great Depression. As we

TABLE 23.4 Value of Building Construction, 1919–1930[a]

	Construction				
Year	*Total*	*Total New*	*Maintenance and Repair*	*Permits (1930 = 100)*	*Cost Index (1967 = 100)*
1919	$ 8.9	$ 6.3	$2.6	81.9	30
1920	9.7	6.7	3.0	87.6	37
1921	8.9	6.0	2.9	107.6	30
1922	10.6	7.6	2.9	167.6	27
1923	12.5	9.3	3.2	212.7	30
1924	13.8	10.4	3.4	213.3	30
1925	15.0	11.4	3.6	252.3	30
1926	15.8	12.1	3.7	239.6	30
1927	16.0	12.0	4.0	214.4	30
1928	15.6	11.6	4.0	199.1	30
1929	15.0	10.8	4.2	187.3	30
1930	12.6	8.7	3.9	100.0	29

[a] Value of construction figures given in billions of dollars.

Source: *Historical Statistics,* series N 1, 61, 111, 118.

will see in the next chapter, this decrease is part of the decline in investment to which Keynesians point as one of the causes of the depression, but the effect was not large enough to create a "great" depression.

THE FINANCIAL SECTOR

Weakness in the farm and construction sectors are "old hat" explanations of events in the 1920s.[22] Although they may signify some deep underlying unsoundness in the economy, scholars have never been willing to pin the immense turnaround in the 1930s on these sectors alone. What is frustrating to economists is the conventional view: that the economy was basically sound but that excessive speculation by the public at large brought old-time American capitalism to grief. This viewpoint is especially galling to the Rational Expectations school of economic thought that believes people cannot systematically err if left in control of their own resources. Hence, in recent years there have been efforts to tag the financial system with major responsibility for 1929 and subsequent events.

The Conventional Explanation

Table 23.5 presents the basic reasons for the conventional view. For purposes of analysis, again the raw data are converted to index-number relatives based upon 1920. In 1929, GNP in *current prices* stood 7.5 percent below the 1920 level, but prices were nearly 40 percent below 1920. The sum of demand deposits and currency in circulation, M_1, was a mere 12.3 percent above 1920. The Federal Reserve's portfolio of securities, plus its outstanding loans and discounts—the measure of Federal Reserve money- creating activity—stood at only 47.9 percent of 1920. Even if the Fed had been willing, the commercial banking system's conservatism hardly could have been a major expansionary source; demand deposits in 1929 were a mere 18.1 percent higher than they had been in 1920.

On the other hand, time deposits had risen by 80.3 percent, the single largest element of potential monetary expansion. Even so, entering time deposits into the larger money supply aggregate, M_2, raises it to a mere 33.9 percent above 1920. Since in 1929 the common stock index had risen by 226 percent over that of 1920, there is something to explain. Wherever the boom in the stock market came from, it is unreasonable to blame it on excess money creation by the banking system. The stock-market price rise of the 1920s remains, as the conventional wisdom always maintained, as the great peculiarity of the 1920s.

What can explain stock-market prices? In general, there is a two-part answer:

1. Until 1929, even with those price increases, stocks were apparently sound purchases for those with money to invest.

TABLE 23.5 Financial Indexes Based on 1920 = 100

Year	*GNP*	*Wholesale Prices*	M_1	*Federal Reserve Loans and Securities*	*Demand Deposits*	*Time Deposits*	M_2	*Common Stock Total*
1919	91.8	89.7	91.8	95.5	92.3	83.3	89.1	143.2
1920	100.0	100.0	100.0	100.0	100.0	100.0	100.0	100.0
1921	76.1	63.2	90.6	47.1	90.8	102.4	94.4	86.0
1922	81.0	62.7	91.3	41.0	93.4	108.9	96.9	105.4
1923	93.0	65.2	96.6	37.4	98.5	123.5	105.2	107.4
1924	92.6	63.4	99.7	38.4	102.4	134.7	110.9	113.4
1925	101.7	67.0	108.1	43.1	112.7	148.1	120.8	139.7
1926	106.0	64.8	110.3	41.3	115.2	158.1	125.5	157.8
1927	103.7	61.9	110.0	49.2	114.9	168.3	128.5	192.2
1928	106.0	62.8	111.2	55.1	116.8	181.0	133.4	250.0
1929	112.7	61.7	112.3	47.9	118.1	180.3	133.9	326.1
1930	98.8	56.0	108.6	41.8	114.4	180.4	131.4	263.5

Source: *Historical Statistics*, series E 23, F 1, X 412–415, 495, 497.

2. In 1929, a bubble on the boom was the final push to the brink of disaster for the stock market.[23]

Since the upper income strata received the lion's share of the increase in income during the 1920s, there was a large stock of saving in search of a return. Because increased stock prices measured increased wealth, people were encouraged to play the market, to make further stock purchases. Such a phenomenon is common in gambling casinos, modern real estate, and commodities markets. The elements usually blamed for the rapid increases in 1920s stocks—reckless loans to brokers by bankers and gambling on insufficient margins—surely played a part, as they always do. However, by conventional measures, investments in stocks must have seemed sound enough, until just at the end.

Why buy common stocks? If a person has a certain sum of money to invest, he or she wants a return on it and a certain amount of security. In general, the less secure the investment, the higher will be the potential yield. In normal circumstances, like the 1920s (apart from crisis periods), bonds will, on average, yield less than stocks. Although bond prices vary (inversely with interest rates), the coupon payment is definite (a certain percentage of the face value) if the firm does not go bankrupt. Even then, bondholders have the first claim on the assets.

Stock dividends are paid according to the distribution of earnings by a firm's management. Stock prices can rise or fall far more than can the bond prices of solvent firms. Thus, in ordinary circumstances the risk-averse investor will prefer bonds to stocks. In general, the climate of business also influences the investor's decisions. In good times, in fact, the investor may be willing to "take a flyer" in stocks. In bad times, he or she may shift to government bonds, the surest thing this side of legal tender itself.

Business Conditions Before the Crash

What were business conditions like before the 1929 crash? There had been the cyclical problems, and ordinary investors were aware of them. They also knew that the economy was growing, and that prices were stable and employment was high.

We can see in Table 23.6 that the number of business firms rose every year until 1929. People were optimistic enough to start up new firms even though failures were occurring. There was a sharp increase in the failure rate in the recession of 1921 (lingering into 1922), but after that time the failure rate was less,

TABLE 23.6 Selected Business Indicators, 1919–1930

					Annual Averages (percentages)				
					Bond Yields		*Stock Yields*		
Year	*Number of Business Firms*	*Failures Per 1,000 Firms*	*Average Liability of Failures ($ thousands)*	*Prime Rate*	*U.S. Govt.*	*Corporate AA*	*Industrials*	*Rails*	*Utilities*
1919	1,711	37	17.6	5.37	4.73	5.49	5.18	6.26	7.37
1920	1,821	48	33.2	7.50	5.32	6.12	5.54	6.81	8.06
1921	1,927	102	31.9	6.62	5.09	5.97	5.84	7.08	8.29
1922	1,983	120	26.4	4.52	4.30	5.10	5.37	5.95	7.62
1923	1,996	93	28.8	5.07	4.36	5.12	5.40	6.29	7.59
1924	2,047	100	26.4	3.98	4.06	5.00	5.25	6.44	7.35
1925	2,113	100	20.9	4.02	3.86	4.88	4.75	5.66	6.13
1926	2,158	101	18.8	4.34	3.68	4.73	5.24	5.52	5.57
1927	2,172	106	22.5	4.11	3.34	4.57	4.72	4.89	4.96
1928	2,199	109	20.5	4.85	3.33	4.55	3.82	4.76	4.09
1929	2,213	104	21.1	5.85	3.60	4.73	3.65	4.29	2.29
1930	2,183	122	25.4	3.59	3.29	4.55	4.45	5.27	3.19

Source: *Historical Statistics,* series V 20, 23, 30, X 445, 474, 477, 480–482.

although it remained at more than double the 1919–1920 rate. Also, the average size of the failures did not rise after 1921. The crisis levels of interest rates of 1920–1921 faded, and, from 1923 to 1929, the prime rate averaged less than 5 percent. Unlike the wild times in the late 1970s and 1980, the low real interest rates in the 1920s were "positive," higher than actual or expected price increases: 4.3 percent in 1926 was more costly to borrowers than 10 percent was in 1980, when prices were rising even faster.

After 1921, when interest rates fell, yields on common stocks generally were higher than yields on bonds. Even in 1928, when interest rates fell back, yields on common stocks were higher than on bonds. In 1928, yields on utilities generally exceeded those on government bonds. A risk-averse investor in 1928 might still have seen stocks as good investments for *their yields alone*, compared to bonds. In addition, the fever for capital gains was building. Stock prices were turning into a new El Dorado (the legendary treasure city of South America), which added to the attractions of stocks and tempted some of the less risk-averse investors to shift into stocks. The yields were good, and the capital gains were outstanding.

Consider the data in Table 23.7. Prices of common stocks recovered quickly from the 1921 downturn. They then rose and, in general, kept rising. By 1928, investors on average had more than doubled their money over 1920 levels. The economy, by nearly every measure, must have seemed sound. Pessimists could have pointed to housing and agriculture or warned that, given the income distribution, further growth of mass consumption was unlikely. However, the signs were mixed.

TABLE 23.7 Average Annual Prices of Common Stocks Indexed on 1920

Year	*Total*	*Industrials*	*Rails*	*Utilities*
1919	143.2	109.7	110.0	100.7
1920	100.0	100.0	100.0	100.0
1921	86.0	78.0	96.6	106.1
1922	105.4	97.7	113.7	130.2
1923	107.4	100.6	112.4	135.6
1924	113.4	105.1	119.9	144.8
1925	139.7	133.7	140.0	174.3
1926	157.8	154.5	156.9	180.5
1927	192.2	192.8	183.0	206.8
1928	250.0	260.3	193.7	275.9
1929	326.1	328.5	221.2	444.1
1930	263.5	252.6	190.9	398.5

Source: *Historical Statistics*, series X 495–498.

Because of Henry Ford's conversion from the Model T to the Model A, auto sales in 1927 had been down—from 3,692,000 autos sold in 1926 to 2,936,000 in 1927—but then shot up to 3,775,000 autos sold in 1928.[24] Steel production in 1928 was 67 million tons, up a million tons from the previous high in 1925. Coal production had fallen (501 million tons in 1928; it had peaked at 573 million tons in 1926), but that decrease in part reflected the booming market in the competitive fuel, oil. Crude oil production, 443 million barrels in 1920, rose to 764 million barrels in 1925 and 901 million barrels in 1928.[25]

Cheap fuel was available for houses, factories, and the mass of autos now crowding the roads. Stocks reached remarkable levels. A buyer of common stocks could look forward to 1929 as a great year for business, and indeed it was, by all our measures, until the plunge.

THE GREAT CRASH

If your tire blew out on the Interstate and then the entire automobile fell apart, you would conclude that something besides the tire was defective. Likewise, many economists believe that somehow or other the economy must have been fundamentally unsound in 1929, despite the abundant evidence to the contrary. The stock-market panic was one of the most interesting and puzzling events in American economic history, and one with the most long-lived and far-reaching consequences. It is worth our attention for a few pages. The tire had failed. That was not unusual. But the auto then fell apart. That *was* unusual. In October 1987, stocks failed again, and again, apparently without warning. On that occasion, however, the economy bounced back. The crash of 1929 could not have caused the Great Depression all by itself.

Stock market crashes are interesting phenomena. What wisdom can we obtain from looking at the 1929 crash? What warning for the future?

Could They See It Coming?

It is fair to say from the general evidence that, if you did not know 1929 was coming, you would not have expected it in 1928. A reasonable analyst would have expected a downturn at *some* point. Every expansion in American economic history has come to an end, just as every recession has come to an end. The great crises swept away wealth, savings, and jobs, and ruined lives. The one that occurred in the 1920s was no different. Yet a remarkable number of people seemed not to believe that it would happen again.

Such faith is what fuels every boom. Unfortunately, booms are like rubbish burning in an incinerator: When *the flame is highest, the acceleration is exhausted.* Hence, the crisis and sudden collapse. The successful speculator gets out before the collapse, or sees it coming and sells short.

Two examples of just such a situation have occurred in the more recent past. In late December 1980, amid the great precious metals boom of that year—when silver was approaching $50 an ounce, and gold, $850—sober professionals were seeing silver at $75 and gold at $1,000 an ounce in "a matter of weeks." Instead, on 21 January 1980, prices crashed: Gold fell 20 percent, and silver fell 25 percent in a few days. Then there were weeks of slower decline until silver approached $10 an ounce, and gold fell to below $500 an ounce. The most sophisticated professionals lost huge fortunes, while others, holding short positions, cleaned up. In October 1987, the stock-market crash saw about a third of its stock values vanish in a few days. Ronald Reagan, like Herbert Hoover before him, immediately opined that the economy was "fundamentally sound." Yet the crash *had* occurred. The economy bounced back in 1987. It did not in 1929.

How can you sense the end of a boom? How can you know that there will be a panic sell-off, that yesterday's plungers will be tomorrow's frightened rabbits? How could you have known in early 1929 that a great disaster was at hand, instead of a significant improvement over the splendid results of 1928? Is such prescience possible?[26]

Let us drop back in history another 80 years and cross the Atlantic. On the night of 5 November 1857, Bonamy Dobrée, Deputy Governor of the Bank of England, wrote in his diary what one of his fellow directors had found: "Hodgson reports a most unpleasant feeling abroad in Lombard Street, a sort of apprehension of insolvency widespread."[27] On that day, the Bank of England's discount rate had been raised to 9 percent, the highest ever, and the great panic of 1857 was about to let loose in London. A week later the Bank rate was 10 percent, the Bank of England's banking department had been *drained* of its own notes, and application had been made to violate the Bank Charter Act of 1844 and issue more Bank of England notes on the basis of government debt.

The crisis of 1857 was one of the most severe in history, spreading financial ruin worldwide. Yet *The Economist*, even then London's most respected financial journal, had written on 4 July 1857, a few months earlier:

> We have neither excessive trade nor numerous new enterprises, nor is there in the public any great and irregular action threatening future convulsion. Our superfluous energy seems … to have blown off in the Russian War.[28]

Late in the summer, bank failures in the United States and failures of firms connected to the American trade in Great Britain caused the Bank of England's Court of Directors to become fearful.

Much of this is similar to the case of 1929. The popular conception was one of unlimited good times. President Coolidge, in his farewell State of the Union message in December 1928, had appraised the "tranquillity and contentment … the highest record of years of prosperity," and had assured the assembled politicians that they could "anticipate the future with optimism."[29] Yet, scholars writing about 1929 report the kinds of preternatural intimations Hodgson had found in Lombard Street. John Kenneth Galbraith quotes Roger Babson's famous address to the Annual National Business Conference on 5 September 1929:

> Sooner or later a crash is coming, and it may be terrific … factories will shut down … men will be thrown out of work … the vicious circle will get in full swing….[30]

Galbraith notes that Babson was widely scoffed at for such foresight.

It is in fact Galbraith's *The Great Crash* that contains the best explanation of one curiosity in Table

23.5, the outlandish growth of common stock prices relative to other measures of monetary activity.

The absence of a general monetary expansion would not necessarily weaken the flow of funds into the stock market if alternative methods developed to *divert* funds there from other uses. Other prices would fall, and stock prices would rise. Galbraith documents the development of such methods after about 1924.[31] There were two major sources of diversion: (a) direct, nonbank loans to brokers and (b) investment trusts.

Brokers' Loans

After the fact, brokers' loans became a villain in the search for an explanation of the stock market bubble. Business firms that ordinarily used their cash surpluses for internal financing, for short-term, self-liquidating loans, or for securities purchases began lending directly to the stock market through loans to brokers. Because the brokers used such funds to finance their own customers, the loans became a major source of credit—leverage in the stock market. Because the loans had maturities at "call," they were instantly retrievable by nonbank lenders, at least in theory, and the earnings were high.

Such loans must have seemed a godsend to corporate treasurers charged with earning interest on temporary surplus cash flows. According to Galbraith, by early 1929, Standard Oil of New Jersey was diverting an average of $69 million a day into call loans; Electric Bond and Share, more than $100 million. Such nonbanking institutions were pouring more funds into the stock market than was the banking system itself.

End-of-year figures for brokers' loans in the 1920s are shown in Table 23.8. According to this evidence, the normal proportion of nonbanking money in such loans in those days (see 1923–1925) was less than 30 percent of the total. However, by 1926, a change was evident. Even at the end of 1929, after the panic, the nonbank proportion of the total stood at nearly 60 percent. In early October 1929, when brokers' loans stood at $8.5 billion, $6.6 billion of that figure, or about 78 percent, came from nonbank sources.[32]

Clearly the nonbanking financial world wanted a share of the speculative action in Wall Street, and, by 1929, it was providing most of it. Even in 1926, when bank loans to brokers dipped, sources outside the banking system continued to increase their supplies of call loans. In 1932, when the dust had really settled over Wall Street, nonbank sources provided less than 6 percent of the depression-level loans to brokers. If stock prices rose from 1926 to 1929 because of "undue speculation," and such undue speculation was fueled by loans to stockbrokers, most of the blame lies outside the banking community.

TABLE 23.8 End of Year, Brokers' Loans, Bank and Nonbank, 1923–1932[a]

Year	*Total*	*New York City Banks*	*Outside Banks*	*Nonbank Sources*	*Percentage Nonbank*
1923	$1,580	$ 720	$ 410	$ 450	28.5
1924	2,230	1,150	530	550	24.7
1925	3,550	1,450	1,550	1,050	29.6
1926	3,290	1,160	830	1,300	39.5
1927	4,430	1,550	1,050	1,830	41.3
1928	6,440	1,640	915	3,885	60.3
1929	4,110	1,200	460	2,450	59.6
1930	2,105	1,280	215	610	29.0
1931	715	540	35	140	19.6
1932	430	335	20	75	17.4

[a] Amounts given are in thousands of dollars unless otherwise indicated.

Source: *Historical Statistics,* series X 547–550.

Investment Trusts

The other popular villain in explaining the stock market bubble is associated with investment trusts, a financial instrument similar to modern mutual funds. A trust sold its own securities, stocks, and bonds to the public, using the proceeds to purchase other stock. The newly acquired stocks could be those of their investment trusts; one trust could therefore own controlling interest in other trusts. Since stocks then (and now) were commonly purchased on **margin** (the buyer puts up some of his or her own cash, and the broker, the rest) and since the market was rising, investment trusts were, for a short time, a remarkable way to make money.

Galbraith's amusing yet carefully researched book describes the affairs of several investment trusts. American Founders Group, started in 1922 with $500, by 1929 grew to 13 companies with holdings in excess of $1 *billion*, "which may well have been the largest volume of assets ever controlled by an original outlay of $500."[33] In 1928, there were perhaps 186 investment trusts; in 1929 alone, 265 new ones were formed. This rapid growth was one manifestation of the bubble on the boom. In 1927, the investment trusts sold $400 million of securities to the public to finance their operations; in 1929, $3 *billion*.[34] The investment trusts were filled with perhaps more than a fair share of chicanery, but they served as a funnel to divert money into stocks and to exhilarate the market.

These two sources of extraordinary diversion—nonbanking money in brokers' loans and investment trusts—added to the amounts put into stocks directly by private investors, banks, and speculators; they served to drive an already powerful stock-market upsurge into a roaring boom in prices. By October 1929, of brokers' loans totaling $8.5 billion, only $1.8 billion came from the banking system.

Great as the stock-market boom had been up to 1928, the first nine months of 1929 provided an impressive balloon, from which the air began to escape in September.

Boom and Crash

If you take July 1926 as a base month, with the monthly stock-market index of prices set at 100, a year later it was 112, and by July 1928, it stood at 148.[35] In two years an investor could have realized a 48 percent capital gain and could have received dividends as well. But there was more to come. From July 1928, the index rose another 45 points to 193. An investor would have nearly doubled his or her money in less than three years from the summer of 1926 *and* realized a gain of 30 percent by midsummer.

Apart from veiled warnings about inevitability, the stock market must have looked very good indeed. After all, as we have seen, the economy seemed sound enough. The market churned around the January 1929 level and then took off again. By September 1929, the index stood at 216, up a further 12 percent in a couple of months. An investor who bought $1,000 worth of those stocks in the summer of 1926 had $2,160 by September 1929. In slightly more than three years, the investor's capital gain alone was 116 percent, and there were dividends as well.

For investment in safe, over-the-counter stocks, the investor's world of 1926–1929 must have seemed hard to beat. True, there were signs of weakness in the "real" economy by September, but those signs and portents were only a few months old (auto sales down, industrial production down), were mixed, and had existed in other years.[36] The highest authorities, from the new president (and the outgoing one) down to the Harvard Economic Society, were touting the general soundness of the economy.[37]

There was a short setback in February 1929 after the Federal Reserve (worried about the scale of brokers' loans) publicly warned that it would not support bank loans for stock speculation nor would it stop British gold losses after the Bank of England discount rate was raised 22 percent, from 4.5 to 5.5 percent in a single step.[38]

On 26 March, there was a paralyzing moment when 8.2 million shares traded *while prices moved down sharply*. The call loan rate hit 20 percent (an average of 1.7 percent a month), but this was not enough to deter a serious speculator who, on recent history, could expect to earn more. However, the moment passed, and stability was regained. Gold was flowing into the New York banks; exports were strong. In August, the Federal Reserve raised its own discount rate to 6 percent, but there was no strong market response to the increase.

Location by Automobile. *Before the automobile, cities and towns were the economic and social centers for the surrounding countryside. People congregated there on Saturdays and holidays to shop and have fun (above). But the availability of the automobile and government-subsidized highways encouraged the development of outlying areas. Communities were replaced with housing tracts, shopping malls, and highway commercial strips. In an attempt to revitalize their communities, some cities rebuilt their downtowns into mall areas, but that failed to bring back commercial vitality. Suburban and exurban development continues to replace older communities.*

New York
Arby's
BURGER
Harlem Av
35
ONLY

macys

Money was tight, if we consider such interest rates against commodity prices or the cost-of-living index. But in the stock market, which had risen nearly 9 percent since January, 6 percent was still a *negative* rate of interest. It still paid to borrow, if you were borrowing from the Fed. For brokers, though, higher interest rates at the peak of the boom no doubt caused some alarm. Galbraith reports that *inside* the Federal Reserve System, as early as August, authorities believed that a crash was coming, but took no further action to offset it. Nor did they probably believe that they should do anything to stop it in those days; a "corrective" in an inflated market was considered a healthy thing.

On 3 September, the market reached its all-time high. Two days later, Babson made his celebrated prediction of a crash, and on that day, 5 September, there was a bad break in the market. It then began to follow a disturbingly wobbly course—in retrospect, a "sure sign" that the boom was over. On Saturday, 19 October, a half-day for trading, the market broke sharply again. On Monday, 21 October, there were more losses. Fear began to build.

On Thursday, 24 October, 12.9 million shares were traded; panic reigned briefly but was stemmed by a flamboyant show of "organized support" from New York financiers. Two more irregular trading days carried U.S. financial history to Monday, 28 October 1929. On that day, more than 9 million shares traded hands, and prices fell more in one day than during the entire previous bad week. Monday was the brink of disaster, which struck the next day.

Raging panic came back on Black Tuesday, 29 October 1929. More than 16 million shares were dumped. The *New York Times* index of stock prices fell 43 points, wiping out in a single day the wealth accumulated in the previous year. By the end of the day, some stocks were down 50 percent from September levels.

Support failed everywhere. **Margin calls** (demands by brokers for more cash from their clients) went out; there were recorded examples of no bids at all for stocks offered for sale. The heavily leveraged firms, the investment trusts, were devastated. Goldman Sachs Trading Corporation, the most glamorous of the investment trusts, was down 42 percent in one day. Tens of thousands of accounts were closed out as margin calls failed, and brokers' loans were called. In U.S. financial history, 29 October 1929 was a day like 7 December 1941 (the attack on Pearl Harbor)—a rare one-day experience that divided one epoch from another.

Partial recoveries came in subsequent weeks, followed by sickening slides. By December, the index (1926 = 100) had fallen to 147, down 32 percent from September. A year later, it was 102, down 53 percent from September 1929. The monthly index found its low of 34 in July 1932, down more than 85 percent from its monthly peak in 1929. An investor who, in September 1929, had $2,116 from a $1,000 investment in September 1926 now had $360. By then, general economic depression had overtaken the country, and Franklin Roosevelt and the New Deal were in the wings of American history.

EXPLANATIONS

Was there any believable explanation for the Great Crash of 1929? Galbraith lists five major sources of weakness that laid the groundwork: (a) unequal income distribution, (b) unstable business organization at the corporate level, (c) weak banking structure, (d) international financial troubles, and (e) ignorance of financial and economic realities by the nation's leaders.[39] But these factors need not have produced a crash in 1929 or at any other time, for that matter. The same may be said of a (similar) list posited by Robert Keller, who also examined technological change and the increasing share of income going to investment capital in the 1920s.[40]

To those who have studied the history of business cycles and the explanations of earlier financial crises and panics, the explanations for the 1929 crash are not new, not unique, not convincing.[41] It happened under the circumstances of the 1920s, but there were other financial panics: 1825, 1836, 1847, 1857, 1866, 1873, 1882, 1893, 1901, 1903, 1907, 1920–1921. They happened under different, but equally compelling, circumstances in the United States and in Europe. Economists have subsequently placed blame on all likely targets for those disasters.[42]

It is frustrating that a single villain cannot be named, once and for all, for 1929 (or any other time). In light of this, it is worthwhile to consider the opinions of Samuel Jones Loyd (later, Lord Overstone) in 1837, and then ask what has been learned.

There had been a financial panic in London in 1836, blamed then upon unsound trading practices with America. The Bank of England had been inept (it had run out of money), and its governor, J. Horsley Palmer, had written and published an essay on the event, *The Causes and Consequences of the Pressure on the Money Market and the Recent Commercial Distress.* Samuel Jones Loyd, an English banker, was moved to answer Palmer's pamphlet with one of his own, *Reflections Suggested by a Perusal of Mr. J. Horsley Palmer's Pamphlet on the Causes and Consequences of the Pressure of the Money Market.* In it Loyd set down his impression of the business cycle in words that have never been surpassed for descriptive generalists:

> The history of what we are in the habit of calling the "state of trade" is an instructive lesson. We find it subject to various conditions which are periodically returning; it revolves apparently in an established cycle. First we find it in a state of quiescence, —next improvement, —growing confidence, —prosperity, —excitement, —overtrading, —convulsion, —pressure, —stagnation, distress, —ending again in quiescence.[43]

The 1929 crash no doubt made investors "feel poor." The losses, sometimes called merely "paper losses," were real enough to those who absorbed them. Even if initially no factory closed because stock prices fell, those who bought stock in such factories immediately following the crash on the basis of secure wealth already accumulated, would come to find in time they were no longer wealthy. In the future, their ability to invest would be impaired.

In October 1929 alone, the reduction in capital value of the nation's stock portfolio was $15 billion, in a year when GNP was $104.6 billion. October 1929 losses were equal to more than 14 percent of that year's GNP. The 1987 stock market meltdown wiped out "paper" wealth of an even greater proportion of 1987 GNP. Yet 1988 proved to be a reasonably good year, with a small rise in real GNP over 1987. History does not necessarily repeat itself. By 1933, the estimated reduction in stock values from the 1929 peak was $85 billion, about 82 percent of the value of 1929 GNP. By 1933, the outcome was an unprecedented economic disaster. More had gone wrong than the bursting of a bubble.

As we will see in the next chapter, there is still considerable debate over what caused the Great Depression. For the present, it is enough to note that the psychological consequences of 1929 ran deep. The "New Era" of the 1920s became a bad joke as the economy ground its way down to 1932. It was replaced by the "New Deal," with its implications that the cards would be shuffled and dealt again and that the game of American economic life would be started afresh.

Cultural historians noted the change from the milieu of *The Great Gatsby* to *The Grapes of Wrath.* Prosperity was not seen again until World War II, when the country's economy, its people, and government had been further transformed by the scourge of the Great Depression. Government policy changes at first attempted to correct some of the weaknesses noted by Galbraith but soon had bigger fish to fry: how to get the American economy to grow. Between 1930 and 1940, the economy could not grow enough to employ its own labor force, something almost unknown in American history over so long a period of years.

NOTES

1. Robert Lampman, *The Share of Top Wealth-Holders in National Wealth 1922–1956* (1962), p. 228, Table 107.
2. *Ibid.*, p. 236, Table 111.
3. Jeffrey Williamson and Peter Lindert, *American Inequality: A Macroeconomic History* (1981), chap. 12.
4. Lampman (1962), p. 235.
5. Charles Holt, "Who Benefited from the Prosperity of the Twenties?" *EEH*, July 1977, p. 283; and Gene Smiley, "Did Incomes for Most of the Population Fall from 1923 Through 1929?," *JEH*, March 1983. Smiley and Richard Keehn, "Federal Personal Income Tax Policy in the 1920s," *Journal of Economic History*, vol. 55, no. 2, June 1995, argue that tax rate reductions in the 1920s successfully minimized tax avoidance by the wealthy, a phenomenon they document for the World War I period. The latest contribution to this dispute is Smiley's "A Note on

New Estimates of the Distribution of Income in the 1920s," *Journal of Economic History*, vol. 60, no. 4, December 2000.

6. George Soule, *Prosperity Decade* (1947).
7. An interesting study of the rate of diffusion of electrical and mechanical appliances is Sue Bowden and Avner Offer, "Household Appliances and the Use of Time: The United States and Britain Since the 1920s," *EHR*, November 1994.
8. Martha Olney, *Buy Now, Pay Later: Advertising, Credit, and Consumer Durables in the 1920s* (1991). Lendol Calder, *Financing the American Dream: A Cultural History of Consumer Credit* (Princeton: Princeton University Press, 1999) is a recent addition to this literature from the viewpoint of consumer culture.
9. Elmus Wicker, "A Reconsideration of Federal Reserve Monetary Policy During the 1920–21 Depression," *JEH*, June 1966.
10. David Brody, *Workers in Industrial America* (1980), p. 62.
11. In "The Upper Turning Point in 1920: A Reappraisal," *EEH*, Spring 1974, the 1920–1921 downturn has been attributed by John Pilgrim mainly to tight money. For an argument that supply bottlenecks played a role in capping the postwar expansion, see K. D. Roose, "The Production Ceiling and the Turning Point of 1920," *American Economic Review*, vol. XLVIII, no. 3, June 1958.
12. For an account of this episode and the Fed's policies at the time, see Wicker (1966).
13. Joseph Swanson and Samuel Williamson, "Estimates of National Product and Income 1919–1941," *EEH*, Fall 1972, show 1922 as the trough year in GNP data, but not in national income, personal income, or unemployment; see Table 3, p. 59.
14. Harry Oshima, "The Growth of U.S. Factor Productivity: The Significance of New Technologies in the Early Decades of the Twentieth Century," *JEH*, March 1984.
15. An interesting discussion of the farmers' appeal to the federal government can be found in Elizabeth Hoffman and Gary Libecap, "Institutional Choice and the Development of US Agricultural Policies in the 1920s," *JEH*, June 1991.
16. Martin Fausold, "President Hoover's Farm Policies 1929–1933," *AgHist*, April 1977.
17. Lee Alston, "Farm Foreclosures in the United States During the Interwar Period," *JEH*, December 1983.
18. For a more detailed analysis of the farm problem in the 1920s, Thomas Johnson, "Postwar Optimism and the Rural Financial Crisis of the 1920s," *EEH*, Winter 1973–1974.
19. Arthur Burns and Wesley Mitchell, *Measuring Business Cycles* (1947).
20. Lloyd Mercer and Douglas Morgan, "Housing Surplus in the 1920s? Another Evaluation," *EEH*, Spring 1973.
21. Household information can be found in *Historical Statistics*, series A 350; the population growth rates are based on series A 7.
22. Soule (1947).
23. Peter Rappoport and Eugene White, "Was There a Bubble in the 1929 Stock Market?" *JEH*, September 1993, argues that, although many economists are skeptical that it is possible to demonstrate the existence of bubbles, their examination of the behavior of the premia demanded on loans for which stock was the collateral suggests, but does not prove, that there was a bubble in 1929. Tung Liu, Gary Santoni, and Courtenay Stone, "In Search of Stock Market Bubbles," *Journal of Economic History*, vol. 55, no. 3, September 1995, is critical of Rappoport and White. White's reply, "Stock Market Bubbles?" is included in the same issue.
24. He simply closed down from May 1927 to January 1928, throwing thousands out of work. Ford had been producing a single car, the Model T, since before World War I. Jonathan Hughes, *The Vital Few* (New York: Oxford University Press, 1986), pp. 335–336.
25. All output data from *Historical Statistics*, series Q 148, P 302; and M 93, 138.
26. Peter Rappoport and Eugene White, "Was the Crash of 1929 Expected?" *AER*, March 1994, argues that the answer is yes. Using options-pricing models, they argue that the crash could have been foreseen more than a year in advance because of a rise in the implied volatility from diffusion models.
27. Jonathan Hughes, *Fluctuations in Trade, Industry and Finance* (Oxford: Clarendon Press, 1960), p. 273.
28. *Ibid.*, p. 20. The "Russian War" is what is now known as the Crimean War.
29. Quoted in John Kenneth Galbraith, *The Great Crash* (1979), p. 1.
30. *Ibid.*, pp. 73–74.
31. *Ibid.*, chaps. II and III.
32. Charles Kindleberger, *The World in Depression, 1929–1939* (1973), p. 113.
33. Galbraith (1979), p. 52.
34. For more history of the investment trusts in the 1920s, see Galbraith's (1979) illuminating Chapter III.
35. Monthly League of Nations data, printed in Kindleberger (1973), p. 111.
36. Lloyd Mercer and Douglas Morgan, "The American Automobile Industry: Investment Demand, Capacity, and Capacity Utilization 1921–40," *JPE*, November/December 1972. The drop in auto sales in the second half of 1929 was not due to market saturation.
37. Galbraith (1979), pp. 127–128.
38. The daily events described here are taken from *ibid.*, pp. 78–112.
39. *Ibid.*, pp. 157–165.

40. Robert Keller, "Factor Income Distribution in the United States During the 1920s: A Reexamination of Fact and Theory," *JEH*, March 1973.
41. For example, see Lance Davis, Jonathan Hughes, and Duncan McDougall, *American Economic History*, (Homewood, IL: Irwin, 1965), 2nd ed., chap. 23, for a round-up of explanations. Also see R. C. O. Matthews, *The Business Cycle* (Chicago: University of Chicago Press, 1959) and Gottfried Haberler, *Prosperity and Depression* (Geneva: League of Nations, 1937).
42. The historian Maury Klein recently published a review of the literature on the crash: "The Stock Market Crash of 1929: A Review Article," *BHR*, Summer 2001.
43. Hughes (1960), p. 229.

SUGGESTED READINGS

Articles

Alston, Lee J. "Farm Foreclosures in the United States During the Interwar Period." *Journal of Economic History*, vol. XLIII, no. 4, December 1983.

Bowden, Sue, and Avner Offer. "Household Appliances and the Use of Time: The United States and Britain Since the 1920s." *Economic History Review*, vol. XLVII, no. 4, November 1994.

Fausold, Martin L. "President Hoover's Farm Policies 1929–1933." *Agricultural History*, vol. 51, no. 2, April 1977.

Hoffman, Elizabeth, and Gary Libecap. "Institutional Choice and the Development of US Agricultural Policies in the 1920s." *Journal of Economic History*, vol. 51, no. 2, June 1991.

Holt, Charles. "Who Benefited From the Prosperity of the Twenties?" *Explorations in Economic History*, vol. 14, no. 3, July 1977.

Johnson, Thomas. "Postwar Optimism and the Rural Financial Crisis of the 1920s." *Explorations in Economic History*, vol. 11, no. 2, Winter 1973–1974.

Keller, Robert. "Factor Income Distribution in the United States During the 1920s: A Reexamination of Fact and Theory." *Journal of Economic History*, vol. XXXIII, no. 1, March 1973.

Klein, Maury. "The Stock Market Crash of 1929: A Review Article." *Business History Review*, vol. 75, no. 2, Summer 2001.

Mercer, Lloyd, and Douglas Morgan. "Housing Surplus in the 1920s? Another Evaluation." *Explorations in Economic History*, vol. 10, no. 3, Spring 1973.

———. "The American Automobile Industry: Investment Demand, Capacity, and Capacity Utilization." *Journal of Political Economy*, vol. 80, no. 6, November/December 1972.

Oshima, Harry T. "The Growth of U.S. Factor Productivity: The Significance of New Technologies in the Early Decades of the Twentieth Century." *Journal of Economic History*, vol. XLIV, no. 1, March 1984.

Pilgrim, John D. "The Upper Turning Point of 1920: A Reappraisal." *Explorations in Economic History*, vol. 11, no. 3, Spring 1974.

Rappoport, Peter, and Eugene White. "Was There a Bubble in the 1929 Stock Market?" *Journal of Economic History*, vol. 53, no. 3, September 1993.

———. "Was the Crash of 1929 Expected?" *American Economic Review*, vol. 84, no. 1, March 1994.

Smiley, Gene. "Did Incomes for Most of the Population Fall From 1923 Through 1929?" *Journal of Economic History*, vol. XLII, no. 1, March 1983.

Swanson, Joseph, and Samuel Williamson. "Estimates of National Product and Income, 1919–1941," *Explorations in Economic History*, vol. 10, no. 1, Fall 1972.

Wicker, Elmus. "A Reconsideration of Federal Reserve Monetary Policy During the 1920–1921 Depression." *Journal of Economic History*, vol. 26, no. 2, June 1966.

Books

Barber, William J. *From the New Era to the New Deal: Herbert Hoover, the Economists, and American Economic Policy, 1921–1933*. New York: Cambridge University Press, 1985.

Brody, David. *Workers in Industrial America*. New York: Oxford University Press, 1980.

Burns, Arthur F., and Wesley C. Mitchell. *Measuring Business Cycles*. New York: National Bureau of Economic Research, 1947.

Galbraith, John Kenneth. *The Great Crash, 1929*. New York: Discus Books, 1979.

Kindleberger, Charles. *The World in Depression, 1929–1939*. Berkeley: University of California Press, 1973.

Lampman, Robert. *The Share of Top Wealth-Holders in National Wealth, 1922–56*. Princeton: Princeton University Press, 1962.

Matthews, R. C. O. *The Business Cycle*. Chicago: University of Chicago Press, 1959.

Olney, Martha L. *Buy Now, Pay Later: Advertising, Credit, and Consumer Durables in the 1920s*. Chapel Hill: University of North Carolina Press, 1991.

Soule, George. *Prosperity Decade*. New York: Holt Rinehart, 1947.

Williamson, Jeffrey, and Peter Lindert. *American Inequality: A Macroeconomic History*. New York: Academic Press, 1981.

CHAPTER TWENTY-FOUR

The Great Depression

After the 1929 crash, the economy began a long descent, year after dismal year, to the bleak winter of 1932–1933. Nine thousand banks failed. Unemployment rose to a quarter of the labor force; millions could find no work. Bread lines, worn-out clothes, destitute living in cardboard hovels in Central Park, roads filled with vagabonds—these are the images of that period in our history.

PERSPECTIVE

What number, or set of numbers, can best describe the impact of the Great Depression of the 1930s? What story most vividly evokes the feeling of it? Between 1929 and 1932, manufacturing output fell by half. Railway passenger car output fell from 2,202 units in 1929 to a mere 7 in 1932; automobile production fell 75 percent (from 4.5 million to 1.1 million). The Great Depression was a time when hamburgers were two for 5 cents, and people could not afford to buy them; when people would work for 10 cents an hour, and employers could not profit from their labor; when the (surviving) banks were filled with idle reserves and borrowing did not occur, although interest rates were below 1 percent per annum; when agricultural produce rotted in the fields, and people went hungry.

Consider Figure 24.1. Marriage rates, birth rates, and even *divorce rates* plunged. The marriage and divorce rates recovered by the mid-1930s; however, because the birth rate was declining in the long run, its recovery was muted. Even so, the low birth rates of 1933 and 1936, 18.4 per 1,000 of population per annum, were not reached again until the 1960s (when the long-term decline quickly resumed, aided by legal abortion). The initial shock of the depression sapped the nation at its vital core. It was disaster.[1]

There is probably no historical subject that can raise so much heat among economists, even to this day, as the Great Depression. A recent National Bureau of Economic Research examination of the period was entitled *The Defining Moment*.[2] Every part of it is still the subject of controversy. What caused the initial downturn? Why did the economy contract for so long (1929 to 1932)? Why did it contract so much? Did government policy help or hinder the recovery attempt? Was the New Deal effort to reorganize the country's economic institutions an admirable act of needed reform or a misguided attempt that derailed the normal processes of adjustment? Was the long depression in employment due to failure of the private sector or a normal response to continuous disruption by government action? Did the New Deal "save" American capitalism or transform it into a permanent **mixed economy** (i.e., an economy in which there are

FIGURE 24.1 Vital Signs 1929–1940

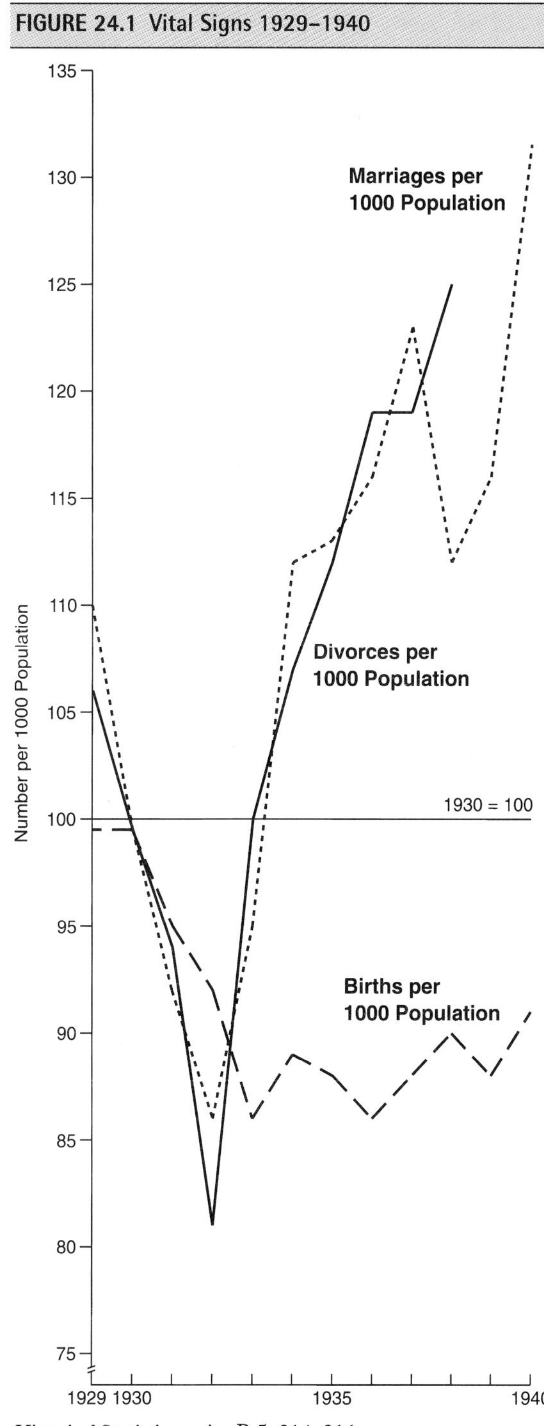

Historical Statistics, series B 5, 214, 216.

elements of both capitalism and socialism, where the government sector plays an important role), forever dependent upon the whims of politics?[3] This chapter will consider the Great Depression. Examination of the New Deal follows in the next chapter.

The peak of the business cycle was reached in the third quarter of 1929, just before the bubble burst on Wall Street. From the data in Table 24.1, we can calculate that between 1929 and 1930 nominal GDP fell 12.0 percent; real GDP fell 8.6 percent. Thus, prices, as measured by the GDP deflator, fell 3.4 percent. These numbers are consistent with a serious downturn, but not yet a "great" depression. To put them in perspective, return for a moment to Table 23.2. Between 1920 and 1921, nominal GNP declined 23.9 percent, but real GNP declined by only 8.7 percent. There was a very sharp price adjustment, a decline of 15.2 percent, in the 1921 recession. As Robert Gordon and James Wilcox argued, in the entire period between the third quarter of 1921 and the third quarter of 1929, eight full years, the GNP deflator varied over a range of only 4.4 percentage points, and the 1929 observation was in the middle of that range.[4] The money supply, as measured by M_2, fell by 2.5 percent during the first four quarters of the downturn. As we can see from Table 23.1, it fell 5.6 percent between 1920 and 1921. Was there anything about the first year of the downturn that would cause people to expect something more than a repeat of 1920–1922–when the economy dropped substantially in 1921 and recovered in 1922?

Skilled observers in 1930 no doubt would have noted the difference in price behavior, but they might not have drawn the conclusion that the real decline in 1929–1930 was more than that of 1920–1921 *because* the price decline was less. This is the "Austrian" view, one of several interpretations to be discussed later.[5] What the observers certainly would not have anticipated was that it would be six years before even the 1930 level of money income would be regained. No one in this country could have anticipated that kind of experience in 1930. It had never been known before.

Instead of suffering a temporary setback in 1930, as had happened in 1920–1921, the American economy teetered on the brink of the Great Depression. The difference was like that between an irrigation ditch and

TABLE 24.1 Unemployment, GDP, and Federal Finance, 1929-1941

Year	Unemployed Percentage of Labor Force	Gross Domestic Product: Current Prices ($ billions)	Gross Domestic Product: 1958 Prices ($ billions)	1958 Prices Per Capita	Federal Receipts ($ billions)	Federal Expenditures ($ billions)	Federal Surplus (+) Deficit (–) ($ billions)
1929	3.2	$103.7	$822.2	$6,744.9	$3.7	$2.6	$+1.1
1930	8.7	91.3	751.5	6,099.8	2.9	2.7	+0.2
1931	15.9	76.6	703.6	5,669.6	1.9	4.0	-2.1
1932	23.6	58.8	611.8	4,898.3	1.6	3.0	-1.3
1933	24.9	56.4	603.3	4,799.5	2.6	3.4	-0.9
1934	21.7	66.0	668.3	5,283.0	3.4	5.5	-2.2
1935	20.1	73.3	728.3	5,716.6	3.7	5.6	-1.9
1936	16.9	83.7	822.5	6,415.8	4.6	7.8	-3.2
1937	14.3	91.9	865.8	6,711.6	6.6	6.3	+0.2
1938	19.0	86.1	835.6	6,427.7	6.0	7.3	-1.3
1939	17.2	92.0	903.5	6,896.9	6.3	8.3	-2.1
1940	14.6	101.3	980.7	7,423.9	8.2	8.5	-0.3
1941	9.9	126.7	1,148.8	8,611.7	14.9	12.7	+2.2

Source: *U.S. Bureau of Economics Analysis, National Income and Product Accounts,* Tables 1.1, 1.2, and 3.2, and *Historical Statistics,* D 86.

the Grand Canyon. The coming experience was as close to a "collapse" as the American economy has ever come. The terrifying slide to 1933 and the failure to find the means of recovery until the recurrence of world war have haunted Americans and their elected representatives ever since. In the 1930s, the forces of expansion, which in the past had seemed ever resilient after each temporary setback, failed. The American people and their government faced a novel problem: an economy that seemed permanently lamed, defective.

1929–1941: THE STATISTICAL BARE BONES

What happened in the early 1930s was extraordinary. In the summer of 1930, the GNP deflator fell below its lowest point in the 1920s. A year later, it was 13.6 percent below what it had been at the peak of the business cycle two years earlier and 11 percent below its lowest value for the 1920s. Between 1929 and 1933, nominal income, measured as GDP, fell 45.6 percent; real income, 26.6 percent (see Table 24.1). By the fall of 1930, it should have been clear that the economy was in desperate straits.

Unemployment

Stanley Lebergott estimated that unemployment was 3.2 percent of the labor force in 1929 and that it reached 24.9 percent in 1933—including those on work-relief programs.[6] It was argued at the time (and still is) that if people had been willing to work for lower wages in the private sector, the federal government's work relief programs would not have been necessary. At this distance in time, such a point has some interesting theoretical attractions. But by 1933, when the first federal work-relief programs were launched, men and women were desperate. They had been promised that prosperity was "just around the corner" for several years. Even with the eventual recovery of output, unemployment stayed high. In real terms, the 1929 level of GDP was regained by 1936. Real income per capita was nearly at 1929 levels in 1937. But unemployment remained at extraordinary levels. Then came a new recession in 1938, in part engendered by the federal government's own incompetence. In 1939, when real per capita GDP at last *exceeded* that of 1929, unemployment was still more than *five times* the 1929 rate.

How many workers remained unemployed if we count *as employed* all those who found jobs in government make-work schemes? We are indebted to Michael Darby for such an estimate.[7] The data in Table 24.2 show the effect of the government's programs on the unemployment rate. Three conclusions emerge. First, government policies were effective to some extent in reducing the percentage of the jobless work force. Second, even with the government's direct federal employment effort (the Works Progress Administration, for example), the 1930s constituted a period of disaster-level unemployment. Third, counting those underemployed—those locked into agricultural seasonal work or in jobs that would have been abandoned for better-paying work except for the terror of long-term joblessness—even Darby's figures for unemployment are undoubtedly underestimated.

TABLE 24.2 Unemployment Rate Estimates (Percentage of Labor Force)

Year	*Lebergott*	*Darby*	*Reduction*
1933	24.9	20.9	4.0
1934	21.7	16.2	5.5
1935	20.1	14.4	6.0
1936	16.9	10.0	6.9
1937	14.3	9.2	5.1
1938	19.0	12.5	6.5
1939	17.2	11.3	5.9

Source: *Historical Statistics,* series D 86; Michael Darby, "Three and a Half Million U.S. Employees Have Been Mislaid," *Journal of Political Economy,* February 1976, 2–76, p. 8.

Wages

What about the really hard-nosed view mentioned earlier—that all workers *could* have been employed had they been willing to accept lower wages? In theory, such would have been the case, *must* have been the case, other things being equal (but they rarely are).[8] We can only speculate on this point. It is true that both money *and* real wages of those with jobs did advance after 1933. Such circumstances *could* indicate that competition over jobs could have been crisper among those without work, although the literary history of the period casts doubt on this purely theoretical proposition.

Again, we have Stanley Lebergott to thank for the numbers in Table 24.3. Real wages, money earnings before and after unemployment, are taken into account, and average hourly earnings all reach their

TABLE 24.3 Annual Earnings for Nonfarm Employees 1929–1941: Employed and Adjusted for Unemployment Deductions

	Annual Money Earnings		*Annual Real Earnings (1914 dollars)*		
Year	*After Deduction for Unemployment*	*When Employed*	*After Deduction for Unemployment*	*When Employed*	*Average Hourly Earnings in Manufacturing (dollars per hour)*
1929	$1,462	$1,534	$855	$898	$.56
1930	1,294	1,494	778	898	.55
1931	1,068	1,406	705	928	.51
1932	807	1,244	593	914	.44
1933	722	1,136	561	882	.44
1934	789	1,146	592	860	.53
1935	851	1,195	623	874	.54
1936	932	1,226	675	888	.55
1937	1,072	1,341	749	937	.62
1938	956	1,303	680	927	.62
1939	1,029	1,346	743	973	.63
1940	1,113	1,392	798	998	.66
1941	1,332	1,561	909	1,066	.73

Source: Stanley Lebergott, "The American Labor Force," in L. E. Davis et al., *American Economic Growth* (New York: Harper & Row, 1972), p. 213, hourly wages from *Historical Statistics,* series D 802.

troughs in 1933. Real wages for the employed had fully recovered to 1929 levels by 1937, and hourly earnings actually had surpassed 1929. Unemployment, together with money wages *times* hours worked, held all other indexes below 1929 levels throughout the 1930s. With money and real wages rising from 1934 onward, conceivably more people could have left the unemployment rolls at lower wages. Conceivably. As Phillip Cagan put it: "We face in the 1930s experience the need to explain a perplexing combination of large-scale unemployment and substantial increases in wages."[9]

The point will always be argued. Business owners would not have welcomed further labor trouble. Wage reductions might have produced that. Roosevelt's policies implanted the idea that *rising* money wages were good for the economy. In any case, would more labor have been employed had it been cheaper once the recovery began in 1933? The evidence shows astounding business conservatism at the time. Business inventories were liquidated from 1929 to 1935. After that, caution reigned in the presence of an antibusiness administration.

Business Conditions

Returning for a moment to Table 24.1, recall that *real* GDP had recovered its 1929 peak by 1936 but that real GDP *per capita* only regained its 1929 level in 1939. *Nominal* GDP did not recover its 1929 level until 1941 when production for World War II was well underway. The depression lingered on, unmoved by the energetic social reconstruction of the New Deal. It is difficult to measure such a thing as business expectations, but most economists consider them to be of fundamental importance in business planning. Several series of data show an extraordinary "down" in business expectations during the 1930s. Consider the five entries in Table 24.4.

Gross private investment nearly vanished between 1929 and 1932, and, in fact, most estimates of net investment (deducting current depreciation) show net *dis*investment of the country's capital stock from 1932 through 1934. The strongest year of the thirties, 1937, was followed by another collapse. Any economic growth that occurs is fueled in part by net investment. Investment in the 1930s was not enough by itself to regain the growth of the 1920s. Year after

TABLE 24.4 Investment, Mergers, Patents, Corporate Issues, and Stock Prices, 1929–1941

Year	*Gross Private Domestic Investment ($ billions)*	*Recorded Mergers*	*Patents Applied for (thousands)*	*New Corporate Issues for Capital[a] ($ millions)*	*Average Prices of Stocks (1941–1943 = 100)*
1929	$16.5	1,245	89.8	$ 8,002	260.2
1930	10.8	799	89.6	4,483	210.3
1931	5.9	464	79.8	1,551	136.6
1932	1.3	203	67.0	325	69.3
1933	1.7	120	56.6	161	89.6
1934	3.7	101	56.6	152(178)	98.4
1935	6.7	130	58.1	(401)	106.0
1936	8.6	126	62.6	(1,062)	154.7
1937	12.2	124	65.3	(1,138)	154.1
1938	7.1	110	66.9	(904)	114.9
1939	9.3	87	64.1	(420)	120.6
1940	13.6	140	60.9	(761)	110.2
1941	18.1	111	52.3	(1,041)	98.2

[a] Series X 367 from 1929–1934 is not consistent with series X 502 thereafter.

Source: *Historical Statistics,* series F 52, V 38, W 96, X 495, 502, 511; see also *Historical Statistics,* 1960, series X 367; U.S. Bureau of Economic Analysis, *National Income and Product Accounts,* Table 1.1.

year, more and more ground was lost. The decline to 1933 was catastrophic in all the indicators in Table 24.4. Even such a basic activity as invention (or at least applications for patents) was dragged down by the slide to 1933. What is equally striking, though, is the failure of business confidence, by these measures, to revive to even close to the levels of 1929 or, in most cases, even back to 1930.

Business confidence was flattened in the Hoover administration even though, since they tended to be Republicans, business owners usually aligned themselves with Hoover. The hero-figure of the 1930s, FDR, and the social and economic activism of his New Deal, may well themselves have been detriments to business hopes. FDR's vigorous characterization of his opponents in the business community as "economic royalists" hardly built confidence.

The stock market was also a barometer of personal expectations. The index shown in Table 24.4 declined 73 percent from 1929 to 1932 and then lingered at prices half or less than the 1929 levels for the rest of the decade. Business mergers are usually associated in the aggregate with periods of economic expansion, periods of big plans and hopes.[10] They fell more than 90 percent from 1929 to 1933 and did not recover until after World War II. New corporate stock issues to raise capital declined 98 percent from the halcyon days of 1929 and lay dead in the water the rest of the decade; the peak of 1937 was about 15 percent of the 1929 level.

Few objective business owners could have found much reason for optimism between 1929 and 1933, when personal consumption expenditures dropped 40 percent (see Table 24.5). No need under those conditions for new orders, and, accordingly, there was net liquidation of business inventories for years. The foreign sector was no help; exports fell in value 67 percent for the years 1929–1933 and then hovered for some years at 50 to 60 percent of 1929 levels.[11]

The banking system, after surviving the blows of 1929, 1930, and 1933, became extraordinarily cash conscious as interest rates fell to subterranean levels. Savers flooded the federal government's Postal Savings System with their hard-earned funds.[12] They did not trust the bankers for more adventures, and the bankers seemed not to trust the public. As we see in Table 24.5, cash reserves as a percentage of deposits had risen in 1936 to 60 percent over the 1929 level, far above any legal requirements, and remained there the rest of the depression years. The interest cost of

TABLE 24.5 Personal Consumption, Cash-Deposit Ratios, and Interest Rates

Year	*Personal Consumption Expenditures ($ billions)*	*National Bank Ratio of Cash to Deposits*	*Prime Interest Rate*	*Rate on 90-Day Commercial Paper*
1929	$77.5	19.8	5.85	5.03
1930	70.2	23.3	3.59	2.48
1931	60.7	22.5	2.64	1.57
1932	48.7	20.0	2.73	1.28
1933	45.9	24.5	1.73	0.63
1934	51.5	28.6	1.02	0.25
1935	55.9	30.5	0.75	0.13
1936	62.2	32.0	0.75	0.15
1937	66.8	31.3	0.94	0.43
1938	64.2	35.3	0.81	0.44
1939	67.2	37.6	0.59	0.44
1940	71.2	42.0	0.56	0.44
1941	81.0	38.9	0.53	0.44

Source: *Historical Statistics*, series F 48, X 445, 446, 643, 648, U.S. Bureau of Economic Analysis, *National Income and Product Accounts*, Table 1.1.

The Great Depression. *In the 1930s, economic depression and natural disasters combined to waste resources on the farm and in the city. Dust bowl farmers abandoned the land (left, above and below). The cities were overwhelmed by an army of the "ill-housed, ill-fed, and ill-clothed." (See Detroit, above right, and Seattle's shantytown, below right.)*

WORK-IS-WHAT-I
WANT-AND-NOT-CHARITY
WHO-WILL-HELP-ME-
GET-A-JOB.-7 YEARS-
IN-DETROIT. NO-MONEY
SENT-AWAY- FURNISH-
BEST-OF-REFERENCES
PHONE RANDOLPH 8381 ROOM
#59.

SEATTLE HARDWARE COMPANY

borrowing money became nearly negligible since stock prices (by past and future standards) were generally rising after 1932 (see Table 24.4). The banks, however, remained stuffed with idle cash.[13] The depression seemed to have an almost unbreakable hold on the private sector. Only after World War II began in Europe, in September 1939, were there sure signs that the glacial conditions might thaw. However, even in 1940, unemployment (not counting make-work jobs) remained at nearly 15 percent of the labor force. The depression had lasted ten long years.

Federal Finance

The flattening of private expectations was due also to real forces. Current federal receipts fell to a low of $1.6 billion in 1932. Income tax rates were *raised* significantly that year across the board.[14] The reason for such a deflationary move in a deep depression was Hoover's forlorn hope of somehow balancing his budget as revenues fell and expenditures rose—his opponent in the 1932 election was critical of the deficit. Consider the data in Table 24.6, which is for federal fiscal years that end on June 30 of the stated year. The largest deficits occurred at the bottom of the cycle, when income and, therefore, tax collections were low. The expenditures were in large part the doing of the outgoing Hoover administration.

Between 1933 and 1937, money income rose by 63 percent, while real income rose by more than 43 percent. Prices made some recovery, making a fear of inflation perhaps not entirely laughable, except that President Roosevelt would go to fantastic (and, ultimately, unconstitutional) lengths from 1933 to 1935 to try to *raise prices*. Just as the highest mountain range on earth lies unnoticed at the bottom of the ocean (in the Philippines), that remarkable expansion of GDP between 1933 and 1937 lay submerged beneath the Great Depression.

With the increase in income, government receipts recovered slowly to 1937 and then leveled off. Expenditures rose through the 1936 fiscal year, then dropped 19 percent the following year. FDR, who had promised to balance the budget if elected, raised taxes after the 1936 election when there were signs of a full recovery at hand. Consequently, the deficits in 1937 and 1938 were sharply reduced. In addition, monetary officials, fearing an inflationary explosion, aided deficit reduction. John Maynard Keynes, upon hearing of it, said, "They profess to fear that which they dare not hope."

The fiscal consequences are treated later; it is enough here to note that the psychological problems of business, in dealing with a federal government whose political stock-in-trade was antibusiness rhetoric, were heightened by a hostile tax climate.

Wholesale prices fell 32 percent between 1929 and 1932, and consumer prices were down 24 percent. They both declined slightly in the 1938 downturn and never recovered their 1929 levels before World War II. Manufacturing production fell a catastrophic 48 percent in that period but then recovered by 1937. In 1937 and 1938, the new Social Security taxes began flowing to the Treasury, substantially raising federal revenues, but reducing consumer expenditures—adding to the forces of contraction. After the sharp setback in 1938, production came back again and, by 1940, had surpassed all earlier levels.

We will consider the issues of monetary policy in more detail later. Here we need only note a few important aspects of the money supply data. M_1, the sum of demand deposits plus currency in circulation,

TABLE 24.6 Expansion Deficit, Money, Prices, and Industrial Production

	Surplus (+) or Deficit (−)[a]	M_1 *($ billions)*	*WPI*	*CPI*	*IMP*[b]
			(1967 = 100)		
1929	+42.3	$26.6	61.9	51.3	23
1930	+7.4	25.8	56.1	50.0	19
1931	−52.5	24.1	47.4	45.6	15
1932	−43.3	21.1	42.1	40.9	12
1933	−26.5	19.9	42.8	38.8	14
1934	−40.0	21.9	48.7	40.1	15
1935	−33.9	25.9	52.0	41.1	18
1936	−41.0	29.6	52.5	41.5	22
1937	+3.2	30.9	56.1	43.0	23
1938	−17.8	30.5	51.1	42.2	18
1939	−25.3	34.1	50.1	41.6	22
1940	−3.5	39.7	51.1	42.0	25
1941	+17.3	46.5	56.8	44.1	32

[a] Surplus (+) or Deficit (−) as percentage of federal expenditures.
[b] IMP = Index of Manufacturing Production.

Source: Table 25.1; *Historical Statistics,* series E 73, 135, P 13, X 414; U.S. Bureau of Economic Analysis, *National Income and Product Accounts,* Table 3.2.

declined slightly more than 20 percent between 1929 and 1932. The majority of this decline occurred after the spring of 1930. This was less than the decline in wholesale prices and just slightly more than the drop in consumer prices. Questions of monetary policy apart, as Peter Temin argues, the money supply was arguably as large in 1933 as it was in 1929![15]

Puzzles

Even with such a cursory introduction, it should be clear that understanding the Great Depression is no simple matter. Prices did come back after 1933, as did manufacturing production. As we can see in Table 24.6, M_1 rose 46 percent between 1933 and 1937, wholesale prices rose 33 percent, and manufacturing rose 64 percent. Moreover, GDP in current prices went up 63 percent, and real GDP went up 43 percent in the same brief period. Thus, Keynes's jibe to the contrary, by 1937 the economy was showing extraordinary strength. Unemployment had fallen more than 42 percent from its peak in 1933. However, much was lost in the 1938 recession.

It seems clear that the 1933–1937 expansion hardly qualified as a return to the flourishing economy of 1929 and that the bitter criticisms of federal policy suggesting the Great Depression was unnecessarily prolonged may have been justified, at least in part. That will be addressed in the following chapter. For the present, we need to address two questions that have sparked significant controversy: What caused the initial downturn? Why did it last so long? There are several different, highly debatable answers to those questions.

EXPLANATIONS OF THE GREAT DEPRESSION

In the 1970s, the debate over the Great Depression was between those who believed the explanation was on the monetary side of the economy (Monetarists) and those who believed it was on the real side (Keynesians). Much of this research was focused on the causes of the initial downturn following the stock market crash of 1929 and the banking crisis of 1930, which was followed by the powerful two-year crash dive ending with massive bank failures and the closing of all the banks in early 1933.[16] There are many explanations of the Great Depression. One that will not be discussed directly is the Schumpeterian view that a slowing in the rate of technological change was a cause of the Great Depression.[17] There are other views to consider as well, especially a newer view that emphasizes the role of the gold standard. Whichever view one adopts, the federal government and its agencies played a crucial and usually negative role.

The Monetarist View

Monetarist arguments naturally depicted a monetary beginning that, if true, helps explain why the depression was so deep and long-lasting. In their monumental *A Monetary History of the U.S.*, Milton Friedman and Anna Schwartz focused attention on why a relatively serious recession became the Great Depression.[18] Friedman and Schwartz documented a downward shift in the deposit-to-reserve and deposit-to-currency ratios at the end of 1930. As the public held a greater share of their money as currency, the deposits, and therefore the reserves, of the banking system shrunk. This decline in the money supply caused aggregate demand to shrink. In addition, aggregate spending decreased, which led to a reduction in output, income, employment, and prices. This, in turn, caused a further reduction in the money supply—and in output and income. As banks attempted to replenish lost reserves by decreasing lending, a subsequent reduction occurred. Monetarists believe that this chain was set in motion by the first bank panic in November 1930. Though the Fed did attempt to put additional reserves into the system, it was a classic case of too little, too late.

The Fed had but two tools with which to fight the bank crisis, only one of which had been included in the Federal Reserve Act of 1913. Officially, it could only reduce the discount rate, the rate at which member banks borrowed from the Fed. The required collateral was short-term, self-liquidating commercial paper, and, as the economy was in a downturn, there was less and less of it. Unofficially, the Federal Reserve Bank of New York under Benjamin Strong had conducted countercyclical open-market operations, but Strong had died, and the power in the system had moved toward the Federal Reserve Board in Washington. Even if Strong had lived, given the location of the banking crisis, there is a question whether an expansionary policy would have been successful in late 1930.

Elmus Wicker found that the 120 banks that failed in November and December of 1930 were all located in the Southeast and tied to the failure of Caldwell and Company in Nashville.[19] Caldwell controlled a large chain of Southern banks as well as many other enterprises. When they encountered financial difficulties in 1929, they sought a partner and merged with Banco Kentucky, a bank-holding chain, in 1930. Banco Kentucky was also in financial straits. The failure of Caldwell and Company spread to all the banks in both chains within a week or two. It seems doubtful the Fed could have localized its policies to prevent this panic.

Friedman and Schwartz emphasized the failure of the private Bank of the United States in December 1930. In part, this is a result of the name, which recalled the public-private ventures of the early 1800s. In part, it was the result of this bank's good reputation. However, a change in management had taken place, from father to son, and the son adopted many questionable practices that led to the bank's being insolvent at the time of its failure. Again, there is very little the Fed could have done about this situation; it is said the bank "deserved" to fail. Further, as Wicker noted, since the bank was located in Brooklyn, if this failure were to be a major part of the story, the effect should have been felt in New York City. Instead, failures continued in the South, where the November failures occurred.

Friedman and Schwartz argued that Strong would not have allowed events to deteriorate to this extent. They believe there was a change in monetary policy regimes shortly after Strong's death. The Fed raised interest rates in 1928, then failed to abort the 1929 stock-market bubble before it burst.[20] The Fed allowed the nominal money supply to fall, actually raised its rediscount rate in 1930 for a time, and then sat idly while thousands of banks failed, to the ruin of their depositors and the desolation of the surrounding economic terrain.

In his study of the stock market in the 1920s, Alexander Field argued that the emphasis on the rise in stock prices (334 percent between August 1921 and the September 1929 peak) has overshadowed an even more remarkable expansion in volume (1,478 percent over the same period).[21] The greater volume reflected increased public participation in the market (and an anticipation of future participation) and produced a major increase in the transactions demand for money. Since wholesale prices fell by an average of 1 percent a year beginning in 1922, *real* interest rates in 1928–1929 reached remarkably high levels, levels that were not seen again until the early 1980s, levels that choked demand in those sectors of the economy dependent on interest financing, new construction and automobiles. Field argues that this started the downturn; the stock market crash reinforced it.

While a dose of expansionary monetary policy may not have been sufficient to turn the tide after the first wave of bank failures in 1930, Field argued that there might have been a softer landing for the economy had an easier monetary policy been followed in 1928–1929. Instead, the Fed concentrated on keeping the bubble in check, and either did not acknowledge or did not recognize this increased transactions demand. As it was, the downturn began in a period of tight money and a liquidity crisis developed in the wake of the first round of bank failures.

A second wave of bank failures began in March 1931, and, by the fall of that year, Federal Reserve policy became even more restrictive—a reason why the depression was so deep and long-lasting. Subsequently, the Fed did little to aid recovery.[22] It did, however, pursue policies in 1936–1937 that were thought to have contributed to the 1938 recession.

Those who disagree with the Monetarists' explanation are quick to note that interest rates did not rise as quickly following the initial decline in the money supply in late 1930 as they had before the stock market crash or in late 1931. This fact suggests that more attention needs to be paid to the demand for money, which may not have been as stable as Monetarists maintain, but may have been declining for reasons associated with real effects.

The Austrian View

The pure neoclassical, or "Austrian," view was set out years ago by F. A. Hayek and Lionel Robbins. It was restated by Murray Rothbard.[23] In this view, the run-up of stock prices to 1929 had its main root in excessive loosening of financial discipline before the crash and then being kept from its normal self-correcting mechanisms by *too much* Federal Reserve effort. Like the Monetarists, the Fed comes out guilty, *but guilty of a different crime.* The Fed expanded its holdings of government securities from $511 million to more than $2.4 billion from 1929 to 1933 in a vain effort to create a greater reserve base for bank loans.[24] Even if the nominal money supply had declined, it had declined too little, according to the Austrians, and not more than prices had. The policy, as far as it succeeded, set back the process of recovery. Had prices fallen far and precipitately, as they did in 1920–1921 in connection with a huge drop in the money supply (see Table 23.1), the recovery might have begun earlier and have sustained a new advance, as it did after 1921, or more viable price-profit ratios. Thus say the Austrians.[25]

The Keynesian View

Among those who disagreed with an exclusively monetary explanation, the Keynesians in particular rushed to protect the importance of their guru, who, after all, published *The General Theory of Employment, Interest, and Money* as a direct result of the failure of classical economics to predict the direction in which the economy seemed headed. Perhaps the most important work here was done by an economic historian. Peter Temin's *Did Monetary Forces Cause the Great Depression?* went to great lengths to answer in the negative.[26] The downward *trend* of interest rates after 1929, together with the lack of evidence that the economy was suffering from any *real* shortage of money for business purposes, left Temin in doubt about the purely monetary explanation. For one thing, as noted earlier, the *real* money supply by 1932 was about the same as it had been in 1929. Temin found that the one factor that had changed fundamentally and independently of the rest was the drop in personal consumption expenditures (see Table 24.5), which dropped more than 9 percent in 1929–1930 (current prices), and then fell another 13.5 percent in 1930–1931, and another 19.8 percent in 1931–1932.[27] Altogether, there was a relentless drop of 41 percent between 1929 and 1933. After the great consumption and stock-market boom of the Roaring Twenties, Americans by the millions closed their wallets and purses and froze their spending from current income.

A limitation of much of the subsequent debate between Monetarists and Keynesians was that the two sides were focused on different dimensions. Temin and the Keynesians were more interested in the first two years of the contraction and the initial decline in private spending, which, they claim, brought the bank failures and monetary collapse in their wake. Thus, they cannot effectively criticize the main thrust of the Friedman-Schwartz analysis, which basically ignored the first year and concentrated on the period following the first wave of bank failures in October 1930. Monetarists were more interested in the unique depth and severity of the depression; thus, they naturally concentrated on the 1931–1933 phase, when the contraction exhibited an unprecedented acceleration.

Temin's conclusions made many economists unhappy. They had not ordinarily thought of consumption as such an independent factor. The volatility of private investment had been their customary target in explaining business cycles.[28] Moreover, if Temin were correct, the Great Depression had been almost an act of God in its inscrutability. There is no simple target, no one to blame. Yet, Gordon and Wilcox independently, and perhaps reluctantly, agree with Temin:

> The stock market collapse precipitated a drastic decline in consumption spending that interacted with and further aggravated the continuing decline in residential construction.[29]

These factors together gave the depression distinct "nonmonetary" origins. In any case, why not hold back on consumption in those conditions? What a fine investment nonconsumption was! As Joel Mokyr argues, suppose that after the 1929 stock-market crash, risk-averse wealthholders decided just to sit on their cash; suppose they did not put it in a bank. In real terms, they would earn nearly 25 percent on their idle money, as measured by the fall in consumer prices to 1933. They would earn nearly 10 percent a year just watching their silver tarnish, as measured against wholesale prices between 1929 and 1932.

It is easier to show that real effects must have been at work in the first two years of the contraction than to determine what those factors were, much less to assign specific quantitative contributions to each of them. As we have seen, beginning in the winter of 1928, the Federal Reserve followed a tight-money policy, and the rate of growth of the money supply slowed. However, similar diminutions had occurred earlier in the 1920s without triggering a major decrease in nominal income. Thus, it is of some interest to consider each of the components of real spending in turn. A decrease in any one of them would lead to a multiplied decrease in income and output in the Keynesian model.

Investment. Most scholars have concentrated their investigations on two sectors of the economy: construction and automobiles. Bert Hickman documented two different effects contributing to a decline in construction investment: overbuilding in the mid-1920s and declining population growth.[30] Between 1923 and 1928, the amount of real residential construction was more than twice what it had been (on average) in the decade leading to World War I. The ratio of real residential construction to real GNP between 1924 and 1927 was as high as it would be during the twentieth century. As late as 1940, the housing-output ratio was still less than half of what it was in the mid-1920s.

Why were there no buyers for these homes? Hickman separated the observed decline in the rate of population growth between the early 1920s and the mid-1930s into two components: (a) that due to a decline in "standardized households" (primarily as a result of the immigration restrictions adopted after World War I), and (b) that due to the decline in income after 1929. How much could this decline in investment have contributed to the decline in income in the Great Depression? Hickman estimated that, under the assumption that income was constant between 1925 and 1930, the decline in the actual number of standardized households would have led to a 49 percent decline in the number of desired housing starts, approximately 4 percent of GNP in 1925.[31] While this might seem small, it is much larger than the percent of federal government expenditures.

Automobile production tripled between 1921 and 1929, and this growth required large additional investments by the producers. The rate of investment was clearly slowing by the end of the 1920s. The industry expanded so fast that it created excess capacity at exactly the time the automobile market became "saturated" (that is, the rate of new car purchases had reached its peak). At the beginning of the 1920s, those who wanted to obtain an automobile were forced to purchase a new one, but, by the end of the decade, a flourishing market in used cars had developed. Allegedly, Henry Ford suddenly realized he was competing against himself.

Lloyd Mercer and Douglas Morgan defined capacity as the minimum point on the short-run average cost curve.[32] Comparing the actual utilization of capital in the automobile industry to this theoretical benchmark, they concluded that, while there was some excess capacity in the late 1920s, it was relatively small. Indeed, there was reason for additional investment as late as the spring of 1929. Similarly, they found that, while the market tended toward saturation in the 1920s, this was not reached until 1930 at the earliest.

In this vein, Alvin Hansen developed the idea of "secular stagnation."[33] The ending of the frontier, the decline in population growth, and, consistent with the Schumpeterian view, the drying up of investment opportunities were forces of fundamental depth that had permanently weakened the stimulus of private investment and, hence, American economic growth. The Great Depression was the end of an era.

A similar, long-run analysis, albeit one that was not so pessimistic, was provided by the British economist Thomas Wilson, in his *Essays in Income and Employment*.[34] Wilson developed a theoretical and empirical argument that the previous investment boom of the 1920s had produced massive excess productive capacity in American industry that had to be utilized (or abandoned) before a new advance could occur. The depression of the 1930s was the result; new investment was not needed in the basic industries suffering from excess capacity. And, echoing Hansen's beliefs, Wilson said that there were insufficient new innovations, as the depression dragged on, to produce entirely new demand for investment in major product departures. The series of data on patents shown in Table 24.4 would tend to support this part of Wilson's thesis.

Of course, not all parts of the economy suffered in the same way, by the same amount, in the 1930s depression. Industries such as chemicals, petroleum, food products, and machinery manufacturing expanded their investments, output, and employment. Michael Bernstein has shown that much of

Urban Growth. *In good times and bad, the economic attractions of southern California produced explosive urban growth. Wilshire Boulevard in Los Angeles is shown in the 1920s (above) and in the 1960s (below).*

New Deal policy toward industry was, in fact, aimed at propping up older basic industries (for example, textiles, lumber, and primary metals), which were saved from innovation by World War II, and again by the Korean War, only to flounder finally in the later decades and require protection from competition. They were the most stagnant industries in the 1930s, and, in fact, were the ones Wilson said were suffering from excess capacity.[35]

In sum, while construction contributed to a downturn in investment in 1927, automobiles did not. The impact of this decline was delayed, but when spending on consumption and inventory investment turned down in 1930, the earlier collapse of construction investment made the contraction more severe. Secular stagnation, the lack of innovation, then contributed to making this a much longer depression than the United States had experienced previously.

Consumption. It appears that the decline in consumption was greater than that of investment. In part, consumption decreased because other components of spending decreased. In part, as Temin argues, some of the decrease has to be attributable to the loss of consumer wealth in the stock market crash. Arguing that proper data do not exist to estimate a contemporaneous macroeconometric model, Rick Mishkin used a postwar model to assess a typical household balance sheet for the years between 1930 and 1941.[36] The reduction in consumer wealth from the crash explains 45 percent of the decline in consumer spending and residential construction during the first year of the downturn. It also explains why the collapse of construction investment did not cause the economy to turn down earlier; it was overshadowed by consumption spending induced by the stock market bubble. The stock market collapse precipitated a drastic decline in consumption spending that interacted with and further aggravated the continuing decline in residential construction.

Decisions to consume and save are supposed by economists to be partly based upon confidence in the future, or lack thereof. Christina Romer argued that the crash created uncertainty about future income and employment, which led to a reduction in expenditures on expensive consumer durables.[37] The effect was most noticeable in the steep drops observable in automobile registrations and department store sales. At the same time, grocery store sales grew. Romer argued this pattern of consumption is the result of consumers' avoiding "irreversible" goods even though they have not changed their estimates of future income. Potential consumers saved from current incomes, causing current demand for output of goods and services to slow down. Savings grew, inventories of unsold goods piled up, new orders dropped, factories closed, and men and women were laid off their jobs.

In his study of personal consumption expenditures, Stanley Lebergott compared expenditures on a sector-by-sector basis during the downturns of 1920–1921 and 1929–1930.[38] About the same number of sectors experienced serious declines in both episodes, but what distinguishes the Great Depression is that almost no sectors experienced a gain. Further, consumption failed to recover in 1930–1931 as it had in the earlier period. Making reference to the same "irreversible" consumer durable purchases as Romer, Lebergott notes that "habits suited to the new high levels of income were not rigidly in place." Indeed, it was the employed portion of the labor force, not the unemployed, that stopped spending during the Great Depression. Lebergott calculates that had those who were unemployed in 1930 refrained from all spending and those who were employed continued to spend at the same rate as in 1929, aggregate consumption in 1930 would have been only 6 percent lower than it had been in 1929.[39]

Government Spending. We examined federal finance earlier in this chapter. Suffice it to note that, in 1929, federal government expenditures were only 2.5 percent of GDP; total state and local spending was a little larger than federal. For all intents and purposes, the federal government almost would have had to double in size simply to counteract the effect of the decline in construction investment. Thus, the federal government budget surpluses of the 1920s were unlikely to have caused the depression, but the tax increases that were passed to remove the deficits that emerged after the economy turned down were likely to have made the depression deeper and longer lasting. Federal taxes were raised in 1932, 1935, and 1937, then the new Social Security taxes were instituted in 1937.[40] During most of the depression, governments at all levels taxed as much as they could. To Keynes, a tax increase during a downturn was just the opposite of what should have been done. In the crudest Keynesian terms, the deficit-reduction tax increases of 1937 plunged the economy into a mid-depression recession in 1938.

The idea of **compensating fiscal policy**, smoothing out the peaks and valleys of the business cycle through compensating tax and spending programs, was mainly the result of Keynes and the depression.[41] If government deficits were run in downswings and surpluses accumulated in expansions, then the government's budget over the entire course of the cycle might be "in balance," even though it was *not* in any given year. Compensating fiscal policy should then satisfy nearly everyone. The policy not only would produce a more even, long-term pattern of growth but incidentally would ease the problems of debt management. Debt would be accumulated at falling interest rates and could be liquidated when interest rates were rising in an expanding economy.

Most important was offsetting the volatility of private investment. Keynes viewed the investment collapse of 1929 through 1933 and the subsequent investment doldrums as a situation that had to be controlled: "I conceive, therefore, that a somewhat comprehensive socialization of investment will prove the only means of securing an approximation to full employment."[42] There was nothing, Keynes argued, in the economic system that would automatically maintain stable full employment. That was the central message of *The General Theory* and its radical heresy from neoclassical economics.

Many economists considered the (relatively) huge spending programs of the New Deal the first fruits of this wisdom, making the depression less severe than it otherwise would have been while at the same time reforming and saving American capitalism from the consequences of its own follies.

A 1956 study by E. Cary Brown gave a rude jolt to this optimistic view. Brown discovered that the increase in federal deficit spending barely offset the decline in other spending, together with the perverse taxing policies by governments at the state and local levels. Brown also noted the possible depressing influence of FDR's antibusiness political stance upon private spending. The result, wrote Brown, was that fiscal policy in the 1930s actually had little expansionary effect. The recovery, such as it was, came primarily from the beleaguered private sector:

> The trend of direct effects of fiscal policy on aggregate full-employment demand is definitely downward throughout the thirties. For recovery to have been achieved in this period, private demand would have had to be higher out of a given private disposable income than it was in 1929. Fiscal policy, then, seems to have been an unsuccessful recovery device in the thirties—not because it did not work, but because it was not tried.[43]

Other economists, notably Alvin Hansen, had earlier suspected the same. The New Deal had not been the Keynesian promised land. Moreover, as a "planned economy" (which people like Rexford Tugwell had wanted), the New Deal was a bust.[44] The planning that did occur was politically motivated, haphazard, and not forcefully pursued. The New Deal did not do what wartime mobilization would do after 1941: end the depression.

Without considering other policies, it is clear that federal spending (a) was not consistently expansionary, and (b) never produced a reduction in unemployment to 1929, or even 1930, levels. The depression was a period of extraordinarily high unemployment throughout. The gyrations of fiscal policy were due in part to sheer ignorance and confusion in policy, as Herbert Stein emphasizes.[45]

While fiscal policy during the Great Depression has escaped much of the censure heaped upon monetary policy, the increase in tax rates was perverse. This was offset to some extent by the increase in expenditures, but present research concludes that, at best, "fiscal policy was no help."

Net Exports. A long-standing argument with roots in the 1932 election campaign maintains that the Smoot-Hawley Tariff Act of June 1930 exacerbated the downturn. The effective tariff rate increased by almost 50 percent between 1929 and 1932. Assuming foreign countries did not retaliate, the tariff increased the price of U.S. imports and close domestic substitutes so that output fell more than it otherwise would have, while prices fell less. Assuming retaliation, the demand for U.S. exports fell; thus, output fell through the standard Keynesian mechanism. In particular, retaliation against U.S. food exports caused a 66 percent decrease between 1929 and 1932 and aggravated the decline in U.S. farm prices. This decline, in turn, initiated a series of rural bank failures in 1930. As we have seen, those bank failures played a pivotal role in aggravating the downturn.

Recent scholarship has been less hard on Smoot-Hawley. It argues that the reduction in trade was more a consequence, not a cause, of the depression. Douglas Irwin recently offered a quantitative assessment. U.S. imports fell a little more than 40 percent between the second quarter of 1930 and the third quarter of 1932. Irwin estimates that approximately a quarter of this decrease is attributable to the increase in the effective tariff rate (Smoot-Hawley plus deflation). Given the small size of the import section (4.9 percent of GDP in 1930), this suggests the effect of Smoot-Hawley was one-tenth that of the decline in building construction.[46] Mario Crucini and James Kahn offer an alternative view. By including retaliation and induced distortions to capital markets, they conclude that Smoot-Hawley could have reduced GDP by as much as two percent, roughly five times greater than Irwin. While this alone is large enough to induce a recession, it should be noted that it is still only half that of building construction.[47]

In sum, Keynesians agree that the Federal Reserve exacerbated the depression, but they don't believe that it had much to do with the start of the depression. That can be traced to the downturn in construction investment in 1928 and the reduction in consumption following the stock market crash in 1929.

The International View

The groups examined thus far have emphasized factors within the U.S. economy. The international view emphasizes factors largely external to the domestic economy, particularly the gold standard. It was gold-standard policies that turned the downturn into the Great Depression in the United States and elsewhere. This view has its origins in a very old literature, one whose tangled trail goes back to the monetary disruptions of World War I.[48]

In the international view, American events are only a part (although a crucial one) of a larger pattern.[49] That pattern may run as deeply in history as the *human* losses in Europe in the period 1914–1918 due to war and influenza that turned the long-range terms of trade against the world's primary producers; so go the arguments of W. Arthur Lewis.[50] Tied to that is the failure of European industry to modernize after the war. This latter argument, presented by Ingvar Svennilson, is a fascinating view of the world depression and a different explanation of its depth and length than is given here.[51]

There is a general consensus that the depression is best explained as a leftward shift of aggregate demand against an upward-sloping aggregate supply curve. The cause of the leftward shift in aggregate demand is the series of shocks that have already been discussed. There remains considerable debate among macroeconomists as to when the aggregate supply curve became upward-sloping. Was it around the turn of the twentieth century or closer in time to the Great Depression? In part, this dispute is tied to the question of when personnel departments (which were replacing foremen as the locus of hiring within a firm) became the effective wage setters.

There is an emerging consensus that the tightening of Federal Reserve policy in 1928 slowed U.S. industrial production in 1929.[52] The Fed was attempting to reduce stock market speculation and to arrest a gold outflow to France after France undervalued gold, but it was unable to accomplish either. Under the gold standard, the appropriate policy is deflation. Lower prices should reduce imports and increase exports, which should improve the balance of trade and attract gold. As we have seen, this tight money policy combined with an increasing transactions demand for money and caused a significant increase in both nominal and real interest rates. As Peter Temin argues in *Lessons from the Great Depression*, the choice was between deflation and devaluation of the exchange rate. A deflationary policy was the preferred choice of most policy-makers and, to Temin, was the most important factor determining the depth of the Great Depression.[53] In the aftermath of World War I, however, it was not easy to deflate wages and prices. Workers expected a voice in policy after their wartime sacrifices, and firms accepting

Hoover's request to maintain wage rates helped reduce wage flexibility as the economy turned down.[54] The relative stability of wages caused production and employment to fall; thus, falling prices and wages did not absorb the full brunt of the fall in demand. Parenthetically, those countries in which the Depression was most severe were those in which real wages were the highest in the mid-1930s.

After gold started flowing into the United States as a result of higher interest rates, the restrictive policy remained. Adherence to the gold standard could not have been the only policy goal. Barry Eichengreen noted that the restrictive U.S. monetary policy induced similar policies in other countries.[55] As Ben Bernanke expresses it:

> ... much of the worldwide monetary contraction of the early 1930s was not a passive response to declining output, but instead the largely unintended result of an interaction of poorly designed institutions, shortsighted policy-making, and unfavorable political and economic preconditions.[56]

Because of World War I, gold stocks in many European countries were at low levels in the mid-1920s. Thus, when U.S. interest rates rose, other countries felt they had to raise their discount rates and restrict domestic credit to protect their gold parities. As Eichengreen argues in *Golden Fetters*, the depression proved to be so severe because the propagation mechanism worked via the fetters imposed by the gold standard. The necessary steps for defending the standard against adverse shocks transformed a serious downturn into a world catastrophe. Indeed, a tendency toward recession was observable in most countries dependent on imported capital before it was evident in the United States:

> while there does not appear to be a satisfactory single factor explanation for the exceptionally rapid contraction of the American economy, a more eclectic approach has considerable explanatory power. The stage was set for the US recession by the turn to contraction in monetary policy.... the shift in Federal Reserve Board policy provoked an even more contractionary shift in policy abroad. Hence US exports weakened. Next the Wall Street crash led consumers to defer spending on expensive items.... In the second half of 1930, another move towards contraction in monetary policy reinforced deflationary tendencies.[57]

Following the first wave of bank panics in 1930, the U.S. economy experienced three more. The first came in the spring of 1931, and the second came in September 1931, when Great Britain abandoned the gold standard. The third came in late winter 1933 at the time FDR was inaugurated. The debate over whether a less restrictive monetary policy might have stemmed the tide of depression before 1931 has been discussed. A crucial assumption in that debate is that the gold standard was not a binding constraint. After mid-1931, this assumption becomes hard to maintain. When Britain abandoned gold, the United States experienced a gold outflow; there was speculation that the United States would have to devalue. At this time, the Federal Reserve sharply raised its discount rate, even though the U.S. economy was contracting rapidly and had massive gold reserves. Eichengreen notes that the gold standard required the Federal Reserve to adopt a tighter monetary policy that would raise interest rates in the hope of preventing the loss of any more gold.[58]

Great Britain resumed gold payments in the mid-1920s at the pre-World War I rates and had to restrict the domestic economy in order to maintain this rate.[59] Because it no longer earned as much from foreign investments as it had before the war, Britain lacked the resources to pay for imports when income was high. If it did not want to lose gold, the Bank of England was forced to raise its discount rate to attract short-term capital. Such adherence to the gold standard (and neglect of the domestic economy) put the British economy in depression long before the rest of the world.[60]

In May 1931, the largest bank in Austria, the Kreditanstalt, failed. This failure pushed the world financial community into a series of banking panics and exchange-rate crises. The Austrian bank, says Peter Temin, operated throughout the 1920s under the assumption that European national boundaries had not changed dramatically following World War I, "as if the Hapsburg empire had not been broken up."[61] An auditor's report that commented on this imprudent assumption caused a run on the bank—and then on to the schilling. Adhering to the rules of the gold standard, the Austrian government quickly ran through its reserves and then invoked foreign exchange controls. The uncertainty engendered by this invocation spread first to Germany, which abandoned the gold standard in July and August, and then to Great Britain, which abandoned the gold standard in September 1931. From Britain, it quickly spread to the United States which, as has been noted, experienced a wave of bank failures following Britain's forsaking the gold standard.[62] By this juncture, the Great Depression is a worldwide phenomenon, and expansionary monetary policy in one country, while potentially helpful, was not going to quell the forces of depression.

As a result of Congressional pleas to do something, the Federal Reserve shifted to a more expansionary policy in the spring of 1932. When Congress adjourned in July, the Fed reverted to its tight money stance. It was not until early 1933, a fourth wave of bank panics, and the abandonment of the gold standard that the Fed began a consistent policy of expansion. And it was not until then that recovery began. As we have seen, that recovery was brisk, but it did not bring the economy back to its level of 1929. As Romer has shown, the recovery was the result of the devaluation of the dollar in 1933 and the inflow of gold from abroad. Bernanke and others show that those who escaped the tight fetters of the gold standard recovered from the depression much faster than those who did not; such countries were better able to initiate expansionary monetary policies. As Romer emphasizes, one reason for the expansion in the United States was that Europeans invested in the U.S. economy to keep their assets safe from Hitler. To do so, they had to trade their gold for U.S. dollars—and with devaluation they received more dollars for their gold.[63]

Among the implications Charles Calomiris draws from the international view is that the effect of a given money supply shock will be greater, depending on how indebted the economy is and what kind of banking system it has.[64] In 1929, the U.S. economy was highly leveraged as a result of the rise of newly available consumer durables that had been purchased on credit and the margin purchases of stock. In addition, the United States had a "poorly diversified, geographically fragmented banking system." The existence of many small, unbranched banks made banking panics much more likely.[65] Further, when the character of financial markets is defined to include nonmonetary channels, the Monetarist argument that expansionary open-market operations may have reversed the downward spiral loses force. Borrowers and bankers lost wealth that open market operations could not replace.

The international view supports the Monetarist argument that a monetary contraction caused real spending reductions at the onset of the depression and that monetary expansion greatly aided the recovery. It does not contradict Romer's assertion that shocks to the domestic U.S. economy were a cause of both the U.S. and worldwide depressions. It reminds us that, even when exports and imports were a very small proportion of U.S. GDP, the United States was firmly tied to the world economy.

WHERE THINGS STAND

Our world never returned to classical American capitalism, largely because of the reaction to the troubles of the 1930s. Whichever view you choose, the events discussed in this chapter created a worldwide loss of faith in a capitalism based on the model of perfect competition. Keynes's *General Theory* was one reflection of the change. Edward Chamberlin and Joan Robinson's models of monopolistic and imperfect competition, respectively, reflect this change in the microeconomic sphere—scale economies were present, products were differentiated, and entry was not completely open. Because perfect competition assumes that the economy is self-adjusting, the first impulse was to see what happened. When the economy continued to decline, the search for some economic "medicine" accelerated. Franklin Delano Roosevelt was elected in 1932 to "do something." That something is the subject of the following chapter.

NOTES

1. Studs Terkel's *Hard Times: An Oral History of the Great Depression* (New York: Pantheon Books, 1970), is particularly recommended for its many vivid recollections of the 1930s from people from all walks of life.
2. Michael Bordo, Claudia Goldin, and Eugene White, *The Defining Moment* (Chicago: University of Chicago Press, 1998). The scope of disagreement on this issue is made clear in Karl Brunner, ed., *The Great Depression Revisited* (1981) in which the "Monetarist" and "real" positions are reasserted and examined.
3. Even staunch Keynesians like Alvin Hansen could see this possibility during the 1930s when Keynesian ideas about fiscal policy were being developed. Alan Sweezey, "The Keynesians and Government Policy, 1933–1939," *American Economic Review*, vol. LXII, no. 2, May 1972, especially p. 122.
4. Robert Gordon and James Wilcox, "Monetarist Interpretations of the Great Depression: An Evaluation and Critique," in Brunner (1981), p. 58.
5. The Austrian view has long been out of fashion. Its most forceful restatement is Murray Rothbard, *America's Great Depression* (1975).
6. Stanley Lebergott, "Annual Estimates of Unemployment in the United States, 1900–1954," in *The Measurement and Behavior of Unemployment* (Princeton: Princeton University Press, 1957).
7. Michael Darby, "Three and a Half Million U.S. Employees Have Been Mislaid," *JPE*, February 1976.
8. Joseph Schumpeter, "The Present World Depression: A Tentative Diagnosis," *American Economic Review*, vol. 21, no. 1, Supplement (1931).
9. Phillip Cagan, "Comments," in Brunner (1981).
10. F. M. Scherer and David Ross, *Industrial Market Structure and Economic Performance*, 3rd ed. (Boston: Houghton Mifflin, 1990), pp. 153–156.
11. In 1929, exports of goods and services stood at $7 billion. This dropped to $2.4 billion in 1933.
12. Under postal savings, a person could deposit money into a fixed-interest account at the post office. During the depression, the low fixed rates offered by the post office proved to be among the highest available to savers. Maureen O'Hara and David Easley, "The Postal Savings System in the Depression," *JEH*, September 1979.
13. By 1944, these extraordinary levels of cash reserves had vanished; the ratio was back to 24.4.
14. Stein, *The Fiscal Revolution in America* (1969), pp. 33–38.
15. Peter Temin, *Did Monetary Forces Cause the Great Depression?* (1976).
16. Brunner (1981) is devoted entirely to the early part of the depression. Brunner's "Introduction" is a summary of the issues. There are outstanding questions about the Federal Reserve's policy in the 1929–1932 period regarding its own warrant as a "lender of last resort." From the evidence, it is doubtful that the Fed's managers considered saving the thousands of failing banks to be a Federal Reserve obligation. Also, their efforts at "reflation," by purchasing government securities in 1931 and 1932 seem to have been thwarted by the caution of commercial bank lending policies, *even had it been the intention of the Fed* to "force" a recovery, or attempt to, by such methods. Jonathan Hughes, "Stagnation Without 'Flation: The 1930s Again," in Barry Siegal, ed., *Money in Crisis: The Federal Reserve, The Economy, and Monetary Reform* (Cambridge, MA: Ballinger, 1984); Gerald Epstein and Thomas Ferguson, "Monetary Policy, Loan Liquidation, and Industrial Conflict: The Federal Reserve and Open Market Operations of 1932," *Journal of Economic History*, vol. XLIV, no. 4, December 1984.
17. Richard Szostak, *Technological Innovation and the Great Depression* (1995), is a book in the Schumpeterian tradition.
18. Milton Friedman and Anna Schwartz, *A Monetary History of the U.S.* (1963). Their long chapter on the depression, later published separately as *The Great Contraction* (Princeton: Princeton University Press, 1965). See also Anna Schwartz's defense of it in Brunner (1981), chap. 1. This volume contains papers by Allan Meltzer, Thomas Mayer, and others defending the Monetarist approach. The Meltzer paper discusses the contractionary consequences of the Smoot-Hawley Tariff of 1931.
19. Elmus Wicker, *The Banking Panics of the Great Depression* (1996).
20. A somewhat different impression can be found in David Wheelock, "The Strategy, Effectiveness, and Consistency of Federal Reserve Monetary Policy, 1924–1933," *EEH*, October 1989.
21. Alexander Field, "A New Interpretation of the Onset of the Great Depression," *JEH*, June 1984. See also James Hamilton, "Monetary Factors in the Great Depression," *Journal of Monetary Economics*, January 1987.
22. If interest rates, which were at 1 percent or less most of the time between 1933 and the coming of war in 1939, were at their minima, that is, they could not have been driven lower by monetary policy, then a Keynesian "liquidity trap" existed. If so, then there was really little or no scope for monetary policy to contribute to a recovery.

Richard Sutch believes that the liquidity trap did in fact exist, "Notes on the Ineffectiveness of Monetary Policy During a Keynesian Depression: The Crises of Liquidation in the United States at Certain Dates in 1932," forthcoming. Cited by permission.

23. F. A. Hayek, *Monetary Theory and the Trade Cycle* (1966); Lionel Robbins, *The Great Depression* (1934); and Rothbard, *America's Great Depression* (1975), chaps. 9–11.
24. *Historical Statistics*, series X 800.
25. For an extended discussion of the Austrian view, see Gene Smiley, *The American Economy in the Twentieth Century* (1994), pp. 148–151.
26. Temin (1976).
27. Temin (1976), p. 64. See also his defense in Brunner (1981) entitled "Notes on the Causes of the Great Depression." An exposition of his thoughts on this subject can be found in his *Lessons from the Great Depression* (1989). For a separate defense of Friedman and Schwartz and a critique of Temin's thesis, see Thomas Mayer, "Money and the Great Depression: A Critique of Professor Temin's Thesis," *Explorations in Economic History*, vol. 15, no. 2, April 1978. Martha Olney's analysis of consumer credit purchases of durable consumer goods supports Temin. Consumers cut new purchases to meet installment payments. Fear of the future also caused them to make fewer new installment contracts as old contracts were paid off. Martha Olney, "Consumer Durables in the Interwar Years: New Estimates, New Patterns," *Research in Economic History*, vol. 12 (1990). Christina Romer also supports Temin for reasons similar to Olney's, "The Great Crash and the Onset of the Great Depression," *QJE*, August 1990.
28. Robert Aaron Gordon, *Economic Instability and Growth: The American Record* (New York: Harper & Row, 1974).
29. Gordon and Wilcox (1981), p. 80.
30. Bert Hickman, "What Became of the Building Cycle?" in Paul David and Melvin Reder, eds., *Nations and Households in Economic Growth: Essays in Honor of Moses Abramovitz* (1973).
31. Alexander Field, "Uncontrolled Land Development and the Duration of the Depression in the United States," *JEH*, December 1992, suggests the haphazard development pattern of the 1920s prolonged depression in the 1930s.
32. Lloyd Mercer and Douglas Morgan, "The American Automobile Industry, Investment Demand, Capacity, and Capacity Utilization, 1921–1940," *JPE*, November/December 1972, and their "Alternative Interpretations of Market Saturation: Evaluation for the Automobile Market in the Late Twenties," *EEH*, Spring 1972.
33. Alvin Hansen stated it in different places and forms, including a book, *Full Recovery or Stagnation* (New York: W. W. Norton, 1939). The shortest statement is his article, "Economic Progress and Declining Population Growth," *AER*, May 1938.
34. Thomas Wilson, *Essays in Income and Employment* (New York: Pitman, 1949).
35. Michael Bernstein, *The Great Depression* (1987).
36. Frederic Mishkin, "The Household Balance Sheet and the Great Depression," *JEH*, December 1978.
37. Romer (1990).
38. Stanley Lebergott, *Consumption Expenditures: New Measures & Old Motives* (1996).
39. *Ibid.*, p. 12.
40. *Ibid.*, pp. 81–90.
41. Stein (1969), pp. 151–168.
42. John Maynard Keynes, *The General Theory of Employment, Interest, and Money* (New York: Harcourt Brace, 1936), p. 378.
43. E. Cary Brown, "Fiscal Policy in the Thirties: A Reappraisal," *AER*, December 1956, p. 863.
44. Otis Graham, Jr., *Toward a Planned Society: From Roosevelt to Nixon* (1976), p. 67.
45. *Ibid.*, chaps. 5–7.
46. Douglas Irwin, "The Smoot Hawley Tariff: A Quantitative Assessment," *REStat*, May 1998.
47. Mario J. Crucini and James Kahn, "Tariffs and Aggregate Economic Activity: Lessons from the Great Depression," *Journal of Monetary Economics*, vol. 38, no. 3, December 1996.
48. Charles Kindleberger, *The World in Depression 1929–1939* (1973); Folke Hilgerdt, *The Network of World Trade* (Geneva: League of Nations, 1942); and Ragnar Nurkse, *International Currency Experience: Lessons of the Interwar Period* (Princeton: League of Nations, 1944). See also Gertrude Fremling, "Did the United States Transmit the Great Depression to the Rest of the World?" *American Economic Review*, vol. 75, no. 5, December 1985. Fremling agrees with Kindleberger on the worldwide origins of the 1930s depression.
49. Christina Romer, "The Nation in Depression," *JEP*, Spring 1993, argues that events within the United States through 1930 can be explained with reference to domestic factors alone.
50. W. Arthur Lewis, *Economic Survey, 1919–1939* (London: Allen and Unwin, 1949).
51. Ingvar Svennilson, *Growth and Stagnation in the European Economy* (Geneva: United Nations, 1954).
52. Hamilton (1987) documents the contractionary open market sale of securities beginning in 1928.
53. Temin (1989).
54. The implications of the aggregate supply side of the international view are discussed in Ben Bernanke, "The Macroeconomics of the Great Depression: A Comparative Approach," *JMCB*, February 1995, pp. 16–25.
55. Barry Eichengreen, "The Origins and Nature of the Great Slump Revisited," *EHR*, May 1992a, is an excel-

lent review of recent scholarship concerning the depression. See also his *Golden Fetters* (1992b) and *Globalizing Capital* (1996). An early version of the argument can be found in Eichengreen and Jeffrey Sachs, "Exchange Rates and Economic Recovery in the 1930s," *JEH*, December 1985.

56. Bernanke (1995), pp. 3–4.
57. Eichengreen (1992a), p. 224.
58. Eichengreen (1992b), pp. 293–298.
59. Peter Temin, "Transmission of the Great Depression," *JEP*, Spring 1993.
60. A particularly astute analysis of this episode can be found in John Maynard Keynes, "The Economic Consequences of Mr. Churchill," reprinted in Keynes, *Essays in Persuasion* (New York: W.W. Norton, 1963).
61. Temin (1993), p. 94.
62. Harold James, "Financial Flows Across Frontiers During the Interwar Depression," *EHR*, August 1992, pp. 603–606, discusses how American decisions following Britain's withdrawal from gold, particularly the announcement on 3 July 1933 that the United States had no intention of stabilizing the dollar, contributed to the effect of the depression on European countries.
63. Christina Romer, "What Ended the Great Depression?," *JEH*, December 1992.
64. Charles Calomiris, "Financial Factors in the Great Depression," *JEP*, Spring 1993.
65. See Richard Grossman, "The Shoe That Didn't Drop: Explaining Banking Stability During the Great Depression," *JEH*, September 1994, for an explanation of the stability of countries such as Britain and Canada. More detail on the Canadian case can be found in Joseph Haubrich, "Nonmonetary Effects of Financial Crises: Lessons from the Great Depression in Canada," *Journal of Monetary Economics*, vol. 25, no. 1, March 1990.

SUGGESTED READINGS

Articles

Bernanke, Ben S. "Nonmonetary Effects of the Financial Crisis in the Propagation of the Great Depression." *American Economic Review*, vol. 73, no. 3, June 1983.

———. "The Macroeconomics of the Great Depression: A Comparative Approach." *Journal of Money, Credit, and Banking*, vol. 27, no. 1, February 1995.

Brown, E. Cary. "Fiscal Policy in the Thirties: A Reappraisal." *American Economic Review*, vol. XLVI, no. 5, December 1956.

Calomiris, Charles W. "Financial Factors in the Great Depression." *Journal of Economic Perspectives*, vol. 7, no. 2, Spring 1993.

Darby, Michael. "Three and a Half Million U.S. Employees Have Been Mislaid." *Journal of Political Economy*, vol. 84, no. 1, February 1976.

Eichengreen, Barry. "The Origins and Nature of the Great Slump Revisited." *Economic History Review*, vol. XLV, no. 2, May 1992a.

———, and Jeffrey Sachs. "Exchange Rates and Economic Recovery in the 1930s." *Journal of Economic History*, vol. XLV, no. 4, December 1985.

Field, Alexander J. "A New Interpretation of the Onset of the Great Depression." *Journal of Economic History*, vol. XLIV, no. 2, May 1984.

———. "Uncontrolled Land Development and the Duration of the Depression in the United States." *Journal of Economic History*, vol. 52, no. 4, December 1992.

Gordon, Robert J., and James A. Wilcox. "Monetarist Interpretations of the Great Depression: An Evaluation and Critique." In Karl Brunner, ed., *The Great Depression Revisited.* Boston: Martinus Nijhoff, 1981.

Grossman, Richard S. "The Shoe That Didn't Drop: Explaining Banking Stability During the Great Depression." *Journal of Economic History*, vol. 54, no. 3, September 1994.

Hamilton, James D. "Monetary Factors in the Great Depression." *Journal of Monetary Economics*, vol. 13, no. 1, March 1987.

Hansen, Alvin. "Economic Progress and Declining Population Growth." *American Economic Review*, vol. 29, no. 1, May 1938.

Hickman, Bert G. "What Became of the Building Cycle?" In Paul David and Melvin Reder, eds., *Nations and Households in Economic Growth: Essays in Honor of Moses Abramovitz.* New York: Academic Press, 1973.

Irwin, Douglas A. "The Smoot-Hawley Tariff: A Quantitative Assessment," *Review of Economics and Statistics*, vol. 80, no. 2, May 1998.

James, Harold. "Financial Flows Across Frontiers During the Interwar Depression." *Economic History Review*, vol. XLV, no. 3, August 1992.

Mercer, Lloyd J., and W. Douglas Morgan. "Alternative Interpretations of Market Saturation: Evaluation for the Automobile Market in the Late Twenties." *Explorations in Economic History*, vol. 9, no. 3, Spring 1972.

———. "The American Automobile Industry, Investment Demand, Capacity, and Capacity Utilization, 1921–1940." *Journal of Political Economy*, vol. 80, no. 6, November/December 1972.

Mishkin, Frederic S. "The Household Balance Sheet and the Great Depression." *Journal of Economic History*, vol. XXXVIII, no. 4, December 1978.

O'Hara, Maureen, and David Easley. "The Postal Savings System in the Depression." *Journal of Economic History*, vol. XXXIX, no. 3, September 1979.

Romer, Christina D. "The Great Crash and the Onset of the Great Depression." *Quarterly Journal of Economics*, vol. 105, no. 3, August 1990.

———. "What Ended the Great Depression?" *Journal of Economic History*, vol. 52, no. 4, December 1992.

———. "The Nation in Depression." *Journal of Economic Perspectives*, vol. 7, no. 2, Spring 1993.

Temin, Peter. "Notes on the Causes of the Great Depression." In Karl Brunner, ed., *The Great Depression Revisited*, Boston: Martinus Nijhoff, 1981.

———. "Transmission of the Great Depression." *Journal of Economic Perspectives*, vol. 7, no. 2, Spring 1993.

Wheelock, David. "The Strategy, Effectiveness, and Consistency of Federal Reserve Monetary Policy, 1924–1933." *Explorations in Economic History*, vol. 26, no. 4, October 1989.

Books

Bernstein, Michael A. *The Great Depression: Delayed Recovery and Economic Change in America, 1929–1939*. New York: Cambridge University Press, 1987.

Brunner, Karl, ed. *The Great Depression Revisited*. Boston: Martinus Nijhoff, 1981.

Chandler, Lester. *America's Greatest Depression: 1929–1941*. New York: Harper & Row, 1970.

Eichengreen, Barry. *Golden Fetters: The Gold Standard and the Great Depression, 1919–1939*. New York: Oxford University Press, 1992b.

———. *Globalizing Capital: A History of the International Monetary System*. Princeton: Princeton University Press, 1996.

Friedman, Milton, and Anna J. Schwartz. *A Monetary History of the United States, 1867–1960*. Princeton: Princeton University Press, 1963.

Garraty, John A. *The Great Depression: An Inquiry into the Case, Course and Consequences of the Worldwide Depression of the Nineteen-Thirties, As Seen by Contemporaries and in the Light of History*. New York: Harcourt Brace Jovanovitch, 1986.

Graham, Otis L., Jr. *Toward a Planned Society: From Roosevelt to Nixon*. New York: Oxford University Press, 1976.

Hayek, F. A. *Monetary Theory and the Trade Cycle*. New York: Kelley, 1966.

Hughes, Jonathan. *The Governmental Habit Redux: Economic Controls from Colonial Times to the Present*. Princeton: Princeton University Press, 1991.

Kindleberger, Charles P. *The World in Depression 1929–1939*. Berkeley: University of California Press, 1973.

Lebergott, Stanley. *Consumption Expenditures: New Measures & Old Motives*. Princeton: Princeton University Press, 1996.

Robbins, Lionel. *The Great Depression*. London: Macmillan, 1934.

Rothbard, Murray. *America's Great Depression*. Kansas City: Sheed & Ward, 1975.

Schumpeter, Joseph. *Business Cycles*. New York: McGraw-Hill, 1939, 2 vols.

Smiley, Gene. *The American Economy in the Twentieth Century*. Cincinnati: South-Western Publishing Co., 1994.

Stein, Herbert. *The Fiscal Revolution in America*. Chicago: University of Chicago Press, 1969.

Szostak, Rick. *Technological Innovation and the Great Depression*, Boulder, CO: Westview Press, 1995.

Temin, Peter. *Did Monetary Forces Cause the Great Depression?* New York: Norton, 1976.

———. *Lessons from the Great Depression*. Cambridge: MIT Press, 1989.

Wicker, Elmus. *The Banking Panics of the Great Depression*. New York: Cambridge University Press, 1996.

CHAPTER TWENTY-FIVE

The New Deal

Franklin Delano Roosevelt came to power in 1933 with the expectation that his new administration would be more aggressive about getting the country out of the depression. In retrospect, it is clear that there was much flailing about (called "experimentation"), giving the appearance, at least, of doing something. The New Deal prescription for electoral success (usually attributed to Postmaster General James Farley): "Tax, tax, tax. Spend, spend, spend. Elect, elect, elect," was scarcely designed to encourage private entrepreneurs or corporate executives to "take a flyer" on the future of American capitalism.

In Chapter 22, we saw that, in the World War I command economy, the needs of defense were combined with an attempt to achieve certain long-standing ambitions of social reformers—for example, the introduction of the eight-hour day, recognition of union bargaining rights, prohibition of child labor, and implementation of minimum wage legislation. The same phenomenon occurred in the 1930s. The idea of recovery was combined with ambitions for extensive reforms of American capitalism and fundamental changes in the concepts of proper federal responsibility so that a 1929 would not happen again—that is, the New Deal.[1]

EMERGENCY MEASURES

It is not easy today to catch the flavor of the Roosevelt administration's first 100 days. Most immediately pressing was the banking crisis.[2]

Banking had been a major growth sector, as we saw in previous chapters. The number of commercial banks had increased from about 13,000 to more than 28,000 between 1900 and 1914. By 1921, there were 31,076 separate commercial banks. Between 1921 and 1934, that number fell by 16,305, of which 14,820 were outright failures. In 1929, 659 banks closed their doors. In 1930, the number doubled to 1,352. After the banking crisis of 1930, more failed, and the number of closures in 1931 rose to 2,294.

In 1932, there was a decline in failures to 1,456, but, as 1933 opened, a new wave of failures threatened, and state governors began declaring bank holidays en masse. People were going into banks and demanding their deposits. With fractional-reserve banking, then as now, deposits are vastly in excess of the currency in the bank that is used to meet the daily outflow. By 4 March 1933, all banks in 38 states had suspended business. Two days later, utilizing powers leftover from World War I legislation, Roosevelt finished the job by declaring a nationwide bank holiday.[3]

When the banks reopened under federal supervision, some 4,000 more were found to be insolvent and were liquidated. Ben Bernanke concluded that so severe were the effects of the banking crisis in the early 1930s (especially in 1931) that the banking system was simply unable to resume as a competent mechanism of intermediation for the rest of the 1930s.[4]

The Roosevelt administration made major changes in the monetary sphere. An Emergency Bank Act, passed 9 March 1933, prohibited specie exports. The Comptroller of the Currency was empowered by executive order to reopen the (solvent) national banks with temporary federal deposit insurance. That stopped the bank runs. Since it was widely believed that "abuses" in Wall Street had created the 1929 stock-market panic and subsequent disasters, an emergency securities act was passed in 1933, placing Wall Street operators under the thumb of the Federal Trade Commission. These changes would be made more permanent in future legislation.

Such temporary measures were preliminary to a devaluation of the dollar. As we know, the United States had been legally a strict gold-standard country since 1900. Now it was believed that many advantages—increased exports, rising commodity prices, a return to full employment—would ensue if the Treasury's gold price were raised.[5] Indeed, "practical people" in this country, as well as theoretical economists, long believed that manipulating the currency could solve broad social and economic problems. As we have seen, Barry Eichengreen argued that the operation of the interwar gold standard was a major cause of the severity of the worldwide depression from 1929 to 1933. The "rules of the game" for defending the gold standard against adverse shocks transformed what otherwise would have been a serious downturn into a worldwide depression.[6]

Roosevelt was standing squarely in the mainstream of American tradition on this particular matter. On 5 April 1933, an executive order was issued forbidding gold hoarding. Arrangements were made to "call in" all U.S. monetary gold in circulation, first to the Federal Reserve Banks, then to the Treasury. On 20 April 1933, another executive order halted Treasury sales of gold for export. The United States was off the gold standard. The Reconstruction Finance Corporation then began buying gold at irregularly increasing prices. Of marginal interest is the fact that Roosevelt was receiving some less-than-expert advice on this policy. George Warren, an agricultural economist at Cornell University, was seized by the idea that you could raise all prices by raising the price of gold.[7] Unfortunately, Roosevelt went along with the professor since that advice was also acceptable to most members of Congress.

Apart from these pressing money matters, the primary emergency was the huge unemployment rate. Local unemployment relief funds were largely exhausted. People looked to the federal government for help, and this dependence introduced the prospect of a departure upon unknown seas. Hoover had not wanted such responsibility to slip to the federal level. Poor relief of nearly all kinds has been, by ancient tradition, a responsibility lodged with state and local authorities. Hoover made federal loan money available to the states for unemployment relief, but he opposed proposals for a permanent federal role that emanated from private business leaders, notably Gerard Swope (president of General Electric). Swope's 1931 plan for federal participation, socializing the problems of unemployment, was characterized by Hoover as "fascist and monopolistic." The "Swope Plan" was destined to reappear, modified, in the Social Security Act of 1935.[8]

Roosevelt rushed in where Hoover had not dared tread. On 20 May 1933, he asked Congress to grant $500 million to the states for emergency relief. The result, the Federal Emergency Relief Agency (FERA), headed by Harry Hopkins, was the predecessor of more permanent agencies to come. Hopkins immediately put millions of dollars into people's hands through "make-work" projects. He would become famous in the New Deal years for imaginative, work-producing, spending programs.

But these were stopgap measures. Soon enough a structure of federal participation and economic intervention emerged. The experience of the World War I command economy now became a handbook of strategies and tactics.

THE FIRST NEW DEAL

The New Deal economic and social programs and institutions are usually treated in two parts, the first and second New Deals, with a dividing frontier at roughly 1936—or 1935 in the opinion of some scholars. Most of the innovative movement appears before 1936, and the U.S. Supreme Court declared a large part of that unconstitutional. The election of 1936 has been considered the dividing line in New Deal history. But, as John Wallis argues, the Wagner Act, Social Security Act, and Emergency Relief Appropriations Act of 1935 were all really part of *renewed* New Deal vigor, and, logically, on an economic basis, the second New Deal really began in 1935.[9]

The NIRA

The National Industrial Recovery Act (NIRA) was the most ambitious part of the first New Deal. It was inspired by the World War I experience, modified by the search for cooperative solutions to business problems that had been pursued by Hoover and others in the 1920s. These people believed that the World War I experience could be made into "industrial self-government" in peacetime, with only a modicum of federal power co-opted. Many economists, business owners, and labor leaders, as well as government officials and politicians, had come to believe that competition among business firms was damaging, that it raised the levels of risk unnecessarily and made business failure and unemployment more likely (and worse) than they needed to be. By 1932, some American leaders were even looking admiringly at the Italian dictator Mussolini for inspiration, strange as that may seem now.

The NIRA was designed to reduce domestic competition.[10] In part, this was a response to businesses that attributed their woes to "unfair competition," particularly to competitors who they believed were "selling below cost." Industrial self-government required that the threat of antitrust prosecution be lifted so that businesses could openly collude on matters of production, price-setting, and employment. The thinking was that business owners themselves could plan production and prices that would be profitable, and a stable, full-employment economy would necessarily result. The NIRA would provide the system that, as we saw earlier, President Wilson ordered abandoned at the end of World War I. Yet there were clear contradictions in the NIRA. Business was forbidden to act collusively to suppress competition and forbidden to act competitively by cutting prices.

One of Bernard Baruch's aides at the old War Industries Board, General Hugh Johnson, was made director of the National Recovery Administration (NRA). Businesses were to organize themselves into identifiable industries, each with its own mutually agreed-upon "code of fair practice." The NRA, like the War Industries Board before it, was to have three advisory boards, representing management, labor (recall the War Labor Board), and "the public."[11] In Section 7A of the NIRA, workers in NRA firms were given the right to bargain collectively with their employers through agents of their own choosing—unions. Once the NRA approved a code, firms in the industry were required to show their acceptance by signing it. Only then were they entitled to display the "Blue Eagle" emblem.

The experiment, although a novel one, was short-lived. It was signed into law 16 June 1933, and within a year 450 codes were written. By May 1935, when the Supreme Court threw out the NIRA (for excessive delegation of power by Congress), 550 industry codes had been adopted.[12] By then, Roosevelt was ready to let it die. The politicians realized that it was an expanding morass of nondirectional regulation. Anderson has documented that the more concentrated industries had a "greater vested interest" in making the NIRA a success.[13] Industrial production only made a significant recovery after the NRA was abolished. About 80 percent of nonagricultural industry was codified, and more than 1,000 "unfair" trade practices (that is, competitive techniques) were identified and prohibited in the codes. General Johnson, a former cavalry officer, stated the spirit of the NRA:

> The very heart of the New Deal is the principle of concerted action, in industry and agriculture, under government supervision, looking to a balanced economy—as opposed to the murderous doctrine of savage and wolfish competition and rugged individualism … dog-eat-dog and devil take the hindmost.[14]

Two parts of the NRA were destined to live, the National Labor Board and the Public Works Administration (PWA). When, in the National Labor Relations Act (Wagner Act) of 1935, Section 7A of the

NIRA was rewritten, the Labor Board became the National Labor Relations Board (NLRB), and it has remained a central force in federal involvement in U.S. labor relations. The PWA, under Harold Ickes, lasted until World War II.

The AAAs of 1933 and 1938

Another New Deal scheme to solve long-standing problems was the 1933 Agricultural Adjustment Act (AAA). It too was thrown out by the Supreme Court (in 1936), but parts were immortalized in 1938 when the second AAA was written without the offending tax on food processors.[15] A central Populist demand in the late nineteenth century had been that the federal government should provide low-interest loans to farmers on the collateral of stored crops.[16]

People were hungry because they lacked money to buy food, even though farm prices actually fell by more than 50 percent between 1929 and 1933. As Roger Ransom pointed out, since the number of farm families did not decline in that short interval, farm income per capita was reduced.[17] The food growers were desperate for income. Lacking any way to raise demand significantly, Congress opted to authorize a massive reduction in supply in order to raise farm income through hoped-for price increases. By 1933, there was already a year's supply of cotton on hand, and wheat inventories were three times the normal amount. The scheme adopted was to restore farm prices to "parity"—to the levels where the ratio of farm to nonfarm prices recovered the average of those prices between 1909 and 1914, one of the most prosperous periods for American farmers in our history. In a famous gesture, 6 million little pigs were slaughtered in 1933 to reduce pork supplies.

In the newly created Commodity Credit Corporation (1933), farmers could get loans on stored crops from a quasi-governmental agency—the Populist "sub-Treasury" scheme at long last. Also, the government bought crops outright to remove food from the markets. Farmers were paid not to grow crops, to take land out of production. Restrictions on output, even for on-the-farm use, were agreed upon.[18]

In addition, other government agencies attempted to help farm families, socially as well as financially. The Farm Credit Act launched the Farm Credit Administration (FCA) in 1934, an agency designed to loan farmers money against the collateral of their real property on more liberal terms than had been achieved by the Federal Land Banks. The FCA would live to become one of the largest lending institutions of any kind in the country. Another project was much less successful. One of Eleanor Roosevelt's favorite ideas was the resettlement of the urban unemployed on farms to achieve partial self-sufficiency. It was tried by the Farm Security Administration, but it did not work well.[19]

An integral part of farm policy was conservation and reclamation, as drought in the 1930s conspired with deficient markets to segment farm misery. The high plains turned into the "Dust Bowl." After the Supreme Court's adverse ruling on the first AAA, Congress passed the Soil Conservation and Domestic Allotment Act, a measure that allowed the Department of Agriculture to pay farmers to restrict planting under the guise of conservation.[20] At the same time, the Tennessee Valley Authority (TVA), organized around the dam built at Muscle Shoals in 1916 on the Tennessee River, became the centerpiece of a nationwide conservation and reclamation effort.[21]

The second Agricultural Adjustment Act was passed in 1938. The crop-control and income-support provisions were even stronger than in the Act of 1933, and this time the U.S. Supreme Court had no objections. Its decision in the test case, *Wickard v. Filburn* (1942), signified its agreement with the proposition that farmers participating in acreage-limitation schemes should not grow a bit extra on their unused land to feed their own livestock.[22] Amended over the years, the 1938 AAA, the "Ever-Normal Granary" act, remains the basis of modern farm policy.

The Financial Reforms

After the first 100 days and the emergency legislation, the Roosevelt administration dug in. Reforms of older institutions remained high on the agenda, but there were some basic new departures, too.

Reform centered on the financial system. The Glass-Steagall Act of 1933 separated commercial banks from most of their securities business.[23] In 1935, the Federal Deposit Insurance Corporation replaced the temporary arrangements of the 1933 act.[24] Marriner S. Eccles, a millionaire Utah banker, was the author of the 1935 Bank Act, which restructured the Federal Reserve System.[25] The (renamed) Board of Governors was given discretionary control over bank reserves and margin requirements for loans against securities. The Governors' Committee, innovated by Benjamin Strong in the 1920s, was moved to Washington; it was renamed the Federal Open Market Committee and had 12 members, seven of whom were the governors themselves. The secretary of the Treasury and the Comptroller of the Currency were removed from the governing of the Fed. The monetary power was now consolidated at the Federal Reserve System's headquarters in Washington.

Moving the Federal Reserve's Open Market Committee to Washington and giving the politically appointed members of the Federal Reserve Board an automatic majority may or may not have been economically wise, but its object was to politicize the Federal Reserve System, to weaken the power of the private sector in the determination of monetary policy. The same goal was true of the board's new powers to alter at will the required reserves of the member banks. Eccles believed that control of the nation's monetary system *should* be politicized in our democracy and control taken away from the New York bankers. He considered their prior domination to have been both undemocratic and incompetent.

Like commercial banking, the securities industry was commonly blamed for the 1929 crash and its contribution to the unfolding miseries of the Great Depression. Whether that industry was reformed or not, it contributed little enough to a business recovery after attempts were made to improve it (refer to Table 24.4). Roosevelt talked grandly of "an end to speculation with other people's money." The money changers had "fled from their high seats in the temple of our civilization." The Truth in Securities Act of May 1933 and the Securities Exchange Act in 1934 were meant somehow to take the risk out of the securities industry and encourage virtue. In 1934, the Securities Exchange Act was passed. The latter set up the Securities and Exchange Commission (SEC) to control the capital markets. They did not yield a recovery in the capital markets. A year later, the Public Utilities Holding Company Act placed federal restrictions for the first time on public utility financial structures and practice and placed them under the SEC's regulation.

The Government as Employer

Direct work relief had been authorized under the FERA. In a sense this was a dramatic departure since it was an overt acceptance by the federal government of responsibility for unemployment. Men and women were set to work on government projects *because* they could not find employment in the private sector.

The Civilian Conservation Corps (CCC) and the Works Progress Administration (WPA) produced benefits for the economy through efforts in conservation, through new sewer and water systems, sidewalks, and roads. Unemployed or underemployed people, to whom society would otherwise have been providing relief support, were put to work in those vast enterprises. Once they were assigned to work on public projects, they were employed at useful labor, *and* society gained the output as a benefit.

The CCC, employing 2.5 million people, lasted from 1933 to 1940. In the desperate conditions of 1933, Harry Hopkins put 4 million people to work on Civil Works Administration (CWA) projects *in two months*. The Public Works Administration (PWA), under Secretary of the Interior Harold Ickes, had been designed under Title II of the NIRA to produce significant public-sector input into the construction industry.

The PWA ultimately spent billions, but the employment effects were deemed insufficient. Thus, in 1935, Congress created the famous WPA under Harry Hopkins to spend money on employment under the Emergency Relief Appropriations Act. Hopkins originally had about $4.9 billion to disperse. By 1941, he had employed 8 million people, an estimated 16 percent of the labor force, on WPA projects, at a cost of $11.4 billion.

That these measures "put people to work," cannot be denied. But at this distance in time, it is not sacrilege to question the net effects. The federal works projects employed people at modest enough wages—supposedly at the "prevailing wage" in the districts where the projects were located. It was no secret, however, that WPA "security" wages, being regular and actually *paid* in cash, were an improvement for the unskilled, even if they were already employed elsewhere.

In 1936, government employment was made more attractive as a result of the Walsh-Healy Act, which fixed standards for hours, wages, and working conditions in all government employments. Some economists at that time (and since) argued that unemployment was kept unusually high throughout the 1930s because *real* wages were kept from falling. In the private sector, firms cut hours and jobs before they reduced the nominal wage; it was "sticky." In the public sector, the federal employment, through its insistence on the prevailing wage, helped wages in general remain above the equilibrium, or full-employment, level. According to the deflationist argument, had wages fallen as freely as prices, full employment *must* have resulted. In addition, there might even have been an advance in real wages, as was true for those people who were able to maintain their employment. If we follow the logic of the argument, the heroic efforts of the federal government were really counterproductive; the public enterprises consumed labor and materials at prices beyond the reach of the private sector. Hence, the private sector remained in a depressed state even though there was a vast expansion of the public enterprise. Whether or not this argument is wholly fantasy, we cannot say.

Table 25.1 shows the primary direct employment vehicles of the New Deal. These expenditures were primarily investments in human capital and remain to this day as models of alternatives to unemployment. Twenty percent of New Deal expenditures were for employment. Although *millions* worked in these projects, they never employed enough people to do more than to moderate the depression unemployment levels. The New Deal make-work schemes, for all their energy and innovation, were never a real substitute for private-sector employment. In 1938, when expenditures were authorized to employ 4 million, that was still a mere 10 percent

A map showing the location of Public Works Administration projects as of fall 1936.

TABLE 25.1 Major New Deal Agencies: Grants to States and Work Relief Earnings, 1933–1939[a]

Agency	*National Grants to States*	*Work Relief Earnings*
FERA	$ 3,017	$ 1,238
CCC	2,622	1,734
CWA	807	718
WPA	6,804	6,586
FSA	273	100
PWA	1,791	—
Total	*15,314*	*10,376*

[a] Amounts given are in millions of dollars.

Sources: U.S. Office of Government Reports, Vol. 10 (Washington, 1941); *Final Statistical Report of the Federal Emergency Relief Administration* (Washington, 1942), Table 10, p. 38; *Security, Relief, and Relief Polices,* National Resources Planning Board (Washington, 1943), Appendix 10, pp. 560–561. We are indebted to John Wallis for this table.

of the civilian labor force. The unemployment rate was 19 percent that year.

FERA was the first federal agency ever to include blanket relief of all kinds to the needy. The federal programs in Table 25.1 were nearly all matching grant schemes with the states, and involved state-level control of expenditures—to whom, how much. As John Wallis points out, the actual counting of Congressional authorizations, grants made to the states, and total expenditures remains to be done. The numbers in Table 25.1 are the best available estimates.[26] The National Youth Administration (NYA) is included in the table as part of WPA grants and earnings; the PWA's construction projects did not employ persons who were on relief. Of the federal grants to the states of $15.3 billion in 1937–1939, only $10.4 billion (about two-thirds) went directly for work relief.

Labor Law

The Wagner Act and the Social Security Act were lasting social innovations of the first New Deal. The Wagner Act (National Labor Relations Act) of 1935 was a federal effort to cut through the mass of conflicting law and practice that was discussed in Chapter 21. The 1931 Norris-LaGuardia Act had restricted the use of court injunctions to halt strikes. Section 7A of the NIRA had mandated collective bargaining in the code industries. The Wagner Act was a rewriting and expansion of NIRA's Section 7A. It produced a wave of unionization in the mass-production industries and the establishment of the Congress of Industrial Organizations (CIO), while setting the basic structure and rights of organized labor for the next half century.[27] Under its terms, labor had the right to organize, elect (by secret ballot) its own bargaining agents, and bargain collectively. Employers were forbidden to interfere with the process—that is, to discharge or otherwise punish employees for union activity. The National Labor Relations Board was established and given the authority to judge and arbitrate the outcomes. So much for the Law of Master and Servant. The Wagner Act was the outcome of a history that goes all the way back to earliest colonial laws rooted in the Elizabethan *Statute of Artificers and Apprentices*. The state was always involved in labor relations; compulsion was always there in some form.

For most of American history, law and the state stood on the side of real property in the wage bargain. The slow transformation to 1935 represented democracy at work.[28] When it paid politicians to shift the supreme political instrument, the apparatus of the state, to the side of labor, they did so. Votes made law, indirectly. Organized labor since 1935 has remained secure under the shield of the Wagner Act (as amended). Complaints heard in the 1970s against union power to raise union wages excessively and contribute to inflationary pressures were at root a complaint against the Wagner Act. Such complaints have been heard less in the last decade as inflation is lower and the strength of private sector unions has eroded. The Wagner Act has protected the rights of organized labor, but not the jobs they once filled.

Social Security

The 1935 Social Security Act was a further federal assumption of power and responsibility. As we know, Anglo-American society had long provided a minimal "security net" for its indigent poor. The technique was traditionally a local affair—township- and county-supported almshouses, poor farms, and so forth.[29] The old system was never exceedingly generous; Stanley Lebergott estimates that, traditionally, such transfer payments made by local governments were from 20 to 30 percent of the income earnings of common labor.[30] Workers injured in their employments had to sue their employers for negligence. The Social Security Act of 1935 was an attempt to correct these defects. It provided (a) an income for the aged, (b) a scheme for unemployment compensation funds to be prepaid by the employers of labor, and (c) categorical relief aids to the aged, blind, and dependent children. These ideas followed in part the Swope Plan of 1931.

The Social Security system has never really been "social insurance;" it is not a contract.[31] Those who pay into it have no legal claim to any benefits. Moreover, it has never been comprehensive in its coverage. Indeed, the United States was the last of the major industrial nations to adopt some form of comprehensive social insurance. The 1935 law was simply a way to get some minimal social protection from an unwilling Congress. Roosevelt, when questioned about the utterly regressive payroll taxes used to launch the system, said, "Those taxes were never a problem of economics. They were politics all the way through."[32]

In subsequent decades the Social Security system was America's main avenue to socialism—collective responsibility for human welfare—without requiring public admission by spread-eagled politicians that the country had departed massively from the old ideal of dynamic, rugged individualism. Millions of Americans have benefited from Social Security payments, which are transfers to former wage-earners from current wage-earners' payments of their special Social Security taxes.

The 1935 Social Security Act was thought to be a great and necessary social improvement, but it was flawed in its beginning. Several attempts have been made to cope with the inadequacies of the current system. Both the tax base and tax rate have been raised; the age at which benefits begin has been increased; and, for some people, a portion of their Social Security benefits has become taxable as ordinary income. None of this has solved the problem—it just postpones the date at which the problem will manifest itself. In addition, new programs like Medicare have been loaded onto it. Social Security remains a vital topic of political discourse; everyone agrees something needs to be done, but there is no consensus on what to do.

THE SECOND NEW DEAL

Reforms in the workplace brought about by federal action were almost impossible to achieve before the 1930s except in wartime or in federal employment itself. As we have seen, the 1916 Child Labor Law was thrown out by the Supreme Court in *Hammer v. Dagenhart* (1918).[33] Efforts to limit hours were overturned in *Adkins v. Children's Hospital* (1923).[34] In the first instance, the doctrine that manufacturing was not interstate commerce was given its strongest support. In the second, the right to freely bargain for wages and working conditions was held to be jeopardized by the District of Columbia's law placing restrictions upon conditions for hiring women and children. (In those days Congress legislated for the District.)

The Supreme Court allowed greater leeway to the states themselves under the traditional doctrines of the police powers.[35] Resistance to escalation of these powers from the state to the federal level was weakened by *Nebbia v. New York* (1934), but inadvertently, since that case involved a state price-fixing law.[36] It sabotaged the doctrine of *Munn v. Illinois* for good, though, leaving only the commerce clause as a barrier to federal regulation. Any business could be regulated, but it must be in interstate commerce to be *federally* regulated. After the 1936 elections, the commerce clause became the open highway to federal regulation. The greatest statement was in *NLRB v. Jones and Laughlin* (1937), which sustained the Wagner Act:

> When industries organize themselves on a national scale, making their relation to interstate commerce the dominant factor in their activities, how can it be maintained that their industrial labor relations constitute a forbidden field into which Congress cannot enter....[37]

The Fair Labor Standards Act

How indeed? In 1938, Congress passed the Fair Labor Standards Act (FLSA), which placed the federal government's power where the colonial township selectmen had been. Federal power to prescribe wages, hours, and working conditions was established.[38] There were exemptions for agricultural laborers (they are still "exempt"), business executives, sailors, and businesses not engaged in interstate commerce of whose labor relations were covered by other federal regulations (for example, railroad employees). Minimum wages were set with provisions to raise them, while maximum hours were prescribed with provisions to lower them. Overtime pay was set at 1.5 times the regular hourly rate, and penalties were laid down for "oppressive child labor." A Wage and Hours Division was established in the Labor Department to enforce all this. What about the sacred division between manufacturing and interstate commerce that had been maintained since *Hammer v. Dagenhart*? The Court ruled in *U.S. v. Darby* (1941), the FSLA test case, that *Hammer v. Dagenhart* "should be and now is overruled."[39] It was as simple as that.

Between the Wagner Act and the FLSA, the New Deal had utterly reversed the traditional position of the state in the wage bargain in this country. In interstate commerce employers *must* negotiate with unionized labor; hours were restricted at their *maximum*, wages at their *minimum*. Old-time capitalists like Henry Ford were stupefied by these changes.[40]

Rural Electrification and Public Power

Although authorized in 1935, the Rural Electrification Administration (REA) brought most of its achievement to fruition after the 1936 elections. By massive organization of rural electric cooperatives, millions of American farms (most of them) were hooked up to central electric power sources for the first time, and a second round of industrialization of American agriculture began, from appliances in farm kitchens to outlets in barns and fields. The private sector had not accepted the challenge of electrification of American agriculture. The REA was criticized by supporters of private utilities, but no one has suggested that "private enterprise" could have done the job better. It did not.

The New Deal did a good job increasing the nation's production and use of electric power. The New Deal motivated a massive increase in energy use through the TVA (Tennessee Valley Authority) system, the great multipurpose dams of the Northwest, the irrigation and power systems created in the plains states (discussed in Chapter 15), and the organization of REA co-ops, which brought power to the country's farms. The power, apart from the REA systems, was largely distributed by private power companies. However, they were now hobbled by the Public Utilities Holding Companies Act of 1935, which had placed them under the control of the Securities and Exchange Commission, restricting their own efforts to be reorganized and prohibiting (profitable) kinds of diversification.

The privately owned utilities had not, in fact, undertaken to provide power sufficiently on a strictly private basis in most rural areas. As a result, the government went ahead with the project, allowing the utilities to participate as junior partners. Only 10 percent of American farms had regular electrical service in 1933, less than was commonly the case in advanced western European countries at the time. The country produced a huge new enterprise in this public- and government-sponsored electric industry. It purposely restricted the private-power sector's growth capacity, while simultaneously pushing the growth of the public-power sector.

The results were ambiguous. Was policy designed to encourage the growth of the electric power industry in general, or merely to create a new public-sector industry? Would greater growth have occurred as a result of a full public-private partnership as in the internal improvements era of the 1830s and 1840s? Without all the antibusiness rhetoric? We will never know.

That such efforts by the federal administration were the product of distinctly mixed motives is no condemnation of the policies. It would be unreasonable to suppose that such great changes in the concept of government responsibility and the implementation of the resulting policies and programs would or could be done without substantial changes in those parts of the economy directly affected. Economically, such changes are the equivalent of technological change in private industry. It is not simply a matter of additional application of the same input combinations. Instead, the production function shifts, and all costs, revenues, and benefits change accordingly. When a Fort Peck or Grand Coulee dam was built, the economic spillovers into the surrounding communities were immense and not calculable in advance.

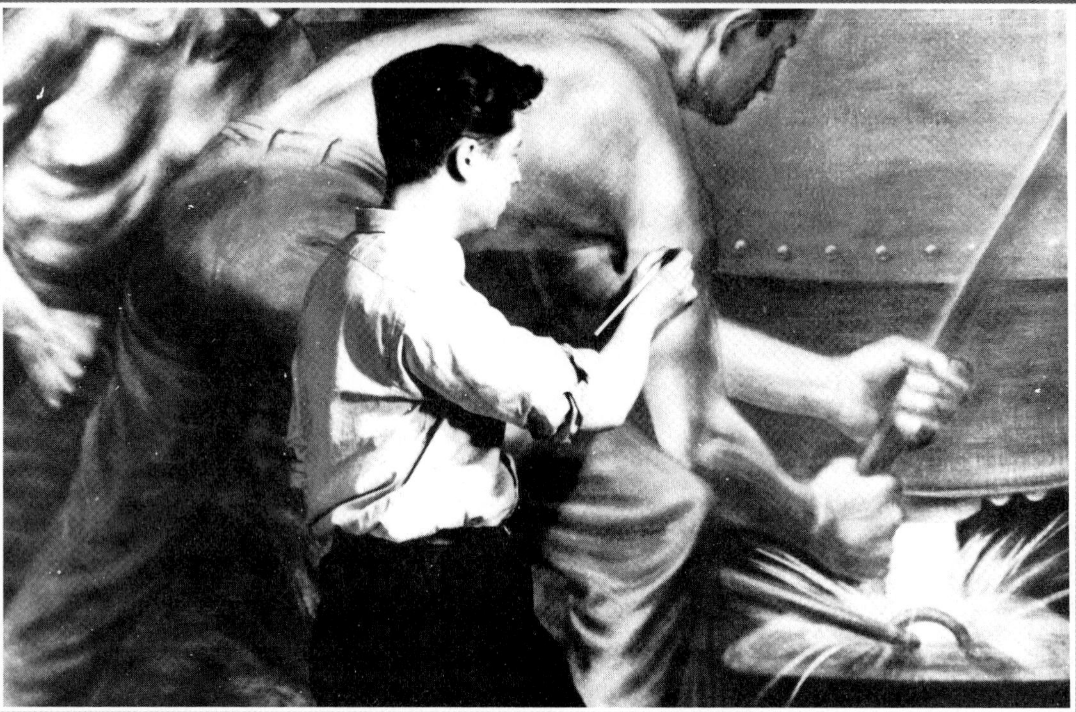

The New Deal Out of Doors. *Activism by the federal government was the hallmark of the New Deal. Artists (above) writers, actors, and musicians all gained from federal projects. Conservation projects (below) restored nature's bounty. Planned cities like this one in Maryland (above right) seemed to be the coming thing. Perhaps the greatest monuments to federal expenditures were water conservation projects such as the Grand Coulee Dam on the Columbia River (below right).*

The Reforms in Retrospect

We have touched only upon the main New Deal measures of reform and change. It cannot be denied that New Deal activism produced great changes, some of them permanent. Three generations of American voters have ratified and re-ratified the permanent New Deal innovations in American society. Most of the New Deal changes were augmentations of lines of government power previously developed in American history, as we know. But there were totally new departures, too. As Charles Cox put it:

> Never before [in peacetime] had Federal regulation promoted the interest of labor unions, or set agricultural prices and production or prescribed statutory decentralization of public utilities.[41]

There was, of course, much more. After all, FDR had promised to do something to relieve unemployment and make business prosper again. Was there any overriding logic to this "something"?

WHAT WERE THEY DOING?

The attack on business leadership was prime political currency from the beginning of the New Deal—indeed, from well before the New Deal; it was present in several election campaigns before 1914. The Pecora Committee had already conducted sensational antibusiness hearings exposing linkages between banking and the stock market before FDR entered the White House. By 1936, Roosevelt was castigating the country's business leadership for being "economic royalists" and won the election by a huge landslide. FDR and his colleagues may well have believed that the nation's business leadership could benefit from a vigorous purge. It is not clear, though, how they imagined that a sound scourging, however morally beneficial to the executive ranks themselves, would aid the processes of recovery.

Policy and Ambiguity

The NIRA was ambiguous in purpose. In the NIRA, Congress granted business freedom from antitrust prosecution—"industrial self-government"—in the hope that cartelization through the NRA codes might produce profitable prices and larger outputs that would put the unemployed back to work. At the same time, it was also a way to encourage the development of organized labor in those industries favored by the industrial codes of the NRA.

Agricultural policies were fashioned from the same sort of mixed motives.[42] In the original Agricultural Adjustment Act, the tax on processors was an attempt to force the "middle man" to pay the cost of loans against stored crops, subsidize the retirement of land from production, and buy farm surpluses outright. The tone of the legislation was antibusiness. Part of the AAA's object was to raise farm incomes by raising farm prices, but other motives were also present. The efforts to reduce supplies by subsidies were offset by other efforts to raise output efficiency on farms through mechanization, financial assistance, improved plowing and cultivation techniques, better fertilizers, improved genetic strains—even to make farm life more pleasant through agricultural extension services. More farming? Less? More output? Less? Higher prices? Lower? All of the above outcomes were implied in the various policies.

The federal government's policy also was inconsistent. The NIRA lifted the antitrust laws in manufacturing industry, but, in 1938, scarcely four years later, the federal government launched a renewed antitrust drive under Thurmon Arnold, and the Temporary National Economic Committee (TNEC) was organized to study the "concentration of economic power" in the American economy with a view to reducing it, if at all possible. If business confidence was thought important to recovery, such policy perambulations as these can have been of little help.

Failure of the Multiplier?

Another view holds that the New Deal, in its vast scope, was, in effect, the construction of a permanent depression, given the institutional nature of the American economy. Most of the employment and output relied upon the private sector, and the private sector was held back by all sorts of government policies (for example, the surtax on incomes in 1935; the drive for a balanced budget in 1937, together with the borrowing of reserves from the commercial banks to demonetize gold flowing into the country and the raising of the required reserve ratios of the commercial banks), which, it is charged, produced an unambiguous return to depression in 1938. The list of possibly counterproductive policies is long. The Wagner Act alone, which suddenly installed a whole new system of labor relations in the manufacturing industry, may have frightened off potential manufacturers.

According to basic macroeconomic theory, the multiplier effect of the public sector should have spilled over into the private sector via consumption expenditures and should have provided the means for recovery. However, according to the argument of E. Cary Brown (discussed in the previous chapter), the New Deal expenditures were insufficient to create the hoped-for income effects via the multiplier process.[43] As Keynesianism, the New Deal was worse than nothing, macroeconomically speaking.

In 1973, Larry Peppers reestimated Brown's work and found fiscal policy in the 1930s even more deficient.[44] By Peppers's calculations of a hypothetical full-employment spending policy, the small federal deficits of the 1930s were actually the equivalents of surpluses at full-employment income levels. The "fiscal drag" noted by Brown was even worse than he had imagined.

Don Reading concluded that the federal government's expenditures may *never* have had recovery as a target. What seems clear from his work is that conservation of natural resources and courting of Senate votes may have been more important targets of federal expenditures than industrial advance.[45]

In retrospect, the New Deal was much like an auto with its wheels spinning, sinking inexorably into the mud. The "reforms" of American capitalism via regulation, like the Public Utilities Holding Company Act and the new public-sector departures like TVA and REA, were merely substitutes for normal private sector activity that now did not occur *because*, in part at least, of the reforms themselves. Given the price level, the great make-work projects of the PWA, CWA, and WPA kept "prevailing wages" too high for employers and prospective employers to hire workers. Agriculture policies to raise prices and farm incomes also raised output, in part canceling out the other actions.

THE NEW DEAL: A SOCIAL REVOLUTION?

Whether it is viewed as savior or destructor, the New Deal must be viewed as very innovative in its time. Very little that is *entirely* new in the way of social policy has been achieved since then. The scope of government has been vastly expanded, but always along lines that were to some extent developed by 1940. Even the federal assumption of responsibility for prices, income, employment, and economic growth (in addition to other objectives) in the Employment Act of 1946 was a formalization of activities and ambitions developing in Washington, D.C., before the depression ended. Indeed, the public perception that the federal power *ought* to be used to pursue such policies was something we saw developing in the late nineteenth century, for example, in the Populist demands.

What Was New?

The pursuit, in peacetime, of policies by the federal government to support any given levels of income, employment, or prices was new. The problem faced by policymakers was partly ideological. Gaston Rimlinger observed that American ideals of individualism formed a "formidable ideological obstacle" to such ideas, even to social insurance.[46] It was not new to utilize the federal power to encourage some industries at the expense of others. Rent creation by government power, as we know, goes back in federalist America to the first tariff; in colonial America, to the first settlements. However, the tradition of private-sector employment, income, wages, and prices was that, police powers apart, these matters were left to free contracting by private parties. President Hoover had resisted the idea that direct federal responsibilities might be extended to such matters, and so, at first, did FDR.

The use of federal power to set up social insurance schemes for nongovernment employees was new. As we saw, the idea originated in large part (for example, the Swope Plan) in the private sector.[47] The 1935 Social Security Act, however, made a new beginning. For employees, participation was mandatory. That removed all the taint of charity from it. Social Security numbers replaced proper names as a means of identification. The system was minimal at first: contributory old-age and retirement benefits for certain classes of employees, inducements for states to liberalize and standardize workers' compensation, and the provision of employer-paid state unemployment compensation funds.

Later expansions of Social Security benefits were not foreseen. The now huge benefit payments for medical assistance, under Medicare and Medicaid, were not envisaged in the original plan. Social Security now is a program of add-ons and adjustments that has never existed as a well-thought-out whole. The result has been a "funding crisis." Given what is currently promised in benefits, and what is (and has been) paid in taxes, the system one day will lack the resources to disburse benefits at the present levels.

As Berkowitz and Wolff have shown, the entire program never recovered from its flimsy institutional origins.[48] Senator Wagner sponsored a national health insurance plan in 1938 that got nowhere in Congress. Harry Truman tried it in his Fair Deal, and that also failed. Every attempt since then has continued to fail because Congress is a creature of special interests, and there are big special interests opposed to national health insurance. That Social Security got through Congress at all was probably due to its minimal coverage. The taxes to pay for it are among our most regressive, and, as we have seen, FDR admitted that the taxes were pure "politics all the way through." The year 1935 was a big one for New Deal legislation. Roosevelt was probably at the height of his power over Congress. Three or four years later a Social Security bill might not have passed at all.[49]

Federal sponsorship of organized labor in the Wagner Act was only partly new, since there already had been federal sponsorship in the Railway Labor Act of 1926. The Norris-LaGuardia Anti-Injunction Act of 1932 was a further federal move in support of organized labor. The Wagner Act was in fact the culmination of labor ambitions for federal support that had seen already two false dawns, one in the World War I command economy and another in the NIRA. A primitive national labor policy was also beginning to evolve out of the Civilian Conservation Corps, the National Youth Administration, and the WPA. War and conscription took care of all that, and nothing reappeared.

Outright and overt federal sponsorship of industrial cartelization in peacetime under the NRA was new, but it failed. The idea was old. In World War I, the government assisted anticompetitive industrial processes in the interests of maximum defense production. When the war ended, President Wilson ordered the connected governmental structures abolished. After the NRA failed to pass the Supreme Court, apart from a revitalization of the Antitrust Division, there really was no continued federal policy of an innovative nature toward manufacturing industry. There were the beginnings of a policy on natural resources and on manpower, but nothing came of them. There was the National Planning Association, which encouraged parallel regional and state planning organizations.[50] Impressive studies were published, and it appeared that a start toward real economic planning might be made, but all that vanished in World War II, and nothing quite like the planning association was ever seen again. Such planning had been based on the assumption that the depression economy was a portent of things to come and that there was an impending need for a greatly expanded federal role if prosperity were ever to be seen again in the land. World War II wiped away all these fears.

What Was Old?

Police-power regulation by the federal government was greatly expanded during the New Deal, as part of the general growth of government activism. But, in principle, it was not new at the federal level, not since 1887. The number of regulatory agencies was so multiplied that it might have seemed to be a "revolutionary" development when it was not. Regularly scheduled air service was something new; to regulate it was not. Two new federal agencies, the Federal Aeronautics Administration and the Civil Aeronautics Board, were applications of time-tested industry-agency regulation. The Interstate Commerce Commission was the beginning of all that.

The creation of government corporations and agencies of all sorts to expand federal financial participation in housing, transportation, and agriculture was a technique already perfected in the World War I command economy. The proliferation of such devices of federal influence and control was fairly stupefying to some observers during the New Deal, and a great many of these agencies, offices, boards, and administrations continue to this day. But they were not new institutional innovations of the New Deal.

Hugh Rockoff examined the publications of economists in the 1920s and earlier and found there were champions for almost all of the New Deal programs. With the arrival of the Roosevelt administration, when the economic doctors were called, microeconomists had what they considered successful prescriptions, things that had been used successfully elsewhere.[51]

Was It a Social Revolution?

If by the word *revolution* one means a radical realignment of social classes or a basic change in the ownership of the means of production, the New Deal was no revolution. Also, one can easily dispute the claim that the New Deal "saved" American capitalism, since it has hardly seemed capable of life independent of government aid and management since the 1930s.

There was no radical change. When the New Deal ended, all constitutions remained. The ownership of property was perhaps subject to more federal regulation than had been true, but that property had not been basically altered. Ben Franklin would have recognized our land tenure in 1940, and so would Governor Bradford of Plymouth. Apart from higher taxes, production by private capital was still designed to yield a profit to be distributed as a reward for private ownership.[52] Industry was still managed by private managers. Food and clothing, shelter, medicine—all were almost entirely private matters in 1940, as had been true in 1929. Economic activity, apart from direct government purchases and police-power regulation, was still almost entirely directed by the "dollar vote" cast by consumers.

Then what was (is) all the excitement about? Why can the New Deal still raise the volume in polite—and not so polite—discussion so easily? Why should FDR and the New Deal be so much more a part of the modern consciousness than Herbert Hoover and the New Era, or even Lyndon Johnson and the Great Society?

The answer really does seem to be commonplace. Some new departures *were* made. In particular, the idea of "community" responsibility for a minimal safety net against personal disaster, always there from colonial times at the local level, was raised to the federal level for the first time and remained there. Not only federal sponsorship of social insurance but also the assumption by the federal government, via fiscal and monetary policy, of the responsibility for prosperity in the aggregate, left the New Deal wearing an aura of bold innovation in history.

Secondly, governmental activism itself got a powerful send-off in the New Deal days with the multiplicity of institutions formed to identify, define, and act upon "social problems." Even though hosts of the New Deal boards, managements, offices, and administrations vanished, others survived, and the idea of a self-starting bureaucracy caught on. Before the 1930s, initiatives for basic social and economic change rarely came from within the permanent federal bureaucracy. During and since the New Deal, such initiatives have become commonplace. The federal bureaucracy was traditionally a body of civil servants whose activities were defined and directed by the elected government. Shifting the power *to set agendas* for national policy from Congress and the executive and private sectors to the permanent government was mainly an achievement of the New Deal. John Wallis and Wallace Oates point out that this rise in the share of federal spending was mainly at the expense of *local* government spending, but local spending as a share of GNP did not fall during the Great Depression. Indeed, it was about the same percentage in 1992 as it had been in 1927.[53] State governments sustained their expenditures because so great a part of the New Deal expenditures consisted of grants, or grants-in-aid to the state governments. In large part, the state governments distributed and administered federal expenditures.[54]

As much as these new departures, the sheer volume of expanded government participation and intervention in the economy coming out of the New Deal created a feeling of "revolution," fundamental change, in the quality of everyday life. The federal government entered most people's lives by 1940, and that was different. It was not new to have the federal government subsidize building construction. It *was* new to have federal finance become a permanent feature of the country's housing industry, supported by a huge network of federal mortgage institutions. Quantity, in the end, appeared to transform quality, and to some extent, that was true. The police-power controls, regulations and regulatory agencies proliferated in the New Deal, and that proliferation continued for decades, despite promises by succeeding presidential candidates to "get the government off people's backs."

As for income and wealth distribution—the alteration of the traditional "class" relations—there has been some narrowing of the range of inequality in the past 50 years (as we will see in Chapter 30), but it remains unclear what the New Deal's real contribution was to this long-run development.

Finally, the number of really new departures in social and economic policy since the New Deal has been so small that the New Deal looks terribly bold in retrospect. Millions of workers receive relatively few benefits from the social insurance programs they pay taxes to support. There was never any national standardization of workers' compensation or unemployment compensation. We have never developed a national system of subsidized higher education based upon *merit*. In spite of years of discussion, the United States does not have universal national health insurance. In other words, its welfare state, expensive as it is, has never been very extensive compared to those of other economically advanced countries.[55] Apart from some huge extensions of particular programs (like the explosion of Aid to Families with Dependent Children expenditures after 1965), the 1930s remains the great era of general innovation.[56] In truth, the permeation of New Deal intervention into the private economy was astonishing.

It is for these reasons that we refer to the New Deal as the one great modern social revolution in the United States. Compared to the civil rights movement of the 1960s and 1970s, the New Deal looms as a moment when elemental forces seemed to have been unleashed. That is partially an illusion. Modern reform movements have concerned themselves with fairly narrow sections of population—those officially defined as minorities or the poor. In these terms, the New Deal was comparatively broad in its reach into American society. That the New Deal *seemed* to embrace the vast majority of Americans was also an achievement. In the panorama of American history, the position (whether positive or negative) of the New Deal and Franklin Delano Roosevelt seems to grow with time.

THE LEGACY OF THE DEPRESSION

After 1933, the American economy was never the same. The apprehensions of that time were burned into the collective memory, and its results were enshrined in the statute books as social insurance and federal responsibility for the poor and unemployed. The nation turned to the federal government for collective solutions to economic and social problems on a scale not known before, except perhaps in the World War I command economy. Faith in unmixed American capitalism was undermined, apparently for good. Even at the top levels of American industry and finance, hope was lost. Herman Krooss, in his book *Executive Opinion*, recorded the shattered capitalist morale and the efforts, replete with overblown oratory, to sustain the faith.[57]

Franklin Delano Roosevelt stayed in the White House for the rest of the 1930s and most of World War II primarily because of the reputation he had gained as the man who "saved the country" from the grip of the depression. As we have seen, the extent of that salvation is ambiguous. What was clear, however, was that the contract of 1789 held; there was no revolution. The economy was changed dramatically, but the political wisdom of the first 150 years held.

The national state constructed by the colonial founders was not destroyed by the economic disaster of the 1930s. This was perhaps the ultimate tribute. And it meant that, however changed by the New Deal, the social contract based upon settled private rights in property and free elections conducted by the calendar would remain the American republic's constitution. It would be tested again and again in succeeding decades, but no test that came in the next half century compared to the one of the 1930s.

This chapter and the previous one present a baffling episode that changed the pre-World War I patterns of economic growth. Even though the New Deal reforms did not end the depression, they were widely approved and were woven into the fabric of American society. The intellectual and institutional baggage of the interwar period was carried into the future. When conditions changed and prosperity returned, the country elected not to return to its former mix of public and private control. The technology of enhanced and expanded politicization of economic decision making, so expanded in the 1930s, was altered and amended in later years and would become a new economic way of life.

NOTES

1. See Jonathan Hughes, *The Governmental Habit Redux* (1991), pp. 159–181, and "Roots of Regulation," in Gary Walton, ed., *Regulatory Change in an Atmosphere of Crisis* (1979); William Leuchtenburg, *Franklin D. Roosevelt and the New Deal 1932–1940* (1963). For an excellent summary, see Robert Higgs, *Crisis and Leviathan* (1987), chap. 8.
2. The best account is still Arthur Schlesinger, Jr., *The Age of Roosevelt* (Boston: Houghton Mifflin 1957, 1959, and 1960), especially vol. II. A good recent account is William J. Barber, *Designs within disorder: Franklin D. Roosevelt, the economists, and the shaping of American economic policy, 1933–1945* (New York: Cambridge University Press, 1996).
3. A run on the dollar, an increase in the foreign demand for gold as the crisis deepened, was a consequence of the anticipation of the devaluation that came when Roosevelt took office. Barrie Wigmore, "Was the Bank Holiday of 1933 Caused by a Run on the Dollar?" *JEH*, September 1981.
4. Ben Bernanke, "Nonmonetary Effects of the Financial Crisis in the Propagation of the Great Depression," *AER*, June 1983.
5. An amusing account of the events of 1933 is in John Kenneth Galbraith's *Money, Whence It Came, Where It Went* (1975), chap. XIV.
6. Barry Eichengreen, *Golden Fetters: The Gold Standard and the Great Depression, 1919–1939* (New York: Oxford University Press, 1992).
7. Galbraith (1975), pp. 210–212.
8. Edward Berkowitz and Kim McQuaid, *Creating the Welfare State* (1988), pp. 92–95.
9. John Wallis, "Why 1933?: The Origins and Timing of National Government Growth 1933 to 1940." *REH*, Supplement 4, 1985.
10. Michael Weinstein, "Some Macroeconomic Impacts of the National Industrial Recovery Act, 1933–1935," in Brunner, *The Great Depression Revisited* (1981). Pamela Pennock, "The National Recovery Association and the Rubber Tire Industry, 1933–1935," *Business History Review*, vol. 71, no. 4, Winter 1997, is an intriguing case study. Pennock argues the tire code led to increased fragmentation and lower prices rather than the expected cartelization and higher prices.
11. There are many parallels between the command economy of World War I and the first New Deal. In addition to those folded into the NRA, the planning activities of the Food Administration reappeared in the two Agricultural Administration Acts. The U.S. Grain Corporation became the Commodity Credit Corporation. The Emergency Fleet Corporation returned as the National Maritime Administration. And the U.S. Housing Corporation became the Federal Housing Administration. Indeed, much of FDR's rhetoric in soliciting support for these institutions was the rhetoric of war.
12. *Schechter Poultry Corp v. U.S.*, 295 U.S. 495 (1935).
13. William Anderson, "Risk and the National Industrial Recovery Act: An Empirical Evaluation," *Public Choice*, vol. 103, no. 2, April 2000. As such, he agrees with Ellis Hawley, *The New Deal and The Problem of Monopoly* (Princeton: Princeton University Press, 1966), who concluded that the codes "reflected the interests of the larger and more highly organized businessmen."
14. George Green, "The Ideological Origins of the Revolution in American Financial Policies," in Brunner (1981), p. 224.
15. *Butler v. U.S.*, 297, U.S. 1 (1936). Barbara Alexander and Gary Libecap argue that the reason why the AAA made a quick comeback lies in the fact that efficient farmers represented by the American Farm Bureau Federation lobbied for the AAA. On the other hand, there was not a similar lobbying effort by industry. See "The Effect of Cost Heterogeneity in the Success and Failure of the New Deal's Agricultural and Industrial Programs," *Explorations in Economic History*, vol. 37, no. 4, October 2000.
16. The federal land banks had been established in 1916 in response to farmers' demands; in the 1920s and 1930s there were fewer foreclosures where those banks were the lending agencies. Lee Alston, "Farm Foreclosure Moratorium Legislation: The Lesson of the Past," *AER*, June 1984.
17. Roger Ransom, *Coping with Capitalism* (1981), pp. 106–108.
18. Frederick Merk, *History of the Westward Movement* (1978), pp. 559–560.
19. The agency was headed by Rexford Tugwell, a member of the original Roosevelt "Brain Trust." Tugwell expresses his views of the New Deal origins in his *The Brains Trust* (1968). The New Deal safety-net for agriculture was resisted in the South whenever it threatened to raise wages or improve conditions for the poorest. Lee Alston and Joseph Ferrie, *Southern Paternalism and the American Welfare State* (1999), chap. 4; and their "Labor Costs, Paternalism, and Loyalty in Southern Agriculture: A Constraint on the Growth of the Welfare State," *JEH*, March 1985.
20. Randal Rucker and Lee Alston estimate that all of the New Deal measures combined saved from 146,000 to just less than 277,000 farms out of the approximately 6.8 *mil-*

lion that existed in the 1930s. They wonder if the effort was worth the price for anyone other than those farm families whose farms were not foreclosed because of the policies, "Farm Failures and Government Intervention: A Case Study of the 1930s," *AER*, September 1987.
21. Merk (1978), chaps. 53–56.
22. *Wickard v. Filburn*, 317 U.S. 111 (1942).
23. Fraud and what would now be called "insider trading" were the motivation for this separation of commercial banking and investment banking. Modern research fails to reveal any evidence that the 1929 crash or the ensuing depression had been aggravated by the relationship the Glass-Steagall Act excised from the nation's institutional structure. Eugene White, "Before the Glass-Steagall Act: An Analysis of the Investment Banking Activities of the National Banks," *EEH*, January 1986. Recent scholarship continues to conclude that Glass-Steagall was unnecessary. See Randall Kroszner and R. G. Rajan, "Is the Glass-Steagall Act Justified?" *AER*, September 1994; and Charles Calomiris, "The Costs of Rejecting Universal Banking," in Naomi Lamoreaux and Daniel Raff, *Coordination and Information* (1995).
24. An interesting perspective on this "solution" can be found in Charles Calomiris, "Is Deposit Insurance Necessary? A Historical Perspective," *JEH*, June 1990. See also Calomiris and Eugene White, "The Origins of Federal Deposit Insurance," in Claudia Goldin and Gary Libecap, eds., *The Regulated Economy* (1994).
25. Jonathan Hughes, *The Vital Few* (1986), pp. 533–539.
26. Estimates of grants for general functions such as education, highways, and relief can be found in John Wallis, "The Birth of the Old Federalism: Financing the New Deal," *JEH*, March 1984, and Wallis (1985).
27. Robert H. Zieger, *The CIO: 1930–1955* (Chapel Hill: University of North Carolina Press, 1955) provides the story of this union prior to the merger with the AFL.
28. Lizabeth Cohen, *Making a New Deal* (1990), is a fascinating account of the multiple ways in which the lives of Chicago's industrial workers changed during the interwar years. In particular, it contrasts their abstinence from national politics and unionism in the 1920s with their involvement in the Democratic party and the emergence of the CIO in the 1930s.
29. Joan Hannon, "Poor Relief Policy in Antebellum New York State: The Rise and Decline of the Poorhouse," *EEH*, July 1985.
30. Stanley Lebergott, *The American Economy: Income, Wealth, and Want* (Princeton: Princeton University Press, 1976), p. 57.
31. Domenico Gagliardo, *American Social Insurance* (New York: Harper, 1949).
32. Quoted in Hughes (1979), p. 52.
33. *Hammer v. Dagenhart*, 247 U.S. 251 (1918).
34. *Adkins v. Children's Hospital*, 261 U.S. 252 (1923).
35. For example, *West Coast Hotel v. Parrish*, 300 U.S. 379 (1937).
36. *Nebbia v. New York*, 291 U.S. 502 (1934).
37. *NLRB v. Jones and Laughlin*, 301 U.S. 1 (1937), pp. 41–42.
38. Andrew Seltzer, "Causes and Consequences of American Minimum Wage Legislation, 1911–1947," *JEH*, June 1995, and his 1994 University of Illinois at Urbana-Champaign doctoral dissertation with the same title, examines the state laws passed prior to 1938 as well as the FLSA.
39. *U.S. v. Darby*, 312 U.S. 100 (1941).
40. Hughes (1986), pp. 334–351.
41. Charles Cox, "Monopoly Explanations of the Great Depression and Public Policies Toward Business," in Brunner (1981), p. 189.
42. An interesting article that combines the NIRA and AAA is Elizabeth Hoffman and Gary Libecap, "Political Bargaining and Cartelization in the New Deal: Orange Marketing Orders," in Claudia Goldin and Gary Libecap, eds., *The Regulated Economy* (1994).
43. E. Cary Brown, "Fiscal Policy in the Thirties: A Reappraisal," *American Economic Review*, vol. XLVI, no. 5, December 1956.
44. Larry Peppers, "Full Employment Surplus Analysis and Structural Changes: The 1930s," *EEH*, Winter 1973.
45. Don Reading, "New Deal Activity and the States, 1933 to 1939," *JEH*, December 1973; and Leonard Arrington, "The New Deal in the West: A Preliminary Statistical Inquiry," *Pacific Historical Review*, August 1969. For a fine-tuning of the issues and analysis, Gavin Wright, "The Political Economy of New Deal Spending: An Econometric Analysis," *REStat*, February 1974.
46. Gaston Rimlinger, "The Historical Analysis of National Welfare Systems," in Roger Ransom et al., *Explorations in the New Economic History: Essays in Honor of Douglass C. North* (New York: Academic Press, 1982), p. 163.
47. Berkowitz and McQuaid (1988).
48. Edward Berkowitz and Wendy Wolff, "Disability Insurance and the Limits of American History," *The Public Historian*, Spring 1986.
49. Certainly this view is supported by Carolyn Weaver's conclusions that normal progress toward private-sector provision of old-age and survivors' insurance was disrupted by the shock of the 1929–1933 recession, and that the New Deal then stepped in, for various reasons, to fill the void. Carolyn Weaver, "On the Lack of a Political Market for Compulsory Old-Age Insurance Prior to the Great Depression: Insights from Economic Theories of Government," *EEH*, July 1983.
50. Otis Graham, Jr., *Toward a Planned Society: From Roosevelt to Nixon* (1976).

51. Hugh Rockoff, "By Way of Analogy: The Expansion of the Federal Government in the 1930s," in Michael Bordo, Claudia Goldin, and Eugene White, eds., *The Defining Moment* (1998).
52. The research of Thomas Renaghan leads one to accept even the much-touted "soak the rich" interpretation of New Deal taxation with a large dose of salt, "Distributional Effects of Federal Tax Policy, 1929–1939," *EEH*, January 1984.
53. John Wallis and Wallace Oates, "The Impact of the New Deal on American Federalism," in Bordo, Goldin, and White, eds., *The Defining Moment* (1998).
54. Wallis (1984); see also Hughes (1979). In "The Political Economy of New Deal Spending Revisited, Again: With and Without Nevada," *Explorations in Economic History*, vol. 35, no. 2, April 1998, Wallis argues that both political and economic effects were important to the determination of how these grants were allocated between the states.
55. Peter Lindert, "What Limits Social Spending?" *EEH*, January 1996, is a comparative view of such expenditures in nineteen countries for the period 1960–1992.
56. AFDC became TANF (Temporary Assistance to Needy Families) as a result of the Welfare Reform Act of 1996.
57. Herman Krooss, *Executive Opinion: What Business Leaders Said and Thought on Economic Issues 1920s–1960s* (New York: Doubleday, 1970), chaps. 5 and 6.

SUGGESTED READINGS

Articles

Alston, Lee J. "Farm Foreclosure Moratorium Legislation: The Lesson of the Past." *American Economic Review*, vol. 74, no. 3, June 1984.

———, and Joseph P. Ferrie. "Labor Costs, Paternalism, and Loyalty in Southern Agriculture: A Constraint on the Growth of the Welfare State." *Journal of Economic History*, vol. XLV, no. 1, March 1985.

Arrington, Leonard J. "The New Deal in the West: A Preliminary Statistical Inquiry." *Pacific Historical Review*, vol. 38, no. 3, August 1969.

Berkowitz, Edward, and Wendy Wolff. "Disability Insurance and the Limits of American History." *The Public Historian*, vol. 8, no. 2, Spring 1986.

Bernanke, Ben S. "Nonmonetary Effects of the Financial Crisis in the Propagation of the Great Depression." *American Economic Review*, vol. 73, no. 3, June 1983.

Calomiris, Charles W. "Is Deposit Insurance Necessary? A Historical Perspective." *Journal of Economic History*, vol. L, no. 2, June 1990.

———. "The Costs of Rejecting Universal Banking: American Finance in the German Mirror, 1870–1914." In Naomi Lamoreaux and Daniel Raff, eds., *Coordination and Information*. Chicago: University of Chicago Press, 1995.

———, and Eugene Nelson White. "The Origins of Federal Deposit Insurance." In Claudia Goldin and Gary D. Libecap, eds., *The Regulated Economy*. Chicago: University of Chicago Press, 1994.

Cox, Charles C. "Monopoly Explanations of the Great Depression and Public Policies Toward Business." In Karl Brunner, ed., *The Great Depression Revisited*. Boston: Martinus Nijhoff, 1981.

Green, George D. "The Ideological Origins of the Revolution in American Financial Policies." In Karl Brunner, ed., *The Great Depression Revisited*. Boston: Martinus Nijhoff, 1981.

Hannon, Joan Underhill. "Poor Relief Policy in Antebellum New York State: The Rise and Decline of the Poorhouse." *Explorations in Economic History*, vol. 22, no. 3, July 1985.

Hoffman, Elizabeth, and Gary D. Libecap. "Political Bargaining and Cartelization in the New Deal: Orange Marketing Orders." In Claudia Goldin and Gary D. Libecap, eds., *The Regulated Economy*. Chicago: University of Chicago Press, 1994.

Hughes, Jonathan. "The Roots of Regulation." In Gary M. Walton, ed., *Regulatory Change in an Atmosphere of Crisis: Current Implications of the Roosevelt Years*. New York: Academic Press, 1979.

Kroszner, Randall, and R. G. Rajan. "Is the Glass-Steagall Act Justified?" *American Economic Review*, vol. 84, no. 4, September 1994.

Lebergott, Stanley. "The American Labor Force." In Lance Davis et al., *American Economic Growth*. New York: Harper & Row, 1972.

Lindert, Peter. "What Limits Social Spending?" *Explorations in Economic History*, vol. 33, no. 1, January 1996.

Peppers, Larry C. "Full Employment Surplus Analysis and Structural Changes: The 1930s." *Explorations in Economic History*, vol. 10, no. 2, Winter 1973.

Reading, Don C. "New Deal Activity and the States, 1933 to 1939." *Journal of Economic History*, vol. XXXIII, no. 4, December 1973.

Renaghan, Thomas M. "Distributional Effects of Federal Tax Policy, 1929–1939." *Explorations in Economic History*, vol. 21, no. 1, January 1984.

Rockoff, Hugh. "By Way of Analogy: The Expansion of the Federal Government in the 1930s." In Michael Bordo, Claudia Goldin, and Eugene White, eds., *The Defining

Moment: The Great Depression and the Twentieth Century.. Chicago: University of Chicago Press, 1998.

Rucker, Randal, and Lee J. Alston. "Farm Failures and Government Intervention: A Case Study of the 1930s." *American Economic Review*, vol. 77, no. 4, September 1987.

Seltzer, Andrew. "Causes and Consequences of American Minimum Wage Legislation, 1911–1947." *Journal of Economic History*, vol. 55, no. 2, June 1995.

Wallis, John J. "The Birth of the Old Federalism: Financing the New Deal, 1932–1940." *Journal of Economic History*, vol. LXIV, no. 1, March 1984.

———. "Why 1933?: The Origins and Timing of National Government Growth 1933 to 1940." *Research in Economic History*, Supplement 4. Greenwich, CT: JAI Press, 1985.

———. "The Political Economy of the New Deal Fiscal Federalism." *Economic Inquiry*, vol. 29, no. 3, July 1991.

———, and Daniel K. Benjamin. "Public Relief and Private Employment in the Great Depression." *Journal of Economic History*, vol. XLI, no. 1, March 1981.

———, and Wallace E. Oates. "The Impact of the New Deal on American Federalism." In Michael Bordo, Claudia Goldin, and Eugene White, eds. *The Defining Moment: The Great Depression and the Twentieth Century.* Chicago: University of Chicago Press, 1998.

Weaver, Carolyn L. "On the Lack of a Political Market for Compulsory Old-Age Insurance Prior to the Great Depression: Insights from Economic Theories of Government." *Explorations in Economic History*, vol. 20, no. 3, July 1983.

Weinstein, Michael M. "Some Macroeconomic Impacts of the National Industrial Recovery Act, 1933–35." In Karl Brunner, ed., *The Great Depression Revisited.* Boston: Martinus Nijhoff, 1981.

White, Eugene Nelson. "Before the Glass-Steagall Act: An Analysis of the Investment Banking Activities of the National Banks." *Explorations in Economic History*, vol. 23, no. 1, January 1986.

Wigmore, Barrie A. "Was the Bank Holiday of 1933 Caused by a Run on the Dollar?" *Journal of Economic History*, vol. XLVII, no. 3, September 1981.

Wright, Gavin. "The Political Economy of New Deal Spending: An Econometric Analysis." *Review of Economics and Statistics*, vol. LVI, no. 1, February 1974.

Books

Achenbaum, W. Andrew. *Social Security: Visions and Revisions.* New York: Holmes & Meier, 1986.

Alston, Lee J., and Joseph P. Ferrie. *Southern Paternalism and the American Welfare State.* Cambridge: Cambridge University Press, 1999.

Berkowitz, Edward, and Kim McQuaid. *Creating the Welfare State: The Political Economy of Twentieth Century Reform*, 2nd ed. New York: Praeger, 1988.

Bordo, Michael D., Claudia Goldin, and Eugene N. White. *The Defining Moment: The Great Depression and the American Economy in the Twentieth Century.* Chicago: University of Chicago Press, 1998.

Brunner, Karl, ed., *The Great Depression Revisited.* Boston: Martinus Nijhoff, 1981.

Chandler, Lester V. *American's Greatest Depression.* New York: Harper & Row, 1970.

Cohen, Lizabeth. *Making a New Deal: Industrial Workers in Chicago 1919–1939.* New York: Cambridge University Press, 1990.

Galbraith, John Kenneth. *Money, Whence It Came, Where It Went.* Boston: Houghton Mifflin, 1975.

Goldin, Claudia, and Gary D. Libecap, eds., *The Regulated Economy: A Historical Approach to Political Economy.* Chicago: University of Chicago Press, 1994.

Graham, Otis L., Jr. *Toward a Planned Society: From Roosevelt to Nixon.* New York: Oxford University Press, 1976.

Higgs, Robert. *Crisis and Leviathan: Critical Episodes in the Growth of American Government.* New York: Oxford University Press, 1987.

Hughes, Jonathan. *The Vital Few: The Entrepreneur and American Economic Progress.* New York: Oxford University Press, 1986 (expanded edition).

———. *The Governmental Habit Redux: Economic Controls from Colonial Times to the Present.* Princeton: Princeton University Press, 1991.

Leuchtenburg, William E. *Franklin D. Roosevelt and the New Deal 1932–1940.* New York: Harper Torchbooks, 1963.

Merk, Frederick. *History of the Westward Movement.* New York: Alfred Knopf, 1978.

Moley, Raymond. *After Seven Years.* New York: Harper, 1939.

Ransom, Roger L. *Coping with Capitalism.* Englewood Cliffs, NJ: Prentice-Hall, 1981.

Shannon, David A. *The Great Depression.* Englewood Cliffs, NJ: Prentice-Hall, 1960.

Sherwood, Robert E. *Roosevelt and Hopkins*, 2 vols. New York: Harper, 1948.

Tugwell, Rexford G. *The Brains Trust.* New York: Viking, 1968.

Walton, Gary M., ed. *Regulatory Change in an Atmosphere of Crisis: Current Implications of the Roosevelt Years.* New York: Academic Press, 1979.

CHAPTER TWENTY-SIX

The "Prosperity" of Wartime

As early as 1940, World War II produced demand for the products of American industry. Before the end of that disastrous summer, after the French sought a truce with the Nazis, it was clear that the United States would be drawn into the conflict, at least as a noncombatant supplier of war goods to the beleaguered British. Conscription was revived in the United States, and orders for war materials increasingly quickened the pace of industry. Unemployment began to drop as workers moved into industrial work stimulated by war output. Indeed, the rate was back down to around 6 percent at the end of November 1941. Studies by economists within the government showed that war production would push the economy back to full employment levels—finally.[1]

In January 1941, FDR asked Congress for the means to arm Americans and the British. In March, the Lend-Lease Act passed in Congress, authorizing the Administration to provide supplies to "any country whose defense the President deems vital to the defense of the United States." The financing would come from debt creation. U.S. exports, already up to $325 million in January 1941, were $460 million by August of that year, compared with $250 million in August 1939. By August 1945, the United States was supplying some $50 billion in war materials to its allies under the Lend-Lease Act ($42 billion net, deducting materials they supplied). Lend-Lease deliveries were greater than the *sum* of all federal expenditures from 1933 to 1939.

But Lend-Lease would be almost a sideline compared to the main American wartime expenditures. In December 1941, with Nazi armies deep into the territory of the USSR, the Japanese attacked American forces in the Pacific, and the Germans declared war on the United States. In the process of another full wartime mobilization, the American unemployment problem vanished at last. Other things being equal, it was as Keynes had suggested; sufficient expenditures by government would stimulate the economy.

Robert Higgs has argued that this view, which he terms the "consensus view," is misleading.[2] After all, the United States was a command economy during the war. Higgs suggests that Simon Kuznets's "peacetime concept" of GDP is a more appropriate measure of the welfare of the average citizen; macroeconomic aggregates that include the war effort are misleading at best. By Kuznets's measure, the economy during World War II did not produce increased consumption or investment; it was rigged to produce increased government expenditures.

> It is difficult to understand how working harder, longer, more inconveniently and dangerously in return for a diminished flow of consumer goods comports with the description that

"economically speaking, Americans had never had it so good."[3]

To Higgs, genuine recovery from the Great Depression did not come with the war, but rather with the end of the war. It was caused not by the government expenditures, but by an increase in financial wealth during the war and the expectation that better times were ahead.

Regardless of which view one adopts, it is clear that the number of Americans earning paychecks increased during the war, albeit not necessarily in jobs they wanted to hold. They were seldom able to spend those paychecks as they would have liked. When the war ended and these constraints were lifted, and a revitalized economy began postwar economic life, it was at levels and growth rates that made the fabled 1920s look small. The depression never returned, but the memory of it lingered.

THE SCOPE OF WAR MOBILIZATION

Once again war required release of output from peacetime uses as well as expanded output. The control apparatus reappeared, but at least with respect to the initial mobilization, Hugh Rockoff notes that the market coordinated what was commanded.[4]

Apparatus

For a command economy to exist, someone must do the commanding. Experience in World War I as well as during the New Deal had driven that lesson home. When war came, the government could temporarily forget the problems of strict constitutionality that had hamstrung its actions in the NRA and AAA episodes.

The president's "war powers" were extraordinary. Following Woodrow Wilson's precedent in 1916, FDR anticipated the war by bringing planners together to chart out the country's possible mobilization patterns. As a result of agitation and enquiry during the New Deal to reorganize the federal government in the interests of economic planning, in September 1939, by Executive Order 8248, the modern Executive Office of the President was established.[5] The president could now expand the executive branch outside the old-line departments and achieve the kind of decisive action war would require, if and when we went to war. In May 1940, FDR appointed members to the National Defense Advisory Commission (NDAC). It was an umbrella organization under which a large part of the wartime administrative apparatus would be constructed. In June 1940, for example, the National Defense Research Council (NDRC) was set up under the NDAC umbrella to mobilize the country's scientific personnel for war. The war effort resembled the New Deal in this regard, and all of it was indebted to Woodrow Wilson's 1917–1918 government for inspiration.[6]

Also under the NDAC umbrella, an institutional framework for the civilian economy was constructed. In 1942, once war had been declared, the War Production Board (WPB) commanded operations

TABLE 26.1 War Expenditures and Manpower Mobilization, 1940–1947

Year	*GDP ($ billions)*	*Total Military Expenditures ($ billions)*	*Numbers in Armed Forces (thousands)*	*Nonagricultural Labor Force (millions)*
1940	$ 101.3	$ 1.8	458	32.4
1941	126.7	6.3	1,801	36.6
1942	161.8	22.9	3,859	40.1
1943	198.4	63.4	9,045	42.5
1944	219.7	76.0	11,452	41.9
1945	223.0	80.5	12,123	40.4
1946	222.3	43.2	3,030	41.7
1947	244.4	14.8	1,583	43.9

Source: *Historical Statistics*, series D 86, 127, F 1, 3, P 13, Y 458, 459, 904; U.S. Bureau of Economic Analysis, *National Income* designed to determine priorities and allocation procedures. That same year, the Office of Price Administration (OPA) was created under control powers set out in the Stabilization Act of 1942.[7] So powerful had the presidency become that, in February 1942, FDR could by mere executive order cause some 115,000 persons with Japanese ancestry living on the West Coast to be forcibly interned in concentration camps, and subsequently to be backed up in this action by Congress and the Supreme Court of the United States.[8] (It was 1988 before the United States apologized to the people who had been interned and Congress agreed to compensate the survivors.)

In 1943, the war effort was intensified by a new bureau, the Office of War Mobilization (OWM), which was set up to coordinate and expedite the efforts of the other agencies.

The complex war effort involved rationing, physical controls, and direct government construction of vast plants and facilities. Leading figures from the New Deal (who had themselves been trained by World War I officials retreaded in the first New Deal) were already available for administrative service in the war effort.[9] In 1943, in any case, Congress canceled out a large part of the New Deal employment-creating bureaucracy; those boards, offices, commissions, and administrations, no longer needed, passed into history. As in World War I and the New Deal, executive talent was recruited from the private sector, and once again these "dollar-a-year" executives (their token government salaries) streamed back to Washington from corporate headquarters, board rooms, and universities across the land. The job at hand was vast, and it was not going to be done by nine-to-five government clerks.

Percentage Unemployed	*Index of Manufacturing Output (1967 = 100)*
14.6	25
9.9	32
4.7	38
1.9	47
1.2	51
1.9	43
3.9	35
3.9	39

and Product Accounts, Table 1.1.

Labor and Materials

As in our other wars, the need was for an *immediate* requisition of labor and materials. In many respects the scale of the World War II mobilization was astonishing to all, friend and foe alike. As can be seen in Table 26.1, the armed forces would hold 12,123,000 men and women by 1945. To train, equip, sustain, and transport them between 1941 and 1945, nearly $250 billion were spent directly, more than $80 billion in the single year 1945. That was a greater sum for military expenditures alone in a single year than the entire GDP had been in any year between 1931 and 1935.

In response to such stimuli between 1940 and the peak war effort, the civilian nonagricultural labor force expanded by 30 percent (see Table 26.1), offsetting, in part, the huge growth of the armed forces. A "worker shortage" existed. The ranks of the unemployed thinned out and then fell to almost meaningless levels, a mere 1.2 percent in 1944. The unemployment levels of the 1930s never returned. In those years, the earnings of teenagers, too young to be drafted, from part-time and summer jobs were commonly more than the annual earnings of their (employed) parents had been just scant years before. Women, teenagers, the disabled, the aged—all were needed to replace the millions gone to foreign fields if output was to be expanded.[10]

Such unknown economic potential astonished even the most knowledgeable and embittered, those who had suffered through the miseries of the 1930s, when it had been argued that greater expenditure efforts to relieve unemployment would endanger the public and cause government bankruptcy. In real terms, full employment GDP in 1944 was three-quarters again that of 1940, the best New Deal year. In current prices, GDP had more than doubled in a scant four years under the stimulus of war spending.

Demobilization

War spending, such a huge shot in the nation's economic arm, seemed to revitalize the economy at last. When demobilization came, the new energy remained. As the veterans returned and reentered the labor force in 1946 and 1947 (and the armed forces and military expenditures shrank accordingly), labor-force expansion picked up again (Table 26.1). Real GDP dipped between 1945 and 1946, but as price controls were lifted, prices rose, and GDP in current prices, down slightly in 1946, rose again. Unemployment resumed the pre-1930s peacetime levels of less than 4 percent. Industrial production in 1943–1944 had been about double the 1940 level. Its decline thereafter reflected reconversion shifts into such areas as housing and services. Housing would finally (in 1949) regain the 1926 level after the long hiatus. In fact, industrial production would not again see the truly extraordinary 1943 levels until 1953, the last Korean War year, when a new wave of peacetime growth began. Demobilization, because of wartime monetization of the economy and pent-up demand for consumer goods, posed few of the problems economists had feared. The worst pessimists supposed the 1930s would return since, by the end of that sorry decade, expert opinion held that, with "secular stagnation" at hand, the country would never experience growth again.

FINANCING THE WAR

With World War I and the New Deal deficits in the immediate background, World War II caused no peculiar financial problems for government authorities except for the matter of sheer volume. As always, for war purposes, the government needed command over resources far in excess of any conceivable taxing power. This demand necessitated enormous federal deficits. Taxation apart, the impact of war finance on prices was reduced to the extent that funds could be borrowed from the public at large. But, necessarily, bonds had to be sold to the Federal Reserve, and that process produced money-supply increases with inflationary potential.

First let us consider the financial picture in very broad strokes (see Table 26.2).[11] Expenditures rose to whatever levels were deemed necessary. It was up to Congress and the monetary authorities to find the means. The problem was to raise expenditures by more than a factor of 8, from $8.5 billion to $70.6 billion, in only five years. Total federal expenditures in 1945 were roughly equal to 80 percent of GDP in the fabled year 1929. Taxes had to be raised to help pay for this increase and were, particularly the rates on income taxes. In addition, withholding was implemented in order for tax revenues to reach the government sooner. But the maximum revenues of 1945 were only about half of expenditures. As the deficits mounted, so did the debt, rising to a (then) staggering $271 billion.[12]

TABLE 26.2 War Finance[a]

	U.S. Government					*Money Supply*		
Year	*Receipts*	*Expenditures*	*Surplus (+) Deficit (–)*	*Gross Federal Debt*	*Individual Income-Tax Receipts*	M_1	M_2	*Commercial Bank Holdings of Federal Debt*
1940	$ 8.2	$ 8.5	$ –0.3	$ 50.7	$ 1.0	$ 39.7	$ 55.2	$ 21.9
1941	14.9	12.7	2.2	57.5	1.6	46.5	62.5	25.9
1942	22.3	31.0	–8.7	79.2	4.2	55.4	71.2	36.5
1943	35.5	52.6	–14.1	142.6	16.1	72.2	89.9	69.3
1944	40.1	67.0	–27.0	204.1	17.0	85.3	106.8	94.6
1945	41.5	70.6	–29.1	260.1	18.7	99.2	126.6	118.0
1946	39.5	44.6	–5.1	271.0	16.4	106.5	138.7	119.3
1947	42.8	37.6	5.2	257.1	18.8	111.8	146.0	105.3

[a]In billions of dollars.

Source: *Historical Statistics,* series Y 339–342, 445, X 414–415, 594; U.S. Bureau of Economic Analysis, *National Income and Product Accounts*, Table 3.2.

Bond Sales and Interest Policy

In World War II, as in World War I, celebrities joined in the patriotic effort, and "bond rallies" were held all over the country (the celebrities functioning as cajoling cheerleaders) to influence patriotic income-earners to loan some of their means to Uncle Sam for the duration. Bonds were sold by financial institutions of all sorts, and a total of 6 million agents were involved in the selling. The effort was unprecedented. As a result, \$157 billion of bonds were sold directly to the public, more than to the financial institutions. In 1946, individual Americans owned 23 percent of the national debt; banks, 40 percent; and nonbank institutions, 37 percent. These proportions were not significantly different from prewar ones, and maintaining the stable distribution of holdings represented a signal achievement.[13]

The Treasury entered the war when interest rates were at all-time lows, and this circumstance allowed the government a degree of control over the war's deadweight costs (interest charges on the borrowing) that it had not enjoyed in World War I. By close cooperation with the Federal Reserve System, the Treasury in 1945 faced only an average of 1.94 percent on its huge debt, compared to 4.2 percent at the end of World War I.

The Federal Reserve authorities announced in April 1942 that they would buy and sell Treasury bills in unlimited quantities at a 0.38 percent discount of maturity values. This step "pegged" the short-term interest on Treasury borrowing at incredibly low rates. Long-term bonds were similarly pegged, at 2.5 percent for the duration, as Figure 26.1 reveals. Indeed, the stability of government rates is the result of coordinated effort by the Treasury and the Federal Reserve to finance the New Deal and World War II. Commercial banks were allowed to buy bonds with "war-loan" accounts that required neither reserve requirements nor deposit insurance. This was interest-bearing money. The banks, like the population at large, bought bonds. The combined portfolios (see Table 26.2) rose from \$21.9 billion in 1940 to \$119 billion by 1946. The banks were stuffed with bonds.[14]

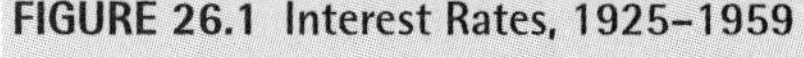
FIGURE 26.1 Interest Rates, 1925–1959

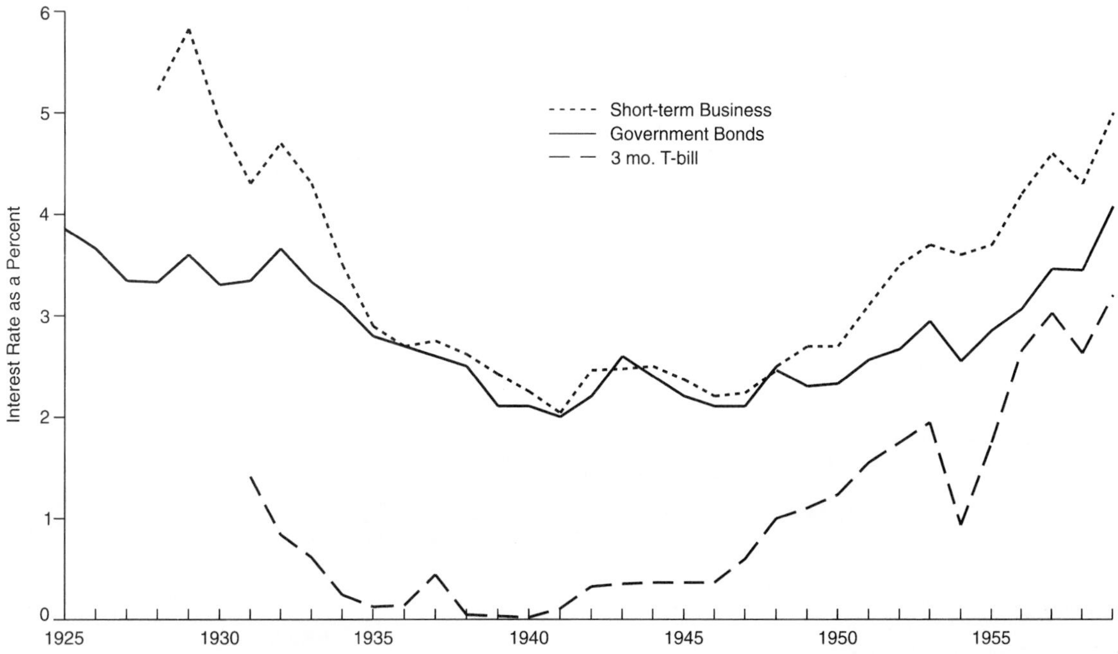

Historical Statistics, series X 450, 466, 474.

Modern War Again. *World War II required a total mobilization of resources. Financial mobilization (above) was not so radical a wartime innovation as was the opening of industrial employment to women workers (above right). On D-Day, Europe began to experience the impact of American industrial power (below left and right).*

Money Supply

The policy of a cheap-money war meant, of course, that the money supply was grossly, and quickly, inflated.[15] Since the country entered the war with vast unemployed resources and capital equipment, the inflationary consequences of the first infusions of money were not greatly feared. After all, the New Deal had wanted nothing more fervently than inflation. Even though production of autos and other consumer durables ceased altogether as plants were shifted to war output, production of nondurables rose. As incomes rose, a nation starved for consumer goods for a decade surged into the markets to buy what *was* available. Retailers' inventories of old goods evaporated. Price controls—together with ticket-rationing of such items as gasoline, meat, and sugar—ensured some facsimile of "fair shares" as the war progressed. To save cloth, cuffs came off men's trousers; woolens became scarce, and nylon stockings for women vanished. Natural crepe soles on men's shoes disappeared. The buying public got used to substitute fabrics and strange combinations of meat and meal. There was plenty, but it was necessarily of different composition.[16]

As Table 26.2 shows, the money supply aggregates were grossly distended. Excess capacity at the beginning allowed output and employment to expand without full inflationary consequences. Nevertheless, the nation was filled with an overhang of potentially inflationary liquidity. But when the war ended, that liquidity, representing both pent-up demand for consumer goods (especially durables, such as new cars and refrigerators) caused by the war and the long depression that preceded it, was met by a burst of physical output. The nation's manufacturing establishment went to work making goods to capture as profits the war-inflated spending power of the public. The results no one predicted. Some economists feared a return of the 1930s; others, runaway inflation. What actually happened looks obvious only in retrospect.

By the war's end, M_1 had grown 150 percent, but wholesale prices were up a mere 35 percent over 1940. By the standard of price inflation alone, the war's management had been a triumph; wholesale prices had doubled in World War I (see Table 23.1).

When price controls were removed in 1946, prices rose powerfully, up 50 percent by 1950 over 1945 levels. The money supply also rose, as part of wartime debt holdings were either cashed in or sold to the Fed. These funds helped finance postwar expansion. But the money supply increase in the period 1945–1950 was only an additional 15 percent. Compared to 1940, by the end of the postwar period, the increased money supply was still far greater than increased prices. Now, the money supply was buying power in the public's hands; prices were the cost of spending it. Not surprisingly, Americans still look back to the war and the first five postwar years fondly: the great prosperity that followed the anguish of the 1930s.[17]

Taxes

The federal government tried to tax away much of the war-inflated income. Taxes divert command over resources to the government. But the United States was still a democracy, and legislators were constrained in their patriotic fervor by the need to be reelected. Thus, taxation was at politically viable levels rather than at the technical maxima to finance the war. It can be seen in Table 26.2 that, in fact, federal revenues grew by nearly a factor of 5 from 1940 to 1945, compared with the eightfold increase of expenditures. It was not a shabby taxing performance, given the electoral constraints.[18]

Excise taxes were raised, and special war taxes were levied upon luxuries (taxes that, typically, remained for decades after the war ended). The key to success was withholding, the pay-as-you-earn individual income tax of 1943. Governments have always had their taxing ambitions restrained by the costs of collection. For example, that marauding soldiers steal grain from peasants is inefficient; the costs are high, and the peasants may well refrain from planting so much the next season. Since most of the nation's income is earned by the nonrich, the problem of seizing part of the incomes of ordinary working people is constrained by the costs of sustaining an army of tax collectors. Already in 1942, the federal government had commandeered the more readily available incomes from visible sources.[19] Employers under the new withholding plan would gather the income taxes from their own employees concurrently with the earning of those incomes. The funds would then be turned over to the Internal Revenue Service. Policing the taxpayers was made easier by this system.

The Social Security taxes of 1937 showed the way. The pay-as-you-earn income tax has been the heart of federal taxation ever since. The tax rates were steeply graduated in the interest of patriotism. Why should individuals at home get rich while "our boys" fought abroad? Naturally, the wartime rates never came back down to peacetime levels.

Individual income taxes, 12 percent of the federal government's tax haul in 1940, grew to 45 percent of revenues by 1945 (see Table 26.2).[20] The pay-as-you-earn income tax gave the federal government an automatic "skim" of the personal income of the entire nation. The New Dealers, living before the Revenue Act of 1943, could never have fantasized such fiscal powers.

In summary, 46.5 percent of the huge war costs were paid for by this taxation. The same figure for World War I had been only 33 percent.[21] Less than perfect, fraught with peril for the future, the tax system of World War II was nevertheless a prodigious achievement. Scaling it down afterward would prove to be a far greater problem than building it up had been in the fervor of wartime patriotism.

THE WAR, LABOR, AND FAMILY INCOME

The war expenditures boosted family incomes decisively, and spending incomes earned from war work provided increased demand for most other goods and services. The Keynesian message had been that, if all other factors remained unchanged, large government expenditures financed by new money creation would lay the foundation for a broad advance. Mean family income, $2,209 in 1941, was up nearly 64 percent in just three years; in current prices it was $3,614 in 1944. Real GDP per capita rose 44 percent in those years. It was an abrupt change from the futility of the 1930s.

Labor Force Participation

As Table 26.1 helps make clear, the depression-era unemployment rates fell dramatically as the war effort gained pace. There quickly developed a labor shortage. With millions under arms, the labor force needed new recruits from those not normally employed. The 1944 labor force was nearly 10 million larger than that of 1940. For the most part, unused sources were tapped for this increase.

Some of the most striking aspects of this development are shown in Table 26.3. The upward draft of expenditures produced extraordinary employment opportunities and pulled into the labor force unusual numbers from the 14–19-years age group. The increase of labor-force participation among teenage females was 80 percent, and for males, 57 percent. Half the nation's males over 65 were gainfully employed, as were a large portion of the females. Retirement at 65 had gone out of fashion, momentarily. There was even a 10 percent increase of females entering the labor force in the prime family-formation years, ages 20 to 24. The total female participation rate rose by 30 percent.

When the war ended, all participation rates declined, as did the labor force itself. The wartime participation rates demonstrated that our conception

TABLE 26.3 Labor Force and Participation

		Percentage Participation Rates						
		Males				*Females*		
Year	*Total Labor Force (in millions)*	*Total*	*16–19 Years*	*20–24 Years*	*65+ Years*	*Total*	*16–19 Years*	*20–24 Years*
1940	56.2	82.5	— 66.4	—	66.9[a]	27.9	— 34.7	—
1944	66.0	88.2	72.2	96.4	49.4	36.3	41.1	55.6
1947	61.8	86.8	67.0	84.9	47.8	31.8	41.1	44.9

[a] The rate for 1940 is for 55+ years.

Source: *Historical Statistics,* series D 1, 30–38.

of "full employment" depends heavily upon assumptions about what are normal participation rates. Obviously, compared to 1944 participation rates, the unemployment levels of the 1930s appear far worse than when more normal participation rates are used. In the 1970s, female participation rates would rise to more than 50 percent under the banner of feminism and the stress of inflation's effect on family living standards. World War II, with its image of "Rosie the Riveter," women doing "men's work," presaged things to come a generation later.

As Claudia Goldin has noted, the war proved to be a boon for older (45–64 years old) married women who, because of the "marriage bar" (see Chapter 28), had been excluded from the labor force for many years. Firms that continued to place restrictions on married women workers put a severe constraint on their ability to acquire labor. This had not been true before the war. Nor did the war benefit other cohorts of women in the same way. Both the oldest and the youngest (ages 14 to 19) groups of women workers showed large increases in employment during the war. The census of 1950, however, documented that, for the youngest cohort, peacetime employment in 1950 was no different from that in 1940, even though wartime employment was 200 percent of that reported in 1940. On the other hand, for the older cohort, the difference was maintained—and even widened. For those in the 20–24-year-old cohort, employment in 1950 was less than it had been in 1940.

"Rosie the Riveter," the woman who entered the labor market just for a war job, reputedly lost that job when the men returned. If she were young, chances are that was true. Goldin reports there is still disagreement whether the young Rosies wanted to continue riveting after the war, but it appears neither their former nor an alternative position was an available option. For the older Rosies, alternative employment became available, and they took it.[22]

Wages

The war's extraordinary demand for the output of manufacturing industry meant demand for factory hands. The nonagricultural labor force rose by nearly one-third between the initial buildup in 1940 and 1944, the peak year of defense employment. Employees in manufacturing, which totaled 10.8 million in 1940, numbered more than 17 million in 1944, an increase of nearly 60 percent. Average weekly earnings in manufacturing rose from $25.20 in 1940 to $46.08 in 1944, a gain of more than 80 percent.[23] Even the nation's farmers (now dwindling in numbers) at last shared in the bonanza. Their prices soared, demand for their output was unprecedented, and the rationing system gave them priority for fuel. The extent of mechanization in the late 1930s helped them raise output even as employment in their industry actually declined. Table 26.4 shows what happened to employee earnings.

In all cases the advance motivated by the war continued in the postwar expansion. Earnings in agriculture, although still low absolutely as well as relatively, actually experienced the greatest wartime increase proportionally. America's perennial surplus of food, as in World War I, now became a core necessity, and the farmers found themselves heroes again. All else depended upon food production. Remember that prices had gone up only by about one-third in the war years; thus, wage earners in nearly all industries experienced considerable gains in real income.

TABLE 26.4 Average Annual Earnings per Full-Time Employee

Year	*All Industries*	*Agriculture Fishing Forestry*	*Mining*	*Contract Construction*	*Manufacturing*	*Services*
1940	$1,299	$ 407	$1,388	$1,330	$1,432	$ 953
1944	2,109	1,021	2,499	2,602	2,517	1,538
1947	2,589	1,276	3,113	2,829	2,793	1,996

Source: *Historical Statistics,* series D 722, 739–741, 745, 755.

Distribution

As was the case in World War I, the income distribution was made more equitable by war expenditures in a mobilized economy. With a great rise in labor force participation and priorities placed upon labor for physical production, the poorest families shared in the good times. The change toward greater equality was not as dramatic as one might suppose, but it was real and a part of the modern trend in this country toward greater equality of income distribution.

As in Table 26.5, the lower 40 percent of families increased their shares slightly, and the shares going to the income earners fell. However, the top 5 percent still received far more income than did the lower 40 percent in 1946. The war had made some better off than others. At least, by 1946, the lower 80 percent together received slightly more than did the top 20 percent. That had not been true before the war.

CONSUMPTION AND INVESTMENT

Personal consumption was constrained by the rationing system that was implemented. The behavior of consumption expenditures during the period contained one small curiosity worthy of note: the rise in the *proportion* spent on food. In addition, the war's impact on consumers' earnings prepared the way for the postwar investment boom.

Increase in Food Consumption

According to Engel's law, as real income rises, the proportion spent on food declines. Americans were already well fed by 1941. But Engel's law assumes some sort of normal distribution of consumption alternatives. When the boom in family incomes came in World War II, expensive new consumer durables, such as autos, household machines, and gadgets, were not being produced. Having already sufficient savings rates, consumers bought more food and drink (in restaurants as well as for home consumption). It was a curious reversal of form, but probably was not due to anything more fundamental than forced saving, the lack of alternatives. Note the changes in Table 26.6.

Rationing, food rationing in particular, arose during the war as a result of the government's attempt to assist the enforcement of price controls, which it knew would result in shortages. Given the rapid shift toward war production, rather than let consumers wrestle over the short supplies in a black market, the government attempted to assure consumers a small amount of each rationed item.[24] There were two principal forms of rationing. For most products other than processed foods, meats, and fats, consumers received a ration ticket permitting the purchase of a specified number of *units* of a particular item. A *point* system was developed for processed foods (blue points) and meats and fats (red points). Consumers received a given number of points to use to purchase goods that carried prices expressed in points. As we might suppose, since ration points functioned as a form of paper money, they had all the problems associated with paper money.[25] Overall, however, Hugh Rockoff argues rationing did help control inflation, especially given the price increases observed in the postwar period.[26]

When the war ended and consumer durables became available again, the consumer expenditure on food declined as purchases of durables increased. The huge postwar demand for durables, in turn, fueled the investment boom of the later 1940s.

TABLE 26.5 Income Distribution

Percentage Distribution of Aggregate Family Personal Income	*1935–1936*	*1946*
Lowest fifth	4.1	5.0
Second fifth	9.2	11.1
Third fifth	14.1	16.0
Fourth fifth	20.9	21.8
Highest fifth	51.7	46.1
Top 5 percent	26.5	21.3

Source: *Historical Statistics,* series G 319–324.

Investment

Conventional wisdom held that the unexampled outpouring of commodities from the wartime economy merely showed dramatically the waste of the 1930s—the unemployment of people and resources, the output and working lives lost forever—and that the slack in the American economy in 1941 had made possible

TABLE 26.6 Personal Consumption Patterns

Year	Total Personal Consumption Expenditures[a]	Food and Drink[a]	Percentage Food and Drink of Total	Household Durables[a]	Percentage Household Durables of Total
1940	$ 71.2	$20.2	28.4	$ 4.9	6.9
1944	108.5	36.7	33.8	6.1	5.6
1945	119.8	40.6	33.9	6.9	5.8
1947	162.3	52.3	32.2	13.6	8.4

[a] Dollar amounts are in billions of dollars. Household durables are furniture, equipment, and supplies.

Source: *Historical Statistics*, series G 419, 434; U.S. Bureau of Economic Analysis, *National Income and Product Accounts*, Table 1.1.

such an expansion of output for war uses with so (relatively) little inflationary pressure.

The data in Table 26.7 for private investment show, in fact, a sharp decline during the war years. The comparison with personal saving is particularly interesting. Note the sharp rise in personal savings during the war—from $4.5 billion in 1940 to almost nine times that amount, $39.0 billion in 1944. Then savings declined precipitately once things to buy entered the market in 1946 and 1947. Americans apparently preferred to buy goods, but would save if they had no alternatives.

The data for gross private domestic investment, on the other hand, fell nearly by half in 1942, once the war was on. By 1943, private investment was only $6.1 billion, a mere 33 percent of the 1941 level. At the end of the war and with it the end of investment priorities, private investment surged to levels never known before, and the great postwar boom was on. But how was the increased output of World War II achieved in the presence of such a sharp decline in private investment?

TABLE 26.7 Personal Savings and Private Investment[a]

Year	Personal Savings	Gross Private Domestic Investment
1940	$ 4.5	$13.6
1941	11.7	18.1
1942	29.0	10.4
1943	34.9	6.1
1944	39.0	7.8
1945	31.4	10.8
1946	16.3	31.1
1947	8.1	35.0

[a] Amounts given are in billions of dollars.

Source: U.S. Bureau of Economic Analysis, *National Income and Product Accounts*, Table 1.1.

As Robert J. Gordon pointed out in a famous essay, a more interesting and unconventional wisdom was concealed in the record of federal wartime expenditures.[27] The Reconstruction Finance Corporation (itself the descendant of World War I's War Finance Corporation) built and equipped industrial buildings largely through its subsidiary, the Defense Plant Corporation. These buildings were made available to private war contractors on favorable terms.[28] After the war, some of the more spectacular installations, like Utah's mammoth Geneva Steel plant at Provo, were sold to private operators. Other buildings and equipment were simply turned over to the wartime users.

Some of the plants used for the atomic bomb project were kept as government property. Others—for example, air bases in the Western deserts—were, like the mothballed fleets of ships and airplanes, of no immediate use and were slowly dismantled, scrapped, or put to imaginative peacetime uses (Camp Stoneman, California, for example, is now an industrial park). Naval supply ships were turned into floating fish canneries; surplus jeeps and trucks lingered for years on farms. Army camps were turned over to private municipalities. Even the miserable barracks buildings and Quonset huts found further life at peacetime locations such as college campuses, where they housed student families.

In any case, the conventional wisdom that the underemployed, depression economy suddenly rose like a phoenix and began to make the planes and tanks needed by wartime America is exaggerated. Just as the labor force had to be expanded by increased participation rates, so the country's industrial plant was enlarged by direct government construction. There was, to be sure, excess capacity in 1941, but it was not the sole source of the great output expansion of the war years.

THE KEYNESIAN LESSON

The war gave economists and politicians everywhere an object lesson in a form of Keynesianism that was not forgotten.[29] Keynes had sketched out the main ideas in his 1941 pamphlet *How to Pay for the War*. It was a powerful application of the analysis developed in his *General Theory of Employment, Interest and Money*. Government-directed expenditures would produce the output necessary to create the material goods for war *and* for civilian consumption and investment. Full use of the economy's productive capacity put a lid on what was possible. Since the money cost of the war goods became spendable income in the economy at large, and since the war products did not enter that economy to absorb those expenditures, taxation, bond sales, and postwar credits (interest-earning deposits made by workers and frozen for the duration) had to absorb the excess income, or else inflation would result. *How to Pay for the War* was also a blueprint for the "national budgets" and planning techniques that became popular in Western Europe after the war, but not here.[30]

Thus the war illustrated, in a sense, the full Keynesian message. Government expenditures, utilizing deficit spending, could and did wipe away the unemployment associated with the depression. But in its full application, monetary measures of a direct nature had to be applied along with physical rationing and other controls to stem the tide of inflation.[31]

American politicians, even the most impeccably conservative ones, could not deny the evidence of their senses—the war had solved the riddle of lingering stagnation and unemployment that had defeated all New Deal efforts. Beginning in the summer of 1941, Americans and their British allies began planning for the postwar world. They embarked upon the grand scheme of world economic recovery and expansion embedded ultimately in the United Nations and the Bretton Woods financial institutions (see Chapter 27). Part of the new international order was, necessarily, the direct assumption by the federal government of the power to control aggregate demand and promote full-employment policies inside the American economy. A new international order would be pointless if the 1930s were going to reappear, as many feared. The war proved, it was argued, that the disaster need not recur. Legislation ultimately appeared (the Employment Act of 1946) that seemed to be justified by the wartime experience—certainly the New Deal itself could not have produced any great confidence in the effectiveness of federal power to produce the full-employment economy.[32]

Whatever the war lesson was, the Employment Act of 1946 was a real revolution in American economic history. Never before had the federal government, the creation of the compromise between the states in the summer of 1787, asserted in law its power and assumed the obligation to "manage" the economy.

NOTES

1. Byrd Jones, "The Role of Keynesians in Wartime Policy and Postwar Planning, 1940–1946," *American Economic Review*, vol. LXII, no. 2, May 1972. Hugh Rockoff argues that the employment of unemployed resources was much more important in the period prior to Pearl Harbor than it was afterward, "From Plowshares to Swords: the American Economy in World War II," National Bureau of Economic Research, Working Paper Series on Historical Factors in Long Run Growth, Historical Paper 77, December 1995.
2. Robert Higgs, "Wartime Prosperity? A Reassessment of the U.S. Economy in the 1940s," *JEH*, March 1992, and

"From Central Planning to the Market: The American Transition, 1945–1947." *JEH*, September 1999.

3. Higgs (1992), p. 53. Higgs is quoting Seymour Melman, *The Permanent War Economy* (New York: Simon and Schuster, 1985), p. 15.
4. Hugh Rockoff, "The Paradox of Planning in World War II," National Bureau of Economic Research, Working Paper Series on Historical Factors in Long Run Growth, Historical Paper 83, May 1996. Rockoff's focus is on the Controlled Materials Plan developed within the WPB in 1943. Although the CMP is often given credit for the success of the mobilization, Rockoff points out the timing indicates that the CMP is, more realistically, an example of too little, too late.
5. Otis Graham, Jr., *Toward a Planned Society: From Roosevelt to Nixon* (1976).
6. Jonathan Hughes, *The Governmental Habit Redux* (1991), pp. 197–199. Hugh Rockoff, *Drastic Measures* (1984), chap. 4; Robert Higgs, *Crisis and Leviathan* (1987), chap. 9.
7. Hugh Rockoff, "The Response of the Giant Corporations to Wage and Price Controls in World War II," *JEH*, March 1981. See also Rockoff and Geofrey Mills, "Compliance with Price Controls in the United States and the United Kingdom During World War II," *JEH*, March 1987.
8. Executive Order 9066, 19 February 1942. *Personal Justice Denied: Report of the Commission on Wartime Relocation and Internment of Civilians* (Washington, D.C.: Government Printing Office, 1982); Peter Irons, *Justice At War* (New York: Oxford University Press, 1983).
9. John Kenneth Galbraith, *A Life in Our Times* (Boston: Houghton Mifflin, 1981), contains his reminiscences of the World War II command economy. His *A Theory of Price Control* (Cambridge: Harvard University Press, 1952) discusses the results of the wartime regime of price and wage controls. In two articles shortly after the war, he laid out his beliefs about price controls, their general superiority as a technique of allocation, and his finding that control of prices was easiest in oligopoly markets, which he found to be fairly general in American business: "Reflections on Price Control," *Quarterly Journal of Economics*, vol. LX, no. 4, August 1946; and "The Disequilibrium System" *American Economic Review*, vol. XXXVII, no. 3, June 1947. Also see Rockoff (1984), chaps. 4–5.
10. See, for example, William J. Collins, "Race, Roosevelt, and Wartime Production: Fair Employment in World War II Labor Markets," *American Economic Review*, vol. 91, no. 1, March 2001.
11. This discussion of war financing is largely derived from Paul Studenski and Herman Krooss, *Financial History of the United States* (1952), chap. 30. For a new and critical evaluation of the processes of organizing the World War II command economy, see Higgs (1986), chap. 9.
12. Lee E. Ohanian, "The Macroeconomic Effects of War Finance in the United States: World War II and the Korean War," *American Economic Review*, vol. 87, no. 1, March 1997, argues that this method of finance led to a larger output and greater economic welfare than the balanced-budget approach used to finance the Korean conflict.
13. In 1940, individuals held 20 percent of all government bonds; commercial banks, 39 percent; and nonbank holders, 44 percent. Nonbank holdings declined as business institutions used their resources to finance new capital outlays. Studenski and Krooss (1952), pp. 454–455.
14. For an account of wartime collaboration between the Fed and the Treasury, see Lester V. Chandler, "Federal Reserve Policy and Federal Debt," *American Economic Review*, vol. XXXIX, no. 2, March 1949.
15. Rockoff (1995) points out that money creation was more important during 1942 than at any other time.
16. The issue of wartime quality deterioration was raised in connection with wage controls. Hugh Rockoff, "Indirect Price Increases and Real Wages During World War II," *EEH*, October 1978.
17. Did price controls really slow inflation down, or merely postpone inflation? See Rockoff (1984), chap. 4. Rockoff argues that the price controls of World War II actually reduced the amount of inflation we had from 1940 to 1950.
18. J. R. Vernon, "World War II Fiscal Policies and the End of the Great Depression," *JEH*, December 1994, argues that the government's fiscal policy in the early years of the war was instrumental in restoring full-employment conditions in 1942. As such, he contradicts the estimates of Bradford DeLong and Lawrence Summers, "How Does Macroeconomic Policy Affect Output?" *Brookings Papers on Economic Activity*, 1988, vol. 2.
19. It should not be construed from the discussion in this section that our modern member of Congress has lost the kind of deep and considered understanding of taxation principles that ruled in 1943. The tax measure *then*, as now, was an outcome of hearings and debates that had little coherence in them. E. D. Allen, "Treasury Tax Policies in 1943," *American Economic Review*, vol. XXXIV, no. 4, December 1944; also Mabel Newcomer, "Congressional Tax Policies in 1943," *American Economic Review*, vol. XXXIV, no. 4, December 1944.
20. Studenski and Krooss (1952), p. 445.
21. *Ibid.*, pp. 295–299.
22. Claudia Goldin, *Understanding the Gender Gap* (1990), pp. 152–154, 175–176.
23. Because of overtime, the increase in earnings was larger than the increase in hourly wage *rates*, which were controlled. D. M. Keezer, "The National War Labor

Board," *American Economic Review*, vol. XXXVI, no. 3, June 1946; and Harry Henig and S. H. Unterberger, "Wage Control in Wartime and Transition," *American Economic Review*, vol. XXXV, no. 3, June 1945.

24. As Rockoff (1996) notes, price controls and rationing helped ameliorate the effects of the rapid mobilization on the distribution of income.
25. In particular, there was considerable counterfeiting of ration point coupons and occasional overissues, both of which led to point inflation.
26. Rockoff (1984), pp. 174–176.
27. Robert Gordon, "$45 Billion of U.S. Private Investment Has Been Mislaid," *AER*, June 1969.
28. Louis Cain and George Neumann, "Planning for Peace: The Surplus Property Act of 1944," *JEH*, March 1981.
29. For a modern summary, see Herbert Stein, *The Fiscal Revolution in America* (1969), chap. 8.
30. Jacob Mosak, "National Budgets and National Policy," *American Economic Review*, vol. XXXVI, no. 1, March 1946.
31. "Disguised" inflation during the war is a further reason why Higgs (1992) questions the Keynesian view of wartime prosperity.
32. For a study of this legislation's misadventures from its earlier version as a "full-employment" act, see S. K. Bailey, *Congress Makes a Law* (New York: Columbia University Press, 1950).

SUGGESTED READINGS

Articles

Cain, Louis, and George Neumann. "Planning for Peace: The Surplus Property Act of 1944." *Journal of Economic History*, vol. XLI, no. 1, March 1981.

Gordon, Robert J. "$45 Billion of U.S. Private Investment Has Been Mislaid." *American Economic Review*, vol. LIX, no. 3, June 1969.

Higgs, Robert. "Wartime Prosperity? A Reassessment of the U.S. Economy in the 1940s." *Journal of Economic History*, vol. 52, no. 1, March 1992.

———. "From Central Planning to the Market: The American Transition, 1945–1947." *Journal of Economic History*, vol. 59, no. 3, September 1999.

Rockoff, Hugh. "Indirect Price Increases and Real Wages During World War II." *Explorations in Economic History*, vol. 15, no. 4, October 1978.

———. "The Response of the Giant Corporations to Wage and Price Controls in World War II." *Journal of Economic History*, vol. XLI, no. 1, March 1981.

———, and Geofrey Mills. "Compliance with Price Controls in the United States and the United Kingdom During World War II." *Journal of Economic History*, vol XLVII, no. 1, March 1987.

Vernon, J. R. "World War II Fiscal Policies and the End of the Great Depression." *Journal of Economic History*, vol. 54, no. 4, December 1994.

Books

Goldin, Claudia D. *Understanding the Gender Gap: An Economic History of American Women.* New York: Oxford University Press, 1990.

Graham, Otis Jr. *Toward a Planned Society: From Roosevelt to Nixon.* New York: Oxford University Press, 1976.

Higgs, Robert. *Crisis and Leviathan: Critical Issues in the Emergence of the Mixed Economy.* New York: Oxford University Press, 1987.

Hughes, Jonathan. *The Governmental Habit Redux: Economic Controls from Colonial Times to the Present.* Princeton: Princeton University Press, 1991.

Rockoff, Hugh. *Drastic Measures: A History of Wage and Price Controls in the United States.* New York: Cambridge University Press, 1984.

Stein, Herbert. *The Fiscal Revolution in America.* Chicago: University of Chicago Press, 1969.

Studenski, Paul, and Herman Krooss. *Financial History of the United States.* New York: McGraw-Hill, 1952.

Vatter, Harold G. *The U.S. Economy in World War II.* New York: Columbia University Press, 1985.

SDSC
SDSC

PART FIVE

BRAVE NEW WORLD? 1945 – PRESENT

MAIN CURRENTS 1945–2002

American involvement in World War II ended in August 1945. The Japanese surrender ended a national collective effort not seen since the end of the American Civil War in 1865. The possibilities seemed boundless in the still air of that wonderful late summer. The Depression and the war—altogether 16 long unremitting years—were at last in the dust of history. Americans could breathe again. They were, it seemed, masters of their own fates. The United States emerged from the long ordeal as the economic colossus of the entire world, and there was no close second. Its industry, science, agriculture and affluence gave its people a heady feeling of superiority. The Constitution had held; the rule of law prevailed; and elections occurred at their appointed intervals. People still spoke of the United States as "young and free." Americans were, in a phrase of the time, on the threshold of "the American Century."

In point of fact, Americans were only about three years from the Berlin Blockade and five from the Korean War and the beginning of the Cold War—never-ending war, never-ending emergency, never-ending peril for what became known as the "national security." The luminous, fragile episode, the "short peace" that began in August 1945 lasted less than five years and vanished without a trace. In fact, given the harsh political campaign of 1948, it may well have been an illusion. Perhaps there really was no peace at all, merely an interlude between wars. Perhaps peace did not really begin until 1989 when the Soviet Union declared bankruptcy, the Berlin Wall crumbled, and "Doonesbury" declared the Cold War over. Whether the "War on Terror" that began in September 2001 returns the U.S. to a long-term state of "cold war" remains to be seen.

After 1950, U.S. economic history became locked in a fateful mixture, the new "welfare state" descended from the New Deal intermingled with continuous, vast military and national security expenditures at home and abroad. For the most part, the wartime tax rates remained, and, soon enough, the federal deficits resumed—at first small, then larger and larger. Economists in 1945–1950 talked seriously of "full employment and price stability" as the legitimate—and achievable—objects of fiscal and monetary policy. By the end of the 1970s, with double-digit inflation, 6 to 7 percent unemployment, and huge deficits at the highest interest rates in all of American history, sober economists spoke of government expenditures as being "out of control" and predicted the end of home ownership for the average American family under the weight of 18 percent mortgages. Economic growth had slowed; the real per-capita GDP of 1979 was not surpassed until 1984. What happened? A popular song in 1945 was "Let the Good Times Roll."[1] Where had they gone? At the turn of the twenty-first century, with inflation and unemployment rates at levels similar to those of the mid- and late-1960s, we believed they had returned.

The post-World War II economic history of the United States has been dominated by perhaps five themes:

1. The American economy has proven resilient during an era of globalization. The time path of GDP suggests that upswings have lasted longer, while downswings have been shorter and milder. The obsolescence of "old economy" plant and equipment and a reduced ability to compete in international markets in many areas of traditional American strength (for example, steel and automobiles) contributed to the "productivity crisis" of the late 1970s and the balance-of-payments problems that emerged in the mid–1980s. After a period of restructuring, the "new economy" of the 1990s, built around computers and the Internet, helped return the economy to strong rates of growth and to retain the economy's dominant international position.
2. The population grew as continued medical advances lowered the death rate and continued economic growth attracted immigrants. The new migrants come from Latin America and Asia more than from Europe. An increasing proportion of the growing labor force was found in tertiary (service) sector as compared to direct employment in the production of food and goods. In addition, there was a movement toward equality in compensation across races and genders.
3. Along with the economy's strong growth, there has been an increase in government expenditures as a share of GDP. The Cold War necessitated vast expenditures for military and quasi-military hardware, labor, foreign aid, and foreign military operations.[2] In addition, despite some deregulation beginning in the late 1970s, the expansion of the regulatory system came to embrace nearly the whole of legal, private economic activity connected to commerce. At the start of the twenty-first century, government plays a larger role in the economy than at any other time in our history.
4. The growth of government expenditures has been accompanied by chronic federal deficits, in both good times and bad, which have contributed to a great deal of political rhetoric. Although there is little evidence that these deficits harm the economy, they have become the symbol of those opposed to the growth of the federal government. In the late 1960s and 1970s, these deficits were argued to have led to steady increases in the money supply and inflation. In the 1980s and 1990s, with significantly less inflation, deficit-reduction, particularly after the Reagan era deficits, remained good politics. Taxes were increased in 1990 and 1993 to help reduce the deficit, and a surplus appeared by the late 1990s. A recession beginning in March 2001, a tax cut, and government expenditures in the wake of the terrorist attack of 11 September 2001 threatened to return the budget to deficit.

5. Growth has enabled the country to address a number of externalities affecting the "quality of life," particularly those connected with the environment. The historically high standard of living provided the funds to help clean our air and water and to eliminate all but a hard core of absolute poverty within the United States.

At the start of a new millennium, some of the problems of the postwar economy have not proven to be as catastrophic as the media once painted them. During the 1970s, it appeared that, as the industries of other nations made the effort to catch up, they began to develop superior techniques of production and distribution, techniques that American industries either could not or would not adopt. The result, as noted, was that economic growth slowed by the late 1970s. This slowdown was short-lived; the growth of per-capita income over the years following 1984 was much faster than during the 20 years preceding it.

In the 1980 presidential election, Ronald Reagan's victory promised a reversal of the "welfare state" trends of nearly a half century, but entitlement expenditures have continued. In 1996, President Bill Clinton, a Democrat, signed a welfare bill passed by a Republican Congress that took a substantial step in the direction of reform. How substantial remains to be seen. Reform of the financially troubled Social Security and Medicare programs has remained beyond the grasp of our politicians. Continued economic growth, as the United States enjoyed into the new millennium, indeed throughout its economic history, will help.

Notes

1. For a clear, if skeletal, summary of events, policy, and opinions of economists, see Robert Gordon, "Postwar Macroeconomics: The Evolution of Events and Ideas," in *The American Economy in Transition*, edited by Martin Feldstein (Chicago: University of Chicago Press, 1980), chap. 2. Also see the comments of Arthur Okun and Herbert Stein immediately following Gordon's article.

2. John Wallis, "American Government Finance in the Long Run: 1790 to 1990," *Journal of Economic Perspectives*, vol. 14, no. 1, Winter 2000. Robert Higgs, "The Cold War Economy: Opportunity Costs, Ideology, and the Politics of Crisis," *Explorations in Economic History*, vol. 31, no. 3, July 1994, surveys the period 1948–1989 with an emphasis on the macroeconomic effects.

CHAPTER TWENTY-SEVEN

From World War II to the New Frontier

From World War II until the 1960s, American economic progress was the envy of the world. By 1960, the American economy had been transformed. The postwar conversion to peacetime production was accomplished relatively quickly and was far less difficult than many people had imagined it would be.[1] Those who had feared a return to a depressed economy were surprised. Those who had feared runaway inflation once price controls were removed also were surprised. The economy stumbled slightly in 1949, but the overall picture was positive. By 1950, consumer prices were only a third or so above the 1945 level, and real GDP had nearly regained its 1945 level—real per-capita GDP was not far behind.

In June 1950, the Korean War broke out. Korea had been divided by the Russians and the Americans into Communist North and non-Communist South Korean governments. After substantial hostility between the two governments, a North Korean tank army swept across the border in June 1950, captured the southern capital, Seoul, and headed farther south, threatening to take the entire peninsula. American ground forces were committed by the president, Harry S. Truman, who called for, and received, United Nations support. General Douglas MacArthur pulled off the last brilliant amphibious landing of his career at Inchon, and United Nations forces drove the Communists north to the Chinese border. Communist China then committed an army, and the war continued. For three years, the battles raged, finally coming to a halt by truce at approximately the original frontiers of the two Koreas.

The 1950s experienced a renewed surge of U.S. economic expansion, which lasted, with small cyclical disruptions, until 1960. By then, overall U.S. industrial output was half again the size of the wartime level of 1945.

THE SHORT PEACE, THE KOREAN WAR, AND ECONOMIC STABILITY

Both the American consumer and the American producer embraced peace in 1945 with a desire to prosper, and they acted accordingly. The "American Century" began with the "short peace"—the conversion and recovery of 1945–1950. Harry Truman was halfway through his second (but first elected) term of office when the war in Korea began. Korea was something different, a limited war that involved only a partial mobilization of resources. Unlike the two world wars, the Korean War produced no significant shortages of materials or manpower. This horrible little war also produced no decisive result. The military mobilization took only a small portion of those who were eligible. The federal deficits were on a small scale, resulting in only a slight money supply increase, and prices remained almost unchanged. Tax revenues covered 100 percent of the expense.[2] Unemployment fell, and business was lively. It was guns *and* butter at home. Economic growth continued apace, literally on a peacetime basis, while the war continued.

Growth with Price Stability

Because the price level rose by about a third between 1945 and 1950, nominal GDP rose, but real GDP did not (see Table 27.1). However, the significant reduction in the amount of military production meant that the fall in real GDP occurred simultaneously with an increase in the production of civilian goods. The 11.1 and 0.7 percent reductions in real GDP in 1946 and 1947 were accompanied by 12.3 and 2.0 percent increases in personal consumption expenditures, a bonanza to the consumer.[3] In this era, for the first time since the 1920s, Americans could indulge their purchasing whims. Unlike the war years, consumers now could find something to own: new cars, refrigerators, soft goods. The same was true for producers.

The country went off on a well-earned spending binge. As the data in Table 27.1 show, consumption expenditures in 1950 were 60 percent higher than those of 1945 in nominal terms and 28 percent higher in real terms. Private investment, operating under the same forces as consumer expenditures, rose to unheard-of levels; in 1950 it was, in fact, equal to over 18 percent of the GDP. Such a high level of private investment was extraordinary, and it produced a healthy, viable level of economic growth. In 1950, private investment was greater than federal government expenditures. This should be contrasted to the experience of the last three decades of the twentieth century when private investment expenditures averaged about 80 percent of the federal government's expenditures.[4]

TABLE 27.1 Selected Postwar Economic Indicators

	Current Prices				*Chained 1996 Dollars*					
Year	*Total GDP*	*Per-Capita GDP*	*Personal Consumption*	*GPDI*	*Total GDP*	*Per-Capita GDP*	*Personal Consumption*	*GPDI*	*Industrial Production (1967=100)*	*Inflation Rate*
1945	$223.0	$1594.0	$119.8	$10.8	$1693.3	$12103.6	$851.8	$69.0	43	2.3
1946	222.3	1572.1	144.2	31.1	1505.5	10647.1	956.9	175.0	35	8.5
1947	244.4	1696.0	162.3	35.0	1495.1	10375.4	976.4	168.6	39	14.4
1948	269.6	1839.0	175.4	48.1	1560.0	10641.2	998.1	215.3	41	7.8
1949	267.7	1794.2	178.8	36.9	1550.9	10394.8	1025.3	164.3	39	-1.0
1950	294.3	1940.0	192.7	54.1	1686.6	11118.0	1090.9	232.5	45	1.0
1951	339.5	2200.3	208.6	60.2	1815.1	11763.4	1107.1	233.2	49	7.9
1952	358.6	2284.1	219.7	54.0	1887.3	12021.0	1142.4	211.1	51	2.2
1953	379.9	2380.3	233.4	56.4	1973.9	12367.8	1197.2	221.0	55	0.8
1954	381.1	2346.7	240.5	53.8	1960.5	12072.0	1221.9	210.8	52	0.5
1955	415.2	2511.8	259.0	69.0	2099.5	12701.1	1310.4	262.1	58	-0.4
1956	438.0	2604.0	271.9	72.0	2141.1	12729.5	1348.8	258.6	61	1.5
1957	461.5	2694.1	287.0	70.5	2183.9	12749.0	1381.8	247.4	61	3.6
1958	467.9	2687.5	296.6	64.5	2162.8	12422.7	1393.0	226.5	57	2.7
1959	507.4	2865.0	318.1	78.5	2319.0	13094.3	1470.7	272.9	64	0.8
1960	527.4	2917.0	332.3	78.9	2376.7	13145.5	1510.8	272.8	65	1.6
1961	545.7	2970.6	342.7	78.2	2432.0	13239.0	1541.2	271.0	66	1.0
1962	586.5	3143.1	363.8	88.1	2578.9	13820.5	1617.3	305.3	71	1.1

Note: *GPDI* = Gross Private Domestic Investment.
Dollar amounts are in billions of dollars.

Source: U.S Bureau of Economic Analysis, *National Income and Product Accounts (NIPA)*, Tables 1.1 and 1.2; *Historical Statistics*, series E 135, P 13.

Table 27.2 indicates that postwar growth advanced on all fronts of the private sector, while the government sector of the national income accounts was actually declining. Building construction led the pace of the advance. Nonresidential structures (factories and offices) stood at 303 percent of the 1945 figure by 1950, while residential investment stood at 1,206 percent. This was the period when decisive suburbanization began, with shopping centers being built away from the central cities to accommodate the expanding suburbs. The flight to the suburbs began and would continue for decades. Manufacturing production was actually half again the 1945 level by 1950, and, by then, it was virtually all civilian goods.

During the years 1950 to 1962, from the Korean War to John F. Kennedy's last full year, the U.S. economy continued to grow without significant inflation. The sources of that growth will be addressed in later chapters. In retrospect, the real drama of those years was the *absence* of drama in the economy. Of course, the usual political hubbub continued; according to politicians and the media, the republic was in constant danger. There were McCarthyism, two presidential heart attacks, and the U2 incident at the end of the Eisenhower administration. So placid was the economic climate that Professor John Kenneth Galbraith was able, in 1958, to send the stock market into a momentary tailspin by reminding a sleepy congressional committee of the events of 1929. Galbraith, who had just finished his book *The Great Crash, 1929*, was invited to testify. A Harvard professor's findings on a piece of economic history were BIG NEWS. No one was more surprised than Galbraith himself.[5]

TABLE 27.2 National Income by Industrial Origin

	1945	*1950*	*1950/1945*
Agriculture and Forestry	$ 15.2	$ 17.6	1.158
Manufacturing	52.2	76.2	1.460
Wholesale and Retail Trade	28.0	40.9	1.461
Contract Construction	4.3	11.9	2.767
Services	14.1	21.8	1.546
Government	36.8	23.6	0.641
Total	181.5	241.1	1.328

Note: Dollar amounts are in billions of dollars.

Source: *Historical Statistics,* series F 226–237.

Look again at Table 27.1 and notice the remarkable stability of the time. The post-World War II recovery continued with only small setbacks. The continuous growth of GDP and industrial production with so little inflation over so long a period was remarkable. There was, to be sure, a gentle updraft in the trend of prices, but few economists either expected or advocated a general *deflation* as a corrective to anything. The experience of 1929–1933 had cured most of them of any desire to see "equilibrium" conditions produced by downward adjustments of prices and wages.

Year by year there was a bit more drama than the table indicates. In 1954 and 1958, for example, the Republican administration received small frights from the sudden appearance of cyclical setbacks. Unemployment, a mere 2.9 percent in 1953 while the Korean War expenditures were still flowing in deficit financing, doubled to 5.6 percent in 1954 when the deficit fell. In 1958, a serious cyclical recession was apparently stemmed, according to Geoffrey Moore, by the "automatic stabilizers" built into the economy by progressive income taxes and unemployment compensation.[6] As incomes decreased, the consequent decline in tax revenues gave President Eisenhower, to his chagrin, a sudden deficit of 5.5 billion, the largest since the end of World War II.

Fiscal and Monetary Concerns

The postwar recovery was one of health and vigor, *and* it was basically unsupported by government expenditure, except for the transfer payments provided by the (still new) Social Security legislation, together with the costs of normal government services. Much of the Truman administration's "Fair Deal" social program had been defeated in Congress, and the New Deal activism in the federal service had not yet been reconstituted.

The United States reduced its military forces to skeletal proportions almost immediately in 1945. The war expenditures fell as contracts were completed, but there were still large leftover expenditures for demobilization and purchases of food and supplies for foreign relief. In the summer of 1947, Secretary of State George Marshall announced a plan for European recovery and cooperation, to be known as the "Marshall Plan," and U.S. involvement in European reconstruction was under way.

Despite the Marshall Plan, federal expenditures dropped by two-fifths between 1945 and 1950 and stayed down (see Table 27.3). Federal tax revenues fluctuated around their 1945 level ending approximately more than a sixth above the 1945 level, but the lower expenditure levels actually produced federal surpluses, largely by accident. Because these surpluses lowered the federal government's financing needs, M_1 (currency plus demand deposits) actually *declined* in 1949, a rare event.

The economy, filled with government securities during the war, suffered no money shortages. The banking system began the process of lending again to private borrowers by selling government securities in the market and to the Federal Reserve System. The rise in interest rates (recall Figure 26.1) exerted a slightly depressing effect upon bond prices, but that did not hinder the process. Potential profits from private lending far exceeded the capital losses of government bonds. Because it was Federal Reserve and Treasury policy to hold down interest rates to ease the problems of debt management (the prime commercial paper rate was only slightly above 1 percent in 1950), the Fed purchased the bank-held securities and produced small net money supply increases.[7] Response on the production side minimized the inflationary impact of the economy's enormous liquidity so that price increases were minimal (see Table 27.1).

Thus, during the "short peace," the economy, by conventional measures, made the transition from its wartime mobilization to peacetime production with impressive stability. The postwar depression so confidently predicted by many economists never came, nor did the inflationary explosion that was supposed to follow the lifting of price controls. After the exhilaration of 1942–1945, contemporaries, remembering 1918–1921, doubted that a smooth transition could be made. Fear of a return of unemployment motivated the presidential campaigns of both Harry Truman and third-party candidate Henry A. Wallace in 1948. Yet, in 1950, with (a) greatly expanded output and investment, (b) stable prices from 1948 onward, and (c) low interest rates and unemployment at 5.3 percent with a stable level of federal spending and taxing, optimists could hardly be blamed for hopes of a promising future. This vision was disrupted by the outbreak of war in Korea.

TABLE 27.3 Government Finance, Money, and Inflation

	Federal Government			
Year	*Receipts*	*Expenditures*	*Net*	M_1
1945	$ 41.5	$ 70.6	$ −29.1	$ 99.2
1946	39.5	44.6	−5.1	106.5
1947	42.8	37.6	5.2	111.8
1948	42.4	38.9	3.5	112.3
1949	37.9	43.6	−5.7	111.2
1950	48.8	43.3	5.5	114.1
1951	62.9	53.3	9.6	119.2
1952	65.8	62.1	3.7	125.2
1953	68.6	66.8	1.8	128.3
1954	62.5	64.2	−1.7	130.3
1955	71.1	65.4	5.7	134.4
1956	75.8	68.3	7.5	136.0
1957	79.3	76.1	3.2	136.8
1958	76.0	81.5	−5.5	138.4
1959	87.0	83.8	3.2	143.3
1960	92.8	85.8	7.0	141.6
1961	94.4	92.0	2.4	143.9
1962	102.3	100.0	2.3	147.0

Note: Dollar amounts are in billions of dollars.

Source: U.S Bureau of Economic Analysis, *National Income and Product Accounts (NIPA)*, Table 3.2; *Historical Statistics*, series X 414.

From 1950 to 1962, the money supply grew by less than a third, about 2.5 percent a year on average, far less than the increase in real production measured by real GDP or industrial production (see Table 27.1). The Federal Reserve System, freed from its automatic support of the federal bond market as the result of the 1951 agreement between it and the U.S. Treasury known as the "Accord," now managed the money market, coaxing here, restraining there. The "supply side" response was an increase of real income of over 50 percent; industrial production rose by 58 percent, and real income per capita (population had risen by 23 percent) stood at $13,820 in 1962, compared with $11,118 in 1950 (chained 1996 prices), a rise of just under 25 percent.

Growing Unemployment

Even though the labor force participation rate remained higher after the war than before it (see Table 26.3), unemployment rates only returned to normal peacetime levels. Unemployment in 1950 was 5.2 percent, more than double the 1.9 percent "overfull-employment" unemployment rate of 1945. And while 5.2 percent was nothing like the 1930s, it was apparently about one-fourth or so higher than had been the case in the 1920s, the last comparable years. Why? A 5 percent unemployment rate was nearly double the economists' notions at *that* time of the "full employment" level of unemployment, somewhere in the neighborhood of 2.5 percent. The 5 percent level gave rise to talk of "structural" unemployment: something new that needed to be coped with by federal action, such as new programs to put the long-term unemployed back into jobs. In fact, the 2.5 percent level, known after 1929 only in the most extraordinary years (and never in the absence of some kind of war effort) was rarely seen again after 1953.

Economists now refer to the "natural" unemployment rate as being at least 5 percent.[8] One reason for the change might be utterly mechanical. With unemployment a less disastrous personal experience by the 1950s than it had been in the days before unemployment compensation, there was, not surprisingly, more of it. Also, the steady growth of an urban population and the availability of unemployment compensation made unemployment visible where it had not been before. The doubling of the "natural" level of unemployment may well have been a statistical mirage.[9]

Summary

The period 1945–1962, apart from the Korean War, was the first chance since 1929 for anything resembling normal economic processes to be decisive in the American economy's growth. The international economy had been set going again, and there was worldwide growth, helped along by aid programs such as the Marshall Plan. The United States did not have to face a stagnating market for its exports, and, although no evidence has been presented on the international balance, suffice it to say for now that merchandise exports, $11.8 billion in 1946 (the first peacetime year), were $21.7 billion in 1962, a rise that almost equaled the expansion of domestic GDP.

Internally, domestic private investment, so long in the doldrums, rose powerfully, from $10.8 billion in 1945 to $78.5 billion by 1959, and stood at $88.1 billion in 1962. From the end of World War II to the New Frontier, no source of growth was stronger. Millions of new homes and factories—together with the supporting infrastructure of highways, roads, water and sewage treatment works, shopping centers, schools, and public buildings—had transformed the domestic aspect of America. All had been achieved with a most moderate general price increase, and real income per capita had grown strongly apace. This is not to say there were *no* social or economic problems, but they seemed manageable, given the flourishing economic activity on all sides. Surely there were grounds for self-satisfied optimism at the end of the 1950s. It was a plodding kind of prosperity, of course. The nation responded by only the narrowest victory margin to John F. Kennedy's call to "get this country moving again"—for the simple reason that for the first time in the memory of most adults, it *had* moved forward in semi-peacetime conditions.

DOMESTIC POLICY IN THE POSTWAR YEARS

Recall that, at the end of World War II, many people expected the economy to return to depression-like conditions. New Deal policies (e.g., unemployment compensation and Social Security) that were intended to provide a safety net had either proved unimportant or were simply ignored during the war, but they were in place as the economy returned to peacetime conditions. The economy performed as well during World War II as during any war in U.S. history, and some of the credit was given to the young economists who came to Washington from their graduate programs where they had studied *The General Theory of Employment, Interest, and Money* by John Maynard Keynes. It was thought that Keynesian principles might provide further insurance against a return of bad times.

The Employment Act of 1946

The Employment Act of 1946 is usually considered in this country to be a New Deal device. It was not. There was an origin much more fundamental than the pure wisdom of Congress. As Richard Gardner explained, the real origin of the 1946 act was an American reaction to British demands in monetary negotiations during World War II.[10] If the U.S. dollar was to become the legal reserve currency of a new international financial order, the United States had to abandon its laissez-faire tradition of not controlling aggregate economic activity *in order to control its balance of payments.*

As discussed, American imports as a proportion of GDP had fallen steadily since the late nineteenth century. Historically, in cyclical slowdowns in the U.S. economy, there was the additional tendency for the U.S. current-account balance of payments to turn even more strongly positive (higher than usual surpluses), thus draining the world of its holdings of U.S. dollar assets. Normal offsets to this problem, foreign lending by Americans, had failed in the 1930s. The British demanded some kind of guarantee that the U.S. economy would be kept, by federal action if necessary, from slipping back into depression.

If the U.S. dollar was to become the main, official "reserve currency" of a new international order, there must be some steady supply of it available—the *United States had to maintain stable imports so that others could earn dollars.* If that caveat did not occur, the United States would "export depression" to the rest of the countries by constraining foreign ability to earn dollars and *thus* maintain their own dollar-backed currencies. The Employment Act of 1946 was a gesture of good faith in response to these reasonable demands. It seems doubtful that such a commitment would have been made *in law* by the U.S. Congress under other circumstances. Federal assumption of responsibility for controlling unemployment was abhorrent, even to FDR. It was one thing to dole out federal aid; it was another to assume the obligation to use the federal power perpetually to intervene in the interests of some given level of employment. As it was, Congress so watered down the act as to make it barely intelligible. If you cut out all the *ifs, ands,* and *buts,* it reads:

> The Congress hereby declares that it is the continuing policy and responsibility of the Federal Government ... to promote maximum employment, production and purchasing power.

Surely the record of the U.S. economy since 1946 adequately illuminates the causes of congressional hesitation. It was a pretense to assume that the promise of the Employment Act could be met. The Act launched the United States into unknown water. Before the 1930s, classically trained economists advised the government to keep "hands off" the economy (and, consequently, there were few economists in Washington). The Employment Act, a Keynesian measure, required the government to put its "hands on" the economy, and that mandated an economic presence. The act required an annual Economic Report of the President, a "state of the economy" report to complement the "state of the union" address. The act created the Council of Economic Advisers to assist in the preparation of such a report and the Joint Economic Committee of the Congress to receive it.

Learning to Live with Deficits

Compared to earlier times, in the 1950s and early 1960s, the United States drifted into a new fiscal state of affairs that seemed to be a temporary aberration, but that can now be seen as more permanent. Even with conservative management, government expenditures tended to exceed revenues in most years. As John Wallis has argued, public finance in the postwar years "only makes sense if we think of Word War II as the beginning of a lengthy shock called the Cold

War that would take 40 years to run its course."[11] The Cold War meant that military expenditures remained a much higher percentage of GDP in peacetime than they had been before the war. To these were added expenditures on New Deal programs such as Social Security, the start of the American welfare system. Wallis refers to what emerged as the "national system" of centralized revenue and decentralized expenditures developed for expanding government expenditures on education, sanitation, transportation, and welfare. The sturdy little string of budget surpluses of the 1920s now seemed less likely.

Consider the Eisenhower years in Table 27.3. The "fiscal policy" argument, as it stood then, was for a compensatory policy—surpluses in expansions, deficits in contractions.[12] In 1953, Republicans faced the prospect of a recession just as they had settled into the White House for the first time in a generation. By August 1953, the signs of a recession were ominously present. Stung by campaign after campaign in which they had been blamed for the Great Depression, these Republicans were understandably nervous. They, in turn, blamed the Democrats for endless deficit spending. Unfortunately for the Republicans, in the face of a recession, Eisenhower's great campaign issue, budget balancing, was out of the question.

Revenues fell in 1954, even though expenditures also fell. One reason for the fall in revenues was a previously scheduled cut in income taxes in January 1954, which the Eisenhower government could not stop. Also, war excise taxes were cut. However, since a tax cut to offset a recession was considered by the enlightened to be compensatory policy, the economists applauded the results the Eisenhower administration did not want. From 1955 to 1957, with the economy expanding, both revenues and expenditures rose. But the General's conservatism—"no new starts"—held back the growth of expenditures, and three small surpluses resulted. The Republicans were triumphant. They had gotten through a recession without the return of 1932 and had then produced budget surpluses.

The 1958 recession produced a deficit again. Eisenhower deplored deficits in any stage of the business cycle, but economists applauded and hoped for a tax cut. Expenditures had risen. In 1959 and 1960, an increase in revenues and a smaller increase in expenditures yielded surpluses. However, by 1960, the economy was slowing down, and unemployment was rising. The result was a decrease in the surplus.

Thus, if we knew nothing of the Eisenhower government except the numbers in Table 27.3, we might consider them well-trained, "modern" fiscal theorists. In fact there was nothing, or nearly nothing, in the results that illustrated motives. The Eisenhower people were fiscal conservatives; they wanted balanced budgets and no inflation. They got little enough inflation. Compared to what was coming, though, the Eisenhower team looks like the rock of "fiscal probity."

That the Eisenhower administration feared inflation might seem surprising to us now. *Nothing* experienced during the entire 1945–1962 period would seem particularly inflationary to those who lived through the late 1970s and early 1980s. But to understand the motives of policymakers historically, we must attempt to see the world through *their* eyes; otherwise, all is incomprehensible. Eisenhower's speeches on inflation, or on the evils of a growing national debt, must be viewed in light of the inflation rates and government deficits that came before, not after. Interest rates of 5 percent seemed crushingly high to the policymakers of the 1950s.

When the Republicans came into office in 1953, it was after a long absence. Democrats had been successful in tagging them with the blame for the Great Depression, and they retaliated by heaping upon the Democrats the responsibility for wars and inflation. Republicans promised peace and price stability, together with economic growth, but they too feared another depression. The Democrats had succeeded brilliantly with their characterization of Herbert Hoover as the man who had fiddled while the nation sank into the 1930s depression. To combat it, the Republicans backed off their anti-inflationary stance in both 1954 and 1958 when the problem became the threat of recession. In addition, expenditures were more difficult to reduce than were revenues. It was hard *not* to have deficits during recessions. After all, by that measure Herbert Hoover had been utterly "Keynesian" in the 1930–1933 fiscal years. His was a predominantly deficit administration, but Hoover's White House years all occurred before arguments had been developed by some economists that perhaps there should be deficits whenever the actual GDP was below the natural employment level.[13]

Prosperity Again. *In the post-World War II era, money supply expansion fueled explosive economic growth. The GI Bill of Rights brought many new students to campus; tents provided additional classrooms at one California college (above). Supermarkets now offered consumers a vast array of frozen foods and other products (below). Urban growth led to moving-day problems that could only have happened in America (above right). One national magazine attempted to depict the American dream circa 1950 (below right).*

PAN AMERICAN VAN AND STORAGE
BEKINS
McCallson VAN & STORAGE CO.
MOVING STORAGE SHIPPING CRATING
PAN AMERICAN VAN AND STORAGE CO.

THE MAN STORAGE & WAREHOUSE COMPANY

POSTWAR INTERNATIONAL REORGANIZATION

In 1950, the international financial system was still recovering from the debacle of the early 1930s. The recovery was due to an extraordinary episode of international politics. World War II gave the British and Americans an opportunity to try again to reconstruct an international financial order after the follies and disasters of the interwar years.

Fixed Exchange Rates

It was traditionally believed that the pre-1914 gold standard, by fixing the mint price of gold among the commercial nations and thus fixing the rates of exchange between currencies, had contributed stability to the old financial system. Whatever the normal risks and hazards of trade were, they were not compounded by fluctuating exchange rates. It was held that international capital movements, in particular, had been facilitated by the absence of exchange-rate risk. In the interwar period, the Gold Exchange Standard had maintained fixed gold prices, but central-bank cover laws were changed to admit gold-backed foreign exchange assets as reserves against central-bank note issues. The collapse of that system between 1929 and 1933 had produced a period of disorder, competitive devaluations, and trading chaos that was only partly stabilized by the Tripartite Agreement of 1936 among the United States, Britain, and France.

World War II disrupted this confusion and ended with the United States holding two-thirds of all the world's monetary gold reserves. The problem was to devise a new system of international monetary agreements with fixed exchange rates, given the extraordinarily lopsided holdings of gold—the ultimate reserve in the thinking of the time. The solution of that problem, at least at first, was the use of gold-backed dollar assets as reserves against postwar expansions of central-bank liabilities—money.

The Bretton Woods Institutions

Even before the entry of the United States into World War II, the reordering of the world by Britain and the United States had begun. In August 1941, Churchill and Roosevelt met on board ship in Placentia Bay, Newfoundland, and issued the Atlantic Charter, a wide-ranging statement of principles and aims that included sections on a revamping of the international system of trade and payments on an expansionist basis—equal access to the world's raw materials, freer (that is, multilateral, not completely free) trade, and the elimination of trading blocs. The 1942 Mutual Aid Agreement (Lend-Lease) restated the principles. All countries "of like mind" were invited to participate in policies directed to:

> ... the expansion by appropriate international and domestic measures, of production, employment and exchange and consumption of goods ... to the elimination of all forms of discriminatory treatment in international commerce, and to the reduction of tariffs and other trade barriers.

In July 1944, as the United Nations (UN) was being planned, financial experts, including Keynes (who had designed the original blueprint) for Britain and Harry Dexter White for the United States, met in Bretton Woods, New Hampshire. The details of these events appear in Richard Gardner's *Sterling-Dollar Diplomacy* and in Sir Roy Harrod's *Life of Keynes*.[14] The problem was to find the means to facilitate three objects of policy, to:

1. Create fixed exchange rates and easy short-term capital movements
2. Provide a method of releasing and augmenting the flow of long-term capital from the restrictions of the 1931–1945 era
3. Create a framework for the lowering of tariffs and the eliminationz of direct barriers to trade

The solution was the **Bretton Woods System,** which established the following:

1. The International Monetary Fund (IMF), which would set a new schedule of international exchange rates and manage that schedule with the aid of short-term credits backed by gold deposits, or *subscriptions*, taken out by each country at the IMF. Payments of the subscriptions were prorated, the United States being the largest subscriber.

Since credit was based on subscription, the IMF has always been known as a "rich man's club."

2. The International Bank for Reconstruction and Development (the World Bank), which would lend at long-term and in other ways assist capital movements by guaranteeing long-term lending from nongovernment sources. The World Bank was undercapitalized and had to devise methods of achieving its ends without impressive resources of its own.[15]
3. The International Trade Organization (ITO), which, as a UN institution, would assume powers to regulate world tariffs. To do so, each country would have to negotiate a treaty with the UN, surrendering those powers to it.

After the war, the United States and its allies put the Bretton Woods System into operation. The new international currency agreements went into effect under the auspices of the International Monetary Fund. In the late 1940s, there was no difficulty with employment and economic expansion, but government policy, apart from its absence, had little to do with that. The dollar-starved world had to receive temporary transfusions *directly* from the U.S. Treasury to sustain itself. The Marshall Plan was the beginning of that process. Decades later, the agreement went sour. As budget appropriations continued for the war in Vietnam, the United States could not maintain full employment and stable prices, too. It began "exporting inflation" instead—the opposite of the original British fears.

The ITO died when the U.S. Senate refused to ratify its charter. But, in 1947, the United States did enter into the General Agreement on Tariffs and Trade (GATT). In 1995, the functions of GATT were folded into a new agency, the World Trade Organization (WTO). From the start, GATT (then WTO) was the substitute for the ITO in the international economic order.

Origins of the European Common Market

By 1947, it was clear that war-devastated Europe (and Japan) faced recovery problems beyond the reach of normal economic processes. The Marshall Plan offered a straightforward grant of resources in return for a coordinated plan of recovery created by the Europeans themselves—including the defeated Germans and Italians—to use the resources efficiently. It is incidental, but worthy of note, that the United States also offered to include the Communist nations of the Soviet sphere in the arrangement, an offer the Soviets declined on Stalin's orders.

The Committee on European Economic Cooperation (first CEEC; then OEEC, when Committee was changed to Organization; now OECD, Organization for Economic Cooperation and Development, to which the United States belongs) was a fantastic success story. For a mere $12 billion of direct aid, Western European recovery was quickly achieved. By 1951, all OEEC countries had surpassed in industrial production their best interwar years.[16] Then began what proved to be stunning economic growth that in a single generation would make the most efficient Western European nations at least equal to the United States itself in per-capita GDP. The Marshall Plan remains one of the signal achievements of intelligent international economic cooperation. It also directly inspired the ensuing tradition of foreign aid given every year by the United States and by its UN partners.

Part of the Marshall Plan included arrangements among the Europeans to grant central-bank credits mutually to facilitate payments to *automatically* supply domestic currencies so that exporting firms and individuals in every participating country could be paid immediately. These *swing credits* were much like the operation of the Interdistrict Settlement Fund within the American Federal Reserve System, which eases the problems of transfers within the U.S. economy. In 1950, these arrangements were formalized by the establishment of the European Payments Union (EPU). The United States made gold available to the Bank for International Settlements (BIS) in Basel, Switzerland (a leftover institution from World War I reparations payments), to fund the EPU credit transfers. Trade among the EPU members boomed with these new arrangements.

Meanwhile, the Europeans wanted to seize the opportunity, while national barriers within Europe were temporarily down, to produce their own version of European integration. Leaders like Robert Schumann of France (an Alsatian who had served both as a German soldier in World War I and in the French army in World War II) and Paul Henri Spaak of Belgium deeply felt the terrible cost of nationalism in Europe. But they also were mindful of other European traditions, the various customs unions, the intra-German *Zollverein* of 1834, the great low-countries customs union BENELUX, and the amount of international cooperation involved in running the old European steel cartel. In 1953, they began European Coal-Steel Community (ECSC), directly reorganizing these basic industries on a supranational basis and establishing the necessary political and social institutions to make the resulting damages to inefficient national firms adjustable.

To make a long story short, in 1958, the ECSC partners signed the Treaty of Rome, and the European Economic Community (EEC)—the famous European Common Market—began its life. By the early 1970s, countries like the United Kingdom that had not been members of the EEC became part of the EEC, and the beginning of European economic integration solidified.

All these alignments were the outcome of enlightened U.S. economic policy during and immediately after World War II, and they would in the end benefit all who had participated. The United States had produced its own "competition" in the world economy, in Europe and Japan, but what an improvement over the past! It now had trading partners in a sense that had rarely been experienced before, and American life was enriched by the use in common everyday activities of the products of those countries. American firms that could not compete generally vanished.

GENERAL CONSIDERATIONS

From the end of World War II through John F. Kennedy's last full year in office, GDP more than doubled, and real GDP rose two-fifths above its 1945 level. Following the eight years of the Eisenhower administration, Kennedy was elected in 1960, and the federal government began a more active redistributive social policy. This era of "fine tuning" of fiscal and monetary policy combined with tax and expenditure programs to encourage stable economic growth—the New Frontier—was aborted by JFK's assassination in 1963. His successor, Lyndon Johnson, began with a pledge to continue the New Frontier. Instead, he and his advisers committed American armed forces *en masse* to shore up the South Vietnamese government, and the U.S. economy was again diverted to war, this time with calamitous consequences from which there still are echoes. When General Eisenhower left the presidency, he was still worried about inflation and the national debt, but those were strictly *ritual* worries. In fact, the ratio of the debt to GDP had been grossly reduced, as can be seen in Table 27.4.[17] Eisenhower also worried about the **military-industrial complex**, the tendency of weapons producers to influence policy and expenditures, to link excessively the overall prosperity of critical regions of the country with that of a continuous Cold War. That problem has never ended—although the combatants changed at the end of the twentieth century. It would have seemed incredible in 1960 that anyone would look back to the 1950s with nostalgia for the "good times."

TABLE 27.4 PERCENTAGE GROSS FEDERAL DEBT OF GNP

Year	*GDP*	*Gross Federal Debt*	*Percentage* $\left(\frac{GFD}{GDP}\right)$
1945	$223.0	$260.1	116.6
1960	527.4	290.5	55.1

Note: Dollar amounts are in billions of dollars.

Source: Bureau of Economic Analysis, *NIPA Tables,* Tables 1.1 and 3.2, and *Statistical Abstract,* 2000, Table 532.

NOTES

1. Robert Higgs, "From Central Planning to the Market: The American Transition, 1945–1947." *JEH*, September 1999, argues that the rapid return to a market economy restored the regime certainty of investors, a necessary condition for the rapid expansion that ensued.
2. See Lee E. Ohanian, "The Macroeconomic Effects of War Finance in the United States: World War II and the Korean War," *American Economic Review*, vol. 87, no. 1, March 1997.
3. The Bureau of Economic Analysis reports a 90.1 percent increase in expenditures on durable goods in 1946 and a 19.0 percent increase in 1947.
4. For the years 2000 and 2001, the two figures are roughly equal.
5. John Kenneth Galbraith, *A Life in Our Times* (1981), pp. 309–310.
6. Geoffrey Moore, "The 1957–1958 Business Contraction: New Model or Old?" *American Economic Review*, vol. XLIX, no. 2, May 1959, p. 305.
7. See Mark Toma, "Interest Rate Controls: The United States in the 1940s," *JEH*, September 1992.
8. It still is unemployment, though, and a worrisome phenomenon when connected with declining labor productivity. Richard Freeman, "The Evolution of the American Labor Market, 1948–1980," in Martin Feldstein, editor, *The American Economy in Transition* (1980), pp. 385–390, and Figure 24.c, p. 153.
9. That is to say, when those unemployed in the more rural economy of the 1930s did not seek work, an illusion of employment existed where there was in fact a lack of it.
10. Richard Gardner, *Sterling-Dollar Diplomacy* (1956).
11. John Wallis, "American Government Finance in the Long Run: 1790 to 1990," *Journal of Economic Perspectives*, vol. 14, no. 1, Winter 2000, p. 77.
12. Herbert Stein, *The Fiscal Revolution in America* (1969), chaps. 9–14, for the Truman-Eisenhower years.
13. *Ibid.*, pp. 443–444, on the development of this view in the mid-1960s. On the other hand, Robert Gordon found that government in the postwar period was the most destabilizing influence in the years 1947–1957. "Postwar Macroeconomics: The Evolution of Events and Ideas," in Feldstein (1980), pp. 121–123.
14. Gardner (1956), and Roy Harrod, *Life of Keynes* (London: Macmillan, 1951).
15. Louis Galambos and David Milobsky, "Organizing and Reorganizing the World Bank, 1946–1972: A Comparative Perspective," *BHR*, Summer 1995, is an interesting examination of how this institution evolved.
16. Jonathan Hughes, *Industrialization and Economic History* (New York: McGraw-Hill, 1970), pp. 268–270.
17. By 1990, both the debt and GDP were approximately ten times the levels of 1960, but the ratio of debt to GDP had risen back to the level of 1960 from a low of 32.5 percent in 1981.

SUGGESTED READINGS

Articles

Bonomo, Vittorio. "International Capital Movements and Economic Activity: The United States Experience, 1870–1968." *Explorations in Economic History*, vol. 8, no. 3, Spring 1971.

Cain, Louis, and George Neumann. "Planning for Peace: The Surplus Property Act of 1944." *Journal of Economic History*, vol. XLI, no. 1, March 1981.

Darby, Michael R. "Postwar U.S. Consumption, Consumer Expenditures, and Savings." *American Economic Review*, vol. LXV, no. 2, May 1975.

Freeman, Richard B. "The Evolution of the American Labor Market, 1948–1980." In Martin Feldstein, ed., *The American Economy in Transition*. Chicago: University of Chicago Press, 1980.

Galambos, Louis, and David Milobsky. "Organizing and Reorganizing the World Bank, 1946–1972: A Comparative Perspective." *Business History Review*, vol. 69, no. 2, Summer 1995.

Gordon, Robert J. "Postwar Macroeconomies: The Evolution of Events and Ideas." In Martin Feldstein, ed., *The American Economy in Transition*. Chicago: University of Chicago Press, 1980.

Higgs, Robert. "From Central Planning to the Market: The American Transition, 1945–1947." *Journal of Economic History*, vol. 59, no. 3, September 1999.

Jacobs, R. L., and R. A. Jones. "Price Expectations in the United States, 1947–1975." *American Economic Review*, vol. 70, no. 3, June 1980.

Toma, Mark. "Interest Rate Controls: The United States in the 1940s." *Journal of Economic History*, vol. 52, no. 3, September 1992.

Books

Brownlee, W. Eliot. *Federal Taxation in America: A Short History*. Cambridge: Cambridge University Press, 1996.

——, ed. *Funding the Modern American State, 1941–1995: The Rise and Fall of the Era of Easy Finance*. Cambridge: Cambridge University Press, 1996.

Feldstein, Martin, ed. *The American Economy in Transition*. Chicago: University of Chicago Press, 1980.

Freeman, Ralph E., ed. *Postwar Economic Trends in the United States*. New York: Harper, 1960.

Galbraith, John Kenneth. *The Affluent Society*. Boston: Houghton Mifflin, 1958.

——. *A Life in Our Times*. Boston: Houghton Mifflin, 1981.

Gardner, Richard. *Sterling-Dollar Diplomacy*. New York: Oxford University Press, 1956.

Hickman, Bert G. *Growth and Stability of the Postwar Economy*. Washington, D.C.: Brookings Institution, 1960.

Stein, Herbert. *The Fiscal Revolution in America*. Chicago: University of Chicago Press, 1969.

Vatter, Harold G. *The U.S. Economy in the 1950s*. New York: Norton, 1963.

CHAPTER TWENTY-EIGHT

Labor and the Tertiary Sector

American economic history, like that of the other advanced economies, shows that economic development—industrialization—can be productive enough to spread a prosperous life through virtually all of a society. The great eighteenth- and nineteenth-century thinkers in economics left two major legacies, one of which has been largely counterproductive. These two great legacies are (a) the theory of market behavior and (b) the belief in diminishing long-run returns to capital. The first legacy, developed from Adam Smith and David Ricardo through Alfred Marshall, lies securely at the base of most subsequent development of the logic of economics. The second legacy anticipated the development of a massive industrial proletariat, in large part unemployed and receiving a mere subsistence income, as the population and labor force grew concomitantly with the industrial structure. Karl Marx is the writer usually associated with the second legacy, but it lay behind the other "classical ideas" of capitalist economic development.[1] The process of industrial development actually has been quite different.

POPULATION

Nineteenth-century economists did not clearly foresee the population, and therefore labor force, changes that would mark the twentieth century. At the turn of that century, a majority of the citizenry still lived in rural areas; 60 percent of the population lived in the Northeast and Midwest. At the start of the twenty-first century, over 75 percent of the population live in urban areas, and close to 60 percent live in the South and West. The Census Bureau reports that the total population in the year 2000 was 281.4 million, 3.7 times more people than a century earlier. Life expectation at birth increased by 63 percent, from 47.3 in 1900 to 77.0 in 2000.[2] The median age increased by almost 50 percent, from 22.9 in 1900 to 35.3 in 2000 (see Table 28.1). In 1900, the average native-born American man was 5 feet, 7½ inches tall; by 1970, he was almost 5 feet, 10 inches in height.[3] We need to examine births, deaths, and immigration to understand the remarkable population growth of the twentieth century.

Births, Birth Rates, and the "Baby Boom"

In Chapters 6 and 16 we discussed four long waves known as Kuznets cycles. Tied to the immigration cycle, they lasted from 16 to 18 years. After World War II, the driving force behind the Kuznets cycle was fertility, not immigration. Consequently, the long-wave lasted roughly 40 years, as can be seen in Figure 28.1, which depicts total births over the

TABLE 28.1 Population, 1900–2000

Year	*Total Population*	*Percent Foreign Born*	*Median Age*
1900	76.0	13.6	22.9
1910	92.0	14.7	24.1
1920	105.7	13.2	25.3
1930	122.8	11.6	26.4
1940	131.7	8.8	29.0
1950	151.3	6.9	30.2
1960	179.3	5.4	29.5
1970	203.3	4.8	28.0
1980	226.5	6.2	30.0
1990	248.7	7.9	32.8
2000	281.4	9.5	35.3

Sources: *Historical Statistics,* series A 57, 69, D 1, 2, 86; *Statistical Abstract, 2000,* Tables 1, 11, and 46.

twentieth century. The upward trend is immediately apparent, as is the extraordinary increase that began shortly after the end of World War II—the baby boom. Figure 28.2 presents the birth rate over the same period. Once again, the trend is immediately apparent, but now it is downward—with the exception of the baby boom. The larger number of births today is a result of a falling birth rate applied to a growing number of young adults, whose parents were in the vanguard of the baby boom.[4]

Richard Easterlin's explanation of this pattern of boom—and bust—is based on what he terms "relative income."[5] The decision to have a child depends on a household's material aspirations relative to its ability to earn income. In simplest terms, the generation that grew up during the Great Depression and fought World War II had relatively low aspirations when they returned home after the war and formed families. Many feared a return of depression. But, as we saw in the previous chapter, potential income in the postwar economy was greater than people expected it to be. In addition, as we will discuss later in this chapter, this was an era that still discriminated against young married women who wanted to work. The generation born after the war bore little of the baggage of depression and war. They grew up in what Galbraith termed "the Affluent Society." Their material aspirations were much higher than the earlier generation, but their potential income was little different. Indeed, as the first generation of male baby boomers entered the labor force, there was a much larger rightward shift of the labor supply curve than what they might have expected. The women's movement, and ultimately public policy, helped to create a

FIGURE 28.1 Births, 1909–1998

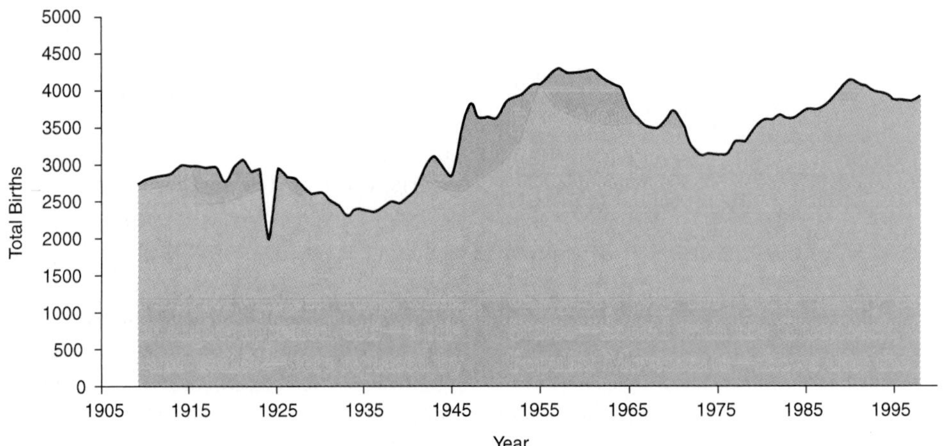

Sources: U.S. Center for Health Statistics, *Vital Statistics of the United States, 1997,* Table 1-1; *Statistical Abstract, 2000,* Table 77.

market that not only welcomed the labor of men but that of their sisters and mothers as well.

Like all simple sketches, this one omits a great deal of detail, some of which is contradictory. What is most important in Easterlin's explanation is that, as the relative price of children rose in the latter half of the twentieth century, the average household demanded fewer of them. The birth rate is an economic variable, but the same is not true of the death rate.

Mortality

Figure 28.2 also displays the death rate from all causes. The general trend is downward, but there are no cycles or waves in this series as there are in the birth rate data. The explanation for the downward trend lies in a large number of technological and scientific discoveries that have dramatically transformed modern medicine. People of all ages have benefited from technological changes that enabled earlier detection and improved treatment and from scientific discoveries that helped to provide cures for many diseases. The effect of prenatal and neonatal care on infant mortality has been enormous. As recently as 1950, the infant death rate was more than three times the total death rate. It was still double in 1970, but, by 1993, the infant death rate fell below the total and has continued to fall relative to the total ever since. When combined with improved healthcare for older Americans, the result has been the 63 percent increase in life expectancy reported above.

Immigration

At the beginning of the twentieth century, immigration was brisk, with 13.6 percent of the population foreign-born. Although the rate would fall over much of the century, particularly as a result of the post-World War I restrictions, it began to increase again at mid-century. However, it has not returned to nineteenth-century levels (see Tables 28.1 and 28.2). For much of this period, immigrants comprised a small proportion of the total population, but they remain a significant contributor to the rate of population growth. In the 1950s, legal immigration was responsible for roughly one-tenth of population growth, but the comparable figure today is roughly one-third.[6]

The Immigration Act of 1965 shifted policy away from geographical quotas toward a set of standards that emphasized labor market skills, the reunification of families, political asylum, and other humanitarian aims. George Borjas argues that, on average, the skill level of the immigrant population has decreased because the proportion of immigrants arriving from developing countries has increased.[7] Yet, it is also true that only about 1 percent of legal immigrants in the first decade of the twentieth century had professional

FIGURE 28.2 Birth and Death Rates, 1909–1998

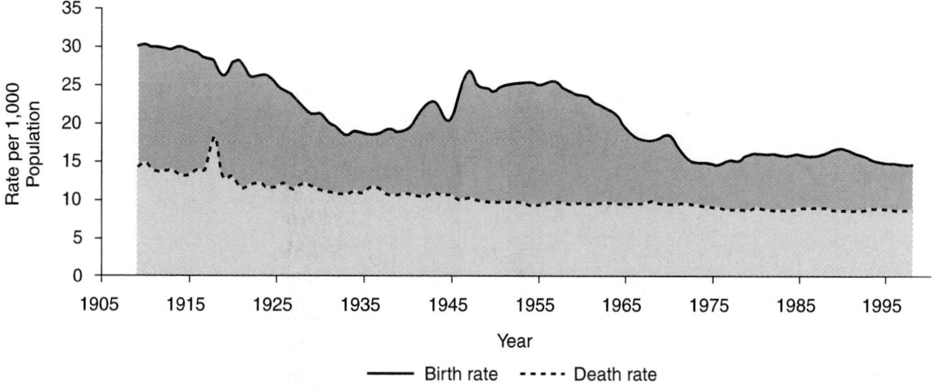

Sources: U.S. Center for Health Statistics, *Vital Statistics of the United States, 1997*, Table 1-3; *Statistical Abstract, 2000*, Table 77; U.S. Center for Health Statistics, *Leading Causes of Death, 1900–1998.*

TABLE 28.2 Immigration, 1931–1998

	Immigrants	*Rate*	*Europe*	*Asia*	*North America*	*Mexico*	*South America*	*Africa*
1931–1940	528	0.4	0.658	0.031	0.303	0.042	0.015	0.003
1941–1950	1035	0.7	0.600	0.036	0.343	0.059	0.021	0.007
1951–1960	2515	1.5	0.527	0.061	0.396	0.119	0.036	0.006
1961-1970	3322	1.7	0.338	0.129	0.517	0.137	0.078	0.009
1971–1980	4493	2.1	0.178	0.353	0.441	0.142	0.066	0.018
1981–1990	7338	3.4	0.104	0.373	0.493	0.226	0.063	0.024
1991-1998	7605	3.6	0.149	0.309	0.497	0.254	0.058	0.037

Note: Immigrants in thousands. Rate in immigrants per 1,000 population. Regional columns report the share of total immigrants coming from each region.
North American data includes Mexico.

Source: *Statistical Abstract* 2000, Table 5, and U.S. Immigration and Naturalization Service, *Fiscal Year 1998 Statistical Yearbook*, Table 2.

occupations; the figure today is close to 25 percent.[8] In the first decade of the twentieth century, roughly 70 percent of immigrants reported their occupation as domestic servant or laborer; the comparable figure today is 20 percent.[9] There also has been a change in the countries of origin of the new immigrants. In the 1930s and 1940s, Europe accounted for over 60 percent of the immigrants, with the balance coming from other North American countries, predominantly Canada. In the last two decades of the twentieth century, only 12 percent came from Europe, while Asia was responsible for 35 percent and the Americas for 49 percent. Mexico alone has contributed 24 percent of the immigrants.

Most economic historians who study immigration have found that, although immigrants initially earn less than native-born Americans, the gap narrows the longer an immigrant remains in the United States.[10] For the period before 1890, Timothy Hatton found that the wages of immigrants who came to the United States as adults grew 0.7 percent faster than those of native-born Americans.[11] Borjas found that those immigrants arriving after 1965 earned somewhat less initially than the immigrants who arrived before that date—the initial gap has grown. One reason for this decrease is the American high school movement, the increasing investment in education made in the United States relative to other countries, which will be discussed shortly. A recent study attempting to explain the declining economic performance of Mexican immigrants relative to the native-born concludes that a good portion of the difference can be explained by the fact the average Mexican receives less schooling than the average American.[12]

Further, the native-born population has migrated internally. Table 28.3 presents data for the percentage of the U.S. population living in four large census regions over the twentieth century. The Northeast held its share of the population until the Depression, but now has only two-thirds the share it had a century ago. The Midwest's share continuously declined throughout the century, while those of both the South and West have grown. The movement of black Americans out of the South is evident; the "Great Migration" will be discussed later. The urbanization of the population, particularly in the South, is also evident. These movements are, in part, a consequence of changes in the labor market.

LABOR

More Americans now participate in the labor force, both in absolute and in percentage terms, than ever before in our history (roughly two-thirds of the population), but the unemployment rate today is in the same range as a century ago (see Table 28.4). The increase in labor force participation is, in part, a result of an increase in health and nutrition. How was it accommodated? What nineteenth-century economists could not foresee were the consequences of technological change and the related rise of the **tertiary sector**. The tertiary, or service, sector consists of teachers, civil servants, hotel workers and

TABLE 28.3 Regional Population, 1900–2000

Region / Year	*Total Population*	*White*	*Black*	*Urban*
Northeast				
1900	27.7	98.1	1.8	66.1
1910	28.1	98.0	1.9	71.8
1920	28.1	97.6	2.3	75.5
1930	28.0	96.5	3.3	77.6
1940	27.3	96.1	3.8	76.6
1950	26.1	94.7	5.1	79.5
1960	24.9	92.9	6.8	80.2
1970	24.1	90.4	8.9	80.4
1980	21.7	86.1	9.9	79.2
1990	20.4	82.8	11.0	na
2000	19.0	na	na	na
Midwest				
1900	34.6	97.9	1.9	38.6
1910	32.5	98.0	1.8	45.1
1920	32.2	97.5	2.3	52.3
1930	31.4	96.3	3.3	57.9
1940	30.5	96.3	3.5	58.4
1950	29.4	94.7	5.0	64.1
1960	28.8	93.0	6.7	68.7
1970	27.8	91.3	8.1	71.6
1980	26.0	88.7	9.1	70.5
1990	24.0	87.2	9.6	na
2000	22.9	na	na	na
South				
1900	32.3	67.4	32.3	18.0
1910	31.9	69.9	29.8	22.5
1920	31.3	72.8	26.9	28.1
1930	30.8	73.1	24.7	34.1
1940	31.6	76.0	23.8	36.7
1950	31.2	78.1	21.7	48.6
1960	30.7	79.1	20.6	58.5
1970	30.9	80.3	19.1	64.6
1980	33.3	78.2	18.6	66.9
1990	34.4	76.8	18.5	na
2000	35.6	na	na	na
West				
1900	5.7	89.9	0.7	39.9
1910	7.7	92.4	0.7	47.9
1920	8.7	93.0	0.9	51.8
1930	10.0	87.7	1.0	58.4
1940	10.9	92.8	1.2	58.5
1950	13.3	92.0	2.8	69.5
1960	15.6	92.1	3.9	77.7
1970	17.1	90.2	4.9	82.9
1980	19.1	80.8	5.2	83.9
1990	21.2	75.8	5.4	na
2000	22.3	na	na	na

Sources: 1900-1970: *Historical Statistics,* Tables A 172, 175, 176, 178. 1980: *Statistical Abstract, 1983,* Tables 19, 22, and 36. 1990: *Statistical Abstract, 1995,* Tables 27 and 31. 2000: U.S. Department of Commerce, U.S. Census Bureau, *Census 2000,* Table 2: Resident Population of the 50 states, the District of Columbia, and Puerto Rico.

TABLE 28.4 Labor Force Characteristics, 1900–2000

	Total Population	*Percent Labor Force*	*Percent Unemployed*	*Labor Productivity (1992=100)*
1900	76.0	55.3	5.0	15.8
1910	92.0	57.2	5.9	17.9
1920	105.7	55.1	5.2	21.1
1930	122.8	54.7	8.7	26.2
1940	131.7	55.5	14.6	33.0
1950	151.3	58.4	5.3	44.2
1960	179.3	58.1	5.5	54.8
1970	203.3	59.0	4.9	72.7
1980	226.5	63.8	7.1	86.0
1990	248.7	66.4	5.5	96.3
2000	281.4	65.3	4.0	118.1

Note: The productivity index reflects output per hour for nonfarm business.

Sources: *Historical Statistics,* series A 57, 69, D 1, 2, 86; *Statistical Abstract, 1995,* Tables 1, 4, 13, 54, 626; *Census 2000:* Labor Force Status and Bureau of Economic Analysis, Series PRS85006093

those of the leisure industry, nurses and other healthcare workers, actors, artists, athletes, and journalists. It is concerned directly with the enhancement of the quality of modern life through professional services—communications, product distribution, education, and the whole host of quality-of-life-enhancing activities characteristic of advanced economies—and only concerned indirectly with the production of food and goods. It is supported by and is nourishing of the enormous rise in productivity in the **primary sector** (agriculture, mining, fishing, forestry) and the **secondary sector** (manufacturing, raw-materials processing).

As discussed in previous chapters, the typical pattern of industrial development among the advanced nations has been characterized by rising productivity that leads to a reduction in the *number* of persons employed in the primary sector and a tapering off of the proportion of the labor force employed in the secondary sector. In some sense, these jobs have been replaced by a massive expansion of the tertiary sector. The tertiary sector, crucial to the development of modern economies, is rooted in education of all kinds. Claudia Goldin refers to the twentieth century as the "human-capital century."[13] In 1940, the white population (both men and women) had completed, on average, slightly more than 8 years of school; by 1970, that had increased to 12 years. This trend toward more education has continued. In 1998, almost half of the white high-school graduates aged 18 to 21, more than a third of black graduates, and almost a quarter of Hispanic graduates were enrolled in some form of higher education.[14]

Goldin has documented what she termed the "Great Transformation" in American education, the period between 1910 and 1940 when secondary education, the high school movement, made education available to far more teenagers than was true in most other countries.[15] The high school movement originated in the late nineteenth century, but, by 1910, only about 10 percent of America's young people graduated from high school. Thirty years later, the percentage of 18-year-olds with a high school diploma exceeded 50 percent. This set the stage for the massive increase in college education that took place in the post-World War II years. The return to education was high at the start; Goldin estimates it to be in excess of 10 percent. This was a time when the demand for young people in manufacturing was declining and the demand for white-collar labor was increasing. By the 1920s, the demand for more educated blue-collar workers was increasing. It is no coincidence that, at the time America began to pull ahead of other countries in terms of income, it also pulled ahead of other countries in terms of education.

As for the industrial proletariat and the "world revolution," Sir John Hicks noted in his book *A Theory of Economic History* that the industrial work forces of the modern economies comprise the solid supports of those systems. The really revolutionary forces in the world today are the poverty-stricken millions of the industrially backward world whose lives are totally outside modern economic development.[16] There is a small example of this in the American economy. It is not the craftspeople and assembly line workers who pose a threat, but those who are unable to find employment *anywhere* in the economy.

Factors Affecting Labor Demand

The market for labor of all kinds is a **derived demand.** The demand for labor depends on its wage rate, and, in turn, its wage rate depends on the productivity of labor and demand for the good or service that labor produces. Demand will increase (shift to the right) if either productivity or the price of output, or both, rises. In addition, any improvements in the circumstances in which labor is used raises demand. Hence, the steady growth and development of urban agglomerations in this country, with their attendant facilities—schools, hospitals, public services, communications systems, governing bureaucracies—will raise the demand for tertiary labor.

Similarly, the development of particular capital products that require tertiary labor for their employment (for example, information systems) raises the demand for the relevant grades of labor. Productivity is also raised by such urban factors as schools and other training facilities, transport systems, and public health. Carmel Chiswick finds, on the demand side, a continuation of the nineteenth-century pattern of substitution of capital for high-priced labor: modern technology involves the expanding employment of "high-level" labor associated with capital equipment that displaces relatively high-priced production labor. Imagine the programming of a robotized manufacturing process rather than a manual manufacturing process. As in the nineteenth century, the wage ratio of this "skilled" (high-level) to "unskilled" (production) labor narrows in the process. Chiswick writes:

> The U.S. economy has been characterized in the twentieth century by dramatic increases in the proportion of the labor force in high-level manpower occupations, together with a decline in their relative wage.

This process over time has produced a

> ...composition of output favoring industries that make relatively intensive use of high-level manpower.[17]

In these conditions, the rightward-shifting demand for labor is increasingly for tertiary employment.

Facing the Environmental Crisis. ***High noon on Liberty Avenue in Pittsburgh, fall 1945 (above). Pollution control and cleaning up produced amazing results as attested by the view of the same street in 1951 (below).***

Factors Affecting Labor Supply

Since supplies of tertiary labor require the entire range of special knowledge, from household labor to nuclear physicists and other technical people, education affects the supply side. In the highly technical parts of the economy, the apparatus of formal education has been of peculiar significance in the creation of supply. In 1997, 45,876 doctorates were conferred. In 1900, there were 382; in 1940, 3,290; and in 1957, 8,752.[18] The supply came from the expansion of those university facilities needed for such education. Most of that expansion was tax supported. Even government is a factor on *both* the demand and the supply side. Government hires Ph.D.s (thus increases demand); it also finances their development (thus helps increase supply). Consequently, both supply and demand have shifted to the right over time. Since personal incomes have risen steadily, the increases in demand have been marginally greater.[19]

Transactions Costs

Another way of looking at tertiary sector employment is in terms of **transactions costs**. In the frictionless economic world of perfect competition, with perfect knowledge, no scale economies, no externalities of any sort, and no government (no taxes or regulation), all resources would be allocated according to consumer demand and production costs. Everyone willing to work would be employed at a wage equal to his or her marginal product times the product price. Business profits above production costs would just compensate the cost of capital and managerial salaries. There would be no barriers to entry or exit in this world for any employment of economic resources. Obviously, there would be no such thing as "market power" in the hands of business firms; they would be competing with each other. Wage and price bargains would be made between any persons or entities with perfect confidence and at zero cost. The world is not like this. Why not?

In an imperfect world there are positive costs involved in completing business transactions, there are externalities, and there are lawyers and accountants, taxes and government, advertising, and attempts to limit or monopolize knowledge (information can be *very* expensive). Such costs as these, lumped together under the transactions costs rubric, are unknown in the elementary economics classroom. However, much tertiary employment is in the world covered by transaction-cost economics, those costs described by John Wallis and Douglass North as "...the costs of capturing the gains from specialization and division of labor."[20] Wallis and North argue that these costs have risen sharply *as a proportion of GDP*; they were an estimated 22.5 percent in 1870 and 40.8 percent in 1970. They should not be thought of as a drag on GDP growth, but rather, the necessary costs, without which growth would not occur. It is, after all, more profitable to have 60 percent of a dollar than 80 percent of a dime.

Job Choice

The choice of occupation depends upon two factors: social mobility and **opportunity cost**, the difference between the income earned from the chosen occupation and the income (potentially higher) that might be earned in another employment. In the long run, an individual receives the wages and benefits available in the particular employment chosen, and today, the choice of employment can become very complicated. For example, a young married woman who has left her position as a bank loan officer to become a full-time mother and household worker faces a major decision once the child reaches, say, age 4. She and her husband must evaluate many factors in trying to decide when, or whether, she will reenter the job market, and no small part of their problem is determining her opportunity cost of returning to work outside the home. They must weigh several new costs against her net salary: the cost of day care and possibly a part-time housekeeper to replace the wife's labor in the home; the possible loss of income from days of work missed due to the child's illnesses or those of the housekeeper; and the increased federal income taxes and higher commuting costs incurred by a two-paycheck family. Of course, none of these factors includes the sociological implications for the family of having a working mother, which must also be considered by the parents. Claudia Goldin's research shows that the mother reentering the labor force will face lower earnings simply due to lack of time and experience on the job, compared with other workers who did not spend time forming families.[21]

Many families have decided that both parents will work. They have decided in favor of the increased income, however small the net increase may be. In 1960, just over 30 percent of married women living with their husbands had opted to enter the regular labor market. By 2000, the participation rate of married women with husbands present was almost double that of 1960. At the start of the twenty-first century, there is little difference between the labor market behavior of men and women.

Figure 28.3 shows the sorts of trade-offs involved. Some fields yield rapidly rising income streams with relatively small initial outlays on education, fields like truck driving or grocery clerking. But marginal annual income increases to additional preparation costs taper off, and little further training occurs after the initial qualification period. Trades, crafts, sales, and clerical work, as well as unskilled jobs, have these characteristics, shown as Occupation 1 in Figure 28.3. Other occupations, such as those involving extensive higher education (neurosurgery, biophysical engineering) yield little for years as the costs mount, measured both as forgone earnings and current outlays. However, such fields tend to pay off handsomely in the long run. They also require steady education of the "refresher" type to maintain the high earnings. The income curve for these is represented by Occupation 2 in Figure 28.3.

Given opportunities, talents, parental ambitions, or whatever, the labor force equips itself to enter the labor market. To be entirely rational, earnings potentials must be traded off against preparation costs (training and education). Years in training are measured in part by the cost of forgone earnings in fields with less elaborate background requirements, in addition to the direct costs of training. The prospect of reaching the higher earning levels must be balanced against such considerations. Opportunities matter. Money constraints keep people away from medicine and the law and from graduate schools. Union restrictions (on race and sex bases, for example) historically limited the entrance to certain crafts and trades. Once a decision is made in favor of a particular field, an individual still will face a certain range of opportunities (e.g., a chemist can work in industry, a university, or private consulting).

FIGURE 28.3 Income and Preparation Costs: Job Options

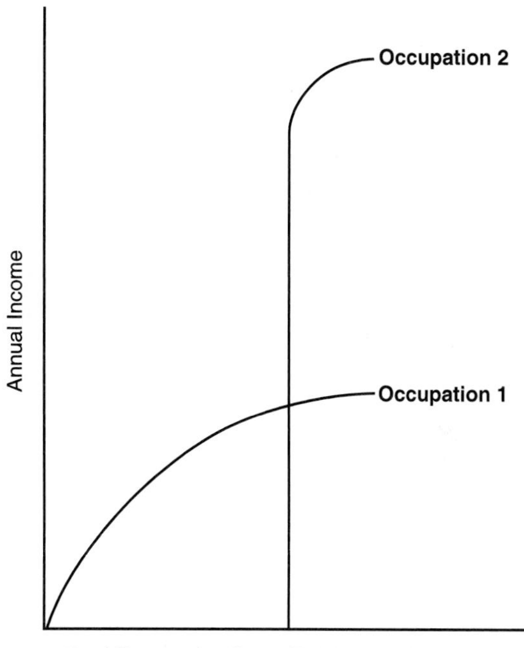

Some employments such as medicine, science, technology, and liberal arts professions (Occupation 2) require long years of preparation, during which they yield little or no income. The payoff comes when education and training end. At that point, incomes rise above those employments that require only on-the-job experience (Occupation 1). Which type of employment offers the highest lifetime earnings depends upon individual circumstances.

Individuals have certain preferences for locational factors—climate, leisure, culture, and family—that can be measured in money terms by the existence of positive opportunity costs and the absence of response to these. A manager in La Jolla, California, may find many nonmonetary reasons to turn down a higher salary in Havre, Montana. She may be surprised by how high the dollar value is, to her, of these "intangible" attributes of La Jolla.

Apart from such implicit valuations of nonpecuniary aspects of employment, the equilibrium of the individ-

Dec 8 **TODAYS MONEY MARKET RATES** Dec 8

TODAY'S BEST INTEREST

CERTIFICATES OF DEPOSIT $1,000 MINIMUM	6 MONTH	DAYS	1-2½ YEAR	2½ YEAR	2½ YEAR	4 YEAR	6 YEAR	8 YEAR
	14.804				NEW 11.75			NEW

CERTIFICATES OF DEPOSIT ($100,000 and Over)	1 MONTH	2 MONTH	3 MONTH	4 MONTH	5 MONTH	6 MONTH	8 MONTH	9 MONTH	ONE YEAR
	18.0	18.0	18.25	17.5	16.5	16.5	16.5	15.0	15.0

SELECTED COMMERCIAL PAPER — RANGE OF RATES

	15-29 DAYS	30-59 DAYS	60-89 DAYS	90-179 DAYS	180-270 DAYS
$10,000-$25,000	17.05 LOW HIGH	17.55 LOW HIGH	16.75 LOW HIGH	15.35 LOW HIGH	13.7 LOW HIGH
$25,000-$100,000	17.3 LOW HIGH	18.0 LOW HIGH	17.2 LOW HIGH	15.65 LOW HIGH	14.05 LOW HIGH
$100,000 or More	17.75 LOW HIGH	18.3 LOW HIGH	17.5 LOW HIGH	16.0 LOW HIGH	14.5 LOW HIGH

9AM GOLD PRICE: 614.00/oz

CAPITAL NOTES

REPURCHASE AGREEMENTS $5,000 MINIMUM	15-29 DAYS	30-59 DAYS	69-89 DAYS
	--- NOT	AVAILABLE	---

TREASURY BILLS $10,000 MINIMUM	15-29 DAYS	30-59 DAYS	60-89 DAYS	90-179 DAYS	180-270 DAYS	271 DAYS OR MORE
	15.5	15.5	15.5	14.6	13.7	13.3

The Information Industry. *An increasing public sophistication in matters such as finance has accompanied the high-tech revolution. The chalkboards (and high interest rates) of the early 1980s (above) gave way to investment centers (and much lower rates) in the early 1990s (below).*

ual is determined by opportunity costs. Since tertiary employment offers such a range of prospects to the sellers of labor, opportunity cost may be more frequently calculated here than by individuals seeking employment in the primary and secondary sectors. This factor may account for the extraordinary mobility of Americans, most of whom are employed in tertiary callings.

LABOR FORCE

Table 28.5 reports the sectoral division of the civilian labor force from 1900 to the present. It clearly depicts the growth of the tertiary sector, according to the census division of occupations. The definition of the tertiary sector underlying the data in Table 28.5 includes only the civilian labor force (it excludes all unskilled labor, all transport workers, all construction workers, and the military forces). The tradition of defining the tertiary sector in terms of output, but measuring it in terms of occupations, is increasingly problematical since vertically integrated firms in the primary and secondary sectors also employ individuals with these occupations. Nonetheless, following tradition, the data in Table 28.5 yield a tertiary sector slightly smaller than data used to make similar calculations elsewhere.[22]

The census data show that, in this century, employment in the tertiary sector, thus defined, more than doubled. As real per-capita income quintupled in the twentieth century, and industrial production and agricultural output rose apace, those workers directly involved in primary and secondary production declined from 73.3 percent to 27 percent of the civilian labor force. If transport and construction workers are added to the sectors considered to be outside direct participation in primary and secondary production, the tertiary sector employs more than three-quarters of the labor force. This is a situation far more like that portrayed in Edward Bellamy's *Looking Backward* than anything foreshadowed in the works either of Karl Marx or Arnold Toynbee.

Table 28.6 reports the absolute numbers underlying Table 28.5. The decline of employment related to primary production is striking. Also note the failure of the unskilled sectors to increase as the other sectors did. As the economy grew, the numbers of skilled crafts workers and operatives in industry and transportation increased. However, note the increases in the number of managers and professionals, technicians, and sales workers. It is these areas that comprise the tertiary sector.

At the bottom of each column is the ratio for that category of employment in 1999 relative to 1900. The structure of occupations in 1999, compared with 1900, embraced a 7.5 million *decrease* in the number of farmers, foresters, and fishermen. In 1900, they were 37.5 percent of the employed labor force; in 1999, a mere 2.3 percent. In 1900, the sum of the MPS and TSAS columns, the occupations normally considered to be white-collar occupations, totaled 5.1 million, or 17.6 percent of the employed civilian labor force. By 1999, their numbers were nearly 79.4 million, 59.5 percent of total employment.

The relative growth in white-collar occupations in Table 28.6 reflects both the growth of the tertiary sector and the fact that those occupations have increased within the manufacturing sector. Today larger numbers of physicists and chemists are employed by universities and by research and development departments of manufacturing corporations. More attorneys are practicing out of their own firms as well as within corporations. That the growth of these occupations accomplished a reversal of the employment structure over the course of the twentieth century explains why

TABLE 28.5 Sectorial Division of the Civilian Labor Force

Year	*Primary*	*Secondary*	*Tertiary*
1900	37.5	35.8	23.6
1910	30.9	38.2	28.5
1920	27.0	40.2	31.1
1930	21.2	39.6	39.2
1940	17.4	39.8	42.8
1950	11.9	41.0	47.1
1960	6.4	39.5	54.1
1970	3.1	36.6	60.3
1980	2.8	31.7	65.6
1990	2.6	26.5	70.9
1999	2.3	24.7	73.0

Sources: *Historical Statistics,* series D 233–682; *Statistical Abstract, 1995,* Table 652; *Statistical Abstract, 2000,* Table 671.

TABLE 28.6 Labor Force Distribution, 1900–1999 (in thousands of workers)

	Primary	*Secondary*		*Tertiary*			*Total*
Year	*FFF*	*PPCR*	*OFL*	*MPS*	*TSAS*	*SO*	*TCLF*
1900	10,888	3,062	7,340	2,907	2,208	2,626	29,031
1910	11,533	4,315	9,919	4,167	3,795	3,562	37,291
1920	11,390	5,482	11,492	5,033	5,496	3,312	42,205
1930	10,322	6,246	13,026	6,786	7,534	4,772	48,686
1940	8,994	6,203	14,393	7,461	8,620	6,069	51,740
1950	6,858	8,205	15,528	9,717	11,536	6,016	57,860
1960	4,132	9,465	16,009	11,956	15,072	7,903	64,537
1970	2,450	11,082	18,086	16,807	21,050	10,251	79,726
1980	2,703	12,529	18,270	25,990	24,819	12,958	97,269
1990	3,001	13,435	17,656	30,823	36,513	15,860	117,288
1999	3,426	14,593	18,167	40,467	38,921	17,915	133,489
1999/1900	0.31	4.77	2.48	13.92	17.63	6.82	4.60
			Percentage Distribution by Group 1999				
Female	19.7	9.0	24.1	49.5	63.8	60.4	46.5
Black	5.0	8.0	15.7	8.0	11.2	18.3	11.3
Hispanic	23.1	12.8	16.6	5.0	8.4	15.2	10.3

FFF Farming, Forestry, and Fishing
PPCR Precision, Production, Craft, and Repair
OFL Operators, Fabricators, and Laborers
MPS Managerial and Professional Specialty
TSAS Technical, Sales, and Administrative Support
SO Service Occupations
TCLF Total Civilian Labor Force

Sources: *Historical Statistics,* series D 233–682; *Statistical Abstract, 2000,* Table 669.

economists and other educational specialists have urged a shift in the national priorities in this country. Employment in these occupations does not involve much in the way of real property ownership or apprenticeship-style training. It does require a broad education for success, and, indeed, unlike the primary and secondary sectors, the tertiary sector is preeminently the sector of educational attainment.[23]

Table 28.6 also shows female and minority participation in 1999. The percentages of women employed in the "technical, sales, and administrative support" and "service occupations" categories are larger than average, while the percentage in the "precision, production, craft, and repair" category is much smaller than average. A greater than average percentage of minorities (black and Hispanic) can be found in the service, laboring, and farming categories. Minority employment in the managerial and professional category is below average.

Do national spending patterns reflect the change? How do federal expenditures on education compare with subsidies for farming, transport, and manufacturing? Are we really facing up to a world in which unskilled factory work, common labor, and agricultural jobs will be as hard to get as were jobs in the tertiary sector in 1900? Does anyone seriously believe that the "reindustrialization" of America will reverse these trends? Is it likely that the United States will return to a labor-intensive factory system? Reindustrialization will no doubt utilize labor-saving methods, such as robots, and, as the labor force continues to increase, newcomers must expect to find work in the tertiary sector or to have the skills (programming, for example) of those in the tertiary sector.

In general, persons entering the tertiary sector have no great opportunity to find suitable work in the primary and secondary sectors. They choose jobs in competition with others like themselves. Since the amount of income available to all tertiary employment is basically determined by productivity increases in the other two sectors (and through foreign trade, of course), the 1970s and early 1980s were times of relative excess of tertiary workers and laggard demand increases. The result was high unemployment. By the late 1980s, due in part to a declining dollar on the foreign exchanges and a consequent export boom, a general expansion in the economy had dropped unemployment to about 5.6 percent by 1990. The decade of the 1990s began with a recession followed shortly thereafter by a long expansion that included the dot.com boom and bust; nonetheless unemployment had fallen to 4.0 percent by 2000—before the economic downturn of 2001.

Women in Tertiary Employment

The importance of employment growth in the tertiary sector is augmented by the consideration that the greatest single change in the composition of the labor force in the twentieth century was in the extent of female participation. One of the more noticeable features of the post-World War II economy was the increased participation of married, adult women with young children. Calculations of the labor force participation of married women over the past two centuries reveal a *U*-shaped relationship; there was a reduction in female labor force participation in the late nineteenth century as wage-work became more common.[24]

In 1900, only 18 percent of the *employed* (that is, wage-earning) labor force was female. By the end of the century, the female proportion had more than doubled. Since women are underrepresented in primary and secondary production, the tertiary sector assumed particular significance.

It is conventionally thought that women enter the labor market, exit to have families, and then reenter. In her study of women in the labor force, *Understanding the Gender Gap*, Claudia Goldin does not find this to be an accurate description. First, in the 1920s and 1930s, the date of exit was that of marriage, not pregnancy. Second, there was very little reentry; those who exited were unlikely to return.[25] More significantly, although few women remained in the labor force their entire working lives, Goldin finds a high rate of work experience among married women still working. The average married clerical worker in 1940 was 33 years old, had 11.3 years of education, and had been working for 13.7 years, including 10.5 years on the current job.[26] This high degree of persistence is evident among all working married women, those who were highly educated and those who weren't.

Only 5 percent of married women officially were in the labor force in 1890 compared with nearly 60 percent today, but this comparison is somewhat misleading. Goldin reports participation rates for married women in 1890 are similar to those in 1940 if farm wives, boardinghouse keepers, and other categories of labor normally excluded from the published census are included. The story gets blurrier the further back you push it. It is clear that, during the preindustrial era, whether on the farm or in their husbands' artisanal shops, married women were active participants. With industrialization, as the relative number of farm households fell and a separation developed between home and urban workplace, the participation of married women shrank, while that of young single women grew. The bottom of the *U* can be associated with the point where the difference in employment between these two categories was greatest, and Goldin places that just after World War I.

Of the entire tertiary sector in 1999, 57 percent of those employed were women, and, of all women in the employed labor force, almost 90 percent were in the tertiary sector. The only nontertiary sector to employ a significant number of women was factory employment, where more than 4 million were employed. As Goldin shows, the employment of women as factory hands in Massachusetts absorbed a full third of all employed white women, even as early as 1850. Women, history tells us, have traditionally provided a pool of relatively cheap labor in manufacturing. Goldin also shows that the clerical employments provided maximum flexibility for a female labor force increasingly able, over time, to come out of the home during and after the necessary chores of child rearing.[27]

The Gender Gap. After 1890, the share of white women working in the clerical and professional sectors began to expand, although for several decades personal service remained the single most important occupation for both white and black women. The movement of white women into clerical occupations was especially rapid in the years before 1930. The rise of white-collar employment for both men and women might have been expected to reduce any difference that existed in their earnings. As capital goods replaced brute strength, as education replaced on-the-job training, as the market expanded, we would expect a narrowing of "the gender gap"—the difference between the wages received by males and females. In a limited way, that appears to be the case. Table 28.7 reports that the ratio of female to male earnings rose from just below 0.30 (Goldin-Sokoloff's estimate for agriculture) in 1815 to roughly 0.5 in 1850 and 0.6 in 1914. The significant narrowing that takes place in the antebellum years to about 1885 is attributable to industrialization. After 1885, the ratio fluctuates with the business cycle, increasing during downturns and falling during upturns. This earnings improvement, however, only affected single, unmarried women; Goldin reports that the wages of married and older women were not affected by these changes.[28] Goldin explains the relative constancy of the hours-adjusted ratio for manufacturing wages after 1885 as a consequence of the growth in diversity as the female labor supply expanded. Manufacturing "attracted those with low levels of human capital, desiring or having to work less than full-time."[29]

TABLE 28.7 Ratio of Female to Male Earnings

Year	*Ratio*
1815	0.228
1820	0.371
1832	0.441
1850	0.460
1885	0.552
1890	0.539
1900	0.554
1905	0.556
1914	0.568
1920	0.559

Source: Claudia Goldin, *Understanding the Gender Gap* (1990), Oxford University Press. Table 3.1, pp. 60–61.

Although the move toward white-collar work extended the period of women's employment, most did not stay long enough to receive promotions. Both men and women started at about the same salary, the men starting as "mail-boys" or messengers; however, the men stayed longer and enjoyed promotion to positions with significantly higher salaries. Occupation segregation barred women from some positions and men from others.[30] Women's jobs involved either no promotion, like those in the secretarial pool, or promotion up a much shorter ladder than that enjoyed by men. The difference in long-term prospects produced the evidence of "wage discrimination" even as the gender gap narrowed.

Goldin finds that discrimination increased in the early years of the twentieth century as the spot labor markets that existed in the manufacturing sector were increasingly replaced by the more formalized wage-setting arrangements practiced by modern firms in which workers are not necessarily paid an amount equal to the value of their current productivity. Since women were expected to leave the workplace sooner rather than later, firms chose not to invest in training for them nor to place them in positions with opportunities for promotion. Notes Goldin:

> Firms in office work and in manufacturing found it profitable to treat women not as individuals, but as a group. As a group, they were less likely to aspire to positions of responsibility; as a group, they were less likely to remain in the labor force.[31]

Since this group was defined to be young women who would be in the labor market for only a short time, reformers felt the need to pass protective legislation. Maximum hour laws and other forms of protection were passed in state after state beginning in the 1880s. In the famous case of *Muller v. Oregon* (1908), the Supreme Court upheld a law mandating a maximum ten-hour workday for women (but not for men) on the argument that work had damaging effects on women and their (potential) children. As a group, however, women were protected only in the workplace, not in the home.

Marriage Bars. Many firms had policies against hiring married women and required their female employees to leave when they married. "Marriage bars" developed after the turn of the twentieth century in those firms (and school districts) where salary scales were correlated with tenure, not productivity. In the early part of the twentieth century, such bars were thought to "protect" women from the rigors of the workplace. Even though sexual discrimination may not have been the motivating factor, Goldin argues that it became a sustaining factor until discrimination became too costly in the 1950s.[32] The cost was lower earlier for two reasons. The first was the fact that older women in 1900 did not have the skills, particularly clerical skills, most in demand. The second was that society considered marriage to be a social arrangement in which the woman's job was to manage the home and family, while the man's was to support his wife and family.

Sectoral Participation. Employment in farming, common labor, and the craft sectors is culturally and historically determined in Western countries. Female participation in those sectors has always been low; the skilled crafts in Western society nearly always have excluded women. American women *can* and *do* farm, but women are involved in farming much more extensively in the rest of the world. The same is true of other unskilled labor. The low participation of women in those areas is due to our lifestyle, and, as a result, those sectors could not be expected to absorb more women in normal circumstances. "Rosie the Riveter" of World War II was an exception; those older, married women who continued to work following the war did not rivet. The young housewives who helped with the harvests in those manpower-short years were also exceptions. In such unskilled areas as migratory farm labor, the participation of women (and children, for that matter) continues to be high.

The managerial and administrative sector has shown remarkable improvement in female participation in the past quarter century; the percentage of women in the managerial and professional category is about the same percent (in fact, a bit larger) as the percentage of women in the civilian labor force. It had been argued that low female participation here is also cultural—"men don't like taking orders from women," and so forth—but there is little evidence to support such arguments. Nevertheless, it remains the case that some of the sectors growing the most since 1900, in addition to management and professional workers—technical workers, sales workers, and service workers—are also those fields that have the largest portions of female workers *and* are in the tertiary sector.

Participation rates for nonwhite, married women have always been considerably higher than those for whites. Nonwhite participation rates were ten times higher in 1890 and three times higher in 1930, but the difference has narrowed in recent years. Much of the closure of the gap is attributable to the increasing participation of white women, but there was some decline among black women during the period between the two world wars.

For most of the twentieth century, the jobs black women held were almost exclusively in agriculture and services, particularly domestic service. Among the potential reasons are the lower income of black families brought on by lower levels of education, higher unemployment among males, and racism. These are the direct effects of slavery. Goldin believes that slavery may also have had an indirect effect: paid labor was less a social stigma among married black women than white.[33]

Although there is a folk wisdom saying that "supply creates its own demand," the supply of female workers was there far too long without demand to take the folk wisdom seriously. The work of Elyce Rotella shows that the rise of female clerical workers, from 2.5 percent of the total clerical work force in 1870 to 52.5 percent by 1930, was the result of the evolution of office machinery.[34] Rotella also emphasizes that the "mechanization" of office work also served initially to separate clerical skills from management functions. Note also that household workers, the traditional employment of women working outside the home, declined between 1900 and 1970. Also by 1970, there were 26 million men, about 52 percent of the male labor force, employed in the tertiary sector. Hence, women, like men, have been drawn into the tertiary sector by the expansion of demand in that sector.

The tertiary sector is not just jobs, but jobs in special locations. The tertiary sector is predominantly urban; it has grown up with the urbanization of the country. Of the 44.3 million employed in that sector by 1970, 37.8 million, or roughly 85 percent, were employed in the central urban areas. Hence, half the men and four-fifths of the women were now in the tertiary sector, and 85 percent of that employment was in cities.[35]

A Statistical Summary. For all workers, and especially white women, expansion of the tertiary sector has provided the majority of net employment opportunities since 1900. Of the net increase of over 100 million jobs over the twentieth century, only a net 14.9 million came outside the tertiary sector. Thus, the tertiary sector accounted for an amazing 85.7 percent of the overall job increase. The large rise in female labor-force participation in the past few decades no doubt explains some of the failure of female wage rates to gain on those of men.[36] But real discrimination against women still accounts for some of the difference.[37] In addition, part-time employment is largely associated with increased female labor-force participation.

Goldin's general survey of female *labor-force* contributions to the economy's growth yields some useful facts in connection with our tertiary sector discussion. Goldin shows that the labor force participation rate for females age 15 to 64 increased from 19.6 percent in 1890 to 59.9 percent in 1980. The female component of the labor force rose from 17 percent to 43 percent in that period. The ratio of female to male full-time earnings increased from 46 percent to 60 percent in that period.[38] Goldin estimates the net contribution of female labor to have been 14 percent—that is, had the female labor force not risen, then GDP would have been 14 percent lower in 1980 than it was. She believes that urbanization added to the rate of increase of female labor force participation, and, as should be clear, urban America is where most of the tertiary sector jobs are to be found.[39]

As Table 28.8 indicates, the gender gap persists, but the ratio is smaller than the 0.60 of recent memory. Among younger workers, "equal pay for equal ability and experience" seems more the rule than the exception; thus further reductions in this gap seem likely.[40]

Black Americans

A significant change in the American economy after World War II was the elimination of sharecropping in cotton. This contributed to the decision of large numbers of rural blacks in the South to migrate to the central cities of the North, a migration that had begun in the years before World War I.[41] William Collins demonstrates that job availability and expected wages played an important role in the "Great Migration." Given that the Civil War ended many years earlier, it is reasonable to ask why was this migration so long in coming. Collins argues that the wave of immigration before World War I, and northern employers' preference for immigrant as opposed to black labor, helps explain the delay.[42]

In the first Census of 1790, 90 percent of the black population was Southern. The percentage in 1910 was similar, but it fell thereafter. It was still 75 percent in 1940, but, by 1970, only 52 percent lived

TABLE 28.8 Median Weekly Earnings, Full-Time Employees, 1994

	Overall	*Male*	*Female*	*Female/Male Ratio*
All Workers	549	618	473	0.77
White	573	638	483	0.76
Black	445	488	409	0.84
FFF		341	283	0.83
PPCR		606	428	0.71
OFL		472	337	0.71
MPS		952	681	0.72
TSAS		626	431	0.69
SO		402	304	0.76

Source: *Statistical Abstract, 2000,* Table 696. See Table 28.6 for abbreviations.

in the South. During the 1970s, many of the industrial jobs held by blacks in the North began to disappear, the victims of increased international competition. Consequently, the percentage of blacks living in the South actually increased slightly over the 1970s and remains around 53 percent today. Nevertheless, as James Smith and Finis Welch have argued, blacks (particularly black males) have made significant progress in closing the earnings gap with respect to whites.[43] Table 28.8 suggests that weekly earnings for blacks with full-time jobs in 1999 were about 78 percent those of whites. Black males earned 76 percent; black females, 84 percent.[44] In 1940, black men earned only 43 percent of whites. Two major reasons for the closing of this racial gap were an increase in the return to education and the migration to the North. Both are associated with a reduction in racial discrimination, as required by law. First, there was an increase in black wages at every schooling level, with the wages of black college graduates growing 45 percent faster than those of whites between 1940 and 1980. Smith and Welch aver, "The two dimensions that served to close the racial wage gap were the narrowing of education disparity between the races and the improving economic benefits from black schooling."[45] Second, until the 1970s, the wages of both races were lower in the South than in the North, whites by 10 percent and blacks by 30 percent. With the migration, this penalty was eliminated. After 1970, the situation improved in the South.

The loss of industrial positions in the North led to a decline in the labor force participation of less-educated black males. Consequently, another reason why the racial wage gap has been closing is the fact that many lower-income males left the labor force in the 1970s. A comparison of the money income of households gives a wage gap of 60.9 percent in 1970, 56.5 percent in 1980, 59.8 percent in 1990, and 62.0 percent in 1998.[46] Many of those households were headed by a working woman, and the tertiary sector was a major employer of black women. Other reasons include an overrepresentation of blacks in the hardest-hit areas, the location of black residences relative to the location of the remaining blue-collar jobs, and increased competition for those jobs due to the increase in immigration.[47] Fairlie and Sundstrom document the emergence of a racial unemployment gap that coincides with the Great Migration. The appearance of this gap appears to be explained by changes in the regions where blacks resided, but its persistence is the other side of the coin of the closing of the wage gap.[48]

In 1999, 72.1 percent of the black labor force was employed in the tertiary sector, and over 85 percent of that was in central cities. While the tertiary sector has expanded more rapidly than the primary or secondary sectors, it also depends more heavily on some sort of noncraft instruction for advancement, most often formal education, but not necessarily so (for example, launderers, maintenance workers). It is also a sector where the racial discrimination characteristic of American society has produced dramatic results. In Figure 28.4, the percentage distribution of the black and white labor forces are listed separately.

According to Figure 28.4, since 1960, the power of the tertiary sector to provide jobs has become ever more apparent. White-collar employment has risen for all races, but the proportion of blacks in white-collar employment has more than doubled. In both racial categories, the proportions in blue-collar employment and agriculture have declined. The mechanization of agriculture has gone hand in hand with that dramatic change. As can be seen, the proportion of white service workers rose slightly (9.9 to 10.1 percent), while black employment in that category declined sharply when measured *as proportions of total black employment*, emphasizing the powerful movement of black workers into white-collar employment in the past three decades.

It should be recalled from Table 28.6 that black workers in 1999 represented 11.3 percent of all workers employed. They are still underrepresented in the white-collar categories. Within the two blue-collar categories, there is a slight underrepresentation in "precision production, craft, and repair" employments, and an overrepresentation among "operators, fabricators, and laborers." The reason for the underrepresentation of blacks among the ranks of crafts workers is fairly straightforward. Until recent years, the craft unions have notoriously discriminated against blacks and other minorities in apprenticeships and memberships.[49] Full representation in this category will take time to achieve, even

FIGURE 28.4 Employed Persons by Occupation and Race, 1960–1999

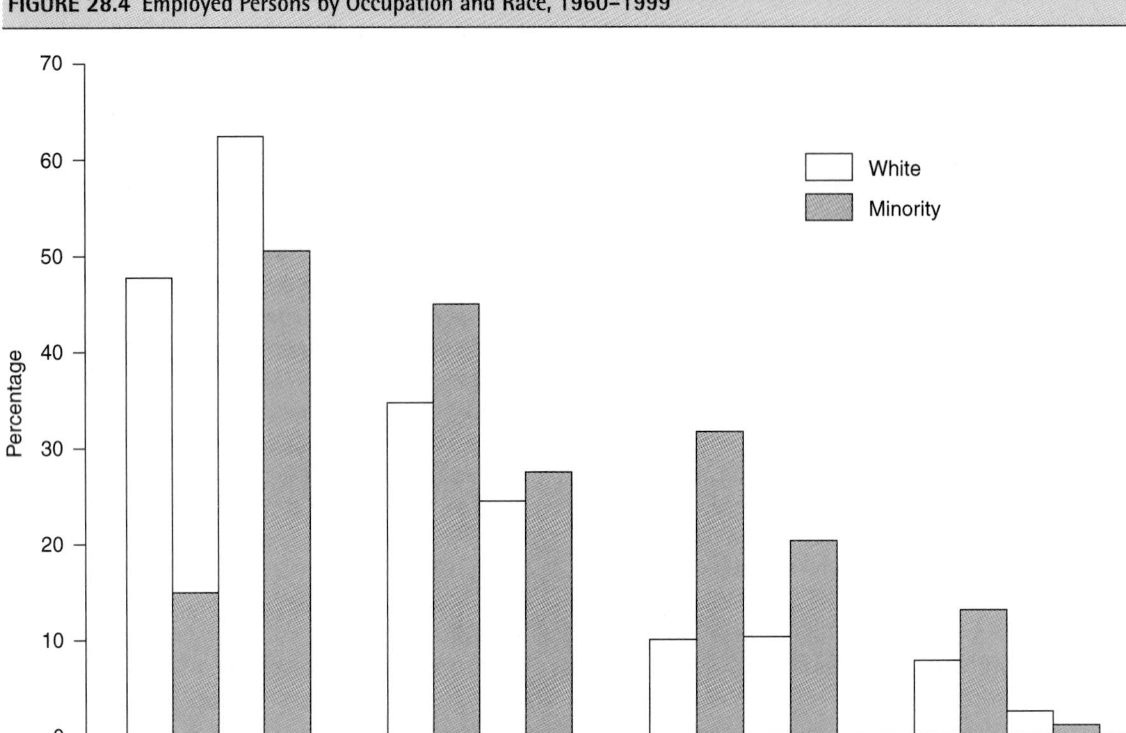

Sources: *Statistical Abstract, 1980*, Table 698; *Statistical Abstract, 2000*, Table 671.

Between 1960 and 1999, black and other minority workers more than doubled the proportions of their total employment in white-collar jobs, while their proportions in service work declined. Among whites, paradoxically, the proportion in service jobs rose slightly, but the main shift among whites was also to white-collar jobs.

though the grosser forms of racial discrimination have ended—they are, after all, now against the law.

To be a competitive farmer today requires a very large capital cost for land, buildings, and equipment. In view of this fact, given our economic and social history, the underrepresentation of blacks in farming is not surprising. Neither is their overrepresentation in "service occupations." These are jobs where poor education and racial discrimination traditionally have placed minorities. Despite the decline of blacks in this category between 1960 and 1999 (see Figure 28.4), they still predominate total employment in a wide range of jobs, everything from sanitation workers to private security personnel.

Organized Labor

One consequence of the growth of the tertiary sector has been the relative decline of organized labor in the private sector, what Leo Troy calls "Old Unionism.[50] The proportion of the labor force now actually working in factories is only about one-fifth. Adding craftspeople, supervisors, and nonfarm workers increases the total to, at most, one-third. As Table 28.5 shows, at the beginning of the twentieth century, the proportion was reversed; the tertiary sector was at most one-quarter of the labor force.

In the 1980s, business leaders proclaimed that far more labor was locked into unionized factory employment by contract work rules than could be supported if the latest automated technologies were introduced. In fact, there still appears to be some job-eliminating technology awaiting introduction to American industry at the start of the twenty-first century. It is wise to consider this subject. From the beginning of this country's industrialization, the emphasis has been upon "labor-saving" technology. Labor has been relatively expensive in American industry, and, as has been discussed repeatedly in previous chapters, there is monumental literature documenting this singular characteristic of American economic development.[51]

Historically, conserving scarce factors by substituting more plentiful factors has helped to shift the production function upward and reduced the real costs of output. Labor traditionally has been the scarce factor of manufacturing because of labor's opportunity costs. At first, it was the pull of American agricultural real incomes that induced inventors from the time of Eli Whitney (1765–1825) to discover new labor-saving technology. In the twentieth century in this country, the tertiary sector was added, with its minimal class structure and relatively easy access to education. Labor unions have attempted to maintain membership, it is often charged, by opposing technical improvements that would reduce their memberships. Featherbedding (requiring more workers than are needed), "bogus" work, soldiering (loafing) on the job, have been the results. Firms like U.S. Steel in South Chicago, Illinois, and the Studebaker company producing automobiles in South Bend, Indiana, collapsed because of their inability to compensate in other ways for such high labor costs. Both these industries will be discussed in some detail in the following chapter.

Just how extensive these practices are in both crafts and unionized manufacturing cannot be estimated overall. It is a matter of looking at every job, every plant. Some people say that union contracts are encrusted with work rules forcing redundant labor to be employed in production. It has been more than 60 years since the Wagner Act (1935) was passed, and it was last seriously amended by the Taft-Hartley Act (1947). As David Sicilia notes, Taft-Hartley did not cripple what the Wagner Act helped create, rather it "gave labor a permanent yet subservient voice in business affairs."[52] Complaints by management of labor-wasting practices imbedded in union contracts continue to be denied routinely by union leaders.

Union leaders plead for higher tariffs and quotas to protect them from "cheap foreign labor" or, perhaps, from new labor-saving technology. Free trade agreements, like the North American Free Trade Agreement (NAFTA), are viewed with suspicion, especially by leaders of industrial unions. Management itself imports foreign competing products (steel, autos) or invests in plants abroad, thus "exporting American jobs," as the saying goes The jobs most likely to be exported are largely in the industrial sector, while those that will be gained are predominately in the tertiary sector. Management argues that the motivation for exporting jobs is not the American pay rates that are too high but the amount of boondoggling protected by contract that makes American labor so expensive. Labor leaders have defended themselves by pointing to management's failures. By the 1970s, the massive invasion of American markets by foreign manufacturers indicated that somehow the American industrial house was not in order. Those manufacturers, many of them devastated during World War II, given the need to become competitive, began to use new technologies that American firms procrastinated in adopting. These problems have not been solved completely, and industrial restructuring has contributed to the decline in union membership.

Restrictive practices by unions are known to European economists as "the English disease." Before Mrs. Thatcher's government, it was widely believed that, because of such practices in the face of technological change, English industry contained as much as twice the locked-in labor that was warranted by current practice in the Common Market countries.[53] Were the disease present, its progress would slowly sap the strength of an economy, and that economy would fall steadily behind other industrial nations in per-capita income produced. The Thatcher government's effort to roll back these developments in Britain during the 1980s produced widespread unemployment in industrial areas. Beginning in the 1970s, Americans faced factory closings in the old industrial towns of the Midwest and Northeast for similar reasons.

Leo Troy noted that the result of these closings is that, "The Old Unionism will end the twentieth century with about the same market share it had at the beginning of the century—7 percent of the nonfarm labor market."[54] The largest percentage was reached in 1953 (26 percent) and the largest membership in 1970 (17 million). In 1999, 9.4 percent of the workers in the private sector (9.4 million people) were members of unions, two-thirds the percentage of 14 years earlier.[55]

The "New Unionism" is public-sector unionism; most of the positions are in the tertiary sector. In 1999, there were over 7 million members of public-sector unions, roughly 37 percent of workers in the public sector.[56] In 1956, only 12.5 percent of the 915,000 government employees were unionized.

A study done by the AFL-CIO in 1983 pinpointed the problems.[57] Manufacturing and construction jobs made up 50 percent of union membership, but only 22 percent of the civilian labor force. Women were 28 percent of union members, but female unionists represented only 15 percent of women workers. Twelve years later, 40 percent of union members would be women, most in the tertiary sector. In 1983, the tertiary sector, with 75 percent of the jobs, was less than 10 percent organized and accounted for only about 20 percent of the membership of the AFL-CIO. AFL-CIO membership in 1993 was 5 percent greater than in 1955, the year of the merger between the AFL and CIO, but the labor force had grown by 107 percent over the same interval.[58] In spite of the efforts by the Old Unionism to retain positions, its relative decline is testimony to the power of the market.

Retirees

Largely because of its relationship to Social Security and the emergence of the modern American welfare system in the late 1930s, the position of elderly workers has become an important research area in recent years. Given the factors we have just discussed with respect to women, we should not be surprised that the available evidence on retirement almost entirely concerns men. The work of Susan Carter and Richard Sutch suggests that, by the turn of the twentieth century, perhaps one-fifth of the men who reached age 55 ultimately behaved in a way consistent with modern notions of retirement; they accumulated assets so that they could withdraw from the labor force and survive on the income generated by the principal and interest on the assets. On average, between 1900 and 1910, men left employment at 66.7 years of age, an age when they had 10.6 years of life left.[59]

This view is in conflict with one that glorifies the Social Security Act by insisting that, before its passage, only wealthy individuals could afford the saving behavior Carter and Sutch found. Further, the work ethic was too strong for an older individual to withdraw from work. Those who were not employed were either ill or disabled. In this view, the increasing number of "retired" men is a result of industrialization, with its demanding work pace that led to significant declines in the supply of labor among older men.

We should recall that the overall savings percentage increased permanently in the 1860s. According to the traditional view, it increased because fathers wanted to support their families, but the evidence suggests that wealth accumulated in this way decreased as the father grew older—an example of what is called life-cycle savings. Brian Gratton found that a substantial increase in the real wages of older workers after 1890 led to positive age-earnings profiles across the life cycle.[60] This, plus the family-based economic strategies of this period, contributed to an increase in financial security for older workers. The fact that intergenerational transfers were part of those strategies is one reason why Social Security legislation proved popular a few decades later. Individually, and in groups, Americans sought whatever advantage could be found in the law.

Dora Costa's study of retirement links current census data back to the Civil War pensions made available to Union Army veterans.[61] She discovered that 70 percent of the decline in the labor force participation of older men up to 1990 was complete by 1960.[62] Indeed today, only a minority of men aged 65 or older remains in the labor force. She demonstrates that much of the increase in retirement through 1950 can be attributed to increases in income and that increases in public pensions were a significant part of that increase. In addition to the Civil War pensions, there was assistance made available to elderly poor by many states in the years before Social Security extended old-age assistance to most Americans. A second important factor in the retirement decision was health. As we have discussed, medical improvements mean that 65-year-old men, on average, have grown healthier over time. Ill health has always been a major factor in the decision to withdraw from the labor force. As Costa argues, technological changes and increases in the public provision of leisure activities have lowered the relative price of leisure to the elderly, so declining incomes are less likely to lead to increases in labor force participation than they once did. Jon Moen's work showed that farmers (and artisans) did withdraw labor services at about the same rate as other workers—quite the opposite of the traditional view.[63] The fact that they continued to live on the farm apparently confused earlier researchers, who assumed that those living on a farm must have been working on a farm.

Income Distribution

It is an axiom of neoclassical economists that economic growth is an effective redistributor of income.[64] Between 1950 and 1977, the United States experienced nearly three decades of well-sustained growth in both money and real terms. It ought to be the case, if the growth axiom holds, that evidence of income distribution will show a trend toward greater equality. This has been the case during wartime when there were short bursts of powerful growth. The years 1950–1977 constitute a longer period, but still one that is underpinned by actual war and big military expenditures. Indeed, in cold-war conditions it may not be reasonable to look for any periods of "peace."

Even so, there was a recession in 1974–1975, then a pickup through 1977. Growth slowed in 1978–1980, and, in 1982, there was a steep recession. In all, the years 1978–1983 were years of stagnation with actual declines in real GDP in 1980 and 1982. Because those on the lower end of the distribution were less able to protect their earnings than were those at the top, it would be expected that the income distribution between 1978 and 1983 would move toward greater inequality.

The official poverty figures in Table 28.9 suggest this outcome. Standards for "poverty" for various-sized households were established by the Social Security Administration in 1964 and have been revised since then. The numbers, imperfect as they are, show the dramatic reduction in poverty one could expect from 1959 to the mid-1970s, when economic growth was relatively strong. The numbers also show the expected turns in the proportions in poverty as the economy's growth slowed. Poverty increased from 1980 to 1983 as the economy faltered, but, from 1984 to 1986, there was a reduction in the proportions of all families below the poverty line as the economy recovered from the 1982 recession. Another downturn in the early 1990s, led to an increase of two points (from 10.3 in 1989 to 12.3 in 1993), but, by 1998, the rate was back to the level it had been in 1989.

The numbers also show the disastrously high poverty levels of Hispanic and black families. Other data show that black families slipped markedly at the end of the 1970s. Median incomes of black families were 54.3 percent of white family incomes in 1950. By 1975, that number had risen to 61.5, but by 1981 it fell back to 56.4. More than 96 percent of the gain since 1950 was lost in just a few years of extremely high inflation. It then began to rise once again, reaching 62.0 in 1998. Stanley Lebergott's study of income and wealth shows why the United States is unlikely ever to eliminate the hard core of poverty by any conventional policies. Lebergott argues that the U.S. economy *generates* poverty along with economic growth by our social processes. Elderly people living alone, divorce, single-parent households, ineffective public education—these and other reasons have increased the number of poor as average income has risen.[65]

The pattern of real wages by industry group suggests that where one worked also made a difference. In the aggregate, real wages fell 5 percent between 1980 and 1995, then rebounded so that, by 1999, they were 1 percent higher than 1980. However, industries

TABLE 28.9 Families Below the Poverty Level

Year	*All*	*White*	*Black*	*Hispanic*
1959	18.5	15.2	48.1	n.a.
1960	18.1	14.9	n.a.	n.a.
1965	11.8	9.3	35.5	n.a.
1970	10.1	8.0	29.5	n.a.
1975	9.7	7.7	27.1	25.1
1980	10.3	8.0	28.9	23.2
1985	11.4	9.1	28.7	25.5
1990	10.7	8.1	29.3	25.0
1998	10.0	8.0	23.4	22.7

Note: Figures are percent in each category.

Source: *Statistical Abstract, 1995,* Table 752; *Statistical Abstract, 2000,* Table 760. Definition of poverty, family of four, 1970, $3,960; changed in 1990 to $13,359.

such as construction, manufacturing, transportation, and retail trade had lower real wages in 1999 than in 1980, while finance, services, and wholesale trade all had higher real wages.[66] Real wages, however, are only part of the story. Employee benefits also increased throughout the period. Real hourly compensation (the sum of wages, salaries, and employers' contributions to social insurance and private benefit plans) in the nonfarm business sector increased by 19 percent between 1980 and 1999.[67]

Table 28.10 shows family incomes divided into quintiles over the half century between 1947 and 1997. The distribution for all family incomes in 1980 was similar to what it had been in 1947, but then the share of income going to the top fifth, particularly the top 5 percent, began to increase. In 1998, the top fifth of all families enjoyed more than 47.2 percent of family incomes, compared with a mere 4.2 percent for the lowest fifth. Observe that *among* black and Hispanic families, income is distributed a bit more unequally than it is among white families. Indeed, racial discrimination and educational disadvantages tend to act more sharply against minority groups, while the payoffs to economic success tend to be equal to those for whites. (At the upper extreme, for example, brain surgeons and NBA stars can expect to receive equal remuneration, regardless of their race.) The table reveals that the top 5 percent of Hispanic families account for a higher percentage of aggregate income than is true for whites; the top 20 percent of black families account for exactly the same percentage as white.

Table 28.11 shows household incomes in 1970, 1980, 1990, and 1998 grouped by percentages in given income brackets. The proportions of households in the very lowest category fell between 1970 and 1998. For black households the proportion rose to 1990 before falling. The median real incomes of black households fell between 1970 and 1980. The proportions of households in the top category rose, regardless of group. Overall, Hispanic households fare better than do black households, but both have larger portions in the lower parts of the distribution than do white households. In 1998, 56.9 percent of white households received $35,000 or more compared with only 40.0 percent for Hispanic households and 37.1 percent for black households. In the lowest category, 8.7 percent of white households received less than $10,000, while the number for Hispanic families was 15.0 and for black households was a disastrous 21.4 percent. For all three groups, the percentages in 1998 were lower than they had been in 1990.

Such numbers are not encouraging for those who want to see greater equality in the distribution of income in this country. Over the long haul, the distributions seem fairly rigid, although the top incomes

TABLE 28.10 Money Income of Families 1947–1997

	Percentage Distribution of Aggregate Income Among Total Population					
Year	*Lowest 20 Percent*	*Next*	*Middle 20 Percent*	*Next*	*Highest 20 Percent*	*Top 5 Percent*
1947	5.0	11.8	17.0	23.1	43.2	17.5
1950	4.5	11.9	17.4	23.4	42.8	17.3
1960	4.8	12.2	17.8	24.0	41.3	15.9
1970	5.4	12.2	17.6	23.8	40.9	15.6
1980	5.3	11.6	17.6	24.4	41.1	14.6
1990	4.6	10.8	16.6	23.8	44.3	17.4
1997	4.2	9.9	15.7	23.0	47.2	20.7
	Percentage Distribution of Aggregate Income by Group 1997					
White	4.6	10.2	15.7	22.8	46.8	20.7
Black	3.4	9.1	15.6	25.1	46.8	17.6
Hispanic	3.9	9.2	14.9	22.8	49.3	21.6

Source: *Historical Statistics,* series G 85–90, *Statistical Abstract, 1999,* Table 751.

TABLE 28.11 Money Incomes of Households in Constant (1990) Dollars

Year	Number of Households	Under $10,000	$10,000–$14,999	$15,000–$24,999	$25,000–$34,999	$35,000–$49,999	$50,000–$74,999	$75,000 and Over	Median Income
All Households									
1970	64,778	13.2	7.5	14.9	15.4	21.5	18.1	9.4	$34,471
1980	88,458	12.2	7.8	15.3	13.9	17.7	18.1	15.0	35,778
1990	94,312	11.4	7.7	14.5	13.8	17.6	18.3	16.7	37,343
1998	103,874	10.3	7.8	14.0	13.2	16.0	18.6	20.1	38,885
White									
1970	57,575	12.0	7.0	14.3	15.4	22.2	19.0	10.1	35,903
1980	71,872	10.6	7.7	15.2	14.1	19.5	19.6	13.4	37,732
1990	80,968	9.6	7.3	14.3	14.0	17.9	19.2	17.8	38,949
1998	87,212	8.7	7.4	13.7	13.2	16.3	19.3	21.3	40,912
Black									
1970	6,180	23.9	12.1	20.7	15.3	15.1	9.6	3.2	21,853
1980	8,847	24.9	12.9	19.0	13.5	14.6	10.5	4.7	21,319
1990	10,671	25.6	11.2	16.2	13.1	15.0	11.7	7.1	23,291
1998	12,579	21.4	10.6	17.4	13.5	14.3	13.2	9.6	25,351
Hispanic									
1970	—	—	—	—	—	—	—	—	—
1975	3,906	15.9	10.5	20.1	16.3	17.2	13.8	6.4	27,037
1980	3,906	15.9	10.5	20.1	16.3	17.2	13.8	6.4	27,037
1990	6,220	16.2	11.3	18.4	15.6	17.2	13.0	8.4	27,848
1998	9,060	15.0	10.9	17.9	16.3	15.8	14.0	10.2	28,330

Note: Blank lines indicate data not available. Figures for all households include other races not shown separately. Persons of Hispanic origin may be of any race.

Source: *Statistical Abstract, 2000,* Table 736.

($50,000 and more) gained markedly in all three categories over the entire period. In part, this gain is a result of Reagan-era tax policies. In part, it may reflect the fact that the most educated, highest-paid workers have increased the numbers of hours they work, while the least educated, lower-paid workers have experienced overall reductions in the numbers of hours they work (e.g., the ten-hour day became the eight-hour day).[68] With significantly lower marginal tax rates, the rich left a greater proportion of their income unsheltered, which made it appear the gap between rich and poor was widening. Realistically, as Alan Blinder puts it, "The central stylized fact about income inequality has been its constancy."[69]

Blinder finds that the U.S. system of cash transfer payments produced a significant impact on equality. The very rich were stripped of some of their funds, and those moneys were given to the poor. The proportion of total family incomes going to the lowest fifth of the distribution in his data (1978) rose about 1.8 percent because of all transfers—cash or in-kind. The proportion of incomes of the highest fifth declined by about the same amount. After all transfers, the lowest fifth in 1978 received 7.21 percent of family income, the highest fifth, 39.35 percent.[70] The richest fifth disposed of 5.5 times as much family income as the lowest fifth, even after the transfers. If we judge from the data in Table 28.10, the income distribution after transfers is about as unequal today as it was almost two decades ago. The transformation of the labor force has seemingly had little effect on the distribution of income.

THE PARADOX OF TERTIARY EMPLOYMENT

Since it was the tertiary sector that was of little consequence, numerically, a century ago, it is not surprising that social theorists like Karl Marx were completely off-target when they predicted that the growth of an underemployed industrial proletariat would swamp capitalism. The "workers" would rise up. Had it not been for the growth of the tertiary sector, who knows?

Since the tertiary sector eats most of the food and employs the machines and other produce of the primary and secondary sectors, it is *primary and secondary sector productivity* that has largely made possible the growth of the tertiary sector, at least at the relative incomes commonly earned by those in tertiary employment. On the other hand, it is the efficiency of the tertiary sector—its science, planning, and organization—that has made such increased productivity in the other sectors possible. The tertiary sector is a paradox in the history of capitalism. *It has been both the creation and possibly the savior of the primary and secondary sectors as the population has grown and the capacity to create food and goods has multiplied.*

It has been a maxim of economics that labor-saving machinery creates more jobs than it destroys. And, overall, this has certainly been true. The enormous increases in the number of jobs, at secularly rising real wages, in the American economy belie the fear that automation will create net unemployment. Productivity creates markets and, hence, employment. But there is no doubt that specific jobs are eliminated. That is the object! Given the history of industrial employment in the twentieth century, it is most likely going to be the tertiary sector that will generate the net increase in numbers of jobs and absorb workers left jobless in industry by rationalization of production in the twenty-first century.

The scenario these changes will produce for the foreseeable future is reminiscent of Edward Bellamy's world in his book *Looking Backward*, in which labor and physical drudgery have been separated.[71] Machines do the distasteful work. Mechanical aids to production of food and goods, centuries in their development, may well end up reducing the industrial proletariat, beloved of Marxist ideologues, to negligible proportions of the employed labor force. Hence, the tertiary options, so many of which are education-intensive, become even more crucial in the future. Hence also, the abandoned folly of those who argue that the labor force in this country is "overeducated." There is obviously no turning back from this need for education, unpleasant as the prospect is for some. An industry that uses inefficient and labor-intensive technology in a competitive world is one that must be subsidized, either directly, by sanctioned monopoly agreements, or by protection from foreign competition, and the American economy already has plenty of these. After all, a nation cannot subsidize *everything*. A subsidy transfers wealth from *A* to *B*. If there is no third party, then it is impossible to subsidize *both A* and *B*. So if American industry becomes technologically backward, it will export those goods in whose creation it is least incompetent—goods embodying low-productivity, "cheap" American labor. At this point in our history, our comparative advantage lies in those goods embodying high-productivity, educated American labor.

NOTES

1. William Baumol, *Economic Dynamics* (1951), chaps. 3 and 4.
2. *Historical Statistics*, series B 107, and *Statistical Abstract of the United States*, 2000, Table 118.
3. The figure for 1900 comes from Dora L. Costa and Richard H. Steckel, "Long-term Trends in Health, Welfare and Economic Growth in the United States," in Richard H. Steckel and Roderick Floud, eds., *Health and Welfare during Industrialization* (Chicago: University of Chicago Press, 1997). The figure for 2000 was supplied by Richard Steckel and is based on the National Health and Nutrition Examination Survey, which is conducted by the National Center for Health Statistics.
4. The fertility of black Americans has been somewhat higher than that of white Americans, but the two series have moved together and the differential has shrunk over time.
5. Richard Easterlin, *Population, Labor Force, and Long Swings in Economic Growth* (1968). See also his *Birth and Fortune* (1987).

6. Timothy J. Hatton and Jeffrey G. Williamson, *The Age of Mass Migration: Causes and Economic Impact* (Oxford: Oxford University Press, 1998), p.6.
7. George Borjas, "National Origin and the Skills of Immigrants in the Postwar Period," *Immigration and the Work Force: Economic Consequences for the United States and Source Areas* (Chicago: University of Chicago Press, 1992). An interesting discussion of current immigration policy can be found in Borjas' *Heaven's Door* (1999).
8. The corresponding figure for employed natives is around 16 percent. See Julian L. Simon, *The Economic Consequences of Immigration.*, 2nd ed. (Ann Arbor: University of Michigan Press, 1999).
9. Illegal immigrants are more likely to be unskilled. It is estimated that the flow of illegal immigrants is roughly 30 percent that of legal immigrants.
10. See George Borjas, "Assimilation, Changes in Cohort Quality and the Earnings of Immigrants." *Journal of Labor Economics*, October 1985; "Assimilation and Cohort Quality Revisited: What Happened to Immigrant Earnings in the 1980s?" *Journal of Labor Economics*, vol. 13, no. 2, April 1995; and Barry Chiswick, "The Effects of Americanization on the Earnings of Foreign-Born Men," *JPE*, October 1978. Chiswick, looking at a cross section of workers in 1970, found that, after 10 to 15 years' residence in the United States, the wages of immigrants eventually exceeded those of native-born workers. This result has been heatedly debated. See, for example, Borjas, "The Economics of Immigration," *JEL*, December 1994.
11. Timothy J. Hatton, "The Immigration Assimilation Puzzle in Late Nineteenth-Century America," *Journal of Economic History*, vol. 57, no. 1, March 1997.
12. See Zadia M. Feliciano, "The Skill and Economic Performance of Mexican Immigrants from 1910 to 1990," *Explorations in Economic History*, vol. 38, no. 3, July 2001.
13. Claudia Goldin, "The Human-Capital Century and American Leadership: Virtues of the Past," *JEH*, June 2001.
14. Corresponding figures for blacks are 5.4 years for males and 6.1 years for females in 1940; 9.8 and 10.3 years respectively in 1970. *Historical Statistics*, series H 609, 617. The current data is taken from *Statistical Abstract*, 2000, Table 292. The white and black percentages for 1998 increased substantially from what they had been in 1975; the Hispanic percentage decreased.
15. See Claudia Goldin, "Egalitarianism and the Returns to Education during the Great Transformation of American Education," *JPE*, December 1999; and "America's Graduation from High School: The Evolution and Spread of Secondary Schooling in the Twentieth Century," *JEH*, June 1998; and with Lawrence Katz, "The Legacy of U.S. Educational Leadership: Notes on Distribution and Economic Growth in the 20th Century," *American Economic Review*, vol. 91, no. 2, May 2001.
16. Sir John Hicks, *A Theory of Economic History* (1969), pp. 156–159.
17. Carmel Chiswick, "The Elasticity of Substitution Revisited: The Effects of Secular Changes in Labor Force Structure," *Journal of Labor Economics*, Fall 1985, p. 492.
18. Over 40 percent of the degree recipients were women as compared to only 14 percent in 1971.
19. These effects slowed in the 1970s. Richard Freeman, "The Evolution of the American Labor Market," in Martin Feldstein, ed., *The American Economy in Transition* (1980), pp. 382–383, and *New York Times*, 17 June 1984, p. F25.
20. John Wallis and Douglass North, "Measuring the Transaction Sector in the American Economy, 1870–1970," in Stanley Engerman and Robert Gallman, eds., *Long-Term Factors in American Economic Growth* (1986).
21. Claudia Goldin, *Understanding the Gender Gap* (1990). In particular, see chap. 4 on "The Emergence of 'Wage Discrimination'."
22. See Jonathan Hughes, "Industrialization: Economic Impact," *International Encyclopedia of the Social Sciences* (1968), vol. 7 and sources cited there.
23. The bulge in tertiary employment in the 1970s *reduced* the returns to education relatively [see Freeman (1980), Table 5.7]. This is not surprising with a stagnant job market and students graduating in record numbers.
24. Goldin (1990). See also Jane Humphries, "'...The Most Free From Objection...' The Sexual Division of Labor and Women's Work in Nineteenth Century England," *JEH*, December 1987. The balance of this section is based on Goldin's book.
25. *Ibid.*, p. 13.
26. *Ibid.*, p. 30.
27. *Ibid.*, chap. 2. For more on women in manufacturing jobs, see Alice Kessler-Harris, *Out to Work: A History of Wage-Earning Women in the United States* (1982).
28. *Ibid.*, p. 67.
29. *Ibid.*, p. 68.
30. Occupational segregation, which has always been high, was probably more severe in the nineteenth than it has been in the twentieth century.
31. Goldin (1990), p. 118.
32. *Ibid.*, p. 173. This is not to say that all discrimination against women ended in the 1950s, just that overt forms such as the marriage bar became too expensive to continue.
33. *Ibid.*, p. 27.
34. Elyce Rotella, "The Transformation of the American Office: Changes in Employment and Technology," *JEH*, March 1981, p. 52. See also Charles Wootton and Barbara Kemmerer, "The Changing Genderization of Bookkeeping in the United States, 1870–1930," *Business History Review*, vol. 70, no. 4, Winter 1996, that discusses how accounting became a male profession while bookkeeping became a female trade.

35. Today, approximately 60 percent of men and 90 percent of women are employed in the tertiary sector.
36. Another consequence of the increased independence of women in American society has been an increase in poverty. See Linda Barrington and Cecilia Conrad, "At What Cost a Room of Her Own? Factors Contributing to the Feminization of Poverty Among Prime-Age Women, 1939–1959," JEH, June 1994.
37. See Francine D. Blau, "Trends in the Well-Being of American Women, 1970–1995," *JEL*, March 1998. While Blau documents substantial progress over her 25-year study period, she notes that some discrimination remains. See also Freeman (1980), pp. 356–363.
38. Goldin finds ambiguity in explanations of persisting wage differentials between men and women, differentials usually explained simply as "discrimination," because there seems to be no other explanation. She conjectures that there has been a persistent underinvestment by women in "job-related skills" by successive cohorts whose idea of their own future participation and work experience was primarily based upon that of their mothers. There are other factors, though, including continuous job experience, that help account for the persisting differentials. Claudia Goldin, "The Gender Gap in Historical Perspective," in Peter Kilby, ed., *Quantity and Quiddity: Essays in U.S. Economic History* (Middletown, CT: Wesleyan University Press, 1987). See also Goldin (1990), Tables 2.1 and 3.1.
39. Claudia Goldin, "The Female Labor Force and American Economic Growth, 1890–1980," in Engerman and Gallman, eds, *Long-Term Factors in American Economic Growth*. Also see Goldin (1990), pp. 186–189.
40. See Goldin (1990), chap. 8.
41. See Craig Heinicke, "African-American Migration and Mechanized Cotton Harvesting, 1950–1960," *EEH*, October 1994.
42. William Collins, "When the Tide Turned: Immigration and the Delay of the Great Black Migration," *JEH*, September 1997. Collins showed that blacks moved at times and to places where immigrants were relatively scarce, suggesting that immigration restrictions such as those adopted after World War I are important in explaining the timing of the Great Migration.
43. James Smith and Finis Welch, "Black Economic Progress After Myrdal," *JEL*, June 1989. See also Thomas Maloney, "Wage Compression and Wage Inequality Between Black and White Males in the United States, 1940–1960," *JEH*, June 1995. Maloney notes almost all the progress occurred in the 1940s.
44. The numbers for Hispanics were even lower, another 10 percent. Median weekly earnings were $324 overall ($343 for males and $305 for females).
45. Smith and Welch (1989), p. 538. The beginning of this improvement is discussed in Robert Margo, *Race and Schooling in the South, 1880–1950: An Economic History* (Chicago: University of Chicago Press, 1990).
46. *Statistical Abstract of the U.S., 2000*, Table 736.
47. See Marcus Alexis, "Assessing 50 Years of African-American Economic Status, 1940–1990," *AER*, May 1998. Alexis also notes there was continued racial discrimination and reduced government enforcement of the anti-discrimination statutes. For the earlier part of the twentieth century, see Price V. Fishback, "Operations of 'Unfettered' Labor Markets: Exit and Voice in American Labor Markets at the Turn of the Century," *JEL*, June 1998, especially section 5. The Fishback article is an excellent review of labor markets in the first part of the twentieth century.
48. Robert W. Fairlie and William A. Sundstrom, "The Racial Unemployment Gap in Long-Run Perspective," *American Economic Review*, vol. 87, no. 2, May 1997.
49. Robert Higgs, "Accumulation of Property by Southern Blacks Before World War I," *American Economic Review*, vol. 72, no. 4, September 1982.
50. Leo Troy, "The End of Unionism: A Reappraisal," *Society*, March/April 1995.
51. For example, H. J. Habakkuk, *American and British Technology in the 19th Century* (1962); Nathan Rosenberg, *Technology and American Economic Growth* (1972), and Rosenberg and David Mowery, *Technology and the Pursuit of Economic Growth* (1989).
52. David B. Sicilia, "Distant Proximity: Writing the History of American Business since 1945," *Business and Economic History*, vol. 26, no. 1, Fall 1997, p. 269.
53. It is thus not accidental that the United Kingdom joins the United States at the bottom of the rankings for productivity increases in the 1960s and 1970s. Belgium, Denmark, France, West Germany, Japan, and the Netherlands all outstripped us by 100 percent between 1967 and 1977 in manufacturing productivity increases [see Freeman (1980), p. 355, Table 5.3].
54. Troy (1995), p. 27.
55. *Statistical Abstract*, 2000, Table 712.
56. *Ibid.* 80 percent of unionized professionals are in the public sector.
57. The study is reported in Walter Galenson, *The American Labor Movement, 1955–1995* (1996), p. 59f. Galenson notes that AFL-CIO membership is roughly 80 percent of total union membership; the vast majority of the remaining 20 percent are members of the National Education Association, the largest single union in the labor movement.
58. Galenson (1996) notes there were parallel trends internationally to those reported here for the United States; the trends were most pronounced in the United States.
59. Susan Carter and Richard Sutch, "Myth of the Industrial Scrap Heap: A Revisionist View of Turn-of-the-Century American Retirement," *JEH*, March 1996, p. 19.
60. Brian Gratton, "The Poverty of Impoverishment Theory: The Economic Well-Being of the Elderly,

1890–1950," *JEH*, March 1996. See also Carole Haber and Brian Gratton, *Old Age and the Search for Security: An American Social History* (1994).

61. Dora Costa, *The Evolution of Retirement: An American Economic History, 1880–1990* (1998).
62. There has been some controversy over the trend in retirement before 1940, one that leads to different interpretations of the role played by the introduction of Social Security. Roger Ransom and Richard Sutch, "The Labor of Older Americans: Retirement of Men On and Off the Job, 1870–1937," *Journal of Economic History*, vol. 46, no. 1, March 1986, argued that labor force participation rates for older men did not decline before Social Security. Their results depend on the assumption that older men who were unemployed for more than six months were really retired, but they were erroneously classified as being in the labor force. Robert Margo, "The Labor Force Participation of Older Americans in 1900: Further Results," *Explorations in Economic History*, vol. 30, no. 4, October 1993, showed statistically that those older Americans who were retired in 1900 were dissimilar to those who were unemployed for more than six months.
63. Jon Moen, "Rural Nonfarm Households: Leaving the Farm and the Retirement of Older Men, 1860–1980," *Social Science History*, vol. 18, no. 1, Spring 1994. This is in agreement with what Costa found.
64. Vilfredo Pareto, the great Italian economist, believed that economic growth, GDP rising more rapidly than population, was the *only* way income distribution could become more equal. Stanley Lebergott, *The American Economy: Income, Wealth, and Want* (1976), p. 144.
65. Lebergott (1976), Part I. Basic poverty data for the period 1960–1993 can be found in *Statistical Abstract*, 2000, Table 760.
66. *Statistical Abstract*, 2000, Table 692.
67. *Ibid.*, Table 689. It should also be noted that the CPI Commission reported that there was a 1.1 percent upward bias in the Consumer Price Index. See Michael J. Boskin, Ellen R. Dulberger, Robert J. Gordon, Zvi Griliches, and Dale W. Jorgenson, "Consumer Prices, the Consumer Price Index, and the Cost of Living," *Journal of Economic Perspectives*, vol. 12, no. 1, Winter 1998. It should be borne in mind that calculations of real variables using the CPI result in underestimates (for example, median income in Table 28.11 and economic growth in general).
68. See, for example, Dora L. Costa, "The Unequal Work Day: A Long-Term View," *American Economic Review*, vol. 88, no. 2, May 1998.
69. Alan Blinder, "The Level and Distribution of Economic Well-Being," in Feldstein (1980), p. 433. Blinder's data show that, between 1952 and 1977, the share of the top 5 percent of family incomes fell, but that of the lowest 20 percent rose only slightly.
70. *Ibid.*, p. 446, and Table 6.18, p. 445.
71. Edward Bellamy, *Looking Backward: 2000–1887* (Boston: Ticknor, 1888).

SUGGESTED READINGS

Articles

Alexis, Marcus. "Assessing 50 Years of African-American Economic Status, 1940–1990." *American Economic Review*, vol. 88, no. 2, May 1998.

Barrington, Linda, and Cecilia A. Conrad. "At What Cost a Room of Her Own? Factors Contributing to the Feminization of Poverty Among Prime-Age Women, 1939–1959." *Journal of Economic History*, vol. 54, no. 2, June 1994.

Blau, Francine D. "Trends in the Well-Being of American Women, 1970–1995." *Journal of Economic Literature*, vol. XXXVI, no. 1, March 1998.

Borjas, George J. "Assimilation, Changes in Cohort Quality and the Earnings of Immigrants." *Journal of Labor Economics*, vol. 3, no. 4, October 1985.

——. "The Economics of Immigration." *Journal of Economic Literature*, vol. XXXII, no. 4, December 1994.

Carter, Susan B., and Richard Sutch. "Myth of the Industrial Scrap Heap: A Revisionist View of Turn-of-the-Century American Retirement." *Journal of Economic History*, vol. 56, no. 1, March 1996.

Chiswick, Barry R. "The Effects of Americanization on the Earnings of Foreign-Born Men." *Journal of Political Economy*, vol. 86, no. 5, October 1978.

Chiswick, Carmel U. "The Elasticity of Substitution Revisited: The Effects of Secular Changes in Labor Force Structure." *Journal of Labor Economics*, vol. 3, no. 4, October 1985.

Collins, William. "When the Tide Turned: Immigration and the Delay of the Great Black Migration." *Journal of Economic History*, vol. 57, no. 3, September 1997.

Fishback, Price V. "Operations of 'Unfettered' Labor Markets: Exit and Voice in American Labor Markets at the Turn of the Century." *Journal of Economic Literature*, vol. XXXVI, no. 2, June 1998.

Freeman, Richard B. "The Evolution of the American Labor Market, 1948–80." In Martin Feldstein, ed., *The American Economy in Transition*. Chicago: University of Chicago Press, 1980.

Goldin, Claudia. "The Female Labor Force and American Economic Growth, 1890–1980." In Stanley Engerman and Robert Gallman, eds., *Long-Term Factors in American Economic Growth*. Chicago: The University of Chicago Press, 1986.

———. "America's Graduation from High School: The Evoution and Spread of Secondary Schooling in the Twentieth Century." *Journal of Economic History*, vol. 58, no. 2, June 1998.

———. "Egalitarianism and the Returns to Education during the Great Transformation of American Education." *Journal of Political Economy*, vol. 107, no. 6, part 2, December 1999.

———. "The Human-Capital Century and American Leadership: Virtues of the Past." *Journal of Economic History*, vol. 61, no. 2, June 2001.

———, and Donald Parsons. "Parental Altruism and Self-Interest: Child Labor among Late-Nineteenth Century American Families." *Economic Inquiry*, vol. XXVII, no. 4, October 1989.

Gratton, Brian. "The Poverty of Impoverishment Theory: The Economic Well-Being of the Elderly, 1890–1950." *Journal of Economic History*, vol. 56, no. 1, March 1996.

Gwartney, James. "Changes in the Nonwhite/White Income Ratio—1939–1967." *American Economic Review*, vol. LX, no. 5, December 1970.

Heinicke, Craig. "African-American Migration and Mechanized Cotton Harvesting, 1950–1960." *Explorations in Economic History*, vol. 31, no. 4, October 1994.

Hughes, Jonathan. "Industrialization: Economic Impact." *International Encyclopedia of the Social Sciences*, vol. 7. New York: Macmillan, 1968.

Humphries, Jane. "'...The Most Free From Objection...' The Sexual Division of Labor and Women's Work in Nineteenth Century England." *Journal of Economic History*, vol. XLVII, no. 4, December 1987.

Maloney, Thomas. "Wage Compression and Wage Inequality Between Black and White Males in the United States, 1940–1960." *Journal of Economic History*, vol. 54, no. 2, June 1994.

Rotella, Elyce J. "Women's Labor Force Participation and the Decline of the Family Economy in the United States." *Explorations in Economic History*, vol. 17, no. 2, April 1980.

———. "The Transformation of the American Office: Changes in Employment and Technology." *Journal of Economic History*, vol. XLI, no. 1, March 1981.

Sexton, Brendon. "The Working Class Experience." *American Economic Review*, vol. LXII, no. 2, May 1972.

Smith, James P., and Finis B. Welch. "Black Economic Progress After Myrdal." *Journal of Economic Literature*, vol. XXVII, no. 2, June 1989.

Troy, Leo. "The End of Unionism: A Reappraisal." *Society*, vol. 32, no. 3, March/April 1995.

Weiss, Thomas. "Urbanization and the Growth of the Service Workforce." *Explorations in Economic History*, vol. 8, no. 3, Spring 1971.

Wallis, John J., and Douglass C. North. "Measuring the Transaction Sector in the American Economy, 1870–1970." In Stanley Engerman and Robert Gallman, eds., *Long-Term Factors in American Economic Growth*. Chicago: The University of Chicago Press, 1986.

Books

Baumol, William. *Economic Dynamics*. New York: Macmillan, 1951.

Benson, Susan Porter. *Counter Cultures: Saleswomen, Managers, and Customers in American Department Stores, 1890–1940*. Champaign: University of Illinois Press, 1986.

Borjas, George J. *Heaven's Door: Immigration Policy and the American Economy*. Princeton: Princeton University Press, 1999.

Costa, Dora L. *The Evolution of Retirement: An American Economic History, 1880–1990*. Chicago: University of Chicago Press, 1998.

Easterlin, Richard. *Population, Labor Force, and Long Swings in Economic Growth: The American Experience*. New York: Columbia University Press, 1968.

———. *Birth and Fortune: The Impact of Numbers on Personal Welfare*, 2nd ed. Chicago: University of Chicago Press, 1987.

Galenson, Walter. *The American Labor Movement, 1955–1995*. Westport, CT: Greenwood Press, 1996.

Goldin, Claudia. *Understanding the Gender Gap: An Economic History of American Women*. New York: Oxford University Press, 1990.

Habakkuk, H.J. *American and British Technology in the 19th Century*. Cambridge: Cambridge University Press, 1962.

Haber, Carole, and Brian Gratton. *Old Age and the Search for Security: An American Social History*. Bloomington: Indiana University Press, 1994.

Hicks, Sir John. *A Theory of Economic History*. New York: Oxford University Press, 1969.

Hughes, Jonathan. *The Vital Few*. New York: Oxford University Press, 1986.

Kessler-Harris, Alice. *Out to Work: A History of Wage-Earning Women in the United States*. New York: Oxford University Press, 1982.

Lebergott, Stanley. *The American Economy: Income, Wealth, and Want*. Princeton: Princeton University Press, 1976.

Owen, John D. *Working Lives: The American Work Force Since 1920*. Lexington, MA: D. C. Heath, 1986.

Rosenberg, Nathan. *Technology and American Economic Growth*. New York: Harper Torchbooks, 1972.

———, and David C. Mowery. *Technology and the Pursuit of Economic Growth*. New York: Cambridge University Press, 1989.

CHAPTER TWENTY-NINE

Postwar Industry and Agriculture

It is easy to "cry wolf" about American manufacturing. As you learned in Chapter 28, most of the expansion of employment opportunities since World War II has been in professions and services. Agricultural employment has declined absolutely, and the expansion of employment in manufacturing has been stagnant in absolute terms and declining proportionally.

Some relevant numbers are shown in Table 29.1. There were a few more production workers in 1999 (12.7 million) than there had been in 1947 (11.9 million). The number had increased to 14 million in the late 1960s and held around 13.5 million for most of the 1970s. The balance of the economy grew. Consequently, while production workers were more than 20 percent of the labor force in 1947, by 1999 their numbers had fallen to below 10 percent. The increase in production was attended by an enormous rise in labor productivity—that is, output per worker.

This trend is not new, of course. American manufacturing has striven to save on expensive labor costs

TABLE 29.1 Manufacturing Employment and the Labor Force, 1947–1999

	Number of Workers (in millions)			*Percentage of Total Labor Force*	
Year	*Total Civilian Labor Force*	*Manufacturing Workers*	*Production Workers*	*Mfg. Workers*	*Production Workers*
1947	59.4	14.5	11.9	24.4%	20.1%
1950	62.2	14.5	11.8	23.3	18.9
1960	69.6	16.2	12.2	23.2	17.5
1970	82.7	18.0	13.5	21.7	16.4
1980	100.9	20.6	13.9	20.5	13.8
1990	126.4	18.8	12.1	14.9	9.6
1999	139.4	18.4	12.7	13.2	9.1

Sources: *Historical Statistics,* series D 14, P 3, 4, 5; *Statistical Abstract, 1992,* Tables 608, 1243; *2000,* Tables 643, 684.

historically. A labor-saving bias has been a determining factor in the choice of technology from very early in the industrial history of the United States. But the post-World War II record in this regard has really been extraordinary. The Federal Reserve System's Index of Industrial Production (1992 = 100) stood at 30.2 in 1955 and reached 143.6 in 2000, an increase of 375 percent, while total manufacturing employment rose a mere 13 percent in the same period, and the number of production workers decreased by 2.3 percent. Over the entire period, then, physical output in manufacturing industries utterly outstripped the increases in the numbers of employed workers. But the increase was not evenly achieved; some periods saw far higher growth than did others.

DISTRIBUTION OF EMPLOYMENT AND VALUE ADDED

In what industries are American manufacturing workers to be found in greatest numbers, and what industries contribute most to the national income? When we consider the clamor about the fate of the "industrial rust belt," the fate of the steel and automobile industries, Table 29.2 may come as quite a surprise. The table shows the composition of employment in 1980 and 1999 and value added in 1980 and 1996. According to Table 29.2, there are almost 1 million fewer manufacturing workers in 1999 than there were in 1980; employment in this sector fell by 4.5 percent over these years. A quick glance at the table indicates

TABLE 29.2 Industrial Distribution of Employment and Value Added in Manufacturing (ranked by ME in 1999)

	1980 Number[a]	*Percent of Total Manufacturing Employment*	*Percent of Value Added by Manufacturing*	*1999 Number*[a]	*Percent of Total Manufacturing Employment*[b]	*Percent of Value Added by Manufacturing*[b]
>5% ME						
35 Machinery, exc Elect	2411	11.7	12.9	2129	11.5	10.7
37 Transportation	1771	8.6	9.9	1855	10.1	10.1
20 Food	1537	7.4	9.7	1685	9.1	10.2
36 Electric Machinery	1963	9.5	9.5	1661	9.0	10.5
27 Printing	1263	6.1	5.7	1553	8.4	7.5
34 Fabricated Metal	1617	7.8	7.5	1489	8.1	6.2
28 Chemicals	910	4.4	9.5	1035	5.6	11.1
30 Rubber	703	3.4	2.9	1019	5.5	4.3
<5% ME						
38 Instruments	616	3.0	3.6	839	4.6	5.6
24 Lumber	698	3.4	2.3	826	4.5	2.4
33 Primary Metal	1096	5.3	6.2	690	3.7	4.0
23 Apparel	1307	6.3	3.0	685	3.7	2.2
26 Paper	645	3.1	3.8	659	3.6	4.1
32 Stone, Clay, Glass	613	3.0	3.1	569	3.1	2.6
22 Textiles	817	4.0	2.5	562	3.0	1.9
25 Furniture	473	2.3	1.5	540	2.9	1.6
39 Miscellaneous	429	2.1	1.6	387	2.1	1.5
29 Petroleum	149	0.7	3.2	137	0.7	1.8
31 Leather	232	1.1	0.6	74	0.4	0.3
21 Tobacco	58	0.3	0.8	39	0.2	1.5

[a] Numbers are in thousands of employees.
[b] The Total Manufacturing Employment data is for 1999; the Value Added by Manufacturing data is for 1996.

Source: *Statstical Abstract, 1982-1983,* Table 1382, *1999,* Table 1233; *2000,* Table 684.

that printing and rubber both experienced greater than 2 percent increases in employment, while apparel suffered a more than 2 percent decrease. Instruments experienced a 2 percent increase in the percent of value added for which it was responsible, while both machinery and primary metals suffered more than 2 percent decreases. In general, Table 29.2 shows that the larger employers are also the larger producers of value added. The machinery industry ranked first in value added in 1910. It still ranks first in employment, and second in value added. The greatest exceptions to the rule are chemicals, petroleum and coal, and tobacco that share the characteristic their contribution to value added far exceeds their shares of employment. The low-wage manufacturing industries are those in which the opposite is true.

STRUCTURE OF RECENT INDUSTRIAL GROWTH

Until the downturn in 1982, there had not been sudden changes in industrial structure for a long time. The recent rates of growth of output for durable and nondurable manufactures are shown in Figures 29.1 and 29.2. In each case the year 1967 is taken as the base year against which the output reached in 1999 is measured. The indexes are weighted by their contributions to value added in the aggregates (all manufacturing, all durables, all nondurables). Among durable goods shown in Figure 29.1, there are several features of note. First, among the sectors growing slower than the average are primary metals and transportation equipment, two areas from which the cries for protection have been loudest, and where, in the cases of steel and automobiles, significant protection has been granted (as will be discussed later in this chapter). The decline of mining in the United States is also clear. Machinery and electronics are among the largest employment groups and producers of value added, and they have also grown the most rapidly. Their growth has exceeded that of durable manufacturing as a whole.

FIGURE 29.1 U.S. Industrial Production Indexes, 1967–1999 (Durable Goods)

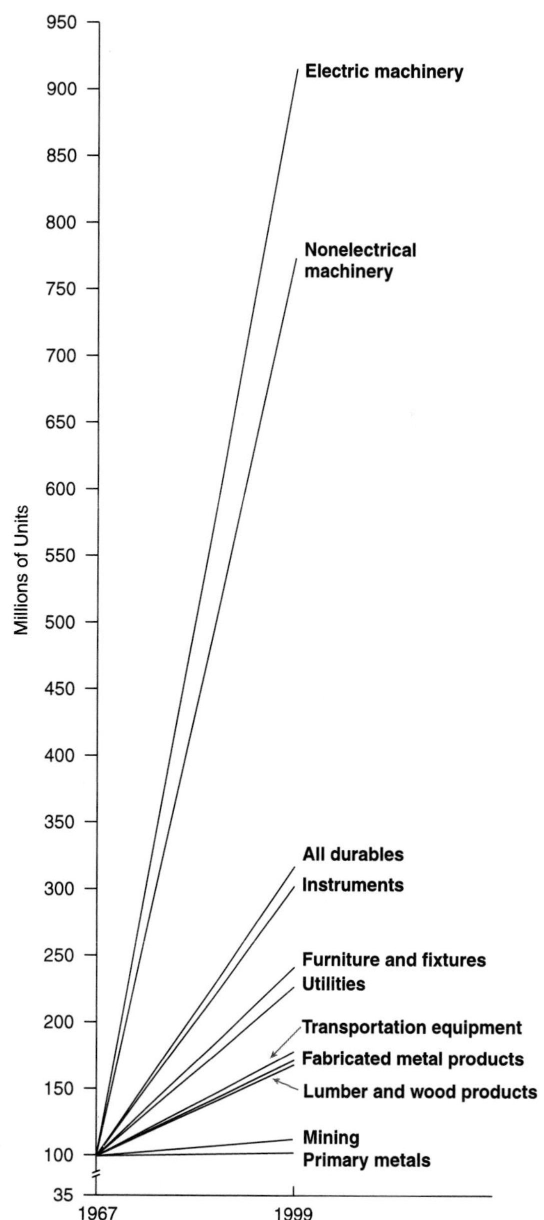

Note: 1967=100.
Source: *Statistical Abstract, 2000,* Table 1238.

Among nondurable manufactures, the modern expansion of rubber and plastics (chemicals) has gone "off the charts" compared with other sectors. All

FIGURE 29.2 U.S. Industrial Production Indexes, 1967–1999 (Nondurable Goods)

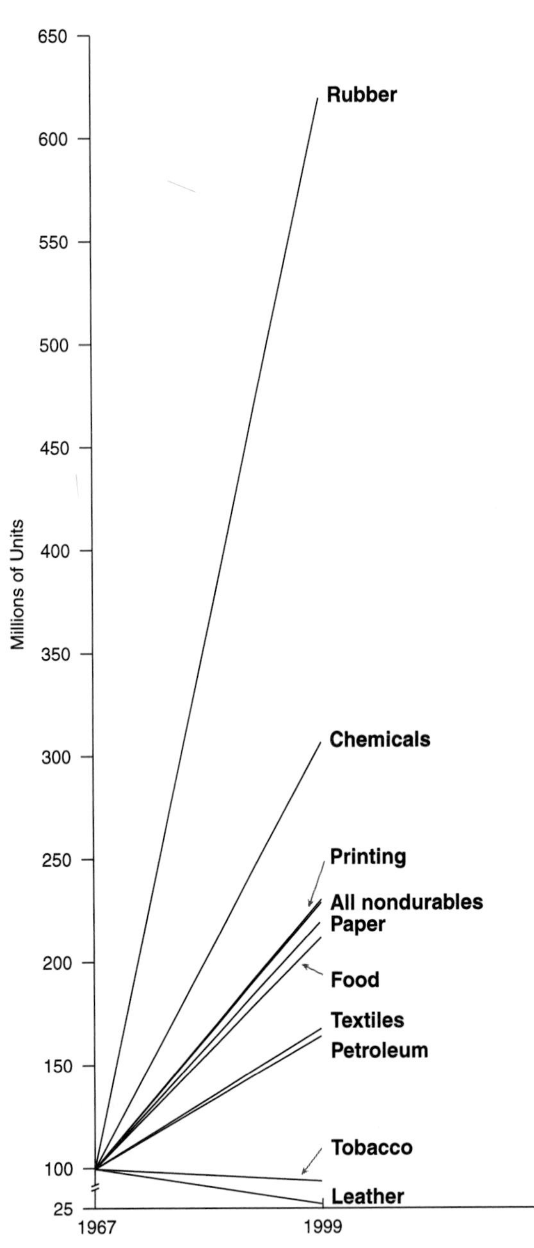

Note: 1967=100.
Source: *Statistical Abstract, 2000,* Table 1238.

major nondurable sectors expanded their output between 1967 and 1999. Only the output of tobacco and leather goods actually declined. Textile mill products has been a relatively slow-growth industry. Like autos and steel, it has encountered significant competition from foreign producers, and, as with autos and steel, the leaders of both capital and labor visited Washington, D.C., in search of protection, and they received it.

THE PRODUCTIVITY ISSUE

Markets are made by productivity, by economic growth; increased income per head is the product, by simple multiplication, of rising output per hour worked. If productivity slows down, so does economic growth. In a simple model like the one in Chapter 3 where the number of furrows plowed per hour changed with no change in the plow, the measurement of productivity was simple enough. But when one is considering whole industries or economies, productivity measurement becomes an arcane business.

From the mid-1960s to the present, American productivity growth rates measured in terms of output per paid hour followed a *U*-shaped path (see Figure 29.3). Growth rates fell in the late 1960s and 1970s, both absolutely and in comparison with other countries. The Department of Commerce estimates that U.S. industrial productivity grew at an annual rate of 3.2 percent in 1948–1965, 2.4 percent in 1965–1973 (a one-third decline in the rate of increase), 1.1 percent in 1973–1978 (a 55 percent decline from 1965–1973) and, finally, −0.8 percent, an absolute decline, in 1978–1980.[1] Such a poor performance would help to explain the gathering stagflation—increasing inflation and unemployment—at the end of the 1970s. In addition, tax revenues declined, and the balance of payments was in deficit. Labor productivity followed a similar downward path; Michael Darby estimates that it rose at an annual rate of 2.6 percent in 1948–1965, 1.9 percent in 1965–1973, and only .05 percent in 1973–1979.[2]

Supporting Bureau of Labor Statistics data for these patterns are given in Table 29.3; the annual data for business is what appears in Figure 29.3. The average annual rate of increase for manufacturing in

FIGURE 29.3 Productivity, 1951–1998

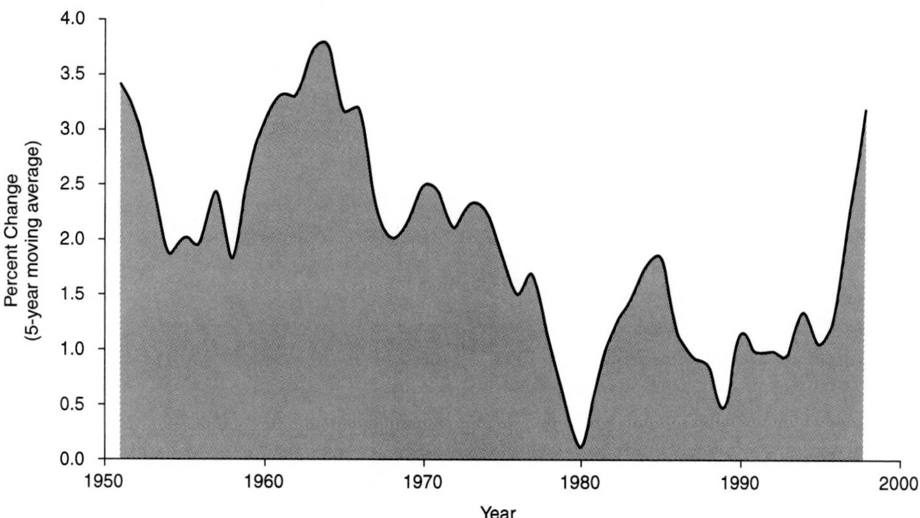

Source: U.S. Bureau of Labor Statistics, business productivity, series PRS84006093.

1975–1980 was only 1.7, only 1.2 for the entire business sector. These growth rates are lower than those for most of the postwar period and certainly are lower than the productivity growth figures for America's major trading partners in Europe and Asia in those years.[3] It has only been in the 1990s that the annual percentage increases for the business sector show an upward trend and a return to the levels of the 1960s.

TABLE 29.3 Indexes of Productivity

	Output Per Paid Hour (1992=100)		
Year	***Business***	***Nonfarm Business***	***Manufacturing***
1950	36.9	41.7	34.0
1955	43.3	47.4	38.8
1960	48.8	51.9	41.8
1965	59.6	62.4	48.5
1970	67.0	68.9	54.2
1975	75.8	77.4	64.3
1980	80.4	82.0	70.1
1985	88.7	89.3	82.3
1990	95.2	95.3	92.9
1995	102.6	102.8	109.0
2000	118.6	118.1	138.5

Source: Bureau of Labor Statistics, Business: series PRS84006093, Nonfarm Business: series PRS85006093, Manufacturing: series PRS30006093

During the 1980s, productivity growth rates began to increase, although they remained at the slower rates of the 1970s in contrast to the much higher rates of the 1960s. During the 1980s, output per hour in the business sector grew at an average rate of 1.7 percent per year. This is slightly higher than the growth rates during the period 1975–1980, but slightly less than those during the period 1973–1978, the period just before the "productivity crisis." Nonfarm business productivity growth peaked in 1978 and then started on a period of slow decline from which it has only recently recovered. Manufacturing productivity in the 1980s was greater than in the 1970s; it recovered from the low that it reached in 1982, and has recently been at very high rates.

What the data reveal is that we experienced a "productivity crisis" in the late 1970s from which we have now largely recovered. The alleged causes of the crisis are numerous—from the loss of the work ethic to excessive government regulation; from too low savings rates to too little emphasis on science and mathematics in the schools. There is a long literature tying the reduction in the investment of manufacturing firms to the reduction in public infrastructure investment.[4] In spite of the fact that the economy has largely recovered, some of the causes (e.g., low savings rates) remain subjects of concern.

When such startling changes occur, it is natural for economists, politicians, preachers, and others to try to explain them. But recall what a range of *different* production experiences these aggregate data cover. As in Figures 29.1 and 29.2, the actual growth of physical output varied widely indeed among industries. The growth of electrical and nonelectrical machinery meant that the index of production for all durable goods production over the period 1967–1999 was a third higher than that for nondurable goods production. As can be seen, primary metal manufacturing production (e.g., steel) was only a little higher (2.9 percent) in 1999 than it had been in 1967; as recently as 1994 it had been lower than in 1967. On the nondurable side, tobacco and leather in 1999 are below the production levels they experienced in 1967. Any statement about production—or productivity—that purports to cover all of industry must be viewed with the greatest caution. Still, there has been a widespread consensus about the decline of American industrial productivity in the late 1970s.

Alfred Chandler, Jr., noted that the productivity slowdown coincided with a leveling of consumer demand, a decrease in the number of new products introduced to the market, and the "unleashing" of global competition.[5] Concern about American competitiveness was accompanied with a renewed burst of merger and acquisition activity that in the 1960s had increased the return on investment and reduced competition.[6] To better understand the "productivity crisis," Chandler assigned manufacturing industries to one of three categories: high-, stable-, and low-tech. High-tech industries were those with the largest expenditures on research and development.[7] Firms in these industries competed by supplying new and improved products. Stable-tech industries continued to supply more or less the same product lines. They competed through product design and product improvements. Lastly, low-tech industries, those with the smallest expenditures on research and development, competed largely through marketing and distribution.

Table 29.4 lists the industries in each of these divisions. Of the high-tech industries, only electronics experienced difficulties in global markets, as we shall see below. The majority of merger activity in this category was for long-term strategic purposes. The majority of such activity in the low-tech industries was to realign firms—to subtract divisions that did not match a company's core business and to add those that did. Since these industries felt little pressure from the international market, these mergers and acquisitions also can be considered as for long-term strategic purposes. Bronwyn Hall discovered that, from the late 1970s to the late 1980s, low-tech firms, as well as those in the short-horizon, stable-tech category, were far more likely to experience a leveraged buyout than other firms.[8]

Long-horizon, stable-tech industries were under the most pressure from the global marketplace, particularly the Germans and the Japanese. Hall found that, on average, twice as many firms in this category assumed large increases in leverage. While firms in this category were under pressure to maintain their investment in research and development, as well as in the capital required to compete with respect to product design and production (e.g., computers), research and development was not as important to them as to firms in the other categories. Indeed, Hall found that firms in this category reduced their investment in both plant and equipment and in research and development. She attributes this to two features of the U.S.

TABLE 29.4 Division of Manufacturing Industries by Category

High-tech	*Stable-tech*	*Low-tech*
Pharmaceuticals	Long-horizon	Food
Electrical equipment	Chemicals	Textiles
Electronics (incl. computers)	Petroleum	Lumber
	Primary metals	
Aircraft-aerospace	Autos and transport	
Instruments		
	Short-horizon	
	Rubber and plastics	
	Stone, clay, and glass	
	Fabricated metals	

Source: Bronwyn Hall, "Corporate Restructuring and Investment Horizons in the United States, 1976–1987," *Business History Review*, Spring 1994, p. 123.

economy in these years: the fact that the corporate tax system was biased toward debt finance and the extremely high interest rates of these years.[9] Firms borrowed what they needed, but, at double-digit interest rates, they didn't borrow much.

Alternatively, consider the idea that there has been no decline attributable to the usual "causes." Michael Darby proposed a series of reasonable adjustments to the labor input that leave doubt about the usual explanations. Darby argued that the adjustments for changes in recent labor force composition were due to (a) *age* (the labor force had gotten younger with the entry of the "baby boom" of the 1950s), (b) *gender* (the big expansion of women reentering the labor force), (c) *immigration* (many more recent arrivals were in the labor force than usual), and (d) *education* (the younger, more female, more foreign workers had yet to achieve the appropriate levels of knowledge to boost their productivity). Thus Darby said that the decline in productivity was "statistical myopia."

Once Darby makes what he construes to be the proper adjustments, employee productivity increased at an average rate of 1.52 percent per annum over the entire period 1900–1979 and by 1.54 percent in 1900–1929, 1.51 percent in 1929–1965, and by 1.53 percent in 1965–1979.[10] Division into other subperiods produced different results, but the point is that "normalization" of the labor input over this century eliminated the big productivity decline. As Darby puts it:

> Thus, it appears that there is no substantial variation in trend private productivity growth over the twentieth century to be explained by variations in regulation growth, oil prices, the failure of American management, labor, or any of the other popular whipping boys.[11]

Observed declines in conventional labor productivity measures are really due to temporary changes in the quality of a single input. There are still declines in conventionally measured physical output per worker-hour. But not to worry, it will pass.

In the cases of steel and autos, the old-time heart of American industrialization, the results of recent economic history are perhaps more easily explained. We can look at these two industries as exemplars on the left side of the *U*-shaped American productivity path. We will look at semi-conductors and computers as exemplars on the right side later.

THE OLD ECONOMY: DECLINE OF AMERICAN PREEMINENCE IN STEEL AND AUTOMOBILES

Beginning in the mid-1970s, the country was alarmed by successive crises involving manufacturing's supposed decline. In the 1992 election campaign, Bill Clinton promised to promote the "reindustrialization" of America through government policy. Others who shared this goal urged that laws be passed to prevent existing industrial plants from closing down or relocating to more salubrious climates, that controls be put on American foreign investment to stop jobs from being "exported," that even more stringent tariffs and quotas be imposed to keep foreign products out of the country. Great and famous industrial plants like Firestone's Dayton, Ohio, tire plant and U.S. Steel's giant Chicago Southworks were left by their owners to rust, with thousands of men and women thrown out of work.[12]

It seemed like a strange nightmare. United States Steel bought an oil company (Marathon) and changed its logo to USX (an attempt to exist incognito?); General Motors cut a deal with Japan's Toyota to manufacture autos of Japanese design in California.[13] Only a generation earlier learned economists had written of the permanent "dollar shortage" brought on by America's invincible industrial superiority, impermeable to any foreign competition. The United States, it was now said, faced inevitable industrial decline, due to superior foreign enterprise. Steel and automobiles, the core industries of the American economy, were in deep trouble.

Since arrangements can be made to lease and buy patent rights (and to manufacture under license to patent holders), and since internationally traded machinery incorporates new technology and the world of technical ideas is essentially unified, it is not too much of an exaggeration to say that the entire world could employ a uniform technology. No single country necessarily has a lock on any set of production techniques and accompanying machinery. Differences in the technologies actually deployed must be due to such phenomena as relative factor proportions, quality of management and labor force, government policies, availability of relevant financial infrastructure, and access to markets.[14] No seasoned observer who has witnessed the rise of manufacturing industry in such places as Hungary, Israel, Taiwan, South Korea, Mississippi, and Idaho would bet against the appearance of significant manufacturing establishments in almost any reasonably situated economy—for example, mainland China.[15] To be sure, the world of manufacturing excellence is still concentrated in those countries that were the leaders in, say 1940, but it is reasonable to expect successful newcomers, and they have appeared. Consider the record of American and world steel output shown in Table 29.5.

Steel was the metal of twentieth-century industrialization—cheap steel for buildings, machinery, roads, bridges, the triumph of the nineteenth-century's "second industrial revolution," starting with Bessemer's converter in 1856 and ending with the banks of open-hearth furnaces in Pittsburgh and along the Great Lakes in the 1890s. Cheap iron ores, superior and cheap coking coals, a gathered and capable labor force, and huge markets linked by rail and water had made steel the "natural" basis of American industrial expansion. After the economic disaster of the 1930s depression, World War II added another burst of demand, which was followed by further expansion in the postwar years. By 1950, nearly 47 percent of world output was made in the United States. Then came another worldwide surge in steel output, and this time, American industry did not expand. By the 1980s, the American share of world output was about one-tenth of the total, and American industry was under siege from import competition, from Japan, Europe, Canada, and even from Brazil.

A similar history may be seen in the record of motor vehicle production shown in Table 29.6. Between 1960 and 1980, world production of motor vehicles more than doubled in response to the general economic expansion of the 1960s and 1970s. But American industry, the largest in the world in 1960, did not participate in that growth. American auto exports grew, but so did imports.

Motor vehicle imports, about 5 percent of domestic sales in 1960, reached 26.7 percent in 1980 and 25.8 percent in 1990, before falling back to 19.3 percent in 1995. Iron and steel imports were less than 7 percent of U.S. consumption in 1960, 14.8 percent by 1990, and 19.1 percent in 1994, despite several protective measures taken to restrict imports. By the end of the 1970s, both steel and automobiles (along with a vast range of related employments) were "in trouble," begging in Washington for protection from foreign competition. Since these two huge industries, dominated by giant firms like United States Steel and General Motors, were to media observers the prime symbols of American industrial power, panic reigned in the media. What had happened? Were the industries that entrepreneurs such as Andrew Carnegie, William Durant, Henry Ford, and Alfred Sloan

TABLE 29.5 World and U.S. Steel Production, 1950–1998

	Crude Steel Production		*Percent*
Year	*World* *(Millions of Net Tons)*	*United States*	*U.S. of World*
1950	207.9	96.8	46.6
1960	379.7	99.3	26.0
1970	654.2	131.5	20.1
1980	790.4	111.0	14.2
1985	792.9	88.3	11.1
1990	849.4	98.9	11.6
1995	829.4	104.9	12.6
1998	856.8	108.8	12.7

Sources: *Historical Statistics,* series P 265; *Statistical Abstract, 1992,* Table 1266; *2000,* Table 1253.

TABLE 29.6 World and U.S. Motor Vehicle Production, 1960–1992

	Production		*Percentage*
Year	*World* *(Million Vehicles)*	*United States*	*United States of World*
1960	16.5	8.0	48.5
1970	29.3	7.9	27.0
1980	38.9	8.0	20.6
1985	43.9	11.7	26.7
1990	48.1	9.7	20.2
1995	49.9	11.9	23.9
1999	54.9	13.0	23.7

Sources: *Statistical Abstract, 1973,* Table 1320; *1982–1983,* Table 1058; *1988,* Tables 990, 1373; *1992,* Tables 1000, 1357; *2000,* Table 1030.

developed going to vanish from the U.S. economy or linger on as protected and parasitic lame ducks?

Steel Making

In the 1950s, two major innovations in steel making occurred. U.S. producers lagged behind in adoption of both (a) the use of basic oxygen furnaces (BOF) and (b) larger-scale plants with continuous slab or billet casting.[16] The latter replaced ingot production followed by rolling at separate slab, billet, and bloom mills. The American producers were deeply committed to open-hearth technology and to separate rolling operations. Their plants, labor forces (and work-rule contracts), and managements were all the products of the older technology.

Our Japanese competitors, meanwhile, scrapped open hearth and changed to continuous-process mills. By 1978, the Japanese, with a 30 to 35 percent cost advantage over American producers, achieved 51 percent of their raw steel output from continuous casting, compared with a mere 15 percent in this country.[17] Magaziner and Reich attribute the initial American backwardness in large part simply to U.S. management's ideas about world trade. Management argued that "... foreign imports were based on cheap labor, dumping, and unfair trade practices, and therefore asked for government protection," which they got.[18]

The Japanese, with no iron ore or coking coal of their own, exporting 40 percent of their steel output (compared to about 3 percent for U.S. producers), had to play the international markets and went for the flexibility of low-cost production based on the best-practice technology.

There were, according to Paul Tiffany, other deep-seated problems in American steel related to big government and big labor, and these led not only to conservative policy regarding plant size, but even to initial refusal to adopt the new BOF technology where it could be done. Tiffany argues that the steel industry's leaders (Big Steel) continuously hoped for a more favorable tax relief and federal subsidy program than they achieved. Their hope was based upon their pivotal position in national defense strategy as the Cold War deepened. During the Korean War, so that steel capacity could be expanded in a hurry, rapid depreciation allowances were granted the steel producer (five years for a new plant), and the resulting extra after-tax profits could be used to expand old or build new facilities. When the war ended, Big Steel's leaders "continuously petitioned" to have these allowances remain in force; however, the Eisenhower administration refused to extend the favorable treatment, arguing that such "... would be unwarranted public meddling into the workings of a free market economy."[19] It was a classic case, following the public relations homilies of Big Steel spokesmen Roger Blough and Benjamin Fairless, of being "hoist by their own petards." Meanwhile, says Tiffany, labor relations in the steel industry were as sour as ever, with Democrats in Congress backing the wage demands of the United Steel Workers while the Truman, Eisenhower, and Kennedy regimes, in succession, resisted the efforts of the industry to pass through the higher wage costs directly to the consumer.

Meanwhile, it was the policy of the federal government throughout the 1950s to extend aid to its European allies and to the Japanese to rebuild their own steel industries with the new technology. By 1959, for the first time in the twentieth century, the United States imported more steel than it exported, as foreign producers easily undercut the domestic industry in price, quality, and delivery schedules.[20]

Huge investments had been made by Big Steel and it was mostly in out-of-date technology. Robert Ankli and Eva Sommer refer to the "mismanagement, sloppy work practices, and waste" at these firms.[21] It is an almost unbelievable record; in the 1950s billions of dollars were sunk into mostly brand-new obsolescence. As two leading students of the industry, Walter Adams and Hans Mueller, phrased it:

> Most of the melt shops were already obsolescent the moment they were installed.[22]

and

> When the expansion ended in the late 1950s, the U.S. industry found itself in a worse competitive position than at the beginning of the decade.[23]

An equally serious problem was the failure to adopt BOF for so long. By 1964, when 12 percent of U.S. production came from oxygen furnaces, the Japanese had already reached 44 percent BOF production, on their way to supremacy. The oxygen converter had been the achievement of a Swiss professor, Robert Durrer, just before the outbreak of World War II. Its first commercial operation was in Austria in 1950. The process was first installed in the United States just four years later by a small producer (McLouth). It took Big Steel another decade to follow suit. Similarly, small American companies began smelting using scrap, with electric furnaces—so-called minimills—in locations far from the production facilities of Big Steel. The commitment to new investments in the old open-hearth technology in the 1950s had been utterly the wrong move by the steel giants.

Consider the data in Table 29.7. Although from 1960 to 1980 net output expanded by a third (and then declined), the production process was undergoing a revolution. BOF and electric furnace production wiped away open-hearth output by 1992, and, with it, the jobs of thousands of steel workers.[24] Empty plants and decaying economic life in the Pittsburgh area, Allentown and Bethlehem, PA, Youngstown, OH, Wheeling, WV, and along the lower reaches of the Great Lakes were the silent monuments of this revolution. The near disappearance of open-hearth output under pressure from BOF and electric furnaces was even more dramatic than the supersession of Bessemer capacity by the new open-hearth plants eight decades or so earlier (Table 17.3). Despite this revolution, by every measurable criterion U.S. steel production is more costly now than that of the international competition; capital, labor, raw materials, all must be expended in greater amounts to get a ton of steel here than in Japan or Western Europe.[25] But the established record was largely the work of Big Steel, not of all U.S. steel makers. After all, both BOF and electric minimill technology were entrepreneured early and profitably by "independent" mills, relatively small firms. By 1963, the six largest steel-makers, operating 50 percent of the total U.S. basic capacity, had not an oxygen furnace among them. Small companies, together operating a mere 7 percent of U.S. basic capacity, made about half of all American BOF output.[26] The technological revolution in steel was here. But not at the top. Why not?

Some blame government for its enterprise-crippling regulations; some blame the unions for their output-crippling work rules and wage demands far in excess of productivity increases; and some blame management for its shortsighted, short-run, bottom-line mentality. Adams and Mueller see the outcome as the natural consequence of Big Steel's history. There is considerable merit in this view. In retrospect, the Big Steel companies have been problem children in American economic development. Once past their earliest stages as dynamic entrepreneurial firms, when the great men of steel made an industry, their corporate descendants became mere bureaucracies, adept at merger, price-fixing, and other oligopolistic behavior.

These giant firms, living decade by decade in a world of oligopoly (and after 1945 of incessant lockstep price increases), protectionism, and periodic bouts with both the huge steel union and its

TABLE 29.7 Raw Steel Production by Process, 1950–1998

Year	Total	*Open Hearth*	*BOF*	*Electric*	*Percentage of Total*		
	(Millions of Net Tons)				*Open Hearth*	*BOF*	*Electric*
1950	96.8	90.8	—	6.0	93.8	—	6.2
1960	99.3	87.6	3.3	8.4	88.2	3.3	8.5
1970	131.5	48.0	63.3	20.2	36.5	48.1	15.4
1980	118.8	13.0	67.6	31.2	11.7	60.4	27.9
1985	88.3	6.4	51.9	29.9	7.2	58.8	33.9
1990	98.9	3.5	58.5	36.9	3.54	59.15	37.31
1995	104.9	—	62.5	42.4	—	58.58	40.42
1998	108.8	—	59.7	49.1	—	57.44	38.97

Sources: *Historical Statistics*, series P 265–269; *Statistical Abstract, 1992*, Table 1266; *2000*, Table 1253.

Congressional supporters, became insensitive to competitive changes both within the United States and in the outside world. As Adams and Mueller phrase it:

> Born of multiple mergers, the large steel companies managed to foster a system of coordinated pricing and orderly growth. No unforgiving rivals forced them to remain in the forefront of organizational and technological efficiency.[27]

By the late 1960s, foreign competition *inside* the American market (imports were 4.7 percent of U.S. consumption in 1960, 16.7 percent by 1968) frightened the leaders of Big Steel back to Washington for a federal protectionist handout. It was granted. From 1969 to 1975, European and Japanese exporters to the United States were under a voluntary restraint agreement (VRA) that gave them quotas in the American market. The VRA ended in 1975 when a private antitrust suit was brought against the system. However, in 1974, a new trade act not only allowed quotas to be imposed against specialty steel imports but also created the Trigger Price Mechanism (TPM) to protect American firms from "dumping"—that is, charging less for steel in the U.S. market than at home. With the TPM, foreign firms could now freely base their offer prices to American customers on high-cost U.S. steel rather than on world-market prices. The consumer was forced to pay the bill. It was a happy outcome for the steel industry, and prices were raised all 'round in celebration.[28] It was admitted that, in these circumstances, the BOF took over within the protected U.S. market more from the pressure of domestic competition—the independents—than from the giant international steel industry growing up overseas.[29] TPM is a case of regulatory capture, with the U.S. government now certifying and publishing the industry's price lists, revised quarterly. When Reagan came in, the VRA was restored.

Primarily because of union pressure, the quotas were imposed to save jobs in the steel mills. The cost of those jobs to everyone else is something to consider. Arthur Denzau estimated that 2,800 jobs were "saved" in steel by the price increases that resulted from the quotas, but at the cost of $750,000 per job and the elimination of 52,000 jobs in steel-using industries.[30] In 1988, the American steel firms reported profits, but they were still protected by the import quotas and were still pleading for extended quotas.

The reduction in basic American steel output in from 1980 to 1985 (Table 29.7) shows the road to survival taken by the American firms. Open hearth production continued to fall as obsolete capacity was junked, while BOF and electric production expanded. By 1999, the industry's capacity was only 80 percent of what it had been in 1980, while only 110,000 steel workers remained of the 399,000 who labored in 1980. What remained of the American steel industry was profitable, especially the smaller firms, although profits were falling as the century came to an end.[31]

To remain competitive in basic steel production, the American steel firms faced the need by the mid-1980s to acquire a world of technical innovation they had ignored in previous decades. In 1985, Chicago's Inland Steel hired the world's largest steelmaker, Nippon Steel Corporation, to consult on installation of new continuous casting equipment and other improvements. In flat steel production the Japanese experts made more than 700 recommendations for technical improvements worth $100 million a year in savings at the Indiana Harbor plant alone.[32] Foreign firms have since bought into the American steel industry, and the international-ownership route now seems the way basic steel is going. It is a worldwide economy, and steel firms are becoming worldwide enterprises.

Automobiles

The steel industry, despite the wooden oligopoly characteristics of Big Steel management, in fact slowly became less concentrated during the twentieth century. The automobile industry, on the other hand, has shown no such tendency, apart from the expansion of the range of choice provided by imports. Three companies—General Motors, Ford, and DaimlerChrysler—sell virtually all domestically produced automobiles, although foreign companies have begun production within the United States. A fourth U.S. company, American Motors, became part of Chrysler following several years during which it was unable to capture more than a negligible share of the market. All other nonspecialized producers vanished from the scene after World War II.[33] New entry is extremely expensive, and, in fact, there have been no successful new entries by American firms for decades. The three remaining American auto firms represent the survivors of more than 1,100 automobile companies that existed at one time or another, some 181 of which appear actually to have produced more than a few demonstration models.[34] Ford Motor Company had once been the giant of the industry but was displaced for good by General Motors in the late 1920s.

Despite notorious nonprice competition among the American auto companies, their proliferation of models and options and the free bargaining between individual buyers and sellers gave the appearance of competitive vigor until the late 1970s. Also, since used cars are competitive with new cars, consumers had plenty of options. Gigantic advertising campaigns attempt to trim consumer tastes to one or the other of the new models each year, but as the Ford Motor Company found out with the failed attempt to introduce a new automobile in 1958, the Edsel, consumer tastes are not so easily manipulated.

Econometric studies show that the auto market is fairly unstable. The price elasticity of demand ranges from −0.5 to −1.5, and the income elasticity from 1.0 to 4.0; thus, demand will fluctuate considerably with respect to income changes and is sensitive, to some extent, to price competition.[35] But because the industry is characterized by price leadership and the other signs of tight oligopoly behavior, direct price competition, model by model, is greatly diminished. In so tightly structured a market, any attempt at direct price competition can be quickly countered by the other producers if there are no great differences among the new models, and there tend not to be. Thus, competition tends to be in styling and product identification through advertising—image! The price element enters into the individual deals between buyers and sellers—a market much like real estate, where "haggling" is still expected behavior. Long dominated by American firms (except for novelties such as luxury cars or sports models), the American automobile industry seemed an unlikely target for a foreign competitor. Table 29.8 shows the market shares from 1937 to 1995.

Since World War II, the Big Three have dominated domestic production, but imports, less than 1 percent as late as 1955, greatly increased in their market share to almost displace American Motors and to cut nearly in half the share of the ill-managed Chrysler Corporation. In 1979, Chrysler nearly went "belly up" with enormous losses and had to get a U.S. Treasury guarantee on its debt—the "Chrysler bailout." In 1981, the Reagan administration acceded to the pleas of the industry and extracted from the Japanese producers a voluntary freeze, a quota, on Japanese imports.[36] Domestic sales then rose, and Chrysler repaid its loans. Also, of course, automobile prices rose dramatically. In 1984, as the economy entered an upswing, the auto companies made record profits domestically, free from increases in foreign imports.

TABLE 29.8 U.S. Auto Market Shares, 1937–1998

Year	*General Motors*	*Ford*	*DaimlerChrysler*	*Other Domestic*	*Foreign*
1937	41.8	21.4	25.4	11.4	—
1946–1950	41.8	21.4	21.6	15.1	0.2
1961–1965	49.7	26.2	12.2	6.0	6.1
1966–1970	46.2	24.3	15.8	2.8	10.6
1971–1975	44.1	24.0	13.4	3.3	15.2
1976–1980	46.8	21.1	10.1	1.8	20.1
1981–1985	43.8	17.8	10.4	2.0	25.9
1986–1990	37.1	20.6	10.7	3.2	28.4
1990–1995	34.6	21.1	9.0	5.9	29.3
1996–1999	31.1	20.0	9.1	7.5	32.3

Sources: Lawrence J. White, "The Automobile Industry," Walter Adams, ed., *The Structure of American Industry* (New York; Macmillan, 1982, 6th ed.), Table 3, p. 147; *Ward's Automotive Yearbook; Ward's Motor Vehicle Facts & Figures 2000.*

TABLE 29.9 U.S. Foreign Trade in Autos, 1950–1995

	Value in Millions of Dollars	
Year	*Exports*	*Imports*
1950	$ 179	$ 21
1960	235	513
1965	393	640
1970	822	3,719
1975	2,852	7,483
1980	3,932	16,675
1985	6,027	36,474
1990	9,708	45,716
1995	14,251	64,526

Sources: *Statistical Abstract, 1992,* Table 1000; *2000,* Table 1030.

As you can see in Table 29.9, the rise in imports far outstripped the impressive expansion of U.S. exports into that booming international market. In fact, U.S. exports rose in value by a factor of 36.3 from 1965 to 1995, but imports went up by a factor of 100.8 (from $640 million to $64.5 *billion*), leaving the country with a deficit of almost $50 billion in its foreign trade in passenger cars. When the Reagan administration put a lid on imports in 1981, foreign producers held slightly more than a one-third share of the U.S. passenger car market, and the American auto industry was headed for panic. The limits on that trade reduced the foreign share to slightly less than one-quarter. Afterward, foreign auto makers, established originally in the American market with cheap and efficient small cars, found their staying power in their reputation for quality. They responded to the quantity restriction by exporting more expensive models to the American market, thus maintaining their revenues—and profits.

At first, for the most part, imports meant subcompacts, a car size not popular with American producers, or consumers, at first. The surge of imports came in the late 1960s. Observe the data in Table 29.10. By 1970, total imports comprised almost 20 percent of the sum of U.S. factory sales of passenger cars plus imports. Imports continued to push upward irregularly until the voluntary freeze by the Japanese in 1981 (in that year the Japanese accounted for 61 percent of all imports). Since total motor vehicle sales include trucks and recreational vehicles, these numbers are not the ones ordinarily quoted; but for the passenger car market, these are the ones that count. In some years, the domestic manufacturers did better than is indicated by the numbers in Table 29.10 (for example, factory sales of 9.2 million units in the boom year 1977). Still, the impression given in the table is the right one; beginning in the late 1960s, foreign autos, for the first time since the domestic industry's beginning, became a major segment of the American market. They captured a larger share than Ford Motors. Why was that?

Most observers noted a combination of price and size. Recall that the income elasticity of demand for new cars was quite high. As inflation picked up in the late 1960s, those whose real incomes lagged behind

TABLE 29.10 Factory Sales and Total Imports, 1950–1995 (Passenger Cars Only)

Year	*Factory Sales*	*Imports*	*Total*	*Percentage Imports of Total*
1950	6,666	21	6,687	0.3
1955	7,920	57	7,977	0.7
1960	6,675	499	7,174	7.0
1965	9,306	569	9,875	5.8
1970	6,457	1,280	7,827	16.4
1975	6,713	1,571	8,284	19.0
1980	6,400	2,398	7,898	27.3
1985	8,002	2,838	10,840	26.2
1990	6,050	2,404	8,454	28.4
1995	6,310	1,506	7,816	19.27

Note: Numbers shown are in thousands.

Sources: *Historical Statistics,* series Q 148; *Statistical Abstract, 2000,* Table 1030; *Ward's Motor Vehicle Facts & Figures 2000.*

Competition Forces Progress. *In modern times, American leadership in basic steel and automobiles has been challenged by foreign competition and has been forced to change to remain competitive. The Chrysler Jefferson assembly plant (Detroit, 1967, above) gave way to the modern Jefferson North plant in 1992, where automobiles on the assembly line are set at a 37-degree angle to reduce worker stress and fatigue (below).*

were willing to pay attention to something besides more expensive, new American cars. The initial volume influx of foreign cars, the VW "bug" and the early Toyotas, were on the low end of the price scale and offered dependable, economical transportation. In university parking lots, where incomes quickly lagged behind the increase in general prices, foreign cars immediately became common.

Also, the foreign cars were small cars, far smaller than the standard American passenger car. This posed a second problem. The American manufacturers were tooled up for and committed to the mass-produced six-passenger sedan. That was the product they made most efficiently and profitably. Small, four-passenger cars were new and not as profitable per unit. American manufacturers tended to scoff at the idea of a seriously rising demand for cars so small that only two adults and a few small children could ride in them comfortably. Also, since the new car market was already filled with standard production, any new small car offered by the domestic producers was mainly just a threat to *their own* market for standard cars. There was a flurry of smaller models in 1959, but, by the 1960s, the American product was bigger than ever.

The imported small cars continued to sell, and, by 1969 and 1970, Ford and GM were offering domestically made subcompacts. These American cars were of poor quality compared with the foreign competition. The 1969 bloodless coup in Libya and the 1973 renewal of the perpetual Arab-Israeli war brought a sharp increase in gasoline prices by 1974, and a new element entered into the demand spectrum—*mileage.*

The small foreign cars, made in countries with high excise taxes on gasoline, were already relatively fuel efficient. The American cars were not. Within a short time, the major U.S. auto companies were importing and selling Japanese cars under various model names. After 1983, as the economy recovered under the cover of protection, and as an international glut of oil reduced and stabilized gasoline prices, the demand for the traditional product of the American auto industry remained strong.

By the late 1970s, imports were no longer "foreign" to American buyers; in the 1980s, foreign manufacturers were assembling cars and producing parts inside the United States. GM and Toyota were engaged in joint U.S. production, as were Chrysler and Mitsubishi. The limit on increases in Japanese imports employed throughout the Reagan-Bush administrations produced the result predicted by the textbooks—a transfer of consumers' money to protected companies. New car prices soared.

It is conceivable that, in the future, more automobile manufacturers will be international conglomerates, that the era of strictly "national" automobile firms is nearly ended. In 1998, what is now called DaimlerChrysler was formed when Chrysler merged with Daimler-Benz. Both GM and Ford have working arrangements with firms from other countries, but there have been no mergers to date. International conglomeration is the way to get "behind" tariff walls. In the past decade, there has been a powerful increase in protectionism, not only in the United States but in other countries as well; protectionism, however, only staves off the inevitable. As it is, the invasion of the U.S. market by foreign producers is the most impressive change in the American automobile industry since the moving assembly line was introduced at Ford's Highland Park plant in 1914.

A Note on Industrial Retardation and Globalization

Economists have long been aware that stagnant industries tend to decline and vanish. When factor proportions change, when tastes change and demand flees from a given product, resources move away to seek employments with higher marginal earnings. Over time, as American economic history demonstrates, change in economic structure is inevitable. Nobel Prize-winner Simon Kuznets described the process this way:

> As we observe various industries within a given national economy, we see that the lead in development shifts from one branch to another. A rapidly developing industry does not retain its vigorous growth forever but slackens and is overtaken by others whose period of rapid development is beginning. Within one country we can observe a succession of different branches of activity in the vanguard of the country's economic development, and within

each industry we can notice a conspicuous slackening of the rate of increase.[37]

Kuznets found that the early stages of an industry's existence tend to present the greatest range of technical possibilities, and competition for the industry's resources will push the most efficient to the front. Later on, especially if there is no fundamental change in the nature of the final product, technological advance and the industry's physical growth slow down. Lack of sufficient market possibilities will contribute to the power of the forces of decline. A lack of new and cheaper raw materials sources, or of dramatic increases in substitute inputs, adds to the tendency toward retardation. The rise of significant foreign competition tends to be an additional retarding factor, on average.

Now, history does not necessarily repeat itself. But if we are to take American economic history seriously at all, we must consider Kuznets's findings, and the modern histories of both the basic steel and auto industries in this country strongly suggest terminal retardation. It is especially ominous in this regard that in neither industry were the major technological advances of the post-World War II era either discovered or pioneered in this country.

In a similar study in the early 1930s, Arthur F. Burns traced the history of retardation in 104 areas of economic activity in the United States and concluded that retardation almost always led to absolute decline.[38] Burns also argued that such retardation in given industries was healthy, overall, for the entire developing organism, as the release of resources from the declining sectors meant an influx into those healthier parts of the economy in expansionary phases. For both Kuznets and Burns, the empirical rule was that industrial retardation, in specific industries, was an inevitable part of economic evolution. Possibly the extraordinary records of the two giants of the American economic past, autos and Big Steel, are manifestations of the Kuznets-Burns rule of industrial retardation. The dynamic, small American steel firms may be the beneficiary of Big Steel's decline.

However, there is one exception to consider, and it is an important one. The very real possibility of internationalization of ownership in both industries is the equivalent of a major new input discovery—in this case, management. Retardation may be overcome.

For some years, foreign investment in American industry has been creating headlines: German, British, French, Japanese, Korean, Chinese (both Taiwan and the mainland), even Canadian. It is nothing new; in the past, foreign investment (ownership) has been vast. Since the 1950s, there has been a more or less steady increase in American equities (stocks) owned by foreigners, in addition to bonds, deposits in American banks, and deposits in foreign branches; foreign banks have even gone into business in main U.S. financial centers. Similarly, Americans, as is well known, have been extending their holdings of foreign assets (as well as lending vast sums, sometimes with disastrous consequences for the lenders). A number of large American banks seemed in the mid–1980s near the edge of a federal bailout from some of their loans in Eastern Europe, Latin America, and elsewhere.

It is "one world," after all. In a world without serious political and military conflicts, nothing would be more natural than these international flows of investment capital. National borders are not put in place by economics but by politics. Investment capital, seeking the highest returns given levels of risk and transactions costs, would, in a perfect world, flow to its most efficient uses. Even in today's perilous world, such flows are taking place on a massive scale. Those who still have "nationalistic" feelings about such matters naturally object, but, as American firms buy into ownership deals even in mainland China, such objections seem both illogical and antique.

International trade has implied and been associated with direct international investment since at least the end of the Napoleonic Wars. In the past such investment was irregular, coming in long waves, as Brinley Thomas emphasized (recall Chapter 16). We seem to be in another such wave. Insofar as it equalizes management skill and application of technology worldwide, it must be welcomed on grounds of economic efficiency. It may help reverse retardation in American steel and automobiles; it has contributed to the growth of American electronics.

THE NEW ECONOMY: AMERICAN PREEMINENCE IN ELECTRONICS

The semiconductor industry emerged in the years after World War II, with the computer and software industries following shortly thereafter.[39] As in steel and automobiles, U.S. firms were faced with competition in the global market, but U.S. firms ultimately proved dominant in all three industries. In the case of semiconductors, they had to regain lost market share.

Semiconductors

The invention of the transistor by John Bardeen, Walter Brattain, and William Shockley at Bell Labs in 1947 is the event that set the modern electronics industry into motion.[40] Shortly thereafter, in response to an antitrust suit, AT&T instituted a policy of disclosure and cross-licensing that facilitated technology transfer to all who might help develop the invention.[41] Indeed, a large number of firms accepted the challenge of discovering ways to commercialize the technology, many of them new, small ventures involving people, including Shockley, who left Bell Labs in the hope of hitting the jackpot in commercial markets.

The military and the space program provided the first major markets for transistors, and their demand was perhaps the most important factor in the industry's growth. Most of the major developments within the private sector were made with the military market in mind. The U.S. government financed a significant portion of the industry's initial research and development.[42] Because the military demand was for specialized, dependable goods, U.S. firms concentrated on the use of silicon, rather than germanium, in making transistors. Silicon was a more expensive material, but the resulting transistors were more stable over a broader range of temperatures. Texas Instruments developed the first commercially successful silicon transistor, which was incorporated into radar and missile systems. In Europe and Japan, where the market was oriented toward consumer electronics, firms concentrated on the use of germanium.

As scientists gained experience with both types of transistors, supply increased much faster than demand, so prices fell. The average amount paid for a germanium transistor in 1957 was $1.85, while a silicon transistor was $17.81. Eight years later, the average germanium transistor was $0.50, while a silicon transistor averaged $0.86. The greater reduction in the price of silicon transistors represents the development of the planar process for silicon, a process for which germanium was unsuitable. The change in relative prices combined with its preferred properties helped to make silicon the standard.

In the late 1950s, Fairchild Semiconductor, led by Robert Noyce, developed a practical integrated circuit based on the planar process. This process, which made it possible to produce batches of semiconductors simultaneously, was developed initially at Bell Labs and perfected at Fairchild. Noyce recognized this process made it possible to place a complete electronic circuit on a single chip.[43] A patent dispute with Jack Kilby of Texas Instruments was resolved by a cross-licensing agreement, and licenses were granted liberally to others, much as AT&T had done with the transistor. Product development was rapid. In the first three decades, the transistor count per integrated circuit increased from 10 (just 10) to 100 million. This was accomplished with almost no change in the average cost of processing the individual circuit. Consequently, the prices of consumer electronics fell dramatically. What students paid for programmable, graphing calculators in the 1990s was about the same amount as their parents paid in the 1960s for simple calculators that did little more than add, subtract, multiply, and divide. The falling relative price of electronic, as compared to mechanical, systems meant rapid growth, and U.S. firms concentrated more on growth than profits.

In 1968, Noyce resigned from Fairchild, and, one month later, he and Gordon Moore founded Intel. They were in competition with such firms as Motorola and Texas Instruments who were focused on the new technology and with older, vertically-integrated firms such as GE, RCA, Sylvania, and Westinghouse. Perhaps because the older firms were involved in such a variety of markets, they devoted less attention to the new technology. By 1975, only RCA among the older firms remained among the top ten semiconductor manufacturers.

By the late 1970s, the U.S. firms held a 59 percent share of worldwide semiconductor sales and 74 percent of integrated circuit sales. A decade later, these shares were 43 and 45 percent, respectively, and Japanese firms held larger shares in both markets. The explanation for this shift lies in the relative decline of the logic and specialty chip market, those for the military and space program, that accounted for only about one-sixth of industry demand by the mid-1970s. Concomitantly, the consumer market was growing

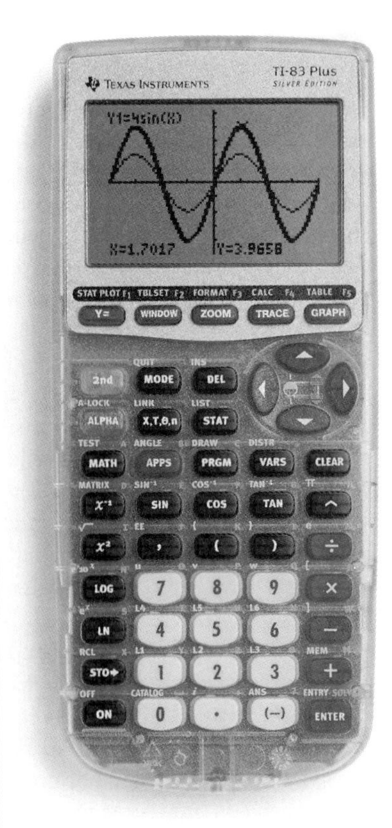

Electronic Calculators. ***Texas Instruments developed the first mini-calculator in 1967 (above). The number of functions it could perform and the amount of information it could display was extremely limited in comparison to a modern TI graphing calculator (right).***

rapidly. The emphasis in that market was on standardized, mass-produced circuitry that favored the larger, more integrated Japanese firms, which were mass-producing calculators and other consumer products. On average, they were much larger than their U.S. counterparts and were able to finance new investment from retained earnings. As in steel and autos, Japanese firms made the decision to enter international markets and made investments in productive capacity and product quality. In particular, the rapidly growing DRAM (dynamic random-access memory) market was ideally suited for the Japanese.

The first 1K DRAM, the Intel 1003, became the industry standard until it was replaced by a 4K chip. U.S. firms, especially Intel, dominated world markets through the mid–1970s. A slowdown in the American economy in the late 1970s delayed the introduction of the 16K DRAM, and Japanese firms seized the opening. They gained a 41 percent share of the 16K market and never looked back. By 1990, the Japanese share of the 4-megabit DRAM market was 98 percent.

By 1985, the American industry was down, way down, but it was not out. As Langlois and Steinmueller observed, "1985 was actually not the beginning of the end but the beginning of a turnaround."[44] Japanese firms retained their competitive advantage in the DRAM market, but the larger market shifted once again. This shift was toward microprocessors as opposed to memory, toward the personal computer (PC). The PC market accounted for 40 percent of integrated circuit sales in 1989; five years later, it had grown to 52 percent. One firm, Intel, was responsible for much of that market. By 1994, it accounted for 31 percent of the world production of microcomponents.[45]

The increased demand for PCs led to an increased derived demand for design-intensive chips, a shift that played to the American strength in these chips. Once again, inventiveness and responsiveness mattered. The growth of the industry enabled small, highly focused U.S. firms to specialize. This led to a separation of design and production. The design was done in the U.S., while the chips often were manufactured in foreign firms that specialized in production. This strategy of globalization was assisted by the U.S. government policy enabling firms to reimport partially-finished products manufactured elsewhere.

TABLE 29.11 Value of Shipments

	Total Computer	*Transistors*	*Integrated Microcircuits*	*Printed Circuit Boards*
1971	1,675.1	—	—	—
1975	2,123.2	—	—	—
1980	8,076.8	599.7	6,605.7	—
1985	19,292.6	655.3	10,910.2	3,490.3
1990	25,630.0	682.3	16,623.3	7,174.5
1995	49,038.1	942.3	48,437.9	8,367.3
1999	62,711.9	810.8	62,829.4	7,976.5

Note: Amounts are in millions of dollars.

Source: Computers: www.census.gov/ftp/pub/industry/1/ma35r99.pdf. Semiconductors: www.census.gov/ftp/pub/industry/1/ma36q99.pdf

It meant that U.S. firms did not have to make significant investments in productive capacity, domestically or internationally. Additionally, U.S. firms began to pay more attention to such matters as manufacturing productivity and product quality, and they arguably had significantly narrowed the gap between themselves and Japanese firms by the mid-1990s.

The resurgence of the American industry stands in stark contrast to the experience in steel and automobiles. Unlike the giant firms of those oligopolistic industries who looked inward, the entrepreneurial firms of the semiconductor industry kept the market in their view and changed with the times. The success of the integrated microcircuit component of the industry is clear in Table 29.11, as is the phenomenal growth of the computer industry.

Computers

The U.S. has dominated the computer industry from its start in the early 1950s. There has been continuous technological change and continuous product innovation. The advances in computer hardware are tied to the advances in semiconductors. Over time, computers have become more powerful, more affordable, and smaller. Bresnahan and Malerba distinguish three distinct types of computer demand: for scientific, engineering and technical research; for business data processing; and for "individual productivity applications."[46] The market for the first has been roughly twice as big as that of the other two. In general, these different demands involve different sized computers that have been supplied by different sized companies. IBM held a dominant position in mainframe computers from the start. New entrants played the key role with respect to minicomputers, PCs, and workstations.

As was true of semiconductors, the public sector helped to underwrite research on computers. While there was some private support, the U.S. military and the Census Bureau were the two agencies most involved. J. Presper Eckert and John W. Mauch of the University of Pennsylvania developed the first U.S. digital electromechanical computer, ENIAC. John von Neumann, an advisor on their second machine, EDVAC, recommended that the computer have stored-programs as opposed to being hardwired, a concept he built into his own computer, the IAS.[47] Eckert and Mauch eventually formed their own company, but it didn't do well and was acquired by Remington Rand, producer of the UNIVAC.

Mainframe computers that could either make calculations or process data were the industry's first commercial products. Given the nature of the demand, producers initially focused on scientific applications but quickly moved to include business applications, particularly accounting. IBM became the market leader, but they faced competition from other office equipment (market-oriented) firms, electronics (technology-based) firms, and entrepreneurial start-ups in both the United States and Europe. The Japanese industry did not get underway until the late 1950s, by which time IBM Japan had a strong position. The interaction in all major producing areas between market-oriented and technology-based firms introduced a strain into the early years of the industry.

IBM's worldwide dominance resulted from its Chandlerian tripartite investment in technology, marketing, and management (see Chapter 18). Throughout the 1950s, IBM introduced ever more powerful families of computers. As the company became more oriented to business applications (and away from those of government), and it did not do so without some misgivings, it invested in the necessary managerial structure to address the demands of its customers. Research and development efforts shifted toward new product development. And given the excess demand for computers, IBM continually improved its manufacturing capabilities.

The most important problem that remained in the early 1960s was the fact that the computers of different families (e.g., 701, 650, and 11401) were incompatible; they were designed to be used for scientific or business purposes, but not both. This was resolved by the introduction in 1964 of the System 360, a truly modular computer. It was this system that consolidated IBM's leadership. The company was able to realize economies of scale through the production of standardized components, which contributed to the upstream integration of computer firms. For example, IBM created its own components division to make semiconductors. This, in turn, enabled it to realize economies of scope between component and computer design. Future generations of computers, such as the System 370 the following decade, enhanced the company's position as the dominant firm. Antitrust pressure led to an unbundling of hardware and system software in the 1970s. While this made it easier for competitors to follow an "IBM-compatible" strategy following the introduction of the System 370, it did little more than reduce IBM's profits. The competitors followed the lead of the dominant firm.

It was at this time that Japan's Ministry of International Trade and Industry (MITI) coordinated the Super High-Performance Computer Project designed to develop a technical capability within Japan. To that end, they were aided by firms such as Nippon Telegraph and Telephone (NTT). The six firms involved in the project made great strides as IBM patents were available as a condition of IBM's presence in Japan. Just before the introduction of the System 370, Japanese firms had close to a 60 percent market share within Japan.[48] The move to a modular system was a boon for the Japanese who could build on their competence in standardized, mass-produced goods. By 1980, Japanese firms were the most important followers of IBM. Their competence, however, was much greater in hardware than in software. They continued to attempt to overtake IBM in the production of mainframes, but the mainframe computer itself was overtaken by the development of much smaller machines.

The first minicomputer was Digital Equipment Corporation's (DEC) PDP-1, introduced in 1960. DEC was a start-up firm with MIT roots. A large number of the firms in this market segment were entrepreneurial start-ups; IBM was not a major presence. The development of the minicomputer and its cousin, the microcomputer, was facilitated by improvements in integrated circuitry. The minicomputer was particularly appropriate for applications in manufacturing establishments and research laboratories. Minicomputer users were computer literate, so suppliers did not face the same problems in marketing their product as IBM did in the mainframe market. A second layer of new firms entered the market to serve as intermediaries between producers and users. Most minicomputer firms concentrated on production; they did not supply significant software support.

Intel introduced the first commercially successful microprocessor in 1971. Up to that point, each new application required the design of a customized set of chips. The microprocessor, a chip that provided general solutions for many applications, conserved on engineering design time and eliminated a bottleneck to technological progress. The most obvious result was the development of the microcomputer (PCs). These were smaller, much less powerful, and much cheaper than minicomputers. Initially, the market was oriented toward hobbyists, who were extremely computer literate. Thus, the initial marketing strategy of firms selling PCs was analogous to that of those selling minicomputers.

There were two main standards for PCs—CP/M and the Apple II. The Apple II system, which was introduced in 1977 and established the PC as a consumer product, involved proprietary architecture and an operating system. The CP/M system was a proprietary product of Digital Research, but it was available on a variety of computers offered by rival companies, most of which were entrepreneurial start-ups. Both systems were open, so software could be, and was, developed by a large number of firms. Again, most such firms were entrepreneurial start-ups. Programs such as the VisiCalc spreadsheet (1979) and the WordStar word processor (1980) brought the PC into the office.

At this point, in August 1981, IBM decided to make its deferred entrance into the PC market. Given the other firms' head start, IBM elected to do so through external linkages, notably Intel microprocessors and Microsoft operating system software. As Langlois has shown, the IBM PC quickly established the 16-bit standard; its only serious competitor in the short run was the Apple Macintosh.[49] But IBM's decision to open its PC architecture involved an important tradeoff. While it set the standard and had its product on the market much sooner than otherwise would have been the case, it opened the door for others to produce "IBM-compatible" PCs. These firms were almost entirely from the United States. In conjunction with IBM, Intel, and Microsoft, they guided the future development of the PC market.

In the 1990s, the two market segments came together as networked mini- and microcomputers could perform many of the functions that were once the exclusive province of mainframes. Computer hardware became more of a commodity; specialized producers hastened the process of vertical disintegration, while software became relatively more profitable than hardware. The United States maintained its position of international dominance because the knowledge required to make profitable innovations was extremely complex, and strong complementarities remain between different segments of the computer market.

Software

The existence of a software industry is a reflection of the growth of specialization in the computer industry, particularly in the years after the introduction of the PC. The comparative advantage of the United States in computers carried over to software from the onset. Software can be divided into three categories—operating systems that control the internal operation of a computer, application tools that support the development of applications, and application solutions that enable users to perform specific tasks such as word processing or spreadsheet calculations.[50] All three can be written to be the same across many users or unique to a particular user. It is possible to produce all three in ways that do not go through the market; indeed, before the PC, either the computer producers or the users themselves supplied most software. In addition, a fair amount of standardized software becomes embedded in products such as control systems and is unavailable as a separate product. While the principles are the same, our discussion will concentrate on traded software that is available as a separate product.

By the mid-1980s, standardized, packaged software accounted for, and continues to account for, a much larger percentage of the U.S. market than elsewhere. This has given the United States "first-mover" advantages in software, particularly for operating systems and application tools, similar to what it has in computers. Application solutions require a much greater degree of "user friendliness," especially the ability to be manipulated in one's native language. It is precisely in this category where the U.S. comparative advantage is weakest.

As noted, there was little commercial software available for purchase before the PC. The ENIAC was hard-wired and did not involve software. As computer architectures became increasingly standardized, particularly following the introduction of IBM's System 360, a market developed for standard operating systems and applications. The firms developing computers under government contracts wrote much of this early software, but users themselves got in the act as standard languages such as COBOL and FORTRAN were available. Thus, some independent software firms made their appearance just before U.S. computer producers began to unbundle hardware and software. This unbundling was only one factor that helped to broaden the market. The System 360, with an operating system that was common to all machines in the family, increased the demand for computers. The introduction of minicomputers in the mid–1960s, a product without bundled software, played an important role. Finally, U.S. trade policy that permitted the foreign production of components, and ultimately some computers, helped to lower the price of computers and, therefore, to increase the derived demand for software.

The introduction of the PC in the late 1970s really opened the door to explosive growth for the software industry. Of particular importance was the emergence of two standard PCs—the IBM and the Macintosh. IBM created an autonomous PC business unit that felt a sense of urgency. It had neither the staff nor the time to develop a unique operating system, so it decided to purchase one externally, Microsoft's MS-DOS system, on the same basis as other customers. Equally important, it did not attempt to restrict Microsoft's ability to sell to other customers.[51] IBM was concerned that its PC be able to run programs written for Microsoft's BASIC operating system as well as MS-DOS, so the field was open to a large number of entrants, and enter they did.[52] Most were new firms that had not been involved in the creation of software for mainframes or even minicomputers.[53] This market separation has remained in the United States

The same was not true in other countries, which have largely been followers. Mainframe computer manufacturers rather than entrepreneurial firms are more likely to be the main supply source. Human and intellectual capital are clearly of much greater importance than physical capital in the production of software. In the United States, human capital development has become institutionalized at the university level where computer science has become an important part of the curriculum, attracting students from all over the world. The private sector (Control Data Corporation and IBM) and the government (National Science Foundation) financed the first steps that were taken in this direction.[54] Intellectual capital involves government policy, and the United States has been more concerned with questions of intellectual property rights in software than have other countries.

Beginning in the 1990s, the industry has been challenged by the growth of networking between PCs and, particularly, by the possibilities the Internet creates. This is still an emerging story and is tied to the property rights question. At the beginning, the Internet was funded by the government. It was originally known as ARPANET; the ARPA stood for Advanced Research Projects Agency, a part of the Department of Defense. In the 1980s, it was run by the National Science Foundation before that agency turned it over to the private sector in 1995.[55] Clearly, the resolution of the government's antitrust suit against Microsoft will condition how the software industry develops in the future, and, as this is being written, that is still a wide open question.[56]

Summary

The United States emerged as the international leader in all three segments of electronics that we examined. U.S. firms were among the earliest entrants in all three, and, in that early period, government money, largely through the Defense Department, was available to facilitate research and development and, more importantly, to purchase the resulting output. The government also funded university training and research that helped to produce scientists and engineers that ultimately became a much larger labor pool than was available elsewhere. The large U.S. market, especially that for mainframe computers, stimulated work in semiconductors and hardware; venture capital made it possible for new entrepreneurial firms to pursue their dreams. The emergence of a large market for PCs stimulated work in software, while the protection afforded by antitrust and a developing system of intellectual property rights made it possible for other new firms to pursue their dreams. It is the growth of the demand for computers in the private sector and the derived demand for semiconductors and software that is at the heart of American preeminence.

Both semiconductor and computer technology benefited from what Nathan Rosenberg called "technological convergence," a process through which the solution to a specific problem contributes to general knowledge that becomes useful in many sectors of the economy. Perhaps the most important of these general purpose technologies was the planar process, but the integrated circuit, standardized memory, microprocessors, stored programs, and modular computers also have proven to be important contributors to the increasing returns these industries have experienced.

Perhaps these three industries will, with age, become oligopolistic, inward-looking, and lose the position of dominance they currently enjoy. The semiconductor industry has responded to the challenge of the international marketplace. Lessons have been learned. Other lessons can be learned from the history of steel and automobiles. One hopes they will be.

DOMESTIC CHANGES IN INDUSTRIAL LOCATION

The much publicized "move to the Sun Belt" of American manufacturing industry in the past 30 years is mainly a myth, the result of a few spectacular relocations during a time when the old industrial cities of the Midwest and Northeast were suffering from a multitude of troubles. Indeed, the data suggest a "Sun Belt" effect in the movement of population and the development of industry for most of the twentieth century. Richard McKenzie's study of regional industrial development shows that, while industrial growth and location changed and while manufacturing employment rose in the Sun Belt and fell in the Frost Belt, this was *not* primarily due to relocation of plants, functions, and people from Frost Belt industries.[57] That is, it has been a rare event that an old Buffalo or Chicago firm has closed down and moved "bag and baggage" to the South, Southwest, or West. The old Frost Belt industries were located in such places as Rochester, New York, and Gary, Indiana, because those locations made good economic sense *for those industries* in their time. Although some old industries moved with the population to the South and West, the increase in employment is the result of the development of *new* industries—with different needs, technologies, transportation costs, and markets—that have located in the South and West.

The present decline of the old metallurgical and engineering industries that grew up and formed the core of Midwestern economic power in the late nineteenth and early twentieth centuries would not matter so much if there were substitutes. Writing in 1984, James Soltow quotes a 1939 study by Glenn McLaughlin and Ralph Watkins of the old steel industry's capital:

> None of the new important industries which have developed in the United States in the past forty years have taken root in Pittsburgh.[58]

In recent years, some areas, like Pittsburgh, have bounced back, while others, like Gary, continue to decline. In many cases, those that have been successful in attracting new activity made use of the science and engineering talent located there. However, they have not generated sufficient jobs to employ all the workers that once toiled in their mills and factories at the wages they once enjoyed.

According to Soltow, the perceived economic plateau in the Midwest was masked by the huge demand of World War II and the postwar expansion for cars, tractors, farm equipment, trucks, steel, machines, earthmoving equipment—the bread-and-butter industries of the Midwest. But the plateau was there. While national employment overall rose 52 percent from 1948 to 1968, and national manufacturing employment rose by more than 26 percent, in the five Great Lakes states, those numbers were merely 37 and 15 percent. Even tertiary-sector employment was growing more slowly than the national average.[59] From 1968 to 1978, manufacturing employment in the Great Lakes states actually declined 1 percent while it managed a 5 percent increase nationally. The old technology would not produce a new expansion of employment in the old locations. Its day has passed. As Soltow puts it:

> In the late 19th and early 20th centuries, the region's economy had been integrated into the national and international economy principally through the creation of the world's most efficient metallurgical-engineering complex.

In the 1960s, foreign competition intensified, while domestic demand rose only moderately. New industries based on petrochemicals and high-tech electronics found homes in places like Houston, Phoenix, and Silicon Valley—not where water transport, iron ore, and coking coal came together. In New England the declining textile industry was to be replaced by high-tech companies.

The social disaster of the old industrial cities and towns was that minority populations had crowded into them during World War II and afterward just when, in fact, their employment growth had ended, at least temporarily, and just when suburbanization had begun in earnest. As Soltow argues, the perception that relatively high unemployment in the old smokestack cities was due somehow to lack of skills, education, and urban blight produced policies that could not touch the real problem—industrial jobs were being created *elsewhere* in industries that had no advantages awaiting them in the smokestack locations.[60]

Finally, modern legislation designed to freeze industrial location, such as the National Employment Priorities acts that were introduced in Congress in the early 1980s, would seem to be curiously misguided. They would merely dissuade firms from locating any place where such legislation applied.[61] This species of legislation is mercantilism, reminiscent of Jean Baptiste Colbert (1619–1683), the French "economic planner" who divided France into compartments to locate and "stabilize" economic development.

As this study of American economic history has emphasized, capital mobility is the basis of economic growth, and policies designed to impede mobility will also impede growth. From the study of steel and autos in this chapter, it should be obvious that more than laws forbidding plant closures would be needed to make those industries internationally competitive. If they were frozen in place *and* all imports were prohibited, the old jobs could be saved, but at what cost to the overall living standards of the American public at large? As Sukkoo Kim and others have demonstrated, over the long run, but especially during the second half of the twentieth century, differences in regional resource endowments diminished as factors became more mobile. This brought about a convergence in regional industrial structures and incomes per capita.[62] Mobility, domestic and international, is the essence of healthy economic growth. However, states and municipalities in this country have a long history of diverting industrial location through tax breaks, subsidies, and other bribes. Questionable as the practice is, it is not new.[63]

MODERN AGRICULTURE

Despite (or possibly because of) almost 75 years of federal intervention and regulation in agriculture and the creation of many institutions to "solve the farm problem," the agricultural sector seems to be frozen beyond hope in its myriad difficulties. Farm output and productivity continued to rise, the family incomes of most farmers lagged behind other sectors, surpluses piled up in government storage facilities, and the number of operating farms continued to decline. Figure 29.4 shows the record of farm population (as a percent of total) from 1820 to 1990, compared with the index of farm output.

At the beginning of the twentieth century, 45.8 million Americans were living on farms; however, by 1991, this figure had fallen to about a tenth (4.6 million), just over 1.8 percent of the total U.S. population.[64] As the farm population and the number of individual farms fell, output in agriculture rose relentlessly. By the end of the 1970s, farm output per hour was four times the level of 1950. The number of persons fed per farm worker at home rose in that period from 15 to 52. In 1920, 6.5 million farms had fed 105.7 million Americans or 16.3 persons per farm. In 1997, there were more than 140 Americans per farm,

FIGURE 29.4 Farm Population vs. Farm Output

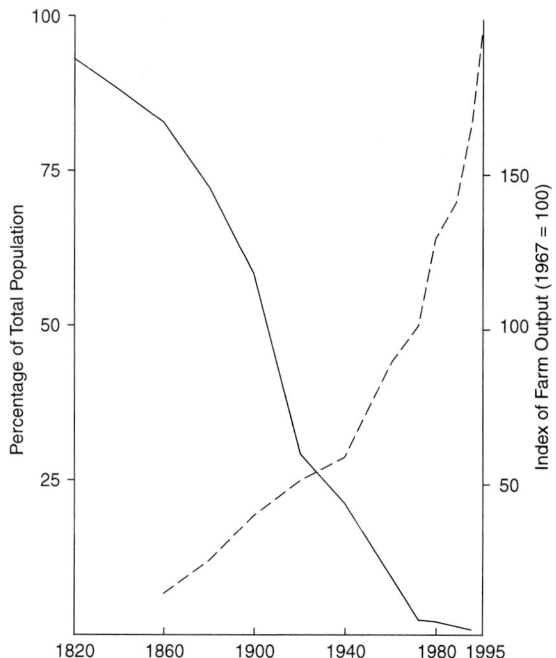

Sources: *Historical Statistics,* series A 2, K 1, 414–429; *Statistical Abstract, 1992,* Tables 1073, 1106; *Statistical Abstract, 2000,* Table 1117.

While farm output soared in the past century, the percentage of the total population engaged in farming declined drastically.

and Americans spent, on average, less than 10 percent of their disposable incomes on farm goods—as late as the 1930s that figure had been 25 percent. In addition, the American farmer was the world's largest exporter of major food crops: 67 percent of world corn (maize) exports, 57 percent of soybean, more than 30 percent of cotton, and 28 percent of world wheat exports came from the United States in 1999. Cotton exports, which were roughly one-third of world exports in 1995, fell to almost half that amount in 1999.

The mechanization of cotton production led to an outmigration of southern farm workers. As Lee Alston and Joseph Ferrie argue, the scientific advances that came at about the same time increased and stabilized yields and reduced the need for laborers with knowledge about farming in a specific locale. Mechanization reduced the cost of monitoring labor and the cost of labor turnover, displacing millions of workers who traveled north and west in search of work. The threat of unemployment maintained the work intensity of those who remained.[65] These technological changes also contributed to a shift toward wage labor and a decline in the institution of sharecropping. The first step was the introduction of the tractor (discussed below). The ability to plow with a tractor meant that a large labor force was needed only for weeding and harvesting. The second step was the adoption of the cotton picker, which harvested almost the entire crop of upland cotton by the end of the 1960s. The largest drop in tenancy occurred in the 1950s. Craig Heinicke's study of black migration notes that the fall in demand during this period was at least as great as the fall in supply. His work suggests the number of acres planted in cotton increased slightly in the 1950s, then fell by almost 50 percent in the 1960s.[66]

As farm families left the countryside, in the North as well as the South, farm amalgamations kept the acreage under cultivation high. By 1997, the average American farm was 434 acres, compared with 147 acres in 1920. Farms of 500 acres and larger (a mere 18.4 percent of all farms) actually contained 79.2 percent of all farmland. A homestead of 160 acres is too small to make a go of it anymore.

This production wonder was one modern outcome of the "industrialization" of American agriculture in recent decades. The application of new fertilizers, herbicides, insecticides, and more efficient machinery had produced an extraordinary increase in labor-hour productivity. The changes wrought by these innovations are illustrated in Figure 29.5.

Much of the previous discussion in this book has highlighted the role of mechanization in improving farm productivity, but biological innovations were just as important.[67] The search for higher-yielding, disease-resistant plants and animals was present from Jamestown on. In the twentieth century, the application of genetics and chemistry accelerated this process and created the "Green Revolution" of the post-World War II years. The best known example is that of hybrid corn. In 1908, George Shull of

FIGURE 29.5 Wheat and Corn Output and Labor Hours Per Acre

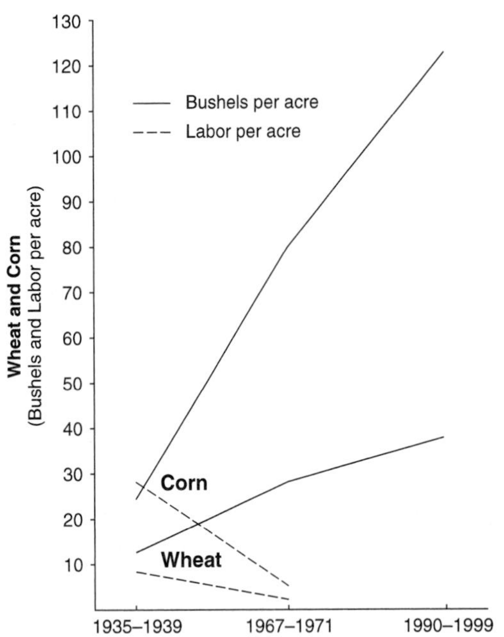

Sources: *Statistical Abstract, 1973,* Table 1012; *Statistical Abstract, 2000,* Table 1126.

Modern farming technology has produced sharply rising yields of wheat and corn per acre, while reducing the labor input per acre farmed by extraordinary amounts.

the Carnegie Institution developed inbred lines of corn by applying genetic theory. A decade later, Edward East and Donald Jones of the Connecticut Experimental Station produced a double-crossed hybrid, as opposed to Shull's single-crossed hybrid. Hybrid corn initially increased yields by 5 to 10 percent over open-pollinated corn. Zvi Griliches's examination of the diffusion of hybrid corn indicated that it diffused according to its economic advantages.[68] In major corn-growing states such as Iowa, it diffused rapidly, with most farmers growing hybrid corn by World War II. Elsewhere, it diffused less rapidly, but, by 1959, the crop was approximately 95 percent hybrid corn.

Yields further increased as a result of the application of chemical fertilizers. By the early years of the twentieth century, soils on northern farms were beginning to become depleted. Between 1910 and 1940, it is estimated that the purchase of fertilizers doubled. In the following 30 years, as the real price of chemical fertilizers fell, purchases increased eight-fold.

The application of genetic theory to animals, the development of artificial insemination in the 1930s, and a better understanding of food chemistry increased livestock yields.

Mechanical improvements continued; none more important than the tractor. Early gasoline tractors were large and used primarily for plowing and harrowing. The Bull (1913) was the first small tractor. The Fordson (1917), a Ford Motor product, was the first mass-produced of the small tractors. But these proved less important than the McCormick-Deering Farmall (1924), the first general-purpose tractor that could cultivate growing crops and tow other equipment. William White estimates that tractors tripled labor productivity and replaced over 24 million work animals.[69] Unlike corn, tractors diffused relatively slowly, but White concludes this was rational by examining quality-adjusted prices, which roughly halved over the period 1918–40 then stabilized as the technology matured.[70] Following Robert Fogel, White estimates the direct *social saving* of the tractor to be 8 percent of GDP in 1954, and substantially higher when the indirect effects, especially the ability to spread chemical fertilizers, are included. This is a substantially higher figure than Fogel or Fishlow calculated for the railroad and illustrates one of the major ways in which the internal combustion engine transformed rural America. The combine (reaper plus threshing) was another, one suggestive of the increased amount of capital required to farm in modern America. The automobile and truck brought farmers and their markets in much closer contact than had ever been the case. The farmer was finally integrated into the rest of American society. On Saturday mornings between mid-summer and late autumn, suburban "farmer's markets" take over commuter parking lots so that farmers from perhaps 150 miles away can sell their wares directly to the consumer.

Since American farms are private business ventures, "industrialization" has led to the usual American phenomena of corporate organization, and, to some extent, scale economies. American agriculture is "efficient" in the sense that it is generally not threatened by foreign competition at the most basic levels, such as the production of wheat, corn, soybeans, peanuts, or raw cotton. But the financing of agriculture, the processing and fabrication of its output, and sales both at home and abroad, have for so long been the consequences of mercurial federal policy making that one would have to be bold indeed to predict its future on the basis of its history, even its recent history. American farming became a technological wonder, and continues now, as in the past, to produce more agricultural output than can be domestically consumed, given the present, or possibly *any* distribution of income. The Populist panaceas of land banks, federal farm mortgages, federal subsidies of exports, domestic food give-away programs, and loans against stored crops have failed to "solve the farm problem." Indeed, in the mid–1980s, American farmers faced bankruptcies and foreclosures in record numbers, and yet another appeal was launched for increased federal aid to "save the family farm." The Reagan administration was threatening, once again, to throw the farmers and their troubles into the "free market," but did not. In fact, 1986 dawned with yet another farm bill full of price supports and other forms of federal subsidies. By 1988, the entire system of federal farm credit faced bankruptcy, and Congress faced the necessity of a bailout that some feared would approach $100 billion.

The Farm Bill of 1996 was intended to be a change in the direction of agricultural policy, a move toward a more market-oriented approach. It removed the tie between income support payments and farm prices and substituted "production flexibility contracts" and a series of fixed annual "transition payments" for a particular set of farmers.[71] These payments were independent of farm prices and specific crop production, the two variables that determined the amount before 1996. The contract requires that, among other things, farmers comply with extant conservation plans and wetland provisions, and that the land be kept in agriculture. The government no longer requires that farmers leave some land idle or that farmers produce the crop they historically produced in order to receive payment. All has not gone smoothly. Between October 1998 and October 2000, low prices for farm commodities led to the passage of four "supplemental emergency assistance packages," and debate continues as to whether the transition should be augmented by some form of income support.

The prospect of resolving the basic farm problem—that a high agricultural quantity is associated with a low price times quantity, a problem that can be identified in the Old Testament—is no brighter today than it was then.

NOTES

1. Ira Magaziner and Robert Reich, *Minding America's Business: The Decline and Rise of the American Economy* (1982), p. 31.
2. M. R. Darby, "The U.S. Productivity Slowdown: A Case of Statistical Myopia," *AER,* June 1984, p. 301.
3. Magaziner and Reich (1982), p. 36.
4. A recent example is Catherine J. Morrison and Amy Ellen Schwartz, "State Infrastructure and Productive Performance," *American Economic Review,* vol. 86, no. 5, December 1996.
5. Alfred Chandler, Jr., "The Competitive Performance of U.S. Industrial Enterprises since the Second World War," *BHR,* Spring 1994, p. 6.
6. An interesting discussion of the merger activity of the 1980s and 1990s, and how it differed over those two decades, can be found in Bengt Holmstrom and Steven N. Kaplan, "Corporate Governance and Merger Activity in the United States: Making Sense of the 1980s and 1990s," *Journal of Economic Perspectives,* vol. 15, no. 2, Spring 2001. This paper is part of a symposium on "Changes in Corporate Structure."
7. See Leonard S. Reich, *The Making of American Industrial Research: Science and Business at GE and Bell, 1876–1926* (Cambridge: Cambridge University Press, 1985), and David A. Hounshell and John Kenly Smith, Jr., *Science and Corporate Strategy: DuPont R&D, 1902–1980* (Cambridge: Cambridge University Press, 1988). Alcoa was another early investor in R&D.
8. Bronwyn Hall, "Corporate Restructuring and Investment Horizons in the United States, 1976–1987," *BHR,* Spring 1994, p. 124. Hall used these categories to undertake a statistical analysis; Chandler used them to present case studies.
9. *Ibid.*, p. 140. Carliss Baldwin and Kim Clark, "Capital-Budgeting Systems and Capabilities Investments in U.S.

Companies after the Second World War," *BHR,* Spring 1994, consider a series of capabilities financial accounting failed to reveal. The problem was not a lack of capital, just the way it was invested (p. 76).

10. Darby (1984), p. 306, Table 4.
11. *Ibid.,* p. 306.
12. Barry Bluestone and Bennett Harrison, *The Deindustrialization of America* (1982); Robert Reich, *The Next American Frontier* (1983); Richard McKenzie, *Fugitive Industry* (1984).
13. Moreover, GM itself imported some 200,000 Japanese autos in 1985 to sell under its own logo.
14. Richard Easterlin, "Why Isn't Everyone Developed?" *JEH,* March 1981.
15. The reader might refer again to Gregory Clark's argument that differences in efficient deployment of labor forces, more than anything else, explain the uneven use of state-of-the-art technology worldwide: "Why Isn't the Whole World Developed? Lessons from the Cotton Mills," *Journal of Economic History,* vol. XLVII, no. 1, March 1987.
16. Baldwin and Clark (1994), pp. 98–101.
17. *Ibid.,* pp. 156–157.
18. *Ibid.,* p. 162.
19. Paul Tiffany, "The Roots of Decline: Business Government Relations in the American Steel Industry, 1945–1960," *JEH,* June 1984, p. 417.
20. *Ibid.,* p. 419.
21. Robert Ankli and Eva Sommer, "The Role of Management in the Decline of the American Steel Industry," *Business and Economic History,* vol. 25, no. 1, Fall 1996, p. 230.
22. Walter Adams and Hans Mueller, "The Steel Industry," in Walter Adams, ed., *The Structure of American Industry,* 6th ed. (1982), p. 76.
23. *Ibid.,* p. 118.
24. *Statistical Abstract, 1995,* Table 1266, reports that open hearth output was essentially zero in this country from 1992 onward.
25. Magaziner and Reich (1982), p. 167; Adams and Mueller (1982), Tables 11, 14A, 14B. In 1981 the net cost per ton combined of employment, coking coal and iron ore were $303 in the United States, $240 in Western Europe, and $187 in Japan. Because of more efficient plants, the costs even of coking coal and iron ore were lower per ton of steel in Japan than in the United States (Table 14B). Japan has no deposits of either. Table 12 of Adams and Mueller shows the U.S. industry to be technologically inferior to the Japanese and the Western Europeans in nearly every measurable dimension.
26. Adams and Mueller (1982), p. 111.
27. *Ibid.,* p. 128.
28. *Ibid.,* pp. 128–133.
29. *Ibid.,* p. 112, n. 84.
30. James Powell, "Steel Import Restraints: Flood the Markets with Choice," *New York Times,* 7 August 1988.
31. Rick Wartzman and Carol Hymowitz, "Uneasy Revival: Big Steel is Back, But Upturn is Costly and May Not Last," *Wall Street Journal,* 4 November 1988.
32. *Chicago Tribune,* 10 February 1986, Section 4, p. 5.
33. Robert Thomas, "Style Change and the Automobile Industry During the Roaring Twenties," in Louis Cain and Paul Uselding, eds., *Business Enterprise and Economic Change* (1973). Two more recent studies are Richard Langlois and Paul Robertson, "Explaining Vertical Integration: Lessons from the American Automobile Industry," *JEH,* June 1989; and Timothy Bresnahan and Daniel Raff, "Intra-Industry Heterogeneity and the Great Depression: The American Motor Vehicles Industry 1929–1935," *JEH,* June 1991.
34. Lawrence White, "The Automobile Industry," in Adams, *The Structure of American Industry* (1982), p. 138.
35. *Ibid.,* p. 146.
36. Baldwin and Clark (1994), p. 90, discusses differences between the U.S. and Japanese automobile industries in their ability to integrate customer preferences into product design.
37. Simon Kuznets, *Economic Change* (1954), p. 254.
38. Arthur Burns, *Production Trends in the United States Since 1870* (1934), p. 279.
39. These three industries, plus the chemical, diagnostic device, machine tool, and pharmaceutical industries are examined in detail in Mowery and Nelson, *Sources of Industrial Leadership* (1999). See also David Mowery and Nathan Rosenberg, "Twentieth-Century Technological Change," in Stanley Engerman and Robert Gallman, editors, *The Cambridge Economic History of the United States. Volume III: The Twentieth Century* (Cambridge: Cambridge University Press, 2000).
40. See Ernest Braun and Stuart Macdonald, *Revolution in Miniature* (Cambridge: Cambridge University Press, 1982).
41. The Justice Department filed the suit in 1949. It was settled through a consent decree signed in 1956 that, among other things, required AT&T to make semiconductor technology widely available, a policy AT&T already had in force. The company hoped that some of the resulting breakthroughs would benefit the telephone business.
42. It should be noted that the federal government, particularly through the military, was a major source of industrial R&D funds in the post-World War II era. The industry also benefited from the emerging venture capital market. See Paul Gompers and Josh Lerner, "The Venture Capital Revolution," *Journal of Economic Perspectives,* vol. 15, no. 2, Spring 2001.
43. See Leslie R. Berlin, "Robert Noyce and Fairchild Semiconductor, 1957–1968," *BHR,* Spring 2001.
44. Richard Langlois and W. Edward Steinmueller, "The Evolution of Competitive Advantage in the Worldwide

Semiconductor Industry 1947–1996," in Mowery and Nelson (2000), p. 48.

45. Other factors were also at work that favored the U.S. firms. The strong position of the yen relative to the dollar through much of this period contributed to a relative decline in Japanese production. Other countries, notably China and Korea, developed their industries with an emphasis on consumer electronics. Finally, there has not been a "blockbuster," rapid-growth electronic device since the VCR in the early 1990s.
46. Timothy Bresnahan and Franco Malerba, "Industrial Dynamics and the Evolution of Firms' and Nations' Competitive Capabilities in the World Computer Industry," in Mowery and Nelson (2000), p. 80.
47. This was named after the Institute of Advanced Study where he was located. Magnetic core memories were developed in part by MIT's Project Whirlwind.
48. With the introduction of the System 370, their share fell to roughly 50 percent.
49. Langlois, "Creating External Capabilities: Innovation and Vertical Disintegration in the Microcomputer Industry," *Business and Economic History,* vol. 19, 1990. See also his "External Economies and Economic Progress: The Case of the Microcomputer Industry," *Business History Review,* vol. 67, no. 1, Spring 1992.
50. There are several definitional problems surrounding the term software. David Mowery, "The Computer Software Industry," in Mowery and Nelson (2000), p. 134, discusses these definitional problems.
51. The same was true of the relationship had with Intel for the purchase of microprocessors.
52. Martin Campbell-Kelly, "Not Only Microsoft: The Maturing of the Personal Computer Software Industry, 1982–1995," *BHR*, Spring 2001, provides a detailed review of this industry. Although its review ends in 1995, the author does include a postscript on the Microsoft case that favors the defense.
53. The "competition" between the OS/2 and Windows operating systems is discussed in *Ibid.*, pp. 122–28. The author notes that once-popular software, Lotus 1-2-3 and WordPerfect in particular, bet on the OS/2 standard and lost market share when Windows proved dominant.
54. Mowery (2000), p. 145, notes that, like other parts of the electronics industry, software benefited from federal monies, especially those that helped finance university-based research centers.
55. See Janet Abbate, *Inventing the Internet* (1999) and "Government, Business, and the Making of the Internet," *Business History Review,* vol. 75, no. 1, Spring 2001.
56. A symposium of the Microsoft case was published in *Journal of Economic Perspectives,* vol. 15, no. 2, Spring 2001. A book written by three economists involved in IBM's defense against antitrust charges is Fisher, McKie, and Mancke, *IBM and the U.S. Data Processing Industry: An Economic History* (1983).
57. McKenzie (1984), chap. 2.
58. James Soltow, "Management, Entrepreneurship, and the Economic Readjustment of the Middle West," *BEH,* 1984, p. 94.
59. *Ibid.,* p. 95.
60. *Ibid.,* p. 97.
61. McKenzie (1984), chap. 4.
62. Sukkoo Kim, "Economic Integration and Convergence: U.S. Regions, 1840–1987," *Journal of Economic History,* vol. 58, no. 3, September 1998. See also Kent James Mitchener and Ian McLean, "U.S. Regional Growth and Convergence, 1880–1980," *Journal of Economic History,* vol. 59, no. 4, December 1999.
63. Harry Scheiber, "State Law and 'Industrial Policy' in American Development, 1790–1987," *California Law Review,* January 1987.
64. Since that time, the federal government has elected not to count the total number of Americans who still live on farms.
65. Lee Alston and Joseph Ferrie, *Southern Paternalism and the American Welfare State* (Cambridge University Press, 1999).
66. Craig Heinicke, "African-American Migration and Mechanized Cotton Harvesting, 1950–1960," *Explorations in Economic History,* vol. 31, no. 4, October 1994.
67. See Alan L. Olmstead and Paul W. Rhode, "Biological Innovation and American Agricultural Development," Institute of Governmental Affairs Working Paper, University of California-Davis, April 2000. See also their, "The Transformation of Northern Agriculture, 1910–1990," in Stanley Engerman and Robert Gallman, eds., *The Cambridge Economic History of the United States. Volume III: The Twentieth Century* (Cambridge: Cambridge University Press, 2000).
68. Zvi Griliches, "Hybrid Corn: An Exploration of the Economics of Technological Change," *Econometrica,* vol. 25, no. 4, October 1957. Griliches wrote a companion paper on tractors: "The Demand for a Durable Input: Farm Tractors in the United States, 1921–1957," in Arnold Harberger, ed., *The Demand for Durable Goods* (Chicago: University of Chicago Press, 1960).
69. William J. White III, "An Unsung Hero: The Farm Tractor's Contribution to Twentieth-Century United States Economic Growth," unpublished Ph.D. dissertation, The Ohio State University, 2000.
70. Olmstead and Rhode consider this process as one of capital replacement, tractors for work animals, and agree that it was rational. Alan Olmstead and Paul Rhode, "Reshaping the Landscape: The Impact and Diffusion of the Tractor in American Agriculture, 1910–1960," *Journal of Economic History,* vol. 61, no. 3, September 2001.
71. Farmers who had participated in the wheat, feed grains, cotton, or rice programs at any time in the previous five years could enter into a seven-year contract.

SUGGESTED READINGS

Articles

Adams, Walter, and Hans Mueller. "The Steel Industry." In Walter Adams, ed., *The Structure of American Industry*, 6th ed. New York: Macmillan, 1982.

Ault, D. "The Continued Deterioration of the Competitive Ability of the U.S. Steel Industry: The Development of Continuous Casting." *Western Economic Journal*, vol. 11, March 1973.

Baldwin, Carliss Y., and Kim B. Clark. "Capital-Budgeting Systems and Capabilities Investments in U.S. Companies after the Second World War." *Business History Review*, vol. 68, no. 1, Spring 1994.

Berlin, Leslie R. "Robert Noyce and Fairchild Semiconductor, 1957–1968." *Business History Review*, vol. 75, no. 1, Spring 2001.

Bresnahan, Timothy F., and Franco Malerba. "Industrial Dynamics and the Evolution of Firms' and Nations' Competitive Capabilities in the World Computer Industry." In Mowery and Nelson, eds. *Sources of Industrial Leadership*. Cambridge: Cambridge University Press, 1999.

———, and Daniel Raff. "Intra-Industry Heterogeneity and the Great Depression: The American Motor Vehicles Industry 1929–1935." *Journal of Economic History*, vol. 51, no. 2, June 1991.

Campbell-Kelly, Martin. "Not Only Microsoft: The Maturing of the Personal Computer Software Industry, 1982–1995." *Business History Review*, vol. 75, no. 1, Spring 2001.

Chandler, Alfred D., Jr. "The Competitive Performance of U.S. Industrial Enterprises since the Second World War." *Business History Review*, vol. 68, no. 1, Spring 1994.

Darby, M.R. "The U.S. Productivity Slowdown: A Case of Statistical Myopia," *American Economic Review*, vol. 74, no. 3, June 1984.

DeVries, Jan. "Is There an Economics Decline?" *Journal of Economic History*, vol. 38, no. 1, March 1978.

Easterlin, Richard. "Why Isn't Everyone Developed?" *Journal of Economic History*, vol. XLI, no. 1, March 1981.

Hall, Bronwyn H. "Corporate Restructuring and Investment Horizons in the United States, 1976–1987." *Business History Review*, vol. 68, no. 1, Spring 1994.

Langlois, Richard, and Paul Robertson. "Explaining Vertical Integration: Lessons from the American Automobile Industry." *Journal of Economic History*, vol. XLIX, no. 2, June 1989.

———, and W. Edward Steinmueller. "The Evolution of Competitive Advantage in the Worldwide Semiconductor Industry, 1947–1996." In Mowery and Nelson, eds. *Sources of Industrial Leadership*. Cambridge: Cambridge University Press, 1999.

Mowery, David C. "The Computer Software Industry." In Mowery and Nelson, eds. *Sources of Industrial Leadership*. Cambridge: Cambridge University Press, 1999.

Scheiber, Harry N. "State Law and 'Industrial Policy' in American Development, 1790–1987." *California Law Review*, vol. 75, no. 1, January 1987.

Soltow, James H. "Management, Entrepreneurship, and the Economic Readjustment of the Middle West." In Jeremy Atack, ed., *Business and Economic History*, second series, vol. 12 (Urbana: University of Illinois Press, 1984).

Thomas, Robert. "Style Change and the Automobile Industry During the Roaring Twenties." In Louis Cain and Paul Uselding, eds. *Business Enterprise and Economic Change*. Kent, OH: Kent State University Press, 1973.

Tiffany, Paul A. "The Roots of Decline: Business Government Relations in the American Steel Industry, 1945–1960." *Journal of Economic History*, vol. XLIV, no. 2, June 1984.

Vatter, Harold. "The Closure of Entry in the American Automobile Industry." *Oxford Economic Papers*, no. 4, October 1972.

White, Lawrence. "The Automobile Industry." In Walter Adams, ed. *The Structure of American Industry*, 6th ed. New York: Macmillan, 1982.

Books

Abbate, Janet. *Inventing the Internet*. Cambridge: MIT Press, 1999.

Adams, Walter, ed. *The Structure of American History*, 6th ed. New York: Macmillan, 1982.

Alston, Lee, and Joseph Ferrie. *Southern Paternalism and the American Welfare State: Economics, Politics, and Institutions in the South, 1865–1965*. Cambridge University Press, 1999.

Bluestone, Barry, and Bennett Harrison. *The Deindustrialization of America: Plant Closings, Community Abandonment, and the Dismantling of Basic Industry*. New York: Basic Books, 1982.

Burns, Arthur F. *Production Trends in the United States Since 1870*. New York: National Bureau of Economic Research, 1934.

Crandall, Robert W. *The U.S. Steel Industry in Recurrent Crisis*. Washington, DC: The Brookings Institution, 1981.

Fisher, Franklin, James McKie, and Richard Mancke. *IBM and the U.S. Data Processing Industry: An Economic History*. New York: Praeger, 1983.

Fuchs, Victor. *Changes in the Location of Manufacturing in the United States.* New Haven: Yale University Press, 1962.

Kuznets, Simon. *Economic Change.* London: William Heineman, Ltd., 1954.

Magaziner, Ira C., and Robert B. Reich. *Minding America's Business: The Decline and Rise of the American Economy.* New York: Harcourt Brace Jovanovich, 1982.

Maxcy, George. *The Multinational Automobile Industry.* New York: St. Martin's Press, 1981.

McKenzie, Richard B. *Fugitive Industry: The Economics and Politics of Deindustrialization.* San Francisco: Pacific Institute, 1984.

Mowery, David C., and Richard R. Nelson, eds. *Sources of Industrial Leadership.* Cambridge: Cambridge University Press, 1999.

Phillips, Richard, et al. *Auto Industries of Europe, U.S. and Japan.* Cambridge, MA: Abt Books, 1982.

Rae, John B. *The American Automobile Industry.* Boston: Twayne Publishers, 1984.

Reich, Robert. *The Next American Frontier.* New York: Time/Life Books, 1983.

CHAPTER THIRTY

From the New Frontier to the New Millennium

The last four decades of the twentieth century, the years between the elections of John F. Kennedy and George W. Bush, witnessed social and economic changes of extraordinary magnitude. Our discussion of the great issues of 1961–2001 takes place against a background of ubiquitous economic change whose larger consequences are yet to be understood in the aggregate.

Following Kennedy's assassination in November 1963, the American republic headed into policies that significantly changed the economy. A modern Rip Van Winkle who went to sleep in 1961 and awoke in 2001 would examine the economy in disbelief. Management, it would seem, had been more than a little careless on more than one occasion in the interim.

At the dawn of the twenty-first century, President Eisenhower's legacy of stable growth was but a dim memory. Impressive real economic growth had been achieved, and the disorder of the early years had given way to a sense of optimism in the 1990s. Budget expenditures had been described as "out of control;" "budget cuts" referred to cuts in the amount of budget increase. Annual federal deficits were huge (between 1967 and 1997 there was a single surplus, in 1969).

On many dimensions, the year 1980 represents a low point in our recent history. Inflation in 1980 was double-digit, nearly 14 percent, while short-term interest rates exceeded 20 percent, the highest in American history, in peace or war. The money supply (measured as M_1) was three times that of 1960, and so was the national debt, which stood at about $850 billion and was headed for the $1 trillion mark. The real incomes of workers were actually declining by 1980, as was labor productivity.[1] The ratio of private saving to national income was the lowest of any advanced economy. Private investment was stagnating; in fact, it was less than half the size of the federal budget. It had been five times federal expenditures in 1929, was still greater than federal expenditures as late as 1951, but then started slipping. Unemployment exceeded 7 percent of the civilian labor force. By the turn of the century, there was a more optimistic view of the future. The economy generally improved after 1980. By 2000, the rate of inflation, interest rates, and the unemployment rate had all decreased. A surplus developed in 1998, but the events of 11 September 2001 make it appear that it will be several more years before we again see a surplus.

Between 1961 and 1980, a whole new set of controversial federal controls came into existence. In 1980, it was widely charged that these controls were significantly reducing the rate of growth of industrial output.[2] Such charges are seldom heard now, but these controls remain controversial.

Between 1961 and 1980, a disastrous war was fought and lost in southeast Asia, one president was assassinated and another was driven from office, and an American embassy was invaded in the Middle East and its employees taken hostage. Racial conflict—erupting in rioting, burning, and looting in New York, Detroit, Chicago, Los Angeles, and elsewhere—shook the nation. Crime was rampant, and huge areas in the inner sections of the large cities became burned-out ruins.

Between 1980 and 2001, things were much more tranquil. After the longest expansion in U.S. history, the economy entered a recession in March 2001, and then came the international terrorist attack of September 11th. A sense of optimism was replaced by a sense of foreboding. The pessimism, then optimism, of the preceding years had been engineered by Americans. Our ability to affect the future was now less certain, yet one expects a sense of optimism will return once the economy enters a new upswing.

As we have seen, the core of U.S. economic growth shifted away from its historic base in heavy industry, a base that had prevailed from the 1870s to World War II. A new lifestyle based upon a range of new industries—electronics, light metals, new chemical compounds, synthetic materials—and a huge influx of women into the labor force impacted American society with elemental force. The benefits to the public of greater safety on the job, cleaner air and water—cleaner than they otherwise would have been—and environmental protection did not enhance the conventional measures of economic growth. Fierce resistance in the early 1980s to a Secretary of the Interior whose actions many believed threatened to degrade the ecological system seemed to underscore the new American devotion to the "quality of life." Through the 1980s, however, there was increasing environmental degradation of all sorts. The scorching "greenhouse summer" of 1988 highlighted the aching environmental problems within the United States and brought louder demands than ever for fundamental changes as crops wilted and East Coast beaches were awash in dangerous garbage. Little progress has been made since. The "Kyoto Protocol" of 1997 that emerged out of a series of international meetings over the 1990s was a declaration that steps would be taken to reduce the problem, but no developed country had ratified the agreement when President Bush, the younger, declared it "fundamentally flawed."[3]

Our attempt to improve our quality of life began with the Kennedy administration.

THE NEW WAVE OF CONTROLS

The 1960s seem destined to be remembered for a new departure in federal controls over the economy. Beginning with the civil rights movement during the early 1960s, American social policy at the federal level was reactivated for the first time since the 1930s.[4] Truman had tried with the "Fair Deal," and Congress had defeated him. Influenced in part by John Kenneth Galbraith's *The Affluent Society* (1958), the Kennedy activists brought to Washington a demand that the *quality* of public expenditures as well as the quantity be increased. River and harbor expenditures would not be enough.

The New Breed

There was an unsubtle change in the nature of federal nonmarket controls. New ideas about the quality of life emerged, along with new concerns about human beings in their living environment as well as in their inanimate physical environment. The traditional method of nonmarket control, apart from the antitrust laws, was that a given agency regulated a *specific* industry or area of economic life. The ICC regulated transportation; the Federal Reserve System regulated banking; the SEC, the securities industry; the FAA, airline industry; the FCC, the communications industry.[5] The great exception was the Sherman Antitrust Act and its amendments, by which the Justice Department, together with the Federal Trade Commission, had power over all infractions of the laws in *whatever* industries those infractions occurred.

Beginning in 1962 with the Food and Drug Amendments (which greatly expanded the Food and Drug Administration's powers) and the Air Pollution Control Act (which laid down national air-pollution standards), a new breed of controls began to appear whose coverage was like the Sherman Act. The regulatory agency involved had its power over *all* violations of the law in whatever areas of economic life they occurred. These new controls have been dubbed *intrusive* because they touch everything, not just specified regulated industries. In fact, *all* industries are regulated by these laws, including those that are subject to other forms of federal regulation as well. Murray Weidenbaum observed in his book *Business and Government in the Global Marketplace*, that there is another difference. In the new regulative mode, the federal regulator has no particular responsibility for the economic impact of his or her rulings on those regulated.[6] If a firm goes out of business because of the regulation, the federal agency involved has no liability for that outcome. In industry-specific regulation, agencies such as the FDA or the Federal Reserve System supposedly have some responsibility to allow life to the regulatees. The new controls thus smacked of autocracy in a way the old methods did not.

Between 1962 and 1972, the majority of the intrusive regulatory structure was founded. The year 1964 saw the Civil Rights Act become law—a federal prohibition against job discrimination on the basis of race—and the establishment of the Equal Employment Opportunity Commission to monitor the act. In 1965, the Water Quality Act required the states to meet standards for the improvement of water quality. A year later, manufacturers were required by the Fair Packaging and Labeling Act to include an expanded range of consumer information on cans and packages. The same year, 1966, children were protected from dangerous toys by the Child Protection Act. Also, the Traffic Safety Act of 1966 set up the National Highway Safety Administration to upgrade and modernize Detroit's ideas about the necessary safety and health features of its products.

Businesses handling farm products were given a mandatory set of standards in 1967 by the Agricultural Fair Practices Act. In that year, the Flammable Products Act set new standards for fire-resistant textiles that manufacturers had to meet in order to be allowed in the nation's markets. Lenders of all sorts were placed under greater borrower scrutiny by the Truth-in-Lending Act of 1968 and made to spell out in detail and simplicity the conditions of all loans made.

Nixon's election in 1968 was not the occasion for any reversal of this expansion of federal nonmarket controls, despite his campaign rhetoric about freedom, laissez-faire, rugged individualism, and the like. The environment received special attention. The Clean Air Act of 1970 had as its basic goal "to protect and enhance the quality of the nation's air so as to promote the public health and welfare and the productive capacity its population." The Water Pollution Control Act was amended in 1972 with an overall goal "to restore and maintain the chemical, physical and biological integrity of the nation's waters." And, the Endangered Species Act of 1973 was designed so that it "would make the taking of endangered species a federal offense, and would permit protection measures to be undertaken before a species is so depleted that restoration is impossible."[7] Indeed, the National Environmental Policy Act of 1969, which required new federally financed projects to submit an environmental impact statement, may well prove to be the single most intrusive piece of economic legislation ever passed.

The federal government in 1970 received permission from Congress to establish general price and wage controls via the Economic Stabilization Act. Securities brokers were required to insure their accounts against loss by the Securities Investors Protection Act. Also in 1970, the National Air Quality Act gave the Environmental Protection Agency authority to administer air-pollution standards. Perhaps the most sensational law of 1970 was the Occupational Health and Safety Act, which created OSHA and endowed it with plenary powers to enforce on-the-job safety standards.[8] In 1972, came the Noise Pollution and Control Act and the Consumer Products Safety Act, whose Consumer Products Safety Commission was placed in charge of the safety features of thousands of manufactured products.

Why All the Regulation?

This burst of regulatory activity introduced a mass of detailed new regulation and regulatory change that was probably unequaled even by the New Deal.[9] Whatever the actual economic impact of these changes (to date no one has measured them with any pretense of accuracy), the motivation was clear enough. Since the free market, left to its own devices, either could not or would not produce a quality of life that satisfied lawmakers, the force of government was placed at the service of broad reform. Very little was left untouched, to the outrage of all those adversely affected and the delight of those whose lives were improved. It was primarily legislation of this kind, the drive for instant reform, instant improvement, that characterized the domestic legislation of Lyndon Johnson's "Great Society" and its spillover into the Nixon era.

In fact, the laws just mentioned are only a sampling, a tip of the iceberg. Public radio and public television, federal funding of the performing arts and the humanities, and change toward broader, "multiple uses" of federal lands and parks, were all parts of a sudden swing toward improvement in the "quality of life." Whatever else it was, the movement was an example of the American ideal. Expressed in the terminology of the arts, it was described by the American painter Mary Buckley as "a shortcut to a masterpiece."

These changes came suddenly with the civil rights movement, the antiwar movement, and the liberation of lifestyles. Time, and politics, will tell whether the quality-of-life movement in this country will persist. Following a trail blazed by Sweden and adopted by the other Western European nations, the United States was attempting to reach for social perfection through government authority. The "traditional" American idea of the welfare state has been merely the provision of basic economic security through state action; but, if the "good life" is seen to include beauty, comfort, convenience, and culture beyond the amounts supplied through private purchase, interested parties will try to achieve requisite supplies of such items as public goods. All that is required is that the people be willing to be taxed, either directly or via inflation. It may not be good for "economic efficiency" in the narrow sense, but it has been good for *votes* for politicians. By the early 1990s, however, Europeans were beginning to question their commitment to what had become more expensive programs than they had envisaged. Similarly, beginning in the 1990s, U.S. politicians paid some attention to the financial problems facing Social Security and Medicare.[10] The tax rates were raised in 1990, and, the following year, the rate and the limits for the Social Security portion were separated from those for Medicare. Later in the decade, a law was passed that ultimately will raise the age at which benefits begin from 65 to 67. While politicians from both parties recognized the popularity of these programs, conservative politicians argued in favor of reducing the subsidies received by seemingly popular programs such as public television and the National Endowment for the Arts. To date, they have not found enough votes to reverse public provision of these goods.

What Professor Galbraith said in *The Affluent Society* was that the American economy was drowning in private goods and was desperately short of positive and uplifting public goods.[11] E. J. Mishan, in *Technology and Growth: The Price We Pay*, added that "natural amenities," like silence, clear air, and pure water, are prescriptive property rights of all people that the market economy has destroyed, without compensation, for the benefit of private profits.[12] According to Mishan, a restoration is in order. For the followers of Galbraith and Mishan, "the new regulation" is merely a down payment on the future. For those opposed to government growth, the new regulation is an unwarranted intrusion into private life, including private business life.

Politics will determine the outcome. After the first Reagan administration, which promised massive deregulation, the issue went into deep background. Indeed, the vast majority of deregulation was accomplished before Reagan took office.[13] Although regulatory relief was one of the major planks of his program to "get the government off our backs," there was relatively little of it during his first term—and less during the second.[14] The amount of attention paid to basic economic principles was much greater for industry-specific regulation than for the new, intrusive social legislation. In a review of health and safety regulation in the 1980s, Kip Viscusi presented examples of Reagan-era rules that could not have passed the simplest benefit-cost test. Viscusi commented that, not only were reforms "never achieved," they were "never attempted."[15] However, Reaganites successfully resisted demands for "reregulation" in banking and transportation, specifically the airlines.

The Transportation Sector

Congress first received a report suggesting an Interstate Highway System in 1939, and, two years later, FDR appointed a committee to refine the concept. In 1944, Congress approved the committee's report, which included the idea of a "national system of interstate highways," but they did not provide any funding at that time because of the war. Several states, noting that limited-access roads were necessary, fell back on eighteenth-century precedent and constructed toll roads. The Pennsylvania Turnpike, which opened in 1940, was the first of these and was built with federal aid from the Works Progress Administration and a loan from the Reconstruction Finance Corporation.[16] The prosperity of the postwar years, and particularly automobile-based suburbanization, increased the demand for new roads.

The 1956 Interstate Highway Act, with a preamble citing national defense, authorized a 42,500-mile system of limited-access, high-speed roadways.[17] It also created the Highway Trust Fund as a way of financing the system. The work was to be done by the states, with $25 billion over 12 years from the federal government paying 90 percent of the tab.[18] It was, in many ways, the culmination of Gallatin's dream of a comprehensive, federal road system connecting all the states.

The Department of Transportation was created in 1968, and with the passing of the Urban Mass Transportation Act two years later, the United States entered what Bruce Seely terms the "golden age of infrastructure development."[19] Our present concern for "crumbling infrastructure," particularly pot-holed streets and see-through bridges, should bring to mind that the original expenditures on much of this capital was made during the Great Depression, and the capital is presently approaching its biblical limit of "three score and ten."

Throughout the 1960s, the railroad industry met with increasing competition and went into a decline from which it has not recovered. The Interstate Highway System and jet aircraft competed with both the passenger and freight sides of rail traffic. For example, in the early 1970s, six East Coast railroads entered bankruptcy. As their freight revenues declined, these railroads began to defer maintenance, and, as service levels deteriorated, more business went to intercity trucks. To save rail freight service in the East, the federal government created Conrail out of these six roads in 1976.[20] The government also assumed responsibility for intercity passenger service in 1970 when it created Amtrak.[21] The interstate highway proved to be a viable competitor for many medium-range passenger trips that might have been a rail journey only a few years earlier, and, at the turn of the twenty-first century, Amtrak remains in financial difficulty.

The first comprehensive regulation of air transportation was established by the Civil Aeronautics Act of 1938. Two years later, the Civil Aeronautics Board (CAB) was split from the Civil Aeronautics Administration (CAA), which became the Federal Aviation Administration (FAA) in 1958 amidst a rapid expansion of commercial aviation. The FAA and the CAB carried out Federal promotion and regulation of civil aviation.

The FAA was one of the original components of the Department of Transportation. Its principal activities include controlling the use of navigable airspace; prescribing regulations dealing with the competence of air personnel, the airworthiness of aircraft, and aircraft control (first established in 1926); and the operation of air route traffic control centers, airport traffic control towers, and flight service stations.[22]

The CAB was involved in setting interstate routes as well as regulating fares for the commercial airlines. With the deregulation of the airline industry in 1978 (firms were free to set their own fares and to develop hub-and-spoke route systems and computerized reservation and yield management systems), the role of the CAB was much diminished; in 1984, the Department of Transportation assumed its residual functions. The responsibility for investigation of aviation accidents, formerly held by the CAB, now resides with the National Transportation Safety Board of the Department of Transportation.

By the end of the 1950s, the race for space transformed the air industry into one concerned with "aerospace." Commercial space launches have become more frequent as the demand for orbiting satellites has increased. This is a worldwide industry, one that functions through agencies of national governments. The 1960s rank among the most dramatic periods in aviation history. The rate of technological change was at an all-time high, but it slowed relatively quickly. With the end of the Vietnam War and the maturation of commercial aviation, aircraft production declined. It would revive somewhat in the 1980s, but not to the level of the early Cold War years. The demand for air transportation has continually increased, but, in the aftermath of the September 11th terrorist attacks, safety issues have arisen that were of little concern before.

Our first industry-specific regulatory body, the Interstate Commerce Commission, was slowly absorbed into the Department of Transportation beginning in 1978. Congress abolished what remained of the ICC on 1 January 1996.

THE FISCAL LEGACY OF CAMELOT

One of the events that marks the transition from the relative calm of the 1950s to a pattern of relatively prolonged upswings in the economy is the Kennedy tax cut of 1964. This dramatic action was decided upon while JFK was still alive, but it was put through Congress by his successor, Lyndon Johnson. According to Herbert Stein, a careful scholar of modern fiscal history, the tax cut was distinctly *not* the first choice of the Kennedy policymakers.[23] They wanted to raise expenditures. A cyclical downturn had been inherited in 1961 from the Eisenhower administration. The economy remained sluggish in the beginning months of the Kennedy administration, what came to be known as "Camelot," and, with unemployment hovering between 6 and 7 percent, the indicated countercyclical policy prescription was for fiscal stimulation. There was fear, however, that a deficit from increased expenditures would be inflationary, and such a result would go against Kennedy's campaign promises.

Kennedy was himself a fiscal conservative. The famous tax cut, according to Stein, emerged from the idea of fiscal drag:

> ... the main lag in the economy since the fall of 1957 had been a lag in private investment ... [due to] the high rate of taxation on the return from investment.[24]

But for a lack of private investment, the economy might indeed have been producing a surplus at full employment. Reduce the taxes, and the deficit would vanish as the economy surged toward full-capacity output, or so the thinking went at the time. The tax cut had to be general, if long-term expectations were to be favorably influenced. It also had to be seen as *permanent*, which it was, but that was a lesson not yet learned. Opposition within the administration came from the desire to build an activist spending policy and fear that a tax cut would weaken the federal government's long-run taxing power. Nevertheless, the fiscal-drag theorists had their way.

The hoped-for response was to come from what we now refer to as the *supply side*—greater production and more employment with the stimulus of an increase in personal disposable incomes. The presumed increase in consumer demand would induce a rise in private investment. Even with reduced tax *rates*, the consequent rise in national income would cause *total* tax yields to increase. Unemployment, which had been 5.5 percent in 1960, fell to 4.5 percent by 1965. Prices rose in 1965 at a rate of 1.6 percent, so the economy was operating at very low levels of unemployment and inflation, as was desired, but a sinister cloud was on the horizon—escalation of the Vietnam War. Camelot and the New Frontier vanished. Johnson's Great Society had to compete with the war, and it failed. Martin Luther King, Jr., said, prophetically, "The bombs we drop on Vietnam will explode in America's cities." Before Johnson fled Washington for Texas, America's cities burned.

By the end of 1968, expenditures were $170 billion, half again the level of 1964. It took 192 years to reach a $118-billion budget, four years to increase it 50 percent, a mere decade to double it. But once again war had "solved" the problem of high unemployment (see Table 28.4), at least for the moment. The deficit of 1967, $8.3 billion, was half again the 1958 Eisenhower deficit of which so much was made by JFK during the 1960 election campaign. Worse was coming, and Lyndon Johnson's administration left its problems to the incoming Nixon administration. The latter experienced a surplus in 1969, and then the bottom fell out on the fiscal theorists. The "American Century" seemingly met an abrupt end.[25]

The legacy of the Kennedy administration—the 1964 tax cut, the policy of budgeting for a full-employment economy even when the economy is underemployed—would have been long forgotten, except that in the 1980 election the idea of a permanent tax cut for fiscal stimulus returned, this time from conservative Republicans. When "supply-side economics" arrived in 1981 with the Reagan administration, the Kennedy legacy was a valuable, if ambiguous, memory.

THE LONG PEACETIME INFLATION

From an era with new controls and tax cuts, perhaps the greatest impression that remains of this time and its dramatic events is inflation. By 1980, the accelerating increase in prices was eating deeply into fixed values of all kinds—into sluggish incomes, old investments, and long-term contracts. It was redistributing income and wealth, changing the American way of life. The comment made about inflation during the Napoleonic wars in England applied to this time as well—that it was a time when "debtors pursued creditors relentlessly and repaid them without mercy."

It was a time to contract new debt, to gamble on the continued rise of prices; it was not a time for the old virtues of hard work and saving. Loans were readily available, and the money was used to pay off debts that had been contracted at a time when prices and wages were lower—but when the real value of money was greater.

Consumer Prices and the Money Supply

The period 1960–1980 was one of general increases in the prices of goods and services, unlike the 1920s when output had advanced with mainly stable prices or as it had during the 1950s. In the 1960s and 1970s, real GDP rose, but not as much as prices did. Of course, consumer prices did not all rise equally, but they rose.

From 1960 to 1965, the **Consumer Price Index** (CPI) rose moderately at 1.3 percent a year; medical care rose twice as fast (see Table 30.1). Then, in the next five years (1965–1970), price increases more than doubled the inflation rate of 1960–1965. In five more years, 1970–1975, the price level rose another 50 percent to more than four times the 1960–1965 rate. From 1975 to 1980, the rate of increase rose again, to 8.8 percent a year on average. Prices more than doubled in a decade, from 38.8 (1982–1984 = 100) in 1970 to 82.4 in 1980. Even more startling was the impression of *acceleration* that existed by 1980.[26] The hyperinflations of history—Germany in 1923, Hungary in 1945—came back into vogue.

Services, medical costs, home ownership, food, fuel—all became more expensive, although apparel prices rose more slowly (clothing and shoes flooded in through the import door from southern Europe and Asia). By 1973, the OPEC cartel had raised the price of crude oil by more than a factor of three. Crude oil prices continued to rise, reaching nearly $40 a barrel in 1980.[27] (The price had been less than $4 a barrel in 1973.) By 1980, all prices except apparel had more than doubled from 1967 levels, and fuel oil and coal prices had more than tripled. The CPI rose 10.3 percent in 1981 and continued to advance in 1982, although at a somewhat slower rate. In 1986, the CPI (see both Table 30.1 and Figure 30.1) stood at 109.6, a full 33 percent more than the 1980 figure, despite the recession of 1982.[28] By 1992, inflation had fallen back into the 2.5 to 3.0 percent range and remained there for the rest of the decade. What was hailed as the removal of inflationary pressure was, in

TABLE 30.1 Annual Rates of Change of Consumer Prices, 1960–1999

Years	*All*	*Food*	*Total Housing*	*Fuel Oil & Coal*	*Gas & Electric*	*Apparel*	*Medical Care*	*All Commodities*
1960–1965	1.3	1.4	1.3	1.2	0.2	0.9	2.6	0.9
1965–1970	4.2	4.0	6.3	3.1	1.5	4.8	7.0	1.5
1970–1975	6.8	8.8	5.7	16.4	9.6	4.5	8.0	7.9
1975–1980	8.8	7.7	13.1	18.8	12.2	5.1	11.5	16.9
1980–1985	5.5	4.0	6.6	2.3	8.4	2.3	10.3	4.5
1985–1990	4.0	4.6	3.6	0.7	0.4	3.4	7.5	3.1
1990–1995	3.1	2.3	2.9	-3.0	1.7	1.2	6.3	2.1
1995–1999	1.8	2.0	2.0	0.4	0.3	-0.1	2.6	1.1

Sources: *Statistical Abstract, 1992,* Tables 738, 740; *2000,* Tables 768, 770.

FIGURE 30.1 Consumer Prices (1982–84 = 100)

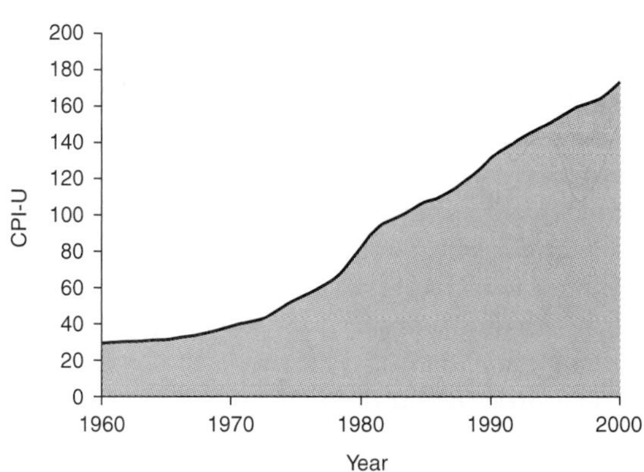

Source: *Statistical Abstract, 2000*, Table 768.

Consumer price increases accelerated in the late 1960s and then zoomed upward in the 1970s, no matter which political party occupied the White House.

fact, a return to the rates of 1966–1967, when the country first began to worry about accelerating inflation. Where did all that inflation come from?

In the long run, *ceteris paribus*, inflation requires an increase in the money supply relative to the output of goods and services—too much money chasing too few goods. In the 1970s and 1980s, it was fashionable to blame OPEC for the inflation—they so grossly raised their oil prices that all other prices rose sympathetically. But, if the money supply is fixed, consumers cannot pay higher prices for all goods. OPEC could not have caused all prices to rise simply by raising the price of its oil.[29]

The sum of all federal deficits between 1960 and 1980 was more than $300 billion. Of that amount, the Federal Reserve System increased its holding of federal bonds by more than $100 billion. The Fed paid for the securities with its own demand liabilities, "high-powered" money whose increase could be multiplied by the commercial banks in their lending operations by more than $500 billion.[30] From 1960 to 1980, M_1 actually rose by some $282 billion (see Table 30.2), an increase by a factor of 3.2, compared with a general rise in prices of a factor of 2.8. Hence, in "Monetarist" terms, the increase in the money supply in response to federal deficit financing was sufficient to account for the inflation. The growth rate of the money supply persisted as an indicator of inflationary trends. As noted, by the end of 1986, the CPI stood at about 33 percent higher than 1980, but M_1 was up 76 percent. At the end of 1994, the CPI was 20 percent higher than 1989, but M_1 was up another 45 percent. It is the economy's ability to expand real output—to sop up some of the money supply increase—that keeps prices from rising as rapidly as the money supply increase.

TABLE 30.2 Securities Prices (Annual Averages of Monthly Averages)

			Bond Yields			
				Standard & Poor		
Year	*Dow-Jones 30 Industrials*	*Standard & Poor, 500 Common Stocks (1941–1943 = 10)*	*U.S. Government Long-Term (10-Year)*	*High Grade Municipals*	*AAA*	*M_1 ($ billions)*
1960	$ 618.0	$ 55.9	$ 4.12	$ 3.73	$ 4.41	$ 127
1965	910.9	88.2	4.28	3.27	4.49	171
1970	753.2	83.2	7.35	6.51	8.04	220
1975	802.5	87.2	7.99	6.89	8.83	295
1980	891.4	118.7	11.43	8.59	11.94	409
1985	1,328.2	186.8	10.62	9.11	11.37	620
1990	2,633.7	330.9	8.55	7.27	9.32	824
1995	5,117.1	614.5	6.57	5.95	7.59	1,127
1999	11,497.1	1,469.3	5.65	5.43	7.05	1,124

Sources: *Statistical Abstract, 1988,* Tables 805, 807; *1992,* Tables 808, 809; *2000,* Tables 821, 823, 831.

The Course of the Price Inflation

The course of the inflation is shown in Figure 30.1. The Vietnam War produced the first acceleration; the second began in 1972 after Richard Nixon's ill-fated attempt to impose price controls. By then, the American public had learned to live with inflationary expectations, and the more they succeeded, the worse the inflation became. The idea was to get rid of money in exchange for real assets, anything with a market value that might rise faster than the inflation rate—real estate and commodities speculation were special favorites.

The Vietnam War began as a "little war." Nothing was done to raise taxes to offset federal expenditures until the summer of 1968. We believed we could fight a war in Vietnam and a "war on poverty" at the same time. The Federal Reserve System did embark upon a policy of tighter money to head off inflation, but it was too little and too late.

The United States still had an obligation to sell gold to foreign central banks at a low, official price ($35 an ounce in the 1960s). In 1968, the country abolished the "gold cover" on Federal Reserve liabilities, making the domestic money supply entirely *discretionary*, as economists used to say. The domestic monetary use of gold was gone, but foreign central banks could and did cash in their dollars at the Fed for gold. Since their inflation rates were far less than the rate in the United States, the real value of those dollars was falling relative to gold. As a result, U. S. holdings of foreign exchange assets fell alarmingly; they declined by nearly 30 percent between 1968 and 1971.[31]

The French, seeing the writing on the wall, pulled out of the Bretton Woods agreement and began cashing in their dollars in 1965—just as they had in the late 1920s, to the detriment of the Gold Exchange Standard. The U.S. balance of payments was in heavy deficit by then, hemorrhaging dollars into the world spending stream. Therefore, on 15 August 1971, President Richard Nixon unilaterally repudiated U.S. obligations in this area of international finance. The official price for gold in the United States was now the high market price, not the fixed "official" price (which already had been raised from $35 an ounce to $42 an ounce in central-bank clearings).

At that point, the Bretton Woods System "collapsed;" it was inoperative as far as gold and dollars were concerned. It had done good service, lasting nearly 26 years—a triumph for such an institution. However, even it could not stand the effusive "gold discoveries" of the time—namely, the huge expansion of Federal Reserve demand liabilities, "high-powered" money; by 1980, the price of gold reached $850 an ounce. That price was a massive world vote of no confidence in the U.S. dollar. Gold prices then collapsed as the speculation against the dollar ended. Interest was once more raised, during the Reagan administration, in a return to some kind of gold standard with (once again) fixed exchange rates, but nothing came of it.

The IMF, the World Bank, and the new institutions and practices spawned by them to continually ease the problems of trade and payments still flourish, to the great benefit of the world economic system.[32] They were the foundation blocks upon which all else rested during the post-World War II decades. The British and Americans had a hard time finding compromises on these two institutions that could get through both Parliament and Congress. Too many vested interests on both sides of the Atlantic were involved for Keynes's original ideas to be adopted. The final formulation was (is), as Keynes quipped at the time: "The Bank is a fund, and the Fund is a bank."[33]

At the same time, the Nixon administration was determined to "do something" about inflation, anything *except* the obvious—stop the deficit spending and consequent borrowing. Congress passed the buck to the president in the Economic Stabilization Act of 1970. Further taxes to finance the war would be highly unpopular, and expenditures were soaring. What to do? The new law read: "The President is authorized to issue such orders and regulations as he may deem appropriate to stabilize prices, rents, wages and salaries...." And what indeed would he deem? What followed were wage and price controls, an attempt to show the world the United States was "doing" something about inflation so that they would stop redeeming dollars for gold. This was a reprise of old ideas, boards, commissions, powers, and offices going back to the World War I command economy. It didn't work; it really wasn't expected to work—only to buy a little time. When the controls were lifted, the inflation rate worsened. In 1972, the Council of Economic Advisers said that the inflation was nearly over.[34] In

1976, they said it again. The inflation continued onward, just as if such forecasts were not made by professional authority.

An interesting sidelight was the failure of the most popular financial instruments to share in the gains. Conventional wisdom *was*, had always been, that common stock prices would rise in anticipation of inflation, "discounting" it in advance. Professors of economics had lulled generations of students to sleep with that wisdom. Anyone who lived by that wisdom in the 1970s lost his or her shirt. Common stocks fluctuated violently, periodically driving past the magical 1,000-mark index on the Dow Jones average of 30 industrials, then falling back again. The index, however, stayed in the range of 850 to 1,000 for the most part, all the way from the mid-1960s to early 1981. The Dow Jones industrials were sinking toward 800 by early 1982. Then, in the fall of 1982, the Dow Jones industrials passed the 1,000 mark once again and peaked at more than 2,700 in August 1987, *after* the slowdown in the growth rate of the money supply that began in 1979, and ultimately precipitated the 1982 recession.

At the beginning of the 1960s, common-stock prices shared in the new price expansion, but the cost of fighting a war in Vietnam, as well as the domestic "war on poverty," added to **cost-push** arguments about inflation; there was *no hope*. Unions, it was feared, would relentlessly push wage increases above productivity increases, and companies would try to pass the increased costs to consumers. Such thoughts drove investors into real property and away from traditional financial investments. As inflation proceeded, interest rates rose, and average bond prices sank. Had stock prices been favored as much as real estate investments after 1960, the Dow Jones industrials would have been pushing 2,000 by 1982. Instead, they lay dead in the water as late as June 1982, below the 1965 level. Note in Table 30.2 the huge increase in M_1 between 1965 and 1980, while stock prices went nowhere. Then recall the late 1920s.

It turns out that such things as stock-market averages are useless as predictors of the future. In the 1920s, it seemed that Americans were overwhelmed with confidence in the American economy's future; the depression of the 1930s followed. In the 1960s and 1970s, as far as the financial markets were concerned, the future seemed dismal. Yet the economy continued to grow overall, even with inflation. After the 1982 recession, massive federal deficits and money supply increases, together with unprecedented foreign investment in the United States, really bolstered a faltering private economy. The stock market boomed.

In the middle of the upswing of the late 1980s, a jarring episode occurred—the stock market "meltdown" of 19 October 1987. After going essentially nowhere in the 1970s and early 1980s, the stock market "took off" after 1983 when inflation rates and interest rates fell. The Dow Jones index of 30 industrial stocks, about 880 in 1982, started rising, and reached 2,000 by 1986. It then soared and, by 27 August 1987, reached a high of 2,746. A slow fade-out then began until, on October 19th—without warning—the Dow fell an astounding 508 points in a single day. A recovery followed, and the index churned around the 1,900 to 2,100 range for the next year. An estimated $1 trillion of wealth had been wiped away, more than a fifth of 1987's GDP figure.

Economists wondered if 1988 would be like 1930. If a negative "wealth effect" after 1929 had contributed to the Great Depression that followed, would history repeat itself? In 1988, at least, it did not. The index passed through the 3,000 barrier in 1991 and continued to soar into the new century.[35]

Inflation and the Financial Sector

Beginning in the 1950s, thrift institutions such as savings and loans (S&Ls) began to vigorously compete with commercial banks. Two Federal Reserve regulations presented difficulties for the banks in this competition—the prohibition of interest payments on checking accounts and Regulation Q, which limited the interest payment on passbook savings accounts. The former led commercial customers to shift funds toward the commercial paper market, and this, in turn, meant the commercial banks more aggressively courted consumer accounts. In this market, they were constrained by Regulation Q and by a 1966 congressional act that allowed S&Ls and other thrift institutions to pay a half-percent higher interest rate than commercial banks.[36] As inflation caused an increase in interest rates in the late 1960s and early 1970s, new alternatives began to develop. Money market mutual funds, introduced in 1972, paid higher interest to consumers and had some features similar to checking accounts. S&Ls and other thrifts developed checking-like accounts (a "negotiable order of withdrawal") that paid interest. Commercial banks introduced automatic transfer services so depositors could store funds in interest-bearing accounts, then move them to their checking accounts when they were needed. As interest rates continued to climb, the nontraditional sources became increasingly popular. Deposits moved out of the banks *and* the S&Ls, a process called *disintermediation.*

This was a particular problem for S&Ls whose historic asset base was long-term, fixed-rate mortgages. The interest they were earning on this asset base was at a lower rate than they had to pay to attract current deposits. It was hoped that the cap on interest rates would minimize this imbalance, but it just led to more disintermediation. Further, with commercial banks constrained to pay lower interest on both savings and checking accounts, the banks began to complain to regulators about unfair competition with S&Ls. Even the 6 percent interest restriction in the Federal Reserve Act on the funds member banks have on deposit with the Fed proved to be a binding constraint for many. State banks began to withdraw from the system; some national banks converted back to state-chartered institutions, then withdrew. The Fed began to worry about its ability to conduct monetary policy, and, as we shall see, they were about to take a quite different approach to monetary policy as the 1980s approached.

By 1980, the disorder in financial markets and the "energy crisis" combined to put several major commercial banks in jeopardy. Among the most infamous episodes, the Penn Square (OK) National Bank closed, and the Continental Illinois National Bank collapsed.[37] Congress responded to the financial crisis by passing two pieces of legislation, the Depository Institutions Deregulation and Monetary Control Act in 1980 and the Garn-St. Germain Depository Institutions Act in 1982. The former said that all depository institutions would face the same reserve requirements and that the Fed would set them.[38] Commercial banks were permitted to offer the interest-bearing, checking-like accounts of the other thrifts, but, in time, the prohibition on interest payments on demand deposits was abolished. Regulation Q was to apply equally to all institutions by 1984 and to disappear altogether at the end of March 1986. In short, there would be little difference between what had been a commercial bank and what had been an S&L. The latter act gave the Federal Home Loan Bank Board (FHLBB) the ability to merge failing and troubled S&Ls with healthier institutions, regardless of the type of institution, further blurring the difference between them. All institutions were allowed to develop money market deposit accounts in order to compete with the money market mutual funds and were successful in doing so.

Inflation and interest rates were still high in 1982, but the new approach to monetary policy had plunged the economy into recession. As had been true in the recession of 1974–1975, this increased the number of failing and threatened institutions. Even when the economy recovered, many S&Ls remained in poor shape due to the erosion of their net worth over the previous decade. In 1987, the General Accounting Office proclaimed the Federal Savings and Loan Insurance Corporation (FSLIC), a wing of the FHLBB, to be insolvent.[39] The Financial Institutions Reform, Recovery, and Enforcement Act of 1989 abolished the FHLBB and the FSLIC and gave the Federal Deposit Insurance Corporation initial responsibility for managing the Resolution Trust Corporation, the agency responsible for bailing out the thrift industry. The current estimate of the actual, ultimate price of the bailout is in the neighborhood of $160 billion, an amount that is lower than the initial estimates. A national commission estimated that it would have cost roughly $25 billion to close insolvent institutions in 1983, an amount roughly equal to four times the assets of the FSLIC at the end of 1982.[40] In retrospect, $25 billion would have been a bargain.[41]

At the state level, the pressure to maintain a healthy commercial banking sector led to a weakening of the historic opposition to branch banking. The federal government also relaxed restrictions on interstate branch banking. The results were dramatic. The traditional independent (unit) bank gave way to the bank holding company, which initially emerged as a way to meet the increasing competition of S&Ls and other thrifts in the 1950s. As recently as 1971, when one-third of the states still had some restrictions on branch banking and another third (especially in the Midwest) prohibited branching altogether, there were 12,063 unit banks in the United States, 153 multi-bank holding companies, and 1,450 one-bank holding companies. This reflected a decrease in the number of unit banks and an increase in the number of both types of holding companies over the 1960s. This trend would accelerate over the next two decades. In 1991, when every state allowed some form of branch banking, the number of unit banks was down to 3,068, while holding companies had increased dramatically (2,025 multi-bank and 5,463 one-bank).[42] The multi-unit form was most likely to be adopted in states that retained restrictions on branch banking since, by its very nature, it is an alternative to branch banking. The commercial banking industry survived the turbulence of the 1970s and 1980s in large part because holding companies were able to absorb weaker institutions. As a consequence, the commercial banking industry today looks quite different than it did at the beginning of the long inflation. The result was consolidation that continues to this day, particularly in the wake of a federal law of 1994 that allowed interstate branching; bank holding companies were permitted to purchase banks in any state.[43] With the demise of the Glass-Steagall Act in 1999, these multistate financial institutions were poised to once again combine banking and securities operations.[44]

GDP, Real Income, Real Wages

With the onset of higher inflation rates in the 1970s, the "national numbers" began to change magnitude in a bewildering way. Was $50,000 a year a higher "real" salary in 1979 than $20,000 a year had been in 1960? Were Americans richer or poorer? It is helpful to try to keep the various relationships in some kind of order.

In 1970, the American GDP passed the $1-trillion mark. It had taken 363 years (from the Jamestown settlement) to get there. The $2-trillion level was reached in 1977, seven years later. There was no celebration because roughly three-quarters of the increase was simple price inflation.

Many American income earners managed to stay ahead of inflation; it was not a constant-sum game. Note in Table 30.3 that, overall, total real GDP (in 1996 prices) continued to rise to 1980, and so did disposable personal income per capita.[45] For the average worker earning wages (outside agriculture), however, real economic advance peaked in the early 1970s; workers could not regain their purchasing power even though their money wages rose nearly by half from 1970 to 1980.

Real GDP rose until 1982, when it fell slightly. Disposable personal income *per capita* in real terms (1996 = 100) continued to increase, but the rate of increase was slowing. It rose at about 3.4 percent per annum between 1960 and 1973, but by only 1.6 percent per annum from 1973 to 1978. By 1980, growth had nearly halted. Between 1970 and 1980, real disposable income per capita grew by 39 percent overall

TABLE 30.3 GDP, Income and Wages 1960–2000

	Total GDP		*Disposable Personal Income Per Capita*		*Average Weekly Wages Nonagricultural*	
Year	*Current Dollars*	*Chained 1996 Dollars*	*Current Dollars*	*Chained 1996 Dollars*	*Current Dollars*	*1982 Dollars*
1960	527.4	2376.7	366.2	1664.8	80.7	183.5
1965	720.1	3028.5	498.9	2131.0	95.5	
1970	1039.7	3578.0	736.5	2630.0	119.8	208.0
1975	1635.2	4084.4	1181.4	3108.5	163.5	214.9
1980	2795.6	4900.9	2019.8	3658.0	235.1	172.7
1985	4213.0	5717.1	3086.5	4347.8	299.1	170.4
1990	5803.2	6707.9	4293.6	5014.2	345.4	259.0
1995	7400.5	7543.8	5422.6	5539.1	394.3	255.0
2000	9963.1	9318.5	6989.8	6511.0	474.4	270.1

Source: U.S. Bureau of Economic Analysis, *NIPA Tables,* Tables 1.1, 1.2, 2.1; *Statistical Abstract, 2000,* Table 692; http://146.4.24/cgi-bin/surveymost

(between 1960 and 1970, the increase had been 58 percent). People who were still ahead of the game in 1980 saw their gains being stopped by inflation, and, of course, many were no longer staying ahead. Real weekly wages (measured in 1982 prices) declined after 1973. By 1980, average weekly real wages were only about 83 percent of the 1970 level. A slow recovery began in 1983–1984, but the recovery could hardly wipe out overnight a decade's losses to inflation. In any case, the recovery in real wages faltered after 1984—nominal weekly wages, of course, rose in every year. There had been real gains for some, but there was fear that the gains would stop as industry after industry ran into trouble with foreign competition and unemployment rose (see Table 28.4)

Consider Figures 30.2 through 30.4. Figure 30.2 shows the Gross Federal Debt in billions of dollars beginning in 1940. It shows the increase in the debt for World War II, the relative constancy of the debt in nominal terms through the 1960s and early 1970s, and the rapid increase beginning in the mid-1970s. One would expect that much of the increase in the 1970s might be due to inflation. Figure 30.3 shows the debt deflated by the consumer price index. The relative constancy of the debt extends from roughly 1950 to 1980 when it, too, begins to increase rapidly. Both these figures are based on absolute data. Figure 30.4 depicts the ratio of Gross Federal Debt to GDP. It shows that this ratio fell into the 1980s. It, too, rose from the mid-1980s through the mid-1990s, but it only rose to the levels in existence just after the end of the Korean War.

FIGURE 30.2 Gross Federal Debt, 1940–2000

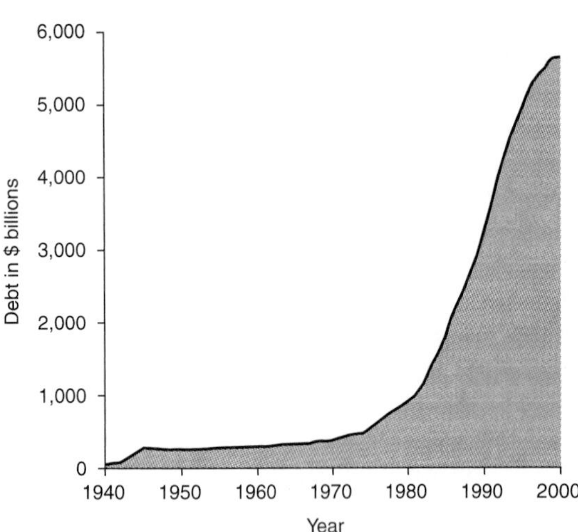

Source: Budget of the U.S. Government, *Historical Tables, Fiscal Year 2002*, pp. 116–117.

FIGURE 30.3 Real Gross Federal Debt, 1945–2000

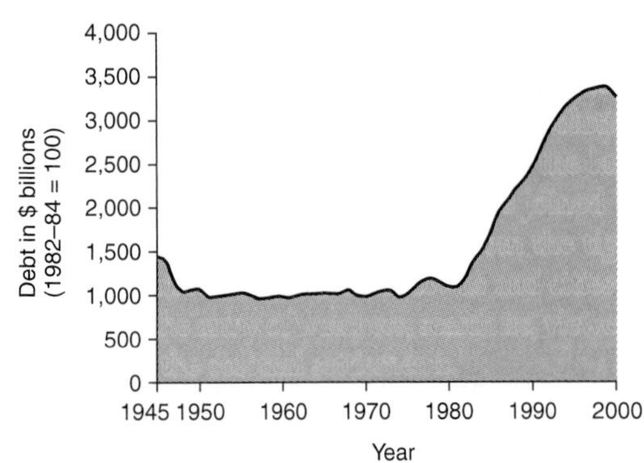

Source: Budget of the U.S. Government, *Historical Tables, Fiscal Year 2002*, pp. 116–117.

FIGURE 30.4 Gross Federal Debt As a Percentage of GDP, 1940–2000

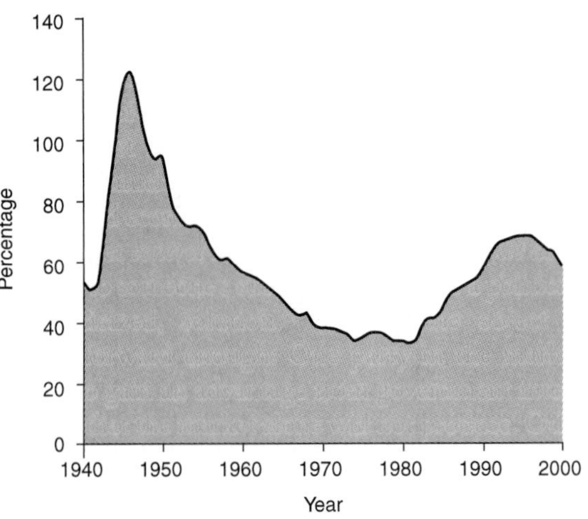

Source: Budget of the U.S. Government, *Historical Tables, Fiscal Year 2002*, pp. 116–117.

Thus, the wild inflationary binge of the 1970s had not "bankrupted the country." In fact, throughout the huge rise in debt from the 1960s, inflation had pushed up wages and prices so that the federal debt was a declining portion of GDP. It was *private* debt that increased dramatically, rising from 82.9 percent of GNP in 1960 to 102.6 percent in 1978.[46] Businesses and individuals who were learning to "live with inflation" increasingly relied on credit, borrowing current dollars knowing they knew they would be repaying with ever "cheaper" dollars. Each year, the money was "worth less" than the year before.

During the buildup of the Vietnam War, unemployment rates dipped into the full-employment range. As Lyndon Johnson told the convention of the AFL-CIO, "You never had it so good." In the 1970s, as growth slowed, the unemployment rate rose. In the recession of 1975, it shot up to more than 8 percent, fell, then rose again to more than 7 percent in 1980. Slowing growth, rising unemployment, industrial troubles, accelerating inflation, high interest rates—these and more spelled electoral disaster for the Democrats in the 1980 elections. By 1982, after two years of slowed money growth, the inflation rate was lower, but interest rates remained high. Unemployment had reached an annual rate of nearly 10 percent, and the economy was suffering from a deep recession. Unemployment fell as the economy recovered, and, by 1988, it was in the neighborhood of 5 percent, *very* low compared with what it had been. The 1990s opened with a resounding recession attributable to a tax increase passed with bipartisan support that year. It ended in 1991, but the ensuing upswing was extremely slow. So slow that, while the trough was marked in July 1991, the 1992 election campaign focused on the ill health of the economy.

The relatively high unemployment rates of the late 1970s and early 1980s masked some remarkable changes in the overall U.S. labor picture. Between 1970 and 1985, population grew by about 16 percent, but the labor force grew more than twice as fast (by about 39.5 percent), and so did employment (about 36 percent). The labor-force participation rate was an amazing 64.8 percent by 1985, actually higher than in World War II, and it has continued to increase (albeit very slowly). Despite all its other troubles, the American economy generated 28.5 million new jobs in those 15 years.[47] As the recovery from the 1982 recession continued, the number of new jobs created continued to grow. Throughout the long peacetime inflation, economic growth continued, albeit with a short reversal here and there.

Between 1985 and 1999, the population again grew by about 16 percent. The labor force and employment both grew at greater rates, but both were much smaller than the previous 15-year period, and employment growth (about 24.6 percent) was greater than labor force growth (about 20.7 percent). The result was that the unemployment rate, 7.2 percent in 1985, fell to 4.2 percent in 1999.[48]

As the idea of real income bore less and less relation to nominal income, interest rates began to be calculated in the media as *real* and *nominal*. How much were interest rates relative to price increases? Ten percent had been a terribly high interest rate in this country historically, but by 1979–1980, a 10 percent nominal rate was actually a negative real rate. It paid to borrow to buy assets on a scale never before known. The real estate market in 1979 was booming like the stock market in 1929.

The Two-Income Family

Much has been written about the profound consequences upon American life of the two-income family, which was created in large part by the fight against inflation. The demand for equal rights for women, changes in home life, the increasing need for day-care centers, the revolution in the frozen and "fast-food" industries—all these reflected the higher proportion of women working outside the home, as we discussed in Chapter 28.

While productivity failed to maintain its historic growth in the 1970s, additional inputs, particularly additional labor inputs from women, propelled increases in total output. The total civilian labor force grew from 72 million persons in 1960 to 105 million in 1980, an increase in 20 years of about 46 percent. More specifically, there were 23 million women in the labor force in 1960 and 45 million in 1980, a rise of more than 90 percent. Of the 33-million-worker increase between 1960 and 1980, some 22 million, or two-thirds of the total increase, were women. By 1999, the labor force was 139.4 million people, with slightly

Alternative Energy. *In the search for alternatives to fossil fuels, Americans are producing energy from many different types of renewable resources such as water (a hydroelectric plant above), the heat in the earth (a geothermal plant below), and wind (turbines above opposite). In spite of ongoing debate, the production of nuclear energy has been increasing (cooling towers below opposite).*

more than 133.5 million of them employed: 64.9 million workers, 46.6 percent of the total, were female.

Aggregate consumption figures also reflected these changes. A *smaller* proportion of consumption expenditures in 1990 went for food than was true in 1960: 15 percent in 1993, compared with 27 percent in 1960, a decline of more than two-fifths. Engel's law alone cannot account for that large a decline. A surprise to some economists was the *decline* in the proportion of expenditures on clothing between 1960 and 1993, from 9.9 to 5.4 percent. In part, this reflects the failure of clothing prices to keep abreast of inflation. It all reflected a world in which the two-income family became more and more the norm in response to the bite of inflation. In the end, however, the force of economic growth more than counterbalanced the force of stagnation, but it was not an easy trip.

STAGFLATION AND "SUPPLY-SIDE" ECONOMICS

By 1976, it had become clear that the cause of continued inflation was not just the continuing deficits; something else, **stagflation**, was at work. The word "stagflation" was a combination of "stagnation" from the increased unemployment rates that had begun to plague the economy and "inflation," which continued unabated. Unemployment rose to 8.5 percent in 1975, then fell only to 7.7 percent during the election year. It was as low as 5.9 percent in 1979, but then rose to 7.2 percent the following year. Inflation, on the other hand, continuously rose, from 5.8 percent in 1976 to 13.5 percent in 1980.

The 1976 presidential election highlighted the problem of attempting to attack stagflation with aggregate demand—monetary and fiscal—policies. Rising oil prices combined with harvest failures in Russia to cause one of the few "supply shocks" to hit the American economy. The increasing unemployment and inflation were caused by a leftward shift of the aggregate supply curve. Any monetary or fiscal policy response to this shift would lead to an improvement in one variable, but a worsening of the other. In the 1976 election, voters were forced to select what many viewed as the lesser of two evils. Republicans argued that inflation was the more serious problem. They recommended restrictive policies that would "Whip Inflation Now" as President Ford's WIN buttons embodied. They admitted this would increase unemployment, but they argued that the victims could be compensated. Democrats argued the opposite. To them, unemployment was the more serious problem. They recommended expansive policies that would increase the inflation rate, but they argued that the victims could be compensated.

The Energy Sector

The supply shock that hit the economy was caused, in part, by upheavals in the petroleum industry. Domestic crude oil output was about 2 billion barrels in 1950, 2.5 billion barrels in 1960. It rose to 3.5 billion barrels in 1970 and then stagnated during the 1970s until some price controls remaining from the controls of the early 1970s were removed. Domestic output, down to 3.2 billion barrels in 1972, was still about 3.3 billion barrels 16 years later. There were differences, however. OPEC, the oil producers' international cartel, found itself in a unique position in the late 1960s and, as noted, increased the price of crude oil by more than a factor of three. By cutting output, they ratcheted oil prices upward in three steps; prices remained level between each step.[49] The result was a price that was nearly $40 a barrel and an "energy crisis" in the United States during the 1970s. OPEC lost its cohesion when faced with new competition from North Sea oil by the early 1980s. By 1988, oil prices had plunged to less than $14 a barrel, back to a level one would have projected had OPEC never flexed its muscles. In the interim, significant adjustments had taken place to conserve energy. Higher-mileage autos were in vogue. Some electrical generating plants switched back to coal, but environmental restrictions on such things as sulfur emissions from coal-fired plants limited this option. Although coal was a lower-cost alternative, the United States chose to burn oil, pay more for the energy, and enjoy cleaner air. It also chose to put a greater reliance on natural gas. What was good for consumers was bad indeed for domestic petroleum producers; the 1980s were hard years in the American oil fields.

Table 30.4 indicates what has happened over time to energy production in the United States. Since 1970, the percentage of energy produced with crude

TABLE 30.4 Energy Production, 1970–1999

		Percentage					
	Total Production	*Crude Oil*	*Natural Gas*	*Coal*	*Nuclear*	*Renewable Energy*	*Natural Gas Liquids*
1970	63.50	32.13	34.13	23.01	0.38	6.41	3.95
1980	67.24	27.14	29.61	27.66	4.07	8.16	3.35
1990	70.85	21.98	25.91	31.70	8.69	8.69	3.08
1999	72.52	17.29	26.61	32.17	10.66	9.90	3.46

Note: Total production is measured in quadrillion British thermal units; the other figures are percentages of total production.

Source: *Statistical Abstract, 2000.* Table 942

oil fell by twice that of natural gas. Coal, nuclear, and renewable energy (hydroelectric, geothermal, and biofuels) have all increased. Much of the 28-fold increase in nuclear power occurred before 1990 when an active political discussion emerged concerning the safety of the technology. Since the three major sources of energy accounted for over three-quarters of energy production in 1999, and since they are all nonrenewable sources, it would appear that nuclear generating plants will continue to be an important part of energy production until such time as alternative technologies prove viable.

The "energy crisis" of the 1970s resulted in part from continued economic expansion with a fairly stagnant base of domestic energy supplies. Between 1960 and 1999, energy used rose by 92 percent, from 43.8 to 96.6 quadrillion British thermal units. As the production data suggest, this growth was achieved in part by imports of fuel, both oil and gas. The net proportion of such imported energy sources rose from 9 percent of total energy consumption in 1960 to 24 percent by 1979. Americans made considerable strides in energy conservation per unit of work in many areas, and, by 1985, the net proportion of imported energy sources to total consumption had fallen to 16 percent. Since then, however, it has risen. Throughout the 1990s, it was at or above the level of 1979.

Despite energy shortages, more installed power than ever was used. Installed *horsepower* (a unit of power equal to 746 watts) of prime movers, which was 4.9 billion units in 1950, stood at 34.9 billion units in 1990. The rate of increase slowed, but, overall, the total increase far outstripped expansions in other areas of economic activity. Much of this power was needed to drive the computers that quickly found their way into American businesses and homes. Since it was primarily the free market that ordered this great change, there was reason to believe electronics would follow the path of older innovations—like steam power, electricity, chemicals, and light metals—in producing higher living standards. The gadgets of the electronic revolution were not adopted for fun only. These things *pay*. By the mid-1980s, Detroit had followed the Japanese auto industry's example of replacing human workers with electronic robots. It is important to recall one of the greatest lessons of economic history: *resources are defined by technology*. Energy had become a critical resource for the American economy.

The Fiscal Record and the Balance of Payments

As the Carter administration assumed responsibility for the economy in 1977, the deficits were big ones that came every year, no matter what the state of the economy (see Table 30.5). Gerald Ford's last full year, 1976, yielded a then-whopping $53 billion federal deficit (down from $69.3 billion the previous year). A balanced federal budget had come to be viewed as a utopian ideal, no longer really achievable—desirable, yes, but not a practical goal. Admittedly, it was *a* policy in a world where there no longer were identifiable fixed fiscal objectives.

It was during the four years of the Carter presidency that the debacle in federal finance reached (then) frightening proportions. There was a feeling that no one was in charge anymore. Between 1975 and 1980, the federal debt rose by 67.7 percent, the money supply (M_1) leapt 38.6 percent, while unem-

TABLE 30.5 Federal Government Finance, 1960–2000

	Current Receipts	*Current Expenditures*	*Surplus (+) or Deficit (-)*
1960	92.8	85.8	7.1
1961	94.4	92.0	2.5
1962	102.3	100.0	2.4
1963	110.2	105.0	5.2
1964	110.2	109.3	0.8
1965	119.3	116.1	3.2
1966	136.3	133.6	2.7
1967	144.9	153.2	−8.3
1968	168.5	169.8	−1.3
1969	190.1	180.5	9.6
1970	184.3	198.6	−14.4
1971	189.8	216.6	−26.8
1972	217.5	240.0	−22.5
1973	248.5	259.7	−11.2
1974	277.3	291.2	−13.9
1975	276.1	345.4	−69.3
1976	318.9	371.9	−53.0
1977	359.9	405.0	−45.2
1978	417.3	444.2	−26.9
1979	478.3	489.6	−11.4
1980	522.8	576.6	−53.8
1981	605.6	659.3	−53.7
1982	599.5	732.1	−132.6
1983	623.9	797.8	−173.9
1984	688.1	856.1	−168.1
1985	747.4	924.6	−177.1
1986	786.4	978.5	−192.1
1987	870.5	1018.4	−147.9
1988	928.9	1066.2	−137.4
1989	1010.3	1140.3	−130.0
1990	1055.7	1228.7	−173.0
1991	1072.3	1287.6	−215.3
1992	1121.3	1418.9	−297.5
1993	1197.3	1471.5	−274.1
1994	1293.7	1506.0	−212.3
1995	1383.7	1575.7	−192.0
1996	1499.1	1635.9	−136.8
1997	1625.5	1678.8	−53.3
1998	1754.0	1705.0	49.0
1999	1874.6	1750.2	124.4
2000	2065.7	1813.9	251.8

Source: U.S. Bureau of Economic Analysis, *NIPA Tables*, Table 3.2.

ployment remained high. The federal deficits seemed huge compared with 1970, but they would grow much larger. Carter's 1976 pledge to balance the federal budget during his administration haunted his presidency with an aura of continuous failure.

In the 1970s, the United States became vulnerable to its foreign balance for the first time in decades. As the dollar plunged in the foreign exchanges, particularly after 1971 when Nixon gave up on the lower "official" price and priced U.S. gold at the higher "market" price, exports earned less per unit, and imports cost more.[50] The inflation-swollen domestic economy demanded more imports. By 1970, deficits began to appear in the merchandise trade balance, the first since the nineteenth century. Because of positive net earnings on invisibles, including foreign investments, the trade balance deficits were muffled and even offset entirely in the current balance until 1982. Then the current account turned powerfully negative, and, by 1988, the sum of the current account deficits had converted the United States, in a mere handful of years, from the world's greatest creditor to the world's greatest debtor nation.

It was an added jolt, however, for Americans to discover that, not only was the federal government unable to control its own fiscal affairs within the American economy, but that the economy no longer enjoyed an unquestioned competitive edge vis-a-vis the rest of the world. Cheaper and superior foreign manufactured goods, from shoes to automobiles, flooded the domestic market. American manufacturers and their unionized labor forces, unable to reduce wages and other costs, raised the cry for protection from foreign competition. It seemed a sad comedown from the idea of the "American Century" of the postwar era.

Actually, such arguments were overly pessimistic. Foreign investment was pouring into the American economy throughout the 1970s, virtually balancing the outflow of American funds seeking productive employment abroad. For example, from 1971 to 1975, American holdings of foreign assets rose by $124 billion, but foreign holdings of U.S. assets rose by $113 billion in return. In 1978 alone, Americans invested $61 billion abroad, but foreigners invested $64 billion in the United States.[51] *Someone* was keeping faith in America, even if Americans seemed to be losing theirs.[52] Foreign investment continued to pour in, financing the deficits, although, by 1988, there were weak knees in American financial circles at the prospect of any potential "loss of confidence" by foreigners and a withdrawal of funds. That catastrophe has remained only a fear as foreigners have kept up their purchases of American assets.

In a way, the United States was merely rejoining the international economy as a trading partner. It was no longer the master in international economic affairs. Americans viewed this development with alarm, but it was in fact the *object* of the postwar international reorganization drafted at Bretton Woods.[53] It just took three decades for those policies to come to fruition. It was a new experience for twentieth-century Americans to find themselves wanting to buy more from the world's market than that market wanted to buy from them, but it was far healthier and viable worldwide than the dependency that countries like Great Britain, Germany, and Japan had upon the United States in the 1950s. They now could compete with the United States on equal terms, and Americans had to get used to competing with them. Americans even had to admit that *foreigners* were now financing *them*. The worm had turned.

By 1980, feelings of the impending chaos in the financial world added to the administration's woes, which by then included the American embassy workers held hostage in Iran. Market interest rates of between 15 and 20 percent brought home-building activity and real-estate markets to a crawl—mortgage rates hit 14 percent. As we have seen, the savings and loan industry, long the steady bulwark of the real-estate market because of its supply of mortgage money, faced collapse. By 1980, international competition forced locally devastating closings of heavy-industrial plants in the traditional production centers of the East and Midwest. The growth of business in the Sun Belt was under way, adding to the woes of rising industrial unemployment. The conventional policy prescriptions seemed to offer no way out from such a sea of troubles. The argument for larger deficits to reduce unemployment was no longer heard. The deficits were already huge, and both unemployment and prices were rising. Carter's economic policy, the reduction of unemployment through economic growth, seemingly required deficits to promote growth. James Buchanan and Richard Wagner, in *Democracy in Deficit*, underlined the unspoken problem with the conventional Keynesian, fiscal-policy tradition.[54] In one basic sense, it really was *depression economics*. It assumed that the economy would rise to the bait of money stimulus and expand real output and employment. The huge increases in deficit-financed money demand, however, raised prices more than output, even with unemployed capacity and unemployed workers.

The policy of the 1946 Employment Act now seemed a dead issue altogether. Buchanan and Wagner argued that it had been a piece of sheer pretense from the beginning:

> This act pledges the government to do something it cannot possibly do, at least so long as our underlying fiscal and monetary institutions are themselves the primary source of instability.[55]

And, said Buchanan and Wagner, if these institutions were stable, there would be no need for the Employment Act.

The old-time liberal Democratic ideal, with such long roots in American history, was stated eloquently by Senator George McGovern in 1980 in his address to Americans for Democratic Action. He argued, according to the *New York Times*, that government was the only "humane" institution in American society:

> Let us insist that Government can and must solve problems, that it can and must eliminate poverty and reduce inflation, that it can and must set goals and define a vision for the nation.[56]

In 1980, he was retired by his constituents, as were leading liberal Democrats.

Jimmy Carter was offered economic advice by a profession that did not fully understand his problems.[57] He experienced essentially the same frustration that Herbert Hoover felt in 1930–1932. In Hoover's case, prices were tumbling and unemployment rose; in Carter's case, prices were soaring and unemployment rose. Economic orthodoxy did not understand the early 1930s, nor did it understand the late 1970s.

Republicans returned to power with conservative Ronald Reagan in 1981. Once again, they pledged to stop inflation, to reduce government "interference" in economic life, and to adopt policies that would revitalize the American economy. They spoke of *capitalism* and *free markets*; Reagan even used the word *entrepreneur* in his inaugural address.

Ending Inflation

What ultimately ended the long inflation was unorthodox. Two months after Carter named Paul Volcker to be chairman of the Federal Reserve Board in August 1979, the Fed announced a major policy change. It would no longer target the Federal Funds rate, the rate at which banks borrow from each other. The Fed would now attempt to target the growth rate of the money supply. In his review of monetary policy in the 1980s, Michael Mussa noted that the motivation was "tactical, psychological, and political;" it was not "a profound religious experience that suddenly converted most members of the FOMC [Federal Open Market Committee] to ... 'monetarism.'"[58] Volcker commented that there was a need to "shake up" the entrenched inflationary psychology. He believed that this new policy had two advantages. First, it seemed a good way to communicate the Fed's intentions to the public. Second, he considered it to be good discipline; it would be hard to rationalize a retreat.[59] Yet, the Fed was forced to retreat by the policies adopted by the Carter administration.

In March 1980, Carter announced new policies designed to combat inflation, including authorizing the Fed to impose consumer credit controls. Ostensibly, there were three reasons for this: (1) to minimize the pressure the deficit placed on interest rates, (2) to limit the increase of consumer credit that Carterites felt contributed to inflation, and (3) to break inflationary expectations. Charles Schultze, who was chairman of the Council of Economic Advisers at the time, considered the rationale absurd.[60] Volcker tried unsuccessfully to talk Carter out of the controls, and, when they were combined with the announced slowing of the money supply, the economy went into recession. The controls were removed a few short months after they were imposed. Monetary policy was eased; the economy recovered; but inflation was still rampant. It is customary to date the imposition of the new policy to October 1979, but Volcker, who had been forced to retreat from that policy, considered 1980 to be a "wasted year" in the fight against inflation.

Immediately following Reagan's election, the Fed returned in earnest to its announced policy of low money supply growth. The policy remained in effect until August 1982, almost a year after it was clear a recession was under way, a recession in which real GDP fell by more than 3 percent and unemployment rose to a postwar high of 10.8 percent. The recession was the worst since the 1930s in terms of unemployment, but by other measures it was relatively mild. Once the recession began, the Fed marginally loosened monetary policy but felt it had to "stay the course," for two reasons: (1) to establish its credibility as an inflation fighter and (2) to persuade households and firms to significantly lower their inflationary expectations. Volcker noted that the Fed believed an expansion would begin in the spring of 1982, but the trough was not reached until November.[61] Indeed, the official record indicates the Fed consistently underestimated both the depth and duration of the recession.

When the Fed finally shifted to an easier policy in the summer of 1982, inflation had fallen from an annual rate of 13.5 percent in 1980 to 3.2 percent in 1983—and it stayed there. In place of targeting the money supply growth rate, the Fed adopted a more eclectic approach—similar to that in the 1950s and early 1960s—in which the Fed determined the "degree of pressure" placed on banks' reserves. Noted James Tobin, "I hope that history will give Paul and his colleagues the praise that they deserve not only for fighting the war against inflation but also for knowing when to stop, when to declare victory."[62] His successor, Alan Greenspan, appointed by President Reagan in 1987, continued the Fed's eclectic approach. Reappointed by Presidents Bush and Clinton, Greenspan was given much of the credit for the economic successes of the 1990s. When the economy slowed in 2000, and turned down in 2001, the Fed undertook a series of interest rate cuts, but it is still too early to judge the effectiveness of that policy.

Reaganomics: Taxes, Expenditures, Cyclical and Structural Deficits

Reagan brought with him a piece of baggage from the 1980 Presidential campaign, **supply-side eco-**

nomics. The idea was simple; Reagan argued that inflation and unemployment could be improved simultaneously by shifting the aggregate supply curve to the right; voters did not have to choose between two evils. The theory was that big, general tax cuts would induce the entrepreneurial classes to reduce their aversion to taxes and allow a greater portion of their actual income to be taxed, thereby increasing tax receipts. At the same time, workers would be induced to increase their efforts, confident in the knowledge they were taking home more per hour from the identical pretax wage. The administration hoped this additional activity, through the Keynesian multiplier process, would put the unemployed and the chronic welfare cases back to work. One piece of evidence cited in support of this theory was the tax cut of 1964, which had been, in part, supported by these same arguments, as Herbert Stein pointed out. It was a gamble in 1981, just as it had been in 1964.[63] The fact that tax cuts were also an expansionary fiscal policy was not part of the rhetoric. In their analysis of the Tax Reform Act of 1986, Alan Auerbach and Joel Slemrod conclude that the labor market was not very responsive to the changes in tax rates, but that investment in equipment was.[64] One large part of the supply-side argument did not hold in practice.

The major changes in fiscal policy can be seen in the big changes of the "full-employment budget" line in Figure 30.5. The Kennedy tax cut of 1964 is at the beginning of a downward trend in the line, while the surtax of the late 1960s cause the line to change to an upward slope. The repeal of this tax led to a decade-long increase in deficits, but these sharply accelerate with the passage of the Reagan tax cuts. The effect of the Tax Reform Act of 1986 appears as an inverted "*U*" in the line during the late 1980s.

The tax cuts passed in 1981 were not those advocated by the supply-siders (a one-time, 33-percent cut across the board), but were strung out over three years, which dampened their impact. Rates were cut 5 percent the first year and 10 percent each of the next two years. The supply-side story made sense for those individuals paying the top marginal tax bracket of the personal income tax. In 1947, when the top bracket was 91 percent, the tax took 9.5 percent of personal income and accounted for 46.5 percent of the federal government's revenues. When the top bracket was reduced to 71 percent in 1971, and again when the top bracket was reduced to 50 percent in 1982, the other percentages remained essentially

FIGURE 30.5 The "Twin" Deficits

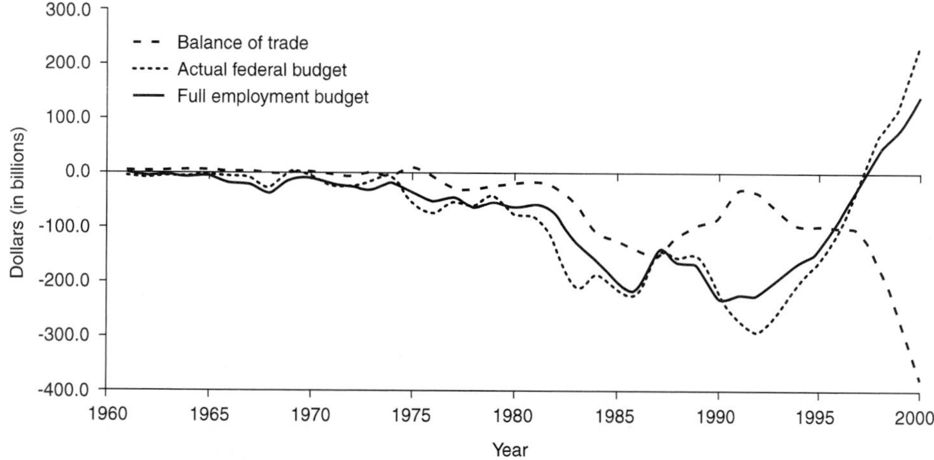

Source: U.S Bureau of Economic Analysis, *NIPA*, Table 1; Congressional Budget Office.

International Markets. *In the early 1980s, President Reagan searched for markets for American products in the booming, and protected, Japanese economy (above). In the 1990s, President Clinton fought to create an open North American market (below).*

unchanged.[65] Why this constancy? At the lower rates, because the affluent were less concerned about sheltering their income in real estate and the like, the lower rate was paid on larger incomes. It may well have been true that tax revenues would have increased, if only the top rate had been cut. But all rates were cut in 1982 because policymakers were concerned with equity and inflation. One cost of this concern was increasing deficits.

As inflation progressed in the 1970s, the federal government found its revenue increased by more than 1 percent for every 1 percent increase in inflation. Taxpayers were paying a larger percentage of their real income in taxes, a phenomenon known as *bracket creep*. Throughout the 1970s, Congress returned these excess revenues to taxpayers through new exemptions and deductions. Reagan's tax proposal was consistent with this approach. However, the bill Congress returned included a provision that tax rates would be indexed beginning in 1985. Henceforth, personal income taxes would be paid on real, not nominal, income. As the deficits increased, there would be no bracket creep to help increase revenues. Congress had to start deleting exemptions and deductions; it had to think about raising taxes.

In 1982, a new fiscal crisis gripped Washington. The tax cuts reduced the amount of revenue the government could expect at any income level. The recession of 1981–1982 reduced tax revenue even more. This reduction, coupled with higher defense expenditures, threatened the fiscal conservatives of the Reagan administration with a deficit for 1982–1983 in excess of $100 billion. Economists refer to the deficit associated with budget rules, with tax and expenditure policies, as the *structural deficit*. The additional revenue shortfall and expenditure increase induced by the recession are referred to as the *cyclical deficit*. The total deficit in 1983, the sum of these two components was $173.9 billion, and the deficits continued to increase until they peaked in 1986 at $192.1 billion. These deficits combined with abundant increases in the money supply, renewed a feeling of Keynesian prosperity of the kind that was never enjoyed in the "pinchpenny" reign of Franklin Roosevelt in the 1930s.

What caused these deficits? One simple answer is wishful thinking. The administration bought into the "Rosy Scenario" that Reagan's first budget director, David Stockman, described as "the most fabulous forecasting error in human history:"

> ... for the relevant period in which these sweeping changes were being made, fiscal 1982–1986, we overpredicted GNP by the precise sum of $2.145 trillion. Now, that was cumulative, but, on a final year basis, 1986, it meant that the forecast of money GNP was $660 billion higher than what actually turned out.[66]

Another simple answer is that, between 1980 and 1983, revenues fell by 1.1 percent of GDP while expenditures rose by 1.9 percent. Thus, the tax cuts can be said to be responsible for about three-eighths of the increase.[67] Three categories of expenditures account for most of the increase. The first Stockman termed "the old people and poor people's budgets," which increased from 4 percent of GDP in 1961 to 10 percent in 1981—with bipartisan support. The second was interest on the public debt. Tight money drove up interest rates dramatically, while the deficits increased the amount that had to be borrowed. The success Reagan's budget-cutters had in trimming the nondefense budget was canceled by this increase in interest payments. The final category was defense. In common with most conservatives, Reagan believed we had let defense expenditures slip to dangerously low levels. He understood increasing defense expenditures would put financial pressure on the Soviet Union, but how large a part this played is not yet known. Given that these expenditures contributed to the fall of communism, they may yet be looked upon more favorably by history than by contemporaries. At a minimum, it was bad public relations to reduce the subsidies for school lunches in order to buy more military hardware.

With the collapse of the Rosy Scenario, tax reform was addressed. The changes passed in 1982 and 1984 did raise revenue, but they were piecemeal. They reduced less than half the increase in the structural deficit caused by the 1981 cuts. In 1983, the president and Congress addressed the problems with Social Security. Real Social Security benefits increased by 25 percent over the 1970s. Tax rates were increased in 1977, but the combination of high inflation and feeble growth raised the specter of insolvency. The 1983 amendments raised taxes once again and reduced the level of benefits.[68]

The other significant change in tax policy got under way in 1982. Don Fullerton discusses four factors leading to this move toward reform.[69] First, in spite of the deficits, supply-siders still had some influence, and they were calling for a "flat-tax," one that involved many fewer brackets. Second, the existing tax system was viewed as inordinately complex; during a television appearance, the head of the Internal Revenue Service confessed that no one knew the U.S. tax code in its entirety. Third, the rates were still sufficiently high to give many corporations and individuals an incentive to shelter their income. Support for the existing system was subverted by a report indicating that many taxpayers were able to avoid paying any tax at all. Lastly, there was concern that the existing system was no longer equitable, that people with about the same income no longer paid about the same amount of tax.

It was Democratic Senator Bill Bradley who, in 1982, first raised the call for a "level playing field." Bradley introduced legislation jointly with Democratic Representative Dick Gephardt. Reagan's political people, fearing that the Democrats would take the tax issue away from Reagan, convinced him to order the Treasury to study the issue. The result was the revenue-neutral Tax Reform Act of 1986, in which marginal rates were cut once again, the number of brackets was significantly reduced, and the number of deductions was severely curtailed. The result was a more equitable tax structure, but not one that reduced the structural deficit.

Consequently, the recovery and expansion of 1983–1988 occurred in the presence of huge deficits—a strictly orthodox Keynesian prescription—and a powerful rise in private investment in response to the tax changes of 1982 and 1984. Not surprisingly, the *rate* of private savings did not increase significantly, and the country was spared the predicted "crowding out" effects of the giant increases in federal debt by foreign investors seeking both safety and high interest rates. Billions of dollars of foreign investment poured into the United States as its fiscal policy moved toward expansion and fiscal policies elsewhere moved toward restraint. This led to an appreciation of the dollar and a worsening of the U.S. current account. The "twin deficits"—the unprecedented federal deficit and the balance of payments deficits—were "financed" by foreign investors (see Figure 30.5).[70] The economy expanded because the trade deficit was less than the increased deficit in the federal budget. The unemployment rate sank back to about 7.5 percent in 1984, the economy continued to generate net increases in total employment, and real wages began to rise again along with real disposable income. By the end of 1988, the unemployment rate dipped to about 5 percent as the expansion continued.

The expansion did not affect all sectors of the economy equally. The falling price of imported goods hit the manufacturing sector hard. While employment was increasing overall, that in the manufacturing sector decreased, and a concern for U.S. "competitiveness" was heard. Also heard was a renewed cry for protection, which, in turn, led politicians to worry more about the deficit in the federal budget.

As noted, one extraordinary outcome of the twin deficits was an appreciation in the U.S. dollar that freely floated on foreign exchanges. Instead of collapsing under the weight of its own excess supply, the dollar rose to astounding strength in 1984–1985 as foreign investors poured billions of their own savings into the United States, driving the dollar up against all currencies in the foreign exchange markets. Once worth 20.5 percent of a British pound, by the spring of 1985, the dollar had soared to about 95 percent of a pound (£1 = $1.05). Then, the dollar caved in and declined to the range of $1.80 to the pound in 1988—$1.60 in the spring of 1997. The huge excess supply of dollars generated by the U.S. balance of payments deficits finally made its impact felt in the foreign exchanges. A devalued dollar was inflationary inside the United States as import prices soared, but exports, now correspondingly cheaper, also soared.

Supporters of "Reaganomics" naturally credited these favorable economic singularities in the whirlwind to "the success of the president's policies." Opponents warned of the dangerous economic threat implied. What if, in the next recession, U.S. interest rates should fall back enough to inspire a mass withdrawal of these hundreds of billions of foreign investment? A recession could be converted into a catastrophic depression, but it was not to be.

Reagan's man, George Bush, won the 1988 election, and Ronald Reagan rode into the sunset as if he had balanced the budget, reduced the national debt, and deregulated the economy, just as he had said he would back in 1980. The Reagan years ended with a note of hope. Employment was full, exports were rising, and both deficits were less in 1988 than they had been in 1987. The Canadians agreed to a free-trade agreement. The wave of leveraged buyouts of American firms with "junk bond" financing resumed after a number of Wall Street operators were imprisoned for misuse of insider information. The 1987 stock market crash had not produced a recession.

AFTERMATH

The Bush administration assumed the burden of the federal fiscal chaos, already shackled by campaign promises to balance the budget without raising taxes. Even the defeated Democrats were hoping that Bush would get lucky. He didn't.

In the presidential campaign of 1988, George Bush exhorted the electorate to "read his lips," he would not raise taxes. As the deficits continued, he relented. A bipartisan package was put in place in 1990 to reduce the structural deficit, a package that soon pushed the economy into recession, thereby enlarging the cyclical deficit. As can be seen in Figure 30.5, the structural deficit decreased in the early 1990s, reversing the general trend of the previous decade. In each of the years 1991 to 1994, the federal budget deficit exceeded $200 billion. In real terms, these were larger than the deficit during 1945, the last year of World War II.

Immediately after his election, Bill Clinton moved to increase taxes as part of a deficit-reduction program, but the rhetoric was to restore the "proper" degree of progressivity to the tax structure, or "soak the rich" as it was called in FDR's day. The tax increase was the same gamble FDR took that caused the recession of 1937. This change in fiscal policy appears as an acceleration in the rate of increase of the full-employment budget line in Figure 30.5. Clinton was luckier; the prolonged upturn that began in June 1991 was sufficiently strong that the tax increase merely dampened the rate of increase and reduced the structural deficit still further. By 1998, the federal budget showed a surplus for the first time since the 1960s. While the federal budget deficit

FIGURE 30.6 Investment As a Percentage of GDP

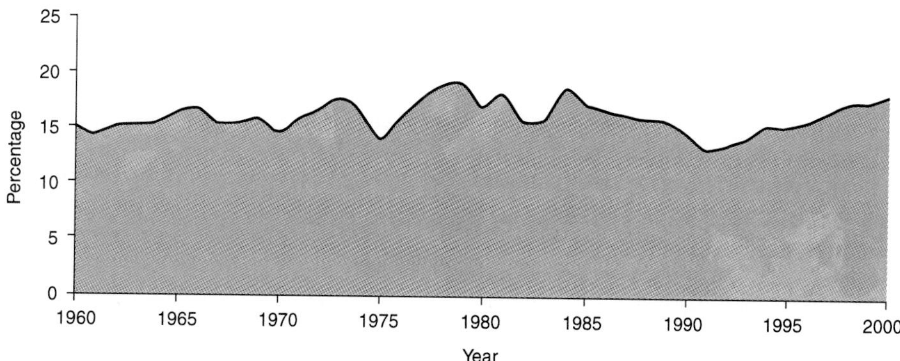

Source: U.S Bureau of Economic Analysis, *NIPA*, Table 1.1.

moved to a surplus, the balance of trade deficit, which improved from the levels of the mid-1980s, suddenly moved to the largest deficits in our history. Part of the stimulus was the "peace dividend" associated with the fall of communism. This dividend was manifested largely as a decrease in defense spending on the Cold War. If, however, the "peace dividend" is defined as an increase in social spending, then, as Hugh Rockoff explains, there was none at the end of the Cold War. After that war, as most other wars, social spending relative to GDP returned to "normalcy," to its prewar trend.[71]

Figure 30.6 shows investment spending as a percentage of GDP. During the years of the productivity crisis in the late 1970s, the percentage actually rose. Beginning in the 1980s, it fell during more years than it rose until it reached a low in 1991. From that time on, the percentage has risen, from 13.4 to 18.4 percent. There are many reasons for the increase during the 1990s, and the Internet figures strongly in two of them. First, firms made the investment in telecommunications equipment so they could make use of the Internet, both to supply and to demand information. Second, Internet firms (dot-coms) entered the industry. One would expect the portion of investment increase attributable to these two sources to slow over time. The initial investment firms made in telecommunications equipment is likely to have been much larger than that they will have to make in the future to maintain their positions, and, as we have already seen, the dot-coms have begun a Schumpeterian process of "creative destruction." A third reason for the increase in the investment percentage is the public's expectation of the future. Those expectations generally remained optimistic through the beginning of the new millennium, former dot-com millionaires notwithstanding.

The United States was a relatively closed economy until the early 1970s, with exports and imports constituting around 5 percent of GDP annually. By the 1980s, these percentages were double those of the 1960s, and, in 2000, imports were almost 15 percent of GDP. During his first term, Clinton signed into law the North American Free Trade Agreement (NAFTA) that brought Mexico into the Canada-U.S agreement.[72] NATO has been expanded, and even Russia is giving signs it would consider an invitation to join. The United States is now an open economy, despite continued calls for protection. While the "American Century" is alleged to have ended in the 1970s, at the end of the second millennium there was only one remaining "superpower"—the United States. It was clear before 11 September 2001 that our economic prospects in the new millennium depend, in part, on how well we learn to live with the rest of the world. That terrible day should have brought into every American home the message that our economic future is inextricably tied to that of the global economy.

NOTES

1. Richard Freeman, "The Evolution of the American Labor Market, 1948–1980," in Martin Feldstein, ed., *The American Economy in Transition* (1980), pp. 351–560. For a general review with international comparisons of recent productivity trends, see Edwin Mansfield, "Technology and Productivity in the United States," in the same volume.
2. An example is David Packard, chairman of Hewlett-Packard Company, "Productivity and Technical Change." in Feldstein (1980), pp. 604–616. Also, Jonathan Hughes, *The Governmental Habit Redux* (1991), pp. 182–201.
3. A second environmental problem, the depletion of the ozone layer due to the discharge of chlorofluorocarbons (CFCs), proved more tractable. The nations responsible for most of the world's production of CFCs agreed in the Montreal Protocol of 1990 to phase out production by 2000.
4. Gavin Wright's presidential address to the Economic History Association, "The Civil Rights Revolution as Economic History," *Journal of Economic History*, vol. 59, no. 2, June 1999, is a personal memoir that argues the movement was both an economic and political revolution.
5. The Civil Aeronautics Board, like the ICC, is now defunct; their remaining functions have been transferred to the Department of Transportation. These are two of the few major federal agencies to be eliminated in modern times.

6. Murray Weidenbaum, *Business and Government in the Global Marketplace* (1995).
7. President Richard Nixon in his Environmental Message of February 1972.
8. OSHA's code book in 1980 contained some 28,000 regulations. See Packard in Feldstein (1980), p. 610, for an industrialist's estimate of the consequences. According to Packard, "Government regulations in fact, may be the largest and most important factor in the decline in productivity in the United States."
9. See Hughes (1991).
10. In a study based on countries that are members of OECD, Peter Lindert, "What Limits Social Spending?" *EEH*, January 1996, argues that such spending "may be governed primarily by the relative sizes of age groups, and by the income distribution, electoral conditions, and the income level." (p. 31).
11. John Kenneth Galbraith, *The Affluent Society* (1958).
12. E. J. Mishan, *Technology and Growth: The Price We Pay* (New York: Praeger, 1973).
13. See Clifford Winston, "Economic Deregulation: Days of Reckoning for Microeconomists," *JEL*, September 1993.
14. See the essay by Paul Joskow and Roger Noll, and the commentary by William Niskanen and Elizabeth Bailey on "Economic Regulation," in Martin Feldstein, ed., *American Economic Policy in the 1980s* (1994).
15. Kip Viscusi, "Health and Safety Regulation," in Feldstein (1994), p. 457.
16. The road made use of the roadbed and seven partially excavated tunnels from a railroad William Vanderbilt and Andrew Carnegie began in the 1880s as a potential competitor to the Pennsylvania Railroad.
17. Mark Rose, *Interstate: Express Highway Politics, 1941–1956* (Lawrence: The Regents Press of Kansas, 1979).
18. The Federal-Aid Highway Act of 1973 allowed urban areas to trade funds earmarked for controversial sections of the interstate system within urban areas for public transportation.
19. Bruce Seely, "A Republic Bound Together," *The Wilson Quarterly*, Winter 1993, p. 35.
20. The six roads were the Central Railroad of New Jersey, Erie Lackawanna, Lehigh & Hudson River, Lehigh Valley, Penn Central, and Reading. Conrail first showed a profit in 1981. In 1987, the federal government sold its interest in the railroad through an initial public offering. Ten years later, the company was sold to CSX Corporation and Norfolk Southern Corporation.
21. Conrail had to provide commuter rail service into the early 1980s.
22. In addition, it is involved in the design, construction, maintenance, and inspection of navigation, traffic control, and communications equipment for the airways, as well as the promotion of air safety.
23. Herbert Stein, *The Fiscal Revolution in America* (1969), chap. 16.
24. *Ibid.*, p. 398.
25. Donald W. White, *The American Century: The Rise and Decline of the United States as a World Power* (New Haven: Yale University Press, 1966) examines America's role in the world in the twentieth century through the eyes of contemporaries.
26. Herbert Stein, commenting on economists' ideas of inflation two decades ago, put it well: "In our naivete we meant by endless inflation an endless rise of the price level, not an endless increase in the rate of increase of the price level." In Feldstein (1980), p. 174.
27. A glut of crude oil appeared in the markets as a result of such advanced *prices*, and by the summer of 1981, OPEC-posted prices were down to $32 a barrel. In 1982, the oil glut continued, and oil prices declined slowly to around $14 a barrel in the fall of 1988. OPEC still tries to restrict the output of crude oil in the hope that the higher prices will result.
28. Readers should recall that the CPI Commission believes that the official CPI numbers are biased by approximately 1.1 percent. See note 67 to Chapter 28.
29. For an analysis of our inflationary adjustment to the "supply shocks" of the 1970s, oil prices and agricultural shortages, see Robert Gordon, "Alternative Responses to External Supply Shocks," *Brookings Papers on Economic Activity*, vol. 6, no. 1, 1975.
30. Given average cash reserve requirements of 20 percent or less.
31. *Statistical Abstract*, 1979, p. 847.
32. See Anne O. Krueger, "Whither the World Bank and the IMF?" *JEL*, December 1998.
33. A "selective review of the Bank and the Fund's current roles" can be found in Krueger, *op. cit.*
34. Carl Christ, "The 1972 Report of the President's Council of Economic Advisers," *AER*, September 1973.
35. At the time the last edition was being written in early 1997, the average was approaching 7,000. As this edition is being written in early 2002, the average is holding at just above 10,000 in spite of two consecutive years in which the Dow Jones average fell.
36. This was reduced to a quarter-percent in 1975. See Gene Smiley, *The American Economy in the Twentieth Century* (Cincinnati: South-Western Publishing, 1994).
37. See Benjamin Klebaner, *American Commercial Banking: A History* (Boston: Twayne Publishers, 1990), chap. 20.
38. The Federal Home Loan Bank Board had been responsible for the S&Ls.
39. There is a large literature on this debacle. See, for example, Edward J. Kane, *The S&L Insurance Mess: How Did It Happen?* (Washington, D.C.: The Urban Institute Press, 1989).

40. The National Commission on Financial Institution Reform, Recovery and Enforcement, *Origins and Causes of the S&L Debacle: A Blueprint for Reform: A Report to the President and Congress of the United States* (Washington, D.C.: Government Printing Office, 1993).
41. See U.S. General Accounting Office, Financial Audit: Resolution Trust Corporation's 1995 and 1994 Financial Statements (1996).
42. James Eliot Mason, *The Transformation of Commercial Banking in the United States, 1965–1991* (New York: Garland, 1997).
43. Eugene N. White, "Banking and Finance in the Twentieth Century," in Stanley Engerman and Robert Gallman, eds., *The Cambridge Economic History of the United States. Volume III: The Twentieth Century* (Cambridge: Cambridge University Press, 2000). This is a useful survey of the whole panoply of financial institutions.
44. Officially, the Gramm-Leach-Bliley Financial Services Modernization Act of 1999 removed the constraints imposed by the Glass-Steagall Banking Act of 1933. It took 66 years for the banks to free the shackles imposed in the wake of the Great Depression.
45. The annual rate of growth of real GDP continued throughout the 1970s in the range of 2.5 percent. As Nathan Rosenberg observed to one of the authors, since productivity was barely rising, the growth was mainly attributable to rising labor-force participation rates among women. In *Wealth and Poverty* (1981), George Gilder argues that this increase in GDP is largely spurious because it depends upon weakening family ties, taking women out of the home where their labor is not counted as GDP, and putting them in a position where it is (pp. 13–16).
46. Benjamin Friedman, "Postwar Changes in the American Financial Markets," in Feldstein (1980), pp. 16–21.
47. 28.5 million is roughly equal to the entire population of Canada; it is more than that of the Scandinavian countries combined.
48. *Statistical Abstract*, 2000, Table 643, p. 403.
49. The three events are the coup d'etat in Libya in 1969, the Arab-Israeli War of 1973, and the coup d'etat in Iran in 1979.
50. Following devaluations from $35 per ounce to $42, which didn't get the desired results, Nixon gave up on the two-tiered gold price system; the market price for gold then being close to $500 per ounce. The result was a shift from a fixed to floating exchange rate regime.
51. *Statistical Abstract*, 1979, p. 847.
52. For a detailed analysis, see William Branson, "Trends in United States International Trade and Investment Since World War II," in Feldstein (1980).
53. When the Nixon Administration abandoned the "official" gold price, the World Bank and the International Monetary Fund, the "Bretton Woods" institutions, were forced to adapt to the new circumstances. In Krueger (1998), the author discusses how these institutions have looked to the needs of both developing economies and those in transition.
54. James Buchanan and Richard Wagner, *Democracy in Deficit* (1977).
55. *Ibid.*, p. 171.
56. *New York Times*, 18 June 1978.
57. See Robert Gordon, in Feldstein (1980), p. 157, for the mercurial record of economists' advice to presidents.
58. Michael Mussa, "Monetary Policy," in Feldstein (1994), p. 96.
59. Paul Volcker's comments on "Monetary Policy," in Feldstein (1994), p. 146.
60. Summary of Discussion, "Monetary Policy," in Feldstein (1994), p. 158. This episode is also discussed by Mussa (p. 98), Volcker (p. 147), and Feldstein in his introduction, "American Economic Policy in the 1980s: A Personal View," p. 6.
61. Volcker in Feldstein (1994), p. 149.
62. James Tobin comments on "Monetary Policy," in Feldstein (1994), p. 152.
63. Stein (1969), pp. 410–411.
64. Alan J. Auerbach and Joel Slemrod, "The Economic Effects of the Tax Reform Act of 1986," *Journal of Economic Literature*, vol. XXXV, no. 2, June 1997.
65. See Don Fullerton, "Tax Policy," in Feldstein (1994), p. 169.
66. David Stockman commentary on "Budget Policy," in Feldstein (1994), p. 274.
67. Between 1983 and 1989 when the deficits shrunk, increased revenues were responsible for about one-third of the shrinkage.
68. Some recipients had to pay income taxes on Social Security benefits; the retirement age was phased upward; and a cost-of-living adjustment was postponed for six months.
69. Fullerton, in Feldstein (1994), p. 190f.
70. See J. David Richardson, "Trade Policy," in Feldstein (1994).
71. Hugh Rockoff, "The Peace Dividend in Historical Perspective," *AER*, May 1998.
72. During his first term, Clinton also signed into law a bill to "change welfare as we know it," but it is too early to determine whether the changes will correct any of the major problems.

SUGGESTED READINGS

Articles

Andersen, Terry L., and Peter J. Hill. "The Race for Property Rights." *Journal of Law and Economics*, vol. XXIII, no. 1, April 1990.

Branson, William H. "Trends in United States International Trade and Investment Since World War II." In Martin Feldstein, ed., *The American Economy in Transition*. Chicago: University of Chicago Press, 1980.

Christ, Carl F. "The 1972 Report of the President's Council of Economic Advisers." *American Economic Review*, vol. 63, no. 4, September 1973.

Freeman, Richard B. "The Evolution of the American Labor Market, 1948–1980." In Martin Feldstein, ed., *The American Economy in Transition*. Chicago: University of Chicago Press, 1980.

Friedman, Benjamin. "Postwar Changes in the American Financial Markets." In Martin Feldstein, ed., *The American Economy in Transition*. Chicago: University of Chicago Press, 1980.

Fullerton, Don. "Tax Policy." In Martin Feldstein, ed., *American Economic Policy in the 1980s*. Chicago: University of Chicago Press, 1994.

Joskow, Paul L., and Roger G. Noll. "Economic Regulation." In Martin Feldstein, ed., *American Economic Policy in the 1980s*. Chicago: University of Chicago Press, 1994.

Krueger, Anne O. "Whither the World Bank and the IMF?" *Journal of Economic Literature*, vol. XXXVI, no. 4, December 1998.

Lindert, Peter. "What Limits Social Spending?" *Explorations in Economic History*, vol. 33, no. 1, January 1996.

Mussa, Michael. "Monetary Policy." In Martin Feldstein, ed., *American Economic Policy in the 1980s*. Chicago: University of Chicago Press, 1994.

Okun, Arthur. "Postwar Macroeconomics Performance." In Martin Feldstein, ed., *The American Economy in Transition*. Chicago: University of Chicago Press, 1980.

Poterba, James M. "Budget Policy." In Martin Feldstein, ed., *American Economic Policy in the 1980s*. Chicago: University of Chicago Press, 1994.

Richardson, J. David. "Trade Policy." In Martin Feldstein, ed., *American Economic Policy in the 1980s*. Chicago: University of Chicago Press, 1994.

Rockoff, Hugh. "The Peace Dividend in Historical Perspective." *American Economic Review*, vol. 88, no. 2, May 1998.

Viscusi, W. Kip. "Health and Safety Regulation." In Martin Feldstein, ed., *American Economic Policy in the 1980s*. Chicago: University of Chicago Press, 1994.

Winston, Clifford. "Economic Deregulation: Days of Reckoning for Microeconomists." *Journal of Economic Literature*, vol. XXXI, no. 3, September 1993.

Books

Anderson, Terry, and Peter J. Hill. *The Birth of a Transfer Society*. Stanford: Hoover Institution Press, 1980.

Buchanan, James, and Richard Wagner. *Democracy in Deficit*. New York: Academic Press, 1977.

Feldstein, Martin. *The American Economy in Transition*. Chicago: University of Chicago Press, 1980.

———, ed. *American Economic Policy in the 1980s*. Chicago: University of Chicago Press, 1994.

Galbraith, John Kenneth. *The Affluent Society*. Boston: Houghton Mifflin, 1958.

Gilder, George. *Wealth and Poverty*. New York: Basic Books, 1981.

Hughes, Jonathan. *The Governmental Habit Redux*. Princeton: Princeton University Press, 1991.

Stein, Herbert. *The Fiscal Revolution in America*. Chicago: University of Chicago Press, 1969.

Weidenbaum, Murray. *Business and Government in the Global Marketplace*, 5th ed. Englewood Cliffs, NJ: Prentice-Hall, 1995.

CHAPTER THIRTY-ONE

Does Our Past Have a Future?

It is inconceivable that a society's future could be made without the influence of its past. This book began with a discussion of the influence of England in colonial America and of the influence of colonial laws and institutions in modern America. There is nothing peculiarly American about this continuity.

The power of the "live hand of the past" astonished the world when, in Iran, a twentieth-century royal dictatorship and its modernized economic and social structures were overthrown by a regime anxious to return to an older way of life. Students of modern Soviet society are amazed by the persistence there of ancient Russian forms and traditions, and how quickly many of them resurfaced with the fall of the Communist state. After all the terrible events of the Communist dictatorship in modern Chinese history, Richard Nixon and others dined in Peking on a sumptuous feast of Mandarin delights. The entire cuisine of that ancient culture survived the Great Leap Forward and the Cultural Revolution.

Complex human institutions live through time; indeed, institutions are the legacy passed between generations in any society. It has been so in the United States, and it doubtless will be so in its future. A country's recent past cannot be tossed aside. The question, "Who will create the future?" is best answered: "To some extent, those who made the past."

ASSETS

This book has traversed a long route, all the way back to the Virginia colony and beyond. It is useful to summarize the principal elements that sustained the country's economic growth, its assets. Similarly, it is useful to examine the liabilities in this history, those parts of its history that have raised problems, that have left its people less well-off than they otherwise might be and, perhaps, threaten them with worse in the future.

The Tradition of Growth

At the beginning the combination of a great natural resource to be exploited, the land, together with a rapidly growing, *able* population, gave Americans a history of unprecedented overall economic growth. That history, the national experience, produced a built-in optimism about the future that induced decision making in anticipation of further growth. It was so when we were a colonial outpost, and it remains so as we have grown to be a major player in a global economy. As J. P. Morgan once put it, anyone who was "bearish" on America's future would surely go broke. Optimism was a self-fulfilling prophecy. The American economy succeeded in part because it had already succeeded. Americans have come to expect economic improvement through growth, and they tend to deal abruptly at election time with those political regimes that fail to deliver it, through errors of either commission or omission—"it is the economy, stupid!"

Social Mobility

Many large, extended American families contain samples of widely different personal incomes, educational achievements, lifestyles, and varieties of economic endeavor—a sister who is a physician, an uncle who works in a factory, a great-aunt who still lives on the family farm, and a distant cousin who lives in a commune in northern California. While such varying lifestyles add variety and excitement to personal experience, they also reflect a very important reality: the country has no readily identifiable or effective system of class barriers. Money—how much you have, not where you got it or what you do with it—remains the main measure of social achievement. While undeniably crass, it is an economically progressive attitude.

The founders forbade "patents of nobility" and thus released the energies of a whole people. The idea was that anybody could be anything. Immigrants still pour across the borders of the United States because of *opportunity*—it is said all over the world that you can be what you achieve in American society. A long string of landed ancestors is of little advantage if the current "bottom line" is financial incompetence. The public educational system that reaches *by law* into every home ensures that, one way or another, every American child can be placed upon the course of personal improvement in a society whose social barriers are fairly porous. Racial and sexual discrimination, legacies of the distant past, have been the major formal barriers to social mobility. For years, reformers have struggled against these anachronisms.

The greater social mobility is within a country, the greater is the chance that talent will not be involuntarily wasted. The more talent is exercised, the nearer the society comes to achieving whatever potential it possesses in its people. While Americans constantly try to increase their social mobility, they already are the "world champions" at this game. It is easier to make it in life if you are born to affluence or are white, but American society, more than any other, has kept the door to personal achievement open through its social mobility. As Stanley Lebergott has shown, the United States still is a nation of the nouveaux riches.[1] However gauche, it is a positive force for economic betterment. The top wealth holders today are not all the same people who were in that category two decades ago.

Acceptance of Technological Change

American history is full of conflict produced by the ready acceptance, even *eager* acceptance, of new ideas, new products, new practices—of innovation in general. Whole towns and settled regions are completely or partially abandoned, populations sent into migration, in the wake of this force. New areas boom; old ones die. New firms expand; old ones fail. The growth of the Sun Belt is a contemporary manifestation of this phenomenon.

This love of the new goes deeply into American life, from the kitchen to the factory. It is both a productive and a disruptive force. Businesses fail when their products lose favor, and families are left without financial support. Schumpeter tied the introduction of innovation to the entrepreneurial function in business growth and referred to the outcome as the "process of creative destruction": The realignment of factors of production to embrace both failure and success generates economic growth. As Burton Klein put it, **macroeconomic stability**—growth at something like full employment through technological change—relies upon **microeconomic instability**—the competitive jostling for markets and control over resources.[2] The dynamic force has been the encouragement and acceptance of innovative technological change. The process maintains a steady element of riskiness in private economic endeavor.

Secure Property Rights

Even though such developments as modern taxation, eminent domain law, zoning, land-use restrictions, and other regulations have reduced the scope of individual control of private property, so strong was the original property-right endowment that Americans still work to acquire private property of all kinds for their personal gain. The lure remains. Historically, the endowment of secure property rights energized the population as much as private interest ever did in any society. People were willing to make extreme sacrifices to acquire property rights, to engage in undertakings with distant payoffs—from clearing farmland to building steel mills—in the hope of personal or family gain from property ownership. In a society with minimal government and no particular centrally directed programs about the shape of its economic future beyond constitutional consensus, secure property rights left the future essentially to the people themselves.

Secure Traditions of Private Contract

All activities founded upon the use of credit, so necessary in any economy dominated by private exchanges of goods and services, require a settled expectation about the security of future commitments. The so-called English legacy was nowhere stronger than in the law of contract and the organization of society to enforce contracts. Americans might well now cringe in horror at the strength of this tradition in earlier times (for example, court enforcement of sales of human beings for life or of their forced labor for terms of years). But such adherence to agreement *in principle* underpinned all private transactions and made the private ownership and control of productive resources all the more powerful as an instrument for economic progress. In the contract clause of the federal Constitution, the power of private contract was elevated above the legislative powers of the sovereign states themselves: thus, *Dartmouth College v. Woodward.*

Calculable Law

Americans have been frustrated at times by the very stability of their legal institutions—for example, the "nine old men" (Supreme Court) who killed the first New Deal. It is not easy to achieve basic legal change. Legislatures may pass laws, but the common-law tradition, together with written constitutions against which all legislation is measured, makes judicial review a necessity for legislation to become law. The very difficulty of achieving radical change through legislation, however, adds substantial stability to private estimates of future values and adds motivation to all contractual agreements designed to yield a distant return. Since investment in real assets and long-term financial settlements must discount the future, the stability of the legal framework greatly eases and reduces the costs of planning private commitments.

Popular Democracy

The fact that Americans as a people collectively create their own disasters as well as triumphs, from the school board to the White House, adds long-term stability to American economic life. It is pointless to advocate violence and upheaval in American life to create social change; the United States *already* has a steady diet of violence and upheaval, together with fundamental social change, and it is all of its own making. Elections come *by the calendar.* Any adult citizen can vote if he or she wants to vote, for whatever candidate, proposal, or political party grabs his or her fancy. Winston Churchill once said of democracy that, while it is an appalling form of government, there is none better. The United States may be faced with carelessness, corruption, abuses of power, and apathy, but it has only itself to blame for them.

However dismaying all these hazards seem at any moment, in the long run they guarantee the permanence of the forms of the American government. Popular democracy adds to long-term political stability even if it is chaotic at any specific point in time. The system can always be improved, always be reformed; however maddening, it is never hopeless. As a result, the American republic of popular democracy goes on, through good times and bad, war and peace, tranquility and upheaval.

The lack of a serious threat of an irregular change of governmental form adds motivation to investment and to economic growth. Government is not just offices and officeholders; it is a form of collective decision making. American government is ordered by rules to an astonishing degree. Reflect for a moment on parliamentary procedure. From the student council meeting to the Senate of the United States, like English-speaking peoples all over the world, Americans live by an accepted set of rules. It is not a matter of law; no one requires *Robert's Rules of Order*. Like the rules of language, these rules are simply accepted as the *only* legitimate form. It is a most extraordinary thing. These rules of democratic decision making prevent both mob rule and dictatorship alike. They also leave the most skilled political demagogues in constant danger of defeat.

Popular democracy is made effective by its settled rules and procedures. In the end, the people can rule themselves because there is a generally accepted machinery with which to do it. *No man, woman, or party could rule in the United States in violation of that machinery*. In American society, parliamentary procedure is the *only* road to legitimate power. Savers and investors can know that radical innovations in the forms of political power cannot come by coup. If the United States were ever to become a "banana republic," it would be through these procedures.

LIABILITIES

The recognition that there is potential for failure forces a consideration of what this history suggests about the methods Americans normally employ that may reduce their potential for growth, that darken their economic future.

Dilution of Property Rights

The classic rights of property are the use, abuse, and fruits of that property. Exploitation of these rights makes ownership desirable, worth struggling to attain. Such rights—and cognate productive motivations—can be weakened in various ways. As the rights weaken, so do the motivations to exploit them.

Since the late nineteenth century, property rights have been weakened for various reasons. Cumulatively, the dilution of property has been powerful, particularly the taxing of its "fruits," the income generated by that property. In extreme cases, as in some inner-city slums, a peculiarly lethal combination of property taxes and regulation has led to the actual abandonment of property by its owners. The result is a socially destructive and profitless wasteland. Taxes, jobs, living space, all are lost. "Urban renewal" condemns property, clears titles, and transfers the property to new owners—a costly procedure.

Moreover, widespread property ownership has traditionally "bonded" the American social community together despite economic and political differences among different owners. As Selig Perlman emphasized in his book *A Theory of the Labor Movement*, the commitment of American labor to peaceable methods and to social stability has always been rooted in accessibility to property ownership, which gave the worker a fixed interest in the established order.[3] In the spirit of reform, the institutions of zoning, land-use rules, and building codes—as well as outright taxation—have diluted ownership. This has been particularly true in inner-city slums, where the desire to acquire and control property has diminished, as has the social stability associated with the ownership of property. One consequence has been the creation of an "underclass," a group that receives little, if any, benefit from economic growth.

The dilution of property rights escalates as governments at all levels have needed revenues and as social reform has created an ever-widening network of restrictions upon the acquisition and uses of property. In the process, the economy has lost some of the motives for economic growth inherent in property ownership. There is a need for greater wisdom in these matters as the incentive to own property is partially responsible for our present wealth. As long as the fabric of American society is rooted in property ownership, it is foolish to weaken it as a mere side effect of other objectives.

Collective Goods and Special Interests

Throughout American history, groups have banded together to achieve the economic gains that they could not realize as individuals operating in the free market. Merchant groups, trade organizations, farmer and industrial lobbies, labor unions, all have tried and succeeded in skewing the benefits of growth by collective action. Tariffs and subsidies (given primarily to business groups), closed entry to competition by law (given to labor unions since the Wagner Act), special privileges from licensing (given to monopoly groups, from public utilities to doctors, lawyers, and teachers), protection of farm cooperatives—all and more are examples from American economic history of special advantages gained by collective action.

The gains from such organization, called **collective goods** by Mancur Olson in his insightful book *The Logic of Collective Action: Public Goods and the Theory of Groups*, are greater than competitive profits.[4] It is characteristic of collective goods that the gains from them can only be captured by the relevant special-interest groups. The consumer pays the bill. Resources are attracted to such noncompetitive employments, and a less than optimal allocation results.

There is a further danger from such noncompetitive groupings of economic power—resistance to change. As Olson points out, where special privilege protected by law makes it possible to resist change and to slack off work efforts, the result will be technological backwardness, low worker productivity, and less economic growth.

Since the American government is a popular democracy where vote-seeking politicians are open to rent-seeking and special-interest pressures, the country's economic future can easily be blighted in what would appear as a perfectly "natural" pattern of responses to economic change. Those who gain collective goods, single-interest groups, are constantly at work seeking the rents derived from special privilege, and the rest of society must be on guard or else be stuck with the bill. Publicity and open debate are the best safeguards.

Big Business and Big Government

Innovation in economic life is the primary cause of growth. Innovation does not just crawl ashore on dark nights like some bizarre mutant. Technological change must be *introduced* by those to whom such innovation is profitable. John Kenneth Galbraith, in his book *The New Industrial State*, makes a useful differentiation between the *entrepreneurial firm* and the bureaucratic ways of present-day giant corporations.[5] Of course, some of the latter were once leaders in progressive technological innovation, and, indeed, for that reason became large firms. The major building block in the 1901 merger that created U.S. Steel was Carnegie Steel, of which it can be said that there never was a more revolutionary competitive innovator; but that was long ago. Run by committees of experts, what Galbraith calls the *technostructure*, today's big businesses tend to be stodgy and conservative.

Taxation, which deals equally with all businesses, differentiating only according to reported profits, adds complications. Heavy income taxes are especially hard on entrepreneurial firms that cannot easily hide behind a portfolio of tax-exempt investments. To grow, they must realize earnings from their major activities, and those earnings are visible and taxable.[6] Thus, demands for transfers of resources from productive activities to government place limits upon the nation's entrepreneurial resources. The efforts by the Reagan administration to reduce those taxes were a straightforward admission that taxes have been excessive.

The problem is a difficult one. Government needs taxes, and entrepreneurial businesses need resources for growth. Judging from past performance, the country's standards in this area of fiscal planning can bear improvement. It is not a problem that has been confronted directly. It first appeared seriously in World War II, and, since that time, government expenditure has come to occupy 40 percent of the GDP in peacetime. It is a problem that ultimately must be solved. Indifference to the problem in an age of Big Government and Big Business has led to a loss of flexibility in the competitive international economy and probably reduced the rate of U.S. economic growth from what it might have been. It is not difficult to be pessimistic about this. It has become an almost automatic response of the political left to accuse the political right of policies that favor big business, and, in the main, big business has supported the political right. While some of these policies may be in the interest of the nation economically, they are generally not in the interest of one of the parties politically.

Jonathan Hughes's work demonstrated how effortlessly and naturally this country is willing (and able) to resort to government to offset unpopular market outcomes. Robert Higgs emphasized how the use of government in the past century to overcome crises (wars, financial panics, depressions) created lingering "ratchet effects," either in intellectual or in institutional forms.[7]

In *The Birth of a Transfer Society*, Terry Anderson and Peter J. Hill argue that the federal power was used by special interests to transfer wealth and income from productive activity to nonproductive activity.[8] As time passed, the transfer power came to dominate the American economy. An entire economic sector grew up that was dependent solely upon the transfer power, either by taxing and spending—or by inflation. The result, said Anderson and Hill, was that the transfer function dominated government; the clamor for more could only be satisfied by an acceleration of transfers. The infestation of lobbyists and single-issue politicians in Washington reflected an ultimate reality. The U.S. Treasury had become the scene of a modern "gold rush" peopled by rent-seeking beneficiaries of government largesse.[9]

Morris Janowitz argued in *Social Control of the Welfare State* that the deficit-financed inflation of the 1970s originated on the supply side as a result of a competition for votes.[10] The result, argued Janowitz, was weak governments that could only perpetuate inflation. Since all political parties were completely in support of extending the welfare state but unwilling to tax its full costs, expenditures ran ahead of revenues, while weak coalition government replaced the more ideologically differentiated, but stronger, governments of former times in the Western democracies. Governments became the helpless puppets of their own pasts. The power to decide, reject, and change course vanished.

Racism, Sexism: The Stumbling Blocks

Even though the United States has been called the "land of opportunity," the door still opens more easily for white males than it does for females and minorities. Racial and sexual prejudices are of ancient and diffuse cultural origins. Only in recent years have concerted, sustained policies based upon new laws (and new interpretations of old laws) at both federal and state levels been implemented in an attempt to suppress and ultimately eliminate their influences from American life.

That distinguished scholars, scientists, writers, artists, jurists, and political and business leaders who are women and/or members of racial minorities now flourish in all walks of American life is proof enough of the sad losses to this nation's economic and intellectual growth that discrimination produced in the past. More than half (women plus minorities) of this nation's distributed ability has been suppressed historically by discrimination. The United States is poorer needlessly in every way as a result. Eliminating systematic discrimination is not a simple matter. Progress had been made, but the problem remains.

Since World War II, great strides have been made in the fight to eliminate racial discrimination. Truman did away with segregated military facilities. The Eisenhower years saw the Supreme Court decision that moved to stop segregated schooling. The Civil Rights Act of 1964 led eventually to the affirmative action quotas of the 1970s. All of this has helped move many American blacks into the economic mainstream.

The legacy of slavery and the 100 years of discriminated "freedom" following the Civil War, however, left behind a huge black population—found in all American cities and in the rural South—many of whom are unable to cope in a competitive free market. Their ancestors moved to the cities, especially northern cities, during the Great Migration to seek (mostly) manufacturing jobs. In most cases, their only qualification was a strong back. Now, these jobs have largely disappeared in the move from an industrial to a service economy. As was discussed in Chapter 28, minimum education requirements now exist for most jobs. At the height of our worst recessions, any Sunday newspaper job section remains full of listings for thousands of unfilled jobs because the minimal education requirements go unmet. In the post-World War II American economy, the number of job seekers has exceeded the number of job vacancies on only a few occasions.

The poorly educated segment of our population is falling economically behind the rest of the nation year by year and threatens to become a permanent underbelly. It is a potential time bomb that periodically has exploded in urban riots. If this country does not reach out to these people with some economic incentives or jobs programs, the ability of the U.S. economy to compete in the international arena will be diminished because the welfare costs of supporting the unemployable will create permanent pressure for budget deficits.

Maintaining the Welfare State

There must be some combination of taxes and transfer payments that is not destructive to the family prospects of the taxpayers and that yet meets the reasonable needs of the aged, ill, infirm, and disabled.

Thus far, the American record for discovering that viable combination has been dismal. The social insurance system, the core of which is Social Security, is the product of more than a half century of building on the legislation of 1935. It has grown piece by piece, with no overall plan to its pattern of development. Needs were met without correct reckoning of their costs.

The entire apparatus of the American welfare state has become of fundamental importance in the American economy. There is no real possibility that the United States will return to the way of life that existed before the Great Depression. That world has largely vanished. Millions of workers have faithfully paid taxes for decades to support the Social Security system. The country's economic future cannot now be separated from the network of the Social Security system. The rest of society has moved on and adapted to Social Security over the decades. Family life has changed in response to it; individual provision for medical insurance, unemployment protection, retirement in old age, all have changed because of Social Security.

Important as the welfare system is, its own impact upon the population has been a mixed blessing. Parts of the system are known to have perverse effects (for example, breaking up families, creating increased dependency and other forms of social incompetence). The United States is the only economically advanced nation with no comprehensive national health system. Although a majority of Americans were reported to favor addressing the issue, they were dissatisfied with what the Clinton administration produced.[11] The American welfare system is inflationary and defective. As noted in the previous chapter, President Clinton signed a bill that was to "change welfare as we know it," but whether the changes will correct any of the major problems remains to be seen.[12]

The Regulated Life

Government regulation now reaches almost everything, from butter to steel. This book has discussed how government regulation has been motivated variously by religion, morals, politics, economics, safety, and public health. The current system, perhaps better called a "nonsystem," from barbershops to nuclear power plants, is totally congenial with American laws and constitutions. It is what *Americans* want. Although technological backwardness through regulation has been imposed purposely at times, that has not usually been the object of regulation, merely a widespread side effect.[13] The result of regulation is rarely the motive for it. As Bruce Owen and Ron Braeutigam point out, the process of regulation tends to be its own outcome.[14]

The regulation of private economic activity by government is as old as government itself on this continent. What can be done is to develop a set of uniform criteria for *deregulation* based on *some* rational basis. What has been developed in the history of the American economy is a regulatory junk pile that makes no general sense at all. Illogical regulation confounds enterprise and economic progress.

Americans, however, have an absolute passion to control economic activity by government, to create social objectives by forcing economic life into regulated patterns. This deeply rooted passion will not likely be eliminated by the processes of popular democracy. Since this passion now is ubiquitous, it is reasonable to try to seek rational criteria for its reform. One might even begin with the simple question: Which parts of the economy, if any, might better serve the commonwealth by *total exclusion* from government regulation? Is the answer *none*? In that case, the "underground economy" will continue to grow and flourish. Even if it is true that there would be no benefit, the legal economy's future would be brighter if some general criteria for regulation could be agreed upon, because Americans will continue to regulate.

Must regulation be destructive of economic growth? If so, enthusiasts for regulation would serve the country's future by explaining *why*. **Sunset laws**, which are regulatory self-destruct systems after some fixed period of time, would be a great contribution. If no system of regulation could last longer than, say, ten years without a renewed warrant, there might be a great transformation. It is possible to improve upon the methods of government regulation.[15] A contemporary accounting must ultimately consider our capability to develop further.

NET WORTH

Net worth is the difference between assets and liabilities. Before investigating the difference itself, it should be noted that there are items that appear on both the asset and liability side of the balance. The most important of these is government. In our summary accounting, government appears as an asset in its role of defining and protecting property rights directly, but it appears as a liability when those rights are diluted indirectly through taxation to generate revenue for other roles. It is an asset when it creates an environment in which technological change can flourish, but it becomes a liability when it allows those changes to be concentrated in the hands of large firms that cease to be entrepreneurial. In these and other examples it should be obvious that the asset carries the potential for the liability; the two are interrelated. There is much in our history American government has done well; whether it has made our net worth larger or smaller is an individual judgment.

On any balance sheet, net worth is a statement of capital and surplus, the ultimate ownership of any going concern. The capital stock and the surplus are invested in the assets of the firm. Pushing the metaphor for a moment, let's apply it to the United States, and to that part of its capital that is human. What generations of Americans have produced is a population that can live voluntarily, peacefully, and productively within its own stable institutional framework. This achievement has been beyond the grasp of many peoples throughout history and remains beyond the grasp of too many of them today.

As Bradford DeLong notes, the twentieth century witnessed the world's material wealth grow far beyond what could have been conceived at the beginning of that century. The global economy is as healthy as it has ever been. The twentieth century also saw the distribution of that wealth between the world's peoples grow more unequal.[16] In the United States and other developed countries our collective production no longer emphasizes the necessities of life such as food, clothing, and shelter. A large portion of that production consists of items that were considered luxuries only a few decades ago. Less-developed countries also grew over the twentieth century, but at a slower rate. Given that the Internet is widely available, given that sophisticated technological information is as near as a few keystrokes, this divergence is somewhat surprising.

Human capital is impossible to measure except for specific tasks at hand. Human capital is the distributed ability to create the material and cultural necessities that are needed to sustain a viable human community and to provide a basis for further development. A wandering desert tribe has sufficient human capital to manage that way of life but not enough to educate doctors, build cities, or launch a space program. Maintaining the complicated and productive culture of modern America and encouraging its economic growth require the ability to adapt institutions and technologies to its changing needs. The United States is one of a small minority of human societies that have produced, thus far, the immense productivity of the economically advanced parts of humanity. Americans have been building their society since 1607, sometimes inadvertently, sometimes with great purpose. The measure of the country's ability to continue this process lies within the brains of its living generations. By this measure, the American economy has a very large capital indeed. With sound management and a little bit of luck, it will continue to grow in the future as it has in the past.

NOTES

1. Stanley Lebergott, *The American Economy: Income, Wealth, and Want* (Princeton: Princeton University Press, 1976), p. 161.
2. Burton Klein, *Dynamic Economics* (Cambridge: Harvard University Press, 1977).
3. Selig Perlman, *A Theory of the Labor Movement* (New York: Kelley, 1949).
4. Mancur Olson, *The Logic of Collective Action: Public Goods and the Theory of Groups* (Cambridge: Harvard University Press, 1971).
5. John Kenneth Galbraith, *The New Industrial State* (Boston: Houghton Mifflin, 1967).
6. Consider the record-breaking numbers of initial public offerings (IPOs) in the past few years. Under SEC rules,

such firms are required to disclose their present financial situation.

7. Jonathan Hughes, *The Governmental Habit Redux: Economic Controls from Colonial Times to the Present* (Princeton: Princeton University Press, 1991); Robert Higgs, "Crises, Bigger Government and Ideological Change: Two Hypotheses on the Ratchet Phenomenon," *Explorations in Economic History*, vol. 22, no. 1, January 1985.
8. Terry Anderson and Peter J. Hill, *The Birth of a Transfer Society* (Stanford: Hoover Institution Press, 1980).
9. Terry Anderson and Peter J. Hill make extensive use of the gold rush analogy in their article, "The Race for Property Rights," *Journal of Law and Economics*, vol. XXIII, no. 1, April 1990.
10. Morris Janowitz, *Social Control of the Welfare State* (Chicago: University of Chicago Press, 1976).
11. The plan proposed by the Clinton administration proved so cumbersome and expensive, the debate so divisive, that the issue has been set aside and allowed to cool. The Kassebaum-Kennedy bill is an attempt to correct some of the most serious problems in the current health insurance system, as is the attempt to find a "Patient's Bill of Rights" acceptable to the George W. Bush administration.
12. See Rebecca M. Blank., *It Takes a Nation: A New Agenda for Fighting Poverty* (Princeton: Princeton University Press, 1997), and David E. Card and Rebecca M. Blank, eds., *Finding Jobs: Work and Welfare Reform* (New York: Russell Sage Foundation, 2000).
13. An example is the Alaskan salmon industry. Douglass C. North and Roger LeRoy Miller, *Economics of Public Issues* (New York: Norton, 1971), pp. 104–108.
14. Bruce Owen and Ron Braeutigam, *The Regulation Game: Strategic Use of the Administrative Process* (Cambridge, MA: Ballinger Publishing Co., 1978).
15. A particularly interesting case study can be found in Peter Temin, with Louis Galambos, *The Fall of the Bell System: A Study in Prices and Politics* (New York: Cambridge University Press, 1987), a case in which antitrust was brought to bear on a regulatory problem; AT&T had become "too big to regulate." The government's lead attorney, William F. Baxter, discusses his role in the case in his comments on "Antitrust Policy," in Martin Feldstein, ed., *American Economic Policy in the 1980s* (Chicago: University of Chicago Press, 1994).
16. J. Bradford DeLong, "The Shape of Twentieth Century Economic History," National Bureau of Economic Research, Working Paper 7569, February 2000. This is the introduction of his forthcoming book available, in part, on his personal website (*www.j-bradford-delong.net*).

GLOSSARY

Aggregate Production Function A mathematical relationship that shows how the factors of production, such as land, labor, and capital, are transformed into national income.

Balance of Payments An accounting system for international payments in which the value of all of a country's exports (including foreign reserves) equals the value of its imports.

Bill of Exchange A dated order to pay (e.g., 90 days after issuance), conventionally drawn by a seller against a purchaser of goods or commodities delivered. An ordinary bank check on a demand deposit is a financial bill of exchange, an order to pay "at sight" unless it is postdated.

Bimetallic Monetary Standard A currency based upon a fixed price for two precious metals at the mint or the central bank, for example, for both gold and silver.

Break-in-Transport A place where one mode of transport ends and another begins, a place of loading and unloading (e.g., a port where goods are taken off a railroad and put aboard a ship).

Bretton Woods System The post-World War II fixed exchange rate system mediated through the International Monetary Fund.

Business Cycle Oscillations over time in aggregate economic activity. Of the several cycles studied, the most commonly recurring nonseasonal one is 36 to 40 months from trough (low point in production and employment) to trough.

Call Loan The species of loan made by financial institutions with potentially the shortest possible maturity—due for repayment when asked for (i.e., "called"). It is a loan most commonly found in money markets like New York and London.

Call-Money Rate The interest rate charged by lending institutions for call loans.

Capital The physical instruments of production: conventionally measured as replacement cost for plant, machines, or tools needed for current production. Capital is also often used as a financial concept, covering all costs of production except labor and raw materials.

Capital Equipment The tools, machinery, and physical plant needed for productive activity. For example, an oven is part of the capital equipment of a bakery.

Capital Gain The net increase in market value of a "capital asset" (e.g., a bond), however conceived, in excess of the purchase cost.

Capital-Output Ratio Expressed as a ratio, the amount of "capital" used to produce output in a given period of time. The amount of capital divided by the national income is the capital-output ratio.

Cliometrics A neologism created by Stanley Reiter in 1960 to describe work done in the 1950s at Purdue University in economic history that utilized computers, economic theory, and mathematical statistics. It is now used to describe quantitative economic history.

Collective Good A term developed by Mancur Olson to describe a privilege from government; see also Public Goods.

Common Law The system of law that originated in England and is based on custom or court decisions.

Comparative Advantage The idea that a person, firm, or economy should specialize in producing those goods and services in which it is relatively more efficient, for which it has lower opportunity costs than others do; this is its comparative advantage.

Compensating Fiscal Policy The idea attributable to Keynes that fiscal policy should be countercyclical; it should be expansionary when the economy is contracting and contractionary when the economy is expanding.

Conservatism The name given to the cautious spirit of Americans by Charles Beard.

Consumer Price Index The weighted average of prices paid by consumers for a representative "market basket" of goods and services. The weights are coefficients that represent the proportion of consumer spending on each item in the index. The CPI is thus different from the Producer Price Index (PPI), which measures prices paid for commodities at the wholesale level.

Cost-Push Inflation The attribution of inflation-producing powers to individual business firms' abilities to "pass along" increases in their own costs to consumers through administered price increases.

Counterfactual A plausible, but not factual, alternative.

Deflation A general decline in prices—the opposite of inflation.

Demand Deposits Bank deposits that are payable on demand, checking accounts.

Depression Economics Theories or explanations of economic events that may be adequate in slack periods but will not usefully explain events during full-capacity employment periods, or during inflations. The phrase commonly is applied to Keynesian economics developed during the 1930s depression.

Deregulation The process of reducing or abolishing the allocation of resources in accord with the rulings of regulatory government bodies, such as the Food and Drug Administration.

Derived Demand Indirect demand. The demand for auto tires is mainly based upon (derived from) the demand for automobiles. If auto sales (or use) decline, so does the demand for tires. Derived demand is thus the market for intermediate goods and factors that are embodied in goods and services that consumers demand.

Devaluation A reduction in the legally specified metallic content of a country's basic monetary unit.

Diminishing Marginal Utility The additional satisfaction derived from the consumption of an additional unit of a good or service is expected to diminish as the quantity consumed increases.

Discretionary Policy As opposed to automatic or mandatory policies. Discretionary policy is action or actions arbitrarily started, stopped, or varied at the will or whim of government.

Double Liability A liability equal to twice the face value of bank stocks was imposed on bank stock owners in New York in 1827 in an effort to encourage prudence.

Dumping Sales of commodities or goods abroad at prices below the cost of domestic production.

Durable Goods Consumer goods meant to last for repeated uses, usually for some years. Autos and refrigerators are counted as consumer durable goods as opposed to food, or even clothing, which vanish relatively quickly in use.

Economic Growth An increase in real income per capita.

Eminent Domain The dominion of the state over all property through which it can condemn private property for public use, but it must pay just compensation to the owner.

Entrepôt A distribution center where goods are warehoused.

Equilibrium Price The market price. The price that is produced by the free interplay of demand and supply, with zero leftover (excess) demand or supply. The equilibrium price will remain unchanged unless there is a shift either of demand or supply.

External Economies Cost reductions produced outside a given productive process, hence "external" to it. Proximity to a railroad is an external economy to a manufacturer since that proximity lowers the cost of transporting both raw materials and finished goods and yet is not part of the manufacturing process itself.

Factors of Production The inputs into the production process. There are three basic factors: labor, capital, and natural resources (including land). In some contexts, entrepreneurship is considered to be a factor of production.

Federal Reserve System The central bank of the United States, designed as a system of 12 district banks, which began operating in 1914.

Fee Simple An estate of direct inheritance in land; what Americans came to call their land tenure.

Fiat Money Currency with no specie backing that is ordered by the issuing government to be full legal tender.

Financial Instruments Bonds, stocks, mortgages, and all other marketable documents of financial transactions and obligations.

Fixed Exchange Rates Exchange rates that do not fluctuate with market conditions, the exchange rates of the gold standard.

Forstall System A Louisiana system that required one-third specie reserves against notes and deposits. It also restricted state bank loans of deposited funds to commercial paper with maturities of 90 days.

Fractional Reserve Banking A system in which banks hold only a fraction of the deposits in reserve in the bank.

Free and Common Socage The basic land tenure of the United States. Among its characteristics are the following: the land is held in perpetuity; it is directly heritable; all the obligations on it are fixed; the owner has the right of waste; and it is freely alienable.

Free Banking A system that originated in New York through which any group of persons could acquire a banking charter by following some general rules to register their group, agreeing to conduct banking business according to state regulations, and, in some states, agreeing to maintain specified reserves.

Free Rider A person, or economic agent, that benefits from an expenditure (usually public) without making a contribution. An economic activity analogous to riding a bus without paying. Any publicly provided service must produce some free riding since all may utilize the service whether taxed for it or not.

Free Silver A movement that sought the free coinage of silver.

Free Trade International trade in which there are no barriers (e.g., tariffs, quotas, embargoes) designed to interfere with purchases or sales in order to protect domestic producers from international competition.

Full Employment Labor market equilibrium in which the number of job seekers is in balance with the number of job vacancies.

Gold Standard An international financial system in which a country's basic monetary unit is defined as a given weight of gold.

Greenbackism The policy platform of the Greenback Party (1875–1876), whose object was to repurchase the national debt (redeem it from its holders) through Treasury issues of paper money, United States Notes ("greenbacks"). The object of the policy was to lower taxes and raise farm prices.

Gresham's Law Gresham's law in its simplest form says that bad money chases out good. In Gresham's original context, it says that money overvalued at the mint generally drives out of circulation money that is undervalued at the mint. The valuations to which he refers compare the official mint prices of, say, gold and silver to their market prices.

Gross Domestic Product (GDP) The market value of goods and services that are not resold during a year and that are newly produced from factors of production located within a country, regardless of who owns them.

Gross National Product (GNP) The market value of goods and services that are not resold during the year and that are newly produced from factors of production owned by citizens of a country, regardless of where they are located.

Human Capital The investment (computed at dollar cost) in human skills, education, and health necessary to maintain or increase the output of goods and services.

Hyperinflation Inflation rates that are extraordinarily high.

Increasing Returns to Scale The case of falling costs at successively rising input levels. For example, the use of assembly lines in the production of some goods helps provide increasing returns to scale.

Indentured Servitude A contract whereby individuals agreed to do certain work for a term of years in return for specified payments, mainly food, clothing, housing, or perhaps some education or training in a craft or skill.

Indexed Data that have been divided by index numbers, thereby showing the relative change between periods.

Infant Industry The argument that some form of protection is necessary for new industries until they mature and are internationally competitive.

Inflation An upward movement in the average of all prices of goods and services. During inflation, prices of many individual items rise while others may fall, and still others may see no change. Inflation is usually measured by a general price index, such as the Consumer Price Index.

Injunction In general, a judicial order requiring those to whom it is directed to take or refrain from certain actions. In particular, it was used as a legal tool against organized labor.

Inputs The ingredients a firm converts to output, conventionally measured as the triad of land, labor, and capital in all their forms. For example, flour and yeast are among the inputs used to make the output, bread.

Intermediation The financial institutions that transform a flow of savings into a flow of investment.

Investment Goods See Capital Equipment.

Joint-Stock Company A partnership in which each partner receives shares of transferable stock equal to the amount of his or her investment. Unlike a corporation, there is no limit on the liability. A suit against (or by) a joint-stock company usually is filed through an officer of the company.

Judicial Instrumentalism The ability of American jurists to stay within the general boundaries of the constitutional settlement and yet modify the substantive content of the law; the freedom to interpret the law.

Labor Movement The attempt of organized labor to obtain legal recognition of unions and other positions favorable to unions.

Labor Productivity The amount of production per unit of labor.

Labor-Saving, Labor-Using Machinery Machines used either to displace labor (in case of labor scarcity) or to employ it (in case of labor abundance).

Laissez-faire This term describes a situation where a government does not interfere in the operation of the economy.

Legal Tender Money that, under the law, may be tendered (offered) in payment of debts and that may not be refused by the creditor.

Long-Run Supply The movement of effective output (supply) capacity over time at various prices.

Macroeconomic Stability Overall economic activity sustained by investment and technological change sufficient to maintain full employment and adequate economic growth.

Malthusian Pressure The case where population increase imposes economic hardship, such as starvation.

Margin The amount a customer has deposited with a broker to provide against loss on transactions. Usually expressed as a percentage of the total, it represents the customer's equity in such an account.

Margin Call The demand by brokers for more cash from their clients; see also Margin.

Marginal Propensity to Import The change in imports relative to the change in GNP over a given time period.

Market Decision The allocation of resources by prices determined in market transactions (e.g., by the establishment of market-clearing equilibrium prices).

Market Failure The price system fails to produce the socially optimal quantity.

Market Overt A system of established market days and sites.

Mercantilism Policies, usually attributed to seventeenth- and eighteenth-century European governments, designed to bias international trade to ensure steady current-account surpluses and thus to accumulate precious metals.

Microeconomic Instability An allusion to the competitive battle in the marketplace between business firms. These battles can produce local business upheavals, even bankruptcies and unemployment, but which, in so doing, ensure the efficient allocation of labor and resources to employment with highest productive returns. Bankruptcies and unemployment "release" workers and resources for more productive uses. It is instability locally, but that instability makes for the most efficient allocation of resources in aggregate.

Military-Industrial Complex The close relationship between the military and the firms that supply goods and services to it.

Mixed Economy An economy in which there are elements of both capitalism and socialism and elements of federal government regulation and control.

Monetarism The school of economic thought that attributes growth of GNP to growth of the stock of money. Monetarists view inflation as a case of money growth exceeding GNP growth.

Money Illusion The confusion of increased money or nominal income with real income.

Negative Externalities Uncompensated damage inflicted on the neighborhood by economic activity. An example would be air pollution.

Nominal Values Nominal values are in terms of the current prices of a time period.

Nonmarket Social Control The allocation of resources by governments, religious bodies, mob action, or other nonmarket forces. The opposite of a market decision. Licensing of professions is nonmarket social control.

Opportunity Cost The maximum income (earnings) foregone as the result of a choice. For example, an account executive in a successful advertising firm has two alternatives—staying on Madison Avenue or chucking it all to raise English Setters in upstate New York (his lifelong dream). If he decides to breed dogs, the higher income he gives up is his opportunity cost.

Perfect Competition A market structure in which there are many buyers and sellers, where access to the market is easy for both buyers and sellers, where no one buyer or seller can influence price, and where price is free to move without restriction.

Police Power The right of government to maintain settled and peaceable conditions, by force if necessary.

Preemption The acquisition of a property right by mere occupancy—"squatting." Preemption rights before 1860 usually meant the right to purchase land previously occupied by squatting. Preemption rights also were called squatters' rights.

Prescriptive Right An individual cannot use his or her property in such a way as to damage the amenity rights of another without being liable for damages.

Price Differentials The same item selling in different places, or times, for different prices.

Primary Sector Agriculture, mining, fisheries, and forestry. The most basic sources of food, raw materials, and energy.

Primogeniture A system of inheritance in which the firstborn son inherits the family estate.

Priority Rights Rights over and above prescriptive rights.

Productivity The amount of output each input factor (or all factors taken together) produce within a given amount of time.

Proprietary Colony Large tracts of land granted to specific individuals by the Crown. Citizens of such colonies retained all their English rights, including the right to representative government.

Public Goods Usually services provided by government whose use by a single consumer does not decrease the total supply (e.g., national defense).

Quit Rents The bundle of fixed incidents combined into a singular periodic payment. These rents eventually became the local property taxes of modern America.

Real Assets Homes, autos, machinery, buildings, as opposed to financial (sometimes called "intangible") assets such as bonds and stocks.

Real Values Real values are calculated in constant prices. Nominal income, wages, or GNP may rise over some period, but if the rise is due strictly to inflation, then real income, real wages, or real GNP has not risen.

Recession The decline in aggregate economic activity following the peak of a business-cycle expansion; officially defined as real GNP falling for two consecutive quarters. It is usually associated with rising unemployment of people and resources.

Redemptioners Largely non-English immigrants who arranged to repay the cost of passage after arrival in the United States. This was often arranged by indenturing a child.

Rent Returns in excess of competitive alternatives to any investment or productive outlay. The income of a concert pianist above the income she could earn doing the next best alternative is her rent.

Rent-Seeking The allocation of resources to the pursuit of rents.

Reservation Price The minimum price at which a seller will agree to sell.

Reserve Ratio The percentage of deposits a bank holds in reserve. A tool of Federal Reserve monetary policy.

Residual Claimant Hypothesis If real wages fall and labor costs decrease, everything else being equal, the real income of the residual claimant, the entity to whom net revenue accrues, will increase.

Royal Colony A colony operated directly by the Crown.

Safety Fund Mandatory deposit insurance in New York State that was the forerunner of the modern Federal Deposit Insurance Corporation (FDIC).

Scale Economies See Increasing Returns to Scale.

Secondary Sector Manufacturing and fabrication; second in line to the primary sector in production of food and goods.

Size Effect The ability of single business firms, by expanding operations over many legal jurisdictions, to evade localized nonmarket control.

Social Savings The difference between the actual cost of a particular activity and the opportunity cost of the next best alternative for accomplishing the identical purpose. It is usually expressed as a percentage of GNP.

Socialism An economic system characterized by central decision making and planning in which the state owns the factors of production.

Specie Gold, silver, and other metals used as coins.

Speculation Purchase or contract for sale of commodities, land, or securities in anticipation of price changes, rather than for use or for mere annual yield.

Stagflation Price inflation accompanied by stagnant real output due to unemployed resources.

Statute Law Law based on legislative enactments.

Suffolk System A plan whereby Suffolk Bank and other Boston banks agreed to accept and pay the notes of those country banks maintaining reserve deposits with the Boston banks.

Sunset Laws A law that imposes regulation for a fixed period of time. For regulation to continue, the law must be renewed.

Supply-Side Economics Analysis of economic activity that concentrates on the elements of production costs and technological change in the determination of GNP. Used in opposition to "demand-side" economics, which focuses on determinants of consumer, business, and government expenditures.

Support Price A government purchase price for any commodity above the market price. For example, many agricultural crops have support prices.

Swing Credits Automatic borrowing rights among European countries associated with the Marshall Plan for European economic recovery in 1947–1950.

Tariff A tax on imported goods (and services) to raise a revenue and/or to prevent or reduce importation of those goods.

Technostructure A word invented by John Kenneth Galbraith to describe the secondary layer of skilled personnel, engineers, scientists, production specialists, sales planners, and so forth in the large modern corporation. This layer lies below top management, yet the technostructure of any firm defines its productive and innovative ability. To Galbraith, it is the technostructure, and not top management, that determines the future.

Tenure The period or terms of holding property, particularly land.

Terms of Trade The ratio of the prices individuals or nations receive for what they produce, to the prices of what they purchase.

Tertiary Sector Services, professions—current economic activity counted as national income that is not directly involved in the production of food, clothing, or shelter. Education, restaurant meals, hotel accommodations, health care, etc. are examples of services.

Transactions Costs The costs associated with bringing buyers and sellers together to complete a transaction.

Transfer Society A society that transfers wealth from the rich to the poor through government.

Unit Banking A banking system in which each bank is a separate business entity unaffiliated with any other bank.

Value Added The revenue received by a firm minus the cost of its materials.

Wealth The sum of net saving over time. Wealth is measured as a stock variable, while saving is a flow from current income.

Zero Sum A situation, such as a game, where the total gains or losses are fixed and the algebraic sum of the gains and losses equals zero. Thus, what someone wins, someone else must lose.

CREDITS

Figures and Tables

p. 92: Figure 5.1. From Charles O. Paullin, *Atlas of the Historical Geography of the United States.* Copyright 1932 by Carnegie Institution of Washington. Reprinted by permission of Carnegie Institution of Washington.

p. 119: Table 6.10. "Regional Income Trends, 1840–1850" by Richard Easterlin from *American Economic History* by Seymour E. Harris (ed.). Copyright © 1961 by the McGraw-Hill Book Company, Inc. Reprinted by permission of the McGraw-Hill Book Company, Inc.

p. 147: Table 8.1. From "The Decline of Steamboating on the Ante-bellum Western Rivers: Some New Evidence and an Alternative Hypothesis" by Erik F. Haites and James Mak, from *Explorations in Economic History,* Fall/1973, Vol. II, No. 1, p. 35. Reprinted by permission of Academic Press, Inc. and James Mak.

p. 165: Table 9.1. Reprinted with permission of Macmillan Publishing Company from *Westward Expansion,* Fifth Edition by Ray Allen Billington and Martin Ridge. Copyright © 1982 by Macmillan Publishing Company.

p. 279: Figure 14.2. From Charles O. Paullin, *Atlas of the Historical Geography of the United States.* Copyright 1932 by Carnegie Institution of Washington. Reprinted by permission of Carnegie Institution of Washington.

p. 296: Figure 15.2. From Charles O. Paullin, *Atlas of the Historical Geography of the United States.* Copyright 1932 by Carnegie Institution of Washington. Reprinted by permission of Carnegie Institution of Washington.

p. 297: Figure 15.3. From Charles O. Paullin, *Atlas of the Historical Geography of the United States.* Copyright 1932 by Carnegie Institution of Washington. Reprinted by permission of Carnegie Institution of Washington.

p. 298: Figure 15.4. From Charles O. Paullin, *Atlas of the Historical Geography of the United States.* Copyright 1932 by Carnegie Institution of Washington. Reprinted by permission of Carnegie Institution of Washington.

p. 299: Table 15.5. Adapted from Albert W. Niemi, Jr., *U.S. Economic History,* Second Edition. Copyright © 1980 Houghton Mifflin Company. Adapted with permission.

p. 344: Table 17.6. From *Manpower in Economic Growth: The American Record Since 1800* by Stanley Lebergott. Copyright © 1964 by the McGraw-Hill Book Company, Inc. Reprinted by permission of the McGraw-Hill Book Company, Inc.

p. 463: Table 24.3. From *Manpower in Economic Growth: The American Record Since 1800* by Stanley Lebergott. Copyright © 1964 by the McGraw-Hill Book Company, Inc. Reprinted by permission of the McGraw-Hill Book Company, Inc.

Photographs

Unless acknowledged otherwise, all photos are the property of Addison Wesley Longman, Inc.

p. xxii: I. N. Phelps Stokes Collection, The New York Public Library, Astor, Lenox, and Tilden Foundations.

p. 22: Prints Division, The New York Public Library, Astor, Lenox, and Tilden Foundations.

p. 30: Library of Congress.

p. 56, all: Smithsonian Institution, NNC, Douglas Mudd.

p. 66t: The Walters Art Museum, Baltimore.

p. 66b: Courtesy The Newberry Library, Chicago.

p. 67t: Joslyn Art Museum, Omaha, Nebraska.

p. 67b: Missouri Historical Society.

p. 73: Library of Congress.

p. 82: Library of Congress.

p. 89: Minnesota Historical Society.

p. 90: From the collections of New Jersey Historical Society.

p. 93: Louis P. Cain.

p. 114: Collection of The New-York Historical Society.

p. 137: Library of Congress.

p. 145t: Collection of The New-York Historical Society.

p. 145b: Carnegie Library, Pittsburgh.

p. 148tl: The Metropolitan Museum of Art, Gift of Mrs. John Sylvester, 1936.

p. 148tr: Courtesy The Bostonian Society, Old State House.

p. 148b: Library of Congress.

p. 149tl: Library of Congress.

p. 149tr: The Metropolitan Museum of Art, Rogers Fund, 1942.

p. 149b: IU Collections, Indiana University Art Museum, Bloomington.

p. 156b: Copelin & Melander/Chicago Historical Society.

p. 157t: Chicago Historical Society.

p. 157b: Chicago Historical Society.

p. 177t: From *The Illustrated Historical Atlas of Bourbon County, Kansas,* 1878. Kansas State Historical Society.

p. 177b: Library of Congress.

p. 194t: Library of Congress.

p. 194b: Courtesy The Newberry Library, Chicago.

p. 209: Collection of the Rensselaer County Historical Society, Troy, NY.
p. 212t: Courtesy American Antiquarian Society.
p. 212cl: The Museum of the City of New York.
p. 212bl: The Museum of the City of New York.
p. 212br: Library of Congress.
p. 213tl: The Museum of the City of New York.
p. 213tr: The Museum of the City of New York.
p. 213bl: The Metropolitan Museum of Art, Rogers Fund, 1942.
p. 213cr: The Museum of the City of New York.
p. 213br: The Museum of the City of New York.
p. 217: Library of Congress.
p. 237: Erich Lessing/Art Resource.
p. 238t: National Maritime Museum, San Francisco.
p. 238b: Library of Congress.
p. 239t: Courtesy of the CA History Rm, CA State Library, Sacramento, CA.
p. 239b: The Bancroft Library, University of California, Berkeley.
p. 243t: Photograph Courtesy of, Peabody Essex Museum, Salem.
p. 243bl: Photograph Courtesy of, Peabody Essex Museum, Salem.
p. 243br: The Henry Francis duPont Winterthur Museum, Delaware.
p. 252: Carnegie Library of Pittsburgh.
p. 257t: Chicago Historical Society.
p. 257b: Library of Congress.
p. 286t: The Bancroft Library, University of California, Berkeley.
p. 286b: Courtesy Southern Pacific Railroad.
p. 287t: Chicago Historical Society.
p. 287b: Culver Pictures.
p. 304, both: Courtesy International Harvester Company.
p. 305t: Caterpillar Inc.
p. 305b: Solomon D. Butcher Collection, Nebraska State Historical Society.
p. 320, both: Library of Congress.
p. 321, both: Library of Congress.
p. 334b: Keystone-Mast Collection, California Museum of Photography, University of California, Riverside.
p. 335t: U.S. War Department, The National Archives.
p. 335b: Courtesy U.S. Steel Corp.
p. 339b: Schnuck Market Inc. Courtesy National Tea Company.
p. 342, both: Chicago Historical Society.
p. 343t: Courtesy Oak Park Public Library, Oak Park, Illinois.
p. 343b: Chicago Historical Society.
p. 348t: Library of Congress.
p. 348b: Collections of Henry Ford Museum and Greenfield Village.
p. 349t: Edison National Historical Site/U.S. Department of the Interior National Park Service.
p. 349b: Chicago Historical Society.
p. 358t: Library of Congress.
p. 358b: Culver Pictures.
p. 366: Library of Congress.
p. 378t: Courtesy of the Massachusetts Historical Society.
p. 378b: Library of Congress.
p. 401, both: Library of Congress.
p. 414t: Albin O. Kuhn Library and Gallery, University of Maryland, Baltimore.
p. 414b: Jacob A. Riis Collection, Museum of the City of New York.
p. 415t: National Archives.
p. 415b: H. J. Heinz Company.
p. 419b: Walter P. Reuther Library, Wayne State Library.
p. 429t: National Archives.
p. 429b: Chicago Historical Society.
p. 442t: Brown Brothers.
p. 442b: Culver Pictures.
p. 454t: Library of Congress.
p. 454bl: Metropolitan Evansville Convention and Visitors Bureau.
p. 454br: Loomis Dean/TimePix
p. 455t: William Garnett.
p. 455cl: Courtesy of U.S. Department of Transportation.
p. 455b: AP/Wide World.
p. 466t: NOAA.
p. 466b: Dorothea Lange Collection/The Oakland Museum of CA, City of Oakland. Gift of Paul S. Taylor.
p. 467t: The Detroit News.
p. 467b: AP/Wide World.
p. 473, both: Spence Air Photos.
p. 488: Library of Congress.
p. 492t: Library of Congress.
p. 492b: U.S. Forestry Service.
p. 493t: Library of Congress.
p. 493b: U.S. Department of the Interior.
p. 508t: Frederick Lewis, Inc.
p. 508b: AP/Wide World.
p. 509t: National Archives.
p. 509b: UPI/Bettman Archives/CORBIS.
p. 518t: From the Collections of University of Pennsylvania.
p. 518b: Milt and Joan Mann/CAMERMANN INTERNATIONAL.
p. 530t: Allan Grant/TimePix.
p. 531, both: J. R. Eyerman/TimePix & E.R. Eyerman/TimePix.
p. 543, both: Allegheny Conference on Community Development.

p. 578, both: Used by permission from DaimlerChrysler Corporation.

p. 582, both: The photos used on page 582 are provided courtesy of Texas Instruments Incorpoated.

p. 610t: Harald Sun/Getty Images.

p. 610b: SuperStock.

p. 611t: Robert Huberman/SuperStock.

p. 611b: Jeff Sherman/Getty Images.

p. 618t: Reprinted with special permission of King Features Syndicate.

p. 618b: Brooks Kraft/SYGMA/Corbis.

NAME INDEX

Page numbers followed by italicized *f* and *t* refer to figures and tables, respectively

SUBJECT INDEX

Page numbers followed by italicized *f* and *t* refer to figures and tables, respectively

GDP 1929–2000[a]

	GDP in billions of current dollars	real GDP in billions of chained (1996) dollars		GDP in billions of current dollars	real GDP in billions of chained 1996 dollars
1929	103.7	822.2	**1965**	720.1	3028.5
1930	91.3	751.5	**1966**	789.3	3227.5
1931	76.6	703.6	**1967**	834.1	3308.3
1932	58.8	611.8	**1968**	911.5	3466.1
1933	56.4	603.3	**1969**	985.3	3571.4
1934	66.0	668.3	**1970**	1,039.7	3578.0
1935	73.3	728.3	**1971**	1,128.6	3697.7
1936	83.7	822.5	**1972**	1,240.4	3898.4
1937	91.9	865.8	**1973**	1,385.5	4123.4
1938	86.1	835.6	**1974**	1,501.0	4099.0
1939	92.0	903.5	**1975**	1,635.2	4084.4
1940	101.3	980.7	**1976**	1,823.9	4311.7
1941	126.7	1148.8	**1977**	2,031.4	4511.8
1942	161.8	1360.0	**1978**	2,295.9	4760.6
1943	198.4	1583.7	**1979**	2,566.4	4912.1
1944	219.7	1714.1	**1980**	2,795.6	4900.9
1945	223.0	1693.3	**1981**	3,131.3	5021.0
1946	222.3	1505.5	**1982**	3,259.2	4919.3
1947	244.4	1495.1	**1983**	3,534.9	5132.3
1948	269.6	1560.0	**1984**	3,932.7	5505.2
1949	267.7	1550.9	**1985**	4,213.0	5717.1
1950	294.3	1686.6	**1986**	4,452.9	5912.4
1951	339.5	1815.1	**1987**	4,742.5	6113.3
1952	358.6	1887.3	**1988**	5,108.3	6368.4
1953	379.9	1973.9	**1989**	5,489.1	6591.8
1954	381.1	1960.5	**1990**	5,803.2	6707.9
1955	415.2	2099.5	**1991**	5,986.2	6676.4
1956	438.0	2141.1	**1992**	6,318.9	6880.0
1957	461.5	2183.9	**1993**	6,642.3	7062.6
1958	467.9	2162.8	**1994**	7,054.3	7347.7
1959	507.4	2319.0	**1995**	7,400.5	7543.8
1960	527.4	2376.7	**1996**	7,813.2	7813.2
1961	545.7	2432.0	**1997**	8,318.4	8159.5
1962	586.5	2578.9	**1998**	8,790.2	8515.7
1963	618.7	2690.4	**1999**	9,299.2	8875.8
1964	664.4	2846.5	**2000**	9,963.1	9318.5

[a] Source: *Bureau of Economic Analysis*, Tables 1.1 and 1.2.